The Univer
Braboeu
Portsmouth Rc
Surrey G

Tort Law

Pearson

At Pearson, we have a simple mission: to help people make more of their lives through learning.

We combine innovative learning technology with trusted content and educational expertise to provide engaging and effective learning experiences that serve people wherever and whenever they are learning.

From classroom to boardroom, our curriculum materials, digital learning tools and testing programmes help to educate millions of people worldwide – more than any other private enterprise.

Every day our work helps learning flourish, and wherever learning flourishes, so do people.

To learn more, please visit us at **www.pearson.com/uk**

Tort Law

Sixth edition

Nicholas J. McBride

Fellow of Pembroke College, Cambridge

and

Roderick Bagshaw

Fellow of Magdalen College, Oxford

Harlow, England • London • New York • Boston • San Francisco • Toronto • Sydney
Dubai • Singapore • Hong Kong • Tokyo • Seoul • Taipei • New Delhi
Cape Town • São Paulo • Mexico City • Madrid • Amsterdam • Munich • Paris • Milan

Pearson Education Limited
KAO Two
KAO Park
Harlow CM17 9NA
United Kingdom
Tel: +44 (0)1279 623623
Web: www.pearson.com/uk

First published 2001 (print)
Second edition published 2005 (print)
Third edition published 2008 (print)
Fourth edition published 2012 (print and electronic)
Fifth edition published 2015 (print and electronic)
Sixth edition published 2018 (print and electronic)

ISBN: 978-1-292-20783-4 (print)
       978-1-292-20784-1 (PDF)
       978-1-292-20785-8 (ePub)

British Library Cataloguing-in-Publication Data
A catalogue record for the print edition is available from the British Library

Library of Congress Cataloging-in-Publication Data
Names: McBride, Nicholas J., author. | Bagshaw, Roderick, author.
Title: Tort law / Nicholas J. McBride, Fellow of Pembroke College, Cambridge
    and Roderick Bagshaw, Fellow of Magdalen College, Oxford.
Description: Sixth edition. | Harlow, United Kingdom ; New York : Pearson
    Education Limited, 2018. | Includes bibliographical references and index.
Identifiers: LCCN 2018000834| ISBN 9781292207834 (print) | ISBN 9781292207841
    (PDF) | ISBN 9781292207858 (ePub)
Subjects: LCSH: Torts—England. | LCGFT: Textbooks.
Classification: LCC KD1949 .M38 2018 | DDC 346.4203—dc23
LC record available at https://urldefense.proofpoint.com/v2/url?u=https-3A__lccn.loc.
gov_2018000834&d=DwIFAg&c=0YLnzTkWOdJlub_y7qAx8Q&r=Q1huLr_hfN5hBmNklTyEbqNkqK
PJUy4ujVI9zNDFILM&m=CI2DfsLx-IIOtRGJiMw7tDNx6ZnPQ7sRZqtN8pGrZ_0&s=w-
poeca5D9DMK_m7_yF8b_QbR-yPoGdtMSbvie0-Aqw&c=

10 9 8 7 6 5 4 3 2
22 21 20 19 18

Cover image © eli77/iStock/Getty Images
Print edition typeset in 9.5/12, ITC Galliard Pro by iEnergizer, Aptara® Ltd.
Printed and bound by CPI Group (UK) Ltd, Croydon, CR0 4YY
NOTE THAT ANY PAGE CROSS REFERENCES REFER TO THE PRINT EDITION

To
Liz, Corin and Arthur
and
Chris, Ben and Damian

Brief contents

Detailed contents

Acknowledgements

We would like to thank all those at Pearson Education who helped with the production of this text, in particular, Melanie Carter, Cheryl Stevart, Jennifer Mair, and Amandeep Kaur. We would both like to acknowledge the huge role played by our students in helping us understand how best to help them understand what can – at first sight – seem like one of the most difficult subjects in English law.

Nick McBride writes. My developing understanding of tort law continues to benefit from conversations with fellow tort lawyers all over the world, especially Rob Stevens, Jason Varuhas, Sandy Steel, James Goudkamp, Ben Zipursky, Paul Davies, Jason Neyers and – of course – Rod. This text could not have been produced without the support provided me by my college, Pembroke College, Cambridge, and Isabel Haskey, and Ines and Luca Anoustis. Large portions of this text were written taking advantage of the opportunities for writing provided by the University of Hong Kong employing me to teach there every August and September.

Roderick Bagshaw writes. I am very fortunate to be able, once again, to thank my wife – Liz – and sons – Corin and Arthur – for their generous support and tolerance during the production of this new edition: I am very grateful for all that you do.

Most of my work on this text was again done using libraries and databases at Magdalen College and the University of Oxford, and I remain grateful to my colleagues at Magdalen and in the Law Faculty at Oxford for all the assistance they provide, directly and indirectly, consciously and unknowingly.

Moreover, as in previous editions, it would be seriously remiss for me to fail to acknowledge the extent to which this text depends on Nick's willingness to go far beyond the conventional role of a co-author. Both of our names appear on the cover, but readers should not infer from that that we share the burdens equally: Nick takes on a far greater share of the writing and of all the other tasks involved in ensuring that this text meets its goals.

Publisher's acknowledgements

We are grateful to the following for permission to reproduce copyright material:

Text

Extract on page 19 from *Van Colle* v *Chief Constable of Hertfordshir* [2009] 1 A.C. 225, at [58]; Extract on page 50 from *Iqbal* v *Prison Officers Association* [2010] QB 732, at [72]; Extract on page 50 from Re F [1990] 2 AC 1, 72; Extract on page 55 from *Re F* [1990] 2 AC 1, 72; Extract on page 70 from *Ashley* v *Chief Constable of Sussex Police* [2008] 1 AC 962, at [22]; Extract on page 70 from *Ashley* v *Chief Constable of Sussex Police* [2008] 1 AC 962, at [29]; Extract on page 92 from *Tomlinson* [2004] 1 AC 46, at [46]; Extract on page 103–104 from *Donoghue* v *Stevenson* [1932] AC 562, 580; Extract on page 138 from *Tai Hing Cotton Mill* v *Liu Chong Hing Bank* [1986] AC 80, at 107 (per Lord Scarman). Extract on page 139 from *Hinz* v *Berry* [1970] 2 QB 40, 42; Extract on page 142 from *McLoughlin* v *O'Brian* [1981] 1 QB 599, 624 (per Griffiths LJ), quoted in Nolan 2004, 20; Extract on page 144 from the House of Lords' decision in *The Aliakmon* (1986), [2011] QB 86, at [132]; Extract on page 146 from *Hunter* v *Canary Wharf* [1997] AC 655, 676 (per Pill LJ); Extract on page 153 from *Spartan Steel & Co Ltd* v *Martin* [1973] 1 QB 27, 38–39; Extract on page 160 from *Candler* v *Crane, Christmas & Co* [1951] 2 KB 164, 183; Extract on page 160 from *Yuen Kun Yeu* v *Attorney-General for Hong Kong* [1988] 1 AC 175, 197; Extract on page 163 from *Arthur J S Hall* v *Simons* [2002] 1 AC 615 (not followed by the High Court of Australia in *D'Orta-Ekenaike* v *Victoria Legal Aid* [2005] HCA 12); Extract on page 163 from *Junior Books Ltd* v *Veitchi Co Ltd* [1983] 1 AC 520; Extract on page 164 from *Vowles* v *Evans* [2003] 1 WLR 1607 (noted, Elvin 2003a); Extract on page 164 from *Henderson* v *Merrett Syndicates Ltd* [1995] 2 AC 145; Extract on page 182 from *Ministry of Housing* v *Sharp* [1970] 2 QB 223, 268; Extract on page 183 from *Cattle* v *The Stockton Waterworks Company* (1875) LR QB 453, 457; Extract on page 189 from *Stovin* v *Wise*, [1996] AC 923, 943; Extract on page 194 from *Capital & Counties plc* v *Hampshire County Council* [1997] QB 1004; Extract on page 195 from *Anns* v *Merton London Borough Council* [1978] AC 728; Extract on page 195 from *Jacqueline Hill*, [1989] 1 AC 53, 63; Extract on page 197 from *Lord Browne-Wilkinson*, [1995] 2 AC 633, 749; Extract on page 206 from *Kent* v *Griffiths* [2001] QB 36, at [47]; Extract on page 213 from *Reeves* v *Commissioner of Police of the Metropolis* [2000] 1 AC 360, 364; Extract on page 233 from *Nettleship* v *Weston* [1971] 2 QB 691, 699; Extract on page 233 from *Nettleship* v *Weston* [1971] 2 QB 691, 700; Extract on page 234 from *Nettleship* v *Weston*, [1971] 2 QB 691, 707; Extract on page 235 from *Wilsher* v *Essex Area Health Authority* [1987] 1 QB 730, 749; Extract on page 238 from *Goldman* v *Hargrave* [1967] AC 645, 663 (per Lord Wilberforce); Extract on page 241 from *Miller* v *Jackson*, [1977] 1 QB 966, 981–2; Extract on page 241 from *Miller* v *Jackson*, [1977] 1 QB 966, 985 (per Geoffrey Lane LJ); Extract on page 243 from *McNair*

J in Bolam v *Friern Hospital Management Committee* [1957] 1 WLR 582, 587; Extract on page 243 from *Bolitho* v *City and Hackney Health Authority*, [1998] AC 232, 241–2 (per Lord Browne-Wilkinson); Extract on page 244 from *Montgomery. In Montgomery* v *Lanarkshire Health Board* (2015] AC 1430, at [90] (per Lord Kerr) [88]. Extract on page 248 from *Biffa Waste Services* v *Maschinenfabrik*, [2009] QB 725, at [78]; Extract on page 248 from *Woodland* v *Swimming Teachers Association* [2014] AC 537, at [6]; Extract on page 249 from *Cassidy* v *Ministry of Health* [1951] 2 KB 343, 362. See also *Gold* v *Essex County Council* [1942] 2 KB 293, at 301–2 (per Lord Greene MR); Extract on page 250 from *Tesco Supermarkets Ltd* v *Natrass* [1972] AC 153, 198; Extract on page 301 from *Commissioners of Police for the Metropolis* v *Reeves*, [2000] 1 AC 360, at 367 (per Lord Hoffmann); Extract on page 302 from *Environment Agency* v *Empress Car Co (Abertilly) Ltd*, [1999] 2 AC 22, 32 (per Lord Hoffmann); Extract on page 317 from *Tremain* v *Pike* [1969] 1 WLR 1556, 1561 (per Payne J); Extract on page 345 from *Edwards* v *Railways Executive* [1952] AC 737, 748; Extract on page 355 from *Ashdown* v *Samuel Williams Ltd* [1957] 1 QB 409, 418 (per Singleton LJ); Extract on page 383 from *League Against Cruel Sports* v *Scott* (1986), QB 240, 251–2; Extract on page 385 from *Southwark London Borough Council* v *Williams*. Ca 1971, [1971] 2 WLR 467; Extract on page 386 from *J A Pye (Oxford) Ltd* v *Graham* [2003] 1 AC 419, at [40]; Extract on page 387 from *Wandsworth Board of Works* v *United Telephone Co Ltd* (1884) 13 QBD 904, 919 (per Bowen LJ); Extract on page 396 from *Hunter* v *Canary Wharf* [1997] AC 655, 706–7; Extract on page 397 from *Hunter* v *Canary Wharf* [1997] AC 655, 676 (per Pill LJ); Extract on page 403 from *Lawrence* v *Fen Tigers Ltd* [2014] AC 822, at [92]); Extract on page 403 from *Barr & Ors* v *Biffa Waste Services Ltd* [2013] QB 455, at [76]; Extract on page 405 from *Adams* v *Ursell* [1913] 1 Ch 269, 270; Extract on page 405 from *Lawrence* v *Fen Tigers Ltd* [2014] AC 822, at [59]; Extract on page 405 from *Lawrence* v *Fen Tigers Ltd* [2014] AC 822, at [181]; Extract on page 407 from *Wheeler* v *JJ Saunders Ltd* [1996] Ch 19, 35; Extract on page 408 from *Lawrence* v *Fen Tigers Ltd* (2014): [2014] AC 822, [94]; Extract on page 408 from *Gillingham BC* v *Medway (Chatham) Dock Co Ltd* [1993] QB 343, 359; Extract on page 408 from *Supreme Court in Lawrence* v *Fen Tigers Ltd* [2014] AC 822, [223]; Extract on page 410 from *Christie* v *Davey* [1893] 1 Ch 316, 326–7; Extract on page 415 from *Hunter* v *Canary Wharf* (1997), AC 655, 721; Extract on page 426 from *Lawrence* v *Fen Tigers Ltd* (2014), AC 822, at [53]; Extract on page 426 from *Lawrence* v *Fen Tigers Ltd* (2014), AC 822, at [56]; Extract on page 427 from *Sedleigh-Denfield* v *O'Callaghan* [1940] AC 880, 886; Extract on page 428 from *Hunter* v *Canary Wharf* [1997] AC 655, at 692; Extract on page 430 from *Hunter* v *Canary Wharf* [1997] AC 655, 693; Extract on page 430 from *Hunter* v *Canary Wharf* (1997), AC 655, at 692; Extract on page 435 from *Shelfer* v *City of London Electric Lighting Co* [1895] 1 Ch 287, 322–3; Extract on page 435 from *Lawrence* v *Fen Tigers Ltd* (2014), AC 822, at [239]; Extract on page 435 from *Shelfer* v *City of London Electric Lighting Co* (1895), 1 Ch 287, 315–6; Extract on page 435 from *Lawrence* v *Fen Tigers Ltd* (2014), AC 822, at [161]; Extract on page 435 from *Lawrence* v *Fen Tigers Ltd* (2014), AC 822, at [168]; Extract on page 436 from *Lawrence* v *Fen Tigers Ltd* (2014), AC 822, at [125]; Extract on page 436 from *Colls* v *Home & Colonial Stores Ltd* [1904] AC 179, 193; Extract on page 437 from *Hunter* v *Canary Wharf* (1997), AC 655, 706–7; Extract on page 439 from *Hunter* v *Canary Wharf* (1997), AC 655, 706; Extract on page 446 from *Cambridge Water Co* v *Eastern Counties Leather plc*, [1994] 2 AC 264, 304; Extract on page 448 from *Cattle* v *Stockton Waterworks Co* (1875), LR 10 QB 453, 457; Extract on page 450 from *Rickards* v *Lothian* [1913] AC 263, 280; Extract on page 451 from *Stannard (t/a Wyvern Tyres)* v *Gore* [2014]

1 QB 1; Extract on page 452 from *Read* v *J Lyons & Co* [1947] AC 156, 173; Extract on page 461 from *Mirvahedy* v *Henley* [2003] 2 AC 491, at [135]; Extract on page 472 from *Jonathan Yearworth & Ors* v *North Bristol NHS Trust* (2010). QB 1, at [45](f); Extract on page 479 from *Kuwait Airways Corpn* v *Iraqi Airways Co* (Nos 4 & 5) (2002), 2 AC 883, at [39]; Extract on page 482 from *TRM Copy Centres (UK) Ltd* v *Lanwall Services Ltd* (2009), 1 WLR 1375, at [10] (per Lord Hope); Extract on page 484 from *Inland Revenue Commissioners* v *Muller & Co's Margarine Ltd* [1901] AC 217, 223–4; Extract on page 488 from *OBG Ltd* v *Allan* [2008] 1 AC 1, at [233] (per Lord Nicholls); Extract on page 488 from *OBG Ltd* v *Allan* [2008] 1 AC 1, at [100]; Extract on page 488 from *OBG Ltd* v *Allan* [2008] 1 AC 1, at [271]; Extract on page 488 from *OBG Ltd* v *Allan* (2008), [2008] 1 AC 1, at [321]; Extract on page 492 from *Lipkin Gorman* v *Karpnale Ltd* [1991] 2 AC 548, 559 (per Lord Templeman); Extract on page 494 from *Kuwait Airways Corpn* v *Iraqi Airways Co* (Nos 4 & 5) (2002), 2 AC 883, at [67]; Extract on page 494 from *Kuwait Airways Corpn* v *Iraqi Airways Co* (Nos 4 & 5) (2002), 2 AC 883, at [82]; Extract on page 507 from *Drummond-Jackson* v *BMA* [1970], [1970] 1 WLR 688; Extract on page 507 from *Stern* v *Piper* [1997], [1997] QB 123; Extract on page 517 from *Jameel (Yousef)* v *Dow Jones & Co Inc* [2005] QB 946, at [39]; Extract on page 520 from *Lewis* v *Daily Telegraph Ltd* [1964] AC 234, 259–60; Extract on page 523 from *Edgington* v *Fitzmaurice* (1885) 29 Ch D 459, 483 (per Bowen LJ); Extract on page 535 from *Reynolds* v *Times Newspapers Ltd* [2001] 2 AC 127, 205; Extract on page 537 from *Jameel (Mohammed)* v *Wall Street Europe SPRL* [2007] 1 AC 359, at [33]. To the same effect, see [51] (per Lord Hoffmann); Extract on page 542 from *Per Gray J, quoted in Purnell* v *BusinessF1 Magazine Ltd* [2008] 1 WLR 1, at [7]; Extract on page 542 from *Broome* v *Cassell & Co Ltd* [1972] AC 1027, 1071 (per Lord Hailsham LC); Extract on page 542 from *Rantzen* v *Mirror Group Newspapers* (1986) Ltd [1994] QB 670, 696; Extract on page 542 from *Cairns* v *Modi* [2013] 1 WLR 1015, at [27]; Extract on page 543 from *Purnell* v *BusinessF1 Magazine Ltd* [2008] 1 WLR 1, at [29]–[30] (per Laws LJ); Extract on page 545 from *Goldsmith* v *Sperrings* [1977] 1 WLR 478, 487; Extract on page 546 from *Derbyshire County Council* v *Times Newspapers Ltd* [1993] AC 534, at 547 (per Lord Keith of Kinkel); Extract on page 547 from *Reynolds* v *Times Newspapers Ltd* [2001] 2 AC 127, 201; Extract on page 559 from *Douglas* v *Hello! Ltd* (No 3) [2006] QB 125, at [105]; Extract on page 560 from *Murray* v *Express Newspapers Ltd* [2009] Ch; Extract on page 563 from *HRH Prince of Wales* v *Associated Newspapers Ltd* [2008] Ch 57, at [36] (per Lord Phillips CJ); Extract on page 564 from *Campbell (Appellant)* v *MGN Limited* (Respondents), at [154]. This was applied in *John* v *Associated Newspapers Ltd* [2006] EWHC 1611 (QB) [2004] 2 AC 457; Extract on page 565 from *Murray* v *Express Newspapers plc* [2009] Ch 481, at [57]; Extract on page 571 from *Lord Woolf CJ* [2003] QB 195, at [43]. See also, for example, Campbell, at [58] (per Lord Hoffmann); Extract on page 571 from *Lord Woolf CJ* [2003] QB 633, at [41]. See also Campbell, at [151] (per Baroness Hale); Extract on page 578 from *Campbell* v *MGN Ltd* [2003] QB 633, at [68]; Extract on page 588 from *Majrowski* v *St Guy's and St Thomas's NHS Trust* [2007] 1 AC 224, at [30]; Extract on page 589 from *Thomas* v *News Group Newspapers* [2001] EWCA Civ 1233, at [29]. In *Levi* v *Bates* [2016] QB 91, at [28]; Extract on page 594 from *O (a child)* v *Rhodes* [2016] AC 219, at [74]; Extract on page 594 from *O (a child)* v *Rhodes* [2016] AC 219, at [87]; Extract on page 594 from *O (a child)* v *Rhodes* [2016] AC 219, at [74]–[76]; Extract on page 596 from *Wainwright* v *Home Office* [2004] 2 AC 406, at [46]; Extract on page 600 from *X* v *Bedfordshire County Council* [1995] 2 AC 633, 747 (per Lord Browne-Wilkinson); Extract on page 601 from *X* v *Bedfordshire County Council* [1995] 2 AC 633,

731–2 (emphasis added); Extract on page 602 from *Morrison Sports Ltd* v *Scottish Power Plc* [2010] 1 WLR 1934, at [37]; Extract on page 602 from *Morrison Sports Ltd* v *Scottish Power Plc* [2010] 1 WLR 1934, at [29]; Extract on page 603 from *Groves* v *Wimborne* [1898] 2 QB 402, 416; Extract on page 603 from *Atkinson* v *The Newcastle and Gateshead Waterworks Company* (1877) 2 Ex D 441, 445–6; Extract on page 604 from *X* v *Bedfordshire County Council* [1995] 2 AC 633, 747; Extract on page 606 from *O'Rourke* v *Camden London Borough Council* [1998] AC 188, 196; Extract on page 613 from *Harper* v *G N Haden & Sons Ltd* [1933] Ch 298, 317 per Romer LJ. See also, *Herring* v *Metropolitan Board of Works* (1865) 19 CB NS 510, 144 ER 886; Extract on page 618 from *R* v *Goldstein* [2006] 1 AC 459, at [39] (per Lord Bingham) and [56] (per Lord Rodger); Extract on page 618 from *Sedleigh-Denfield* v *O'Callaghan* [1940] AC 880, 904–5; Extract on page 619 from *Sedleigh-Denfield* v *O'Callaghan* [1940] AC 880, 902; Extract on page 620 from *Mint* v *Good* [1951] 1 KB 517, 526–7, per Denning LJ; Extract on page 630 from *Freedom In Wainwright* v *Home Office* (2004), 2 AC 406, at [46]; Extract on page 633 from *British Motor Trade Association* v *Salvadori* (1949), Ch 556, 565; Extract on page 636 from *OBG Ltd* v *Allan* [2008] 1 AC 1, at [39] (per Lord Hoffmann); Extract on page 637 from *Emerald Construction Co* v *Lowthian*: CA 1965, [1965] AC 269; Extract on page 639 from *South Wales Miners' Federation* v *Glamorgan Coal Company*: HL 1905, [1905] AC 239; Extract on page 645 from *Merkur Island Corp* v *Laughton*: HL [1983] 2 AC 570; Extract on page 645 from *Merkur Island Corp* v *Laughton*: HL [1983] 2 AC 570; Extract on page 646 from *OBG Ltd* v *Allan* (2008), 1 AC 1, at [48] (per Lord Hoffmann); Extract on page 647 from *OBG Ltd* v *Allan* (2008), 1 AC 1, at [49] (per Lord Hoffmann); Extract on page 647 from *OBG Ltd* v *Allan* (2008), 1 AC 1, at [162] (per Lord Nicholls); Extract on page 648 from *OBG Ltd* v *Allan* (2008), 1 AC 1, at [269] (per Lord Nicholls); Extract on page 648 from *OBG Ltd* v *Allan* (2008), 1 AC 1, at [61] (per Lord Hoffmann); Extract on page 649 from *OBG Ltd* v *Allan* (2008), 1 AC 1, at [61] (per Lord Hoffmann); Extract on page 655 from *Mogul Steamship Co Ltd* v *McGregor, Gow & Co* [1892] AC 25, 42; Extract on page 655 from *Mogul Steamship Co Ltd* v *McGregor, Gow & Co* [1892] AC 25, 42; Extract on page 658 from *Lonrho Ltd* v *Shell Petroleum Co Ltd* (No 2): HL 1 Apr 1981, [1982] AC 173; Extract on page 664 from *Edgington* v *Fitzmaurice* (1885), (1885) 29 Ch D 459; Extract on page 670 from *OBG Ltd* v *Allan* (2008), 1 AC 1, at [47] (per Lord Hoffmann); Extract on page 670 from *OBG Ltd* v *Allan* (2008), 1 AC 1, at [56] (per Lord Hoffmann); Extract on page 672 from *Ajinomoto Sweeteners Europe Sas And Asda Stores Limited* [2011] Qb 497, At [28]; Extract on page 677 from *Glinski* v *Mciver*: HL [1962] AC 726; Extract on page 679 from *Jones* v *Swansea City Council*: CA [1990] 1 WLR 54; Extract on page 703 from *Smith* v *Linskills*: CA [1996] 1 WLR 763; Extract on page 720 from *Stubbings* v *Webb and Another*: HL 10 Feb [1993] 2 WLR 120; Extract on page 756 from *Thompson* v *Commissioner of Police of the Metropolis* [1998] QB 498, 516; Extract on page 756 from *Sutcliffe* v *Pressdram Ltd* [1991] 1 QB 153, 184; Extract on page 758 from *AB* v *South West Water Services Ltd* [1993] QB 507, 532; Extract on page 788 from *A* v *Bottrill* [2003] 1 AC 449, at [29]; Extract on page 789 from *Mediana (Owners of Steamship)* v *Comet (Owners of Lightship)* [1900] A.C. 113; Extract on page 789 from *Mediana (Owners of Steamship)* v *Comet (Owners of Lightship)* [1900] A.C. 113; Extract on page 801 from *Bonnard* v *Perryman*: CA 2 Jan [1891] 2 Ch 269; Extract on page 804 from *Ashdown* v *Telegraph Group Ltd* [2002] Ch 149, [27]; Extract on page 826 from *Fish & Fish Ltd* v *Sea Shepherd UK* [2015] AC 1229, at [21] (per Lord Toulson); Extract on page 840 from *Viasystems (Tyneside) Ltd* v *Thermal Transfer (Northern) Limited* [2006] QB 510, at [79].

Preface to the sixth edition

The Preface to the fifth edition of this text expressed the hope that tort law was in for a period of relative quietude in terms of future developments, as most of the important questions relating to the law of tort had seemed to be answered (whether well or badly is another matter) and it was hard to see any appetite for reopening those questions. While followers of this text will generally have found it reliable in its predictions – both in relation to how the courts will decide concrete cases, and as to the future development of tort law – we must confess to having missed the mark with this one.

The past couple of years have seen the UK Supreme Court resurrect the tort in *Wilkinson* v *Downton* from the grave in which Lord Hoffmann sought to bury it (*O (a child)* v *Rhodes* (2015)), expand the law on vicarious liability in such a violent and unexplained manner that it is now extremely difficult to state what limits exist on that form of liability (*Mohamud* v *Morrison Supermarkets plc* (2016), *Armes* v *Nottinghamshire County Council* (2017)), recognise a new tort of maliciously instituting civil proceedings against another (*Willers* v *Joyce* (2016)), and attempt in an unprecedented manner to rewrite the entire law on when a defendant to a civil claim will be able to raise a defence of illegality to the claimant's claim in a case that had nothing to do with tort law (*Patel* v *Mirza* (2016)). We have also seen, in *ABC* v *St George's Healthcare NHS Trust* (2017), the Court of Appeal ignore the UKSC's very clear decision in *Michael* v *Chief Constable of South Wales Police* (2015) as to what approach the courts should adopt in cases where a public body is sued for failing to save someone from harm; while in *Wilkes* v *DePuy International Ltd* (2016), Hickinbottom J muddied the waters as to when a product will be regarded as being defective under the Consumer Protection Act 1987 by ruling that such an inquiry should not be affected by any categorisation of the kind of defect the product is supposed to be suffering from and should instead rest on a consideration of all the circumstances 'no more and no less' (though it is hard to see what 'more' the courts could take into account).

In so far as it is possible to detect a trend underlying these developments, it may be captured by Lord Neuberger's remarkable address on 'Some Thoughts on Principles Governing the Law of Torts' – delivered to a conference in Singapore on 'Protecting Business and Economic Interests' on 19 August 2016 and available on the UK Supreme Court website – where Lord Neuberger (sadly now retired as President of the UK Supreme Court) expressed himself sceptical as to whether judges could or 'should decide tort cases by applying well established principles to the facts of those cases' and instead proposed a much larger role for judges' deciding tort cases 'by reference [to] what they see as the appropriate policy considerations as applied to those facts'. Such words may be seized upon as manna from heaven by students who would wish for nothing more than to be released from the necessity of studying the hundreds of pages making up this text and told instead that all tort cases can be resolved in accordance with the law by simply applying a range of a hundred or so policy factors to the facts of the case. Perhaps the future of tort law texts is to compete in compiling lists of such policy factors, together with cases that are taken as demonstrating such factors at work. However, we reject such a vision of what a tort law text should look like, as well as Lord Neuberger's assertions that tort law is 'innately incoherent', that the law of tort provides 'unfertile ground for any clear, general underlying philosophy', that the 'analysis of tort cases, at least in the United Kingdom, appears to demonstrate a notable degree of disarray and a marked lack of reliable principle', that the fact that it is much easier to sue public bodies for a failure to act under the Human Rights Act 1998 than the common law of negligence is 'symptomatic of such issues being driven by policy considerations rather than any great principle' (on which, see McBride 2016a[1]), and that there are no 'reliable principles by which allegations of professional negligence or of other torts are to be assessed'. Of course, there may an element of self-fulfilling prophecy about Lord Neuberger's remarks: the more judges think along the above lines, the more it will come to be the case that it is correct to think along these lines. However, the core of sound principle that underlies the law of torts as an intelligible and distinct area of law remains, for the time being, discernible and we have tried, as in all previous editions, to provide students with a clear guide as to how to make sense of this area of law.

We have sought in this edition to ensure that the guidance provided by this text occupies significantly fewer pages than in the previous edition, so that the task of properly mastering tort law remains within the grasp of the average, hard-working student. The fifth edition comprised 38 chapters; whereas this edition comprises 32. In terms of page length, this edition is about ten per cent shorter than the previous one. However, we hope that readers of this edition will find that we have managed to do more with less: providing just as complete an account of the law of tort as the previous edition while fully explaining any and all recent developments in the law that have occurred since the last edition, including those mentioned above.

Nicholas J. McBride
Roderick Bagshaw

1 October 2017

---

[1] All citations of articles and papers in this text follow the Harvard system, where a complete citation for the article or paper cited can be found at the back of this text.

Table of cases

Table of statutes, statutory instruments and conventions

Statutes

Statutory Instruments

Conventions

Chapter 1
The basics

Aims and objectives

Reading this chapter should enable you to:

(1) Understand what a civil wrong is, and that a tort is a form of civil wrong.

(2) Begin to understand what forms of behaviour will amount to torts.

(3) Understand what remedies will be available when a tort has been committed.

(4) Come to grips with various different views of what tort law is 'about'.

(5) Distinguish tort law from other areas of law, such as criminal law or property law.

(6) Understand what role insurance plays in tort claims and the way tort cases are decided.

1.1 The function of tort law

Tort law is one of the most fundamental legal subjects that you can study. This is because the function of tort law is to determine what legal rights[1] we have against other people, free of charge and without our having to make special arrangements for them, and what remedies will be available when those rights are violated.

In *Donoghue* v *Stevenson* (1932), Mrs Donoghue and a friend of hers went to a café in Paisley, Scotland. Donoghue's friend ordered an ice cream 'float' for Donoghue. Francis Minchella, the café owner, served Donoghue with a tumbler of ice cream and an opaque bottle of ginger beer. Minchella poured some of the beer over the ice cream to create the 'float' and left the bottle – now half full – on Donoghue's table. After Donoghue had eaten some of the 'float', she topped it up by pouring onto it some more ginger beer.

---

[1] From now on, whenever we use the word 'right', we mean by that a legal right, not a moral right.

As she did so, the decomposing remains of a snail slid out of the ginger beer bottle. Donoghue was taken ill. She brought a claim in tort against David Stevenson, the manufacturer of the ginger beer. She argued that Stevenson had been careless in allowing a snail to get into the bottle, and as a result he should be held liable in tort to compensate her for the illness she had suffered after drinking the bottle's contents (dead snail remains and all).

In bringing her claim against Stevenson, Donoghue faced an uphill battle. The available authorities that applied to her case indicated that:

(1) If Donoghue wanted to sue Stevenson in tort, she had first of all to show that she had a right against Stevenson that he take care that the ginger beer in her bottle was safe to drink. If she could not show this, then even if Stevenson had been careless in allowing a snail to get into the ginger beer bottle, he would have done no wrong – committed no tort – to Donoghue in being careless.

(2) Donoghue could only have had a right against Stevenson that he take care that the ginger beer in the bottle was safe to drink if she and he had entered into a contract – a legally binding agreement – under which Stevenson undertook to take such care in manufacturing the ginger beer.[2] Obviously, this requirement was not satisfied in this case. Donoghue and Stevenson were complete strangers. Donoghue did not even have a contract with Minchella, the café owner who had served her the ginger beer, as the ginger beer had been bought from Minchella by her friend, and not her.

When the case came to the House of Lords, the Law Lords decided – by a 3:2 majority – that (2) was incorrect. It decided that even though Donoghue and Stevenson were complete strangers, Donoghue still had a right that Stevenson take care that the ginger beer in her bottle was safe to drink. *Donoghue* v *Stevenson* established that a consumer would *not* have to enter into a contract with a manufacturer if she wanted to have a right that the manufacturer take care that his goods were safe for the consumer to use. Instead a consumer would have such a right automatically.

What the House of Lords did in *Donoghue* v *Stevenson* was exactly what tort law does generally. Tort law tells us what rights we have against other people automatically – free of charge and without us having to make any special arrangements for them – and what remedies will be available when those rights are violated. To save words, let's call these rights that tort law gives us, *basic rights*. So the function of tort law is to determine what basic rights we have against other people, and what remedies will be available when those rights are violated.[3] The major task of a tort text is to set out what these basic rights are, and what remedies will be available when they are violated.

1.2 Rights and duties

Because lawyers use the word 'right' in different ways, saying – as we do – that tort law determines what basic rights we enjoy against other people can create confusion. Lawyers use the word 'right' in at least three different ways:

(1) To describe what A has when A has a power to perform some kind of legal act, such as suing someone for damages, or terminating a contract. So if A has the power to sue B for

---

[2] *Winterbottom* v *Wright* (1842) 2 M & W 109, 152 ER 402.
[3] For an excellent presentation of this view of tort law, see Tettenborn 2000a.

damages, lawyers say that A has a 'right' to sue B for damages. Similarly, if A has the power to terminate a contract that A has with B because B has failed to perform her side of the contract in some serious way, then we say that A has a 'right' to terminate his contract with B.

(2) To describe what A has when the law imposes a legal duty on B to do *x*, and the law imposes that duty on B for A's benefit. In such a situation, lawyers will say that A has a 'right' against B that B do *x*. This right is correlative to the duty that (lawyers say) B *owes* A to do *x*. The right does not arise out of the duty. The duty does not arise out of the right. The duty and the right are two sides of the same coin.

So, for example, we said above that the issue in *Donoghue* v *Stevenson* was whether Donoghue had a right against Stevenson that he take care that the ginger beer in her bottle was safe to drink. But an exactly identical way of expressing this point is to say that the issue in *Donoghue* v *Stevenson* was whether Stevenson owed Donoghue a duty to take care that the ginger beer in her bottle was safe to drink. And that was the way the case was argued in the House of Lords – in terms of duties, not rights. But it makes no difference whether you discuss that case in terms of Stevenson owing a duty of care to Donoghue, or in terms of Donoghue having a right against Stevenson that he take care. It comes to the same thing.

(3) To describe what A has when the law takes steps to protect some freedom or interest of A's from being interfered with by other people. So, for example, it is correct to say that you have a 'right' to freedom of speech. This is because the law takes special steps to protect your freedom of speech – in two ways.

First, the Human Rights Act 1998 makes it unlawful for a public body to interfere with your freedom of speech if doing so serves no legitimate purpose,[4] or if doing so does serve a legitimate purpose but would have a disproportionate effect on your freedom of speech.

Secondly, the law grants you immunities, or exemptions, from certain legal rules that would otherwise have the effect of allowing other people to unacceptably interfere with your freedom of speech. For example, it is normally the case that if you defame someone else – say something bad about them – then the person you have defamed will be entitled to sue you for damages. But applying that rule across the board would have the effect of unacceptably interfering with your freedom of speech – for example, when what you have to say about someone else is damaging but true, or when you occupy some position that makes it important that you be able to say what you think about someone else without fear of being sued. In order to prevent people's freedom of speech being unacceptably interfered with in this way, the law grants us certain immunities, or exemptions, from the law on defamation.

So if you say something bad about A, but what you say about A is substantially true, then you will almost always have a defence to being sued by A for defamation. Again, if a journalist in good faith publishes an article that makes damaging allegations about B, then the journalist will have a defence to being sued by B for defamation if the article was on a matter of public interest, and the journalist acted responsibly in publishing the article. And again, a Member of Parliament who makes damaging allegations against C on

---

[4] Article 10(2) of the European Convention on Human Rights provides that it may be legitimate to limit freedom of speech 'in the interests of national security, territorial integrity or public safety, for the prevention of disorder or crime, for the protection of health or morals, for the protection of the reputation or rights of others, for preventing the disclosure of information received in confidence, or for maintaining the authority and impartiality of the judiciary.'

the floor in Parliament cannot be sued at all by C – and this is so even if the MP in question knew that what he was saying about C was untrue when he said it.

When we say that the function of tort law is to determine what basic rights we have against other people, and what remedies are available when those rights are violated, we are using the word 'right' in the *second* sense above. This is a very important point, because people often mix up the second and third types of rights and say things like – 'In *Donoghue* v *Stevenson*, Donoghue was entitled to sue Stevenson because he violated her right *to* bodily integrity'. No – Donoghue was entitled to sue Stevenson because she had a right *that* he take care that the ginger beer in her bottle was safe to drink, and he (we can suppose) violated that right.[5]

Remedies in tort law are based on the violation of a 'right *that* . . .', not a 'right *to* . . .'. Tort law does not do what it does because we have various 'rights to . . .' (bodily integrity, freedom of speech, reputation, property, trade, vote, freedom from discrimination, and so on).[6] On the contrary: our 'rights to . . .' (bodily integrity, freedom of speech, reputation, property, trade, vote, freedom from discrimination, and so on) exist because tort law does what it does in giving us particular rights against other people that they not act in particular ways. It is because we have *those* rights that we can say we have rights to bodily integrity, freedom of speech, reputation, and so on.[7]

In *Allen* v *Flood* (1898), Allen represented ironworkers who were employed by the Glengall Iron Company to repair a ship. The ironworkers were employed on a 'day to day' basis. In other words, if they were working on the ship one day, the Glengall Iron Company had no contractual duty to employ them to work on the ship the next day. But equally, they had no contractual duty to turn up to work on the ship the next day. So each day, the ironworkers would present themselves at the yard for work, and see if they would be taken on for that day. Flood and Taylor were also employed on a 'day to day' basis by the Glengall Iron Company to work on the ship, repairing its woodwork. The ironworkers objected to working alongside Flood and Taylor because Flood and Taylor had previously done some ironwork on another ship, and the ironworkers regarded such work as exclusively theirs to do. So Allen told the Glengall Iron Company that if the company carried on employing Flood and Taylor, the ironworkers would no longer work on their ship. The result was that the next day, Flood and Taylor were told they were no longer needed to work on the ship.

Flood and Taylor sued Allen. They won at first instance, and in the Court of Appeal. When the case reached the House of Lords, nine Law Lords heard the case. Such was the importance of the case, the nine Law Lords asked eight judges to sit in on the hearings and advise them as to what decision they should give in the case. Of those eight judges, six (Hawkins, Cave, North, Wills, Grantham and Lawrance JJ) said that Flood and Taylor were entitled to sue Allen, and only two (Mathew and Wright JJ) said they were not. However, the nine Law Lords decided by six (Lords Watson, Herschell, Macnaghten,

---

[5] In fact, the issue of whether Stevenson failed to take care that Donoghue's ginger beer was safe to drink was never tried. The only issue the House of Lords had to decide was whether Stevenson owed Donoghue a duty of care. The case was then sent back down to a lower court to resolve the issue of whether Stevenson breached that duty of care. But the case was settled – Stevenson paid Donoghue damages out of court – before that issue came to court.

[6] Again, it should be remembered (see fn 1, above) that we are talking of legal rights here, not moral rights.

[7] See McBride 2011 for a much more detailed exposition of this basic point.

James, Shand and Davey) to three (Lord Halsbury LC, and Lords Ashbourne and Morris) that Flood and Taylor had no claim in this case. All in all, 21 judges heard arguments in *Allen* v *Flood* (including one judge at first instance, and three in the Court of Appeal) – 13 found for Flood and Taylor, and only 8 for Allen.

Allen v *Flood* illustrates just how important it is to bear in mind that you can only sue someone in tort for doing *x* if you can show that you had a right against them *that* they not do *x*. This point was overlooked by the 13 judges who ruled for the claimants in *Allen* v *Flood*. Those judges all took the view that Flood and Taylor should be allowed to sue Allen because they had a 'right to trade' that had been unjustifiably interfered with by Allen. But whether or not Flood and Taylor had a 'right to trade' was irrelevant. The real issue was whether Flood and Taylor had a right against Allen *that* he not persuade the Glengall Iron Company not to re-employ them the next day by threatening that if the company did so, the ironworkers represented by Allen would no longer work on the company's ship. The House of Lords decided that Flood and Taylor had no such right against Allen.

The only (relevant) rights that Flood and Taylor did have against Allen were: (1) a right that Allen not persuade the Glengall Iron Company to breach any contract it had with Flood and Taylor, and (2) a right that Allen not intentionally cause Flood and Taylor loss using means that were independently unlawful. Flood and Taylor could not sue Allen because neither of those rights had been violated in this case. Right (1) was not violated because the Glengall Iron Company was under no contractual obligation to employ Flood and Taylor the next day. Right (2) was not violated because the means by which Allen caused Flood and Taylor loss in this case was to threaten that the ironworkers that he represented would not turn up to work the next day. As the ironworkers were under no contractual duty to turn up for work the next day, it was not independently unlawful for Allen to make this threat.

1.3 The range of torts

In principle, there are as many different torts as there are different basic rights that tort law gives us against other people.[8] In practice, this is not true as there is one tort, *negligence*, that encompasses the violation of a large number of different rights that we have against other people that they take care not to harm us in some way, or take care to help us in some way. The range of torts recognised under English law can be divided up into a number of different groups:

(1) *Torts of trespass to the person*. These include battery (unlawfully touching another), assault (unlawfully making someone think that they are about to be touched), and false imprisonment (unlawfully confining someone's movements to a particular area).

(2) *Negligence*. This tort covers any situation where a defendant has breached a duty of care owed to a claimant. There are a large number of different duties of care recognised under the law, and a large number of different situations in which one person will owe another a

---

[8] Rudden 1991–1992 provides us with a list of over 70 torts which have been recognised at one time or another in the common law jurisdictions. But it is doubtful whether some of the listed 'torts' are actually torts – for example, 'homicide' or 'products liability'.

duty of care. As we will see,[9] periodic attempts have been made to come up with a master formula that will tell us in any given situation whether or not one person will owe another a duty of care, and if so, what sort of duty. In truth, all such attempts to come up with such a master formula have failed. Either the formula has been wrong or the formula has amounted to nothing more than saying 'A will owe B a duty of care if it would be "fair, just and reasonable" for him to do so' – which may be true, but is hardly informative.

(3) *Torts to land.* This group of torts includes the tort of trespass to land (unlawfully going on to someone else's land) and the tort of private nuisance (unlawfully interfering with the amenity value of land in someone else's possession), as well as any forms of the tort of negligence that involve breaching a duty to take care not to do something that is liable to damage someone else's land or a duty to take care to do something to protect someone else's land from being damaged.

(4) *Torts to goods.* Again, the tort of negligence is relevant here, in that anyone whose goods have been destroyed, damaged or stolen due to another's carelessness might be able to claim that that other owed her a duty of care to protect her goods from being harmed. Other torts that belong to this group are trespass to goods (unlawfully touching another's goods) and conversion (treating another's goods as though they are your own to dispose of). A further tort, detinue (which involved refusing to hand over goods to the person entitled to them), was abolished in 1977, and this type of wrong is now treated as a form of conversion.

(5) *Personality torts.* These torts involve acting in ways that impinge on someone's ability to function as a person, or to interact with other people. They include defamation, harassment and the new tort of invasion of privacy (or, more accurately, unlawful disclosure of private information to a third party).

(6) *The economic torts.* The torts that belong to this group are so-called because they all involve inflicting some kind of economic harm on someone else. This group includes the tort of inducing a breach of contract, the intentional infliction of economic loss using unlawful means to do so, conspiracy, deceit (intentionally or recklessly lying to someone so as to get them to act in a particular way), passing off (trading on the goodwill attached to someone's name or business, or trading in a way that might endanger the goodwill attached to someone's name or business), and malicious falsehood (deliberately telling a third party lies about someone with the object of causing that someone loss). In theory, this group also includes any form of the tort of negligence that involves a breach of a duty to take care not to harm, or to safeguard, someone else's economic welfare.

(7) *Abuse of power torts.* This group includes misfeasance in public office (which either involves a public official unlawfully and intentionally causing someone loss, or involves a public official knowingly doing something unlawful that he knew would cause someone loss) and malicious prosecution (which involves A instituting criminal proceedings against an innocent person for no legitimate reason).

(8) *Statutory torts.* We will discuss these in more detail shortly,[10] but for the time being: A will commit a statutory tort if: (1) he breaches a duty that Parliament has imposed on him for the benefit of B; and (2) Parliament intended that a breach of that duty should be actionable in tort – that is, Parliament intended that the same remedies that are available against someone who commits one of the torts set out above should also be available against A.

---

[9] See below, §4.2.
[10] See § 1.11, below.

The range of torts recognised under English law expands and contracts over time, to reflect changing social notions as to what basic rights we should have against other people. We have already seen how in *Donoghue* v *Stevenson*, the House of Lords was confronted with the question: Should a consumer automatically have a right against the manufacturer of a product she is using that the manufacturer take care that that product is safe to use? Previous decisions had indicated that a consumer should not: that if a consumer wanted such a right, she would have to go to the manufacturer and bargain for it. Such decisions reflected a desire not to impose too many burdens on businesses and expose them to the risk of a multiplicity of lawsuits:

> The only safe rule is to confine the right to recover [for harm caused by a defective product] to those who enter into [a] contract [with the manufacturer]; if we go one step beyond that, there is no reason why we should not go fifty.[11]

But by the time *Donoghue* v *Stevenson* was decided, the pendulum had swung, and the majority in the House of Lords was more concerned to enhance the degree of protection enjoyed by consumers than it was to protect businesses from too many lawsuits.

Donoghue v *Stevenson* was an example of changes in society triggering an expansion in the basic rights we enjoy against each other; but social change can also result in a contraction in our basic rights. For example, it used to be the case that if a man was married, he would normally have a right against other men that they not sleep with his wife,[12] that they not encourage his wife to leave him, and that if his wife did leave him, that they not give her a place to stay.[13] As McCardie J frankly admitted in *Butterworth* v *Butterworth and Englefield* (1920), the reason for this was that a 'wife was in substance regarded by the common law as the property of her husband'[14] – so interfering with a man's wife was regarded as being akin to interfering with his property. Now that society has rejected the idea that a man's wife is his property, the idea that a married man will have a right against other men that they not interfere with his marriage has also been rejected.[15]

1.4 Torts and wrongs

A tort is often said to be a form of *civil wrong*.[16] We agree: a tort is a form of *wrong*, and that it is appropriate to classify that kind of wrong as being a *civil* wrong.

A wrong involves the breach of a legal duty.[17] All wrongs can be divided up into *private* wrongs and *public* wrongs, according to the type of legal duty that has been breached.

---

[11] *Winterbottom* v *Wright* (1842) 2 M & W 109, at 115 (per Alderson B).

[12] Matrimonial Causes Act 1857, s 33.

[13] *Winsmore* v *Greenbank* (1745) Willes 577, 125 ER 1330.

[14] [1920] P 126, 130.

[15] See the Law Reform (Miscellaneous Provisions) Act 1970, ss 4 (abolishing the right to sue someone for committing adultery with your wife) and 5 (abolishing the right to sue someone for inducing your wife to leave you). Section 2 of the Administration of Justice Act 1982 provides that '[no] person shall be liable in tort . . . to a husband on the ground only of having deprived him of the services or society of his wife'. The last remaining traces of the idea that a man's wife is his property were removed from the law by the House of Lords in *R* v *R* [1992] 1 AC 599, ruling that a man is *not* allowed to have sexual intercourse with his wife without her consent.

[16] See Birks 1995.

[17] From now on, whenever we use the word 'duty' we mean by that a legal duty, not a moral duty.

Breach of a legal duty that has been imposed on someone for the benefit of a specific individual is a private wrong; while breach of a duty that has been imposed on someone for the benefit of society as a whole is a public wrong. So, for example, if A beats B up, he commits a private wrong – A had a duty not to beat B up and that duty was imposed on A for B's benefit. We mark the fact that the duty that A breached in this case was imposed for B's benefit by saying that the duty A breached was *owed to B* and that A committed a wrong *in relation to B* in beating B up. By contrast, if you damage or destroy the breeding site or resting place of a wild animal that belongs to a 'European protected species', you will commit a public wrong. The duty that you had not to do such a thing[18] was imposed on you not for the benefit of a particular individual, but for the benefit of society as a whole.

With that all said, let us now turn to civil wrongs. There are two popular ways of defining what a civil wrong is:

(1) A private wrong. That is, a breach of a duty owed to another, or – to put it another, exactly equivalent way – the violation of a right that one person had against another.[19]

On this definition, we would agree that a tort is a form of civil wrong. Clearly, everything we have said so far indicates that we take the view that someone who commits a tort commits a private wrong.

(2) Any kind of wrong – private or public – that is capable of giving rise to a right to bring an action (known as a 'civil action') against the person who committed that wrong for damages.[20]

On this definition, we would again agree that a tort is a form of civil wrong. Someone who commits a tort commits a wrong, and one of the remedies that *may* be made available against them is an order to pay damages to someone else. But strong emphasis needs to be placed on the word 'may'. If someone commits a tort, it is not necessarily the case that they will *always* have to pay damages to someone else. In Chapter 22, we will see that there are a large number of situations where someone who has committed a tort will be able to raise a *defence* to being sued for damages in respect of that tort.

1.5 The importance of being a victim

When a tort has been committed, usually only the victim of the tort will be entitled to seek a remedy. (If he does so, he is known in English law as a 'claimant', and as a 'plaintiff' in all other countries whose legal systems derive from English law. English courts stopped using the term 'plaintiff' after 1999 in an attempt to make the process of suing someone else more 'user-friendly'.)

Now – suppose that A has committed a tort by doing *x*. Who is the victim of A's tort? It's the person who had a right that A not do *x*. Or to put it another way – exactly equivalent – it's the person to whom A owed a duty not to do *x*. By doing *x*, A has committed a tort *in relation to* that person. And that person will normally be the only person entitled to bring a claim against A for what he has done. Consider, for example, the **Gullible Lovers Problem**:

---

[18] Under the Conservation of Habitats and Species Regulations 2010, reg 41(d).
[19] See Birks 1995, at 33.
[20] See Birks 1995, at 40.

Envy hates *Handsome* because *Handsome* is going out with *Beauty*, *Envy*'s ex-girlfriend. *Envy* keeps his feelings to himself, and pretends to be *Handsome*'s friend. One day, he hits on a plan to hurt *Handsome*. He tells *Handsome* that he has found out from a friend that X Corp is just about to announce that it has discovered a cure for AIDS. This is not true. In fact, *Envy* has found out that X Corp is about to announce that it is insolvent. *Envy* urges *Handsome* to buy as many shares in X Corp as he can afford. *Handsome* spends £20,000 of his own money on X Corp shares. *Handsome* also tells *Beauty* about the news about X Corp, and she spends £75,000 of her own money on X Corp shares. A week later, X Corp announces that it is insolvent, and both *Handsome* and *Beauty*'s shares become worthless.

In this situation, *Envy* has committed a tort – it was a tort for *Envy* to lie to *Handsome* with the object of getting *Handsome* to act in a particular way and with the result that *Handsome* did act in that way. The tort *Envy* committed was the tort of deceit (or fraud). Now – who was the victim of *Envy*'s tort? Who had a right against *Envy* that he not lie to *Handsome* with the object of getting *Handsome* to act in a particular way and with the result that *Handsome* did act in that way? To put it another way, the duty *Envy* had not to lie to *Handsome* etc etc – for whose benefit was that duty imposed on *Envy*? The answer is obvious: *Handsome* had a right that *Envy* not lie to him etc etc; the duty *Envy* had not to lie to *Handsome* etc etc was imposed on him for the benefit of *Handsome*. So *Handsome* was the victim of *Envy*'s tort. It follows that *Handsome* will be entitled to sue *Envy* for compensation for the losses he suffered as a result of *Envy*'s lies.

If *Beauty* wants to sue *Envy* for compensation for the losses *she* has suffered, it is not enough for her to show that she suffered those losses as a result of *Envy*'s committing a tort in relation to *Handsome*. She will have to show that *Envy*, in acting as he did, *also* committed a tort in relation to *her*, and not just a tort in relation to *Handsome*. *Beauty* will find it very hard to do this. She will find it very hard to establish that *she* had a right against *Envy* that *Envy* not lie to *Handsome*. To put it another way, she will find it very hard to show that *Envy* owed *her* a duty not to lie to *Handsome*.

There are plenty of cases that make it clear that only the victim of a tort will normally be entitled to a remedy for the fact that that tort has been committed. The most famous of them is an American case, *Palsgraf v Long Island Railroad* (1928). In that case, a traveller, T, attempted to get onto a train as it was moving away. A porter standing nearby, D, tried to help T onto the train. In doing so, D carelessly knocked a package that T was carrying to the ground. Unfortunately, the package contained fireworks, and when the package hit the ground, the fireworks exploded. The plaintiff (this was an American case, and in America people who bring legal actions are known as plaintiffs, not claimants) in the *Palsgraf* case was a woman called Helen Palsgraf, who was standing some way away. The shock of the explosion caused a weight scale, that Helen Palsgraf was standing next to, to fall over and hit her. She sued for compensation. The New York Court of Appeals dismissed her claim. As Cardozo CJ explained, D had not committed a tort *in relation to Palsgraf* in knocking T's package to the ground. He had owed T a duty to take care not to knock the package to the ground, as it was reasonably foreseeable that doing so would damage the package. But he had not owed Palsgraf a duty to take care not to knock the package to the ground as it was not – the contents of the package not being apparent to a person in D's position – reasonably foreseeable that Palsgraf would suffer any harm as a result of the package being knocked to the ground. So as Palsgraf was not the victim of any tort committed by D, she could not sue for damages.

The English version of the *Palsgraf* case is *Bourhill* v *Young* (1943). In that case, John Young was riding too fast on his motorbike and crashed into a car driven by a third party. Young died of the injuries that he suffered in the crash. At the time of the crash, Mrs Bourhill was about 50 feet away: she was on a tram and was about to get off. By the time she reached the scene of the accident, Young's body had been taken to hospital and all she could see was some of his blood on the road. Bourhill fell ill – either because of the shock of hearing the crash, or the shock of seeing the blood, or a combination of the two – and later miscarried a baby she was eight months pregnant with at the time of the accident. She sued Young's estate for damages. Her claim was dismissed by the House of Lords. It held that Young had not owed Bourhill a duty to take care not to crash his bike. It had simply not been foreseeable that doing so would result in someone like Bourhill – someone standing 50 feet away – being injured as a result of Young's crashing his bike. Of course, in carelessly crashing his bike, Young committed a tort in relation to the third party into whose car he crashed. But it was not enough for Bourhill to show that she had suffered harm as a result of Young's committing a tort in relation to that third party. She had to show that Young, in acting as he did, also committed a tort in relation to *her* – and this she could not do, for the reasons just explained.

This is a point that students always need to bear in mind whenever they consider cases where a defendant is employed to protect the interests of a person, or class of people, and then fails to do that job properly: cases like *Hill* v *Chief Constable of West Yorkshire* (1989) (where the police failed to catch the serial killer known as the 'Yorkshire Ripper' in time before he could kill his last victim, Jacqueline Hill), or *X* v *Bedfordshire County Council* (1995) (where social workers failed to investigate adequately allegations that the five children in that case were being abused or neglected) or *Capital and Counties plc* v *Hampshire County Council* (1997) (where, in two of the situations considered in that case, a fire brigade failed to put out a fire on business premises effectively, with the result that the fire later flared up again and burned the premises down), or *Kent* v *Griffiths* (2000) (where the claimant, who was having an asthma attack, stopped breathing and suffered brain damage – something that could have easily been prevented had the ambulance workers who had been summoned to take the claimant to hospital not taken so long to get to her house). There is no doubt that the defendants in all these cases failed to do their jobs properly. In so doing they did something wrong *to their employers*. But for a tort lawyer, that is irrelevant to the question of whether the claimants in these cases should have been allowed to sue the defendants. That question depends on whether the defendants, in failing to do their jobs properly, did anything wrong *to the claimants*. In other words, did the *claimants* (as opposed to the defendants' employers) have a basic right that the defendants take reasonable steps to protect their interests? And the answer is normally 'no' – tort law does not normally give us a basic right that other people save us from harm.

So students must always be on guard against the temptation to think, 'The defendants did something wrong here, and the claimants suffered loss as a result, so the claimants must be entitled to sue.' This is an easy mistake to fall into: and one from which our judges are not immune. For example, some judges are fond of beginning their judgments in cases analogous to the ones we have just mentioned by invoking, 'the rule of public policy that has first claim on the loyalty of the law: that wrongs should be remedied.'[21]

---

[21] See *X* v *Bedfordshire CC* [1995] 2 AC 633, at 663 (per Sir Thomas Bingham MR); *Gorringe* v *Calderdale MBC* [2004] 1 WLR 1057, at [2] (per Lord Steyn); *A* v *Essex CC* [2004] 1 WLR 1881, at [43] (per Hale LJ); *D* v *East Berkshire Community NHS Trust* [2005] 2 AC 373, at [24]–[25] (per Lord Bingham).

But the fact that A has committed a wrong does not tell us anything about whether B – who has suffered a loss as a result of A's actions – should be entitled to a remedy. What is crucial is to determine whether B is a victim of A's wrong – and no amount of braying that 'wrongs should be remedied' will get us any closer to understanding whether B can claim to have been a victim of A's wrong.

There is hardly any rule in English law that does not have an exception to it, and the rule that it is only the victim of a tort who will be entitled to a remedy is no exception. The most important exception to this rule applies in *wrongful death* cases – where A has committed a tort in relation to B and B has died as a result. In such a case, B's estate will be entitled to sue for damages for the actionable losses that B suffered before he died. But B's *family* will also usually be entitled to sue A for damages under the Fatal Accidents Act 1976. This is so even though it was B who was a victim of A's tort, and not B's family. B's family will, first of all, be able to sue A for 'loss of support' – that is for any loss of economic support that they would have received in the future from B had he not been killed as a result of A's tort. If B was married, then B's wife will also be able to sue A for the fixed sum of £12,980 as damages for 'bereavement'. If B was a child then B's parents will be able to sue for bereavement damages. B's funeral costs will also be recoverable from A at the suit of his estate.

1.6 The loss compensation model of tort law

Let us now turn to consider, in this section and the next, two alternative views of tort law that can be found in other texts and articles about tort law.

By far the most dominant alternative view of tort law is the *loss compensation model* of tort law, according to which tort law determines, in a case where A has caused B some kind of loss, when A will be entitled to sue B for compensation for that loss. So, for example, Lord Bingham remarked in the case of *Fairchild* v *Glenhaven Funeral Services Ltd* that, 'The overall object of tort law is to define cases in which the law may justly hold one party liable to compensate another.'[22]

On this view, tort law does not just cover the case where A commits a private wrong in relation to B, and B suffers some loss as a result, and B is entitled to sue A for compensation for that loss. Tort law *also* covers the case where A causes B to suffer some loss *without having done anything wrong* but A is still held liable to compensate B for that loss. For example, we saw earlier that the House of Lords' decision in *Donoghue* v *Stevenson* established that the manufacturer of consumer goods will owe a consumer using one of his products a duty to take care that that product is safe to use. What happens if a modern-day David Stevenson manufactures glass bottles using the safest bottle production line in the world, but nevertheless one in every million of the bottles that he produces is liable to fracture because of microscopic and undetectable impurities in the glass? If A is injured as a result of one of these bottles fracturing, A will not be able to sue the manufacturer in negligence – as he took all reasonable steps to see that the bottle would be safe to use – but A will *still* be entitled to sue the manufacturer for compensation for his injuries under the Consumer Protection Act 1987, which makes manufacturers *strictly liable* for harm done to persons as a result of their products being dangerously defective. This is an

---

[22] [2003] 1 AC 32, at [9].

example of 'compensation without wrongdoing' – even though it is impossible to say that the manufacturer did anything wrong in making glass bottles on the safest production line in the world, he is still liable to pay compensation in those one in a million cases where a bottle leaves his production line with an infinitesimally small flaw in it, and as a result fractures and injures someone.

We reject the loss compensation model of tort law, for a number of different reasons:

(1) The loss compensation model of tort law completely ignores the many non-compensatory remedies that are standardly available in tort cases. The most important of these non-compensatory remedies is the *injunction*, which is a court order requiring someone who is continually committing a tort to stop doing it. Another non-compensatory remedy that is available in some tort cases is *disgorgement damages*, which require someone who has committed a tort to give up some gain which he has obtained as a result of committing that tort.

(2) The loss compensation model of tort law cannot account for the existence of torts that are actionable *per se*: that is, torts that can be committed without causing anyone else any loss. For example, suppose that while A is on holiday, B – A's neighbour, and to whom A has given a spare key – watches the TV in A's house because hers is broken. A is not aware of this. In this situation, B has committed the tort of trespass to land – she went onto A's land without his permission. The fact that A has suffered no loss as a result of B's trespass is irrelevant: trespass to land is a tort that is actionable *per se*. The fact that B can be held liable for committing a tort in this situation is something that the loss compensation model of tort law simply cannot comprehend.

(3) The loss compensation model of tort law simply does not fit the way we think and speak about tort law.

For example, we have just seen that under the loss compensation model of tort law, liability arising under the Consumer Protection Act 1987 is counted as a form of tort liability. But no one would ever seriously say that a manufacturer who is held liable under the 1987 Act has committed a *tort* – and that is because, at the very deepest level, we must subscribe to the idea that committing a tort involves doing something wrong to someone else.

Similarly, what is called 'the rule in *Rylands* v *Fletcher*' says that if A brings onto his land something that is liable to do damage to his neighbour B's land if it escapes from A's land, then if that thing does escape and damage B's land, A will be held liable to compensate B for the damage – and this is so even if A took all due care to prevent the thing escaping. On the loss compensation model of tort law, liability arising under the rule in *Rylands* v *Fletcher* counts as a form of tort liability. But there is some significance in the fact that we talk about the *rule* in *Rylands* v *Fletcher* – hardly anyone ever talks about the *tort* in *Rylands* v *Fletcher*. Again, that must be because we subscribe at a very deep level to the idea that committing a tort involves doing something wrong to someone else – and someone who is held liable under the rule in *Rylands* v *Fletcher* has not necessarily done anything wrong to anyone else.

Again, if the government lawfully expropriates someone else's land (say) to build a new motorway, it is required to pay the landowner the fair value of the land. Interestingly, this is not an example of 'compensation without wrongdoing' that has ever gotten into the tort texts. When one of us once asked an extremely distinguished writer on tort law why this was, the response was, 'Well, it's a liability that only the State is subject to'. Surely the more convincing answer is that no one thinks that the government has committed a tort in this situation. This is again because we subscribe at a very deep level to the idea that committing a tort involves doing something wrong to someone else – and the government does no wrong when it lawfully expropriates other people's property.

Despite its fundamental flaws, the loss compensation model of tort law has proved highly influential in determining the current shape of tort law texts. Liability under the Consumer Protection Act 1987, and liability under the rule in *Rylands* v *Fletcher* are both in. The availability of injunctions in tort cases is not mentioned, or downplayed. Gain-based damages are not mentioned or reconceptualised as really compensatory in nature. Torts that are actionable *per se* are relegated to one chapter at the end of the text. Tort law in these texts becomes a ragbag of causes of action, which are treated as having nothing in common except the remedy – compensation – that you get at the end. It is no wonder that such texts confess that tort law is very difficult to understand, that it is impossible to ascribe any one aim or function to tort law, and that it is impossible to define with any precision what a tort actually is. But if tort law as presented in the texts is in a mess, it is a mess that the academics have created by subscribing to the loss compensation model of tort law. The reality is that: (i) tort law – if looked at right – is quite simple to understand, and (ii) it is possible to say clearly what the aim or function of tort law is in one sentence, and (iii) it is perfectly easy to define what a tort is.

Having said that, we have not sought to expel all forms of 'compensation without wrongdoing' from this text. It would be odd not to discuss liabilities arising under the Consumer Protection Act 1987 and under the rule in *Rylands* v *Fletcher* in a tort text as such liabilities are intended to supplement, and indeed supplant, liabilities arising under the conventional law of tort. And examiners who ask a student to discuss what liabilities 'in tort' arise out of a given situation will certainly expect the student to be willing and able to discuss, if appropriate, whether the situation gives rise to someone being held liable under the Consumer Protection Act 1987 or under the rule in *Rylands* v *Fletcher*.

1.7 The residual wrongs model of tort law

The second alternative view of tort law that we need to discuss is the *residual wrongs model of tort law*, according to which tort law is made up of all civil wrongs that are not dealt with under some other area of law – such as the law of contract, or the law of equity. (We will discuss both of these areas of law very shortly.)[23] On this view, it makes no sense to talk of tort law as having a 'function' or to think that the various torts recognised in English law have anything in common. The only function 'tort law' performs is to provide us with a title under which we can group the civil wrongs that are left over once we deduct the civil wrongs that we can make sense of as belonging to some determinate area of law such as the law of contract, or the law of equity. And the only thing that the various torts recognised in English law have in common is their orphan status as wrongs that cannot be classified as belonging to some such determinate area of the law. As Tony Weir has joked, 'Tort is what is in the tort texts and the only thing holding it together is the binding.'[24]

We disagree. The various torts gathered together in the tort law texts are not orphans, and nor are they unrelated to each other. The very fact that their daddy is not the law of contract or the law of equity tells us something about who their daddy actually is.

---

[23] See §§ 1.9, 1.10, below.
[24] Weir 2006, ix.

The torts gathered together in the tort law texts owe their status as wrongs to a consensus, evolving over time, among our lawmakers as to what the law should do by way of requiring each of us to look out for the interests of other people.[25] This consensus underlies *all* of the torts that are gathered together in the tort texts: it is imprinted on their DNA. It could hardly be otherwise. The courts could hardly draw on one moral-political vision as to what the law should do by way of requiring us to look out for each other's interests in deciding a negligence case, and then draw on a completely different vision in deciding a false imprisonment case.[26]

Some might argue, against what we have said in the preceding paragraph: 'But what about public nuisance? That is a completely different kind of tort to all the other torts gathered together in the tort law texts. Surely that shows that the residual wrongs view of tort law is correct, and that the various torts gathered together in the texts really have nothing in common?' Indeed, public nuisance is a very strange 'tort'. To explain: there are many different ways of committing a public nuisance, but for our purposes, you should just consider the case where A blocks the highway for a long time, or dumps oil into the sea. In such a case, A will be guilty of committing a wrong – the wrong of public nuisance. Now, suppose various people have suffered loss as a result of A's actions. In such a case, only those who have suffered 'special damage' as a result of A's actions – that is, damage that is significantly worse than that suffered by everyone else – will be entitled to sue A for damages. This is a very different rule from the normal rule that applies when A has committed a tort – where, as we have seen, only the victim of A's tort will normally be entitled to sue A for damages, and this is so even if the victim of A's tort has suffered a comparatively trivial loss as a result and someone else has suffered a devastating loss.

But does this show that the residual wrongs view of tort law is correct? Not really. It could be argued – and we would argue – that public nuisance is not a tort at all. It is not a private wrong. Rather, it is a public wrong – involving the breach of a duty imposed for the benefit of society as a whole – akin to the wrong of disturbing a protected animal's habitat. The only reason it has gotten into the tort texts is because they are wedded either to the loss compensation model of tort law (under which claims for compensation for loss under the law on public nuisance count as part of the law of tort) or to the residual wrongs model of tort law (under which public nuisance counts as a tort because it is a wrong that is capable of giving rise to a civil action for damages and cannot be classified as arising under the law of contract or the law of equity).

So the strangeness of the law on public nuisance does not, of and in itself, establish that the residual wrongs view of tort law is correct. Proponents of such a view would be on firmer ground if they could show that the various well-established torts – such as negligence,

---

[25] There are, at the moment, at least three rival accounts as to what private law – the bit of the law that requires us to look out for other people's interests – should do. There is the increasingly influential view (advanced by Weinrib 1995, and Ripstein 2006a, 2006b, 2007b, 2009, 2015) that private law should give effect to the demands of *Kantian right*, according to which each of us is entitled to determine for ourselves – independently of anyone else – what purposes we will pursue, and private law should prevent people from acting in ways that subvert our independence as persons. There is the *Rawlsian/contractualist* view (originating in Rawls 1971) that private law should give effect to whatever legally enforceable rights we would all agree that we should have against each other if we made such an agreement under fair conditions. And there is the *natural law view* (originating in Finnis 1980, now Finnis 2011) according to which private law should, by giving us legally enforceable rights against each other, aim to enable each of us to live a flourishing life; that is, a life which participates in a full range of objective human goods.

[26] Though this is not to deny that their understanding of these matters can evolve over time.

or the various forms of trespass to the person, or the various torts to property – have *nothing* to do with each other. But no one has ever convincingly managed to do this.

1.8 Tort law and human rights

English law has had a law on human rights as long as it has had a law of tort. That is because most of the rights that tort law recognises us as having are enjoyed by us by virtue of our humanity. The reason why we have rights under the law of trespass not to be touched without our consent, and not to be threatened with imminent violence, and not to be falsely imprisoned is because our basic dignity as human beings means that it would be wrong to treat us in those ways. And the reason why the English law of tort developed *beyond* the law of trespass was because the law of trespass – with its emphasis on the direct interference with another's person – was inadequate to give effect to the full range of rights that our humanity deserves. Of course, there are some rights that tort law gives us that cannot be said to rest on our basic dignity as human beings; for example, rights emerging out of 'assumptions of responsibility' by one person to another.[27] But if we ask, in relation to most of the rights we have under the law, 'Why do we have *these* rights, and not some inferior set of rights?' the answer will invariably be, 'Because all human beings should have at least *these* rights.'

Perhaps it sounds odd to claim that the law of tort, for the most part, rests on a vision of what human rights we have.[28] If it does sound surprising then this is probably due to the fact that when the language of 'human rights' entered popular culture[29] the human rights concerned were primarily thought of as rights that individuals had, or ought to have had, against their governments. Thus in the 1970s dissidents in Eastern Europe argued that their governments were violating their 'human rights', and anti-Communist politicians and journalists in the West beat out a similar message. Similarly, when in the 1980s, politicians and journalists on the left also started talking the language of human rights, it was usually to argue that governments in the West were also guilty of human rights violations, particularly in relation to the way intelligence agencies and police forces

---

[27] See below, §§ 5.9–5.10.

[28] The idea occasionally peeps through in the caselaw, such as *Ilott* v *Wilkes* (1820) 3 B & Ald 304, 106 ER 674, holding that an occupier of premises who sets a spring gun on his premises to deter trespassers must give trespassers as much notice as possible of the existence of the spring gun on the ground that 'Humanity requires that the fullest notice possible should be given, and the law of England will not sanction what is inconsistent with humanity' (per Best J, at 319 (B & Ald), 680 (ER)). Also the great judgment of Lord Mansfield in *Somerset* v *Stewart* (1772) Lofft 1, 98 ER 499, holding that a slave who has arrived in England cannot be held against his will by his purported master: 'The state of slavery is. . . so odious, that nothing can be suffered to support it, but positive law. Whatever inconveniences, therefore, may follow from a decision, I cannot say this case is allowed or approved by the law of England . . .' (at 19 (Lofft), 510 (ER)).

[29] It is not easy to date when the notion of 'human rights' entered general discourse. Thus while the United Nations proclaimed the Universal Declaration of Human Rights in 1948, George Orwell's classic anti-totalitarian work *1984* – written in the same year – contains plenty of references to humanity, the importance of 'staying human' and the significance of the 'human mind' as a vehicle for grasping and hanging onto the truth; but not one reference to 'human rights'. Many commentators would argue that the relevant date was during the 1970s: for example, Moyn 2010 reports (at p. 4) that in 1977 the *New York Times* used the phrase 'human rights' approximately five times more frequently than in any previous year. See also Moyn 2014.

operated. Of course since then the language of human rights has been used in a much wider range of contexts. Indeed, today it is plausible to argue that 'if the discourse of peacetime global society can be said to have a common moral language, it is that of human rights.'[30] But it is still the case that most of the plethora of pleas, demands and complaints, which are made using the language of human rights, are directed at governments. Nonetheless, while this means that we most often *hear* human rights invoked in contexts where the key issue is the relationship between individuals and their governments, there is no reason why we cannot acknowledge that most of the rights that individuals have against other individuals are similarly founded on the equal dignity and freedom of all human beings. Moreover, as we will see, there are important connections between the rights that individuals can invoke against their governments and the rights that they can rely on in a tort claim.

For your purposes, the most important document on human rights that you have to know about is the European Convention on Human Rights (or 'ECHR', for short). This Convention was drawn up in 1950, in the aftermath of the Second World War, and set out a number of different 'human rights' that states signing the Convention pledged to observe. They include the right to life (Article 2), the right not to be subjected to torture or to inhuman and degrading treatment (Article 3), the right not to be enslaved or compelled to perform forced labour (Article 4), the right to liberty and security of person (Article 5), the right to a fair trial (Article 6), the right not to be retrospectively convicted of committing an offence (Article 7), the right to respect for private and family life (Article 8), the right to freedom of thought, conscience and religion (Article 9), the right to freedom of expression (Article 10), the right to freedom of peaceful assembly and freedom of association (Article 11), the right to marry (Article 12), the right not to be discriminated against in the enjoyment of the other rights and freedoms (Article 14), the right to peaceful enjoyment of possessions (First Protocol, Article 1), the right to education (First Protocol, Article 2), and the right to free elections (First Protocol, Article 3).

All the member states of what is called the 'Council of Europe' are signatories to the ECHR. This now comprises 47 states – virtually all of the European states, including Russia and other states from the former Soviet Union. Importantly, the ECHR is not a product of the European Union (comprising 28 states) – a point sometimes lost on journalists who regularly ascribe responsibility for decisions of the European Court of Human Rights (ECtHR) to the European Union.[31] Students should be careful not to fall into the same error. The ECtHR – which sits in Strasbourg, France – is a wholly different institution from the Court of Justice, often called the European Court of Justice (or 'ECJ', for short) by English lawyers,[32] which sits in Luxembourg and interprets and applies the law of the European Union.

---

[30] Beitz 2009, 2.

[31] For example, the *Yorkshire Post* of 3 November 2010 carried the headline: 'EU court ruling means prisoners will have right to vote.' The article under the headline referred to a 2005 decision of the European Court of Human Rights – *Hirst* v *UK (No 2)* (2006) 42 EHRR 41 – that a blanket ban on prisoners being allowed to vote was inconsistent with Article 3 of the First Protocol to the ECHR. (Article 3 provides that 'The High Contracting Parties undertake to hold free elections at reasonable intervals by secret ballot, under conditions which will ensure the free expression of the opinion of the people in the choice of the legislature.') And the *Guardian* on 4 January 2015 apologised for making the same mistake in the previous day's headline, 'PM backs 100-year jail sentences to avoid EU ruling on whole-life tariffs' – the ruling concerned was one made by the European Court of Human Rights in Strasbourg, not by the EU!

[32] Officially, the Court of Justice is one of three parts of an institution called the Court of Justice of the European Union.

Although English lawyers played a large part in drafting the original text of the ECHR, there are two major inconsistencies between that text and the centuries-old understanding of what human rights we enjoy against each other that was developed under the English law of tort.

(1) *Exigibility.* The ECHR only imposes obligations on the states that have signed it. It does not impose obligations, directly, on private individuals. This is understandable. The lawyers who drafted the ECHR had in mind the state-sponsored atrocities that took place in Nazi Germany after 1933, and wanted to put the ECHR in place to prevent such atrocities ever taking place again. But the idea of human rights only being exigible against the state is a paradoxical one, and one that did not form part of the traditional understanding of human rights as developed under the English law of tort. On that understanding, the rights we were given by the English law of tort were exigible against *everyone*.

(2) *Acts and omissions.* The ECHR – as it has been subsequently interpreted by the ECtHR – does not only impose *negative* obligations on the states who are bound by it, that is obligations not to do something positive that would violate someone's rights under the ECHR, such as the right to life (Article 2), or the right not to be subjected to torture or to inhuman or degrading treatment or punishment (Article 3). It also imposes *positive* obligations on signatory states to take reasonable steps to protect people's rights under the ECHR, such as the right to life, and the right not to be subjected to inhuman or degrading treatment. So a state – or representative of the state – that fails to respond adequately to reports that it has received that *Bethan* is in imminent danger of being killed by an ex-boyfriend, or that *Benedict* is being sexually abused by his parents, may be found to have violated their rights under the ECHR as a result of its failure to act. The idea that we might have a human right to be saved from harm by the state, or by its representatives, is inconsistent with the English law of tort's traditional understanding of what rights we have against each other. That understanding is summed up by the old saying: 'Not doing is no trespass'. Under the law of trespass, if you did not do anything, you could not be found to have done anything wrong to anyone else. While the law of tort has expanded beyond the law of trespass, it has not abandoned the idea that, absent special circumstances, there is nothing wrong with failing to save someone else from harm. Even today, strangers are allowed to walk past people lying unconscious in the street without any legal sanction at all.

These inconsistencies between the ECHR and the indigenous understanding of what rights we have proved relatively unproblematic for the first 45 years of the ECHR's existence. This is because the ECHR was unenforceable in UK courts. So the UK courts only had to apply one understanding – the indigenous understanding – of what rights we have against each other when deciding whether or not a particular defendant had wronged a particular claimant. If an individual wanted to complain that the United Kingdom had not granted her the rights that it undertook to provide when it signed the ECHR then she had to head to Strasbourg, and bring a claim against the United Kingdom there, before the ECtHR. That all changed with the enactment of the Human Rights Act 1998 ('HRA' for short), which made the ECHR enforceable in UK courts, and came into effect on 2 October 2000.

The *direct* effect of the HRA is to make it unlawful (under s 6) for 'a public authority to act in a way which is incompatible with a Convention right' and to confer on the courts the power (under s 8) to 'grant such relief or remedy, or make such order, within its powers as it considers just and appropriate' when a public authority has acted in a way which was incompatible with a Convention right. As a result, a claimant who wants to sue a public body in an English court for damages for something it has done after 2 October 2000 need no longer rely exclusively on the law of tort to bring her claim; she could try instead to argue that the public body has violated her rights under the ECHR and obtain a remedy that way. In cases where a public body is merely guilty of an omission – a failure to save the claimant from harm – this is a boon for claimants. As we will see,[33] claimants cannot normally sue a public body for an omission under the law of tort, but as we have just seen, it *is* possible in certain circumstances for claimants to argue that a public body has violated their Convention rights through a mere omission.

The *indirect* effects of the HRA have been twofold. First, in situations where the scope of tort law depends on statutes the UK courts are now obliged to interpret those statutes, so far as it is possible to do so, to make them compatible with Convention rights.[34] Secondly, in situations where the rules of tort law are part of the common law the courts have been put under pressure to develop and reshape those rules to make them more 'Convention-friendly'. This pressure takes a variety of different forms.

(1) *Negative obligations.* Under s 6(3) of the HRA, 'a court or tribunal' counts as a 'public authority' for the purposes of s 6 of the HRA. This has the effect of subjecting UK courts to the ECHR, including the *negative* obligations it imposes on states not to do something *positive* that would violate someone's rights under the ECHR. So, since the HRA was enacted, the UK courts have had to be careful not to decide tort cases in a way that could allow the losing party to say that the court directly violated his rights under the ECHR in the way it decided the case. The courts have been particularly mindful, in the way they decide tort cases, of the possibilities: (i) that, by dismissing a claimant's claim too peremptorily, they might violate the claimant's rights under Article 6 of the ECHR to 'a fair and public hearing' in 'the determination of his civil rights and obligations'; and (ii) that, by sanctioning something a defendant has said, or by preventing through an injunction a defendant from saying something he wants to say, they might violate the defendant's rights under Article 10 to 'freedom of expression'. How the courts have reacted to these possibilities will be discussed further below.

(2) *Positive obligations.* Because 'a court or tribunal' counts as a 'public authority' for the purposes of s 6 of the HRA, it has been argued that the HRA has the effect of imposing on the courts the *positive* obligations that the ECHR imposes on states to take reasonable steps to protect people's enjoyment of the rights they have under the ECHR. Some have argued that the courts are, as a result, legally required under the HRA to develop and expand the law of tort to give greater protection (in tort) to the rights that people are granted by the ECHR.[35] If this view is correct – and one of us is very firmly of the view that it is not[36] (and the other fully agrees) – then it might be argued that the courts are duty-bound under the HRA to revise the well-established tort rule that absent special circumstances there is no liability for omissions, at least in cases where life or freedom from cruel treatment is at stake. The argument is based on the premise that the existence of such a rule means that the law of tort is not doing as much it could and should to protect people's rights to life and to be free from cruel treatment under the ECHR, and that therefore the courts are in breach of their obligations under the HRA by maintaining such a rule.

---

[33] See below, Chapter 6.

[34] HRA, s 3.

[35] See, in particular, Hunt 1998.

[36] See Bagshaw 2011b.

While the judges might deny this, it is hard to avoid the impression that it was arguments such as these that led them, soon after the enactment of the HRA, to sweep away the traditional tort law rule that there is no free-standing right not to have one's privacy invaded, with the result that the legal protection for people's Article 8 rights 'to respect for [their] private and family life, [their] home and [their] correspondence' was considerably enhanced.[37]

(3) *Pressure for harmony.* Even in situations where the courts are not *obliged* to develop the law in some way it would be surprising if the courts did not feel some awkwardness or embarrassment when faced by a claimant who can sue a defendant under the HRA but not under the law of tort. If tort law cannot help those who have been badly treated or let down by public officials or state institutions then this tends to make the home-grown law of tort seem fusty and undeveloped compared with the newer and more vigorous HRA. If the claimant's rights were actually violated (as a claim under the HRA demonstrates), why does the law of tort not recognise this?

Twice in recent years – first in *Van Colle* v *Chief Constable of Hertfordshire Police, Smith* v *Chief Constable of Sussex Police* (2009), and then in *Michael* v *Chief Constable of South Wales Police* (2015) – it was argued that in a case where the police had failed to save someone from being killed or seriously injured by an attacker, the judges should eliminate any distinction between the law of negligence and the HRA and allow the police to be sued in negligence if the police's failure to act violated the deceased's right to life under Article 2 of the ECHR. And twice the UK's highest court (by a substantial majority both times: 4:1 in *Van Colle, Smith* and 5:2 in *Michael*) has rejected this argument, on the basis that there was no necessity to bring the law of negligence into line with the HRA and that doing so would undermine the special limits that Parliament had placed on when claims under the HRA could be brought.[38]

However, the fact that in these two cases combined, the Law Lords and Supreme Court Justices ruled by nine to three that the law of negligence should not be brought into harmony with the scope of claims under Article 2 does not mean that other judges will not be subject to *pressure* to make other parts of the law of tort harmonious with other Convention rights. Many lawyers share the sentiment expressed by Lord Bingham in *Van Colle* (2009): '. . . one would normally be surprised if conduct which violated a fundamental right or freedom of the individual did not find reflection in a body of law as sensitive to human needs as the common law.'[39]

1.9 Tort law and contract law

As we have seen, it is tort law that determines what basic rights we enjoy against other people, and what remedies will be available when those rights are violated. It is contract law that provides us with the facility to alter the rights that tort law provides us with – either by entering into contracts that give us extra rights against other people that tort law does not give us (contracting *on top of* tort law) or by entering into contracts that reduce the rights that tort law gives us against other people (contracting *out of* tort law).

---

[37] See below, Chapter 17.
[38] For further discussion of this point, see below, § 6.1(C), and Nolan 2013b.
[39] [2009] 1 AC 225, at [58].

Tort law draws a fundamental distinction between acts and omissions – that is, between doing something that makes someone worse off than they would have been if you had done nothing, and failing to do something that would have made them better off than they would have been if you had done nothing. Tort law is far more willing to give us rights that people not make us worse off, than it is to give us rights that other people make us better off. Generally speaking, if you want to have a right that someone do something for you that will make you better off, then you need to enter into a contract with them that provides that they will act in that way. But to obtain such a right, you will normally need to pay. Promises are not normally contractually binding unless something – called *consideration* by the lawyers – has been given in return for them. So tort rights come free of charge, but are limited in what they will do for you; contract rights can do far more for you, but you normally need to pay for them.

The need to contract on top of tort law, and the iron distinction between tort rights and contract rights, has been lessened in the past 30 years or so by the increasing willingness of the courts to recognise that if A 'assumes a responsibility' to B, then B will have a right in tort that A take care to do whatever it is that he 'assumed a responsibility' for doing. It is not entirely clear what 'assuming a responsibility' to someone else involves – but the available authorities indicate that A will 'assume a responsibility' to B if he indicates to B (or reasonably appears to be indicating to B) that she can rely on him to act in a particular way, and she does so rely on him. So tort rights arising out of 'assumptions of responsibility' do not have to be paid for, but they only arise in special circumstances – to establish such a right against someone else, you have to show that they encouraged you to rely on them and you did so rely.

Turning to the topic of contracting out of tort law, it is an interesting question whether any of the basic rights that tort law gives us are *inalienable* – that is, they simply cannot be given up, no matter how much you might want to give them up. In considering this question, we need to draw a distinction between giving up a right here and now, and giving up rights in the future. So far as giving up a right here and now is concerned, the law recognises that '*volenti non fit injuria*' – no wrong (*injuria*) is done to the willing (*volenti*). If you are happy for someone to lock you up or beat you up, you cannot later turn round and complain that your rights have been violated. (Though the courts will require clear evidence before they will accept that you were genuinely *volenti* as to what was done to you.)

But how far can you contract to give up your basic rights in the future – so that someone would be allowed in the future to lock you up or beat you up, even if you were *not* happy to be treated that way at the time they were locking you up or beating you up? It is now recognised that a cinema that sells you a ticket to watch a film on its premises does thereby, and for the duration of the film, surrender the right that it would normally have as a landowner that you not stay on its premises if you have been asked to leave. (Though the cinema will still have a right that you leave the premises if you start being a nuisance to other customers.) At the opposite extreme, a contract of slavery will be void – so if you agreed with a TV production company to be locked up in a house for six months and have your doings in the house continuously televised, it seems highly unlikely that they would be allowed to keep you locked in if you demanded to be let out after three weeks.

So far, we have been looking at how people can contract on top of tort law to give themselves contractual rights that tort law will not provide them for free, and how far people can contract out of tort law to modify the rights and remedies for violation of those rights that tort law would otherwise give them. But the very act of entering into a contract can give rise to rights in tort:

(1) If *Worker* undertakes in a contract with *Homeowner* to install a new kitchen in *Homeowner*'s house, *Worker* will almost invariably be found by the courts to have 'assumed a responsibility' to install the kitchen with a reasonable degree of care and skill – with the result that he will owe *Homeowner* a duty in tort to install that kitchen with a reasonable degree of care and skill.[40] So if he carelessly fails to do a good job, *Homeowner* can not only sue him for committing a breach of contract; she can also sue him (concurrently) in tort (under the tort of negligence) for failing to do a good job in installing the kitchen.

(2) If *Magician* undertakes in a contract with *Mother* to perform at a birthday party *Mother* is throwing for her son, then *Mother* will have a right against everyone else that they not persuade *Magician* to breach his contract with *Mother* unless they have a really good reason for doing so. Anyone who violates this right will commit the tort of *inducing a breach of contract* in relation to *Mother*.

1.10 Tort law and equity

Before the end of the nineteenth century, the English legal system could be roughly divided into three parts. There was, first of all, Parliament, which changed the law by enacting *statutes* that all English courts were and are required to give effect to under the doctrine of *Parliamentary supremacy*, or *sovereignty*. Secondly, there were the Courts of Common Law, from which the *common law* emerged, made up of the rules and principles given effect to by the common law judges deciding cases argued before them. Thirdly, there was the Court of Chancery, which would in its judgments supplement or modify the common law as given effect to by the Courts of Common Law. The rules and principles given effect to by the Court of Chancery were known as *equity*. Equity modified and supplemented the common law in three significant ways:

(1) *Enforcing common law rights.* Where a claimant's rights at common law were being violated, or in danger of being violated, by a defendant but damages (the only remedy he would be able to get from the Courts of Common Law for the violation of his rights) would be an inadequate remedy, the Court of Chancery would grant the claimant an *injunction*, requiring the defendant not to violate the claimant's rights and threatening him with imprisonment if he did.[41]

(2) *Recognising equitable rights.* Where a claimant had no rights that were enforceable in the Courts of Common Law, but the Court of Chancery thought that justice demanded that they should recognise that the claimant had a right against someone else, the Court of Chancery would recognise that the claimant had such a right – called an *equitable right* – and grant the claimant remedies – *equitable remedies* – when that right was violated (which violation would be known as an *equitable wrong*). The most obvious example of such rights are the equitable rights that the beneficiary under a *trust* was recognised as having,

---

[40] Though see the strange decision of the Court of Appeal in *Robinson* v *Jones (Contractors) Ltd* [2012] QB 44, which seems hostile to finding an 'assumption of responsibility' here.

[41] This is where we get the saying 'Equity acts *in personam*' from: '*in personam*' here means 'against the body'. If you didn't do what the Court of Chancery told you to do, you would be thrown into prison, rather than having your goods seized (which was the way the Courts of Common Law would enforce their judgments).

that the trust property be applied for the benefit of the beneficiary by the trustee of the trust, the legal owner of the trust property.

(3) *Modifying common law rights.* If a claimant did have rights that were enforceable in the Courts of Common Law, but the Court of Chancery took the view that it would be unjust – or *unconscionable* – for the claimant to be allowed to exercise those rights, then the Court of Chancery would prevent the claimant enforcing those rights by issuing an injunction against the claimant. This created tensions between the Courts of Common Law and the Court of Chancery that were only resolved by a declaration of King James I in 1615 that in any conflict between the common law and equity, equity was to prevail.

Tort law was a creation of the Courts of Common Law. Claims in tort were brought in the Courts of Common Law, and could only succeed if the claimant had a right that was recognised under the common law. As we have just seen, the Court of Chancery was willing to grant injunctions to tort claimants for whom damages were an inadequate remedy, but that was the Court of Chancery's only involvement in the law of tort. The equitable rights that were recognised in the Court of Chancery and enforced by the Court of Chancery had nothing to do with the law of tort. To say that an equitable wrong was a tort would have been regarded as complete nonsense by a nineteenth-century lawyer.

At the end of the nineteenth century, the formal distinction between the Courts of Common Law and the Court of Chancery was abolished by the Judicature Acts, which created one unified court system, known as the 'Supreme Court of Judicature'.[42] No longer would claimants have to choose which court to plead their case in. All courts would from now on practise the same law. But that law was made up of three parts, corresponding to the three parts of the legal system before the Judicature Acts: statute law, common law, and equity. Fusion of the courts did not abolish the distinction between common law and equity; and those branches of the law continued evolving along their own paths. While claimants now all go to the same court to have their cases heard, those cases are still presented as being 'a claim at common law' or 'a claim in equity' or even 'a claim at common law and in equity', and the remedies that are available to a claimant do still vary – at least in language, if not in substance – depending on whether he or she is making 'a claim at common law' or a 'claim in equity'.

The fact that fusion did not eliminate the difference between common law and equity means that among lawyers the concept of a 'tort' has retained its roots in the common law. You would still get some very funny looks from practising lawyers if you attempted to assert that a breach of trust is a tort. A breach of trust is a wrong, but because it is a wrong that has its roots in the law of equity, practising lawyers do not think of it as being a tort. And they are right to do so. It is dangerous to use old words in new ways: associations that have built up around the old word may infect the new usage in undesirable ways. Perhaps one day this text will evolve into one on 'The Law of Wrongs' (or 'Wrongs Law'), and will treat of all the rights we have against each other and what remedies will be available when those rights are violated, without making any distinction between which rights, historically, are 'legal' in nature and which 'equitable'. That would be a more rational development than trying to assert, as a matter of linguistic *fiat*, that 'all wrongs are torts' and that a tort text will deal with all wrongs.

---

[42] Renamed the 'Supreme Court of England and Wales' by s 1(1) of the Supreme Court Act 1981, and then re-renamed the 'Senior Courts of England and Wales' by s 59 of the Constitutional Reform Act 2005, to avoid confusion with the 'Supreme Court of the United Kingdom', which replaced the House of Lords as the highest court in the UK on 1 October 2009.

One wrong which, because of its history, escapes clear classification as a tort or an equitable wrong is the wrong of *invasion of privacy* – or, more accurately, the wrong of *unauthorised disclosure of private information to another*. It has its formal roots in the equitable wrong of breach of confidence, which involves disclosing to a third party secrets that you have been told by someone else. As a result, most judges regard the wrong of invasion of privacy (to use the simpler expression for the moment) as being an equitable wrong and not a tort. However, the wrong of invasion of privacy seems to have very little in common with the equitable wrong of breach of confidence: you can sue someone for committing the wrong of invasion of privacy even if what they are disclosing was not told to them by you or anyone else, and even if what they are disclosing is not secret anymore. Moreover, the remedies available for the wrong of invasion of privacy seem to have more in common with the remedies available for a tort than an equitable wrong. For example, you can claim compensatory damages if someone invades your privacy – when the idea of compensatory damages being available for equitable wrongdoing is one that is still alien to most equity lawyers. Given this, there does not seem to be any danger involved in calling the wrong of 'invasion of privacy' a tort – and indeed, we do deal with that wrong in this text. In any case, given the close links between the law on privacy and other well-established areas of tort law, such as the law of defamation, the law of malicious falsehood, the law on trespass to land, and the law on passing off, it would be strange not to deal with actionable invasions of privacy in a tort text.

1.11 Tort law and statute law

While tort law has its origins in the decisions of the Courts of Common Law, statute law does have an effect on tort law in a number of different ways:

A. Creating new torts

Parliament can create *statutory torts*, by endowing people with statutory rights and making it clear that the violation of those rights is to be *actionable in tort* – that is, remedied in the same way as a normal common law tort.

Parliament creates a statutory right whenever it imposes a duty on someone for the benefit of a particular individual. For example, s 1 of the Protection from Harassment Act 1997 provides (with certain exceptions) that if you know or ought to know that your doing *x* would amount to harassment of a particular individual, you must not do *x*. That duty is imposed on you for the benefit of the particular individual who would be harassed by your doing *x*, and so that individual has a statutory right that you not do *x*. Violation of that right will amount to a statutory tort as s 3 of the 1997 Act provides that 'an actual or apprehended breach of s 1 may be the subject of a claim in civil proceedings by the person who is or may be the victim of the course of conduct in question.'

What if Parliament creates a statutory right and makes it clear that a violation of that right is to be remedied in a particular way, but not in the same way as a normal common law tort? This is the case with the Human Rights Act 1998, which gives each of us a right that public bodies not act in ways that are inconsistent with our rights as set out in the European Convention on Human Rights (ECHR). Section 8 of the 1998 Act sets down specific rules as to how a breach of the Act is to be remedied: a 'just and appropriate' remedy is to be awarded, and such a remedy is not to include an order to pay damages unless such an award 'is necessary to afford just satisfaction to the person in whose favour it is made'. This is a very different set of remedial rules from those that obtain when a normal common law tort is committed, under which the victim of a tort can normally expect to obtain damages for any losses caused by the tort that are not too remote a consequence of that tort's being committed. Given the remedial regime set out in s 8 of the 1998 Act, it would be wrong (because liable to create confusion) to say that a public body will commit a 'tort' if it acts inconsistently with someone's rights as set out in the ECHR. It will commit a private wrong (a breach of statutory duty), but not a tort.

What if Parliament creates a statutory right but does not make it clear one way or the other whether or not violation of such a right is to be actionable in tort? Unfortunately, this is often the case – either because of Parliamentary *optimism* (Parliament may assume no one would ever fail to do what Parliament tells them to do) or because of Parliamentary *cowardice* (imposing statutory duties is an easy way of gaining popularity with the people who benefit from those duties, while specifying what unpleasant consequences should follow if the duty is breached is an easy way of losing popularity with those who are subject to those duties). The most straightforward solution would be to say that when such a right is violated the only remedy is to seek a declaration that it has been violated, or when it is clear that such a right might be violated, the only remedy is to seek an injunction to prevent the violation. Unfortunately, the courts have bravely decided that even in such cases, it should be possible – if one looks hard enough – to determine whether or not Parliament intended that a violation of such a right should be actionable in tort, thus generating a huge amount of very uninteresting caselaw on whether the violation of a particular statutory provision does or does not amount to a statutory tort.

B. Modifying tort law

The second way statute law can have an effect on tort law is by modifying or extending: (1) the rights that we enjoy under tort law; and (2) the remedies that may be obtained when someone commits a tort.

For example, under the common law, an occupier of premises would only owe a trespasser on his land a duty to take steps to protect him from some danger on his land if 'common humanity' demanded that he offer him such protection. This rule was replaced by the Occupiers' Liability Act 1984, which provided that an occupier would owe a trespasser a duty to take steps to protect him from some danger on his land if: (i) the occupier knew or ought to know of the danger; (ii) the occupier knew or ought to know that a trespasser might come into the vicinity of that danger; and (iii) the danger was one which the occupier reasonably could be expected to offer some protection against.

A common law rule that affected the remedies available to the victim of a tort went like this: if *Fool* committed the tort of negligence in relation to *Victim* by breaching a duty of care owed to *Victim*, and *Victim* was partly to blame for the losses she suffered as a result of *Fool*'s breach, then *Victim* could not sue *at all* for compensation for those losses. This very strict rule was replaced by the Law Reform (Contributory Negligence) Act 1945, which provided that *Victim* should be allowed to sue for compensation for her losses, but the damages recoverable should be reduced so far as is 'just and equitable having regard to' how far *Victim* was to blame for the fact that she suffered those losses.

C. Preventing contracting out of tort law

The third way that statute law can have an effect on tort law is by preventing people 'contracting out' of tort law. The most obvious example of this is s 65 of the Consumer Rights Act 2015, which provides that any contractual provision which purports to prevent an individual or his estate suing a business in negligence for killing or injuring him is automatically of no effect.

D. Requiring the courts to develop tort law in certain ways

The fourth way that statute law can have an effect on tort law is by imposing duties on the courts to develop tort law in certain ways. There is only one example of this, and it is arguable how far this example goes.

Under the Human Rights Act 1998, the courts count as public bodies, and therefore have a duty under the 1998 Act – like other public bodies – not to act in ways that are inconsistent with individuals' rights as set out in the ECHR. So the courts have a duty under the 1998 Act to make sure that tort law – as it is applied in the UK courts – does not work in ways that violate individuals' rights under the ECHR to freedom of speech (Article 10), or to a fair trial of their civil rights and obligations (Article 6), and so on. That is not controversial.

What is more controversial is the argument that the courts have a duty under the Human Rights Act 1998 to develop tort law as it applies *between private individuals* so as to give greater protection to people's rights under the ECHR to life (Article 2), not to be subjected to inhuman or degrading treatment (Article 3), and to respect for their private and family life (Article 8) than they have at the moment. The argument is that just as a police officer would be acting inconsistently with an individual's right to life under Article 2 of the ECHR if he watched that individual being stabbed to death and did nothing to intervene,[43] the courts also act inconsistently with people's rights to life under Article 2 when they sit on their hands and fail to develop tort law so that it does more to protect people from being killed, by – for example – failing to get rid of the rule that there is normally no liability in tort for failing to save a stranger from drowning. The argument is very strained, for two reasons. First of all, it is clear in the case of the police officer that if he intervened, then the stab victim's life would probably be saved. It is not at all clear that making people liable in tort for failing to save strangers from drowning would have the net effect of saving more people's lives. Secondly, even if UK law could do more than it does at the moment to protect people's rights to life, it is not clear why the burden of doing more to save people's lives should fall on *tort* law, rather than some other area of the law, such as the criminal law.

Perhaps because of the weakness of this argument, the Human Rights Act 1998 has only had a patchy effect in terms of inducing the courts to develop tort law so as to give people greater protection against their various rights under the ECHR being violated:

(1) We start with *Article 2(1)*, which provides that 'Everyone's right to life shall be protected by law. No one shall be deprived of his life intentionally . . .' This Article has not, so far, had much of an indirect effect on English tort law. As we have seen, in *Van Colle* v *Chief Constable of Hertfordshire Police*, *Smith* v *Chief Constable of Sussex Police* (2009), and

---

[43] *Osman* v *United Kingdom* [1998] EHRR 101.

in *Michael* v *Chief Constable of South Wales Police* (2015), the House of Lords and the UK Supreme Court rejected attempts to argue that the police's liabilities in negligence should be expanded so as to make them liable in negligence for failing to protect someone whom they know is in danger of being killed or injured by someone else. Given this, it seems impossible that – for the foreseeable future at least – the courts will accept that their obligations under the Human Rights Act require them to modify the general rule in English tort law against liability for omissions (absent special circumstances) so as to protect more effectively people's rights to life under Article 2.

(2) Turning to *Article 3*, this provides that 'No one shall be subjected to torture or to inhuman or degrading treatment or punishment.' Unlike Article 2, Article 3 has had a very significant indirect effect on English tort law. The story is told in more detail below,[44] but briefly: until the HRA came into effect, the English courts had maintained that local authorities could not be sued in negligence for failing properly to investigate allegations that children were in danger of being abused or neglected. The courts could have justified this rule by reference to the general rule in English tort law against liability for omissions.[45] Instead, the courts held that it was necessary for local authorities not to be held liable in negligence for their failures to protect children from abuse or neglect because the prospect of their being held liable might cause them to adopt a very defensive mindset and take a lot of children into care who were not in fact in any danger of being abused or neglected.[46] However, after the HRA came into force it became clear that local authorities that had failed to take steps to protect children whom they knew were in danger of being abused or neglected could be sued *under the 1998 Act* for violating those children's rights under Article 3.[47] Given this, the courts no longer thought there was any point in ruling that local authorities could not be sued *in negligence* for failing to protect children from being abused or neglected and in 2004, the Court of Appeal held that a local authority that received a report that a child was in danger of being abused or neglected *would* owe that child a duty to take care to investigate that report properly.[48] Had the HRA never been enacted, it is very doubtful that this development in the law of negligence would have happened.

(3) *Article 5(1)* provides that:

Everyone has the right to liberty and security of person. No one shall be deprived of his liberty save in the following cases and in accordance with a procedure prescribed by law:

(a) [imprisonment after conviction];

(b) [arrest or detention for disobeying a court order];

(c) [arrest or detention of a person to bring him to court on reasonable suspicion of having committed an offence, or to prevent him committing an offence, or fleeing the scene of an offence];

(d) [detention of a minor for educational supervision];

(e) [detention of persons to prevent spreading of infectious diseases, or persons of unsound mind, alcoholics, drug addicts or vagrants];

(f) [detention of persons to stop them entering into the country illegally, or to deport or extradite them].

---

[44] See below, § 6.11.

[45] Though this would not have been sufficient in those cases where a local authority caused damage (usually psychiatric harm) by intervening and removing a child from its parents unnecessarily.

[46] See *X* v *Bedfordshire CC* [1995] 2 AC 633, 650.

[47] See *Z* v *United Kingdom* [2001] 2 FLR 612.

[48] *D* v *East Berkshire Community Health NHS Trust* [2004] QB 558.

It is uncertain how far the courts will take into account Article 5(1) in developing the common law on when someone is allowed to deprive someone of their liberty. It was conceded in *Austin* v *Commissioner of Police of the Metropolis* (2009) that the police powers to detain people in order to prevent a breach of the peace could not be invoked to justify 'kettling' a mixed crowd of demonstrators and West End shoppers if such detention violated Article 5(1). However, it was held that Article 5(1) was not engaged on the facts of *Austin*.[49] So far as *private* persons are concerned, it is not yet clear whether the courts will be tempted severely to restrict the circumstances under which acts of imprisonment can be justified so as to ensure the better protection of people's Article 5(1) rights not to be deprived of their liberty save in the very limited circumstances set out in Article 5(1).

(4) *Article 6(1)* provides that 'In the determination of his civil rights and obligations or of any criminal charge against him, everyone is entitled to a fair and public hearing within a reasonable time by an independent and impartial tribunal established by law . . .' Like Article 3 and Article 5 – and unlike the next two Articles we will be looking at – this Article gives people an *unqualified* right: that is, a right that cannot be abridged under any circumstances. However, the ECtHR has interpreted this right in a qualified way, holding that state actions which prevent A's civil rights and obligations being determined at a fair and public hearing in court will not violate A's Article 6(1) rights provided those actions serve a legitimate purpose and do not have a disproportionate effect on A's interests.

It was thought at one time that Article 6(1) would have a major impact on the English law of tort. In the case of *Osman* v *Ferguson* (1993), it was claimed that the police were liable for the tort of negligence because they had failed to take sufficient steps to protect a schoolboy and his family from a deputy headmaster at the boy's school who had developed an obsession with the boy. The deputy headmaster ended up injuring the boy and killing the boy's father. The Court of Appeal dismissed the family's claims against the police on the basis that even if the police were as incompetent as the family alleged, the police could still not be sued as they had not owed the boy or the rest of his family a duty of care to protect them from the deputy headmaster. Disturbed by the perception that the Court of Appeal was here giving effect to a blanket ban on the police being sued in negligence, regardless of the merits of the case, the ECtHR found, in the case of *Osman* v *UK* (1999), that the Court of Appeal's finding that the police had not owed a duty of care in this case violated the family's rights under Article 6(1).

The immediate effect of the *Osman* decision was to make the courts very cautious about striking out negligence claims on the basis that no duty of care was owed to the claimant.[50] However, in the later case of *Z* v *United Kingdom* (2001), the ECtHR confessed that in *Osman* it had misunderstood the English law of negligence, and that it now realised that no one under English law enjoyed the benefit of a blanket ban from being sued under the law of negligence.[51] Given this, the English courts would not violate people's rights under Article 6(1) if, after having seriously considered the allegations made by a claimant, they dismissed the claimant's claim on the basis that even if those allegations

---

[49] See below, § 2.1.

[50] See *Barrett* v *Enfield LBC* [2001] 2 AC 550 (refusal to strike out a claim that a local authority had owed a boy in care a duty of care to raise him properly and not shuffle him from school to school); *Phelps* v *Hillingdon LBC* [2001] 2 AC 619 (refusal to strike out a claim that a local authority had owed special needs children a duty of care to provide them with an education appropriate to their needs).

[51] Five of the 17 judges in the ECtHR dissented, and continued to insist that the ECtHR had been correct to find a violation of Article 6(1) in *Osman* v *UK* (1999).

were true, the claimant would still have no case because no duty of care was owed to him. Since then, the English courts have not been troubled by any suggestions that dismissing claims in negligence on the basis that no duty of care was owed to the claimant would result in their violating the claimant's Article 6(1) rights.

(5) *Article 8* provides that:

1. Everyone has the right to respect for his private and family life, his home and his correspondence.
2. There shall be no interference by a public authority with the exercise of this right except such as is in accordance with the law and necessary in a democratic society in the interests of national security, public safety or the economic well-being of the country, for the prevention of disorder or crime, for the protection of health or morals, or for the protection of the rights and freedoms of others.

There is no doubt that this Article has had a major indirect effect on English tort law, in encouraging the courts to abandon the long-standing rule that there was no free-standing right to sue a defendant in tort for invading your privacy.[52] Over the last 20 years, the courts have developed the law on when someone can be sued for breaching another's confidence so as to give better protection to people's Article 8(1) rights to respect for their private and family life. Indeed this area of the law has developed so far from its roots that we think that the new cause of action should be treated as an independent tort: 'wrongful disclosure of private information'. Our detailed discussion of this tort, and the even more recently recognised wrong of 'wrongfully obtaining access to private information', is below, in our chapter on 'Invasion of Privacy'.[53]

It has also been argued[54] that the courts are required by the combined effect of the HRA and Article 8 to develop the law on private nuisance so that non-owners of land are allowed to sue in nuisance when their quiet enjoyment of the land they are living on is interfered with by someone else. There are severe problems with this argument, which we will address in our chapter on 'Private Nuisance'.[55]

(6) *Article 10* provides that:

1. Everyone has the right to freedom of expression. This right shall include freedom to form opinions and to receive and to impart information and ideas without interference by public authority and regardless of frontiers . . .
2. The exercise of these freedoms, since it carries with it duties and responsibilities, may be subject to such formalities, conditions, restrictions or penalties as are prescribed by law and are necessary in a democratic society, in the interests of national security, territorial integrity or public safety, for the prevention of disorder or crime, for the protection of health or morals, for the protection of the reputation or rights of others, for preventing the disclosure of information received in confidence, or for maintaining the authority and impartiality of the judiciary.

---

[52] See Arden 2010, at 147: 'Convention rights have had a powerful influence and they have led to the development of a right of action for breach of confidence, but not for invasions of privacy generally. The right of action for breach of confidence has been developed along the lines of Convention rights, not because English judges were compelled to do this, but because it was generally felt that the law did not provide adequate remedies against the intrusions by the paparazzi. The English courts chose to accept the Convention value of privacy as interpreted by the Strasbourg court.'

[53] See below, Chapter 17.

[54] See, for example, Hunt 1998.

[55] See below, § 13.11.

In developing the law on invasion of privacy, the courts have had to be careful not to develop the law in such a way that defendants' rights under Article 10 are violated. So the courts have ended up saying that in order to decide whether or not to find liability in a 'wrongful disclosure of private information' case, they have to weigh the claimant's interests in having their privacy protected against the defendant's interests in being allowed freely to talk about the claimant's private life. The complexities of this weighing process are explained more fully below.[56]

More generally, the courts' obligations under the HRA – together with the existence of Article 10 – mean that they have a continual obligation to monitor the law of defamation to ensure that that area of law does not have a disproportionately adverse effect on freedom of expression. The question of whether the law of defamation, as it stands at the moment, does have such an impact on freedom of expression is, again, a question we will address later on.[57]

1.12 Tort law and criminal law

We have already seen one link between tort law and criminal law. If Parliament makes it a criminal offence for A to harm B, we can normally say (assuming that Parliament made it unlawful for A to harm B in order to protect B's interests) that B has a statutory right that A not harm B (or, in other words, that A owes B a statutory duty not to harm B). It may be that a violation of that right will be actionable in tort: it will depend on whether Parliament intended that a violation of that right should be actionable in tort.

However, there is a deeper link between tort law and criminal law in that the core of the criminal law – made up of offences such as murder, manslaughter, rape, assault, theft, and criminal damage to property – exists to punish people who deliberately or recklessly violate the basic rights that we are supplied with by tort law. In this way, the criminal law helps protect our rights from being violated. So there are many cases where someone who commits a tort – known in legal parlance as a *tortfeasor* – will commit a crime as well. If A hits B for no good reason, that is a tort and a crime – battery, in both cases. If a man has sexual intercourse with a woman without her consent, that is a tort – battery. If he had no reasonable grounds for believing that she was consenting to have sex with him, then he will also have committed a crime – rape. If a doctor fails to treat a patient properly with the result that the patient dies, the doctor will have committed a tort – negligence. If the doctor's failure to treat the patient properly was so culpable as to be worthy of punishment, then the doctor will also have committed a crime – gross negligence manslaughter. If A drives off B's car without B's consent, he will have committed two torts – trespass to goods (touching someone else's property without their permission) and conversion (treating someone else's property as your own to dispose of). If A, in driving away B's car, acts dishonestly and with the intent permanently to deprive B of the car, he will also commit a crime – theft.

The overlap between tort law and criminal law often leads students into blunders in the way they talk about claims in tort. If A has committed a tort in relation to B, it would be wrong to say that B can *prosecute* A for committing that tort. No – B can *sue* A for

---

[56] See below, § 17.2(H).
[57] See below, § 16.13.

committing that tort. If A is going to be prosecuted for what he has done, it will be by the State, and only if his actions amounted to a crime. If A has committed a crime in acting as he did, it would be wrong to say that A can be held *liable* for committing that crime. People are held liable for committing torts, not crimes. Getting back to the tort that A has committed in relation to B, it would be inappropriate to say that A is *guilty* of committing a tort in relation to B. The language of 'guilt' and 'innocence' should be confined to the criminal sphere.

While the core of the criminal law exists to protect the rights that tort law supplies us with from being violated by other people, by threatening to punish people who intentionally or recklessly violate those rights, tort law performs much the same role in making awards of exemplary (or punitive) damages against tortfeasors who deliberately violate other people's rights. Under English law, such awards can only be made against public officials who have acted in an 'oppressive, arbitrary or unconstitutional way' in committing a tort, or against someone who has deliberately committed a tort figuring that the gain he will make from committing that tort will exceed what he will have to pay by way of compensatory damages for committing that tort.[58] In order to avoid the risk of a tortfeasor whose tort also amounts to a crime being punished twice over for his actions, exemplary damages may not be awarded against a tortfeasor whose actions have already been the subject of a criminal prosecution.[59]

1.13 Tort law and property law

In order to teach students law, law schools are forced to divide the law up into digestible subjects – contract law, tort law, criminal law, land law, constitutional law, administrative law, and so on. One unfortunate side effect of this need to divide up the law is that it creates the impression that there is a clear cut division between these different areas of law. So it is with tort law and property law. Many academics seem to be under the impression that a given legal rule or principle can be allocated either to the realm of tort law, or the realm of property law, but cannot belong to both.[60] The reality is that there is a substantial overlap between tort law and property law.

In terms of a Venn diagram, tort law and property law are two intersecting circles within a rectangle that represents the entirety of English law. The area covered by both

---

[58] *Rookes* v *Barnard* [1964] AC 1129.

[59] Though see the strange case of *AT* v *Dulghieru* [2009] EWHC 225 (QB), criticised below, § 24.3(A)(4).

[60] Calabresi and Melamed 1972 may have helped to create this impression, by suggesting that tort law was a matter of 'liability rules' (making people pay money for the losses caused by their acting in a particular way) and property law was a matter of 'property rules' (requiring people to act in a particular way), and that all private nuisance cases (where B complains that her use and enjoyment of land is being interfered with by the way A is using his land) could be solved either by the application of a liability rule (allowing A to use his land as he likes so long as he compensates B for the interference that this will cause to her use and enjoyment of land) or a property rule (requiring A not to use his land in a way that will interfere with B's use and enjoyment of her land) or no rule at all (allowing A to use his land as he likes without requiring him to compensate B for the interference that this will cause to her use and enjoyment of land). The problem with this 'view of the cathedral' of the common law, as Calabresi and Melamed put it, is that tort law does not deal in liability rules. In Calabresi and Melamed's terms, it deals in property rules – it tells people to act in certain ways, and provides a variety of remedies when people fail to do what tort law tells them to do.

the tort law circle and the property law circle is made up of rules and principles that belong to both areas of law. These rules and principles define what basic rights someone with a given interest in property will have against other people, and what remedies will be available when those rights are violated. These rules and principles belong to tort law, because it is tort law that defines what basic rights we have against other people, and what remedies will be available when those rights are violated. But these rules and principles also belong to property law, because they concern what rights are enjoyed by people who have a particular interest in property, and what remedies will be available when those rights are violated.

So what rules and principles belong exclusively to tort law and do not have anything to do with property law? And what rules and principles belong exclusively to property law and have nothing to do with tort law? On the tort law side, if we have a basic right against someone else but we are given that right not because we have some kind of interest in property, but for some other reason – then that right has nothing to do with property law. So, for example, the right A will have that B not lie to him and induce him to act in a particular way (the violation of which amounts to the tort of deceit, or fraud) has nothing to do with property law – he does not have that right because he has a particular interest in property, but because he is a human being whose autonomy (or freedom to choose what to do, free from other people's manipulations) is deserving of respect.

On the property law side, all the rules and principles that define what can amount to property, what interests someone can have in property, and how those interests may be acquired and lost, belong exclusively to property law and have nothing to do with tort law. Tort law only comes in after someone has acquired an interest in property, to define what rights that interest-holder has against other people by virtue of his holding that interest. Tort law has nothing to say about what sort of interests people can have in property, and how those interests may be acquired and lost. It is a rule of property law, and not tort law, that no more than four people can own land as joint tenants, and that if Blackacre is conveyed to A, B, C, D, E and F in undivided shares, then Blackacre will be legally owned by A, B, C and D as joint tenants, and held on trust by them for A, B, C, D, E and F.[61] Where tort law comes in, and where tort law and property law overlap, is in determining what rights these various people have against other people by virtue of the interests they have in Blackacre. (Though because Blackacre is in this situation held on trust for A, B, C, D, E and F, equity will also have something to say about what rights – in equity's case, equitable rights – these various individuals will have against other people by virtue of the fact that they each have a *beneficial interest* in Blackacre.)

1.14 Tort law and strict liability

Strict liability exists when the fact that a particular event has occurred means that a claimant can obtain a remedy against a defendant, but the defendant was not necessarily at fault, or to blame, for that event occurring. There is strict liability both within, and outside, tort law.

Strict liability within tort law is not usually objectionable where the remedy being sought against a defendant is an *injunction* or some sort of specific order that the defendant

---

[61] Law of Property Act 1925, s 34.

act in a particular way. For example, suppose that *Dealer* acquires an antique watch that was stolen from *Owner*. If *Owner* finds out that *Dealer* has her watch, and cannot get *Dealer* to hand over the watch voluntarily to her, *Owner* will usually be able to obtain an order that *Dealer* hand the watch over to her.[62] The fact that *Dealer* was not at fault for the fact that *Owner*'s watch has come into his hands makes no difference. It is *Owner*'s watch and *Dealer* must now give it back. In this case, strict liability is unobjectionable.[63]

Where strict liability within tort law becomes more questionable is where the remedy being sought against the defendant is *damages*. For example, suppose that *Hiker* is going for a walk along a public pathway marked out on a map that he is carrying. But suppose the map is wrong and leads *Hiker* onto *Rich*'s land. In this case, *Hiker* will have committed a tort (the tort of trespass to land) in relation to *Rich*. The fact that *Hiker* was not at fault for walking on to *Rich*'s land does not affect the matter. The map maker's mistake cannot abridge the right *Rich* had against *Hiker* that *Hiker* stay off her land. Now: the English courts are strongly committed to the idea that if A has committed a tort in relation to B, and B has suffered loss as a result, then B should in principle be entitled to recover damages from A – and they will not give A a defence to being sued for damages by B in cases where A was not at fault, or not to blame, for the fact that he committed that tort. The upshot is that *Hiker* may be held liable to pay *Rich* damages for trespassing on her land, even though he was not at fault for going onto her land.

Instances of strict liabilities to pay damages *outside* tort law (properly understood) are, strangely enough, easier to justify. We have already come across a couple of examples:

(1) A producer of a dangerously defective product will be held liable for the harm done by that product under the Consumer Protection Act 1987 even if he was not necessarily to blame for the fact that the product was dangerously defective.

(2) If A, in the course of using his land in a non-natural way, brings onto his land, or collects on his land, something that is liable to do damage if it escapes, then if that thing does escape and damages B's land, B will be entitled to sue A under the rule in *Rylands* v *Fletcher* for compensation for that damage even if A was not necessarily at fault for the fact that that thing escaped off his land.[64]

Both examples of strict liability can be explained as being based on an *enterprise risk* rationale. That is: if you engage in some enterprise for your own benefit which involves some inherent risk of harm to others, then if that risk materialises, you should compensate those others for the harm you have suffered. It's only fair: if you want to keep the benefits from your enterprise, then you should shoulder the burdens associated with that enterprise.

---

[62] Such an order – for what is called *specific restitution of goods* – will only be available if being paid the value of the watch would be an inadequate remedy for *Owner*. We have made the watch an antique watch in order to satisfy this condition. If this condition were not satisfied, *Dealer* would be given the option of either returning the watch, or paying *Owner* its value.

[63] Things become tougher on *Dealer* if he bought the watch or spent money in the belief that it was his to keep (perhaps on a display case for it) or if *Dealer* has given away something of value in the belief that the watch was his to keep (perhaps another, inferior, example of the same sort of antique watch). In such situations, *Dealer* will be left out of pocket if he is required to hand over *Owner*'s watch. But *Dealer* will still be required to hand over the watch. There is no defence of what is called *change of position* to a proprietary claim: *Foskett* v *McKeown* [2001] AC 102.

[64] These *are* examples of liability rules in Calabresi and Melamed's terminology (see above, n 60), in that they attach a cost to something that someone is allowed to do (manufacturing products, bringing dangerous things onto his land in the course of using that land in a non-natural way).

Such an enterprise risk rationale may underlie a very well-established rule of strict liability associated with tort law. This is the rule of *vicarious liability* that says: If *Employee* commits a tort in relation to *Victim* in the course of *Employee*'s employment by *Employer*, then *Victim* will be entitled to sue *Employer* for whatever sum in damages she is entitled to recover from *Employee*; and this is so even if *Employer* was not necessarily at fault for the tort committed by *Employee*. This is one of the most important rules associated with tort law as tortfeasors rarely have enough money to be worth suing. It is only companies and public bodies that usually have pockets deep enough to satisfy tort claimants seeking damages – and it is the law on vicarious liability that allow those pockets to be picked. If there were no law on vicarious liability, the law reports would contain very few instances of tort claims. However, it is possible to argue that the law on vicarious liability exists to do more than keep tort lawyers in employment, and give tort claimants someone to sue. It can be argued that if *Employer* seeks to profit from having *Employee* work for him, and there is a risk associated with the work that *Employee* is employed to do that he will commit a particular tort, then it is only fair that if that risk materialises, *Employer* should be held liable for the losses suffered by the victim of *Employee*'s tort.

1.15 Insurance[65]

Insurance has a role to play at both ends of a tort claim – the claimant's end and the defendant's end.

A. Claimants

At the claimant's end, the claimant may have suffered loss that is covered by an insurance policy (under what is called 'first party insurance'). If the loss takes the form of a physical injury, then the law allows the claimant to sue the defendant in tort for compensation for her injury *and* claim from her insurance company the sum payable under her insurance policy for that injury. The law does not regard this as a form of 'double recovery'. It takes the view that people may put a special value on their bodies and if the special value that they put on their bodies has led them to take out insurance to cover harm to their bodies (such as a pianist insuring his hands, or a model insuring her legs and her face), then they should be allowed to claim on that insurance policy in full if their bodies are harmed, whatever rights they might simultaneously have under tort law to claim damages for the harm that they have suffered.

If the loss suffered by the claimant takes some other form – such as damage to property or an economic loss – then the law says that the claimant's right to sue the defendant in tort for compensation for that loss will *not* be affected if she has already recovered compensation for that loss under her insurance policy. The defendant cannot take advantage of arrangements that the claimant put in place to protect herself, and for which the claimant paid good money, in order to reduce his liability to the claimant. *However*, if the claimant has already recovered compensation for the loss she has suffered under her insurance policy then:

(1) If she subsequently sues the defendant in tort for compensation for that loss, she must hand over the damages she wins to her insurance company.[66]

---

[65] See, generally, Merkin 2010 and Merkin 2012.
[66] *Lord Napier and Ettrick* v *Hunter* [1993] AC 713.

(2) If she – having claimed on her insurance policy – is not interested in suing the defendant in tort for compensation for the loss she has suffered, her insurer can bring a claim in tort against the defendant *in the claimant's name* for such compensation and can keep any damages that it recovers.

It is a little puzzling why insurance companies have this right, which arises under the law of subrogation (under which the insurance company, having paid out on the claimant's insurance policy, is said to be *subrogated to* the claimant's rights to sue the defendant). The law is clear that an insurance company that has had to pay out to the victim of a tort cannot bring a claim *in its own name* against the person who committed that tort for the loss it has suffered as a result of that tort being committed.[67] So why do the courts allow an insurance company to bring effectively the same claim *in the name of the victim of the tort*? Three possible explanations may be given:

(a) The terms of the contract between the insurer and insured may provide that the insurer can do this, and the courts are simply giving effect to this contract;

(b) Public policy demands that the loss suffered as a result of a tortfeasor's conduct should ultimately fall on the tortfeasor, so as to penalise him for what he has done – and allowing the insurer to sue in the insured's name where the insured has been compensated by the insurer is a good way of ensuring this happens;

(c) This whole area of law represents an unprincipled concession to the insurance industry, designed to help keep their costs (and the costs of premiums) down.

B. Defendants

At the defendant's end, the defendant may be carrying liability insurance (called 'third party insurance'), which will cover him if he is held liable to the claimant. Officially, the fact that a liability insurer, and not the defendant, will end up paying the bill for any damages awarded to the claimant is not supposed to have any effect on whether the defendant is held liable to pay damages to the claimant. However, it is hard to imagine that the existence of liability insurance has not played a role in shaping the following features of tort law:

(1) The courts will readily find that a motorist has breached the duty he will owe nearby drivers and pedestrians to take care not to drive dangerously if he is guilty of a momentary lapse of attention – even though experiments have shown that no driver can be humanly expected to keep his eyes on the road all the time. The fact that it is not the driver, but his liability insurer, that will foot the bill for any claim made against the driver for harm done as a result of his momentary lapse of attention may explain why the courts are happy to adopt such a strict attitude in negligence cases involving motorists.

(2) Staying with motorists, the Road Traffic (NHS Charges) Act 1999 provides that if A is liable to compensate B for injuries that B has suffered as a result of a motor vehicle accident, and B's injuries have been treated by the National Health Service, then A will be liable to compensate the government for the money spent on B's care. Again, the fact that A will almost always be carrying liability insurance must account for why Parliament is happy to impose such a liability on A.

---

[67] *La Société Anonyme de Remourquage à Hélice* v *Bennetts* [1911] 1 KB 243. This case provides another example of the principle discussed in the previous section, that where a tort has been committed, it is normally only the victim of the tort who is allowed to sue.

(3) The same fact makes it easy to understand the otherwise strange provision in s 2 of the Congenital Disabilities (Civil Liability) Act 1976, that a pregnant woman who is driving will owe her unborn child a duty to take care to drive carefully – so that if she breaches that duty and her child is, as a result, born disabled, the child can sue its mother for compensation for its disability. A right to sue for such compensation could not help the child if its mother were paying the compensation out of her own pocket – the compensation payment would merely represent money that the mother would have to spend on her child's care anyway. However, as the child's injuries were sustained as a result of a motor accident, the compensation payment will not come from the mother, but her motor liability insurer – so giving the child a right to sue its mother will provide a way of tapping into the mother's liability insurance policy so as to cover the future costs of catering for the child's disabilities.

(4) The fact that private defendants (whether the defendant is a company or an individual) almost invariably carry liability insurance – it is, after all, the 'deep pockets' that their liability insurance gives them that make them a target for litigation – means that the courts have never had to give any thought to whether successful claimants in tort cases should recover anything other than full compensation for the actionable losses that they have suffered.[68] As a result, damages awarded in tort cases can easily run up to hundreds of thousands of pounds – amounts way beyond the ability of a normal individual to pay. If liability insurance were not allowed to exist our courts would have long ago switched to a system where the damages payable in tort cases would be much smaller on average, and would reflect what individuals could afford to pay.

The fact that there may be an insurance company at both ends of a tort claim – so that an award of damages in a tort case may represent nothing more than a payment from one insurance company (a liability insurer) to another insurance company (a property insurer) – should make anyone wonder whether tort law is worth retaining in its current form. Do we pay too high a price for the benefits we obtain from having a system of tort law?

1.16 Paying for tort law

At first sight, it seems to be employers (through the law on vicarious liability) and insurance companies (through liability insurance policies) who pay the price for tort law's existence. It is they, predominantly, who have to meet the cost of the (justified) damages claims that are made by tort victims. However, a second look at the situation tells us that it is in fact the general public that pays the cost of meeting those claims through higher prices for the goods and services that employers exist to provide, and through higher insurance premiums. In that sense, the cost of meeting the claims made by tort claimants is 'spread' throughout the population. At the same time, the general public does not just cover the cost of meeting those claims, but also the costs involved in paying for the courts and the lawyers that are needed to keep the tort system functioning. So tort law can be seen as a system for taking money out of the pockets of the general public and funnelling it into the hands of: (1) tort victims; (2) tort lawyers; and (3) the civil court bureaucracy.

---

[68] Goldberg 2006 argues that *fair* compensation, rather than *full* compensation, should be (and once was) the standard remedy for committing a tort.

But none of that matters to the task of assessing whether we pay too high a price for having a system of tort law. From the point of view of society as a whole, it is impossible to tell whether the redistribution of income effected by tort law has – of and in itself – a negative or a positive effect. So in order to assess whether it is worth having a system of tort, we need to look at the social benefits and social costs of having a system of tort law that exist independently of tort law's redistributive effects.

The social benefits are, it seems to us, *potentially* threefold:

(B1) Vesting people with basic rights gives people *more control* over their lives than they would have otherwise. Under a system of law where there was no tort law, people would become wholly dependent on the criminal law, and what security they could purchase out of their own pockets, to protect them from being harmed by other people.

(B2) People *feel better* if they are vested with basic rights. They feel that the state is, first of all, respecting them enough to give them a certain minimum level of protection that they are entitled to simply by virtue of who they are, and is, secondly, respecting them enough to give them the ability to control whether or not they take advantage of that minimum level of protection.

(B3) People are *better protected* in a legal system that includes a system of tort law than one that does not. Tort law gives people another layer of protection, above and beyond what protection they might enjoy under the criminal law. Moreover, because tort law is a self-administered system of protection, tort law is likely to provide a more reliable level of protection than will the criminal law, which depends for its effectiveness on the competence, concern, and integrity of public officials.

These social benefits are only potential in nature. The less use people make of tort law, and the less relevant it is to their daily life and the way they are treated by other people, the more attenuated these benefits will be. In a country where tort law is perceived to be something that only rich people can take advantage of, these social benefits will be virtually zero.

The social costs from having a system of tort law that exist independently of its redistributive effects are, it seems to us, also threefold:

(C1) The fact that you might be sued if you fail to conform to tort law's demands means that people will often do much more than tort law requires them to do in order to ensure that they will not incur the risk of being sued. This 'overkill' response to tort law's demands represents a social cost because it is wasteful – but it is something that is an unavoidable by-product of the existence of a system of tort law. People do not like to be sued, and will always go out of their way to avoid the risk that they might be sued.

(C2) The 'overkill' response to the existence of tort law becomes even more costly when it takes the form of avoiding doing things that are socially beneficial, or getting in the way of other people doing things that are socially beneficial. The classic example of this is provided by the case of *Tomlinson v Congleton Borough Council* (2004).

That case centred around a lake in a park run by the defendant council. There were a number of beaches around the lake which hundreds of people would relax on during the summer. When it got very hot, some people would go for a swim in the lake, ignoring the 'No Swimming' signs that the council had posted all around the lake. The council became concerned that if someone got injured while swimming, they would sue the council for compensation. The council decided that to avoid this risk, it would turn the beaches around the lake into swampland, so that no one would ever want to go near the lake. But before the council got the chance to put its plans into action, John Tomlinson dived into the lake, hit his head on the bottom, and was paralysed. The council's worst fear was realised: Tomlinson sued the council, arguing that they had owed him a duty to do more than they had done to stop him endangering himself.

The House of Lords dismissed his claim. They ruled that tort law did not demand that the council destroy the valuable social amenity represented by the beaches around the lake so as to save people like Tomlinson from harming themselves.[69] The House of Lords' decision in *Tomlinson* was intended to reassure local councils that all the law of negligence required them to do by way of protecting people from harm on their land was to act reasonably. However, the House of Lords missed the point as to why the council in *Tomlinson* was happily proposing to destroy the beaches around the lake before Tomlinson's accident. To *win* a negligence case, all you may have to show is that you acted reasonably. (Though it is worth pointing out that the council in *Tomlinson* lost in the Court of Appeal.) To *avoid being sued at all*, you *may* have to go beyond what is reasonable and take *unreasonable steps* to minimise the risk of people being injured on your watch. And it is the desire to avoid being sued at all that motivates actors like the council in *Tomlinson* – not the desire to give yourself a good chance of winning if you are sued – and attempting to avoid being sued at all can involve acting in ways that are contrary to the public interest.

(C3) The third potential social cost associated with tort law lies in the fact that anyone who is continually exposed to a risk of being sued in tort needs to carry liability insurance. This gives insurance companies a huge amount of power over the insured, to dictate to the insured what they must and must not do – threatening that if the insured do not do as they are told, they will lose their liability insurance. This transfer of power to insurance companies represents a considerable social cost because of the loss of autonomy, responsibility and accountability involved in transferring to insurance companies the power to make decisions as to what precautions the insured should take to avoid harm to others. If we lived in a rational world, there is simply no way an insurance company would be given the power to decide, for example, whether a teacher needed to be on duty at a school on a Saturday when the school hall was being used for a wedding reception, or whether a play area in a park should have a merry-go-round on it. But that is the world we live in at the moment.

It does not seem to us that these are merely potential costs of having a system of tort law. They are costs that are *always* present whenever a system of tort law exists, and so far as the size of these costs are concerned, they seem to loom very large at present.

The conclusion we are moving towards is a pessimistic one: that the social costs of having a system of tort law seem at the moment to outweigh the social benefits. However, this conclusion does not necessarily suggest that we should *abolish* tort law. *Reforming* tort law so as to reduce the social costs associated with its existence and maximise its social benefits would seem a more sensible, and promising, option. Such a programme of reform would involve both cutting tort law down to size and strengthening its application. Rolling back the scope of tort law would reduce the power of liability insurance companies to dictate to individuals, companies and public bodies what they should do. The need to carry liability insurance might also be lessened by reducing the size of damages awards and relating them to

---

[69] See, in particular, [2004] 1 AC 46, at [46] (per Lord Hoffmann) and [81] (per Lord Hobhouse).

individual defendants' ability to pay. Simplifying tort law in this way would also help to strengthen tort law's application – a simpler tort law would help individuals re-connect with tort law, and understand what it is here for, and what it does for them. Simplifying and speeding up the procedures for bringing tort claims would also help individuals feel that tort law is not just a rich man's luxury, but an area of law that exists to protect everyone.

1.17 Tort law as a foreign country

Our survey of the basics of English tort law is now over. To a novice student reading this chapter, tort law must seem like a foreign country. People who live in this country speak an unfamiliar language, full of strange terms and phrases like 'conversion', '*volenti non fit injuria*', 'duty of care', and 'misfeasance in public office'. The boundaries of the country are hard to make out – it is hard to know when you are still in tort law, and when you have strayed beyond tort law into some other area of law. It is also hard to know what the relations between tort law and its neighbours are like. The country has its strange customs, which take some getting used to – such as only allowing people to sue if they are 'victims' of a tort; or allowing the victim of a tort not only to sue the person who committed that tort, but also her employer. The layout of the country seems so complicated, it is easy to get confused, and go wrong, and lose your way.

The reaction is understandable, but it is important that newcomers to tort law do not get put off. The longer you spend in this country, the more familiar it becomes, and the easier it gets. So, for example, we would suggest that if you have gotten this far in reading this text, that you turn back to page one and start reading again. You can't expect to have learned in one go everything we have been trying to tell you in this first chapter. As well as spending time getting used to tort law and its ways, it is also important that you start trying as soon as possible to talk like a tort lawyer, by writing essays and problem answers and conducting moots. Of course, like any beginner in a foreign language, you are likely to get some things wrong. But getting things wrong is the first step towards getting things right.

Before we go further in exploring the difficult terrain of tort law, we would like to suggest one analogy that it might be worth keeping a hold of, so as to make tort law seem a bit less unfamiliar and a bit easier to understand. Tort law, stripped down to its essentials, is something you have been familiar with since you were a child playing at school. At school, there were lots of rules designed to make the school run smoothly: get into school and be in class by 9 am, no pushing in line in the lunch queue, no playing dangerous games in the playground. If you broke those rules and were caught, you would be liable to be punished by the school in some way. There were other rules that were aimed to help you do your best as a student – no submitting homework late, no copying other children's work, no talking during tests. Again, if you broke those rules you were liable to be punished. Finally, there was a third set of rules that were more concerned with placing limits on what you could do to other children – no fighting, no bullying, no stealing. If you broke those rules, then you were again liable to be punished – but you would also be required to make things up with the child who you had maltreated, usually by saying sorry and shaking their hand. Doing that would get your relationship with the child you had maltreated back to normal, and allow both of you to put the past behind you and get on with your life. Tort law is like the third set of school rules. It tells you how you should treat other people and specifies what you must do to make things up to them if you fail to treat them right. Tort law is simply playground morality, writ very large indeed.

Further reading

John Goldberg's 'Ten half-truths about tort law' (2008) 41 *Valpairiso University Law Review* 1221 provides the reader with a wonderful overview of the history of tort law, and contending views about the nature and function of tort law. The same author's **'Unloved: tort law in the modern legal academy'** (2002) 55 *Vanderbilt Law Review* 1501 is also highly recommended.

For particular views of tort law, see **Lord Bingham, 'The uses of tort'** (2010) 1 *Journal of European Tort Law* 3 (tort law exists to discourage undesirable behaviour); **Jolowicz, 'Civil litigation: what's it for?'** (2008) 67 *Cambridge Law Journal* 508 (tort law exists to provide people with a peaceful means of obtaining redress for the wrongs done to them and to resolve disputes in a just manner); and **Tettenborn, 'Professional negligence: free riders and others' in Economides** *et al* **(eds),** *Fundamental Values* (Hart Publishing, 2000), **Chapter 17** (tort law exists to determine what basic rights we have against each other and what remedies will be available when those rights are violated). The Tettenborn piece may be hard to get hold of: an alternative and extended summary of this last view of tort law can be found in **McBride, 'Rights and the basis of tort law' in Nolan and Robertson (eds),** *Rights and Private Law* (Hart Publishing, 2011), **Chapter 12**.

John Goldberg and Benjamin Zipursky are the academics who are nowadays most strongly associated with the view that tort law exists to provide the victims of wrongs with a peaceful means of obtaining redress for the wrongs they have suffered, but an early statement of this view can be found in **J.M. Kelly, 'The inner nature of the tort action'** (1967) 2 *Irish Jurist (New Series)* 279.

The view that tort law exists to provide people who have unjustly suffered loss a means of obtaining compensation for that loss (condemned as long ago as 1971 by Tony Weir as encouraging tort law to go 'a-whoring after false gods' (see **Veitch and Miers, 'Assault on the law of tort'** (1975) 38 *Modern Law Review* 139, fn 35)) is gradually falling out of favour but **Patrick Atiyah's** *The Damages Lottery* (Hart Publishing, 1997) provides a good example of (1) someone who takes such a view of tort law; and (2) the despair, and the desire to abolish tort law and come up with something better in its stead, that adopting such a view of tort law promotes. Atiyah's book is well summarised and criticised in **Ripstein, 'Some recent obituaries of tort law'** (1998) 48 *University of Toronto Law Journal* 561.

The extent to which our system of tort law inflicts a social cost in the form of creating a 'compensation culture' is addressed in **Williams, 'State of fear: Britain's compensation culture reviewed'** (2005) 25 *Legal Studies* 499; Lewis, Morris and Oliphant, 'Tort personal injury claims statistics: is there a compensation culture in the United Kingdom?' (2006) 14 *Torts Law Journal* 158; and Morris, 'Spiralling or stabilising? The compensation culture and our propensity to claim damages for personal injury' (2007) 70 *Modern Law Review* 349. Political attempts to come to grips with our 'compensation culture' (if we have one) are summarised and assessed in **Mullender, 'Blame culture and political debate: finding our way through the fog'** (2011) 27 *Professional Negligence* 64 and Morris, '"Common sense common safety": the compensation culture perspective' (2011) 27 *Professional Negligence* 82.

If we have a compensation culture in the UK, its existence is often blamed on the ability claimants now have to bring claims financed on a 'no win, no fee' basis, a system of funding tort litigation that has long existed in the United States as a means of enabling impecunious claimants to obtain some justice from those who have wronged them. **Jonathan Harr's book** *A Civil Action* **(Century, 1996)** provides a fascinating account of a real-life American case fought on a 'no win, no fee' basis.

The relationship between tort law and insurance is excellently explored in **Rob Merkin's** two papers **'Tort and insurance: some insurance law perspectives' (2010) 26** *Professional Negligence* **194** and **'Tort, insurance and ideology: further thoughts' (2012) 75** *Modern Law Review* **301**, and Tom Baker's 'Liability insurance as tort regulation: six ways that liability insurance shapes tort law in action' (2005) 12 *Connecticut Insurance Law Journal* 1.

Chapter 2
Trespass to the person

Aims and objectives

Reading this chapter should enable you to:

(1) Understand when someone will commit the torts of assault, battery, and false imprisonment.

(2) Understand the distinctions between these various torts, in particular with regard to how much at fault someone has to be before they will be found to have committed one of these torts.

(3) Get a good overview of the situations where a defendant will be held *not* to have committed the torts discussed in this chapter because the defendant can establish that his conduct was justified in some way.

(4) Understand the debates over whether, and when, the courts should find that a defendant did *not* commit the torts discussed in this chapter because the defendant mistakenly believed that his conduct was justified in some way.

(5) Understand what remedies are available when someone commits one of the torts set out in this chapter.

2.1 The basics

We begin our exploration of the torts recognised by English law with some of the oldest forms of wrongdoing for which claimants would be able to obtain a remedy from the English courts. These are the torts that are known, collectively, as torts involving a 'trespass to the person'.

The name of these torts goes back to the birth of the common law – a general system of law administered by the King's courts. A claimant seeking a remedy for some wrong that he or she alleged they had suffered could only gain access to the King's courts with the aid of a *writ*, which was an order issued by the King's representative that the claimant's case be heard in the King's court. Originally, the only writ that the sort of claimant that we would nowadays classify as a 'tort' claimant could obtain was a *writ of trespass*. Writs of trespass came in a variety of different forms: the writ of *trespass de vi et armis* (available where the claimant claimed that he or she had suffered personal injury as a result of the defendant's direct and forceful misconduct), the writ of *trespass quare clausum fregit* (available where the claimant claimed that the defendant had gone onto the claimant's land), and the writ of *trespass de bonis asportatis* (available where the claimant claimed that the defendant had damaged his or her goods by carrying them away).

For some time, claimants who wanted to sue for some other kind of wrong in the King's court would not be able to have their case heard because their case simply was not covered by the writ of trespass. However, in the fourteenth century, the King's representatives were granted the power to issue new writs of *trespass on the case* if they thought a particular case, while not covered by the writs of trespass, was sufficiently similar to a trespass case as to be deserving of a remedy. Much of the law of negligence – which we will start to look at in the next chapter – has its origins in the power to issue writs of trespass on the case. But the law of trespass came first. And rightly so: no legal system worthy of the name could allow the sort of wrongs originally dealt with by the writs of trespass to go unremedied. The minimum aim of any decent legal system – which is to preserve a certain degree of stability in the lives of the people governed by that system – could not be achieved if people were free to beat each other up, or imprison each other without cause, or steal their property, or go onto their land.[1]

We will look later on at the trespass torts that protect people's property.[2] For the moment, we are concerned with the trespass torts that protect people's persons. There are three of them: *battery, assault,* and *false imprisonment.* A will commit the tort of battery in relation to B if he touches her when he has no lawful justification for doing so. A will commit the tort of assault in relation to B if he makes her think he is about to touch her when he has no lawful justification for doing so. A will commit the tort of false imprisonment in relation to B if he does something to limit her freedom of movement to a confined space when he has no lawful justification for doing so.

The existence of these torts confers on each of us a certain zone of liberty, within which we enjoy some freedom from interference with our bodily integrity and our ability to move about. However, this zone of liberty becomes weakened and attenuated the more occasions the law allows other people to intrude into it, arguing that they have a lawful justification for doing so. Those who would seek to violate this zone of liberty do not just include the wicked and selfish and ill-disposed, but also those who claim that they are acting in the *public interest* by depriving us of freedoms that the common law would otherwise give us. So the courts, in dealing with trespass cases, are often called upon to decide when it would be lawful for a representative of the State to interfere with someone else's liberty. These cases – dealing as they do with fundamental political questions about the relative importance of the individual and the collective – are some of the most interesting a law student can study.

For example, on 1 May 2000, the police suffered a major humiliation when anti-capitalist demonstrators ran riot through London, destroying a branch of McDonalds and defacing the Cenotaph and the statue of Winston Churchill in Whitehall. The following year, the police were better prepared. Acting on intelligence that the demonstrators were planning to assemble in Oxford Circus before dispersing around the capital, at 2 pm on 1 May 2001, the police set up a cordon at the junction at Oxford Circus, trapping within the cordon a large number of would-be demonstrators as well as a lot of people who were simply out shopping. About 3,000 people were trapped within the cordon, and they were held there until 9.30 pm, at which point the police judged that the steam had gone out of

---

[1] For a discussion of the minimum aims of a legal system, see Hart 1994, 193–200.
[2] See below, Chapter 12 and § 14.4.

the would-be demonstrators and that it was safe to let them go. Lois Austin – a would-be demonstrator – was one of the people trapped within the cordon. When she requested the police to let her out, so that she could pick her baby up from a crèche, her request was denied. She was told that she and everyone else were being held in order to 'bore you into submission' and was told that she only had herself to blame if she was unable to pick up her baby. Lois Austin sued the police, arguing that they had acted unlawfully in holding her in the cordon; a tactic that has become known as 'kettling'.

At first instance and in the Court of Appeal, it was held that the police tactic of kettling demonstrators at Oxford Circus had been lawful.[3] Even though innocent shoppers had been caught up in the police cordon, it was still lawful to hold people within the cordon for almost eight hours because doing so was necessary to prevent a breach of the peace. By the time the case reached the House of Lords, Lois Austin's lawyers were reduced to arguing that holding within the cordon was unlawful, not under the common law, but under the Human Rights Act 1998, which – among other things – requires public bodies not to violate people's rights to liberty under Article 5 of the European Convention on Human Rights. Under Article 5, everyone has a 'right to liberty and security of person' and someone can only be deprived of their liberty in certain exceptional circumstances, which did not apply on the facts of the case in *Austin*. The House of Lords held that Article 5 had not been violated as holding someone in a cordon for almost eight hours did not amount to depriving someone of their liberty.[4] As a result, they upheld the lawfulness of kettling as a police tactic for handling demonstrations that are liable to become violently out of control.[5]

It is surprising that of the nine judges who ended up considering the case of *Austin* v *Commissioner of Police of the Metropolis*, not one could be found to speak for the idea that it is unlawful to imprison an innocent person, whether or not doing so is necessary in order to prevent a breach of the peace.[6] This is surprising for two reasons. First, the courts have traditionally struck a more individualistic note in determining where the line is to be drawn between protecting individual liberty and promoting collective security.[7] The traditional position is well represented by Tony Weir, who has observed that 'no one in Britain, *no one*, can justify deliberately touching even a hair on [a claimant's] head, or entering her garden – much less depriving her of her liberty – merely on the ground that it was reasonable to do so . . . '.[8]

---

[3] [2005] EWHC 480 (QB) (Tugendhat J); [2008] 1 QB 660.

[4] [2009] 1 AC 564.

[5] The House of Lords' judgments were handed down on 28 January 2009. They bore immediate, and bitter, fruit on 2 April 2009, when the police used kettling as a tactic for handling demonstrators at the G20 economic summit in London. The police tactics were widely blamed for turning an initially peaceful anti-bankers demonstration outside the Bank of England into a violent confrontation between demonstrators and police that resulted in windows being smashed in at branches of HSBC and the Royal Bank of Scotland, and the death of a newspaper vendor, Ian Tomlinson, who was pushed over by a policeman in the aftermath of the demonstration. Widespread criticism of the police tactics at the G20 summit led to their initiating a review of the practice of kettling demonstrators. Supporters of kettling may have taken some grim comfort from the events in late 2010, when – in the absence of kettling – demonstrators against plans to raise student university fees were allowed to run riot in London, smashing in windows at the Conservative Party headquarters, and threatening the Prince of Wales and Duchess of Cornwall.

[6] It is less surprising that the European Court of Human Rights (ECtHR) upheld the House of Lords' decision in *Austin* v *United Kingdom* (2012) 55 EHRR 14: the ECtHR is wary of interfering too much with decisions taken at a national level that are of some political importance or sensitivity.

[7] See, for example, *Beatty* v *Gillbanks* (1882) 9 QBD 308 (it is not unlawful to organise a march just because the march will be met with violence by the organisers' opponents).

[8] Weir 2004, 322 (emphasis in original).

Secondly, in cases like *Austin* it is not easy to decide which set of values should prevail – those of individual liberty, or those of collective security. It is simply not possible to say that whenever the public interest conflicts with individual liberties, individual liberties must give way. Human fallibility on the issue of what is actually in the public interest guarantees that every society that has been founded on the principle of the supremacy of the collective over the individual has eventually descended into a charnel house. A due concern for individual liberty must sometimes be allowed to trump our desire to protect and advance the public interest. But it is very hard to say when that should be the case. *Austin* certainly does not seem to be an easy case where it was obvious that the public interest should have been allowed to prevail over the interests of individual liberty. Given this, it is surprising that none of the judges who decided *Austin* seemed to feel much discomfort about finding that the 'kettling' in *Austin* was lawful.[9]

2.2 Conduct requirements

Each of the torts under discussion in this chapter has two different aspects: a conduct requirement, and a fault requirement. A defendant who is sued for committing a particular trespass tort has to satisfy both before he can be found to have committed the tort. In this section, we look at the conduct requirements for each of the trespass to the person torts.

A. Battery

For the tort of battery to be committed, a defendant must have *directly* and *voluntarily* applied *force* to the claimant's body. Let us take each of these italicised terms in turn, in reverse order.

(1) *Force.* This requirement will obviously be satisfied if the defendant touches the claimant. It will also be satisfied if (i) the claimant is hit by something thrown by the defendant, whether or not the defendant intended to throw the thing *at* the claimant,[10] or (ii) the defendant removes something that the claimant is sitting on, with the result that the claimant falls to the ground.[11]

(2) *Voluntariness.* This requirement will *not* be satisfied in cases where the defendant was not in control of his body at the time he touched the claimant (or otherwise directly applied force to the claimant's body). So, for example, if A and B are both standing in a train and the train suddenly brakes, with the result that A is thrown against B, A will not have committed the tort of battery in relation to B.

(3) *Directly.* The requirement that the defendant directly apply force to the claimant's body is a major limit on the scope of the tort of battery. The requirement of directness is

---

[9] Since the decision in *Austin*, the courts have sought to restrict its impact, ruling – for example – in *R (Moos)* v *Commissioner of Police of the Metropolis* [2012] EWCA 12 at [95] that it is only 'when the police reasonably believe that there is no other means whatsoever to prevent an imminent breach of the peace that they can as a matter of necessity curtail the lawful exercise of their rights by third parties.'

[10] *Scott* v *Shepherd* (1773) 2 Black W 892, 96 ER 525 (defendant threw a lighted firework into a marketplace and the firework was thrown from trader to trader in an attempt to get rid of it, and ended up exploding in the claimant's face; held that the defendant was liable for battery).

[11] *Dodwell* v *Burford* (1670) 1 Mod 24, 86 ER 703 (defendant struck claimant's horse with the result that it bolted and the claimant was thrown from the horse; held that the defendant was liable for battery).

better explained by example, rather than by definition. If A pushes B into a hole, that is a battery. If A digs a hole in the road and B later on falls into it, that is not a battery. If A injects a poison into B's body, that is a battery. If A puts poison in B's drink and B later drinks it, that is not a battery.

B. Assault

For the tort of assault to be committed, a defendant must have performed a positive act that made the claimant *think* that someone is *about* to apply force directly and voluntarily to their body. Again, let us take these italicised terms in turn, in reverse order.

(1) *About.* There is no assault on a claimant unless the claimant is made to think that they are in *imminent danger* of being attacked.

In *Tuberville* v *Savage* (1669), it was held that Tuberville did not commit an assault when he drew his sword on Savage and said, 'If it were not assize-time I should not take such language from you.' As it *was* assize time (that is, the time when the courts had set up in town to hear any criminal or civil cases), Tuberville's words did *not* lead Savage to believe that Tuberville was about to strike him with his sword.

In *Thomas* v *National Union of Mineworkers (South Wales Area)* (1986), the claimants were coal miners who wished to go to work during the miners' strike. As they entered, the colliery where they worked they suffered abuse and threats from massed pickets at the colliery gates. They sought to obtain an injunction against the massed picketing, claiming among other things that the pickets were committing the tort of assault in abusing and threatening them as they entered the colliery. This claim was rejected by Scott J on the ground that the claimants were always driven into the colliery and were separated from the pickets by ranks of policemen – given this, it could hardly be said that the abuse and threats the claimants received when they entered the colliery put them in fear that they were *about* to be beaten up by the pickets.

It is not clear *how* imminent the threat of an attack has to be for an assault to have been committed. In *R* v *Ireland* (1998) (a criminal case), the defendant made a series of malicious telephone calls to three women – when they answered he would remain silent. The women all developed psychiatric illnesses as a result of their treatment at the hands of the defendant. The defendant was charged with committing the offence of assault occasioning actual bodily harm and was convicted. The House of Lords upheld the conviction, holding that his silent telephone calls could have led the women in question to believe they were about to be attacked by whoever was on the other end of the line. This was so even though there would have been some interval of time before the defendant could get from wherever he was phoning the women from to their houses. It seems that it was enough, for the assault to be established, that the women were put in *uncertainty* as to whether they were *about* to be attacked. That is, they were made to think that they *might* be *about* to be attacked.

(2) *Think.* For an assault to be committed, the claimant must be made to *think* that she is about to be attacked. So if A creeps up on B from behind and hits her on the head with a plank of wood, that is a battery, but not an assault. At no point was B made to think that she was about to be attacked. It is enough, for an assault to be committed, that the claimant was made to *think* that she was about to be attacked. It does *not* (repeat *not*) have also to be shown either: (i) that the claimant *was* about to be attacked; or (ii) that the claimant was *afraid* of being attacked. So, for example, if A points a fake gun at B and says 'I'm going to shoot you' and B is unaware that the gun is fake, that is an assault. It does not matter that A was incapable of shooting B with the gun, and nor will it matter if B would actually welcome being shot because he is suicidally depressed.[12]

C. False imprisonment

For the tort of false imprisonment to be committed, a defendant must have performed a *positive act* that *directly resulted* in the claimant's freedom of movement being *completely restricted or restricted to a defined area*. Let us take each of the italicised terms in turn, in reverse order.

(1) *Restriction*. If *Policeman* wrongfully arrests *Innocent* and drags *Innocent* to a nearby police station, *Innocent* is falsely imprisoned while she is being taken to the station: her freedom of movement has been completely restricted by *Policeman*. Once *Innocent* is placed in a police cell, she is still falsely imprisoned, but this time because her freedom of movement has been restricted to a defined area. The requirement that a claimant's freedom of movement be completely restricted, or restricted to a defined area, was not satisfied in *Bird v Jones* (1845), where the claimant was prevented from walking along a public right of way by the defendants, who had set up an enclosure on the right of way for the purpose of viewing a boat race. The claimant had not been falsely imprisoned because his freedom of movement had only been restricted in one direction (the direction he wanted to go). He had been free to go back where he came from and so his freedom of movement had not been completely restricted to a defined area.

(2) *Directly resulted*. It does not have to be shown that the defendant *himself* restricted the claimant's freedom of movement – it just has to be shown that the defendant did something positive that *directly resulted* in the claimant's freedom of movement being restricted. But the defendant's actions must have the *direct* effect of restricting the claimant's freedom of movement. For example, in a case where A tips off the authorities that B may be guilty of wrongdoing, with the result that B is arrested, the Court of Appeal has held that A can only be found guilty of false imprisonment if A *persuaded, encouraged,* or *requested* the authorities to arrest B.[13] Given this, it is unlikely that *Mule* could sue *Smuggler* for false imprisonment just because he planted drugs in her luggage that resulted in her being arrested by the police.

(3) *Positive act*. The requirement that for the tort of false imprisonment to be committed, a positive act has to be performed was reaffirmed by the Court of Appeal in *Iqbal* v *Prison*

---

[12] In *Mbasogo* v *Logo Ltd* [2006] EWCA Civ 1370, the Court of Appeal said of the *Thomas* v *NUM* case (at [75]) that: 'The threats made by pickets to those miners who sought to go to work were not an assault because the pickets had no capacity to put into effect their threats of violence whilst they were held back from the vehicles which the working miners were within.' This suggests that if A threatens to shoot B if B does not do as he says, then A's threat will *not* amount to an assault if A did not have the capacity to shoot B at the time he made his threat. This cannot be right.

[13] *Davidson* v *Chief Constable of North Wales* [1994] 2 All ER 597. Though see now *Westcott* v *Westcott* [2009] QB 407, holding that someone reporting a crime to the police enjoys absolute immunity from being sued for doing so.

Officers Association (2010).[14] In that case, a number of prison warders failed (in breach of their contracts of employment) to turn up to work, with the result that the claimant prisoner could not be let out of his cell at the time he would normally be let out. It was held that the prison warders' *failure* to turn up to work did not make them liable to the claimant for false imprisonment.

In *R v Bournewood Community and Mental Health NHS Trust, ex parte L* (1999), a patient, L, was staying at a mental health ward at Bournewood Hospital. He was, in theory, free to leave the ward when he liked, but the medical staff had decided that if L attempted to leave, they would section him under the Mental Health Act 1983 and prevent him from leaving. The House of Lords held that L was not falsely imprisoned while he was on the ward – the fact that the staff had decided to stop L leaving if he attempted to leave could not, of and in itself, mean L was imprisoned as the staff could not imprison L just through having a certain mental state.[15]

(4) *No requirement of awareness.* It should be noted that there is *no* (repeat *no*) requirement that the claimant be *aware* that he has been imprisoned for him to be able to sue for false imprisonment.[16] So if A locks a room in which B is sleeping and then unlocks the room before B awakes, A may be liable for falsely imprisoning B – the fact that B was unaware that she was sleeping in a locked room will be completely immaterial.[17]

2.3 Fault requirements

As we have already seen Tony Weir observe, if you are being sued for committing one of the trespass torts, it is no defence simply to say that 'I acted reasonably under the circumstances.' To that extent, the trespass torts are torts of strict liability: the fact that you were not at fault for what happened will not necessarily absolve you of liability. Having said that, before we can find a defendant liable for committing one of the trespass torts, we do need to inquire into his or her mental state at the time he or she acted. But what sort of mental state a defendant needs to have been in to have committed one of the trespass torts varies from tort to tort.

---

[14] This requirement also provides a possible explanation of the Privy Council decision in *Robinson v Balmain New Ferry Company Ltd* [1910] AC 295. The claimant in that case wanted to take a ferry from a wharf operated by the defendants. Entrance or exit from the wharf was through a turnstile and anyone wanting to use the turnstile had to pay a penny to the defendants. The claimant paid his penny, went through the turnstile and waited for the ferry. He then changed his mind about catching the ferry and demanded to be let back through the turnstile without paying another penny for the privilege. The defendants refused to let him through. A claim for false imprisonment against the defendants failed. One possible explanation is that the defendants did not do anything *positive* in this situation to imprison the claimant: they merely failed to release him from the situation in which he had put himself.

[15] There was however evidence that the staff had taken positive steps to make it *harder* for L to leave the ward, in that they kept him constantly sedated and dissuaded family members and friends from visiting him. The European Court of Human Rights found that the staff's conduct had violated L's right to liberty under Art 5 of the European Convention on Human Rights (*HL v United Kingdom* (2005) 40 EHRR 32 (noted, Pedain 2005)). Had greater emphasis been placed on the staff's conduct, rather than their mental state, in the House of Lords, it is hard to imagine they would not also have been found liable for false imprisonment.

[16] The same point would apply to battery: if A has sex with B while she is passed out, and she has no awareness of what he is doing, and feels no ill effects from what he has done, he has still committed the tort of battery.

[17] Most jurisdictions in the United States take the view that a claim for false imprisonment could *not* be made here.

A. Battery

Diplock J's decision in *Fowler* v *Lanning* (1959) established that merely showing that the conduct requirements for a battery have been satisfied is not enough to show that a defendant has committed the tort of battery. In that case, the claimant sued the defendant for damages. His statement of claim said, 'on November 19, 1957 at Vinyard Farm, Corfe Castle, in the county of Dorset the defendant shot the [claimant]. [As a result] the [claimant] sustained personal injuries . . .' The defendant applied to have the claimant's claim struck out on the ground that the statement of claim did not disclose a good cause of action against the defendant. Diplock J agreed, holding that in this kind of case it would have to be shown at the very least that the defendant *carelessly* shot the claimant before he could be sued.

At first sight, this seems to make the tort of battery redundant. Were it established that the defendant either carelessly or, worse, intentionally shot the claimant, the claimant would of course have been able to sue the defendant in negligence for his injuries. So what role is there for the tort of battery? We would submit that battery still has a useful role to play in dealing with cases where a defendant *intentionally* touched the claimant, and (i) the defendant's touching the claimant caused the claimant to suffer no loss, or no loss that the law of negligence could compensate the claimant for (such as pure distress); or (ii) the defendant's touching the claimant was reasonable under all the circumstances. If either (i) or (ii) is true, a claim in negligence will not help the claimant, and the only way the claimant will be able to sue the defendant is by bringing a claim for battery. Where a defendant *carelessly* touched the claimant and either (i) or (ii) is true, there is nothing in *Fowler* v *Lanning* that would prevent the claimant suing the defendant in battery, but we are doubtful whether the courts would allow the claimant to evade the limits on when someone can sue another in negligence by that route.

So the decision in *Fowler* v *Lanning* has effectively limited the tort of battery to cases of *intentional* touchings (or other direct applications of force to the claimant's body).[18] Since *Fowler* v *Lanning*, various attempts to tighten up still further the ambit of the tort of battery have been made, but with no success. In *Letang* v *Cooper* (1965), Lord Denning MR suggested that a defendant could only commit the tort of battery if he *intended to injure* the claimant.[19] This suggestion was disapproved in *Wilson* v *Pringle* (1987): '[an] intention to injure is not essential to an action for [battery]'.[20] But in the very same case – in

---

[18] It need not be shown that the defendant intended to apply the force to the *claimant's* body, so long as he intended to apply force to *someone's* body and ended up applying force to the claimant's body. So A will also commit the tort of battery in relation to B if he directly applies force to B's body with the intention of applying that force to C's body: *Bici* v *Ministry of Defence* [2004] EWHC 786 (QB), at [68]–[71] (soldiers operating in Kosovo committed tort of battery in shooting MB even though they were aiming to hit FB when they opened fire). Beever 2009 criticises the reasoning of the judge in *Bici* (which involves transplanting the criminal doctrine of 'transferred malice' (under which A will be guilty of murder if he intends to kill C and accidentally ends up killing B instead) to tort law. But he supports the result in *Bici* on the basis that 'the soldiers intended to shoot the occupants of the car and that class of persons included [MB]' (at 416). But he can only make this argument by endorsing a *very* wide view of intention whereby what you intend is not restricted to what your 'aim, want or purpose' is, but also covers whatever you are aware will happen as a result of your actions 'in the ordinary course of events' (415). This very wide concept of intention has no support in the modern day law. Goldberg 2006 argues (at fn 81) that if A aims to shoot at B and accidentally ends up shooting C instead, C's cause of action against A should be in negligence, not in a battery.

[19] [1965] 1 QB 232, 239.

[20] [1987] 1 QB 237, 249.

which a schoolboy playfully pulled on a schoolbag that a friend was carrying over his shoulder, with the result that the friend fell to the ground and injured his hip – the Court of Appeal held that a defendant could not be held to have committed the tort of battery unless he had acted in a *hostile* way.[21] They accordingly declined to find that a battery had been committed on the facts of *Wilson* v *Pringle* and sent the case back down for a hearing to determine whether the defendant, in acting as he did, had acted with the requisite degree of hostility. Tony Weir has remarked of this decision that 'it is perfectly clear that this is nonsense'[22] and indeed in *Re F* (1990), Lord Goff disapproved the Court of Appeal's suggestion in *Wilson* v *Pringle* that a touching has to be 'hostile' before it can amount to a battery:

> I respectfully doubt whether that is correct. A prank that gets out of hand; an over-friendly slap on the back; surgical treatment by a surgeon who mistakenly thinks that the patient has consented to it – all these things may transcend the bounds of lawfulness, without being characterised as hostile. Indeed the suggested qualification is difficult to reconcile with the principle that any touching of another's body is, in the absence of lawful excuse, capable of amounting to a battery . . .[23]

B. Assault

Suppose that *Paranoid* thinks that anyone who rubs their nose in front of her is indicating that they are about to attack her. *Fidget* rubs his nose while he is talking to *Paranoid*, and as a result *Paranoid* thinks that *Fidget* is about to attack her. The conduct elements for an assault are satisfied here, but has *Fidget* assaulted *Paranoid*? To discuss this issue, we need to distinguish the following cases:

(i) *Fidget* knew about *Paranoid*'s belief about the significance of nose rubbing and he rubbed his nose in front of her with the intention of making her think that she was about to be attacked.

(ii) *Fidget* knew about *Paranoid*'s belief and he intentionally rubbed his nose in front of her, but not in order to make her think that she was about to be attacked but in order to stop his nose itching. At the time he rubbed his nose, he realised the effect his rubbing his nose would have on *Paranoid*, but thought it was a price worth paying for relieving the itch on his nose.

(iii) *Fidget* knew about *Paranoid*'s belief but was so distracted by an itch on his nose that he rubbed his nose in front of her without even thinking about what effect this might have on *Paranoid*.

(iv) *Fidget* was not aware of *Paranoid*'s belief but ought to have been aware of it (he had been warned about it before by *Fidget*'s friends and family, but had either forgotten or not paid attention).

(v) *Fidget* was not aware of *Paranoid*'s belief and had no reason to know about it.

---

[21] [1987] 1 QB 237, 250: 'for there to be . . . a battery there must be something in the nature of hostility.'
[22] Weir 1998a, 109.
[23] [1990] 2 AC 1, 73.

There is clearly an assault in situation (i), and we think it follows from *Fowler* v *Lanning* (1959) that there is clearly not an assault in situation (v). We think that (ii) would also amount to an assault, unless *Fidget* could argue that he had a lawful justification for rubbing his nose under the circumstances. (iii) and (iv) are examples of 'careless assaults' and – as we have seen – there is nothing in *Fowler* v *Lanning* to rule out the possibility that a claim in trespass could be made against a defendant who is merely careless. But it must be doubtful whether the courts would allow a claim for assault to be made against a defendant who was merely careless as to what effect his conduct would have on the claimant.[24]

C. False imprisonment

In *Iqbal* v *Prison Officers Association* (2010), Smith LJ took the view that 'with false imprisonment . . . the claimant must show . . . an intention to deprive the claimant of his liberty.'[25] If this is right, then an *intention to imprison* is an essential element to any claim for false imprisonment: it will not be enough for a claimant to show that the defendant intentionally did something that resulted in the claimant being imprisoned.

2.4 Consent

In *Re F* (1990), Lord Goff remarked that 'as a general rule physical interference with another person's body is lawful if he consents to it; though in certain limited circumstances the public interest may require that his consent is not capable of rendering the act lawful.'[26] Lord Goff's qualification to his 'general rule' was designed to cover cases where consent is no defence to someone being charged under criminal law with an offence against the person. For example, in *R* v *Brown* (1994), a group of sado-masochists who inflicted various wounds on each other for sexual pleasure were convicted of assault occasioning actual bodily harm, contrary to s 47 of the Offences Against the Person Act 1861. However, if A invites B to wound him for their mutual sexual pleasure, it is very doubtful – if B takes up A's invitation – whether A could sue B, claiming that B had violated his rights in wounding him. Given this, we can amend Lord Goff's *dictum* to say that 'physical interference with another person's body is *always* lawful *for the purposes of tort law* if he consents to it; though in certain limited circumstances the public interest may require that his consent is not capable of rendering the act lawful *for the purposes of the criminal law*.' But this simple statement conceals a host of difficulties, which we will now explore.

A. Validity of consent

If A has touched B in some way, B will obviously not have validly consented to A's touching her in the way he did if B did not agree that A could touch her in the way he did. So suppose *Patient* went to hospital for a tonsillectomy but *Surgeon* – due to an administrative

---

[24] In *Bici* v *Ministry of Defence* [2004] EWHC 786 (QB), Elias J held that for a defendant to be held liable to a claimant in assault, it has to be shown that the defendant intended to put the claimant 'personally in fear of imminent violence . . . The fact that [putting someone in fear of imminent violence] may have been the consequence of [the defendant's] actions, even a foreseeable consequence, is not enough to fix [him] with liability in trespass' (at [77]).

[25] [2010] QB 732, at [72].

[26] [1990] 2 AC 1, 72.

mix-up – performed an appendectomy instead. In such a case, it could not be said that *Patient* validly consented to *Surgeon*'s touching her in the way he did.[27]

Even if B formally agreed that A could touch her in the way he did, it still cannot be said that she validly consented to A's touching her in that way, if, when she agreed, she did not really understand what A was proposing to do. So suppose *Doctor* proposed to *Patient* that he treat her condition by giving her an 'intrathecal injection of phenol solution nerve block'. If *Patient* agreed that *Doctor* could do this but did not actually understand what *Doctor* was proposing to do – because *Doctor* did not bother to explain to *Patient* what such an injection involved – then it cannot be said that *Patient* validly consented to *Doctor*'s giving her such an injection.[28]

A difficult issue is whether B has validly consented to A's touching her if she understood what A was doing in touching her, but had been misled as to A's *motives* in touching her. For example, in *KD* v *Chief Constable of Hampshire* (2005), the claimant became distressed while she was being interviewed by a police constable about her sexual history with a former boyfriend (who, it was alleged, had sexually abused the claimant's daughter). The constable hugged the claimant – but not, as the claimant thought, with the intention of cheering her up, but because he was attracted to her. It was held that the constable committed a battery in hugging the claimant – so while the claimant consented to being hugged by the constable, her consent must have been rendered invalid by her being misled as to the reasons why the constable was hugging her.[29]

B. Vitiation of consent

An apparently valid consent will be vitiated, and rendered invalid, if it was procured through illegitimate pressure or through the illegitimate exercise of some influence over the person giving their consent. Suppose, for example, that *Surgeon* performed an abortion on *Girl* but *Girl* only agreed to the abortion because her father threatened to kill her if she did not have it. In this case, it cannot be said that *Girl* validly consented to *Surgeon*'s performing the abortion on her. This is not to say that *Girl* could sue *Surgeon* for battery in this case. But if *Surgeon* is to establish a lawful justification for what he did, he cannot do so by claiming that *Girl* consented to the abortion. The topic is further explored below.[30]

It is well established that an apparently valid consent will *not* be vitiated merely because it is not *informed*. So, for example, if *Beauty* consents to have sex with *Handsome*, a man she has met through an Internet dating site, her consent to have sex with *Handsome* will not be rendered invalid merely because he turns out to be HIV+ and she would never have agreed to have sex with him had she known of that fact.[31] In *Chatterton* v *Gerson* (1981), the claimant had an operation which left her with an extremely painful scar. The claimant

---

[27] *Chatterton* v *Gerson* [1981] 1 QB 432, 443.

[28] Ibid. Cf. *R* v *Williams* [1923] 1 KB 340 where the defendant – who had been engaged to give singing lessons to one Vera Howley – persuaded Howley to allow him to have sexual intercourse with her by pretending that he was performing a surgical operation on her to improve her voice. He was convicted of rape; she had not validly consented to the defendant's having sex with her as she did not really understand what he was proposing to do when she agreed that he could have sex with her.

[29] Cf. *R* v *Tabassum* [2000] 2 Cr App Rep 328 (defendant persuaded a number of women to let him touch their breasts by pretending to be a doctor who was advising the women how to check their breasts for lumps; he was convicted of indecent assault).

[30] See below, § 2.7(A).

[31] *R* v *Dica* [2004] QB 1257, at [39].

consulted the defendant – who was a specialist in treating pain – and he suggested that she have an operation to block the sensory nerve behind the scar which was transmitting pain signals to her brain. The claimant agreed and the defendant carried out the operation. After the operation, the claimant discovered that the area around her scar was numb and she had suffered a loss of muscle power in that area. The claimant's attempt to sue the defendant in battery was rejected on the ground that the fact she was unaware there was a risk she would suffer numbness and loss of muscle power if she had the operation did not mean she had not validly consented to the operation being carried out, as she still understood perfectly well the nature of the operation the defendant was carrying out. Nowadays, the claimant would be advised to sue the defendant in negligence instead for his failure to inform her properly of the risks attached to the operation.[32]

C. Withdrawal of consent

A continuing interference with someone's person may be initially consented to, but what happens if consent is subsequently withdrawn? The general rule is that withdrawal of consent will render any further interference unlawful. So if A is having sex with his girlfriend, B, with her consent and she tells him to stop having sex with her, he will commit a battery if he ignores her and carries on having sex with her.

There is an important exception to this general rule, which applies where it would not be reasonable to expect the initially consented-to interference to stop immediately once consent has been withdrawn. In such a case, once consent is withdrawn, the defendant will be given a reasonable period of time to bring the interference to an end, and will only be held liable for continuing the interference if it carries on beyond that period of time. So, for example, suppose *Beauty* is giving *Handsome* a lift on the back of her motorbike, with *Handsome* holding onto her leather jacket, when she suddenly remembers that *Handsome*'s hands will be really filthy from doing some work on the bike before they set off. If *Beauty* tells *Handsome* to stop touching her jacket, it will be lawful for *Handsome* to continue holding on until *Beauty* has stopped the bike and it is safe for him to let go.

In *Herd* v *Weardale Steel, Coal and Coke Company Ltd* (1915), the claimant was a miner who descended to the bottom of a pit at the start of his shift. He then refused to do certain work and asked to be lifted up to the surface. The claimant was only allowed to go back up to the surface at the end of the morning shift and even then he was only permitted to go back up once all the miners on the morning shift had been taken to the surface. The claimant sued, claiming that he had been falsely imprisoned. The House of Lords dismissed his claim. One explanation of the decision is that this was a withdrawal of consent case where the claimant initially consented to be left at the bottom of the pit, and then withdrew his consent.[33] Given this, under the law, the defendants were allowed a reasonable period of time to release the claimant from the bottom of the pit, and on the facts of the case, it was reasonable for the defendants to wait until the end of the shift to release the claimant: there was no reason why they should go to the trouble and inconvenience of arranging for the claimant to be taken back to the surface on his own.

---

[32] See §§ 7.4(C)(2) and 8.10.
[33] See Tan 1981 for this explanation of the decision in *Herd*, though he doubts whether the case was correctly decided on the facts.

D. Possibility of consent

Some people are incapable of giving a valid consent to having their person interfered with in a given way. If B's level of maturity, intelligence and understanding was not such that B could be safely left to decide for herself whether or not A could touch her in the way he did, any consent that B gave to A's touching her will not be valid.

If, at the time B agreed that A could touch her in the way he did, B was an adult (over 18) and not mentally unstable or acting under the influence of drugs or alcohol, it will be automatically presumed that B's level of maturity, intelligence and understanding was such that she could be safely left to decide for herself whether or not A could touch her in the way he did.

Section 8 of the Family Law Reform Act 1969 provides that 'the consent of a minor who has attained the age of [16] years to any surgical, medical or dental treatment which, in the absence of consent, would constitute [a battery], shall be as effective as it would be if he were of full age . . .' The effect of this is that if *Doctor* treated *Child* with *Child*'s agreement and *Child* was between 16 and 18 at the time, it will be automatically presumed that *Child* was of a level of maturity, intelligence and understanding that she could be safely left to decide for herself whether or not *Doctor* could treat her in the way he did – just as would have been the case if *Child* had been over 18 when she agreed to being treated by *Doctor*.

If, when B agreed A could touch her in the way he did, B was less than 16 years old then no fixed rules will apply – all the circumstances will have to be looked at to determine whether, when B agreed A could touch her in the way he did, B's level of maturity, intelligence and understanding was such that she could be safely left to decide for herself whether or not A could touch her in the way he did. If B was of such a level of maturity, intelligence and understanding, she is known as being *'Gillick* competent', after the case in which the rule for determining B's competence to give consent was laid down.[34]

E. Consent on behalf of others

In a case where an under 16 year old is not *Gillick* competent to consent to medical treatment, medical treatment will still be lawful if it is carried out with the consent of one of the child's parents.

A much more difficult situation is where *Child*, who is over 16 or *Gillick* competent, is *refusing* treatment that one of *Child*'s parents is consenting to – is it lawful in that situation to treat *Child*? The available *dicta* are confused.[35] The issue is most likely to arise in

---

[34] *Gillick* v *West Norfolk and Wisbech Area Health Authority* [1986] AC 112.

[35] *Dicta* in favour of the view that it would be lawful to treat *Child* despite their positive refusal to be treated can be found in *Re R (a minor) (wardship: consent to treatment)* [1992] Fam 11, 23–5 (per Lord Donaldson MR); *Re W (a minor) (medical treatment)* [1993] Fam 64, 76 (per Lord Donaldson MR), 87 (per Balcombe LJ). *Dicta* in favour of the view that it would be unlawful to treat *Child* if they are positively refusing to be treated can be found in *Re R (a minor) (wardship: medical treatment)* [1992] Fam 11, 27 (per Staughton LJ). The latter view rests heavily on some *obiter dicta* of Lord Scarman's in *Gillick* v *West Norfolk and Wisbech Area Health Authority* [1986] AC 112, 188–189: '. . . I would hold that as a matter of law the parental right to determine *whether* or not their minor child below the age of 16 will have medical treatment *terminates* if and when the child achieves a sufficient understanding and intelligence to enable him or her to understand fully what is proposed' (emphasis added).

two situations: (i) where *Child* has moral beliefs not shared by his or her parents (for example, where a 15-year-old refuses to have an abortion when her parents want her to have one); and (ii) where *Child* is engaging in short-term thinking about what is in their best interests while his or her parents are engaging in long-term thinking about what is in the child's best interests (for example, where a 10-year-old is refusing to have braces fixed on his teeth to adjust them because it will ruin his last year in primary school). One way of resolving the conflict between *Child* and parent in these kind of situations might be to let the parent's wishes prevail where the treatment is medically important but not radically invasive, but only allow radically invasive treatment (for example, an abortion) against *Child*'s wishes when it is necessary to save *Child*'s life.

F. Consent to risks

In principle, a valid consent to the *risk* of having one's person interfered with in some way should afford just as much a defence to being sued in trespass as a valid consent to the *fact* of one's person being interfered with does. And so it proves, for the most part.

For example, in *Blake* v *Galloway* (2004), the claimant was a 15-year-old who joined a group of similarly aged children who were playfully throwing twigs and bits of bark at each other. The claimant threw a bit of bark at the defendant, that hit the defendant in the chest. The defendant threw the bark back in the direction of the claimant. Unfortunately, the bark hit the claimant in the face, injuring one of his eyes. The claimant sued for damages for the injury in negligence and battery. His claim was dismissed. While he had not consented to being hit in the eye by the bark thrown by the defendant, he *had* consented to the *risk* of being hit in the eye by the sort of playful throwing of the bark that the defendant had engaged in. Of course, if the defendant had intentionally aimed the bark at the claimant's eye or had thrown it at him at very high velocity, not caring where it hit the claimant, it could not be said that the claimant consented to the risk of being hit by a piece of bark that was thrown like that – such a throw would have been well outside the expectations of the participants in the game. But as the defendant's throw was purely playful and not reckless, the claimant had consented to the risk of being hit in the eye by that kind of throw.

The idea that consent to the risk of one's person being interfered with affords a lawful justification for that interference may also be seen to underlie Goff LJ's suggestion in *Collins* v *Wilcock* (1984) that an application of force to another's person that is 'generally acceptable in the conduct of daily life'[36] will not amount to a battery. So if A and B are at a noisy party, and A grabs B's arm to get her attention, then that will not amount to a battery. If you go to a noisy party, you consent to the risk of that sort of thing happening to you.[37] In *Collins* v *Wilcock* itself, a policewoman grabbed a prostitute by the arm to stop her from walking away when she was trying to question her. The Court of Appeal held that the policewoman committed the tort of battery in restraining the prostitute – the policewoman's conduct went well beyond what is 'generally acceptable in the conduct of daily life'.

The idea that consenting to the risk of one's person being interfered with in some way provides a lawful justification for that interference runs into difficulty in cases where people

---

[36] [1984] 1 WLR 1172, 1177.
[37] It should be noted that in *Re F* [1990] 2 AC 1, Lord Goff thought that this rationalisation of his suggestion in *Collins* v *Wilcock* was 'artificial' (at 72).

try to exploit that idea to subvert the monopoly of violence that the State is supposed to possess in enforcing people's rights. Consider the **Restaurant-Dungeon Problem**:

> *Rich* goes to a very exclusive and expensive restaurant for a meal. He is warned when he makes the reservation at the restaurant that people who do not pay for their meals will be kept in a dungeon underneath the restaurant until someone comes to pay their bill. There are also numerous notices to this effect at the entrance to the restaurant and on the menu. *Rich* enjoys an excellent meal, but when he comes to pay the bill, he discovers he has left his wallet at home. He is forcibly dragged into the underground dungeon by the kitchen staff and has to wait there for 36 hours, until his ex-wife comes to pay the bill.

If *Rich* tries to sue the restaurant for false imprisonment, can they argue that they had a lawful justification for imprisoning him based on the fact that he consented to the risk that he might be imprisoned if he did not have enough money on him to pay the bill? In principle, the restaurant should be able to argue this. However, such an argument runs up against the argument that debts should be enforced through the courts, and not through private force. It is likely that this latter argument would prevail, and the courts would find that the restaurant was liable for false imprisonment in this case.[38]

2.5 Necessity

Returning to Lord Goff's judgment in *Re F* (1990), immediately after the couple of sentences quoted at the start of the last section, Lord Goff observed, 'There are also specific cases where physical interference without consent may not be unlawful – chastisement of children, lawful arrest, the prevention of crime, and so on.'[39] We will be grouping these specific cases under the heading of 'necessity'.

The term 'necessity' needs some explanation here. Normally, the word 'necessity' is used to describe the plea of someone who claims 'I *had* to act as I did'. Normally, such a plea is unconvincing: very few people *had* to act as they did. Even if someone has been made an offer 'he can't refuse', he can actually refuse the offer and face the consequences. However, in this section we intend to give the word 'necessity' a much wider meaning, under which someone relies on a necessity defence whenever they say that it was, on balance, *good* for them to do as they did. Necessity – in this sense – is not, of and in itself, a defence to being sued for trespass to the person. Merely saying 'I did a good thing in acting as I did' is no more of a defence than merely saying 'It was reasonable for me to act as I did.' However, there are plenty of situations where the law does allow one person to interfere with another's person on the basis that it is good for them to act in that way.

---

[38] See Tan 1981, 167: 'a creditor cannot imprison his debtor in the absence of statutory authority' (quoting Glanville Williams). The only authority on point does not really tell us very much. In *Sunbolf* v *Alford* (1838) 3 M & W 248, 150 ER 1135, the claimant was forcibly restrained from leaving the defendant's restaurant when he failed to pay the bill. It was held that the defendant was liable for false imprisonment. But in that case, there were no notices telling people that they might be detained if they tried to leave without paying.

[39] [1990] 2 AC 1, 72.

Such situations can be grouped into four categories. First, *self-interested interference*: A interfered with B in order to protect himself from being harmed in some way. Secondly, *paternalistic interference*: A interfered with B in order to protect B from being harmed in some way. Thirdly, *interference to protect third parties*: A interfered with B in order to protect a third party from being harmed in some way. Fourthly, *interference based on the public interest*: A interfered with B because it was generally in the public interest to do so. We will now look at each of these categories in turn.

A. Self-interested interference

Under the law on *self-defence*, if B poses an unjustified threat to A's life or person, A is allowed to use reasonable force against B in order to protect himself. In such a case, B will have a lawful justification for his actions.

Are there are any limits on what can amount to 'reasonable force'? Consider the **Dead Man Walking Problem**:

Evil invites *Patsy* round to his house, and serves her with a glass of wine when she arrives. When *Patsy* drinks the wine, she remarks that it has a funny taste. *Evil* tells *Patsy* that he poisoned it with a toxin that invariably proves fatal within two hours of being drunk. *Evil* further tells *Patsy* that he has left the antidote to the poison at a location within a 15 minute drive of the hotel where *Patsy*'s best friend is currently staying. *Evil* hands *Patsy* a gun and says that he will tell *Patsy* where the antidote is once *Patsy* visits her best friend in his hotel room and shoots him dead. *Patsy* refuses to do any such thing.

Is *Patsy* allowed to torture *Evil* in this situation to extract the information as to where the antidote is?[40] Would torture count as 'reasonable force' in this situation? It seems doubtful that the courts could ever countenance regarding torture as 'reasonable force'. Doing so would open the door to the State torturing suspected terrorists to extract information about terrorist plots. The point is reinforced by Article 3 of the European Convention on Human Rights, which provides that 'No one shall be subjected to torture or to inhuman or degrading treatment or punishment.' This is one of the few rights laid down by the European Convention that is completely unqualified – there are no exceptions to it.[41] Even the right to life (Article 2) may be abridged 'if it results from the use of force which is no more than absolutely necessary . . . in defence of any person from unlawful violence'. However, refusing to allow *Patsy* to torture *Evil* in this situation does create a paradox. If *Evil* came at *Patsy* with a syringe full of deadly poison, *Patsy* would be allowed under the

---

[40] Slapping or punching *Evil* would probably not be regarded as torture, at least if not prolonged. Putting needles under *Evil's* fingernails or ripping out *Evil's* fingernails certainly would be.

[41] A Grand Chamber of the European Court of Human Rights held in *Gäfgen v Germany* (2011) 52 EHRR 1 (noted, Bjorge 2011) that Article 3 forbade the torturing of a kidnapper to find out the location of a child he had kidnapped: 'the prohibition on ill-treatment of a person applies irrespective of the conduct of the victim or the motivation of the authorities. Torture, inhuman or degrading treatment cannot be inflicted even in circumstances where the life of an individual is at risk. No derogation is allowed even in the event of a public emergency threatening the life of the nation. Article 3, which has been framed in unambiguous terms, recognises that every human being has an absolute, inalienable right not to be subjected to torture or to inhuman or degrading treatment under any circumstances, even the most difficult' (at [107]).

law to shoot *Evil* dead in order to protect herself. But not killing *Evil* and merely putting *Evil* through excruciating pain instead is not regarded as an acceptable way of saving *Patsy*'s life.

B. Paternalistic interference

The law does not allow you to interfere with someone else on paternalistic grounds if they are an adult, capable of making up their own mind what they want, and want to be left alone. But it is different in the case of adults who cannot be asked what they want, or are not mentally fit to decide for themselves what they want. For example, it is well established that if B is in danger of being hit by some moving object, A will commit no battery if he drags B out of the way,[42] Similarly, it is well established that if B is brought unconscious into hospital, A, the attending doctor, will commit no battery if he gives B the medical treatment she needs to bring her back to good health.[43]

In *Re F* (1990), the House of Lords gave formal expression to the principle underlying this last example and ruled that: if A has medically treated B, an adult, without her consent, A will not have committed a battery in so treating B if: (i) it was in B's best interests for A to treat her in the way he did; (ii) B did not validly decline to be treated by A in the way he treated her; and (iii) B was incapable of validly consenting to be treated by A in the way he treated her (either because she was drunk or because she was mentally unstable or because she was unconscious at the time she was treated by A).[44]

Parliament has now intervened to put the area of law governed by *Re F* on a statutory footing. Under s 5 of the Mental Capacity Act 2005, D will act lawfully in doing

an act in connection with the care or treatment of another person ("P") . . . if –

(a) before doing the act, D takes reasonable steps to establish whether P lacks capacity in relation to the matter in question, and
(b) when doing the act, D reasonably believes –
   (i) that P lacks capacity in relation to the matter, and
   (ii) that it will be in P's best interests for the act to be done.

provided that P is not under 16.[45]

Under s 2 of the 2005 Act, 'a person lacks capacity in relation to a matter if at the material time he is unable to make a decision for himself in relation to the matter because of an impairment of, or a disturbance in the functioning of, the mind or brain'. And s 3(1) provides that, 'For the purposes of [s] 2, a person is unable to make a decision for himself if he is unable – (a) to understand the information relevant to the decision, (b) to retain

---

[42] *Re F* [1990] 2 AC 1, 74.
[43] Ibid.
[44] In *Re F*, F was a voluntary in-patient in a mental hospital. She was 36 years old but had the mental age of a small child. When she showed signs that she was about to become sexually active, F's mother sought to have her sterilised on the grounds that it would be harmful to F's mental health if she became pregnant. The House of Lords held that the hospital staff at F's mental hospital would commit no battery if they sterilised F without her consent: it would be in F's best interests to be sterilised; F had not validly declined to be sterilised; and F's mental age meant that F was incapable of validly consenting to be sterilised.
[45] This is a consequence of s 2(5) of the 2005 Act, which provides that 'No power which a person ("D") may exercise under this Act – (a) in relation to a person who lacks capacity, or (b) where D reasonably thinks a person lacks capacity, is exercisable in relation to a person under 16.'

that information, (c) to use or weigh that information as part of the process of making the decision, or (d) to communicate his decision.'

Section 6 of the 2005 Act places an important limit on the scope of s 5. It deals with the situation where D 'restrains' P – that is, the situation where D 'uses, or threatens to use, force to secure the doing of an act which P resists, or' the situation where D 'restricts P's liberty of movement, whether or not P resists'. Section 6 provides that if we want to establish that D is acting lawfully in 'restraining' P, it will not be enough to show that the conditions set out in s 5, above, are satisfied. It will *also* have to be shown that: 'D reasonably believes that it is necessary to do the act in order to prevent harm to P' *and* 'the act is a proportionate response to – (a) the likelihood of P's suffering harm, and (b) the seriousness of that harm'.[46]

We can illustrate how the 2005 Act works by considering two cases that were decided under the old law, as set out in *Re F*.

In *B* v *An NHS Hospital Trust* (2002), spinal problems meant that the claimant was paralysed from the neck down and could not breathe without the assistance of a ventilator. Operations to allow the claimant to breathe unaided were unsuccessful and the claimant, deciding that she did not wish to live any more, asked for her ventilator to be switched off. The claimant's doctors declined to do this, and so the claimant took them to court. It was held that *Re F* did not apply and that the doctors were acting unlawfully in continuing to treat the claimant. Even if it were in the claimant's best interests to be kept alive, the claimant was old enough and intelligent enough to decide for herself whether she wanted to continue being treated, and so her refusal to be treated any more was perfectly valid. It is likely that the same result would be reached under the 2005 Act, given s 1(4) of the 2005 Act which provides that, 'A person is not to be treated as [being] unable to make a decision merely because he makes an unwise decision.'

In *Re T* (1993), T was injured in a car accident when she was 34 weeks pregnant. She was admitted into hospital where she went into labour. She was told that the baby would have to be delivered by Caesarean section and that it might be necessary to give her a blood transfusion to replenish her blood after the operation. T told the hospital staff that she was a Jehovah's Witness and did not want to have a blood transfusion after her Caesarean. After the Caesarean was carried out – and before T had regained consciousness – T's condition suddenly deteriorated and she was transferred to an intensive care unit where she was put on a ventilator and paralysing drugs were administered. She was then given a blood transfusion at the behest of T's father and boyfriend. The Court of Appeal had to decide whether the hospital had committed a battery in doing so.

The court thought that the House of Lords' decision in *Re F* established that the hospital did *not* commit a battery in treating T in the way it did: the court thought that it had been in T's best interests to give her a blood transfusion (she might have died without it); T had not validly declined to be given a blood transfusion *in the circumstances in which she was given it*; and at the time the blood transfusion was administered T was incapable of validly consenting to its being given to her. It is, again, likely that the same result would be reached

---

[46] Even if all these conditions are satisfied, this will not authorise D to do anything to P which would deprive P of his liberty: s 4A of the 2005 Act (as amended by the Mental Health Act 2007, s 50) provides that subject to certain narrow exceptions, 'This Act does not authorise any person . . . to deprive any other person . . . of his liberty'; and s 6(5) of the 2005 Act provides that 'D does more than merely restrain P if he deprives P of his liberty within the meaning of Article 5(1)' of the European Convention on Human Rights.

under the 2005 Act. One important difference between the law under the 2005 Act, and the old law as stated in *Re F*, is that to establish that their treatment of T was lawful under the 2005 Act, her doctors would merely have to show that they reasonably believed that T lacked capacity at the time they gave her a blood transfusion, and that giving her a blood transfusion was in her best interests. There is no doubt that T lacked the capacity to decide whether or not to have a blood transfusion at the time it was administered, and it is highly likely that T's doctors would have been able to establish that they reasonably thought giving her a blood transfusion was in her best interests at the time it was administered. Section 4(6) of the 2005 Act does provide that in determining what is in a person's ('P's') best interests, the person making that determination ('D') must consider 'so far as is reasonably ascertainable – (a) [P]'s past and present wishes and feelings . . ., [and] (b) the beliefs and values that would be likely to influence his decision if [P] had [the] capacity [to make that decision] . . .' However, even taking these factors into account, T's doctors would be able to argue convincingly that they reasonably thought that it was in T's best interests to have a blood transfusion: the fact that she did not want a blood transfusion to replenish her blood did not mean that she did not want a blood transfusion to save her life.

C. Interference to protect third parties

The law on when someone can interfere with another's person in order to protect a third party from harm is still developing. The law on self-defence will apply to allow you to use force against someone who poses an unjustified threat to someone else's life or person in order to protect the threatened person.[47] And we have already seen in the *Austin v Commissioner of Police of the Metropolis* (2009) case that the courts are prepared to accept that the police can imprison even completely innocent people who pose no danger to anyone else if there is no other way of preventing a breach of the peace. In *Re S* (1993), the President of the Family Division, Sir Stephen Brown, ruled that a doctor who performs a Caesarean section on a pregnant patient in order to save the life of her foetus will commit no battery even if the patient has validly declined to undergo a Caesarean section.[48] However, in *St George's Healthcare NHS Trust v S* (1999), the Court of Appeal held that this was wrong: if a pregnant patient validly declines to undergo a Caesarean section, a doctor who performs such an operation on the patient will commit a battery even if it is necessary to perform the operation in order to save the life of the patient's foetus.

D. Interference based on the public interest

There are a number of different occasions where the law gives people the power to interfere with other people's persons on the basis that it is in the public interest for people to have that power.

---

[47] Cf. *Re A* [2001] Fam 147, where the Court of Appeal held that it would be lawful to operate on two conjoined twins, Jodie and Mary, to separate them even though the operation would result in Mary's death, as Mary (by relying on Jodie's heart and lungs to keep her alive) posed a (passive) threat to Jodie's life and removing Mary from Jodie was the only way to save Jodie's life as Jodie was not strong enough to keep both her and Mary alive on one heart and one set of lungs.

[48] In so holding he was following a suggestion of Lord Donaldson MR's in *Re T (adult: refusal of medical treatment)* [1993] Fam 95, 102: 'An adult patient who . . . suffers from no mental incapacity has an absolute right to choose whether to consent to medical treatment, to refuse it or to choose one rather than another of the treatments being offered. The only possible qualification is a case in which the choice may lead to the death of a viable foetus.'

(1) *Public defence.* Section 3 of the Criminal Law Act 1967 provides that '[a] person may use such force as is reasonable in the circumstances in the prevention of crime, or in effecting or assisting in the lawful arrest of offenders or suspected offenders or of persons unlawfully at large'.[49] So if A runs out of a store with some goods which he has stolen, B – one of the store's security guards – will commit no battery if she chases A and wrestles him to the ground in an attempt to apprehend him.

(2) *Lawful chastisement.* If A hits B to punish her for misbehaving, A will not usually be able to argue that he acted lawfully in hitting B. It used to be that there were two exceptions to this general rule. *First*, parents were allowed to use reasonable force to discipline their children. This exception has now been qualified by s 58(3) of the Children Act 2004, which provides that 'Battery of a child causing actual bodily harm to the child cannot be justified in any civil proceedings on the ground that it constituted reasonable punishment.' *Secondly*, a schoolteacher, acting *in loco parentis*, was allowed to use reasonable force to punish the children in his care if they misbehaved. This second exception no longer survives: s 548 of the Education Act 1996 provides that 'Corporal punishment given by, or on the authority of, a member of staff to a child . . . cannot be justified in any proceedings on the ground that it was given in pursuance of a right exercisable by the member of the staff by virtue of his position . . .'[50]

(3) *Powers of arrest.* In granting people powers to arrest others, ss 24 and 24A of the Police and Criminal Evidence Act 1984 draw a distinction between ordinary citizens (effecting a 'citizen's arrest') and the police.

Generally speaking, only the police can make a *preventative* arrest, arresting someone who is *about* to commit an offence or who the police reasonably think is about to commit an offence – but even then, the police can only effect such an arrest when they have reasonable grounds for believing that the arrest is necessary (a) to identify the arrestee; or (b) to prevent physical injury or damage to property or a public nuisance; or (c) to protect a child from the arrestee; or (d) to aid the investigation or prosecution of the offence the arrestee is, or is thought, to be about to commit.

In the case where *Suspect* is *committing* or *has committed an offence* – or is reasonably thought to be committing or have committed an offence – the police can arrest *Suspect* if one of conditions (a)–(d) are satisfied. But a private citizen can only arrest *Suspect* in the case where *Suspect* is committing – or is reasonably thought to be committing – (i) an indictable offence; *and* (ii) it is reasonable to believe that arresting *Suspect* is necessary to prevent physical injury or damage to property or to give the police a chance to take *Suspect* into custody *and* (iii) it is not reasonably practicable to allow the police to arrest *Suspect*. A private citizen can only arrest *Suspect* for committing an offence *in the past* if conditions (i)–(iii) are satisfied *and* the offence in question was actually committed (though not necessarily by *Suspect*).

---

[49] See also the Education Act 1996, s 550A, which provides that 'A member of the staff of a school may use, in relation to any pupil at the school, such force as is reasonable in the circumstances for the purpose of preventing the pupil from doing (or continuing to do) any of the following, namely – (a) committing any offence, (b) causing personal injury to, or damage to the property of, any person (including the pupil himself), or (c) engaging in any behaviour prejudicial to the maintenance of good order and discipline at the school or among any of its pupils, whether that behaviour occurs during a teaching session or otherwise.'

[50] In *R (Williamson)* v *Secretary of State for Education and Employment* [2005] 2 AC 246, the House of Lords rejected a claim that this provision violated the applicants' rights to manifest their religion or beliefs under Art 9 of the European Convention on Human Rights and Art 2 of the First Protocol to the Convention.

(4) *Prisons.* Section 12(1) of the Prison Act 1952, provides that '[a] prisoner, whether sentenced to imprisonment or committed to prison on remand or pending trial or otherwise, may be lawfully confined in any prison'. This is so even if it is subsequently established that the prisoner was wrongly convicted of the offence for which he was imprisoned. In such a case, the prisoner will not be able to sue anyone *in tort* for imprisoning him – for no one did him any legal wrong in locking him up – but he may be entitled to some statutory compensation under s 133 of the Criminal Justice Act 1988 for the fact that he was detained in prison for an offence he did not commit. We will deal in the next section with what the position is where a prisoner is held in jail longer than he should have been, but we should note at this stage the decision of the House of Lords in *R v Deputy Governor of Parkhurst Prison, ex parte Hague.*[51]

That decision actually dealt with two cases – the *Hague* case and *Weldon v Home Office*. In the *Hague* case, the claimant – a prisoner at Parkhurst Prison – claimed he had been falsely imprisoned because he had been kept in isolation for 28 days, contrary to the Prison Rules 1964. In the *Weldon* case, the claimant – a prisoner at Leeds Prison – claimed he had been falsely imprisoned because he had been detained in a strip cell. Lord Bridge remarked that the 'primary and fundamental issue' raised by the *Hague* and *Weldon* cases was:

> [Does] any restraint within defined bounds imposed upon a convicted prisoner whilst serving his sentence by the prison governor . . . but in circumstances where the particular form of restraint is not sanctioned by the prison rules, amounts for that reason to the tort of false imprisonment.[52]

The House of Lords answered this question in the negative on the basis that a governor's authority to detain a prisoner under s 12(1) of the 1952 Act did not come with any limits attached to it. So a governor could not act unlawfully in detaining a prisoner under s 12(1) of the 1952 Act merely because the *way* in which he chose to imprison the prisoner breached the Prison Rules 1964. The House of Lords therefore dismissed the claims of both the claimant in the *Hague* case and the claimant in the *Weldon* case.

However, s 12(1) only makes it lawful for the *prison governor* (and those acting with the governor's authority) to detain a prisoner, however he happens to be detained. The House of Lords was very clear that if A, a fellow prisoner of B's, locks B in a prison shed, then A will have committed the tort of false imprisonment.[53] Similarly, the House of Lords held that if A, a prison officer, locks B in a cell and does so in bad faith – knowing that he has no authority from the governor of the prison to do so – then A will have committed the tort of false imprisonment.[54]

The decision in the *Hague* case seems quite legalistic, resting as it does on a wide interpretation of the powers granted to a prison governor under s 12(1) of the 1952 Act. However, it may be that the real basis of the decision in *Hague* was that the House of Lords was simply trying to avoid the government being swamped with claims for compensation from prisoners, each alleging that their detention was unlawful because it technically breached the Prison Rules 1964.

(5) *Mental health.* People suffering from various mental disorders may in certain circumstances be arrested or detained in hospital.[55]

---

[51] [1992] 1 AC 58.

[52] Ibid, 162.

[53] [1992] 1 AC 58, 164, 166, 178.

[54] [1992] 1 AC 58, 164.

[55] See, for example, Mental Health Act 1983, s 136.

2.6 Statutory authority

The above section gave us a number of different examples where people are given *statutory powers* to interfere with other people's persons. The position of a defendant who wishes to rely on the fact that he was given a statutory power to interfere with another's person in order to establish he had a lawful justification for acting as he did is complicated by the fact that the *valid* exercise of a statutory power will normally be subject to a number of conditions. These conditions are of two types:

A. Statutory conditions

These conditions are expressly or impliedly laid out in the statute. They take the form: 'If *x* is true, then D will have the power to [interfere with C's person]' If *x* is not satisfied, then the statute will not give D a power to interfere with C's person and D will not be able to rely on the statute to justify his interfering with C's person.

For example, s 34(1) of the Police and Criminal Evidence Act 1984 provides that 'A person arrested for an offence shall not be kept in police detention except in accordance with the provisions of . . . Part [IV] of this Act.' One of those provisions[56] provides that the custody officer of a police station where an arrestee is being detained should periodically review the arrestee's detention to see whether 'his detention without being charged is necessary to secure or preserve evidence relating to an offence for which he is under arrest or to obtain such evidence by questioning him.'[57] This condition was not observed in the case of *Roberts* v *Chief Constable of the Cheshire Constabulary* (1999), where the claimant was arrested on suspicion of conspiracy to burgle and held in police custody for eight hours and 20 minutes before his detention was reviewed by the custody officer. Because the statute provided that his detention should have been reviewed no more than six hours after it was initially authorised, it was held that he had been falsely imprisoned for at least the extra two hours and 20 minutes that he was detained in custody before having his detention reviewed.[58]

B. Public law conditions

Where a statutory power to interfere with other people's persons has been created, the courts will readily infer that Parliament intended that the exercise of that power should be subject to a number of different conditions:

(1) that the power not be exercised for an *improper purpose*; (2) that the power only be exercised after the power-holder has considered all *relevant considerations* (and has put out of his mind any *irrelevant* considerations); (3) that the power not be exercised in a way that is *wholly unreasonable*; (4) that (in certain cases) that the grantee of the power not exercise it before having given the person against whom the power is exercised a *fair hearing*; (5) that the grantee of the power not

---

[56] Police and Criminal Evidence Act 1984, s 40(1).
[57] Police and Criminal Evidence Act 1984, s 37(1).
[58] See also *Christie* v *Leachinsky* [1947] AC 573 (arrest of claimant without warrant declared unlawful as statute under which he was arrested gave no power to arrest without warrant); and *Langley* v *Liverpool City Council* [2006] 1 WLR 375 (police constable had no power to take child into custody in order to protect child from harm under Children Act 1999 unless there were compelling reasons to do so, which did not exist in this case).

exercise it in a way that would disappoint for no good reason other people's *legitimate expectations* as to how that power would be exercised; (6) that the grantee of the power be *open about the reasons* why he has exercised the power in the way he has; (7) that the grantee of the power exercise that power in a way that is not inconsistent with the *European Convention on Human Rights*.[59]

The courts will infer that Parliament intended that the exercise of a statutory power to interfere with other people's persons should be subject to such conditions because they assume that Parliament is committed to the idea that statutory powers should only be exercised in a responsible manner; and all of the above conditions are designed to ensure that is the case.

If D is granted a statutory power[60] to interfere with C's person and he exercises that power in a way that violates one or more of the above conditions, he is said to have exercised the power in breach of a *public law duty*.[61] The question of whether, and if so when, the breach of a public law duty will prevent a defendant claiming that he had a lawful justification for interfering with the claimant's person was addressed by the Supreme Court in the recent case of *Lumba* v *Secretary of State for the Home Department* (2011).[62]

That case had its roots in the revelation in April 2006 that 1,023 foreign nationals who had been imprisoned in the UK for committing various criminal offences – including five who had committed sex offences against children – had not been considered for deportation after they were released from prison. This caused a media outcry and the Home Secretary, Charles Clarke, was subsequently replaced by John Reid, who declared the Home Office 'unfit for purpose'. Eager to avoid further bad publicity, the Home Office revised its policy on when it would exercise its powers under the Immigration Act 1971 to detain a foreign national prisoner (FNP) who had been released from prison. (The 1971 Act allows the Home Office to deport from the UK anyone who is not a British citizen if his 'deportation [is deemed] to be conducive to the public good' and allows a foreign national who has been designated for deportation to be detained pending his deportation.) At the time, the Home Office's *official* policy was that they would only detain an FNP who had been released from prison if it was necessary to do so. But in order to avoid the media outrage that would inevitably result if an FNP was not detained after having been released from prison and took advantage of his freedom to commit a serious criminal offence, the Home Office instituted a *secret* policy that *any* FNP who was released from prison should be detained pending deportation.

---

[59] See any text on constitutional or administrative law for a more in-depth discussion of these conditions and the key authorities that establish that the valid exercise of a statutory power is subject to these conditions. It should be noted that these conditions can only really apply to powers that the power-holder has some *choice* about exercising. In the case of a power such as the power to imprison under s 12(1) of the Prisons Act 1952 (discussed above, § 2.5(D)(4)), where a prison governor really has *no choice but* to detain a prisoner, it makes no sense to say that the valid exercise of that power is conditional on requirements (1)–(7) being observed. That is why in the *Hague* case (ibid), the House of Lords ruled that there were no limits on the power to detain under s 12(1).

[60] It should be noted that the valid exercise of a power under the *common law* to interfere with someone else's person is also subject to the above conditions. For example, it was assumed in *Austin* v *Commissioner of Police of the Metropolis* [2009] 1 AC 564 that the police would not have validly exercised their powers to prevent a breach of peace if in doing so they had violated Art 5 of the European Convention on Human Rights.

[61] The word 'duty' may be a bit of a misnomer here. It is not so much that a power holder has a *duty* to exercise the power in accordance with conditions (1)–(7), but that the power holder will *not be entitled* to exercise that power unless he abides by conditions (1)–(7).

[62] The case is reported at [2012] 1 AC 245 and will be referred to below simply as '*Lumba*'.

The claimants in *Lumba* were detained after being released from prison pursuant to this secret policy; though it was not disputed that the seriousness of the offences for which the claimants had been imprisoned meant that they would have been detained even under the Home Office's official policy. The Supreme Court agreed in *Lumba* that the Home Office had breached a public law duty – the requirement that they be open about the reasons why they were detaining the claimants – in exercising their powers under the Immigration Act 1971 to detain the claimants. However, the Supreme Court divided over the issue of whether that breach meant that the claimants had been falsely imprisoned. Of the nine Supreme Court Justices who decided *Lumba,* six took the view that the claimants had been falsely imprisoned (but for different reasons), and three took the view that they had not been falsely imprisoned.

In the majority, Lords *Dyson* and *Collins* and Lady *Hale* took the straightforward position that there was no lawful justification for imprisoning the claimants in *Lumba* because the Home Office's decision to detain the claimants was invalid as a matter of public law.[63] The decision to detain the claimants was made in pursuance of a policy that the Home Office was not entitled to pursue. It did not matter – so far as the claim that the claimants had been falsely imprisoned was concerned – that the Home Office *could* have lawfully detained the claimants under its official policy.[64] The fact that the claimants *might* have been lawfully detained did not mean that they *had* been lawfully detained.[65]

The other members of the majority in *Lumba* (and, indeed, the minority) were more cautious about adopting the line that *any* breach of a public law duty that had a bearing on, and was relevant to,[66] the decision to exercise a statutory power to interfere with a claimant's person would mean that there was no lawful justification for that interference. Lord *Kerr* took the view that there was no lawful justification for detaining the claimants in *Lumba* because the reasons for detaining them frustrated the purpose for which the Home Office had been given the power to detain foreign nationals like the claimants.[67] The fact that the claimants had been detained pursuant to a secret policy made it much harder (if not impossible) for the claimants to determine whether their detention was justified. Lords *Hope* and *Walker* argued that there was no lawful justification for detaining the claimants because their detention amounted to a serious 'abuse of power'.[68]

In the minority, Lord *Brown* (with whom Lord *Rodger* agreed) objected to the majority's finding that the claimants in *Lumba* had been falsely imprisoned on the basis that 'not every decision to detain affected by a public law breach necessarily carries in its wake an unanswerable claim for false imprisonment.'[69] Where the public law breach 'consists of applying, in place of [the government's] published policy, an unpublished policy less

---

[63] *Lumba*, at [68]–[69] (per Lord Dyson), [207] (per Lady Hale). Lord Collins expressed agreement with Lord Dyson's judgment at [219], but perhaps departed from the spirit of Lord Dyson's judgment by emphasising at [219] that 'the *serious* breach of public law in this case has the result that the detention of the [claimants] was unlawful. Any other result would negate the rule of law.'

[64] Though this feature of the case had the effect of reducing the damages payable to the claimants to a nominal level: see below, § 9.2.

[65] *Lumba*, at [71] (per Lord Dyson), [208] (per Lady Hale), [221] (per Lord Collins); also [175] (per Lord Hope), and [239]–[241] (per Lord Kerr).

[66] *Lumba*, at [68] (per Lord Dyson): 'the breach of public law must bear on and be relevant to the decision to detain.' Lady Hale held (at [207]) that 'the breach of public law duty must be material to the decision to detain and not to some other aspect of the detention and it must be capable of affecting the result.'

[67] *Lumba*, at [250]-[251].

[68] *Lumba*, at [170] (per Lord Hope), and [193] (per Lord Walker).

[69] *Lumba*, at [358].

favourable to those subject to the detaining power'[70] Lord *Brown* took the view that only a claimant who would have been entitled to be released under the published policy could sue for false imprisonment.[71] He pointed out the paradox involved in saying that the claimants had been falsely imprisoned when had they 'sought to challenge [their] continued detention by judicial review (or habeas corpus), the court would have been likely to [decline] in its discretion to order the [claimants'] release.'[72] How then, he asked, could one justify awarding 'damages to those conceded to have been rightly detained?'[73]

None of these positions is particularly satisfactory. The position taken by Lord *Dyson et al* gives rise to the problem that the House of Lords may have been trying to avoid in the *Hague* case: the problem of technical breaches of public law requirements resulting in the government being held liable for false imprisonment.[74] But at least their position has the virtue of making the law reasonably certain, which is more than can be said of Lords *Kerr*, *Hope* or *Walker*'s judgments. On the other hand, Lord *Brown*'s judgment would create an unsustainable distinction between cases where a defendant exercises a statutory power to interfere with a claimant's person in breach of an expressed or implied condition on its exercise in the statute (in which case Lord *Brown* would be in favour of finding liability, even if the defendant could have exercised his power to interfere with the claimant's person without breaching any condition)[75] and cases where a defendant's exercise of a statutory power to interfere with a claimant's person breached a public law condition on the exercise of a statutory power.

2.7 Mistakes

We have already quoted Tony Weir as saying that 'no one in Britain, *no one*, can justify deliberately touching even a hair on [a claimant's] head, or entering her garden – much less depriving her of her liberty – merely on the ground that it was reasonable to do so . . .' In the same passage, Tony Weir immediately went on to say:

> . . . or on the more insidious ground that he reasonably thought he was entitled to do so. Trespass trips up the zealous bureaucrat, the eager policeman and the officious citizen; indeed, punitive damages can be awarded against the first two. It is not enough to *think* you are entitled; you must actually *be* entitled.[76]

The quote suggests there is no room for a defendant to escape liability in trespass by claiming they mistakenly believed they were entitled to interfere with the claimant's person. The reality is more complex, and requires very careful discussion.

---

[70] *Lumba*, at [353].

[71] *Lumba*, at [355]. Lord Phillips, also in the minority, took the view (at [321]–[323]) that where there was a disparity between the government's official policy as to how it would exercise its detention powers and its actual policy, only those who had a 'legitimate expectation' that they would not be detained under the official policy could claim they had been falsely imprisoned, and the claimants in *Lumba* did not fall into that category.

[72] *Lumba*, at [359].

[73] *Lumba*, at [361].

[74] See the subsequent case of *Kambadzi v Secretary of State for the Home Department* [2011] UKSC 23, where the detention of a foreign national who was being held pending deportation – having served time in prison for sexual assault – was rendered unlawful merely because his continued detention had not been reviewed as regularly as the Home Office had said it would review it in a policy document.

[75] *Lumba*, at [347](2).

[76] Weir 2004, 322 (emphasis in original).

A. Mistaken belief in consent

Let us first take the case where a defendant mistakenly believes that the claimant has consented to his touching her in some way. Consider the **Gullible Student Problem**:

> *Hopeful* attends a party at *Beauty*'s house. As the party finishes very late, *Beauty* agrees that *Hopeful* and some other friends can sleep over in the front room, while she goes to bed. *Hopeful*'s friends tell him that *Beauty* has told them that she would like *Beauty* to wake her with a kiss. *Hopeful* has always liked *Beauty* and is very happy to hear this. He wakes himself up at 6.30 am, goes upstairs to *Beauty*'s room and kisses her on the lips. *Hopeful*'s kissing *Beauty* wakes her up, and *Beauty* – who never said that she wanted *Hopeful* to kiss her awake – is disgusted to find *Hopeful* kissing her.

It is very likely in this case that *Beauty* could sue *Hopeful* for what he has done. Even though *Hopeful* is completely innocent, it cannot be the case that what *Hopeful*'s friends told him deprived *Beauty* of the right she had not to be subjected to unwelcome physical attentions from people like *Hopeful*. Only *Beauty* could waive that right. But what should we say about the **Changing Mind Problem**?

> *Beauty* and *Hopeful* are both at a party. *Beauty* tells *Hopeful* that she would like him to kiss her. *Hopeful* has always liked *Beauty* and is very happy to hear this. *Hopeful* leans in to kiss *Beauty*, but before he does, *Beauty* has a sudden change of heart. *Beauty* decides that she does not want *Hopeful* to kiss her, but before she has a chance to say anything, *Hopeful* has kissed her on the lips.

In this situation, *Beauty* did not consent to *Hopeful*'s kissing her at the time he actually did kiss her, any more than she did in Gullible Student. The only difference between the two situations is that in Gullible Student, *Hopeful*'s friends made *Hopeful* think *Beauty* wanted him to kiss her; in Changing Mind, *Beauty* made *Hopeful* think she wanted him to kiss her. Should it make a difference who told *Hopeful* that *Beauty* wanted him to kiss her? We think it should and that *Beauty* should not be entitled to sue *Hopeful* in Changing Mind.

One elegant way of reaching this result is by invoking the law on *estoppel*. The law on estoppel now has many different branches, but it originated as a part of the law of evidence. Under the law on estoppel, *Beauty* would be prevented (or estopped) from claiming that she did not consent to *Hopeful*'s kissing her in Changing Mind. This is because she represented to *Hopeful* that she wanted him to kiss her, and he relied on that representation by kissing her. Given this, she cannot now go back on her representation and say in court that, actually, when *Hopeful* kissed her, she was not consenting. It would be different if, when *Hopeful* leaned in to kiss *Beauty*, he saw the confusion in her eyes and realised she was hesitating about kissing him, and decided to quickly steal a kiss before it was too late. In such a case, *Hopeful* could not argue that he relied on *Beauty*'s representation that she wanted him to kiss her. When he kissed her, he was no longer acting in good faith on the basis of her representation, and was simply trying to take advantage of the situation. In such a case, *Beauty* would not be estopped from claiming that she did not consent to the kiss, and would be able to sue *Hopeful* for battery.

B. Mistaken belief in self-defence

The issue of whether a defendant to a trespass claim could rely on a mistaken belief that he was being attacked by the claimant to defeat that claim was considered by the House of Lords in the case of *Ashley* v *Chief Constable of Sussex Police* (2008).

In that case, Ashley was shot dead by PC Christopher Sherwood, who was part of a group of armed police officers that conducted a drugs raid on Ashley's house at 4.20 am on 15 January 1998. Sherwood had been briefed that Ashley might be dangerous and was first into Ashley's bedroom where Ashley – having been woken by the sound of the raid – was standing naked in the middle of the room with no light on. Sherwood was found not guilty of murdering Ashley on the ground that he honestly thought that Ashley might be about to fire a gun at him. Under the criminal law, a defendant who honestly (though mistakenly) acts on facts which, if they had been true, would have given him a defence of self-defence is entitled to be acquitted.[77]

When Ashley's family brought a claim in tort against the police, the police argued that a similar rule should apply under the civil law, and that the courts should find that Sherwood did no wrong in shooting Ashley if he honestly (though mistakenly) thought his life was in danger. The House of Lords unanimously rejected this argument, and quite rightly too. Ashley could not suddenly have lost the rights he would otherwise have had not to be shot just because Sherwood decided that his life was in danger. It would have been different if Ashley had *done something* to give Sherwood reasonable grounds for believing that his life was in danger. In such a case, Ashley's actions would have deprived him of his rights not to be shot: people who play with fire can expect to be burned.[78]

But would Sherwood have had a defence had he *reasonably* thought his life was in danger, and he shot Ashley for that reason? Sherwood had, after all, been briefed before the raid by his commanders that Ashley was a dangerous individual and that might have made his belief that his life was in danger a reasonable one to have. Three of the Law Lords who decided *Ashley* left the question open as to whether, in such a case, Sherwood would have done anything wrong in shooting Ashley.[79] Lord Carswell thought that any kind of reasonable belief that Sherwood's life was in danger would have entitled Sherwood to shoot Ashley.[80] Lord Bingham said nothing on the issue.

The concern about allowing a defence in this type of case – where Sherwood reasonably believed his life was in danger, but not because of anything Ashley did – is that allowing such a defence suggests that what was said in a briefing room some miles away from Ashley's house could deprive Ashley of his rights not to be shot. This would seem counter-intuitive. If what *Hopeful*'s friends said to him in the Gullible Student could not strip *Beauty* of her rights that she would otherwise have had not to be kissed by someone she was repulsed by, then a police briefing could not have stripped Ashley of the rights that he would otherwise have had not to be shot. Given this, we favour the view that it would only have been lawful (under the law of tort) for Sherwood to shoot Ashley if *Ashley* had done something to make it reasonable for Sherwood to believe his life was in danger. If *someone else* had done something to make it reasonable for Sherwood to believe this, that would not give him a defence.

---

[77] *R* v *Williams (Gladstone)* [1987] 3 All ER 411.

[78] Though see Lord Scott in the *Ashley* case ([2008] 1 AC 962, at [20]), who seems to have taken the view that in this sort of case, Ashley's family would still have been entitled to sue Sherwood, subject to a discount in the damages for contributory negligence.

[79] [2008] 1 AC 962, at [20] (per Lord Scott), [55] (per Lord Rodger), and [90] (per Lord Neuberger).

[80] [2008] 1 AC 962, at [76] (per Lord Carswell).

C. Mistaken belief in validity of byelaw

In *Percy v Hall* (1997), the claimants were arrested over 150 times for trespassing on land in the vicinity of a military communications installation in North Yorkshire in breach of the HMS Forest Moor and Menwith Hill Station Byelaws 1986. These byelaws were actually invalid at the time the claimants were arrested because they were insufficiently precise. When this was discovered, the claimants sued the constables for false imprisonment. The claimants' claims were dismissed by the Court of Appeal: the fact that the constables had mistakenly believed the byelaws were valid, and would have been failing in their duties had they not enforced those apparently valid byelaws, was enough to give them a defence to being sued for false imprisonment. Tony Weir calls the decision 'disgraceful'.[81] It certainly seems inconsistent with the next set of cases.

D. Unduly prolonged detention in prison

Suppose that someone makes a mistake in determining how long *Prisoner* should spend in prison and as a result he is imprisoned for three months longer than he ought to have been. Can *Prisoner* sue his prison *Governor* on the ground that he was falsely imprisoned for those three months? If it was the *courts* that made the mistake in calculating *Prisoner*'s sentence, then *Prisoner* will *not* be able to sue *Governor* for falsely imprisoning him.[82] *Governor* will be able to argue that he was duty-bound to imprison *Prisoner* for as long as he did, and that he therefore had a lawful justification for imprisoning *Prisoner* for the extra three months that *Prisoner* should not have served.

If, however, it was *Governor* who made the mistake in calculating *Prisoner*'s sentence, then *Prisoner will* be able to sue *Governor* for falsely imprisoning him – and this is so even if the *Governor*'s mistake was an entirely reasonable one to make. This was established by the House of Lords' decision in *R v Governor of Brockhill Prison, ex parte Evans (No 2)* (2001).[83] In that case, the claimant was a woman named Evans who was sent to prison to serve several terms of imprisonment, running concurrently. At the time Evans was sent to prison, the Divisional Court had ruled – in a case called *R v Governor of Blundeston Prison, ex parte Gaffney* (1982) – that the release date of a prisoner serving several concurrent sentences should be calculated in a certain way (call this 'Method X'). The governor, abiding by the decision in *Gaffney*, applied Method X to determine when Evans should be released. However, while Evans was still in prison, she went to court and persuaded the Court of Appeal to rule that the governor should have used a different method for calculating her release date – let's call this method 'Method Y'.[84] The Court of Appeal thereby overruled the decision of the Divisional Court in *Gaffney*. According to Method Y, Evans should have *already* been released 59 days previously and, accordingly, she was released on the same day as the Court of Appeal overruled *Gaffney*. Evans sued the prison governor, claiming that she had been falsely imprisoned in being detained for those extra 59 days. The House of Lords allowed her claim.

---

[81] Weir 2004, 354.

[82] *Quinland* v *Governor of Swaleside Prison* [2003] QB 306. A will not be able to sue the *courts* for falsely imprisoning him by virtue of s 2(5) of the Crown Proceedings Act 1947, which provides that 'No proceedings shall lie against the Crown by virtue of this section in respect of anything done or omitted to be done by a person whilst discharging or purporting to discharge any responsibilities of a judicial nature vested in him, or any responsibilities which he has in connection with the execution of judicial process.'

[83] Noted, Cane 2001a.

[84] *R v Governor of Brockhill Prison, ex parte Evans* [1997] QB 443.

It is hard to reconcile this decision with the decision in *Percy* v *Hall*. If the constables in *Percy v Hall* had a lawful justification for arresting the claimants in that case based on the fact that they were duty-bound to arrest the claimants when they did, it is hard to see why the governor of Evans's prison did not have a similar lawful justification for detaining Evans for as long as he did. After all, until *Gaffney* was overruled, the governor of Evans's prison was – for all practical purposes – *required* to calculate Evans's release date using Method X and to detain Evans in prison until that date.[85]

2.8 Remedies

The victim of a trespass to the person will normally be able sue for compensation for any actionable losses that the tort caused her to suffer.[86] (An exception exists under s 45 of the Offences Against the Person Act 1861, which prevents someone who has brought a private prosecution against someone for assault or battery in the magistrates' court subsequently suing the same person in tort for assault or battery.)[87] Aggravated damages and exemplary (or punitive) damages may also be available if the tortfeasor acted in a sufficiently outrageous way in committing the tort.[88] Even if the victim has suffered no loss as a result of the trespass tort being committed, he or she will still be able to sue for *nominal* damages (about £5) to mark the fact that his or her rights have been violated.

It has been suggested that the mere violation of a right should attract a more substantial award than merely nominal damages, and that consequently someone whose rights have been violated should be able to sue – in the absence of any other remedy being available to them – for something known as *vindicatory damages*: damages designed to mark the fact that someone's rights have been violated.[89]

The possibility that the victim of a trespass tort might be able to sue for such damages was first raised by Lord Scott in the case of *Ashley* v *Chief Constable of Sussex Police* (2008), the facts of which have already been set out above.[90] In that case, Ashley's family were not only claiming that Sherwood had acted unlawfully (under the law of tort) in shooting Ashley. They also claimed that the police officers who had organised the raid had acted negligently in failing to brief properly the officers conducting the raid (including Sherwood) and that their negligence had contributed to Ashley's death, in the sense that had Sherwood been briefed properly, he might not have been so quick to fire at Ashley when he went into Ashley's bedroom. The defendant – the Chief Constable of Sussex Police – was prepared to admit negligence, and had offered to settle the family's claim and pay them all the damages they were seeking on the basis that the officers who had organised the raid were negligent. But the defendant was not prepared to admit that Sherwood had acted unlawfully (under the law of tort) in shooting Ashley. Ashley's family therefore

---

[85] See Judge LJ's remarks in the Court of Appeal in *R* v *Governor of Brockhill Prison, ex parte Evans (No 2)* [1999] QB 1043, 1071: 'The governor was blameless. Indeed if he had not continued to detain [Evans] he would have been acting in defiance of the earlier decisions of the Divisional Court . . . So in detaining [Evans] for as long as he did the governor was responsibly performing his duties.'

[86] See below, Chapter 8, for the law on causation, and Chapter 9, for the law on actionability.

[87] A case where this provision was applied to stop the claimant suing for battery was *Wong* v *Parkside NHS Trust* [2003] 3 All ER 932.

[88] Aggravated and exemplary damages are discussed in more detail below, Chapter 24.

[89] Vindicatory damages are discussed in more detail below, Chapter 26.

[90] See above, § 2.7.

declined the Chief Constable's settlement offer and wanted the case to go to trial, in order
to have it publicly established that Sherwood had done something wrong (under the law
of tort) in shooting Ashley.

The issue the House of Lords was asked to resolve was whether Ashley's family could do
this, or whether their continuing attempts to sue the Chief Constable should be struck out
on the basis that they amounted to an abuse of process, given that the Chief Constable had
already admitted negligence and was prepared on that basis to pay the family all the damages they could possibly recover by taking their claim to trial. The House of Lords decided,
by three to two, that Ashley's family should be allowed to proceed with their claim against
the Chief Constable. Lord Rodger and Lord Bingham thought that as Ashley's family had
an arguable claim that a battery had been committed against Ashley, there was no basis for
striking out an attempt to have that claim tried in court, whatever the motives of Ashley's
family in wanting to take their case to court. Lord Scott (with whom Lord Rodger agreed)
went further, arguing that it was entirely legitimate for Ashley's family to want to have it
publicly established that Ashley had been (under the law of tort) wrongfully killed.[91] Furthermore, Lord Scott thought that if it were established that Ashley had been unlawfully
killed (under the law of tort), Ashley's estate might be entitled to 'vindicatory damages',
which were 'essentially rights-centred, awarded in order to demonstrate that the right in
question should not have been infringed at all.'[92] The fact that vindicatory damages might
be available to Ashley's estate was, for Lord Scott, an additional reason why the claim for
battery in *Ashley*'s case had to be allowed to continue: 'The chief constable has conceded
compensatory damages. He has not conceded vindicatory damages and he cannot do so
unless he concedes liability on the assault and battery claim.'[93]

In the subsequent case of *Lumba* v *Secretary of State for the Home Department* (2011),
the Supreme Court was radically divided over the issue of whether vindicatory damages
would be available in a trespass case, with three Supreme Court Justices ruling that vindicatory damages had no place in the law of tort, and four Supreme Court Justices indicating their willingness to allow such damages to be claimed, at least in some circumstances.
This aspect of the *Lumba* decision is discussed in much more detail below.[94]

The emphasis placed in some of the judgments in *Ashley* and *Lumba* on the vindicatory
element of the remedies that are available for the trespass torts finds strong echo in the work
of Tony Weir, who argues that in thinking about what remedies should be available when A
commits a trespass to the person in relation to B, we should separate out *compensatory* remedies from *vindicatory* remedies. B, he argues, should only be able to sue A for compensation if she has a claim in negligence against A for compensation. On the other hand,
vindicatory remedies – such as an injunction, or a declaration that A acted wrongfully in
relation to B – should be available to B whether or not A was at fault for what happened:

> where the [claimant] is seeking compensation for harm, the rules of negligence seem so appropriate
> nowadays as to be almost mandatory, whereas they have, or ought to have, no place where the [claim-
> ant] is seeking, not compensation for harm, but rather vindication of the rights by whose infringe-
> ment he is aggrieved. It is not a great step to move from the proposition that no harm need be
> established in a trespass claim to the position that if harm is alleged, the rules of negligence apply.[95]

---

[91] [2008] 1 AC 962, at [23].
[92] [2008] 1 AC 962, at [22].
[93] [2008] 1 AC 962, at [29].
[94] See below, §26.3(B).
[95] Weir 1998a, 1092–110. See also Weir 2006, 134–5.

One problem with this suggestion is that the law on trespass to the person protects some interests that are not well protected under the law of negligence – such as an interest in being free to move about, or being free from threats of harm. Weir's proposal would make it harder for a claimant who was falsely imprisoned or assaulted to recover compensation for the frustration of having one's liberty taken away, or any distress caused by being threatened with imminent attack. Another, more philosophical, problem with this proposal is that it is not clear that it is possible to separate out compensation from vindication. As we will see,[96] some academics argue that the reason why the victim of a tort (B) can sue the person who committed that tort (A) for compensation is to vindicate B's rights against A. The award of compensation is meant to give B the monetary equivalent of whatever right of B's it is that A violated in acting as he did. If these academics are right, then compensation should be payable whenever a right has been violated, whether or not the violator was at fault for the violation.

Further reading

The modern-day dominance of the law of negligence within tort law – and in particular, tort law as it is taught in the universities – means there is not much decent writing on the torts dealt with in this chapter. What writing there is is usually flawed by characterising these torts as *intentional* torts – which confuses these torts with a separate set of torts (dealt with in the chapter on 'Economic Torts', below) which require for their commission that the defendant acted with an *intention to harm* the claimant. See, for example, **David Howarth's 'Is there a future for the intentional torts?' in Birks (ed),** *The Classification of Obligations* **(OUP, 1997), 233–281,** which groups *together* assault, battery, false imprisonment *and* the economic torts under the heading 'intentional torts'.

Tony Weir's views on the torts discussed here have been summed up above, but are well worth reading in the original: **Weir,** *An Introduction to Tort Law,* **2nd edn (Clarendon Press, 2006), Chapter 9**. He takes the view that the torts discussed here are very different in function from the tort of negligence that we are just about to look at in detail. The trespass torts are concerned with vindicating rights; negligence is concerned with compensating for harm. For similar views, see **Peter Cane, 'Justice and justifications for tort liability'** (1982) 2 *Oxford Journal of Legal Studies* 30; and **Jason Varuhas, 'A tort-based approach to damages under the Human Rights Act 1998'** (2009) 72 *Modern Law Review* 750.

---

[96] See below, § 23.7(B).

Chapter 3
Claims in negligence

Aims and objectives

Reading this chapter should enable you to:

(1) Understand the basic elements that have to be made out for a claim in negligence to be made.

(2) Understand the relationships between negligence and other types of civil wrong.

(3) Understand what remedies will be available when someone commits the tort of negligence.

3.1 The basics

If a claimant wants to sue a defendant in negligence, he will have to show four things:

1. that the defendant owed the claimant *a duty of care*;

2. that the defendant *breached* that duty of care;

3. that the defendant's breach *caused* the claimant to suffer some kind of loss; and

4. at least one of the losses that the defendant's breach caused the claimant to suffer is *actionable*.

For those who find it hard to remember the above, it might be useful to note that these four requirements correspond with the first four letters of the alphabet: D (for duty of care), B (for breach), C (for causation) and A (for actionability).

Duty comes *first*:

The law takes no cognizance of carelessness in the abstract. It concerns itself with carelessness only where there is a duty to take care and where failure in that duty has caused damage. In such circumstances carelessness assumes the legal quality of negligence and entails the consequences of negligence.[1]

---

[1] *Donoghue* v *Stevenson* [1932] AC 562, 618–619 (per Lord Macmillan). See also *Bourhill* v *Young* [1943] 1 AC 92, 116 (per Lord Porter).

Some university lecturers on the law of negligence prefer to leave the topic of duty to the end, after they have dealt with the law on breach of duty (usually lectured on under the heading 'fault'), and causation, and actionability (usually lectured on under the heading 'remoteness of damage'). We have two reasons for not following their example.

First, in a negligence case, the courts do not simply ask – Was the defendant careless? They ask – Did the defendant breach a duty of care owed to the claimant? And what factors the courts take into account in answering that question will depend crucially on what *sort* of duty it was that the defendant owed the claimant. For example, the duty of care a landowner owes his neighbours to protect them from dangers arising on his land requires him simply to do his best, given the resources he has, to deal with any such dangers.[2] In contrast, the duty of care a driver owes nearby users of the road to take care not to drive dangerously does not just require him to do his best to drive safely, but to drive to the standards of a normal, qualified driver – even if he is incapable of reaching that standard.[3] So you simply cannot understand the authorities on when the courts will find that a defendant breached a duty of care owed to the claimant without a good prior understanding of what sort of duties of care we owe each other.

Secondly, just as there is no such thing as carelessness in the abstract, neither is there such a thing as causation in the abstract. Whether or not a defendant's breach of a duty of care will be held to have caused the claimant to have suffered a particular kind of loss will depend on what sort of duty of care the defendant is supposed to have owed the claimant. Consider the **Unfortunate Rock Star Problem**:

> *Star* goes everywhere with his *Bodyguard*. *Driver* carelessly runs over *Star* while *Star* is crossing the road. *Envy* – who suspects that *Star* is having an affair with his wife and who has been following *Star* to confirm his suspicions – takes advantage of the fact that *Star* is lying in the middle of the road to go up to *Star* and kick him in the head (something which causes *Star* to suffer severe brain damage). *Bodyguard* does nothing to stop *Envy* doing this, because he is unhappy with *Star* for sleeping with *Bodyguard*'s latest girlfriend.

In this case, we have two people – *Bodyguard* and *Driver* – who owed *Star* duties of care (in *Driver*'s case, a duty to take care not to drive dangerously, and in *Bodyguard*'s case, a duty to take reasonable steps to save *Star* from being attacked). *Driver* and *Bodyguard* each breached the duties of care they owed *Star*. *Star* would not have suffered the brain damage that he did had *Driver* and *Bodyguard* not *each* breached the duties of care that they respectively owed him. But only *Bodyguard*'s breach of his duty of care will be held to have *caused Star*'s brain damage. That is because of the nature of the particular duty of care that *Bodyguard* owed *Star* – a duty to prevent the very kind of attack that brought about *Star*'s brain damage.[4] But it is impossible to appreciate this point if you have no idea what sort of duties of care *Driver* and *Bodyguard* owed *Star* in this case.

---

[2] *Goldman* v *Hargrave* [1967] AC 645. See below, § 7.5.
[3] *Nettleship* v *Weston* [1971] 2 QB 691. See below, § 7.2(D)(2).
[4] See below, § 8.11.

3.2 Negligence and intention

Sir Percy Winfield once suggested that someone would commit the tort of negligence if, and only if, he 'breach[ed] a legal duty to take care by an *inadvertent* act or omission'.[5] This seems wrong. Suppose *Driver* drives down a street at 80 miles an hour and as a result runs over *Pedestrian*. *Pedestrian* attempts to sue *Driver* in negligence for compensation for her injuries. Could *Driver* really rebut *Pedestrian*'s claim by arguing that while he admittedly owed *Pedestrian* a duty to take care not to drive dangerously, he did not commit the tort of negligence in relation to *Pedestrian* in driving as he did because he *deliberately* drove down the road at 80 miles an hour? The answer must be 'no'. A breach of a duty of care is still a breach, even if the breach was committed intentionally.

Perhaps acknowledging this point, Winfield later suggested that someone would commit the tort of negligence if: (1) he breached a duty of care owed to another *and* (2) when he breached that duty he did not intend to harm that other.[6] Again, there does not seem any reason for this limitation on the scope of the tort of negligence. Suppose, for example, that *Mother-in-Law* visited *Husband* in his house. While she was in the house, she put her foot through a rotten floorboard on the staircase which *Husband* had neglected to replace and as a result twisted her ankle. Now suppose that *Mother-in-Law* sues *Husband* in negligence, claiming that her injury happened as a result of *Husband*'s breach of the duty of care that he owed her as an occupier to take reasonable steps to see that she would be reasonably safe while she was on his premises. Could *Husband* really defeat *Mother-in-Law*'s claim by arguing that 'When I found out that the floorboard was rotten and liable to give way, I deliberately left it untouched in the hope that when my *Mother-in-Law* came visiting she would put her foot through it'? Surely not[7] – the fact that *Husband* breached the duty of care he owed *Mother-in-Law* as his visitor with the intention of harming her would not stop any court from concluding that *Husband* had committed the tort of negligence in this case.[8]

3.3 Negligence and other wrongs[9]

Negligence is one of very few torts that is not, on its face, geared towards protecting people from suffering a particular *kind* of harm. Unlike torts such as defamation (which protects reputation) or battery (which protects someone's physical integrity) or false imprisonment (which protects someone's freedom of movement), negligence seems simply to focus on what the defendant *did*, rather than on what harm he caused. This gives negligence, as a tort, the potential to range very wide indeed. In any case where a defendant acted unreasonably and a claimant suffered harm as a result, the claimant *might* be able to

---

[5] Winfield 1926, 184 (emphasis added).

[6] Winfield 1934, 41.

[7] Cf. *New South Wales* v *Lepore* (2003) 212 CLR 511, at [162] (per McHugh J): '[a claimant] may, if he or she chooses, sue in negligence for the intentional infliction of harm'; also *Blake* v *Galloway* [2004] 1 WLR 2844, at [17] (per Dyson LJ): 'If the defendant . . . [had] deliberately aimed the piece of bark at the claimant's head, then [the claimant might have been able to sue the defendant in negligence].'

[8] This position was endorsed – though without citing this text – by Arden LJ in *Dunnage* v *Randall* [2016] QB 639, at [150] (using the example of a defendant who deliberately allows the claimant to use a path across the defendant's garden, knowing that the path is dangerous to use).

[9] See Weir 1998a.

argue that the defendant is liable in negligence to compensate him for the harm he has suffered, on the basis that the defendant owed him, and breached, a duty to take care not to act as he did, and the harm suffered by the claimant resulted from that breach.

Lawyers have not been slow to seize on negligence's potential to provide a remedy in any case where unreasonable conduct has resulted in harm being suffered. As Lord Templeman remarked in *CBS Songs* v *Amstrad plc* (1988), when making a negligence claim 'it is always easy to draft a proposition which is tailor-made to produce the desired result.'[10] And the courts have sometimes allowed lawyers to make claims in negligence for compensation in respect of harms which other areas of the law of tort are concerned to protect people against. All of which means there is now some overlap between the law of negligence and a range of other wrongs. In this section, we want to chart the areas of overlap and see how far they go:

(1) *Battery.* Unlike negligence, battery is a tort that is actionable *per se*. So a claimant suing in battery has no need to show that he has suffered any loss. Nor does he have to show that the defendant acted unreasonably in touching him – all he has to do is show that the defendant intentionally or carelessly touched him. This means that battery, rather than negligence, will be the tort a claimant will sue under if he has suffered no tangible harm as a result of being touched by the defendant or if the defendant acted reasonably in touching him. But in cases where a defendant *carelessly* touched a claimant, and physical injury or a psychiatric illness resulted, a claim in negligence may well be available, as well as a claim in battery. In practice, such cases tend to be pleaded as negligence cases, rather than battery cases. Certainly, in a case where *Driver* has carelessly run down *Pedestrian* in the street, it would be regarded as peculiar for *Pedestrian* to sue *Driver* in battery, rather than in negligence.

(2) *False imprisonment.* In theory, false imprisonment can only be alleged where a defendant intentionally locked up a claimant.[11] So if a defendant carelessly did something that resulted in a claimant being imprisoned, negligence is the only tort that might provide the claimant with a remedy – provided, of course, that the imprisonment resulted in the claimant suffering some tangible harm. (If the defendant is a public authority, a claim under the Human Rights Act 1998 might also be available.) This was the case in *Al-Kandari* v *Brown* (1988), where the defendant firm of solicitors was acting for the claimant's husband in a child custody dispute between the claimant and her husband. Because the husband had a record of violence and kidnapping his and the claimant's children, the courts had ordered that the husband's passport be held by the defendants. Due to the defendants' carelessness, the husband was allowed to get his passport back, and he promptly kidnapped the claimant and their children. The claimant was left tied up in the back of a van, and the claimant's children were spirited out of the country and she never saw them again. The claimant successfully sued the defendants in negligence for damages for the physical and psychiatric injuries she had suffered as a result of being kidnapped.

(3) *Defamation.* A substantial overlap between the law of negligence and the law of defamation was created by the House of Lords' decision in *Spring* v *Guardian Assurance* (1995). In that case, the claimant was seeking a job selling life insurance policies. His prospective employer contacted the firm for which he used to work for a reference. The firm responded that the claimant was 'a man of little or no integrity and could not be

---

[10] [1988] 1 AC 1013, 1059.
[11] See above, § 2.3.

regarded as honest'. This was doubly unfortunate: first, the reference resulted in the claimant not getting the job; second, the reference was extremely unfair. Had the claimant sued his old firm in defamation, his claim would have been dismissed as the firm would have had a defence of 'qualified privilege' to his claim.[12] So the claimant sued the firm in negligence instead, and won. It is surprising that claimants have – post-*Spring* – not attempted to make more attempts to circumvent the rules on when someone can sue in defamation by invoking the law of negligence. But the result is that it is still very unclear how far the law of negligence can help protect people from suffering loss as a result of having their reputation besmirched.

(4) *Breach of statutory duty.* We have already seen,[13] that if A breaches a statutory duty imposed on him for the benefit of B, and B suffers loss as a result, B may be able to bring a claim (a claim for 'breach of statutory duty') for compensation for that loss. But he will only be able to do so if Parliament intended that a breach of that statutory duty be actionable in tort. But what if it is clear that Parliament did not so intend? In such a case, B might be tempted to bring a claim in negligence against A instead, arguing that A owed him a duty to take care not to act as he did. Due to the almost single-handed efforts of Lord Hoffmann, it seems that this option is now closed off to B unless there are special circumstances in B's case that would justify the courts in finding that A owed B a duty of care. The mere fact that A was subject to a statutory duty not to act as he did will not be enough on its own to justify the courts in finding that A owed B a duty to take care not to act as he did:

> If a statute actually imposes a duty, it is well settled that the question of whether it was intended to give rise to a private right of action depends upon the construction of the statute. . . If the statute does not create a private right of action, it would be, to say the least, unusual if the mere existence of the statutory duty could generate a common law duty of care.[14]

(5) *Private nuisance.* As we will see, the tort of private nuisance – very roughly speaking – exists to protect the value of a claimant's land as something to be used and enjoyed.

The tort extends far enough to allow *Owner* to sue *Neighbour* when he knows or ought to know that a problem has arisen on his land that creates a foreseeable risk that *Owner*'s land will be damaged, and fails to take reasonable steps to deal with that problem, with the result that *Owner*'s land is in fact damaged. (*Neighbour*'s liability in this case is known as liability for 'adopting or continuing' a nuisance.) In such a case, *Owner* can sue *Neighbour* in private nuisance for the harm done to his land, but there is authority that he can choose to sue in negligence as well.[15] However, nowadays the claim would usually be made in nuisance,[16] and there seems no advantage in bringing the claim in negligence instead: *Owner* would still have to prove fault on the part of *Neighbour* for what happened, and would probably only be able to recover damages for the harm done to his land, just as would be the case in nuisance.[17]

One potential overlap between the law of private nuisance and the law of negligence has been eliminated by the House of Lords' insistence that claims cannot be brought in

---

[12] See below, § 16.10(1).
[13] See above, § 1.11.
[14] *Gorringe* v *Calderdale MBC* [2004] 1 WLR 1057, at [23] (per Lord Hoffmann).
[15] *Goldman* v *Hargrave* [1967] AC 645.
[16] See *Leakey* v *National Trust* [1980] QB 485 and *Holbeck Hall Hotel Ltd* v *Scarborough BC* [2000] QB 836.
[17] See below, § 13.9(C).

private nuisance for personal injury.[18] As a result, a landowner who suffers physical injury as a result of inhaling smoke coming from his neighbour's land can only sue in negligence, rather than private nuisance. It is unclear what the position is if it is the landowner's cattle that are poisoned as a result of inhaling the smoke from the defendant's land. In such a case, it may be that a claim in private nuisance will be available,[19] thus giving the landowner the option of suing his neighbour either in negligence or in private nuisance.

(6) *Breach of contract.* Moving away from tortious wrongs and into other wrongs, some overlap between the tort of negligence and the wrong of breach of contract was created by the House of Lords' decision in *Henderson* v *Merrett Syndicates Ltd* (1995), which ruled that if A has, in a contract with B, 'assumed a responsibility' to B to perform a certain task carefully, and then fails to perform that task carefully, B will not only be able to sue A for breach of contract; he will also be able to sue A in negligence (provided, of course, that A's carelessness has caused B to suffer an actionable loss).

(7) *Equitable wrongs.* While a trustee who holds money on trust for a beneficiary will owe that beneficiary a duty to invest that money carefully,[20] that duty is equitable in nature. As such, breach of that duty will amount to an equitable wrong, rather than a tort. The courts have generally set their face against allowing those with a merely equitable interest in property to take advantage of the law of tort to obtain remedies when that property is misapplied.[21] As a result, there is no real overlap between the law of negligence and the law of equitable wrongs. However, where a third party carelessly damages property that is held on trust for the claimant, the Court of Appeal has now allowed that the claimant might be able to sue the third party for damages.[22]

3.4 Remedies for negligence

Negligence seems to be a peculiar tort in that most people think that compensatory damages are the *only* remedy available to a claimant in a negligence case.

In *Kralj* v *McGrath* (1986), Woolf J held that in a negligence case, aggravated damages (damages designed to assuage a claimant's feelings of outrage at the way the defendant has treated him) will *never* be available. It is hard to see why: there is no other tort for which aggravated damages will never be available. Woolf J held that allowing such damages to be awarded in negligence cases would 'be wholly inconsistent with the general approach to damages in this area, which is to compensate the [claimant] for the loss that she has actually suffered'.[23] But that begs the question of whether compensatory damages *should* be the only type of damages available in negligence cases.

In principle, exemplary damages (damages designed to punish a defendant who has flouted the law by deliberately committing a tort) should be available in negligence cases so long as the defendant's breach of a duty of care was sufficiently culpable, has not been

---

[18] *Hunter* v *Canary Wharf* [1997] AC 655, 696 (per Lord Lloyd) and 707 (per Lord Hoffmann).
[19] The question is discussed further below, § 13.12.
[20] Trustee Act 2000, ss 1, 2 and Sched 1.
[21] See below, § 15.3(B)(5).
[22] For further discussion, see below, § 5.8.
[23] *Kralj* v *McGrath* [1986] 1 All ER 54, 61.

punished under the criminal law, and falls within the rules laid down in *Rookes* v *Barnard* (1964) for when exemplary damages may be awarded. There is one New Zealand case – *A* v *Bottrill* (2003) – where exemplary damages were awarded against a doctor who was negligent in adopting a completely out of date method for examining the claimant's cervical smear tests for cancer. The New Zealand Court of Appeal declined to award exemplary damages against the doctor, on the ground that he was not conscious of doing anything wrong when he acted as he did. The Privy Council held that in principle exemplary damages could be awarded so long as it was established that the defendant's conduct was so outrageous as to be worthy of punishment. The case shows a willingness on the part of at least some English judges to allow exemplary damages to be awarded in appropriate negligence cases – but there is, at the moment, no authority where such damages *were* awarded by an English court.

There is, similarly, no English precedent where an injunction has ever been awarded against a defendant to stop him breaching a duty of care.[24] Indeed, there seems to be no precedent anywhere in the common law world, apart from two obscure American cases where an injunction was awarded against an employer, forcing him to comply with the duty of care he owed his employees to take care to protect them against risks of injury arising in the workplace.[25] (In both cases, the risk was of developing cancer from being exposed to second hand smoke in the workplace.) The lack of authority does not, we think, indicate that we are not actually required by the courts to observe the duties of care we owe other people. (There are, for example, plenty of cases where the courts are willing to distort the rules on when a person can sue another in negligence in order to ensure that a defendant suffers some kind of sanction for breaching a duty of care that he owed someone else and isn't allowed to 'get away with' breaching that duty.)[26] The difficulty lies in the fact that duties of care are rarely breached on a continuing basis. When a duty of care is breached, it tends to be a one-off event that happens without warning to the person who is owed the duty of care. As a result, there is never any chance for a claimant to seek an injunction, to force a defendant to comply with a duty of care that he owes the claimant. By the time the claimant finds out about the breach, it is too late – it has already happened.

---

[24] See *Miller* v *Jackson* [1977] QB 966, at 980: 'there is no case, so far as I know, where [an injunction] has been granted to stop a man being negligent' (per Lord Denning MR). In *CBS Songs plc* v *Amstrad* [1988] AC 1013, 'damages and an injunction for negligence [were] sought' (ibid, at 1060) against the defendants, but no duty of care was found to be owed in that case: see below, § 5.3.

[25] *Shimp* v *New Jersey Bell Telephone Co*, 368 A 2d 408 (1976) and *Smith* v *Western Electric Co*, 643 SW 2d 10 (1982).

[26] Notable examples are: *White* v *Jones* [1995] 2 AC 207 (discussed below, § 5.12); *Reeves* v *Commissioner of Police of the Metropolis* [2000] AC 360 (§ 6.4); *Fairchild* v *Glenhaven Funeral Services Ltd* [2003] 1 AC 32 (§ 8.5); and *Chester* v *Afshar* [2005] 1 AC 134 (§ 8.10).

Chapter 4
Duty of care: introduction

Aims and objectives

Reading this chapter should enable you to:

(1) Become acquainted with the history of various tests that have been proposed as ways of determining whether a defendant owed a claimant a duty of care in a given case.

(2) Understand the kinds of factors that the courts will take into account in determining whether a duty of care was owed in a particular case.

(3) Come to grips with various debates that surround the concept of a duty of care; in particular, over what someone who owes another a duty of care is actually required to do.

4.1 The basics

As we have seen, the first thing a claimant needs to establish – if he or she wants to bring a claim in negligence against a defendant – is that the defendant owed him or her a duty of care of some kind. Three points need to be made at this stage about duties of care:

A. Different types of duty

There are many different kinds of duty of care that people can owe each other. We can categorise the duties of care that we might owe each other in three different ways: (1) according to what they require someone to do; (2) according to what sort of interest they are designed to protect; and (3) according to how they arise.

Looking at (1) first, we can begin by splitting the various duties of care recognised in English law into *negative duties* and *positive duties*. A negative duty of care requires a defendant to take care *not to act* in a certain way. A positive duty of care requires a defendant *to act* in a certain way. We can then split up our positive duties of care into two groups. Some positive duties of care require a defendant to take reasonable steps to ensure a particular outcome. An example is an occupier's duty to take reasonable steps to see that a visitor on her premises is reasonably safe for the purposes for which she is on those premises.[1] Other positive duties of care require a defendant to perform a particular task with a reasonable degree of care and skill. An example is the duty a doctor will owe his patient to treat her with a reasonable degree of care and skill.

Turning to (2), the various duties of care that we might owe each other are designed to protect a variety of interests: physical, mental, and economic. For example, suppose that a driver carelessly crashes into a bus shelter, killing most of the people waiting at the bus shelter. The driver will have owed the people waiting at the bus shelter a duty to take care not to crash into the bus shelter. That duty will have been designed to protect those people's physical integrity. But he will also have owed anyone who puts themselves in danger rescuing people in the aftermath of the accident a duty to take care not to crash into the bus shelter. That duty of care will have been imposed on him to protect potential rescuers from the mental scars they might suffer as a result of what they see during the course of their rescue efforts. And the driver will also have owed the company that owns the bus shelter a duty to take care not to crash into the bus shelter. That duty is designed to protect the company's economic interest in not having its property damaged.

With regard to (3), some duties arise merely because it is foreseeable that acting in a particular way will result in someone else suffering harm of some kind. A driver's duty to take care not to act dangerously is one such duty – a driver has that duty merely because it is reasonably foreseeable that if he drives dangerously, other people nearby will get hurt. For other duties, foreseeability of harm is not enough. There are some duties that a defendant will only be subject to if he has 'assumed a responsibility' to someone else. For example, in giving advice to someone else as to what is the best way of investing their money, I will only owe them a duty to take care not to give them bad advice if I 'assume a responsibility' to them not to give them bad advice – which requirement will only be satisfied if I do something to make them think that they can safely rely on my advice and don't need to get anyone else's opinion.

B. The duty–harm relationship

As we will see later,[2] if a claimant wants to sue a defendant in negligence for compensation for a particular harm that she has suffered, then she has to show that the defendant owed her a duty of care that was geared towards protecting her from suffering *that kind of harm*. As Lord Bridge of Harwich observed in *Caparo Industries plc* v *Dickman* (1990): 'It is never sufficient simply to ask whether A owes B a duty of care. It is always necessary to determine the scope of the duty by reference to the kind of damage from which A must take care to hold B harmless.'[3]

As a result of this, a claimant has to be quite selective about what sort of duty of care she will use to base her claim against the defendant on. Consider, for example, the **Forgetful Investor Problem**:

One morning, *Commuter* reads something in the newspapers that makes her think that she needs to sell all her shares in *Dodgy plc*. She then takes a train to work, resolving that once she gets into work, she will call her broker and have him sell her shares. Unfortunately, due to the carelessness of the *Train Driver*, *Commuter*'s train de-rails. *Commuter* is unharmed, but is so shaken by the accident that she completely forgets to sell her shares in *Dodgy*. By the time she remembers, the value of shares in *Dodgy* has plummeted.

---

[1] Occupiers' Liability Act 1957, s 1.
[2] See below, § 9.3.
[3] [1990] 2 AC 605, 627.

Commuter may want to sue *Train Driver* in negligence for the money she has lost as a result of forgetting to sell up her interest in *Dodgy*. But in order to get her claim off the ground, she cannot rely on the fact that *Train Driver*'s negligence in breaching the duty he owed her – and each of the other people on the train – to take care not to drive the train dangerously caused her to lose a lot of money (in that had he not been negligent, she would have remembered to sell her shares and would have done so at a much higher price than she can now get for her shares). This is because the duty *Train Driver* owed *Commuter* to take care not to drive dangerously was designed to protect *Commuter* from suffering some kind of physical harm, not economic harm. If *Commuter* wants to sue *Train Driver* in negligence for the economic loss that she has suffered, she will have to show that he owed her a duty of care that was geared towards protecting her from suffering *that kind of loss*. This she will not be able to do. Duties of care that exist to protect people from suffering some kind of pure economic loss – that is a loss not consequent on physical injury or property damage – generally only exist between people with some kind of special relationship between them; which is obviously not the case between *Commuter* and *Train Driver*.

In cases where a claimant suffers two *independent* (that is, not causally related to each other) harms as a result of a defendant's actions, if she wants to sue the defendant in negligence for compensation for each of those harms, she will have to show that the defendant owed her *two* duties of care: the first geared towards protecting her from the first kind of harm she wants to sue for, the second geared towards the second kind of harm. The duties of care in question could be identical in content – they could each require the defendant to do exactly the same thing – but they will be distinct in respect of the reason why they exist.

For example, in *Spartan Steel & Alloys Ltd* v *Martin* (1973), the defendants carelessly cut through a power line that supplied electricity to the claimants' factory. The power cut had two independent effects on the claimants. First of all, it stopped the claimants from working on some 'melts' that they were processing – with the result that the 'melts' were damaged. Secondly, it stopped the claimants doing any work at all for a number of hours. The claimants wanted to sue the defendants in negligence for compensation for these harms they had suffered – the harm to the melts, and the harm to their business. The Court of Appeal held that the claimants could recover for the first harm, but not the second. Why?

Well, the defendants *had* owed the claimants a duty to take care not to cut through the power line. But this duty was imposed on the defendants because it was reasonably foreseeable that cutting through the power line might cause people like the claimants to suffer some kind of property damage. So the defendants had owed the claimants a property-protecting duty of care, and the claimants could rely on that to sue the defendants in negligence for the harm done to their 'melts'. But in order to sue for the harm to their business, the claimants had to establish that the defendants owed them a business-protecting duty to take care not to cut through the power line. And this they could not do. Such a duty – which would have the effect of protecting the claimants against suffering a form of pure economic loss – generally only exists between people in some kind of special relationship, and no such relationship existed between the claimants and the defendants in *Spartan Steel*.

C. Duties of care and public policy

There are three views on the relevance of public policy – in other words, the public interest – in determining whether one person owes another a duty of care.

(1) *Policy minimalists* take the view that question of whether A owed B a duty of care should be decided without any reference at all to public policy.[4] An early statement of the policy minimalist position can be found in the judgment of Lord Scarman in *McLoughlin* v *O'Brian* (1983), in which he argued,

> The distinguishing feature of the common law is [the] judicial development and formation of principle. Policy considerations will have to be weighed: but the objective of the judges is the formulation of principle. And, if principle inexorably requires a decision which entails a degree of policy risk, the court's function is to adjudicate according to principle, leaving policy curtailment to the judgment of Parliament.[5]

Lord Scarman thought that principle demanded that the courts should find that A owed B a duty to take care not to injure C if it was reasonably foreseeable that A's injuring C would result in B suffering a psychiatric illness. He wondered at the same time whether such a position would be 'socially desirable':

> I foresee social and financial problems if damages for [psychiatric illnesses] should be made available to persons other than parents and children who without seeing or hearing the accident, or being present in the immediate aftermath, suffer [a psychiatric illness] in consequence of it. There is, I think, a powerful case for legislation [to restrict claims in this area] . . .[6]

Why, then, Lord Scarman asked, should the courts not try to draw the line and come up with some rule on when a duty of care would be owed that would work in a socially acceptable way? His answer was:

> Simply, because the policy issue as to where to draw the line is not justiciable. The problem is one of social, economic, and financial policy. The considerations relevant to a decision [as to where to draw the line] are not such as to be capable of being handled within the limits of the forensic process.[7]

(2) *Policy maximalists* take the view that the public interest is *always* relevant to the question of whether A owed B a duty of care. Policy considerations can be invoked as a reason for *denying* that A owed B a duty of care; and they can be invoked as a reason for *claiming* that A owed B a duty of care. For example, in *Hill* v *Chief Constable of West Yorkshire* (1989) the House of Lords had to decide whether the police had owed a murder victim a duty to take reasonable steps to apprehend her killer before he got a chance to kill her. The House of Lords found that the police had not owed the murder victim a duty of care. *Part*[8] of their reason for denying that a duty of care was owed in *Hill* was that finding that the police owed the potential victims of crime a duty of care would be contrary to the public interest:

> The general sense of public duty which motivates police forces is unlikely to be appreciably reinforced by the imposition of . . . liability so far as concerns their function in the investigation and suppression of crime. From time to time they make mistakes in the exercise of that function, but it is not to be doubted that they apply their best endeavours to the performance of it. In some

---

[4] See Stevens 2007 and Beever 2007 for two policy minimalist presentations of the law of negligence.

[5] [1983] AC 410, at 430.

[6] [1983] AC 410, at 431.

[7] Ibid.

[8] It is almost always forgotten that in Lord Keith of Kinkel's leading speech in the *Hill* case, the policy reasons that he gave for refusing to find a duty of care was owed occupy *one* paragraph at the end of a 14 paragraph judgment, and that last paragraph begins 'That is sufficient for the disposal of the appeal' – thus clearly indicating that there were sufficient reasons to dismiss the claim that a duty of care was owed in *Hill* without needing to rely on the public interest at all.

instances the imposition of liability may lead to the exercise of a function being carried on in a detrimentally defensive frame of mind . . . Further it would be reasonable to expect that if potential liability were to be imposed it would be not uncommon for actions to be raised against police forces on the ground that they had failed to catch some criminal as soon as they might have done, with the result that he went on to commit further crimes. While some such actions might involve allegations of a simple and straightforward type of failure – for example that a police officer negligently tripped and fell while pursuing a burglar – others would be likely to enter deeply into the general nature of a police investigation, as indeed the present action would seek to do . . . A great deal of police time, trouble and expense might be expected to have to be put into the preparation of the defence to the action and the attendance of witnesses at the trial. The result would be a significant diversion of police manpower and attention from their most important function, that of the suppression of crime. Closed investigations would require to be reopened and retraversed, not with the object of bringing any criminal to justice but to ascertain whether or not they had been competently conducted.[9]

A policy maximalist would think it entirely legitimate to take such concerns into account in deciding a case like *Hill*. But a policy maximalist would also think it legitimate to take into account policy considerations as a reason, not for *denying* that a duty of care was owed in a case like *Hill*, but as a reason *for* finding that a duty of care was owed in a case like *Hill*.

For example, suppose that Lord Keith was wrong in the first two sentences of the above quote. Suppose that it could be established that the police are generally lazy and uninterested in catching criminals and preventing crime, and a useful way of galvanising them into action would be to hold over them the prospect that if they failed to do their jobs properly, they could be sued in negligence by victims of crimes that would never have occurred if the police had not been incompetent. A policy maximalist would think it legitimate to take that into account as a positive reason for finding that a duty of care was owed in a case like *Hill*.

(3) Finally, there is *our position*,[10] which is that if *everything else* indicates that it would be *wrong* for the law to impose a particular duty of care on a class of people, the public interest cannot make it *okay* for the law to impose that duty of care on that class of people. But if *everything else* indicates that the law *should* impose a particular duty of care on a class of people, it would still be *wrong* for the law to impose that duty of care on that class of people if doing so would be contrary to the public interest.

For example, let's suppose there are lots of reasons that indicate that it would be wrong for the law to impose on the police a duty of care to catch criminals, which duty would be owed to potential victims of those criminals' crimes. (To save words, we'll call such a duty a *criminal-catching* duty of care.) For example, it might be objected that imposing a criminal-catching duty of care on the police would result in the law subjecting the police to a special disadvantage that they had done nothing to deserve. If it would be wrong to impose a criminal-catching duty of care on the police for reasons like this, then it would still be wrong to impose such a duty of care on the police even if doing so would result in their doing a better job.

By way of contrast, a case could be made for saying that the law should impose on the social services a duty to take care not to take a child out of the family home when there is no good reason to, where that duty would be owed to the parents of the child. But even if

---

[9] [1989] 1 AC 53, 63 (per Lord Keith of Kinkel).
[10] See McBride 2011, 364-5; also Robertson 2011, text at n 26.

that were true, it might still be wrong for the law to impose such a duty of care on the social services, if doing so would impair their efficiency in protecting children at risk of harm.

4.2 Duty of care tests

Over the years, a number of different judges have attempted to come up with 'tests' that can be applied to determine whether or not a given defendant owed a claimant a duty of care of some description:

The *Heaven* v *Pender* test (1883):

> whenever one person is by circumstances placed in such a position with regard to another that every one of ordinary sense who did think would at once recognise that if he did not use ordinary care and skill in his own conduct with regard to those circumstances he would cause danger of injury to the person or property of the other, a duty arises to use ordinary care and skill to avoid such danger.[11]

Lord Atkin's 'neighbour principle' (1932):

> You must take reasonable care to avoid acts or omissions which you can reasonably foresee would be likely to injure your neighbour. Who, then, in law is my neighbour? The answer seems to be – persons who are so closely and directly affected by my act that I ought reasonably to have them in contemplation as being so affected when I am directing my mind to the acts or omissions which are called in question.[12]

The *Anns* test (1978):

> in order to establish that a duty of care arises in a particular situation, it is not necessary to bring the facts of that situation within those of previous situations in which a duty of care has been held to exist. Rather the question has to be approached in two stages. First one has to ask whether, as between the alleged wrongdoer and the person who has suffered damage there is a sufficient relationship of proximity or neighbourhood such that, in the reasonable contemplation of the former, carelessness on his part may be likely to cause damage to the latter – in which case a prima facie duty of care arises. Secondly, if the first question is answered affirmatively, it is necessary to consider whether there are any considerations which ought to negative, or to reduce or limit the scope of the duty or the class of person to whom it was owed or the damages to which a breach of it may give rise . . .[13]

The 'incremental test' (1985):

> It is preferable, in my view, that the law should develop novel categories of negligence incrementally and by analogy with established categories, rather than by a massive extension of a prima facie duty of care restrained only by indefinable 'considerations which ought to negative, or to reduce or limit the scope of the duty or the class of the person to whom it is owed.'[14]

The *Caparo* test (1990):

> in addition to . . . foreseeability of damage, necessary ingredients in any situation giving rise to a duty of care are that there should exist between the party owing the duty and the party to whom it is owed a relationship characterised by the law as one of 'proximity' or 'neighbourhood' and that the situation should be one in which the court considers it fair, just and reasonable that the law should impose a duty of a given scope upon the one party for the benefit of the other.[15]

---

[11] *Heaven* v *Pender* (1883) 11 QBD 503, 509 (per Brett MR).
[12] *Donoghue* v *Stevenson* [1932] AC 562, 580 (per Lord Atkin).
[13] *Anns* v *Merton LBC* [1978] AC 728, 751–752 (per Lord Wilberforce).
[14] *Sutherland Shire Council* v *Heyman* (1985) 127 CLR 424, 481 (per Brennan J).
[15] *Caparo Industries plc* v *Dickman* [1990] 2 AC 605, 617-618 (per Lord Bridge of Harwich).

A number of different points need to be made about these tests for finding whether or not a duty of care was owed in a given case.

A. The need for tests

Lower courts only need to use a test to determine whether or not a defendant owed a claimant a duty of care in a novel case – where the issue of whether or not the defendant owed the claimant a duty of care has not yet been settled. If it has been settled, then they simply apply the law as it stands at the moment. As a result, there are fewer and fewer occasions when the lower courts – courts of first instance and the Court of Appeal – have to use these tests to determine whether or not a duty of care was owed. This is because, as more and more cases are decided on whether a duty of care was owed in a given situation, fewer and fewer cases can be genuinely said to raise a genuinely novel issue as to whether or not the defendant owed the claimant a duty of care.

It is different for the UK Supreme Court (UKSC), which is not bound by the decisions of the lower courts, or by its own decisions, or by the decisions of the House of Lords, which was the UKSC's predecessor as the highest court in the UK. So even in a case where the law on whether the defendant owed the claimant a duty of care seems to be settled, the UKSC is free to 'unsettle' the law, and find (or refuse to find) that a duty of care was owed when all the precedents indicated that a duty of care was not owed (or was owed). In reaching its decision, the UKSC may want to employ a test for whether or not the defendant owed the claimant a duty of care, both to focus its mind on what it should take into account in determining whether the settled law on this issue is satisfactory or needs changing, and to give everyone the impression that the UKSC is not free to decide the case however it likes, but is instead bound by rules that it has to observe in reaching that decision.

It is an interesting question whether a student answering a problem question that raises the issue of whether the defendant owed the claimant a duty of care should do so from the perspective of a lower court judge or a Justice of the UKSC. We think most students would be expected to answer the question as though they were a lower court judge and *should therefore have very little need to draw on any tests for whether or not the defendant owed the claimant a duty of care.* Unless the problem question raises a genuinely novel issue, there should be ample authorities available to the student to be able to say – without need for recourse to any tests – whether or not a duty of care was owed in the situation under consideration.

B. The fate of the tests

Both Brett MR's test in *Heaven v Pender* and Lord Atkin's 'neighbour principle' were inspired by the idea that the existing authorities on when a defendant would owe a claimant a duty of care must have something in common – and if that 'common element' could be identified, then that would provide the courts with a guide as to what they should be looking for in future cases that raised the question of whether or not a defendant owed a claimant a duty of care. So Lord Atkin argued in *Donoghue v Stevenson*: 'in English law there *must* be, and is, some general conception of relations giving rise to a duty of care, of which the particular cases found in the books are but instances.'[16] But it soon became clear that the 'common element' that they both seized on – foreseeability of harm – was not a

---

[16] [1932] AC 562, 580 (emphasis added). To similar effect, see Brett MR in *Heaven v Pender* (1883) 11 QBD 503, 509.

satisfactory criterion for determining whether or not a duty of care was owed in any given case; in particular, cases where the defendant had *failed to save* the claimant from suffering some kind of harm, and cases where the defendant had done some positive act that resulted in the claimant suffering some kind of *pure economic loss.*[17] As a result, Lord Atkin's 'neighbour principle' had very little impact in terms of being used by the courts after *Donoghue* v *Stevenson* to determine whether or not a defendant owed a claimant a duty of care.[18]

And there the matter rested until the 1970s, when litigants became more determined to test the scope of the tort of negligence – in particular, by bringing claims in negligence against public bodies – and the courts felt the need to come up with a test for whether or not a duty of care was owed in a given case that would help them deal with all the novel duty claims that were being made to them. The test that the House of Lords provided the courts with was the *Anns* test – a duty of care will be owed if it is reasonably foreseeable that the defendant's conduct would result in the claimant suffering harm, and there are no policy considerations that would weigh against finding that such a duty was owed. The *Anns* test quickly came under fire[19] for making it too easy for the courts to find that a duty of care was owed in a particular case, and for making the law on when one person would owe another a duty of care intolerably uncertain.

The 'incremental test' suggested by Brennan J in the High Court of Australia and the *Caparo* test (sometimes referred to by the courts as the 'threefold test') were both reactions against the *Anns* test. Requiring that a claimant show that his case was analogous to cases where it had already been established that a duty of care would be owed, and requiring that the claimant show that there existed a relationship of 'proximity' between him and the defendant and that it was 'fair, just and reasonable' that the courts find a duty of care between the claimant and the defendant were simply ways of making it harder for claimants to convince the courts to recognise that a duty of care was owed in a novel case, and thereby reintroducing some kind of stability into this area of the law.

It is not clear that either of these tests were intended to do anything more than that. Certainly their authors could not have thought that either of these tests provided the courts with any concrete *guidance* as to what they should look for in determining whether

---

[17] As Brett MR himself acknowledged, when – having become Lord Esher MR – in *Le Lievre* v *Gould* [1893] 1 QB 491, he declined to apply his *Heaven* v *Pender* test to a case where a surveyor's carelessness had resulted in the owner of land losing money that he had paid in advance to a builder for the construction of buildings on that land (the advance payments being made on the strength of the surveyor's certificates that the work was going as planned).

[18] For example, in the most important negligence case that was decided between 1940 and 1970 – *Hedley Byrne* v *Hellers & Partners Co Ltd* [1964] AC 465 – counsel for the claimants placed great reliance on *Donoghue* v *Stevenson* (arguing (at 472) that 'it should apply to words as well as deeds') but when the case was decided, Lord Reid only cited *Donoghue* v *Stevenson* to say that it was of no assistance (ibid, at 482: 'I do not think it has any direct bearing on this case') and Lord Devlin cited *Donoghue* v *Stevenson* as authority in favour of his not deciding the case in a way that would leave the law in a defective state (at 516: 'The common law is tolerant of much illogicality, especially on the surface, but no system of law can be workable if it has not got logic at the root of it') while going on to hold that counsel for the claimants had gone too far in trying to apply *Donoghue* v *Stevenson* 'literally to a certificate or a bankers' reference' (at 525). He held that 'The real value of *Donoghue* v *Stevenson* . . . is that it shows how the law can be developed to solve particular problems . . . As always in English law, the first step in such an inquiry is to see how far the authorities have gone, for new categories in the law do not spring into existence overnight' (at 525).

[19] Particularly from Lord Keith of Kinkel: *Peabody Donation Fund* v *Sir Lindsay Parkinson & Co Ltd* [1985] AC 210, 240–1; *Yuen Kun Yeu* v *Att-Gen for Hong Kong* [1988] AC 175, 190–4; *Rowling* v *Takaro Properties Ltd* [1988] AC 473, 501; and *Hill* v *Chief Constable of West Yorkshire* [1989] AC 53, 60.

a duty of care was owed in a novel case. A court seeking to apply the 'incremental test' to determine whether or not a duty of care was owed in a novel case would inevitably end up asking: *How close* does this case have to be to a situation where it is established that a duty of care was owed before we can find that a duty of care was owed in this case? But the incremental test does not tell them. And even at the moment the *Caparo* test was set out by Lord Bridge of Harwich in *Caparo Industries plc* v *Dickman*, he admitted that:

> the concepts of proximity and fairness embodied [in this test] are not susceptible of any such precise definition as would be necessary to give them utility as practical tests, but amount in effect to little more than convenient labels to attach to the features of different specific situations which, on a detailed examination of all the circumstances, the law recognises pragmatically as giving rise to a duty of care of a given scope.[20]

C. The *Caparo* test

Despite its vagueness, the *Caparo* test still to this day provides the courts with a formula that they will invariably invoke if they need to resolve a debate over whether or not a defendant owed the claimant a duty of care in a given case. It is worth, then, looking at the *Caparo* test in more detail. The *Caparo* test essentially says that a defendant will have owed the claimant a duty of care in a given case if: (1) it was reasonably foreseeable that the claimant would suffer harm as a result of the defendant's actions or inaction; (2) there was a relationship of proximity between the defendant and the claimant; and (3) it would be 'fair, just and reasonable' to find that the defendant owed the claimant a duty of care.

The key leg of this formula is the last one. Essentially, the *Caparo* test tells the courts: find that A owed B a duty of care if, and only if, it would be 'fair, just and reasonable' to do so.

In some cases (usually involving A doing something positive that foreseeably resulted in B's person or property being harmed), this requirement will be satisfied merely by showing that it was reasonably foreseeable that A's actions would result in B suffering some kind of harm. In such cases, the courts will say that because (1) is true, (2) and (3) are also true – the fact that it was foreseeable that B would suffer harm as a result of A's actions also establishes that there was a sufficient relationship of 'proximity' between them, and that it would be 'fair, just and reasonable' to find that A owed B a duty of care.

But in other cases (such as cases where A has failed to save B from harm, or has done something positive that foreseeably resulted in B suffering some kind of pure economic loss or psychiatric illness), the mere fact that it was foreseeable that B would suffer some kind of harm if A acted as he did will *not* make it 'fair, just and reasonable' to find that A owed B a duty of care. Something more will be required – some kind of special relationship, or special circumstances, that would justify the courts in finding that A owed B a duty of care. In such cases, the courts will not find that (2) and (3) are made out unless such a special relationship, or special circumstances, are made out.

In each type of case, the courts' decision as to what needs to be established in order to show that there was a sufficiently 'proximate' relationship between A and B (mere foreseeability of harm, or a special relationship or special circumstances) will be driven by its view as to when it would be 'fair, just and reasonable' to find that A owed B a duty of care. The same point was made by Lord Oliver of Aylmerton in *Caparo Industries plc* v *Dickman*:

---

[20] [1990] 2 AC 605, 618.

it is difficult to resist a conclusion that what have been treated as three separate requirements are, at least in most cases, in fact merely facets of the same thing, for in some cases the degree of foreseeability is such that it is from that alone that the requisite proximity can be deduced, whilst in others the absence of that special relationship can most rationally be attributed simply to the court's view that it would not be fair and reasonable to hold the defendant responsible. 'Proximity' is, no doubt, a convenient expression so long as it is realised that it is no more than a label which embraces not a definable concept but merely a description of circumstances from which, pragmatically, the courts conclude that a duty of care exists.[21]

The fact that the *Caparo* test amounts to nothing more than an instruction to the courts to act reasonably in determining whether or not a defendant owed a claimant a duty of care not only establishes that the *Caparo* test does not really function as a 'test' for determining when a duty of care will be owed. It also means that the *Caparo* test does not really provide us with any kind of concrete guidance that will help us predict when the courts will and will not find that a defendant owed a claimant a duty of care. For that, we need to abandon all talk of 'tests' and focus instead on what kind of *factors* the courts will take into account in determining whether or not a duty of care was owed in a particular case.

4.3 Duty of care factors[22]

So what sort of factors will the courts take into account in deciding whether or not it would be 'fair, just and reasonable' to find that a duty of care was owed in a particular case? This is a list of the more important factors:

A. Reasonable foreseeability of harm

As we have already seen, the courts will not find that A owed B a duty of care if it was not reasonably foreseeable that B would be affected by A's actions. This is because the law of negligence would become unduly uncertain if it simply said, 'You must not do *x* if someone somewhere will be harmed by your doing *x*.' If the law did say this then A would never know whether he was allowed to do *x* or not because he could never be certain whether or not his doing *x* would harm someone somewhere in the world. So the law of negligence allows A to do *x* if it is not reasonably foreseeable that someone else will be harmed by A's doing *x*. If A wants to know whether he is allowed to do *x*, all he has to do is take reasonable steps to check and see if anyone will be harmed by his doing *x*, and if it does not look as though anyone will be, he will know he is free to go ahead and do *x*.

B. Reasonableness

One of the differences between the law of trespass and the law of negligence is that you can't be held liable in negligence for acting reasonably.[23] So the courts will not find that A owed B a duty of care not to do *x* if it was reasonable for A to act in that way; nor can A be said to have owed B a duty of care to do *x* if it would have been unreasonable for A to do *x*.

---

[21] [1990] 2 AC 605, 633.

[22] See Stapleton 1998, Stanton 2007b, Hartstone 2008.

[23] See above, §§ 2.3, 2.5, 2.7, for examples of situations where someone can be held liable in trespass despite acting reasonably.

We have already seen an example of this principle at work in the case of *Tomlinson* v *Congleton BC* (2004),[24] where it was contended that the defendant local council owed people who might endanger themselves by swimming in a lake in the council's park a duty to turn the beaches around the lake into marshland so that no one in their right mind would ever want to go anywhere near the lake. As we have seen, the House of Lords rejected in the strongest terms the idea that the council was subject to a duty to do something so ridiculous.[25]

For the same reason, an employer will not owe an ex-employee a duty to hide the truth about that ex-employee's performance at work when writing a reference for the ex-employee, even if it is reasonably foreseeable that telling the truth about the ex-employee will stop him getting the job.[26]

C. Acts and omissions

English law draws a fundamental distinction between acts and omissions – between cases where A does something that makes B worse off than she would have been had A done nothing, and cases where A fails to do something that would have had the effect of making B better off than she currently is. So if A pushes B into a lake, then that is an 'act'. If someone else pushes B into the lake, and A fails to rescue B, that is an omission.[27]

The courts are far more willing to find that a duty of care was owed in an 'act' case than in an 'omission' case. We will fully explore the reasons for this in Chapter 8, but for the time being it suffices to point out that a duty not to do *x* is far less intrusive on individual liberty (because it leaves the person subject to it free to do anything but *x*) than a duty to do *x* is (because the person subject to a duty to do *x* is not free to do anything except *x*). The courts will usually only find that A owed B a duty of care to make B better off in some way if there existed some kind of 'special relationship' between A and B. If there was not, they will usually deny that A owed B a duty of care on the ground that there was no 'proximity' between the parties. For example, in *Hill* v *Chief Constable of West Yorkshire* (1989), the police failed to save Jacqueline Hill from being killed by the 'Yorkshire Ripper', Peter Sutcliffe. But as there existed no special relationship between Jacqueline Hill and the police, the House of Lords found that the police did not owe Jacqueline Hill a duty to take reasonable steps to catch Peter Sutcliffe before he could kill again. There was not a sufficient relationship of 'proximity' between them to warrant finding that a duty of care was owed.

---

[24] Discussed above, § 1.16.

[25] Ibid.

[26] *Lawton* v *BOC Transhield* [1987] 2 All ER 608.

[27] There are some cases where the distinction between an act and an omission can be difficult to apply. Take the case – considered *obiter* in *Candler* v *Crane, Christmas & Co* [1951] 2 KB 164, at 183 and 194 – of the marine hydrographer who omits a reef from a map of the seabed. A ship's captain, using the map, steers his ship in such a way that it collides with the reef. This looks like an omission case – the hydrographer failed to save the ship from colliding with the reef because he failed to alert the captain to the existence of the reef. If it is, then the members of the Court of Appeal who considered this case in *Candler* were right to think that the hydrographer did not owe the ship's owner a duty of care in preparing his map of the seabed: there was no 'special relationship' between the two that would justify finding that a duty of care was owed. But we might be able to say that this case is an act case if, had the map not been drawn up, the ship's captain would have relied on his own eyes or other charts, spotted the reef and steered the ship clear of it. If this is the case, then we can say that the marine hydrographer made things worse by drawing up his map – had he not drawn up his map, the ship would not have been damaged. If this is the case, then it could be said that the hydrographer owed the ship's owner a duty of care in drawing up his map, even in the absence of a 'special relationship' between the two: see below, § 5.2.

D. Seriousness of harm

In an 'act' case, whether the courts are willing to find that A owed B a duty of care not to act as he did will turn on a number of factors. One of the most important is the seriousness of the harm that B stood to suffer if A acted as he did. If it was reasonably foreseeable that B would suffer *physical injury* or *damage to his property* as a result of A's actions, then the courts will readily find that A owed B a duty of care not to act as he did.

If, on the other hand, it was *merely* foreseeable that B would suffer *pure economic loss* as a result of A's actions, the courts will not find that A owed B a duty of care not to act as he did. The loss that B stood to suffer if A acted as he did was not serious enough[28] to warrant the law's intervening to require A to look out for B's interests.[29] This is not to say

---

[28] For an interesting argument that cases of someone's suffering pure economic losses are always more trivial than cases of someone's suffering property damage (because property is more important to our personalities than stocks of wealth), see Witting 2001.

[29] Cases where a duty of care was denied because the only ground for imposing it would have been that it was foreseeable that the defendant would suffer economic loss as a result of the claimant's actions include: *Cattle* v *Stockton Waterworks Co* (1875) LR 10 QB 453 (no duty of care owed to contractors not to delay them in their work, thereby making their contract to do that work less profitable); *Simpson & Co* v *Thomson* (1877) 3 App Cas 279 (no duty of care owed to insurer not to damage insured property); *Société Anonyme de Remourquage à Hélice* v *Bennetts* [1911] 1 KB 243 (no duty of care owed by defendants not to sink ship being towed by tug, thereby preventing the tug earning a fee for towing the ship); *Weller & Co* v *Foot and Mouth Disease Research Institute* [1966] 1 QB 569 (virus causing foot and mouth disease escaped from defendants' premises and caused outbreak of foot and mouth disease in area with the result that claimants' business as cattle auctioneers was temporarily suspended; no duty of care not to release virus owed by defendants to claimants); *Candlewood Navigation Corporation Ltd* v *Mitsui OSK Lines Ltd, The Mineral Transporter* [1986] AC 1 (no duty of care owed to claimants not to damage ship which claimants did not have proprietary interest in but which the claimants had to pay hire for even if the ship was damaged); *Leigh & Sillavan Ltd* v *Aliakmon Shipping Co Ltd, The Aliakmon* [1986] AC 785 (no duty of care owed to claimant not to damage goods which the claimant had contracted to pay for but which he had not yet acquired ownership or possession of); *Simaan General Contracting Co* v *Pilkington Glass Ltd (No 2)* [1988] QB 758 (job of constructing building in Saudi Arabia given to claimant; building was to include a green glass curtain wall and the job of constructing the wall was subcontracted to F; job of constructing the glass that would make up the wall was sub-subcontracted to defendant; defendant's glass panels were not the right shade of green with the result that the fee payable to the main contractor for constructing the building was reduced; held, that defendant had not owed the claimant a duty of care in constructing the panels); *CBS Songs* v *Amstrad Consumer Electronics plc* [1988] AC 1013 (no duty of care owed to claimant recording company whose royalties might be reduced as a result of defendants' marketing tape-to-tape recording machine which would allow illegal copies of cassette tapes to be made); *Van Oppen* v *Clerk to the Bedford Charity Trustees* [1990] 1 WLR 235 (no duty of care owed by school to pupil to arrange insurance on his behalf against his being injured playing rugby at the school); *Pacific Associates* v *Baxter* [1990] 1 QB 993 (no duty of care owed by engineers employed to judge whether contractors should be paid for the work they have done to use reasonable skill and care in making those judgments); *Islington LBC* v *University College London Hospital NHS Trust* [2005] EWCA Civ 596 (no duty of care owed to local authority that foreseeably would have to spend money providing residential care to person who suffered stroke as a result of defendant hospital's negligence); *WBA* v *El-Safty* [2005] EWHC 2866 (doctor does not owe football club a duty of care to treat one of their footballer's injuries properly); *Customs and Excise Commissioners* v *Barclays Bank* [2007] 1 AC 181 (where A is suing B and has obtained a 'freezing order' over B's bank account to stop B transferring money from the account out of the country and beyond A's reach, B's bank will not owe A a duty of care to stop B withdrawing money from his account). It is customary to mention, alongside these cases, cases such as *D & F Estates* v *Church Commissioners* [1989] AC 177 and *Murphy* v *Brentwood DC* [1991] 1 AC 398 (held in both cases, no action maintainable in negligence against builders of a dangerously defective house for the cost of repairing the defects in the building). However, in those cases a duty of care *was* owed (see below, § 5.2): the real significance of those cases was that they set a limit on the losses that someone would be liable for if he or she breached that duty of care. An explanation of the House of Lords' rulings in *D & F Estates* and *Murphy* is set out below, at § 9.3.

that the courts will always refuse to find that A owed B a duty of care in a case where he did something that merely made B economically worse off. It is merely to say that the *mere* fact that it was reasonably foreseeable that B would lose money as a result of A's actions will not be enough to justify a finding that A owed B a duty of care. Something more will be required, such as the existence of a 'special relationship' between A and B.

Similarly, if the only loss that it could be foreseen that B would suffer as a result of A's actions was that B would suffer *distress*, the courts will not find that A owed B a duty of care not to act as he did unless there existed some kind of 'special relationship' between A and B.[30] The mere fact that it was reasonably foreseeable that B would suffer distress as a result of A's actions will not be enough to warrant finding that A owed B a duty of care not to act as he did.[31]

So – *Driver* will owe nearby pedestrians a duty of care not to drive dangerously because it is reasonably foreseeable that they will be physically injured if she drives dangerously. She will not owe a nearby pedestrian's *Employer* a duty of care not to drive dangerously. This is because the only loss that it is foreseeable *Employer* will suffer if *Driver* drives dangerously and runs down the pedestrian is economic loss – the disruption his business will suffer as a result of his employee being run down – and there exists no 'special relationship' between *Driver* and *Employer* that would tip the scales in favour of a finding that *Driver* owes *Employer* a duty of care not to drive dangerously. Similarly, *Driver* will not owe the nearby pedestrian's uncles and aunts a duty of care not to drive dangerously – the only loss that it is foreseeable they will suffer if she drives dangerously and runs down the pedestrian is distress.

E. Fairness

One factor that the courts will always take into account in determining whether a duty of care was owed in a given situation is the need to be 'fair'. 'Fairness' is a slippery term, but best encapsulates the reason why the courts will sometimes refuse to find that a duty of care was owed in a particular case if doing so might expose a defendant to a 'liability in an indeterminate amount for an indeterminate time to an indeterminate class'.[32] If there is a danger that finding that A owed B a duty of care will result in A's liability for the harm he caused B getting out of all proportion to his fault in causing that harm, the courts may well refuse to find that a duty of care was owed.

For example, in *The Nicholas H* (1996), a classification society certified that a ship was fit to sail when it was not. When the ship sank with all its cargo on board, the cargo owners sued the classification society in negligence for compensation for the loss of the cargo, claiming that the defendant had owed them a duty of care not to certify the ship as being fit to sail when it was not. The House of Lords held that the classification society had not owed a duty of care to the cargo owners. This was so even though *The Nicholas H* was an 'act' case (without the certificate from the classification society the ship could not have sailed, so issuing the certificate made the cargo owners worse off than they were before the certificate was issued) and it was plainly foreseeable that the cargo owners would suffer property damage if the ship was certified as being fit to sail when it was not. Part of the reason for denying that a duty of care was owed in this case may have been that if a duty

---

[30] See below, § 5.7, for an account of when someone may sue in negligence for compensation for mere distress.

[31] See *Rothwell* v *Chemical & Insulating Co Ltd* [2006] EWCA Civ 27, at [63]: 'The law does not recognise a duty to take reasonable care not to cause anxiety.'

[32] *Ultramares Corporation* v *Touche*, 174 NE 441 (1931), at 444, per Cardozo CJ.

of care was found in this case, the classification society's liability could have run into millions of pounds – depending on the value of the cargo on board the ship – and got out of all proportion to the society's initial fault in approving the ship as being fit to sail.

F. Individual responsibility

If finding that a duty of care was owed in a particular case might tend to undermine people's sense of individual responsibility, then that is a factor which will weigh heavily (though not conclusively) against a finding that a duty of care was owed. There are two ways in which a finding of a duty of care might undermine people's sense of individual responsibility.

(1) Finding a duty of care might allow a responsible adult to escape some or all of the consequences of his own foolhardiness by giving him the right to sue someone else in negligence for compensation for self-inflicted injuries. For example, in *Vellino* v *Chief Constable of Greater Manchester Police* (2002), the police arrested the claimant, a habitual thief, in his flat. He attempted to escape arrest by jumping out of his kitchen window. He fell very badly and was severely injured. The Court of Appeal held that the police had not owed the claimant a duty to take reasonable steps to stop him escaping from police custody. Similarly, in *Barrett* v *Ministry of Defence* (1995), a soldier died after he had too much to drink at a party held in his barracks. It was argued that the soldier's commanding officer owed the soldier a duty to take reasonable steps to ensure that he did not drink too much at the party. The Court of Appeal rejected this claim, holding that it would not be 'fair, just and reasonable' to find that the commanding officer had owed the soldier such a duty.[33] *Tomlinson* (2004) is another case in the same vein, with Lord Hoffmann holding in that case that:

> A duty to protect against obvious risks of self-inflicted harm exists only in cases in which there is no genuine or informed choice, as in the case of employees whose work requires them to take the risk, or some lack of capacity, such as the inability of children to recognise danger . . . or the despair of prisoners which may lead them to inflict injury on themselves . . .[34]

(2) The second way in which finding that a duty of care was owed in a particular case might undermine people's sense of individual responsibility is if finding that a duty was owed might allow an admitted wrongdoer to escape being held liable to compensate the victim of his wrong for the harm that he did her. For example, in *Mitchell* v *Glasgow City Council* (2009), Mitchell was killed by a 'neighbour from hell' about whom he had complained to the council. The council had held a meeting with the neighbour – who had a history of violence – and disclosed to him at the meeting that Mitchell had made a video of the neighbour threatening Mitchell. The neighbour became very angry and left the meeting. The council made no attempt to warn Mitchell that he might be in danger from his neighbour; and sadly, shortly after the meeting ended, the neighbour attacked and killed Mitchell with an iron bar. The House of Lords held that the council had *not* owed Mitchell a duty to warn him that he might be in danger – despite the fact that one of the situations where A will owe B a duty to save him from harm is where A has put B in danger of suffering that harm.[35]

---

[33] However, once the soldier fell into a drunken stupor and the officers in charge undertook to look after him, they owed him a duty to look after him with a reasonable degree of care and skill: [1995] 1 WLR 1217, 1223. See below, § 6.4.

[34] [2004] 1 AC 46, at [46].

[35] See below, § 6.3, where the *Mitchell* case is discussed in further detail.

It is hard to avoid the impression that at least part of the reason for the House of Lords' decision was that they thought that if they held that the council had owed Mitchell a duty of care in this case, that would have the effect of diluting the neighbour's liability for what he did to Mitchell. Instead of suing the neighbour, who was primarily responsible for what happened to Mitchell, Mitchell's estate would be encouraged to target the council instead, which was – at best – secondarily responsible for the tragic turn of events. Moreover, even if Mitchell's estate did sue the neighbour, the neighbour would have been allowed – if the council had owed Mitchell a duty of care – to seek to make the council share some of the cost of compensating Mitchell's estate under the law on contribution. The law of contribution applies in cases where *Defendant One* and *Defendant Two* are *both* liable in tort to compensate *Victim* for some loss that she has suffered, and *Victim* successfully sues *One* for compensation for that loss. *One* can then make a claim in contribution against *Two*, arguing that as *Two* was also liable to *Victim*, he should be made to contribute towards the cost of compensating *Victim* by paying *One* a 'just and equitable' sum that reflects *Two*'s responsibility for what happened to *Victim*.[36] So here: if Mitchell's estate had sued his neighbour for damages for the injuries he suffered before he died, and the House of Lords had held that the council had owed Mitchell a duty of care and was therefore potentially liable in negligence for what happened to Mitchell, Mitchell's neighbour might have been able to escape some of the burden of compensating Mitchell's estate for what he did to Mitchell by making a claim in contribution against the council.

G. Divided loyalties

The courts will often refuse to find that a duty of care was owed in a specific case because doing so would harm the public interest. The most obvious way in which this might happen is where the prospect of being sued might cause a public official to 'take his eye off the ball' and not do his job properly because he is more concerned about avoiding litigation that he is with performing his responsibilities in the way they should be performed.

There are many situations where the courts will refuse to find that a duty of care is owed because they fear that the existence of such a duty will tempt a public official not to do his job properly and opt instead to do whatever will expose him to the least risk of being sued:

(1) *Judges.* A judge deciding a civil case will not owe the parties to the case a duty to decide the case with a reasonable degree of care and skill.[37] If a judge feared he might be sued by the losing party in a civil case, he might be less concerned about giving the right decision and more concerned about 'splitting the difference' between the parties so as to avoid annoying either of them with his decision.

(2) *Military commanders.* A military officer will not owe a duty of care to the soldiers under his command in the heat of battle.[38] If he did, he might be tempted not to put them in harm's way – so as to avoid being sued later by soldiers injured in the battle and the families of soldiers who were killed – when doing so is required to achieve his military objectives.

---

[36] Civil Liability (Contribution) Act 1978, ss 1, 2.

[37] *Rondel* v *Worsley* [1969] 1 AC 191, 270 (per Lord Pearce); *Sirros* v *Moore* [1975] QB 118; *FM (a child)* v *Singer* [2004] EWHC 793.

[38] *Mulcahy* v *Ministry of Defence* [1996] QB 732; *Smith* v *Ministry of Defence* [2014] AC 52.

(3) *Police.* If the police suspect A of committing a crime, they will not owe A a duty of care in carrying out their investigations into whether or not he committed that crime.[39] Moreover, if A presents himself to the police as being a witness to a crime, the police will *not* owe A a duty of care to treat him properly as a witness, and a potential victim of crime.[40] The courts fear that finding that the police are subject to either of these duties of care will divert them from their central task of investigating crime.

(4) *Health and safety inspectors.* The Court of Appeal ruled in *Harris* v *Evans* (1998) that a health and safety inspector did *not* owe a duty of care to a claimant whose business was severely disrupted by the health and safety inspector making what turned out to be unjustified demands on the claimant. The Court of Appeal was fearful that if it found that health and safety inspectors owed duties of care to businesses affected by their findings and decisions, inspectors would – out of a desire to avoid being sued – become very cautious about making any decisions or findings that might adversely affect someone's business.[41]

(5) *Social services.* In *D* v *East Berkshire Community NHS Trust* (2005), the House of Lords held that if the social services investigate allegations that *Parent* is abusing his *Daughter*, the *only* person the social services will owe a duty of care to in carrying out their investigations is *Daughter*. They will *not* owe *Parent* a duty to carry out their investigations with a reasonable degree of care and skill.[42] Their Lordships feared that if the social services owed *Parent* such a duty of care, they would become excessively cautious about taking *Daughter* into care, for fear that they might be sued by *Parent* if they made a mistake and took *Daughter* into care when she was not actually at risk. So if a duty of care were owed to *Parent*, it might cause the social services to neglect their fundamental responsibility to safeguard *Daughter*'s interests.[43]

(6) *Councils.* A concern not to do anything that might cause public officials to neglect their core responsibilities may also explain why the House of Lords refused to find that a duty of care was owed in the *Mitchell* case, discussed above. Some of the Law Lords expressed themselves concerned that if they found that a duty of care *was* owed by the council to Mitchell in this case, that might have the effect of discouraging councils generally from tackling the problem of 'neighbours from hell' on the basis that if someone made a complaint about their neighbour, the council would be taking a risk of getting sued if it addressed the complaint but would not if it ignored it.[44]

---

[39] *Calveley* v *Chief Constable of Merseyside Police* [1989] AC 1228.

[40] *Brooks* v *Commissioner of Police of the Metropolis* [2005] 1 WLR 1495.

[41] [1998] 1 WLR 1285, 1298 (per Sir Richard Scott V-C). See also *Jain* v *Trent Strategic HA* [2009] 1 AC 853. Both *Harris* and *Jain* are discussed below, § 5.12.

[42] See also *Lawrence* v *Pembrokeshire County Council* [2007] 1 WLR 2991. The position is the same in Australia (*Sullivan* v *Moody* (2001) 207 CLR 562, at [62]) and New Zealand (*B* v *Attorney General* [2003] 4 All ER 833).

[43] Though see now *MAK* v *United Kingdom* (2010) 51 EHRR 14 holding that *Parent*'s rights under Article 8 of the European Convention on Human Rights will be violated if the social services unreasonably reach the wrong conclusion that *Daughter* is being abused and as a result take her into care. If the UK courts follow *MAK*, *Parent* will be entitled to sue the social services under the Human Rights Act 1998 for unreasonably taking *Daughter* into care. If this happens, the divided loyalty argument against finding that the social services owed *Parent* a duty of care under the common law will fall away as the potential for being sued under the Human Rights Act 1998 will mean that the social services' loyalties will *already* be divided.

[44] [2009] 1 AC 874, at [27]–[28] (per Lord Hope), and at [77] (per Baroness Hale).

One of the reasons why *policy minimalists* think that considerations of public policy should *not* be taken into account in determining whether or not a defendant owed a claimant a duty of care is that – they argue – judges are simply *not competent* to determine correctly whether or not deciding a case one way or the other would be contrary to the public interest. If this is right, then one implication is that whether or not a particular judge is convinced by a public policy argument that he should decide a case in a particular way will become a matter of *chance* – as there is no guarantee that the objective strength of that argument will determine whether or not the judge accepts it or not. While we have criticised *policy minimalism* above, it must be admitted that it does seem that it is just a matter of chance whether or not the courts will deny a duty of care on the basis of what we might call a *divided loyalty* argument. There are plenty of cases where the courts have not been convinced by such arguments to deny that a duty of care was owed in a particular case, and it is very difficult to say why *divided loyalty* arguments won the day in the situations above, but were dismissed in the situations discussed below.

(1) *Doctors.* The courts have never hesitated to find that doctors owe duties of care to their patients in treating them, despite widely expressed fears that doing so only encourages doctors to practise 'defensive medicine', giving patients excessive tests and treatments in an attempt to demonstrate publicly that everything has been done for the patient and avoid litigation.[45]

(2) *Referees.* In *Spring* v *Guardian Assurance* (1995), the House of Lords dismissed fears that if they found that an *Employer* will owe an *Ex*-employee a duty of care in writing a reference for him, *Employer* would become excessively cautious about saying anything negative about *Ex* in his reference. This was so even though *Employer* will normally owe the *Prospective Employer* to whom the reference is sent a duty to take care to provide an accurate reference and admitting that he *also* might owe a duty to *Ex* in writing a reference might create a real conflict between *Employer*'s desire to perform his primary duty to provide *Prospective Employer* with an accurate reference and *Employer*'s desire not to say anything that might result in his being sued by *Ex*. Moreover, in the law of defamation, references are protected by qualified privilege precisely because it is feared that if they were not, referees would become unduly cautious about expressing themselves frankly in their references.[46]

(3) *Barristers.* It used to be the law that a barrister would not owe a duty to his or her client to conduct that client's case in court with a reasonable degree of care and skill. One of the reasons for this was that 'A barrister has an overriding duty to the court to act with independence in the interests of justice: he must assist the court in the administration of justice and must not knowingly or recklessly mislead the court'[47] and it was feared that if barristers owed their clients a duty of care, a desire to avoid 'the possibility of being sued in negligence would at least subconsciously lead some counsel to undue prolixity which would not only be harmful to [his or her] client but against the public interest in prolonging trials.'[48] However, in *Arthur J S Hall* v *Simons* (2002)[49] the House

---

[45] American studies estimate the cost of defensive medicine in the United States as being in the tens of *billions* of dollars: see, for example, US Congress Office of Technology Assessment, *Defensive Medicine and Medical Malpractice*, OTA-H-602 (1994); Kessler & McClellan 1996.

[46] For an account of the law on qualified privilege, see below, § 16.9(B).

[47] Code of Conduct of the Bar of England and Wales, para 302.

[48] *Rondel* v *Worsley* [1969] 1 AC 191, 229 (per Lord Reid).

[49] Noted, Seneviratne 2001.

of Lords was less concerned about this and as a result swept away the no-duty rule in relation to barristers.

(4) *Expert witnesses.* Almost ten years later, in *Jones* v *Kaney* (2011) the UKSC also swept away the rule that an expert witness who was hired (or volunteered) to give evidence in court on behalf of a claimant or a defendant would not owe their client an actionable duty of care in giving that evidence. Under the Civil Procedure Rules, such witnesses have an overriding duty to the court 'to help the court on matters within their expertise'. The UKSC dismissed fears that finding that an expert witness owed a duty of care to his client might tempt the witness to breach this overriding duty by not saying anything that might prove damaging to the client's case for fear that if he did so, he might end up being sued by his client.

H. Waste of resources

Another way in which finding that a duty of care was owed in a concrete case may harm the public interest is when doing so would encourage a lot of groundless litigation against a public body, which would in turn take up *valuable time and resources* to deal with. As we have seen, this was one of the reasons why, in the *Hill* case, the House of Lords thought that it would *not* be 'fair, just and reasonable' to find that the police owed potential victims of a criminal on the loose a duty to take reasonable steps to arrest him.[50]

In other cases, this argument for finding that it would not be 'fair, just and reasonable' to find that one person will owe another a duty of care has been less successful. In *Phelps* v *London Borough of Hillingdon* (2001), Lord Nicholls – with the agreement of Lord Jauncey of Tullichettle – suggested that the time had come to recognise that teachers owe their students a duty to teach them with reasonable skill and care. He acknowledged some would be concerned that taking such a step would adversely affect the public interest. However, Lord Nicholls felt able to dismiss these concerns: 'I am not persuaded by these fears.'[51]

I. Parliament's intentions

The courts are subordinate to Parliament. It follows that the courts cannot find that A owes B a duty of care if to do so would undermine Parliament's intentions in passing a particular piece of legislation.

For example, imagine that Parliament placed the Identity and Passport Service (IPS, for short) under a statutory duty to process people's passport applications within eight weeks of their being submitted. Imagine also that Parliament provided that breach of this statutory duty should *not* be actionable in tort. So if *Traveller* received a new passport 12 weeks after submitting her application for a new passport, she would *not* be able to bring an action for breach of statutory duty against the IPS. Could she instead argue that the IPS owed her a duty of care in negligence to process her application within eight weeks of its being submitted? The answer is, 'Without more – no. If the *only* basis for saying that the IPS owed *Traveller* a duty of care in this case is the fact that it was under a statutory duty to process her application within eight weeks of its being submitted, then the courts cannot find that the IPS owed *Traveller* a duty of care in processing her application.'

---

[50] See above, § 4.1.
[51] [2001] 2 AC 619, 667.

The reason why the courts cannot do this is that to do so would undermine Parliament's intention that the IPS's breach of statutory duty in *Traveller*'s case should not be actionable in tort. If the courts were to find that the IPS owed *Traveller* a duty of care in processing her application based *only* on the fact that the IPS owed *Traveller* a statutory duty to process her application speedily, then the courts would effectively be making the IPS's breach of statutory duty actionable in tort. The statutory duty that the IPS was under to process *Traveller*'s passport application speedily would give rise to a parallel duty of care, and *Traveller* would be able to bring a claim in negligence against the IPS if the IPS breached its statutory duty to process her passport application speedily. It is for this reason that Lord Hoffmann, in particular, has repeatedly insisted that:

> If [a public authority's failure to perform a statutory] duty does not give rise to a private right to sue for breach, it would be unusual if it nevertheless gave rise to a duty of care at common law which made the public authority liable to pay compensation for foreseeable loss caused by the duty not being performed. It will often be foreseeable that loss will result if, for example, a benefit or a service is not provided. If the policy of the Act [imposing the statutory duty in question was] not to create a statutory liability to pay compensation, the same policy should ordinarily exclude the existence of a common law duty of care.[52]

J. Separation of powers

The courts' concern not to undermine the will of Parliament in finding whether a defendant owed a claimant a duty of care is based on a deeper concern to respect the *separation of powers* – the idea that different government bodies (these bodies are usually identified as the judiciary, the executive, and the legislature) have different jobs to do and their effectiveness at doing those jobs would be undermined were one body to do another body's job.

Finding that a particular public body owed a claimant a duty of care threatens to undermine the separation of powers because doing so allows and requires the courts to dictate to that public body in what manner it should do its job. For this reason, the courts have traditionally steered well clear of finding that public bodies owe other people duties of care in making *policy* decisions as the courts have felt that to do so would give them too much power to dictate how such decisions were made. So the courts will never find that the Treasury owes anyone a duty of care in fixing the UK's budget; or that a police force owes anyone a duty of care in deciding how to set about hunting down and catching a criminal on the loose. In the terminology, the issue of what 'taking care' in performing these functions would involve is *non-justiciable* – something that it is not for the courts to decide. The courts are much more comfortable finding that a public body owes a duty of care when it is guilty of some *operational* failure,[53] where the issue of what the public

---

[52] *Stovin* v *Wise* [1996] AC 923, 952–3. See also Lord Hoffmann's judgments in *Gorringe* v *Calderdale MBC* [2004] 1 WLR 1057, at [23] ('If the statute does not create a private right of action, it would be, to say the least, unusual if the mere existence of the statutory duty could generate a common law duty of care'); and in *Customs and Excise Commissioners* v *Barclays Bank plc* [2007] 1 AC 181, at [39] ('you cannot derive a common law duty of care directly from a statutory duty'). To the same effect, see Lord Scott in *Gorringe* v *Calderdale MBC* [2004] 1 WLR 1057, at [71]: 'if a statutory duty does not give rise to a private right to sue for breach, the duty cannot create a duty of care that would not have been owed at common law if the statute were not there.'

[53] For the distinction between failings at a policy and operational level, see *Anns* v *Merton LBC* [1978] AC 728, 754 (per Lord Wilberforce), and *X* v *Bedfordshire CC* [1995] 2 AC 633, 736–38 (per Lord Browne-Wilkinson).

body should do has been determined by the powers that be, and there is some lower-level failure to follow through the line of direction set for the public body at a higher level – though it cannot be emphasised enough[54] that it is *far from the case* that the courts will always find that a public body owed a duty of care to those affected by an operational failure on its part; many of the other factors mentioned in this section will militate against finding such a duty of care, particularly where the public body was guilty of a failure to save someone from harm.[55]

The decision of the UKSC in *Smith* v *Ministry of Defence* (2014) shows these kinds of concerns at play. The case concerned a number of incidents where British soldiers serving in Iraq had been killed or injured because, it was alleged, the Ministry of Defence ('MoD') had not done enough to protect those soldiers by, for example, equipping them with vehicles that were properly armoured against improvised explosive devices or providing the British Army with training to avoid killing soldiers on their side in 'friendly fire' incidents. With respect to Lord Carnwath, who said that the claims in *Smith* involved extending 'the law of negligence . . . into a new field'[56], there was nothing novel about the claims in *Smith* – employees routinely sue their employers under the law of negligence for carelessly failing to provide them with safety equipment or for failing to take care to protect them from being harmed by their fellow employees. What was troubling about *Smith* was the identity of the employer being sued – the MoD – and the possibility that finding that it owed a duty of care in respect of the manner in which it trained and equipped its soldiers might involve the courts in having to make decisions about how much money the MoD ought to spend on such things.

The majority in *Smith* (four Supreme Court Justices, led by Lord Hope) held that while there could be no question of finding that a duty of care was owed in respect of decisions taken 'at a high level of command and closely linked to the exercise of political judgment and issues of policy'[57] a duty of care might be owed in respect of lower-level 'decisions about training or equipment that were taken before deployment'.[58] What kind of decisions were ultimately to blame for the deaths and injuries suffered in the *Smith* case, and therefore whether a duty of care could be said to have been owed in making those decisions, could only be determined after a full hearing of the facts of the case. The majority therefore declined to find that no duty of care *could* have been owed in the *Smith* case and declined to strike out the claims in that case. The minority in *Smith* (three Supreme Court Justices, led by Lord Mance) thought that even to contemplate that a duty of care was owed in the kinds of cases raised by *Smith* would involve the courts in intractable difficulties:

> The claims that the ministry failed to ensure that the army was better equipped and trained involve policy considerations . . . They raise issues of huge potential width, which would involve courts in examining procurement and training policy over years, with senior officers, civil servants and ministers having to be called and to explain their decisions long after they were made.[59]

---

[54] See *Rowling* v *Takaro Properties* [1988] AC 473, 501 (per Lord Keith of Kinkel).

[55] See, most recently, the decision of the UKSC in *Michael* v *Chief Constable of South Wales Police* [2015] AC 1732, refusing to find that a duty of care was owed in a case where operational failures meant that the police took too long to get to the house of a woman who was calling 999 to say that her ex-partner was going to kill her – by the time he turned up the woman was dead. See § 6.1(C), below, for an in-depth discussion of the *Michael* case.

[56] [2014] AC 52, at [157].

[57] [2014] AC 52, at [76] (read in conjunction with [99]).

[58] [2014] AC 52, at [99].

[59] [2014] AC 52, at [128] (per Lord Mance).

K. Novelty

The more novel a claim that a duty of care was owed in a particular case, the less likely it is that the courts will accept it. There are two reasons for this.

First of all, while the courts do sometimes act as legislators and create new law with their decisions, they do not like to advertise this fact for fear of attracting accusations that they are acting undemocratically and usurping the role of Parliament. So when the courts are invited in a particular case to create new law, they are unlikely to accept the invitation unless they can dress up the innovation that they will be introducing into the law as a marginal, or incremental, development of the existing law.

Secondly, just as Parliament can make mistakes in reforming the law, so can the courts. Indeed, the courts are more prone than Parliament in one respect to making mistakes in reforming the law. This is because when the courts are invited to reform the law in some way, they will often be unable to tell what the full effects will be of reforming the law in the way proposed. As a result, the courts will often find it difficult to tell whether a given reform of the law will be beneficial in the long run. Given this, the courts are rightly wary of using their powers to reform the law in radical ways, and are happier to make small changes in the law, where the effects of those changes can be more easily estimated and assessed.

These concerns about the wisdom of the courts' developing the law on when one person will owe another a duty of care underlay Brennan J's adoption of the 'incremental test' for when a defendant will owe a claimant a duty of care in *Sutherland Shire Council* v *Heyman* (1985), which was set out above.[60] However, there are problems with applying the incremental test in practice.

First of all, it can be argued that it places too tight a constraint on the courts' ability to find a duty of care in a novel case. Secondly, it is often arguable whether one case is genuinely analogous to another. Thirdly, it is unclear – as we have already observed – how close a given case needs to be to an already established duty situation for the incremental test to be satisfied in that case. For these reasons, in *Customs and Excise Commissioners* v *Barclays Bank plc* (2007), Lord Bingham dismissed the 'incremental test' for determining whether a duty of care was owed in a novel case as 'of little value as a test in itself'.[61]

The same case does, however, provide a great deal of support for Brennan J's view that the courts should be wary of making radical changes in the law on when one person will owe another a duty of care. So Lord Bingham conceded that 'The closer the facts of the case in issue to those of a case in which a duty of care has been held to exist, the readier a court will be [to find a duty of care in the case in issue] . . . The converse is also true.'[62] And Lord Mance made it clear that he viewed 'incrementalism' as an 'important cross-check'[63] on finding a duty of care in a novel case, on the basis that 'caution and analogical reasoning are generally valuable accompaniments to judicial activity, and this is particularly true in the present area'.[64]

---

[60] See above, § 4.2.
[61] [2007] 1 AC 181, at [7].
[62] Ibid.
[63] [2007] 1 AC 181, at [93].
[64] [2007] 1 AC 181, at [84].

L. The importance of remedying wrongs

In our list of factors that the courts will take into account in deciding whether A owed B a duty of care in a novel case, we have left until last a factor that some judges like to mention *first* in deciding whether a duty of care was owed in a novel case. This factor is: 'the rule of public policy that has first claim on the loyalty of the law: that wrongs should be remedied.'[65]

As a factor to be taken into account in judging whether A owed B a duty of care in a novel case, this is very puzzling. The very reason we want to know whether A owed B a duty of care is to find out whether or not A *wronged* B in acting as he did. So to say that one of the things we should take into account in judging whether A owed B a duty of care is the fact that A *did* wrong B, and that that wrong needs to be remedied by allowing B to sue A for damages, seems to be a fairly spectacular case of putting the cart before the horse. As Lord Rodger observed in the case of *D* v *East Berkshire Community NHS Trust* (2005):

> In [inquiring into whether a defendant owed a claimant a duty of care] I do not actually find it helpful to bear in mind – what is in any event obvious – that the public policy consideration which has first claim on the loyalty of the law is that wrongs should be remedied. Harm which constitutes a 'wrong' in the contemplation of the law must, of course, be remedied. But the world is full of harm for which the law furnishes no remedy. For instance, a trader owes no duty of care to avoid injuring his rivals by destroying their long-established businesses. If he does so and, as a result, one of his competitors descends into a clinical depression and his family are reduced to penury, in the eyes of the law they suffer no wrong and the law will provide no redress – because competition is regarded as operating to the overall good of the economy and society. A young man whose fiancée deserts him for his best friend may become clinically depressed as a result, but in the circumstances the fiancée owes him no duty of care to avoid causing this suffering. So he too will have no right to damages for his illness. The same goes for a middle-aged woman whose husband runs off with a younger woman. Experience suggests that such intimate matters are best left to the individuals themselves. However badly one of them may have treated the other, the law does not get involved . . .[66]

We agree, and do not think that this factor should play any part in a court's decision as to whether or not a duty of care was owed in a novel case.[67]

4.4 Duty-scepticism[68]

A sceptic is someone who harbours doubts about the truth of some proposition. There are people who are sceptical about the truth of the following two propositions about duties of care:

---

[65] See *X* v *Bedfordshire CC* [1995] 2 AC 633, at 663 (per Sir Thomas Bingham MR); *Gorringe* v *Calderdale MBC* [2004] 1 WLR 1057, at [2] (per Lord Steyn); *A* v *Essex CC* [2004] 1 WLR 1881, at [43]; *D* v *East Berkshire Community NHS Trust* [2005] 2 AC 373, at [24]–[25] (per Lord Bingham).

[66] [2005] 2 AC 373, at [100].

[67] See Robertson 2013 for a defence of the idea that the only point of negligence law is to afford a remedy where someone has seriously wronged someone else, so whether or not A has seriously wronged B is the *key* factor to determine whether we should find that A owed B a duty of care. But why bother then with finding that A owed B a duty of care – why not just give B a remedy against A?

[68] This section and the following section are quite theoretical. A student seeking simply to understand how negligence cases are decided in the courts does not need to read either of these sections. However, a student who wants to gain a deeper understanding of *why* negligence cases are decided the way they are should read on – but slowly.

(1) *That it is an essential element of the law of negligence that a claimant in negligence show that the defendant owed her a duty of care.* We can say that people who are sceptical about this proposition are sceptics about the *essentiality* of the notion of a duty of care to the law of negligence.

(2) *That when the courts find that a defendant owed the claimant a duty of care, the defendant was actually legally required to act carefully in some respect.* We can say that people who are sceptical about this proposition are sceptics about the *reality* of duties of care in negligence.

Let's now look at each of these forms of duty-scepticism in detail, to see if there is anything to them.

A. Essentiality sceptics

Sceptics of this kind fall into two camps.

There are, first, those who think that a claimant who is suing a defendant in negligence should not need to show that a defendant owed her a duty of care because the defendant will *always* have owed the claimant a duty not to cause her to suffer foreseeable harm by acting carelessly. So if the claimant can establish that the defendant acted carelessly in some way, and that the claimant suffered some kind of foreseeable harm as a result of the defendant's carelessness, then we can *take it as read* that the defendant did something wrong to the claimant in acting as he did. To ask then, 'Did the defendant owe the claimant a duty of care not to act as he did?' seems to be wholly redundant. Of course he did. On this view, then, the duty of care requirement acts as a 'fifth wheel on the coach', in William Buckland's memorable phrase.[69] So let's call people who think like this, *fifth wheelers.*[70]

There are, second, those who think that a claimant who is suing a defendant in negligence should not need to show that a defendant owed her a duty of care because the outcome of the claimant's case should not depend on whether or not the defendant did anything *wrong* to the claimant in acting as he did. For the claimant to win her case, it should be enough for her to show that the defendant was careless and she suffered loss as a result. If she can show this, then it is only just that the claimant should be able to sue the defendant for compensation. As between the defendant and the claimant, the defendant was to blame for the loss suffered by the claimant, and the claimant was not. So the loss suffered by the claimant should fall on the defendant, not the claimant. Let's call people who think like this, *fault fans* – in that, they think that the courts should focus on fault rather than wrongdoing in determining whether a defendant is liable to a claimant in negligence.

There are plenty of tort academics who are either fifth wheelers or fault fans. But we are neither. We are not fifth wheelers because it seems to us impossible to say that, as a matter of positive law, A will *always* owe B a duty to be careful if it is reasonably foreseeable that B will suffer some kind of harm if A is careless. As Lord Rodger pointed out in *D v East Berkshire Community NHS Trust* (2005), there are plenty of times when the law allows people to be careless, even though doing so may foreseeably cause harm to others.[71] We are not fault fans because a system of law that was genuinely based on a 'fault principle'

---

[69] See Buckland 1935, at 641.

[70] The great tort lawyer Sir Percy Winfield was a fifth wheeler, arguing in Winfield 1934 (at 66) that the duty requirement in negligence was 'superfluous' and 'might well be eliminated from the tort of negligence'.

[71] [2005] 2 AC 373, at [100].

that losses should fall on those who were at fault for causing them would destabilise society – both because people would be paralysed from doing anything by the fear that if their conduct was judged to have fallen below the standard of a 'reasonable man' they might be fixed with a huge bill for damages, and because the normal business of the courts would collapse under the weight of the claims for compensation with which they would be flooded by claimants arguing that someone else was to blame for their misfortunes.

B. Reality sceptics[72]

Sceptics of this kind think that when the courts *say* that A owed B a duty of care, they don't really *mean* that A was under a duty to B to act carefully in some respect. Rather, when the courts say that A owed B a duty of care, they are simply saying that A will be held liable to pay B compensation if A's lack of care results in B suffering some kind of harm. And – more importantly – when the courts say that A did *not* owe B a duty of care, they are simply saying that, for one reason or another, B will *not* be allowed to sue A for compensation if A's lack of care results in B suffering some kind of harm. On this view, then, the duty concept in negligence acts as a convenient 'control device' which helps to stop the scope of claims for compensation in negligence getting out of control.[73]

There are, again, plenty of tort academics who are sceptics about the reality of duties of care in negligence. But we are not. It seems to us that there is plenty of evidence that the courts mean what they say when they say that a defendant owed a claimant a duty to act carefully in some respect. For example, we have already seen that the courts are willing to distort the rules on causation to make sure that a defendant who is in admitted breach of a duty of care is not allowed to 'get away' with breaching that duty, but instead will incur some kind of sanction for his breach.[74] If the courts do not mean people to abide by the duties of care that the courts say that people owe others, why would they do this? Similarly, the fact that, in theory, exemplary damages may be available in a case where someone has deliberately breached a duty of care owed to another (provided, of course, that various other conditions are satisfied),[75] and the fact that someone can be convicted of the criminal offence of gross negligence manslaughter if their breach of a duty of care owed to another results in that other's death, indicates that when the courts say we owe someone else a duty of care, we are meant to abide by that duty, and not meant to think that the courts are simply putting us on notice that if we are careless, we will be held liable to pay compensation.

4.5 Risk and harm

There is a saying that 'damage is the gist of negligence'.

Some people interpret this as meaning that the duty of care that *Driver* owes nearby *Pedestrian* is a duty not to injure *Pedestrian* by driving carelessly. So if *Driver* is drunk at the wheel and his car is veering madly across the road, he will not do anything wrong to

---

[72] For in-depth explorations of this topic, see McBride 2004, Goldberg & Zipursky 2006 and Priel 2014.

[73] See Fleming 1998, 135–6: 'The basic problem in the "tort" of negligence is that of limitation of liability. One or more control devices were required to prevent the incidence of liability from getting out of hand. Among these, "duty of care" occupies today a paramount position.'

[74] See above, § 3.1; also below, §§ 8.5, 8.11.

[75] See above, § 3.4.

Pedestrian if he just misses hitting *Pedestrian*. He may have been driving carelessly, but his duty was not to *injure* Pedestrian by driving carelessly and *Driver* did not injure her. So in the case where *Driver* just avoids hitting *Pedestrian* despite driving really badly, *Pedestrian* cannot complain that he has been negligent towards her.

On this view, the only duty *Driver* owes *Pedestrian* is *conduct plus result-focused* (or 'CPR-focused' for short). We reject this view. We think that *Driver* owes *Pedestrian* a duty to take care not to drive dangerously. This duty of care is purely conduct-focused (or 'C-focused' for short). Whether he *also* owes *Pedestrian* a CPR-focused duty not to injure *Pedestrian* by driving badly is a matter of debate.[76] But we think the view that the *only* duty of care *Driver* owes is a CPR-focused duty is untenable, for the following reasons:

(1) In the case where *Driver* is drunk at the wheel, and veering madly across the road, but just misses hitting *Pedestrian*, most people would think that *Driver* has done something morally wrong to *Pedestrian* in driving as he did. He took a huge chance with *Pedestrian*'s life. The risk that he created may not have materialised; but he still took a risk, and that was a bad thing to do. It would be strange if the law of negligence – which (as we have said before) is based, in part, on a moral vision of what we can legitimately demand that other people do for us – took a completely different view of *Driver*'s conduct and said that, in law, *Driver* did nothing wrong to *Pedestrian* in driving as he did.

(2) The point of legal duties is to guide people's behaviour. Only legal duties that are C-focused can do this effectively. Legal duties that are CPR-focused leave people uncertain as to what they can do. They tell people: 'You can drive as carelessly as you like down the road, just so long as you don't hit anyone.' But if you do not know whether you are going to hit anyone or not before you start driving, such 'guidance' amounts to no guidance at all. There is a reason why parents tell their children to go to bed at 7 pm on the dot, and don't tell them, 'You can stay up as long as you like, so long as you are not tired in the morning.'[77]

(3) The courts frequently find that a given defendant has breached a duty of care owed to the claimant, but that the breach has not caused the claimant any harm. It would not be possible for them to come to this conclusion if causation of harm had to be shown as a precondition of establishing that a defendant breached a duty of care owed to a claimant.

(4) The most famous statement in English law as to what duties of care we owe each other is Lord Atkin's 'You must take reasonable care to avoid acts or omissions which you can reasonably

---

[76] Ripstein & Zipursky 2001 argue (at 220) that *Driver* owes *Pedestrian* a C-focused duty to take care not to drive dangerously *and* a CPR-focused duty not to injure *Pedestrian* by breaching the C-focused duty that he owes *Pedestrian*.

[77] Nolan 2013a makes the duty-sceptical assertion (at 561) that 'the so-called "duty of care" is not a duty after all, so that the term is a confusing misnomer.' However, his real position seems to be that duties of care do actually exist, but they take the CPR form of requiring us not to cause other people harm by acting carelessly. So in any given case where it is asserted that a defendant breached a duty of care owed to a claimant, you do not have to ask whether the defendant owed the claimant a duty of care: you just have to ask whether the claimant caused the defendant relevant harm by acting carelessly. But Nolan makes the important point that if duties of care do take the CPR form then they are not really duties – in the sense of legal rules that are capable of guiding behaviour. He rejects the idea that duties of care take the C form of simply requiring us not to engage in certain forms of conduct on the basis that someone who does not cause any harm by engaging in those forms of conduct cannot be sued (at 561–62). However, the idea that a legal duty can only exist if there is a sanction for its breach has been discredited since at least 1961: see McBride & Steel 2014, Chapter 2, or Smith 2011.

foresee would be likely to injure your neighbour.'[78] That statement is unambiguously C-focused. Lord Atkin did *not* say 'You must avoid injuring your neighbour by failing to take reasonable care to avoid acts or omissions that reasonably foreseeably would have that effect.'

(5) As we will see,[79] in cases where it is uncertain whether A's breach of a duty of care owed to B has caused B harm, the courts will sometimes hold A liable for that harm because they think that A should not 'get away' with breaching his duty of care, but should instead incur some kind of sanction. And there are other cases[80] where the normal rules on causation indicate that A's breach did *not* cause B harm, but the courts will distort the normal rules on causation to ensure that A's breach incurs some kind of sanction. The only way of explaining these cases is to adopt a C-focused view of the duties of care we owe each other. A CPR-focused interpretation of our duties of care is unable to explain these cases. If we are uncertain whether A's actions have caused B harm, or we know that A's actions have *not* caused B harm, then – if the CPR-focused view of the duties of care we owe each other is correct – it is not possible to say that A has done anything wrong to B; in which case, why are we twisting the law to ensure that he is held liable to B?

Further reading

On the utility of 'tests' to determine whether we owe another a duty of care, see **Smith & Burns, 'Donoghue v Stevenson – the not so golden anniversary' (1983) 46 Modern Law Review 147**, and **Morgan, 'The rise and fall of the general duty of care?' (2006) 22 Professional Negligence 206**.

It might be an interesting idea to compare our list of factors that judges take into account in determining whether one person owed another a duty of care with Jane Stapleton's (**Stapleton, 'Duty of care factors: a selection from the judicial menus' in Cane and Stapleton (eds), The Law of Obligations: Essays in Honour of John Fleming (OUP, 1998)**) and consider what accounts for the differences.

The idea that our duties of care really exist is defended in **McBride, 'Duties of care – do they really exist?' (2004) 24 Oxford Journal of Legal Studies 417**, and **Goldberg and Zipursky, 'The Restatement (Third) and the place of duty in negligence law' (2001) 54 Vanderbilt Law Review 657** and, by the same authors, **'Seeing tort law from the internal point of view: Holmes and Hart on legal duties' (2006) 75 Fordham Law Review 1563**. In response to these arguments, David Howarth concedes that duties of care really exist, but argues that we are all subject to just one duty of care, a duty to take not to harm others: see **Howarth, 'Many duties of care – or a duty of care? Notes from the underground' (2006) 26 Oxford Journal of Legal Studies 449**. Donal Nolan's **'Deconstructing the duty of care' (2013) 129 Law Quarterly Review 559** is deconstructed by us at fn 77, above. For a more full frontal assault than either Howarth or Nolan attempts on the idea that duties of care actually exist see **Dan Priel's 'Tort law for cynics' (2014) 77 Modern Law Review 703**.

---

[78] *Donoghue* v *Stevenson* [1932] AC 562, 580. See also Diplock LJ in *Doughty* v *Turner Manufacturing Co Ltd* [1964] 1 QB 518, 531: 'the law of negligence . . . is the application of common morality and common sense to the activities of the common man. He must take reasonable care to avoid acts or omissions which he can reasonably foresee would be *likely* to injure his neighbour . . .' (emphasis added).

[79] See below, § 8.5.

[80] See below, § 8.11.

Chapter 5
Duty of care: acts

Aims and objectives

Reading this chapter should enable you to:

(1) Understand, in a case where a defendant has carelessly caused a claimant to suffer harm by doing something positive, when the courts will find that the defendant owed the claimant a duty of care not to act as he did.

(2) Understand, in particular, that the courts take a much more restrictive approach to finding a duty of care in cases where the claimant suffered a psychiatric illness than they do in cases where the claimant suffered a physical injury as a result of the defendant's actions, and why this is.

(3) Understand when a claimant will be able to argue that the defendant's actions resulted in him suffering damage to his property and in what situations the claimant will be confined to arguing that the defendant's actions caused him pure economic loss, and why the law takes a much more restrictive stance to finding a duty of care in the latter kind of situations.

(4) Understand the full range of situations where the courts have found that a defendant owed a claimant a duty of care in cases where the defendant caused the claimant to suffer pure economic loss, and the range of different explanations that might be offered as to why the courts found a duty of care in those situations.

5.1 The basics

We are mainly concerned in this chapter with cases where a defendant has performed a *positive* act that has resulted in the claimant suffering some kind of harm. It must be emphasised that – unless the contrary is made clear – everything we say in this chapter (and especially in this introductory section) as to when a defendant will owe a claimant a duty of care will *only* apply to cases where a defendant has performed a positive act that has resulted in a claimant suffering harm. The law on when a defendant will owe a claimant a duty to save her from suffering some kind of harm, with the result that a defendant can be held liable for a *failure to act*, will be dealt with in the next chapter.

So – a defendant has performed a positive act that has resulted in the claimant suffering some kind of harm, and the claimant wants to sue the defendant in negligence for what he has done. As we have seen, in order to get her claim off the ground, the claimant will have to show that the defendant breached a duty of care that he owed to her in acting as he did. But – as we have also seen, when discussing the Forgetful Investor Problem[1] – it will not be enough for the claimant to show that the defendant breached any old duty of care in acting as he did. The claimant has to show that the defendant breached a duty of care that was geared towards protecting her from the harm for which she wants to sue the defendant. So in a case where the defendant's act has resulted in the claimant suffering some kind of physical injury, she needs to show that the defendant – in acting as he did – breached a duty of care that was geared towards protecting her from suffering physical injury. In the same way, in a case where the defendant's act has resulted in the claimant suffering some kind of pure economic loss, she needs to show that the defendant – in acting as he did – breached a duty of care that was geared towards protecting her from suffering pure economic loss.

It is a lot harder to establish that a defendant owed a claimant a duty of care that was geared towards protecting her from suffering pure economic loss than it is to establish that a defendant owed the claimant a duty of care that was geared towards protecting her from suffering physical injury. The table below gives a rough summary of what a claimant will have to show if she wants to show that the defendant owed her a duty of care geared towards protecting her from suffering a particular kind of harm. The different kinds of harm in the first column are arranged according to how easy it is to establish that a defendant owed a claimant a duty of care geared towards protecting the claimant from suffering that kind of harm:

Duty of care geared towards protecting claimant from –	What has to be established
Physical harm	It was reasonably foreseeable that the defendant's actions would result in the claimant suffering some kind of physical injury.
Property damage	It was reasonably foreseeable that the defendant's actions would result in property being damaged, and the claimant had a sufficient interest in the property at the time it was damaged as a result of the defendant's actions.

---

[1] See above, § 4.1(B).

Duty of care geared towards protecting claimant from –	What has to be established
Psychiatric illness	It was reasonably foreseeable that the defendant's actions would result in the claimant suffering some form of psychiatric illness, and there was a sufficient degree of proximity between the defendant's actions and the claimant's suffering psychiatric illness (where what counts as a sufficient degree of proximity depends on how the claimant's psychiatric illness was triggered).
Pure economic loss	There was a special relationship between the defendant and the claimant, or special circumstances that would make it 'fair, just and reasonable' to find that the defendant owed the claimant a duty of care geared towards protecting the claimant from suffering some kind of pure economic loss.
Pure distress	There was a contractual relationship between the defendant and the claimant, under which the defendant undertook to perform some task for the claimant with reasonable skill and care, and an important object of the defendant's undertaking was to secure some mental satisfaction for the claimant, or save the claimant from some sort of mental distress.

If we look down the list of harms in the first column, we will see that – as a general rule – the law makes it harder for a claimant to establish that a defendant owed her a duty of care that was geared towards protecting her from suffering a particular kind of harm, the less serious the harm in question is. But there is an important exception to this rule. It is easier for the claimant to establish that the defendant owed her a duty of care geared towards protecting her property from being damaged, than it is for a claimant to establish that a defendant owed her a duty of care that was geared towards protecting her mind from being damaged. It is a difficult question whether the restrictive stance of the law towards finding duties of care designed to protect people from being made mentally ill is justified. (As we have already seen,[2] Lord Scarman in *McLoughlin* v *O'Brian* (1983) was in favour of the courts simply finding such a duty of care whenever it was reasonably foreseeable that a defendant's actions would result in a claimant suffering a psychiatric illness – though he also acknowledged that such a position might create social problems that it would be up to Parliament to deal with.) We will attempt to address that question later on, after you have gained a better appreciation of what the law currently says as to when a defendant will owe the claimant a duty of care that is geared towards protecting her from suffering some kind of psychiatric illness.

Psychiatric illness cases are also special in another respect. Consider the facts of *Page* v *Smith* (1996). The defendant carelessly ran into the claimant's car while the claimant was sitting in it. The claimant was uninjured, but the experience caused him to suffer a renewed onset of chronic fatigue syndrome (CFS) – a condition that the claimant had suffered from in the past, but which he had managed to overcome. The claimant sued the defendant in negligence for compensation for his CFS. This was a claim for damages for psychiatric illness. Given this, we would expect the claimant to have to show that the defendant breached a duty of care that was geared towards protecting the claimant from suffering a psychiatric illness. But the House of Lords held that this was unnecessary. It was enough

---

[2] See above, § 4.1(C)(1).

if the claimant could establish that his psychiatric illness resulted from the defendant's breaching a duty of care that was geared towards protecting the claimant from suffering a *physical injury*. The claimant was easily able to satisfy this condition. The defendant had owed him a duty to take care not to crash into the claimant's car based on the fact that it was reasonably foreseeable that doing so would result in the claimant suffering some kind of physical injury. The defendant breached this duty when he carelessly crashed into the claimant's car, and the claimant's psychiatric illness resulted from that breach of duty.

Page v *Smith* (1996) is unorthodox in that it allows a claimant to sue for one kind of harm based on the breach of a duty of care geared towards protecting the claimant from suffering another kind of harm. Given this, in *Rothwell* v *Chemical & Insulating Co Ltd* (2007), the House of Lords sought to limit *Page* v *Smith* to cases where a claimant has suffered a psychiatric illness as an *immediate* result of the defendant breaching a duty of care owed to the claimant that was geared towards protecting the claimant from suffering a physical injury.[3] So *Page* v *Smith* did not apply to a case like *Coleman* v *British Gas* (2002) where the defendant installed a gas heater in the claimants' house. The gas heater was defective: it leaked carbon monoxide. The problem with the heater was only discovered seven years later. Amazingly, the claimants suffered no physical ill effects from breathing in carbon monoxide for so many years. But after the problem with the heater was discovered, they each developed a psychiatric illness as a result of worrying that they *had* been poisoned by the carbon monoxide leaking from their heater. It was held that the claimants could not sue the defendant for their psychiatric illness. The defendant had owed the claimants a duty to take care not to install a defective gas heater in their house. This duty of care arose because it was reasonably foreseeable that installing a defective heater in the claimants' house would result in their being physically injured. So this duty of care was geared towards protecting the claimants from suffering a physical injury. But the claimants had not suffered any physical injury as a result of the defendant's breaching this duty of care. They had, instead, suffered a psychiatric illness: the wrong kind of loss. *Page* v *Smith* did not apply to save the claimants' claim because the claimants' psychiatric illness was not an *immediate* consequence of the defendant's negligence, in the same way as the psychiatric illness of the claimant in *Page* v *Smith* had been immediately triggered by the defendant in that case crashing into the claimant's car. The claimants' psychiatric illness in the *Coleman* case resulted from their worrying, seven years after their heater had been installed, that they had been poisoned. If the claimants wanted to recover for their psychiatric illnesses, they would have to establish, in the normal way, that the defendant had breached a duty of care owed to the claimants that was geared towards protecting them from psychiatric illness. This the claimants could not do. As the above table indicates, in order to do this they would have had to show (at the very least) that it was reasonably foreseeable that installing a defective heater in the claimants' house would result in the claimants suffering some kind of psychiatric illness. And they could not do this.

Clearly, the concept of reasonable foreseeability plays a major role in determining whether or not a defendant owed the claimant a duty of care in the sort of cases we are concerned with in this chapter – cases where a claimant has suffered harm as a result of a defendant's positive act. (Though, as we have seen, it does not play a deciding role in cases where a claimant has suffered a psychiatric illness or pure economic loss or mere distress as a result of a defendant's positive act.) So how do we determine whether it was reasonably

---

[3] [2008] 1 AC 281, at [55] (per Lord Hope), [77] (per Lord Scott), [95] (per Lord Rodger), and [104] (per Lord Mance).

foreseeable that a defendant's actions would result in a claimant suffering some kind of harm? Some guidance is provided by the decision of the Privy Council in *The Wagon Mound (No 2)* (1967) (the facts of which we need not worry about for the time being).[4]

In that case, Lord Reid – delivering the judgment of the Privy Council – indicated that questions of reasonable foreseeability can be resolved by asking whether the possibility of the claimant being harmed in some way by the defendant's action would, before the event, have been regarded as being so 'fantastic or far-fetched that no reasonable man would have paid any attention to it'.[5] If, before the event, a reasonable person would have thought that there was a 'real . . . risk'[6] that the claimant would be harmed in some way as a result of the defendant's actions, then it will have been reasonably foreseeable that the defendant's actions would result in the claimant suffering that kind of harm. Applying that standard to the *Coleman* case, we have to ask whether, when the defendant installed the heater in the claimants' house, a reasonable person would have thought that there was a real risk that if the heater turned out to be defective, the claimants would suffer a psychiatric illness as a result, or would have dismissed such a possibility as being 'far-fetched or fantastic'. On this approach, we have little doubt that the judge reached the right decision that it was *not* reasonably foreseeable that the claimants would develop a psychiatric illness if the defendant installed a defective gas heater in their house.

Other cases are more difficult. In *Bhamra* v *Dubb* (2010), the issue was whether the defendant caterer in that case had owed a guest at a Sikh wedding reception a duty to take care not to serve food that contained egg. The guest suffered from an egg allergy and died as a result of eating a dish ('ras malai') that was served by the defendant at the reception and which contained egg. The guest never asked anyone whether the dish contained egg, because Sikhs are prohibited from consuming meat, fish or eggs – so he must have thought that there was no chance he would be served a dish made out of eggs at the reception. The question of whether the defendant caterer owed the guest a duty of care came down to whether it was reasonably foreseeable that serving a dish made out of eggs at the reception would result in one of the guests falling ill. Statistical evidence was introduced to show that one in every 1,000 people suffers from an egg allergy. That meant that if 100 people attended the wedding reception, there was a 10 per cent chance (approximately) that at least one of them would suffer from an egg allergy.[7] If 500 people attended the reception, that probability rises to 40 per cent (approximately).[8] So, clearly, there was a real risk – and not a 'far-fetched or fantastic possibility' – that someone with an egg allergy would attend the wedding reception. But that is not enough to establish that it was reasonably

---

[4] For a summary of the facts, see below, § 9.2 fn 13.

[5] [1967] 1 AC 617, at 641.

[6] [1967] 1 AC 617, at 642. Lord Reid actually spoke of a 'real *and substantial* risk' (emphasis added), but the following paragraph of his judgment indicated that he thought that in a case where it was established that the defendant's regularly acting in a particular way (here, playing cricket) would result in harm to someone like the claimant (someone passing outside the defendant's cricket ground – who might be hit on the head by a ball hit out of the ground) once every thousand years counted as a risk that was 'plainly foreseeable' and was not 'fantastic or far-fetched', even though it was 'infinitesimal' (ibid). Given this, we think the qualifier 'substantial' can be dropped.

[7] We calculate this probability by saying that the chance that any one guest would *not* suffer from an egg allergy is 0.999. So the probability that every single guest did not suffer from an egg allergy at a wedding reception attended by 100 guests is 0.999 x 0.999 x 0.999 . . . etc until we have done 100 multiplications. In other words 0.999^{100}. This comes to 0.905 (rounding up to three decimal places). So the probability that at least one guest would suffer from an egg allergy is 0.095 – that is, just under 10 per cent.

[8] $1 - 0.999^{500} = 0.394$ (rounded up to three decimal places).

foreseeable that serving an egg dish at the reception would result in one of the wedding guests being harmed. The crucial issue – once it is accepted that someone with an egg allergy could be expected to attend the wedding reception – is: How could someone with an egg allergy be expected to behave at the reception? Could he be expected to keep his guard up, to refuse to rely on the wedding caterer to observe the religious prohibitions on serving meat, fish or eggs at a Sikh wedding, and to turn away any dishes that looked suspicious (or at least not to eat from them without having first obtained assurances that they were egg-free)? Or could he be expected to let his guard down, and partake freely of all the dishes on offer at the reception, confident that the caterer would do everything required to observe the religious prohibition on serving egg at a Sikh wedding reception? If the first, then we might conclude that there was no real risk that serving an egg dish at the reception would result in harm to one of the guests – any guests that suffered from an egg allergy could have been expected to guard against the possibility that they would be served an egg dish at the wedding. If the second, then there would obviously be a real risk that serving an egg dish at the reception would result in harm to one of the guests – anyone who suffered from an egg allergy attending the reception would be a sitting duck, so to speak, if an egg dish were served at the reception.

The courts (at first instance, and in the Court of Appeal) held that a guest suffering from an egg allergy could be expected to let his guard down at the reception, and eat from all the dishes served at the reception without worrying about whether they contained egg. This conclusion is questionable given: (1) the potential extreme downside for a guest who had an egg allergy of eating a dish containing egg; and (2) the lack of any prior, or special, relationship between the guests and the caterer, that might have encouraged a guest who suffered from an egg allergy to think that the caterer would not cut any corners in what dishes he served at the reception. However, the decision of the courts in the *Bhamra* case is *only* questionable – it is not clear what the right answer is in this case.

The use of statistical evidence in the *Bhamra* case shows just how extraordinary the 'reasonable person' (from whose perspective we determine what is reasonably foreseeable) can be. The 'reasonable person' is someone who can not only afford to take the time to contemplate questions such as 'Is there a real risk that someone with an egg allergy might be at the wedding reception?', but is also armed with the statistical information required to answer that question. The fact that the 'reasonable person' is endowed with superpowers of forethought, insight and knowledge that could not reasonably be expected to be shared by any ordinary member of the public creates a danger for the law of negligence. By making the existence of our duties of care dependent on what such an abstract 'reasonable person' could have been expected to foresee, there is a danger that people may end up being fixed with duties of care that they could not reasonably be expected to have known that they were subject to at the time they acted. This seems unfair, though the unfairness is mitigated by the consideration that the bill for paying damages to a claimant in a negligence case is usually not ultimately borne by the person who was negligent, but by his or her employer or insurance company.

5.2 Physical injury (1): the basic rule

Before *Donoghue* v *Stevenson* (1932) was decided, there were plenty of cases where a defendant had been held liable in negligence for carelessly performing a positive act that resulted in a claimant suffering physical injury.

Examples of such cases that were mentioned in Lord Atkin's judgment in *Donoghue* v *Stevenson* are: *Dixon* v *Bell* (1816) (where the defendant asked a very young maidservant to fetch a gun for him, and while she was carrying the gun, she fired it, with the result that the claimant was injured); *Grote* v *Chester and Holyhead Railway* (1848) (where the claimant was a train passenger who was injured when a bridge over which the claimant's train was passing collapsed; the bridge had been built by the defendant); *George* v *Skivington* (1869) (where the claimant was injured using a shampoo that was manufactured by the defendant and that contained harmful ingredients); *Hawkins* v *Smith* (1896) (where the claimant dock worker was injured as a result of using a defective sack which had been supplied by the defendants); *Dominion Natural Gas Co Ltd* v *Collins* (1909) (where the defendants supplied gas to some business premises, installing a pressure safety valve that allowed gas that was building up in the system to escape into the premises, rather than the open air; as a result, a quantity of gas built up inside the premises and an explosion occurred in which the claimant was injured); and *Oliver* v *Saddler & Co* (1929) (where a dock worker was killed when a sling that was supplied by the defendants, and that was being used to lift a load from a ship to the dockside, broke).

What Lord Atkin did in his judgment in *Donoghue* v *Stevenson* was to suggest that the decisions in all these cases rested on a common principle, that applied to determine when one person will owe another a duty of care.[9] As we have already seen, the 'neighbour principle' that Lord Atkin formulated to explain the outcome of the decisions in all these cases was seriously inadequate in that it failed to distinguish between cases where a defendant had caused a claimant harm by performing a positive act and those involving an omission, and failed to note that in cases where a defendant's actions resulted in a claimant suffering less serious harm – such as pure economic loss – foreseeability of harm alone cannot ground a duty of care.[10] However, a narrower formulation of Lord Atkin's neighbour principle does, we think, adequately explain both the outcome of the above cases and many other cases decided since *Donoghue* v *Stevenson*. According to this narrower formulation: A will *normally* owe B a duty to take care not to do a positive act *x*, if it is reasonably foreseeable that A's doing *x* will result in someone like B suffering some kind of physical injury. Such a formulation explains, we think, why there is a duty of care in the following cases:

(1) If A sells goods to B, A will normally owe B a duty to take care not to sell him goods that are unsafe to use or consume in the way they are intended to be used or consumed.[11]

(2) If A manufactures a product that is being used by B, A will normally owe B a duty to take care to see that that product is reasonably safe to use.[12]

(3) If A is out driving, A will owe other users of the road in the vicinity a duty to take care not to drive dangerously; similarly, if A is parking his car, A will owe other users of the road a duty to take care not to park the car in a dangerous fashion.[13]

(4) If A and B are playing football and A attempts to tackle B, A will owe B a duty to take care not to execute the tackle in an unnecessarily dangerous manner.[14]

---

[9] For a series of papers celebrating the 80th anniversary of the decision in *Donoghue* v *Stevenson*, see Thomson 2013; also published in (2013)(3) *Juridical Review*.

[10] See above, § 4.3(D).

[11] *Langridge* v *Levy* (1837) 2 M&W 519, 150 ER 863; *Abouzaid* v *Mothercare (UK) Ltd, The Times*, 20 February 2001.

[12] *Donoghue* v *Stevenson* [1932] AC 562.

[13] *Maitland* v *Raisbeck* [1944] KB 689; *Parish* v *Judd* [1960] 1 WLR 867.

[14] *Condon* v *Basi* [1985] 1 WLR 866.

(5) If A is in possession of a dangerous thing – such as a loaded firearm, a poison, or an explosive[15] – and B is incapable of handling that thing properly, A will normally owe B and anyone else who might be harmed by the thing's improper use a duty not to entrust it to B's care.[16]

(6) If A owns a car and B – who is obviously drunk – asks A for the keys to his car, intending to go for a drive in it, A will owe users of the highway a duty not to give B the keys to his car.[17]

(7) If A, a highway authority, places signs alongside a highway, A will owe each driver on that highway a duty to take care not to position those signs in such a way that that drivers will be unreasonably endangered.[18]

(8) If A is building a house, A will normally owe any future occupants of that house a duty to take care not to build the house in such a way that it will become unreasonably dangerous to live in.[19]

(9) If it is reasonably foreseeable that C will be put in danger if A sets a building on fire, and that someone like B will attempt to rescue C if this happens, thereby putting himself in danger, A will owe B a duty to take care not to set that building on fire.[20]

---

[15] *Dominion Natural Gas Co* v *Collins* [1909] AC 640, 646.

[16] *Dixon* v *Bell* (1816) 5 M & S 198, 199, 105 ER 1023, 1024; *Attorney-General for the British Virgin Islands* v *Hartwell* [2004] 1 WLR 1273.

[17] *P Perl (Exporters) Ltd* v *Camden LBC* [1984] QB 342, 359; *Yetkin* v *London Borough of Newham* [2010] EWCA Civ 776.

[18] *Levine* v *Morris* [1970] 1 WLR 71; also *Yetkin* v *London Borough of Newham* [2010] EWCA Civ 776 (bush planted by defendant authority allowed to grow to such an extent that it obstructed drivers' line of sight, with the result that there was accident in which claimant was injured).

[19] *Dutton* v *Bognor Regis United Building Co Ltd* [1972] 1 QB 373, overruling *Bottomley* v *Bannister* [1932] KB 458 and *Otto* v *Bolton & Norris* [1936] 2 KB 46. The decision in *Dutton* was subsequently affirmed by the House of Lords in *Anns* v *Merton LBC* [1978] AC 728. The House of Lords has now disapproved both *Dutton* and *Anns*. *D & F Estates* v *Church Commissioners* [1989] AC 177; *Murphy* v *Brentwood DC* [1991] 1 AC 398. The better view of those decisions, we submit, is that they did *not* disapprove of the view taken in *Dutton* and *Anns* that if A builds a house he will owe B, a subsequent occupier of that house, a duty to take care to ensure that he does not build that house in such a way that it will become dangerous to live in. In *D & F Estates* and *Murphy* the House of Lords disapproved the view taken in *Dutton* and *Anns* that if (1) A builds a house and in doing so breaches the duty he owes B, a subsequent occupier of that house, to take care not to build the house in such a way that it will become dangerous to live in and (2) as a result, B is put to expense making the house safe to live in then, other things being equal, (3) B will be entitled to sue A in negligence so as to be reimbursed for the expense she was put to. The reason why B will not be able to sue A in negligence is that there is no relation between the harm that B has suffered here (pure economic loss) and the harm that A's duty was imposed on him in order to avoid (physical injury, and damage to B's possessions): see above, § 4.1(B), and below, § 9.3. The fact that B will not be entitled to sue A *in negligence* to recover the money she spent on repairing her house does not, of course, mean that B will not be entitled to sue A *at all* to recover that money. She may have an action under the Defective Premises Act 1972 (on which, see below, § 18.5). For an interesting argument that she would be entitled to bring a claim in restitution against A to recover the expense incurred by her in making her house safe to live in, see Moran 1997.

[20] *Ogwo* v *Taylor* [1988] AC 431. More difficult is the situation where A owes C a duty to save him from harm, A breaches that duty, and B attempts to save C instead, thereby endangering himself. One cannot use the formula discussed here to establish that A owed *B* a duty to rescue C because A is merely guilty of an omission and it is not clear why the fact that A owed *C* a duty to rescue her should mean that he also owed *B* a duty to rescue C. That A *will* have owed B a duty to rescue C in this situation is established by the decision of the Court of Appeal in *Baker* v *T E Hopkins* [1959] 1 WLR 966, though the Supreme Court of Canada took a different view in *Horsley* v *MacLaren, The Ogopogo* [1971] 2 Lloyd's Rep 410.

(10) If A is labelling bottles of medicine, he will owe B a duty to take care that he does not mislabel those bottles of medicine if it is reasonably foreseeable that someone like B will suffer some kind of physical injury if those bottles are mislabelled.[21]

(11) If B's mother asks A, a local authority, whether T would make a suitable child-minder for B, A will owe B a duty not to tell B's mother that T would make a suitable child-minder for B if A knows, or ought to know, that such advice will be acted on and that T has violent tendencies that mean that B will in fact be in danger of being killed or injured if she is looked after by T.[22]

(12) If B wants to adopt a child through A, an adoption agency, A will normally owe B a duty not to place with her a child which A knows or ought to know suffers from a personality disorder which means that the child is very likely to injure B if he is placed with B.[23]

(13) If A is asked to certify that an aircraft is ready to fly, he will owe those who are due to fly on the aircraft a duty not to say that the aircraft is ready to fly if he knows or ought to know that the aircraft is not fit to fly.[24]

A number of different aspects of the formula we advanced above – that A will *normally* owe B a duty to take care not to do a positive act *x*, if it is reasonably foreseeable that A's doing *x* will result in someone like B suffering some kind of physical injury – need further explanation.

A. Normally

A will not *always* owe B a duty of care not to do something that foreseeably will result in B's being injured. The exceptions to the normal rule that a duty of care will be owed in this kind of situation can be grouped under three headings: (1) *volenti non fit injuria*; (2) reasonable conduct; (3) public policy.

(1) *Volenti.* We have already come across the concept of *volenti non fit injuria* – the idea that 'no wrong is done to the willing'.[25] For example, if A is HIV+, it is reasonably foreseeable that B will become HIV+ if A has unprotected sex with her. But if B – in full knowledge of A's condition – wants to have unprotected sex with him, then A will do no wrong to B by having unprotected sex with her.[26] The maxim that *volenti non fit injuria* will be discussed more fully below, in our chapter on 'Defences'[27] – though it should be noted that, technically, the maxim does not operate in this context as a defence (that protects an admitted wrongdoer from being sued) but as a way of establishing that the defendant did not commit a tort at all in the way he behaved.

(2) *Reasonable conduct.* We have also already seen that a defendant cannot be sued in negligence for acting reasonably.[28] So if it was reasonable for A to act in a particular way, B cannot argue that A owed her a duty to take care not to act in that way even if A's acting

---

[21] *Caparo Industries plc* v *Dickman* [1990] 2 AC 605, 636C.
[22] *T* v *Surrey County Council* [1994] 4 All ER 577.
[23] *A* v *Essex CC* [2004] 1 WLR 1881.
[24] *Perrett* v *Collins* [1998] 2 Lloyd's Rep 255 (discussed, Witting 2000a).
[25] See above, § 2.4.
[26] *R* v *Dica* [2004] QB 1257.
[27] See below, Chapter 22.
[28] See above, § 4.3(B).

in that way exposed her to a reasonably foreseeable risk of being physically injured. For example, in *Bolton* v *Stone* (1951), the claimant was standing outside the defendants' cricket ground when she was hit by a cricket ball that had been hit for six out of the ground. The House of Lords dismissed the claimant's claim for damages. The defendants had acted quite reasonably in carrying on playing cricket on their ground without taking any special precautions to avoid the risk of people outside the ground being hit by flying cricket balls. This was because the risk of someone being hit by a cricket ball while standing outside the defendants' ground was infinitesimally small.[29] Given this, it was reasonable for the defendants not to do anything about the risk.

It was different in *Miller* v *Jackson* (1977), which was also a case involving claimants being harmed by flying cricket balls. In that case, the claimants' property adjoined the defendants' cricket ground and the risk that the claimants would be harmed by a cricket ball that was knocked out of the ground was quite substantial. The only way to avoid this risk was for the defendants to stop playing cricket on their ground. Two of the three judges who decided the case in the Court of Appeal – Geoffrey Lane and Cumming-Bruce LJJ – took the view that it was not reasonable for the defendants to carry on playing cricket on their ground. The risk of injury created by the defendants' activity was too high. Accordingly, these two judges were happy to find that the defendants owed the claimants a duty not to carry on playing cricket on their ground – though they disagreed over whether it would be right to grant an injunction to *force* the defendants to stop playing cricket. The third judge was Lord Denning MR, who took the view that the social value involved in the defendants' playing cricket was such that it was reasonable for them to carry on, despite the risks involved for the defendants' neighbours.

Miller illustrates how judging whether it was reasonable for a defendant to act in a particular way can often require us to weigh the costs and benefits of the defendant's actions. Sometimes that weighing exercise has already been done by Parliament, in deciding whether or not to make a particular activity illegal. If Parliament has made a particular activity illegal (for example, driving at 50 miles per hour in a built-up area), the courts will accept Parliament's judgment that the costs associated with that activity outweigh its benefits, and that acting in that way is unreasonable. As a result, if it is reasonably foreseeable that B will be physically injured if A acts in a way that Parliament has made illegal, the courts will readily find that A owes B a duty to take care not to act in that way.

This piece of common sense is often distorted by academics and judges, who sometimes say things like 'a breach of statutory duty is evidence of negligence' or 'a breach of statutory duty amounts to negligence *per se*'. This is not true. Suppose that A is driving down the road and B is walking beside the road some way up ahead. The speed limit applying to the road is 30 mph. In such a situation, we can argue that A owes B a duty to take care not to drive at more than 30 mph. It is, of course, reasonably foreseeable that A's driving faster than 30 mph will result in B's being injured, in the sense that it would not be 'fantastic or far-fetched' to suggest that A's breaking the speed limit will create a risk of B's being injured. The fact that it is independently unlawful for A to drive faster than 30 mph will mean that A cannot argue that it would be reasonable for him to drive faster than 30 mph, and that it would therefore be wrong for the courts to find that he owed B a duty to take care not to

---

[29] In *Overseas Tankship (UK) Ltd* v *The Miller Steamship Co Pty Ltd, The Wagon Mound (No 2)* [1967] 1 AC 617, 642 Lord Reid estimated that the risk of someone being hit by a ball hit out of the defendants' ground was such that it would only happen once every thousand years or so.

drive faster than 30 mph. However, A's duty in this situation will be *to take care* not to break the speed limit. So if A does end up breaking the speed limit, that does not show that he has breached the duty of care that he owes B. It still has to be shown that A's breaking the speed limit was a result of lack of care on his part, and was not – for example – because a faulty speedometer led A to believe he was under the speed limit when he was not.

(3) *Public policy.* Considerations of public policy will rarely result in A being exempted from the duty he would normally have to take care not to do something that foreseeably would result in B being physically injured. One example of such an exemption is the rule of *combat immunity*, under which 'While in the course of actually operating against the enemy, the armed forces are under no duty of care to avoid causing loss or damage to those who may be affected by what they do.'[30] The reason for the rule is to avoid the decisions made by military commanders and soldiers in the field of battle being adversely affected by the prospect of being sued by those harmed by their decisions.[31] However, the UK Supreme Court has recently made it clear in *Smith* v *Ministry of Defence* (2014) that the scope of the rule of combat immunity should be 'narrowly construed' and does not extend to military decisions made before armed forces were involved in 'actual or imminent armed conflict':[32]

> At the stage when men are being trained, whether pre-deployment or in theatre, or decisions are being made about the fitting of equipment to tanks or other fighting vehicles, there is time to think things through, to plan and to exercise judgment. These activities are sufficiently far removed from the pressures and risks of active operations against the enemy for it . . . not to be unreasonable to expect a duty of care to be exercised, so long as the standard of care that is imposed has regard to the nature of these activities and to their circumstances.[33]

B. Positive act

It cannot be emphasised enough that the formula for when one person will owe another a duty of care under discussion here applies only in cases where it is foreseeable that A's performing a *positive act* will result in B being made worse off than she is at the moment. The fact that it is foreseeable that B will suffer harm if A does not intervene to save B from that harm is not, on its own, enough to justify A's owing B a duty of care to rescue B. This is a point we will discuss further below.[34]

C. Reasonable foreseeability

We have already discussed in outline when we can say that it was reasonably foreseeable that A's acting in a particular way would result in B's suffering some kind of harm. Here we want to flesh out that idea a bit more.

---

[30] *Smith* v *Ministry of Defence* [2014] AC 52, at [93] (per Lord Hope). For an example of the rule of combat immunity at work, see *Mulcahy* v *Ministry of Defence* [1996] QB 732 (soldier not allowed to sue in respect of deafness caused as a result of being in front of a howitzer when it was fired in the course of operations in the Gulf War – what made the case worse was that the soldier was only in front of the howitzer when it was fired because he had been ordered by his superior officer to fetch some water from in front of the howitzer and the same superior officer then ordered the howitzer to be fired).

[31] See above, § 4.3(G).

[32] [2014] AC 52, at [92] (per Lord Hope).

[33] [2014] AC 52, at [95] (per Lord Hope).

[34] See below, § 6.1.

If A knew that his actions could have the effect of harming B, then the requirement of reasonable foreseeability is automatically satisfied. If A did not know, the issue of whether it was or was not reasonably foreseeable that A's actions would result in B's being harmed depends on what a *reasonable person in A's position* could have been expected to foresee at the time A acted. This raises the further issue of – what attributes do we give this reasonable person in determining what he or she could have been expected to foresee?

The authorities are clear that the reasonable person should be given the same *age* as A. So we judge what was reasonably foreseeable from the perspective of someone who was the same age as the defendant. In *Mullin* v *Richards* (1998), two 15-year-old school children – Teresa Mullin and Heidi Richards – were playfully fencing with plastic rulers when one of the rulers snapped and a fragment of plastic from the snapped ruler entered Mullin's right eye, blinding her in that eye. Mullin sued Richards in negligence. The Court of Appeal dismissed the claim, holding that Richards had not owed Mullin a duty of care in fencing with her. This was because, judged from the perspective of a *reasonable 15-year-old*, it was not reasonably foreseeable that the fencing match would result in Mullin suffering some kind of harm. (Though presumably the result would have been different if the fencing match had been a particularly violent one.)

It does not seem that the law makes any further concessions to A's frailties and imperfections in determining what characteristics the reasonable person has. It is established that if A is particularly stupid, that will not be taken into account in judging what he or she could reasonably be expected to have foreseen.[35] The consensus of academic opinion is that the same position holds even in the case where A suffers from some disability which means that A has a much lower mental age than his or her physical age. That, too, will not be taken into account in judging what a reasonable person in A's position could have been expected to foresee.[36] To take any other line, it seems, would open up the door to stupid and thoughtless defendants claiming that, like one's mental age, their stupidity or thoughtlessness is a genetic condition which should be taken into account in judging what a reasonable person in their position would have realised.[37]

Whether or not A owed B a duty of care under the formula discussed here depends crucially on what was reasonably foreseeable *at the time A acted*. For example, in *Roe* v *Minister of Health* (1954), each of the claimants went into hospital for an operation. In both cases, their spines were injected with nupercaine at the start of the operation to anaesthetise them. Unfortunately, the nupercaine in question had been stored in ampoules which had, in turn, been stored in phenol, a disinfectant. Some of this phenol passed through tiny invisible cracks in the ampoules and contaminated the nupercaine which was injected into the claimants' spines. As a result, the claimants were permanently paralysed. Before the nupercaine was injected into the claimants' spines the ampoules had been inspected for cracks but none was visible and as a result the claimants' doctors thought that it was safe to inject the claimants' spines with the nupercaine; at the time, nobody realised that it was possible that ampoules of nupercaine might suffer from invisible cracks as a result of which the nupercaine contained in those ampoules might become contaminated.

It follows that, once the claimants' doctors had inspected the ampoules of nupercaine for visible cracks and found that there were none, the doctors did *not* owe the claimants a duty not to inject their spines with nupercaine under the physical danger principle. *At that*

---

[35] *Vaughan* v *Menlove* (1837) 3 Bing NC 468, 132 ER 490.
[36] See Moran 2003, 18–26.
[37] For criticism of this argument, see Moran 2003, 28–31; also Mullender 2000.

time (when the injections were administered), a reasonable person in the position of the claimants' doctors would not have thought that there was a real risk that the claimants would suffer some form of physical injury if their spines were injected with nupercaine. Of course, thanks to the experience of people like the claimants in *Roe* we now know better – we now know that if you inject someone's spine with nupercaine which comes from an ampoule which has no visible cracks, there is still a real risk that that nupercaine is contaminated and that someone will suffer some form of physical injury as a result of being injected with that nupercaine. However, the crucial thing in *Roe* was that at the time the claimants were operated on, nobody realised this – as a result, it was not possible to argue that the claimants' doctors in *Roe* had owed the claimants a duty not to inject their spines with nupercaine on the basis that it was reasonably foreseeable *at that time* that doing so would result in harm to the claimants.

Similarly, in *Abouzaid* v *Mothercare (UK) Ltd* (2001), the claimant was a 12-year-old boy who attempted to attach a sleeping bag to a pushchair. The sleeping bag was attached to the pushchair by passing two elasticated straps attached to either side of the sleeping bag around the back of the pushchair and buckling them together using a metal buckle attached to the end of one of the straps. Unfortunately, when the claimant attempted to buckle the straps together, they slipped from his grasp and the strap with the metal buckle at the end recoiled, hitting the claimant in his left eye. (Presumably the claimant was standing in front of or beside the pushchair when he let go of the straps; had he been standing behind the pushchair, the straps would have recoiled away from him when he let go of them.) The claimant's left eye was blinded as a result and he sued the defendants, who sold the sleeping bag through their stores, for compensation.

His claim in negligence was dismissed: he could not establish that the defendants had owed him a duty not to market the sleeping bag.[38] The reason was that *at the time the defendants marketed the sleeping bag*, a reasonable person in the position of the defendants would not have realised that there was a real risk that people like the claimant might suffer some form of physical injury as a result of the sleeping bag being designed the way it was. Before the claimant was injured, there was no reason for anyone to think that someone using the sleeping bag could suffer this kind of accident – presumably because everyone assumed that anyone attaching the sleeping bag to a pushchair would do so by standing behind the pushchair and pulling the straps attached to the sleeping bag towards them; not by standing beside or in front of the pushchair and pulling the straps away from them. Of course we now know better and, as a result, it may well be that stores nowadays owe their customers (and their customers' children) a duty not to market sleeping bags designed in the same way as the sleeping bag in the *Abouzaid* case.

D. Someone like

It would be difficult for any claimant to show that it was reasonably foreseeable at the time the defendant acted that the defendant's actions would result in that *particular* claimant being injured. Instead, all the claimant has to show is that it was reasonably foreseeable that *someone like* the claimant would be injured as a result of the defendant's actions. To see whether this condition is satisfied, we focus in on a particular feature of the claimant

---

[38] The claimant was, however, allowed to sue for compensation under the Consumer Protection Act 1987: see below, § 11.3.

that played a part in the claimant's being injured as a result of the defendant's actions and ask whether it was reasonably foreseeable that the defendant's actions would result in someone with that feature being injured. Depending on the particular circumstances of the case, we might end up asking whether it was reasonably foreseeable that the defendant's actions would injure someone who was using the defendant's products;[39] or someone who was in the vicinity of the defendant's vehicle;[40] or someone who was blind;[41] or someone who suffered from an egg allergy.[42]

E. Physical injury

The duty formula under discussion here only applies in cases where it is foreseeable that B will suffer some kind of *physical injury* as a result of A's doing *x* – where the term 'physical injury' covers death or lesser harms that any normal person would regard as forms of 'physical injury', such as wounds or bruises.[43] It should be noted that the term 'physical injury' does *not* cover any form of *psychiatric illness.*[44] As we are about to see, mere foreseeability that one's actions will result in someone else suffering a psychiatric illness is not usually enough to give rise to a duty of care. Something extra usually has to be established before the courts will accept that A owed B a duty to take care not to act in a way that foreseeably resulted in B suffering a psychiatric illness.

5.3 Physical injury (2): harm caused by a third party

A difficult issue is whether the duty formula under discussion in the previous section applies in a case where A has done something unreasonable that has resulted in B's either physically harming *herself* or physically harming a *third party*, C.

In cases where B is – to borrow a term from the criminal law – an 'innocent agent' who was not really responsible for the harm she did to herself or C, there is no real problem: if it was reasonably foreseeable that A's actions would have the result they did, then the courts will readily find that A had a duty to take care not to act as he did, with that duty being owed either to B (in the case where B harmed herself) or to C (in the

---

[39] As in *Donoghue* v *Stevenson* [1932] AC 562.

[40] As in *Farrugia* v *Great Western Railway Co* [1947] 2 All ER 565, where the claimant was injured by a load falling off the defendant's lorry.

[41] As in *Haley* v *London Electricity Board* [1965] AC 778, where the claimant fell into a hole dug in the street by the defendants.

[42] As in *Bhamra* v *Dubb* [2010] EWCA Civ 13, discussed above, § 5.1.

[43] It also seems to cover getting pregnant, which not many people would regard as a form of physical injury: see *Walkin* v *South Manchester HA* [1995] 1 WLR 1543; *Richardson* v *LRC Products* [2000] Lloyd's Rep Med 280; *Parkinson* v *St James and Seacroft NHS Hospital* [2002] QB 266; though the House of Lords was more equivocal in *McFarlane* v *Tayside Health Board* [2000] 2 AC 59, with Lords Steyn (at 81) and Millett (at 107) saying that pregnancy is a form of physical injury, Lord Slynn saying that it is not (at 74), and Lords Hope (at 86–87) and Clyde (at 102) saying that pregnancy is *analogous* to a physical injury. If pregnancy is a form of physical injury, then if A has sexual intercourse with B using contraception that he knows or ought to know is unreliable and B gets pregnant as a result and carries the child to term, will she be entitled to sue A for damages on the basis that he owed her, and breached, a duty to take care that he did not use unreliable contraception in having sex with her?

[44] Though the courts in other contexts do sometimes treat a psychiatric illness as though it were a form of physical injury: see *Page* v *Smith* [1996] AC 155, discussed above, § 5.1.

case where B harmed C). We have already seen an example of this in the case of *Dixon* v *Bell* (1816), where the defendant asked a very young maidservant to fetch a gun for him, and while she was carrying the gun, she fired it, with the result that the claimant was injured. The defendant was held to have owed a duty of care to the claimant in this case because it was reasonably foreseeable that giving the gun to such a young girl who had no experience of safely handling such things might result in someone like the claimant being shot.

Much more difficult are cases where B is *not* an innocent agent, and was responsible for the harm that she did either to herself or to C. Two examples of 'harm to self' cases raising the issue of whether a duty of care was owed to the claimant by a defendant who had put the claimant in a position to harm himself are *E (a child)* v *Souls Garages* (2001) and *Barrett* v *Ministry of Defence* (1995).

In the *E* case, a petrol station manager broke the law by selling petrol in a can to the claimant, a 13-year-old boy. Unknown to the manager (though he could have guessed, had he thought about it), the claimant wanted to get high by sniffing the petrol. The claimant and a friend of his spent some time sniffing the petrol, in the course of which they managed to spill a fair amount of petrol on their clothes. After a while, they decided to smoke a cigarette, with the predictable consequence that the claimant's clothes were set alight. The claimant ended up with burns on 56 per cent of his body. It was held that the petrol station manager could be sued for the claimant's injuries: as it had been reasonably foreseeable that selling the claimant the petrol would have the result it did, the manager had owed the claimant a duty not to sell him the petrol.

It was different in *Barrett*. In that case, a soldier got drunk at a Hawaiian party that had been organised by the defendants at the soldier's barracks. It was the soldier's birthday and he had recently been promoted, so he had a double reason to celebrate. He ended up drinking so much that he collapsed and eventually died from choking on his own vomit. A claim that the defendants had owed the soldier a duty to stop serving him alcohol when it became clear he had had too much was rejected by the Court of Appeal:

> I can see no reason why it should not be fair, just and reasonable for the law to leave a responsible adult to assume responsibility for his own actions in consuming alcoholic drink. No one is better placed to judge the amount that he can safely consume or to exercise control in his own interest as well as in the interest of others. To dilute self-responsibility and to blame one adult for another's lack of self-control is neither just nor reasonable and in the development of the law of negligence an increment too far.[45]

The fact that the soldier in *Barrett* was an adult, and the claimant in *E* a child may account for the difference in the two cases: the child's responsibility for his harming himself in *E* may not have been as great, because of his immaturity, as the soldier's responsibility for harming himself in *Barrett*. Similarly, if B were *already* drunk, and then A did something unreasonable that resulted in B's harming himself, the courts may be more ready to find that A owed B a duty of care not to give B a chance to harm himself. B's drunkeness will dilute (though not negate) his responsibility for the harm he did to himself. This may explain the result in the Canadian case of *Crocker* v *Sundance Northwest Resorts* (1988),

---

[45] [1995] 1 WLR 1217, 1224 (per Beldam LJ). A claim that the defendants had owed the dead soldier a duty of care *after* he collapsed, to see that he did not choke on his own vomit, did succeed (at 1225), and is explained below, § 6.4.

where the defendant was held liable for supplying the claimant – who was obviously drunk – with ski equipment, with the result that the claimant, in his drunken state, injured himself in a subsequent ski race.

What about the case – which Robert Rabin calls an 'enabling tort' case[46] – where A's unreasonable act contributes in some way to B's harming C, and B is responsible for what has happened to C? John Goldberg and Benjamin Zipursky provide us with some examples of this sort of case:

> A person cosigns a friend's application for a car loan, knowing that the friend has the propensity to be overcome by 'road rage' . . . [T]he friend carelessly runs into [someone] during a bout of rage. A fertilizer manufacturer is aware that its product can be converted into a powerful bomb by determined terrorists . . . [It fails] to take steps to reduce the risk of such misuse [with the result that its fertilizer is used in a bombing]. A woman is aware of her ex-boyfriend's violent jealousy, as well as his occasional appearances at a bar located in their small town. She nonetheless agrees to meet a date for a drink at the bar . . . [H]er ex-boyfriend shows up and proceeds to pummel her date . . . A website permits users to create individual accounts and to post messages offering and seeking goods and services, but it declines to monitor the type of transactions being consummated. One account holder maintains a posting offering 'full body massage therapy'. Another takes up the offer, agreeing to pay for a hotel room in which they will meet. The buyer, in fact, uses the occasion to assault and rob the masseuse . . .[47]

In such cases, C will face two formidable obstacles in the way of his establishing that A owed him a duty to take care not to 'enable' B to harm C:

(1) C would obviously have to show that it was reasonably foreseeable that A's actions would result in B harming C. But the authorities indicate that in this kind of case, the requirement of reasonable foreseeability will *not* be satisfied merely by showing that a reasonable person would have thought there was a 'real risk' that if A did what he did, B would end up harming C. Instead, it will have to be shown – these authorities indicate – that it was *very likely*[48] or *probable*[49] that B would harm C if A did what he did. In *Topp v London Country Bus (South West) Ltd* (1993), the defendants left a bus outside a pub with the keys in the ignition, with the result that someone took the bus for a joyride and ended up running over and killing the claimant's wife. It was held that the defendants had not owed the claimant's wife a duty to take care not to act as they did because it was not reasonably foreseeable – in the sense of *very likely* or *probable* – that their actions would result in this kind of harm occurring.

(2) In a case in which B has committed a tort in relation to C, the courts will hold that A *also* committed that tort if he was an *accessory* to B's tort. Under the law on accessory liability in tort,[50] *assisting* someone to commit a tort will *not* make you an accessory to that tort. Given this, it seems unlikely that the courts would undermine this aspect of the law on accessory liability by finding that someone who has 'enabled' someone else to commit a tort will be liable in negligence instead. In *CBS Songs plc v Amstrad* (1988), the claimants sued the defendants for breach of copyright, arguing that they were liable as an accessory

---

[46] Rabin 1999.
[47] Goldberg & Zipursky 2009, 1217.
[48] *Lamb* v *Camden LBC* [1981] QB 625, 642 (per Oliver LJ).
[49] *Smith* v *Littlewoods LBC* [1987] AC 241, 258 (per Lord Mackay).
[50] This area of the law is set out below, in Chapter 30.

for the millions of acts of breach of copyright that had been committed by people using the defendants' stereos to make copies of cassette tapes that had been bought in shops. The claim was dismissed: the defendants could not be held liable as accessories to those acts of breach of copyright merely because they had enabled those acts to be performed. As an alternative, the claimants sued the defendants in negligence. Lord Templeman dismissed the claim in scathing terms:

> Since *Anns* v *Merton London Borough Council* [1978] AC 728 put the floodgates on the jar, a fashionable [claimant] alleges negligence. The pleading assumes that we are all neighbours now, Pharisees and Samaritans alike, that foreseeability is a reflection of hindsight and that for every mischance in an accident-prone world someone solvent must be liable in damages . . . In the present proceedings damages and an injunction for negligence are sought against Amstrad for a breach of statutory duty which Amstrad did not commit and in which Amstrad did not participate . . . Under and by virtue of that [statute] Amstrad owed a duty not to infringe copyright and not to authorise an infringement of copyright. They did not owe a duty to prevent or discourage or warn against infringement.[51]

Even if C can overcome these hurdles (and it is not clear whether hurdle **(2)** can ever be overcome), it is submitted – in line with the decision of the Court of Appeal in *Barrett*, above – that A will only have owed C a duty to take care in an 'enabling tort' case where B's responsibility for the harm he did C is attenuated by some lack of capacity, such as B's being a child, or B's being drunk.

If this is right, then it is unlikely that a UK court would find that a duty of care would be owed in any of the cases described by Goldberg and Zipursky, as the principal wrongdoers in those cases (the road rage driver, the terrorists, the jealous boyfriend, and the robber) are all substantially responsible for the harm they did their victims. Closer to the line is a situation such as the one in *West* v *East Tennessee Pioneer Oil Co* (2005), where two of the defendants' employees helped an obviously drunk driver fill his car up with petrol.[52] The driver then drove onto the wrong side of the road, and after driving south on a northbound carriageway for two miles, hit the claimants' car head-on, causing the claimants to suffer serious injuries. The Supreme Court of Tennessee held that the defendants' employees had owed the claimants a duty of care not to 'enable' the drunk driver to drive any further. The fact that the driver was *already* drunk, with the result that his responsibility for what happened after he went back onto the road was diluted (though, obviously, not negated), may mean that a UK court would reach the same conclusion.

5.4 Psychiatric illness (1): general principles in accident cases

There are many different ways in which a defendant's positive act might result in a claimant suffering a psychiatric illness. In this section, we will focus on cases where a defendant carelessly performs a positive act that results in an *accident* occurring, in which someone

---

[51] [1988] AC 1013, 1059, 1060.
[52] Our thanks to Kyle Lawson for bringing this case to our attention.

is injured or almost injured, and the claimant suffers a psychiatric illness as a result. Three such cases can be distinguished:

A. Injury to the claimant

B was injured in an accident brought about by A's carelessly doing x. B's injuries result in B later on developing a psychiatric illness.

This is the most straightforward case, and the one which troubles the courts the least. In this sort of case, B should find it relatively easy to establish that A owed her a duty to take care not to do x, arguing that it was reasonably foreseeable that someone like her would suffer injury as a result of A's doing x. If A did owe B a duty of care on that basis, then A's breach has initially resulted in B suffering the right kind of loss – physical injury. In suing for damages for that physical injury, she can also recover compensation for any psychiatric illness that she suffered as a result of being injured, no matter how unforeseeable.[53] So, as long as it was reasonably foreseeable that A's doing x would result in B suffering some kind of physical injury, B should be able to sue A in negligence for compensation for her psychiatric illness.

B. Almost injury to the claimant

A caused an accident as a result of carelessly doing x, and B was almost injured as a result. The experience resulted in B developing a psychiatric illness.

We have already seen an example of this sort of situation in the caselaw: *Page* v *Smith* (1996).[54] In this case, the claimant – whose chronic fatigue syndrome had revived as a result of the defendant's carelessly crashing into the claimant's car while the claimant was in it – was able to establish that the defendant had owed him a duty of care not to crash into the claimant's car by relying on the fact that it was reasonably foreseeable that crashing into the claimant's car would result in the claimant being injured. Although the claimant did not suffer any physical injury as a result of the defendant's breaching this duty of care, it was held that the claimant could still sue for the psychiatric illness resulting from the defendant's breach. The claimant did not even have to prove that the psychiatric illness was a foreseeable consequence of the defendant's breach – it was enough that some physical injury could be foreseen as resulting from the breach.

Page v *Smith* indicates that in the general situation set out above, B will be able to sue A in negligence for his psychiatric illness provided he can show that A owed him a duty to take care not to do x based on the fact that it was reasonably foreseeable that A's doing x would result in B's being physically injured.

---

[53] *Simmons* v *British Steel plc* [2004] UKHL 20 (accident at work resulting in physical injury and consequent severe depressive illness caused by employee's anger at employers' failure to heed his warnings that his working conditions were dangerous).

[54] See above, § 5.1. See also *Schofield* v *Chief Constable of West Yorkshire* [1999] ICR 193 (claimant police officer suffered post-traumatic stress disorder when colleague unexpectedly discharged gun three times in her presence, thus exposing her to foreseeable risk of physical injury); *Donachie* v *Chief Constable of Greater Manchester Police* [2004] EWCA Civ 405 (claimant police officer was given the job installing a tracking device on the bottom of a car owned by a criminal gang; unfortunately the batteries in the tracking device did not work properly, and the claimant had to go back to the car nine times to replace the tracking device, an experience that both exposed him to a foreseeable risk of physical injury and caused him to develop post-traumatic stress disorder).

C. Injury or almost injury to a third party

A's carelessly doing *x* resulted in an accident in which C was killed or injured, or almost killed or injured, and B suffered a psychiatric illness as a result.

This sort of psychiatric illness-resulting-from-an-accident situation is the one that the courts have found most troublesome to resolve, and the one that dominates the case law on when a claimant can sue a defendant in negligence for a psychiatric illness. Two reasons can be given for why these kinds of cases have proved so difficult to resolve.

First, unlike the first two accident situations considered above, the courts will not usually be able to find that A owed B a duty to take care not to do *x* based on the fact that it was reasonably foreseeable that *B* would suffer some kind of *physical injury* if A did *x*. While it may have been reasonably foreseeable that C (who is known in the caselaw as the 'primary victim' of A's conduct) would suffer some kind of physical injury as a result of A's doing *x*, the same will not usually be true of B (who is known in the caselaw as the 'secondary victim' of A's conduct). So if the courts want to find that A owed B a duty of care in this situation, they will have to base that duty of care on something other than foreseeability of physical harm to B.

Secondly, in searching for some rule or formula that they can apply to decide whether or not A owed B a duty of care, the courts have had to be wary of employing a rule or formula that could have the effect of exposing A to lawsuits from a substantial number of people, with the result that the scope of the liabilities incurred by A as a result of his killing or injuring (or almost injuring) C could get out of all proportion to his fault.

The rule or formula that the courts have ended up employing in these kinds of situations is a very complex one. First of all, it has to be shown that it was reasonably foreseeable that A's actions would result in B's developing a psychiatric illness. This requires B to show that:

(1) B was in a 'close and loving relationship' with C, and what happened to C was sufficiently serious as to make it reasonably foreseeable that someone like B would suffer a psychiatric illness as a result; OR

(2) In the aftermath of the accident carelessly caused by A's doing *x*, B helped to assist C, and what B saw or experienced in trying to assist C made it reasonably foreseeable that B would suffer a psychiatric illness as a result; OR

(3) B reasonably, but wrongly, felt responsible for what happened to C, and what happened to C was sufficiently serious as to make it reasonably foreseeable that B would suffer a psychiatric illness as a result; OR

(4) B saw what happened to C, and what B saw was so horrific that it was reasonably foreseeable that B would suffer a psychiatric illness as a result.

But foreseeability of a psychiatric illness is not enough to establish a duty of care. In order to keep the scope of A's liabilities within manageable bounds, the courts will require B to establish something more before they will find that A owed B a duty of care. What this 'something more' ('SM') is depends on the basis on which B is arguing that it was reasonably foreseeable that she would suffer a psychiatric illness as a result of A's actions.

(1–SM) If B is basing her claim on the fact that she was in a 'close and loving relationship' with C, she has to show that her psychiatric illness was triggered by the shock of *witnessing*

the accident in which C was killed or injured or almost injured, or seeing C in the *immediate aftermath* of that accident.[55]

(2–SM) If B is basing her claim on the fact that she helped to assist C in the aftermath of the accident caused by A, B will have to show that she was, or thought she was, in danger at the time she was trying to help C.

(3–SM) If B is basing her claim on the fact that she felt responsible for what happened to C, B will have to show that she was present at the scene of the accident in which C was killed or injured or almost injured.

(4–SM) If B is basing her claim on the fact that she witnessed what happened to C, and what B saw was so horrific that someone like her – a mere bystander – could have been expected to develop a psychiatric illness as a result, the courts seem to have taken the position that A will not have owed B a duty of care – no matter how foreseeable B's psychiatric illness might have been.

5.5 Psychiatric illness (2): the caselaw on accident cases

In this section, we will look in more detail at the case law dealing with when a claimant can recover for psychiatric illness in an 'injury or almost injury to a third party' case. We will divide up the caselaw according to the four different types of 'injury or almost injury to a third party' situations in which a claimant might be able to establish that it was reasonably foreseeable that the defendant's actions would result in her developing a psychiatric illness. Having looked at these situations, we will consider a fifth situation (the case where a defendant foreseeably caused the claimant to develop a psychiatric illness by injuring, or almost injuring, *himself*) which deserves separate consideration.

A. Close and loving relationship

The leading case in this area is *Alcock* v *Chief Constable of South Yorkshire* (1992). That case arose out of the Hillsborough disaster where 96 football fans were crushed to death and hundreds more were injured at the Leppings Lane end of Hillsborough Football Stadium in Sheffield before an FA Cup semi-final between Liverpool and Nottingham Forest. The immediate cause of the disaster was the decision of the police to open an

---

[55] So if B's psychiatric illness is triggered by her grief at C's dying, or as a result of the strain of tending to C after he is injured in the accident, she will not be able to establish that A owed her a duty of care: see *Alcock* v *Chief Constable of South Yorkshire* [1992] 1 AC 310, 396 (per Lord Keith), 400 (per Lord Ackner). And if B's psychiatric illness is triggered not by C's initial injury, but by C's subsequently dying as a result of that initial injury, then she will not be able to establish that A owed her a duty of care: *Taylor* v *A Novo (UK) Ltd* [2014] QB 150. The requirement that B's psychiatric illness be triggered by the *shock* of witnessing some horrifying *event* in which C was injured, or seeing C in the immediate aftermath of that event, proved fatal to the claimant's claim in *Liverpool Women's NHS Trust* v *Ronayne* [2015] EWCA Civ 588 where B's wife, C, ended up in intensive care after suffering complications caused by a negligently carried out hysterectomy – the fact that B suffered mental problems as a result of learning from C's doctors that she might die and subsequently seeing her in intensive care was not enough to establish that the hospital had owed B (as well as C) a duty of care in operating on C.

outer gate to the Leppings Lane end of the Hillsborough Stadium without cutting off access to spectator pens 3 and 4 at that end, which were already full. Football fans rushed through the opened gate into pens 3 and 4 with the result that those at the front of those pens were crushed. The claimants in *Alcock* were relatives of the dead who had developed various forms of post-traumatic stress disorder in the aftermath of the disaster. None of the claimants whose cases were decided by the House of Lords in *Alcock* succeeded in their claim for compensation; none of them could establish that the police owed them a duty to take care not to cause the disaster at Hillsborough.[56]

Most of the claimants in *Alcock* failed to establish that the police owed them a duty of care because they could not show that it was reasonably foreseeable that they would develop a psychiatric illness as a result of the accident at Hillsborough occurring. The only way they could show that it was reasonably foreseeable that they would develop a psychiatric illness as a result of the Hillsborough tragedy occurring was by showing that they were in a close and loving relationship with someone killed or injured at Hillsborough. But the House of Lords held that most of the *Alcock* claimants had not established that they were in a close and loving relationship with anyone killed or injured at Hillsborough. For example, Brian Harrison suffered post-traumatic stress disorder when he lost his two brothers at Hillsborough. His claim that the police owed him a duty to take care not to cause the accident at Hillsborough failed because there was nothing in the evidence before the House of Lords to suggest that he enjoyed a sufficiently close and loving relationship with his brothers as to make it reasonably foreseeable that he would develop a psychiatric illness as a result of their being killed and the House of Lords was not prepared to presume that Brian Harrison enjoyed such a relationship with his brothers.

It was different in the case of Mr and Mrs Copoc, who lost their son at Hillsborough and subsequently suffered post-traumatic stress disorder. In their case, the House of Lords *was* prepared to presume – in the absence of any evidence going the other way – that they enjoyed such a close and loving relationship with their son that it was reasonably foreseeable that they would develop a psychiatric illness in the aftermath of the Hillsborough disaster. Their claims that the police owed them a duty to take care not to cause the accident at Hillsborough failed because they could not establish that their psychiatric illnesses were triggered by their witnessing the Hillsborough disaster unfold or its immediate aftermath. They *did* see live pictures of the Hillsborough disaster unfolding on television but the fact that broadcasting guidelines forbade the transmission of live pictures showing scenes of recognisable human suffering led the House of Lords to think that what the Copocs saw on television could not have accounted for their subsequently developing post-traumatic stress disorder. The pictures they saw were insufficiently shocking – they gave rise to anxiety, but nothing more. Nor could the Copocs establish that they developed their psychiatric illnesses as a result of seeing their son in the *immediate* aftermath of the Hillsborough tragedy. Only one of the Copocs – Mr Copoc – travelled to Sheffield after the disaster and he only saw his son's body the next day, long after the

---

[56] One claimant succeeded in his claim for compensation at first instance: William Pemberton, who went by coach with his son to the match. His son had a ticket to watch the match; Pemberton stayed on in the coach, intending to watch the match on the coach's television. Pemberton watched the disaster unfold on the television and then searched for his son. His son had in fact died in the disaster and Pemberton identified his body at around midnight. No appeal was made against the first instance judge's decision that the police had owed Pemberton a duty to take care not to cause the accident at Hillsborough: [1992] 1 AC 310, 339, 348, 351, 365.

disaster had occurred. The real reason why the Copocs suffered post-traumatic stress disorder in the aftermath of the Hillsborough disaster was because of what they *imagined* their son had gone through – not because of what they *saw*.

The House of Lords was only prepared to presume that one other *Alcock* claimant enjoyed a close and loving relationship with someone killed or injured in the Hillsborough tragedy. This was Alexandra Penk. She lost her fiancé, Carl Rimmer, at Hillsborough and subsequently suffered post-traumatic stress disorder.[57] But again, Alexandra Penk's claim that the police owed her a duty to take care not to cause the accident at Hillsborough to occur failed because she could not establish that her psychiatric illness was caused by her witnessing the Hillsborough tragedy unfold or its immediate aftermath. All Alexandra Penk saw were live pictures of the tragedy unfolding – and they were insufficiently shocking for her post-traumatic stress disorder to be attributed to her witnessing them.

The fact that the claims of the Copocs and Alexandra Penk failed in *Alcock* leads some unwary students to conclude that in a 'close and loving relationship' case, it is not enough – for the purposes of establishing that the defendant owed the claimant a duty of care – to show that the claimant's psychiatric illness was triggered by watching live television pictures of the claimant's loved one being killed or injured. Not so:[58] the crucial element in the *Alcock* case was that the television pictures the Copocs and Alexandra Penk saw were not clear enough for them to be able to say that they saw their son and fiancé, respectively, being killed or injured. But what if the television companies had breached broadcasting guidelines and zoomed in on scenes of identifiable human beings being crushed to death? If such television scenes would have shown the Copocs and Alexandra Penk what was happening to their loved ones, it is submitted that the police *would* have been found to have owed the Copocs and Alexandra Penk a duty of care – but their claims would still have failed. This is because the police would have been able to argue that their breach of duty to the Copocs and Alexandra Penk did not *cause* their psychiatric illnesses. Those illnesses were caused by the deliberate, voluntary, informed and unreasonable decision of the television companies to breach broadcasting guidelines and show scenes of identifiable people suffering. That decision would have broken the chain of causation between the police's negligence and the psychiatric illnesses suffered by the Copocs and Alexandra Penk, and absolved the police of responsibility for those illnesses. It may be that, in such a case, the Copocs and Alexandra Penk would have been able to sue the television companies, arguing that they owed them a duty to take care not to broadcast such distressing pictures. The issue will be discussed in the next section, when we look at cases where a defendant causes a claimant to suffer a psychiatric illness by doing something other than causing an accident.

---

[57] Would the House of Lords have been prepared to presume that she was in a close and loving relationship with Carl Rimmer had they actually been married at the time of the Hillsborough tragedy? One would have thought so, but see Lord Keith's remarks in *Alcock*: '[the] kinds of relationship which may involve close ties of love and affection . . . may be present in family relationships or those of close friendship and may be stronger in the case of engaged couples than in that of persons who have been married to each other for many years': [1992] 1 AC 310, 397.

[58] [1992] 1 AC 310, 405 (per Lord Ackner: 'simultaneous broadcasts of a disaster cannot in all cases be ruled out as providing the equivalent of the actual sight or hearing of event or of its immediate aftermath'), 417 (per Lord Oliver: 'there may well be circumstances where the element of visual perception is provided by witnessing the actual injury to the primary victim on simultaneous television'). Lord Jauncey of Tullichettle declined to express a view: [1992] 1 AC 310, 423.

Let's now take a closer look at Mr Copoc. How soon after the Hillsborough tragedy unfolded would he have had to have seen his son's dead body for him to be able to argue that his psychiatric illness was triggered as a result of seeing his son in the immediate aftermath of the Hillsborough tragedy? In *McLoughlin* v *O'Brian* (1983), the claimant's daughter was killed and her husband and other two children were injured in a car accident. The claimant was at home when the accident happened, and was only told of it two hours later.[59] She was driven to the hospital (which would have taken about thirty minutes, according to Google maps) where her husband and surviving children were being looked after. The House of Lords was happy to accept in this case that the claimant's subsequent psychiatric illness had been triggered by her witnessing the 'immediate aftermath' of the accident involving her husband and children. So two and a half hours is not too long. Lords Ackner and Jauncey of Tullichettle expressed doubt in *Alcock* as to whether someone who identified a loved one's body eight or nine hours after the accident in which they were killed could be said to have been witnessed the *immediate* aftermath of the accident.[60]

B. Rescue

The decision in *Alcock* to reject all of the claims made by relatives of those who had died in the Hillsborough tragedy created some difficulty for the House of Lords seven years later when, in *Frost* v *Chief Constable of South Yorkshire Police* (1999),[61] five police officers who had been on duty on the day of the Hillsborough tragedy sought to sue their police force for the psychiatric illnesses they claimed to have suffered as a result of witnessing what happened that day.

The police officers' claim for damages was based on an earlier authority – *Chadwick* v *British Transport Commission* (1967) – where a claimant suffered a psychiatric illness as a result of what he saw and heard in attending to the survivors of a train crash that happened 200 yards from his house, and that was caused by the defendant train company's carelessness. It was held that the defendants had owed the claimant a duty to take care not to cause the train crash on the basis that it was foreseeable that if such a crash did occur, a rescuer like the claimant would suffer a psychiatric illness as a result. The police officers claimed that they were rescuers, like the claimant in *Chadwick*, and given that it had been reasonably foreseeable that their rescue activities on the day of the Hillsborough tragedy would result in their suffering a psychiatric illness, their senior officers had owed them a duty to take care not to cause the disaster at Hillsborough.

It would have been very embarrassing for the House of Lords to allow the police officers' claims in *Frost*.[62] The blameless relatives in *Alcock* would have been outraged to have their claims for compensation turned down while members of the police – which bore sole responsibility for what happened at Hillsborough – had their claims allowed.

---

[59] The House of Lords had it that she was told an 'hour or so' after the accident ([1983] AC 410, 417 (per Lord Wilberforce), but the Court of Appeal judgment is clearer that the accident happened at 4 pm, and the claimant was told about it at about 6 pm: [1981] 1 QB 599, 603 (per Stephenson LJ).

[60] [1992] 1 AC 310, 405 (per Lord Ackner) and 424 (per Lord Jauncey of Tullichettle). Lord Oliver seems to have been of the same view: 410.

[61] The case is also known as '*White* v *Chief Constable of South Yorkshire Police*'. Some of the complications in the decision are very well discussed in Case 2010.

[62] As Lords Steyn and Hoffmann frankly acknowledged in *Frost*: [1999] 2 AC 455, at 499, and 510 respectively.

As a result, the Law Lords must have been on the look-out for any feature of the facts in *Frost* that would allow them to distinguish that case from *Chadwick*. They found it in the element of physical danger. In *Chadwick*, the claimant had spent nine hours crawling through wreckage from the train crash, trying to get people out from under the wreckage. In contrast, in *Frost*, two of the claimants helped carry the dead, two of the claimants tried unsuccessfully to resuscitate injured spectators in the stadium, one of the claimants assisted at a mortuary to which the dead were taken: and none of them was ever in any physical danger at all.

The House of Lords seized on this aspect of the case in *Frost* as a reason for dismissing the claimants' claims, ruling that in a case where A carelessly causes an accident and B suffers psychiatric illness trying to rescue the victims of that accident, A will only have owed B a duty to take care not to cause that accident if B was, or thought he was, in physical danger at some point in his rescue effort. Lord Goff dissented, thinking that this was a profoundly unsatisfactory basis on which to determine whether a defendant who had caused an accident owed a duty of care to a rescuer who had suffered a psychiatric illness in that accident:

> Suppose that there was a terrible train crash and that there were two Chadwick brothers living nearby, both of them small and agile window cleaners distinguished by their courage and humanity. Mr A. Chadwick worked on the front half of the train, and Mr B. Chadwick on the rear half. It so happened that, although there was some physical danger present in the front half of the train, there was none in the rear. Both worked for 12 hours or so bringing aid and comfort to the victims. Both suffered [post-traumatic stress disorder] in consequence of the general horror of the situation. [According to the decision of the majority], Mr A. would recover but Mr B. would not. To make things worse, the same conclusion must follow even if Mr A. was unaware of the existence of the physical danger present in his half of the train. This is surely unacceptable.[63]

C. Responsibility

This category of case where a duty of care might be owed to a claimant who suffered a psychiatric illness as a result of a defendant's carelessness was first recognised in *Dooley* v *Cammell Laird & Co Ltd* (1951).

In that case, the claimant was a crane driver. The claimant was in his crane and was lowering a sling-load of materials into a hold when the rope which attached the sling-load to his crane snapped. The sling-load of materials fell into the hold where several of the claimant's colleagues were working. Fortunately, no one was injured. However, the claimant, sitting high up in his crane, did not know that and, thinking he was responsible for the accident that had occurred, developed a psychiatric illness at the thought of what he had done. In fact the accident was the fault of the claimant's employers – who had failed to check that the rope was strong enough for lifting purposes – and the firm that had manufactured the rope. The claimant sued both of them for damages. His claim was allowed. It was held that the defendants had owed the claimant a duty to take care not to cause the accident that had occurred on the ground that because the claimant thought he was responsible for the accident that occurred, it was reasonably foreseeable that the claimant would develop a psychiatric illness as a result of that accident's occurring.

---

[63] [1999] 2 AC 455, 487.

However, just as the decision in *Chadwick* was substantially qualified by the decision of the House of Lords in *Frost*, so the decision in *Dooley* has been substantially qualified by the decision of the Court of Appeal in *Hunter* v *British Coal Corp* (1999). In that case, the claimant was employed by the defendants to work at their coal mine. He was driving a vehicle along a track when he became aware of a water hydrant protruding into the track. The claimant tried to manoeuvre the vehicle round the hydrant but the track was too narrow and the claimant managed to strike the hydrant, causing water to flow from it. The claimant stopped his vehicle and got out and tried to stop the flow of water from the hydrant with the assistance of a fellow employee, one Tommy Carter. The claimant ran off, looking for a water hose that he could use to channel the flow of water from the hydrant, while Carter continued to attempt to shut the hydrant off. When the claimant was 30 metres away from the hydrant, it burst and Carter was killed in the explosion. The claimant only learned that Carter had died on his way back to the scene of the accident. Feeling responsible for Carter's death, the claimant developed a deep depression. In fact, the defendants were responsible for the accident that occurred: it was their fault the track down which the claimant had been driving had been too narrow with the result that the claimant's vehicle struck the hydrant, with tragic consequences.

The claimant sued the defendants. The Court of Appeal turned down his claim, holding that the defendants had not owed the claimant a duty of care not to cause the accident that had triggered his depression because the claimant had not *witnessed* the accident. The Court of Appeal may have wanted to limit the scope of *Dooley* by imposing a requirement that a *Dooley*-style claimant witness the accident for which he felt responsible out of a fear that in the absence of such a requirement, someone who caused an accident might end up being found to have owed duties of care to a wide range of people who felt responsible for it. For example, if a motorist ran down a little girl in the street, it is conceivable that quite a few people might feel responsible for the girl's death and develop psychiatric illnesses as a result: the parents who let their girl go out on her own, the people who the little girl was on her way to visit, the policeman who did not ask the little girl where she was going and take her there himself. If the motorist were to be held to have owed all of these people a duty to take care not to run down the little girl, then his eventual liability would grow out of all proportion to his fault in running her down. (Though it should be noted that that liability would be borne by his insurance company.)

Hunter may not contain the last word on the issue of what has to be established before a duty of care will be found in a *Dooley*-type case. In *W* v *Essex CC* (2001), the claimant foster parents each developed a psychiatric illness when a boy who had been placed with them sexually abused their children. They sued the local authority who had placed the boy with them. The House of Lords refused to strike out the claimants' claims, holding that it was arguable that the local authority had owed them a duty not to place the boy with them. The House of Lords thought that a duty of care might have been owed to the claimants in this case because they *felt responsible* for what had happened to their children.[64] If so, then the decision in *W* casts doubt on whether *Hunter* was correctly decided as, of course, the claimants were not present when their children were sexually abused.

---

[64] [2001] 2 AC 592, 601.

D. Bystanders

In *McLoughlin* v *O'Brian* (1983), Lord Wilberforce observed that in 'injury or almost injury to third party' cases, where the

> possible range [of people who might want to make claims in such cases goes from] the closest of family ties – of parent and child, or husband and wife – [to] the ordinary bystander . . . [e]xisting law recognises the claims of the first: it denies that of the second, either on the basis that such persons must be assumed to be possessed of fortitude sufficient to enable them to endure the calamities of modern life, or that defendants cannot be expected to compensate the world at large.[65]

However, some of the Law Lords in *Alcock* v *Chief Constable of South Yorkshire* (1992) took the view that in the right kind of case – where A has caused an accident that was so horrific that it was reasonably foreseeable that B, a mere bystander witnessing the accident, would develop a psychiatric illness as a result – B might be able to argue that A owed him a duty to take care not to cause the accident that triggered B's psychiatric illness:

> Psychiatric injury to [a mere bystander] would not ordinarily, in my view, be within the range of reasonable foreseeability, but could not perhaps be entirely excluded from it if the circumstances of a catastrophe occurring very close to him were particularly horrific.[66]

> As regards [bystanders], while it may be very difficult to envisage the case of a stranger, who is not actively and foreseeably involved in a disaster or its aftermath, other than in the role of rescuer, suffering shock-induced psychiatric injury by the mere observation of apprehended or actual injury of a third person in circumstances that could be considered reasonably foreseeable, I see no reason why he should not, if in the circumstances, a reasonably strong-nerved person would have been so shocked. In the course of argument your Lordships were given, by way of example, that of a petrol tanker careering out of control into a school in session and bursting into flames. I would not be prepared to rule out a potential claim by a passer-by so shocked by the scene as to suffer psychiatric illness.[67]

> I would not exclude the possibility . . . of a successful claim, given circumstances of such horror as would be likely to traumatise the most phlegmatic spectator, by a mere bystander.[68]

Despite these *dicta*, both the Court of Appeal – in *McFarlane* v *E E Caledonia Ltd* (1994)[69] – and the House of Lords – in *Frost* v *Chief Constable of South Yorkshire* (1999)[70] – have held that the House of Lords decided in *Alcock* that someone who suffers a psychiatric illness simply as a result of witnessing an accident occur will *only* be able to sue in negligence for compensation for that illness if he or she was in a sufficiently 'close and loving relationship' with someone involved in the accident. On this reading of *Alcock*, the decision of the House of Lords in that case establishes that in a case where a bystander has developed a psychiatric illness as a result of witnessing an accident carelessly caused by A, the bystander will *never* be able to argue that A owed her a duty of care not to cause the

---

[65] [1983] AC 410, 422.
[66] [1992] 1 AC 310, 397 (per Lord Keith of Kinkel).
[67] [1992] 1 AC 310, 403 (per Lord Ackner).
[68] [1992] 1 AC 310, 416 (per Lord Oliver).
[69] [1994] 2 All ER 1, 14. See also *French* v *Chief Constable of Sussex* [2006] EWCA Civ 312 (ruling that police officers could not sue in negligence for psychiatric illness that resulted from shooting of a third party).
[70] [1999] 2 AC 455, 462 (per Lord Griffiths), 472 (per Lord Goff), 496–497 (per Lord Steyn), 502 (per Lord Hoffmann). Lord Browne-Wilkinson, the other judge in *Frost*, agreed with the judgments of Lords Steyn and Hoffmann: [1999] 2 AC 455, 462.

accident that traumatised her: she will not have been in a sufficiently 'close and loving relationship' with anyone involved in the accident.

This reading of *Alcock* is simply wrong and completely inconsistent with the *dicta* from *Alcock* cited above. In fact, this reading of *Alcock* gets *Alcock* backwards. *Alcock* did *not* say that a bystander who develops a psychiatric illness as a result of witnessing an accident occur will only be able to sue in negligence for compensation for her illness if she was in a 'close and loving relationship' with someone involved in the accident. What *Alcock* said was that someone who develops a psychiatric illness because she was in a 'close and loving relationship' with someone who was involved in the accident will only be able to sue in negligence for compensation for her illness if her illness was triggered by her witnessing the accident or the immediate aftermath.

So what went wrong? How could the courts get *Alcock* so wrong? The fault lies, we suggest, in the fact that some judges seem to take the view that whether or not a duty of care was owed to a claimant who suffers a psychiatric illness as a result of an accident occurring will depend on whether the claimant was a 'primary' or 'secondary' victim of that accident. The idea being that one rule will apply to determine whether or not a duty of care was owed to you if you are a 'primary victim' and another rule will apply to determine whether or not a duty of care was owed to you if you are a 'secondary victim'.

Now – the claimants in *Alcock* were 'secondary victims' of the Hillsborough tragedy. The House of Lords ruled in *Alcock* that the defendants in that case could only have owed the claimants a duty of care if: (1) the claimants were in a 'close and loving relationship' with the primary victims of the defendants' carelessness; and (2) the claimants' psychiatric illnesses were triggered as a result of their witnessing the primary victims being killed or injured or almost injured, or the immediate aftermath thereof. If you think that there is *one* rule that determines when a duty of care will be owed to the 'secondary victim' of an accident who has developed a psychiatric illness as a result of that accident occurring, then you will naturally think that the House of Lords was laying down in *Alcock* – a 'secondary victim' case – what that rule was: you have to show a 'close and loving relationship' and proximity in 'space and time' to the accident in which the primary victims of the accident were killed or injured or almost injured. And such a rule would rule out a duty of care ever being owed to a bystander who suffers a psychiatric illness as a result of witnessing an accident occur, as the bystander is also – like the claimants in *Alcock* – a 'secondary victim' but not in a 'close and loving relationship' with anyone involved in the accident.

But the truth is there is no *one* rule that determines when a 'secondary victim' can sue. As we observed above, the law in this area is much more complex. The simplistic view that there is *one* rule introduces all sorts of complications into our understanding of the law. How, for example, are we to account for the fact that a duty of care *was* owed to the claimant in *Dooley* v *Cammell Laird & Co Ltd* (1951) and to the claimant in *Chadwick* v *British Transport Commission* (1967), even though those claimants were obviously not in a 'close and loving relationship' with the primary victims of the defendants' carelessness in those cases? The only way is to reclassify those claimants as 'primary victims'.[71] But if

---

[71] Lord Oliver suggested in *Alcock* that the claimant in *Dooley* was a 'primary victim' ([1992] 1 AC 310) and Lord Slynn seemed to endorse this suggestion in *W* v *Essex CC* ([2001] 2 AC 592, 601). Other Law Lords have tried to stick with the sensible (and intelligible) view that you only count as a 'primary victim' of A's causing an accident if A owed you a duty to take care not to cause that accident because it was reasonably foreseeable that doing so would cause you to suffer some kind of physical injury: see Lord Lloyd's judgment in *Page* v *Smith* [1996] AC 155, and Lord Steyn in *Frost* v *Chief Constable of South Yorkshire* [1999] 2 AC 455, 496.

we do this, the distinction between 'primary victims' and 'secondary victims' becomes meaningless and consequently useless as a means of organising, and discussing, this area of the law.[72]

E. Self-harm

Let us now look at the situation where B foreseeably suffers a psychiatric illness because A's actions result in *A* being killed or injured or almost injured. In such a case, could B argue that A owed B a duty to take care not to kill or injure or almost injure *himself* (A)?

The issue came up in *Greatorex* v *Greatorex* (2000). In that case, the claimant's son was out driving in a friend's car when he crashed it and was injured as a result. The claimant – acting in his capacity as a fire officer – attended the scene of the car crash and saw his son unconscious, injured and trapped in the car. As a result of seeing this, the claimant developed a psychiatric illness. The claimant then sued his son for damages. (This was not as heartless as it seems. While the son was not insured to drive his friend's car, the Motor Insurers' Bureau would have covered any judgment entered against the son.) The claimant argued that his son owed him a duty to take care not to crash the car he was driving, on the basis that it was reasonably foreseeable that if he did so, the claimant would suffer a psychiatric illness as a result. Now, on the basis of what has already been said, one would expect the court to have ruled that the son *did* owe the claimant a duty to take care not to crash the car. The claimant was in a close and loving relationship with his son and developed his psychiatric illness as a result of attending the immediate aftermath of the accident in which his son was injured. However, Cazalet J ruled that no duty of care had been owed to the claimant in this case, for two reasons.

First of all, Cazalet J thought that the son's 'right of self-determination' would have been unacceptably limited if he had owed the claimant a duty to take care not to crash the car he was driving.[73] It is not clear that this is correct. If someone *wants* to kill himself, there is a case for saying that he will *not* owe those members of his family who might be affected by his death a duty not to kill himself – the existence of such a duty would, it is true, completely take away his 'right of self-determination'.[74] But the claimant's son was not *trying* to kill himself when he crashed his friend's car. Given this, it is not clear why his 'right to self-determination' would have been infringed if he had owed C a duty to take care that he did not crash his friend's car.

---

[72] Cf. Teff 1998, 113–14: 'preoccupation with a victim's "primary" or "secondary" status only adds a further layer of obfuscation, distracting attention from the central issue . . . The primary/secondary divide . . . is . . . a recipe for more litigation and further confusion.' Regrettably, some judges seem to regard the distinction between 'primary' and 'secondary' victims as of *crucial* importance for the purpose of determining whether a duty of care was owed in *any* case (including cases where no one has been involved in an accident) where someone has suffered a psychiatric illness as a result of someone else's actions. See, for example, *Hatton* v *Sutherland* [2002] 2 All ER 1, at [19]–[22] and *In Re Organ Retention Group Litigation* [2005] QB 506 (also known as *AB* v *Leeds Teaching Hospital NHS Trust*), at [197].

[73] [2000] 1 WLR 1970, 1984.

[74] It is submitted that the would-be suicide will still owe other people a duty not to commit suicide in such a way that, it can reasonably be foreseen, will result in their suffering some kind of physical injury. So someone who wants to commit suicide will have a duty not to do it by taking a plane flight and blowing it up in mid-flight. Similarly, he will have a duty not to commit suicide by throwing himself off the top of a skyscraper if it is reasonably foreseeable that people walking around the base of the skyscraper will suffer some kind of physical injury if he does so.

Cazalet J's second reason for denying that a duty of care was owed in this case was that to find a duty of care in this kind of case would 'open up the possibility of a particularly undesirable type of litigation between the family, involving questions of relative fault as between its members'. He continued:

> To take an example, A, while drunk, seriously injures himself. B, his wife, [develops a psychiatric illness as a result of seeing A injure himself]. What if A raises, by way of a defence, the fact that he had drunk too much because B had unjustifiably threatened to leave him for another man or had fabricated an allegation of child sexual abuse against him? Should the law of tort concern itself with this issue? In a case where A's self-harm is deliberate, the possibility that B's claim may be met by a defence of contributory negligence, alleging that B's behaviour caused A to harm himself, is an alarming one.[75]

Once again, this is not wholly convincing. Suppose, to take Cazalet J's example, A – in his drunken state – carelessly set fire to the family home and B only escaped the fire after she had been severely burned. In this case, the law will not prevent B from suing A in negligence in respect of her burns – even though allowing her to bring such an action will give rise to the same sort of difficulties as Cazalet J thought would arise if, in his example, B were allowed to sue A in negligence in respect of her psychiatric illness.

5.6 Psychiatric illness (3): non-accident cases

So far, we have been looking at cases where a defendant performs a positive act that causes an accident that in turn results in a claimant suffering a psychiatric illness, either because the claimant is injured or almost injured in the accident, or because a third party (or even the defendant) is killed or injured or almost injured in the accident. There are, however, other ways that a defendant can cause a claimant to suffer a psychiatric illness:

(1) *Bad news.* A tells B some bad news and as a result B develops a psychiatric illness.

(2) *Humiliating or degrading treatment.* A treats B in a way that is particularly humiliating or degrading and B develops a psychiatric illness as a result.

(3) *Stress at work.* A makes his employee, B, do work that is so stressful or difficult for B that B ends up suffering a psychiatric illness.

(4) *Fear of future harm.* A has done something to put B in danger of suffering some kind of physical harm. B has not yet actually suffered any physical harm as a result of A's actions, but develops a psychiatric illness as a result of worrying that he will suffer physical harm in the future.

In each of these cases, there would be little fear of A's liability getting out of all proportion to his fault if A were found to owe B a duty of care. B is, after all, the only one in a position to sue A in these kinds of situations. However, the courts have still had to be cautious about developing the law on when a duty of care will be owed in some of these situations, for fear that being too ready to find that a duty of care was owed will deter people from acting in ways that are desirable or, at least, reasonable.

For example, people do sometimes need to be told bad news – and the bearers of that bad news should not be put off saying what they need to say for fear that what they say will

---

[75] [2000] 1 WLR 1970, 1985.

result in their being sued. Again, while no one is in favour of people being treated in a humiliating or degrading way, saying that A will owe B a duty to take care not to humiliate or degrade B may have the effect of discouraging people from engaging in behaviour that is on the borderline of being humiliating or degrading – for example, a chef bawling out a trainee who has messed up a dish, or a football manager giving the 'hairdryer treatment' to a footballer who has played particularly badly. Finally, if the courts are too willing to find that an employer owes his employee a duty to take care not to make the employee do work that is too stressful or difficult for him, on the basis that it is reasonably foreseeable that doing so will result in the employee suffering a nervous breakdown, they could add considerably to the costs of an employer's enterprise (in that the employer will need to take on more workers to handle the work, or reduce the workload, of employees who cannot cope with the work they are expected to do) and could discourage employees from employing people with poor mental health records.

With that in mind, let us now look at how the courts approach the task of finding whether or not a duty of care was owed in each of the above four situations.

A. Bad news

In *Alcock* v *Chief Constable of South Yorkshire Police* (1992), Lord Ackner observed that, 'Even where the nervous shock and the subsequent psychiatric illness could have been reasonably foreseen, it has generally been accepted that damages for merely being informed of, or reading, or hearing about the accident are not recoverable.'[76] However, there he was thinking of a claimant who was trying to sue the defendant who *caused* the accident.[77] But could a claimant ever sue a defendant who had caused her to develop a psychiatric illness by telling her bad news?

For the claimant's claim to succeed, it would first of all have to be shown that her psychiatric illness was in response to what the defendant *said*, rather than the *event* that the defendant was telling the claimant about. So it would have to be shown that:

(1) the claimant's psychiatric illness was triggered by the *insensitive* way in which the defendant broke some bad news to her (for example, telling someone whose daughter has been run over and killed, 'You're never going to see your brat again'); *or*

(2) the claimant's psychiatric illness was triggered by her being *misinformed* that something bad happened, when in fact it had not (for example, telling someone 'I'm sorry to tell you that your daughter died this morning at school', when in fact the daughter is absolutely fine and it was her schoolmate who died).

With regard to situation (1), in *Mount Isa Mines Ltd* v *Pusey* (1970), a decision of the High Court of Australia, Windeyer J was hostile to the suggestion a duty of care might be owed in that kind of situation:

> If the sole cause of shock be what is told or read of some happening then I think, unless there be an intention to cause a nervous shock, no action lies against . . . the bearer of the bad tidings. There is no duty in law to break bad news gently . . .[78]

---

[76] [1992] 1 AC 310, 400.
[77] The same point could be made of similar *dicta* by Lord Wilberforce in *McLoughlin* v *O'Brian* [1983] AC 410, 423 and Lord Keith in *Alcock* [1992] 1 AC 310, 398.
[78] (1970) 125 CLR 383, 407.

However, times have changed and in *AB* v *Tameside & Glossop Health Authority* (1997), a case where a health authority informed 114 patients by letter that they may be HIV+ because they had been treated by a HIV+ health worker, it was conceded by counsel for the defendant health authority – which was being sued by patients who complained that they had developed a psychiatric illness as a result of the way they were told this news – that the defendant health authority had owed the patients a duty to take care not to break this news to them in an insensitive way. The claim against the health authority was still dismissed by the Court of Appeal, but on the ground that the health authority had not really acted in such an insensitive manner by writing to the patients to let them know they were at risk before they had sorted out any counselling facilities that could be made available to patients who were worried about their health. So breach, rather than duty, was the focus of the decision in *AB*.

Allin v *City and Hackney HA* (1996) was an example of situation (2). The claimant gave birth at the defendants' hospital. The baby was delivered, after a protracted labour, through an emergency Caesarean. The baby was in a very poor condition after it was born, having lost 80 per cent of its blood. After the mother was taken back to the pregnancy ward of the hospital from the operating theatre, two doctors told her that her baby had died. This was not true, as the claimant discovered six hours later. The good news that her baby was alive came too late to prevent the claimant subsequently developing post-traumatic stress disorder. It was held at first instance that the claimant could sue the defendants in negligence for damages for her psychiatric illness. The issue of whether the claimant had been owed a duty of care not to misinform her of the fate of her baby was not explicitly addressed: the judge seems to have assumed that such a duty existed.

Nicholas Mullany, in discussing the above cases, says that, 'Foreseeability of psychiatric injury is what matters . . .'[79] It may be doubted how often it will be the case that it will be reasonably foreseeable that someone will develop a full-blown psychiatric illness simply as a result of being treated insensitively or thinking temporarily that a tragedy has occurred. Given this, we could expect duties of care to arise rarely in 'liability for giving bad news' cases.

B. Humiliating or degrading treatment

In *Wainwright* v *Home Office* (2004), a man named Patrick O'Neill was arrested and taken into custody on a charge of murder. His mother and his brother went to visit him in prison. When they arrived at the prison they were strip-searched to check that they were not carrying any drugs that they could hand over to O'Neill. The strip-search was conducted by ordering the mother and the brother to undress; though the prison guards did touch the brother in the course of the strip-search. The mother was very distressed by the whole experience. The consequences of the strip-search for the brother were more serious: it was found that the strip-search had caused him to suffer a psychiatric illness.

The mother and the brother sued the prison authorities for damages. The mother could not sue the prison authorities in negligence because it is well established that you cannot normally sue in negligence for damages for pure distress.[80] And the brother did

---

[79] Mullany 1998, 384. This is in line with the general view taken in Mullany & Handford 1993, that psychiatric illness should be treated as a form of physical injury, with the result that foreseeability of psychiatric harm should normally give rise to a duty of care.

[80] See below, § 5.7.

not need to rely on the law of negligence to sue the prison authorities: he could argue that the prison guards committed the tort of battery in touching him, and sue them for damages on the basis that his psychiatric illness was triggered by their committing that tort. The interesting question for our purposes is whether the brother *could* have sued the prison authorities in *negligence* for compensation for his psychiatric illness, by arguing that they owed him a duty of care not to subject him to the distressing and humiliating experience of being strip-searched. Let's assume for the purposes of discussing this question that: (1) it was reasonably foreseeable that strip-searching the brother would result in his suffering a psychiatric illness; and (2) the prison authorities acted unreasonably in strip-searching the brother.

Given these two assumptions, could the brother have argued that the prison authorities owed him a duty of care not to order him to undress? The House of Lords' decision in *Wainwright* is frustratingly unclear on the issue.[81] In favour of the answer 'yes' is Lord Hoffmann's treatment in *Wainwright* of the case of *Janvier* v *Sweeney* (1919). In that case, the claimant was made physically sick as a result of the defendants' threatening her. She sued the defendants for damages and was allowed to recover on the ground that the defendants had committed a tort in relation to her in threatening her – the tort in *Wilkinson* v *Downton*.[82] Lord Hoffmann made it clear that he thought: (1) that the claimant in *Janvier* v *Sweeney* could have sued the defendants in negligence; and (2) that the claimant would have been entitled to succeed against the defendants even if she had merely suffered a psychiatric illness as a result of their threats.[83]

But if this is right, and the claimant in *Janvier* could have argued that the defendants in that case owed her a duty of care not to threaten her, then the claimant in *Wainwright* could equally well have argued that the defendants in that case owed him a duty of care not to order him to undress, and he could have sued the defendants in negligence for the psychiatric illness that he developed as a result of the defendants' breach of that duty. However, there is a *dictum* in *Wainwright* that goes against this. In his judgment, Lord Scott observed, 'I agree with the Court of Appeal [in *Wainwright*], and with your Lordships, that if there had been no touching, as there was not in [the mother's] case, no tort would have been committed.'[84] If this is right then if no one had touched the brother, the brother would *not* have been able to sue the prison authorities in negligence or anything else – and this is so even if the whole experience of being strip-searched caused the brother to suffer a psychiatric illness.

Our own view, for what it is worth, is that Lord Scott was wrong and that the brother in *Wainwright* could have sued the prison authorities in negligence had he chosen to do so.[85]

---

[81] This is perhaps understandable given the way *Wainwright* was argued.

[82] For an account of the tort in *Wilkinson* v *Downton*, see below, §§ 17.1(C) and 17.4.

[83] [2004] 2 AC 406, at [40]: 'By the time of *Janvier* v *Sweeney* . . . the law was able comfortably to [deal with this kind of case] in the law of *nervous shock caused by negligence*' (emphasis added).

[84] [2004] 2 AC 406, at [60].

[85] In support of this it may be observed that Lord Scott seemed completely to forget that the brother in *Wainwright* suffered a psychiatric illness: see [2004] 2 AC 406, at [57]: 'The essence of the complaint of each claimant is that he or she was subjected to conduct by the prison officers . . . that was calculated to, and did, cause humiliation and distress' (this was of course *not* the essence of the brother's complaint); and at [58]: 'there is an important difference between the case of [the brother] and that of [the mother]. In the course of, and as part of, the strip-search . . . one of the prison officers [touched the brother] . . .' (the other important difference, unnoted by Lord Scott, is of course that the brother suffered a psychiatric illness and the mother did not).

C. Stress at work

We are concerned here with the situation where B develops a psychiatric illness as a result of the stress created by the type of work that her employer, A, makes her do. In order to establish that A owed her a duty of care not to make her do that work – or at least not to make her do that work without some kind of help that would make the work less stressful – the very first thing that B has to establish is that it was *reasonably foreseeable* that she would develop a psychiatric illness if she were made to do that kind of work. But even if B can do this, that may not be enough to show that A owed B a duty of care not to make her do the work that triggered her psychiatric illness.

In *Walker* v *Northumberland County Council* (1995), the claimant was employed by the defendant local authority as an area social services officer from 1970 to 1987. He was responsible for managing teams of social services fieldworkers in an area which had a high proportion of child care problems. In 1986 the claimant had a nervous breakdown as a result of the stress his job was putting on him. When he came back to work, he discovered that there was a considerable backlog of work waiting for him to clear up and within six months he had another nervous breakdown which led to his stopping work permanently. When he was dismissed by the defendant local authority on grounds of permanent ill health, the claimant sued the defendant local authority in negligence so as to be compensated for the loss of income resulting from his second, irremediable, nervous breakdown. Coleman J allowed the claimant's claim, holding that when the claimant came back to work, the defendant local authority had owed the claimant a duty of care which required them to provide the claimant with some kind of assistance to perform his work. The basis for finding that the local authority had owed the claimant such a duty of care was that it had been reasonably foreseeable when the claimant came back to work that he would suffer a second breakdown if the local authority insisted that he perform his duties without giving him any kind of assistance.

It was crucial to the outcome of the case that the claimant in *Walker* had *already* suffered a nervous breakdown. It was that first breakdown that made his second breakdown reasonably foreseeable. The decision of the Court of Appeal in *Hatton* v *Sutherland* (2002) makes it clear that an employee who suffers a nervous breakdown as a result of being made to do particularly stressful work without any assistance or counselling will find it *very* difficult to show that her breakdown was reasonably foreseeable if nothing was done or nothing happened before her breakdown to alert her employers to the fact that she was having difficulty coping with the amount or type of work that she had to do. In that case, the Court of Appeal was hostile to the idea that the mere nature of an employee's work may be enough to make it reasonably foreseeable that she will develop a psychiatric illness if she is made to do that work without any kind of assistance or counselling.[86] The court went on to observe that, '*Unless he knows of some particular problem or vulnerability, an employer is entitled to assume that his employee is up to the normal pressures of the job.*'[87]

---

[86] [2002] 2 All ER 1, at [12] and at [24].

[87] [2002] 2 All ER 1, at [29] (emphasis in original). In *Barber* v *Somerset County Council* [2004] 1 WLR 1089, the House of Lords expressed broad agreement with this statement: ibid, at [5] (per Lord Scott: '[The Court of Appeal's decision in *Hatton* succeeds] in succinctly and accurately expressing the principles that ought to be applied') and, more tepidly, at [64] (per Lord Walker: '[The Court of Appeal's decision in *Hatton* provides] useful practical guidance, but it must be read as that, and not as having anything like statutory force').

The decision of Coleman J in the *Walker* case seems to suggest that if it is reasonably foreseeable that an employee will develop a psychiatric illness if her employer makes her do some kind of work, then the employer will owe her a duty of care not to make her do that kind of work without giving her some kind of assistance. However, since *Walker* was decided, the courts have shown themselves uneasy at the idea that an employee can demand to be excused from, or given assistance to perform, some or all of her contractual duties merely because it is reasonably foreseeable that if she performs those duties without assistance, she will develop a psychiatric illness. As Lord Rodger observed in *Barber* v *Somerset County Council* (2004):

> The contract of employment will usually regulate what is to happen if an employee becomes unable, due to illness or injury, to carry out his duties. There may be provision for a defined period on full pay, followed by a further defined period on reduced pay, followed by termination of the contract. At the end of the process the employer is free to make new arrangements. While the timetable is likely to be definite, the exact legal analysis of the employee's position when off work under such provisions is by no means free from difficulty. Whatever the position, however, the introduction of a tortious duty of reasonable care on the employer to provide assistance so that the employee can return to work and draw his normal pay, but do less than his full duties for an indefinite period, does not sit easily with such contractual arrangements. Nor does it seem likely to promote efficiency within the enterprise or department.[88]

In *Koehler* v *Cerebos* (2005), the High Court of Australia went further, holding that

> An employer may not be liable for psychiatric injury to an employee brought about by the employee's performance of the duties originally stipulated in the contract of employment . . . Insistence upon performance of a contract cannot be in breach of a duty of care.[89]

If this is right, it severely narrows the scope of situations where an employee who has suffered a perfectly foreseeable psychiatric illness as a result of being made to do stressful work can sue in negligence for compensation for that illness. In effect, she would only be able to sue if she did not originally agree to do that kind (or level) of work when she started working for her employer, but her employer subsequently required her to do that kind (or level) of work.[90]

It is still unclear whether the English courts will follow these *dicta*. However, it may be suggested that, given the scope of the powers enjoyed by the courts to imply terms into contracts of employment to protect the interests of employees when it would be fair, just and reasonable to do so, this is one of those occasions when there is no point 'in searching for a liability in tort where the parties are in a contractual relationship'.[91] In other words, if the law of contract does not protect an employee who has developed a psychiatric illness as a result of the work she was made to do, it is hard to understand why the law of negligence should do any more for her.[92] The reasons why the employee cannot bring a claim

---

[88] [2004] 1 WLR 1089, at [34].

[89] (2005) 222 CLR 44, at [29].

[90] (2005) 222 CLR 44, at [37]. This was the case in *Daw* v *Intel Corporation (UK) Ltd* [2007] EWCA Civ 70, where the claimant worked for the defendants as a mergers and acquisitions payroll integration analyst and suffered a nervous breakdown when poor management resulted in her being loaded with more and more responsibilities with which she could not cope.

[91] *Tai Hing Cotton Mill* v *Liu Chong Hing Bank* [1986] AC 80, at 107 (per Lord Scarman).

[92] See, to similar effect, in the context of a claim for pure economic loss against an employer in tort, *Greenway* v *Johnson Matthey plc* [2016] 1 WLR 4487, at [49]–[51].

in contract for her psychiatric illness will apply with equal force to stop the employee bringing a claim in negligence for that illness.

D. Fear of future harm

Here we are concerned with cases that are like *Page* v *Smith* (1996),[93] in that the defendant in these cases has carelessly done something that foreseeably might have resulted in the claimant being physically injured, but unlike *Page* v *Smith* in that the claimant did not develop a psychiatric illness as a result of being almost injured by the defendant's carelessness but as a result of worrying that the defendant's carelessness will result in her being injured *in the future*.

In such cases, the House of Lords has made it clear that the claimant will *not* be able to rely on *Page* v *Smith* to recover damages for her psychiatric illness.[94] So, in suing the defendant, the claimant will not be able to rely on the fact that her psychiatric illness resulted from the breach of a duty of care that the defendant owed her and that was geared towards protecting her from being *physically injured*. She will have to show that the claimant owed her an independent duty of care not to act as he did that was geared towards protecting her from suffering a *psychiatric illness*. For that – it is submitted – she will have to show that it was reasonably foreseeable that the defendant's actions would cause her to develop a psychiatric illness centred on her fear that she would suffer physical harm in future as a result of what the defendant did.[95]

5.7 Pure distress

In this section, we are looking at situations where A's positive act has resulted in B's suffering, not a psychiatric illness, but pure distress. By 'pure distress', we mean distress (which can take the form of grief, fear, upset, anger, embarrassment, humiliation or sorrow – and that is not meant to be an exhaustive list) that is not consequent on B's being injured, or B's property being damaged. In such a case, can B ever establish that A owed her a duty to take care not to act as he did?

In *Hinz* v *Berry* (1970), Lord Denning MR held that: 'in English law, no damages are awarded for grief or sorrow caused by a person's death. No damages are to be given for the worry about the children, or for the financial strain or stress, or the difficulties of adjusting to a new life.'[96] In *Alcock* v *Chief Constable of South Yorkshire* (1992),

---

[93] See above, § 5.1.

[94] See *Rothwell* v *Chemical & Insulating Co Ltd* [2008] 1 AC 281; above, § 5.1.6.1

[95] This requirement was held to be satisfied in *Group B Plaintiffs* v *Medical Research Council* [2000] Lloyd's Rep Med 161 (discussed, O'Sullivan 1999), and *Andrews* v *Secretary of State for Health*, June 19 1998, unreported, where the claimants developed psychiatric illnesses as a result of worrying that human growth hormone (hGH) injections that they had received from the government as children (when the government should have known such injections were unreasonably dangerous) would result in their developing Creutzfeldt-Jakob Disease in the future. But note Nolan 2004 who observes (at 15) that in California, a claim for a 'fear of future harm' psychiatric illness could only be brought if it was more likely than not that the claimant would suffer physical harm as a result of the defendant's negligence in the future: *Potter* v *Firestone Tire and Rubber Co*, 863 P 2d 795 (Cal. 1993) (claim for psychiatric illness as a result of fear of developing cancer in the future from exposure to dump filled with carcinogenic waste by the defendants). It is unlikely that the claimants in the hGH cases could have satisfied this requirement, given a rate of 40 deaths from 1,800 people who were treated with hGH.

[96] [1970] 2 QB 40, 42.

Lord Ackner was similarly negative about the possibility of suing in negligence for pure distress: 'Mere mental suffering, though reasonably foreseeable, if unaccompanied by physical injury, is not a basis for a claim for damages.'[97]

These *dicta* were borne out by the decision of the House of Lords in *Hicks* v *Chief Constable of South Yorkshire* (1992), which was another case that arose out of the Hillsborough tragedy. That case concerned two sisters – Sarah and Victoria Hicks – who were crushed to death at the Leppings Lane end of the ground. The defendant police force had, of course, owed the Hickses a duty to take care not to cause the spectator pens where they were standing to become overcrowded as it was reasonably foreseeable that spectators like the Hickses would be physically injured if those pens did become overcrowded. However, the *Hicks* case was decided on the basis that the defendants' breach of this duty of care did not ever cause the Hickses to suffer physical injury – that what physical injuries they did suffer as a result of being crushed to death were suffered at the same moment as their death. The only loss that the Hickses suffered before they died – it was supposed – was the terror they went through as they were slowly crushed to death. The House of Lords held that damages for this form of pure distress were not recoverable in negligence.[98] Although the distress felt by the Hickses as they were crushed to death resulted from the defendants' breach of a duty of care that they owed the Hickses, that duty of care was geared towards protecting the Hickses from suffering physical injury, not pure distress. And there was – evidently – nothing in the facts of the *Hicks* case that led the House of Lords to think that the defendant police force owed the Hickses a duty to take care not to put them through such a 'truly terrifying experience'.

In *Wainwright* v *Home Office* (2004) – which was a case, as we have seen, where the defendants caused one of the claimants to suffer pure distress by making her strip before allowing her to see her son in prison – Lord Hoffmann expressed himself open to the possibility of 'abandoning the rule that damages for mere distress are not recoverable' but made it clear that if such a step in the law were to be taken, it could not be taken via the law of negligence, where the mere careless infliction of harm can give rise to liability: 'The defendant must have acted in a way which he knew to be unjustifiable and either intended to cause harm or at least acted without caring whether he caused harm or not.'[99] And Lord Hoffmann went on to express doubts whether even that might justify a claim in tort for pure distress:

> In institutions and workplaces all over the country, people constantly do and say things with the intention of causing distress and humiliation to others. This shows lack of consideration and appalling manners but I am not sure that the right way to deal with it is always by litigation.[100]

Hicks and *Wainwright* were cases where there was no 'special relationship' between the claimants and the defendants.[101] Could such a 'special relationship' give rise to a duty of care geared towards protecting a claimant from suffering mere distress?

---

[97] [1992] 1 AC 310, 401.

[98] [1992] 2 All ER 65, 69.

[99] [2004] 2 AC 406, at [45].

[100] [2004] 2 AC 406, at [46].

[101] See also *Al-Kandari* v *Brown* [1988] 1 QB 665, where it was held (at 675) that the trial judge had been right to hold that 'he was not entitled to award damages for grief or sorrow' in a case where the defendant firm of solicitors – who were not in any kind of 'special relationship' with the claimant – carelessly allowed the claimant's husband to get hold of his passport from the defendants, with the result that he immediately kidnapped the claimant's children and left the country. But the claimant could sue for the physical injury and psychiatric illness she had suffered as a result of the defendants' breach of the duty of care that they owed the claimant.

Vernon v *Bosley (No 1)* (1997) seems to indicate a negative answer. In that case, the defendant was a nanny who was charged with the job of looking after the claimant's two children. One day, the defendant was driving a car with the children in it. She carelessly lost control of the car, and it crashed down a 30 foot bank into a river that flowed alongside the road. The defendant managed to escape from the car, but the children were trapped. The claimant – who was working at a nearby factory – was called to the scene of the accident by the police. There, he and his wife watched the attempts to rescue their children. The attempts were unsuccessful, and the children died. The claimant suffered a recognised psychiatric illness – pathological grief disorder – in the aftermath of his children's deaths. The majority of the Court of Appeal accepted that the claimant's illness was a consequence of his being on the scene of the accident (as opposed to the loss of his children) and as a result found, in line with the authorities we have already discussed, that the defendant owed the claimant a duty of care on which he could base a claim for his psychiatric illness.

There was, in fact, no need to invoke authorities like *McLoughlin* v *O'Brian* (1983) and *Alcock* v *Chief Constable of South Yorkshire* (1992) to establish that the defendant owed the claimant a duty of care here. As we will see,[102] the fact that the defendant 'assumed a responsibility' to the claimant to look after his children meant that she owed the claimant a duty to look after those children with a reasonable degree of care and skill. What, then, would have happened had the claimant not suffered a recognised pathological grief disorder as a result of the defendant's breach of this duty of care, but merely grief? Would he have been entitled to sue for damages for that grief, given that there was in this case a 'special relationship' between the parties? The Court of Appeal was clear that mere grief would not have been actionable in *Vernon* v *Bosley*: 'Damages for mental injury do not include compensation for feelings of grief and bereavement which are not themselves symptomatic of illness.'[103]

As against this must be set *Hamilton Jones* v *David & Snape (a firm)* (2004), where the defendant firm of solicitors were employed by the claimant to represent her in custody proceedings against the husband. The claimant told the defendants she was worried her husband – a Tunisian national – would attempt to take her children to Tunisia with him. To stop this happening, in February 1994 the defendants informed the UK Passport Agency that the claimant's husband was prohibited from removing the children from the claimant's care, and the Passport Agency undertook that for the next 12 months they would do their best to ensure that the claimant's husband was not issued with a British passport, and told the defendants to tell them at the end of the 12 months if they wanted the Passport Agency to renew this undertaking for the next 12 months. This the defendants failed to do. As a result, the claimant's husband – who had by now become a British citizen – had no trouble obtaining a British passport in June 1996. Shortly after that, he added the claimant's children's names to the passport. And shortly after *that*, he took the children to Tunisia. The claimant sued the defendants for damages for the distress she felt at losing her children. Neuberger J held that the claimant could sue the defendants for such damages either by bringing a claim against the defendants for breach of contract or by suing them in negligence. (The relevant duty of care that was breached in this case was a duty to represent the claimant with reasonable

---

[102] See below, § 6.2.
[103] [1997] 1 All ER 577, 604.

skill and care, which duty was based on the contractual 'assumption of responsibility' that the defendants made to the claimant when they took on her case.)

Andrew Burrows has sought to sum up the effect of the *Hamilton Jones* decision by saying that:

> . . . mental distress damages are recoverable in [negligence] provided they would be recoverable in that situation for breach of contract. In other words, mental distress damages will be recoverable provided one can show that an important object of the services was to provide mental satisfaction or freedom from distress . . .'[104]

(In contract law, the 'object of the contract' is an important limit on the availability of damages for pure distress resulting from a breach of contract.)[105] But where does that leave *Vernon* v *Bosley*? There must have been a contract in that case, and an important object of that contract would have been to relieve the claimant from having to worry about his children and to give him the mental satisfaction of knowing they were safe. Perhaps grief is special and is simply non-actionable under any circumstances, for two reasons. First, grief for the loss of a loved one is something that the claimant may have had to go through anyway at some stage in his life, and so should not be actionable even if a defendant has accelerated the moment at which the claimant has to go through that experience. Secondly, a couple of judges have expressed concern at the effect that litigation may have on the depth and duration of a claimant's psychiatric illness:

> Both at the bar and on the bench I have listened to doctors and particularly psychiatrists saying in cases of psychiatric illness that no further recovery is to be expected until the litigation is finished. I have often heard medical opinion suggest that litigation prolongs symptoms of psychiatric illness, making it more deep-seated and difficult to treat. May we not by giving the remedy aggravate the illness? Surely health is better than money.[106]

> Where there is generally no prospect of recovery, such as in the case of injuries sustained in sport, psychiatric harm appears not to obtrude often. On the other hand, in the case of industrial accidents, where there is often a prospect of recovery of compensation, psychiatric harm is repeatedly encountered and often endures until the process of claiming compensation comes to an end . . . The litigation is sometimes an unconscious disincentive to rehabilitation.[107]

It may be that the courts are wary of the effect that the prospect of litigation might have on the grieving process, turning something that can be healing into something pathological.

5.8 Harm to property

We are concerned here with the situation where a defendant has performed a positive act that has resulted in an item of property P being harmed. If a claimant wants to show that the defendant owed her a duty of care not to act as he did, the claimant will have to show that: (1) she had a sufficient interest in P at the time it was harmed as a result of the defendant's act; and (2) it was reasonably foreseeable that the defendant's act would result in property like P being harmed. If (1) and (2) are made out, the courts will normally find

---

[104] Burrows 2004, 337–8.
[105] *Farley* v *Skinner* [2002] 2 AC 732.
[106] *McLoughlin* v *O'Brian* [1981] 1 QB 599, 624 (per Griffiths LJ), quoted in Nolan 2004, 20.
[107] *Frost* v *Chief Constable of South Yorkshire* [1999] 2 AC 455, 494 (per Lord Steyn).

that the defendant owed the claimant a duty of care, geared towards protecting P from being harmed. All this raises a number of issues.

A. Property

The above formula for establishing that a defendant owed a claimant a duty of care will only apply in the case where the defendant's positive act has resulted in a *tangible* item of property – an item of property you can touch, such as a computer or a book or a house or a piece of land – being harmed.

Intangible items of property – items of property that you cannot touch, such as a patent (giving the holder a monopoly over a particular idea) or an easement (a right over someone else's land) or a charge (a right to the proceeds of the sale of an item of property) – are not protected by the above formula. Mere foreseeability that A's acting in a particular way will destroy, or get in the way of B's exploiting, an intangible item of property that B has an interest in will not give rise to a duty of care on A's part not to act in that way.[108]

B. Sufficient interest

In a case where A has done something positive that has resulted in an item of property P being harmed, and it was reasonably foreseeable that A's actions would have that kind of effect, then A will normally have had a duty to take care not to act as he did. But that duty is only owed to – in other words, imposed for the benefit of[109] – people who had a *sufficient interest* in P *at the time it was harmed*. But what counts as a sufficient interest?

Until the recent decision of the Court of Appeal in *Shell UK Ltd* v *Total UK Ltd* (2010), it had been thought – on very high authority[110] – that A's duty would only have been owed to those who had a *legal* interest in P, or were in *possession* of P, at the time it was harmed. However, the Court of Appeal ruled in *Shell* that:

1. A's duty will *also* have been owed to anyone for whom P was held on trust at the time it was harmed;

2. *but* anyone for whom P was held on trust at the time it was harmed will *not* be able to sue in their own right for the losses they have suffered as a result of P being harmed *unless* they make the legal owner of P at the time it was harmed a party to their claim against A.

---

[108] *Esser* v *Brown* (2004) 242 DLR (4th) 112 (a notary who destroyed the claimant's interest in a ranch she owned with her husband when he executed a sale of the ranch to a third party which the claimant had not agreed to (her husband had forged her signature on the contract of sale) had not owed the claimant a duty of care not to destroy her interest in the ranch). Though see the decision in *Ministry of Housing* v *Sharp* (1970) 2 QB 223 (discussed below, § 5.13), where it was held that the defendant – whose carelessness in informing the purchaser of land that there were no charges over the land meant that the claimant lost his charge over the land when it was purchased – had owed the claimant a duty of care.

[109] See above, § 1.2.

[110] See *Leigh & Sillavan Ltd* v *Aliakmon Shipping Ltd, The Aliakmon* [1986] AC 785 (K-M shipped steel coils to be delivered to L&S, price to be paid in full on delivery (whatever condition the coils were in) and L&S only to acquire title to the goods once they had paid for them; the coils were damaged in transit as a result of D's carelessness; L&S still had to pay in full for the coils and sought to recover their loss from D; held, D had not owed a duty of care to L&S not to damage the coils as L&S was not the legal owner of the coils at the time they were damaged; nor was it in possession of the coils at that time).

Shell was concerned with the aftermath of the explosion at the Buncefield oil depot on 11 December 2005. The oil depot – which was owned by Total UK – was capable of carrying 60m gallons of fuel. A gauge on a storage tank that was being filled with unleaded fuel stopped working, which meant that no one could tell the tank was full. As a result fuel kept on being pumped into the tank, and soon overflowed the tank. The overflowing fuel gave rise to a vapour cloud which ignited, for reasons never identified. The resulting explosion was the largest in peacetime Europe. It damaged numerous pipelines leading away from Buncefield. These pipelines were owned by a shell company, WLPS Ltd, and were held on trust for four oil companies, including Shell, that used the pipelines to supply oil to their customers.[111] Shell sued Total in negligence, claiming that Total had owed Shell a duty to take care not to damage the pipelines owned by WLPS Ltd, and seeking to recover the loss of profits that Shell had suffered when the pipelines were damaged, as a result of being unable to supply their customers with oil, and having to supply what oil they could through more expensive means of transport.

Shell's claim was dismissed at first instance, but was allowed in the Court of Appeal. The Court of Appeal could see no problem in allowing Shell's claim, holding that 'it is legalistic to deny Shell a right to recovery . . . It is, after all, Shell who is (along with BP, Total and Chevron) the "real" owner, the "legal" owner being little more than a bare trustee of the pipeline.'[112] The 'high authority' adverted to above (the House of Lords' decision in *The Aliakmon* (1986)) was distinguished as merely requiring a claimant who wanted to sue a defendant in negligence for damaging property that was held on trust for the claimant to join the legal owner of the property in the claim. Once this is done, the claimant's action will be able to proceed and she will be able to recover damages for the losses that *she* has suffered as a result of the property being damaged.[113]

The decision of the Court of Appeal has come in for some fierce academic criticism.[114] Four criticisms can be made of the decision.

(1) Claims in negligence are claims under the common law, and it is not clear why the common law *should* get involved with protecting the beneficiary under a trust from losses that he or she has suffered as a result of the trust property being damaged. It is also not clear whether the common law *can* get involved with protecting the beneficiary without unacceptably disrupting and confusing the existing equitable rules on when a beneficiary can sue for losses suffered as a result of a third party interfering with trust property.[115]

---

[111] The pipelines were owned by a shell company because of the rule of law mentioned above, in § 1.13, that no more than four people can own land legally as joint tenants (Law of Property Act 1925, s 34). As there were originally more than four oil companies that wanted to have an interest in the pipelines leading away from Buncefield, it was thought best to vest legal ownership in a shell company and have that company hold the pipelines on trust for the oil companies that would be using those pipelines.

[112] [2011] QB 86, at [132].

[113] [2011] QB 86, at [129]-[130]. Strangely, a point of law (as to whether a beneficiary for whom property is held on trust can sue for *his own* loss if he joins the legal owner in his claim) that was 'not resolve[d]' (by the decision in *The Aliakmon*) in para [131] becomes 'clear' by para [137] ('it is clear that the beneficial owner can sue if he joins the legal owner').

[114] See Low 2010; Turner 2010.

[115] A consideration which led the Court of Appeal in *MCC Proceeds Inc v Lehman Bros International (Europe)* [1998] 4 All ER 675 (discussed below, § 17.2(D)(5)) to refuse to allow B to sue in conversion where trust property which is held on trust for B by A is interfered with by C. (*MCC Proceeds* was cited to the Court of Appeal in argument in *Shell* but not referred to in its judgment.)

(2) There is an argument to be made that where A holds property on trust for B, B does not actually have an interest in the trust property. All B has are rights *in* or *against* the rights A holds over the trust property.[116] If this is correct, then the Court of Appeal was wrong to think in *Shell* that Shell was (along with the other oil companies who used the pipelines at Buncefield) the 'real' owner of the pipelines that were damaged in this case. The *only* owner was WLPS Ltd; and all Shell had were rights against WLPS. If this is right, then Shell's claim was, in effect, one for pure economic loss, and one that could not have been allowed without overturning the restrictive rules on when a duty of care will be owed in a pure economic loss case.[117]

(3) If Total *had* owed Shell a duty of care in this case, it is not clear why Shell had to join *WLPS* to its claim against Total in order for *Shell* to sue Total in negligence for the losses suffered by *Shell* as a result of Total's breach of a duty of care owed to *Shell*. The requirement that Shell join WLPS to its claim was intended to get round the inconvenient authority of *The Aliakmon* (1986). But the Court of Appeal might have done better if, instead of distinguishing *The Aliakmon* on utterly specious grounds, they had complied with the rules of precedent and dismissed Shell's claim as being inconsistent with *The Aliakmon*.

(4) The Court of Appeal confessed itself in *Shell* as having been influenced by 'the impulse to do practical justice'.[118] One can see why 'justice' might have seemed to dictate that Shell be afforded a remedy here. It was only s 34 of the Law of Property Act 1925[119] that led Shell and the other oil companies that used the pipelines at Buncefield to vest legal title to the pipelines in WLPS. Had s 34 not existed, Shell and the other companies might have made themselves joint legal owners of the pipelines, and there would then have been no obstacle in the way of Shell suing for the economic losses it suffered as a result of those pipelines being damaged and destroyed. However, one virtue of s 34 is that it limits the number of legal owners of a piece of land to *four*. By holding in *Shell* that a defendant who has damaged trust property will have owed a duty of care not only to the legal owner of that property, but also anyone for whom the property was held on trust, the Court of Appeal opens the defendant to the possibility of claims being made against him by a potentially unlimited number of claimants, as there is no limit on how many people for whom property can be held on trust. Suppose, for example, that a *hundred* different oil companies had used the pipelines at Buncefield, and those pipelines were held on trust for all of them. It is not clear whether it would be just to hold a defendant liable to a hundred different claimants, each suing for losses running into hundreds of thousands or millions of pounds, when the defendant was guilty of a trivial fault that resulted in the pipelines blowing up.

The Supreme Court allowed Total's application for leave to appeal the Court of Appeal's decision in *Shell*.[120] However, Total subsequently settled with Shell, and the Supreme Court was deprived of the chance to reverse the Court of Appeal's decision in *Shell* and restore order to this area of law. Until another such case reaches the Supreme Court, the position is that in the case we are considering – where it was reasonably foreseeable that property P would be harmed as a result of A's doing *x* – A will have owed a duty to take care not to do *x not just* to whoever legally owned P or possessed P at the time it was

---

[116] See Low 2010, 507, and references cited therein.
[117] See below, § 5.9.
[118] [2011] QB 86, at [143], quoting Lord Goff in *White* v *Jones* [1995] 2 AC 207, 259–60.
[119] See above, fn 111.
[120] [2011] QB 86, 105.

harmed, *but also* to whomever P was held on trust for at the time it was harmed. (Though a claimant for whom P was held on trust at the time it was harmed will only be able to sue A in negligence if the claimant joins the legal owner of P to the claim.)

C. Harm

What counts as 'harming' property for the purposes of the duty formula discussed here?

Obviously, destroying or damaging an item of property P will amount to harming it.[121] Property will count as having been damaged if it undergoes 'a physical change which renders [it] less useful or less valuable.'[122] So, in *Hunter* v *Canary Wharf* (1997), the Court of Appeal held that the deposit of excessive dust on a carpet could amount, of and in itself, to damage to the carpet. And in *Blue Circle Industries* v *Ministry of Defence* (1999), the Court of Appeal was willing to hold that the intermingling of plutonium with soil so that it could not be removed amounted to a form of property damage. In *Pride & Partners* v *Institute of Animal Health* (2009), Tugendhat J held that farmers whose pigs became overweight and therefore less valuable because of movement restrictions on animals during an outbreak of foot and mouth disease 'have a real prospect of succeeding in the contention that that is physical damage'.[123]

What about cases of interferences with property that fall short of damaging or destroying it? Consider the **Lost Ring Problem**:

> *Bride* has just been married in a picturesque country house, and is leaning against a wishing well on the house grounds, talking to *Friend*. *Friend* asks to see *Bride*'s wedding ring and *Bride* hands it over. While *Friend* is holding the ring up to the light, *Bridesmaid* rushes excitedly up to *Friend* to get a look at the ring, and is unable to stop herself from crashing into *Friend*, with the result that *Friend* drops the ring and it falls into the well.

Can we say that the ring has been harmed here – even though its fall to the bottom of the well has almost certainly not destroyed or damaged it? We think if the ring is effectively irretrievable then *Bride* could claim that the ring has been harmed,[124] and argue on that basis that *Bridesmaid* owed her a duty to take care not to crash into *Friend* (it being reasonably foreseeable that *Bridesmaid*'s doing this would result in the ring dropping to the bottom of the well). The **Useless T-Shirts Problem** is different:

> *Chancer* manufactures 10,000 T-shirts which he is planning to sell to people attending the opening of the London Olympics. The T-shirts carry the official Olympics logo and say 'July 27 2012 – I Was There'. On the day of the opening ceremony, a major accident caused by *Driver*'s carelessness results in *Chancer* being unable to transport the T-shirts to the stall that he has set up outside the Olympic Stadium in Stratford. *Chancer* subsequently tries to sell the T-shirts over the Internet, but no one is interested in buying them.

---

[121] See Weston 1999 for a useful discussion as to when someone who has lost computer data can argue that they have suffered a form of damage to property for the purposes of the duty formula discussed here.

[122] *Hunter* v *Canary Wharf* [1997] AC 655, 676 (per Pill LJ).

[123] [2009] EWHC 685 (QB), at [75].

[124] In *The Nicholas H* [1996] AC 211, cargo belonging to the claimant was lost at sea when the ship that was carrying it sank. No one would disagree that in this case the cargo was harmed for the purposes of duty formula under discussion here.

Here the T-shirts are as useless to *Chancer* as the ring is in Lost Ring. But we do not think *Chancer* can argue that the T-shirts have been harmed as a result of *Driver*'s carelessness. He still has the T-shirts and they are physically unaffected by what *Driver* did.

D. Time of harm

In order to argue that a defendant owed her a duty of care under the duty formula discussed here, a claimant has to show that she had a sufficient interest in an item of property that the defendant harmed *at the time it was harmed*. So it can be very important in certain cases to identify the time at which a given item of property was harmed. For example, consider the **Cracked Vase Problem**:

> *Rich* wants to sell a vase of hers at auction. The day before the auction, all the auction items are on display at the auction house for potential buyers to look at. During the viewing hours, *Clumsy* picks up the vase to look at it, and puts it back down a bit too heavily, with the result that the vase develops an invisible crack at its base. The next day, *Owner* buys the vase and takes it home. Within a week, the crack at the base of the vase spreads and becomes visible and the vase shatters.

Can *Owner* argue that *Clumsy* owed her a duty of care under the duty formula under discussion here? The answer is no – *Owner* did not have a legal interest in, or possession of, the vase at the time *Clumsy* harmed it. Admittedly, the vase did shatter when it belonged to *Owner*. But that shattering was merely an extension of the initial harm that it suffered in the auction house when *Clumsy* put it back down. And at that time, *Owner* did not have a sufficient interest in the property.

The vase in the above example was initially sound and was subsequently made unsound by *Clumsy*'s rough handling of it. What about a case where an item of property was *always* unsound because it was manufactured in a way that meant that it was doomed to blow up or shatter or fall apart at some point in the future? The duty formula under discussion here will have no application to such a case. The reason is that the property was never harmed by the manufacturer.

Suppose, for example, that *Blower* manufactures window glass and carelessly introduces a contaminant into the molten glass from which he makes his windows. As a result, a window pane that is subsequently installed in *Owner*'s house suffers from a flaw that causes it to shatter a couple of years later. *Owner* may be able to point to the shattered window and say 'My property has been damaged by *Blower*'s carelessness'. But appearances deceive: *Blower* has not really harmed *Owner*'s window in this case. The window came into the world in a flawed state, and the shattering is merely an outward manifestation of the internal weakness from which that window always suffered. So *Blower* has not done anything here to make the window worse than it once was.

If *Owner* wants to sue *Blower* in negligence here, it cannot be for the damage suffered by the window, because *Blower* did not really damage the window. Instead, *Owner* will have to sue *Blower* for the *cost of replacing the window* or the *money Owner wasted on purchasing the window*. This is a form of pure economic loss. The issue of when a claimant can establish that a defendant owed her a duty of care in a pure economic loss case will be discussed below. However, we can briefly anticipate the discussion below by saying here that the fact that it is foreseeable that A's actions will result in B suffering a form of pure economic loss will not be enough to establish that A owed B a duty of care. Usually, it will have to be shown that there existed some kind of special relationship between A and B, based on A's 'assuming a responsibility' to B. In the case we are discussing here, no such special relationship will exist between *Blower* and *Owner*. The result is that *Owner* will have no remedy in negligence against *Blower* for the fact that his window has shattered.

E. Differentiating property

Suppose that *Maker* manufactures beer bottles that suffer from an internal flaw which means that they are liable to shatter if kept in cold conditions. *Owner* buys one of these beer bottles and puts it in his fridge. Two days later, the bottle shatters, spilling beer all over the inside of the fridge and a joint of meat that *Owner* was keeping in the fridge.

If *Owner* wants to sue *Maker* in negligence for the damage to the fridge or the joint of meat, then she should have no problem using the duty formula discussed here to establish that *Maker* owed her a duty of care geared towards protecting those items of property from being harmed. *Maker* has performed a positive act – putting flawed beer bottles into circulation – that has resulted in *Owner's* fridge and joint of meat being harmed, and it was reasonably foreseeable that *Maker's* putting flawed beer bottles into circulation would have that kind of effect. So if *Owner* wants to sue *Maker* in negligence for the damage to the fridge or the joint of meat, she will have no problem arguing that *Maker* owed her a duty to take care not to put flawed beer bottles into circulation. The only issue will be whether *Maker* breached that duty: whether he was at fault for the flaw from which the beer bottles suffered.

But what if *Owner* isn't content just to sue for the damage to the fridge or the joint of meat, but wants to sue as well for the *loss of the beer* that spilled all over the fridge when the beer bottle shattered? Can *Owner* establish that *Maker* owed her a duty of care geared towards protecting her from suffering *that* kind of harm? It depends on how we look at the bottle of beer that *Owner* stored in her fridge. Was that *one* item of property – a bottle-containing-beer. Or was it *two* items of property – a bottle, and a quantity of beer?

If it was just one item of property, then *Owner* cannot invoke the duty formula under discussion here to recover damages for the loss of the beer. *Maker's* positive act in putting flawed beer bottles into circulation harmed *Owner's* fridge and joint of meat. But it did not harm the other item of property in *Owner's* fridge – the bottle-containing-beer. That is because that item of property was already damaged, even before *Maker* put it into circulation. Even if we suppose that the bottle-containing-beer was at some point initially sound, but *Maker* did a positive act that resulted in that item of property becoming flawed before it left *Maker's* factory (for example, by storing the bottle improperly after it rolled off *Maker's* production line), that postive act harmed *Owner's* bottle-containing-beer long before it became *Owner's* property. So *Owner* can use the duty formula under discussion here to establish that *Maker* owed her a duty of care geared towards protecting her fridge or her joint of meat from being harmed; but not in order to establish that *Maker* owed her a duty of care geared towards ensuring that *Owner's* bottle-containing-beer did not shatter when it was stored in *Owner's* fridge.

But what if we can say that when *Owner* put the bottle of beer in her fridge, she was putting *two* items of property into the fridge – a bottle, and a quantity of beer? In such a case, *Owner could* use the duty formula under discussion here to launch a negligence claim against *Maker* for the loss of the beer. *Owner* could argue that *Maker's* positive act of storing beer in a defective bottle has resulted in harm to the beer, and that that beer was harmed when it belonged to *Owner*, in that the beer was perfectly sound up until the moment when the bottle in which it was stored shattered.

So – which is it to be? One item of property, or two?[125] In *Aswan Engineering* v *Lupdine* (1987), Lloyd LJ (with whom Fox LJ agreed) took the 'provisional view'[126] that in this case, the answer is that *Owner* had two items of property – a bottle, and a quantity of beer. So *Owner* would be able to rely on the duty formula under discussion here to sue *Maker* not only for the damage to her fridge and her joint of meat, but also the loss of the beer.[127] It may seem quite a trivial question whether or not *Owner* can sue *Maker* for the loss of the beer in this case. But there are other cases that raise the same issue where the stakes will be a lot higher.

For example, suppose that *Maker* manufactures a car and carelessly installs a tyre on the car which is dangerously defective. A year later, *Owner* buys the car from a car dealer. Some time after that, *Owner* is driving the car when the tyre blows out and the car crashes. *Owner* is unharmed, but the car is a write-off. Can *Owner* sue *Maker* in negligence[128] for the loss of her car? Whether *Owner* can use the duty formula under discussion here to establish that *Maker* owed her a duty of care, that was geared towards protecting her car from being damaged, depends on whether we think that *Owner* obtained *one* item of property when she bought the car manufactured by *Maker* (a car), or *more than one* item of property (a car and a set of tyres). If only *one* item of property, then *Maker* did not do anything to harm *Owner*'s car. That car was brought into the world in a flawed state, and the twisted remains of the car lying at the side of the road are merely an extension of that initial flaw. If *more than one* item of property, then we can say that *Maker* did a positive act (installing a defective tyre on the car that was eventually bought by *Owner*) that harmed *Owner*'s car (which was until that moment, perfectly sound) when the tyre on *Owner*'s car blew out. Lloyd LJ's provisional view in *Aswan* was that the second analysis is preferable. If this is right, then *Owner* will be able to argue in this case that *Maker* owed her a duty to take care not to put a defective tyre on the car that she ended up buying, because: (1) his positive act of putting that tyre on the car harmed an item of property (the car) that belonged to her at the time it was harmed (that is, it was perfectly sound up until the tyre blowing out); and (2) it was reasonably foreseeable that putting a defective tyre on the car would result in its being harmed at some point in the future.

---

[125] Tettenborn 2000b suggests that if a component part of a chattel can be removed without damaging the other parts of the chattel, the component and the rest-of-the-chattel should be regarded as being two separate items of property. But it is not clear how this test would apply in this case. In theory, the beer could be separated from the bottle without damaging the beer (by pouring it into another container, for example). On the other hand, the beer will spill and be spoiled if it is suddenly deprived of its bottle.

[126] [1987] 1 WLR 1, 21.

[127] In the *Aswan* case itself, the claimants ordered some waterproofing compound from L. L, in turn, ordered some pails from the defendants to store the compound in when shipping it to the claimants. Having obtained the pails from the defendants, L filled them with the compound and L shipped them to the claimants in Kuwait, where they were left in the blazing sun. Eventually the heat caused the plastic pails to collapse and the compound was lost. The claimants sued the defendants in negligence, claiming that the defendants had owed them a duty not to supply L with the pails that they did because it was reasonably foreseeable that doing so would result in the compound sold by L to the claimants being lost. Lloyd and Fox LJJ dismissed the claim on the ground that as the defendants had no idea the pails would be shipped to Kuwait, it was not reasonably foreseeable that the compound sold by L to the claimants would be lost if it was shipped to the claimants in the pails that the defendants supplied to L. Nicholls LJ dismissed the claim on the ground that the manufacturer of a container will not owe a duty of care in manufacturing the container to anyone who loses his or her property as a result of the container being insufficiently sturdy.

[128] *Owner* will not be able to sue *Maker* under the Consumer Protection Act 1987 for the damage done by the tyre to the car: s 5(2). See below, § 11.5.

Again, suppose that *Builder* constructs a house, and in the course of building that house he instals electrical wiring around the house. The wiring is defective, but the problem is not detected initially, or even by the time *Owner* buys the house a few years later. Some time after *Owner* buys the house, the defective wiring causes a fire to start which results in the house being burned down. *Owner* wants to sue *Builder* in negligence for the loss of her house. Whether she can use the duty formula under discussion here to launch a claim against *Builder* will depend on whether what *Owner* bought when she bought the house was *one* item of property (a house), or *more than one item of property* (a house, and an electrical wiring system that goes with the house). If just one item, then she will not be able to establish that *Builder* did anything to harm the house in this case – the house came into the world in a flawed state, and its charred remains are merely an extension of that initial flaw. If more than one, then *Owner* can rely on the formula under discussion here. She can say that *Builder*'s positive act in wiring the house with defective wiring resulted in a separate item of property – the house – being harmed at the time it belonged to her.

In *Murphy* v *Brentwood DC* (1990), Lord Keith of Kinkel took the view that in the case we have just described – where the entire house, including the wiring, is built by A – it would be 'unrealistic' to separate out the house from its wiring: 'In that situation the whole package provided by the contractor would . . . fall to be regarded as *one* unit rendered unsound as such by a defect in the particular part.'[129] On the other hand, he thought that if the electric wiring had been installed by a third party, *Contractor*, then in that kind of case it could be argued that the house and wiring were separate items of property, so that *Owner* could argue that *Contractor* owed her a duty to take care not to install wiring that was defective, because the act of installing such wiring resulted in a separate item of property (the house) being harmed at a time when it belonged to *Owner*.[130]

In the same case, Lord Bridge of Harwich took a different approach, drawing a distinction between a case where:

> some part of a complex structure . . . does not perform its proper function in sustaining the other parts and a case where some distinct item incorporated in the structure . . . positively malfunctions so as to inflict positive damage on the structure in which it is incorporated.[131]

In the first type of case, one could not say that there were two separate items of property, one (defective item) harming the other (previously sound item). There is just one piece of property that was brought into the world in a defective state and is now falling apart under its own flaws. But in the second type of case, a claimant could argue that a previously sound item of property belonging to her ('the structure') has been harmed by defects in a 'distinct item' of property for which the defendant is responsible. It was not clear on which side of the line Lord Bridge would have thought our example fell. He said that:

> if a defective central heating boiler explodes and damages a house or a defective electrical installation sets the house on fire, I see no reason to doubt that the owner of the house, if he can prove that the damage was due to . . . negligence . . . can recover damages . . . But the position in law is entirely different where, by reason of the inadequacy of the foundations of the building to support the weight of the superstructure, differential settlement and consequent cracking occurs.[132]

---

[129] [1991] 1 AC 398, 470 (emphasis added).
[130] Ibid: '[In such a case] it might not be stretching ordinary principles too far to hold the electrical subcontractor liable for the damage.'
[131] [1991] 1 AC 398, 478.
[132] Ibid.

But it is not clear whether Lord Bridge's reference to an 'electrical installation' was meant to cover the case of electrical wiring that is inside the walls of a building.[133]

F. Normally

We said at the start of this section that if A has harmed an item of property P by doing some positive act, and B can show that: (1) she had a sufficient interest in P at the time it was harmed, and (2) it was reasonably foreseeable that A's actions would result in property like P being harmed, then the courts will *normally* find that A owed B a duty of care not to act as he did. The same exceptions to the usual practice of finding a duty of care when physical injury is foreseeable also apply in this area. That is, even if (1) and (2) are shown to be true, A will still *not* be found to have owed B a duty of care if: (i) B was happy for A to do what he did, despite the dangers for P; (ii) it was reasonable for A to do what he did; or (iii) it would be contrary to the public interest to find that A owed B a duty of care.

(iii) will be rarely made out, but probably underlies the decision of the House of Lords in *The Nicholas H* (1996). In that case, the eponymous ship, which was carrying the claimant's cargo, developed a crack in its hull while it was travelling from South America to Italy. The ship anchored off Puerto Rico and was inspected by the defendant classification society. The defendants told the shipowners that they would be willing to pass *The Nicholas H* as seaworthy – and thus allow it to continue on its way – if the shipowners temporarily repaired its hull and then repaired it properly as soon as possible after it discharged its cargo. The temporary repairs were done and *The Nicholas H* went on its way. However, it sank a week later when the temporary repairs failed. The claimant's cargo, which was worth $6,200,000, was lost. The claimant could recover only $500,000 from the shipowner by way of compensation for the loss of his cargo due to a limitation clause in the contract between the claimant and the shipowner.

The claimant sued the defendants for the balance of his loss, claiming that they had been negligent in allowing *The Nicholas H* to proceed on its way. The House of Lords dismissed the claim, holding that the defendants had not owed the claimant a duty of care not to approve the ship as seaworthy when it was not. This was so even though it had been perfectly foreseeable that the claimant's cargo would be harmed if the defendants approved the *Nicholas H* as seaworthy when it was not. So why did the House of Lords not give effect to the duty formula under discussion here?[134] The reason was that the House of

---

[133] For another case raising this kind of problem, see *Bellefield Computer Services Ltd* v *E Turner & Sons Ltd* [2000] BLR 97 (noted, Duncan Wallace 2000). A wall separating a storage area within a building from the rest of the building was badly constructed with the result that when a fire broke out in the storage area, it spread to the rest of the building. It was held that this was a case of one item of property – a building divided up into different areas by a wall – suffering from a defect from the moment of its creation, with the defect manifesting itself in eventual fire damage. It was not a case of a sound item of property – the area of the building outside the storage area – being damaged because another item of property – the wall separating the storage area from the rest of the building – was defective.

[134] Lord Lloyd, dissenting, thought that a duty of care should have been found: 'All that is required is a straightforward application of *Donoghue* v *Stevenson*': [1996] 1 AC 211, 230. It seems likely that had anyone on board the *Nicholas H* been drowned when it sank, the House of Lords would not have hesitated to find that the defendants owed the people on board the *Nicholas H* a duty to take care not to approve the ship as being seaworthy when it was not, on the basis that it was reasonably foreseeable when the *Nicholas H* was in dock that those on board the *Nicholas H* would suffer some kind of physical injury if the defendants approved it as being seaworthy when it was not. But of course, that duty of care would have been geared towards protecting people on board the *Nicholas H* from being killed or injured, and could not be prayed in aid of the claimants' case here for damages for the loss of their cargo.

Lords thought it would be contrary to the public interest to rule that a classification society will owe the owners of cargo aboard a ship a duty to take care not to say that a ship is seaworthy when it is not. Lord Steyn, giving the leading judgment, gave two reasons why such a ruling would be contrary to the public interest.

First, classification societies act in the general public interest in certifying whether or not ships are seaworthy – their doing so helps to save lives, ships and cargo at sea. If classification societies could be sued in negligence when their surveyors carelessly passed as seaworthy ships that were not seaworthy, then they would not – Lord Steyn thought – be able to carry out their functions as efficiently. They would be exposed to a large number of claims; their surveyors would be overly inclined to label ships as unseaworthy if there was any doubt on the matter; classification societies' staff and resources would be tied up in dealing with claims made against them instead of being used for the main task of classifying ships.[135]

Secondly, Lord Steyn thought that if classification societies could be sued in negligence when their surveyors carelessly passed as seaworthy ships that were not seaworthy, then they would, before passing a ship as seaworthy, demand that the shipowner agree to indemnify them against any negligence liability they might incur as a result of passing the ship as seaworthy. So, in the end, any liabilities incurred by the classification societies in negligence would be passed on to shipowners – thus bypassing the limitations of liability that shipowners insert into their contracts of carriage with cargo owners. As a result, shipowners would no longer be able to predict for insurance purposes the extent of the liabilities they would incur if their ships sank and merchant shipping would as a result be disrupted.

5.9 Pure economic loss (1): *Hedley Byrne*: the basic principle[136]

Until 1964, it was thought that a claimant could not sue a defendant in *negligence* if a defendant's positive act resulted in the claimant suffering pure economic loss – that is, economic loss not resulting from the claimant's being injured (physically or mentally), or the claimant's property being harmed.[137]

In a long series of cases[138] decided both before and after the House of Lords' decision in *Donoghue* v *Stevenson* (1932), the courts made it clear that the mere fact that it was reasonably foreseeable that the defendant's conduct would result in a claimant suffering some form of pure economic loss would *not* be enough to ground a duty of care, owed by

---

[135] For much the same reason, it has been held that the Civil Aviation Authority will *not* owe the owner of an aircraft a duty of care not to certify an aircraft as being fit to fly when it is not: *Philcox* v *Civil Aviation Authority*, *The Times*, 8 June 1995.

[136] See, generally, Barker, Grantham & Swain 2015.

[137] Actions for pure economic loss had long been available where the defendant committed the tort of *deceit* in relation to the claimant (by deliberately inducing the claimant to act in a particular way by telling the claimant a lie when the defendant knew what he was saying was a lie, or didn't care whether it was true or not), or where the defendant committed the tort of *intentional infliction of harm using unlawful means* or the tort of *conspiracy* in relation to the claimant. These torts were (and are) known as the *economic* torts precisely because they can form the basis of a claim for pure economic loss. The economic torts are discussed below, Chapter 24. A claim in negligence for pure economic loss *was* allowed in the odd case of *Morrison Steamship Co* v *Greystoke Castle* [1947] AC 265, but that case remained an isolated precedent until 1964.

[138] See above, § 4.3, fn 30.

the defendant to the claimant. The reasons why in this context foreseeability of harm is not enough to give rise to a duty of care were well set out by Lord Denning MR in the 'relational' economic loss case of *Spartan Steel & Co Ltd* v *Martin* (1973).

A 'relational' economic loss case is one where a defendant has carelessly harmed a third party's person or property and the claimant has suffered pure economic loss as a result of his relationship with that third party's person or property. So it was in the *Spartan Steel* case: the defendants had carelessly cut through a power supply line that fed power to, among others, the claimants' factory. The claimants' power was cut off for about 14 hours. The claimants wanted to sue the defendants for the profits they could have made had they been allowed to work during those 14 hours. But to do that, they had to show that the defendants owed them a duty of care not to cut off their power supply, that was geared towards protecting them from suffering an interruption to their business activities.[139] The Court of Appeal held that no such duty of care had existed in this case. Lord Denning MR explained:

> the cutting of the supply of electricity . . . is a hazard we all run . . . [W]hen it does happen, it affects a multitude of persons: not as a rule by way of physical damage to them or their property, but by putting them to inconvenience, and sometimes to economic loss. The supply is usually restored in a few hours, so the economic loss is not very large. Such a hazard is regarded by most people as a thing they must put up with – without seeking compensation from anyone. Some there are who install a stand-by system. Others seek refuge by taking out an insurance policy against breakdown in the supply. But most people are content to take the risk on themselves. When the supply is cut off, they do not go running round to their solicitor. They do not try to find out whether it was anyone's fault. They just put up with it. They try to make up the economic loss by doing more work next day. This is a healthy attitude which the law should encourage . . . [Another] consideration is this: if claims for economic loss were permitted for this particular hazard, there would be no end of claims. Some might be genuine, but many might be inflated, or even false. A machine might not have been in use anyway, but it would be easy to put it down to the cut in supply. It would be well-nigh impossible to check the claims . . . Rather than expose claimants to such temptation and defendants to such hard labour – on comparatively small claims – it is better to disallow economic loss altogether, at any rate where it stands alone, independent of any physical damage.[140]

So mere foreseeability of harm could not, in this context, ground a duty of care because: (1) a claimant's interest in not suffering pure economic loss was generally not *important* enough to justify subjecting the defendant to a duty of care; and (2) there was a *floodgates* fear that if foreseeability of pure economic loss was enough to ground a duty of care, the courts would be flooded with claimants arguing that a defendant was liable for some pure economic loss the claimant had suffered because it was foreseeable the defendant's actions would have that effect.

While everyone acknowledged foreseeability of pure economic loss was not enough to give rise to a duty of care, it seemed until 1964 that in pure economic loss cases, there was

---

[139] The claimants could establish that the defendants owed them an identical duty of care that was geared towards protecting them from having their property harmed as a result of their power being cut off. This was because the defendants' act in cutting off the claimants' power supply *did* cause harm to some 'melts' that were being processed by the claimants at the time the power went off, and it was reasonably foreseeable that cutting off the power supply would cause people like the claimants to suffer that kind of property damage. But that duty of care could not be relied on by the claimants to sue for the quite independent loss of profits from their not being able to do any work for 14 hours.

[140] [1973] 1 QB 27, 38–39.

nothing else that could give rise to a duty of care either. In *Candler* v *Crane, Christmas & Co* (1951), Denning LJ suggested that accountants who were drawing up accounts for a company would not only owe a contractual duty to the company to draw up those accounts with reasonable skill and care, but also a duty in negligence to any claimant who they knew would be shown the accounts and who would rely on those accounts in a particular transaction.[141] But that suggestion was rejected by the other two members of the Court of Appeal in the *Candler* case, who reaffirmed the general rule that there was no liability in negligence for pure economic loss.

But then along came the great[142] case of *Hedley Byrne & Co Ltd* v *Heller* (1964). Hedley Byrne, a firm of advertising agents, wanted to find out whether a company called Easipower Ltd was creditworthy or not before they placed some advertising orders on Easipower's behalf. Hedley Byrne were personally liable for the cost of these advertising orders and were therefore understandably concerned to know whether they could recoup the cost of placing those orders from Easipower. Hedley Byrne's bankers approached Heller & Partners, Easipower's bankers, for a reference as to Easipower's creditworthiness. Heller gave Easipower a favourable reference, on the strength of which Hedley Byrne placed a number of advertising orders on Easipower's behalf. Soon afterwards, Easipower went into liquidation and Hedley Byrne were unable to recover from Easipower the money they had laid out on Easipower's behalf in placing those advertising orders.

Hedley Byrne sued Heller, claiming that Heller had owed them a duty to take care that it did not mislead them as to Easipower's creditworthiness and that Heller breached that duty when it supplied them with a positive reference as to Easipower's creditworthiness. The House of Lords dismissed Hedley Byrne's claim on the ground that Heller's advice to Hedley Byrne as to Easipower's creditworthiness had been given 'without responsibility'.[143] But the House of Lords made clear that had Heller not done this, it *would* have owed Hedley Byrne a duty to take care not to mislead them as to Easipower's creditworthiness.

But why would Heller have owed Hedley Byrne a duty of care? Their Lordships came up with a number of different explanations. Lord *Reid*: Heller would have 'accepted a responsibility' for the accuracy of their advice or would have 'accepted a relationship' with Hedley Byrne which required them to take care in advising Hedley Byrne.[144] Lord *Morris*: Heller would have 'assumed a responsibility' to tender Hedley Byrne 'deliberate advice'.[145] Lord *Morris* (with the agreement of Lord *Hodson*): Heller would have known or ought to have known that their advice would be relied upon by Hedley Byrne.[146] Lord *Hodson*: there would have existed a 'sufficiently close'[147] or 'special'[148] relationship between Heller and Hedley Byrne which would have given rise to a duty of care owed by Heller to Hedley Byrne. Lord *Devlin*: there would have existed a 'special relationship' between Heller and Hedley Byrne that was 'equivalent to contract'. In other words, Heller would have

---

[141] [1951] 2 KB 165, 179–184.
[142] Not so great in the view of Campbell 2015, who subjects *Hedley Byrne* to withering criticism. See also Campbell 2016, and Whittaker 1997.
[143] [1964] AC 465, 492, 504, 511, 532–3, 539–40.
[144] [1964] AC 465, 486.
[145] [1964] AC 465, 494.
[146] [1964] AC 465, 503, 514.
[147] [1964] AC 465, 509.
[148] [1964] AC 465, 511.

'assumed a responsibility' towards Hedley Byrne in circumstances where, if Heller had been paid by Hedley Byrne to assume that responsibility, there would have existed a contract between Hedley Byrne and Heller.[149] Lord *Pearce*: there would have existed a 'special relationship' between Heller and Hedley Byrne which gave rise to an 'assumption that care as well as honesty' was demanded when Heller advised Hedley Byrne.[150]

Given the vagueness and variety of these statements it is understandable that there has been a great deal of debate as to when exactly one person will owe another a duty of care under the decision in *Hedley Byrne*. Subsequent caselaw establishes that Lords Morris and Hodson's view that if A knows or ought to know that B will rely on some advice of his, A will owe B a duty of care in rendering that advice is too wide to be acceptable.[151] Something more is required before A will be found to have owed B a duty of care. But what is that 'something more'? The speeches of Lords Reid, Devlin and Morris in *Hedley Byrne* suggest that it needs to be shown that A 'assumed a responsibility' towards B for the quality of his advice. But when will A be held to have done this? There are essentially two schools of thought on this issue.

(1) *'Assumption of responsibility' is an empty concept.* According to this school of thought, the concept of an 'assumption of responsibility' is essentially meaningless. In other words, the courts will be free to find that A 'assumed a responsibility' towards B for the quality of his advice *whenever* they *want* to find that A owed B a duty of care in giving that advice. This was the line taken by Lord Griffiths in the case of *Smith* v *Eric S Bush* (1990):

> I do not think . . . assumption of responsibility is a helpful or realistic test of liability [under *Hedley Byrne*] . . . The phrase 'assumption of responsibility' can only have any real meaning if it is understood as referring to the circumstances in which the law will deem the maker of the statement to have assumed responsibility to the person who acts upon the advice.[152]

In *Phelps* v *Hillingdon LBC* (2001), Lord Slynn made essentially the same point: 'The phrase ['assumption of responsibility'] means simply that the law recognises that there is a duty of care. It is not so much that responsibility is assumed as that it is recognised or imposed by law.'[153]

(2) *Assumption of responsibility' is not an empty concept.* According to this second school of thought, the concept of an 'assumption of responsibility' is meaningful. In other words, it is only possible to say truthfully that someone has 'assumed a responsibility' to another in *certain definable circumstances*. Of course, the courts may have in the past found that a defendant 'assumed a responsibility' to a claimant outside those circumstances, but in those cases the courts were guilty of abusing the concept – in those cases the courts wanted to find that the defendant owed the claimant a duty of care for such-and-such a reason and they simply *said* that the defendant 'assumed a responsibility' to the claimant in order to provide themselves with some legal justification for their finding that the defendant owed the claimant a duty of care.[154]

---

[149] [1964] AC 465, 528–9, 530.

[150] [1964] AC 465, 539.

[151] See, in particular, the decision of the House of Lords in *Williams* v *Natural Life Health Foods Ltd* [1998] 1 WLR 830, discussed below.

[152] [1990] 1 AC 831, 862.

[153] [2001] 2 AC 619, 654. See also the judgment of Lord Roskill in *Caparo Industries plc* v *Dickman* [1990] 2 AC 605 at 629; Stapleton 1998, 64–5; Barker 1993.

[154] See Lord Goff's judgment in *White* v *Jones* [1995] 2 AC 207 for a particularly transparent example of this happening.

Lord Steyn took this view of the concept of an 'assumption of responsibility' in *Williams* v *Natural Life Health Foods Ltd* (1998): 'There was, and is, no better rationalisation for [this] head of tort liability than assumption of responsibility . . . There is nothing fictional about this species of liability in tort.'[155] Lord Bingham took the same view in *Customs and Excise Commissioners* v *Barclays Bank plc* (2007) when he remarked that 'there are cases in which one party can *accurately* be said to have assumed responsibility for what is said . . . to another';[156] as did Lord Hoffmann in the same case when he said that:

> In . . . cases in which the loss has been caused by the claimant's reliance on information provided by the defendant, it is critical to decide whether the defendant (rather than someone else) assumed responsibility for the accuracy of the information to the claimant (rather than to someone else) . . .[157]

We prefer the second view, not least because it seems that in *Hedley Byrne*, Lords Reid, Devlin and Morris must have had *something* in mind when they talked of a defendant owing a claimant a duty of care if he 'assumed a responsibility' to her.[158] We would go further and say that if A takes on the job of advising B on a particular matter, A will 'assume a responsibility' to B for the quality of his advice if and only if *he indicates to B that she can safely rely on his advice*. If this is right then we can say that the House of Lords' decision in *Hedley Byrne* establishes that: If A takes on the job of advising B on a particular matter and he indicates to B that B can safely rely on that advice, then A will owe B a duty to take care that he does not give B any incorrect advice on that matter. Let us call this the *basic principle* in *Hedley Byrne*.[159] We can now look at a number of different kinds of situations to see this principle in action.

A. Advice given 'without responsibility'

The decision of the House of Lords in *Hedley Byrne* makes it clear that if A takes on the job of advising B on a particular matter but makes it clear that his advice is given 'without responsibility', he will normally not owe B a duty of care in giving that advice. By making it clear that his advice is given 'without responsibility', he is making it clear to B that his advice cannot be safely relied on.

It was necessary to say in the above paragraph that A will not *normally* owe B a duty of care in advising her if he has made it clear to her that his advice is given without responsibility. This is because under s 2(2) of the Unfair Contract Terms Act 1977, if A was acting

---

[155] [1998] 1 WLR 830, 837. See also the judgment of Lord Browne-Wilkinson in *White* v *Jones* [1995] 2 AC 207, at 273–4.

[156] [2007] 1 AC 181, at [4] (emphasis added).

[157] [2007] 1 AC 181, at [35].

[158] The second view has recently been endorsed by Lord Toulson in *Michael* v *Chief Constable of South Wales Police* [2015] UKSC 2, at [100], warning against the tendency 'for courts to use the expression "assumption of responsibility" when in truth the responsibility has been imposed by the court rather than assumed by D. It should not be expanded artificially.'

[159] It is worth noting that this basic principle cannot explain the House of Lords' finding in *Smith* v *Eric S Bush* [1990] 1 AC 831 that a duty of care was owed in that case: see below, § 5.12. It is hardly surprising, then, that Lord Griffiths should have poured scorn in that case on the idea that an assumption of responsibility was a prerequisite to a duty of care being owed under *Hedley Byrne*: had he found that an assumption of responsibility *was* required, he would not have been able to rely on the decision of the House of Lords in *Hedley Byrne* as authority for the view that a duty of care was owed in *Smith* v *Eric S Bush*.

'in the course of business' in advising B, and due to his carelessness in advising B she suffered some form of economic loss, A will not be allowed to rely on the fact that he gave his advice 'without responsibility' so as to deny that he owed B a duty of care in advising her, if it would be 'unreasonable' to allow him to rely on that fact to deny that he owed B a duty of care. So it is possible that if A was advising B 'in the course of business' he might still be held to have owed B a duty of care in giving her that advice even if that advice was formally given 'without responsibility'.

B. Advice given directly to advisee knowing that the advice will be relied on

In *Hedley Byrne*, Lord Reid observed that:

> A reasonable man, knowing that he was being trusted or that his skill or judgment were being relied on, would, I think, have three courses open to him. He could keep silent or decline to give the information or advice sought: or he could give an answer with a clear qualification that he accepted no responsibility for it or that it was given without that reflection or inquiry which a careful answer would require: or he could simply answer without any such qualification. If he chooses to adopt the last course he must, I think, be held to have accepted some responsibility for his answer being given carefully, or to have accepted a relationship with the inquirer which requires him to exercise such care as the circumstances require.[160]

It follows from this that if *Anxious* asks *Guru* to advise her on some matter, and *Guru* knows that *Anxious* will rely on whatever he says, then if *Guru* undertakes to advise *Anxious* on that matter, he will owe her a duty of care in giving her that advice. The reason for this is that when he takes on the job of advising *Anxious*, *Guru* will implicitly indicate to *Anxious* that she can safely rely on his advice. *Anxious* will think – and will be entitled to think – that, '*Guru* knew that I would rely on his advice unless I was discouraged from doing so. Given that he knew this, he surely would have discouraged me from relying on his advice if his advice could not be safely relied on. But he did not do this – he gave me his advice and did nothing to discourage me from relying on it. Surely, then, his advice can be safely relied on.'

This was the position in *Welton* v *North Cornwall District Council* (1997). In that case, the claimants owned a guest house which constituted food premises for the purpose of the Food Act 1984 and the Food Safety Act 1990. The claimants were visited by one E, a health inspector. E said that the claimants' kitchen was not up to scratch. He could have closed the claimants' kitchen down – effectively putting their guest house out of business – but instead took it upon himself to advise the claimants as to what they needed to do to their kitchen to bring it up to a satisfactory standard. Acting on this advice, the claimants made numerous alterations to their kitchen, 90 per cent of which – they subsequently discovered – were completely unnecessary. The claimants sued, claiming that E had owed them a duty of care in advising them as to what they needed to do to their kitchen to bring it up to scratch. The Court of Appeal allowed their claim. When E took on the job of advising the claimants as to what they needed to do, he knew that they would rely on whatever he said, and so by undertaking to advise the claimants, he implicitly indicated to them that his advice could be safely relied on.

It should be noted that in the situation we are considering, *Guru* will be held to have 'assumed a responsibility' to *Anxious*, irrespective of whether or not he *subjectively* wanted to indicate to *Anxious* that she could safely rely on his advice. The duty of care that *Guru*

---

[160] [1964] AC 465, 486.

will owe *Anxious* in this situation will arise out of the fact that *Guru* gave *Anxious* the *impression* that his advice could be safely relied upon. So whether or not the courts will find that *Guru* 'assumed a responsibility' to *Anxious* will not depend on whether *Guru* *intended* to 'assume a responsibility' to *Anxious*, but will instead depend on whether *Guru* *gave Anxious the impression* that he intended to 'assume a responsibility' to *Anxious*. As Lord Hoffmann observed in *Customs and Excise Commissioners* v *Barclays Bank plc*:

> The answer [to the question of whether the defendant assumed responsibility to the claimant] does not depend on what the defendant intended but . . . upon what would reasonably be inferred from his conduct against the background of all the circumstances of the case.[161]

C. Advice given on a social occasion

Suppose that *Money* and *Fool* are drinking together in the pub, and *Money* asks *Fool* whether he thinks she should invest her savings on the stock market. *Fool* says, 'Definitely – this is a good time to buy.' *Money* acts on *Fool*'s advice and invests all of her savings in the stock market, and loses most of it when the stock market subsequently crashes. Let us assume that *Fool* was careless in his advice: at the time he talked to *Money* the stock market had reached a record high and there were widespread warnings that a correction in stock market levels was overdue. But did *Fool* owe *Money* a duty of care in advising her whether or not to invest in the stock market? The answer will normally be 'no'. *Fool* did nothing to indicate to *Money* that she could safely rely on his advice – that is, rely on his advice without seeking any further advice from anyone else. The casual context in which *Money* sought *Fool*'s advice meant that he had no reason to think that she would rely on whatever he said, and so *Money* could not have been entitled to infer from the fact that *Fool* gave *Money* his opinion on what she should do that he was indicating to her that she could rely on his advice without consulting anyone else.

So the normal rule is that someone giving advice on a social occasion will not owe a duty of care to the advisee.[162] However, the rule will be displaced if A gives B advice on

---

[161] [2007] 1 AC 181, at [35]. See also [5] (per Lord Bingham): 'it is clear that the assumption of responsibility test is to be applied objectively . . . and is not answered by consideration of what the defendant thought or intended'; *Henderson* v *Merrett Syndicates* [1995] 2 AC 145, at 181 (per Lord Goff): 'it must be expected that an objective test will be applied when asking the question whether, in a particular case, responsibility should be held to have been assumed by the defendant . . .'; *Michael* v *Chief Constable of South Wales Police* [2015] UKSC 2, at [135] (per Lord Toulson).

[162] See *Hedley Byrne & Co Ltd* v *Heller & Partners Ltd* [1964] AC 465, 482–3 (per Lord Reid); *Howard Marine & Dredging Co* v *A Ogden (Excavations) Ltd* [1978] QB 574, 592–3 (per Lord Denning MR). The same will be true if John rang Mary out of the blue for her advice without making it clear that he was going to be relying on her advice: *Tidman* v *Reading Borough Council* [1994] Times LR 592; *Fashion Brokers Ltd* v *Clarke Hayes* [2000] PNLR 473. Or if the circumstances of John's inquiry were generally such as not to put Mary on warning that John was going to rely on her advice: see *James McNaughton Paper Group Ltd* v *Hicks Anderson & Co* [1991] 2 QB 113 (held, no liability for an off-the-cuff statement made by accountant as to profitability of a company in the course of negotiations to take over the company). A different result would have been reached if it had been made clear to the accountant that his statement would be relied upon: *Galoo* v *Bright Grahame Murray* [1994] 1 WLR 1360; *Law Society* v *KPMG Peat Marwick* [2000] 1 WLR 1921. Puzzlingly, it has been held that a solicitor working for someone selling a house will *not* owe the purchaser of the house a duty of care in answering the purchaser's inquiries even if it is made abundantly clear to him that those answers will be relied upon by the purchaser: *Gran Gelato Ltd* v *Richcliff (Group) Ltd* [1992] Ch 560 (Nicholls V-C). For criticisms of the decision in *Gran Gelato*, see Reed 1996, 69–73.

a social occasion and in doing so explicitly assures B that she *can* safely rely on his advice. In such a situation, A will owe B a duty of care in advising her. This was the situation in *Chaudhry* v *Prabhakar* (1989). In that case, Chaudhry was thinking of buying a Golf car that her friend Prabhakar had spotted was for sale. Chaudhry obviously wanted to know whether the car was in good condition before buying it. Prabhakar advised her that the car was in good condition and told her that she did not need to get a qualified mechanic to look at it. Chaudhry subsequently bought the car on the strength of this advice. The car subsequently proved to be unroadworthy and Chaudhry sued Prabhakar in negligence for compensation. The Court of Appeal held that Prabhakar had owed Chaudhry a duty of care in advising her as to the condition of the car: he had discouraged her from seeking anyone else's opinion on the condition of the car and had therefore explicitly indicated to her that his advice – that the car was in good condition – could be safely relied on.

D. Advice given by a non-expert

It was suggested by the majority of the Privy Council in *Mutual Life and Citizens' Assurance Co Ltd* v *Evatt* (1971) that if A undertakes to advise B on some matter, A will not owe B a duty of care in giving that advice if A did not hold himself out as being an expert on the matter advised upon. This seems too strong, and the decision in the *Evatt* case – denying that a duty of care was owed by a defendant company advising the claimant investor on whether its sister company's finances were sound – has been criticised by the domestic courts.[163]

The better view, we would submit, is that if A makes it obvious that he is not an expert on the matter on which he is advising B, that is something that should be taken into account in deciding whether or not A indicated to B that his advice could be safely relied on. If A makes it clear to B – or B knows already – that he is not an expert on the matter on which B is seeking A's advice, then the courts will usually find that A did *not* indicate to B that his advice could be safely relied on.

But it would be different if *Anxious* said to *Dabbler*, 'I know you are not a financial expert, but you're more of an expert than me, and I don't trust anyone else to give me good advice, so I'll do whatever you tell me to do – do you think I should invest in the stock market?' If *Dabbler* gives *Anxious* his advice without urging *Anxious* to seek out more opinions, then it will be hard not to find that *Dabbler* – in giving *Anxious* his advice – implicitly indicated to *Anxious* that she could safely rely on his advice. Similarly, it would be different if *Dabbler* said to *Anxious*, 'I'm not a doctor, but even I know that you are as fit as a fiddle. You are going to look stupid if you ask a doctor if you should be concerned about a silly lump on your arm. Take it from me – it's nothing.' In such a case, *Dabbler* will have explicitly indicated to *Anxious* that she could safely rely on his advice as to the

---

[163] See *Esso Petroleum Co Ltd* v *Mardon* [1976] QB 801; *Howard Marine & Dredging Co* v *A Ogden (Excavations) Ltd* [1978] QB 574; *Spring* v *Guardian Assurance plc* [1995] 2 AC 296, 320 (per Lord Goff); *Commissioner of Police of the Metropolis* v *Lennon* [2004] 2 All ER 266. Though see *Robinson* v *Jones (Contractors) Ltd* [2012] QB 44, which in its eagerness to prevent a claim being made under the extended principle in *Hedley Byrne* (below §5.10) against a building firm for defects in a flat that they sold off-plan (before it was built) to the claimants, the Court of Appeal held that claims under *Hedley Byrne* were limited to '*professional persons* . . . [who] give advice, prepare reports, draw up accounts, produce plans and so forth . . . [and who] expect their clients and possibly others to act in reliance upon their work product . . .' (at [75] (per Jackson LJ, emphasis added)).

state of her health. So in both these alternative scenarios, the courts will – and should – find that *Dabbler* owed *Anxious* a duty of care in advising her, even though *Dabbler* has no expertise (and professes no expertise) in the matter on which he was advising *Anxious*.

E. Advice given in a published work

In *Candler* v *Crane, Christmas & Co* (1951), Denning LJ observed that, 'a scientist or expert . . . is not liable to his readers for careless statements made in his published works.'[164] This seems correct, even after the decision of the House of Lords in *Hedley Byrne*. If A writes a text or an article, he cannot be taken to have invited his readers to think that the information in that article can be relied upon without seeking further advice.

F. Official registers

Oftentimes, the law will require someone to be officially registered before they are allowed to trade, for example, as a child-minder. If A is in charge of maintaining such an official register, does A invite people looking at the register to think that they can rely on him to have taken care to ensure that C – someone who is on the register – is a fit and proper person to deal with?

The Privy Council said the answer is 'no' in *Yuen Kun Yeu* v *Attorney-General for Hong Kong* (1988). The register in that case was a register of deposit-taking companies. The claimants lost the money they had deposited with a company that was on the register, but had been run fraudulently and with little regard for investors' interests. The claimants sued the defendant – who was in charge of maintaining the register – on the ground that by allowing the company's name to appear on the register, he had represented that people like the claimants could safely rely on him to have taken care to ensure that the company was a fit and proper company to accept deposits. The Privy Council rejected this argument: the existence of the procedure for registering deposit-taking companies did not 'warrant an assumption that all [registered] deposit-taking companies were sound and fully creditworthy'.[165]

G. Advice given by a third party

Suppose that *Money* wants some advice as to whether she should invest in a particular company, *Dodgy* plc. *Money*'s *Friend* asks *Investor*, a self-professed expert on the industry in which *Dodgy* operates, whether it would be a good idea to invest in *Dodgy*. *Investor* assures *Friend*, 'You should buy as many shares as possible. They are working on something at the moment that will quadruple the share price when it's announced.' *Friend* then goes to *Money* and says, 'Take it from me – you won't go wrong if you invest in *Dodgy*.' *Money* then invests a large sum in *Dodgy* and loses all of it when *Dodgy* announces a few months later that it is insolvent. *Money* then finds out from *Friend* that *Investor* was the source of the bad advice to invest in *Dodgy*. *Money* sues *Investor*, claiming that he owed *her* a duty of care in advising *Friend* whether it was a good idea for her to buy

---

[164] [1951] 2 KB 164, 183.
[165] [1988] 1 AC 175, 197.

shares in *Dodgy*. Her claim will fail. *Investor* did not 'assume a responsibility' to *Money* in giving that advice – he never indicated to *Money* that *she* could safely rely on that advice. There was, in fact, no kind of contact between *Investor* and *Money* that could ground a finding that *Investor* 'assumed a responsibility' to *Money* for the quality of his advice.

That this is correct is confirmed by the decision of the House of Lords in *Williams* v *Natural Life Health Foods Ltd* (1998).[166] Natural Life Health Food Shops Ltd was a company which provided the following service. People who were interested in opening a health food shop could approach Natural Life for an assessment as to how successful the health food shop was likely to be. If, on the basis of that assessment, they were still interested in opening the shop, Natural Life would, for a fee, allow them to open their shop using the Natural Life Health Foods trade name and would advise them as to how to run their shop. The claimants approached Natural Life because they were interested in opening a health food shop in Rugby. The managing director of Natural Life, Richard Mistlin, prepared some reports which predicted that the health food shop the claimants were proposing to open would enjoy a healthy turnover. Even though he prepared the reports, Mistlin never actually had any dealings with the claimants – they dealt with another employee of the company, Ron Padwick. On the strength of Mistlin's reports, the claimants opened a health food shop in Rugby under the Natural Life trade name. However, the shop enjoyed less success than Mistlin's reports indicated it would and the claimants, after trading at a loss for 18 months, were finally forced to close the shop.

The claimants sued Natural Life in negligence. Unfortunately, Natural Life was not worth suing; it was wound up a couple of years after the claimants commenced proceedings against Natural Life. Mistlin, on the other hand, did have substantial assets – so the claimants then tried to sue him in negligence. They argued that he had owed them, and breached, a duty to take care that he did not mislead them as to how successful the Rugby health food shop was likely to be; and that had he not breached this duty, he would have told them that the Rugby health food shop was unlikely to be a success and they would never have invested their money in it.

The House of Lords rejected the claimants' claim. Lord Steyn, giving the only judgment, ruled that Mistlin had not owed the claimants a duty of care in preparing his reports as to how profitable the Rugby health food shop was likely to be under the basic principle in *Hedley Byrne*. While Mistlin *did* take on the job of preparing the reports given to the claimants on the potential profitability of the Rugby health food shop, the lack of contact between Mistlin and the claimants meant that *Mistlin* did not at any point indicate to the claimants that they could safely rely on his advice. In contrast, Natural Life – a separate person from Mistlin – *did* indicate to the claimants that they could safely rely on the advice Natural Life gave them as to how profitable the Rugby health food shop was likely to be. So Natural Life *did* owe the claimants a duty under the basic principle in *Hedley Byrne* to take care that they did not supply the claimants with any incorrect advice as to how profitable the Rugby health food shop was likely to be. However, as has already been observed, this was of little comfort to the claimants as Natural Life was not worth suing.

---

[166] Discussed, Armour 1999.

5.10 Pure economic loss (2): *Hedley Byrne*: the extended principle

It is now well acknowledged that *Hedley Byrne* is not *just* authority in favour of the proposition that someone who takes on the task of advising another on a particular matter will, in certain circumstances, owe that other a duty of care in giving that advice. Certain *dicta* in *Hedley Byrne* suggest that if A has indicated to B[167] that B can safely rely on him to perform a particular task with a certain degree of care and skill and B has so relied on A, A will owe B a duty to perform that task with that degree of care and skill.[168]

Many cases, decided before and after *Hedley Byrne*, seem to support this suggestion. (A suggestion which, it should be noted, can not only be relied on in cases where A has performed a *positive act* that has resulted in harm to B, but also in cases where A has *failed to save* B from suffering some kind of harm, when he indicated to B that he could be relied on to act carefully to save B from that harm, and B did so rely.)[169] Most of them deal with the following kind of situation:

1. A is a professional – that is, he holds himself out as being able to perform a particular task T with a 'professional' degree of care and skill;

2. as a result, B is led to believe that A can be safely relied on to perform task T with a 'professional' degree of care and skill;

3. B asks A to perform task T for her;

4. A knows that B's request is made in the belief that A can be safely relied on to perform task T with a 'professional' degree of care and skill and B knows that A knows this;

5. A agrees to perform task T for B.

In such a case, B will think – and she will be entitled to think – that, by agreeing to do task T without warning her that she can't expect him to perform that task to his usual high standards, A has indicated to B that she can safely rely on him to perform that task with a 'professional' degree of care and skill. And B will have relied on A to do exactly that by asking him to perform task T. So A's holding himself out to be a professional, and B's asking A to work for her, and A's agreeing to work for B without telling her that she can't trust him to be competent – all combine together to establish that A owes B a duty to perform task T

---

[167] By 'B' we mean either B or B's agent, acting on B's behalf.

[168] [1964] AC 465, 502–3 (per Lord Morris): 'it should now be regarded as settled that if someone possessed of a special skill undertakes, quite irrespective of contract, to apply that skill for the assistance of another person who relies upon such skill, a duty of care will arise'; 531 (per Lord Hodson): 'those who hold themselves out as possessing a special skill are under a duty to exercise it with reasonable care'; 531 (per Lord Devlin): 'If a defendant says to a [claimant]: "Let me do this for you; do not waste your money in employing a professional, I will do it for nothing and you can rely on me", I do not think he could escape liability . . .'; 538 (per Lord Pearce): 'if persons holding themselves out in a calling or situation or profession take on a task within that calling or situation or profession, they have a duty of skill and care.'

[169] See further, § 6.2, below.

with a 'professional' degree of care and skill under what we can call the *extended principle in Hedley Byrne*.

A lot of cases support the idea that in this kind of situation, a duty of care will be owed. These cases variously hold that:

(1) A doctor will owe his patient a duty to treat his patient with the care and skill that a reasonably competent doctor would exercise in treating a patient.[170]

(2) A dentist will owe his patient a duty to treat that patient with the care and skill that a reasonably competent dentist would exercise in treating a patient.[171]

(3) A vet who treats an animal at the owner's request will owe that owner a duty to treat that animal with the care and skill that a reasonably competent vet would exercise in treating that animal.[172]

(4) A solicitor who handles a case or transaction on behalf of a client will owe that client a duty to handle that case or transaction with the care and skill that a reasonably competent solicitor would exercise in handling that case or transaction.[173]

(5) A barrister who handles a client's case in court will owe that client a duty to conduct that case in court with the care and skill that a reasonably competent barrister would exercise in conducting that case.[174]

(6) A surveyor will owe a client of his who has asked him to value a house or piece of land that he is thinking of purchasing a duty to survey that house or land with the care and skill that a reasonably competent surveyor would exercise in surveying a house or a piece of land.

(7) An architect will owe a client who has commissioned him to design a building or supervise the construction of a building a duty to design that building or supervise the construction of the building with the care and skill that a reasonably competent architect would exercise in carrying out that kind of task.

(8) A subcontractor who is employed by a main contractor to carry out building work because the subcontractor assured the client on whose behalf the work is being carried out that they could be relied on to perform the work with a certain degree of care and skill, and the client relied on those assurances by requesting the main contractor to

---

[170] *Pippin* v *Sherrard* (1822) 11 Price 400, 147 ER 512; *Gladwell* v *Steggal* (1839) 5 Bing NC 733, 132 ER 1283; *Barnett* v *Chelsea & Kensington Hospital Management Committee* [1969] 1 QB 428. The concept of a doctor–patient relationship was stretched *very* far by Gage J in *A* v *Leeds Teaching Hospital NHS Trust* [2004] EWHC 644 (QB), holding that the parents of a baby that had died in hospital enjoyed a doctor–patient relationship with the baby's doctor, so that the doctor owed the parents a duty to act towards them with reasonable skill and care – particularly in relation to explaining to them what the baby's post-mortem would involve and whether any of the baby's organs would be retained.

[171] *Edwards* v *Mallan* [1908] 1 KB 1002; *Fish* v *Kapur* [1948] 2 All ER 176.

[172] *Chute Farms* v *Curtis*, *The Times*, 10 October 1961.

[173] *Nocton* v *Lord Ashburton* [1914] AC 465; *Midland Bank* v *Hett, Stubbs and Kemp* [1979] Ch 383.

[174] *Arthur J S Hall* v *Simons* [2002] 1 AC 615 (not followed by the High Court of Australia in *D'Orta-Ekenaike* v *Victoria Legal Aid* [2005] HCA 12).

employ the subcontractor, will owe the client a duty of care to carry out the work with that degree of care and skill.[175]

(9) An engineer who has been engaged to undertake some building work by a client will owe that client a duty to execute that work with the care and skill that a reasonably competent engineer would exercise in doing that sort of work.[176]

(10) An accountant will owe a client who has commissioned him to draw up a set of accounts a duty to draw up those accounts with the care and skill that a reasonably competent accountant would exercise in drawing up a set of accounts.

(11) The referee of a game will owe the participants in the game a duty to referee the game with a reasonable degree of care and skill.[177]

(12) Someone who runs an investment syndicate will owe a member of that syndicate a duty to make decisions about what investments the syndicate makes with a reasonable degree of care and skill if that member joined the syndicate on the basis of assurances made by the manager to him, or his representatives, that the manager would run the syndicate's affairs with a reasonable degree of care and skill.[178]

Three points about the duty of care arising under the extended principle in *Hedley Byrne* should be noted:

(1) *Degree of care and skill.* If A – implicitly or explicitly – indicates to B that he can be safely relied on to perform a particular task T with a certain degree of care and skill and B did so rely on him, he will *not* owe B a duty to perform that task T with any *more* care and skill than he (objectively) indicated he could be safely relied on to exercise in performing task T.[179]

So – in *Philips* v *William Whiteley Ltd* (1938), the claimant asked the defendants, a firm of jewellers, to pierce her ears. The claimant suffered some ill effects from the operation and sought to recover compensation for those ill effects by suing the defendants in negligence. The court dismissed the claimant's claim: it held that the defendants had owed the claimant a duty to pierce her ears with the skill and care that a reasonably competent jeweller would exercise in piercing someone's ears and that the

---

[175] *Junior Books Ltd* v *Veitchi Co Ltd* [1983] 1 AC 520, as explained in *D & F Estates* v *Church Commissioners* [1989] 1 AC 177, 215 (per Lord Oliver) and in *Murphy* v *Brentwood DC* [1991] 1 AC 398, 466 (per Lord Keith). See also Perry 1992, 302–8. The actual decision in *Junior Books* was so widely stated that it triggered a backlash against it, a backlash that carried over into the decision of the Court of Appeal in *Robinson* v *Jones (Contractors) Ltd* [2012] QB 44, at [92], where *Junior Books* is condemned as 'aberrant, indeed as heretical' (at [92], per Burnton LJ). But on its facts, the finding of a duty of care in *Junior Books* can easily be explained as warranted under the extended principle in *Hedley Byrne* and had the case originated in England (rather than Scotland, where the notion of a collateral contract between a client and a subcontractor is not accepted), the courts could easily have found that a full-blown contract existed between the defendants and the claimants: *Shanklin Pier Ltd* v *Detel Products Ltd* [1951] 2 KB 854.

[176] *Congregational Union* v *Harris and Harris* [1988] 1 All ER 15; *Ketteman* v *Hansel Properties* [1987] AC 189.

[177] *Vowles* v *Evans* [2003] 1 WLR 1607 (noted, Elvin 2003a).

[178] *Henderson* v *Merrett Syndicates Ltd* [1995] 2 AC 145.

[179] *Vowles* v *Evans* [2003] 1 WLR 1607, at [28], holding that it is arguable that someone who volunteers to referee a game as a replacement for a referee who has not turned up will not be expected to referee the game with as much skill and care as someone who has been trained to act as a referee: 'the volunteer cannot reasonably be expected to show the skill of one who holds himself out [to be a] referee, or perhaps even to be fully conversant with the [l]aws of the [g]ame.'

defendants had not breached that duty. The claimant's claim that the defendant had owed the claimant a more stringent duty of care – a duty to pierce her ears with the skill and care that a reasonably competent surgeon would exercise in piercing some-one's ears – was dismissed: the defendants had never indicated to the claimant that they could be safely relied on to pierce her ears with the skill and care that a surgeon would exercise in piercing someone's ears.

Similarly, in *Wilsher* v *Essex Area Health Authority*,[180] the Court of Appeal held that if A treats B, a hospital patient, A will owe B a duty to treat B with the skill and care that a reasonably competent person *in A's post* would exercise in treating that patient. It would be unreasonable to take A as indicating that he will exercise any higher degree of care and skill in treating B. So a junior house officer who treats a patient will owe that patient a duty to treat that patient with the skill and care that a reasonably competent junior house officer would exercise in treating a patient; a level of skill and care which would, presum-ably, be lower than the level of skill and care that a reasonably competent consultant would exercise in treating a patient.[181]

(2) *Fair, just and reasonable.* It used to be thought that if A assumed a responsibility to B under the extended principle in *Hedley Byrne* it would be *automatically* 'fair, just and reasonable' to find that A owed B a duty of care.[182] After all, if A did not want – for whatever reason – to owe B a duty of care, he could have easily avoided doing so by not assuming any responsibility to B; so if he did assume such a responsibility to B, he can hardly complain if the courts take him at his word and find that he did owe B a duty of care.

However, a recent case that puts that in question is *An Informer* v *A Chief Constable* (2013), where a confidential police informant's handlers failed to step in and stop him being prosecuted by other police officers for money laundering offences. This failure resulted in the informant suffering considerable financial losses, as his assets were fro-zen as part of the prosecution process. The informant sued, claiming that when he had agreed to act as an informant, the police had 'assumed a responsibility' towards him to protect his personal safety *and his livelihood* and had therefore owed him a duty of care to protect him from the kind of financial loss that he had suffered. The majority in the Court of Appeal thought that the police had assumed such a wide-ranging responsibil-ity to the claimant,[183] but still declined to find that the police had owed the claimant a duty of care to protect him from being prosecuted by other police officers as the exist-ence of such a duty would undesirably impinge on the ability of the police to decide for themselves how to investigate suspected crimes.

(3) *Concurrent liability.* It will be observed that in all 12 of the situations set out above where a duty of care has been found to exist between a defendant and a claimant under

---

[180] [1987] 1 QB 730, reversed on other grounds by the House of Lords: [1988] 1 AC 1074.

[181] Of course, one way in which a reasonably competent junior house officer might act negligently would be in failing to seek assistance from a more qualified physician when it ought to have been clear to a reasonably competent junior house officer that such assistance was necessary.

[182] *Henderson* v *Merrett Syndicates Ltd* [1995] AC 145, 181: 'once the case is identified as falling within the *Hedley Byrne* principle, there should be no need to embark upon any further enquiry whether it is "fair, just and reasonable" to impose liability for economic loss' (per Lord Goff).

[183] [2013] QB 579, at [113] and [117] (per Arden LJ), [168] and [174] (per Pill LJ). The third judge (Toulson LJ) thought that the police's duty of care to the claimant only extended to safeguarding his physical welfare: [64]–[67].

the extended principle in *Hedley Byrne*, a contract might well also have existed between them, requiring the defendant to take care of the claimant or the claimant's affairs. If such a contract did exist, then a lack of care on the part of the defendant would not only result in the defendant breaching a duty of care owed to the claimant under *Hedley Byrne* with the result that the claimant might be able to sue the defendant in *negligence*; the defendant's lack of care would also amount to a breach of contract, allowing the claimant to sue the defendant for *breach of contract*. So when A and B enter into a contract where A expressly or impliedly undertakes to deal with B, or B's affairs, with a reasonable degree of care and skill, a breach of that undertaking will not only amount to a breach of contract but could also render A liable in negligence to B under the extended principle in *Hedley Byrne*. If this is the case, then A will be *concurrently liable* to B in both contract and tort, and B will be free to choose how to frame her claim against B, depending on which cause of action – contract or tort – is more advantageous for her. That *Hedley Byrne* has the effect of creating the potential for a defendant to be held concurrently liable in contract *and* tort for breaching a contractual undertaking to take care of the claimant, or the claimant's affairs, was acknowledged by the House of Lords in *Henderson* v *Merrett Syndicates Ltd* (1995) with Lord Goff observing that:

> in the present context, the common law is not antipathetic to concurrent liability, and . . . there is no sound basis for a rule which automatically restricts the claimant to either a tortious or a contractual remedy. The result may be untidy; but . . . I do not find it objectionable that the claimant may be entitled to take advantage of the remedy which is most advantageous to him . . .[184]

5.11 Pure economic loss (3): *Hedley Byrne*: two misconceptions

Before concluding our discussion of *Hedley Byrne*, we should briefly pause to note and dismiss two common misconceptions about that case.[185] Both arise out of the twin facts that: (1) in *Hedley Byrne* the claimants suffered a form of pure economic loss; and (2) it was in *Hedley Byrne* that the House of Lords first countenanced the possibility that a claimant might be entitled to sue a defendant in negligence for compensation for some form of pure economic loss that she had suffered as a result of the defendant's actions.

(1) *Hedley Byrne only relevant in pure economic loss cases.* The first misconception is that *Hedley Byrne* is only ever relevant in establishing that a duty of care was owed in a case

---

[184] [1995] 2 AC 145, 193–94.

[185] A third possible misconception which some students might entertain is that a duty to take care not to mislead others can only exist in a *Hedley Byrne*-type case. This is obviously incorrect. In the right circumstances, the House of Lords' decision in *Donoghue* v *Stevenson* [1932] AC 562 can operate to impose on someone a duty to take care not to mislead someone else. For example, if a blind man asks you if it is safe to cross the road, you will owe him a duty to take care that you do not tell him that it is safe to cross the road when it is not (it being reasonably foreseeable that if you do so, he will suffer some kind of physical injury as a result). See *Haseldine* v *Daw* [1941] 2 KB 343 (discussed below, § 6.1) for an example of a decision which could be explained on the basis that the defendant breached a duty to take care not to mislead someone else which arose under *Donoghue* v *Stevenson*.

where a claimant has suffered a form of pure economic loss as a result of a defendant's actions. On this view, in cases where a claimant has suffered some other kind of harm – such as physical injury or psychiatric illness – as a result of a defendant's actions or non-actions, the decision in *Hedley Byrne* will be irrelevant to the inquiry as to whether or not the defendant owed the claimant a duty of care. This is nonsense: there is no sign that the Law Lords in *Hedley Byrne* meant their remarks as to when one person will owe another a duty of care to be confined to cases where a defendant has caused another to suffer a form of pure economic loss.[186]

(2) *Recovery for pure economic loss only allowed in Hedley Byrne cases.* The second misconception is that if a claimant has suffered a form of pure economic loss as a result of a defendant's actions, the claimant will *only* be able to establish that the defendant owed her a duty of care not to act as he did if the House of Lords' decision in *Hedley Byrne* covers her case. So if *Hedley Byrne* does not cover the claimant's case, then the defendant will not have owed the claimant a duty of care.[187] This is, again, nonsense: there is no reason to think that the Law Lords in *Hedley Byrne* were seeking to lay down for all time an exhaustive set of rules as to when a duty of care will be owed in a pure economic loss case. As the House of Lords made clear in *Customs and Excise Commissioners* v *Barclays Bank* (2007), to establish that A owed B a duty of care in a case where B has suffered pure economic loss as a result of A's carelessness, it will be sufficient, *but not necessary,* to show that A assumed a responsibility to B not to be careless.[188]

Unfortunately, the misconception that a claimant can only recover in negligence for pure economic loss if *Hedley Byrne* covers her case is now quite widespread and has given rise to the further misconception that *any* pure economic loss case in the law reports in

---

[186] For examples of *physical injury* cases where a claimant will be able to invoke *Hedley Byrne* to establish that a defendant owed her a duty of care, see any medical negligence case that involves a failure to treat a patient with reasonable skill and care; also the case of *Swinney* v *Chief Constable of the Northumbria Police* [1997] QB 464, discussed below, § 6.2. For examples of *property damage* cases where the claimant was allowed to invoke *Hedley Byrne* to establish that the defendant owed her a duty of care see the Canadian case of *Densmore* v *Whitehorse* [1986] 5 WWR 708 and *Stansbie* v *Troman* [1948] 2 KB 48 (both discussed below, § 6.2) and *Bailey* v *HSS Alarms Ltd, The Times,* 20 June 2000 (failure to protect business from being burgled). A *psychiatric illness* case where *Hedley Byrne* could have been used to establish that the defendant owed the claimant a duty of care is *McLoughlin* v *Grovers* [2002] QB 1312, where the claimant developed a psychiatric illness as a result of being wrongfully convicted of robbery and causing grievous bodily harm; he sued his solicitors for compensation for his illness claiming that he would not have been convicted had they conducted his case with reasonable skill and care; held, that the claimant had an arguable claim against the defendants and his claim should not be struck out.

[187] For an example of this misconception at work, see the Court of Appeal's decision in *Phelps* v *Hillingdon LBC* [1999] 1 WLR 500, where the claimant sued for compensation for the harm done to her prospects as a result of the defendant's failure to diagnose her as being dyslexic while she was at school. As this was regarded in the Court of Appeal as being a pure economic loss case, it was conceded on all sides that the defendant could *only* have owed the claimant a duty of care in treating her if the decision in *Hedley Byrne* applied to the claimant's case: ibid, 513–14. It was found that it did not as the defendant had not 'assumed a responsibility' to the claimant. The claimant in *Phelps* appealed to the House of Lords, and their Lordships found that a duty of care *was* owed to the claimant: [2001] 2 AC 619. For an explanation of the House of Lords' decision in *Phelps,* see below: § 5.13

[188] [2007] 1 AC 181, at [4] (per Lord Bingham), [52] (per Lord Rodger), [73] (per Lord Walker), and [93] (per Lord Mance).

which the courts found that a duty of care was owed is a '*Hedley Byrne* case'.[189] Anyone labouring under this further misconception will find it quite impossible to come up with an intelligible account as to when one person will owe another a duty of care under *Hedley Byrne*. The reason is that while *most* of the pure economic loss cases in the law reports in which the courts have found that a duty of care was owed *are Hedley Byrne* cases, *not all of them are* – some of those cases rest on quite different principles, which we will explore below. So there is no *single* principle underlying all of the pure economic loss cases in the law reports in which the courts have found that a duty of care was owed and any attempt to discover such a principle will be doomed to failure.

5.12 Pure economic loss (4): some difficult cases

There are a number of pure economic loss cases where the courts found that the defendant(s) owed the claimant(s) a duty of care, but it is not possible to say that the duty of care was based on a *Hedley Byrne*-style 'assumption of responsibility'.

A. Property surveys

These cases[190] are concerned with the following kind of situation. *Poor* – who was not particularly well-off – wanted to buy a house. She managed to find a fairly cheap house at the bottom end of the property market and applied to *Lender* – a bank or building society or local authority – for a loan to help her buy the house. *Lender* appointed *Surveyor* to survey the house for them to check that the house would provide them with adequate security for the loan. *Surveyor* surveyed the house and reported back that it was worth at least as much as the loan for which *Lender* was applying.

Unfortunately, *Lender* failed to survey the house properly and failed to spot some defects in the house which meant that it was worth much less than *Poor* was proposing to pay for it. *Poor* was too poor to afford her own survey, but was reassured that the house was in good condition when *Lender* approved the loan to her – after all, she thought, if *Lender*'s surveyor had spotted any problems with the house, *Lender* would hardly have agreed to loan her the money she needed to buy it. So *Poor* went ahead and purchased the house with the assistance of the loan from *Lender*. She then discovered that the house was worth much less than she agreed to pay for it.

It is now well established that in this sort of situation, *Surveyor* will have owed *Poor* a duty to survey the house with a reasonable degree of care and skill. It is impossible to explain this result by reference to the extended principle in *Hedley Byrne* because the

---

[189] One of the authors of this text has not been immune to this misconception in the past: see McBride & Hughes 1995. This second misconception seems to have originated in a misreading of some of the speeches in the House of Lords in *Murphy* v *Brentwood DC* [1991] AC 398. Lord Bridge, for instance, stated (at 475) that 'purely economic [losses are] . . . not recoverable in tort in the absence of a special relationship of proximity . . .' and some have misread this as meaning that purely economic losses are not recoverable in tort in the absence of a special relationship of the kind involved in *Hedley Byrne*-type cases.

[190] *Smith* v *Eric S Bush* [1990] 1 AC 831; *Merrett* v *Babb* [2001] QB 1174.

existence of the duty of care owed by *Surveyor* to *Poor* does not depend on *Surveyor's* having had any contact with *Poor*.[191]

B. References

In *Spring* v *Guardian Assurance plc* (1995), Spring was employed as a sales director and office manager by Corinium Ltd. Corinium sold life assurance policies on behalf of Guardian Assurance, the defendants. When Corinium was taken over by the defendants, Spring was dismissed. Spring attempted to go into business on his own selling life assurance policies for Scottish Amicable. When he approached Scottish Amicable, that company asked the defendants to supply them with a reference for Spring. Scottish Amicable was obliged to do this under the rules of the Life Assurance and Unit Trust Regulatory Organisation (Lautro), of which Scottish Amicable was a member. The defendants supplied Scottish Amicable with a reference for Spring that stated, among other things, that Spring was 'a man of little or no integrity and could not be regarded as honest'. Unsurprisingly, Scottish Amicable declined to allow Spring to sell life assurance policies on its behalf. The same thing happened when Spring approached two other life assurance companies and for the same reason.

Spring sued the defendants in negligence, arguing that the defendants had owed him, and breached, a duty to use reasonable skill and care in supplying his prospective employers with references about him. The House of Lords found that the defendants had owed Spring such a duty of care. Why was this? It is impossible to explain this result on the basis that the defendants owed Spring such a duty under the extended principle in *Hedley Byrne*.[192] The defendants never indicated to Spring that he could safely rely on them to use reasonable skill and care in preparing references about him for prospective employers;

---

[191] This has been made crystal clear by the decision of the Court of Appeal in *Merrett* v *Babb* [2001] QB 1174. In that case, the claimant, Merrett, lost a lot of money purchasing a defective house with the assistance of a loan from a building society. The building society asked a firm of surveyors to value the house for them and an employee of the firm, Babb, valued the house as being worth at least as much as Merrett was wanting to borrow to buy the house. Before Merrett had a chance to sue the firm of surveyors in negligence, they went out of business. So instead she sued Babb – who had substantial assets – claiming that *he* personally had owed her a duty to survey the house with a reasonable degree of care and skill. By the time *Merrett* was decided, the decision of the House of Lords in *Williams* v *Natural Life Health Foods Ltd* [1998] 1 WLR 830 had made it clear that the existence of contact between a defendant and claimant is essential for a duty of care to arise between the defendant and claimant under *Hedley Byrne*. (See also, on this point, *Mills* v *Winchester Diocesan Board of Finance* [1989] Ch 428, *Mariola Marine Corp* v *Lloyd's Register of Shipping* [1990] 1 Lloyd's Rep 547 and *A & J Fabrication (Batley) Ltd* v *Grant Thornton (a firm)* [1999] PNLR 811.) However, there had been absolutely no contact between Merrett and Babb at the time Babb surveyed the house that Merrett ended up purchasing; indeed, she was not even aware of his identity at that time. Despite this, the Court of Appeal still found that Babb *had* owed Merrett a duty of care in valuing the house and the House of Lords refused leave to appeal: [2001] 1 WLR 1859. So the duty of care in *Merrett* v *Babb* and the other survey cases *cannot* be explained by reference to the extended principle in *Hedley Byrne*. Of course, those who have fallen into the trap of thinking that *all* pure economic loss cases where a defendant has been held to have owed a claimant a duty of care are *Hedley Byrne* cases cannot but think that there is some conflict between the decisions in *Williams* v *Natural Life* and *Merrett* v *Babb*. There is, of course, no conflict: the *Williams* case was concerned with when one person will owe another a duty of care under *Hedley Byrne*; the duty of care in *Merrett* v *Babb* arose for some other reason.

[192] Admittedly, Lord Goff thought that this *was* a *Hedley Byrne* case ([1995] 2 AC 296, at 316) and Lord Lowry agreed with him (at 325). However, none of the other Law Lords agreed.

and even if they did Spring never did anything in the expectation that they would act in that way. It would have been different if Spring had asked the defendants if he could give his prospective employers their name as a possible source of references and the defendants had agreed that he could. The defendants, by agreeing to supply Spring with a reference, would have implicitly indicated to him that he could safely rely on them to supply his prospective employers with references that were prepared with a reasonable degree of care and skill and Spring would have so relied on them by telling his prospective employers that they could ask the defendants for a reference about him. But this was not the case here. In *Spring*, the references supplied by the defendants were asked for, and supplied, over Spring's head.

C. Diagnosis of special needs

In *Phelps* v *Hillingdon London Borough Council* (2001), the claimant suffered from (undiagnosed) dyslexia and as a result suffered severe learning difficulties at school. In an attempt to find out what was wrong, the claimant was sent at age 11 to an educational psychologist to be tested. The psychologist failed to notice that the claimant was dyslexic; she reported that the claimant suffered from no specific weaknesses and suggested that the source of the claimant's learning difficulties was a lack of confidence. She recommended that action be taken to boost the claimant's confidence in her abilities. With her dyslexia undiagnosed, the claimant continued to experience learning difficulties and left school at age 16 with no GCSEs.

Shortly after the claimant left school, her parents paid for her to be tested again and this time around the claimant's dyslexia was diagnosed. The claimant sued the defendants, the psychologist's employers, claiming that the psychologist had owed her, and breached, a duty to test her with a reasonable degree of care and skill and that the defendants were vicariously liable in respect of the psychologist's negligence. The House of Lords held that the educational psychologist had indeed owed the claimant a duty to test her with a reasonable degree of skill and care.

It is impossible to explain this result by reference to *Hedley Byrne*. As Stuart-Smith LJ observed when deciding the case in the Court of Appeal:

> [The first instance] judge did not ask himself the question whether [the educational psychologist] had voluntarily assumed responsibility for advising the [claimant] through her parents. [The educational psychologist's] duty was to advise the school and the local authority. Merely because the [claimant] was the object of that advice and the parents were told in effect what the advice was, does not in my judgement amount to such an assumption of responsibility.[193]

The House of Lords' finding that a duty of care was owed in *Phelps* must have rested on some other basis than that the educational psychologist 'assumed a responsibility' to the claimant.[194]

---

[193] [1999] 1 WLR 500, 519. Otton LJ agreed (at 527): 'the [claimant] has not shown that [the educational psychologist] assumed responsibility to the [claimant] to prevent her from sustaining such loss or damage as may be recoverable.'

[194] Perhaps for that reason, Lord Slynn criticised in *Phelps* the idea that 'there has to be an assumption of responsibility by the person concerned. That phrase can be misleading in that it can suggest that the professional person must knowingly and deliberately accept responsibility . . . The phrase means simply that the law recognises that there is a duty of care. It is not so much that responsibility is assumed as that it is recognised or imposed by the law': [2001] 2 AC 619, 654.

D. Wills

In *White* v *Jones* (1995),[195] B quarrelled with his two daughters over his deceased wife's will. As a result, he made a will in which he left them nothing. Three months later – in June 1986 – he was reconciled with his daughters and resolved to make a new will under which his two daughters would receive £9,000 each. On 17 July 1986, he instructed the defendant solicitors to draw up a new will in those terms. By 14 September 1986, when B died, the defendant solicitors had still not got around to drawing up B's new will, so the daughters received nothing from B's estate. B's daughters sued the defendant solicitors in negligence, arguing that the defendants had owed them a duty to draw up B's new will with a reasonable degree of care and skill; that the defendants had breached that duty in taking so long over drawing up the will; and that had the defendants not breached that duty, they would have inherited £9,000 each from B's estate. By a bare majority, the House of Lords allowed the daughters' claim.

It is impossible to explain the House of Lords' decision that the defendant solicitors owed B's daughters a duty of care by reference to *Hedley Byrne*. Of course, the defendant solicitors owed *B* a duty to draw up his will with a reasonable degree of care and skill, as he had asked them to draw up the will, in the full expectation that they would do so competently, and the defendant solicitors had agreed to take on the job. But the defendants never indicated to the *claimants* that they could be relied on and indeed the claimants did not rely on the defendants to draw up the will with a reasonable degree of skill and care; the claimants, for example, did not both go out and buy new cars in the expectation that they would receive £9,000 each under B's will. There was in fact no contact between the defendants and the claimants. So there was no 'assumption of responsibility' by the defendants to the claimants that would have justified a finding that the defendants owed the claimants a duty of care under *Hedley Byrne*.

E. Loss of land rights

In *Ministry of Housing* v *Sharp* (1970), the owner of some land was refused permission to develop his land by the Ministry of Housing, and was awarded £1,828 in compensation. (This would be the equivalent of about £30,000 today.) The refusal of permission to develop the land was later reversed, which meant the Ministry of Housing acquired a charge over the land for the money it had paid the owner, and which was now liable to be repaid. Before the money was repaid, the land was sold to developers. The developers who were buying the land asked the defendants to do a search of the local land charges register and tell them what charges existed over the land. The defendants did not inform the developers of the Ministry of Housing's charge over the land. This meant that when the land was sold to the developers, it came to them free of the Ministry of Housing's charge. The Ministry of Housing sued the defendants in negligence for compensation for the loss of their charge. The Court of Appeal held that the defendants had owed the Ministry a duty of care in responding to the developers' query about land charges. The decision cannot be explained on the basis of *Hedley Byrne* as the defendants never assumed a responsibility to the Ministry of Housing to act carefully in responding to the developers' request for information about what charges existed over the land they were buying.

---

[195] Criticised, Weir 1995; also Klar 1998, 317–19.

F. Sterilisation of business

In a number of cases, a local authority or public official has carelessly misused its powers with the result that a business has not been allowed to carry on trading.

In *Harris* v *Evans* (1998), Harris used a mobile telescopic crane to provide bungee jumping facilities to members of the public. Evans was a health and safety inspector who inspected the crane when it was on a site in Devon. Evans recommended to the local council that Harris not be allowed to use the crane until it had been certified as fit to be used for bungee jumping. The council acted on Evans' recommendation and forbade Harris to use his crane until he had obtained such a certificate. It was, in fact, impossible – and also completely unnecessary for the purposes of ensuring the public's health and safety – for Harris to obtain such a certificate, and so Harris found himself unable to offer bungee jumping facilities at the site in Devon. Nor could he do so anywhere else: on Evans's initiative, a neighbouring council warned Harris not to offer bungee jumping facilities at any site within their jurisdiction until he had obtained the right certificate for his crane; and when Harris tried to set up shop at another site, the local council that was in charge of that site forbade Harris from doing so (again, presumably at Evans's instigation). Harris went to court and it was held that Harris need not obtain a certificate saying that his crane was suitable to be used for bungee jumping in order to use the crane. At that stage, Harris had been put out of business for roughly three months.

Harris sued Evans in negligence for compensation for the economic loss he had suffered as a result of Evans' incompetence. The Court of Appeal rejected his claim, holding that Evans had not owed Harris a duty of care. The Court of Appeal held that it would be contrary to the public interest to find that a duty of care was owed in this situation:

> The duty of enforcing authorities, whether inspectors or local authorities, is to have regard to the health and safety of members of the public. If steps which they think should be taken to improve safety would have an adverse economic effect on the business enterprise in question, so be it. A tortious duty which rendered them potentially liable for economic damage to the business enterprise caused by the steps they were recommending to be taken would, in my judgment, be very likely to engender untoward cautiousness and the temptation [to postpone making a decision until further inquiries have been made in the hope of getting more concrete facts].[196]

For much the same reason, the House of Lords denied that a duty of care was owed in *Jain* v *Trent Strategic HA* (2009), where the defendant local authority convinced a judge to withdraw a nursing home's registration – effectively closing down the home – by making misleading allegations about the safety of the residents in the home in the course of a 25-minute *ex parte* hearing at which the claimant owners of the home were not present. The claimants applied to have the judge's order set aside, and this was done by the Registered Homes Tribunal, which made some scathing criticisms of the conduct of the defendants. By then four months had passed and it proved to be impossible to get the nursing home up and running again. The claimants sued the defendant local authority in negligence. The House of Lords dismissed the claim, finding that it would be contrary to the public interest to find that a duty of care was owed in this case, for precisely the same reason as the Court of Appeal had declined to find a duty of care in the *Harris* case: if local authorities knew that they could be sued if they improperly closed down a nursing

---

[196] [1998] 1 WLR 1285, 1298 (per Sir Richard Scott V-C). The passage in square brackets is a quote from Lord Browne-Wilkinson's judgment in *X* v *Bedfordshire CC* [1995] AC 633, 750 to which Scott V-C referred at the end of this passage.

home on health and safety grounds, that could have the effect of making local authorities over-cautious in discharging their main function, that of protecting the health and welfare of residents of nursing homes.

While *Harris* and *Jain* were cases where the courts denied that the defendants owed the claimants a duty of care, what is interesting about those cases for our purposes here is that the courts in these cases refused to find a duty of care because they thought it would be contrary to the public interest to find such a duty. That implies that they *would have been willing* to find that a duty of care was owed if such a finding did not have any negative implications for the public interest. The impression is reinforced by the fact that four of the Law Lords who decided *Jain* went out of their way to express their 'regret' that they could not find a way that the claimants could sue the defendants under the law of negligence,[197] and attempted to point out possible arguments that the claimants could make in the European Court of Human Rights if they wanted to pursue a claim that the defendants had infringed their rights under the ECHR in that court.[198]

Given this, it is interesting to note another 'business sterilisation' case where the defendant was not a public body, but a company. This was the Australian case of *Perre* v *Apand Pty Ltd* (1999). That case concerned a set of potato farms located in South Australia. The potatoes grown on these farms would be exported to Western Australia, where the price of potatoes was particularly high. One of the farms was occupied by the Sparnon family. The defendants sold the Sparnons potato seed that the defendants ought to have known was diseased. The potatoes that grew from the seed on the Sparnon farm suffered from a disease called 'bacterial wilt'. Under the Plant Diseases Act 1914, potatoes could not be imported into Western Australia from any farm within 20 km of an outbreak of bacterial wilt for five years. As a result, when bacterial wilt was detected on the Sparnon farm, the claimants – whose farms were based about 3 km from the Sparnon farm – found themselves cut off from the lucrative Western Australia potato market for five years.[199] The claimants sued the defendants in negligence for compensation for their loss of profits. The High Court of Australia allowed the claim. In finding that the defendants had owed the claimants a duty to take care not to sell the Sparnons diseased potato seed, the High

---

[197] [2009] 1 AC 853, at [40] (per Lord Scott), [48] (per Baroness Hale), [52] (per Lord Carswell), and [53] (per Lord Neuberger).

[198] [2009] 1 AC 853, [38]–[39] (per Lord Scott), [43]–[45] (per Baroness Hale), [54] (per Lord Neuberger). The claimants could not bring a claim under the Human Rights Act 1998 in this case, as the 1998 Act only came into force on 2 October 2000, some time after the events in this case (which occurred in September 1998).

[199] This fact makes *Perre* different from *Jain*, and a weaker case than *Jain* for the imposition of a duty of care: the claimants lost their business in *Jain*, whereas the claimants' business was merely made less profitable in *Perre*. The same distinction marks the difference between the *Jain* case and the case of *Neil Martin Ltd* v *Commissioners for Her Majesty's Revenue and Customs* [2007] EWCA Civ 1041, where the claimant subcontractor sued the defendant tax authorities for failing to give him a tax certificate promptly enough, which certificate would have enabled contractors to pay him without deducting tax. Because deducting tax from payments made to subcontractors and handing that deducted tax over to the government involved a lot of hassle for contractors, the lack of such a tax certificate made contractors less willing to hire the claimant to work for them. The claimant's claim was dismissed on the ground that when Parliament set up the scheme for awarding tax certificates, it imposed a duty on the defendants to award tax certificates to those qualifying for them, *not* a duty to award those certificates promptly. The Court of Appeal held that it was not within their power to do what Parliament had chosen not to do, and impose on the defendants via the law of negligence a duty to award the claimant his tax certificate within a reasonable period of time.

Court emphasised the claimants' degree of vulnerability to having their business interfered with if the defendants sold diseased potato seed to one of the claimants' neighbours.[200]

The decision in *Perre* can be compared with the decision of Tugendhat J in *Pride & Partners* v *Institute of Animal Health* (2009), where the claimants were farmers who suffered business losses as a result of an outbreak of foot and mouth disease (FMD) and consequent government-imposed restrictions on the movement of farm animals. The claimants alleged that the FMD virus that was responsible for the outbreak of FMD had escaped from the defendants' laboratories. The claimants cited *Perre* as authority in favour of the proposition that the defendants had owed the claimants a duty to take care not to allow the FMD virus to escape from their laboratories. The defendants conceded that they did owe the claimants such a duty of care, but argued that that duty was geared towards protecting the claimants' animals from being harmed.[201] The defendants denied that they owed the claimants an equivalent duty of care that was geared towards protecting the claimants' businesses from being harmed. Tugendhat J agreed with the defendants. He distinguished the *Perre* case from the *Pride & Partners* case on the basis that the duty of care in *Perre* was only owed to farmers based within 20 km of the Sparnon farm, whereas the suggested duty of care in *Pride & Partners* would have been owed to *every livestock farmer in Britain* whose living was affected by FMD-triggered movement restrictions.[202] Clearly, a finding that the defendants owed a duty of care to the claimants that was geared towards protecting the claimants' businesses would have exposed the defendants to a huge number of claims, and their liability would have spiralled out all proportion to their (supposed) fault in allowing the FMD virus to escape the confines of their laboratory.

That the UK courts might be more willing to find that a duty of care is owed in a 'business sterilisation' case where no consideration of public policy militates against finding a duty of care, and where liability would be limited to a particular claimant or group of claimants is confirmed by the recent decision of Edis J in *Sebry* v *Companies House* (2016), holding that an employee at Companies House owed the claimant company a duty of care not to register the claimant company as being in liquidation (which meant that no one was willing to deal with the claimant company or lend it money and the claimant company eventually went into administration) when it was not.

Taken together, all of the above cases *may* be taken as indicating that in a 'business sterilisation' case, the UK courts *may* be willing to find that a duty of care was owed if: (i) the defendant has wrecked the claimant's business through a positive and illegitimate act, (ii) the claimant was powerless to protect himself against what the defendant did, (iii) finding that the defendant owed the claimant a duty of care would not expose the defendant to 'liability in an indeterminate amount for an indeterminate time to an indeterminate class'[203] and (iv) finding that the defendant owed the claimant a duty of care not to act as he did would not be contrary to the public interest.[204] Naturally, if the UK courts did find a duty of care was owed in such a case, that finding could not be explained by reference to the extended principle in *Hedley Byrne*.

---

[200] (1999) 198 CLR 180, at [10]–[15] (per Gleeson CJ), [38] (per Gaudron J), [50] and [123]–[124] (per McHugh J), [216] (per Gummow J), [296] (per Kirby J).
[201] [2009] EWHC (QB) 685, at [110].
[202] [2009] EWHC (QB) 685, at [115]-[116].
[203] *Ultramares Corporation* v *Touche*, 174 NE 441 (1931), per Cardozo CJ.
[204] For further discussion, see Bagshaw 2009a.

5.13 Pure economic loss (5): explanation of the difficult cases

Having set out these exceptions to the normal rule that there is no duty of care in a pure economic loss case absent an 'assumption of responsibility' by the defendant to the claimant, we could simply move on and stop discussing these exceptions. Some students will be tempted to wish that we would do this, and start talking about when A will owe B a duty of care to *save* B from suffering some kind of harm (the topic of the next chapter). But it would be remiss of us not to attempt to explain *why* a duty of care will be owed in the above cases. Such an explanation is needed for two reasons.

First of all, we cannot understand how far these cases go, and what they *actually* tell us about when one person will owe another a duty of care, without an explanation of why a duty of care will be owed in these cases. For example, in *Goodwill* v *British Pregnancy Advisory Service* (1996), the claimant was a woman who had been made pregnant as a result of having unprotected sex with a man who was supposed to have had a vasectomy performed upon him by the defendants. Counsel for the claimant sought to argue that the House of Lords' decision in *White* v *Jones* (1995) indicated that the defendants owed the claimant a duty to carry out the vasectomy with a reasonable degree of care and skill. In order to see whether that argument is right or wrong, we have to be able to explain *why* a duty of care will be owed in a *White* v *Jones*-type situation. Once we can do this, we can see whether that explanation also applies to indicate that a duty of care will also be owed in a *Goodwill*-type case.

Secondly, we won't be able to tell whether or not the courts were right to find that a duty of care was owed in the above cases unless we can first come up with a convincing explanation as to why the courts might have found that a duty of care was owed in these cases. Once we have come up with such an explanation, then we will be in a position to see whether there is *actually* a good reason for finding a duty of care in these cases, or whether the best reason we can come up with for finding a duty of care in such cases is simply not good enough.

In trying to come up with an explanation as to why a duty of care will be owed in the cases set out above, we need to follow certain rules of thumb:[205]

(1) Our explanation should fit the decided cases. We should try to avoid coming up with an explanation of why a duty of care was owed in *Spring* v *Guardian Assurance Ltd* (1995) that suggests *Spartan Steel & Co Ltd* v *Martin* (1973) was wrongly decided. Of course, some cases may be wrongly decided. But we should have a prejudice in favour of explanations that do not require us to conclude that the judges have gone wrong in large numbers of cases.

(2) Our explanation should be morally appealing. We should have a prejudice in favour of explanations that do not require us to conclude that a large number of judges are vicious, or mercenaries, or prejudiced, or class warriors. If we have to choose between an explanation of the decision in *White* v *Jones* (1995) which says the ex-barrister Law Lords who decided the case were biased against solicitors, and the explanation of that decision offered below, then we should prefer the explanation offered below.

---

[205] The first two rules are heavily indebted to that part of Ronald Dworkin's theory of law that explains how courts spell out from the decided cases underlying 'principles' that guide their decisions in other cases. See, generally, Dworkin 1986.

(3) The judges' own explanations as to how they reached their decisions are no more worthy of respect than anyone else's. The correct explanation as to why a duty of care will be owed in a *Smith* v *Eric S Bush*-type case may be very different from the explanation that any of the judges who decided that case may have offered. Lord Goff, speaking extra-judicially, has characterised the 'judicial act . . . as an educated reflex to facts . . .'[206] But a judge who experiences a certain reflex to a certain set of facts may not be in the best position to explain *why* he or she experiences that reflex. It depends on the judge's degree of insight and articulacy – and some judges are less insightful and articulate than others.

(4) We should not think that *all* of the above cases can be explained in the *same* way. It is just as likely that *some* of them can be explained in one way, and others can be explained in another way. We should not fall foul of what Lord Goff – speaking extra-judicially on another occasion[207] – called 'the temptation of elegance': of finding *one* rule, *one* principle, *one* idea that can account for *everything*. In fact, the best explanation we can come up with for the above cases is a complex one, where different cases are explained in different ways. Our explanation goes as follows:

A. Severe dependency as a basis for a duty of care

Some of the above cases can be explained on the basis that if A knows that B's future will be ruined if A does a positive act *x*, then A will owe B a duty to take care not to do *x*. This – we would contend – is the best explanation of why a duty of care will be owed in the survey cases, in a *Spring*-type situation, and a *Phelps*-type situation. In each of these cases, the claimant's future was in the defendant's hands, and the defendant knew it, and the defendant ruined their future by doing something positive. In *Smith* v *Eric S Bush* (1990), and the other survey cases, it was reporting back to the building society that the house the claimant was thinking of buying needed no essential repairs, when it did. In *Spring* (1995), it was telling the claimant's prospective employer that the claimant was 'a man of little or no integrity and could not be regarded as honest'. In *Phelps* (2001), it was reporting back to the claimant's school that the claimant was not dyslexic but was merely suffering from confidence problems.

In each of these cases, the claimant could not afford for the defendant to do what the defendant did, and the defendant knew it. This was literally the case in *Smith* v *Eric S Bush*, where the claimant was (as the defendant well knew) buying a house at the lower end of the property market and could therefore have been expected by the defendant both to have not enough money to employ his own surveyor, and to be financially ruined if he ended up buying a house that turned out to be worth a lot less than he paid for it, or that needed a lot of money spending on it to make it habitable. This was also the case in *Spring*, where the claimant simply could not get a job in the industry where he made his living without the support of the defendants, as under the rules of the life insurance industry, he could not be employed without his employer soliciting a reference from the defendants. And this was obviously the case in *Phelps*, where the claimant's prospects of leaving school with a decent set of qualifications crucially depended on her getting a correct diagnosis of her educational difficulties from the defendant psychologist.

---

[206] Goff 1986, 4.

[207] Goff 1983, 174.

If this explanation of these cases is right, two things follow. *First*, a duty of care should only be owed in a survey case where the surveyor knew that his survey would be relied on by the purchaser,[208] and that the purchaser would suffer a devastating financial loss if the survey turned out to be wrong.[209] Both conditions should be satisfied in a case where the surveyed property is a house, at the bottom end of the market. Neither condition will be satisfied if the surveyed property is a block of offices, or an expensive house: in such a case, the surveyor could expect the purchaser to employ someone to survey the property, and will have no reason to expect that his survey will be relied upon, or reason to think that if he gets his survey wrong, the purchaser will suffer a devastating economic loss.[210] That this is correct has been confirmed by the Court of Appeal in *Scullion v Bank of Scotland plc* (2011). In that case, the claimant was an investor who bought a flat, intending to let it out to tenants. He did not bother to have a surveyor assess the flat's capital value and for how much he could realistically expect to rent it out. Instead, he relied on the report on these matters prepared by the defendants for the bank that lent the claimant the money he needed to buy the flat. When the investment turned out to be a bad one, the claimant sued the defendants in negligence, arguing that their report had been carelessly prepared. His claim was dismissed: the defendants had had no reason to think that the claimant would rely on their report, and had therefore not owed the claimant a duty of care.

Secondly, the Court of Appeal was *wrong* to rule in *Kapfunde v Abbey National plc* (1999) that the decision of the House of Lords in *Spring v Guardian Assurance plc* (1995) had no application to a case where the claimant was sent by her prospective employers for a medical check-up and lost the job that would otherwise have been hers because the doctor told her prospective employers (wrongly) that the claimant was likely to have a higher than average rate of absence from work.[211] The Court of Appeal thought *Spring* had no application in *Kapfunde* because the basis of the duty of care in *Spring* was the prior relationship between the claimant and defendant as employee and employer. In fact, a close reading of *Spring* reveals that the defendant was not technically ever the claimant's employer, because there was no contractual relationship between them.[212]

---

[208] *Smith v Eric S Bush* [1990] 1 AC 831, at 865 (per Lord Griffiths): 'The necessary proximity arises from the surveyor's knowledge that the overwhelming probability is that the purchaser will rely upon his valuation . . .'; to the same effect, see *Smith v Eric S Bush* [1990] 1 AC 831, at 844 (per Lord Templeman) and 871–2 (per Lord Jauncey of Tullichettle), and also *Caparo Industries plc v Dickman* [1990] 2 AC 605, at 638–9 (per Lord Oliver of Aylmerton) and 657, 661 (per Lord Jauncey of Tullichettle).

[209] Cf. Hoffmann J in *Morgan Crucible Co v Hill Samuel Co* [1991] Ch 295, at 303: 'the typical plaintiff in a *Smith*-type case is a person of modest means and making the most expensive purchase of his or her life.'

[210] Stapleton 1991 seems to think (at 277–83) that it is hard to understand why a duty of care will be owed in a survey case when a builder of a house will *not* owe a subsequent purchaser of the house a duty to build that house with a reasonable degree of care and skill. In fact, as Stapleton 1995 seems to recognise (at 335–7) there is no contradiction here. The reason why a builder will not owe a subsequent purchaser of a house a duty to build that house with a reasonable degree of care and skill is that the builder – at the time he was building the house – will not *know* that if he does a bad job, a subsequent purchaser will definitely be made drastically worse off as a result. This is because there are ways that a subsequent purchaser of a house can protect herself against the risk that the house will turn out to be no good – for example, by having the house surveyed or by taking out insurance.

[211] Contrast the case of *Everett v Griffiths* [1920] 3 KB 163, where it was suggested (at 182) that a doctor examining a patient on behalf of the authorities to determine whether or not the patient should be committed for psychiatric treatment will owe the patient a duty to take care not to diagnose him as in need of treatment when he is not in need.

[212] [1995] 2 AC 296, 315 (per Lord Goff).

The true basis of the decision in *Spring*, it is suggested, was identified by Lord Lowry in *Spring* as lying in

> the probability, often amounting to a certainty, of damage to the individual [resulting from a bad reference] which in some cases will be serious and may indeed be irreparable. The entire future prosperity and happiness of someone who is the subject of a damaging reference which is given carelessly but in perfectly good faith may be irretrievably blighted.[213]

Given this, there seems no reason why *Spring* should not extend to:

1. The set of facts presented in *Kapfunde*.

2. The set of facts presented in *McKie v Swindon College* (2011), where the claimant had enjoyed a number of happy years working at Swindon College and had just been appointed to a job at the University of Bath, when – for no reason anyone could ever fathom – two employees at Swindon egged on Swindon's human resources manager to warn his counterpart at Bath that there had been a number of concerns about the claimant (both in terms of student safety and his relationship with colleagues) while he worked at Swindon. There had not been. The result of the warning was that the claimant was summarily dismissed from his job at Bath. It was held that Swindon College had owed the claimant a duty of care not to ruin unnecessarily his relationship with the University of Bath, and had been put in breach of that duty by the foolish actions of its employees.

3. The set of facts presented in the Canadian case of *Haskett v Trans Union of Canada* (2003), where the claimant was denied credit because the credit reporting agency wrongly reported that the claimant was a bad credit risk. The Ontario Court of Appeal invoked *Spring* as authority for finding that the credit reporting agency had owed the claimant a duty of care in this case, observing that

   > Credit is an integral part of everyday life in today's society. Not only people seeking loans, mortgages, insurance or car leases, but those who wish, for example, to rent an apartment or even obtain employment may be the subject of a credit report . . . Without credit, one is unable to conduct any financial transactions over the telephone or on the internet.[214]

Having said that, *Haskett* has *not* been followed in the UK. In *Smeaton v Equifax plc* (2013), it was held that a credit reference agency did *not* owe the claimant a duty of care not to tell other people that the claimant had been made bankrupt (which he had not) on the basis that harm to the claimant was not foreseeable (as the claimant could be expected to correct the inaccurate information on his credit record) and finding that a duty of care was owed to the claimant would expose credit reference agencies to potentially indeterminate liabilities and cut across schemes laid down by Parliament for regulating those agencies.[215] However, when these sorts of considerations do not apply, the UK courts have shown themselves willing to find a duty of care not to damage someone's credit rating. For example, in *Durkin v DSG Retail Ltd* (2014), it was conceded by counsel – and the UK Supreme Court did not question it – that a bank that had loaned a claimant money owed the claimant a duty of care not to make untrue statements about him to credit reference agencies.[216]

---

[213] [1995] 2 AC 296, 326.
[214] (2003) 224 DLR (4th) 419, at [29].
[215] [2013] EWCA Civ 108, at [75].
[216] [2014] 1 WLR 1148, at [32].

By contrast, the Court of Appeal was *right* to rule that *Spring* did *not* extend to the facts of *Greenway* v *Johnson Matthey plc* (2016).[217] In that case, the claimant employees were prevented from doing any more high-paid work for the defendant employers handling platinum because tests showed that they had become sensitised to platinum with the result that allowing the claimants to continue to handle platinum might result in their developing various physical ill-effects in the future. The claimants argued that the defendants had owed them a duty of care under *Spring* to take greater precautions against their become sensitised to platinum, so that they would not lose their high-paying jobs handling platinum. Sales LJ held that the 'nexus' between the defendants' failings in exposing their employees to excessive quantities of platinum and 'the impact on the employees' future employability [was] more indirect and remote' than it was in *Spring*.[218]

B. Business sterilisation

It may be that our rationale for the decision of the House of Lords in *Spring* (and *Phelps*, and *Smith* v *Eric S Bush*) also explains why a duty of care *might* be found in a business sterilisation case where (1) the defendant has wrecked the claimant's business through a positive and illegitimate act, (2) the claimant was powerless to protect himself against what the defendant did, (3) finding that the defendant owed the claimant a duty of care would not expose the defendant to 'liability in an indeterminate amount for an indeterminate time to an indeterminate class' and (4) finding that the defendant owed the claimant a duty of care not to act as he did would not be contrary to the public interest. On this view, just as finding a duty of care in *Spring* protects people's significant interests in being allowed to make a living by being employed *by someone else*, finding a duty of care in a 'business sterilisation' case protects people's significant interests in being allowed to make a living through *self-employment*.

If this is right, then a duty of care should only be owed in a 'business sterilisation' case where the claimant is a *real* person who has been deprived of his living by someone else's carelessness. It is noticeable that in all of the 'business sterilisation' cases mentioned above, this condition was satisfied: the claimant was a real person (or a company with a real person, or a small group of real people, as the sole owner)[219] whose living was dependent on his business not being interfered with by the defendant. And it is hard to imagine that the High Court of Australia would have gone out of its way to find a duty of care in *Perre* v *Apand Pty Ltd* (1999) if the claimant had been a multi-national company, one of whose potato farms had become a temporarily less lucrative operation because diseased potato seed had been planted in a neighbouring farm.

One of us has suggested a more limited rationale for finding a duty of care in at least some 'business sterilisation' cases.[220] On this view, having your business made illegal can be treated as a distinct form of damage from pure economic loss, in that a claimant whose

---

[217] The Court of Appeal was also right to find (without, though, citing *Spring*) that it was *arguable* that a duty of care was owed to the claimant police officers in *James-Bowen* v *Commissioner of Police of Metropolis* [2016] EWCA Civ 1217, who found themselves being labelled as violent thugs by the defendant police commissioner in announcing the settlement of a claim for damages that had been made against the commissioner arising out of alleged misconduct by the claimants. On whether the courts should *ultimately* find that a duty of care was owed on the facts of *James-Bowen*, see McBride 2017.

[218] [2016] 1 WLR 4487, at [45].

[219] By all media accounts, the company at the heart of the *Sebry* litigation (above § 5.12(F)) was a family-run company.

[220] See Bagshaw 2009a.

business has been made illegal has not just suffered a pure economic loss, but has had his freedom under the law limited. Such an explanation provides a nice fit with the 'business sterilisation' cases, but its moral appeal remains to be established. Is a case where someone is legally not allowed to carry on his business more deserving of the law's intervention than a case where someone is legally allowed to carry on his business, but simply cannot because someone has unlawfully cut off his power supply?

C. Intermeddling

Whether or not the 'business sterilisation' cases can be explained by reference to the same ideas that – we argue – underlie decisions such as the ones in *Smith* v *Eric S Bush* (1991), *Spring* (1995) and *Phelps* (2001), those ideas *cannot* work to explain the decision of the House of Lords that a duty of care was owed in *White* v *Jones* (1995). As the claimants in that case only stood to inherit £9,000 each under their father's will, it can hardly be said that the solicitor who took on the job of drawing up that will knew that the claimants' future was in his hands when he did so.[221] The best[222] explanation of the decision in *White* v *Jones* that we can come up with goes as follows.

White v *Jones* applies in a case where A wanted to confer a benefit on B, and C undertakes to assist A in conferring that benefit on B,[223] but C's carelessness in assisting A ends

---

[221] A subtle argument that might be made in favour of thinking that the duty of care in *White* v *Jones* could be based on such an idea goes as follows: 'Had the claimants been left *a house* under the will, the solicitors would have known *in that case* that if they performed the job of drawing up the will badly, the future well-being of the claimants would have been radically impaired, and we could have found that the solicitors owed the claimants a duty of care in that case on the basis of authorities like *Spring* and *Phelps* and *Smith* v *Eric S Bush*. Now – the law would become intolerably uncertain if it said that a solicitor will owe a duty of care in drawing up a will to those who are due to inherit a "large" legacy under the will, but not to those who are due to inherit a "small" legacy. So the only thing we can do in a *White* v *Jones* situation is to say that if A is instructed to draw up a will under which B is due to inherit a legacy, A will owe B a duty to draw up that will with a reasonable degree of care and skill, whatever the size of the legacy B is due to receive under the will.' The problem with this argument is that it rests on an unjustified premise: even if the claimants in *White* v *Jones* had been due to receive a house under their father's will, it is hard to see why the claimants' future well-being would have been radically *impaired* had the solicitors done a bad job of drawing up that will. They would merely have missed out on a large bonus.

[222] Lord Browne-Wilkinson suggested in *White* v *Jones* that the basis of the defendant's duty was the fact that when the defendant took on the job of drawing up the will, he knew that the claimants' future economic welfare was dependent on his doing that job properly: [1995] 2 AC 207, 275. However, that explanation is palpably too wide as the same could be said of many of the 'relational economic loss' cases (see above, § 4.3, fn 29) where a duty of care was denied. Lord Goff suggested that a duty of care needed to be found in *White* v *Jones* because 'practical justice' demanded that the House of Lords close the 'loophole' or 'lacuna' that would otherwise exist in this case, whereby the only person the defendant owed a duty of care to (the father) suffered no loss as a result of the defendant's breach of that duty and therefore could not sue, while the only person who suffered a loss (the claimants) was owed no duty and therefore could not sue: [1995] 2 AC 207, 259. But that presupposes that we should find the defendant liable to *someone* in a *White* v *Jones* case – but why? If the desire is to ensure that the defendant does not 'get away' with being negligent without incurring some kind of sanction from the law, then a complaint to the Law Society should have ensured that 'practical justice' would be done in this case.

[223] The undertaking to assist has to be voluntary, so as to prevent a defendant who is dragooned into a third party's scheme to help the claimant suddenly being fixed with an onerous duty of care to see that he does not screw things up for the claimant. See *Rowley* v *Secretary of State for Work and Pensions* [2007] 1 WLR 2861, holding that the defendant Secretary of State – who had been fixed with a statutory duty to assess, through the Child Support Agency, how much a single mother should be paid in child support maintenance payments – did not owe the claimant (a single mother) a duty to take care not to get the assessment wrong.

up *preventing* A from conferring that benefit on B.[224] In such a case, C will be found to have owed B a duty to be careful in assisting A. The basis of the duty is the fact that B would have had the benefit that A wanted to confer on her but for C's intermeddling. As a result, C's unhelpful assistance amounted to a kind of theft, or destruction, of a benefit that – morally, though not legally – belonged to B.

If this is right, then a number of things follow:

1. *White* v *Jones* will *not* apply in a case where A employs C to convey a parcel of land to B, but due to C's incompetence, the conveyance does not go through, and A subsequently changes his mind and refuses to try again to convey the land to B.[225] In such a case, C's carelessness will not have *prevented* A from conveying the land to B; it will merely have given A a chance to change his mind.

2. *White* v *Jones* does not just apply in wills cases, but applies in any case where A wants to confer a benefit on B, and is prevented from doing so by C's unhelpful assistance. This was confirmed by the Court of Appeal decision in *Gorham* v *British Telecommunications plc* (2001). In that case, G, a married man with two young children, wanted to set up a pension which would provide some financial security for his wife and children should he predecease them. He went to Standard Life for some advice and they failed to advise him properly. They advised him to take out a Standard Life pension when in fact G's wife and children would have been far better off had G joined the occupational pension scheme run by his employer, British Telecom. When G died, G's wife and children sued Standard Life claiming that Standard Life had owed them, and breached, a duty to take care that they did not give G bad pensions advice. The Court of Appeal held that Standard Life had owed G's wife and children such a duty of care under *White* v *Jones*. Rightly so, if we accept the analysis of *White* v *Jones* advanced here. G wanted to provide his wife and children with as much financial security as possible after he died. Standard Life undertook to assist him in doing that but they in fact prevented him from doing that by giving him bad pensions advice. So – on the analysis of *White* v *Jones* advanced here – Standard Life owed G's wife and children a duty to take care that they did not give G bad pensions advice.

3. The Court of Appeal was right to reject counsel for the claimant's argument in *Goodwill* v *British Pregnancy Advisory Service* (1996) that *White* v *Jones* indicated that a duty of care was owed to the claimant in that case. In that case, the claimant became pregnant after having sex with M, who was supposed to have been sterilised by the defendants. The Court of Appeal held that *White* v *Jones* did not apply here because it was hardly realistic to say that, in being sterilised, M was attempting to confer a benefit on women such as the claimant (the benefit of not getting pregnant).[226] It might have been different, though, if

---

[224] In *White* v *Jones*, Lord Mustill (dissenting) thought that some such principle had to underlie the decision in *White* v *Jones* and on that basis condemned the majority decision as going 'far beyond anything so far contemplated by the law of negligence': [1995] 2 AC 207, 291.

[225] *White* v *Jones* [1995] 2 AC 207, 262 (per Lord Goff). See also *Hemmens* v *Wilson Browne* [1995] Ch 223 (held: no duty owed by firm of solicitors to claimant in drawing up deed under which claimant would have had the right to call on A at any time to pay her £110,000); *Wells* v *First National Commercial Bank* [1998] PNLR 552 (held: bank that agrees to refinance company and, as part of the deal, agrees to pay off some of the company's debts will not owe the debtors a duty to pay off those debts); and *Briscoe* v *Lubrizol* [2000] ICR 694 (held: underwriters of company's health insurance scheme owe no duty of care to employee claiming under that scheme when they assess whether his claim is genuine or not; even if they turn down his claim when it is genuine, that will not prevent the employee obtaining what he is entitled to under the scheme).

[226] [1996] 1 WLR 1397, 1403.

the claimant had been M's wife – in such a case, it would have been possible to argue that M wanted to confer a benefit on the claimant in being sterilised. So if the claimant had been M's wife, it might have been possible to argue that the defendants owed the claimant a duty under *White* v *Jones* to take care that they did not botch M's operation.[227]

D. Interference with intangible property

This leaves the decision of the Court of Appeal in *Ministry of Housing* v *Sharp* (1970) – the hardest case to explain, in our view.

In that case, Lord Denning MR held that the House of Lords' decision in *Hedley Byrne* v *Heller* (1964) indicated that the defendant (who was answering the inquiry as to whether there were any charges over some land some developers were going to purchase) owed the claimant (who had a charge over that land which would be lost if the defendant answered the developers' question in the negative and the developers subsequently bought that land) a duty of care. Counsel for the defendant argued that this was not true – that a duty of care would only be owed in a *Hedley Byrne* situation if the defendant 'assumed a responsibility' to the claimant, and there had been no such 'assumption of responsibility' here. Lord Denning denied that an 'assumption of responsibility' was required for liability to arise under *Hedley Byrne* and held that 'the duty to use due care in a statement arises . . . from the fact that the person making it knows, or ought to know, that others . . . would act on the faith of his statement being accurate.'[228] However, we now know this is not true, as the House of Lords held that mere knowledge that someone would rely on your statement would not be enough to give rise to a duty of care in *Williams* v *Natural Life Health Foods Ltd* (1998).

Salmon LJ seemed to rest his decision that a duty of care was owed in *Ministry of Housing* v *Sharp* (1970) on the basis that it was reasonably foreseeable that a mistake on the part of the defendant would result in the claimants' 'legal rights [being] taken away'.[229] This seems to identify a more satisfactory basis for the decision that a duty of care was owed in *Sharp* than Lord Denning MR's judgment did. However, once you start saying that A will owe B a duty to take care not to do something that will foreseeably interfere with B's legal rights to something, you have a tiger by the tail, as there is no limit to the number of legal rights to something that claimants can argue they have (such as rights to trade, marry, walk down the street, watch TV, go to a football match, and so on) and that could be foreseeably interfered with by a defendant. As McHugh J observed in *Perre* v *Apand Pty Ltd* (1999):

> Nor do I think that this Court should accept that a defendant should owe a duty of care merely because its conduct may defeat or impair 'a precise legal right' of the [claimant] in circumstances where the defendant is in a relationship with the [claimant] and in a position to control the enjoyment of that right . . . To impose duties of care in such situations would extend the liability of defendants, perhaps massively . . . The Perres no doubt had a right to trade, and that is a right that in various circumstances the law will protect, but not by imposing duties of care on others simply because they are in a position to control the enjoyment of the plaintiff's right to trade.[230]

Given this, it would be better to say that it was reasonably foreseeable that a mistake on the part of the defendant would cause the claimants to lose a *proprietary interest* that the claimants had in the land which the developers were going to purchase, and it was that which gave rise to a duty of care in *Sharp*. Seen in this way, the decision in *Sharp* is an

---

[227] Ibid.
[228] [1970] 2 QB 223, 268.
[229] [1970] 2 QB 223, 280.
[230] (1999) 198 CLR 180, at [84]–[85].

extension of the rule that if it is reasonably foreseeable that A's actions will result in property that B has a sufficient interest in being harmed, then A will normally owe B a duty to take care not to act in that way – with the rule being extended here to a case where the property was intangible in nature (you can't touch a charge). Whether such an extension is justified or not is another matter.

E. Another explanation

This ends our explanation of all the 'difficult cases' that were the subject of the previous section. But you should not think that our explanation is the only one on offer. Other explanations are possible – though in our view, they do not provide as good an explanation of these 'difficult cases' as ours does. But so that you can make up your own mind on this, here is a brief alternative explanation[231] of the above 'difficult cases':

> In cases where A's positive actions have foreseeably resulted in B suffering a form of pure economic loss, the *only* general reason why the courts hesitate to find that A owed B a duty of care not to act as he did is a fear that if they do so, A may be exposed to a multitude of claims, and that his liability will spiral out of all proportion to his fault in acting as he did. So in a 'relational economic loss' case where A has carelessly damaged property belonging to C, and B has suffered economic loss as a result, the reason why the courts will only normally find that A owed C a duty of care in this case is that if they find that A also owed B a duty of care, there may be no end to the number of claims that might be made against A, as more and more people come forward, claiming that they too suffered some form of economic loss as a result of C's property being damaged.
>
> For example, in *Cattle* v *Stockton Waterworks* (1875), Blackburn J justified his refusal to find that the defendants in that case – who had carelessly flooded K's land and disrupted work that the claimant was doing on that land – had owed the claimant a duty of care on the basis that the effect of such a finding would be to allow not only the claimant to sue, but also 'every workman and person employed [by the claimant to work on K's land], who in consequence of [the] stoppage [of that work] made less wages than he would otherwise have done.'[232] Blackburn J acknowledged that this objection to finding a duty of care was 'technical and against the merits, and we would be glad to avoid giving it effect'[233] but felt that he had no alternative but to refuse to find a duty of care in that case. More recently, in *The Mineral Transporter* (1986), Lord Fraser of Tullybelton took the same line, arguing that the rule against a duty of care being owed to a claimant in a 'relational economic loss case' was 'a pragmatic one dictated by necessity'.[234]
>
> It follows that in cases where the courts can find that A owed B a duty to take care not to act in a way that foreseeably caused B to suffer pure economic loss without exposing A to a multitude of claims, they should do so (provided, of course, that there are no other special objections that can be made to finding a duty of care in such a case). This will be the case where A knew or ought to have known that B 'individually, and not merely as a member of an unascertained class, [was] likely to suffer economic loss as a consequence of his negligence . . .'[235] In all of the 'difficult cases' discussed above – and, indeed, in *Hedley Byrne* itself – this requirement is satisfied and as a result, the courts' basic objection to finding a duty of care in a pure economic loss case is removed. In all of the above cases, the defendant knew that the claimant was especially likely to suffer pure economic loss as a result of his actions, and there was no danger that the defendant's actions would cause a wider class of people to suffer pure economic loss.

---

[231] See Yap 2009 for an example of this sort of way of thinking about the cases.
[232] (1875) LR 10 QB 453, 457.
[233] Ibid.
[234] [1986] AC 1, 16.
[235] *Caltex Oil Pty Ltd* v *The Dredge 'Willemstaad'* (1976) 136 CLR 529, 555 (per Gibbs J).

We think this explanation suffers from the flaw that is not particularly appealing. It misses the fact that it is often not that important to protect B from suffering pure economic loss at A's hands, because pure economic loss is – viewed in abstraction – not a particularly serious harm that we need to protect people (let alone companies) against suffering. It is only if the pure economic loss that B stands to suffer as a result of A's actions is of a *type* that is particularly serious, that the balance shifts in favour of intervention – and our explanation of the 'difficult cases' set out in this section has been concerned to identify what those types of economic loss might be.

Further reading

For an excellent overview of the law on recovery in negligence for psychiatric illness, see **Handford, 'Psychiatric injury in breach of a relationship' (2007) 27** *Legal Studies* **26. Rachael Mulheron** criticises the need – in a 'psychiatric illness' case – to establish that a claimant suffered a 'recognised psychiatric illness' (as opposed to something falling just short of this) in her **'Rewriting the requirement for a "recognised psychiatric injury" in negligence claims' (2012) 32** *Oxford Journal of Legal Studies* **77.**

Christian Witting wrote a very stimulating article on why tort law might distinguish between harm to property cases and pure economic loss cases in **'Distinguishing between property damage and pure economic loss in negligence: a personality thesis' (2001) 21** *Legal Studies* **481. Peter Benson** wrote the classic article on how we could explain the distinction as based on the fact that in a pure economic loss case, the claimant cannot argue that his rights have been violated: **'The basis for excluding liability for economic loss in tort law' in Owen (ed),** *The Philosophical Foundations of Tort Law* **(Clarendon Press, 1995)** but – as all such articles do – mixed up his 'rights that . . .' (the violation of which can give rise to tort liability) with his 'rights to . . .' (the existence of which is a product of tort law, and does not underlie tort law). Just because you don't have a 'right to' a certain level of business does not mean that you cannot claim that you had a 'right that' a defendant not carelessly do something that had the effect of damaging your business: see **McBride, 'Rights and the basis of tort law' in Nolan and Robertson (eds),** *Rights and Private Law* **(Hart Publishing, 2011).** Stapleton, **'Comparative economic loss: lessons from case-law-focused "middle theory"' (2002) 50** *UCLA Law Review* goes to the opposite extreme of being too wide, but is still on the right lines, and has the signal virtue of being extremely clear and comprehensive (having been written for an American audience which – apparently – pays little attention to issues about the recovery of pure economic loss).

Stevens, **'***Hedley Byrne* v *Heller*: **judicial creativity and doctrinal possibility' (1964) 27** *Modern Law Review* **121** is an *incredible* article – written just weeks or months after *Hedley Byrne* was decided, and anticipating a huge amount of its future development as a ground of liability. **Whittaker, 'The application of the "broad principle of *Hedley Byrne*" as between parties to a contract' (1997) 17** *Legal Studies* **169** is disapproving of a lot of that development.

Kit Barker is much more skeptical than we are of the possibility that the notion of an 'assumption of responsibility' can make sense of the scope of liability under *Hedley Byrne*: **'Unreliable assumptions in the law of negligence' (1993) 109** *Law Quarterly Review* **461.** He returns to the subject of recovery for economic loss in **'Economic loss and the duty of care: a study in the exercise of legal justification' in Rickett (ed),** *Justifying Private Law Remedies* **(Hart, 2008),** but the paper may be too advanced for most students.

Chapter 6
Duty of care: omissions

Aims and objectives

Reading this chapter should enable you to:

(1) Understand the distinction between an act and an omission and why it is much harder to establish in an omission case that a defendant owed a claimant a duty of care to save the claimant from harm than it is in the case where a defendant carelessly caused the claimant harm through a positive act.

(2) Understand the history of the development of the law on when a public body will owe a claimant a duty of care to save the claimant from harm that the public body is in a good position to save the claimant from, and what the law currently says on that issue.

(3) Understand the range of different situations where a defendant will owe a claimant a duty of care to save the claimant from harm.

6.1 The basics

In this chapter, we cross over a fundamental divide in English law – between acts and omissions. It is simply not possible to understand tort law properly without understanding the significance English law attaches to the distinction between acts and omissions. In this context, the significance of the distinction lies in this: while foreseeability of harm may – as we have seen – ground a duty to take care not to act in a particular way, foreseeability of harm is never enough to give rise to a duty of care to come to someone else's assistance. Something more than mere foreseeability of harm must be shown before a duty to save someone else from that harm will arise.

As a result, the rule in English law is that if A is in a position to save B from harm, A will *not* owe B a duty to rescue B unless there exist some special circumstances that would warrant imposing a duty on A to rescue B, such as that: (1) A assumed a responsibility to look after B; or (2) A put B in danger of suffering harm; or (3) A interfered with either B or someone else's saving B from suffering harm; or (4) A was in control of a dangerous thing that posed a foreseeable threat to B, or A was in a control of a dangerous person and B was at special risk of being harmed by that person.[1] (This is not meant to be an exhaustive list: you will need to read the whole of this chapter to understand *all* the situations where the law makes an exception to the general rule that people do not owe other people duties of care to save them from harm.)

The case of *Sutradhar* v *Natural Environment Research Council* (2006) provides an example of this rule at work. That case arose out of what the World Health Organisation has called 'the largest mass poisoning of a population in history.' From the 1970s onwards, the Bangladeshi government – with the assistance of foreign aid from governmental organisations like the UK Overseas Development Agency – had sought to provide drinking water for its citizens by sinking millions of tube wells all over the country, to access underground water supplies. Unfortunately, in many cases the ground in which the tube wells were sunk was contaminated with arsenic, which in turn contaminated the water coming out of those wells. It is estimated that tens of millions of Bangladeshis have suffered arsenic poisoning as a result of drinking water from these tube wells. The claimant in *Sutradhar* was one of them.

The defendants in the *Sutradhar* case were an organisation that had been commissioned by the Overseas Development Agency to do a study on how far the Bangladeshi tube wells (which no one suspected at the time of being anything but a good thing) were standing up to the strain of repeated use. On their visit to Bangladesh to carry out the study, the defendants found that the tube wells they were looking at had not deteriorated at all. So they proposed to use the remaining money allocated for that study to carry out a study of the chemistry of water in the area, so as to see whether the water could support fish farms. In carrying out that study – the results of which were distributed around various Bangladeshi governmental and non-governmental organisations – the defendants failed to test the water they were studying for arsenic. Had they done so, they would have spotted the problem of arsenic contaminating water supplies coming from tube wells, and something could have been done about it. But as it was, everyone continued to think that tube wells were perfectly safe.

The claimant (who lived in the area being tested by the defendants) sued the defendants in negligence, arguing that they had owed him a duty of care in carrying out their study. The House of Lords dismissed the claim as 'hopeless'.[2] The reason was that the defendants had not done anything to make the claimant worse off: they had merely failed to do something that would have saved the claimant from being made ill. As a result, it was not possible to find that the defendants owed the claimant a duty of care – there being no special circumstances attaching to the case that would have made it 'fair, just and reasonable' to find that a duty of care was owed.

Three issues remain to be dealt with in this introductory section before we can go on to set out the exceptional situations where a defendant will owe a claimant a duty of care to save her from harm: (1) What is the difference between an act and an omission? (2) Why do private persons not normally have a duty of care to save other people from harm when they are in a good position to do so? (3) What is the attitude of the law towards imposing duties of care on public bodies to save other people from harm?

---

[1] *Yuen Kun Yeu* v *Attorney-General for Hong Kong* [1988] AC 175, 192; *Stovin* v *Wise* [1996] AC 923, 931; *Michael* v *Chief Constable of South Wales Police* [2015] UKSC 2, at [97].
[2] [2006] 4 All ER 490, at [2] (per Lord Hoffmann).

A. Acts and omissions

The basic difference between acts and omissions can be put as follows. In an act case, a defendant makes a claimant worse off by doing something positive. In other words, in an act case, the claimant is worse off than she would have been had the defendant done nothing at all. By contrast, in an omissions case the claimant is no worse off than she would have been had the defendant done nothing at all. Consider, for example, the **Falling Sign Problem**:

> One winter, *Highway Authority* put up a sign by the side of a road to warn drivers of treacherous black ice ahead. The sign was south-facing. Unfortunately, the highway authority did not do enough to secure the sign from being blown over by the strong winds that were common at that time of year.
>
> In Scenario (1), a wind blowing in a south-westerly direction blew the sign over so that it fell into the road, where it lay flat on the road. *Driver* ran over the sign at full speed, lost control of her car, and was severely injured in the ensuing crash.
>
> In Scenario (2), a wind blowing in a north-easterly direction blew the sign over so that it fell backwards and lay flat by the side of the road and was invisible to passing motorists. Unaware of the black ice ahead, *Unlucky* drove onto it at full speed, lost control of his car, and was severely injured in the ensuing crash.

In Falling Sign (1) we are dealing with an 'act' case: *Highway Authority*, through its positive act of putting the sign by the side of the road without securing it from being blown over, made *Driver* worse off than she would have been had the highway authority done nothing.[3] In Falling Sign (2) we are dealing with an 'omission' case: *Highway Authority*, by failing to secure the sign by the side of the road, failed to save *Unlucky* from the danger of crashing on the black ice on the road up ahead.[4]

It may seem paradoxical that whether we are dealing with an 'act' or 'omission' case in the Falling Sign Problem depends on the direction the wind was blowing in that case. But the paradox is more apparent than real. In the first scenario, we are holding *Highway Authority* liable for its positive act in putting up a sign by the side of the road (which was then blown into the middle of the road). In the second scenario, we are not holding *Highway Authority* liable for putting a sign up; we are holding *Highway Authority* liable for failing to make sure that the sign it put up stayed up (with the result that the sign was not visible when *Unlucky* came driving along).

In *Haseldine* v *Daw* (1941), a firm of engineers were employed by a landlord to maintain a lift in a block of flats owned by the landlord. On one of the firm's monthly visits to maintain the lift, an engineer, having cleaned the lift's machinery, failed to put a component part in the lift's machinery back properly in place. As a result, the next day, when the claimant used the lift, the lift fell to the bottom of the lift shaft, and the claimant was injured.

---

[3] Cf. *Levine* v *Morris* [1970] 1 WLR 71; also *Yetkin* v *Mahmood* [2011] QB 827 (bush planted by defendant authority allowed to grow to such an extent that it obstructed drivers' line of sight, with the result that there was accident in which claimant was injured).

[4] Cf. *Gorringe* v *Calderdale MBC* [2004] 1 WLR 1057.

The Court of Appeal held that the firm of engineers was liable in negligence for the claimant's injuries. This was pretty clearly an act case. A lift that was basically sound in condition (though somewhat worn and battered, the evidence showed) was rendered unsound by the engineer's positive act in removing a component part from the lift's machinery and then failing to replace it properly after he had cleaned it. As it was reasonably foreseeable that this positive act would result in someone like the claimant suffering a physical injury, the engineer was rightly held to have owed a duty of care to the claimant.

But what if *Engineer* had – on his monthly visit – simply failed to spot that there was a problem with the lift that would make it dangerous to use, with the result that *Visitor*, who subsequently used the lift, was injured? Would that be a case of an act, or an omission? If an act, then *Engineer* could be held liable to *Visitor*, based merely on the fact that it was foreseeable that leaving the lift in a dangerous state would result in someone like *Visitor* being injured. If an omission, then *Engineer* could only be held liable to *Visitor* if there was some special relationship between *Engineer* and *Visitor*, or some special circumstances that would warrant imposing a duty on *Engineer* to take positive steps to protect *Visitor* from harm – which requirement would not have been satisfied in the case here.

We think that this scenario is an 'act' case. Presumably, when *Engineer* arrived to inspect the lift, the lift was put out of commission. And when *Engineer* indicated to the landlord at the end of his inspection that *the lift could be used again*, the lift was put back into use. By indicating to the landlord that the lift could be used again, *Engineer* performed a positive act that made *Visitor* worse off than he would have been had *Engineer* done nothing. This is because, if *Engineer* had done nothing and not indicated to the landlord the lift could be used again, the lift would have been permanently out of commission, and *Visitor* could not have used the lift, and would not have been injured as a result of using it.

It was different in *Anns* v *Merton LBC* (1978). In that case, a block of flats were constructed on inadequate foundations. The plans for the building – which were deposited with the defendant local authority – specified that the foundations should be at least three foot deep. As it turned out, the building's foundations were shallower than that, by about six inches. The result was that cracks started developing in the building. The claimants were leaseholders of parts of the building. They sued the defendant local authority for failing to exercise its powers under the Public Health Act 1936 to ensure that the building was constructed in accordance with the plans for its construction. This was clearly an 'omission' case. The defendant local authority – by doing nothing – had failed to save the claimants from suffering harm (in this case, the cost of making the building safe). It would have been different, we suggest, if at some stage in the building work, that work could not have continued until the defendants had first issued a certificate, indicating that they were satisfied that the building's foundations were of an adequate depth. Issuing such a certificate would have amounted to a positive act that had the effect of making the claimants worse off, in that had such a certificate not been issued and the defendants had done nothing instead, the building could never have been completed and the claimants would not have had to incur the expense of making it safe.[5]

---

[5] Compare the facts of *The Nicholas H* [1996] AC 211 (discussed above, § 5.8), which was an 'act' case precisely because the ship could not have sailed without a certificate from the defendant society.

B. Private persons

Why does the law draw a distinction between acts and omissions so that it is unusual for private persons to owe other people a duty of care to save them from harm? *Kantian* theorists of tort law – that is, academics who think that tort law basically gives effect to the Doctrine of Right set out in the first part of Immanuel Kant's *Metaphysics of Morals* (1797)[6] – argue that 'Tort duties protect each person's ability to use his or her means as he or she sees fit, secure from the interferences of others.'[7] Tort duties do not seek to do anything but protect people's abilities to decide what to do with the means at their disposal because, at base, each of us enjoys a *right to independence* which means that the only time the law is justified in interfering with *your* independence (that is, your ability to decide what to do with the means at your disposal) by coercing you in some way is in order to protect *someone else*'s independence (that is, their ability to decide what to do with the means at their disposal). So in the stock situation where A comes upon a pond in which B, a drunk, is drowning, on the *Kantian* account, it would be *wrong* for the law to impose a duty on A to fish B out of the pond because doing so would interfere with A's right to independence – A would no longer be free to decide what to do with his bodily strength – when doing so is not necessary to protect B's independence; that is, B's ability to decide what to do with the means at his disposal. If A leaves B to drown in the pond, then A has not interfered with B's independence – in fact, the complaint against A would be that A has respected B's independence *too much* by leaving B to his fate!

Many people find Kantian justifications of tort law's failure to impose on people general duties of care to rescue other people from harm too chilly to be acceptable; and indeed, Kant himself never tried to provide any proof that we all enjoy a right to independence.[8] However, we do not need to sign up to Kant's views to see that a number of arguments can be made in favour of the law's only imposing on private persons duties of care to rescue other people from harm in very limited circumstances:

(1) *Intrusiveness.* As Lord Hoffmann pointed out in *Stovin* v *Wise* (1996), 'it is less of an invasion of an individual's freedom for the law to require him to consider the safety of others in his actions than to impose upon him a duty to rescue or protect.'[9] If A has a duty *not* to do *x*, he is free to do anything but *x*. If A has a duty to do *x*, he is not free to do anything other than *x*. The severe limits on someone's freedom that someone experiences when they are subjected to a duty to do something positive mean that such duties always require very strong justification.

---

[6] The two most prominent such academics are Ernest Weinrib (Weinrib 1995, Weinrib 2012) and Arthur Ripstein (Ripstein 2006b, Ripstein 2007b, Ripstein 2009, Ripstein 2015).

[7] Ripstein 2007b, 15.

[8] For criticisms of the idea that we have such a right, see Bird 2007 and Tadros 2011.

[9] [1996] AC 923, 943.

(2) *Certainty.* A concern to avoid uncertainty or lack of clarity in the law may be one of the reasons why the courts have so far been unwilling to recognise the existence of a general 'duty to rescue' in English law.[10] As Richard Epstein points out:

> Once one decides that . . . an individual is required under some circumstances to act at his own cost for the exclusive benefit of another, then it is very hard to set out in a principled manner the limits of social interference with individual liberty.[11]

He asks, for example: If we admit that someone crossing a bridge has a duty to throw a rope to someone drowning in the waters below, would someone who is asked to donate a very small amount of money to charity to help save a life have a legal duty to make that donation? If a patient needed a life-saving operation which only one surgeon in the world could perform, would that surgeon come under a legal duty to travel to the patient's bedside and perform that operation – assuming of course that someone could be found who would be willing to cover his travel expenses?[12]

Rather than get the law involved in trying to answer these difficult questions, the English courts have preferred to adopt the *simpler, clearer and more certain* position[13] that A is under no duty to attempt to rescue a stranger, B, from a danger if A played no role in creating the danger and is not otherwise responsible for it – and this is so no matter how easy the rescue might be and no matter how serious and imminent the danger B is in.

(3) *Moral crowding out.* Tony Weir observes that, 'The understandable urge to bring legal standards up to those of delicate morality should be resisted, or there would be no room for generosity or for people to go beyond the call of legal duty.'[14] The conservative commentator Dinesh D'Souza explains why this is so important:

> [Suppose] that I am walking down the street, eating a sandwich, when I am approached by a hungry man [who] wants to share my sandwich. Now if I give him the sandwich, I have done a good deed, and I feel good about it. The hungry man is grateful, and even if he cannot repay me

---

[10] See Tomlinson 2000 (demonstrating the uncertainty afflicting French law as a result of its recognising a general 'duty to rescue'). The law in Vermont states that a 'person who knows that another is exposed to grave physical harm shall, to the extent that the same can be rendered without danger or peril to himself or without interference with important duties owed to others, give reasonable assistance to the exposed person unless that assistance or care is being provided by others' (12 Vt. Stat. Ann. §519). It is easy to think up hypothetical situations where it is very uncertain whether someone would have a duty of care under this provision. For example, suppose B has fallen in the street and is bleeding from his head. Some people gather round B and ask him whether he is okay. A, a doctor, comes along. Is B exposed to 'grave physical harm' in this situation? – perhaps he is: perhaps his bleeding will worsen and he will die unless he is given treatment. Is A able to give him that assistance without danger or peril to himself? – perhaps he can't: perhaps B has AIDS and A will expose himself to the risk of infection by treating B's wounds. Is B already being provided with assistance or care by others? – perhaps not, if the people around him are not doing anything effective to help him. Weinrib 1980 suggests (at 268–79) that a general duty to rescue can be recognised without making the law uncertain if it is limited to cases where the potential rescuer could not, or could not easily, *charge* the person in danger for rescuing him. However, this assumes that the law on when someone can charge someone else for rescuing him from danger is relatively clear; but it is not.

[11] Epstein 1973, 198.

[12] Epstein 1973, 198–9. The examples involving the bridge and the life-saving operation are both found in Ames 1908.

[13] See Weinrib 1980, 247: 'No observer would have any difficulty outlining the current state of the law throughout the common-law world regarding the duty to rescue. Except when the person endangered and the potential rescuer are linked in a special relationship, there is no such duty.'

[14] Weir 2006, 1.

for my kindness, possibly he will try to help someone else when he has the chance. So this is a transaction that benefits the giver as well as the receiver. But see what happens [if the law *requires* me to give the hungry man my sandwich]. The government takes my sandwich from me by force. Consequently, I am a reluctant giver. The government then bestows my sandwich upon the hungry man. Instead of showing me gratitude, however, the man feels entitled to this benefit. In other words, the involvement of the [law] has utterly stripped the transaction of its moral value, even though the result is exactly the same.[15]

So compelling people to do the right thing gives people less space to engage in random acts of kindness that may result in them developing positive relationships with people that they do not otherwise know.[16] Of course, this does not mean that the law should be abolished and that everyone should be left free to choose in all circumstances whether or not to do the right thing. But it does mean that people need to be left *some* space to choose whether or not to do the right thing.[17]

(4) *Preserving autonomy.* There is another reason why it is important that there are some areas in people's lives where they are left alone to do what they like, without having to convince any legal official that what they have done or what they are proposing to do is reasonable. If the law required people to act reasonably *all the time*, then people would be deprived of any sense that their lives were genuinely their own. Instead of feeling that they were in some respects authors of their own lives, people would instead feel that they were simply living out their lives along lines that had been pre-programmed according to someone else's dictates. So – in order that people retain some sense of themselves as autonomous beings – there are some areas of people's lives that simply have to remain private and free from legal regulation.

(5) *Deterring rescue.* If the law is going to impose a duty on A to save B from harm, it has to be shown – at the very least – that imposing such a duty on A will actually benefit B. This may not always be the case.[18] Suppose that *Drunk* is drowning in a lake, and *Rambler* walks by and sees *Drunk*'s plight. If *Rambler* knows that he can be sued if he fails to rescue *Drunk*, that may not encourage him to try to save *Drunk*. It may have the opposite effect, of encouraging *Rambler* to walk on, and not do anything for *Drunk*, for fear that if he does try to help *Drunk*, he will merely bring attention to himself and expose himself to the risk of a lawsuit if anyone is unhappy with how quick or efficient his rescue efforts were. Better to walk on and disappear into the shadows where no one will be able to find him and blame him for what has happened to *Drunk*.

It is not fanciful to suggest that the existence of legally enforceable duties to rescue may actually put people off rescuing others. The need to allay the fears of would-be rescuers

---

[15] D'Souza 2002, 81–2.

[16] See, further, McBride 2006a, 29–31.

[17] For an identical argument in favour of the law's *not* enforcing all seriously made promises, see Kimel 2003.

[18] Hyman 2005 investigated whether the absence of a general duty to rescue in American law had an adverse effect on people's willingness to help others out. He counted only 16 examples of bystanders failing to rescue (in the absence of a statutory duty) in the United States between 1994 and 2004. (He combed the accounts in law texts, over 100 relevant law review articles, and all newspaper and magazine stories on LexisNexis®.) Hyman also sought to measure the relative incidence of voluntary rescue and non-rescue in the United States. Using data from organisations which provide awards for rescues he found that confirmed rescues outnumber non-rescues by about 740:1, and the risk of dying as a result of attempting a voluntary rescue is approximately 70 times higher than the risk of dying as a result of bystanders failing to offer assistance.

that 'no good deed goes unpunished' has led many American states to enact 'Good Samaritan laws' which typically provide that:

> Any person who, in good faith, renders emergency medical care or assistance to an injured person at the scene of an accident or other emergency without the expectation of receiving or intending to receive compensation from such injured person for such service, shall not be liable in civil damages for any act or omission, not constituting gross negligence, in the course of such care or assistance.

However, it is not clear that the existence of such laws would provide sufficient reassurance to would-be rescuers, particularly given that such laws do not apply in cases of 'gross negligence'.

(6) *Unfairness.* In *Stovin* v *Wise* (1996), Lord Hoffmann observed that one argument against the existence of general duties to rescue takes the form of a 'why pick on me?' argument.[19] This argument applies particularly strongly in the case where a large class of people were in a position to help B, but no one did. In this situation, if B suffers harm as a result of the fact that no one would come to his rescue, he will be entitled to sue *any* member of that class for *full* damages for the harm he has suffered. But if B chooses to sue A, a particular member of the class of people who failed to come to B's assistance, A will be entitled to think that it is unfair that he has been picked on to be sued, rather than anyone else who could have helped B. Of course, A could – after he has been held liable in full to B – bring a claim in contribution against everyone else who failed to help B. But this will be scant consolation if those people are untraceable or judgment-proof. In such a case, A will be entitled to think that the law has worked in a completely arbitrary way to fix him with a large part of the bill for what has happened to B. Such arbitrariness is avoided under a system where the mere fact that someone is in a position to save B from harm is not sufficient to give rise to a duty to rescue B.

(7) *Individual responsibility.* In cases where a human being is responsible for B's being in danger of suffering some kind of harm, the courts may be unwilling to recognise that a third party is under a duty to save B from that harm because doing so may end up allowing whoever was primarily responsible for putting B in harm's way to dilute his responsibility for what has happened.

Suppose, first of all, that it was B who put himself in danger of suffering some kind of harm. For example, suppose that *Curious* took some drugs and suffered a bad reaction to them. *Curious*'s *Housemate* failed to call for an ambulance because he was scared of getting into trouble with the authorities. As a result, *Curious* ended up brain-damaged. If we say that *Housemate* owed *Curious* a duty of care in this situation to summon assistance for him, *Curious* will be allowed to sue *Housemate* for compensation for his brain damage, subject to a deduction – for 'contributory negligence'[20] – to take account of the fact that *Curious* is partly responsible for the harm he has suffered. But – it might be argued – *Curious* should not be allowed to sue *Housemate at all* in this situation, because *Curious* is *wholly* to blame for what happened to him.

Suppose, secondly, that it was a third party who put B in danger of suffering some kind of harm. For example, suppose that *Vicious* and *Innocent* were walking home together by

---

[19] [1996] AC 923, 944.
[20] See below, § 23.5.

a river, and they got into an argument, and *Vicious* pushed *Innocent* into the river. *Innocent* could not swim and soon got into difficulties. *Vicious* called on *Passer-By*, to dive in and drag *Innocent* to shore, but *Passer-By* refused to do so. *Innocent* drowns. If we say that *Passer-By* owed *Innocent* a duty of care in this situation to go to his assistance, then if *Vicious* is held liable in a wrongful death action to compensate *Innocent*'s dependants for the loss of support that they suffered as a result of *Innocent*'s death,[21] *Vicious* will be able to bring a claim in contribution against *Passer-By*, arguing that as *Passer-By* is also liable for *Innocent*'s death, *Passer-By* must contribute his fair share to *Vicious*'s liability in this case. But – it might be argued – *Vicious* should not be allowed to sue *Passer-By at all* in this situation, because *Vicious* is *wholly* to blame for what happened to *Innocent*.

These arguments, taken together, make a compelling case for the law's refusing to find that private persons owe other people duties of care to rescue them from harm outside the exceptional circumstances that we will be setting out in the rest of this chapter.

C. Public bodies

While the law on when a private person will owe another a duty of care to rescue them from harm has been clear for many years, the same cannot be said of the law on when a *public body* will owe someone a duty of care to save them from harm. Until very recently, the law on this issue was very unsettled. Two different approaches to determining whether or not a public body owed a claimant a duty of care in an omissions case could be discerned in the caselaw.

(1) The first approach we will call the *uniform approach*. Under this approach, a public body should *not* be held to have owed a claimant a duty of care to save her from some harm *unless* a private person, equivalently situated, would have owed the claimant such a duty of care. This approach is most closely associated with Lord Hoffmann.[22] Speaking extra-judicially, he said:

> unless [a] statute creates an immunity from suit, expressly or by necessary implication, a public body owes a duty of care in such circumstances, and only in such circumstances, as a private body would have owed a duty. There are two sides to this coin. On the one side, if a public body does something which, if undertaken by a private body, would have created a duty of care, it will owe a similar duty of care. On the other side, the fact that a public body has statutory powers to do something, or even a public law duty, does not create a duty of care in circumstances in which a private body would have owed no such duty.

> public bodies owe no duty of care by virtue only of the fact that they have statutory powers or public law duties. An actual relationship with the claimant, such as would give rise to a duty of care on the part of a private body, is required. The effect is to take out of the law of negligence most questions of whether a public body has made the right decisions about how it should exercise its powers, that is to say, questions of administration.[23]

---

[21] See above, § 1.5, and below, § 28.1.

[22] See also constitutional scholar Albert Venn Dicey's articulation of the ideal of the 'rule of law', which meant (among other things): 'equality before the law, or the equal subjection of all classes to the ordinary law of the land administered by the ordinary law courts; the "rule of law" in this sense excludes the idea of any exemption of officials or others from the duty of obedience to the law which governs other citizens or from the jurisdiction of the ordinary tribunals' (Dicey 1908, 198).

[23] Hoffmann 2009, paras 6 and 15.

An excellent example of the *uniform approach* at work is the Court of Appeal's decision in *Capital & Counties plc* v *Hampshire CC* (1997). That case combined together four different appeals.

The first two appeals concerned a case where a fire brigade was called to put out a fire at a set of offices. When the fire brigade turned up, the fire was being kept under control by the sprinkler system in operation at the office building – but for some reason, the chief fire officer ordered that the sprinkler system be turned off. This resulted in the fire spreading rapidly and the building being destroyed. The Court of Appeal held the fire brigade *had* owed the lessees of the offices a duty of care not to turn off the sprinklers. Anyone else would have owed the same duty of care, given the foreseeable effect that the positive act of turning off the sprinklers would have on the spread of the fire, and there was no reason for exempting the fire brigade from that duty of care.

The final two appeals dealt with in *Capital & Counties* concerned cases where firefighters had failed to deal effectively with fires that started on the claimants' premises, with the result that the fires destroyed buildings on those premises. In dealing with these appeals, the Court of Appeal held that the firefighters had *not* owed the claimants a duty to take reasonable steps to put the fires out and as a result dismissed the claimants' claims in negligence for compensation for the loss of their buildings. As the Court of Appeal observed,

> In our judgment the fire brigade are not under a common law duty to answer the call for help, and are not under a duty to take care to do so. If, therefore, they fail to turn up, or fail to turn up in time, because they have carelessly misunderstood the message, got lost on the way or run into a tree, they are not liable.[24]

The decision is perfectly understandable under the *uniform approach*. Had the claimants asked their neighbours to help them put out the fires that had started in their buildings, the neighbours would not have owed the claimants a duty of care to help put out the fires. So, under the *uniform approach*, there was no basis for finding that the fire brigades in the last two appeals dealt with in *Capital & Counties* owed the claimants a duty of care to help save their buildings from being destroyed by fire.

(2) We will call the second approach the *policy approach*. Under this approach, the courts *will* find that a public body owed a claimant a duty of care to save her from harm *unless* there is some reason of public policy why it would be undesirable to find that the public body was subject to such a duty of care.

The *policy approach* first made an appearance in English law in the case of *Anns* v *Merton LBC* (1978). As we explained above,[25] *Anns* was clearly an 'omission' case. The defendant local authority in that case – by failing properly to inspect the foundations of the claimant's building while it was being constructed – had failed to save the claimants from suffering harm (in this case, the cost of making their building safe).

Lord Wilberforce suggested that the question of whether the defendant local authority had owed the claimants a duty of care to save them from the expense of putting their building right could be dealt with using a two-stage test:

> First one has to ask whether, as between the alleged wrongdoer and the person who has suffered damage there is a sufficient relationship of proximity or neighbourhood such that, in the reasonable contemplation of the former, carelessness on his part may be likely to cause damage to the

---

[24] [1997] QB 1004, 1030.
[25] § 6.1(A).

latter – in which case a prima facie duty of care arises. Secondly, if the first question is answered affirmatively, it is necessary to consider whether there are any considerations which ought to negative, or to reduce or limit the scope of the duty or the class of person to whom it was owed or the damages to which a breach of it may give rise . . .[26]

Obviously the first stage was easily satisfied: it was obvious that failing to ensure that the foundations were properly constructed would result in harm to the claimants. So everything turned on whether there were any policy considerations that militated against recognising that the local authority in *Anns* had owed the claimants a duty of care. Not being able to find any, Lord Wilberforce held that the defendants had owed the claimants a duty of care properly to inspect the foundations.

As we have already observed,[27] in the 1980s, the courts disowned the *Anns* test for determining whether or not a defendant owed the claimant a duty of care, and the fall of the *Anns* test meant that the *policy approach* to determining whether or not a public body owed a claimant a duty of care to save her from suffering some kind of harm was eclipsed. However, legal academics – who, for some reason, were generally in love with the idea of holding public bodies liable for omissions across the board[28] – would not let the *policy approach* die, and insisted on interpreting all cases subsequent to *Anns* that refused to hold public bodies liable in negligence for omissions as 'really' giving effect to the *policy approach* and as 'really' based on policy concerns. The academic treatment of the House of Lords' decision in *Hill* v *Chief Constable of West Yorkshire* (1989) provides a good example of this.

In the *Hill* case, the House of Lords had to decide whether the police were liable in negligence for failing to catch the 'Yorkshire Ripper' (Peter Sutcliffe) before he killed Jacqueline Hill, the last of 13 women that Peter Sutcliffe killed. The leading judgment (which three of the other four Law Lords deciding the case agreed with), denying that the police owed Jacqueline Hill a duty of care to apprehend Peter Sutcliffe, was delivered by Lord Keith of Kinkel. His decision is made up of 15 paragraphs. The first 14 paragraphs denied that the police had owed Jacqueline Hill a duty of care on the basis that in *Hill* there existed no

> special characteristics or ingredients beyond reasonable foreseeability of likely harm which may result in civil liability for failure to control another man to prevent his doing harm to a third.[29]

As a basis for denying that the police owed Jacqueline Hill a duty of care, this is perfectly explicable under the *uniform approach* – just as a private individual would not have owed Jacqueline Hill a duty of care to save her from being killed by Peter Sutcliffe in the absence of special circumstances, neither could the police have owed her such a duty of care in the absence of such special circumstances.

Lord Keith could not have made it clearer that it was the absence of such special circumstances that was the reason why he was denying that the police owed Jacqueline Hill a duty of care: in the first sentence of the last paragraph of his speech, he expressly said, 'That is sufficient for the disposal of the appeal.'[30] However, he then went on to observe that there were various policy reasons why it would be undesirable to allow the police to be sued for failing to catch criminals: (1) doing so would add nothing to the current incentives the police have to do a good job of catching criminals; (2) the possibility of being sued might

---

[26] [1978] AC 728, 751–752.
[27] See above, § 4.2(B).
[28] Weir 1989 was an outstanding exception.
[29] [1989] 1 AC 53, 62.
[30] [1989] 1 AC 53, 63.

result in the police acting 'defensively' in investigating crimes; (3) holding the police liable in negligence for failing to catch criminals might result in the courts having to deal with issues about the adequacy of a police investigation that they were incompetent to deal with; and (4) resolving such issues would take up a great deal of the police's time and money.

The legal academic reception of the *Hill* decision was revealing. The decision in *Hill* was taken: (1) to rest entirely on policy considerations; and (2) to establish that the police had an 'immunity' from being sued in negligence for failing to investigate crime properly. As we have just seen, (1) was not true. Neither was (2): there was nothing for the police to be immune from: there was no rule that would ordinarily make them liable to Jacqueline Hill that they were being exempted from. However, someone who believes that we should adopt the *policy approach* to determining whether a public body owed a claimant a duty of care to save her from harm will end up endorsing both (1) and (2). Under the *policy approach*, policy considerations could have been the only basis for refusing to find that the police owed Jacqueline Hill a duty of care. And under the *policy approach*, in denying that the police had owed Jacqueline Hill a duty of care, the House of Lords *was* exempting the police from the duty of care that they *would* have owed her had considerations of policy not intervened to let them off the hook.

The *policy approach* was kept alive by the academics throughout the 1980s and re-entered the judicial mainstream in the mid-1990s via Sir Thomas Bingham MR (as he then was), who in a Court of Appeal case – that went on to be heard by the House of Lords under the name *X* v *Bedfordshire CC* (1995) – concerning a local authority's errors when seeking to protect a child from being sexually abused, remarked that in determining whether the local authority owed the child a duty of care

> it would require very potent considerations of public policy, which do not in my view exist here, to override the rule of public policy which has first claim on the loyalty of the law: that wrongs should be remedied.[31]

We have already noted how question-begging this is, as a factor to be taken into account in determining whether or not a defendant owed a claimant a duty of care, because the whole issue at stake in such an inquiry is whether the defendant has actually done anything wrong to the claimant.[32] However, Sir Thomas Bingham MR's statement effectively revived the *policy approach* to determining whether or not a public body owed a claimant a duty of care to save her from harm: any judge who invoked Sir Thomas Bingham MR's statement in deciding such a case was basically proclaiming that the claimant should be allowed to sue the public body (and therefore that the public body should be held to have owed the claimant a duty of care) unless there existed 'very potent considerations of public policy' why the claimant's claim should be turned down. The very first example of this happening was provided by *X* v *Bedfordshire County Council* itself when it went to the House of Lords.

The case could have been decided on the *uniform* basis that if a private individual who was in a position to know that a child (say, living next door) was being sexually abused did not owe the child a duty of care to save it from being abused, then the local authority in whose area the child lived could not owe that child a duty of care either. However, Lord Browne-Wilkinson, delivering the leading judgment, expressed his agreement with Lord Bingham that

---

[31] [1995] 2 AC 633, 663.
[32] See above, § 4.3(L). See also Hoffmann 2009, at para 20: 'I yield to no one in my admiration for Lord Bingham, but I am bound to say that is as question-begging a statement as you could find.'

the public policy consideration which has first claim on the loyalty of the law is that wrongs should be remedied and that very potent counter-considerations are required to override that policy . . . However, in my judgment there are such considerations in this case.[33]

As we will see, the decision to deny that a duty of care was owed in *X* v *Bedfordshire CC* on grounds of public policy was later on to have fateful implications for the scope of local authorities' duties of care towards children who were being sexually abused in their area.[34]

The table below sets out a timeline of cases which dealt with the issue of whether a public body owed a claimant a duty of care to save her from harm, and classifies them according to whether they the court's approach to that question was based on the *uniform approach* or on the *policy approach*.

Uniform approach	Policy approach
East Suffolk Rivers Catchment Board v *Kent* (1941) (river authority that takes on the job of repairing a sea wall owes no duty to repair the wall expeditiously to farmer whose land will be flooded until the sea wall is properly repaired)	
	Anns v *Merton LBC* (1978) (local authority that decides to inspect foundations of building has duty to inspect them with reasonable skill and care)
Yuen Kun Yeu v *Att-Gen for Hong Kong* (1988) (Commissioner maintaining register of deposit-taking banks does not have a duty of care to ensure that only well-run banks are on register)	
Hill v *Chief Constable of West Yorkshire* (1989) (no duty of care on police in investigating crimes)	*X* v *Bedfordshire CC* (1995) (no duty of care on local authorities to save children from being abused because important they should be left free to decide how to deal with such cases without threat of being sued hanging over them)
Stovin v *Wise* (1996) (no duty of care on highway authority to flatten roadside bank of earth that obscured line of vision at junction)	
Capital & Counties plc v *Hampshire CC* (1997) (no duty of care to fight fires effectively or even turn up to fight them after having accepted 999 call)	
	Hussain v *Lancaster CC* (2000) (no duty of care on local authority to prevent tenants racially harassing claimant as proving fault on the part of the local authority would involve courts in intractable issues)
	Kent v *Griffiths* (2001) (duty of care on ambulance service that has accepted 999 call to pick up and take patient to hospital reasonably quickly)
Gorringe v *Calderdale MBC* (2004) (no duty of care on highway authority to tell motorists to slow down at bend in the road)	

---

[33] [1995] 2 AC 633, 749.
[34] See below, § 6.11(3).

Uniform approach	Policy approach
	D v *East Berkshire NHS Trust* (CA) (2004) (finding of no duty of care in *X* v *Bedfordshire CC* overturned as prospect of being sued under Human Rights Act 1998 now means decisions about whether to intervene and what to do with at-risk children are always being made under cloud of potential litigation)
	Van Colle v *Chief Constable of Hertfordshire Police, Smith* v *Chief Constable of Sussex Police* (2009) (in *Smith* case, no duty of care on police to protect man against being attacked by ex-lover as finding such a duty of care would unduly bias police towards prioritising cases where an identified person claimed they might be the victim of violence over other cases)
Furnell v *Flaherty* (2013) (no duty of care on Heath Protection Agency or district council to protect visitors to animal petting zoo against outbreak of e. coli disease)	
	Smith v *Ministry of Defence* (2014) (policy concerns about courts dictating to military how much it should spend on safety equipment and training do not make it unarguable that military owed duty of care to soldiers injured due to alleged lack of proper armour or training)

As you can see, the caselaw was fundamentally divided over the issue of whether the *uniform approach* or the *policy approach* was the right approach to adopt in determining whether a public body owed a claimant a duty of care to save her from harm. Finally, in one of the handful of negligence cases that truly deserves the appellation 'great' – *Michael* v *Chief Constable of South Wales Police* (2015)[35] – the UK Supreme Court had the chance to rule on which approach was the correct approach.

In *Michael*, Joanna Michael – who lived in a town called St Mellons, near the south coast of Wales – made a 999 call to the police at 2.29 am. Her ex-partner, Cyron Williams, had discovered her in bed with another man, had hit her, taken the man away to drive him into town, and had said he would be coming back. Joanna's call was misrouted and was picked up by a police operator, Ms Mason, who was working for Gwent Police, in the county neighbouring the county where Joanna was based. Joanna explained what had happened, and at some point said that Williams was going to kill her. Mason told Joanna that she would let the police force in Joanna's area know about her call, and that she should stay off the phone as the police would want to call her back. Joanna hung up. Mason logged the call as a 'Grade 1' call, requiring an 'immediate' response, which would mean the police getting to Joanna's front door within five minutes of Joanna's hanging up. But when Mason talked to the call handler – a Mr Gould – who was dealing with 999 calls in the South Wales area, where Joanna was based, Mason failed to mention that Joanna was in fear of her life. Gould therefore logged the call as a 'Grade 2' call, requiring a 'priority' response, which meant the police should aim to get to Joanna's

---

[35] [2015] AC 1732 (henceforth, '*Michael*').

front door within an hour of her calling the police. As a result, the police had still not arrived at Joanna's by the time she made another 999 call at 2.43 am, which was also misrouted to the Gwent police, rather than the South Wales police. This time, screaming was heard on the line and Joanna's case was upgraded to one requiring an 'immediate' response. However, by the time the police arrived at Joanna's house at 2.51 am (22 minutes after Joanna's first call), they found that she had been stabbed to death by Williams.

Joanna's family sued the South Wales and Gwent police forces, alleging – among other things – that they had owed Joanna a duty of care in the way they handled her call. The case was tailor-made for a final showdown between the *uniform* and *policy approaches* to whether a public body will owe someone a duty of care to save them from harm. On the *uniform approach*, it was hard to make a case for saying that Joanna was owed a duty of care in *Michael*. As we will see, none of the established categories of situation where a private person would owe someone else a duty of care seemed to exist in Joanna's case. By contrast, on the *policy approach*, it seemed obvious that Joanna *was* owed a duty of care. The operational nature of the failures in Joanna's case – the fact that by the police's own procedures, they failed Joanna – meant that it was hard to see a policy reason why the police should *not* be found to have owed Joanna a duty of care.

By a 5:2 majority, the UK Supreme Court ruled decisively and clearly in favour of adopting the *uniform* approach, and declined to find that the police had owed Joanna Michael a duty of care. Lord Toulson gave the majority judgment and immediately established his *uniform* credentials by deprecating as 'unfortunate'[36] the habit of saying that the decision of the House of Lords in *Hill* v *Chief Constable of West Yorkshire Police* (1989) meant that the police enjoy some kind of 'immunity' from being sued in negligence when they fail to protect a victim of crime. As he pointed out: 'An "immunity" is generally understood to be an exemption based on a defendant's status from liability imposed by the law on others'.[37] He went on to observe that:

> The refusal of the courts to impose a private law duty on the police to exercise reasonable care to safeguard victims or potential victims of crime, except in cases where there has been a representation and reliance, does not involve giving special treatment to the police . . . The question is not whether the police should have a special immunity, but whether an exception should be made to the ordinary application of common law principles which would cover the facts of the present case.[38]

Lord Toulson declined to find that the police owed Joanna Michael a special duty of care, based either on the fact that they were aware that her life was in danger,[39] or that Joanna had given the police information that meant that they were aware that there was a 'specific and imminent' threat to her safety.[40] Lord Toulson thought that finding that the police

---

[36] *Michael*, at [44].

[37] Ibid.

[38] *Michael*, at [115]–[116].

[39] Lord Toulson called this the 'intervener's liability principle' in *Michael*, at [18](1). Lady Hale favoured finding a duty of care on this basis in her dissenting judgment in *Michael*, at [197].

[40] This was the basis on which Lord Bingham would have found a duty of care in the *Smith* case in the conjoined appeals of *Van Colle* v *Chief Constable of Hertfordshire Police*, *Smith* v *Chief Constable of Sussex Police* [2009] 1 AC 225, but which was rejected by his fellow four Law Lords on policy grounds; it was also the basis, with some changes in language, on which Lord Kerr would have favoured finding a duty of care in his dissenting speech in *Michael* at [144], read with [168].

had owed Joanna Michael a duty of care on either of these bases would be arbitrary.[41] But his more fundamental objection to finding that the police had owed a duty of care in *Michael* when an equivalently situated private person would not have owed such a duty of care was that:

> it is one thing for a public authority to provide a service at the public expense, and quite another to require the public to pay compensation when a failure to provide the service has resulted in a loss. Apart from possible cases involving reliance on a representation by the authority, the same loss would have been suffered if the service had not been provided in the first place, and to require payment of compensation would impose an additional burden on public funds.[42]

> It does not follow from the setting up of a protective system from public resources that if it fails to achieve its purpose, through organisational defects or fault on the part of an individual, the public at large should bear the additional burden of compensating a victim for harm caused by the actions of a third party for whose behaviour the state is not responsible.[43]

The decision in *Michael* represents a shattering defeat for the *policy approach* to determining whether a public body owed a claimant a duty of care to save her, an approach which undoubtedly underlay the judgments of the two dissentients in *Michael*, Lord Kerr and Lady Hale.[44] The *Michael* case has settled for a generation[45] to come that the correct approach in determining whether a public body owed a claimant a duty of care to save her from harm is the *uniform* approach: you simply ask whether the case falls into one of the categories of situation where a private person would owe a claimant a duty of care to save them from harm. If it does not, then – absent absolutely compelling grounds for finding a duty of care and creating a new category of situation where a duty of care will be owed – then the public body will not have owed the claimant a duty of care. However, two questions remain.

---

[41] *Michael*, at [119]–[120], [129], and [137].

[42] *Michael*, at [110], summarising the reasoning of Lord Hoffmann in *Stovin v Wise* [1996] AC 923.

[43] *Michael*, at [114].

[44] See, for example, *Michael*, at [161] (per Lord Kerr): 'Put bluntly, what one group of judges [namely, the four majority Law Lords in the conjoined *Van Colle* and *Smith* appeals in [2009] 1 AC 225] felt was the correct policy answer in 2009, should not bind another group of judges even as little as five years later' and at [189] (per Lady Hale): 'In what circumstances can the police owe a duty of care to protect an individual member of the public from harm caused by a third party? There are said to be two objections to imposing such a duty' – so no need to make any case *for* finding a duty of care; the only issue is whether there is an objection to finding a duty. Some indication of just how intellectually shattering the defeat of the policy approach in *Michael* was can be gleaned from the fact that neither of the 'objections' listed by Lady Hale to finding a duty of care in a *Michael*-type case are actually objections: they are simply statements as to when one person will owe another a duty of care.

[45] Though some seem not to have received the message. See the egregious – in light of the decision in *Michael* – decision of the Court of Appeal in *ABC v St George's Healthcare NHS Foundation Trust* [2017] EWCA Civ 336 where the claimant sued the defendant health authority for failing to tell her that her father – who was being treated by the defendants – had Huntington's Disease and that she therefore had a 50 per cent chance of having it herself. As it turned out, the claimant *did* have Huntington's Disease and sued the defendants, claiming that had she known she had the disease, she would never have had a child as a single parent because her diagnosis meant that the child was very likely to be orphaned at a young age. Egged on by counsel for the *defendants*, the Court of Appeal resolved the question of whether the claimant's claim should be struck out by considering nine policy reasons why the defendants should *not* be found to have owed the claimant a duty of care (and held that the claim should not be struck out because none of the policy considerations were convincing). On the uniform approach, the claim should have been dismissed in the absence of proof of any special circumstances existing between the claimant and the defendants – an ordinary individual who found out about the claimant's father's condition would not have owed the claimant a duty of care to tell her, so why should the defendants?

(1) *Why the uniform approach?* If you go back through the various reasons advanced above[46] in favour of the law's restrictive approach to finding that private persons owe other people duties of care to rescue them from harm, it is a striking fact that none of them seem to apply with any or much force when a public body, such as the police in *Michael*, is in a position to save someone from harm. For example, finding that the police owed a duty of care in *Michael* would not have unacceptably intruded on the police's freedom as the police are not supposed to be free to ignore the plight of people like Joanna Michael.[47] So why should we apply the rules that determine when a private person will owe another a duty of care to save someone from harm to a public body, when the reasons for refusing to find that private people owe general duties of care to save people from harm do not apply to public bodies?[48]

A variation on Lord Hoffmann's 'why pick on me?' argument can be made in favour of treating public bodies and private persons the same, even though the reasons for the law's treating private persons in the way it does do not apply to public bodies. The argument is that it would be wrong for the law to treat public bodies and public servants worse than it does private persons. If the law did that, then it would be effectively punishing the state for trying to do good, and employees of the state for choosing a life of public service over one of self-interest. The cynical saying 'no good deed goes unpunished' would become a legal principle. If, for example, *Michael* had gone the other way and found that Mason owed Joanna Michael a duty of care to handle her call properly, Mason might have been entitled to ask, 'Why pick on me? – Why subject me to a legal duty and possible legal action if people are unhappy with my efforts to save others from harm, when the law does not touch all those people who have, unlike me, decided to dedicate their lives to pursuing their own self-interest?'[49]

(2) *What about the Human Rights Act 1998?* We have already seen that public bodies can be routinely sued under the Human Rights Act 1998 ('HRA') if they carelessly fail to save an identified individual who they know or ought to know is in imminent danger of being killed or injured or being subjected to inhuman or degrading treatment.[50] Indeed, in *Michael*, the UK Supreme Court allowed a claim by Joanna Michael's family against the police under the HRA to proceed on precisely that basis.[51] So if public bodies can be sued for omissions under the HRA, why should they not also be liable for omissions under the law of negligence? Three points can be made about this.[52]

First, it can be argued that the European Court of Human Rights made a mistake in developing an understanding of the human rights that we enjoy against the state that not only means we have rights against the state that it not do evil to us, but also

---

[46] See above, § 5.1(B).

[47] Indeed, both of the call operators who dealt with Joanna Michael's case were put on disciplinary charges after her death; in Ms Mason's case, she was charged with gross misconduct.

[48] It is not clear whether even on a Kantian approach we could justify refusing to impose widespread duties of care to rescue people from harm on public bodies: if public bodies have no right to independence, then the usual Kantian objection to coercing defendants to help other people out does not apply to public bodies.

[49] The point becomes even more acute when it is realised that if Mason had been found to have owed Joanna Michael a duty of care, she might have been exposed to the possibility of being prosecuted for gross negligence manslaughter and imprisoned.

[50] See above, § 1.8

[51] *Michael*, at [139] (per Lord Toulson).

[52] See, further, Nolan 2013b.

rights that the state do good things for us. If this is a mistake, it would compound the mistake to allow claimants to sue in negligence for omissions that are actionable under the HRA.

Secondly, when Parliament enacted the HRA, it must have done so on the understanding that it was thereby committing the UK state to being held liable in certain circumstances for its failures to save people from harm. So when the courts find a public body liable under the HRA for a failure to act, it is at least giving effect to Parliament's intentions in doing so. But the judges, in developing the common law of negligence, are acting on their own initiative and cannot claim any Parliamentary *imprimatur* for what they are doing. Given this, the existence of liability for omissions under the HRA cannot give the courts any warrant for extending the scope of liability under the common law of negligence.

Thirdly, when Parliament enacted the HRA, it placed strict limits on the ability of claimants to bring claims under the HRA. Most importantly, such claims normally have to be brought within one year of the 'date on which the act complained of took place.'[53] This limit on the ability of claimants to sue the state under the HRA would be completely undermined if the courts developed the law of negligence (to which more generous limitation periods apply)[54] to allow claimants to sue in negligence for failures to act which are actionable under the HRA. This last consideration has led the UK's highest court twice to refuse point-blank to develop the common law of negligence to allow claims in negligence to be brought for omissions in parallel to claims under the HRA. As Lord Toulson observed in the *Michael* case:

> On orthodox common law principles I cannot see a legal basis for . . . gold plating the claimant's Convention rights by providing compensation on a different basis from the claim under the Human Rights Act 1998.[55]

We will now set out the various situations in which one person *will* owe another a duty of care to save them from harm.

In setting out these situations, we will not only be drawing on tort cases, but criminal law cases as well. This is because while criminal liability normally only attaches to *acts*, a *wrongful failure to act* will be treated as the equivalent of an act under the criminal law, and criminal lawyers' notions of when a criminal defendant will be under a duty to act are drawn from the law of tort, and the law of negligence in particular.[56] Some academics who specialise in the criminal law are resistant to the idea that the criminal law owes anything to the law of tort. But in cases where the issue is raised whether the defendant was under a duty to act, what other area of law can the criminal lawyers look to, to tell them the answer to this question?

The dependence of this area of the criminal law on the law of tort is made clear by the Corporate Manslaughter and Corporate Homicide Act 2007, which provides that a corporation will commit an offence 'if the way in which its activities are managed or

---

[53] Human Rights Act 1998, s 7(5)(a).

[54] See below, § 22.11.

[55] *Michael*, at [125]. See also the earlier remarks in *Van Colle* v *Chief Constable of Hertfordshire Police, Smith* v *Chief Constable of Sussex Police* [2009] 1 AC 225, at [82] (per Lord Hope), [104] (per Lord Carswell), [138]–[139] (per Lord Brown).

[56] See *R* v *Adomako* [1995] 1 AC 171, at 187 (per Lord Mackay): 'the ordinary principles of the law of negligence apply to ascertain whether or not the defendant has been in breach of a duty of care towards the victim who has died.'

organised – (a) causes a person's death, and (b) amounts to a gross breach of a relevant duty of care owed by the organisation to the deceased'[57] and a 'relevant duty of care' is defined as any of a limited range of 'duties owed by it under the law of *negligence*'.[58] But it is not the relatively recent 2007 Act that tends to provide the richest source of criminal caselaw on when one person will owe another a duty to save that other from harm. It is, rather, the much more well-established offence of *gross negligence manslaughter* that provides that. A defendant will be held to have committed the offence of gross negligence manslaughter if he causes another's death by breaching a duty of care owed to that other and his conduct in breaching that duty of care was so outrageous that it is worthy of punishment.[59] Clearly, in *any* case where a defendant is charged with gross negligence manslaughter for *failing* to assist someone who was in danger of dying, his guilt will crucially depend on whether the courts are willing to find that he owed the deceased a duty of care – and the courts, in deciding that issue, will inevitably have to fall back on the law of negligence's conception of when one person will owe another a duty to save them from harm.[60]

6.2 Assumption of responsibility

The first situation where the courts will find that one person will owe another a duty to act should be very familiar to us: it is the situation where A 'assumes a responsibility' to B to protect B's welfare in some way.

Such an 'assumption of responsibility' will characteristically take one of two forms. *Either* A will have indicated to B that B can rely on A to look after B's interests with a reasonable degree of care and skill and B will have relied on A to do this. *Or* A will have indicated to B that B can rely on A to take reasonable steps to protect B from some kind of harm and B will have relied on A to do this.

It is the first kind of assumption of responsibility that underlies a doctor's duty to treat his patient with a reasonable degree of care and skill.[61] The UK Supreme Court declined to find that the second kind of assumption of responsibility existed on the facts of *Michael* v *Chief Constable of South Wales Police* (2015) on the ground that 'The only assurance which the call handler gave to Ms Michael was that she would pass on the call to the South Wales Police. She gave no promise as to how quickly they would respond.'[62]

---

[57] Section 1(1).

[58] Section 2(1) (emphasis added).

[59] *R* v *Adomako* [1995] 1 AC 171.

[60] For general discussion of how the courts determine whether or not a duty of care was owed in a gross negligence manslaughter case, see Herring and Palser 2007.

[61] It was held in *Airedale NHS Trust* v *Bland* [1993] AC 789 that a doctor's positive duty to treat his patient with reasonable skill and care did not extend to requiring the doctor to feed and keep a hydrated a patient in a permanent vegetative state (that is, a patient who has enough brain functioning to keep his organs functioning but not to maintain consciousness) where being kept alive is not in the patient's 'best interests'. The same does not apply to a patient who is conscious and has expressed a wish to be given food and water – except in the situation where the patient is on the brink of death anyway, a doctor cannot conclude that it is in the patient's 'best interests' to be allowed to slip away and not give the patient any food or water: see *R (Burke)* v *General Medical Council* [2006] QB 273.

[62] *Michael*, at [138] (per Lord Toulson).

However, there are a number of cases where the second type of assumption of responsibility has given rise to a duty of care to save someone from harm:[63]

1. *Stansbie* v *Troman* (1948): the defendant decorator (in breach of undertakings he had made to the claimant) left the claimant's front door unlocked when he went to the shops to buy some wallpaper, thereby allowing thieves to enter the house and steal valuables worth almost £10,000 in today's money.

2. *Welsh* v *Chief Constable of Merseyside Police* (1993): the claimant was arrested for failing to attend the magistrates' court to be tried for two theft offences that he had already told the Crown Prosection Service ('CPS') he had committed and asked to be taken into account in sentencing him for some other criminal offences he had been found guilty of. It was held that it was strongly arguable that the CPS owed the claimant a duty of care to tell the magistrates that they were dealing with the theft offences given that the claimant had been given to understand the CPS would do this.[64]

3. *Swinney* v *Chief Constable of the Northumbria Police* (1997): the claimant informed on T to the police, telling them that T was involved in killing a police officer. The claimant was assured by the police that his identity would be kept secret but T learned of the claimant's identity when documents including the claimant's name were stolen from a police car. T then threatened the claimant and the claimant developed a psychiatric illness. It was held it was strongly arguable that the police had owed the claimant a duty of care to keep his identity secret.[65]

4. *Densmore* v *Whitehorse* (1986):[66] a fire started in the claimant's house. The claimant rang the fire department and was told a fire engine would be on its way; but none was actually sent and the claimant's house and its contents were destroyed. The Yukon Territory Supreme Court held that the fire department had owed the claimant a duty to take reasonable steps to get a fire engine to her house because she had relied on the fire department to take such steps by not doing anything to save the contents of her house – by, for example, throwing selected items out of the window or carrying them out of the house – while she was waiting for the fire engine to turn up.[67]

A crucial feature of the Yukon Territory Supreme Court's willingness to find a duty of care in *Densmore* was the fact that the claimant had *relied* on the fire department to send

---

[63] In addition to the cases cited in the text, see also *Personal Representatives of the Estate of Biddick (Deceased)* v *Morcom* [2014] EWCA Civ 182 (defendant undertook to hold entry hatch to loft in place while the claimant fixed some insulating material to the other side of the hatch; defendant then left his position to take a phone call and the claimant fell through the hatch; held that the defendant had owed the claimant a duty of care to hold the hatch door in place).

[64] It is quite clear that if the CPS had *not* indicated to the claimant that they could be safely relied on to take reasonable steps to inform the magistrates of his conviction, they would not have owed him a duty to take any steps to inform the magistrates of his conviction: *Elguzouli-Daf* v *Commissioner of the Police of the Metropolis* [1995] QB 335.

[65] When the case went to trial, the judge (Jackson J) found that the police had indeed owed the claimant a duty to take reasonable steps to see that T did not find out that she had informed on him. However, the claimant's claim was dismissed on the ground that the police had not breached that duty of care. See *Swinney* v *Chief Constable of Northumbria Police (No 2)*, The Times, 25 May 1999.

[66] Discussed, Bagshaw 1999.

[67] But query whether she should have been confined to suing the defendant fire department for the value of the items she could have saved but for the fire department's misleading assurance: see, ibid.

a fire engine to her house. This element of reliance will be missing in most fire cases – if your house is burning down, there is very little you yourself will be able to do about it, and so an assurance that a fire engine is on its way will make very little difference to what you do after you receive that assurance. But could a duty to act arise simply in response to the fact that a defendant has *undertaken* or *promised* to do something for the claimant, where that undertaking or promise has *not* induced the claimant to rely on the defendant in any way?

Robert Stevens thinks the answer is 'yes': 'Doctors are entitled to walk past the sick, but if a sign is put up saying "Public Hospital" a duty has been assumed that care will be taken of those who turn up expecting treatment.'[68] The example is not a good one: those who have turned up expecting treatment might have gone elsewhere but for the sign saying 'Public Hospital'. They have therefore relied on the hospital's general indication to all and sundry that the hospital will take reasonable steps to treat them. A clearer case of non-reliance is presented by the **Unconscious Man Problem**:

> *Doctor*, is on his way to meet his girlfriend for dinner. As he passes by an alleyway, he sees *Drunk*, lying unconscious on the ground. *Doctor* goes to attend to *Drunk*, but after he has taken *Drunk*'s pulse and checked that he is breathing regularly, *Doctor*'s mobile phone goes off. It is *Doctor*'s girlfriend, demanding to know where he is. *Doctor* rushes off to meet his girlfriend without doing anything more to look after *Drunk*. Half an hour later, *Drunk* throws up and chokes on his own vomit and dies because he has not been placed in the right position to stop this happening.

Did *Doctor* owe *Drunk* a duty to take reasonable steps to make him better? Robert Stevens thinks he did: 'the duty of a doctor who assumes responsibility towards a patient [can arise] even though the [patient] is wholly ignorant of the undertaking.'[69] There are some *dicta* which support this position.[70] The decision of the Court of Appeal in *Kent* v *Griffiths* (2001) could also be taken as supporting Stevens' position.

In that case, the claimant suffered an asthma attack. Her doctor came to see her and it was decided that she had to be taken to hospital. The doctor rang the London Ambulance Service (LAS) and they told her they would send an ambulance along to take the claimant to hospital. No ambulance had arrived 13 minutes later, so the claimant's husband rang the

---

[68] Stevens 2007, 11, citing *Barnett* v *Chelsea & Kensington Hospital Management Committee* [1969] 1 QB 428. In that case, three workmen presented themselves to a casualty department, complaining that they were feeling sick. The nurse on duty rang the doctor on call, and he advised that they should go home and consult their own doctors. They were in fact suffering from arsenic poisoning from drinking contaminated tea and one of them died five hours later. There is nothing in the facts of this case that supports Stevens' radical position: the nurse and doctor on duty clearly assumed a responsibility to the men to treat them with reasonable skill and care.

[69] Stevens 2007, 12.

[70] *Banbury* v *Bank of Montreal* [1918] AC 626, 689 (per Lord Atkinson): 'It is well established that if a doctor proceeded to treat a patient gratuitously, even in a case where the patient was insensible at the time and incapable of employing him, the doctor would be bound to exercise all the professional skill and knowledge he possessed, or professed to possess, and would be guilty of gross negligence if he omitted to do so'; *Hedley Byrne & Co Ltd* v *Heller and Partners* [1964] AC 465, 495 (per Lord Morris): 'A medical man may unexpectedly come across an unconscious man, who is a complete stranger to him, and who is in urgent need of skilled attention: if the medical man, following the fine traditions of his profession, proceeds to treat the unconscious man he must exercise reasonable skill and care in doing so.'

LAS to be told that the ambulance would be another seven or eight minutes. But still no ambulance came. Twenty-nine minutes after the original call, the claimant's doctor rang the LAS and was told the ambulance would be there in a couple of minutes. It took five more minutes for the ambulance to turn up. The claimant arrived in hospital 46 minutes after the original call, and promptly suffered a respiratory arrest which resulted in her suffering a miscarriage, a change of personality, and serious memory impairment. A shameful tale, made worse by the fact that had the LAS gotten the claimant to hospital within a reasonable period of time, the treatment she would have received there would have prevented her suffering a respiratory arrest. The Court of Appeal held that the LAS had owed the claimant a duty to take reasonable steps to get her to hospital reasonably quickly. Lord Woolf MR held that 'The acceptance of the call in this case established the duty of care.'[71]

On the other hand, in *The Ogopogo* (1970), Schroeder JA, in the Ontario Court of Appeal, said that 'even if a person embarks upon a rescue and does not carry it through, he is not under any liability to the person to whose aid he had come so long as discontinuance of his efforts did not leave the other in a worse condition than when he took charge.'[72] And in *Capital & Counties Plc* v *Hampshire CC* (1997), Stuart-Smith LJ held that: 'If [a passing doctor] volunteers his assistance [to help the victim of a traffic accident], his only duty as a matter of law is [to take care] not to make the victim's condition worse.'[73]

We prefer Schroeder JA's and Stuart-Smith LJ's view, for a reason which should by now be familiar. If we find that the mere undertaking to act to help someone else gives rise to a duty of care to make good on that undertaking, the effect will be to penalise those who try to help others. It cannot be right to say that, in Unconscious Man, *Doctor* owed *Drunk* a duty of care to make him better when, if *Doctor* had ignored *Drunk* and not done anything to help him, he would not have owed *Drunk* a duty of care at all. Lords Morris and Atkinson were simply wrong. The better view of *Kent* v *Griffiths* (2001) is that Lord Woolf MR was *not* saying in that case that a bare undertaking to assist someone else can give rise to a duty of care. Lord Woolf was a liberal judge who was instinctively in favour of finding that the emergency services owe people in need a duty to save them from harm, unless some good reason can be shown why such a duty should not be recognised. For Lord Woolf, the acceptance of the call in *Kent* v *Griffiths* was not a reason *for* finding that there existed a duty of care in that case; the acceptance of the call meant there was *no* reason why a duty of care should *not* be found in that case:

> An important feature of this case is that there is no question of an ambulance not being available or of a conflict in priorities . . . [O]nce there are available, both in the form of an ambulance and in the form of manpower, the resources to provide an ambulance on which there are no alternative demands, the ambulance service would be acting perversely . . . if it did not make those resources available. Having decided to provide an ambulance an explanation is required to justify a failure to attend within reasonable time.[74]

---

[71] [2001] QB 36, at [49].

[72] [1970] 1 Lloyd's Rep 257, 263. The case was appealed to the Supreme Court of Canada, but the Supreme Court found it unnecessary to deal with the issue raised by Schroeder JA's *dictum*: [1971] 2 Lloyd's Rep 410.

[73] [1997] QB 1004, 1035. See also the case of *X and Y* v *London Borough of Hounslow* [2009] EWCA Civ 286, where it was held that the defendant council had not assumed a responsibility for the safety of the two claimants in that case (both adults with learning disabilities who were bullied and sexually abused by strangers whom they had welcomed into their flat), even though the council's social services department was regularly visiting the claimants, and generally trying to take steps to secure their welfare.

[74] [2001] QB 36, at [47].

This kind of reasoning was completely repudiated by the UK Supreme Court in *Michael* v *Chief Constable of South Wales Police* (2015). However, that does not mean the Court of Appeal was *wrong* to find that a duty of care was owed in *Kent* v *Griffiths*. An alternative explanation of why a duty of care was owed in that case is set out below.[75]

6.3 Creation of danger

A number of authorities support the idea that if A knows or ought to know that he has done something to put B in danger of suffering some kind of harm, A *may* owe B a duty to take reasonable steps to protect B from that danger.

This idea will be of no relevance in a case where A has *wrongfully* put B in danger of suffering some kind of harm, and that danger materialises. In such a case, B can sue A for compensation for the harm she has suffered by focusing on A's initial wrong, and will have no need to try to establish that A owed her a duty of care to protect her from the danger he put her in. For example, suppose *Driver One* carelessly runs over *Pedestrian* and as a result she is lying in the middle of the road, unable to move because her legs are broken. *Driver One* sees what has happened but does not do anything to assist *Pedestrian*. She is subsequently run over by another car driven by *Driver Two*. The second impact causes *Pedestrian* to suffer severe brain damage. *Pedestrian* will be able to sue *One* for that brain damage because *One*'s initial act of negligence in running her down contributed to her suffering that brain damage in the sense that, had *One* not run *Pedestrian* down, she would not have been subsequently run over by *Two*. In this case, *Pedestrian* will not need to argue that *having run her down*, *One* owed her a duty to go to her assistance. No doubt he did; but *Pedestrian* will not need to rely on that fact in order to sue *One* for damages for her brain damage.

The duty formula under discussion in this section comes into its own where A has *innocently* put B in danger of suffering some kind of harm, or where A has acted perfectly *reasonably*, but the result of his actions has been to put B in danger of suffering some kind of harm. For example, in the American case of *Hardy* v *Brooks* (1961), the defendant was driving along the highway when a cow wandered into his path. The defendant was unable to avoid crashing into the cow, and the cow died on the spot. The cow's carcass was lying in the middle of the road and posed a clear danger to oncoming traffic. The defendant failed to do anything about this danger, that he had, unwittingly, played a part in creating. He did not try to alert the authorities to try to get them to move the cow out of the road, and did not put up any warning signs to alert oncoming traffic that there was an obstruction up ahead. He simply drove around the cow and proceeded on his way. The claimant subsequently crashed into the cow and was injured. It was held that the defendant had owed the claimant a duty to take reasonable steps to protect the claimant from the danger that he had played a part in creating.

A number of aspects of this duty formula need careful examination.

A. Creating danger

There is clearly a distinction between creating a danger and providing an occasion for danger to arise. For example, if A threatens to kill B, no one would suggest that A's

---

[75] See below, § 6.4.

mother owes B a duty to take reasonable steps to ensure her safety from A because A's mother 'created' the danger B is in by giving birth to A.

But it is difficult to know where to draw the line between conduct that creates a danger and conduct that has merely provided an occasion for danger to arise. On one side of the line – the 'creation of danger' side – lie cases like *Kane* v *New Forest DC* (2002) and *Watson* v *British Board of Boxing Control* (2001). In *Kane*, the defendant council approved the creation of a right of way passing over a main road. There was nothing wrong with that. Unfortunately, the right of way crossed over the main road at a bend in the road, so some motorists would not be able to see a pedestrian using the right of way to cross the road until it was too late. And that is how the claimant ended up being injured. The Court of Appeal held that the defendant council had owed the claimant a duty to take reasonable steps to protect the claimant from the danger created by their approving the creation of a right of way at such a dangerous junction. In *Watson*, Michael Watson spent 40 days in a coma and six years in a wheelchair because he did not receive proper medical attention after a particularly brutal boxing match with Chris Eubank. Watson sued the British Board of Boxing Control (BBBC), which had been involved in putting on and promoting the fight. The Court of Appeal held that the BBBC had owed Watson a duty to take reasonable steps to protect him from the danger that he would suffer lasting injuries as a result of his fight with Eubank by seeing to it that there were adequate medical facilities at ring-side.

On the other side of the line – seemingly – are cases like *Mitchell* v *Glasgow City Council* (2009) and the Canadian case of *Childs* v *Desormeaux* (2006). In *Mitchell*, a 'neighbour from hell' called James Drummond attacked and killed James Mitchell after the defendant council – which rented neighbouring council flats to both Drummond and Mitchell, and which was trying to deal with the problems created by Drummond's anti-social behaviour – informed Drummond in a meeting with him that Mitchell had videoed Drummond threatening him. It was argued that after Drummond became visibly angry and stormed out of the meeting, the defendant council had owed Mitchell a duty to take steps to warn him that he might be in danger. The House of Lords rejected this contention. At least two of their Lordships took the view that the council had not done enough here for it to be correct to say that it had *created* a danger to Mitchell. As Lord Brown observed, 'by threatening a disruptive tenant with eviction a landlord cannot sensibly be said to be creating the risk of personal violence towards others . . .'[76]

In *Childs* v *Desormeaux*, the defendants hosted a New Year's party which was attended by Desmond Desormeaux. The party was a 'bring your own bottle' party. Desormeaux had far too much to drink at the party, and by the time he left, the level of alcohol in his blood was three times the legal limit for drivers. Desormeaux drove home from the party in his drunken state and ended up colliding with another car. One of the passengers in the other car was killed, and the claimant was paralysed. The claimant was obviously entitled to sue Desormeaux in negligence for compensation for her injuries, on the basis that he had owed her a duty to take care not to drive home drunk. The difficult question that the Supreme Court of Canada had to resolve was whether the defendants had owed the claimant a duty to take reasonable steps to stop Desormeaux driving home drunk, on the basis that, by hosting the party at which he got drunk, they had played some part in creating

---

[76] [2009] 1 AC 874, at [82]. Lord Scott seemed to take much the same view.

the danger that people like the claimant would be exposed to if Desormeaux drove home drunk. The Canadian Supreme Court ruled that the defendants had not owed the claimant a duty of care in this case:

> Holding a private party at which alcohol is served – the bare facts of this case – is insufficient to implicate the host in the creation of a risk sufficient to give rise to a duty of care to third parties who may be subsequently injured by the conduct of a guest. The host creates a place where people can meet, visit and imbibe alcohol, whether served on the premises or supplied by the guest. All this falls within accepted parameters of non-dangerous conduct. More is required to establish a danger or risk that requires positive action. It might be argued that a host who continues to serve alcohol to a visibly inebriated person knowing that he or she will be driving home has become implicated in the creation or enhancement of a risk sufficient to give rise to a prima facie duty of care to third parties. We need not decide that question here.[77]

What accounts for the difference between *Kane* and *Watson* on the one hand, and *Mitchell* and *Childs* on the other? It is tempting to locate the difference in the fact that in *Mitchell* and *Childs* the ultimate source of the danger to the claimant was the deliberate, voluntary, informed and unreasonable act of a third party (Drummond's attacking Mitchell; Desormeaux's drunk driving), and that kind of act 'breaks the chain of causation' between whatever the defendant has done and the danger to the claimant.[78] However, there are some cases that make it difficult to argue that a defendant cannot be held to have created a danger to a claimant if something has happened to 'break the chain of causation' between the defendant's conduct and the danger the claimant is in.

First, it has been held in both England[79] and Australia,[80] that if it is reasonably foreseeable that a prisoner, A, will attack a fellow prisoner, B, if he is given the chance, the prison authorities will owe B a duty to take reasonable steps to keep A away from B. The existence of this duty of care can be best seen as arising out of the duty formula discussed here – by imprisoning B within the same walls as A, the prison authorities have helped to create a danger that B will be attacked by A. But, it should be noted, it could be argued that there exists a 'break in the chain of causation' between the prison authorities' imprisoning B, and the danger resulting from B's being imprisoned – B's being imprisoned only gives rise to a danger of B being attacked because A has deliberately, voluntarily and unreasonably decided that he wants to attack B.

Secondly, in *R v Evans* (2009), the defendant gave some heroin to her half-sister Carly. Carly injected herself with the heroin and subsequently complained to the defendant that she was feeling hot. The defendant saw that Carly was 'in a mess' – her lips were blue and she had lost colour in her skin – and realised that there was a danger Carly was overdosing on the heroin. Instead of calling for an ambulance, the defendant put her to bed, hoping that she would recover spontaneously. Unfortunately, Carly died during the night. The defendant was charged with gross negligence manslaughter. It was argued that she had owed Carly a duty to call her an ambulance and that the defendant's breach of that duty had contributed to Carly's death and was so outrageous as to be worthy of punishment. A very strong Court of Appeal – five

---

[77] [2006] 1 SCR 643, at [44].
[78] On the concept of a 'break in the chain of causation', see below, § 8.11.
[79] *Ellis* v *Home Office* [1953] 2 All ER 149.
[80] *New South Wales* v *Budjoso* (2005) 222 ALR 663.

judges – held that the defendant had owed Carly a duty of care in this case, based on the fact that:

> when a person has created or contributed to the creation of a state of affairs which he knows, or ought reasonably to know, has become life threatening, a consequent duty on him to act by taking reasonable steps to save the other's life will normally arise.[81]

But, it should be noted, the defendant's act of supplying Carly with heroin only put Carly in danger of dying through an overdose because Carly deliberately, voluntarily and unreasonably injected herself with the heroin, when she knew what the effect of doing this might be on her. Given this, Carly's act would normally be held to have 'broken the chain of causation' between the defendant's supplying her with heroin, and Carly's being in danger of dying from an overdose. However, the Court of Appeal still held that the duty formula under discussion here applied to the defendant in this case.

Perhaps the best that can be said is that there are no iron rules in this area. In a situation where A has done something that has played a part in B being exposed to a danger of being harmed either by herself, or a third party, C, the greater the part A has played in B's being put in danger, the more likely the courts are to find that A has 'created a danger' and has a duty to take reasonable steps to protect B from that danger. In *Childs* v *Desormeaux*, the defendants had very little to do with Desormeaux's drunk driving – they merely hosted an event, but were not the ones who supplied the alcohol at that event.[82] Likewise, the defendants in *Mitchell* v *Glasgow City Council*. While their lack of caution in confronting Drummond with the evidence that Mitchell had made a video of him may have played a part in Drummond's subsequently attacking Mitchell, Drummond could well have seized on some other excuse to attack Mitchell, as he had in the past. But in *R* v *Evans*, Carly simply could not have overdosed without the assistance of the defendant. As a result, it was fair to find that the defendant in *Evans* helped to create the danger that Carly would die of a heroin overdose.

---

[81] [2009] 1 WLR 1999, at [31].

[82] The lack of any iron rules in this area explains why, when the defendant *did* supply the alcohol and did so on a commercial basis, different courts in different countries have come to different conclusions as to: (1) whether the defendant will owe a duty of care to *road users* who might be injured by the drinker's drunken driving, to stop the drinker driving home; and (2) whether the defendant will owe a duty of care to the *drinker* to see that he gets home safely. In Canada, the courts have answered 'yes' to (1) and (2): *Jordan House Ltd* v *Menow* [1974] SCR 239 (claimant got drunk at defendants' bar and wandered off into the night and was hit by a car; held that the defendants had owed the claimant a duty to arrange for some way to get him home safely) and *Stewart* v *Pettie* [1995] 1 SCR 131 (two couples – the Stewarts and the Petties – went to the defendants' establishment to have something to eat and watch a play; they all had a fair amount to drink and when Stuart Pettie drove them all home, there was an accident in which the Stewarts were injured; held that in principle the defendants might have owed the Stewarts a duty of care to see that they were not injured by Pettie's drunk driving, but on the facts they could not have known that Pettie was not fit to drive). In Australia, the High Court has recently made it clear that a duty of care would only be owed in (2) in very extreme cases: *CAL No 14* v *Motor Accidents Board* (2009) 239 CLR 390 (noted, Guy, Richardson & Hocking 2010). In that case, the claimant had been drinking at the defendant's pub for three hours on his way home from work, and at one point had given the defendant the keys to his motorbike to ensure that he was not tempted to drive home drunk. But he eventually asked for the keys back. The defendant gave them to him and the claimant was injured when he drunkenly fell off the bike driving home. Held, that the defendant had not owed the claimant a duty of care to see that he got home safely, or at least that he did not drive home. For further discussion of 'social host' and 'commercial host' liability for injuries caused by drunkenness, see Orr 1995, Solomon & Payne 1996, Dalphond 2002, Fordham 2010 (at 33–42).

B. What kind of harm?

All of the cases we have discussed so far have involved a defendant putting a claimant in danger of suffering some kind of physical harm. In *Butchart* v *Home Office* (2006), the defendant prison authorities put the claimant in danger of suffering a psychiatric illness by placing him in the same cell as a prisoner with suicidal tendencies, when they knew or ought to have known that the claimant was in a similarly fragile mental state and there was a real risk he would suffer a mental breakdown (as he did) if his cellmate killed himself. The Court of Appeal held that the prison authorities had owed the claimant a duty to take reasonable steps to monitor the claimant's cellmate to make sure that he did not kill himself.

There is, so far as we know, no tort case where the issue has been addressed as to whether A will owe B a duty to take reasonable steps to protect B's property if A has done something that has put that property in danger of being harmed. (For example, suppose that A is in the park playing with his son, and he attempts to throw a tennis ball to his son. He misses his aim, and the tennis ball falls into a nearby lake. B's dog rushes into the lake to retrieve the ball and starts to struggle . . .) However, the criminal case of *R* v *Miller* (1983) suggests that creating a foreseeable danger to property *can* give rise to a duty to act.

In that case, the defendant fell asleep in someone else's house while he was still smoking a cigarette. He dropped the lit cigarette onto the mattress on which he was lying. Soon after, the claimant woke up and realised the mattress was on fire. However – because he was very drunk and not thinking straight – he did not attempt to do anything about the fire but simply moved to another room to find another place to sleep. The fire subsequently spread to the rest of the house. The defendant was charged with arson under the Criminal Damage Act 1971. He could not be convicted on the basis of his initial act of dropping the lit cigarette. This is because arson is a crime of recklessness, and when the defendant dropped the cigarette he was not aware that that act might result in property being damaged by fire. But if the defendant acted *wrongfully* in *failing to do anything about the fire* when he woke up, then he could be convicted, as he was aware at that stage that if he did not do anything about the fire, property might be damaged by fire. The House of Lords found that the defendant had been under a duty to act in this case, based on the fact that he had (albeit unwittingly) created a foreseeable risk of harm to property by dropping his lit cigarette on the mattress.

C. What sort of steps?

In a case where the duty formula under discussion here applies, and A owes B a duty to take reasonable steps to protect B from some danger that he has created, how much is A actually required to do for B? The question has not been at all well explored, either in the case law or in academic articles.

In *E Hobbs (Farms) Ltd* v *Baxenden Chemicals* (1992), it was held that the manufacturer of foam insulation installed in the claimant's farm buildings owed the claimant a duty to *warn* him that the foam was combustible when the manufacturer realised that this was the case: 'a manufacturer's duty of care does not end when the goods are sold. A manufacturer who realises that omitting to warn past customers about something which might result in injury to them must take reasonable steps to attempt to warn them, however lacking in negligence he may have been at the time the goods were sold.'[83]

But in this sort of case, a warning would not have completely protected the claimant against the risk of his farm buildings burning down if the foam insulation caught fire. Could the defendant have been required to do more, and strip the insulation out of the buildings, at the defendant's own expense? We would suggest that it would depend on how far the defendant was at fault for creating the danger to which the claimant's buildings are now exposed. If the defendant was not at fault at all – there was no reason why he should have known about the risk posed by this insulation at the time he installed it – then, we would suggest, a warning is all the defendant has to give the claimant. Once that has been given, the defendant could justifiably claim that he had done enough, and further protection against the risk of fire damage was a matter for the claimant to provide. If the defendant was very culpable for installing such dangerous insulation in the claimant's buildings, then he could be required to do more – but, of course, in such a case, if the risk of fire damage materialised, the claimant would simply be able to sue the defendant for that damage on the basis that he acted negligently in *installing* the insulation, and not worry about arguing that the defendant acted negligently in *failing to remove* the insulation.

In a number of American cases, defendants who have created dangers that claimants will suffer some kind of physical harm *in the future* have been ordered to set up 'medical monitoring funds' which would cover the expense of giving the claimants regular check-ups to ensure that they get medical treatment as soon as their physical condition seems to be deteriorating as a result of what the defendants did.[84] Whether a defendant's duty to take reasonable steps to look after the health of a claimant who he has put in danger of suffering physical harm in the future extends so far as to require him to set up a 'medical monitoring fund' for the claimant would, we suggest, again depend on the circumstances.[85] More specifically, it will depend on how blameworthy the defendant was for putting the claimant in danger of suffering physical harm in future, and how easily the defendant could afford to cover the cost of setting up such a fund.

---

[83] [1992] 1 Lloyds Rep 54, 65.

[84] *Friends for All Children* v *Lockheed Corporation Inc*, 746 F 2d 816 (1984) (Lockheed ordered to create fund to pay for Vietnamese children – who were involved in a plane crash which was Lockheed's fault – to undergo regular neurological exams to check for any incipient brain disorder caused by the decompression they had experienced in the crash); *Ayers* v *Jackson*, 525 A 2d 287 (1987) (company that polluted residents' water with carcinogenic chemicals was ordered to create a fund to pay for the residents to undergo regular medical tests in the future to detect whether or not the pollution had caused them to develop cancer); *Potter* v *Firestone Tire & Rubber Co*, 863 P 2d 795 (1993) (medical monitoring award made against tyre company that dumped hazardous waste next to claimants' land, thus putting them in danger of developing cancer); *Hansen* v *Mountain Fuel Supply Co*, 858 P 2d 970 (1993) (defendant who exposed contractors to excessive quantities of asbestos dust while they were working for defendant could be ordered to create a fund to pay for contractors' health to be monitored – but only if the contractors were in danger of developing a serious disease as a result of being exposed to the asbestos 'for which a medical test for early detection exists . . . and for which early detection is beneficial, meaning that a treatment exists that can alter the course of the illness' (ibid, at 979)).

[85] So far as we know, John Goldberg and Benjamin Zipursky were the first to suggest (brilliantly) that orders to set up 'medical monitoring funds' could be rationalised as the courts' enforcing a defendant's duty to take reasonable steps to deal with a danger that he had played some part in exposing the claimant to: see Goldberg & Zipursky 2002, 1709–15.

6.4 Interference

A number of cases can be taken as suggesting that if A knows or ought to know that B is in need of help to avoid some harm, and A knows or ought to know that he has done something to put off or prevent someone else helping B, then A will owe B a duty to take reasonable steps to give B the help she needs.

The duty of care that the ambulance service owed the claimant in *Kent* v *Griffiths* (2001)[86] can be explained on this basis. As Lord Woolf MR observed in that case: 'If wrong information had not been given about the arrival of the ambulance, other means of transport could have been used.'[87] By telling the claimant's doctor and husband that an ambulance was on its way and would be arriving imminently, the ambulance service put them off finding some other way to get the claimant to hospital (for example, in a taxi).[88]

In *Costello* v *Chief Constable of the Northumbria Police* (1999), the claimant was a woman police officer who was attacked by a prisoner when she took the prisoner down to the cells in a police station. Another officer, H, accompanied the claimant in taking the prisoner down to the cells in order to help her out if there was any trouble. However, when H saw B – a police inspector – standing by the cells, H went back upstairs, assuming that B would assist the claimant if she was attacked by the prisoner. When the claimant was attacked, B – contrary to expectation – stood by and did nothing. The Court of Appeal found that B had owed the claimant a duty to take reasonable steps to save her from being attacked. The Court of Appeal said that the duty of care arose because B 'assumed a responsibility' to the claimant.[89] However, it seems clear that he did not – B never indicated to the *claimant* that she could rely on him to look after her if she got into trouble. A more satisfactory explanation of the case is that B owed the claimant a duty of care because he indicated to *H* that he would take care of the claimant if she got into trouble, and thereby dissuaded H from sticking around to make sure he would be on hand if anything happened to B.

In *Reeves* v *Commissioner of Police of the Metropolis* (2000), a man named Martin Lynch was remanded in police custody on charges of credit card fraud; he was also under investigation for handling stolen vehicles. He was known to be a suicide risk, having tried to kill himself twice before while in police custody. This time he succeeded. He took advantage of the fact that the police had left the spyhole into his cell open, and tied a shirt around the metal bars on the outside of his door, over the spyhole, and hanged himself. It was accepted on all sides of the case that the police had owed Lynch a duty to take reasonable steps to see that he did not kill himself. While counsel for the claimant (Lynch's partner) argued that 'The duty . . . arose . . . from the well-known fact that custody has a depressive effect on people who are not otherwise suicidal'[90] – which would indicate that the duty in this case arose out of some 'creation of danger' idea – it seems likely that the police would have owed Lynch a duty of care even if their taking him into custody was not

---

[86] See above, § 6.2.

[87] [2001] QB 36, at [49].

[88] [2001] QB 36, at [17]: 'But for the acceptance of the 999 call the [claimant] would have been driven to the hospital and would have arrived prior to her "arrest".' See also *Michael*, at [138], which explains the duty of care in *Kent* v *Griffiths* as being based on the 'misleading assurances that an ambulance would be arriving shortly.'

[89] [1999] 1 All ER 550, 564.

[90] [2000] 1 AC 360, 364.

the reason why he felt suicidal.[91] Given this, a more satisfactory explanation as to why a duty of care was owed in *Reeves'* case was that, by taking him into custody, the police cut him off from sources of support that might have helped him overcome his suicidal tendencies. Having done this, they owed him a duty to take reasonable steps to stop him committing suicide themselves.[92]

The same idea, that cutting someone off from alternative sources of support gives rise to a duty to act, probably underlies the finding of a duty of care in *Barrett* v *Ministry of Defence* (1995). In that case, it will be recalled, a soldier got so drunk at a Hawaiian party that had been organised by the defendants at his barracks that he collapsed and later died from choking on his own vomit. The Court of Appeal refused to find that the defendants had owed the soldier a duty of care not to serve him so many drinks that he collapsed. However, it was found at first instance – and not disputed on appeal – that after the soldier collapsed, the defendants had owed the soldier a duty to take reasonable steps to see that he got through the night safely, and had breached that duty by failing to summon a doctor to see him.[93] This duty arose because after the soldier collapsed, the officer in charge of the barracks had the soldier taken to his cabin and put in his bunk. In so doing, the officer cut the soldier off from other sources of support that might have been able to intervene to see that he did not die during the night.

Viewed this way, *Barrett*'s case is strongly analogous to the American case of *Zelenko* v *Gimbel Bros* (1935). In that case, Mary Zelenko collapsed in the defendants' department store. The defendants took her into the store infirmary to look after her, but then failed to do anything for her for six hours. Zelenko died as a result of not being treated quickly enough. While it could not be shown that any particular individual had been dissuaded or prevented from looking after Zelenko as a result of the defendant's taking charge of her, the court was satisfied that it was 'beyond doubt [that if the defendant had left Zelenko alone] some bystander . . . would have summoned an ambulance'[94] and as a result found that the defendant had owed Zelenko a duty to take reasonable steps to give her the medical attention she needed.

The idea that interfering with someone's helping another who is in need or danger can give rise to a duty of care may also underlie the otherwise very difficult to explain case of *Chandler* v *Cape plc* (2012). In that case, the claimant developed asbestosis having been carelessly exposed to asbestos dust 40 years before while working for Cape Building Products Ltd ('Cape Products'). Unfortunately, by the time the claimant's asbestosis developed, Cape Products had gone out of business and could not be sued. So the claimant sued Cape Products' parent company, Cape plc, instead arguing that *Cape plc* had owed him a duty of care to protect him from being exposed to asbestos dust. The Court of

---

[91] There is a hint that this was the case in counsel for the defendants' observation in the course of argument that 'The suicidal tendencies of the deceased arose from his concern about his pending criminal trial and his unwillingness to face the possibility of going to prison': [2000] 1 AC 360, 365.

[92] The duty of care that doctors owe their patients with known suicidal tendencies to stop them killing themselves (see *Savage* v *South Essex Partnership NHS Foundation Trust* [2009] 1 AC 681, at [47] (per Lord Rodger) and [99] (per Baroness Hale)) can probably be best rationalized as arising as a result of an 'assumption of responsibility' to the patient under § 6.2, above.

[93] [1995] 1 WLR 1217, 1223.

[94] 287 NYS 134, 135 (1935).

Appeal held Cape plc had indeed owed the claimant such a duty of care. Arden LJ held that the crucial elements establishing that such a duty of care was owed were:

(1) the businesses of the parent and subsidiary are in a relevant respect the same; (2) the parent has, or ought to have, superior knowledge on some relevant aspect of health and safety in the particular industry; (3) the subsidiary's system of work is unsafe as the parent company knew, or ought to have known; and (4) the parent knew or ought to have foreseen that the subsidiary or its employees would rely on its using that superior knowledge for the employees' protection.[95]

Taken together, these factors suggest that the duty of care in *Chandler* v *Cape* was generated by the fact that Cape Products was looking to its parent company, Cape, to tell it how to look after its employees' health and safety and Cape knew or ought to have known that was the case. Given this, it could be said that Cape interfered with Cape Products' protecting the claimant from developing asbestosis with the result that Cape owed the claimant such a duty of care. Subsequent caselaw indicates that in the absence of such interference a *Chandler* v *Cape* style duty of care will not be owed by a parent company to the employees of one of its subsidiary companies.[96]

In all of the cases we have discussed so far, the defendant either dissuaded or prevented *someone else* from helping someone in need. What about the situation where A has dissuaded or prevented B from *helping themselves?* In such a situation, there will usually be no need to rely on the idea that interference gives rise to a duty to act in order to establish that A owed B a duty of care. In a 'dissuasion' case, it will usually be possible to find that A 'assumed a responsibility' to B, and base a duty to act on that. In a 'prevention' case, it will usually be possible to argue that A had a duty to take care not to stop B helping herself to avoid the danger she was in, on the basis that it was reasonably foreseeable that if he did so, B would suffer physical harm as a result. However, there may be some cases where neither of these analyses will really work to show that a duty of care was owed. And in such cases, recourse to the idea that interference gives rise to a duty to act may be necessary.

For example, in *Mercer* v *South Eastern & Chatham Railway Companies' Managing Committee* (1922), the claimant was hit by a passing train as he crossed a railway line. The gate to the path over the railway line was usually locked by the defendant when a train was due to come by, but the defendant had on this occasion left the gate unlocked and this had led the claimant to believe that it was safe to cross the railway line. It was held that the defendant had owed the claimant a duty to take reasonable steps to ensure that he locked the gate to the path over the railway line when a train was due to come by.

The finding of a duty of care in this case cannot easily be explained without recourse to the idea that interference gives rise to a duty to act. The defendant did not 'assume a responsibility' to anyone by regularly locking the gate when a train was due to come by: he never indicated to people like the claimant that they could rely on him to take care to do this.[97] And mere foreseeability of physical harm to someone like the claimant could not give rise to a duty on the part of the defendant to take the *positive* step of locking the gate

---

[95] [2012] 1 WLR 3111, at [80].

[96] See *Thompson* v *The Renwick Group plc* [2014] EWCA Civ 635, especially at [36]–[37].

[97] For example, the philosopher Immanuel Kant was well-known in his home town of Königsberg for going for a daily walk at exactly the same time every day. So much so, that people would set their watches and clocks according to what time Kant passed their houses. But no one would say that in this case Kant 'assumed a responsibility' to the townsfolk of Königsberg that he would take care to go for a walk at exactly the same time every day. Regularity of behaviour does not give rise to an assumption of responsibility.

when a train was due to go by. But it could be argued that the defendant was aware – or ought to have been aware – that his regular custom of locking the gate as a train was due to go by was having the effect of encouraging people like the claimant to think that if the gate was unlocked, they could cross the railway line *without having to worry about whether a train was coming along*. Having encouraged people like the claimant to let their guard down in this way, the defendant owed them a duty to take reasonable steps to protect them from the risk that they might be run down by a train as they crossed the railway line.

While the idea that interference gives rise to a duty to act seems to be well-established in the law, the potential ambit of that duty formula was limited by the first instance decision in *OLL Ltd* v *Secretary of State for Transport* (1997).[98] In that case, a party of eight children and one teacher got into severe difficulty on a canoeing trip in the sea off Lyme Regis. The coastguard was mobilised but bungled the rescue operation, directing a lifeboat and a Royal Navy helicopter to search for the party in the wrong area. As a result, all the members of the party suffered severe hypothermia and four of the children died. It was claimed in the subsequent litigation that the coastguard had owed the members of the party a duty to take reasonable steps to rescue them.

It was arguable that the idea that interference gives rise to a duty to act applied in this case. It could have been argued that the coastguard prevented the lifeboat crew and the Royal Navy from rescuing the stricken party by giving them wrong directions, and as a result the coastguard owed the party a duty to take reasonable steps to rescue them. However, May J refused to find that a duty of care was owed by the coastguard here, holding that it would be 'artificial'[99] to distinguish between the coastguard and other rescue organisations that were attempting to save the teacher and children at sea. This was a case of one person getting in his own way in attempting to rescue the canoeing party; not a case of someone getting in the way of *someone else* who was trying to rescue the party.[100]

The case of *Poppleton* v *Trustees of the Portsmouth Youth Activities Committee* (2008) might be taken as placing another limit on the idea that interference gives rise to a duty to act. In that case, the defendants ran some indoor climbing premises that were used by the claimant. The claimant attempted to jump from one climbing wall to another. His attempt failed, and he fell to the ground and was severely injured. He sued the defendants, arguing that they had owed him a duty to warn him that the matting at the base of the climbing walls was not very thick and did not offer much protection to falling climbers: had he known this, he would not have attempted to jump from one wall to another. Although it could be said that the defendants lulled the claimant into a false sense of security here by providing safety matting that was not as safe as it might have looked, the Court of Appeal rejected the claim that a duty to warn the claimant was owed by the defendants here as the

---

[98] Discussed, Bagshaw 1999.

[99] [1997] 3 All ER 897, 907.

[100] So in the case of Loraine Whiting – whose estranged husband broke into her house, shot her, and then killed himself, and who then died from loss of blood with the police actively preventing the ambulance services from going into the house because they feared (despite 30 calls from Loraine Whiting telling them that her husband was dead) that the husband might still be in the house waiting to shoot at anyone coming in – the *OLL* decision would seem to prevent interference being used as the basis of an argument that the police owed Loraine Whiting a duty of care to come to her aid, having stopped the ambulance services coming to her assistance. The police and ambulance services should be bundled together into one unit, 'the emergency services', which unit did not owe Loraine Whiting a duty of care because it did not 'assume a responsibility' to her, or put her in danger, or stop anyone else outside 'the emergency services' coming to her assistance.

claimant was still aware that there was *some* risk attached to attempting to jump from one wall to another. So lulling a claimant into a false sense of *relative* security might not be enough to allow a claimant to invoke the idea that interference gives rise to a duty to act.

6.5 Control

It seems to be well established that if A is in control of a dangerous *substance or animal,* and it is reasonably foreseeable that someone like B will be harmed by that substance or animal if A allows it to escape his control, then A will owe B a duty to take reasonable steps to keep that thing or that animal under his control.[101]

What is controversial is what the position is where A is in control of a *human being* and it is foreseeable that someone like B will be harmed if that human being escapes A's control. In a case where B has been harmed by C – who was under A's control – whether or not A owed B a duty of care to keep C under control seems to depend on how responsible C was for the harm he did B. If he was not at all responsible, A will have owed B a duty of care if it was merely foreseeable that C's escaping A's control would result in B being harmed. If C was responsible for the harm he did B, something more will be required before the courts will find that A owed B a duty of care to keep C under control. In order not to dilute C's responsibility for what he did to B too much, the courts will only find that A owed B a duty of care to control C if B was in *special danger* of being harmed by C if C escaped A's control.

In *Carmarthenshire County Council* v *Lewis* (1955), a four-year-old boy attending nursery school wandered off the school premises and onto the road running alongside the nursery school. The claimant's husband, who was driving along the road, swerved to avoid the boy and crashed into a tree and died. The claimant sued, claiming that the defendant county council – which owned the school – and the teachers at the school had owed her husband, and breached, a duty to take reasonable steps to keep control of the children at the school. The House of Lords agreed that the defendant county council and the teachers at the school had owed the claimant's husband such a duty of care. As the boy was not at all responsible for what happened to the claimant's husband, mere foreseeability that someone like the claimant would be harmed if the boy escaped the defendants' control was enough to give rise to a duty of care to keep the boy under control. And it was, of course, eminently foreseeable that children at the school would wander into the road outside the school and cause accidents if defendants did not keep control of them.[102]

It was different in *Dorset Yacht Co Ltd* v *Home Office* (1970). In that case, seven 'Borstal boys' – young offenders who were in custody – were on a training exercise on Brownsea Island in Poole Harbour. They were under the supervision of three officers. One night the boys escaped, taking advantage of the fact that all three officers had, contrary to instructions, gone to bed. They boarded one of the vessels in the harbour and set sail in it but it

---

[101] If the substance or animal escapes A's control without any negligence on his part and B is harmed as a result, B may still be entitled to sue A for compensation under either the rule in *Rylands* v *Fletcher* or the Animals Act 1971 (see below, Chapter 14).

[102] See also *Palmer* v *Cornwall County Council* [2009] EWCA Civ 456 (claimant schoolboy was hit in the eye by a large rock thrown by another schoolboy during a lunch break; defendant local authority held liable for failing to have enough staff on the ground supervising children playing at lunchtime to see that this sort of thing did not go on).

collided with the claimant's yacht. They then boarded the claimant's yacht and did further damage to it. The claimant sued the Home Office for compensation, arguing that the officers had owed him a duty to take reasonable steps not to let the boys escape. The House of Lords found that such a duty had been owed to the claimant.

There was no problem showing that it was reasonably foreseeable that someone like the claimant would suffer harm if the boys were allowed to escape the officers' control. This is because it was reasonably foreseeable – very likely or probable – that if the boys were allowed to escape the officers' control, they would commandeer one of the boats in the harbour in an attempt to get off the island and make good their escape, and in so doing would damage the boat. It followed that it was reasonably foreseeable that someone like the claimant – someone who owned a boat in the harbour – would suffer harm if the boys were allowed to escape their officers' control.

However, as the boys were responsible for what happened to the claimant's yacht, foreseeability of harm was not enough to give rise to a duty of care. It had to be shown that the claimant was *especially* at risk of suffering harm if the boys in this case escaped the defendants' control. This requirement of 'special danger' to the claimant was satisfied here because people like the claimant – people who owned boats in the harbour – were at greater risk of suffering harm as a result of the boys' escape than other members of the population such as shopkeepers or owners of bikes on the island. Their boats would be especially valuable to the boys if they were allowed to escape – so their boats were especially likely to be targeted by the boys on escape as compared with other items of property such as groceries or bikes. It follows that the result of the case would have been different had the boys, on escaping, robbed a shop on the island.[103] No duty would have been owed to the shopkeeper to take reasonable steps to prevent the boys escaping as there would have been no special risk that the shopkeeper's wares would be targeted by the Borstal boys on escape.

In line with the position taken here in the text, Lord Morris suggested in the case of *Dorset Yacht Co Ltd* v *Home Office* that 'If a person who is in lawful custody has made a threat, accepted as seriously intended, that, if he can escape, he will injure X . . . a duty [will be] owed to X to take reasonable care to prevent escape.'[104] This requirement was not satisfied in *K* v *Secretary of State for the Home Dept* (2002). In that case, M, a Kenyan citizen, was imprisoned for sexual assault and then for burglary. He was detained, awaiting deportation, but was released on order of the Home Secretary. M subsequently raped the claimant. The claimant sued the Home Secretary in negligence, claiming that he had owed her a duty not to release M. The Home Secretary applied to have the action struck out. For the purposes of hearing the striking out claim, it was assumed against the Home Secretary that he had acted unreasonably in ordering M to be released and that it was reasonably foreseeable that if M was released, he would attack someone like the claimant. It made no difference: the Court of Appeal still refused to find that the Home Secretary had owed the claimant a duty not to release M. The special danger requirement was not satisfied here. The claimant was at no greater risk of being attacked by M on release than the rest of the population or the rest of the female population.

'Control' in this context classically means 'physical' control. In *Tarasoff* v *Regents of the University of California* (1976), one of the defendants' psychiatric patients – Prosenjit Poddar – killed the claimants' daughter, Tatiana Tarasoff. Poddar had confided to the

---

[103] [1970] AC 1004, 1070 (per Lord Diplock).
[104] [1970] AC 1004, 1039.

defendants in the course of treatment that he was intending to kill Tarasoff. It was held that, in these circumstances, the defendants had owed Tarasoff a duty to warn her of the danger she was in. John Goldberg and Benjamin Zipursky have suggested that the decision can be rationalised on the basis that control of a dangerous person can give rise to a duty to act:

> Although the defendant-therapists in *Tarasoff* did not have custody over the dangerous patient, they had previously ordered his confinement and in any event enjoyed the authority under state law to order confinement of persons posing a danger to themselves or others.[105]

It is not clear whether in the UK, the notion of control giving rise to a duty to act would extend to 'power to control' cases. The closest the UK has come to a *Tarasoff*-type case is *Palmer* v *Tees Health Authority* (1999), where the claimant's four-year-old daughter, Rosie, was kidnapped, sexually assaulted, and murdered by a man called Armstrong. Armstrong was being treated by the defendants for various psychiatric problems as an in-patient, and subsequently as an out-patient. A claim that the defendants had owed Rosie a duty to take reasonable steps to diagnose and treat his tendencies to sexually assault children was dismissed by the Court of Appeal on the basis that Rosie (as opposed to any other child) had not been in special danger of being attacked by Armstrong. The question of whether the defendants would have owed Rosie a duty of care had she been in special danger of being attacked by Armstrong did not therefore arise. We think it is unlikely that such a duty of care would have existed. To base such a duty merely on the power to control someone, rather than the fact of control, would go too far towards undermining the rule against there being a general duty to rescue people who you are in a position to save from harm.

6.6 Occupiers

The idea that control of a dangerous thing or person may give rise to a positive duty of care to protect other people from that thing or person finds fresh application in the law on occupiers' liability, where someone who is in control of premises that are in a dangerous state may owe people on or near those premises a duty to take reasonable steps to safeguard them from being harmed by the state of those premises.

Some academic lawyers are resistant to the idea that the law on occupiers' liability is part of the law of negligence. It is hard to see why. The occupier of land is subject to duties of care and when he breaches one of those duties, the remedies for his breach are exactly the same as would be awarded against anyone else who breached a duty of care owed to another. However, out of respect for those academics who expect to see the law on 'occupiers' liability' dealt with separately from the law of negligence, we have gathered together the relevant materials on occupiers' liability into a separate chapter in this edition of this text. Having said that, students will find it useful to be informed at this stage of the various positive duties of care that an occupier of land will owe to other people:

(1) Under the *Occupiers' Liability Act 1957*, an occupier will normally owe his visitors, and other people lawfully on his land, a duty to take reasonable steps to see that they are reasonably safe for the purposes for which they are on the premises.

(2) Under the *Occupiers' Liability Act 1984*, an occupier will owe a *trespasser* a duty to take reasonable steps to safeguard him or her against a danger arising on his land if: (a) he knows

---

[105] Goldberg & Zipursky 2009, 1240 n 121.

or ought to know of the danger; (b) he knows or ought to know that a trespasser on his land might go into the vicinity of that danger; and (c) that danger is one he could reasonably be expected to do something about.

(3) Under the *general law of negligence*, an occupier will owe a range of positive duties of care to a range of different people. For example, he will owe his neighbours a duty to take reasonable steps to put out any fires on his land that are liable to spread onto his neighbours' land. And he will owe people passing by his land a duty to take reasonable steps to see that any fixtures on his land – for example, a sign or a tree – that overhang the road will not fall on them.

The law on occupiers' liability is dealt with in much more detail in Chapter 10, below.

6.7 Landlords

If *Landlord* lets premises to *Tenant* and *Landlord* knows or ought to know that the premises suffer from a defect[106] that *Landlord* is obliged[107] to repair under the contract of tenancy, then s 4 of the Defective Premises Act 1972 provides that *Landlord* will *normally* owe:

> all persons[108] who might reasonably be expected to be affected by defects in the state of the premises a duty to take such care as is reasonable in all the circumstances to see that they are reasonably safe from personal injury or from damage caused to their property by [that] defect.[109]

6.8 Employers

It has long been well established that if A employs B, A will *normally* owe B a duty to take reasonable steps to see that she is not killed or physically injured in working for him. So A will *normally* owe B a duty to take reasonable steps to ensure: (1) that B's fellow employees are competent and are therefore not likely to act in ways which would unreasonably endanger B's health and safety; (2) that B's place of work is reasonably safe to enter and work in; (3) that B and B's fellow employees will do their work in a way that will not unreasonably endanger B's health and safety; and (4) that B is provided with the necessary plant and equipment to enable her to do her work without unreasonably endangering her health and safety and that that plant and equipment is reasonably safe to use.

---

[106] Defective Premises Act 1972, s 4(2). The Court of Appeal has made it clear that it need not be shown, for the purposes of this requirement, that *Landlord* had actual knowledge of the existence of the defect or of facts which indicated that the defect existed: it is enough to show that a reasonable man in *Landlord*'s position would have discovered the existence of the defect. See *Sykes* v *Harry* [2001] QB 1014 (leave to appeal refused by the House of Lords: [2002] 1 WLR 2286).

[107] Under s 4(4), if the contract of tenancy merely gave *Landlord* the *power* to repair the defect, *Landlord* is to be regarded for the purposes of s 4 of the 1972 Act as having a *duty* under the contract of tenancy to repair that defect *unless* the contract of tenancy clearly placed the responsibility for repairing that defect on *Tenant*.

[108] Including the tenant(s) of the let premises: *McAuley* v *Bristol City Council* [1992] 1 QB 134; *Sykes* v *Harry* [2001] QB 1014, at [21].

[109] Section 4(1).

This duty will rarely be displaced on the grounds that *volenti non fit injuria*. For example, the mere fact that B goes to work every day knowing that her workplace is not a reasonably safe place to work in does not establish that she is willing to work for A in a place of work that is not reasonably safe for her to work in.[110] In such a case – where B's only alternative to turning up for work is to quit her job and seek alternative employment on an uncertain job market – it cannot be said that B *willingly* chooses to work for A in a dangerous workplace when she continues to turn up for work in the knowledge that her workplace is not a reasonably safe place to work in.[111] Similarly, if A warned B before employing her that her future place of work would not be reasonably safe to work in and B agreed to work for A on that basis, B cannot be said to have *willingly* chosen to work for A in a dangerous workplace if her only reason for taking such a risk with her life or health was that she needed a job. So, in the case just described, A, having employed B, will – despite his warning to B – still owe B a duty to take reasonable steps to ensure that B's workplace is reasonably safe for her to work in.

How far does the duty that A will owe B to take reasonable steps to see that she will not be killed or injured working for him go? For example, suppose that A employs B to do a particular kind of work and it becomes clear that B is very likely to suffer injury if she is made to carry on doing that kind of work. No doubt in such a case it would be good practice for A to reassign B to some other kind of work which is less dangerous. But what if there is no other work available? Will A owe B a duty to dismiss her? For a long time, the courts took the view that A could not owe B such a duty.[112] However, in *Coxall* v *Goodyear GB Ltd* (2003), Simon Brown LJ took the view that if the risk that B will be injured if she carries on working for A is serious enough then A may well owe B a duty to dismiss her.[113]

So far we have discussed the duty an employer will owe his employee to see that she is not *killed or injured* while working for him. Will he also owe her a duty to take reasonable steps to see that she will not suffer *other kinds of harm*? The decision of the House of Lords in *Frost* v *Chief Constable of South Yorkshire* (1999) seems to establish that an employer will not owe his employees a *general* duty to take reasonable steps to see that they do not suffer any kind of *psychiatric illness* in working for him.[114] However, we have already seen that it is well established that if it is reasonably foreseeable that an employee will suffer a nervous breakdown if she is made to do a certain kind of work without any kind of assistance or counselling, then the employer will owe his employee a duty to take

---

[110] *McCafferty* v *Metropolitan Police District Receiver* [1977] 1 WLR 1073.

[111] *Smith* v *Baker* [1891] AC 325.

[112] See *Withers* v *Perry Chain Co Ltd* [1961] 1 WLR 1314, 1317 (per Sellers LJ): 'I cannot believe that the common law requires employers to refuse to employ a person who is willing to work for them simply because they think that it is not in the person's best interests to do the work. That would be imposing a restriction on the freedom of the individual which I think is foreign to the whole spirit of the common law of our country.'

[113] [2003] 1 WLR 536, at [29]. In *Barber* v *Somerset County Council* [2004] 1 WLR 1089, Lord Rodger of Earlsferry took much the same view, acknowledging that in cases where an employee would be exposed to a substantial risk of injury if he carried on working, his employer might owe him a duty to sack him: ibid, at [30].

[114] See also *French* v *Chief Constable of Sussex Police* [2006] EWCA Civ 312 (no duty to give police officers adequate training in running operations involving firearms even if it was foreseeable – which it was not – that failure to do so would result in police officers who were involved in a wrongful shooting suffering psychiatric illnesses as a result being subjected to criminal and disciplinary proceedings).

reasonable steps to see that she gets that assistance or counselling.[115] Furthermore, the House of Lords has held that it is strongly arguable that if A employs B and A knows or ought to know that B is being harassed to such an extent by her fellow employees that there is a danger she will suffer a breakdown, A will owe B a duty to take reasonable steps to stop the harassment.[116]

Turning to harms to property and economic harms, it seems that an employer will not owe an employee a duty to take reasonable steps to see that her property is not harmed while she is working for him;[117] neither will he owe her a duty to take reasonable steps to see that she does not suffer some kind of pure economic loss in working for him.[118]

6.9 Bailees

If A holds B's goods on a bailment for B, A (who is known as a 'bailee') will owe B (who is known as a 'bailor') a duty to take reasonable steps to safeguard those goods from being destroyed, damaged or stolen.

Some academics are resistant to regarding the breach of this duty of care as *negligence*. Unlike those academics who dislike the idea that the law on occupiers' liability is part of the law on negligence, these academics have a point.

First, s 2(2) of the Torts (Interference with Goods) Act 1977 provides that 'An action lies in conversion for loss or destruction of goods which a bailee has allowed to happen in breach of his duty to his bailor'. It seems, then, that conversion (another tort entirely) and not negligence is the appropriate cause of action when goods are lost or destroyed as a result of a bailee's breach of the duty of care he owes the bailor.

Secondly, in the recent case of *Yearworth* v *North Bristol NHS Trust* (2010) – where the defendants were being sued for failing to take reasonable steps to preserve sperm deposited with them by the claimants, who were undergoing treatment for cancer and might have been made infertile by that treatment – the Court of Appeal expressed itself 'strongly attracted' to the idea that the liability of a bailee who has failed to safeguard goods that have been bailed to him arises neither in contract, nor in tort, but is '*sui generis*' and 'where the gratuitous bailee has extended, and broken, a particular promise to his bailor, for example that the chattel will be stored in a particular place or in a particular way, the measure of damages may be more akin to that referable to breach of contract rather than to tort.'[119]

In light of all this, we will defer a detailed discussion of the law of bailment until our chapter on 'Torts to Personal Property'.[120]

---

[115] See above, § 6.6.

[116] *Waters* v *Commissioner of Police of the Metropolis* [2000] 1 WLR 1607 (held that it was strongly arguable that this principle applied in the case where the defendant commissioner occupied a status analogous to an employer in relation to the claimant policewoman, who suffered a breakdown as a result of being subjected to severe harassment from her fellow police officers for reporting that she had been raped by a fellow police officer).

[117] *Deyong* v *Shenburn* [1946] KB 227 (no duty to prevent theft of clothes from dressing room). However, if an employee's property is destroyed or damaged while she is working in her employer's factory, she may be able to bring a claim in negligence against her employer under the Occupiers' Liability Act 1957. See below, § 10.2.

[118] *Reid* v *Rush & Tompkins Group plc* [1990] 1 WLR 212 (no duty to advise employee of advisability of taking out insurance when working for defendant abroad).

[119] [2010] QB 1, at [48] ((h) and (i)).

[120] See below, § 15.4(C).

6.10 Carriers

If A gives B a lift in his car, A will normally owe B a duty under the Occupiers' Liability Act 1957 to take reasonable steps to ensure that the condition of his car is such that B will be reasonably safe in taking a lift in his car. This is because the law on occupiers' liability does not just cover occupiers of land but anyone 'occupying or having control over any fixed or moveable structure, including any vessel, vehicle or aircraft'.[121] But A will, in any case, owe B a more general duty to take reasonable steps to ensure that B will not be killed or injured in taking a lift in his car.

For example, in *Jebson* v *Ministry of Defence* (2000), the claimant was a soldier who went to Portsmouth with some fellow soldiers for a night out. Anticipating that the claimant and his companions would be in no condition to get back to their barracks after their night out, the defendants – the claimant's employer – sent a lorry to take them back home. The claimant – who was considerably the worse for wear after his night out – attempted to climb onto the roof of the lorry as it took him back to barracks. Unfortunately for the claimant, he failed in his attempt and fell off the lorry and into the road, suffering various injuries in the process. He claimed that the defendants had owed him a duty to take reasonable steps to ensure that he would not suffer any kind of injury in travelling in their lorry and that they had breached that duty in failing to have someone in the back of the lorry to supervise him and his companions and to make sure that they did not – in their drunken state – try to climb out of the lorry while it was travelling along. The Court of Appeal allowed the claimant's claim.

6.11 Child carers

Cases involving children seem to bring out the judges' most protective instincts. The courts will readily find that people involved with looking after children will owe those children a range of positive duties of care:[122]

A. Parents

Paradoxically, our opening statement is *least* true in cases involving those closest to a child: his or her parents. In cases involving parents, the courts have been wary of finding that parents owe their children duties of care, for fear of fostering litigation between family members, and intruding into difficult issues about what constitutes 'good parenting' and 'bad parenting'.[123]

---

[121] Occupiers' Liability Act 1957, s 1(3)(a).

[122] See, generally, Bagshaw 2001.

[123] Cf. *Woodland* v *Swimming Teachers Association* [2014] AC 537, at [25](6) (per Lord Sumption): 'the custody and control which parents exercise over their children is not only gratuitous, but based on an intimate relationship not readily analyzable in legal terms. For this reason, the common law has always been extremely cautious about recognizing legally enforceable duties owed by parents on the same basis as institutional carers.' See also the decision of the Court of Appeal in *OPO* v *MLA* [2014] EWCA Civ 1277 refusing to find (at [57]) that a parent owed his child a duty of care not to write a book about the parent's miserable childhood, which might foreseeably cause the child to suffer psychiatric illness (Not challenged on appeal: [2016] UKSC 32). For an extended discussion of how far parents should be held to owe their children legally enforceable duties to raise them properly, see Shmueli 2010.

Having said that, it seems clear that a parent will owe her child any duty of care that she would owe someone who was not her child. So a parent who is driving a car with her child in the back seat will owe the child a duty to take care not to drive dangerously.[124] She will also owe him a duty to take reasonable steps to feed him. So in *R v Gibbins and Proctor* (1919), a father who had starved his child with the aim of killing her was convicted of murder on the ground that his failure to feed the child was a wrongful omission. In *Surtees v The Royal Borough of Kingston upon Thames* (1991), Stocker LJ was prepared to accept that a parent who is looking after their child *for a particular period of time* will owe the child a duty 'to take such care as in all the circumstances was reasonable to ensure that the [child is] not exposed to unnecessary risk of injury, the standard of care being that of a careful parent in the prevailing circumstances.'[125]

In *XA v YA* (2010), Mrs Justice Thirlwall was doubtful whether it would be 'fair, just and reasonable' to find that a mother owed her son a duty to take reasonable steps to protect him from being continually assaulted by his father, for two reasons: (i) in such a case, the mother would probably be the subject of domestic violence as well, and it would be unfair to burden her with a duty of care when she was in such a vulnerable state; and (ii) it would not be desirable to get the civil courts involved in second-guessing a mother's decisions as to how best to protect her child from being harmed by an abusive partner.[126] And in *Barrett v Enfield LBC* (1998), Lord Woolf MR held that a parent would *not* owe a child a duty to make decisions about his or her future with a reasonable degree of care and skill:

> parents are daily making decisions with regard to their children's future and it seems to me that it would be wholly inappropriate that those decisions, even if they could be shown to be wrong, should be ones which give rise to a liability in damages.[127]

B. Teachers

It seems well established that a teacher will owe the students in his charge a duty to take reasonable steps to see that those students do not come to any harm while on the school premises.[128] As Lord Clyde observed in *Phelps v Hillingdon London Borough Council* (2001):

> [there] is no question that a teacher owes a duty of care for the physical safety of a child attending school under the charge of that teacher. The teacher has a duty to take reasonable care that the child does not come to any harm through any danger which may arise during the course of the child's attendance at the school.[129]

It also seems to be accepted that if a student has 'special needs' or suffers from learning difficulties, his teachers will owe him a duty to take reasonable steps to ensure that that student is not disadvantaged as a result of the fact that he suffers from those special needs or learning difficulties. So in *X v Bedfordshire County Council* (1995), Lord Browne-Wilkinson

---

[124] *Barrett v Enfield LBC* [1998] QB 367, 377; *XA v YA* [2010] EWHC 1983, at [140].

[125] [1991] 2 FLR 559, 569.

[126] [2010] EWHC 1983 (QB), at [143].

[127] [1998] QB 367, 377.

[128] The duty does not extend to seeing that the child does not come to any harm off the school premises: *Bradford-Smart v West Sussex County Council* [2002] EWCA Civ 7 (discussed, Elvin 2003b).

[129] [2001] 2 AC 619, 670. See also *Van Oppen v Clerk to Bedford Charity Trustees* [1990] 1 WLR 235, 250 (per Balcombe LJ). The same is true of educational authorities: see *New South Wales v Lepore* (2003) 212 CLR 511.

held – with the agreement of the other Law Lords deciding the case – that if 'it comes to the attention of [a] headmaster that a pupil is under-performing, he does owe a duty to take such steps as a reasonable teacher would consider appropriate to try to deal with such under-performance'.[130] In the *Phelps* case, the House of Lords refused to strike out a number of claims which were premised on the basis that the teachers of a student who suffers from special needs or learning difficulties will owe him a duty to take reasonable steps to ensure that that student is not disadvantaged from the fact that he suffers from those special needs or learning difficulties. The House of Lords held it was *arguable* that the teacher of a student who suffers from special needs or learning difficulties would owe him such a duty of care. Lord Nicholls – with the agreement of Lord Jauncey of Tullichettle – went further and held that 'a teacher [*will*] owe a duty of care to a child with learning difficulties . . . A teacher must exercise due skill and care to respond appropriately to the manifest problems of such a child, including informing the head-teacher or others about the child's problems and carrying out any instructions he is given.'[131]

The cases do not go so far as to say that the teachers of a *normal* student will owe him a duty to teach him with reasonable skill and care. Lord Nicholls held that the teachers of a normal student would owe him such a duty of care in *Phelps*[132] but only one of the other six Law Lords who decided *Phelps* indicated that he agreed with Lord Nicholls on this point.

C. Social services

In *Barrett* v *Enfield LBC* (2001), the claimant had been taken into care by a local authority when he was 10 months old. He stayed in care until he was 18 years old. In that time – the claimant alleged – he was placed with two foster families, and was moved into six different homes in 12 years. The claimant further alleged that the authority made no proper attempt to have someone adopt him, or to reunite him with his mother. The claimant sued the authority in negligence, claiming that they had owed him a duty to raise him with a reasonable degree of care and skill, and that he had developed psychological problems as a result of the authority's breaching that duty of care. The House of Lords unanimously held that it was *arguable* that the defendant local authority had owed the claimant a duty of care once they had taken him into care.

Given the endorsement that the decision in *Barrett* subsequently received from the House of Lords in *Gorringe* v *Calderdale MBC* (2004),[133] it may be that there is no longer any doubt that a local authority will owe a duty of care to someone in the position of the claimant in *Barrett*. This is so even though, as we have seen, a parent would not owe a child a duty of care of the type contended for in *Barrett*. The House of Lords did not think that this was an insuperable objection to the claimant's claim in *Barrett*: they thought that it should be easier to sue a *substitute* parent – like the social services in *Barrett* – than an *actual* parent. Lord Hutton suggested in *Barrett* that this was partly because some of the decisions that the local authority had to make were very different from those that a natural parent would normally have to make and partly because the local authority employs expert staff and advisers to assist it in making decisions about the future of the children in its care.[134]

---

[130] [1995] 2 AC 633, 766.
[131] [2001] 2 AC 619, 667.
[132] Ibid.
[133] [2004] 1 WLR 1057, at [39] (per Lord Hoffmann), [73] (per Lord Scott), [100] (per Lord Brown).
[134] [2001] 2 AC 550, 587–588.

It was at least arguable in *Barrett* that the social services had assumed a responsibility to the claimant in that case, and that the social services' duty of care to the claimant could be explained on that basis.[135] No such explanation can be offered of the decision of the Court of Appeal in *D* v *East Berkshire Community NHS Trust* (2004), which held that if a local authority receives reports that a child is being abused or neglected and the authority decides to investigate those reports, the authority will owe the child in question a duty to investigate the reports with a reasonable degree of care and skill.[136] The decision is incompatible with the *uniform approach* to determining whether or not a public body owed a claimant a duty of care to save them from harm that was endorsed by the UK Supreme Court in *Michael* v *Chief Constable of South Wales Police* (2015); after all, a neighbour who suspected that a child was at risk of being abused would not owe that child a duty of care to report their suspicions to the authorities.

Given this, it should come as no surprise that the history of how *D* v *East Berkshire NHS Trust* came to be decided was contaminated by the *policy approach* that was rejected in *Michael*. The roots of the decision in *D* lie in the decision of the House of Lords in *X* v *Bedfordshire County Council* (1995), where the House of Lords was asked to decide whether the social services could owe a duty of care to save a child that was at risk of being abused. As we have seen, the House of Lords held that the social services did not owe the child such a duty of care, but – influenced by Sir Thomas Bingham MR's judgment in the Court of Appeal in the same case – Lord Browne-Wilkinson based his decision on policy grounds, arguing that if the social services did owe a duty of care, then they would be vulnerable to being sued if they failed to save a child from being abused and the prospect of being sued for failing to save children from abuse would make the social services excessively cautious and overactive in investigating and acting on allegations of child abuse.[137] However, when the Human Rights Act 1998 ('HRA') came into force, that meant the social services could be sued *under the HRA* if they carelessly failed to protect an identified child who they knew was at risk of being abused[138] – and as a result the desire to protect local authorities from the prospect of being sued for failures to save children from being abused that lay at the root of Lord Browne-Wilkinson's refusal to find a duty of care in *X* could no longer be satisfied. Given this, the Court of Appeal in *D* v *East Berkshire* felt free to hold that the decision in *X* could not 'survive the Human Rights Act 1998'[139] and ruled that the social services *will* owe a duty of care to a child that is suspected of being at risk of abuse at home.

---

[135] This was Lord Hoffmann's explanation of *Barrett* in *Gorringe* v *Calderdale MBC* [2004] 1 WLR 1057, at [39]. The one difficulty with it is the lack of reliance (in the sense of doing something different that he would not otherwise have done) by the claimant on his carers.

[136] [2004] QB 558, at [83]. It is quite clear that the assertion in that paragraph that a duty of care is owed to a child who is suspected of being at risk of being abused at home extends to cases where the social services carelessly decide to leave the child in the family home as well as cases (such as that presented in *D* itself) where the social services carelessly decide to take the child out of the family home. A positive duty of care to save children at risk of abuse is also owed by the social services in New Zealand: see *Attorney-General* v *Prince* [1998] 1 NZLR 262 (NZCA) and *B* v *Attorney-General* [2003] 4 All ER 833 (PC).

[137] [1995] 2 AC 633, 650. This fear seems not to have been unfounded. After the 'Baby P' scandal, where a child was killed in his family home, despite being the subject of regular visits by the social services, the resulting opprobrium towards social workers generally triggered a huge increase in the number of applications to court by local authorities to take 'at risk' children into care.

[138] This was confirmed by the European Court of Human Rights in *Z* v *United Kingdom* [2001] 2 FLR 612, applying *Osman* v *UK* [1999] FLR 193: see above, § 1.11.

[139] [2004] QB 558, at [83].

It is highly doubtful that the decision in *D* v *East Berkshire NHS Trust* can survive the reasoning of the UK Supreme Court in *Michael* v *Chief Constable of South Wales Police* (2015).[140] However, it may be that no branch of the social services will want to incur the opprobrium of trying to overthrow it – and, in any case, the possibility of a claim under the HRA in cases where the social services carelessly fail to save a child from being abused in the family home makes it unlikely a case will come up where the issue of whether a duty of care was owed by the social services in negligence will have to be squarely confronted. So it may be that *D* v *East Berkshire NHS Trust* will be able to hang on – a relic of a way of thinking about the duties of care of public bodies that has now been firmly repudiated in *Michael*.

Further reading

For detailed expositions of the law in this area, see **Nolan, 'The liability of public authorities for failure to confer benefits' (2011) 127** *Law Quarterly Review* **260;** **Bagshaw, 'The duties of care of emergency service providers' [1999]** *Lloyd's Maritime and Commercial Law Quarterly* **71**; and **Fordham, 'Saving us from ourselves – the duty of care in negligence to prevent self-inflicted harm' (2010) 18** *Torts Law Journal* **22**, brilliantly synthesising the UK, Australian and Canadian authorities on when (if ever) defendants will owe claimants a duty of care to protect them from: (i) killing themselves; (ii) drunkenly injuring themselves; (iii) injuring themselves while engaging in dangerous sports; and (iv) gambling their money away.

Tom Cornford's *Towards a Public Law of Tort* **(Ashgate, 2008)** proposes that the law of negligence should be reformed to give effect to a principle ('Principle I') that a claimant who suffers harm as a result of a public authority's unreasonable failure to treat the claimant in the way that the law requires should be entitled to sue that public authority for compensation. The proposal assumes that negligence law is fundamentally about compensating for loss rather than vindicating rights. In **David Howarth's** casenote **'Poisoned wells: "proximity" and "assumption of responsibility" in negligence' (2005) 64** *Cambridge Law Journal* **23**, the former Lib Dem MP is acute (and disapproving) in pointing out that the common law regards decent public services as not something we have a *right* to; but he does not pursue that insight and instead concludes that decisions against holding public bodies liable for omissions are just a matter of 'policy' (no). What gives us a right to decent public services? Those who pay for those services might think they had a right to decent public services. But would we be happy with a law that said that taxpayers have a right to be protected by the police, but non-taxpayers must go hang? And how much of an individual taxpayer's money actually goes into the pocket of a policeman who is in a position to save that taxpayer from a beating?

In its 2008 Consultation Paper *Administrative Redress: Public Bodies and the Citizen*, the Law Commission proposed that a public authority should be held liable for harm

---

[140] Lady Hale will have done the case (which she was party to deciding when she was a member of the Court of Appeal) no favours by pointing out in *Michael* the 'striking' parallels (*Michael*, at [195]) between *D* v *East Berkshire NHS Trust* and the *Michael* case. The parallels are, indeed, striking, and not in favour of the decision in *D* v *East Berkshire NHS Trust*.

caused or not averted as a result of the authority acting unlawfully but only if the authority was seriously at fault in acting (or not acting) as it did. The effect of the proposal would have been to radically expand public bodies' liability for failing to prevent harm, and radically contract their liabilities for causing others to suffer harm. The paper was widely criticised and the proposal has not been implemented.

Academics gave a generally warmer welcome to the decision of the New South Wales Court of Appeal in *Lowns* v *Woods* (1996), holding a GP liable for failing to come to the assistance of a boy having an epileptic fit: see **Williams, 'Medical Samaritans: is there a duty to treat?' (2001) 21** *Oxford Journal of Legal Studies* **393, Gray and Edelman, 'Developing the law of omissions: a common law duty to rescue?' (1998) 6** *Torts Law Journal* **240**, and **Haberfield, '*Lowns* v *Woods* and the duty to rescue' (1998) 6** *Tort Law Review* **56**.

Chapter 7
Breach of duty

Aims and objectives

Reading this chapter should enable you to:

(1) Understand the factors that the courts will take into account in determining whether or not a defendant breached a duty of care owed to a claimant.

(2) Come to grips with the concept of a non-delegable duty of care, when a defendant will be held to have breached a non-delegable duty of care, and what sort of duties of care are non-delegable.

(3) Understand when a claimant will be able to establish that a defendant breached a duty of care by relying on a plea of *res ipsa loquitur*.

7.1 The basics

We have now finished discussing when one person will owe another a duty of care. In this chapter, we turn to the issue of when a duty of care will be held to have been breached. It is an obvious point, but one which is often overlooked by students, that a duty of care is not a duty to *ensure* that something happens or does not happen. The fact that A has crashed his car into B's car does not necessarily mean that A breached the duty of care that he owed B to *take care* not to crash into B's car. To show that A breached this duty of care we have to establish that . . . And at this point the law gets very difficult.

Most people would say that we have to establish that A's driving failed to come up to the standards of a *reasonable* driver, and more generally that we establish whether or not a defendant has breached a duty of care owed to a claimant by seeing whether the defendant failed to do what a *reasonable person* would have done, in the circumstances. Such formulations do emphasise an important point about duties of care. In most situations where it is alleged that a defendant breached a duty of care owed to the claimant, it is not enough for a defendant to say 'I did my best!' So, in the case we are considering, A cannot argue that he took care not to crash into B's car by merely saying he did his best not to crash into B's car. The duty of care that drivers owe other drivers requires drivers to live up to an *objective* standard of care in their driving, one which makes no allowances for the individual idiosyncrasies of a particular driver.

But at the same time, saying that we determine whether A breached the duty of care he owed B not to crash into B's car by seeing whether A's driving came up to the standards of a reasonable driver leaves too much open. How do we determine what those standards are? Suppose that A crashed into the back of B's car because his attention was momentarily distracted by a picture of a half-naked model on a billboard beside the road, and he failed to spot that B had unexpectedly braked in front of him. Would a *reasonable* driver's attention have been distracted in this way? How can we tell? If it could be established that 75% of male drivers would have taken their eye off the road when faced with such a distraction, would that show that a *reasonable* driver would have taken his or her eye off the road? Or do we follow the American judge Learned Hand's line that:

> in most cases reasonable prudence is in fact common prudence; but strictly speaking it is never its measure . . . Courts must in the end say what is required; there are precautions so imperative that even their universal disregard will not excuse their omission.[1]

The truth is – it is not possible to come up with any single rule, or standard, by which to determine whether a given defendant has breached a duty of care owed to a claimant. Many people have tried to come up with some such rule or standard. For example, the same American judge we have just quoted came up with a very famous formula for determining whether or not a failure to take a certain precaution meant that a defendant had breached a duty of care. In the case of *United States* v *Carroll Towing Co* (1947), the issue came up as to whether the owner of a barge that was tied up at a pier should have had someone on the barge during normal business hours to look after the barge if (as happened) it became untied from its moorings. Learned Hand J said:

> Since there are occasions when every vessel will break from her moorings, and since, if she does, she becomes a menace to those about her; the owner's duty, as in other similar situations, to provide against resulting injuries is a function of three variables: (1) The probability that she will break away; (2) the gravity of the resulting injury, if she does; (3) the burden of adequate precautions. Possibly it serves to bring this notion into relief to state it in algebraic terms: if the probability be called P; the injury, L; and the burden, B; liability depends upon whether B is less than L multiplied by P: i.e., whether $B < PL$.[2]

Learned Hand J applied the formula to find that the barge owner in the *Carroll Towing* case should have had someone on board during normal business hours: the cost of taking such a precaution was outweighed by the *magnitude of the risk* of something going wrong if someone was not on board at such a time. (Where the magnitude of the risk is assessed by multiplying the probability of something going wrong by the harm that will be done if something goes wrong.)

However, as we will see, the 'Hand Formula' for determining whether someone has breached a duty of care owed to another may not always apply.[3] For example, suppose that a car company discovers that a particular line of cars manufactured by the company suffers from a dangerous defect. As a result, the company will come under a duty to take reasonable steps to prevent that defect injuring those who might foreseeably be affected by the defect.[4] But what does taking such 'reasonable steps' require? Suppose that recalling and

---

[1] *The TJ Hooper*, 60 F 2d 737 (1932).

[2] 159 F 2d 169, 173 (1947).

[3] Richard Wright is the most vocal critic of the Hand Formula: see Wright 1995 and Wright 2003. See also Zipursky 2007.

[4] This is under the 'creation of danger' principle discussed above, § 6.3.

fixing the cars affected by the defect would cost £700m, and the prospective losses that would be suffered if the company did nothing (discounted by the probability of the defect in question causing harm) only came to £250m. In such a case, the Hand Formula might suggest that doing nothing is the reasonable thing to do as B > PL. However, were the company to do nothing in this situation,[5] it seems clear it would not just be held to have acted negligently – its negligence would be regarded as so serious that it might warrant an award of exemplary (or punitive) damages being made against it if and when the company was sued by any victims who suffered harm as a result of the defect that it did nothing to rectify.

Given that it is not possible to come up with a *single* rule, or standard, that we can employ to determine whether or not a given defendant has breached a duty of care that he owed to a claimant, the way we will proceed in this chapter is to set out a number of *different* rules that will govern this enquiry, but in relation to each rule explain the exceptions that exist to those rules (and, in some cases, the exceptions that exist to the exceptions). Those rules and their exceptions are briefly set out below:

(1) *Objectivity.* The *rule* is – as we have already seen – that the fact that a defendant did his or her personal best to avoid something happening will not necessarily mean that he or she did not breach a duty of care owed to the claimant. The standard of care that a defendant is expected to exercise in the interests of a claimant is *objective.* The *exceptions* to this rule are too complicated to set out here, but are set out in the next section.

(2) *Balancing.* The *rule* is laid out in the Hand Formula. If A owed B a duty to take reasonable steps to avoid X happening, and failed to take a given precaution P to avoid X happening, we determine whether A's failure to take precaution P put him in breach of the duty of care that he owed B by *balancing* the *cost* of taking precaution P against the *magnitude* of the *foreseeable* risk that X would happen if precaution P were not taken.

A possible *exception* to this rule is where the magnitude of the foreseeable risk that X would happen if precaution P were not taken was *very serious.* As the example considered above of the defective car shows, in such a case balancing the cost of taking precaution P against the magnitude of the risk that X would happen if that precaution were not taken may be inappropriate, and the courts may refuse to excuse A's failure to take precaution P on cost grounds. A possible *exception to this exception* is where taking precaution P would have *social costs* – that is, costs to society at large. In such a case, it might be that failing to take precaution P could be justified on grounds of the social cost involved in taking that precaution, even if the risk that X would happen if that precaution were not taken was relatively serious.

(3) *Common practice.* The *rule* is that pleading 'everyone (or most people) would have done the same as me' does *not* work to establish that you have not breached a duty of care owed to someone else. So the fact that 75 per cent of male motorists would have taken their eyes off the road to look at a poster of a half-naked model will not excuse a defendant who ran into the claimant's car because his attention was distracted by such a poster.

---

[5] Something that Ford is alleged to have done in the famous 'Ford Pinto case' (*Grimshaw* v *Ford Motor Co*, 119 Cal App 3d 757 (1981)), where – it is claimed – Ford decided against repairing a defect in the protection around the fuel tank in its Pinto range of cars on the ground that the repairs would cost more than it would have to pay out if the inadequate protection resulted in an accident. For a measured view of the Ford Pinto case, see Schwartz 1991.

The *exception* is where a professional is under a duty to exercise a reasonable degree of care and skill in looking after a client's interests. In such a case, the courts will normally allow the professional to plead that he did exercise such care and skill in looking after the client's interests by showing that there is a significant body of opinion within his profession that would regard it as proper for him to treat his client in the way he did. (This is known as the '*Bolam* test' for professional negligence, after the case of *Bolam* v *Friern Hospital Management Committee* (1957), in which it was first set out.)

However, there are a couple of *exceptions to the exception* where (i) the courts regard the 'significant body of opinion' as being plainly wrong-headed or irrational, or (ii) a doctor is alleged to have acted negligently in failing to tell a patient of a risk associated with a proposed course of treatment – the doctor will not be able to save herself from an allegation of negligence by pointing to a 'significant body of opinion' that favours not telling the patient of that particular risk.

(4) *Personal fault.* The *rule* is that in determining whether a defendant breached a duty of care owed to a claimant, we look at the defendant's *own* conduct and see whether *that* conduct fell short of the standard of care that the defendant was expected to live up to. There are two *exceptions* to this rule.

First of all, in the case where A owed B a *non-delegable duty of care* to take reasonable steps to avoid X happening, and A gave the job of avoiding X happening to C, if C failed to take reasonable steps to avoid X happening, then *A* will be held to have breached the duty of care *he* owed B to take reasonable steps to avoid X happening.

Secondly, as a company does not do anything itself, but instead operates through people who work for it, in determining whether a company has breached a duty of care, we look at the conduct of the people whose conduct can be fairly *attributed* to the company.

(5) *Proof.* The *rule* is that the burden of proving that a defendant has breached a duty of care owed to the claimant falls on the claimant. The burden of proof shifts to the defendant in a case where the maxim '*res ipsa loquitur*' ('the thing speaks for itself') applies. If what has happened to the claimant was unlikely to have happened had the defendant taken care, what has happened to the claimant will count as evidence that the defendant has breached his duty of care, and the burden of proof will then fall on the defendant to show that, in fact, he did *not* breach his duty of care and that what happened to the claimant has some other explanation.

We will now look at each of these rules and their exceptions in much more detail.

7.2 Objectivity

A. The rule

That a defendant cannot claim to have discharged a duty of care that he owed the claimant by merely saying 'I did my best' has been established in English law ever since the case of *Vaughan* v *Menlove* (1837).

In that case, the defendant constructed near the claimant's property a hay-rick (a pile of hay that has been left out in the sun to dry). The hay-rick spontaneously ignited in the sunshine, and the fire spread to the claimant's land, and the claimant's house burned down as a result. The claimant sued the defendant, claiming that the defendant had acted negligently either in the way he constructed the hay-rick, or in choosing to locate it so close to the claimant's land. The defendant was held liable at first instance, but argued that the case should be tried again to determine 'whether he had acted bona fide to the best of his judgment' on the ground that 'if he had, he ought not to be responsible for the misfortune of not possessing the highest order of intelligence.'[6] The Court of Common Pleas dismissed the application, on the ground that whether 'the Defendant had acted honestly and bona fide to the best of his own judgment' was irrelevant to the case. Inquiring into such matters:

> would leave so vague a line as to afford no rule at all, the degree of judgment belonging to each individual being infinitely various . . . Instead, therefore of saying that the liability in negligence should be co-extensive with each individual, which would be as variable as the length of the foot of each individual, we ought rather to adhere to the rule which requires in all cases a regard to caution such as a man of ordinary prudence would observe.[7]

The court's justification for adopting an objective approach to questions of whether a defendant has breached a duty of care owed to a claimant found a strong echo in the decision of the Court of Appeal in *Nettleship* v *Weston* (1971), almost 150 years later.

In that case, the claimant agreed to give a friend's wife, the defendant, some driving lessons. During the third lesson, the defendant panicked while taking the car round a corner, failed to straighten up the car, and it mounted the pavement and struck a lamp-post. The claimant's knee was injured in the collision, and he sued the defendant in negligence. Lord Denning MR held that the defendant owed *other road users* a duty to take care to drive 'in as good a manner as a driver of skill, experience and care, who is sound . . . in limb, who makes no errors of judgment, had good eyesight and hearing, and is free from any infirmity'.[8] He went on to hold that the *same* duty of care was owed to the claimant instructor – the fact that he got into the car, knowing that the defendant was only capable of driving to the standard of a learner driver, made no difference:

> The driver owes a duty of care to every passenger in the car, just as he does to every pedestrian on the road: and he must attain the *same* standard of care in respect of each. If the driver were to be excused according to the knowledge of the passenger, it would result in *endless confusion and injustice*. One of the passengers may know that the learner driver is a mere novice. Another passenger may believe him to be entirely competent . . . Is the one passenger to recover and the other not? Rather than embark on such inquiries, the law holds that the driver must attain the same standard of care for passengers as for pedestrians.[9]

Applying that standard of care to the facts of *Nettleship* v *Weston*, the Court of Appeal found the defendant liable in negligence for the claimant's injury.

---

[6] (1837) 3 Bing NC 468, 471; 132 ER 490, 492.

[7] (1837) 3 Bing NC 468, 475; 132 ER 490, 493 (per Tindal CJ).

[8] [1971] 2 QB 691, 699.

[9] [1971] 2 QB 691, 700. The High Court of Australia originally disagreed with this, holding in *Cook* v *Cook* (1986) 162 CLR 376 that a lesser duty of care would be owed to a passenger who knew the driver was inexperienced. However, the High Court reversed that position in *Imbree* v *McNeilly* (2008) 82 AJLR 1374 (noted, Allen 2009) and adopted *Nettleship* v *Weston* as good law in Australia.

B. Justifications for the rule

The cases justify holding people to an *objective* standard of care – a standard of care that makes no allowances for a particular defendant's incapacity to meet that standard – on *practical* grounds. As Megaw LJ observed in *Nettleship* v *Weston*:

> if [a] doctrine of varying standards were to be accepted as part of the law . . . it could not logically be confined to the duty of care owed by learner drivers. There is no reason in logic why it should not operate in a much wider sphere. The disadvantages of the resulting unpredictability, uncertainty and, indeed, impossibility of arriving at fair and consistent decisions outweighs the advantages. The certainty of a general standard is preferable to the vagaries of a fluctuating standard.[10]

However, more *principled* justifications for the objective standard of care may be also offered.

(1) In a case where *Professional* has voluntarily assumed a responsibility to *Client*, it is *fair* to hold *Professional* to the standard of care that *Professional* indicated to *Client* that she could be expected to live up to when she assumed a responsibility to *Client*. If *Professional* has persuaded *Client* to allow her to work for him by holding herself out as having the expertise of a consultant, she cannot complain at then being expected to treat *Client* with the degree of care and skill that a reasonable consultant would apply in working for *Client*.[11]

(2) In a case where *Inexpert* and *Expert* simultaneously owe each other duties of care – for example, in the case where *Inexpert* and *Expert* are both driving in each other's vicinity – it might be thought *unfair* if *Inexpert* owed *Expert* a lesser degree of care than *Expert* owed *Inexpert*. Holding that *Expert* owes *Inexpert* more than *Inexpert* owes *Expert* would seem to punish *Expert* for his expertise, and reward *Inexpert* for her inexperience.

(3) In a case where *Inexpert* and *Other People* each owe A a duty of care, it might be thought *unfair* if *Inexpert* owed A a lesser duty of care than *Other People* did. Holding that *Other People* are subject to a more stringent duty of care than *Inexpert* might be thought to punish *Other People* for not being *Inexpert*, and reward *Inexpert* for not being like *Other People*.

(4) In a case where *Dangerous* could avoid exposing anyone to danger by simply doing *nothing*, if *Dangerous* chooses to put other people at risk of harm by *acting*, it is *not unfair* to require *Dangerous* to take a great deal of care to ensure that his choice to act does not result in those other people suffering harm, even if *Dangerous* is incapable of meeting that standard of care. If *Dangerous* had not wanted to be subjected to such a demanding standard of care, he could have avoided it by simply *not acting*.

Holding a defendant to an objective standard of care is hardest to justify in a *principled* way in a situation where none of the above four factors apply. That is: in a case where a defendant owes a claimant a duty of care that: (1) has not been voluntarily assumed; (2) is not matched by a corresponding duty of care that the claimant owes the defendant; (3) is only owed to the claimant by the defendant and not by other people; and (4) does not arise out of a defendant's choice to act in a way that has put the claimant in danger of being harmed. As it happens, in at least two situations where (1)–(4) are true, the courts

---

[10] [1971] 2 QB 691, 707.
[11] See *Wilsher* v *Essex Area Health Authority* [1987] 1 QB 730 (if A treats B, a hospital patient, A will owe B a duty to treat B with the skill and care that a reasonably competent person in A's *post* would exercise in treating the patient).

do *not* apply an objective standard of care to the defendant, and require him instead to do his best with what he has to protect the claimant from harm. But before we get on to those situations, we will first look at how the objective standard of care is applied in practice.

C. Application of the rule

The objective standard of care takes no account of the defendant's personal circumstances, but it is not *inhumane*. It does *not* require a defendant to demonstrate *superhuman* levels of care for the claimant. Two features of the way the objective standard of care is applied demonstrate this.

(1) *Emergencies and other stressful situations.* It is well known that people tend to react sub-optimally in emergencies and other stressful situations. It would be unreasonable to require people in such situations to do whatever a reasonable person would do in the cool light of day, and the objective standard of care is tempered to take that into account. This principle has been most recently acknowledged by s 4 of the Social Action, Responsibility and Heroism Act 2015 which says that in determining whether a defendant breached a duty of care:

> The court must have regard to whether the alleged negligence . . . occurred when the person was acting heroically by intervening in an emergency to assist an individual in danger.

However, s 4 adds nothing to the law: the same principle has long been given effect to by the courts.[12] For example, in *Surtees* v *Kingston-upon-Thames Borough Council* (1991), Sir Nicolas Browne-Wilkinson V-C warned that the court:

> should be wary in its approach to holding parents in breach of a duty of care owed to their children . . . The studied calm of the Royal Courts of Justice, concentrating on one point at a time, is light years away from the circumstances prevailing in the average home. The mother is looking after a fast moving toddler at the same time as cooking a meal, answering the telephone, looking after the other children and doing all the other things that the average mother has to cope with simultaneously, or in quick succession, in the normal household. We should be slow to characterise as negligent the care which ordinary loving mothers are able to give individual children, given the rough-and-tumble of home life.[13]

Similarly, in *Wilsher* v *Essex Area Health Authority* (1987), Mustill LJ held that, in considering whether or not a doctor or a nurse had failed in his or her duty to treat a patient with the degree of care and skill that a reasonably competent doctor or nurse occupying the same post would exercise in treating a patient:

> full allowance must be made for the fact that certain aspects of the treatment may have [had] to be carried out in what [one may call] 'battle conditions.' An emergency may overburden the

---

[12] See, in addition to the quotes in the text, *Smith* v *Ministry of Defence* [2014] AC 52, at [64] (per Lord Hope): 'A court should be very slow to question operational decisions made on the ground by commanders . . .' and at [99] (also per Lord Hope): 'Great care needs to be taken not to subject those responsible for decisions at any level that affect what takes place on the battlefield . . . to duties that are unrealistic or excessively burdensome.'

[13] [1991] 2 FLR 559, 583-4. See also *Carmanthenshire County Council* v *Lewis* [1955] AC 549 (held, teacher did not breach duty of care not to allow child to escape into the road outside the school merely because her attention was momentarily distracted by the need to bandage up another child's wounds).

available resources, and, if an individual is forced by circumstances to do too many things at once, the fact that he does one of them incorrectly should not lightly be taken as negligence.[14]

The same point applies where a player in a game makes, in the heat of the moment, an error of judgment with the result that another player is injured. It would be unreasonable for the law to expect people playing games to avoid making any such errors. Given this, a player will only be held to have breached a duty of care not to injure other players in the game if he made a mistake that demonstrated a *wanton or reckless disregard* for another player's safety.[15]

(2) *Automatism.* If the defendant is not responsible for what his body is doing – in the sense that his body is beyond his control or it is very difficult for him to control what his body is doing – he will *not* be found to have breached an objective standard of care merely because he has failed to bring his body under control.

For example, in *Mansfield* v *Weetabix* (1998), the defendant was a driver who was unaware that he suffered from malignant insulinoma – a condition which meant that, if he did not eat properly, his brain would be starved of the quantities of glucose necessary for it to function properly. One day, the defendant set out on a 40-mile journey without eating properly and, as a result, his driving became more and more erratic, culminating in his driving off the road and into the claimants' shop. The claimants sued the defendant, claiming that he had breached the duty he owed them to take care not to drive dangerously. The Court of Appeal dismissed the claim.[16] The defendant's malignant insulinoma meant that he could not have helped driving the way he did. Of course, it would have been different if the defendant had been aware of his condition and gone out driving without taking care to eat properly. His failure to take reasonable steps to ensure that his driving would not be affected by his condition would have put him in breach of the duty he owed to all those on or near the roads used by him – including the claimants – to take care not to drive dangerously.

It was different in *Dunnage* v *Randall* (2016) where the defendant, a paranoid schizophrenic, poured petrol on himself and attempted to set himself on fire using a lighter. When the claimant tried to stop the defendant, the lighter ignited and the claimant was severely burned in the resulting conflagration. The Court of Appeal held unanimously that the defendant had breached a duty of care owed to the claimant in acting as he did. He was not acting as an automaton – he knew what he was doing and was acting perfectly deliberately in so acting[17] – and the fact that it may have been very difficult for the

---

[14] [1987] 1 QB 730, 749. To the same effect, in relation to soldiers conducting peace-keeping operations, see *Bici* v *Ministry of Defence* [2004] EWHC 786 (QB), at [46].

[15] See *Wooldridge* v *Sumner* [1963] 2 QB 43 (spectator injured when defendant rode his horse too fast); *Condon* v *Basi* [1985] 1 WLR 866 (footballer injured as a result of foul tackle by defendant); *Caldwell* v *Fitzgerald* [2001] EWCA Civ 1054 (jockey injured in race as a result of actions of two other jockeys); *Blake* v *Galloway* [2004] EWCA Civ 814 (claimant struck in eye by piece of bark thrown at him by defendant in course of good natured horseplay). See also *Orchard* v *Lee* [2009] EWCA Civ 295, where the claimant was a teacher who was injured when a 13 year schoolboy who was playing tag ran into her: held that as the boy was playing 'within a play area, not breaking any rules . . . [and] not acting to any significant degree beyond the norms of the game', he was not liable.

[16] In so doing, they disapproved Neill J's judgment in *Roberts* v *Ramsbottom* [1980] 1 All ER 7, which suggested that a driver who drove his car dangerously due to the fact that he suffered some personal failing would be held to have breached the duty he owed others to take care not to drive dangerously if, at the time he was driving, he enjoyed some *limited* control of the car.

defendant to resist acting as he did, did not justify relaxing the objective standard of care that he was expected to exercise in the interests of the claimant.[18]

(3) *Isolated mistakes.* 'To err is human'; 'We all make mistakes'. So far, these consoling and commonplace bits of wisdom do not seem to be taken into account in applying the objective standard for determining whether a defendant breached a duty of care. For example, if A momentarily takes his eyes off the road ahead and as a result fails to notice that B's car in front of him has braked, so that A then crashes into the back of B's car, A will be found to have breached the duty of care that he owed B – the fact that it is actually quite normal for drivers to take their eyes off the road from time to time will be no excuse. However, s 3 of the Social Action, Responsibility and Heroism Act 2015 *might* have the effect of moderating the harshness with which the objective standard for determining whether someone has breached a duty of care is applied to people who make isolated mistakes. This section provides that in determining whether a person has breached a duty of care:

> The court must have regard to whether the person, in carrying out the activity in the course of which the alleged negligence . . . occurred, demonstrated a predominantly responsible approach towards protecting the safety or other interests of others.

It remains to be seen whether this provision will encourage the courts, in applying the objective standard to determine whether a defendant has breached a duty of care, to be more indulgent towards defendants who are guilty of merely isolated mistakes.

D. Exceptions to the rule

There are two principal exceptions to the objective standard of care.

(1) *Assumption of responsibility.* In a case where A owes B a duty of care arising out of an 'assumption of responsibility' by A to B, A's duty of care will only require her to live up to the standard of care that she indicated to B she could be relied upon to apply in dealing with B. Sometimes this works against A, if she holds herself out to B as being capable of working for B to a higher standard of care than A is in fact capable. But if A has made it clear to B that B cannot expect very much of her, but B has – notwithstanding that – still put her trust in A, all A will have to do is live up to that very modest standard of care.

(2) *Duties to act.* We said above that the objective standard of care was hard to justify in a *principled* way in a situation where a defendant owes a claimant a duty of care that: (a) has not been voluntarily assumed; (b) is not matched by a corresponding duty of care that the claimant owes the defendant; (c) is only owed by the defendant and not by other people; and (d) does not arise out of a defendant's choice to act in a way that has put the claimant in danger of being harmed. But we also said that in at least two situations where (a)–(d) are true, all the defendant would be required to do for the claimant was *his best*, given his circumstances.

The first situation is where a landowner owes his neighbours a duty to take reasonable steps to deal with a naturally occurring hazard (such as a fire) arising on his land. The duty of care owed by the landowner in this case will be 'measured' in the sense that all it

---

[17] [2016] QB 639, at [111]–[112], [135], [145].
[18] Ibid, at [107], [130], [147].

requires the landowner to do is to do *his best* to deal with the hazard, given his circumstances:

> [L]ess must be expected of the infirm than of the able-bodied: the owner of a small property where a hazard arises which threatens a neighbour with substantial interests should not have to do as much as one with larger interests of his own at stake and greater resources to protect them: if the small owner does what he can . . . he may be held to have done his duty: he should not be held liable unless it is clearly proved that he could, and reasonably in his individual circumstances should, have done more.[19]

The same sort of reasoning applies in the case where a prisoner is in police custody, with the result that the police owe him a duty to take reasonable steps to protect him from killing himself. That duty of care will only require the police to do their best, with the resources that they have, to save the prisoner from killing himself.[20]

7.3 Balancing

A. The rule

In a case where A owes B a duty to take reasonable steps to avoid X happening, and has failed to take a precaution P against X happening, *the rule* is that we determine whether A's failure to take precaution P has put him in breach of the duty of care he owed B by balancing the *cost* of taking precaution P against the *magnitude of the foreseeable risk* that X would happen if precaution P were not taken. (The magnitude of the foreseeable risk is given by multiplying the probability that X would happen if precaution P were not taken by the extent of harm B would suffer if X happened – with the probability and extent of harm being assessed according to what a reasonable person in A's position would have assessed them as being at the time A failed to take precaution P.)

COST OF PRECAUTION	MAGNITUDE OF FORESEEABLE RISK	
	High	Low
High	*Miller* v *Jackson* (1977) (negligence)	*Bolton* v *Stone* (1951) (no negligence)
		Latimer v *AEC* (1953) (no negligence)
		Tomlinson v *Congleton BC* (2004) (no negligence)
Low	*Paris* v *Stepney BC* (1951) (negligence)	*Scout Association* v *Barnes* (2010) (negligence)
		Harris v *Perry* (2009) (no negligence)

The above table, and the cases below, demonstrate this rule in action.

---

[19] *Goldman* v *Hargrave* [1967] AC 645, 663 (per Lord Wilberforce). If dealing with the hazard effectively was beyond the landowner, given his resources, he may still be held to have breached the duty of care that he owed his neighbours to take reasonable steps to deal with the hazard if he did not warn his neighbours of the danger and invite them to join with him in dealing with it: see *Holbeck Hall Hotel Ltd* v *Scarborough BC* [2000] QB 836.

[20] *Knight* v *Home Office* [1990] 3 All ER 237.

(1) *High risk–low cost.* Where there is a high degree of foreseeable risk to the claimant if a given precaution is not taken, and it would not cost very much to take that precaution, it would be negligent not to take that precaution. This was the case in *Paris* v *Stepney BC* (1951), where the defendant employers failed to provide the claimant with goggles to protect his one remaining good eye while he removed a bolt on a rusty vehicle. While the probability that doing such 'bolt work' would result (as happened) in a chip of metal flying up and damaging the claimant's one remaining good eye was low, the seriousness of the harm that would result from that eye being damaged was such that the magnitude of the foreseeable risk of harm that the claimant would be exposed to if he were not given goggles was very high. Given that it would not have been very expensive to supply the claimant with goggles, the House of Lords held that defendants had breached the duty of care they owed the claimant to see that he would be reasonably safe in working for them by failing to provide him with goggles.[21]

(2) *Low risk–high cost.* Where things are the other way around, and it would cost a lot of money to eliminate a risk of harm to the claimant that is of a low magnitude, it will not be negligent to allow the risk to stand and not do anything about it. This was the case in *Bolton* v *Stone* (1951) (not negligent on the part of a cricket club not to do anything about the very small risk that someone might be hit by a cricket ball flying out of the ground given the cost involved in reducing that risk, either by putting higher fences around the ground or by stopping playing cricket at the ground altogether), *Latimer* v *AEC* (1953) (where an employer was held not to have been negligent in merely spreading sawdust over an oil spill at work to make the floor less slippery; eliminating the remaining possibility that someone might have slipped on the oil would have cost too much relative to the risk posed by the oil now that it had sawdust scattered over it), and *Tomlinson* v *Congleton BC* (2004) (not negligent to fail to protect people who disregarded 'no swimming' signs around a lake in a public park from the small risks of harm to which they exposed themselves by swimming in the lake given that the only way to stop those people endangering themselves would have been to destroy the beaches around the lake and turn them into swamp-land, thereby discouraging anyone from going near the lake).

(3) *Low risk–low cost.* Cases where the magnitude of the risk of harm R that the claimant would have been exposed to if the defendant did not take a particular precaution P was low, but the cost of taking that precaution would also have been low, are marginal. An assessment of whether the defendant's failure to take precaution P was negligent will depend on a fine assessment of the magnitude of the risk R and the cost of precaution P. It is no surprise, then, to find that in a recent 'low risk-low cost' case – *The Scout Association* v *Barnes* (2010) – the Court of Appeal divided 2:1 on whether to find that the defendant had acted negligently.

In that case, a group of boy scouts played a game known as 'Objects in the Dark', where *n* scouts run about a hall in the dark, each trying to find and pick up one of *n-1* blocks of wood. The unlucky scout who has been unable to pick up a block of wood is eliminated from the game, and the game starts again with one less scout and one less block of wood, until the final round where there are only two scouts left, searching in the dark for one block of wood. The claimant fell over a bench near a wall while playing this

---

[21] See also *Hudson* v *Ridge Manufacturing Co Ltd* [1957] 2 QB 348 (negligent not to take more serious action than merely reprimanding an employee who had a long history of playing dangerous pranks on his fellow employees).

game and was injured. It was found that the risks associated with playing this game in the dark (as opposed to in the light) were quite small – no one in the claimant's scout group had ever been injured before playing this game. But at the same time, the cost involved in playing the game in the light rather than in the dark was not that great. Playing the game in the dark added some spice of excitement to the game, but it was not essential to the playing of the game (which was called 'Grab' if played in the light). Jackson LJ found that it had *not* been negligent to play the game in the dark:

> Obviously the risks of this particular game were increased by turning off the main lights. But I do not see how it could possibly be said that these increased risks outweighed the social benefits of the activity. Children and teenagers have played games with an element of risk, including games in the dark, since time immemorial. The game played by the claimant and his fellow scouts . . . was much safer than many games which children might play, if left to their own devices . . . It was a game which has been played on many occasions before and since that date without mishap.[22]

Smith and Ward LJJ disagreed, preferring to trust the judgment of the first instance judge who had taken a different view of the relative balance of risk and cost in this case. He had asked himself: 'Is the benefit of added fun worth the added risk? [and] decided it was not worth it. Scouting would not lose much of its value if the game was not to be played in the dark.'[23]

In another low risk–low cost case, *Harris* v *Perry* (2009), the Court of Appeal found for the defendant. In that case, the claimant was a child who suffered very serious head injuries when he was hit by another child doing a somersault on a bouncy castle on which they were both playing. The defendants were a husband and wife who had had triplets. They had put the bouncy castle up in their back garden for children to play in as part of a birthday party they were holding for the triplets. The wife stood in front of the bouncy castle and an inflatable bungee run, keeping an eye on what was happening on both inflatables. The accident to the claimant happened while the wife's attention was distracted helping a child on the bungee run. It was held that the defendants had not been negligent in not having someone spend all the time watching what was happening on the bouncy castle. Although the cost involved in having someone supervise the bouncy castle full time might not have been that high, it was still not unreasonable to have someone look after both inflatables at the same time given that the magnitude of the foreseeable risk of a child's being injured on the bouncy castle was very low. (Even though injury might have been quite probable, the extent of the injury that a child would foreseeably suffer as a result of playing on a bouncy castle was not serious.)

B. Exceptions to the rule

There are two potential exceptions to the above balancing approach to determining whether it is negligent not to take a given precaution against a particular risk.

(1) *High risk–high cost cases.* In a *high risk–high cost* case, it would cost a lot to guard against a risk of a high degree of magnitude. In such a case, it might be improper for a defendant not to do anything about the risk on the ground that it would cost too much to deal with it. Allowing a defendant to ignore such a risk on grounds of cost would – it

---

[22] [2010] EWCA Civ 1476, at [32].
[23] [2010] EWCA Civ 1476, at [59] (per Ward LJ).

could be argued – violate the ideal of the *separateness of persons*: the idea that harming A, or exposing A to a serious risk of harm, cannot be justified simply by reference to the benefit B will obtain from harming A or exposing A to a serious risk of harm.

A case which supports the idea that balancing is not allowed in *high risk–high cost* cases, and that in such a case it would be negligent not to guard against the possibility of the claimant being injured no matter how expensive it might be to guard against that possibility, is *Miller* v *Jackson* (1977). In that case, the claimants lived so near to a cricket ground that it was very likely that a ball hit out of the ground might end up flying into their house; and it was quite common for cricket balls to be hit out of the ground. So the magnitude of the risk of harm to which the claimants were exposed as a result of living next to the cricket ground was very high. But the cost of averting that risk – essentially, closing down the cricket ground – would also have been very high, in terms of loss of enjoyment for the cricketers and their spectators. It was for this reason that Lord Denning MR refused to find that the cricket club was doing anything wrong in continuing to play cricket on their ground:

> There is a contest here between the interest of the public at large; and the interest of a private individual. The *public* interest lies in protecting the environment by preserving our playing fields in the face of mounting development, and by enabling our youth to enjoy all the benefits of outdoor games, such as cricket and football. The *private* interest lies in securing the privacy of his home and garden without intrusion or interference by anyone . . . As between their conflicting interests, I am of [the] opinion that the public interest should prevail over the private interest. The cricket club should not be driven out.[24]

But the other two judges in the Court of Appeal disagreed: no matter how great the cost might have been of closing down the cricket club, that could not justify exposing the claimants to such a high degree of risk: 'The risk of injury to person and property is so great that on each occasion when a ball comes over the fence and causes damage to the [claimants], the defendants are guilty of negligence.'[25]

However, a balancing approach might be justified in a *high risk–high cost* situation where the issue is whether the defendant has breached a duty of care requiring him to take *positive steps* to save the claimant from harm. If the claimant is in a great deal of danger, but it would also carry a high cost to save her from harm, a court might decline to find a defendant liable in negligence if, on grounds of that cost, he fails to rescue the claimant.[26] Refusing to find the defendant liable in negligence in this kind of case would not violate the ideal of the *separateness of persons* as failing to save someone from harm never violates that ideal: the complaint against A, in a case where A has failed to save B from harm, is always that A regarded B as *too* separate from him, and not that A has failed to respect B's separateness as a person.

---

[24] [1977] 1 QB 966, 981–2.
[25] [1977] 1 QB 966, 985 (per Geoffrey Lane LJ).
[26] An example of such a situation would be a *Tomlinson*-type situation where it is clear that people will not pay any attention to signs around a public lake telling them it is dangerous to swim there and there is a very high risk that swimming in the lake will cause an individual swimmer to contract Weil's Disease (a possibly fatal disease contracted by contact with animal urine in water), but each individual swimmer discounts this risk as 'not going to happen to me' and the only way of effectively stopping swimmers running such a risk would be to turn the beaches around the lake into swampland, thus ruining a valuable public amenity.

(2) *Public benefit.* Parliament has twice made it clear in recent years that it wants the courts, in determining whether or not someone has breached a duty of care, to be more indulgent to defendants who are acting for the public benefit. Parliament's first stab at making this clear was contained in s 1 of the Compensation Act 2006, which provides that:

> A court considering a claim in negligence or breach of statutory duty may, in determining whether the defendant should have taken particular steps to meet a standard of care (whether by taking precautions against a risk or otherwise), have regard to whether a requirement to take those steps might –
>
> (a) prevent a desirable activity from being undertaken at all, to a particular extent or in a particular way, or
> (b) discourage persons from undertaking functions in connection with a desirable activity.

Parliament's second go at reassuring people who act for the public benefit that the courts will not, or should not, too easily find that they have breached a duty of care is contained in s 2 of the Social Action, Responsibility and Heroism Act 2015 which says that in determining whether a person has breached a duty of care:

> The court must have regard to whether the alleged negligence . . . occurred when the person was acting for the benefit of society or any of its members.

How should we read these provisions? One way of interpreting them is to say that they add nothing to the existing common law – that they merely restate the balancing approach that is already employed by the courts to determine whether a failure to take a given precaution was negligent.[27]

However, an alternative reading is possible. On this alternative reading, these provisions are intended to *bias* the courts *against* finding that a defendant breached a duty of care in cases where: (1) the defendant was acting for the public benefit, *and* (2) it is difficult to tell whether, on a balancing approach, the defendant should have taken a particular precaution against the claimant suffering a particular harm. In such cases – this reading suggests – the courts should refuse to find that the defendant breached a duty of care that he owed to the claimant. So, for example, on this reading of these provisions, the Court of Appeal was *wrong* to rule in *Scout Association* v *Barnes* (2010) that playing 'Objects in the Dark' was negligent. The case was a marginal one (as it was a *low risk-low cost* situation) and the defendant scout master was acting for the public benefit in running the scout group and having them play games together.

So far, all the indications are that the courts will adopt the first reading of these provisions, and not the second.[28] However, if they were ever to adopt the second reading, then these provisions would create a second exception to the normal balancing process adopted by the courts in determining whether a defendant has breached a duty of care.

---

[27] *The Scout Association* v *Barnes* [2010] EWCA Civ 1476, at [34] (per Jackson LJ): '[The] principle . . . enshrined in section 1 of the Compensation Act 2006 . . . has always been part of the common law'; *Uren* v *Corporate Leisure* [2011] EWCA Civ 66, at [13] (per Smith LJ): 'section 1 of the Compensation Act 2006 [does] not add anything to the common law position.'

[28] See ibid, and also the comments made by Lord Pannick at the report stage in the House of Lords on what was then clause 2 of the Social Action, Responsibility and Heroism Bill 2014: 'I cannot remember a more pointless, indeed fatuous, piece of legislation than Clause 2 of this Bill, with the possible exception of Clauses 3 and 4 of this Bill . . . Clause 2 will not change the law. Courts already have regard to whether the alleged negligence or breach of statutory duty occurred when the person was acting for the benefit of society or any of its members.'

7.4 Common practice

A. The rule

The rule in this area is so well established, there is no real authority to demonstrate it:[29] the fact that people generally might be expected to act in a particular way does not, of and in itself, establish that acting in that way is a reasonable thing to do. So a defendant cannot argue that he or she discharged a duty of care owed to a claimant merely by showing that everyone else or most people could have been expected to act in the same way that he or she did.

B. The exception to the rule

There is an exception to the above rule in cases where A owes B a duty to perform some task with the skill and care that a reasonably competent professional would have exercised in performing that task. As a general rule, in judging whether or not A's performance was up to scratch, the courts will allow themselves to be guided by the opinion of professionals in the field. The general rule traces its origin to the direction of McNair J in *Bolam* v *Friern Hospital Management Committee* (1957):

> A doctor is not guilty of negligence if he has acted in accordance with a practice accepted as proper by a responsible body of medical men skilled in that particular art . . . Putting it the other way round, a doctor is not negligent, if he is acting in accordance with such a practice, merely because there is a body of opinion that takes a contrary view.[30]

The general rule is, as a result, known as the '*Bolam* test for negligence'. The case of *Maynard* v *West Midlands Regional Health Authority* (1984) illustrates the test in action. In treating the claimant, the defendants subjected the claimant to a diagnostic procedure called a mediastinoscopy which damaged the claimant's vocal cords. The claimant sued the defendants, claiming that they had breached the duty they owed her to treat her with a professional degree of skill and care. The claim failed: the defendants could show that a substantial body of medical opinion would have supported the claimant's being subjected to a mediastinoscopy given her condition.

C. Exceptions to the exception

We can identify two exceptions to the rule that the courts will absolve a professional of acting negligently if the professional's actions were supported by a body of opinion within the professional's profession.

(1) *Bolitho*. In *Bolitho* v *City and Hackney Health Authority* (1998), the House of Lords ruled:

> the court is not bound to hold that a defendant doctor escapes liability for negligent treatment or diagnosis just because he leads evidence from a number of medical experts who are genuinely of [the] opinion that the defendant's medical treatment or diagnosis accorded with sound medical practice . . . the court has to be satisfied that the exponents of the body of opinion relied upon can demonstrate that such opinion has a logical basis. In particular in cases involving . . .

---

[29] Though see the quote of Learned Hand J, above, at fn 1.
[30] [1957] 1 WLR 582, 587.

the weighing of risks against benefits, the judge . . . will need to be satisfied that, in forming their views, the experts have directed their minds to the question of comparative risks and benefits and have reached a defensible conclusion on the matter.[31]

So in a case where the court is convinced that a particular body of opinion within a profession as to how a professional should conduct himself is not 'responsible, reasonable and respectable'[32] because that body of opinion is 'not capable of withstanding logical analysis',[33] a defendant will *not* be allowed to rely on that body of opinion to establish that he discharged the duty of care that he owed the claimant as a professional.

In an excellent survey of the caselaw on when a body of opinion within the medical profession will fall foul of *Bolitho*,[34] Rachael Mulheron has identified six grounds on which the courts might find that a particular body of opinion is 'not capable of withstanding logical analysis':[35] (1) if the body of 'opinion has overlooked that a "clear precaution" to avoid the adverse outcome for the patient was available'; (2) if the body of opinion has failed to weigh 'the comparative risks and benefits of the chosen course of conduct'; (3) if the body of opinion contravenes 'community expectations of [what amounts to] acceptable medical practice'; (4) if the body of opinion 'cannot be correct when taken in the context of the whole factual evidence'; (5) if the body of opinion 'is not internally consistent' – for example, because it says that it would be both improper and proper to conduct a certain procedure; and (6) if the body of opinion is directed at whether performing a particular procedure would involve a *gross* or *wanton* lack of care on the part of the doctor performing it.[36]

(2) *Montgomery.* In *Montgomery* v *Lanarkshire Health Board* (2015), the UK Supreme Court held that the question of whether or not a doctor had breached the duty of care he owes his patient to treat her with reasonable skill and care by failing to tell her of a risk associated with the way he was proposing to treat her should *not* be resolved by asking whether there was a responsible body of opinion within the medical profession that would support not telling the patient about that risk. Instead, the doctor's failure to explain the risk, in comprehensible language,[37] to his patient would normally put him in breach of the duty of care he owes the patient if: (i) the risk was 'material' – that is, a risk that a reasonable person in the patient's position would regard as significant; and (ii) the doctor knew or ought to have known that the risk would be so regarded.[38] However, the failure to explain might be justified if the doctor 'reasonably consider[ed] that its disclosure would be seriously detrimental to the patient's health' or if the doctor had no chance to explain the risk to the patient because the patient required 'treatment urgently but [was] unconscious or otherwise unable to make a decision.'[39]

---

[31] [1998] AC 232, 241–2 (per Lord Browne-Wilkinson).

[32] [1998] AC 232, 241.

[33] [1998] AC 232, 243.

[34] Mulheron 2010.

[35] ibid, 620–35.

[36] A seventh (actually, the second in her list) factor identified by Mulheron (ibid, 623) – that the court will be *unwilling* to apply *Bolitho* to override a body of medical opinion if that body of opinion is directed at balancing conflicting demands on a doctor or a hospital's resources – is omitted from the above list as this factor identifies a situation where the courts will *not* apply the *Bolitho* exception to the *Bolam* test, rather than a situation where the courts *will* apply *Bolitho*.

[37] Explaining the risk in an incomprehensible way will also put the doctor in breach of his duty of care: [2015] AC 1430, at [90] (per Lord Kerr).

[38] Ibid, at [87].

[39] Ibid, at [88].

The UK Supreme Court justified its departing from *Bolam* in the context of failures to disclose risks of treatment to patients on the ground that patients are entitled to be empowered – by being told about the risks associated with their treatment – to decide for themselves how they should be treated, 'accepting responsibility for the taking of risks affecting their own lives, and living with the consequences of their choices.'[40] However, it is not clear whether this will be the consequence of the decision in *Montgomery*. A doctor who is encouraged by *Montgomery* to tell a patient of a remote risk attached to a proposed course of treatment, with the result that the patient irrationally shies away from undergoing that treatment, could well end up being sued by the patient for failing to take reasonable steps to change her mind and get her to see that the proposed course of treatment is the 'right' one. It is also not clear how far *Montgomery* might apply in other contexts – for example, in the realm of financial advice where claimants who have lost money as a result of making a particular investment would be very interested in being able to sue their financial advisers for failing to inform them of a 'material' risk associated with that investment.

7.5 Breach through others

A. The rule

As a general rule, a defendant who owes a claimant a duty of care can only be held to have breached that duty of care if he *personally* failed to live up to the standard of care required of him by that duty. For example, in *Gwilliam v West Hertfordshire Hospitals NHS Trust* (2003), a hospital organised a fund-raising fair within its grounds. As one of the activities laid on at the fair, the hospital hired a 'splat wall' from a firm called 'Club Entertainments'. Someone using the splat wall would don a Velcro suit, bounce on a trampoline and then launch themselves from there at a wall, to which they would stick. Unfortunately, the splat wall in *Gwilliam* was not properly set up by the Club Entertainments staff that provided the wall, and Ethel Gwilliam's foot got stuck in the trampoline as she tried to jump off it, with the result that she was permanently disabled. She sued the hospital for compensation, claiming that it had breached the duty of care that it owed her as a visitor to its premises under s 2(2) of the Occupiers' Liability Act 1957 to 'take such care as in all the circumstances of the case is reasonable' to see that she would be 'reasonably safe in using the premises for the purposes for which [she was] invited or permitted . . . to be there.' Her claim failed: the *hospital* had personally taken such care. Club Entertainments seemed like a reputable company, and there was no reason to think that the staff had not set up the trampoline properly.[41] The fact that *Club Entertainments* had not taken care to see that Gwilliam would be safe in using their trampoline had no effect on whether the hospital had breached its duty of care to her.

B. The first exception to the rule: non-delegable duties

The first exception to the above rule arises out of the existence of *non-delegable* duties. A non-delegable duty works as follows. If A owes B a duty to take reasonable steps to see

---

[40] Ibid, at [81].
[41] It was argued the hospital's duty of care to Gwilliam required it to check that Club Entertainments had adequate liability insurance. This aspect of the case is discussed in detail in § 9.2(A)(9), below.

that X does not happen, and A gives the job of seeing that X does not happen to C, if A's duty is *non-delegable*, then if C fails to take reasonable steps to see that X does not happen,[42] then *A* will be held to have breached the duty of care that A owed B.[43]

The duty of care that an occupier owes his visitors under the Occupiers' Liability Act 1957 is *delegable*. This is made clear by s 2(4)(b) of the Act, which provides that:

> where damage is caused to a visitor by a danger due to the faulty execution of any work . . . by an independent contractor employed by the occupier, the occupier is *not* to be treated without more as answerable for the danger if in all the circumstances *he* had acted reasonably in entrusting the work to an independent contractor and had taken such steps (if any) as *he* reasonably ought in order to satisfy himself that the contractor was competent and that the work had been properly done.[44]

So the fact that Club Entertainments failed to take reasonable steps to ensure the safety of Ethel Gwilliam did not put the hospital in *Gwilliam* in breach of the duty of care that it owed her under s 2(2) of the 1957 Act.

The following duties of care *are* non-delegable:

(1) *Employment.* The most important example of a non-delegable duty of care is the duty an employer owes his employees to see that they are not killed or injured in working for him.[45] So if *Boss* gives *Foreman* the job of supervising the work done by *Boss's* employees, to see that they will be reasonably safe in doing that work, and *Foreman* fails to give *New Boy* adequate instructions as to how to use a particular machine, with the result that *New Boy* is injured, *New Boy* will be able to sue *Boss* in negligence for breaching the duty of care that *Boss* owed *New Boy* as his employee to take care to see that *New Boy* would be reasonably safe in working for him. *Foreman's* lack of care will have put *Boss* in breach of *his* duty of care.[46]

---

[42] C will be found to have failed to take reasonable steps to see that X does not happen if C *deliberately* brings about X: *Armes* v *Nottinghamshire County Council* [2017] UKSC 60, at [51] (disapproving the suggestion in *New South Wales* v *Lepore* (2003) 212 CLR 511 that A can only be put in breach of a non-delegable duty of care by C's *carelessly* failing to see that X does not happen).

[43] Morgan 2015 adopts a different analysis (at 118), according to which a defendant who owes a claimant a non-delegable duty of care does not actually owe the claimant a duty of care at all, but a *strict* duty to *ensure* that *care is taken* with regard to the claimant's relevant interests. One problem with this analysis is that it is not everyone's carelessness that will put the defendant in breach of the duty of care that he owes the claimant; but only the carelessness of someone that the defendant has given the job of looking after the claimant's interests. But if the defendant's duty is to *ensure* that *care is taken* it is not clear why this limit on the defendant's liability exists.

[44] Emphasis added.

[45] *Wilsons & Clyde Coal Co Ltd* v *English* [1938] AC 57; *McDermid* v *Nash Dredging & Reclamation Co Ltd* [1987] 1 AC 906.

[46] But note that this is only so because *Foreman* was *given the job* of seeing that employees like *New Boy* would be reasonably safe in working for *Boss*. See *Davie* v *New Merton Board Mills Ltd* [1959] AC 604 (employee injured by defective tool unable to sue employer on ground that manufacturer's negligence in manufacturing tool put employer in breach of non-delegable duty of care that he owed employee because employer never gave manufacturer job of ensuring that employees would be safe; note, however, employee would now be able to sue employer under s 1 of the Employers' Liability (Defective Equipment) Act 1969); and *O'Reilly* v *National Rail & Tramway Appliances Ltd* [1966] 1 All ER 499 (employee injured as a result of fellow employees' negligence in handling live shell that was in a pile of scrap metal being processed by employees unable to sue employer on ground that employees' negligence put employer in breach of the non-delegable duty of care that he owed employee because employees not given job of ensuring employee's safety).

(2) *Bailment.* If A hands over some goods to B to look after for her, B is said to hold those goods on a bailment for A (with B being referred to as the 'bailee' of those goods, and A the 'bailor'), and as a result B will owe A a duty to take reasonable steps to protect the goods from being lost, damaged or stolen. That duty of care is non-delegable. So if B subsequently gives the goods to C to look after, and C fails to take reasonable steps to protect the goods, then C's carelessness will put B in breach of the duty of care that she owed A.

For example, in *Morris* v *C W Martin & Sons Ltd* (1966), the claimant gave her fur coat to a firm of furriers to be cleaned. The furriers sent the coat to the defendant cleaners. The defendants were bailees of the coat for the claimant and as such they owed her a duty to take reasonable steps to safeguard the coat. Unfortunately, the defendants gave the job of looking after the coat to one of their employees, who promptly stole it. Lord Denning MR held[47] that the employee's theft of the coat put the defendants in breach of the duty of care that they owed the claimant to safeguard her coat and accordingly held the defendants liable to the claimant for the loss of her coat.[48] The fact that it was the employee *who had been given the job* of looking after the coat who stole it was crucial to the finding that the defendants had breached the duty of care that they owed the claimant. Had it been some other employee who stole the coat, the defendants would not have been held liable unless they, or the employee who was given the job of looking after the coat, were personally at fault for the occurrence of the theft.[49]

(3) *Extra-hazardous activities.* We have already seen that if A is going to engage in some activity that creates a danger for B, A will owe B a duty to take reasonable steps to see that

---

[47] [1966] 1 QB 716, 725, 728.

[48] Note that there is some dispute as to whether the true basis of the defendants' liability in this case was that: (a) the defendants' employee put them in breach of the non-delegable duty that they owed the claimant to safeguard her coat; or (b) the defendants were vicariously liable in respect of the tort committed by their employee (the tort of conversion) when the employee stole the coat. Lord Denning MR's judgment supports view (a). Diplock LJ's judgment in the same case supports view (b). Salmon LJ's judgment straddles both views. In *Lister* v *Hesley Hall Ltd* [2002] 1 AC 215 it was assumed without any debate that *Morris* v *C W Martin* was a vicarious liability case: ibid, at [19] (per Lord Steyn), [46] (per Lord Clyde), [57] (per Lord Hobhouse), [75]–[76] (per Lord Millett). In *Dubai Aluminium Co Ltd* v *Salaam* [2003] 2 AC 366, Lord Millett once again assumed without debate that *Morris* was a vicarious liability case (at [129]). Lord Nicholls was less dogmatic (at [29]), noting that there was some debate over the basis of liability in *Morris*. However, he thought it unnecessary to express his views on the issue. The High Court of Australia was divided in *New South Wales* v *Lepore* (2003) 212 CLR 511 over the issue of how best to analyse the basis of liability in *Morris*. Gleeson CJ (at [48]) and Kirby J (at [312]) held that *Morris* was a vicarious liability case; Kirby J going so far as to deride alternative explanations of the case as 'feeble' (ibid). However, Gaudron J (at [127]) and McHugh J (at [147], [161]) both viewed the defendants' liability in *Morris* as resting on the fact that their employee had put them in breach of a non-delegable duty of care that they owed the claimant. Tony Weir is in no doubt that the latter analysis is correct, pointing out that the defendants would have been just as liable in *Morris* to the claimant had they given her fur coat to an independent contractor to look after, which he then stole: Weir 2006, 112. (Had that happened, of course, there would have been no possibility of the defendants being held vicariously liable for the tort committed by the contractor in stealing the coat because one should not be held vicariously liable in respect of torts committed by one's independent contractors: see below, § 31.1.) This seems to us the clinching argument and establishes that the liability in *Morris* is more satisfactorily viewed as arising out of the fact that the defendants' employee's actions put them in breach of the non-delegable duty of care that they owed the claimant to safeguard her coat.

[49] [1966] 1 QB 716, 740–1, per Salmon LJ.

that danger does not materialise.[50] In *Honeywill & Stein* v *Larkin Bros* (1934), the Court of Appeal held that if A's activity was *extra-hazardous* in nature (in *Honeywill & Stein* itself, taking photographs by setting off magnesium flashes), the duty of care that A owed B to take reasonable steps to see that B was not harmed by that activity would be non-delegable in nature.

The decision in *Honeywill & Stein* was severely criticised by the Court of Appeal in *Biffa Waste Services* v *Maschinenfabrik* (2009)[51] on the grounds that the decision was unsupported by authority, and it was very difficult to tell when an activity should be classified as 'ultra-hazardous'.[52] The Court of Appeal made it clear that it would have liked to overrule *Honeywill & Stein* if it could, but as the Court of Appeal is bound by its own decisions, all it could say was that:

> the doctrine enunciated in . . . *Honeywill* . . . is so unsatisfactory that its application should be kept as narrow as possible. It should be applied only to activities that are exceptionally dangerous whatever precautions are taken.[53]

In the subsequent UK Supreme Court case of *Woodland* v *Swimming Teachers Association* (2014), Lord Sumption also expressed doubts about this category of non-delegable duties of care, observing that it rests on 'arbitrary distinctions between ordinary and extraordinary hazards which may be ripe for re-examination.'[54]

(4) *Educational authorities.* As we have seen, an educational authority will owe children at a school under its control a duty to take reasonable steps to see that they do not come to any physical harm while they are at school.[55] The UK Supreme Court held in *Woodland* v *Swimming Teachers Association* (2014) that that duty of care is non-delegable.[56] So in *Woodland* itself, the claimant schoolchild suffered a severe brain injury as a result of spending too long knocked out underwater during a swimming lesson organised by the claimant's school but run by an independent contractor, Direct Swimming Services ('DSS'). The UK Supreme Court held that if DSS had been careless in the way it conducted the swimming lesson, then that would put the school in breach of the duty of care it owed the child to take reasonable steps to see that she did not suffer any physical harm while she was in their care.

(5) *Assumption of responsibility.* There are numerous authorities that seem to indicate that if A owes B a duty of care under the extended principle in *Hedley Byrne* because she has 'assumed a responsibility' to B to do some work with a reasonable degree of care and skill,

---

[50] See above, § 6.3.
[51] Noted, Stanton 2009.
[52] [2009] QB 725, at [70]–[75].
[53] [2009] QB 725, at [78].
[54] [2014] AC 537, at [6].
[55] See above, § 6.11.
[56] By contrast, in *Armes* v *Nottinghamshire County Council* [2017] UKSC 60, the UK Supreme Court held that any duty of care the social services owed a child that has been taken into its care is *delegable* so that if the social services placed that child in foster care, they will not be held to have breached any duty of care they owed the child merely because the foster family carelessly fails to look after the child properly. Lord Reed justified the decision on the basis that finding that the social services' duty of care was non-delegable might discourage social services from acting in the best interests of the children in their care by placing those children with foster carers (at [45]).

or to take reasonable steps to see that X does not happen, that duty of care will be non-delegable in nature.

For example, in *Cassidy* v *Ministry of Health* (1951), Lord Denning MR said that:

> when hospital authorities undertake to treat a patient, and themselves select and appoint . . . the professional men and women who are to give the treatment, then they are responsible for the negligence of those persons in failing to give proper treatment, no matter whether they are doctors, surgeons, nurses or anyone else.[57]

Similarly, it was held in *Philips* v *William Whiteley Ltd* (1938) that the defendant firm of jewellers in that case owed the claimant a non-delegable duty to pierce her ears with the degree of care and skill that a reasonably competent jeweller would exercise in piercing someone's ears. The defendants had summoned an employee of another firm to perform the operation but, fortunately for the defendants, the employee in question pierced the claimant's ears with the requisite degree of care and skill and did not therefore put the defendants in breach of the duty of care that they owed the claimant.

It may be that the decision in *Lloyd* v *Grace, Smith & Co* (1912) can also be explained on this basis.[58] The claimant in that case consulted a firm of solicitors with a view to increasing the income she received from her investments. Her affairs were entrusted to the care of the firm's managing clerk, who used his position to defraud the claimant of two cottages that she owned. The firm was held liable for the loss suffered by the claimant. The case is often viewed as one where the firm was held vicariously liable in respect of the managing clerk's deceit.[59] However, it is possible to argue that the true basis of the firm's liability in this case was that the firm owed a non-delegable duty to the claimant to handle her affairs with a reasonable degree of care and skill and that the managing clerk – who was given the job of handling the claimant's affairs – put the firm in breach of that duty of care when, far from handling her affairs with a reasonable degree of care and skill, he defrauded her of her cottages.[60]

---

[57] [1951] 2 KB 343, 362. See also *Gold* v *Essex County Council* [1942] 2 KB 293, at 301–2 (per Lord Greene MR).

[58] Other difficult cases that might also be explained on this basis are *Rogers* v *Night Riders* [1983] RTR 324 (mini-cab firm that responded to the claimant's call for a mini-cab held liable for defective door on mini-cab that caused claimant injury; maybe the mini-cab firm could be said to have 'assumed a responsibility' to the claimant to take reasonable steps to see that the mini-cab they recommended was safe to travel in, and had been put in breach of the resulting duty of care by the driver's failure to check that the car was safe to travel in?) and *Photo Production* v *Securicor* [1980] AC 827. In *Photo Production*, the defendant security company in that case was employed to patrol the claimants' factory at night to see that it was not burned down or broken into during the night. The job of patrolling the factory was given to one of the defendants' security guards who, one night, deliberately started a fire in the factory with the result that the factory burned down. The defendant security company was held *prima facie* liable for the fire damage. (In fact, there was an exclusion clause in the contract between the defendants and the claimants that absolved the defendants of liability.) There are *dicta* in the case (ibid, at 846 (per Lord Wilberforce) and 852 (per Lord Salmon) which indicate that the source of the defendants' *prima facie* liability in this case was that they were vicariously liable for the tort committed by their employee in starting the fire. However, it is possible to argue that the real source of the defendants' liability in this case was that their employee's lack of care put them in breach of a non-delegable duty of care that they owed the claimants: see *New South Wales* v *Lepore* (2003) 212 CLR 511, at [146]–[148] (per McHugh J).

[59] *Lister* v *Hesley Hall Ltd* [2002] 1 AC 215, at [19] (per Lord Steyn), [73] (per Lord Millett).

[60] See *New South Wales* v *Lepore* (2003) 212 CLR 511, at [127] (per Gaudron J).

Students often ask whether there is any test by which we can determine whether a given duty of care is delegable or non-delegable. John Murphy has argued that far from being just *one* category of situation where a duty of care will be non-delegable in nature, 'assumption of responsibility' is the keystone concept underlying *all* non-delegable duties of care. In other words, in all cases where a duty of care is non-delegable, the duty is non-delegable because it is based on an 'assumption of responsibility' by the defendant to the claimant.[61] In *Woodland* v *Swimming Teachers Association* (2014), Lord Sumption identified 'two broad categories of case'[62] in which a D will owe a C a non-delegable duty of care: (1) where D is engaged in an ultra-hazardous activity; and (2) where C is a 'patient or child, or for some other reason is especially vulnerable or dependent on the protection of [D] against the risk of injury' and C is in D's custody or care and D has thereby assumed 'a positive duty to protect [C] from harm' and C 'has no control over how [D] chooses to perform' that duty.[63]

Neither Murphy nor Sumption's analyses of the basis of non-delegable duties of care seem particularly satisfactory. Murphy's analysis cannot account for why duties of care arising out of someone's engaging in an 'ultra-hazardous' activity are non-delegable. Sumption's analysis acknowledges this, but as a result he ends up giving us a list of situations where a duty of care will be non-delegable akin to the list which we have just presented rather than providing us with a key to unlock the mystery of why some duties of care are delegable and some are non-delegable. Sumption's 'two broad categories of case' are also in danger of overlooking bailment – one of the most elementary situations where a duty of care will be non-delegable. Finally, neither Murphy nor Sumption can really explain why the duty of care that an occupier owes his visitors under the Occupiers' Liability Act 1957 is delegable, rather than non-delegable, as that duty has as much claim as an employer's duty to his employees to be based on an 'assumption of responsibility' by the defendant to the claimant.

C. The second exception to the rule: companies and other artificial legal persons

A company is an artificial legal person. As such, as Lord Diplock remarked in *Tesco Supermarkets Ltd* v *Natrass* (1972), 'it is incapable itself of doing any physical act or being in a state of mind'.[64] If a company is to act, then, it can only do so through natural persons – people who are, of course, capable of performing physical actions. This creates a problem when we want to determine whether or not a *company* breached a duty of care that it owed to someone else.[65] *Whose* actions should we look at in order to determine whether or not that duty of care was breached? The law in this area is confused.[66]

---

[61] Murphy 2007a, 379-90.

[62] [2014] AC 537, at [6].

[63] [2014] AC 537, at [23].

[64] [1972] AC 153, 198.

[65] Of course, this issue only comes up if we want to establish whether a company is *personally* liable to compensate a claimant for some loss that he or she has suffered. If it is not personally liable to pay such compensation it may still be *vicariously liable* to pay such compensation if one of its employees caused the claimant to suffer the loss in question by committing the tort and there was a sufficiently close connection between what the employee was employed to do and the tort committed by the employee: see below, § 31.2.

[66] For a full survey of the authorities, see Ferran 2011.

The traditional rule is that one determines what a company has done by looking at the actions of those who represent the company's '*directing mind or will*'.[67] In the 1990s, it was suggested – principally by Lord Hoffmann – that *how* we ascertain what a company did depends very much on the *nature and purpose* of the legal rule that requires us to find out what that company did.[68] However, this approach is difficult to apply in the context that we are concerned with here – determining whether a company has breached a duty of care that it owes to someone else. The reason is that the sort of duties of care we are concerned with in this text are not targeted specifically at companies, and so the creators of those duties of care – usually judges, sometimes legislatures – will have had *no* intentions as to what approach we should adopt in determining whether a company has breached that duty of care. Moreover, since the decision in *Meridian Global Funds*, both the Court of Appeal and the House of Lords have taken the position that the 'directing mind or will' approach to determining what a company did should be adopted unless there is a good reason why a different approach should be adopted (such as that Parliament intended that a different approach should be adopted in the context of determining whether a company committed a particular statutory offence).[69]

So to sum up: in every case where an artificial legal person owed someone else a duty we are confronted with the problem – Whose actions should we look at to determine whether or not that person breached that duty? In the case of companies that problem is solved, we suggest, by adopting the 'directing mind or will' principle according to which we ascertain what a company did at a particular time by looking at what those who represented that company's 'directing mind or will' at that time did. The same approach should be adopted in relation to artificial legal persons that are not companies, such as local authorities.

---

[67] See, for example, *Tesco Supermarkets Ltd* v *Natrass* [1972] AC 153. The traditional rule traces its origin to the judgment of Viscount Haldane LC in *Lennard's Carrying Co Ltd* v *Asiatic Petroleum Co Ltd* [1915] AC 705, 713: 'My Lords, a corporation is an abstraction. It has no mind of its own any more than it has a body of its own; its active and directing will must consequently be sought in the person of somebody who for some purposes may be called an agent, but who is really the directing mind and will of the corporation, the very ego and centre of the personality of the corporation.' Denning LJ found a characteristically colourful way to express the principle in *Bolton (Engineering) Co Ltd* v *Graham & Sons Ltd* [1957] 1 QB 159, 172: 'A company may in many ways be likened to a human body. It has a brain and a nerve centre which controls what it does. It also has hands which hold the tools and act in accordance with directions from the centre. Some of the people in the company are mere servants or agents who are nothing more than hands to do the work and cannot be said to represent the mind or will. Others are directors and managers who represent the directing mind or will of the company, and control what it does. The state of mind of these managers is the state of mind of the company and is treated by the law as such. So you will find that in cases where the law requires personal fault as a condition of liability in tort, the fault of the manager will be the personal fault of the company.'

[68] *Re Supply of Ready Mixed Concrete (No 2)* [1995] 1 AC 456; *Meridian Global Funds Management Asia Ltd* v *Securities Commission* [1995] 2 AC 500.

[69] See *Attorney-General's Reference (No 2 of 1999)* [2000] QB 796, 814, 816: 'the primary "directing mind and will" rule still applies though it is not determinative in all cases' and *Stone & Rolls Ltd* v *Moore Stephens* [2009] 1 AC 1391 (company cannot sue for losses resulting from auditor's negligent failure to detect the company sole director's misappropriations of company funds as the company – through the director, as its 'directing mind and will' – was party to the illegal acts that resulted in those losses occurring).

7.6 Proof

A. The rule

The general rule is that it is up to the claimant in a negligence case to prove that the defendant breached a duty of care owed to her. So, for example, in *Knight* v *Fellick* (1977), the claimant was run down by the defendant driver. The claimant was so badly injured in the accident that she had no memory of how it happened. The claimant sued the defendant in negligence for compensation but her claim failed: she could not prove that the defendant was driving without due care and attention at the time he hit the claimant.

B. *Res ipsa loquitur*

The burden of proof shifts to the defendant – who will then have to show that he did *not* breach a duty of care owed to the claimant – if the facts of the case are such that the most natural explanation of what happened is that the defendant was careless.[70] In such a case the facts of the case will indicate ('*res ipsa loquitur*' means '*the thing speaks for itself*') that the defendant breached his duty of care, and it will be up to the defendant to show that he was not, in fact, careless.

So a *res ipsa loquitur* argument would have been available to the claimant in *Knight* had the accident happened in broad daylight: one would not usually expect a driver to run someone down when visibility is perfect unless the driver was careless in some way. Unfortunately for the claimant in *Knight*, the accident happened at night, on a road which had no lighting, and the claimant was wearing dark clothes at the time. So the fact that the claimant had been run down did not, of and itself, indicate that the defendant had been careless in running her down.

Res ipsa loquitur has been applied to help establish that the defendant breached a duty of care owed to the claimant in the following types of cases: (1) the defendant performed a minor operation on the claimant's hand and after the operation was over the claimant lost the use of his hand;[71] (2) the claimant was working in the defendant's factory and an electrical panel fell on his head;[72] (3) the claimant was injured when a coach driven by the defendant suddenly veered across the road into the claimant's path;[73] (4) the defendant cleaned a suit belonging to the claimant and the claimant suddenly developed dermatitis on wearing the suit again.[74] A plea of *res ipsa loquitur* was not allowed in the case where a

---

[70] The requirements that had to be satisfied before a *res ipsa loquitur* argument could be made in favour of the view that the defendant had breached a duty of care owed to the claimant were first set out by Erle CJ in *Scott* v *London and St Katherine Docks Company* (1865) 3 H & C 595, 601; 159 ER 665, 667: 'where the thing [which caused the accident complained of] is shewn to be under the management of the defendant . . . and the accident is such as in the ordinary course of things does not happen if those who have the management use proper care, it affords reasonable evidence, in the absence of explanation by the defendants, that the accident arose from want of care.'

[71] *Cassidy* v *Ministry of Health* [1951] 2 KB 343.

[72] *Bennett* v *Chemical Construction (GB) Ltd* [1971] 1 WLR 1571.

[73] *Ng Chun Pui* v *Lee Chuen Tat* [1988] RTR 298 (note that no finding of negligence was ultimately made in this case – even though it looked at first as if the defendant had been careless in driving the coach, he had an explanation for his driving into the claimant's lane: he was trying to avoid a car that had cut in front of him).

[74] *Mayne* v *Silvermere Cleaners* [1939] 1 All ER 693.

door on a moving train operated by the defendant suddenly opens and the claimant falls out.[75] The fact that the door opened suddenly did not of itself indicate that the defendant was careless in operating the train: the door could just as well have opened because of the fault of another passenger.

C. Exceptions to the rule

The law on *res ipsa loquitur* does not create a genuine exception to the rule as to burden of proof set out above: the burden of proving carelessness still starts with the claimant, who is then allowed to shift it onto the defendant by pleading *res ipsa loquitur*. But there are a couple of genuine exceptions to the rule as to burden of proof as to carelessness in a negligence case:

(1) *Bailment.* If A holds goods on a bailment for B and those goods are lost, damaged, or stolen, it will be presumed – unless A can prove otherwise – that A breached the duty of care that he owed B to take reasonable steps to safeguard those goods.[76]

(2) *Criminal conviction.* If A owed B a duty of care and has been convicted of a criminal offence which A could not have committed had he fulfilled the duty of care that he owed B, in any civil proceedings between A and B it will be conclusively presumed – unless A can prove otherwise – that A breached the duty of care that he owed B.[77]

Further reading

The law on breach of duty of care does not excite academics very much. Except for adherents to the law and economics school, who think that the 'Hand Formula' for determining whether or not a duty of care has been breached indicates a commitment on the part of the judges to maximising economic efficiency (the idea being that you only have to take a precaution against a given risk if taking that precaution can be justified on cost-benefit grounds). For more, see **Posner, 'A theory of negligence' (1972) 1** *Journal of Legal Studies* **29**; and for responses to Posner, see **Wright, 'Hand, Posner and the myth of the "Hand Formula"' (2003) 4** *Theoretical Inquiries in Law* **145** and **Zipursky, 'Sleight of Hand' (2007) 48** *William and Mary Law Review* **1999**.

Of course, legal economists – and many tort lawyers who have nothing to do with law and economics – see 'fault' as being the foundational concept in the law of negligence, and 'duty' as something that could easily be dispensed with. On this view, liability in negligence is justified on the basis that the defendant was *at fault* for the harm suffered by the claimant. For a lecture delivered from within that kind of world view see **Tunc, 'Tort law and the moral law' (1972) 30** *Cambridge Law Journal* **247**. One problem with this view is that in requiring people to live up to an objective standard of care, the law of negligence frequently holds people liable for harms for which they were *not* personally to blame. For an explanation as to why it might be *not unfair* to hold someone liable for the outcome of their actions even though they were not personally to blame for those outcomes, see

---

[75] *Easson* v *London and North Eastern Railway Company* [1944] 1 KB 421.
[76] *Houghland* v *R R Low (Luxury Coaches) Ltd* [1962] 1 QB 694; *Port Swettenham Authority* v *T W Wu & Co* [1979] AC 580.
[77] Civil Evidence Act 1968, s 11. On which, see *Stupple* v *Royal Insurance Co Ltd* [1971] 1 QB 50.

Honoré, 'Responsibility and luck: the moral basis of strict liability' (1988) 104 *Law Quarterly Review* 530.

Mayo Moran criticises the objective standard of care as potentially discriminatory in her monograph *Rethinking the Reasonable Person* (**OUP, 2003**). The book is too long and complex for students to be reasonably expected to read it, but it is well-reviewed from a tort lawyer's perspective by **Richard Mullender in 'The reasonable person, the pursuit of justice, and negligence law' (2005) 68** *Modern Law Review* **681**. Moran's 'The reasonable person: a conceptual biography in comparative perspective' (2010) 14 *Lewis & Clark Law Review* 1233 also supplies a good summary of her views on the objective standard care in tort law at 1238-49.

For an excellent exploration of whether negligence law asks too much of us, see **Mullender, 'Negligence law and the concept of community' (2008) 16** *Tort Law Review* **85**, and for an account of situations where negligence law asks less of us than it does other people see **Nolan, 'Varying the standard of care in negligence' (2013) 72** *Cambridge Law Journal* **651**.

Chapter 8
Causation

Aims and objectives

Reading this chapter should enable you to:

(1) To understand the basic criteria that the courts take into account in determining whether a defendant's wrong caused the claimant to suffer a particular harm: (a) the 'but for' test, (b) whether the claimant or a third party broke the chain of causation between the defendant's wrong and the harm suffered by the claimant, (c) whether the defendant's wrong materially increased the risk that the claimant would suffer that harm, or whether that harm was merely a coincidental result of the defendant's actions.

(2) To understand when the courts will find that a defendant's wrong caused the claimant to suffer a particular harm even though the 'but for' test is not satisfied; that is, in (a) cases of overdetermination, and (b) cases where the *Fairchild* exception applies.

(3) To understand in what situations, and why, the courts will find that a defendant's wrong caused the claimant to suffer a particular harm even though we would normally say that (a) there was a break in the chain of causation between the defendant's wrong and the harm suffered by the claimant, or (b) that the harm suffered by the claimant was merely a coincidental result of the defendant's wrong.

(4) To come to grips with some of the alternative approaches to determining whether a defendant's wrong has caused the claimant to suffer harm that have been advanced in the academic literature and evaluate the strengths and flaws in these alternative approaches.

8.1 The basics

The victim of a breach of a duty of care will not be able to sue in negligence unless she can show that the breach *caused* her to suffer an *actionable* loss. This chapter is about causation; the next chapter is about actionability. However, it is important for the student reader to remember that the law on causation and actionability is not just relevant to the law on negligence. It is relevant in *every* case where the victim of a tort – *any* tort – wants to sue for compensatory damages. In such a case, he will always have to show that the commission of that tort *caused* him to suffer some kind of *actionable* loss. If it did not, then compensatory damages will simply not be available.[1] And the law on causation is not just relevant in cases where the victim of a tort wants to sue for compensatory damages. It is also relevant to:

(1) Wrongful death claims, where the dependants of the victim of a tort will only be allowed to sue under the Fatal Accidents Act 1976 if they can show that that tort *caused* the death of the victim of the tort.[2]

(2) Cases where a claimant wants to bring a claim for compensation under some liability rule which entitles him to sue for compensation for losses *caused* by a certain event (for example, the manufacture of a dangerously defective product, under the Consumer Protection Act 1987).

(3) Cases where a defendant is being prosecuted under the criminal law for *causing* some harm (for example, in a murder case, where the prosecution has to show that the defendant caused another's death).

Whatever the context, the rules and principles of the law of causation remain the same.[3] The basic starting point is the 'but for' test – would *x* have happened but for what A did? If *x* would have happened anyway, that would normally count against finding that what A did caused *x* to happen. If *x* would not have happened at all, that would normally count in favour of finding that what A did caused *x* to happen. But the 'but for' test is notoriously inadequate as a test for determining causation issues. Sometimes it produces paradoxical results, indicating that *no one* caused *x* to happen, when we know someone must have. Sometimes it is overbroad: it will indicate that A caused *x* to happen, when such a finding will seem counter-intuitive to ordinary people. As an example of a paradox produced by the 'but for' test, consider the **Water Bottle Problem**:

The night before *Traveller* is due to make a trip into the desert, her camel is loaded up with provisions, including a very large and very full water bottle. During the night, *Malice* empties the water bottle and fills it with poison, so that the next day, when *Traveller* needs to have a drink from the water bottle, she will drink the poison, and die. A couple of hours later (and unaware of what *Malice* has done), *Envy* makes a tiny hole in the bottom of the water bottle, so that the contents of the water bottle start dribbling out of the hole. *Envy*'s plan is that the water bottle will still seem fairly full in the morning, when *Traveller* starts out on her journey, but by the time she needs a drink, the bottle will be completely empty, and *Traveller* will die of dehydration. The next morning, *Traveller* gets up, checks her camel, sees nothing wrong with the water bottle, and rides out into the desert. By the time she needs a drink, the water bottle is empty. *Traveller* dies of dehydration in the desert.

Who caused *Traveller*'s death here? If we apply the 'but for' test we reach a paradoxical conclusion. Looking at *Malice* first, *Malice* can argue that had he not done what he did, *Traveller* would have died in exactly the same manner and at exactly the same time as she

---

[1] Though some other form of damages such as nominal damages (see below, Chapter 26) or disgorgement damages (see below, Chapter 25) might be.

[2] See below, § 28.1.

[3] Though some would question whether that is true: see the discussion of Lord Hoffmann's views below, § 8.13.

actually did. *Malice*'s replacing *Traveller*'s water with poison turned out to have zero effect on how *Traveller* died. Turning to *Envy*, *Envy* can argue that had she not done what she did, *Traveller* would have died a lot more quickly than she actually did. *Traveller* would have dropped down dead from being poisoned as soon as she had a drink from the water bottle. As a result of what *Envy* did, *Traveller* instead got a chance to live for a few more days before finally collapsing from dehydration. So rather than causing *Traveller*'s death, *Envy* actually saved *Traveller*'s life.

So applying the 'but for' test in this context produces the paradoxical conclusion that *neither Malice nor Envy* caused *Traveller*'s death. The conclusion seems[4] paradoxical because we know that had *Malice* and *Envy* not messed around with *Traveller*'s water bottle, she would not now be lying dead in the desert.

Here are two situations where applying the 'but for' test seems to produce a 'false positive' result (in other words, the 'but for' test indicates that someone's actions caused something to happen, when our intuitions tell us that such a finding is incorrect):

1. *Footballer* scores a last-minute winner in an important World Cup game. *Gambler* had a bet that the game would end in a draw, and is so angered at losing his bet that later on that evening, he gets into a fight in a pub, and ends up stabbing *Drinker*. No ordinary person would say that *Footballer*'s scoring a last-minute goal caused *Drinker* to be stabbed, even though *Drinker* would not have been stabbed but for *Footballer*'s last-minute winner.

2. *Happy* puts on a new dress to go to a party. At that party, *Drunk* carelessly spills wine over the dress, and it is permanently stained. No ordinary person would say that *Happy*'s wearing her new dress to the party caused the dress to end up with a wine stain on it, even though that would not have happened but for *Happy*'s wearing the dress to the party.

In cases where application of the 'but for' test produces paradoxical results, or 'false positives', the 'but for' test needs to be modified or supplemented by additional tests for causation. The main additional tests that the courts use are the *break in the chain of causation* test and the *material increase in risk* test.

The *break in the chain of causation* test is what we have to appeal to in order to explain why *Footballer*'s scoring a last-minute winner did not cause *Drinker* to be stabbed. In between *Footballer*'s scoring a last-minute winner and *Drinker*'s being stabbed, something else happened that contributed to *Drinker*'s being stabbed: *Gambler* lost his temper, got into a fight, and got out a knife. Because *Gambler*'s actions were *deliberate* (he was in control of what he was doing), *voluntary* (he was not acting under pressure), *informed* (he knew what the effects of his actions would be) and *unreasonable* (it was stupid of him to do what he did), they amount to what lawyers call a *novus actus interveniens* – a new and intervening act, that has the effect of breaking the chain of causation between *Footballer*'s goal and *Drinker*'s being stabbed.

We cannot use the break in the chain of causation test to explain why *Happy*'s wearing her new dress to the party did not cause it to end up stained. While *Drunk*'s carelessness in spilling the wine over *Happy*'s new dress undoubtedly contributed to its being stained, the fact that *Drunk* was not acting *deliberately* in spilling wine over the dress means that what *Drunk* did, did not break the chain of causation between *Happy*'s wearing her new

---

[4] We will suggest later on that this conclusion may not be as paradoxical as it seems: see below, § 8.13.

dress to the party and its ending up stained. (It would have been different if *Lecher* intentionally spilled wine all over *Happy*'s dress to encourage her to get out of it.) Instead, we explain why *Happy*'s wearing her new dress to the party did *not* cause it to end up being stained by reference to the *material increase in risk* test – wearing a new dress to a party does not materially increase the risk that it will end up being stained. Of course, *Happy*'s dress would not have been at *any* risk of being stained if she had left it in her wardrobe. But *Happy* did not increase the risk to the dress of its being stained to any *substantial* extent by taking it out of the wardrobe and putting it on. (It would have been different if *Happy* was going to a Bugsy Malone theme party where it was contemplated that the guests would have a big custard pie fight: in that case, one could say that *Happy* did cause any damage that her clothes sustained in the fight by choosing to wear those clothes to the party.)

But even these tests need modification and supplementation where *they* threaten to produce undesirable conclusions. This is particularly the case where the application of tests like the break in the chain of causation test and the material increase in risk test would mean that a breach of a particular duty of care would *never* give rise to a liability to pay compensatory damages to the victim of the breach, because the defendant breaching the duty of care could *always* rely on these tests to say that his breach did not cause the victim of the breach to suffer any loss, and thereby escape any kind of sanction for his breach.

For example, we have seen that if the police take someone into custody who they know or ought to know is suicidal, then they will have a duty to take reasonable steps to see that he does not kill himself.[5] If they breach that duty, and their prisoner takes advantage of their breach to kill himself, they could always argue – if they were sued for damages – that they are not liable because the prisoner's *deliberate, voluntary, informed* and *unreasonable* decision to kill himself broke the chain of causation between their breach and his death. If such an argument were successful, then the police's duty of care to suicidal inmates would become meaningless – they would be free to breach it with impunity. In order to avoid this result, the House of Lords ruled in *Reeves* v *Commissioner of Police of the Metropolis* (2000) that in this kind of case, the police would not be allowed to rely on the 'break in the chain of causation' test to say that their negligence did not cause the death of someone who killed themselves in custody.

Three more points need to be made about the law of causation before we can move on to look at it in more detail:

(1) It is possible for more than one person to cause something to happen. For example, suppose *Driver One* carelessly runs into *Pedestrian* while she is crossing the road. *Pedestrian* flies through the air onto the opposite side of the road, where she is run over for a second time by *Driver Two*, who is too busy arguing with his wife to pay any attention to the drama playing out in front of him. In this second collision, *Pedestrian* suffers serious spinal injuries that mean she will be paralysed for life. In this situation, *both One and Two*'s careless driving has caused *Pedestrian*'s paralysis. Had *One* not been driving badly, *Pedestrian* would not have been run over by *Two* and been paralysed; and *Two*'s bad driving did not break the chain of causation between *One*'s bad driving and *Pedestrian*'s paralysis because *Two* was not *deliberately* driving badly. Had *Two* not been driving badly, *Pedestrian* would obviously not have been run over by *Two* and been paralysed.

---

[5] See above, § 6.4.

(2) Academics try to express the distinction between the 'but for' test for causation and tests that are designed to modify or supplement the 'but for' test by saying that the 'but for' test is concerned with *factual causation*, while tests like the 'break in the chain of causation' test and the 'material increase in risk' test are concerned with *legal causation*. We are not fans of this distinction, for three reasons.

First, it does not seem right to say that issues such as 'Was there a break in the chain of causation between what the defendant did and the outcome of his actions?' and 'Did the defendant's actions materially increase the risk that this outcome would occur?' have *no bearing* on the issue of whether the defendant's actions *in fact* caused a particular outcome to occur. It is not only lawyers who might be expected to be attentive to such issues in trying to determine who was responsible for something that has happened.

Secondly, saying that there is a distinction between issues of *factual* causation and *legal* causation does not seem to contribute anything to our understanding of the law. How is our understanding of the law enhanced by saying that the 'but for' test is concerned with *factual* causation and other tests for causation are concerned with *legal* causation? In fact, the use of such language could well get in the way of our understanding what lawyers are doing when they deal with causation issues. It suggests that lawyers are prone to *lying* about causation issues – refusing to find *in law* that the defendant's actions caused a particular outcome when *in fact* the defendant's actions *did* cause that outcome.

Thirdly, once one starts down the road of saying that there is a relative disconnect between the *law* on causation and ordinary people's views on causation, there is literally no limit on how many rules or principles one could see as being rules about *legal* causation. All the rules and principles set out in the next chapter (on 'Actionability') could be recharacterised as rules and principles that say 'There is no liability in this kind of case because the defendant's actions were not a *legal* cause of the loss suffered by the claimant.' A concept that can be abused so easily has nothing to recommend it.

(3) The presentation of the law on causation in this chapter is pretty conventional – it corresponds with the way most lawyers approach causation issues. However, some academics think that the conventional approach to causation should be abandoned. They think that asking, 'Would this have happened but for what the defendant did?' is the wrong place to start. We continue to think that the best way for students to get a good working understanding of the law of causation is to adopt the conventional approach to the law on causation set out in this chapter.[6] But in deference to the critics of the conventional approach, and in order to deepen students' understandings of the law on causation, one of the sections towards the end of this chapter is devoted to alternative approaches to the law on causation.

---

[6] As Green 2014 acknowledges (at 3–4), alternative academic accounts of causation are so complex that they are very difficult for judges (let alone students) to come to terms with and apply. Some of the difficulties involved in presenting such an alternative account are shown by Green 2014 itself, which attempts to present a new 'robust and practical' and 'consistently effective' analysis of causation called the 'Necessary Breach Analysis' (NBA) which asks in a given negligence case where a claimant is suing a defendant for compensation for harm that she suffered (1) whether it is established that it is more likely than not the claimant would not have suffered that harm when she did had no one being negligent, and if so, (2) whether the effect of the defendant's negligence was *operative* when the claimant suffered the harm she did. However, the definition (offered at 46–47) of when we can say that a defendant's negligence was operative is really hard to understand and makes the NBA as hard to apply as any of the alternative academic accounts of causation that we will canvass below.

8.2 The 'but for' test

According to the 'but for' test for causation, if we want to see whether A's tort caused B to suffer some kind of loss, we must first ask whether that loss would not have occurred but for A's committing that tort.

In *Barnett* v *Chelsea & Kensington Hospital Committee* (1969), three nightwatchmen presented themselves at a hospital casualty department, complaining that they had started vomiting after drinking some tea. The casualty officer on duty told the men to go to bed and call their own doctors. The men followed his advice and five hours later one of them died from arsenic poisoning. It was held that the casualty officer's failure to treat the man who died (in breach of the duty of care he owed him to treat him with a reasonable degree of care and skill) did not cause his death; he would have died anyway, even if he had been treated by the casualty officer.

In *McWilliams* v *Sir William Arrol & Co* (1962), the claimant's husband was working for the defendant, his employer, on a steel lattice tower when he fell to his death. It was found that the defendant's failure to provide the husband with a safety belt (in breach of his duty under s 36(2) of the Factories Act 1937) did not cause the husband's death. If the defendant had supplied the husband with a safety belt he would not have worn it so it could not be said that but for the defendant's failure to supply the husband with a safety belt, the husband would not have fallen to his death.[7]

In *Jobling* v *Associated Dairies Ltd* (1982), the claimant was employed by the defendants in their butchers' shop. In 1973 he slipped on the floor of the shop because the defendants had failed (in breach of their duty under the Offices, Shops and Railway Premises Act 1973) to keep the floor free from slippery substances. The claimant suffered a back injury which was somewhat disabling. In 1976 the claimant's back became completely disabled because he developed a condition called myelopathy. The myelopathy was completely unconnected with the claimant's accident in 1973. It was held that while the defendants' failure to keep the floor of their shop free from slippery substances had caused the claimant's disablement between 1973 and 1976, that failure had not caused any of the claimant's disablement after 1976. If the defendants had kept the floor of their shop free from slippery substances, the claimant would still have been completely disabled from 1976 onwards.

In *Calvert* v *William Hill Ltd* (2008), the claimant lost about £2m, gambling money with the defendants, using a special telephone betting account that they had set up for him. The claimant had asked the defendants to close the account down, so as to put a brake on his gambling habit. However, the claimant's instruction was never acted on, with the result that when the gambling bug next hit him and he picked up the phone and rang the defendants, they continued to accept his bets. It was found that the defendants had 'assumed a responsibility' to the claimant to close the account down, and as a result,

---

[7] It might have been different if the defendant had owed the claimant's husband a duty not only to supply him with a safety belt but *also* to take steps to ensure that he wore it. In that case, it could have been argued that had the defendant supplied the claimant's husband with a safety belt *and* taken steps to ensure that he wore it, the claimant's husband would have worn a safety belt while he was working and would not have fallen to his death. It could therefore have been argued that the defendant's breach of the duty he owed the claimant's husband to supply the claimant's husband with a safety belt *and* to take steps to ensure that he wore it caused the claimant's husband to die. See, for example, *Nolan* v *Dental Manufacturing Co Ltd* [1958] 1 WLR 936.

they owed him a duty of care from then on not to accept bets on that account. However, at first instance, Briggs J found that had the defendants not breached this duty of care, the claimant would still have suffered the same loss in any case, except perhaps at a slower rate:

> had [the claimant] been excluded from telephone betting by [the defendants] . . . he would have sought other avenues for large scale betting, whether on the telephone or on the internet, and would have continued his gambling, albeit on a lesser daily scale than that in which he indulged with [the defendants] . . . even if deprived of the opportunity to pursue his telephone gambling with [the defendants] . . . the claimant would ultimately have ruined himself financially, albeit at a slower rate because of the reduced scale of gambling which would have been available to him.[8]

It is important to note that in a tort case, the question we ask in applying the 'but for' test is – Would B have suffered the loss she did 'but for' A's *tort*? Tortfeasors are not held liable in tort for the losses caused by their bare acts or omissions, but for the losses caused by their *wrongs*.[9]

The difficulty this sometimes creates in applying the 'but for' test is illustrated by the case of *The Empire Jamaica* (1957). In that case, the defendants' ship collided with, and damaged, the claimants' ship. At the time of the accident, the defendants' ship was sailing in breach of regulations that said that the first and second mate of the ship should be certified: in fact only the first mate on the defendants' ship was certified. Did the defendants' breach of regulations cause the accident? Applying the 'but for' test to this question produces an ambiguous answer. This is because there were two ways the defendants could have complied with the regulations that they breached.

The first way of complying with the regulations was to ensure that when the ship sailed, the first and second mates on the ship were certified. The defendants failed to do this, but this failure did *not* cause the accident that damaged the claimants' ship according to the 'but for' test. The accident would still have happened, even if the second mate on the defendants' ship was certified. However, the second way of complying with the regulations was not to allow the defendants' ship to sail at all, given that the second mate on board was not yet certified. Again, the defendants failed to do this. Now – we can say that the accident which damaged the claimants' ship would not have happened but for this failure. Had the defendants' ship not sailed at all, it would never have been in a position to collide with the claimants' ship.

---

[8] [2008] EWHC 454 (Ch), at [203]. The Court of Appeal decided the case on slightly different grounds, which are dealt with below, § 8.8.

[9] The decision of the Court of Appeal in *Robbins* v *Bexley LBC* [2013] EWCA Civ 1233 (noted, Steel 2014) is inconsistent with this and looks wrong. The defendant council failed to do anything to prune the roots of the poplar trees in its park and some of these roots eventually spread and undermined the foundations of the claimant's house. It was conceded that the defendants had owed the claimants a duty of care to prune the roots but it was found that (1) if the defendants had done the bare minimum that their duty of care required, they would not have pruned the roots by enough to avoid the damage that the roots ended up doing to the claimants' house; and (2) if the defendants had acknowledged that they owed the claimants a duty of care to prune the roots, they would have in fact pruned them by a lot more than the bare minimum their duty required them to do, and this would have avoided the damage done to the claimants' house. The Court of Appeal held the defendant council liable for the damage done to the claimants' house. This does not seem to be a case of holding the defendants liable for the damage caused by their *breaching* the duty of care that they owed the claimants, but rather a case of holding the defendants liable for the damage caused by their *failing to try* to comply with the duty of care that they owed the claimants.

So – whether we say that the claimants' ship would not have been damaged but for the defendants' breach of regulations depends on how we characterise that breach. Do we say that the defendants' breach consisted in their sailing their ship without having a certified second mate on board? Or do we say that the defendants' breach simply consisted in their sailing their ship? It seems that the approach we should adopt in cases like this is to characterise the defendants' breach in the way that is most favourable to the defendants. This is what the House of Lords did in *The Empire Jamaica* case – they characterised the defendants' breach as consisting in their sailing their ship without having a certified second mate on board and consequently found that the defendants' breach of regulations did not cause the accident in which the claimant's ship was damaged.

Consider, in light of this, the **Learner Driver Problem**:

> *Learner* is learning to drive. One day, he goes out driving in his car without having a qualified driver sitting beside him in the car. While *Learner* is driving along – *and driving perfectly carefully* – *Child* suddenly runs out into the middle of the road without looking to see if there is any oncoming traffic and is hit by *Learner*'s car. The accident happened so suddenly that there was nothing *Learner* – or any other driver, however careful and experienced – could have done to avoid it. *Child* is injured as a result of the accident and wants to sue *Learner* in negligence for compensation for her injuries.

Can she do so? There is no problem in finding that *Learner* owed someone like *Child* a duty not to go out driving without having a qualified driver sitting beside him. This is because it was reasonably foreseeable that if he did this, someone like *Child* – a nearby pedestrian – would be injured.[10] But *Learner* could have complied with this duty in one of two ways:

(1) *Learner* could have stayed at home and not gone out driving (in which case, *Child* would not have been injured).

(2) *Learner* could have gone out driving with a qualified driver sitting beside him (in which case, *Child* would still have been injured because the qualified driver would not have been able to do anything to avoid the accident, any more than *Learner* could have done).

So this gives us two different ways of characterising *Learner*'s breach of the duty that he owed *Child* in this case. We can say that *Learner* breached that duty by: (1) going out driving; or (2) going out driving without having a qualified driver sitting beside him. Characterising *Learner*'s breach in the way that is most favourable to him, we will say that *Learner*'s breach of duty to *Child* consisted in his going out driving without having a qualified driver sitting beside him – and consequently find that *Learner*'s breach of duty did *not* cause *Child*'s injuries. Had *Learner* gone out driving with a qualified driver sitting beside him, *Child* would still have been injured in the way she was.

The case of *Lumba* v *Secretary of State for the Home Department* (2011) demonstrates the above principles in action. In that case, the claimants were held by the Supreme Court to have been falsely imprisoned. They had been detained by the Home Office under the Immigration Act 1971 pursuant to a policy that the Home Office was not entitled to pursue because it was a *secret* policy that did not accord with the Home Office's *official* policy

---

[10] See above, § 5.2.

on when it would detain people like the defendants.[11] However, it was conceded that even under the Home Office's official policy, the claimants would have been eligible to be detained. It followed that there were two ways the Home Office could have avoided falsely imprisoning the claimants:

(1) It could have let the claimants go.

(2) It could have applied its official policy to the claimants and detained them under that policy.

Characterising the Home Office's wrong in the way that was most favourable to it, we can say that their wrong in this case involved a failure to apply its official policy to the claimants' case. But that wrong caused the claimants no harm: had the official policy been applied, the claimants still would have been detained. Given this, the Supreme Court found that the claimants in *Lumba* were not entitled to sue for compensation for the fact that they had been falsely imprisoned by the Home Office.[12]

Ernest Weinrib has argued that the House of Lords' decision in *McGhee* v *National Coal Board* (1973)[13] can be explained by reference to the above principles.[14] The claimant in that case had developed dermatitis as a result of being employed by the defendants to clean out some brick kilns. This was hot and dirty work which exposed the claimant to clouds of abrasive brick dust. The defendants failed to provide the claimant with any on-site washing facilities which would allow him to wash off the brick dust as soon as he knocked off work. Instead, the claimant had to cycle home and wash there. After some days of working in the brick kilns, the claimant was found to be suffering from dermatitis. The House of Lords held that the claimant could sue the defendants in negligence for compensation for his dermatitis. The defendants were admittedly in breach of the duty of care that they owed the claimant to take reasonable steps to see that he did not suffer any physical harm as a result of working for them, but there were two ways the defendants could have avoided breaching that duty of care:

(1) The defendants could have provided the claimant with a shower at the end of the day.

(2) The defendants could have avoided asking the claimant to work on cleaning out brick kilns until they were able to provide him with a shower at the end of the day.

It is not clear that breach (1) was a but for cause of the claimant's dermatitis as he might still have developed dermatitis from the brick dust that settled on his skin during the working day, but breach (2) was definitely a but for cause of the claimant's dermatitis – had the defendants avoided asking the claimant to work on cleaning out brick kilns, the claimant would not have developed dermatitis. The difficulty with saying that the House of Lords in *McGhee* found the defendants' negligence caused the claimant's dermatitis because it took the view that the defendants breached the duty of care that they owed the claimant by doing (2) rather than (1) is that this involves construing the defendants' breach in the way that is most favourable to the *claimant*, rather than the defendants. This seems inconsistent with the result in both *The Empire Jamaica* and *Lumba*. As we will see, other explanations of *McGhee* are available to us.

---

[11] This aspect of the *Lumba* case is discussed in more detail above, § 2.6.
[12] [2012] 1 AC 245, at [95] (per Lord Dyson).
[13] Discussed, Hope 2003.
[14] Weinrib 2016, 152–55.

The point that defendants are held liable in tort for the losses caused by their *wrongs*, not their bare acts or omissions, helps solve a problem that puzzles Michael Moore, a well-known writer on causation issues. He cannot understand how any defendant could be said to have caused another person's loss through an omission, when 'omissions . . . are literally no things at all.'[15] He argues that in cases where A is held liable in tort for failing to save B from suffering some kind of harm, A's liability is 'non-causal in nature': 'we should be upfront about it. [A is] liable in such cases because [he] failed to prevent harm, not because [he] caused harm.'[16] This is the sort of confusion academics fall into when they cease to make wrongdoing the central focus of tort law, and start to think of it as a system for allocating responsibility for loss. In the sort of case Moore is talking about, A is held liable not for a bare failure to prevent harm, but because he has done something wrong when, had he not done wrong, B would not have suffered the harm for which she is seeking damages. While it may make no sense to think of a bare omission as causing harm,[17] a *wrong* that involves a failure to act can perfectly well be said to have caused harm, in the case where had that wrong not occurred, the harm would not have been suffered.

8.3 Divisible and indivisible harm

A *divisible* harm is a harm that may be suffered to a greater or lesser extent. An *indivisible* harm is one that does not vary in extent. An example of a divisible harm is a disease affecting the proper functioning of the lungs such as asbestosis or silicosis. An example of an indivisible harm is death or the loss of a hand. Applying the 'but for' test to determine whether a defendant's tort caused the claimant harm produces different results if the harm in question was divisible or indivisible. It is also arguable that an exception to the 'but for' test now exists in indivisible harm cases.

A. Divisible harm

In a case where a claimant has suffered a divisible harm, the claimant will be able to sue a defendant in tort for compensation for that harm if she can establish that but for the defendant's tort the harm suffered by the claimant would not have been *as bad* as it is at the moment. This was arguably the basis of the House of Lords' decision in *Bonnington Castings* v *Wardlaw* (1956). The claimant in that case was suffering from pneumoconiosis – a form of lung disease. In the claimant's case, he had developed the disease from inhaling silica dust at work. Some of the dust he inhaled he should have been protected from inhaling by his employer. The rest of the dust the employer could do nothing about. The House of Lords held that the employer's negligence in failing to protect the claimant from silica dust had made a 'material contribution' to his lung disease. The fact that the claimant's lung disease was a divisible harm allowed them to reach that conclusion. It seemed obvious

---

[15] Moore 2009, 129.

[16] Moore 2009, 142.

[17] So it is almost certain that right at this moment, a baby is dying in the Third World who could have been saved had you chosen to live your life differently. But no one in their right mind would say that your choice to live your life in the way you do has *caused* that baby's death.

that the claimant's lung disease would not have been as bad as it was had his employer protected him from inhaling silica dust at work.

If the claimant's employer was being held liable in this case on the basis that his negligence had made the claimant's lung disease *worse*, it would seem to follow that he should only have been held liable to compensate the claimant for the *extent* to which he had made the claimant's lung disease worse. However, this did not happen in *Bonnington*: the claimant's employer was held liable for *all* of the claimant's lung disease.[18] This was because the House of Lords was not asked in *Bonnington* to decide what the extent of the claimant's employer's liability should be – just whether the claimant's employer was liable. Had they been, it is generally acknowledged that the claimant's employer should only have been liable for that proportion of the claimant's lung disease that was attributable to the employer's negligence.[19]

The courts have adopted this approach to assessment of damages in other divisible harm cases since *Bonnington*. For example, in *Holtby* v *Brigham & Cowan (Hull) Ltd* (2000), the claimant developed asbestosis after working for a number of different employers, including the defendants. It was found that the defendants' negligence had caused the claimant's asbestosis to be 75 per cent worse than it would otherwise have been. Accordingly, the defendants were held liable to pay the claimant compensation for 75 per cent of his asbestosis. (This sum was assessed by figuring out what sum would fully compensate the claimant for his asbestosis, and then knocking 25 per cent off this figure.)

B. Indivisible harm

In an indivisible harm case, the claimant cannot sue the defendant by claiming, 'Your tort caused the harm I suffered to be worse than it otherwise would have been!' Under the 'but for' test, a claimant suffering an indivisible harm has to show that she would not have suffered that harm *at all* but for the defendant's tort because an indivisible harm is either suffered or not. This creates real problems for claimants. For example, the dermatitis suffered by the claimant in *McGhee* counted as an indivisible harm: you either suffer dermatitis or you don't. Now if we characterise the breach of duty in *McGhee* (discussed in the previous section) as being a failure to provide the claimant with a shower at the end of the day, it was very hard for the claimant to show that had he been provided with such a shower and not been forced to cycle home caked in brick dust and wash there, he would not have developed dermatitis.

However, the courts seem to have recently cleared away some of the obstacles that a strict application of the 'but for' test places in the way of a claimant recovering compensation in tort for an indivisible harm. In *Williams* v *Bermuda Hospitals Board* (2016), the Privy Council effectively created an exception to the 'but for' test for causation in the situation where a defendant's tort *contributed to the existence of a state of affairs* that was a but for cause of the claimant's suffering an indivisible harm. In such a case, the Privy Council ruled, the defendant's tort will be held to have caused the harm suffered by the

---

[18] This feature of *Bonnington* may be why some judges regard that case as an exception to the normal 'but for' test for causation rather than an application of it (in the sense that the claimant's employer ended up being held liable for harm that would have been suffered anyway, even if the employer had not been negligent): see, for example, *Sienkiewicz* v *Greif (UK) Ltd* [2011] 2 AC 229, at [17] (per Lord Phillips).
[19] See Bailey 2010, 174; *Sienkiewicz* v *Greif (UK) Ltd* [2011] 2 AC 229, at [176] (per Lord Brown).

claimant *even if* it is strongly arguable that had the defendant not committed that tort, the claimant still would have suffered that harm. The facts of *Williams* demonstrate this principle at work. The claimant in that case suffered temporary damage to his heart and lungs – an indivisible injury. That damage was caused by the claimant suffering sepsis – a condition where antibodies that have been released in someone's body to deal with an infection start actually harming the body. Two things contributed to the claimant's suffering sepsis: (1) the defendant hospital negligently failed to diagnose quickly enough that the claimant was suffering from acute appendicitis when he was taken into hospital complaining of feeling unwell, and (2) during the delay in treating the claimant, the claimant's appendix ruptured with the result that pus started leaking around his pelvic region. The Privy Council held that (1) was a cause of the temporary[20] damage to the claimant's heart and lungs even though it was not shown that had the defendant hospital been quicker about diagnosing the claimant's appendicitis, the defendant's appendix would not have ruptured, and the defendant would not have suffered the sepsis that caused the damage to his heart and lungs.

The decision in *Williams* is not free from difficulty: (1) *Bonnington Castings* was the main authority quoted in favour of the rule applied in *Williams*[21] even though that was a divisible harm case; (2) the Privy Council seemed to think that in finding in favour of the claimant they were simply applying the 'but for' test for determining whether a defendant's tort caused a claimant to suffer a particular harm,[22] when they were not; (3) in the absence of a finding that the claimant's appendix would not have ruptured had the defendants not negligently delayed in diagnosing his appendicitis, it is hard to see a basis for finding that the defendants' negligence materially contributed to the sepsis that was the immediate cause of the damage suffered by the claimant to his heart and lungs.[23] However, there is some judicial[24] and academic[25] support for the rule applied in *Williams*, and the rule in *Williams* has the advantage of being able to deal with a notorious weak spot in the 'but for' test for determining whether a defendant's tort caused a claimant to suffer a particular harm: the fact that the 'but for' test finds that there was no causation in an *overdetermination* case. (Cases of overdetermination are discussed below, in §8.8.)

---

[20] The damage was eventually repaired through further hospital treatment.

[21] [2016] AC 888, at [26].

[22] Ibid, at [47].

[23] For an excellent discussion of what amounts to a 'material contribution' to a state of affairs, see Bailey 2010.

[24] See *Bailey* v *Ministry of Defence* [2009] 1 WLR 1052, where the claimant was in a weakened state post-surgery, was given a drink, vomited, inhaled some of the vomit and suffered brain damage as a result. The claimant's weakened state was a consequence both of the claimant's having pancreatitis but also the lack of care that she had received from the defendants whilst staying at their hospital. The Court of Appeal held that the defendants were liable to compensate the claimant for her brain damage on the basis that their negligence had materially contributed to the weakened state that was a 'but for' cause of the claimant's brain damage.

[25] In particular, Jane Stapleton: see Stapleton 2013; Stapleton 2015, 709–13; and Stapleton and Steel 2016. But note that Stapleton does *not* believe that if a defendant's tort is found to have caused a claimant to suffer harm under the rule applied in *Williams*, that the defendant should be held liable in full to compensate the claimant for that harm. If the same harm would have occurred had *no one* committed a tort in relation to the claimant, then Stapleton would absolve the defendant tortfeasor of liability (while still finding that the defendant's tort *caused* the harm suffered by the claimant).

It is questionable, though, whether the rule applied in *Williams* can explain the finding of liability in *McGhee*. The rule only works where we know that a particular state of affairs was a 'but for' cause of the claimant's suffering a particular harm and the defendant's tort 'materially contributed' to the existence of that state of affairs. On the one hand, it could be said that: (1) the state of affairs that was a 'but for' cause of the claimant's dermatitis in *McGhee* was that the defendant's skin was exposed to brick dust; and (2) the defendant's negligent failure to provide the claimant with a shower at the end of the work day materially contributed to the defendant's skin being exposed to brick dust in that the defendant would not have been exposed to brick dust for as long as he was had he been allowed to shower at the end of the work day. On that basis, the rule in *Williams* would apply to find that the defendant's negligence caused the claimant's dermatitis in *McGhee*. But on the other hand, it could also be said that we don't know which state of affairs was a 'but for' cause of the claimant's dermatitis: (1) the defendant's being exposed to brick dust at work; or (2) the defendant's being exposed to brick dust at work *and* on the cycle home – and in the absence of knowing *that* we cannot tell whether the defendants' negligent failure to provide the claimant with a shower at the end of the day materially contributed to the state of affairs that caused the claimant's dermatitis.

8.4 Evidential difficulties (1): the standard approach

As the *McGhee* case shows, applying the 'but for' test often gives rise to evidential difficulties because what the test requires us to do is engage in a *counterfactual* inquiry, where we try to imagine what the world would be like had something *not* happened that *did* happen. All of us will have had the experience of thinking, 'What would have happened had I not . . .' ('. . . gone to that party where I met my wife', '. . . missed that appointment for a job interview', '. . . had that argument with my friend') and being left completely uncertain what the answer is. The courts are faced with the same difficulty. It can often be very difficult to tell what would have happened to the victim of a tort had that tort not been committed.

In physical injury cases, the standard approach that the courts adopt to resolve these evidential difficulties is to ask is it *more likely than not* that the claimant would not have suffered a particular injury but for the defendant's tort? If the claimant can show that the *probability* that she would *not* have suffered a given injury had the defendant not committed his tort is *greater* than 50 per cent, then the courts will decide the case on the basis that the claimant would *not* have suffered that injury but for the defendant's tort. If she can do this, the courts will say that the claimant has established *on the balance of probabilities* that she would not have suffered the injury but for the defendant's tort.

So, for example, in *Chester* v *Afshar* (2005),[26] Chester was suffering from back pain. She consulted the defendant doctor, Afshar, who recommended that she have an operation to remove three discs from her back. Unfortunately, he failed to warn her that there was a very small risk (1–2 per cent) that she would suffer nerve damage in her back as a result of the operation. Chester agreed that Afshar could operate on her and three days later, on 21 November 1994, Afshar carried out the operation. Although Afshar carried out the operation with all due care and skill, Chester suffered nerve damage and was partially paralysed as a result of the operation. Chester sued Afshar in negligence for compensation for the harm she had suffered.

---

[26] Noted, Stevens 2005.

There was no doubt in this case that Afshar breached the duty he owed Chester, as her doctor, to treat her with reasonable skill and care. Afshar should have told Chester of the risk of nerve damage associated with the operation he was proposing to carry out on her. But was it the case that Chester would not have been paralysed but for Afshar's breach of the duty of care that he owed her? To answer that question, we have to think about what would have happened had Afshar told Chester about the risk of nerve damage associated with the operation. It was established that had he done this, Chester would have taken a few days to think over whether she should go ahead with the operation. As a result, the operation would probably have taken place on something like the 25 November 1994. Had the operation been carried out *then*, it was more likely than not (in fact, it was 98–99 per cent likely) that the operation would have passed off without incident, and Chester would not have suffered any nerve damage or paralysis in her back. So, on the balance of probabilities, Chester would not have been paralysed had Afshar not breached the duty of care that he owed her. Given this, the House of Lords accepted that the 'but for' test for causation was satisfied in Chester's case.

It was different in *Hotson* v *East Berkshire HA* (1987) and *Wilsher* v *Essex AHA* (1988). In *Hotson*, the claimant fell when climbing a tree and one of his hips sustained an acute traumatic fracture. He was taken to hospital but the defendants (in breach of the duty of care they owed him) failed to diagnose his injury and sent him home. After five days, the claimant was taken back to the hospital and this time his injury was correctly diagnosed. As things turned out, the hip fracture resulted in the claimant being permanently disabled. The claimant claimed that the defendants' breach of the duty of care they owed him when he first went to the hospital caused him to be permanently disabled. It was impossible to tell with any certainty whether or not the claimant would have been permanently disabled even if the defendants had correctly diagnosed and treated his injury when he first went to the hospital. If the claimant's fall had damaged a certain proportion – call it x per cent – of the blood vessels in his hip then the claimant would have been permanently disabled whatever the defendants had done when he first went to hospital. If the fall had damaged less than x per cent of the blood vessels in his hip then the defendants would have been able to prevent the claimant becoming permanently disabled had they acted promptly when the claimant first went to hospital. No one could tell with any degree of certainty what proportion of blood vessels in the claimant's hip were damaged by his fall and therefore no one could tell with any degree of certainty whether or not the claimant would have been permanently disabled even if the defendants had treated his injuries when he first came to the hospital.

The courts in *Hotson* resolved this uncertainty by asking – Was it more likely than not that the claimant's fall damaged *less than* x per cent of the blood vessels in his hip? If the answer was 'yes' then they would have held that the claimant would *not* have become permanently disabled but for the defendants' negligence. But if the answer was 'no' then the courts would have held that the claimant was doomed to become permanently disabled even if his hip had received impeccable treatment when he first went to hospital. As things turned out, the answer was 'no'. It was found that the probability that the claimant's fall damaged less than x per cent of the blood vessels in his hip was only 25 per cent. It was therefore more likely than not that the claimant's fall damaged at least x per cent of the blood vessels in his hip and therefore more likely than not that the defendants' negligence made no difference to the claimant's becoming permanently disabled. The claimant's claim for damages therefore failed: he could not show that the defendants' negligence caused him to become permanently disabled.

In *Wilsher*, the claimant was a baby that was born prematurely. Shortly after he was born, he developed a serious eye condition called retrolental fibroplasia (RLF for short) and was blinded as a result. The claimant was exposed to excess oxygen by the defendants' employees when he was in hospital, being looked after in an incubator. This excess oxygen may have caused him to develop RLF. However, the claimant also suffered from four medical conditions that could also have accounted for his developing RLF. Given this, he could not show that it was more likely than not that he would not have developed RLF but for the defendants' employees' breaching the duty of care they owed him to treat him with reasonable skill and care. As a result, the House of Lords dismissed the claimant's claim in negligence against the defendants for compensation for the fact that he was blind: he could not show that the defendants' employees' negligence had caused him to go blind.

It is fashionable nowadays to express the 'more likely than not' rule in terms of 'doubling the risk'. That is, the courts ask: 'Did the defendant's tort more than double the risk that the claimant would suffer the harm that he did?' If so, it is more likely than not that the defendant's tort caused the claimant to suffer that harm. An example drawn from Lord Mackay's judgment in the *Hotson* case will make this clear. In talking about the *McGhee* case, Lord Mackay presented the following hypothetical:

> say that it was established that of 100 people working under the same conditions as the [claimant] and without facilities for washing at the end of their shift 70 contracted dermatitis: of 100 people working in the same conditions as the [claimant] when washing facilities were provided for them at the end of the shift 30 contracted dermatitis.[27]

In this hypothetical, the nature of the work done by the claimant in *McGhee* meant he had a 30 per cent risk of contracting dermatitis. However, the failure to provide him with washing facilities raised that risk of contracting dermatitis to 70 per cent – more than doubling the risk that the claimant would contract dermatitis. Now that the claimant *has* contracted dermatitis, we can say that there was a 3 in 7 chance that it was due to his being exposed to brick dust while at work and a 4 in 7 chance that it was due to the lack of washing facilities. It was therefore more likely than not that it was the failure to provide washing facilities that caused the claimant to develop dermatitis.

While it did not disapprove of the use of statistical information like this to resolve evidential difficulties over causation, the Supreme Court in *Sienkiewicz* v *Greif (UK) Ltd* (2011)[28] counselled caution over the use of such statistics as a way of proving whether or not a given event caused a particular outcome. Lord Rodger, in particular, emphasised:

> the point made by *Phipson on Evidence*, 17th edn (2010), para 34–27, that, unless a special rule applies, 'Where there is [statistical] evidence of association [between a particular event and a particular outcome], the court should not proceed to find a causal relationship without further, non-statistical evidence.' In other words, since, by its very nature, the statistical evidence does not deal with the individual case, something more will be required before the court will be able to reach a conclusion, on the balance of probability, as to what happened in that case. For example, where there is a strong [statistical] association between a drug and some condition which could have been caused in some other way, that evidence along with evidence that the claimant developed the condition immediately after taking the drug may well be enough to allow the judge to conclude, on the balance of probability, that it was the drug that caused the claimant's condition.[29]

---

[27] [1987] AC 750, 786.
[28] [2011] 2 AC 229 ('*Sienkiewicz*').
[29] *Sienkiewicz*, at [163].

Lady Hale agreed with Lord Rodger, arguing that 'the existence of a stastically significant association between factor X and disease Y does not prove that in the individual case it is more likely than not that factor X caused disease Y'.[30] For example, just because there is (let's suppose) a statistically significant association between going to the opera and developing gout, that does not mean that going to the opera causes gout. The association of gout with opera-going (if there is one) is due to the fact that opera-goers are likely to drink more than people who do not go to the opera, and has nothing to do with their attending the opera.

Lords Mance and Kerr took a slightly softer line than Lord Rodger and Lady Hale, holding that statistical information can only be relied upon as the *sole* source of evidence as to whether a defendant's tort caused a claimant harm in 'the rarest of cases'.[31] On the other hand, Lords Phillips and Dyson thought that there was no fundamental reason why the courts should not rely on statistical information to establish that the defendant's tort had caused the claimant to suffer a particular harm, on the basis that the defendant's tort 'doubled the risk' of the claimant suffering that harm.[32] However, Lord Phillips counselled that in cases where statistics indicate that the probability that the defendant's tort caused the claimant harm only slightly exceeded the probability that something else did, such statistics should probably not be relied on. They would provide a 'tenuous basis' for concluding that the defendant's tort caused the harm because 'the balance of . . . probability is a very fine one . . . [and] the [statistical] data may not be reliable.'[33]

Despite these disagreements over whether statistical information could be used in a case where we have *no doubt* that event X and event Y have occurred and we want to know whether event X *caused* event Y to happen, *all* of the Supreme Court Justices who expressed a view on this issue were hostile to the use of *general* statistical information to establish that *a particular event actually happened*. So, for example, they considered the hypothetical situation of 'a town in which there were only two cab companies, one with three blue cabs and the other with one yellow cab.'[34] Assuming that a claimant has been knocked down by a cab whose colour has not been observed, the Supreme Court Justices in *Sienkiewicz* agreed that the fact that there was a 75 per cent probability that a blue cab knocked the claimant down, did not provide a sufficient basis for finding that a blue cab *did* knock the claimant down.[35] (However, statistical information *specific* to the claimant's situation *might* still be relevant. For example, if someone saw the claimant being knocked down by a blue cab, and two out of the three drivers employed by the blue cab company were observed an hour beforehand drunkenly staggering out of a pub and getting into their respective cabs, that *might* be taken as evidence that the blue cab that knocked down the claimant was being driven by a drunk driver.)

---

[30] *Sienkiewicz*, at [172].

[31] *Sienkiewicz*, at [192] (per Lord Mance). See also [205] (per Lord Kerr): 'the use of [statistical] data to seek to establish any specific proposition in an individual case requires to be treated with great caution.'

[32] *Sienkiewicz*, at [78], [90]–[93] (per Lord Phillips) and at [222] (per Lord Dyson). The only other Supreme Court Justice to sit in the *Sienkiewicz* case – Lord Brown – expressed no view on these issues.

[33] *Sienkiewicz*, at [83].

[34] *Sienkiewicz*, at [95].

[35] *Sienkiewicz*, at [96] (per Lord Phillips), [156] (per Lord Rodger), [171] (per Lady Hale), [216]–[217] (per Lord Dyson).

The standard ('more likely than not', or 'doubling the risk') approach to resolving evidential difficulties can be productive of injustice. Consider the **Two Hunters Problem**, which is based on a real case, the Canadian case of *Cook* v *Lewis* (1951):

> *Shooter One* and *Shooter Two* are both out hunting with shot guns. They simultaneously hear some rustling in the bushes and simultaneously fire in the direction of the noise. *Beater* was hit in the leg by one of the shots, but forensic analysis is unable to tell from whose gun the shot was fired.

In this case, both *One* and *Two* have clearly been negligent in relation to *Beater*. They each owed him a duty to take care not to fire their guns in the way they did – as it was reasonably foreseeable that doing so would result in physical injury to someone like *Beater* – and they each breached that duty of care. But if we apply the 'more likely than not' rule to *Beater*'s case, he will not be able to sue *either One or Two* for compensation for his wound. The reason is that he will only be able to show that it is 50 per cent likely that *One* shot him, and 50 per cent likely that *Two* shot him. He will not be able to reach the magic figure of 51 per cent in relation to either of them. In *Cook* v *Lewis* itself, the Supreme Court of Canada thought that such a result would be very unfair, and ended up finding that, in the case we are considering, *both One and Two* would be liable *in full* to compensate C for his injury.[36] In the case of *Fairchild* v *Glenhaven Funeral Services Ltd* (2003), the House of Lords indicated that it agreed with this solution.[37]

8.5 Evidential difficulties (2): the *Fairchild* exception

The decision of the House of Lords in *Fairchild* v *Glenhaven Funeral Services* (2003)[38] is a good example of the maxim, 'The road to hell is paved with good intentions'. *Fairchild* actually concerned three cases. In each of them, an employee (C) was

> employed at different times and for differing periods by both A and B . . . A and B were both subject to a duty to take reasonable care to prevent C inhaling asbestos dust because of the known risk that asbestos dust (if inhaled) might cause a [form of cancer called] mesothelioma . . . [Both] A and B [breached] that duty . . . during the periods of C's employment by each of them with the result that during both periods C inhaled excessive quantities of asbestos dust.[39]

C subsequently developed mesothelioma and sought to recover damages from either A or B for his mesothelioma. Mesothelioma is a cancer that is always fatal in those who contract it. It is also a cancer about which we know very little. It is associated with exposure to asbestos dust: the more asbestos dust you inhale, the higher your risks of developing mesothelioma. But we do not know how asbestos dust causes mesothelioma to develop. So if C inhales a particular quantity of asbestos dust while working for A, we cannot say how probable it is that *that* exposure to asbestos dust will result in C developing

---

[36] To the same effect, see the American case of *Summers* v *Tice*, 199 P 2d 1 (1948).
[37] [2003] 1 AC 32, at [39] (per Lord Nicholls), [169] (per Lord Rodger).
[38] The case is reported at [2003] 1 AC 32, and we will henceforth refer to it as '*Fairchild*'.
[39] *Fairchild*, at [2] (per Lord Bingham).

mesothelioma. It might be 0 per cent – C may already be doomed to develop mesothelioma because of the asbestos dust he has already inhaled while working for other people, or from the general atmosphere. It might be 100 per cent – the asbestos dust that C inhaled while working for A might have doomed C to develop mesothelioma (either all by itself or in combination with other dust that C had already inhaled). We just don't know.[40]

Given this, in the cases dealt with in *Fairchild*, C could not rely on the standard ('more likely than not', or 'doubling the risk') approach to resolving evidential difficulties about causation to determine *whose* negligence caused him to develop mesothelioma. It was impossible to say whether it was more likely than not that C developed mesothelioma because of A's negligence or B's negligence. Despite this, the House of Lords held in *Fairchild* that C *would* be entitled to sue *both* A *and* B for compensation for his mesothelioma. Why was this? Two arguments seem to have led the House of Lords to reach this conclusion:

(1) *The fairness argument* goes as follows. If we applied the standard approach to resolving evidential difficulties about causation to cases such as C's, then it seems that employees who worked for *one* bad employer and contracted mesothelioma as a result would be much better off than employees who worked for *two or more* bad employers and contracted mesothelioma as a result. An employee who worked for *one* bad employer would have no problem establishing that it was his employer's negligence that triggered his mesothelioma and would therefore have no problem obtaining full compensation for his mesothelioma from that employer. An employee who worked for two or more bad employers would find it very difficult to establish which of his employers' negligence caused his mesothelioma and would therefore find it very difficult to identify anyone whom he was entitled to sue for compensation for his mesothelioma. This is unfair: why should an employee who worked for one bad employer be in a much better position to obtain compensation for his mesothelioma than an employee who worked for two or more bad employers?[41] To avoid this unfairness, we have to waive the normal rules on causation in the case where an employee who has contracted mesothelioma worked for two or more employers and allow the employee to sue his employers for compensation for his mesothelioma even though we cannot establish *which* of his employers' negligence caused that mesothelioma to develop.[42]

(2) *The sanction argument* goes as follows. If we do not allow C to sue A and B for compensation for his mesothelioma in this sort of case, then the duties that employers owe their employees to take reasonable steps to see that they do not inhale asbestos dust will become essentially empty. An employer will know that if he breaches that duty and one of his employees subsequently develops mesothelioma, he will not be held liable so long as he can show that that employee was also exposed to asbestos dust during the course of his

---

[40] See, further, Stapleton 2002b, 280–1, 299.

[41] *Fairchild*, at [36]: '[Holding that C could not obtain compensation for his mesothelioma] would be deeply offensive to instinctive notions of what . . . fairness demands' (per Lord Nicholls).

[42] It could be argued against this that it is unfair to hold a negligent employer liable for mesothelioma developed by a claimant when it was more likely than not that his negligence did not cause that mesothelioma to develop. However, their Lordships were able to overcome this objection, arguing that if they had a choice between being unfair to an innocent claimant and being unfair to a negligent employer, they would rather be unfair to the wrongdoing employer: *Fairchild*, at [33] (per Lord Bingham), [39]–[42] (per Lord Nicholls), [155] (per Lord Rodger).

working life while working for someone else.[43] We have to ensure that employers do not feel free to breach the duties of care that they owe their employees – and so in this sort of case we have to make it clear that an employer who has negligently exposed an employee to asbestos dust will be held liable to pay that employee compensation if the employee subsequently develops mesothelioma and this is so even if it cannot be shown that it was the employer's negligence that caused the employee to develop his mesothelioma, because the employee was also exposed to asbestos dust while working for other people.[44]

In holding in *Fairchild* that C could sue *both* A *and* B in negligence for compensation for his mesothelioma, the House of Lords left two questions unanswered:[45]

(1) *The extent of liability question*. For how much are A and B liable? Are they each liable *in full* to compensate C for his mesothelioma – so that C can then recover full compensation from *either* A *or* B? (Lawyers call this 'liability *in solidum*'.) Or are A and B each liable only to compensate C for a *proportion* (or what lawyers call an '*aliquot* share') of C's mesothelioma – so that C will have to sue *both* A *and* B if he wants to recover full compensation for his mesothelioma?

(2) *The single wrongful exposure question*. Does the *Fairchild* exception to the standard approach to resolving evidential difficulties in causation (the 'more likely than not' – or

---

[43] *Fairchild*, at [33]: 'Were the law [not to allow C's claim in the kind of case we are considering], an employer exposing his employee to asbestos dust could obtain complete immunity against mesothelioma . . . claims by employing only those who had previously been exposed to excessive quantities of asbestos dust. Such a result would reflect no credit on the law' (per Lord Bingham); at [62]: 'a rule requiring proof of a link between the defendant's asbestos and the claimant's disease would, with the arbitrary exception of single-employer cases, empty the duty of content. If liability depends upon proof that the conduct of the defendant was a necessary condition of the injury, it cannot effectively exist' (per Lord Hoffmann); at [155]: 'if the law did [here] impose a standard of proof that no [one claiming compensation for mesothelioma] could ever satisfy, then, so far as the civil law is concerned, employers could with impunity negligently expose their workmen to the risk of . . . mesothelioma. The substantive duty of care would be emptied of all practical content so far as victims are concerned' (per Lord Rodger).

[44] This argument is actually quite weak in this context. This is for two reasons. First, the argument's success in this context depends on a verbal sleight of hand. The argument only works in this context if one says that the duty of care that C's employers owed him, and breached, was a duty to take reasonable steps to see that he did not inhale asbestos dust – the argument being that if C were not allowed to sue A and B here, then employers generally would be left free to breach this duty of care. But if one characterises the duty of care that C's employers owed him, and breached, in wider terms – as a duty to take reasonable steps to see that he did not come to any physical harm in working for him – then not allowing C to sue *in this situation* would not mean that employers generally would be free to breach this wider duty of care. Secondly, even if *Fairchild* had gone the other way, employers would hardly have had *carte blanche* to expose their employees to excessive amounts of asbestos dust. An employer acting in this way would be: (1) subject to criminal sanctions; and (2) held liable to an employee who contracted asbestosis after working for him (the idea being that the employer's negligence in exposing the employee to asbestos will have either caused the employee to develop asbestosis or made the asbestosis 'worse' – in which case the employer will be held liable to compensate the employee for that 'part' of the asbestosis which is attributable to the employer's negligence).

[45] A third question – of only academic importance now – was whether A and B were being held liable to C under the *Fairchild* exception because (1) the effect of the *Fairchild* exception was to hold that both A and B *caused* C's mesothelioma, or because (2) the effect of the *Fairchild* exception was to hold both A and B liable for exposing C to the *risk* of contracting mesothelioma. The UK Supreme Court held in *Durham* v *BAI Run Off Ltd* (popularly known as the '*Trigger Litigation*' case) [2012] 1 WLR 867 (noted, McBride & Steel 2012b) that (1) is correct: the *Fairchild* exception is a rule about when we can find that a claimant caused a defendant harm, not a rule creating a wholly new category of liability in negligence for exposing someone to the risk of suffering harm.

'doubling the risk' – approach) also apply in cases where *only* one employer has wrongfully exposed C to asbestos dust, and C's mesothelioma might also be due to asbestos dust that he has been innocently exposed to (for example, from the general atmosphere) or that he has exposed himself to (for example, by doing some DIY work at home)?

The House of Lords got the chance to answer these questions in the subsequent case of *Barker* v *Corus UK Ltd* (2006).[46] In that case, the House of Lords said:

(1) *In response to the extent of liability question.* In a case where A and B have each wrongfully exposed C to asbestos dust, and C has subsequently developed mesothelioma, A and B will each be liable only to compensate C for a proportion of his mesothelioma, with their proportionate shares being assessed according to how much each of them did to expose C to the risk of developing mesothelioma.[47]

(2) *In response to the single wrongful exposure question.* In a 'single wrongful exposure' case, the *Fairchild* exception will apply, and C will be entitled to sue an employer who has wrongfully exposed him to asbestos dust for damages, even though C's mesothelioma might be attributable to asbestos dust that C has been innocently exposed to, or that C has exposed himself to.[48]

The House of Lords' answer to the 'extent of liability' question was severely criticised by trades unions and MPs who represented the interests of employees who had developed mesothelioma as a result of being exposed to asbestos dust at work. The reason is that the House of Lords' decision in *Barker* made it much harder for employees in mesothelioma cases to recover *full* compensation for their mesothelioma. To recover full compensation, they would have to sue *all* of their employers who had exposed them to asbestos, and hope that those employers were still in existence and still worth suing.

The then Labour government immediately responded to this criticism by enacting s 3 of the Compensation Act 2006. This provides that if: (1) C has contracted mesothelioma as a result of being exposed to asbestos dust, and (2) A is liable under *Fairchild* to compensate C for the fact that he has contracted mesothelioma, then (3) A will be liable to compensate C *in full* for his mesothelioma, though the damages payable may be reduced for any contributory negligence on C's part.

Unfortunately, at least two of the Law Lords who decided *Barker* had answered the 'single wrongful exposure' question in the affirmative *because* they thought that an employer who had wrongfully exposed an employee to asbestos dust would *only* be liable to compensate that employee for a proportion of the mesothelioma that he had subsequently developed.[49] So suppose C has developed mesothelioma after having been

---

[46] This case is reported at [2006] 2 AC 572, and is referred to below as '*Barker*'.

[47] See *Barker*, at [48] (per Lord Hoffmann): 'The damages which would have been awarded against a defendant who actually caused the disease must be apportioned to the defendants according to their contributions to the risk. It may be that the most practical method of apportionment will be according to the time of exposure for which each defendant is responsible, but allowance may have to be made for the intensity of exposure and the type of asbestos.'

[48] *Barker*, at [16]–[17] (per Lord Hoffmann), [59] (per Lord Scott), [97]–[99] and [101] (per Lord Rodger), [117] (per Lord Walker), [128] (per Baroness Hale).

[49] *Barker*, at [117] (per Lord Walker), [128] (per Baroness Hale). See also Lord Rodger at [101], holding that *in solidum* liability should *not* apply where there is a single wrongful exposure and self-exposure to asbestos dust. Also see Lord Brown in *Sienkiewicz*, at [182]: 'It is to my mind quite clear that the preparedness of the majority of the court in *Barker* to extend the reach of the *Fairchild* principle [to cases of single wrongful exposures] was specifically dependent on their being aliquot liability only.'

exposed to asbestos dust: (1) for two weeks while working for A; and (2) for six months while doing DIY work in his house. Two of the Law Lords who decided *Barker* thought it would not be unfair to hold A liable to pay damages to C here *because* A's liability would be limited to take account of the extent to which he had increased the risk that C would develop mesothelioma.

So s 3 of the Compensation Act 2006 made it unclear again what the answer was to the 'single wrongful exposure' question. Would the courts hold that there was liability in a single wrongful exposure case such as the one we have just been discussing if they knew that the effect of holding A liable to pay C damages was that A would be held liable *in full* to compensate C for his mesothelioma – and this is so even though A only exposed C to asbestos for two weeks, and C was exposed to asbestos from other sources for six months?

The Supreme Court supplied the answer in the case of *Sienkiewicz* v *Greif (UK) Ltd* (2011), holding that the *Fairchild* exception to the standard approach for resolving evidential uncertainties *did* apply in single wrongful exposure cases. This was so even though applying the *Fairchild* exception in such cases – in conjunction with s 3 of the Compensation Act 2006 – could have the 'draconian' effect of holding an employer liable in full for a claimant's mesothelioma when he was 'responsible for only a small proportion of the overall exposure of [the] claimant to asbestos dust'.[50] In such a case, the only way an employer could moderate his liability would be either: (1) to show that the amount of asbestos to which he exposed the claimant was so small that it exposed the claimant to an 'insignificant' or '*de minimis*' risk of developing mesothelioma (in which case the employer would not be liable at all);[51] or (2) to show that the claimant culpably exposed himself to asbestos dust (in which case the damages payable to the claimant would be reduced for contributory negligence).[52]

The facts of *Sienkiewicz* itself illustrate the point. In that case, Enid Costello was wrongfully exposed to a moderate amount of asbestos dust over 18 years while working for the defendant employers. She subsequently developed mesothelioma, and died. Her daughter brought a wrongful death claim under the Fatal Accidents Act 1976, alleging that the defendants' negligence had caused her mother's death. The judge at first instance found that everyone runs a risk of developing mesothelioma from breathing air that has asbestos dust in it. He quantified that risk in Costello's case as being 24 cases per million.[53] He found that the asbestos dust that the defendants had wrongfully exposed Costello to increased the risk that she would develop mesothelioma to 28.39 cases per million. This represented an increase in risk of 18 per cent. As this increase in risk was not insignificant or *de minimis*, the Supreme Court held the defendants liable *in full* to compensate the claimant for the losses flowing from Costello's death.

As Lord Brown observed, *Sienkiewicz* was a very different case from the sort of case that the House of Lords was considering in *Fairchild*.[54] Because *Sienkiewicz* was a case where there was only one wrongful exposure, it was not a case where the *fairness argument*

---

[50] *Sienkiewicz*, at [58] (per Lord Phillips); also at [184] (per Lord Brown).

[51] *Sienkiewicz*, at [107] (per Lord Phillips), [176] (per Lord Brown).

[52] Compensation Act 2006, s 3(3)(b).

[53] This is higher than the normal risk we all run of developing mesothelioma from the environment because the area where Costello lived had high levels of asbestos in the air (probably due to undetected torts – though this was not a point that anyone made an issue of in *Sienkiewicz*).

[54] *Sienkiewicz*, at [178].

demanded that the defendants be held liable for the deceased's mesothelioma.[55] But in *Sienkiewicz*, the Supreme Court identified a new basis for the *Fairchild* exception to the standard ('more likely than not', or 'doubling the risk') approach to resolving cases of evidential uncertainty about causation. This we can call the '*rock of uncertainty*'[56] *argument*. According to this argument, the reason why the standard approach to resolving evidential difficulties about causation was not applied in *Fairchild* (and the claimants' claims in that case dismissed) was because in mesothelioma cases, it is impossible at the moment to say with any certainty what is the probability that a claimant developed mesothelioma because of a given exposure. It is to prevent claimants' cases foundering on this impossibility that the *Fairchild* exception was developed (or so the Supreme Court claimed in *Sienkiewicz*). Given this, the Supreme Court thought that there was no logical reason why the *Fairchild* exception should not also apply in a case like *Sienkiewicz*: the 'rock of uncertainty' posed just as much of an obstacle to bringing a claim in *Sienkiewicz* as it did in *Fairchild*.[57]

While confirming that *Fairchild* applied in a single wrongful exposure case like *Sienkiewicz*, the Supreme Court was very keen to place a limit on the scope of *Fairchild*. Lord Brown seemed to suggest that the *Fairchild* exception to the standard approach to resolving evidential difficulties about causation *only* applied in mesothelioma cases. He remarked that, 'Mesothelioma cases are in a category all their own'[58] and that 'Save only for mesothelioma cases, claimants should henceforth expect little flexibility from the courts in their approach to causation.'[59] The general emphasis placed in *Sienkiewicz* on the *Fairchild* exception having been created to assist claimants who – because of our general level of scientific ignorance about the links between asbestos dust and mesothelioma – were simply unable to satisfy the standard approach to resolving evidential uncertainties about causation also seems to support the idea that the *Fairchild* exception only applies in mesothelioma cases; and will only apply in such cases so long as we remain ignorant as to how asbestos dust triggers mesothelioma.[60]

Having said that, there is *one* non-mesothelioma case where we think *Fairchild* would *still* apply after the decision of the Supreme Court in *Sienkiewicz*. That is the kind of case presented by the Two Hunters Problem:[61] where two or more people have committed a wrong in relation to the claimant, and we know that the claimant has suffered harm as a result of one of those wrongs, but the probability that a particular wrong caused the claimant to suffer that harm is 50 per cent or less. Applying the standard approach to resolving evidential uncertainties about causation would result in the claimant *not* being able to sue *anyone* for compensation for the harm he has suffered when the *sanction argument* and the *fairness argument* that underlay the original decision in *Fairchild* indicate that this would be unsatisfactory.

---

[55] Though the *sanction argument* might still apply: not applying *Fairchild* to a single wrongful exposure case might allow defendants to expose claimants to small, but still unacceptable, levels of asbestos and escape liability for mesothelioma on the basis that other, environmental, factors could have caused the mesothelioma.

[56] The phrase is from *Fairchild*, at [7] (per Lord Bingham). The phrase appears 15 times in the Supreme Court judgments in *Sienkiewicz*.

[57] *Sienkiewicz*, at [106] (per Lord Phillips), [141]-[142] and [160] (per Lord Rodger), [167] (per Lady Hale), [184] (per Lord Brown), [189] (per Lord Mance), [200] and [203] (per Lord Kerr), [208] and [212] (per Lord Dyson).

[58] *Sienkiewicz*, at [174].

[59] *Sienkiewicz*, at [187]. See also [189] (per Lord Mance: '[we should learn] the lesson of caution that history may teach in relation to future invitations to depart from conventional principles of causation.')

[60] That the *Fairchild* exception may disappear as our knowledge of how mesothelioma is triggered develops was explicitly contemplated by Lord Phillips (at [103]), Lord Rodger (at [142]), and Lord Dyson (at [208]).

[61] See above, § 8.4.

Some support for the idea that the claimant would be allowed to sue for compensation in the Two Hunters Problem is provided by Lord Phillips' judgment in *Sienkiewicz*.[62] In para [105] of his judgment, he said:

> even if one could postulate with confidence . . . the extent of the contribution of a defendant to the victim's exposure to asbestos . . . there would still be justification for the application of the *Fairchild* rule where *all the exposure was wrongful*. Imagine four defendants each of whom had contributed 25% to the victim's exposure so that there was a 25% likelihood in the case of each defendant that he had caused the disease. The considerations of fairness that had moved the House in *Fairchild* would justify holding each of the defendants liable, notwithstanding the impossibility of proving causation on the balance of probability.[63]

Were each of the defendants to be held liable in this case, s 3 of the Compensation Act 2006 (assuming it was still in force) would kick in to make each of the defendants liable *in full* for the claimant's mesothelioma. However, s 3 only applies to mesothelioma cases. In any other case where *Fairchild* applies, the House of Lords' decision in *Barker* v *Corus (UK) Ltd* remains good law. So in the Two Hunters Problem itself, we could expect the courts to hold *both One and Two* liable to pay damages to *Beater* (who has been shot either by *One*'s gun or *Two*'s gun, but we cannot tell which). But *Barker* would apply to limit *One* and *Two*'s liability so that they would each only be held liable for 50 per cent of the harm suffered by *Beater*.

Beyond the sort of non-mesothelioma case presented by the Two Hunters Problem, *Sienkiewicz* makes it unsafe to go.[64] The Supreme Court decision in *Sienkiewicz* makes it highly unlikely that *Fairchild* would ever be applied in a case like *Wilsher* v *Essex AHA* (1988), where a baby that had been delivered prematurely was blinded, possibly by a single wrongful exposure to excess oxygen but also possibly because of a range of other, innocent, factors. Unlike in the Two Hunters Problem or the situation contemplated by Lord Phillips above, a range of different agents[65] might have caused the harm in *Wilsher*, and only one of those agents was wrongful. While the *rock of uncertainty* argument might apply in a *Wilsher*-type scenario – it may be impossible to tell with any

---

[62] See also *Heneghan* v *Manchester Dry Docks Ltd* [2016] 1 WLR 2036, which – in applying the *Fairchild* exception to a case where the deceased contracted lung cancer (not mesothelioma) as a result of being exposed to excessive quantities of asbestos dust by various employers, including the defendant, but applying *Barker* to ensure that the defendant was only held liable for a proportion of the claimant's lung cancer – is completely consistent with the position taken in the text.

[63] Emphasis added.

[64] Steel 2012 argues (at 245) that *Fairchild* will *also* apply in the non-mesothelioma case where our understanding of how a particular disease develops makes it impossible to tell whether the proportion of a toxic agent that A wrongfully exposed C to caused C to develop the disease. However, this regards the decision in *Sienkiewicz* as intended to be more principled than was perhaps the case.

[65] In both *Fairchild* and *Barker*, *Wilsher* was distinguished on the basis that the harm in that case might have been caused by *different* agents, operating in *different ways* on the baby: see *Fairchild*, at [22] (per Lord Bingham), [118] (per Lord Hutton), [170] (per Lord Rodger); and *Barker*, at [23] (per Lord Hoffmann). Hoffmann 2017 is persuaded by Steel 2015 (at 237–39) to feel nothing 'but embarrassment at ever having espoused' a *single agent* limit on the *Fairchild* exception. The embarrassment is unjustified. There are only three ways of reconciling *Fairchild* with *Wilsher*: (1) limit the *Fairchild* exception to single agent cases; (2) hold that *Fairchild* only applies to multiple wrongful exposure cases; (3) hold that *Fairchild* only applies in a single wrongful exposure case where the claimant is suffering from mesothelioma. At the time *Barker* was decided, the House of Lords was unwilling to adopt options (2) or (3), so that left only option (1). Our view is that the law has now adopted option (3) (while holding that *Fairchild* might still apply in a multiple wrongful exposure case even if mesothelioma is not involved), with the result that the single agent limit on *Fairchild* is now redundant. For a different view, see Green 2017.

certainty what the probabilities were that a given agent caused the baby's blindness – the House of Lords made it clear in *Sienkiewicz* that the *rock of uncertainty* argument will only be allowed to subvert the normal causation requirements in mesothelioma cases.

Similarly, it seems unlikely that *McGhee* v *National Coal Board* (1973) would be decided the same way today – at least if we see *McGhee* as a forerunner of the decision in *Fairchild* and based on similar concerns to the ones that motivated *Fairchild*.[66] (Though there is nothing in the judgments in *Sienkiewicz* that would allow us to say that it has been overruled.) *McGhee* was – like *Wilsher* – another case of a single wrongful exposure (to brick dust that the defendants should have allowed the claimant to wash off at work before going home). It was uncertain whether *that* exposure (as opposed to the (non-wrongful) exposure to brick dust at work) had caused the claimant to suffer the harm (dermatitis) for which he sought compensation. Unlike in *Wilsher*, the claimant was allowed to sue for damages in *McGhee*. Lord Brown made it clear in *Sienkiewicz* that he thought *McGhee* was 'undoubtedly a problematic case'.[67] Lord Phillips took much the same view, describing *McGhee* as a 'puzzling case' on the ground that:

> no other workman had ever contracted dermatitis at the defendants' brick kiln, so one wonders what the basis was for finding that the lack of shower facilities was potentially causative. Had there been [statistical] evidence, it seems unlikely that this would have demonstrated that the extra ten or fifteen minutes that, on the evidence, the pursuer took to cycle home doubled his risk of contracting dermatitis, or came anywhere near doing so.[68]

Plainly Lord Phillips thought that in *McGhee*, recovery could only be justified on the presentation of statistical evidence that supported the inference that it was more likely than not the claimant would not have suffered dermatitis had he been provided with washing facilities.

8.6 Evidential difficulties (3): loss of a chance cases

So far, we have been looking at how the courts handle cases where a claimant wants to sue for compensation for a *physical injury* that she claims the defendant's tort has caused her to suffer, and it is uncertain whether or not the claimant would not have suffered that injury but for the defendant's tort. The courts adopt a quite different approach in economic loss cases, where the claimant is suing for compensation for some form of economic loss that she claims the defendant's tort has caused her to suffer. Suppose, for example, that *Applicant* wants to sue for compensation for the fact that she did not get a job as a skiing instructor which, she claims, she would have obtained but for *Defendant*'s tort.

Not getting a job is a form of economic loss. In *Applicant*'s case, the economic loss could be pure (which would be the case where *Applicant* didn't get the job because *Defendant* gave her an unfairly bad reference) or the economic loss could be consequent on physical injury (which would be the case where *Applicant* didn't get the job because *Defendant* negligently injured her so badly that she could no longer be considered for a

---

[66] For other possible explanations of *McGhee* (and the difficulties with those explanations), see above, §§ 8.2 and 8.3(B).

[67] *Sienkiewicz*, at [177].

[68] *Sienkiewicz*, at [92].

job as a skiing instructor). It doesn't matter. In either case, the courts do *not*: (a) require *Applicant* to show that it was at least 51 per cent likely that she would have gotten the job as a skiing instructor but for *Defendant*'s tort, and if *Applicant* can show this, (b) hold that *Defendant*'s tort *caused Applicant* not to get the job as a skiing instructor. Instead, the courts simply find out what (if any) was the *chance* that *Applicant* would have gotten the job as a skiing instructor had *Defendant* not committed his tort, and if there was a chance that *Applicant* would have gotten the job but for *Defendant*'s tort, they will award *Applicant* compensation for the loss of that chance of getting the job.[69]

Why do the courts do this? Why don't they adopt the 'all or nothing' approach that they adopt in physical injury cases, and say that the *only* thing *Applicant* can sue for is the loss of the job, and she can sue for that, *in full*, if she can show that it was at least 51 per cent likely that she would have gotten the job but for *Defendant*'s tort? The reason they do not, it seems, is that adopting such an approach would either *overcompensate* or *undercompensate Applicant*. If all *Defendant*'s tort deprived *Applicant* of was the *chance* of getting a job, then why should she get damages assessed on the basis that *Applicant* would *certainly* have gotten the job but for *Defendant*'s tort if the chance that she would have gotten the job was still only 55 per cent, or 60 per cent, or 70 per cent? And if *Defendant*'s tort *did* deprive *Applicant* of the chance of getting a job, why should she not get damages for the loss of that chance even if the chance she would have gotten the job was only 45 per cent, or 30 per cent, or even 15 per cent?

But then the question must be asked – So why don't the courts adopt the same approach in physical injury cases? Instead of adopting an 'all or nothing' approach, and saying that in a physical injury case the *only* thing a claimant can sue for is compensation for that injury, and she can sue for that, *in full*, if she can show that it was at least 51 per cent likely that she would not have suffered that injury but for the defendant's tort – why can't the claimant simply sue for the chance (however big or small the chance might have been) that she would not have suffered that injury but for the defendant's tort, and recover damages designed precisely to compensate her simply for the loss of that chance? There are two large obstacles in the way of the claimant's making a claim for damages for loss of a chance in the context of a physical injury case.

A. Proof

In the case where *Applicant* is applying for a job as a skiing instructor, it is easy to see why we might say that *Applicant* has a *chance* of getting the job. The reason is that whether she gets the job or not is down to the decision of the employer, and human beings enjoy free will. There is always a chance that the decision *could* go your way when you apply for a job.

In the case where a claimant wants to sue for damages for the loss of a chance of avoiding a physical injury, it is much more difficult for the claimant to show that the defendant's tort deprived her of a *genuine chance* of avoiding that injury. This is an obstacle the claimant in *Hotson* was not able to overcome. In that case, it will be recalled, the claimant fell

---

[69]See, for example, *Brown v Ministry of Defence* [2006] EWCA Civ 546, holding that first instance judged erred in awarding claimant 100 per cent compensation for loss of pension rights that she would have earned had she worked continuously for 22 years in army, on basis that it was probable she would have served those 22 years. He should instead have awarded her damages tailored to compensate her for the chance that she would have earned the pension payable after 22 years' service. (The Court of Appeal assessed that chance as being 30 per cent and therefore ordered she be awarded damages equal to 30 per cent of the pension she would have obtained had she retired after 22 years' service.)

out of a tree and suffered a hip fracture which resulted in him eventually becoming permanently disabled. The House of Lords found that it was 75 per cent likely that when the claimant fell out of the tree, he damaged so many blood vessels in his hip that he was doomed to become disabled, no matter how well he was treated by the defendant. But this not only means it was more likely than not that the defendant's failure to treat him properly did not make any difference to his becoming disabled. It *also* means that it was more likely than not the defendant's failure to treat the claimant properly did not *even* deprive him of a chance of avoiding disability: it was more likely than not that the claimant had *no chance* of avoiding disability when he was first seen by the defendant.

Students who have trouble appreciating this point should consider the **Lottery Ticket Problem:**

> *Friend* went to a birthday party for *Ungrateful* at her house and included inside her birthday card a ticket for the National Lottery® draw that was due to take the place the same evening as *Ungrateful*'s party. *Friend* could not remember what numbers he had picked for the ticket. *Ungrateful* accepted the card and saw the ticket (without noting the numbers), but quickly put both the card and ticket aside and did not even bother to watch the National Lottery draw being made to see if she had won. *Friend* was so angry that *Ungrateful* did not seem at all excited by his present that, when her back was turned, he ripped up the ticket and threw the pieces of the ticket away. Due to a computer breakdown, there is no record of where the winning tickets for the draw on the evening of *Ungrateful*'s birthday were bought, and indeed there is no record of whether there was any winning ticket for that draw.

Did *Friend* deprive *Ungrateful* of a chance of winning the National Lottery when he ripped her ticket up? Most students will be tempted to say 'Yes – though it was a very small chance.' The temptation should be resisted. Either *Friend* picked the winning numbers or he did not. If he did, *Ungrateful* won the Lottery. If he did not, *Ungrateful could not have won* the Lottery with the ticket *Friend* gave her. Which is it – was *Ungrateful* a winner, or a loser? The only way of resolving that question is through consulting the balance of probabilities. And when we do this, we will obviously conclude that it is more likely than not that *Ungrateful could not have won* the National Lottery with the ticket *Friend* gave her.[70]

It was the same with the claimant in *Hotson*. He could not prove, on the balance of probabilities, that when he was wheeled into the defendant's hospital, that he had *any* chance of avoiding permanent disability. As a result, it was simply not possible to make a claim for damages for loss of a chance of avoiding disability in *Hotson*.[71] However, there do seem to be cases where the courts are willing to accept that Nature gives everyone a

---

[70] The chance that *Friend* actually came up with the winning numbers for the weekend National Lottery draw was 1 in 14 million.

[71] Though some academics do insist that damages for loss of a chance could have been awarded in *Hotson*: see Peel 2003b, 627, and references contained therein. An amazing number of academics argue that the fact that the House of Lords awarded the claimant in *Hotson nothing* means that *Hotson* is authority for the proposition that damages for loss of a chance of avoiding physical injury cannot be claimed in negligence: see Porat & Stein 2003, 679; Weir 2004, 214–15. As the majority of the Court of Appeal recognised in *Gregg* v *Scott* [2002] EWCA Civ 1471 (at [39], per Latham LJ and at [78], per Mance LJ) this is incorrect – the facts of the case in *Hotson* were such that the claimant simply could not bring a claim for loss of a chance against the defendants. See, to the same effect, Reece 1996; also Hill 1991. Fleming 1997 puts the point quite well (at 69): '[A] 25% probability that there was a chance [of avoiding injury cannot] be conflated into a 25% chance [of avoiding injury].'

genuine chance of avoiding harm. For example, if A negligently dislocates B's knee, the courts recognise that in such a case we can say B has a *chance*, but no more than a *chance*, of developing arthritis in his knee in the future as a result of what A has done. The courts do not approach that kind of case on the basis that B is either inevitably doomed to develop arthritis, or is inevitably fated to get better with proper treatment – and ask B to establish, on the balance of probabilities, which it is going to be in his case.

B. Type of loss

The second big obstacle in the way of a claimant suing for damages for loss of a chance of avoiding injury[72] is the fact that the courts seem to regard a loss of a chance of avoiding physical injury as *economic* in nature. It is understandable that the courts should have taken such a position. A loss of a chance of avoiding physical injury is not to be equated with a physical injury. There is a big difference between having your leg broken, and losing a chance to avoid having your leg broken. But if a loss of a chance of avoiding physical injury is not a physical injury, what kind of loss is it? Because chances are economically valuable – for example, people are willing to pay good money to enhance their chances of avoiding injury by buying expensive safety equipment – it seems only natural to regard the loss of a chance of avoiding physical injury as an economic loss.[73]

But this has an important implication. Because they seem to think of losses of a chance of avoiding physical injury as being economic in nature, the courts tend to only allow claims for such losses of a chance to be made in cases where claims for economic loss can be made. There is no problem where the loss of a chance is consequent on a physical injury, or harm to property – in such cases, it has long been recognised that damages for economic loss flowing from the physical injury or harm to property may be recoverable. So where A's tort physically injures B, and as a result, B's chances of avoiding some further injury (such as arthritis) in the future are diminished, B may be able to recover damages for the loss of those chances.[74] Similarly, where A's tort damages B's property, and as a result, B's chances of selling that property for a good price in future are diminished, B can recover damages for the loss of those chances.[75]

---

[72] To save words, the term 'avoiding physical injury' here and below should be taken as including the case where a claimant loses the chance to recover from some physical injury.

[73] Though compensation for the loss of a chance of avoiding physical injury would not just be limited to the economic consequences of being injured, but would include damages for the loss of a chance of avoiding the pain and suffering consequent on being injured.

[74] To save words, we are of course assuming that B is the victim of A's tort, and that B's physical injury is an actionable consequence of A's tort. The same applies to the immediately following sentence about harm to property.

[75] See *Blue Circle Industries plc* v *Ministry of Defence* [1999] Ch 289. The claimants owned land next to land owned by the Atomic Weapons Establishment (AWE). The claimants were in negotiations to sell the land for about £10.5m to a third party when it was discovered that the land was contaminated with nuclear waste from the AWE's land. The third party broke off negotiations and the claimants set about cleaning up their land. The property market collapsed in the meantime and once the claimants' land was cleaned up and marketable again, it was only worth £5m. The claimants sued the defendants for damages, claiming that the defendants had committed a tort in contaminating their land. The trial judge found that there was a 75 per cent chance that had the defendants not committed their tort, the third party would have bought the claimants' land for £10.5m and therefore that there was a 75 per cent chance that but for the defendants' tort, the claimants would have been £5.5m better off than they were. Consequently, he awarded the claimants 75 per cent of £5.5m as compensation for the fact that the defendants' tort deprived the claimants of the chance of selling their land for £5.5m more than they ended up obtaining for it.

But where B is suing A for damages for a *pure* loss of a chance, that seems to count in the eyes of the courts as a pure economic loss and – as we have seen – damages for pure economic loss are only recoverable in negligence where the duty of care that A owed B, and breached, was geared towards protecting B from suffering some form of pure economic loss. The idea that damages for a pure loss of a chance will only be available in negligence where the defendant assumed some responsibility for the claimant's financial welfare seems to explain the cases quite well. In particular, it explains the difference between *Allied Maples Group Ltd* v *Simmons & Simmons* (1995) on the one hand, and *Gregg* v *Scott* (2005) and *Rothwell* v *Chemical & Insulating Co Ltd* (2008) on the other. The defendants in the *Allied Maples* case owed the claimants a duty of care to protect their financial welfare. They were very different from the defendants in *Rothwell* (employers) and *Gregg* v *Scott* (doctors), who owed the claimants in their respective cases a duty of care to protect the claimants' physical well-being, not their financial welfare.

In the *Allied Maples* case, the claimants bought the share capital of K, a subsidiary of G, in order to acquire leases held by K. The claimants' solicitors – the defendants – conducted the negotiations with G over the terms of the share deal. The defendants negligently failed to tell the claimants that the terms of the share deal did not protect them against the risk that they would have to meet any liabilities incurred by K's subsidiaries. The claimants successfully argued that had they been told this, there was a chance they would have successfully renegotiated the deal with G to obtain such protection. As a result, they were allowed to sue the defendants for damages to compensate them for the fact that they lost that chance to renegotiate the deal with G as a result of the defendants' negligence.

In *Rothwell*, the claimants were negligently exposed to asbestos fibres by the defendant employers, but were not allowed to sue the defendants for damages to compensate them for the chance that they might develop asbestos-related diseases in the future as a result of the defendants' negligence. It was crucial to the Court of Appeal's reasoning in this case that the defendants' negligence had not so far caused the claimants to suffer any kind of physical injury.[76] So the claimants had lost a *pure* chance of avoiding developing an asbestos-related disease in the future as a result of the defendants' negligence, and the Court of Appeal ruled that damages could not be recovered for the loss of that chance. A similar claim for a *pure* loss of a chance – of recovering permanently from cancer – was dismissed in *Gregg* v *Scott*. In that case, the claimant's doctor negligently failed to spot that the claimant was presenting with symptoms of cancer. As a result, his treatment was delayed by eight months. The claimant wanted to sue for the loss of a chance of going into permanent remission that – he claimed – that eight month delay in treatment had cost him. A 3:2 majority in the House of Lords dismissed the claim.

Gregg v *Scott* is a case where the facts are hard to understand, and the judgments in the House of Lords are even harder to assimilate. By way of a postscript – or appendix – to this section, we will do our best in the following section to make the House of Lords' decision

---

[76] The claimants had developed what are called 'pleural plaques' – small, smooth plates – on their lungs as a result of being exposed to the asbestos fibres, but both the Court of Appeal and, subsequently, the House of Lords ([2008] 1 AC 281) ruled that these were not serious enough to count as a physical injury. The Scottish Parliament responded to the decision in *Rothwell* by passing the Damages (Asbestos-related Conditions) (Scotland) Act 2009, which provides that 'Asbestos-related pleural plaques are a personal injury which is not negligible' and that 'Accordingly, they constitute actionable harm for the purposes of an action of damages for personal injuries' (ss 1(1) and 1(2), respectively).

in *Gregg* v *Scott* easy to understand for readers who want, or need, to know what was said in that case. But the normal student reader need not worry unduly about reading the following section. Most readers should aim to skip forwards to the section on 'Overdetermination'. After they have read and mastered the remainder of this chapter, from 'Overdetermination' onwards, they can then come back to the section on 'Gregg v Scott' – but only if they have the time and inclination to do so.

8.7 *Gregg v Scott*[77]

In order to understand the facts of *Gregg* v *Scott* (2005), it is first necessary to understand some points of terminology relating to the treatment of cancer patients. Someone suffers from cancer if they have at least one malignant tumour in their body. A cancer patient is said to go into remission if all the malignant tumours that were in their body have been killed. A cancer patient who is in remission is said to have suffered a relapse if a new malignant tumour is detected in their body. This new tumour will almost always have developed from a cancer cell that was secreted by one of the tumours that were formerly in the cancer patient's body. A cancer cell can take years to develop into a tumour, so a cancer patient who is in remission can suffer a relapse some years after they went into remission. A cancer patient is said to be 'cured' if they have been in remission for 10 years. The reason for this is that if a cancer patient has been in remission for 10 years it is unlikely that they are still carrying any cancer cells that were secreted by the tumours that were in their body 10 years ago: if they were, one would expect the cancer cells to have developed into tumours by now, thus causing the patient to suffer a relapse.

Now we can make sense of the facts of *Gregg* v *Scott*. In 1994, the claimant developed a lump under his left arm. He consulted his doctor, the defendant, and the defendant told him not to worry about it. Had the defendant treated the claimant with a reasonable degree of skill and care, he would have referred the claimant to hospital, where they would have discovered the lump was cancerous, and treatment of the lump would have started in April 1995. Had the lump been treated at that stage there was a 42% chance that the claimant's cancer would have been 'cured'. However, the lump went untreated and the claimant's cancer spread. A year later, the claimant consulted another doctor, the cancer was detected and treatment started in January 1996. However, because the cancer was more advanced, the treatment that the claimant underwent was much more intensive, and his chances of being 'cured' were now only 25 per cent. The claimant did go into remission after treatment commenced, but he subsequently suffered two relapses. However, he went into remission after the second relapse, and by the time the House of Lords heard the claimant's claim for damages against the defendant – that is, in May 2004 – he had been in remission for six years.

The claimant could not establish that had the defendant doctor not been negligent he would have been 'cured'. Had the defendant doctor not been negligent, and treatment of the claimant's cancer commenced in April 1995, it was still more likely than not at that stage that the claimant's cancer would not have been 'cured'. So, on the balance of probabilities, the claimant's cancer would not have been 'cured' even if the defendant doctor had not been negligent. Instead, then, of suing the defendant doctor for damages for the fact that he

---

[77] Reported at [2005] 2 AC 176; referred to below as '*Gregg*'.

had not been 'cured', the claimant sought to sue the defendant for damages to compensate him for the fact that, as a result of the defendant doctor's negligence, his chances of being 'cured' had gone down by 17 percentage points, from 42 per cent to 25 per cent.

By a majority of 3:2, the House of Lords dismissed the claimant's claim for damages. Only Lord Nicholls was in favour of allowing the claimant to make a claim for a 'pure' loss of a chance of being cured. He advanced three basic arguments in favour of his position:

(1) *The sanction argument.* If claims for the loss of a chance of being cured cannot be brought under English law, then a doctor who is presented with a patient with a very poor chance of being cured will have no incentive to treat the patient properly.[78] If he fails to treat the patient properly and the patient's condition worsens, he will always be able to argue that he should not be held liable to the patient because it was more likely than not that the patient's condition would have got just as bad had he treated the patient with a reasonable degree of care and skill.

(2) *The fairness argument.* If claims for the loss of a chance of being cured are not allowed in English law, then the law will unfairly discriminate between different kinds of patients.[79] For example, suppose that *Patient One* and *Patient Two* both independently consult *Doctor* because they have been feeling unwell. In fact, both of them are – without knowing it – HIV+. *One*'s condition is more advanced than *Two*'s and he has only a 45 per cent chance of avoiding developing AIDS, even if he receives proper treatment. *Two*, on the other hand, has a 55 per cent chance of avoiding developing AIDS, if she receives proper treatment. Unfortunately, neither of them receive proper treatment because *Doctor* negligently fails to diagnose that they are HIV+. *One* and *Two* both subsequently develop AIDS.

In this situation, *Two* will be able to claim full compensation from *Doctor* for the fact that she has developed AIDS.[80] She will be able to argue that it was more likely than not that had *Doctor* not been negligent she would not have developed AIDS and so *Doctor*'s negligence caused her to develop AIDS. In contrast, *One* will not be able to argue that *Doctor*'s negligence caused him to develop AIDS because it was more likely than not that he would still have developed AIDS even if *Doctor* had treated him properly. Now – if *One* is *not* allowed here to sue *Doctor* for damages for the fact that as a result of her negligence he lost a 45 per cent chance of avoiding developing AIDS, then the result is that *Two* will be allowed to sue for compensation for the fact that she has developed AIDS, and *One* will not be allowed to sue for anything. And this is so even though the difference between *One* and *Two*'s chances of avoiding developing AIDS with proper treatment was only 10 per cent.

(3) *The argument from authority.* The law already allows claims for pure losses of a chance in other contexts.[81] For example, if a court throws out A's claim for damages because his solicitor negligently failed to file the claim in time, A will be able to sue his solicitor in negligence for compensation for the loss of the chance that he might have won his case. So why not allow a claim for the pure loss of a chance here? Why should doctors be treated more favourably than solicitors?

---

[78] *Gregg*, at [4].

[79] *Gregg*, at [3].

[80] Though the courts will reduce the compensation somewhat to take account of the possibility that *Two* would have developed AIDS anyway even if *Doctor* had not been negligent.

[81] *Gregg*, at [15]–[19].

Lord Hoffmann and Baroness Hale advanced the following arguments against awarding damages for the pure loss of a chance of being cured:

(1) *The Hotson*[82] *problem.* In cases such as *Gregg* v *Scott*, it may well be that the claimant never had a chance of being cured, and if this is the case it would be inappropriate to award him damages on the basis that his doctor's negligence deprived him of a chance of being 'cured'.[83] The statisticians tell us that of 100 patients presenting with a lump like the claimant's in *Gregg* v *Scott*, 42 will be 'cured' if they are treated immediately. One way of interpreting this statistic is to say that each of those 100 patients has a 42 per cent chance of being 'cured'. If this is right, then it would be correct to say that the claimant in *Gregg* v *Scott* had a 42 per cent chance of being 'cured' when he saw the defendant doctor. But there is a different way of reading the statistics. It may be that of 100 patients presenting with a lump like the claimant's in *Gregg* v *Scott*, the varying genetic make-ups of the 100 patients mean that 42 of them are certain to be 'cured' so long as the lump is treated immediately, and 58 of them have no chance of being 'cured' no matter how much treatment they receive. If this is right, then it was more likely than not that the claimant in *Gregg* v *Scott* had *no chance* of being 'cured' and it would therefore be inappropriate to award him damages on the basis that he did have a chance of being cured.

(2) *Administrative difficulties.* Even if this problem could be overcome, and the claimant in Gregg v Scott did genuinely have a chance of being 'cured' when he saw the defendant doctor – though it is hard to know how that could be established – allowing claimants to bring claims for the pure loss of a chance of being cured would create a number of administrative difficulties.

First, the number of claims that could be brought against doctors would be hugely increased, with 'enormous consequences for insurance companies and the National Health Service'.[84] Doctors would, in effect, become liable to pay damages to their patients every time it was established that they had failed to treat their patients with reasonable skill and care. This is because in every such case the doctor's patient would be able to argue that his or her doctor's negligence had diminished his or her chances of being cured and that he or she was therefore entitled to compensation for the loss of that chance of being cured.[85]

Secondly, personal injury claims arising out of medical negligence would become much more complicated to process. In the case we were just discussing above, if *One* were allowed to sue *Doctor* for the fact that her negligence deprived him of a chance of avoiding developing AIDS, the law could no longer justifiably hold *Doctor* liable to compensate *Two in full* for the fact that she had developed AIDS based only on the fact that *Two* had a 55 per cent chance of avoiding developing AIDS with proper treatment when she saw *Doctor*. *Two* would instead be confined to suing *Doctor* for the loss of the 55 per cent chance of avoiding AIDS that she was deprived of as a result of *Doctor*'s negligence. So all personal injury claims arising out of medical negligence would become loss of a chance claims, involving 'expert evidence [that] would have to be far more complex than it is at present. Negotiations and trials would be a great deal more difficult. Recovery would be much less predictable . . .'[86]

---

[82] See above, § 8.6.
[83] *Gregg*, at [79]–[81] (per Lord Hoffmann).
[84] *Gregg*, at [90] (per Lord Hoffmann).
[85] *Gregg*, at [215] (per Baroness Hale).
[86] *Gregg*, at [225] (per Baroness Hale).

(3) *Lord Nicholls' arguments.* Finally, none of Lord Nicholls's arguments in favour of allowing recovery for a pure loss of a chance in *Gregg* v *Scott* stands up.

First, as to the sanction argument, it is not necessary to allow claims for a pure loss of a chance of being cured to be made against doctors in order to encourage them to treat patients who have poor prospects of recovering properly. The doctor's natural desire to do his or her best for his or her patients, the General Medical Council, and the criminal law provide sufficient encouragement.[87]

Secondly, as to the fairness argument, any unfairness in the way the law currently treats patients in terms of the remedies they are provided with when their doctors let them down is justified on the grounds of the administrative difficulties, described above, that would arise under any other remedial regime.

Thirdly, as to the argument from authority, there may be a difference between a case like *Gregg* v *Scott* and cases where the law currently allows claims for a pure loss of a chance to be made.[88] A pure loss of a chance may count in the law's eyes as a form of pure economic loss and is thus only claimable in cases where A has hired B to safeguard or promote his economic welfare, which is not the case in a medical negligence case.

As to the other two judges who decided *Gregg* v *Scott*:

(1) *Lord Hope* would have allowed the claimant's claim for damages, not on the ground that it was a claim for a pure loss of a chance, but on the basis that the defendant doctor's negligence had caused the claimant to suffer a physical injury – the spreading of his cancer. The claimant, Lord Hope argued, was entitled to be compensated for this injury, and such compensation would include a sum for the chance that, because of the spread in the cancer, the claimant's cancer would not be cured in future. (In the same way, if A has tortiously caused B to suffer a hip injury, A will not only be held liable to compensate B for the hip injury, but also for the chance that B will develop arthritis in the future as a result of the hip injury.) The problem with this approach is that it assumes that the defendant's negligence caused the claimant's cancer to spread – but, on the balance of probabilities, it is far from clear that the claimant's cancer would not have spread in any case, even if the defendant had not been negligent.

(2) *Lord Phillips MR* indicated that he would be willing to allow a claim for damages for a loss of a chance in a case – such as the case, discussed above, where *One* develops AIDS after his HIV+ status is not diagnosed by *Doctor* – where a patient has suffered an 'adverse outcome' and there was a chance that it could have been avoided had the patient been treated with a reasonable degree of care and skill by his or her doctor.[89] However, it was not clear whether the claimant in *Gregg* v *Scott* had suffered an 'adverse outcome' – which in this case would mean *not being cured*. Given that at the time of the House of Lords' hearing, the claimant had been in remission for six years, and the fact that the official definition of being cured of cancer is being in remission for ten years, there was every chance that the claimant would in fact finally be cured. So Lord Phillips concluded that *Gregg* v *Scott* was simply not an appropriate case in which damages for the loss of a chance of avoiding an 'adverse outcome' could be awarded.

---

[87] *Gregg*, at [217] (per Baroness Hale).
[88] *Gregg*, at [218]–[220] (per Baroness Hale).
[89] *Gregg*, at [190].

Lord Phillips' judgment means that there was a technical majority in *Gregg* v *Scott* in favour of allowing a claim for damages for the loss of a chance of getting better to be made in the case where a patient who had a 40 per cent chance of avoiding developing AIDS with prompt diagnosis and proper treatment subsequently developed AIDS when his case was not properly handled by his doctors. However, in reality, *Gregg* v *Scott* has been interpreted as effectively ruling out – for the time being – claims for loss of a chance of getting better being made against a negligent doctor. As Lord Neuberger MR observed in the Court of Appeal in *Wright* v *Cambridge Medical Group* (2011):

> I accept that the reasoning of the House of Lords [in *Gregg* v *Scott*] . . . does not conclusively shut out . . . this court from applying a loss of a chance approach . . . However, certainty and consistency are of great importance in this difficult area and, while the question would be appropriate for reconsideration by the Supreme Court, I consider that, at this level, we should probably not expand the loss of a chance doctrine into the realm of clinical negligence.[90]

8.8 Overdetermination

We can say that a loss or event is *overdetermined* if a defendant's tort would have been sufficient to bring about that loss or event, but that loss or event would have happened anyway even if the defendant had never committed his tort. Consider, for example, the **Double Poison Problem**:

> *Husband* and *Wife* are deeply unhappy; *Wife* because she loves another man, and *Husband* because *Wife* does not love him anymore. *Husband* decides to kill himself and puts a cyanide pill in a cup of coffee that he has made for himself. While his back is turned, *Wife* – who is unaware of what *Husband* has done – puts some poison in *Husband*'s coffee cup. The poison has the side effect of neutralising the cyanide in the coffee. *Husband* subsequently drinks the coffee and drops down dead.

Did *Wife*'s putting poison in *Husband*'s coffee cause his death? If we apply the but for test, we run into a problem. Had *Wife* not put poison in *Husband*'s coffee, *Husband* would have died from poison anyway. *Husband*'s death is overdetermined in this situation. *Wife*'s putting poison in *Husband*'s coffee would have been sufficient to bring about *Husband*'s death. But *Husband* would still have died from poisoning had *Wife* not put poison in his coffee. So does this mean that *Wife*'s putting poison in *Husband*'s coffee did *not* cause his death? The conclusion is counter-intuitive. It was, after all, *Wife*'s poison that flooded *Husband*'s system when he drank the coffee. So we would say in this situation that *Wife* caused *Husband*'s death. At the same time, we would *not* say that *Wife* caused any of the *losses* (for example, to *Husband*'s dependants) flowing from *Husband*'s death, as those losses would have been suffered anyway, even if *Wife* had never poisoned *Husband*.

In the **Double Poison Problem Reversed**, we would *not* say that *Wife* caused *either Husband*'s death, *or* any of the losses flowing from *Husband*'s death:

---

[90] [2013] QB 312, at [84].

> *Husband* and *Wife* are deeply unhappy; *Wife* because she loves another man, and *Husband* because *Wife* does not love him anymore. *Husband* decides to kill himself, but *Wife* is unaware of this decision. *Wife* presents *Husband* with a cup of coffee that she has secretly laced with poison. *Husband* thanks her for the cup of coffee, and secretly puts a cyanide pill in the cup, which has the side effect of neutralising the poison that *Wife* put in the cup. *Husband* then drinks the coffee and drops down dead.

In these situations, there does not seem to be any problem with saying that *Wife* did not cause the losses flowing from *Husband*'s death. But consider the **Two Fires Problem**:

> A and B both negligently start fires at an equal distance from C's house. The fires spread at an equal pace and engulf C's house at exactly the same time.

In this case, if we apply the 'but for' test, we will end up saying that neither A nor B's negligence caused C's house to burn down: had A not been negligent, C's house would still have burned down as a result of B's negligence; and had B not been negligent, C's house would still have burned down as a result of A's negligence. But in this situation, it would be unjust to allow both A and B to escape being held liable for what has happened to C's house. A variant on the Two Fires Problem is the **Three References Problem**:

> A, B and C are each requested by D – a former student of theirs – to write a reference for him for a job that he is applying for. A, B and C each mix D up with E, a student who had a history of drug use and petty theft. A, B and C each write a bad reference for D, who had an excellent record as a student. D does not get the job.

Again, if we apply the 'but for' test, we will end up saying that none of A, B or C caused D to lose the chance of getting the job for which he was applying: had A not been negligent, B and C's bad references would have put paid to D's chances; had B not been negligent, A and C's bad references would have ensured D didn't get the job; and had C not been negligent, A and B's bad references would have crushed D's hopes. Again, it would be unjust to apply the 'but for' test to allow each of A, B and C to rely on the other two's negligence to each escape liability for what has happened to D here.

It might be suggested that although *Fairchild* v *Glenhaven Funeral Services Ltd* (2003) was *not* a case of overdetermination,[91] we could invoke that case as authority for finding the wrongdoers liable for the harms suffered by the claimants in cases like Two Fires and Three References. After all, the same sort of arguments about fairness and the need to sanction wrongdoing that might motivate us to find liability in cases like Two Fires and Three References also underlay the House of Lords' decision in *Fairchild*. However, there are two problems with this. First of all, the decision of the Supreme Court in *Sienkiewicz* v *Greif (UK) Ltd* (2011) has made it clear that *Fairchild* is intended to help claimants in certain cases – predominantly mesothelioma cases – where *evidential* difficulties get in the way of their suing a defendant for compensation.[92] However, the problem the claimants

---

[91] It was *not* the case in *Fairchild* that had one of the defendants not been negligent, the claimant would have contracted mesothelioma anyway as a result of one of the other defendants' negligence. The claimant might well not have contracted mesothelioma at all. The problem in *Fairchild* was not knowing *whose* negligence caused the claimant's mesothelioma.

[92] See above, § 8.5.

face in making out causation in overdetermination cases are more *conceptual or philosophical*, than evidential. Secondly, the House of Lords' decision in *Barker* v *Corus (UK) Ltd* (2006) will apply to any non-mesothelioma case where *Fairchild* applies to limit a defendant's liability to a proportion of the harm suffered by the claimant. However, it is not clear that in an overdetermination case like the Two Fires Problem, C should be forced to sue A *and* B in order to recover *full* compensation for the loss of her house.

Most writers on causation would reject the suggestion that we should invoke *Fairchild* in overdetermination cases like Two Fires or Three References. They would argue instead that recovery in cases like these is justified on the basis that the wrongdoers in these cases *have* caused harm to the claimant. Some support this argument by adopting a qualified form of the 'but for' test for causation, according to which A will have caused C to suffer some kind of harm if that harm would not have been suffered *in the way it was* but for A's actions. So in Two Fires, *both* A *and* B caused C's house to burn down because it would not have burned down *in the way it did* had A and B not lit their fires. Others[93] argue that the rule applied by the Privy Council in *Williams* v *Bermuda Hospitals Board* (2016)[94] applies in cases like Two Fires and Three References in that in Two Fires, C's house burned down because of a state of affairs – the house's being engulfed by fire – that both A and B contributed to, and that in Three References, D didn't get the job because of a state of affairs – D's getting some bad references – that A, B and C all contributed to. A third school of thought argues that causation is established in cases like Two Fires and Three References under the 'NESS' test for causation, which we will discuss in detail later on.[95] On this test, A *and* B *and* C caused D not to get a job in Three References because there is a set of circumstances in which A's failing to give D a good reference would have been sufficient to produce the result that D did not get his job, and the same could be said of B and C.

We do not need to get involved in the debates (which tend to be interminable, anyway) as to which of these approaches to overdetermination cases should be preferred. What is important is that *everyone agrees* that in overdetermination cases like Two Fires and Three References, the wrongdoers involved should each be held liable, and held liable *in full*, for the harm suffered by the claimant. If this is right, then it would be dangerous to apply *Fairchild* – and, by necessary implication, *Barker* – to these kinds of overdetermination cases. Instead we should simply say that in cases like Two Fires and Three References a causal link *will* be found between a wrongdoer's conduct and the harm suffered by the claimant, even though that harm would have been suffered anyway as a result of the conduct of other wrongdoers.

In the situations we have looked at so far, had the defendant not done what he did, the same harm would have occurred anyway, *at the same time* as it occurred in real life. But the problem of overdetermination also arises when, had the defendant not done what he did, the same harm would have occurred *a bit later* than it did in real life. We have already seen a couple of examples of this: *Jobling* v *Associated Dairies Ltd* (1982) and *Calvert* v *William Hill Ltd* (2008).[96] In *Jobling* the claimant suffered from a condition that would have disabled his back three years after it was disabled due to the defendants' tort. The claimant was only allowed to sue for damages for three years' worth of disability, on the basis that after that time, the defendants' tort did not cause any of the losses flowing from the claimant's disability as those losses would have happened anyway. In *Calvert*, the claimant was allowed to use a telephone gambling account with the defendants that should have been disabled. He was not allowed at first instance to sue for any of the losses

---

[93] See above, n 25.
[94] Discussed above, § 8.3(B).
[95] See below, § 8.12(A).

that he suffered using that telephone account as those losses would have eventually been suffered anyway, even if the account had been disabled.

While these decisions seem unexceptionable, problems again rear their head when a third party's wrong would have eventually caused the claimant to suffer the same losses that he has suffered as a result of the defendant's tort. In *Baker* v *Willoughby* (1970), the defendant negligently ran over the claimant As a result of the accident the claimant suffered fairly severe injury to his left leg and ankle. The accident occurred in 1964. The claimant sued the defendant so as to be compensated for the fact that the defendant's negligence had caused him to lose the use of his left leg. In 1967 – before the claimant's case against the defendant had been tried – the claimant was shot in the left leg during an armed robbery and the claimant's left leg had to be amputated immediately.

If we apply the 'but for' test to determine the respective liabilities of the defendant and the armed robbers for the claimant's loss of the use of his left leg, we reach a paradoxical conclusion. Had the defendant not committed his tort, the claimant would have had the use of his left leg for three years, before it was shot in the armed robbery and amputated. So the defendant should be liable to pay damages for the loss of the use of the claimant's left leg for three years. Turning to the armed robbers, had they not shot the defendant's leg, he would have carried around a useless leg for the rest of his life. So it is hard to see that the armed robbers caused the defendant any loss – according to the 'but for' test – by shooting his left leg. (In fact, they may have benefited him by saving him years of pain and strain in trying to get around on a left leg that was so severely damaged.)

So if we apply the 'but for' test to this situation, we will end up concluding that the claimant should be able to recover from the defendant damages for the loss of his leg for three years *and that is it*. Nothing else will be recoverable, even though in 1964, the claimant had a perfectly sound left leg, and since then he has not been able to use his left leg and that will be the case until he dies. Applying the 'but for' test in this situation would therefore result in the claimant being severely undercompensated. He would get nothing for the fact that from 1967 to the end of his life, he would have to manage without a left leg.

To avoid this paradox, the House of Lords in *Baker* awarded damages against the defendant on the basis that the defendant's negligence had caused the claimant to lose the use of his left leg *for the rest of his life*. So the defendant was not just liable for the loss of the use of the claimant's left leg from 1964 to 1967, but from 1967 onwards as well – even though, had the defendants not committed their tort, the claimant would still have lost the use of his left leg from 1967 onwards. No injustice was done to the defendant by the House of Lords in so holding. It was just a matter of luck that the claimant was shot in the armed robbery, and there is no reason why the claimant's bad luck (where it is due to someone else's wrong) should turn into good luck for the defendant, in terms of reducing his liability from a liability to compensate the claimant for the loss of the use of his left leg for the rest of his life into a liability just to compensate the claimant for the loss of the use of his left leg before it was shot.

The table below sums up how the courts handle cases of overdetermination:

Unrelated event . . .	. . . was innocent	. . . was wrongful
. . . would have produced same harm same time or before	No Damages (Double Poison Problem)	Both Wrongdoers Caused Harm (Two Fires Problem; Three References Problem)
. . . would have produced same harm later	Damages Reduced (*Jobling*; *Calvert*)	Original Wrongdoer Held Fully Liable (*Baker*)

---

[96] See above, § 8.2.

To see how the table works, let us apply it to the Water Bottle Problem, where *Traveller* died in the desert after *Malice* poisoned *Traveller*'s water bottle, and *Envy* ensured that it was empty before *Traveller* could have a drink from it. As we saw above,[97] applying the 'but for' test to this situation suggests that neither *Malice* nor *Envy* caused *Traveller*'s death: had *Malice* not done what he did, *Traveller* would have died in exactly the same way and at exactly the same time as she did in real life; and had *Envy* not done what she did, *Traveller* would have died a lot sooner than she did in real life. However, as both *Malice* and *Envy* are wrongdoers, the courts will find that *both Malice and Envy* caused *Traveller*'s death in this situation.

8.9 Another solution to overdetermination?

In *Cook* v *Lewis* (1951), Rand J suggested that each of the hunters who shot in the direction of the claimant in that case should be held liable because their negligence in shooting had destroyed the claimant's ability to sue the person who had actually shot him:

> What, then, the culpable actor has done by his initial negligent act is, first, to have set in motion a dangerous force which embraces the injured person within the scope of its probable mischief; and next, in conjunction with circumstances which he must be held to contemplate, to have made more difficult if not impossible the means of proving the damaging results of his own act or the similar results of the act of another. He has violated not only the victim's substantive right to security, but he has also culpably impaired the latter's remedial right of establishing liability.[98]

Cook v *Lewis* was not an overdetermination case – it was an evidential uncertainty case – but some people think that Rand J's idea that a claimant can sue a defendant not for injuring her, but for depriving her of the right to sue someone else for damages, can be applied to solve overdetermination problems where two wrongdoers have each done something that was independently sufficient to cause a claimant to suffer a particular loss for which the claimant wants to sue.

For example, in the Two Fires Problem – where A and B each negligently start fires that engulf C's house – we could straightforwardly say that because the loss of C's house is overdetermined by A and B's negligence C cannot sue either A or B for the fire damage to his house. However, had A not been negligent, C would have had a perfectly good claim against B for the fire damage to his house – so C can sue A in negligence for compensation for the fact that he does not now have a right to sue B for that fire damage. And – on the same basis – C can sue B in negligence for the fact that, had B not been negligent, C would now have a perfectly good claim against A for the fire damage to his house.

In *Wright* v *Cambridge Medical Group* (2011), the Court of Appeal endorsed the idea that overdetermination problems could be solved by allowing a claimant to sue a defendant for depriving him of the right to sue a third party for damages. In *Wright*, the Court of Appeal considered what the position would be in the **Two Negligent Doctors Problem**:

---

[97] § 8.1.
[98] [1951] SCR 830, 832.

Ill presents herself at *GP*'s surgery, complaining that her leg hurts. She is in fact suffering from a deep vein thrombosis (a blood clot) in her leg, but *GP* tells her not to worry, and that the pain will probably go away if she just rests her leg for a couple of days. *GP* had no reasonable basis for making that diagnosis, and should have referred *Ill* to a hospital, where she could have been seen by *Consultant*. In fact, *Ill*'s leg pains do not go away, and two days later she suffers severe brain damage when the thrombosis in her leg travels to her brain. There is evidence that even if *GP* had referred *Ill* to *Consultant* when she first presented herself at *GP*'s surgery, *Consultant* would have culpably failed to diagnose *Ill*'s deep vein thrombosis (DVT), as he was at the time telling all his patients that their problems were 'all in your mind' and that 99 per cent of medical problems could be solved through prayer and meditation.

If *Ill* tries to sue *GP* for compensation for her brain damage, he might try to argue that his negligence in treating her did not cause her brain damage because even if he had referred her to *Consultant*, her DVT would have still gone undiagnosed, and she would have still suffered her brain damage. In *Wright*, both Lord Neuberger MR and Elias LJ thought that *Ill* would still be entitled to sue *GP*, not for her brain damage, but for the fact that had *GP* referred her to *Consultant*, she would then have been entitled to sue *Consultant* for substantial damages for failing to diagnose her DVT properly.[99] So *Ill* could sue *GP* for the fact that his negligence resulted in her suffering an economic loss – the loss of the money she would have been able to recover from *Consultant* had she been referred to him, and had he failed to treat her properly.

Elegant though this may seem as a solution to the problem of overdetermination, as a matter of legal principle, it is untenable. This is for three reasons.[100] First, a claim for losing the right to sue someone for damages is a claim for economic loss, and damages for pure economic loss are not ordinarily available in cases like Two Negligent Doctors or Two Fires. A claim for pure economic loss could not normally be made in Two Fires as there is no kind of special relationship between the claimant and the defendants. There is a special relationship in Two Negligent Doctors, but it is one that is geared towards protecting *Ill* from physical injury, not pure economic loss.

Secondly, in a lot of overdetermination cases, the loss of a right to sue someone for damages will count as being an unforeseeable consequence of a defendant's negligence, and will therefore be non-actionable as too remote. For example, in Two Fires it will not – in the ordinary course of things – have been reasonably foreseeable that A's negligently starting a fire near C's house would result in C suffering the loss of 'being unable to sue B for damages for the fire damage to his home'. So that loss will be too remote a consequence of A's negligence for it to be actionable.[101]

Thirdly, this 'solution' to problems of overdetermination has the potential in certain cases to plunge the law into unsolvable paradoxes akin to the paradox of Protagoras.[102] For example, suppose that in Two Fires, C sues A for compensation for depriving C of the right to sue B for the fire damage to his house. If C does this, it is not clear why A cannot argue: 'You can't sue me. My negligence in starting a fire has caused you no effective loss, as you can still sue B for depriving you of the right to sue *me* for the fire damage to your house.' But if C sues B for compensation for depriving C of the right to sue A for the fire damage

---

[99] [2013] QB 312, at [58] (per Lord Neuberger MR) and at [98] (per Elias LJ).
[100] See McBride & Steel 2012a; also Nolan 2009, 177.
[101] See below, § 9.2.

to his house, it seems that B could make a similar reply to C's claim. So C cannot sue either A or B because each can rely on the fact that C can sue the other to deny that he is liable to C. The fact that each is liable to C is a reason why neither can be liable to C. The only way for the law to avoid becoming trapped by this paradox in cases like Two Fires[103] is to reject outright the suggestion that in overdetermination cases, it might be possible for a claimant to sue a defendant for depriving him of the right to sue a third party in tort.

8.10 Coincidences

Consider the **Healed Victim Problem**:

> *Driver* negligently runs over *Unlucky* and she suffers various injuries to her head and chest as a result. She spends a month in hospital being treated for her injuries and is largely healed of those injuries by the time she leaves hospital. As *Unlucky* is walking out of the hospital front door, she is hit by a car that is being negligently driven by *Careless*. Her leg is broken in the collision.

Has *Driver*'s tort caused *Unlucky* to suffer a broken leg in this case? Most people would instinctively say 'no', even though *Unlucky*'s leg would not have been broken had *Driver* not negligently run her over. Most people would say that it is just a *coincidence* that *Unlucky* broke a leg leaving the hospital where she was being treated for the injuries she sustained as a result of being run over by *Driver*. They would say the same thing in the **Careless-Careful Driver Problem**:

> *Driver*, angered by an argument that he has had with his wife, drives very fast to a junction. But he quickly realises how irresponsible he is being and as he approaches the junction, he slows down and keeps a proper look out for nearby traffic and pedestrians. *Teen* tries to cross the road at the junction and steps out right in front of *Driver*'s car, which she has not seen because she is distracted by a conversation she is having on her mobile phone. *Driver* is unable to avoid *Teen* and runs into her, breaking her leg.

Let's assume that *Driver* committed a tort (negligence) in relation to *Teen* by driving very fast to the junction: it was reasonably foreseeable that doing so might result in someone waiting at the junction being injured,[104] and so *Driver* owed *Teen* a duty to take care not to drive very fast up to the junction. Now – if *Driver* had not committed this tort, it seems very likely that *Teen* would not have been injured in the way she was. Had *Driver*

---

[102] Protagoras, a famous lawyer, took on a pupil, Euathlus, on the understanding that E would pay P for his instruction once E won his first case. Before E had won any case, P sued for his fee, arguing that if his claim was turned down on the basis that E had not yet won his first case, E should be ordered to pay up anyway as he would – by definition – have just won his first case. E argued in response that if he were ordered to pay up then he would – by definition – still not have won his first case, and so should not be ordered to pay up.

[103] The paradox does not arises in Two Negligent Doctors as there is only one possible defendant (*GP*) who can be sued by *Ill* in that situation.

[104] There was a real risk, for example, that *Driver* might lose control of the car when he was driving at such a speed and end up ploughing into pedestrians who were waiting to cross the road at the junction.

not driven so fast up to the junction, his car would not have been in the wrong place at the wrong time when *Teen* stepped out into the road. His car would have been some way away from *Teen*, and *Driver* would have had time to brake and stop the car before he collided with *Teen*. Despite this, most people would feel unease about saying that *Driver*'s negligence caused *Teen*'s injuries in this case. It is just a *coincidence*, they would say, that *Driver*'s negligence resulted in his car being in the exact place it needed to be to hit *Teen* when she unthinkingly walked out into the middle of the road.

These examples have been carefully constructed so that we cannot say in either case that there was a break in the chain of causation between *Driver*'s torts and the broken legs suffered by *Unlucky* and *Teen*. *Careless*'s negligent driving in Healed Victim, and *Teen*'s carelessness in stepping out onto the road in Careless-Careful Driver, are not sufficiently serious as acts to break the chain of causation between what *Driver* did and what happened to *Unlucky/Teen*.[105] Instead, what makes the broken leg a *coincidental result* of *Driver*'s wrong in each of the above cases is that *Driver*'s wrong did not *materially increase the risk* that *Unlucky/Teen* would suffer a broken leg in the way she did. In Healed Victim, *Driver*'s running over *Unlucky* did not materially increase the risk that she would be run over again in leaving the hospital, after having made a full recovery from the injuries she suffered as a result of being hit by *Driver*. In Careless-Careful Driver, *Driver*'s driving fast up to the junction did not materially increase the risk that *Teen* would be hit by *Driver*'s car once *Driver* had slowed the car down and started keeping a proper look out for nearby people and traffic.[106]

In *Carslogie Steamship Co Ltd* v *Royal Norwegian Government* (1952), the claimants' ship, the *Heimgar*, was damaged in a collision with the *Carslogie*, which was owned by the defendants. The collision occurred because of the defendants' negligence. The *Heimgar* was on its way to port to have the damage it had suffered in the collision with the *Carslogie* repaired permanently when it was involved in a violent storm which rendered the *Heimgar* unseaworthy. The *Heimgar* limped into port where it spent 30 days having both the storm damage and the damage done in the collision with the *Carslogie* repaired simultaneously. If the *Heimgar* had not suffered any storm damage it would have taken ten days to repair the damage done in the collision with the *Carslogie*. It was held that the defendants' negligence did not cause the *Heimgar* to suffer the storm damage which resulted in its being detained in port for 30 days. In previous editions of this text, we explained this result by saying that the storm broke the chain of causation between the defendants' negligence and the storm damage. It now seems to us that a better explanation is that the defendants' negligence did not materially increase the risk that the *Heimgar* would suffer storm damage on its way to be repaired. It was just a coincidence that a violent storm broke out over the path the *Heimgar* was taking to port, to be repaired.

We have already mentioned *Chester* v *Afshar* (2005), as an example of a situation where the courts applied a balance of probability test to determine whether the claimant (Chester)

---

[105] See below, § 8.11.

[106] Contrast *Gray* v *Botwright* [2014] EWCA Civ 1201. The claimant driver entered a junction without looking to see whether there was any approaching traffic because he assumed all such traffic had been stopped by a red light. Unfortunately, the defendant had run the red light and crashed into the claimant's car. The defendant argued that his negligence did not cause the accident on the ground that his case was analogous to the Careless-Careful Driver Problem. The Court of Appeal disagreed, and rightly so: by running the red light the defendant had materially increased the risk of precisely the kind of accident occurring that occurred in *Gray* (ibid, at [31]).

would have suffered paralysis had the defendant (Afshar) not breached the duty of care he owed her as his patient in failing to inform her that there was a 1–2 per cent risk that the operation he was proposing to perform on her back would result in her being paralysed.[107] It was found that had Chester been told this she probably would have delayed having the operation, as she considered her options, but having done so she probably would gone ahead with the operation. But the probability that she would *not* have been paralysed as a result of having that later operation was 98–99 per cent. So it was (overwhelmingly) more likely than not that had Afshar informed Chester of the risks associated with her operation, that she would not have been paralysed.

The 'but for' test indicates, then, that Afshar's negligence caused Chester's paralysis. But it was just a coincidence that Afshar's negligence had this effect. Afshar's negligence in failing to disclose to Chester that there was a risk of paralysis associated with her operation did not materially increase the risk that when she went under the knife, she would end up paralysed. The risk was always the same, whatever Afshar said or didn't say to Chester. It was just Afshar's bad luck that the one time (we can suppose) he did not tell his patient that there was a risk of paralysis associated with her operation, that that risk materialised. Given this, we cannot say that Afshar's negligence caused her paralysis.[108]

Despite this, the House of Lords held – by a 3:2 majority – that Afshar *should* be held liable to compensate Chester for her paralysis.[109] The majority so ruled because they were concerned that, if Afshar were not held liable, then every time a doctor advised a patient to have an operation and failed – in breach of the duty of care he owed the patient – to inform her of the risks associated with the operation, his breach of duty would go unsanctioned by tort law. If the patient agreed to have the operation and suffered harm as a result, even though the operation was carried out impeccably, the doctor could argue that he should not be held liable for that harm because his breach of duty in failing to inform the patient of the risks associated with that operation had not caused the harm suffered by the patient. The doctor's duty to inform his patient of the risks associated with a particular operation would then become empty – the doctor would be free to breach that duty with impunity.

In order, then, to vindicate the patient's 'right to know', the majority felt[110] that it was necessary to create a special exception to the rules on causation in *Chester* v *Afshar* and hold that: (1) if a doctor wrongfully failed to inform a patient of a risk associated with an operation that it was proposed the patient undergo; and (2) had the patient been informed of this risk, she would probably have either refused to undergo the operation or delayed having the operation so as to think it over whether she should undergo it;[111] and (3) in

---

[107] See above, § 7.4.

[108] [2005] 1 AC 134, at [13]–[22] (per Lord Steyn); [30]–[32] (per Lord Hoffmann); and [61] and [81] (per Lord Hope).

[109] For criticism, see Clark & Nolan 2014.

[110] [2005] 1 AC 134, at [22]–[24] (per Lord Steyn); [56] and [87] (per Lord Hope); and [101] (per Lord Walker).

[111] There is an issue as to whether this requirement has to be satisfied in order for an award of damages to be made under *Chester* v *Afshar* [2005] 1 AC 134. The argument is that if the object of such an award of damages is to vindicate a patient's 'right to know' such damages should be available even if telling the patient of the risks associated with her operation would have had no effect on the timing of her operation. However, of the majority judges, both Lord Steyn (ibid, at [19]) and Lord Hope (at [61] and [81]) attached importance to the fact that had Chester been told of the risk of nerve damage associated with her operation, her operation probably would not have gone ahead when it did. In light of this, it seemed to us correct to say that damages will only be awarded to a patient under *Chester* v *Afshar* if requirement (2) is satisfied.

the course of the operation, this risk materialised with the result that the patient suffered harm; then (4) the doctor should be held liable in negligence to compensate the patient for that harm.[112]

In dissent, Lord Hoffmann held that if (1), (2) and (3) were established, then there might be a case for awarding the patient a 'modest solatium'[113] to compensate her for the fact that her right to know the risks associated with her operation so as to make an informed decision whether or not to undergo the operation had been violated. However, he failed to see why the compensation payable to a patient whose 'right to know' had been violated should depend on whether the risk which the patient was not informed of had materialised, and how much harm had been suffered by the patient as a result of that risk's materalising.[114] Lord Bingham also dissented. He dismissed the majority's justification for allowing Chester's claim on the ground that 'in the current legal and social climate' few doctors would 'consciously or deliberately violate' a patient's 'right to be appropriately warned' of the risks associated with her operation. He saw no reason why 'the law should seek to reinforce that right by providing for the payment of very large damages by a defendant whose violation of that right is not shown' to have caused the claimant to suffer the injury for which she is seeking compensation.[115]

The case of *Wright* v *Cambridge Medical Group* (2011) illustrates how tricky it can be, to apply the idea that a tort does not cause a particular outcome that would not have happened but for that tort being committed if the tort did not materially increase the risk of that outcome occurring – and serves as a salutary warning to students who might be tempted to apply this idea promiscuously in answering problem questions. In *Wright*, when the claimant was a baby she developed an infection in her hip. She was taken to see the defendant doctor on a Wednesday, and he negligently failed to refer her to a hospital for further examination. Her condition grew worse, and a different doctor referred her to hospital on the Friday. Unfortunately, the hospital failed to treat the claimant's condition properly, with the result that her hip became permanently damaged. The Court of Appeal held that the claimant could sue the defendant doctor for damages: had he referred her to hospital on the Wednesday, it was more likely than not that she would have been properly treated and avoided permanent damage to her hip. Elias LJ dissented on the ground that had the claimant been treated properly in hospital on the Friday, she would have avoided any permanent damage to her hip. So, he argued, the negligent delay in referring the claimant to the hospital did not materially increase the risk that she would end up suffering permanent damage to her hip, and could not therefore be said to have caused her to suffer that damage.[116] However, as Smith LJ pointed out, this argument was incorrect. The delay in referring the claimant to hospital *did* materially increase the risk that the

---

[112] It is crucial that the *very* risk that the doctor was under a duty to warn the patient about materialise. So there would be no recovery in a case where *Patient* was not advised by *Doctor* that there was a 2 per cent risk of her being paralysed as a result of her operation, and *Patient* went ahead with the operation, and it went perfectly well, but as she left the hospital, she was run over by *Driver*. Although the *Doctor*'s failure to warn *Patient* of the risk of paralysis might have been a but for cause of her being run over – had he warned *Patient*, she might have taken a couple of days before agreeing to the operation, and never encountered *Driver* on the way out of hospital – the risk that *Doctor* was under a duty to warn *Patient* about did not materialise in this case.

[113] [2005] 1 AC 134, at [34].

[114] [2005] 1 AC 134, at [35].

[115] [2005] 1 AC 134, at [9].

[116] [2011] EWCA Civ 669, at [106].

claimant would suffer permanent damage to her hip as it shortened the period that was available to the hospital to diagnose and treat the claimant's hip problem and correct any initial incorrect diagnosis and treatment of that problem.[117]

8.11 Break in the chain of causation

Where *Victim* would not have suffered *Harm* but for *Defendant*'s tort, *Defendant*'s tort will still not be held to have caused *Harm* to occur if something happened *after Defendant*'s tort that also contributed to *Harm* occurring and that was *sufficiently serious* as to 'break the chain of causation' between *Defendant*'s tort and *Harm* occurring.

As a working hypothesis, we will suggest that the only sort of event that can break a chain of causation is a *positive act* that is *deliberate, voluntary, informed* and *unreasonable*. (Such an act is often referred to in the case law as a '*novus actus interveniens*'.) You need all five (as well as showing that the positive act contributed to the harm suffered by the claimant) to establish a break in the chain of causation between the defendant's tort and the harm suffered by the claimant. The following cases seem to support the idea that *positive acts* will break a chain of causation if, and only if, they are *deliberate* (that is, the act was done intentionally . . .), *voluntary* (. . . not under pressure or mental incapacity . . .), *informed* (. . . knowing the consequences of acting in that way . . .) and *unreasonable*.

In *Haynes* v *Harwood* (1935), the defendant left some horses unattended in a street. The horses bolted and the claimant, a policeman, dashed out and attempted to stop the horses. He was injured in doing so. It was held that the defendant's negligence in leaving the horses unattended in the street had caused the claimant to be injured. True, the claimant was only injured as a result of the defendant's negligence because he deliberately ran out and attempted to stop the defendant's horses bolting. However, it had been reasonable for the claimant to do this.

In *Hyett* v *Great Western Railway Company* (1948), a fire broke out in a train wagon which had been left by the defendants – the wagon's owner – in a railway siding. The fire broke out because of the defendants' negligence in leaving a number of leaking paraffin drums in the wagon. The claimant – who was employed to do work on the wagons in the railway siding – saw the fire and tried to deal with it. While a friend of his went for assistance, the claimant attempted to remove a number of the paraffin drums from the wagon. While he was doing so one of the drums exploded and the claimant was injured. It was held that the defendants' negligence had caused the claimant to be injured. While the claimant was only injured as a result of the defendants' negligence because he deliberately chose to try to remove some of the paraffin drums in the wagon, as it was reasonable for the claimant to do this, this deliberate act of his did not break the chain of causation between the defendants' negligence and his being injured.

In *Knightley* v *Johns* (1982), the defendant drove his car dangerously down a tunnel, in breach of the duty of care he owed other users of the tunnel. As a result, the car overturned near the exit to the tunnel. The police turned up but failed to close the entrance to the tunnel to oncoming traffic. A police inspector at the exit to the tunnel realised the omission and told the claimant – a police constable on a motorcycle – to ride through the tunnel to the entrance and close off the entrance to oncoming traffic. The claimant did

---

[117] [2011] EWCA Civ 669, at [131].

so, travelling against the traffic coming through the tunnel, and was hit by a car as he came round a bend in the tunnel.

It was held that the defendant's dangerous driving did not cause the claimant's accident, even though the accident would not have happened but for the defendant's dangerous driving. The defendant's dangerous driving only resulted in the claimant being injured because the police inspector deliberately and unreasonably instructed the claimant to ride back through the tunnel against the flow of the traffic. Given this, the defendant's dangerous driving did not cause the claimant's injury – the police inspector's instruction broke the chain of causation between the defendant's dangerous driving and the claimant's accident. It would have been different, of course, if the inspector's instruction had been a reasonable one to give: in that case, the giving of the instruction would not have broken the chain of causation between the defendant's dangerous driving and the claimant's accident.

In *The Oropesa* (1943), two steam vessels, *The Manchester Regiment* and *The Oropesa* collided. The collision was, in part, due to the negligence of the defendants, who were in charge of *The Oropesa*. Although *The Manchester Regiment* was badly damaged in the collision, its master thought it could be salved and set out in a boat with 16 men to go to *The Oropesa* and to discuss what could be done to rescue *The Manchester Regiment*. Before the boat could reach *The Oropesa* it capsized in rough weather and nine of the men in the boat were drowned. It was held that the collision between *The Manchester Regiment* and *The Oropesa* had caused the death of the nine men in the boat. While the defendants' negligence only resulted in the nine men dying because the master of *The Manchester Regiment* voluntarily set out to sea with those nine men – and seven more – the master acted reasonably in doing so and therefore his voluntarily setting out to sea did not break the chain of causation between the negligence of the defendants and the men's deaths.

In *Wieland* v *Cyril Lord Carpets Ltd* (1969), the claimant was injured in a traffic accident caused by the defendant's negligence. She was taken to hospital where a collar was fitted to her neck. The collar made it difficult for the claimant to move her head and as a result she was unable to use her bifocal glasses with her normal skill. The result was that shortly afterwards, when she was descending some stairs with the assistance of her son, she became confused as to the position of the stairs and fell. Her ankles were damaged in the fall. It was held that the defendant's negligence had caused the damage to the claimant's ankles. Admittedly, the defendant's negligence only resulted in the claimant's ankles being fractured because: (1) the hospital put a collar on the claimant which made it difficult for the claimant to use her bifocals; and (2) the claimant chose to walk down a flight of steps while it was difficult for her to use her bifocals. However, it was obviously reasonable for the hospital to do (1) and it was reasonable for the claimant to do (2) given that she walked down the stairs with the assistance of her son and so there was no break in the chain of causation between the defendant's negligence and the claimant's ankles being fractured.

It was different in *McKew* v *Holland & Hannen & Cubitts (Scotland) Ltd* (1969). In that case, the claimant was employed by the defendants. The claimant suffered certain injuries as a result of the defendants' negligence. The claimant's injuries meant, among other things, that his left leg was prone to give way suddenly. A few days later, the claimant and a few members of his family inspected a flat which he was thinking of renting. On leaving the flat, the claimant, unassisted, walked down some steep stairs which had no handrail. The claimant's left leg suddenly gave way and he fell down the stairs with the result that he fractured one of his ankles. The House of Lords held that the defendants' negligence did not cause the claimant's ankle fracture. The defendants' negligence only resulted in the claimant suffering an ankle fracture because the claimant chose to walk down a steep staircase which had no handrail without any assistance. This was an unreasonable thing to do and so the claimant's decision to walk down the staircase without any assistance broke the chain of causation between the defendants' negligence and the claimant's ankle fracture.

In *Lynch* v *Knight* (1861) – a defamation case – the defendant warned the claimant's husband that the claimant was a 'notorious liar', that she took 'delight in causing disturbances' wherever she went and that her behaviour could be attributed to one Dr Casserley who 'all but seduced' the claimant. The claimant's husband reacted to these words by divorcing the claimant. The claimant sued the defendant in slander for compensation for the fact that her husband had divorced her. It was admitted that the defendant's words amounted to slander, but it was held that the husband's decision to divorce the claimant had broken the chain of causation between the defendant's words and the break-up of the claimant's marriage: it had not been reasonable for the claimant's husband to react to the defendant's words in the way he did.

A number of points need to be made about the law on what sort of events will break a chain of causation.

A. Omissions

It is clear that an omission – however wrongful, deliberate, voluntary, informed and unreasonable – will *not* break a chain of causation. Suppose, for example, that *Malice* pushes *Drunk* into a lake, where *Drunk* starts drowning. *Bystander* could very easily save *Drunk*'s life, but does not do so. If *Drunk* drowns, *Malice* will not be able to say that *Bystander*'s failure to save *Drunk*'s life broke the chain of causation between his pushing *Drunk* into the lake and *Drunk*'s death through drowning. This will be so even if *Bystander* was under a legal duty to save *Drunk*'s life – as would be the case if *Bystander* were *Drunk*'s bodyguard.

However, the fact that omissions do not break chains of causation does not mean that a claimant will be able to sue if she *allows* a defendant's tort to cause her some kind of harm that the claimant could easily have avoided. In such a case, the claimant might be barred from suing for that harm, not because the defendant's tort did not cause her that harm, but because the claimant was under a *duty to mitigate* the harm she suffered as a result of the defendant's tort.[118] For example, in *McAuley* v *London Transport Executive* (1958), the claimant suffered an accident at work as a result of the defendants' negligence. The claimant's left wrist was cut in the accident. The claimant was taken to hospital but he refused to have an operation on his wrist that would have gone some way towards restoring the claimant's left hand and wrist to full working order. Without an operation, the condition of the claimant's left wrist deteriorated and he lost the use of his left hand. In this case, the defendants' negligence caused the claimant to lose the use of his left hand: the claimant's failure to agree to the operation that would have saved his hand did not break the chain of causation between the defendants' negligence and the claimant's losing the use of his left hand. However, the claimant was still barred from suing for compensation for the loss of the use of his left hand: he only lost the use of his left hand because he failed to mitigate the losses suffered by him as a result of the defendants' negligence.

---

[118] See below, § 9.6.

B. Natural events

It is often contended that a *natural* event that is *unforeseeable* – such as an earthquake – can have the effect of breaking the chain of causation between a defendant's tort and a harm suffered by a claimant.[119] Such a rule, it is argued, explains the lack of causation in the **Lightning Problem**:

> *Thug* stabs *Unlucky*. As *Unlucky* is being taken to hospital in an ambulance, the ambulance is struck by lightning and *Unlucky* is electrocuted to death.

Thug has not caused *Unlucky*'s death in this case, it is argued, because the lightning strike that contributed to *Unlucky*'s death broke the chain of causation between *Unlucky*'s stabbing and *Unlucky*'s death. However, such a case could easily be explained away as an example of a *coincidence*: *Thug*'s stabbing *Unlucky* did not materially increase the risk that he would die from electrocution. Given this, it is submitted there is no need for the hypothesis that unforeseeable natural events break chains of causation: all examples of such cases can be explained on the basis that the harm suffered by the claimant is merely a coincidental result of the defendant's actions.

C. Foreseeability

It is clear that the foreseeability of someone's acting in a particular way is *not* relevant – of and itself – to the issue of whether that someone's act has had the effect of breaking a chain of causation. No one contends that an unforeseeable act cannot have the effect of breaking a chain of causation. (For example, if *Distracted* carelessly sets a house on fire, and *Strange* is burned because he walks into the house while it is ablaze because he is curious to see what it feels like to be in a burning building, *Distracted* has not caused *Strange*'s burns.) So academics who contend that the foreseeability of an act *is* relevant to the issue of whether that act has broken a chain of causation must be taken to be arguing that a foreseeable act will *never* break a chain of causation. That is plainly not true. If *Curious* wants to take heroin and injects himself with a needle full of heroin that *Supplier* has supplied him with, and *Curious* dies of overdosing on the heroin, *Supplier* has not caused *Curious*'s death.[120] The fact that it was plainly foreseeable that *Curious* would take the heroin that *Supplier* gave him does not prevent *Curious*'s deliberate, voluntary, informed and unreasonable act of taking the heroin from breaking the chain of causation between *Supplier*'s giving *Curious* the heroin and *Curious*'s death.

D. Medical expenditure

If A tortiously injures B and B opts to have her injuries privately treated, can A argue that B's decision to 'go private' broke the chain of causation between his tort and B's medical expenditure, as B's injuries could have been treated on the National Health Service? The answer is 'no'. Section 2(4) of the Law Reform (Personal Injuries) Act 1948 provides that in 'an action for damages for personal injuries . . . there shall be disregarded, in determining the reasonableness of any expenses, the possibility of avoiding those expenses or part of them by taking advantage of facilities available under the National Health Service . . .'

---

[119] Hart & Honoré 1985.
[120] *R v Kennedy* [2008] 1 AC 269.

E. Exceptions

There are a number of occasions where the courts will *not* find that a deliberate, voluntary, informed and unreasonable act broke a chain of causation. To save words below, let us called a deliberate, voluntary, informed and unreasonable act a 'DIVU' act.[121] The main situation in which the courts will refuse to give effect to the idea that DIVU acts break chains of causation is where doing so would deprive a defendant's duty of care of any force.

For example, in *Stansbie v Troman* (1948),[122] the defendant decorator owed the claimant a duty to take reasonable steps to lock up her house if he went out, as he had 'assumed a responsibility' to the claimant to do so whenever she was away from the house. The defendant breached this duty of care by leaving the house unlocked for two hours while he went shopping for some wallpaper. A thief took advantage of the defendant's negligence to steal some valuables from the claimant's house. If the defendant were allowed to say in this case that the thief's DIVU act of stealing from the claimant broke the chain of causation between the defendant's negligence in leaving the house unlocked and the claimant's losing her valuables, then the defendant's duty of care would become meaningless. He would be free to leave the house open all day to thieves, safe in the knowledge that he could never be held liable for any thefts resulting from his negligence: he would always be able to plead that the thieves' DIVU acts in stealing from the claimant broke the chain of causation between his negligence and her losses.

In *Reeves v Commissioner of Police of the Metropolis* (2000), a man named Lynch hanged himself while in the defendants' custody. Lynch was known to be a suicide risk and the defendant police force therefore owed him a duty to take reasonable steps to ensure that he did not commit suicide.[123] The defendant police force breached this duty. Lynch – who was of sound mind and knew what he was doing – took advantage of the defendants' negligence to hang himself. The claimant brought a wrongful death action against the defendants, claiming that their negligence had caused Lynch's death and that the defendants were therefore liable to compensate her for the loss of support that she and her child by Lynch suffered as a result of Lynch's death. It was argued that the defendants' negligence had not caused Lynch's death: there was a break in the chain of causation between the defendants' negligence and Lynch's death because Lynch performed a DIVU act in hanging himself.[124]

The House of Lords refused to find that the defendants' negligence had not caused Lynch's death:

> [If] the law [has imposed] a duty [on someone] to guard against loss caused by the free, deliberate and informed act of a human being . . . [it] would make nonsense of the existence of this duty if the law were to hold that the occurrence of the very act which ought to have been prevented negatived [the existence of a] causal connection between the breach of duty and the loss.'[125]

---

[121] Students who over-estimate the popularity of this text among tort law academics should be warned that if they use the term 'DIVU act' in their essays or problem answers, their teachers and examiners will probably not know what they are talking about.

[122] Discussed above, § 6.2.

[123] See above, § 6.4.

[124] Had it been shown that Lynch was acting under some pressure or depression in hanging himself, such an argument would have immediately failed: *Pigney v Pointer's Transport Services Ltd* [1957] 1 WLR 1121; *Kirkham v Chief Constable of the Greater Manchester Police* [1990] 2 QB 283; *Corr v IBC Vehicles Ltd* [2008] 1 AC 884.

[125] [2000] 1 AC 360, at 367 (per Lord Hoffmann).

In other words, if the normal rules on when there will be a break in the chain of causation were applied in this case, then the defendants could never have been held liable for breaching the duty of care they owed Lynch to take reasonable steps to see that he did not kill himself. If Lynch took advantage of their breach of duty to kill himself, the defendants would always be able to argue that their breach did not cause Lynch's death because his DIVU act in killing himself broke the chain of causation between their breach and Lynch's death.[126]

Another example of a situation where the courts will refuse to give effect to the idea that DIVU acts break chains of causation is provided by the criminal law case of *Environment Agency* v *Empress Car Co (Abertilly) Ltd* (1999). In that case, the defendant company owned a diesel tank in a yard that drained directly into a river. Diesel was taken from the tank by turning a tap. When the tap was turned on, diesel would flow down a pipe into another tank. On 20 March 1995, someone unknown turned the tap on, the diesel started flowing, filled up the other tank and overflowed into the yard. The diesel then drained away into the river. The defendant company was charged with committing an offence under s 85(1) of the Water Resources Act 1991 which says that a defendant will commit an offence if 'he causes . . . any poisonous, noxious or polluting matter . . . to enter any controlled waters.'

The defendants argued that they had not caused the diesel to enter the river. The DIVU act of the unknown person who had turned the tap on had broken the chain of causation between whatever they did and the diesel polluting the river. The House of Lords held that this argument did not work. As a matter 'of statutory construction, having regard to the policy of the Act'[127] it was intended that people like the defendants should be held responsible for an escape of polluting matter from their land into controlled waters where that escape was the result of the defendants doing something on their land that played a part in the escape, and where the escape was not also attributable to a natural event or an intervention of a third party that was wholly unexpected and abnormal.

8.12 Alternative approaches to causation

We have now said enough to give the reader a good working knowledge of how the courts will approach cases where they have to decide whether a defendant's tort caused a claimant to suffer some kind of harm. However, there are a number of people who disagree with the approach we have adopted to presenting the law on causation in this chapter. In this section, we will take a look at their views.

A. Richard Wright

Richard Wright is an American academic who argues that what he calls the 'NESS test' provides a superior basic test of causation to the 'but for' test.[128] The NESS test says that event X causes event Y if event X is a Necessary Element in a Set of circumstances that were Sufficient to bring about event Y.

---

[126] It is for this reason B will be held liable for A's brain damage in the Unfortunate Rock Star Problem: see above, § 3.1.

[127] [1999] 2 AC 22, 32 (per Lord Hoffmann).

[128] See Wright 2011a.

What seems to make the NESS test superior to the 'but for' test, is that – unlike the 'but for' test – the NESS test can handle cases of overdetermination. For example, consider again the Two Fires Problem:

> A and B both negligently start fires at an equal distance from C's house. The fires spread at an equal pace and engulf C's house at exactly the same time.

As we have seen, the 'but for' test suggests that neither A's negligence nor B's negligence caused C's house to be destroyed: had A not been negligent, C's house would still have been destroyed by the fire negligently started by B; had B not been negligent, A's negligence would still have resulted in C's house being destroyed. The NESS test avoids such a seemingly paradoxical conclusion.

Under the NESS test, we ask whether A's negligence was a necessary element in a set of circumstances that was sufficient to bring about the damage to C's house that actually happened in this case. The answer is 'yes' – the set of circumstances 'A negligently started a fire, the fire spread, the fire reached C's house, C's house was sound and intact at the time the fire reached the house' describes a set of circumstances that are sufficient to produce the result 'C's house burns down' and A's negligently starting the fire is a necessary element of that set. So we conclude under the NESS test that A's negligence was a cause of C's house burning down. But the NESS test also allows us to say that B's negligence was a cause of C's house burning down. B's negligence also forms a necessary part of a set of circumstances ('B negligently started a fire, the fire spread, the fire reached C's house, C's house was sound and intact at the time the fire reached the house') that were sufficient to produce the result 'C's house burns down'. So both A's negligence and B's negligence caused C's house to burn down under the NESS test.

The NESS test also produces a positive finding that A caused B's death in the **Murder on the Orient Express Problem:**[129]

> *Tycoon* is stabbed in his sleep by 13 people, including *Butler*. Each of the 13 only stabs *Tycoon* once and no stab affects a vital organ. *Tycoon* dies of blood loss from his 13 stab wounds.

The 'but for' test tends to suggest that *Butler* did not cause *Tycoon*'s death here: had *Butler* not stabbed *Tycoon*, *Tycoon* would still have died of blood loss from the 12 other stab wounds he received. The NESS test reaches an opposite conclusion. Assume that six stab wounds were the bare minimum number of stab wounds *Tycoon* would have had to suffer to die of loss of blood in the way he did. Given this, we can describe a set of circumstances, which include as a necessary part *Butler*'s stabbing *Tycoon*, that were sufficient to give rise to *Tycoon*'s dying through loss of blood: '*Butler* stabbed *Tycoon*, *Tycoon* received five other stab wounds'. As a result, we can say – under the NESS test – that *Butler*'s stabbing *Tycoon* was a cause of *Tycoon*'s death. (The same would be true of any of the other 12 people who stabbed *Tycoon*: under the NESS test, each of them caused *Tycoon*'s death because their stabbing *Tycoon* was sufficient (in conjunction with five other people stabbing *Tycoon*) to bring about *Tycoon*'s death.)

---

[129] This problem is named after the famous Agatha Christie novel *Murder on the Orient Express* where an American businessman is stabbed to death while sleeping on the Orient Express.

In applying the NESS test, two things are very important: (1) you have to accurately describe the event the causes of which you are asking about; and (2) a set of circumstances can only count as having been sufficient to bring about a particular event if *every single element* of that set *actually existed* to bring about that event.

The **Julius Caesar Problem** illustrates point (1):

> On 15 March 44 BC, Julius Caesar was attacked in the Roman Senate by over 60 Roman notables who had decided to kill him. He was stabbed 23 times, including by his close friend Brutus. According to the historian Suetonius, only the second stab wound, to Caesar's chest, was lethal.

Did Brutus cause Caesar's death by stabbing him? The answer is 'no'. While the stab wound inflicted by Brutus may have been sufficient – along with an unspecified number of the other stab wounds inflicted on Caesar – to bring about Caesar's death through loss of blood, Caesar did not die of loss of blood. He died from the injury to his chest triggered by the second stab wound that he suffered. If Brutus did not inflict that second stab wound, he did not cause Caesar's death.

The Double Poison Problem and the Double Poison Problem Reversed illustrate point (2). In the Double Poison Problem,[130] *Husband* poisons a cup of coffee so that he can kill himself. Before he can drink the coffee, *Wife* poisons it in order to kill *Husband*. *Wife*'s poison has the side effect of neutralising the poison *Husband* has put in the cup. *Husband* subsequently drinks the coffee and drops down dead. The NESS test has no problem reaching the conclusion that *Wife* caused *Husband*'s death here. *Wife*'s putting poison in *Husband*'s coffee cup formed a necessary part of a set of circumstances ('*Wife* put poison in *Husband*'s coffee cup, *Husband* drank the coffee, the poison was still active at the time the coffee touched *Husband*'s lips') that were sufficient to bring about *Husband*'s death.

In the Double Poison Problem Reversed, *Wife* poisoned *Husband*'s cup of coffee first, and *Husband* slipped some poison into his coffee second, with the side effect that it neutralised *Wife*'s poison. *Husband* then drank the coffee and died. In this case, the NESS test indicates that *Wife* did *not* cause *Husband*'s death. We *can* envisage of set of circumstances where *Wife*'s putting poison in *Husband*'s coffee *would* have been sufficient to bring about *Husband*'s death: '*Wife* put poison in *Husband*'s coffee cup, *Husband* drank the coffee, the poison was still active at the time the coffee touched *Husband*'s lips'. However, the third element in that set of circumstances did not exist in this case: the poison was no longer active at the time the coffee touched *Husband*'s lips.

So should we adopt the NESS test as our basic test for causation? We think people should be cautious about adopting the NESS test for the following reasons.

(1) Richard Wright argues that the NESS test 'captures the essence of causation and gives it a comprehensive specification and meaning.'[131] While the NESS test may be better than the but for test of causation at handling problems of overdetermination, it shares with the but for test of causation a basic flaw that should make anyone doubt whether *either* test is an adequate basic test of causation. The flaw is this: under the NESS test (as well as the 'but for' test) a huge range of circumstances count as causes of any particular event. Any list of the set of circumstances that were sufficient to bring about the event of your reading this

---

[130] See above, § 8.8.
[131] Wright 2011a, 322.

text at this particular moment would include: 'the universe coming into existence', 'the Earth settling into a stable orbit around the Sun'; 'trees growing on the surface of the Earth'; 'human beings coming into existence'; 'Julius Caesar being stabbed on 15 March 44 BC' – all these things count as causes of your reading this text at this particular moment under the NESS test.[132] But there is something odd about any view of causation which counts such a huge range of events, stretching back over unimaginably huge periods of time, as causes of your reading this text at this particular moment in time. The same point could be made in the context of the case where A throws a stone at B's window, shattering it. The presence of the window is a necessary element in the set of circumstances sufficient to bring about the consequence of the window being shattered. But would anyone normally argue that the existence of the window was a cause of its being shattered?

(2) It may be questioned whether the NESS test *is* actually better at handling problems of overdetermination than the 'but for' test. The issue is this: In a case like the Two Fires Problem,[133] is it *obvious* that *each* of A *and* B have caused C's house to burn down? Or is it the case that it is not at all obvious that each of A and B have caused C's house to burn down, but we do not wish to *say* that *neither* of them caused C's house to burn down because doing so would produce results that are unacceptable or paradoxical? If it is obvious that each of A and B have caused C's house to burn down, then the NESS test is superior to the 'but for' test – it, unlike the 'but for' test, identifies who has caused C's house to burn down. If it is not at all obvious that *each* of A *and* B have caused C's house to burn down in the Two Fires Problem, then the 'but for' test is better than the NESS test[134] – it identifies the Two Fires Problem as a genuinely problematic case for the law on causation, while the NESS test just waves the problem away.

Richard Wright argues that if we say that *neither* A *nor* B *caused* C's house to burn down then we must say that C's house burning down was an 'unexplained miracle'.[135] But this is too quick. We can perfectly well explain why C's house burned down: 'A negligently started a fire some way away from C's house and B independently did the same thing. The two fires converged on C's house and it burned down.' The real issue is whether we can honestly reduce *that* explanation down to the formula: 'A and B each caused C's house to burn down.' Or would it be more *accurate* to say that while *neither* A *nor* B *caused* C's house to burn down (as the but for test indicates), each *played a part in*, or was *involved in*, or *had something to do with* C's house burning down?

The point becomes extremely pressing when we consider the Water Bottle Problem.[136] Richard Wright argues that under the NESS test the Water Bottle Problem is not a problem at all.[137] *Malice* (who put poison in *Traveller*'s water bottle) did not cause *Traveller*'s death in this case as *Malice*'s poisoning *Traveller*'s water bottle was not a necessary element in a set of circumstances that would have been sufficient to bring

---

[132] Julius Caesar's being stabbed counts as a cause under the NESS test as had Julius Caesar not been assassinated, history would have been so different that you, the writers of this text, and this text itself would almost certainly not have come into existence but for that event. So Julius Caesar *had* to die for you to read this text at this particular time.

[133] See above, § 8.8.

[134] And is better than a modified form of 'but for' test under which A can only be said to have caused event X to occur if event X would not have occurred *in the way it did* had A not done what he did.

[135] Wright 2011a, 299.

[136] See above, § 8.1.

[137] See Wright 2011a, 298.

about *Traveller*'s death *from dehydration*.[138] But the NESS test tells us that *Envy* (who put a hole in the bottom of *Traveller*'s water bottle, which was by then filled with poison) *did* cause *Traveller*'s death here as we can describe a set of circumstances ('*Envy* put a hole in the bottom of *Traveller*'s water bottle, *Traveller* did not notice the hole when she inspected her water bottle, by the time *Traveller* wanted a drink the contents of her water bottle had completely dribbled out of the hole that *Envy* put in the water bottle') which include what *Envy* did and which would have been sufficient to bring about *Traveller*'s death from dehydration.

What do you think? Do you think it is *easy* to say here that *Envy*, and not *Malice*, caused *Traveller*'s death in this situation? Our view is that it is not easy at all, and the 'but for' test works better than the NESS test in that it makes clear that this is a situation that is genuinely problematic for the law on causation. In our view, it is not possible confidently to explain what happened here as '*Envy*, and not *Malice*, caused *Traveller*'s death'. And we see no reason why we cannot say that while neither *Envy* nor *Malice* caused *Traveller*'s death, each of them *played a part in*, or *was involved in*, or *had something to do with*, *Traveller*'s death.

B. Lord Hoffmann

Lord Hoffmann delivered a lecture at Oxford on 'Causation' in May 2005 that was subsequently published in the *Law Quarterly Review*.[139] In that lecture, he argued that there is no *one* approach to questions of causation that should be applied across the board to all cases where we have to determine whether A's actions caused B to suffer some kind of harm. What approach should be adopted in any given case is a matter for the law to decide. Once one has ascertained 'what causal connection the law requires . . . one then decides, as a question of fact, whether the claimant has satisfied the requirements of the law. There is, in my opinion, nothing more to be said.'[140]

The trouble with this *non-essentialist* approach to the law on causation is that it seems to leave it up to the judges to determine what rules on causation they will adopt in particular types of case. (Assuming, of course, that Parliament has not pre-empted their decision by dictating what rules they should adopt in a particular type of case.) This raises the possibility that the judges may adopt rules on causation that are counter-intuitive or bear no relation to the way ordinary people think about the notion of causation. For example, if Lord Hoffmann is right what is there to stop the judges adopting a rule that says that if 'A does *x* with the object of producing effect Y, and Y occurs after A has done *x*, A's doing *x* will have caused Y to happen'? Such a rule seems counter-intuitive. How can A's intention – a mental state – in doing *x* have any effect on whether A's doing *x* caused Y to happen? And, unsurprisingly, the application of such a counter-intuitive rule would produce odd results – for example, that *Wife* caused *Husband*'s death by poisoning his coffee in *both* the Double Poison Problem (right) *and* the Double Poison Problem Reversed (wrong). Lord Hoffmann's non-essentialist approach to causation opens the door to the judges falling into these kinds of errors.

It may be that Lord Hoffmann would deny that this is the case and argue that by 'causal connection' he meant *valid* causal connection – so in a case where A is alleged to

---

[138] It would be different if the poison had been so foul smelling that as soon as A lifted the water bottle to his lips, he would have known something was up and would not have drunk the water.

[139] Hoffmann 2005.

[140] ibid, 603.

have caused B to suffer some kind of harm, A *cannot* be held liable for that harm if a finding that A caused B to suffer that harm would, for example, violate some natural law (for example, that something you do now cannot cause the death of someone who is already dead). But if one concedes that, then the question arises – What counts as a valid causal connection? Can we validly say that A's doing *x* caused B harm if there is only a coincidental connection between A's doing *x* and the harm suffered by B? Can we validly say that A's doing *x* caused B harm if that harm would have been suffered anyway (and in exactly the way it was suffered, and at the exact same time too) had A not done *x*? On these sorts of questions it is far from true that there is 'nothing more to be said.'

C. Roderick Bagshaw

Roderick Bagshaw has started to sketch out a very different view of causation than any we have looked at so far.[141] On this view, instead of seeking to trace out *lines* of causation between different events, we should instead see events as carrying with them *fields of influence* on subsequent events. The stronger the influence event A has on a subsequent event B, the greater its *causal potency*, and the more likely we are to say that event A was *a cause* of event B occurring.

To take an example given by Bagshaw:

> Suppose that Trevor is walking up a stony beach when he decides to pick up a stone and throw it through Claire's window. He then does this. Did the presence on the beach of the stone he threw 'cause' the breaking of the window?[142]

Richard Wright would apply the NESS test here to say that the presence of the stone on the beach *was* a cause of the breaking of the window. Bagshaw disagrees, appealing to the relative 'causal potency' of the presence of the stone on the beach:

> The stone's 'inert presence' on the beach [was] clearly not wholly irrelevant to the breaking of the window. It was, after all, only by being present on the beach that *that* stone (eventually) came to strike the window. But . . . the mere presence of the stone is a very *weak* 'cause' when set alongside Trevor's choice [to throw the stone through the window].[143]

In another example considered by Bagshaw, he imagines a pond full of fish, and that 50 units of poison need to be introduced into the pond to kill all the fish. Suppose that A carelessly spills 40 units of poison into the pond, B carelessly spills 30 units of poison into the pond, and C carelessly spills 10 units of poison into the pond. All the fish die. Who caused their death? The NESS test tells us that *each* of A, B and C caused the death of the fish. We can construct a set of circumstances which was sufficient to bring about the death of the fish, and which actually occurred, where each of A, B and C's putting poison in the pond was a necessary element of that set of circumstances.[144] But on Roderick Bagshaw's approach, this is too crude an answer.

If A, B and C *simultaneously* spilled the poison in the pond, on a 'causal potency' approach, we would say that 'A was more *causally involved* in killing the fish than B, who

---

[141] Bagshaw 2011a.
[142] ibid, 379.
[143] ibid.
[144] For example: A puts 20 units of poison in the pond, B puts 20 units of poison in the pond, C puts 10 units of poison in the pond. This actually happened: the fact that A *also* put *another* 30 units of poison in the pond, and B *also* put *another* 10 units of poison in the pond is irrelevant under the NESS test.

was *more involved* than C.'[145] But despite the different levels of influence that A, B and C's spillages had on the subsequent death of the fish, we would probably still say that each of them caused the death of the fish as their *degree of contribution* was relatively strong in each case. But it might be different if A and B spilled their poison into the pond *first* and then C only spilled his poison into the pond later (but before the poison spilled by A and B into the pond had begun to do its work). In such a case, C's spilling the poison into the pond had very little influence on what happened later. The fish were already doomed by the time C came along. While C's spilling the poison into the pond will have had a physiological effect on some of the fish – it is hard to imagine that some of the fish did not absorb some of the molecules of poison spilled by C[146] – the degree of influence that C's spillage had on what happened to the fish was so weak that we might well, in this case, say that C did *not* cause the death of the fish.

Unsurprisingly, we would contend that this 'analogue' account of causation (where an event only counts as a cause of a subsequent event if it has a *strong* influence on that subsequent event occurring) has a lot going for it, and may well give a better account of how we intuitively think about causation than more traditional 'digital' accounts of causation (which attempt to provide us with tests that can give a simple yes/no answer to whether an event was a cause of a subsequent event). However, it must be questioned whether such an account of causation can be successfully employed in a *legal* context, where understandable importance is placed on the law's being clear and predictable in its application.

8.13 Fact and policy

We will conclude our discussion of the law on causation by considering the issue of how far inquiries into causation are simply inquiries into matters of fact, and how far those inquiries are affected by policy considerations. As so often, the truth lies in between two opposing extremes.

The first extreme view is that in a case where A has committed a tort and B has suffered some kind of harm, our conclusion as to whether A's tort caused B to suffer that harm will *always* turn on policy considerations. This seems too extreme. If A punches B in the face, breaking B's nose in the process, our conclusion that A's battery caused B to suffer a broken nose does not seem to rest on any considerations of public policy. One way of rescuing this *policy-based* view of causation might be to argue that public policy considerations account for why we are content to find that it was *A's tort* that caused B's nose to break in the above case, instead of focusing our attention on A's upbringing, or his genetic make-up, or anything B might have done to provoke A into hitting him. It might be argued that the reason why we do this is that we do not want to make it *too easy* for tortfeasors to escape liability for the consequences of their actions, by blaming their upbringing or their genetic makeup or the victim of the tort for what they did. But it might equally be argued that the reason why we do not allow tortfeasors to do this is that, *as a matter of fact*, those factors do not prevent us from finding that A's tort caused B's nose to break. In any explanation of why B's nose broke, A's punching B in the face will loom very large; so large that whatever the chain of events leading up to the punch, the punch will still remain *a* cause of B's nose breaking.

---

[145] ibid (emphasis in original).
[146] A point acknowledged in Bagshaw 2011a, 373.

The second extreme view is that in a case where A has committed a tort and B has suffered some kind of harm, if we ask whether A's tort caused B to suffer that harm, we are always asking a question of fact. Allan Beever takes this extreme view, arguing that:

> to say that causation is, even in part, a normative or policy matter is to imply that our judgments or preferences for deciding liability determine the fundamental nature of the universe; as if, were human beings not to exist, or were even just law to be abolished, the fundamental nature of the universe would change. This is, of course, nonsense.[147]

Beever is right to point out that questions of causation are relevant to scientific inquiries into 'the fundamental nature of the universe' and that it is nonsense to suggest that the scientists' approach to questions of causation might be affected by public policy considerations. But Beever goes too far in denying that causation is not '*even in part*, a normative or policy matter' (emphasis added). It seems undeniable that public policy considerations do play *a role* in the courts' deliberations as to whether or not A's tort caused B to suffer some kind of harm.

In taking this view, we do not go so far as to say that any part of the law of causation that does not involve the basic and straightforward application of the 'but for' test, or NESS test, of causation rests on public policy considerations. We do not accept, for example, that the law on what amounts to a *novus actus interveniens* rests on public policy considerations.[148] But it seems obvious that the courts *do* monitor the outcomes of the application of what Lord Hoffmann calls 'the standard criteria'[149] for determining what was a cause of what, and will adjust those outcomes if they consider them to be contrary to the public interest.

So in a case where A allows B to kill herself, or even encourages B to kill herself, we would *normally* say that B and only B caused her own death. But where A was under a duty to take reasonable steps to save B from killing herself and application of the normal rules on causation would allow A to breach that duty of care with impunity, the courts will refuse to apply the normal rules and will find that A's breach of duty *did* cause B's death.[150] In a case where A, B and C each employed D to work for them for five years, and they each exposed D to excessive quantities of asbestos while he worked for them, and D subsequently developed mesothelioma, we would *normally* find that *none* of A, B or C could be said to have caused D's mesothelioma. However, the courts will instead find that *each* of A, B and C caused D's mesothelioma so as to ensure that an employer's duty of care not to expose his employees to dangerous substances such as asbestos is not rendered nugatory, and in order to ensure that D gets the compensation that we know is due to him from someone.[151]

It seems, then, that inquiries into causation are neither exclusively a matter of fact nor exclusively a matter of policy. They are, at base, inquiries into questions of fact – but the courts will adjust the outcome of those inquiries where they threaten to work injustice, or harm the public interest.

---

[147] Beever 2007, 413.
[148] In *support* of this view see Lord Bingham in *Corr* v *IBC Vehicles Ltd* [2008] 1 AC 884, at [15]: 'the rationale of the principle that a *novus actus interveniens* breaks the chain of causation is fairness.' *Against* this view, see Lord Bingham (!) in *R* v *Kennedy* [2008] 1 AC 269, at [14]: 'The criminal law generally assumes the existence of free will . . . generally speaking, informed adults of sound mind are treated as autonomous beings able to make their own decisions how they will act . . . Thus D is not to be treated as causing V to act in a certain way if V makes a voluntary and informed decision to act in that way rather than another.'
[149] Hoffmann 2005.
[150] See above, § 8.11.
[151] See above, § 8.5.

Further reading

We think we have summed up the various academic views about causation well enough above, but for those interested in reading those views at first hand, see: **Hoffmann, 'Causation' (2005) 121** *Law Quarterly Review* **592; Wright, 'The NESS account of natural causation: a response to criticisms' and Bagshaw, 'Causing the behaviour of others and other causal mixtures', both in Richard Goldberg (ed),** *Perspectives on Causation* **(Hart Publishing, 2011).** The *Perspectives on Causation* book is the result of a special conference on causation in Aberdeen and is well worth looking at as it represents the current state of the art in academic thinking about causation. A review of the book is provided by one of us in **(2013) 29** *Professional Negligence* **136**.

Elsewhere, **Sandy Steel and David Ibbetson's article 'More grief on uncertain causation in tort' (2011) 70** *Cambridge Law Journal* **451** provides a very good and readable summary of the state of the law after the Supreme Court's decision in *Sienkiewicz*, as does **Steel, 'Causation in English tort law: still wrong after all these years' (2012) 31** *University of Queensland Law Journal* **243**. Stephen Bailey's **'Causation in negligence: what is a material contribution?' (2010) 30** *Legal Studies* **167** helps sort out a lot of the confusions implicit in the cases' attempting to resolve causation issues by asking whether the defendant's actions materially contributed to the harm suffered by the claimant. **Jane Stapleton's** latest thoughts on causation are to be found in **'Unnecessary causes' (2013) 129** *Law Quarterly Review* **39** and **'An "extended but-for test" for causal relations in the law of obligations' (2015) 35** *Oxford Journal of Legal Studies* **697**.

Three recent monographs on the law on causation are **Green,** *Causation in Negligence* **(Hart Publishing, 2014), Steel,** *Proof of Causation in Tort Law* **(Cambridge University Press, 2015), and Turton,** *Evidential Uncertainty in Causation in Negligence* **(Hart Publishing, 2016).**

Chapter 9
Actionability

Aims and objectives

Reading this chapter should enable you to:

(1) Understand when a claimant will be prevented from a suing a defendant for compensation in respect of harm that the defendant's wrong caused her to suffer on the ground that: (a) the harm was too remote; (b) the harm was the wrong kind of loss (that is, not the kind of harm that the duty breached by the defendant was imposed on him in order to avoid); (c) the public interest or the proper administration of justice requires that the claimant not be allowed to sue the defendant for compensation for that harm; (d) the harm suffered by the claimant was one which the claimant could have been expected to avoid suffering.

(2) Understand when a claimant who has suffered harm as a result of a defendant's breaching a duty of care owed to her under the basic or extended principle in *Hedley Byrne* will be prevented from suing for compensation for that harm under the *SAAMCO* principle.

9.1 The basics

Many academics would name this chapter 'Remoteness of Damage', and discuss in this chapter when a claimant will be prevented from suing a defendant in tort for compensation for a loss that the claimant has suffered on the ground that that loss was a *remote* consequence of the defendant's tort. However, the law on remoteness of damage is only one aspect of a more fundamental area of tort law: the law on when a loss that a defendant's tort has caused a claimant to suffer will be *actionable*. That is the concern of this chapter. Again, it should be emphasised that this chapter (despite its location in this text) is relevant to *all* cases where the victim of a tort wants to sue for compensatory damages – not just negligence cases.

The law on actionability will be briefly laid out here:

(1) *Remoteness.* Some losses that are suffered by the victim of a tort will be non-actionable because they are too remote a consequence of that tort being committed. There are different rules for determining whether or not a loss is 'too remote', depending on what sort of tort has been committed.

The normal rule in *negligence* cases is that unforeseeable losses are too remote to be actionable. But there are exceptions. For example, if A negligently injures B, and B is entitled to sue A in negligence for that physical injury, then B will *also* be entitled to sue A for any economic losses or psychiatric illnesses flowing from that physical injury, no matter how unforeseeable those losses or illnesses might have been.

The rule that unforeseeable losses are too remote to be actionable applies to all *non-intentional torts* – that is, torts which can be committed by a defendant without his having any intention to injure someone else, or some other form of very culpable intent. Though, again, there may be an exception where someone commits a non-intentional tort *intentionally* – for example, where someone intentionally breaches a duty of care, or trespasses on someone's land, or defames someone's reputation. There are *dicta* in the cases suggesting that the remoteness rule that applies to *intentional torts* will also apply in cases where someone has intentionally committed a non-intentional tort.

The remoteness rule that applies to intentional torts says that *any* losses suffered by the victim of an intentional tort as a *direct* consequence of that tort being committed will not be too remote to be actionable, no matter how unforeseeable they were.

(2) *Scope of duty.* Some losses will be non-actionable because they fall outside the 'scope of the duty' that the defendant owed the claimant. The best example of this is actually a case about breach of statutory duty rather than negligence. In *Gorris* v *Scott* (1874), the claimant's sheep were transported to a foreign port on the defendant's ship. Under the Contagious Diseases (Animals) Act 1869, the defendant had a statutory duty to ship the claimant's sheep in pens. However, he did not bother doing this. As a result, the claimant's sheep were swept out to sea when a wave crashed onto the defendant's ship; had they been placed in pens at the time, the sheep would have been perfectly safe. The claimant sued the defendant for compensation for the loss of his sheep but his claim was dismissed. The reason was that the duty that the defendant owed the claimant was imposed on him *not* in order to stop the claimant's sheep from drowning but in order to help ensure that if some of the claimant's sheep contracted some kind of disease mid-voyage, the disease would not spread to the rest of the claimant's sheep; if the claimant's sheep were kept separated in pens the sheep in one pen would not be able to pass on any disease they were suffering from to the sheep in the other pens. So the loss suffered by the claimant in this case fell outside the 'scope of the duty' that the defendant had owed the claimant. In other words, the loss suffered by the claimant in this case was non-actionable because it was the *wrong kind of loss.*

The idea that a loss may be non-actionable because it is the wrong kind of loss applies in negligence cases, and indeed in all cases where someone is suing in tort for compensatory damages. We saw an example of this idea applying in a (hypothetical) negligence case when we considered the **Forgetful Investor Problem**:

> One morning, *Commuter* reads something in the newspapers that makes her think that she needs to sell all her shares in *Dodgy* plc. She then takes a train to work, resolving that once she gets into work, she will call her broker and have him sell her shares. Unfortunately, due to the carelessness of the *Train Driver*, *Commuter*'s train de-rails. *Commuter* is unharmed, but is so shaken by the accident that she completely forgets to sell her shares in *Dodgy*. By the time she remembers, the value of shares in *Dodgy* has plummeted.

In this case, the loss suffered by *Commuter* as a result of *Train Driver*'s negligence is the wrong kind of loss. The duty that *Train Driver* owed *Commuter* was imposed on him in order to help ensure that *Commuter* did not suffer some kind of physical injury, not in order to help ensure that *Commuter* was not distracted from some business that she had to do when she got into work.

It is because losses will be non-actionable if they fall outside the 'scope of the duty' that the defendant owed the claimant that in negligence cases, a claimant has to be quite selective about what sort of duty of care she will claim the defendant owed her. As we have already observed:[1] it is not enough for a claimant to show that the defendant owed her, and breached, a duty of care. The claimant has to show that the defendant owed her, and breached, a duty of care that was geared towards saving her from suffering the kind of harm for which she wants damages.

(3) *Other reasons.* Finally, there are a whole host of losses that a claimant might have suffered as a result of a defendant's tort that are non-actionable not because they are too remote, or because they are the wrong kind of loss, but for some other reason.

Sometimes considerations of *public policy* dictate that a claimant should not be able to sue for a particular loss. Public policy concerns can explain the result in *Gray* v *Thames Trains Ltd* (2009). In that case, the defendants' negligence resulted in the claimant suffering a psychiatric disorder that resulted in him killing a stranger. He pleaded guilty to manslaughter on the grounds of diminished responsibility and was ordered to be detained in hospital under the Mental Health Act 1983. Had the defendants not been negligent, the claimant would have been working and earning good money during the period that, in real life, he was going to be detained in hospital because of his manslaughter conviction. The House of Lords held that the claimant could not sue for the money that, but for the defendants' negligence, he would have earned during the span of time he was going to be locked up in hospital. To allow him to do so would have been to allow him to evade one of the normal, and intended, consequences of detaining someone under the criminal justice system, which is to hit the detainee in the pocket by preventing them earning the money they would have been able to earn had they obeyed the law and remained at liberty.

Other times, the courts will hold that a particular loss is non-actionable because allowing a claim for that loss would *bring the law into disrepute*. This was the reason why the House of Lords ruled in *McFarlane* v *Tayside Health Board* (2000) that in a case where a doctor's negligence resulted in a claimant having a baby that she would not otherwise have had, the claimant will not be allowed to sue for the cost of bringing up that baby. To rule otherwise would have sent out a message that the courts regarded having a baby as a harm rather than a benefit, and would have required the courts to make unacceptable distinctions between rich families (that could afford to have their child privately educated and would then seek to recover that cost from the defendant whose negligence was responsible for that child being born in the first place) and poor families (that could never afford to have their child privately educated and so could not then put themselves in a position to claim damages for that kind of loss).

---

[1] See above, § 4.1.

9.2 Remoteness of damage

Suppose A has committed a tort in relation to B and B has suffered some kind of loss as a result. *Normally* that loss will count as a remote consequence of A's tort if it was *not* reasonably foreseeable at the time A committed his tort that someone like B would suffer *that kind of loss* as a result of A's committing that tort. Let's call this the *foreseeability test* for determining whether a loss suffered by the victim of a tort was a remote consequence of that tort.

The foreseeability test may seem straightforward to apply, but it is not. The reason is that in cases where the courts have applied the foreseeability test to determine whether a loss suffered by a claimant was a remote consequence of a defendant's tort, they have emphasised that neither 'the precise *manner* [in] which the injury occurred nor its *extent* [have] to be foreseeable.'² So what does have to be foreseen? In *Jolley* v *Sutton LBC* (2000), Lord Hoffmann observed that:

> what must have been [foreseeable] is not the precise injury that occurred but injury of a given description. The foreseeability is not as to the particulars but the genus. And the description is formulated by reference to the nature of the risk which ought to have been foreseen.³

But the courts enjoy a great deal of leeway in determining *how to describe* what type of injury could have been reasonably foreseen would result from the defendant's tort.

In *Jolley* v *Sutton LBC* itself, a council owned a piece of amenity land near a block of flats. A boat had been left lying on this land for about two years. The boat was in a poor condition and anyone playing about on the boat was liable to put a foot through the rotten timbers of the boat and suffer an injury. Given this – and given the fact that children playing on the amenity land were liable to clamber onto the boat and run the risk of being injured – the council owed children going onto the amenity land a duty under the Occupiers' Liability Act 1957 to take reasonable steps to remove the boat from the land. The council breached this duty when they did nothing about the boat for two years. In that time, the claimant and a friend of his – two 14-year-old children – saw the boat and decided to repair it; they had a wild dream that if they did this, they would one day be able to go sailing in it. They used a car jack to elevate one side of the boat and, crawling underneath, repaired some of the holes in the hull of the boat. Unfortunately, one day when the claimant was working under the boat, the car jack gave way and the boat fell on the claimant's back, causing him severe spinal injuries. The claimant sued the council for damages. The case turned on whether the claimant's injuries were a remote consequence of the council's admitted negligence under the foreseeability test.

Now whether or not you think that the foreseeability test was satisfied here will depend a great deal on how you describe what kind of loss it was reasonably foreseeable might be suffered if the council left the boat on its land. If we say that the type of loss was simply 'Physical injury from meddling with the boat', then the foreseeability test was plainly satisfied here: the claimant suffered that kind of loss here as a result of the council's breach of the duty of care it owed him. However, if we say that it was only reasonably foreseeable that leaving the boat on the council land would result in 'Physical injury from the boat's rotting floorboards giving way' then the foreseeability test was not satisfied in *Jolley*: the claimant did *not* suffer that kind of loss as a result of the council's breach of the duty

---

² *Jolley* v *Sutton LBC* [2000] 1 WLR 1082, 1090 (per Lord Steyn).
³ [2000] 1 WLR 1082, 1091.

of care it owed him. The trial judge and the House of Lords adopted the first description of what kind of loss it was reasonably foreseeable might be suffered as a result of the council's negligence in leaving the boat on its land, and allowed the claimant's claim for damages. In contrast, the Court of Appeal adopted the second description of what kind of loss it was reasonably foreseeable would be suffered if the council left the boat on its land, and as a result dismissed the claimant's claim for damages.[4] What accounts for the difference?

At a formal level, we determine whether it was reasonably foreseeable that a defendant's tort would result in a claimant suffering a particular type of loss by asking whether at the time the defendant acted, there was a 'real risk' that the claimant would suffer that kind of loss as a result of the defendant's conduct. A risk that a reasonable person would have brushed off as 'fantastic or far-fetched' will not satisfy this requirement.[5] It may be that the trial judge and the House of Lords thought that a reasonable person in the position of the defendant council would have recognised that if they left the boat on their land, there was a real risk that a child like the claimant could be injured in more ways as a result of being attracted to the boat than by simply putting his leg through a rotting floorboard; whereas the Court of Appeal may have been less imaginative in its approach to the question of what risks of injury a reasonable person in the position of the council could have foreseen.

However, it may be that the *only* real risk in this situation was that a child like the claimant would put his foot through a rotting floorboard in clambering over the boat, but sympathy for the claimant and the fact that the council was a 'deep pockets' defendant may have led the trial judge and the House of Lords to describe *that* risk in relatively wide terms – 'It was reasonably foreseeable that someone like the claimant would suffer physical injury from meddling with the boat' – so as to enable the claimant's injury to slip under the foreseeability test.

Something like this seems to have happened in *Hughes* v *Lord Advocate* (1963), where the defendants opened a manhole in the street in order to work on some telephone cables, about 9 feet under the road. A paraffin lamp provided them some illumination in doing their work. The area around the manhole was covered by a tent. The defendants went for a 15-minute tea break at 5 pm. They left the manhole open and the tent around the manhole unattended. The claimant – another child, this time eight years old – took advantage of the defendants' absence to enter the tent and see what was inside. The defendants had owed the claimant a duty of care not to leave the tent unattended because it was reasonably foreseeable that someone like the claimant would be attracted into the tent, and might fall into the hole, or be burned by the paraffin lamp being knocked over, or some combination of these events. What *actually* happened was something that could not have been foreseen. The claimant stumbled over the lamp, knocking it into the hole. The lamp broke, and paraffin vapour escaping from the lamp ignited through contact with the lamp flame, creating an explosion that threw the claimant into the hole, where he was severely burned.

The House of Lords held that it did not matter that the *manner* in which the claimant was injured was unforeseeable. Instead, they adopted a wide definition of the kind of risk of harm that it could be foreseen the claimant was exposed to in this case – 'It was reasonably foreseeable that leaving the tent unattended would result in a child like the claimant suffering burns from playing about in the tent' – which allowed the injuries that the claimant did suffer in this case to slip under the foreseeability test.

---

[4] [1998] 1 WLR 1546.
[5] *The Wagon Mound (No 2)* [1967] 1 AC 617, 641–2 (per Lord Reid).

Lord Reid held that it was enough that 'The accident was caused by a known source of danger'[6] (the lamp). Lord Jenkins thought that distinguishing between injuries due to burning (foreseeable) and injuries due to explosion (unforeseeable) involved drawing a 'distinction . . . [that] is too fine to warrant acceptance.'[7] He thought that what was reasonably foreseeable in this case was 'a danger of fire of some kind' and so the claimant's injuries fell within the range of injuries that were reasonably foreseeable consequences of the defendants' leaving the tent unattended. Lord Morris held that:

> it could reasonably have been foreseen that a boy who played in and about the canvas shelter and played with things that were thereabouts might get hurt and might in some way burn himself. That is just what happened. The [claimant] did burn himself, though his burns were more grave than would have been expected. The fact that the features or developments of an accident may not reasonably have been foreseen does not mean that the accident itself was not foreseeable. The [claimant] was . . . injured as a result of the type or kind of accident or occurrence that could reasonably have been foreseen.[8]

Lord Guest agreed that it would be wrong in this case to say that the accident here was of a type that was not reasonably foreseeable: 'An explosion is only one way in which burning can be caused. Burning can also be caused by the contact between liquid paraffin and a naked flame. In the one case paraffin vapour and in the other case liquid paraffin is ignited by fire. I cannot see that these are two different types of accident.'[9] Lord Pearce also took the view that the fact that the claimant's burns were caused by an explosion was irrelevant: 'The resulting damage, though severe, was not greater than or different in kind from that which might have been produced had the lamp spilled and produced a more normal conflagration in the hole.'[10]

In other cases not involving children, the courts have not been so expansive in defining the type of loss that it was reasonably foreseeable a claimant might suffer as a result of a defendant's tort.

In *Doughty* v *Turner Manufacturing Co* (1964), the defendants' factory contained two cauldrons full of molten liquid; the defendants' employees would dip metal parts into the cauldron to heat them up. Each cauldron had an asbestos cover that would sit on top of the cauldron, to conserve its heat. The claimant was injured when one of the asbestos covers was carelessly knocked into the cauldron on which it was sitting: the molten liquid unexpectedly reacted with the asbestos and exploded, and the claimant – who was standing nearby – was severely burned as a result. The Court of Appeal was doubtful whether anyone had been negligent in this case (given that it was unforeseeable that knocking the asbestos cover into the cauldron would result in an explosion) but held that even if negligence were made out, the claimant would still not be able to recover for his injuries as it was not reasonably foreseeable that knocking the asbestos cover into the cauldron would result in the claimant suffering the kind of injury that he did. While it was reasonably foreseeable that knocking the asbestos cover into the cauldron might result in the claimant being burned from molten liquid splashing on him, 'it would be quite unrealistic to describe this accident as a variant of the perils from splashing.'[11]

---

[6] [1963] AC 837, 847.
[7] [1963] AC 837, 850.
[8] [1963] AC 837, 852.
[9] [1963] AC 837, 856.
[10] [1963] AC 837, 858.
[11] [1964] 1 QB 518, 527 (per Lord Pearce).

In *Tremain* v *Pike* (1969), the claimant worked for the defendant on a farm that had a rat infestation. He contracted Weil's Disease from handling hay on which the rats had urinated. The judge trying the claimant's claim for damages was – like the Court of Appeal in *Doughty* – doubtful whether the defendant had been negligent in failing to take steps to control the rat infestation on the farm. But the judge went on to say that even if negligence could be established, the claimant could still not sue for damages for contracting Weil's Disease as Weil's Disease did not fall within the class of injuries that it was reasonably foreseeable the claimant might suffer as a result of a rat infestation:

> The kind of damage suffered here was a disease contracted by contact with rats' urine. This, in my view, was entirely different in kind from the effect of a rat bite, or food poisoning by the consumption of food or drink contaminated by rats. I do not accept that all illness or infection arising from an infestation of rats should be regarded as of the same kind.[12]

It should be clear from the above cases that the foreseeability test for remoteness of damage is not a self-executing test. Judges enjoy some freedom of manoeuvre in characterising what type of harm was a reasonably foreseeable consequence of the defendant's tort. This, and the fact that any finding as to whether the foreseeability test is satisfied in a given case will always turn on a detailed scrutiny of the facts of that case,[13] means that cases like those we have discussed above provide very limited guidance as to whether the

---

[12] [1969] 1 WLR 1556, 1561 (per Payne J).

[13] An example of a situation where this was true is provided by the *Wagon Mound* litigation. The litigation arose out of a fire that started when the defendants negligently allowed a lot of oil to spill into Sydney Harbour. The oil spread and drifted close to the first claimants' wharf, where the first claimants were doing some welding work on a ship called the *Corrimal*, which belonged to the second claimants. A piece of molten metal from the welding work dropped into the oil and set it on fire. The wharf and the *Corrimal* suffered severe fire damage. The first claimants sued the defendants in negligence for compensation for the fire damage done to their wharf in *Overseas Tankship (UK) Ltd* v *Morts Dock & Engineering Co Ltd, The Wagon Mound* [1961] AC 388. Their claim failed because it was held that it was not reasonably foreseeable at the time that if the defendants spilled any oil into the harbour it would ignite and set the first claimants' wharf on fire. (Why then did the defendants owe the first claimants a duty to take care that they did not spill any oil into the harbour? The reason is that it *was* reasonably foreseeable that if the defendants spilled any oil into the harbour it would spread and foul the first claimants' wharf.) When the second claimants subsequently sued the defendants for compensation for the fire damage done to the *Corrimal* (in *Overseas Tankship (UK) Ltd* v *Miller Steamship Co Pty, The Wagon Mound (No 2)* [1967] 1 AC 617) they introduced a lot of scientific evidence to show that it *was* reasonably foreseeable at the time the defendants spilled the oil into Sydney Harbour that it could ignite and start a fire. As a result, they convinced the courts that the fire damage to the *Corrimal was* a reasonably foreseeable consequence of the nuisance the defendants created by spilling oil into Sydney Harbour. Why didn't the first claimants press this evidence on the courts in the original *Wagon Mound* case? Two reasons can be given. First, they did not think that they had to: they assumed that if they showed that the defendants were negligent, the defendants would be held liable for *all* the losses that were a *direct* result of the defendants' negligence, however unforeseeable. This was the rule laid down by the Court of Appeal in *Re Polemis* [1921] 3 KB 560. This rule was, however, overturned in the first *Wagon Mound* case, with the Privy Council ruling that a negligent defendant could not be held liable for a loss suffered by a claimant if that loss was not a reasonably foreseeable consequence of the defendant's negligence. Secondly, it would have harmed the first claimants' claim for compensation if they had admitted that it was reasonably foreseeable that the oil that the defendants spilled into Sydney Harbour could ignite. If it *was* reasonably foreseeable, then the first claimants would have been partly to blame for the fire damage done to their wharf, having carried on doing welding work on the *Corrimal* while oil was lapping around their wharf. And if the first claimants were partly to blame for the fire damage done to their wharf, the damages payable to compensate them for that fire damage would have been reduced on the grounds of contributory negligence.

foreseeability test will be satisfied in a particular case. As Lord Steyn observed in the *Jolley* case: '[In] this corner of the law the results of decided cases are inevitably very fact-sensitive. Both counsel nevertheless at times invited your Lordships to compare the facts of the present case with the facts of other decided cases. That is a sterile exercise.'[14]

We will now turn to note a number of exceptions that exist to the foreseeability test for remoteness of damage.

A. The eggshell skull rule[15]

This rule (otherwise known as the '*thin skull rule*') says that if it was foreseeable that A would suffer some kind of physical injury as a result of B's tort, but because A has a pre-existing condition, A suffers a much worse injury as a result of B's tort, that much worse injury will *not* count as a remote consequence of B's tort.

In *Smith* v *Leech Brain* (1962), the defendant employed the claimant's husband to work with molten metal. Due to the defendant's failure to take adequate measures to protect the claimant's husband, he was struck on the lip by a piece of molten metal. The ensuing burn caused the tissues in the husband's lip to turn cancerous and the husband eventually died from the cancer. The claimant brought a wrongful death action against the defendant. It was held that the husband's death was not a remote consequence of the defendant's negligence. It had been reasonably foreseeable that the husband would suffer some kind of physical injury as a result of the defendant's negligence, and he ended up suffering a much worse injury because he had a pre-existing condition.

The same rule applies to cases where the victim of a tort has what is sometimes called an 'eggshell personality' and develops a very serious psychiatric illness as a result of that tort being committed when only a much less serious psychiatric illness was foreseeable. In such a case, the very serious psychiatric illness will *not* count as a remote consequence of the defendant's tort.

For example, in *Brice* v *Brown* (1984), the claimant was involved in a car accident that was caused by the defendants' negligence. The claimant had suffered from a hysterical personality disorder from early childhood and developed a severe mental illness as a result of the accident. Stuart Smith J held that the claimant's illness was not a remote consequence of the defendants' negligence even though it had not been reasonably foreseeable that the claimant would suffer a psychiatric illness as severe as the one she developed as a result of the accident in which she was involved. It was enough that it had been reasonably foreseeable that the claimant would develop *a* psychiatric illness as a result of the accident.[16]

B. Economic loss consequent on physical injury

A rule analogous to the eggshell skull rule says that if A has committed a tort in relation to B, and B has suffered some kind of physical injury as a result, if B can recover

---

[14] [2000] 1 WLR 1082, 1089.

[15] For an excellent discussion, see Stigglebout 2009.

[16] It should be noted that nowadays, under the House of Lords' ruling in *Page* v *Smith* [1996] AC 155 (discussed above, § 5.1, and below) the claimant would not even need to show that it was reasonably foreseeable that she would suffer a psychiatric illness as a result of being involved in the accident: it would be enough for her to show that it was reasonably foreseeable that she would suffer some kind of physical injury as a result.

compensation for the physical injury that she has suffered as a result of A's tort, B will be able to sue A for compensation in respect of *any* loss of income or other economic losses flowing from that injury whether or not those economic losses were a foreseeable consequence of A's tort.[17] Scrutton LJ made the point graphically in *The Arpad*:

> In the cases of claims in tort, damages are constantly given for consequences of which the defendant had no notice. You negligently run down a shabby-looking man in the street, and he turns out to be a millionaire engaged in a very profitable business which the accident disables him from carrying on [you will be held liable for the economic loss so caused].[18]

The same rule does not apply in property damage cases. *However*, if you negligently damage someone else's property, you must compensate them for the full value of that property, no matter how unforeseeable it might have been that that property would be worth that much. As Scrutton LJ went on to observe in *The Arpad*, if 'you negligently and ignorantly injure the favourite for the Derby'[19] you have to compensate the owner of *that* horse for the damage done to *that* horse, even though you may have had 'no notice' of its value at the time it was injured. Consider, for example, the **Hollywood Dog Problem**:

Trainer owns a dog that is used in a lot of TV series and films because it is so well-trained. *Trainer* earns about £3m a year from allowing his dog to be used in this way. One day, *Unlucky* carelessly runs the dog down in the street as it is crossing the road.

In this case, *Trainer* might not be able to sue directly for the loss of the £3m a year income resulting from his dog's death: that economic loss was an unforeseeable consequence of the dog being killed. But what he can do is sue for damages to compensate him for the loss of his dog, and those damages will equal the value of the dog. Given that the dog was capable of producing an income stream of £3m a year, that value will have been considerable, and would have run into millions of pounds.

---

[17] However, see now *Haxton* v *Philips Electronics Ltd* [2014] 1 WLR 1271, where the defendant employers negligently exposed the claimant's husband to asbestos dust at work, and the claimant was in turn exposed to that asbestos dust when she washed her husband clothes when he came home from work. Both the claimant and her husband developed mesothelioma as a result. The husband died and the claimant was allowed to bring a claim for loss of support under the Fatal Accidents Act 1976 (see above, § 1.5, and below, § 28.4). However, the damages that she could recover under that head were reduced to take account of the fact that due to the defendant's negligence, her life expectancy had been reduced and as a result the amount of support she could have expected to have received in her lifetime from her husband had he not died was correspondingly reduced. So the claimant then sued in negligence for this economic loss, that she had suffered as a result of the defendants' negligence in relation to *her* by negligently exposing *her* to asbestos dust, with the consequence that she had developed mesothelioma. The claim was allowed, but some time was spent discussing whether the economic loss suffered by the claimant was too remote to be recoverable on the grounds of lack of foreseeability (at [22]–[23]). If the law as stated in the text is correct, the foreseeability of the loss suffered by the claimant in *Haxton* should have been irrelevant to the issue of whether it was too remote to be recovered.

[18] [1934] P 189, 202. To the same effect, see *Smith* v *London and South Western Railway Co.* (1870) LR 6 CP 14, 22–3 (per Blackburn J).

[19] [1934] P 189, 202–3.

C. *Page* v *Smith* (1996)[20]

In this case, the defendant negligently ran into the claimant's car while the claimant was in it. As a result,[21] the claimant developed chronic fatigue syndrome (CFS).[22] The House of Lords held, by a bare majority, that the claimant's CFS was *not* a remote consequence of the defendant's negligence. Two of the Law Lords who made up the majority in *Page* v *Smith* held that it was reasonably foreseeable at the time the defendant negligently ran into the claimant's car that if he did so the claimant would develop a psychiatric illness as a result.[23] But they *also* expressed their agreement with the opinion of Lord Lloyd, the third member of the majority, and *he* said that the claimant would be entitled to recover for his psychiatric illness even if it was *not* reasonably foreseeable at the time the defendant crashed into the claimant's car that the claimant would suffer a psychiatric illness as a result.[24]

Lord Lloyd's view is hard to justify. He seemed to take the view that even if the claimant's psychiatric illness was not a reasonably foreseeable consequence of the defendant's negligence, the claimant's psychiatric illness would *not* count as a remote consequence of the defendant's negligence under the foreseeability test because psychiatric illness counts as a form of physical injury[25] and it *was* reasonably foreseeable that the claimant would suffer *that kind of loss* if the defendant crashed into the claimant's car.[26] However, it is hard to see why we should treat psychiatric illnesses and physical injuries as being the same kind of loss in this context when in almost every other context we recognise that there is a distinction between them.[27] Perhaps recognising this, the courts have made it clear that *Page* v *Smith* will only apply in cases where a claimant's psychiatric illness was triggered by the experience of being almost injured by a defendant's negligence.[28]

---

[20] For discussion, see Bailey and Nolan 2010.

[21] It was found in *Page* v *Smith* (*No 2*) [1996] 1 WLR 855 that the claimant's CFS was indeed attributable to his being involved in the crash.

[23] [1996] AC 155, 170 (per Lord Ackner), 181–2 (per Lord Browne-Wilkinson).

[22] The collision was quite trivial but the claimant – having suffered from CFS in the past – was liable to develop CFS again as a results of incidents such as these.

[24] Though he too thought that at the time the defendant crashed into the claimant's car, it was reasonably foreseeable that the claimant would develop a psychiatric illness as a result: [1996] AC 155, at 197. The two dissenting Law Lords in *Page* v *Smith* thought that the crash had not been serious enough as to make it reasonably foreseeable that the claimant would suffer a psychiatric illness as a result: [1996] AC 155, at 169–70 (per Lord Keith of Kinkel), 180 (per Lord Jauncey of Tullichettle).

[25] [1996] AC 155, at 197: 'There is no justification for regarding physical and psychiatric injury as "different kinds of damage".'

[26] That was after all the main reason why the defendant owed the claimant a duty to take care not to run into his car in the first place.

[27] See above, § 5.4.

[28] See above, § 5.1. Though see *Essa* v *Laing* [2004] EWCA Civ 2, where the defendant committed the statutory tort of racial discrimination (discussed below, § 22.6) in relation to the claimant and the claimant suffered a psychiatric illness as a result. Held, on the basis of *Page* v *Smith*, that the claimant could sue for damages in respect of his psychiatric illness even if it was not a foreseeable consequence of the defendant's tort: it was enough that it was reasonably foreseeable that the claimant would suffer distress as a result of the defendant's tort. Rix LJ dissented on this point. Also see *Donachie* v *Chief Constable of Greater Manchester* [2004] EWCA Civ 405, where *Page* v *Smith* was applied to allow a claimant police officer to sue for the hypertension that he had suffered as a result of being made by the defendants to make nine trips to a suspect's car to attach a tagging device to the underside of the car (the tagging device was faulty and it took nine trips to make it work). It was held that the defendants had owed the claimant a duty of care not to make him make so many trips to the car because it was reasonably foreseeable that he would suffer some kind of physical injury at the hands of the suspect if he were made to do so. It was held that the claimant could sue for the psychiatric illness that he had suffered as a result of the defendants' breach of this duty of care even though it was not foreseeable that he would suffer such an illness as a result of the defendants' breach; it was enough that it was reasonably foreseeable that the claimant would suffer some kind of physical injury as a result of the defendants' carelessness.

D. *Hedley Byrne* (1964)

The normal rule on remoteness of damage that applies in breach of contract cases – known as 'the rule in *Hadley* v *Baxendale*'[29] – is slightly different from the one that applies in negligence cases. While the rule that normally applies in negligence cases says that a negligent defendant will not be liable for any losses that it was not reasonably foreseeable that the claimant would suffer at the time the defendant *breached* the duty of care that he owed the claimant, the rule in *Hadley* v *Baxendale* says that a defendant who has committed a breach of contract will not be liable for any losses that it was not reasonably foreseeable that the claimant would suffer at the time the defendant *contracted* with the claimant. So what is foreseeable at the time the defendant *breached* his contract with the claimant is irrelevant under the rule in *Hadley* v *Baxendale*. What is important is what was reasonably foreseeable at the time the defendant contracted with the claimant – the reason being that it would be very unfair on the defendant to hold him liable for losses that he could not have anticipated would be suffered by the claimant when he contracted with the claimant, as had he anticipated that he might be held liable for such losses he might have declined to contract with the claimant or would have demanded more advantageous terms for contracting with the claimant.

The Court of Appeal has now sensibly ruled in *Wellesley Partners LLP* v *Withers LLP* (2015) that where a defendant is sued for breaching a duty of care that he owed the claimant under the basic or extended principle in *Hedley Byrne*[30] the rule on remoteness of loss that should apply to the defendant is that supplied by the rule in *Hadley* v *Baxendale*, and not the rule that normally applies in negligence cases. The ruling is sensible because the rationale of the rule in *Hadley* v *Baxendale* applies just as strongly in cases where the basis of the claimant's claim against the defendant is that the defendant 'assumed a responsibility' to the claimant. It would be very unfair on the defendant to hold him liable to the claimant for losses resulting from the defendant's failure to live up to the responsibility he assumed to the claimant if he had no chance to know that the claimant might suffer those losses at the time he assumed a responsibility to the claimant, and had he known, he might have declined to assume such a responsibility or would have done so under conditions as to how much he would be liable for on failing to live up to that responsibility. The ruling is also sensible in that in cases where a defendant is concurrently liable to a claimant for committing a breach of contract and in negligence under the extended principle in *Hedley Byrne*,[31] the ruling in *Wellesley Partners* reduces the difference it makes whether the claimant sues the defendant in contract or tort: the same rule on remoteness of damage will apply, however the claimant chooses to frame her claim.

E. Intentional torts

The foreseeability test for determining whether the loss suffered by the victim of a tort was a remote consequence of that tort does not seem to apply to cases where someone commits an *intentional tort*.

An intentional tort is *not* a tort that is committed intentionally. An intentional tort is a tort that can *only* be committed intentionally – that is, by someone who knows what he or she is doing. So the torts we have looked at so far – negligence, assault, battery, and false imprisonment – are examples of *non-intentional torts*. All these torts can be committed

---

[29] After *Hadley* v *Baxendale* (1854) 9 Exch 341.
[30] Discussed above, §§5.9–5.10.
[31] See above §5.10.

unintentionally or inadvertently.[32] So are private nuisance and defamation. In contrast, malicious falsehood is an example of an intentional tort: it can only be committed intentionally – by *maliciously* making a false statement about someone to a third party which results in that someone suffering loss. Other examples of intentional torts are: the intentional infliction of harm using unlawful means, conspiracy, deceit and malicious prosecution.

The cases indicate that the foreseeability test applies to determine what losses are a remote consequence of a defendant's tort when the tort that the defendant has committed is a non-intentional one.[33] But a different remoteness rule applies where the defendant's tort is an intentional one. This remoteness rule goes as follows. If A has committed an intentional tort in relation to B and B has suffered some kind of loss as result, that loss will *not* have been a remote consequence of A's tort if it was a *direct*[34] consequence of A's tort.[35] So A may be held liable to compensate B for the loss she has suffered even if it was *not* reasonably foreseeable at the time A committed his tort that B would suffer that kind of loss as a result. Why is this? Why do the courts treat people who commit unintentional torts more favourably than they do people who commit intentional torts?

The reason must be that the courts recognise that people can commit non-intentional torts quite innocently, and accordingly attempt to ensure that the liability of someone who commits a non-intentional tort does not get out of all proportion to his fault for committing that tort. In contrast, someone who commits an intentional tort will always be very wicked and there is no reason why we should try to put a limit on such a person's liabilities. Accordingly, someone who commits an intentional tort will be held liable for all the losses that were suffered by the victim of his tort as a direct result of that tort being committed – however unforeseeable those losses were.

Of course, if A has *deliberately* committed a non-intentional tort, it is hard to see why the courts should treat him any more indulgently than it does people who commit intentional torts. Given this, there is a strong case for saying that the remoteness rule which applies to people who commit intentional torts should also be applied to people who deliberately commit non-intentional torts.[36] Under this approach, if A has deliberately committed a non-intentional tort in relation to B and B has suffered some kind of loss as a direct result of A's committing that tort, that loss would not be a remote consequence of A's tort – even if it was not reasonably foreseeable that B would suffer that kind of loss when A committed his tort.

---

[32] Though of course they can also be committed intentionally. See above, § 3.2, for a discussion of whether the tort of negligence can be committed intentionally.

[33] See *Overseas Tankship (UK) Ltd v Morts Dock & Engineering Co Ltd, The Wagon Mound* [1961] AC 388 (negligence); *Overseas Tankship (UK) Ltd v Miller Steamship Co Pty, The Wagon Mound (No 2)* [1967] 1 AC 617 (nuisance); *Slipper v British Broadcasting Corpn* [1991] 1 QB 283 (libel).

[34] 'Direct' here probably means 'without the intervention of any other cause'. So the fire damage that resulted from the defendant's parking his car without authority in the claimants' car park in *Mayfair Ltd v Pears* [1987] 1 NZLR 459 (discussed below, § 12.6, fn 51) was not a direct consequence of the defendant's intentional trespass on the claimants' land: the defendant's trespass only resulted in the claimants' car park suffering fire damage because the car caught on fire.

[35] *Doyle v Olby (Ironmongers) Ltd* [1969] 2 QB 158 and *Smith New Court v Scrimgeour Vickers (Asset Management) Ltd* [1997] AC 254 confirm that this is the position in relation to the tort of deceit. Lord Lindley confirmed that this is the position in regard to conspiracy in *Quinn v Leathem* [1901] AC 495, 527.

[36] See Gordley 1998.

There is some authority in favour of the view that the remoteness rule that applies to people who commit intentional torts should also be applied to people who intentionally commit non-intentional torts. Lord Nicholls indicated he thought that a defendant who intentionally converted another's goods should be held liable for all the losses suffered by that other as a direct result of the defendant's act of conversion in *Kuwait Airways Corpn* v *Iraqi Airways Co (Nos 4 & 5)*:

> as the law now stands, the tort of conversion may cause hardship for innocent persons. This suggests that foreseeability, as the more restrictive test [for remoteness of damage], is appropriate for those who act in good faith. Liability remains strict, but liability for consequential loss is confined to types of damages which can be expected to arise from the wrongful conduct . . .
>
> Persons who knowingly convert another's goods stand differently. Such persons are acting dishonestly. I can so no good reason why the remoteness test of 'directly and naturally' applied in cases of deceit should not apply in cases of conversion where the defendant acted dishonestly.[37]

F. Statutory torts

In *Essa* v *Laing* (2004), the Court of Appeal held that if A has committed a tort by breaching a statutory duty owed to B and B has suffered some kind of loss as a result, the foreseeability test will *not* necessarily apply to determine whether the loss suffered by B was a remote consequence of A's tort. To see whether the test will apply or not, one simply has to interpret the Act or Regulations that created the statutory duty breached by A.[38]

In *Essa*, the defendant committed a tort under the Race Relations Act 1976 by racially abusing the claimant. The claimant developed a psychiatric illness as a result of the abuse he had suffered. Pill and Clarke LJJ held that – given the language of, and policy underlying, the 1976 Act – the foreseeability test should *not* be applied to determine whether the claimant's psychiatric illness was a remote consequence of the defendant's tort. It seems that Pill LJ might have taken a different view had the defendant's tort been committed unintentionally,[39] whereas Clarke LJ took the view that the foreseeability test should *never* apply in race discrimination cases. The third judge in the *Essa* case – Rix LJ – thought that the foreseeability test should apply in race discrimination cases: there was no reason to adopt a more relaxed remoteness rule given that a tort can be committed under the 1976 Act even if one has no intention of doing so.[40]

In the subsequent case of *Jones* v *Ruth* (2011), the Court of Appeal had to decide what remoteness rule would apply in cases where a defendant harassed a claimant, contrary to the Protection from Harassment Act 1997. The Court held that in such a case, the claimant could recover for harm suffered as a result of the harassment even if it was not foreseeable. In reaching this conclusion, Patten LJ placed stress on two factors: (a) there

---

[37] [2002] 2 AC 883, at [103]-[104]. The New Zealand Court of Appeal held in *Mayfair Ltd* v *Pears* [1987] 1 NZLR 459 that a defendant who intentionally trespasses on another's land should be held liable for all the losses suffered by that other as a direct result of the defendant's trespass. See also Pill LJ's judgment in *Essa* v *Laing* [2004] EWCA Civ 2, discussed below.

[38] [2004] EWCA Civ 2, at [46], [48] (per Clarke LJ)

[39] [2004] EWCA Civ 2, at [39].

[40] [2004] EWCA Civ 2, at [98], [105]. Rix LJ was unenthusiastic (at [106]) about the idea that the foreseeability test should apply in cases of non-intentional racial discrimination but not in cases of intentional race discrimination.

was nothing in the provisions of the 1997 Act that suggested that damage had to be foreseeable before it would be actionable under the Act; and (b) harassment is a form of 'deliberate conduct of a kind which the defendant knows or ought to know will amount to harassment of the claimant.'[41]

9.3 Scope of duty

We said above that the reason why the courts have adopted the foreseeability test for remoteness of damage in non-intentional tort cases is to help ensure that a tortfeasor's liability does not get out of all proportion to his fault. As Viscount Simonds observed in *The Wagon Mound* (1961) (the first tort case to adopt the foreseeability test for remoteness of damage):

> it does not seem consonant with current ideas of justice or morality that for an act of negligence, however slight or venial, which results in some trivial foreseeable damage the actor should be liable for all consequences however unforeseeable and however grave, so long as they can be said to be 'direct'. It is a principle of civil liability . . . that a man must be considered to be responsible for the probable consequences of his act. To demand more of him is too harsh a rule . . .[42]

However, Viscount Simonds' judgment identified an *additional* reason why, in a negligence case at least, a defendant's liability should be limited to the reasonably foreseeable consequences of his actions:

> Just as . . . there is no such thing as negligence in the air, so there is no such thing as liability in the air. Suppose an action brought by A for damage caused by the carelessness (a neutral word) of B, for example, a fire caused by the careless spillage of oil. It may, of course, become relevant to know what duty B owed to A, but the only liability that is in question is the liability for damage by fire. It is vain to isolate the liability from its context and to say that B is or is not liable, and then to ask for what damage he is liable . . . If . . . B's liability (culpability) depends on the reasonable foreseeability of the consequent damage, how is that to be determined except by the foreseeability of the damage which in fact happened – the damage in suit?[43]

Some find these words of Viscount Simonds hard to understand. But they seem to suggest that loss suffered as a result of a breach of a duty of care is not actionable unless that duty of care was imposed in order to help ensure that the claimant would not suffer that kind of loss. So it is useless for A to establish that B owed him a duty of care not to do *x* because it was reasonably foreseeable that B's doing *x* would cause A to suffer one kind of loss, if A actually suffered a quite different loss as a result of B's breach. A must show that B's duty of care not to do *x* was imposed on her because it was reasonably foreseeable that B's doing *x* would cause A to suffer the kind of loss that she *actually* suffered. But A will not be able to do this if it was, in fact, *not* reasonably foreseeable that B's actions would result in A suffering *that kind of loss*. In such a case, the loss suffered by A will be outside the scope of whatever duty of care B did owe A, and therefore non-actionable.[44]

---

[41] [2011] EWCA Civ 804, at [32].

[42] [1961] AC 388, 423.

[43] [1961] AC 388, 425.

[44] See, to the same effect, Lord Hoffmann in *Jolley* v *Sutton LBC* [2000] 1 WLR 1082, 1091: 'unless the injury [suffered by the claimant] is of a description which was reasonably foreseeable, it is (according to taste) "outside the scope of the duty" or "too remote."' See also Machin 1954 and Stauch 2001, both of whom advance 'scope of duty'-type arguments in favour of a foreseeability test of remoteness in negligence.

We have already seen, in looking at the law of negligence, plenty of examples of this principle, that a loss will be non-actionable if the duty of care that the defendant owed the claimant, and breached, was not geared towards protecting the claimant from suffering that kind of loss.

First, if A carelessly causes B to be crushed to death, but before she dies she does not suffer any physical injury, but simply pure distress, the distress is not actionable: *Hicks* v *Chief Constable of South Yorkshire* (1992). The duty of care A will have owed B, and breached, in this case was imposed on A to help ensure she did not suffer physical injury, not to help her avoid being distressed.

Secondly, if A carelessly shuts off the power to B's factory, and the power cut has two independent effects – damaging some products B was processing at the time of the power cut, and preventing B doing any further work – the damage to the products will be actionable, but not the pure economic loss resulting from B's not being able to do any more work: *Spartan Steel & Co Ltd* v *Martin* (1973). The duty of care A will have owed B in this case was imposed on A in order to help ensure his property was not harmed, not in order to prevent B's business being interfered with.

Thirdly, if A carelessly constructs a dangerously defective building, and B – a subsequent occupier of the building – has to spend money having the building made safe, B will not be able to sue A in negligence for compensation for the money he has spent if there is no *Hedley Byrne*-type relationship between A and B: *D & F Estates* v *Church Commissioners* (1989), *Murphy* v *Brentwood DC* (1991). In the absence of an 'assumption of responsibility' by A to B for the quality of his building work, the only duty of care A will have owed B, and breached, (a duty to take care not to construct a dangerously defective building, arising under *Donoghue* v *Stevenson*) in this situation will have been imposed on A to help ensure that B's person and property was not harmed from A's building falling down, not in order to help ensure that B would not have to spend money making A's building safe.[45]

Fourthly, if A carelessly exposes B to excessive quantities of asbestos dust, but B has not yet suffered any physical ill effects from this, B will not be allowed to sue A for the chance that he might develop an asbestos-related disease in the future: *Rothwell* v *Chemical & Insulating Co Ltd* (2006, CA). The duty of care A will have owed B in this case (to take

---

[45] The position taken by the House of Lords in *Murphy* and *D & F Estates* is not without its critics (see, for example, Cooke 1991; Fleming 1997, 59–60) and it is clear that in other common law jurisdictions B *would* be entitled to sue A in negligence for compensation for the cost of making the building safe, even in the absence of a special relationship between them: see *Bryan* v *Moloney* (1995) 182 CLR 609 (Australia); *Winnipeg Condominium Corporation No 36* v *Bird Construction Co. Ltd* [1995] 1 SCR 85 (Canada). It may be that the criticism of the House of Lords' stance rests on a false premise. The critics say that in the situation we are considering B *ought* to be able to sue A for the money she has spent on making the building safe; *therefore* she ought to be able to sue A in *negligence*. But this assumes that the *only* cause of action available to B in this situation is a claim in negligence. There is no reason to think that this is true. See Moran 1997 for an interesting argument that B would be able to bring a claim in *restitution* against A to recover the money she has spent in making the building safe to live in; also Stevens 2007, 30–1. There are a number of American cases which support Moran's argument: see *City of New York* v *Keene Corp*, 505 NYS 2d 782 (1986) (aff'd, 513 NYS 2d 1004 (1987)) (claimants allowed to sue defendants in restitution for cost of removing potentially toxic asbestos which defendants had installed in claimants' schools); *Adams-Araphoe School District No 28-J* v *Celotex Corp*, 637 F Supp 1207 (1986) (ditto); *Drayton Public School District No 19* v *WR Grace & Co*, 728 F Supp 1410 (1989) (ditto); *City of New York* v *Lead Industries Ass'n, Inc*, 644 NYS 2d 919 (1996) (claimants allowed to sue manufacturers of potentially toxic paint in restitution for cost of removing paint from their city buildings).

reasonable steps to see that B's place of work is a safe place to work in) was imposed on A to help ensure that B did not suffer physical injury, not in order to maximise B's chances of avoiding physical injury in the future.

Now – suppose that A's breach of a duty of care that he owes B results in B suffering some kind of loss L that A's duty of care *was* designed to help ensure that B did not suffer. In suing A for compensation for loss L, B will *also* be entitled to sue A for compensation for *any consequential losses* flowing from loss L, so long as those losses are not too remote a consequence of A's negligence. This is so even if those consequential losses are of a different type from loss L.

For example, if *Driver* negligently runs over *Pedestrian*, and *Pedestrian*'s knee is dislocated as a result, *Pedestrian* will not only be entitled to sue for the physical injury he has suffered as a result of *Driver*'s negligence, but also the chance that because his knee has been dislocated, he might develop arthritis in the future. The fact that a loss of a chance of avoiding physical injury in future is a very different kind of loss from actual physical injury does not matter in this context: because, in this case, the loss of a chance of avoiding an arthritic knee in future flows from the injury to *Pedestrian*'s knee, the loss of that chance can be sued for as part of *Pedestrian*'s claim to be compensated for the injury to his knee.

In *Attia* v *British Gas* (1988), the defendants were installing some central heating in the claimant's home. In the course of so doing, they negligently started a fire. It took fireman four hours to get the fire under control, and the house and its contents suffered extensive damage. While the fire was blazing away, the claimant came home and saw what was happening. She claimed to have developed a psychiatric illness as a result of the shock of seeing her house going up in flames. The Court of Appeal held that so long as the claimant's psychiatric illness was a reasonably foreseeable consequence of the defendants' negligence, it was actionable. The decision can be supported on the basis that the defendants had owed the claimant a duty to take care not to set her house on fire, which duty was geared towards protecting the claimant's house and possessions from being damaged. The defendants' breach of this duty caused exactly the type of loss that the duty of care was designed to avoid – damage to the house and contents. In suing for compensation for the damage to the house and contents, the claimant could also recover for any non-remote consequential losses flowing from that damage. Provided the claimant's psychiatric illness was reasonably foreseeable, it counted as a non-remote consequential loss flowing from the damage done to her house and contents, and would therefore be actionable.

The principle of non-actionability under discussion here does not just apply in negligence cases, but across the board in all tort cases. We have already seen its application in a breach of statutory duty case, *Gorris* v *Scott* (1874), where the claimant was not allowed to sue for the loss of his sheep that resulted from the defendant's breach of statutory duty to keep them in pens while they were being transported by ship, because that duty was imposed on the defendant to stop disease spreading among the sheep, not to stop them being drowned. As the defendant's breach had resulted in the sheep drowning, and not becoming diseased, then the claimant's loss was non-actionable.

Another example of the same principle at work in the context of a breach of statutory duty is provided by the case of *Nicholls* v *F Austin (Leyton) Ltd* (1946), where the claimant was hit and injured by a piece of wood flying out of a piece of machinery that had been inadequately fenced, in breach of s 14(1) of the Factories Act 1937. It was held that the claimant could not sue her employer for damages because s 14(1) was designed to prevent the claimant coming into contact with dangerous machinery, not to prevent her being hit by something that had been ejected from a machine.

9.4 The *SAAMCO* principle

The '*SAAMCO* principle' is an off-shoot of the idea, discussed in the previous section, that a loss will not be actionable if it falls outside the 'scope of the duty' that the defendant owed the claimant, and breached. The principle was introduced into the law in the case of *South Australia Asset Management Corp* v *York Montague Ltd* (1997)[46] – hence, '*SAAMCO*'. The principle affects how much A can sue B for by way of damages if A breaches a *Hedley Byrne*-type duty of care that A owed to B because he 'assumed a responsibility' to B.

The *SAAMCO* principle has been described as being 'easier to formulate than to apply'.[47] This is not true: the *SAAMCO* principle is *both* extremely difficult to formulate *and* extremely difficult to apply.[48] The basic idea behind it seems to go like this.[49] If A has 'assumed a responsibility' to B in performing some task, and as a result A owes B a duty of care in performing that task, B will only be able to sue for compensation for a loss caused by A's breach if A's 'assumption of responsibility' to B was designed to safeguard B from suffering that kind of loss.

In the *South Australia* case, Lord Hoffmann – the originator of the *SAAMCO* principle – gave an example of a situation where the principle would bite:

> A mountaineer about to undertake a difficult climb is concerned about the fitness of his knee. He goes to a doctor who negligently makes a superficial examination and pronounces the knee fit. The climber goes on the expedition, which he would not have undertaken if the doctor had told him the true state of his knee. He suffers an injury which is an entirely foreseeable consequence of mountaineering but has nothing to do with his knee.[50]

In this case, the doctor will have 'assumed a responsibility' to inspect the climber's knee properly, and will as a result have owed the climber a duty of care under *Hedley Byrne* to inspect the knee with a reasonable degree of care and skill. The climber has been injured

---

[46] Noted, O'Sullivan 1997a. The case is otherwise known as *Banque Bruxelles Lambert SA* v *Eagle Star Insurance Ltd*.

[47] *Nykredit Plc* v *Edward Erdman Ltd* [1997] 1 WLR 1627, 1631 (per Lord Nicholls).

[48] A couple of cases illustrate the difficulties that the courts have experienced in applying the *SAAMCO* principle. See *Platform Home Loans* v *Oyston Shipways Ltd* [2000] 2 AC 190 (discussed below, § 28.5(E)), where the House of Lords reversed a unanimous Court of Appeal's application of the *SAAMCO* principle, but not without dissent from one Law Lord (Lord Cooke); and *Aneco Reinsurance Underwriting Ltd* v *Johnson & Higgins Ltd* [2001] UKHL 51 where neither the House of Lords nor the Court of Appeal below could reach a unanimous decision as to how the *SAAMCO* principle applied in that case. Consensus was achieved in *Hughes-Holland* v *BPE Solicitors* [2017] UKSC 21, where the Court of Appeal and the UKSC agreed that the *SAAMCO* principle ruled out the claimant from suing his solicitors for negligently drawing up legal documents that misrepresented how money that the claimant was lending a property developer would be used (the claimant thought the money was being used to fund the development; the developer actually planned to use the money to purchase the property that was to be developed). This was right: the responsibility that the claimant's solicitors assumed to him was geared towards ensuring that the claimant had a legal right to be repaid the money he was lending the developer, and not towards ensuring that the claimant did not make a bad loan because he was muddled about how the loan money was to be used or had miscalculated how financially successful the development he thought he was funding was going to be.

[49] For more detailed treatments of the *SAAMCO* principle and how it operates, see Dugdale 2000, Evans 2001, Peel 2003a; Butler 2003. The originator of the *SAAMCO* principle talks about it extra-judicially at Hoffmann 2005, 596.

[50] [1997] AC 191, 213.

(let's assume in an avalanche that he was caught up in) as result of the doctor's breach of this duty of care, in the sense that had the doctor inspected the knee properly, he would have told the climber that his knee was knackered, and the climber would have abandoned his plans to go mountaineering. But the injury suffered by the climber in this case was unrelated to the reason why the doctor 'assumed a responsibility' to the climber in the first place. The doctor 'assumed a responsibility' to the climber to safeguard the climber from suffering a knee-related injury while climbing. But the injury the climber suffered here was not knee-related, and was therefore non-actionable under the *SAAMCO* principle.[51]

The *South Australia* case itself was concerned with the following kind of situation. *Customer* applies to *Bank* for a loan of £200,000 and offers certain properties – call them 'security properties' – as security for the loan. *Bank* gets *Surveyor* to value them and *Surveyor* values the properties as being worth £220,000. In fact, *Surveyor* failed to value the security properties with a professional degree of care and skill, thereby breaching the duty of care he owed *Bank* in valuing the properties. The security properties were in fact worth only £180,000. Unaware of this, *Bank* lends *Customer* the £200,000 requested. Come the time for repayment, *Customer* defaults on the loan. *Bank* then seeks to get his money back by selling the security properties but – due to a fall in the market – the properties are now worth only £110,000. So *Bank* makes a net loss of £90,000 on the loan – the difference between the value of the loan and what he has managed to claw back by selling the security properties.

Bank discovers that *Surveyor* was negligent in valuing the security properties and he sues *Surveyor* for compensation for the £90,000 he lost on the loan to *Customer*. *Bank* argues that if *Surveyor* had not been negligent, *Surveyor* would have told *Bank* that the security properties were worth only £180,000 and so *Bank* would not have loaned *Customer* anything – *Customer* would have been unable to offer him sufficient security for the loan. It follows that had *Surveyor* not been negligent, *Bank* would not have lost £90,000. However, *Bank* will only be able to sue *Surveyor* for £40,000 in damages under the *SAAMCO* principle. Why is this? The reason is *Surveyor*'s 'assumption of responsibility' to *Bank* was designed to safeguard *Bank* from suffering loss *as a result of lending money to Customer on inadequate security.*

Now – how much of the loss suffered by *Bank* here is suffered *because it lent money to Customer on inadequate security?* Well, the fact that *Bank* was willing to lend *Customer* £200,000 on security that was valued at £220,000 shows that it thought that security *worth that much* was adequate security for the loan. Had *Bank* lent *Customer* £200,000 on

---

[51] There is another way of getting to this result. If we characterise the duty of care the doctor owed the climber in this case as a duty to take care not to tell the climber that his knee was sound when it was not, there were two ways the doctor could have discharged that duty: (1) he could have told the climber that his knee was not sound (in which case, the climber would not have gone on the expedition and would not have been injured); or (2) the doctor could have treated the knee and made it sound, before passing the climber as fit to climb (in which case, the climber would still have gone on the expedition and still have been injured). Characterising the doctor's breach in the way that is most favourable to him (see above, § 8.2) we say that the doctor breached his duty to the climber in this case by failing to make his knee sound – and consequently find that the doctor's breach did *not* cause the climber to be injured, as that injury would still have been it was even if the doctor had not breached his duty to the climber. Having said that, it is not possible to explain all instances of the application of the *SAAMCO* principle as resting on such reasoning: in a lot of the cases covered by *SAAMCO* there is only one way of characterising the defendant's breach of his duty of care.

security worth that much, that security would have been worth £150,000 when the time came for *Customer* to repay. (We assume here that the security would have declined in value by £70,000 as a result of a fall in the market, just like the security properties that *Customer* actually offered to *Bank* as security for *Bank*'s loan to him.) So had *Bank* lent money to *Customer* on adequate security, it would still have lost £50,000 on his loan to *Customer*. It follows that of the £90,000 loss suffered by *Bank* in this case, only £40,000 of that loss was suffered by it as a result of its lending money to *Customer on inadequate security*. So, under the *SAAMCO* principle, *Bank* will only be able to sue *Surveyor* for compensation for that £40,000 loss.[52]

A pre-*SAAMCO* case which can, in its result, be seen as giving effect to the *SAAMCO* principle is *Caparo Industries plc* v *Dickman* (1990). In that case, Caparo Industries plc were a company that held shares in Fidelity plc. Touche Ross, the defendants, audited Fidelity's accounts before they were circulated to Fidelity's shareholders. Touche Ross stated that the company's accounts gave a 'true and fair' representation of the company's financial position. This was not correct and Touche Ross should have known it. The accounts showed that Fidelity enjoyed a pre-tax profit of £1.3m. The true position was that Fidelity had suffered a loss of over £400,000. Caparo launched a takeover bid for Fidelity, relying on the fact that Touche Ross had given the company's accounts their seal of approval. The takeover bid was successful but when Caparo took a closer look at the books it discovered that it had paid too much for Fidelity.

Caparo sued Touche Ross in negligence, arguing that Touche had owed them, as one of Fidelity's shareholders, a duty of care in auditing the accounts. Had Touche not breached that duty of care, Caparo argued, Touche would have uncovered the truth about Fidelity's financial position and as a result Caparo would not have taken over Fidelity or Caparo would have paid a much smaller price for Fidelity. Caparo's claim for compensation was dismissed. It was conceded that Touche *had* owed Caparo a duty of care in auditing Fidelity's accounts – but Touche had only owed Caparo that duty *in their capacity as shareholders*. The loss that Caparo suffered as a result of Touche's negligence was suffered by Caparo in a quite different capacity – in their capacity as corporate raiders. Given this, Caparo could not sue Touche for compensation for the loss, by analogy to the rule that if A commits a tort in relation to B and C suffers some kind of loss as a result, C will not normally be entitled to sue A for compensation for that loss. Touche committed a tort in relation to Caparo *qua* shareholders in auditing Fidelity's accounts but it was Caparo *qua* corporate raiders who suffered a loss as a result.

Nowadays, Caparo's claim for compensation could be dismissed by reference to the *SAAMCO* principle. When Touche 'assumed a responsibility' to Caparo and the other shareholders in Fidelity when auditing Fidelity's accounts, Touche did so in order to help Caparo and the other shareholders in Fidelity decide whether to reward or punish Fidelity's board of directors for their performance over the previous financial year. Touche did

---

[52] It would have been different if the fall in the property market had been more modest: say the security properties were actually worth £170,000 when *Customer* defaulted, having been originally worth £180,000. In that case, *Bank*'s loss on the loan would have come to £30,000 and the loss it would have suffered had it lent *Bank* £200,000 on adequate security (that is, security worth £220,000) would have been £0 – the security properties would have declined in value from £220,000 to £210,000 but that would still have afforded enough security to allow *Bank* to get back all the money that it loaned *Customer*. So *all* of the £30,000 loss suffered by *Bank* in this scenario would have been attributable to the fact that it loaned *Customer* money on inadequate security and *Surveyor* would therefore be liable to compensate *Bank in full* for the loss suffered by it as a result of *Surveyor*'s negligence.

not 'assume a responsibility' to Caparo in order to help ensure that Caparo did not bid too much for Fidelity on taking it over. So any losses suffered by Caparo in bidding too much for Fidelity were non-actionable under the *SAAMCO* principle.[53]

In light of this, let's now consider the **Misdiagnosed Patient Problem**:

> *Patient* visits *Doctor*, complaining of headaches. *Doctor* sends *Patient* for some scans and tells *Patient* that, sadly, her headaches are being caused by an inoperable and cancerous brain tumour. He tells her that she has, at most, six months to live. *Patient* reacts to this news by quitting her job and spending all her savings (£100,000) on holidays and extravagant parties for her friends. Six months later, *Patient* is still extremely healthy. Puzzled, *Patient* goes back to *Doctor* for another check-up. *Doctor* apologises and says that due to his mixing up *Patient*'s scans with *Another Patient*'s, he gave *Patient* the wrong diagnosis. He tells *Patient* that she is in fact completely healthy and that her headaches were probably due to watching too much television.

While *Patient* has suffered a considerable loss here as a result of *Doctor*'s breach of the duty of care he owed *Patient* to treat her with a reasonable degree of care and skill, it is strongly arguable that *Patient*'s loss is non-actionable under the *SAAMCO* principle. *Doctor* 'assumed a responsibility' to *Patient* in order to help *Patient* get better, not in order to help *Patient* decide how to spend her savings.[54]

A comparison can be drawn with the case of *Stevens v Bermondsey & Southwark Group Hospital Management Committee* (1963). In that case, the defendant's negligent diagnosis of the extent of the injuries suffered by the claimant as a result of a third party's negligence caused the claimant to settle his claim for damages against the third party for £125, when he would have been entitled to sue for much more. The claimant sued the defendant for the extra amount he would have demanded from the third party had the defendant not been negligent. It was held that the claimant's claim failed. The *SAAMCO* principle explains the result. The defendant 'assumed a responsibility' to the claimant in this case to help the claimant get better, not in order to help him determine how much he should sue a third party for by way of compensation for his injuries.

---

[53] See also *Reeman* v *Department of Transport* [1997] 2 Lloyd's Rep 648, where the claimant bought a boat which had been certified as being seaworthy by the defendant. In fact, the boat was not seaworthy and was, as a result, practically valueless. The claimant's action for damages was dismissed: the defendant had been employed to determine whether or not it would be safe for people to travel on the boat, not to ensure that the claimant did not make a bad bargain in buying a boat. The *Caparo* case was distinguished in *Morgan Crucible Co plc* v *Hill Samuel & Co Ltd* [1991] Ch 295 where, it was claimed, the defendant representatives of a company made various representations to the claimants, who were thinking of taking over the company, as to the financial health of the company with the object of persuading the claimants to increase their bid for the company. The claimants subsequently discovered that they had bid too much for the company and sued for compensation. It was held that if these facts were made out, the claimants had an arguable claim against the defendants.

[54] In *Hedley Byrne & Co Ltd* v *Heller* [1964] AC 465, Lord Devlin suggested (at 517) that it would be 'nonsense' for the law not to give a remedy in the case where a doctor negligently advises a patient 'that he cannot safely pursue his occupation when in fact he can and he loses his livelihood'. (Our thanks to Sandy Steel for bringing this *dictum* to our attention.) Such a case would not, we think, be caught by the *SAAMCO* principle as the whole point of consulting the doctor here is to determine whether it would be a good idea for the patient to carry on working as he does, and the doctor's advice deprives him of the opportunity to carry on working when it would in fact be a good idea to carry on.

A more difficult case is presented by the **Second Misdiagnosed Patient Problem:**[55]

> *Patient* visits *Doctor*, complaining of headaches. *Doctor* sends *Patient* for some scans and tells *Patient* that, sadly, her headaches are being caused by an inoperable and cancerous brain tumour. He tells her that she has, at most, six months to live. *Patient* does some research on the Internet and discovers that there is a group of doctors in the United States working on cures for the type of brain tumour that *Doctor* has diagnosed her as having. She requests *Doctor* to send her scans to the American doctors, and the doctors tell *Patient* that they are willing to treat her. *Patient* pays a deposit for her treatment, and travels to the United States at great expense. The American doctors examine *Patient* and tell her that she is perfectly healthy; *Patient* cannot recover the deposit for her treatment.

In this case, it is much more difficult to tell whether the economic losses suffered by *Patient* as a result of *Doctor*'s misdiagnosis are non-actionable under the *SAAMCO* principle. *Doctor* 'assumed a responsibility' to *Patient* to help *Patient* get better, and *Patient*'s expenses here have been incurred in an attempt to get better. But it is likely that a claim for these expenses will still fail under the *SAAMCO* principle. *Doctor* did not 'assume a responsibility' to *Patient* in order to save her money from consulting alternative doctors to obtain the treatment she needed. *Doctor*'s reasons for 'assuming a responsibility' to *Patient* were purely non-pecuniary in nature: they were to help *Patient* get better, and she is not physically in worse shape as a result of *Doctor*'s misdiagnosis.

9.5 Wrongful pregnancy/birth

Suppose *Doctor* committed a tort in relation to *Mother* and *Mother* ended up giving birth to a child that she would not otherwise have had. This simple sentence covers a number of different situations:

(1) *Wrongful pregnancy.* *Mother* did not want to become pregnant, and *Doctor* 'assumed a responsibility' to *Mother* for sterilising her or her permanent partner. *Doctor* carelessly failed to carry out the sterilisation operation properly, with the result that *Mother* became pregnant and carried her baby *Son* to term.

(2) *Wrongful birth (1).* *Mother* becomes pregnant accidentally but *Doctor* fails to spot that she is pregnant in time for her to have an abortion, which she probably would have had, had she been told about her pregnancy in time.[56] *Mother* carries her baby *Son* to term.

(3) *Wrongful birth (2).* *Mother* becomes pregnant intentionally but does not want to have a disabled baby. *Doctor* fails to spot that the baby in *Mother*'s womb is disabled. Had *Mother* been told this, she probably would have had an abortion.[57] *Mother* carries her baby *Son* to term.

---

[55] We are grateful to Kirsty Mills for suggesting this variation.

[56] Section 1(1)(a) of the Abortion Act 1967 allows an abortion to be performed if the pregnancy 'has not exceeded its twenty fourth week and . . . continuance of the pregnancy would involve risk, greater than if the pregnancy were terminated, of injury to the physical or mental health of the pregnant woman . . .'

[57] Section 1(1)(d) of the Abortion Act 1967 allows an abortion to be performed 'if there is a serious risk that if the child were born it would suffer from such physical or mental abnormalities as to be seriously handicapped.'

It seems to be well established that in all of these situations, *Mother* will be entitled to sue *Doctor* for compensation in respect of the inconvenience that she suffered in the run-up to giving birth, the pain and suffering that she went through in labour, any economic losses that she suffered before giving birth as a result of taking time off work, having to spend money on new clothes to fit her as she grew larger, and so on.[58]

But if *Mother* attempts to sue *Doctor* for compensation in respect of the money she is going to have to spend on bringing up *Son*, she will usually find that that loss is regarded as being automatically non-actionable by the courts.[59] In order to understand *when* this loss will be held to be non-actionable, we have to distinguish between the case where *Son* is healthy and the case where *Son* is born disabled.

A. Healthy child

The House of Lords ruled in *McFarlane* v *Tayside Health Board* (2000)[60] that if *Mother* and *Son* are both healthy then the cost of bringing up *Son* will be automatically non-actionable.[61] In a subsequent case – *Rees* v *Darlington Memorial Hospital NHS Trust* (2004)[62] – the House of Lords placed a 'gloss' on the ruling in *McFarlane*, holding that while *Mother* would not be entitled to sue *Doctor* for damages representing the cost of bringing up *Son*, *Mother would* be entitled to sue *Doctor* for a fixed sum of £15,000 to compensate her for the disruption to her life that bringing up *Son* will involve.

Two issues arise out of this: (1) Why is *Mother not* allowed to sue *Doctor* for the cost of bringing up *Son*? (2) Why *is Mother* allowed to sue *Doctor* for a fixed sum of £15,000 to compensate her for the disruption to her life that bringing up *Son* will involve?

(1) On the first issue, a number of reasons were advanced by the Law Lords in both *McFarlane* and *Rees* as to why the cost of bringing up *Son* should be held to be non-actionable.

---

[58] *McFarlane* v *Tayside Health Board* [2000] 2 AC 59, 74 (per Lord Slynn), 81 (per Lord Steyn), 87 (per Lord Hope), 102 (per Lord Clyde). It is unclear why, in either of the *wrongful birth* situations, *Mother* will be entitled to sue *Doctor* for compensation in respect of these losses – it could be argued (particularly in the case of the second wrongful birth situation) that she willingly took the risk that she would suffer these losses when she became pregnant. See, on this, Mason 2002, 50.

[59] The cost of bringing up *Mother*'s child will be regarded as actionable in Australia: *Cattanach* v *Melchior* (2003) 215 CLR 1 (noted, Cane 2004).

[60] [2000] 2 AC 59 ('*McFarlane*').

[61] For criticisms of this ruling, see Hoyano 2002. An attempt to get round this ruling was made in *Greenfield* v *Irwin* [2001] 1 WLR 113, where the claimant – who had given birth to a baby that she would not have had but for the defendants' negligence – did not sue the defendants for the cost of bringing up the baby, but rather sued to be compensated for the loss of income she had experienced as a result of giving up work to look after the baby full time. The claim was dismissed on the ground that if it were allowed, a coach and horses would be driven through the House of Lords' ruling in *McFarlane*. Another attempt to get round *McFarlane* was made in *Rees* v *Darlington Memorial Hospital NHS Trust* [2004] 1 AC 309, where a woman who was near-blind decided that she would be incapable of bringing up a baby properly and as a result had the defendants perform a sterilisation operation on her. The defendants performed the operation incompetently and the claimant subsequently conceived, and gave birth to, a healthy baby boy. It was argued that while the claimant's boy was perfectly healthy, the fact that the *claimant* was disabled meant that *McFarlane* did not apply, and that the claimant should at the very least be allowed to recover the *extra* cost of bringing up the boy that was attributable to the fact that *she* was disabled. The House of Lords rejected this claim by 4:3, holding that *McFarlane* applies across the board to *all* cases where someone gives birth to a healthy child as a result of another's negligence.

[62] [2004] 1 AC 309 ('*Rees*').

First, it would be wrong, in assessing the damages payable to *Mother* to disregard the benefits *Mother* would reap from bringing up *Son*. These benefits must be taken as *at least equalling* the cost of rearing *Son* – either because thinking anything else would be morally offensive[63] or because the only fair way of taking these benefits into account is to *assume* that they at least equal the cost of bringing up *Son*.[64] Given this, it must be taken that the benefits of bringing up *Son* at least equal the costs and therefore no claim can be made for the cost of bringing up *Son*.

Secondly, to make *Doctor* liable for the cost of bringing up *Son* would impose on *Doctor* a liability far out of proportion to his fault in either causing *Mother* to become pregnant or failing to bring her pregnancy to an end.[65]

Thirdly, if *Doctor* were required to compensate *Mother* for the cost of bringing up *Son*, the funds would in all probability come out of the hard-pressed coffers of the National Health Service; and the general public would think it wrong for that money to be used to subsidise the upbringing of *Son*, as opposed to using it to treat patients.[66]

Fourthly, were *Mother* to be compensated for the cost of bringing up her child, then the amount payable to *Mother* would depend on how rich she is – the richer she is, the more she could be expected to spend on bringing up *Son* and therefore the greater the damages that would be payable to *Mother*. It would be 'unseemly' for the law to allow *Mother*'s award to depend on how rich or poor she is.[67]

(2) Moving on to the second issue, why will *Mother* be allowed to sue *Doctor* for a fixed sum of £15,000 in the situation we are considering? The House of Lords divided 4:2 in *Rees* over the issue of whether *Mother* should be allowed to make such a claim against *Doctor*.[68] The majority thought that it would be wrong if the law did nothing to compensate *Mother* for the 'loss of autonomy' that she had suffered as a result of giving birth to a child.[69] They thought that awarding *Mother* £15,000 would afford her some compensation for this 'loss of autonomy'.[70]

Lords *Steyn* and *Hope* criticised the majority ruling on this issue. Lord *Steyn* took the view that the courts simply did not have the power to make awards designed to compensate individuals for intangible fancies such as 'loss of autonomy' – let alone to rule that such awards would be fixed across the board at £15,000, whatever the circumstances of a claimant who gave birth to an unwanted healthy baby as a result of someone else's negligence.[71] Lord *Hope* said he could not understand why the majority was proposing to compensate for the 'loss of autonomy' suffered by a claimant who gave birth to an

---

[63] *McFarlane*, at 82 (per Lord Steyn), 111 (per Lord Millett); *Rees*, at [28] (per Lord Steyn), [112] (per Lord Millett).

[64] *McFarlane*, at 97 (per Lord Hope); *Rees*, at [51] (per Lord Hope), [138] (per Lord Scott).

[65] *McFarlane*, at 91 (per Lord Hope); *Rees*, at [16] (per Lord Nicholls).

[66] *Rees*, at [6] (per Lord Bingham).

[67] *McFarlane*, at 82 (per Lord Steyn).

[68] Lord Hutton, sitting in *Rees*, did not express an opinion on the issue.

[69] *Rees*, at [8] (per Lord Bingham), [17] (per Lord Nicholls), [123] (per Lord Millett); [148] (per Lord Scott).

[70] Though Lord Bingham took the view that the award of £15,000 is not designed to *compensate* B for any loss that she has suffered: *Rees*, at [8]. For a possible alternative explanation of the nature of this award, see below, § 26.3(A).

[71] *Rees*, at [45].

unwanted healthy baby as a result of someone's negligence through the award of a *fixed* sum of £15,000. If such an award is meant to be compensatory, then why should such a claimant not be entitled to say, 'The value of *my* loss of autonomy comes to much more than £15,000, and so I should be awarded much more than the fixed sum the majority in *Rees* said I should be given.'[72]

B. Disabled child

Let's now consider what the position is if, in the situation we are considering, *Son* is *disabled*. The House of Lords' decision in *McFarlane* did not deal with that issue at all – it was purely concerned with what the position would be if *Son* were healthy.

After *McFarlane* was decided, the Court of Appeal ruled in *Parkinson v St James and Seacroft University Hospital NHS Trust* (2002)[73] that if, in the situation we are considering, *Son* was disabled, *Mother* would be entitled to sue *Doctor* for the *extra cost of raising Son that is attributable to the fact he was born disabled.* So, on this view, the normal costs of raising *Son*, that *Mother* would have incurred whether or not *Son* was disabled, would still be non-actionable. But any *extra* expenses that *Mother* would have to incur in raising *Son* because he is disabled would be actionable.

In *Rees*, the House of Lords found themselves split on the issue of what the position should be in the case where *Son* is disabled. Lords Steyn, Hope and Hutton took the view that *Parkinson* was correctly decided.[74] Lords Bingham and Nicholls took the view that *Parkinson* was wrongly decided and that in the situation we are considering, *Doctor*'s liability to *Mother* should not depend on whether *Son* was born healthy or disabled. In *both* cases, *Mother* should not be allowed to claim *anything* for the cost of bringing up the child: instead, all she will be entitled to sue *Doctor* for (in addition to damages for the pain of pregnancy and so on) is a fixed sum of £15,000 to compensate her for her 'loss of autonomy'.[75]

Lord Scott took the view that we may have to distinguish between: (1) the case where *Doctor* was employed to stop *Mother* becoming pregnant, or continuing with her pregnancy, because she was fearful that any baby she had would be disabled; and (2) the case where *Doctor* was employed to stop *Mother* becoming pregnant because she did not want to have another baby. He thought that the Court of Appeal's ruling in *Parkinson* should only be allowed to apply in case (1). So he thought that if (2) were true, *Mother* should not be allowed to sue for *anything* in respect of the cost of her disabled *Son*.[76]

As the issue of whether *Parkinson* was rightly decided did not arise for decision in *Rees*, Lord Millett preferred to leave the question 'open'.[77] He went on to observe that while in 'strict logic', a claimant who gave birth to a disabled child should not be allowed to claim

---

[72] *Rees*, at [71]–[73].

[73] [2002] QB 266 ('*Parkinson*').

[74] *Rees*, at [35] (per Lord Steyn), [57] (per Lord Hope), [91] (per Lord Hutton).

[75] *Rees*, at [9] (per Lord Bingham), [18] (per Lord Nicholls).

[76] *Rees*, at [145].

[77] *Rees*, at [112].

[78] Because – following the logic underlying Lord Millett's judgments in *McFarlane* and *Rees* on the issue of whether a claim for the cost of bringing up a healthy child should be allowed – if one did allow such a claim to be made in the case where a claimant gave birth to a disabled child, one *would* be saying that bringing up a disabled child *is* more trouble than it is worth; which can hardly be right.

anything for the cost of bringing up the child,[78] he himself did not think that the Court of Appeal's ruling in *Parkinson* was 'morally offensive'. At the same time, he expressed himself fearful that allowing *Mother* to sue for the extra cost of bringing up *Son* that was attributable to the fact that *Son* was born disabled might 'prove difficult to achieve without introducing nice distinctions and unacceptable refinements of a kind which tend to bring the law into disrepute'.[79]

What a mess! However, as *Parkinson* was not overruled in *Rees*,[80] *Parkinson* will remain binding on all courts up to and including the Court of Appeal until the UK Supreme Court readdresses the issue of whether *Parkinson* was correctly decided. As this is not likely to happen any time soon, we can safely assume that for the foreseeable future, the Court of Appeal's decision in *Parkinson* will determine how much a claimant is entitled to sue a defendant for in a disabled child case. So in the situation we are considering – where *Mother* has given birth to a disabled *Son* because of *Doctor's* negligence – *Mother* will be entitled to sue *Doctor* for compensation in respect of any extra expenses that she will have to incur in raising *Son* because he is disabled.[81] This ruling gives rise to a couple of complications that need to be addressed.

First of all, what is the difference between a disabled child and a healthy child? Suppose, for example, that due to *Doctor's* negligence, *Mother* gives birth to a baby *Girl*. As *Girl* grows up, it becomes clear that she is short-sighted and will need to wear glasses. Will *Mother* be able to sue *Doctor* for the cost of providing those glasses? It depends on whether *Girl* counts as being 'disabled' or not: if she is a 'healthy' child, then *Mother* will not be able to recover *any* of the costs of raising *Girl*, including the cost of providing her with spectacles. In the *Parkinson* case, Hale LJ suggested that a child will be held to be disabled if 'he is blind, deaf or dumb or suffers from mental disorder of any kind or is substantially and permanently handicapped by illness, injury or congenital deformity . . .'[82] On this definition, *Girl* would probably not count as being disabled and so *Mother* would not be able to sue *Doctor* for the cost of providing her with glasses.

Secondly, what is the position in the following case? *Doctor* negligently performs a vasectomy on *Husband*. Thinking (incorrectly) that the operation has been a success, *Wife* and *Husband* have unprotected sex. As a result *Wife* becomes pregnant. She decides to carry the child to term but six months into her pregnancy, she is involved in a car accident due to the negligence of *Driver*. *Wife* survives the car accident but her doctors tell her that, as a result of the accident, her baby is liable to be severely brain-damaged when he is born. Nevertheless *Wife* decides to carry on with the pregnancy and three months later she gives birth to *Girl*, who suffers from severe brain damage.[83] Will *Doctor* be liable for the extra cost that *Wife* will have to incur in raising *Girl* that is attributable to the fact that she has been born brain-damaged? One would have thought not, but in

---

[79] *Rees*, at [112].

[80] Nor could it have been as the correctness of the Court of Appeal's ruling in *Parkinson* was not at issue in *Rees*.

[81] Though this point was not addressed by any of the Law Lords in *Rees*, it is presumably the case that B would *also* be entitled to sue A for a fixed sum of £15,000 to compensate her for the 'loss of autonomy' suffered by her as a result of A's negligence.

[82] *Parkinson*, at [91] (quoting s 17(11) of the Children Act 1989).

[83] In this situation, *Driver* will be liable to compensate *Girl* for the fact that she was born disabled under the Congenital Disabilities (Civil Liability) Act 1976: see below, § 29.2.

Parkinson the Court of Appeal held that *Doctor would* be liable so long as *Driver*'s negligence did not break the chain of causation between *Doctor*'s negligence and *Wife*'s giving birth to *Girl*.[84] As *Driver*'s negligence will not have had that effect, *Doctor* will be liable.[85]

9.6 Mitigation

Suppose that A has committed a tort in relation to B and B has suffered some kind of loss as a result. That loss will be non-actionable if B could have done something after A committed his tort to avoid suffering that loss but she *unreasonably* failed to do so. B has a 'duty to mitigate'[86] the losses suffered by her as a result of A's tort and will be barred from suing A for damages in respect of any losses that she has only suffered as a result of A's tort because she breached that 'duty'.[87]

We have already seen an example of this principle at work in the case of the workman who unreasonably refused to have an operation which would have saved his left hand, the hand having been originally injured by the defendants' negligence.[88] He was not allowed to sue the defendants for compensation in respect of the loss of his left hand because the loss of that hand was attributable to his failure to mitigate the losses suffered by him as a result of the defendants' negligence. Let's now look at how the duty to mitigate applies in a couple of concrete situations:

A. Avoidable births

What is the position in the following case? Suppose *Husband* and *Wife* asked *Surgeon* to carry out a vasectomy on *Husband* so that *Husband* and *Wife* could have sexual relations without using contraceptives. *Surgeon* performed the operation but (in breach of the duty of care he owed *Wife* and *Husband*) he failed to carry it out properly and the operation was as a

---

[84] *Parkinson*, at [53] (per Brooke LJ) and [92] (per Hale LJ).

[85] *Driver*'s negligence was not a *novus actus interveniens* because it was not deliberate. Could it be argued that *Wife*'s failure to have an abortion when she was told that *Girl* would be born severely brain-damaged broke the chain of causation between *Doctor*'s negligence and *Wife*'s giving birth to *Girl*? No – it must be remembered that omissions do not break chains of causation (see above, § 9.12). Could it be argued, alternatively, that *Wife* is barred from suing *Doctor* for the extra cost of raising *Girl* that is attributable to the fact that she has been born with brain damage because by failing to have an abortion she failed to mitigate the losses suffered by her as a result of *Doctor*'s negligence? The answer is 'no' – see below, § 9.6(A).

[86] This is, of course, not a real duty – B cannot be compelled to mitigate the losses suffered by her as a result of A's tort or sued if she fails to mitigate those losses.

[87] It seems, in light of the decision of the Privy Council in *Geest plc* v *Lansiquot* [2002] 1 WLR 3111, that the burden of proving that B has breached this 'duty' will fall on A. So if B has suffered some kind of loss as a result of A's tort that she could have avoided, B will still be able to claim compensation for that loss unless A can show that B acted *unreasonably* in failing to avoid that loss. In an earlier case, the Privy Council took the opposite view, holding that in the situation just described, B would not be able to claim compensation for the loss that she has suffered unless *she* could show that she acted *reasonably* in failing to avoid that loss: *Selvanayagam* v *University of West Indies* [1983] 1 WLR 585. There is something to be said for the position taken by the Privy Council in *Selvanayagam*: it will surely be easier for B to demonstrate that she acted reasonably in failing to avoid the loss in question than it will be for A to show that B acted unreasonably in failing to avoid that loss.

[88] See above, § 8.11(A).

result ineffective. Thinking, however, that the operation had been a success, *Wife* and *Husband* began to have unprotected sexual intercourse and *Wife* eventually became pregnant. Nine months later, *Wife* gave birth, experiencing a lot of pain and suffering in doing so. *Wife* also had to take time off work during the pregnancy and spent money on new clothes that would fit her in the latter stages of her pregnancy. Suppose she wants to sue *Surgeon* for damages in respect of these forms of economic loss and the pain and suffering experienced by her in labour, arguing that *Surgeon*'s negligence caused her to suffer these forms of loss.

Could *Surgeon* argue that *Wife* is barred from suing him for damages in respect of these losses on the ground that she could have avoided these losses by having an abortion? Obviously, the answer is 'no'. It cannot be argued that *Wife* acted *unreasonably* in not having an abortion – so it cannot be said that her failure to have an abortion put her in breach of her 'duty to mitigate' the losses suffered by her as a result of *Surgeon*'s negligence. Astonishingly, in *Emeh* v *Kensington Area Health Authority* (1985), Park J, at first instance, took the opposite line and suggested that in the case we are considering, *Wife* *might* be barred from suing *Surgeon* for damages in respect of the losses that her pregnancy caused her to suffer on the ground that she could have avoided those losses by having an abortion. Fortunately, good sense has prevailed in the courts: Park J's views have been firmly rejected by both the Court of Appeal in *Emeh*'s case and by the House of Lords in *McFarlane* v *Tayside Health Board* (2000).[89]

Having said that, in the case of *Richardson* v *LRC Products Ltd* (2000), Ian Kennedy J suggested that if *Wife* was warned by *Surgeon* that *Husband*'s vasectomy had been unsuccessful the day after *Husband* impregnated her, then *Wife* might be barred from suing *Surgeon* for damages in respect of the losses suffered by her as a result of her pregnancy if she failed to bring that pregnancy to a halt by taking a 'morning-after' pill. In such a case, he thought it could be said that *Wife* had failed to mitigate the losses suffered by her as a result of *Surgeon*'s negligence.[90]

B. *White* v *Jones* (1995)[91]

An unusual case which raised a 'duty to mitigate' point – though it was not argued as such in the case – was *Gorham* v *British Telecommunications plc* (2000).[92] That case, it will be recalled, concerned a man, G, who was given some bad pensions advice by the defendants.

---

[89] *McFarlane*, 74 (per Lord Slynn), 81 (per Lord Steyn), 104 (per Lord Clyde), 112–13 (per Lord Millett).

[90] The case actually concerned a claim under the Consumer Protection Act 1987: a married couple claimed that the wife had become pregnant as a result of their using a defective condom which split while they were making love. Ian Kennedy J rejected the claim that the condom was defective but held that even if it were, the claimants still had no case because the wife – knowing that the condom had split – could have easily avoided suffering any loss as a result by taking a 'morning-after' pill. The decision is not easy to reconcile with the views expressed by the Court of Appeal in *Emeh* and the House of Lords in *McFarlane*. Is there a distinction between taking a 'morning-after' pill and having an abortion? Munby J thought there was in *R (Smeaton)* v *Secretary of State for Health* [2002] EWHC 610 (Admin) (*not* a tort case), ruling that the 'morning-after' pill was not an abortifacient under the Abortion Act 1967.

[91] For a straightforward *White* v *Jones* case which raised a duty to mitigate point, see *Walker* v *Medlicott & Son* [1999] 1 WLR 727, where the defendant firm of solicitors failed to draft a will properly with the result that the claimant was not left a house in the will which the testatrix had intended to leave to the claimant; the claimant's claim for compensation was dismissed because he could have applied to have the will rectified under s 20(1) of the Administration of Justice Act 1982 and so had failed to mitigate the loss suffered by him as a result of the defendants' negligence.

[92] Discussed above, § 5.13.

As a result, the claimants, G's wife and two young children, were left worse off after G's death then they would have been had the defendants advised G properly. Had the defendants advised G properly, G would have joined his employer's pension scheme, instead of taking out a pension plan with the defendants. And had G joined his employer's pension scheme, the claimants would have obtained a lump sum on his death.

The claimants sued the defendants for compensation and it was held that the defendants had owed them a duty of care in advising G under the principle in *White* v *Jones* and that the defendants had breached that duty of care. However, it was held that the claimants could not sue for the lump sum that they would have received on G's death had he been properly advised by the defendants. The reason was that some time after being badly advised by the claimants, G discovered that his employer's pension scheme was superior to the pension plan that he had taken out with the defendants, but he then failed to join his employer's pension scheme. Had he done so, the claimants would have received the lump sum on G's death that they were suing the defendants for not receiving. In other words, G failed to mitigate the loss that the defendants' negligence caused the claimants to suffer on G's death.

It is not surprising that G's failure to mitigate the claimants' loss should have been held against the claimants. If the principle in *White* v *Jones* is (as we contend)[93] concerned with situations where A has been *prevented* by B's actions from conferring a benefit on C no action should be available to C under *White* v *Jones* if B's actions did not actually *prevent* A from conferring that benefit on C.

9.7 No double recovery

The principle against double recovery (the victim of a tort recovering twice for the same loss) applies in a number of different contexts to make a loss suffered by the victim of a tort non-actionable:

(1) *Compensation from another tortfeasor.* If *Defendant One* and *Defendant Two* are both liable in tort to compensate *Victim* for some loss that she has suffered, and *Victim* has recovered *full* compensation for that loss from *One*, *Victim* cannot – of course – subsequently sue *Two* for compensation for that loss. The effect of *One*'s payment is to make *Victim*'s loss non-actionable with regard to *Two*. *One* will, however, be entitled to bring a claim in contribution against *Two* under the Civil Liability (Contribution) Act 1978, requiring *Two* to pay him a 'just and equitable'[94] sum as a contribution towards *One*'s compensation payment to *Two*.

(2) *Legal costs.*[95] It is well established that in a case where *Defendant* has committed a tort in relation to *Victim*, *Victim* will *not* be able to sue *Defendant* for damages in respect of the legal costs that she has incurred in bringing a claim in tort against *Defendant*, even though *Defendant*'s tort undoubtedly caused *Victim* to incur those costs and those costs were an obviously non-remote consequence of *Defendant*'s tort.

Traditionally, this has been said to be because the law already provides *Victim* with a way of recovering those costs from *Defendant* – through an action for costs, under the

---

[93] See above, § 5.13.
[94] Section 2(1).
[95] See, generally, Merrett 2009.

Civil Procedure Rules – and does not want that mechanism for recovering costs to be subverted by a claim for costs being made under cover of a claim for damages in tort. However, this traditional explanation is nowadays weakened by the fact that recent reforms (known as the 'Jackson reforms')[96] to the civil justice system mean that a claimant whose case is litigated under a *conditional fee agreement* (that is, on a 'no-win, no-fee' basis) will *not* recover all of her costs from the defendant even if her claim is successful. Her lawyer will customarily include, as part of those costs, a 'success fee' designed to compensate him for taking on the risk that he might lose the case and not get anything for his efforts on the claimant's behalf. This 'success fee' – capped at 25 per cent of the damages recoverable by the claimant in personal injury cases – will not be recoverable as part of an order for costs in cases where the claimant wins her case against the defendant.

In personal injury cases, successful claimants were supposed to be 'compensated' for losing the ability to recover any 'success fees' that they had to pay their lawyers through the damages for non-pecuniary losses such as mental distress or loss of amenity or physical discomfort being increased by 10 per cent.[97] However, this still leaves successful claimants in personal injury cases short-changed; and successful claimants represented on a 'no-win, no-fee' basis in cases not involving personal injury are left substantially out of pocket. Despite this, it seems unlikely that an attempt to challenge the traditional rule that legal costs cannot be recovered through an action for damages by the victim of a tort (at least where those costs were incurred under a conditional fee agreement) would succeed; were it to do, the Jackson reforms would completely unravel.

(3) *Damage to property.* In a case where *Defendant* has tortiously damaged *Owner*'s property, *Owner* will be entitled, as of right, to compensation for that damage, assessed on either a 'cost of repair' or 'cost of replacement' basis. Whether *Owner* gets 'cost of repair' damages or 'cost of replacement' damages will depend on which sum is more reasonable, under the circumstances.[98] But the fact that *Owner* has a right to sue *Defendant* for compensation for the damage to his property on either a 'cost of repair' or 'cost of replacement' basis, means that *Owner cannot* sue *Defendant* for the *actual* costs that he has incurred either repairing or replacing the damaged property. If he could, he would then recover the cost of repairing or replacing his property from *Defendant* twice over – once as compensation for the damage to his property, and once as compensation for the consequential loss that he has suffered as a result of his property being damaged.

9.8 Public policy

There are a residual number of cases where losses suffered by the victim of a tort will be regarded as non-actionable because it would be contrary to public policy to allow recovery for those losses.

For example, in *Pritchard* v *J H Cobden Ltd* (1988), the claimant suffered some brain damage in a road traffic accident caused by the defendant's negligence. The brain damage

---

[96] After Sir Rupert Jackson LJ, and his report (Jackson 2009) recommending reforms to the law on the recovery of civil litigation costs.

[97] This aspect of the 'Jackson reforms' was implemented by the decision of the Court of Appeal in *Simmons* v *Castle* [2013] 1 WLR 1239.

[98] See below, § 23.3(C).

had the effect of changing the claimant's personality for the worse. As a result, the claimant's marriage broke down and his wife divorced him. The claimant sued the defendant, seeking to be compensated for the economic loss that he had suffered when his assets were divided up between him and his wife in the divorce. The Court of Appeal held that this loss was not actionable, on the ground that it would be contrary to public policy to allow the claimant to recover for this loss.

There were a number of reasons why this was so. First, allowing this sort of claim could lead to abuse. Suppose *Husband* and *Wife* were a married couple who were going to divorce when *Husband* was involved in an accident negligently caused by *Driver*. If the sort of claim made by the claimant in *Pritchard* were allowed, *Husband* and *Wife* could easily collude with each other and claim that, when they divorced each other, they did so because of the effects of the accident. *Husband* would then be allowed to recover from *Driver*, and split with *Wife*, the value of the assets that he lost in the divorce.

Secondly, allowing this sort of claim could undermine marriages. Suppose that *Husband* was happily married to *Wife* when he was involved in an accident that was negligently caused by *Driver*, and that the injuries sustained by *Husband* in the accident had a damaging effect on his personality. If the sort of claim made by the claimant in *Pritchard* were allowed then *Husband* would know that if *Wife* divorced him because of his change in personality he would suffer no financial prejudice whatsoever: he would be able to claim the value of any assets he lost in the divorce. He would then have less incentive to try and moderate the effect of the accident on his personality for the sake of preserving his marriage.

Thirdly, if this sort of claim were allowed, then in the case we have just been considering – where *Husband* was happily married to *Wife* when he was negligently injured by *Driver* – if *Wife* wanted to divorce *Husband* because of the effect that his injuries have had on his personality, *Driver* would be entitled to be represented in any proceedings dealing with how *Husband* and *Wife*'s assets should be divided. This is because such proceedings would have an effect on *Driver*'s legal liabilities. So the divorce court dealing with *Husband* and *Wife*'s divorce would have to have regard not only to their interests, but also to *Driver*'s interests, in deciding how *Husband* and *Wife*'s assets should be divided between them.

Further reading

On remoteness, see **Stauch, 'Risk and remoteness of damage in negligence' (2001) 64** *Modern Law Review* **191**. On *McFarlane* and *Rees*, see **Hoyano, 'Misconceptions about wrongful conception' (2002) 65** *Modern Law Review* **883**; **Bagshaw, 'Children as actionable damage' (2004) 15** *King's College Law Journal* **117**; and **Priaulx,** *The Harm Paradox: Tort Law and the Unwanted Child in an Era of Choice* **(Routledge, 2007)**.

Chapter 10
Occupiers' liability

Aims and objectives

Reading this chapter should enable you to:

(1) Understand who counts as being an occupier of premises.

(2) Understand what sort of dangers can be said to have arisen on a particular set of premises because of the state of the premises.

(3) Understand when an occupier will owe someone a duty of care to protect that person from a danger arising because of the state of the premises under (a) the Occupiers' Liability Act 1957, and (b) the Occupiers' Liability Act 1984.

(4) Understand when an occupier will be allowed to rely on (a) a disclaimer of duty, (b) an exclusion clause, and (c) a warning to avoid being held liable to a claimant under the 1957 Act or the 1984 Act.

(5) Understand when an occupier will be held to owe someone a duty of care under the general law of negligence to protect that person against a danger not arising as a result of the state of the premises.

10.1 The basics

The law has long taken the view that the occupation of land gives rise to positive duties of care to protect the interests of other people who might be affected by hazards arising on that land. In this chapter, we will split up the liabilities incurred by an occupier who fails to protect someone from a hazard arising on that land according to whether they arise:

(1) *Under the Occupiers' Liability Act 1957* ('OLA 1957') – under which an occupier will owe his visitors, and other people lawfully on his land (though not by virtue of using a right of way over his land), a duty to take reasonable steps to see that they are reasonably safe for the purposes for which they are on the land.

(2) *Under the Occupiers' Liability Act 1984* ('OLA 1984') – under which an occupier will owe trespassers on his land (and those using a right of way over the land) a duty to take reasonable steps to protect them against dangerous features of his land when: (i) he knows or ought to know about the dangerous feature; and (ii) he knows or ought to know a trespasser (or someone using a right of way) might come into the vicinity of that dangerous feature; and (iii) he can reasonably be expected to offer some protection against that danger.

(3) *Under the general law of negligence* – under which an occupier will owe a variety of people a range of duties of care: (i) to his visitors, a new duty – only recently established – to take reasonable steps to protect them against being harmed by fellow visitors; (ii) to his neighbours, a duty to take reasonable steps to abate hazards arising on his land that threaten to damage his neighbours' land; (iii) to people passing by his land, a duty to take reasonable steps to avoid their being injured as a result of any fixtures on his land falling into the road outside his land.

An important issue is whether an occupier of land can rely on a notice he has put up on his land to escape being held liable to someone who has been injured on his land. To address this issue, we need to distinguish between three types of notice. The first type of notice is a *disclaimer* notice, making it clear that the occupier does not accept that he has any duty to look out for the safety of people on his land. An example of a disclaimer notice is:

> No responsibility accepted for the safety of people or their property on these premises

The second type of notice is an *exclusion* notice, where the occupier accepts that he has a duty to look out for the safety of people on his land, but puts people on notice that if they want to come onto his land, they have to agree that they will not sue him (or only sue him for a limited amount of money) if he fails in that duty and they suffer harm as a result. An example of an exclusion notice is:

> No liability accepted to anyone suffering harm on these premises

The third type of notice is a *warning* notice, telling people coming onto the occupier's land of a particular danger on that land. An example of a warning notice is:

> Warning! Risk of death or injury beyond this point

The following table provides a rough guide to the law on when an occupier of premises can rely on one of the above types of notices to escape being held liable to a claimant who has been harmed on his premises; we will discuss this issue in much more detail in § 10.4:

Type of notice the occupier tries to rely on as against . . .	Disclaimer	Exclusion	Warning
Visitor	Domestic occupiers can rely on notice, but businesses cannot in death or personal injury cases and can only do so in other cases where reasonable to do so.	Domestic occupiers can rely on notice, but businesses cannot in death or personal injury cases and can only do so in other cases where reasonable to do so.	Can always be relied on if it enabled visitor to be reasonably safe (because occupier will have discharged the duty of care to visitor by giving warning).
Trespasser	Can never be relied on.	Domestic occupiers can rely on notice, but businesses cannot in death or personal injury cases and can only do so in other cases where reasonable to do so.	Can always be relied on if it enabled trespasser to be reasonably safe (because occupier will have discharged the duty of care to trespasser by giving warning).

As we have said, the above table provides only a rough guide to the law, but already some distinctions are obvious:

(1) *Visitors* v *trespassers.* In one way, visitors to *Occupier*'s land are in a better position than trespassers on that land. Under OLA 1957, *Occupier* will automatically owe his visitors a duty of care, while he will only owe trespassers a duty of care to protect them against certain dangers on his land so long as certain conditions (set out in (2), above) are satisfied in respect of those dangers. But the 1957 Act allows *Occupier* to disclaim the duty of care that it imposes on him for the benefit of his visitors, while there is no equivalent provision in the OLA 1984. So if you are faced with an obdurate and callous *Occupier* who makes it clear to you that he is not accepting any responsibility for your safety, you are actually better off being a trespasser on his land as opposed to a visitor. This is very odd.

(2) *Domestic occupiers* v *business occupiers.* The oddness of the law is somewhat mitigated by statute law which places limits on the ability of businesses to rely on a disclaimer or an exclusion notice to escape being held liable to a claimant who has suffered harm on their land: they can never rely on a disclaimer or exclusion notice where the claimant has been killed or injured (Consumer Rights Act 2015 ('CRA'), s 65 (where the claimant counts as a 'consumer'), and Unfair Contract Terms Act 1977 ('UCTA'), s 2(1) (where the claimant does not)[1]). In cases where the claimant suffers some other kind of loss (such as damage to his property) the business cannot rely on the disclaimer or exclusion notice to avoid being held liable to the claimant if the disclaimer or notice was 'unfair' (where the claimant counts as a 'consumer': CRA, s 62) or 'unreasonable' (where the claimant does not: UCTA, s 2(2)). But UCTA does not place any limits on the abilities of ordinary householders to rely on a disclaimer or exclusion notice to escape being held liable to a visitor who has been harmed in their home.

(3) *Disclaimers/exclusions* v *warnings.* The law is therefore quite hostile to businesses trying to escape being held liable to people harmed on their land by relying on disclaimer or exclusion notices that they placed on their property. But there is nothing wrong at all with a business (or any other kind of occupier) trying to rely on a warning notice to avoid being held liable to a claimant who has been injured on the occupier's land. In doing so, the occupier will be trying to argue: 'I know I owed the claimant a duty of care to protect her against a particular danger arising on my land, but I was careful to protect her: I warned her against the danger, and my warning was sufficient to allow her to avoid that danger.' If that plea is made out, there is no basis for holding the occupier liable to the claimant: the occupier took all the care he was required to take to protect the claimant from harm.

10.2 Occupiers' Liability Act 1957

A. Establishing a duty under the Act

Nine points need to be borne in mind, in considering whether or not a defendant owed a claimant a duty of care under the 1957 Act.

---

[1] A person who has been killed or injured on business premises will *not* count as being a 'consumer' if, in being on those premises, he was *not* 'acting for purposes that [were] wholly or mainly outside [his or her] trade, business, craft or profession' (CRA, s 2(3)).

(1) *The common duty of care.* Section 2 of OLA 1957 provides that:

1. An occupier of premises owes the same duty, the 'common duty of care', to all his visitors, except in so far as he is free to and does extend, restrict, modify or exclude his duty to any visitor or visitors by agreement or otherwise.

2. The common duty of care is a duty to take such care as in all the circumstances of the case is reasonable to see that the visitor will be reasonably safe in using the premises for the purposes for which he is invited or permitted to be there.

(2) *Premises.* Section 1(3) of OLA 1957 provides that the 'common duty of care' will extend not just to occupiers of land, but also any person 'occupying or having control over any fixed or moveable structure, including any vessel, vehicle or aircraft.' But for the purposes of the discussion below, we will disregard this point and focus on the 'common duty of care' that an occupier of land will owe other people under OLA 1957.

(3) *Occupier.* The term 'occupier' is not defined in OLA 1957, but in *Wheat v E Lacon & Co Ltd* (1966), Lord Denning suggested that:

> . . . wherever a person has a sufficient degree of control over premises that he ought to realise that any failure on his part to use care may result in injury to a person coming lawfully there, then he is an 'occupier' . . . In order to be an occupier it is not necessary for a person to have entire control over the premises. He need not have exclusive occupation. Two or more people may be 'occupiers'.[2]

We can distinguish four situations: (a) where *Owner* – or no one[3] – lives in the house owned by *Owner*; (b) where *Owner* has leased the house he owns to *Tenant*; (c) where *Owner* is not living in the house he owns, but is permitting *Licensee* to live there on a casual basis; (d) where *Owner* is not living in the house he owns because *Contractor* is currently doing work renovating the house. *Owner* will be an occupier of the house in (a) and (c) because he has control over the house.[4] He will not be an occupier of the house in (b) because *Tenant* will have control over the house; so *Tenant* will be the occupier of the house in (b).[5] In (d), *Owner* will be an occupier of the house because he has control over it; but *Contractor* might *also* be an occupier, depending on how much control he has over who comes into the house.

(4) *Visitor.* Not everyone who goes onto someone's premises does so as the occupier's 'visitor'. If B enters premises occupied by A, B will do so as A's 'visitor' if: (i) B was *invited* or *permitted* to enter those premises by A; or (ii) B was invited or permitted to enter those premises by someone who had the ostensible authority to issue such an invitation or permission on A's behalf.[6]

---

[2] [1966] AC 552, 577.

[3] See *Harris* v *Birkenhead Corporation* [1976] 1 WLR 279 (an abandoned house which was compulsorily purchased by the defendant local authority was occupied by the defendant local authority even though it never took possession of the house).

[4] Cf. *Wheat* v *E Lacon & Co Ltd* [1966] AC 522 (defendants still counted as occupiers of first floor of pub despite letting manager of pub use first floor as private accommodation).

[5] Where *Owner* only leases part of the house to *Tenant*, *Owner* will still count as being an occupier of the parts of the premises that are not leased to *Tenant*: *Ribee* v *Norrie* (2001) 33 HLR 777 (sitting room of hostel occupied by owner of hostel).

[6] For a discussion of the concept of 'ostensible authority' in this context, see *Ferguson* v *Welsh* [1987] 1 WLR 1553, 1563 (per Lord Goff).

(5) *Estoppel*. It will generally not be difficult to establish whether (i) or (ii), above, are true.[7] But even if they are not, A may still be prevented (or estopped) from denying that B entered his premises as his 'visitor' if he (or someone with ostensible authority to act on his behalf) reasonably led B to *believe* that A had invited or permitted her to be on those premises. As Lord Oaksey observed in *Edwards v Railway Executive* (1952):

> in considering the question whether a licence can be inferred, the state of mind of the suggested licensee must be considered. The circumstances must be such that the suggested licensee could have thought and did think that he was not trespassing but was on the property in question by the leave and licence of its owner.[8]

For example, in *Lowery v Walker* (1911), members of the public had for about 35 years taken a short cut across the defendant's field to get to a railway station. In all that time, the defendant never started legal proceedings to try and get people to stop crossing his field. The House of Lords found that by acting in this way the defendant had led members of the public to believe that they were permitted to cross his land to access the railway station and could not therefore now argue that they were trespassing on his land when they cut across his land for that purpose.

(6) *Ceasing to be a visitor*. A claimant who enters a defendant's premises as a visitor may cease to be a visitor if he goes beyond the bounds within which he is permitted (or has been led to believe he is permitted) to be there. As Scrutton LJ famously observed in *The Calgarth* (1927): 'when you invite a person into your house to use the staircase, you do not invite him to slide down the bannisters.'[9]

Until very recently, this *dictum* had always been interpreted as meaning that as *Guest* slid down the bannisters in *Host*'s house, *Guest* would no longer be a visitor, but a trespasser. So at the moment he was sliding down the bannister, he would no longer be protected by OLA 1957 against (for example) the risk of being cut by a splinter of wood sticking out of the bannister, but he might be protected instead by OLA 1984 (which governs the duties of care an occupier owes trespassers). However, in *Harvey v Plymouth City Council* (2010), Carnwath LJ (with whom the other two members of the Court of Appeal agreed) entertained the novel proposition that as *Guest* was sliding down the bannisters, he might still be a visitor, but would not be protected by OLA 1957's 'common duty of care', which only requires an occupier to take steps to see that a visitor is reasonably safe 'for the purposes for which he is invited or permitted to be there'.[10] We think this suggestion is dangerous, as it threatens to consign *Guest* to a legal limbo: neither protected by OLA 1957 (because he is a visitor, but not protected by the 'common duty of care' in sliding down the bannisters) nor by OLA 1984 (because he is a visitor, and not a trespasser). The safest view is that in the situation we are considering, *Guest* is a trespasser at the moment he is sliding down the bannisters.

In the *Harvey* case, the claimant was injured when drunkenly running about in the dark on a piece of council land adjoining and overlooking a supermarket car park: he tripped over the chain link fence at the boundary of the land and fell about 18 feet into the car park below. He suffered brain damage as a result of the fall. The Court of Appeal

---

[7] Though see the extraordinary facts of *R v Collins* [1973] QB 100, where the defendant climbed up to the window of a young lady's bedroom and she invited him in for sex, in the mistaken belief that he was her boyfriend.

[8] [1952] AC 737, 748.

[9] [1927] P 93, 110.

[10] [2010] EWCA Civ 860, at [22].

found that the defendant council had not owed the claimant a 'common duty of care' under OLA 1957 as he was drunkenly running about. The land had been used for a long time – without any objection from the council – by teenagers wanting somewhere to hang out or fool around with each other. The Court of Appeal held that such teenagers 'had every reason to think that they were there with the licence of the owners' and were therefore 'visitors' for the purpose of OLA 1957.[11] However, no one using the land could have thought that the council was permitting people to use it for activities that carried an 'obvious risk of accident'.[12] So, by drunkenly running about in the dark, the claimant ceased to be a visitor for the purposes of OLA 1957.[13]

(7) *Persons lawfully on the premises.* Section 2(6) of OLA 1957 provides that the 'common duty of care' that an occupier of premises owes his visitors will also be owed to someone who enters the premises 'in the exercise of a right conferred by law'. There is, however, an important exception to this. Section 1(4) of OLA 1957 provides that 'a person entering any premises in exercise of rights conferred by . . . the Countryside and Rights of Way Act 2000, or . . . the National Parks and Access to the Countryside Act 1949' will not be protected by OLA 1957; such a person comes under OLA 1984.

(8) *State of the premises.* Although section 1(1) of OLA 1957 provides that OLA 1957 'regulate[s] the duty which an occupier of premises owes to his visitors in respect of dangers due to the state of the premises *or to things done or omitted to be done on them*',[14] it is now generally accepted that the duties of care imposed on occupiers by both OLA 1957 and OLA 1984 are duties to protect people from being harmed as a result of the *state of the premises* being in a dangerous condition.[15]

The key case – although it deals with OLA 1984, rather than OLA 1957 – is *Tomlinson* v *Congleton BC* (2004). In that case, it may be recalled, the claimant was injured when he went swimming in a lake on the defendant council's land. He had no permission to go swimming in the lake and so was trespassing on the council's land when he went into the lake. The claimant sued the council for compensation under OLA 1984 but his claim was dismissed: the claimant had not been harmed as a result of the state of the council's premises being in a dangerous condition. As Lord Hoffmann observed of the lake in the *Tomlinson* case:

> There was nothing special about [the lake]; there were no hidden dangers. It was shallow in some places and deep in others, but that is the nature of lakes. Nor was the council doing or permitting anything to be done which created a danger to persons who came to the lake. No power boats or jet skis threatened the safety of either lawful windsurfers or unlawful swimmers.[16]

---

[11] [2010] EWCA Civ 860, at [18].

[12] [2010] EWCA Civ 860, at [27].

[13] [2010] EWCA Civ 860, at [28]. Note that Carnwarth LJ's conclusion on this point is in line with the traditional reading of Scrutton LJ's *dictum* in *The Calgarth*, and inconsistent with his suggestion (at [22]) that a visitor who exceeds the bounds for which he is permitted to be on another's premises might remain a visitor, but will not be protected by the 'common duty of care'.

[14] Emphasis added.

[15] *Fairchild* v *Glenhaven Funeral Services Ltd* [2002] 1 WLR 1052 (CA), at [109]–[133]; *Everett* v *Comojo (UK) Ltd* [2011] EWCA Civ 13, at [33] ('the relationship between the parties already carries with it an established duty, under the Occupiers' Liability Act 1957, in relation to *the condition of the premises*' (emphasis added)).

[16] [2004] 1 AC 46, at [26]. In *Lear* v *Hickstead* [2016] EWHC 528 (QB), Picken J held (at [40]) that a duty of care could arise under the 1957 Act in respect of *any* activity conducted on the defendant's premises other than 'an activity carried out by a claimant'. This seems too strong: only activities that *make use of* the premises in a *continuous* fashion can be said to have affected the *state* of the premises.

Could the claimant have argued that the lake *itself* was a dangerous feature of the land on which it was located and that he had therefore been injured because the council's land had a dangerous feature? Not on the facts of *Tomlinson*, where the claimant was a mature adult: the mere existence of the lake did not pose any kind of danger to *him*.[17] However, it might have been different if the claimant in *Tomlinson* had been a *small child* who fell into the lake and was injured.

The decision of the Court of Appeal in *Keown* v *Coventry Healthcare NHS Trust* (2006) makes it clear that in such a case the lake *itself* would have counted as a dangerous feature of the land – with regard to the child – if the child was unaware of the danger of drowning that it was incurring by going near the lake. So if the child in our imagined case was too young to appreciate the danger posed by going near the lake on the council's land, the council would have owed the child a duty to take reasonable steps to protect him from that danger.[18] In the *Keown* case itself, the claimant was a child who was injured when he fell from a fire escape attached to the defendants' accommodation block; the claimant had been climbing the fire escape to impress his friends. The Court of Appeal held that the defendants had not owed the claimant a duty under the 1984 Act to take reasonable steps to protect him from the danger of falling from the fire escape. As the claimant well knew how dangerous it was to climb the fire escape, the mere presence of the fire escape did not pose any danger to *him*; it was what he chose to do on the fire escape that put him in danger.

(9) *Property*. So far we have been assuming that an occupier's duty under OLA 1957 will be to take reasonable steps to protect visitors on his land from being physically injured. However, s 1(3) of OLA 1957 makes it clear that the 'common duty of care' extends to taking reasonable steps to see that *property* that is lawfully on the premises is not damaged or destroyed as a result of the occupier's premises being in a dangerous condition, which duty will be owed to whoever happens to own the property at the time it is on the premises (whether the owner is a visitor or not).

B. Establishing a breach of a duty under the Act

All of the principles set out in Chapter 7 of this text will be relevant to the inquiry as to whether an occupier of premises breached the 'common duty of care' he owed a visitor. However, OLA 1957 makes a number of specific points about when we can find this 'common duty of care' has been breached, which we will consider below.

(1) *Children*. Section 2(3)(a) provides that an occupier 'must be prepared for children to be less careful than adults'. So an occupier must do more to protect children from dangers on his land than he might have to do to protect adults: while a warning might be enough for an adult, fencing-off a danger might be necessary for a child. At the same time, children do normally come with adults (in the form of their parents, or carers) in tow, and if

---

[17] See *Donoghue* v *Folkestone Properties Ltd* [2003] QB 1008, at [36]: 'An expanse of water, be it a lake, pond, river or the sea, does not normally pose any danger to a person on land'; also *Baldacchino* v *West Wittering Council* [2008] EWHC 3386 (QB), holding (at [70]) that no danger due to the state of the premises existed in case where claimant dived into the sea off the defendants' beach from a navigation beacon at a time when (unknown to the claimant) that the tide was going out and the waters around the beacon were becoming shallow.

[18] If the child had been allowed to come onto the council's land then the said duty would have been owed under OLA 1957; if he had not been, then the duty would have been owed under OLA 1984 (assuming of course that all the other conditions required for a duty to have been owed under the 1984 Act were satisfied in this case).

an occupier can expect a child to be accompanied by an adult who can protect them from harm, a warning to the adult might be enough to protect the child. For example, in *Phipps* v *Rochester Corporation* (1955),[19] a boy fell into an unprotected trench that had been dug across some grassland for the purpose of laying a sewer. It was held that the defendant occupiers of the land had not breached the duty of care they owed the boy in doing nothing to protect children from falling into the trench: they could have reasonably expected the boy to have his parents with him and to protect him from this danger. However, note the date of the case: what might have been reasonable to expect in 1955 may be very different nowadays.[20]

(2) *Known risks.* An occupier will not be under a duty to take special steps to protect a visitor against a risk that the visitor knows about and can easily avoid given that he or she knows about it. Two provisions in OLA 1957 reflect this point. First, s 2(3)(b) provides that:

> an occupier may expect that a person, in the exercise of his calling, will appreciate and guard against any special risks ordinarily incident to it, so far as the occupier leaves him free to do so.

Secondly, s 2(4)(a) provides that:

> where damage is caused to a visitor by a danger of which he had been warned by the occupier, the warning is not to be treated without more as absolving the occupier from liability, unless in all the circumstances it was enough to enable the visitor to be reasonably safe . . .

(3) *Accepted risks.* Section 2(5) provides that the 'common duty of care' does not require an occupier to protect a visitor against 'risks willingly accepted as his by the visitor'. The maxim *volenti non fit injuria* will apply in such a case.

For example, in *Simms v Leigh Rugby Football Club* (1969), the defendant rugby club's ground had a concrete barrier running around the pitch, 7 feet from the touchline, in order to keep the spectators from going onto the pitch. It was held that S, a rugby player who played on the defendant rugby club's ground, took the risk that he would be injured by being thrown against this concrete barrier when he stepped onto the pitch – the existence and location of the barrier being permitted under the byelaws of the game, as laid down by the Rugby Football League. So the defendant rugby club did not owe S a duty to take care to ensure that he was not injured by being thrown against the concrete barrier around the pitch.

But *scienter* is not *volens* (knowing is not willing), and it is clear that when a visitor enters premises in the knowledge that she might be harmed in a particular way, she will not be held to have willingly taken the risk that she would be harmed in that way if she had no choice but to enter premises. For example, in *Burnett v British Waterways Board* (1973), B was employed to work on a barge which was being towed into the defendant's lock. B was injured when the rope towing the barge snapped and hit B. Even though B knew this might happen, it was not held that he had willingly taken the risk of being injured in this way. This is because B had no choice but to stay on the barge as it was towed into the defendant's lock.

(4) *Independent contractors.* We have already seen that the 'common duty of care' that an occupier of premises owes his visitors is *delegable*.[21] That is, an occupier can only be held

---

[19] [1955] 1 QB 450.

[20] Having said that, see *Bourne Leisure Ltd v Marsden* [2009] EWCA Civ 671, where the owners of a caravan site were *not* held liable for the drowning of a two-year-old in a pond on the caravan site based on their failure to warn the parents of the boy of the presence of the pond as it would have been obvious to the parents that it would be dangerous to let a two-year-old boy wander around the site unaccompanied.

[21] See above, § 7.5(B).

to have breached that duty of care if he *personally* failed to take reasonable steps to see that his visitors would be reasonably safe for the purposes for which they were on his premises. Section 2(4)(b) makes this clear:

> where damage is caused to a visitor by a danger due to the faulty execution of any work of construction, maintenance or repair by an independent contractor employed by the occupier, the occupier is not to be treated without more as answerable for the danger if in all the circumstances *he had acted reasonably* in entrusting the work to an independent contractor and had taken such steps (if any) as *he reasonably ought* in order to satisfy himself that the contractor was competent and that the work had been properly done.[22]

In *Gwilliam* v *West Hertfordshire Hospitals NHS Trust* (2003), the Court of Appeal suggested that an occupier might not have done as much as he reasonably ought in order to satisfy himself that the contractor was *competent* if he had not taken reasonable steps to reassure himself that the contractor carried *liability insurance*: the idea being that if a contractor did not carry liability insurance, that might raise a question mark over whether the contractor was actually that reputable, and therefore competent.[23] Sedley LJ dissented on this point in *Gwilliam*, observing that there is a big difference between reassuring yourself that a contractor is competent, and reassuring yourself that a contractor will be worth suing if he proves to be incompetent.[24]

Since *Gwilliam*, the Court of Appeal has twice said that it prefers Sedley LJ's reasoning on this point.[25] However, there may be one way of saving the majority's reasoning in *Gwilliam*. Going back to a point made much earlier in this text,[26] the need to carry liability insurance will place a substantial constraint on *Insured*'s behaviour: *Insured*'s *Insurer* will be in a strong position to dictate to *Insured* how he should conduct himself by holding over *Insured* the threat that if he does not do what *Insurer* tells him to do, his liability insurance will be withdrawn. So requiring a contractor to carry liability insurance may be a good way of ensuring that his work is 'properly done', by effectively subcontracting the job of ensuring that the contractor is competent to his liability insurer, who will have a substantial incentive (in the form of wanting to avoid having to pay out on the contractor's liability insurance policy) to ensure that the contractor performs his duties properly.

C. Wrong kind of loss

Even if *Occupier*'s breach of the 'common duty of care' that he owes to *Visitor* has caused *Visitor* injury, *Visitor* will be barred from suing *Occupier* for damages if the injury *Visitor* has suffered is the 'wrong kind of loss' – not the sort of injury the *Occupier* was supposed to be guarding against when he breached the 'common duty of care' that he owed *Visitor*.

The case of *Darby* v *National Trust* (2001) makes the point. In that case, the claimant's husband drowned swimming in a pond maintained by the defendants. The defendants breached the 'common duty of care' that they owed the husband under OLA 1957 in failing to warn him of the risk that he might contract Weil's Disease in swimming in the

---

[22] Emphasis added.
[23] [2003] QB 443, at [15] (per Lord Woolf CJ).
[24] [2003] QB 443, at [56].
[25] *Naylor* v *Payling* [2004] EWCA Civ 560; *Glaister* v *Appleby-in-Westmorland Town Council* [2009] EWCA Civ 1325.
[26] See above, § 1.15.

pond. Had they done so, the husband probably would not have gone swimming, and would not have drowned. However, the husband's *drowning* was the 'wrong kind of loss' to ground a claim for damages against the defendants here. *That* sort of harm – having nothing to do with Weil's Disease – was not the sort of harm that the defendants were duty-bound to protect the claimant's husband against suffering.

10.3 Occupiers' Liability Act 1984

A. Antecedents to the Act

Until 1984, the law drew a big distinction between an occupier's liability to his visitors and an occupier's liability to trespassers on his land. Reasonable care had to be taken to protect visitors from injury to their persons or property. In contrast, an occupier would only owe a trespasser a duty to take reasonable steps to protect them from harm when 'common humanity' demanded it.[27] This may have been acceptable when an adult was *deliberately* trespassing on someone else's land, but less so when a child went onto someone else's land to play, or a hiker lost his way and ended up trespassing on someone else's land. So OLA 1984 was passed in order to enhance the protection available to trespassers.

B. Establishing a duty under the Act

The following points should be borne in mind in determining whether a defendant owed a claimant a duty of care under the 1984 Act.

(1) *The basic rule* underlying OLA 1984 is that an occupier of premises will owe a duty:

> to persons other than his visitors in respect any risk of their suffering injury on the premises by reason of any danger due to the state of the premises or to things done or omitted to be done on them[28] . . . if –
>
> (a) he is aware of the danger or has reasonable grounds to believe that it exists;
> (b) he knows or has reasonable grounds to believe that . . . [someone who is not his visitor] may come into the vicinity of the danger; and
> (c) the risk is one against which . . . he may reasonably be expected to offer [someone who is not his visitor] some protection.[29]

If (a)–(c) are satisfied in relation to a particular danger, the occupier will owe someone who is not his visitor a duty to take reasonable steps to see that that someone 'does not suffer injury on the premises by reason of the danger concerned.'[30]

(2) *State of the premises.* As has already been observed, this duty is a duty to protect trespassers from being injured as a result of an occupier's premises being in a dangerous state.[31]

(3) *Protected persons.* The duty owed under OLA 1984 is to 'persons other than [the occupier's] visitors'. This does not just include trespassers but also, by virtue of s 1(4) of OLA 1957, 'a person entering any premises in exercise of rights conferred by . . . the Countryside

---

[27] *British Railway Board* v *Herrington* [1972] AC 877.
[28] Section 1(1)(a).
[29] Section 1(3).
[30] Section 1(4).
[31] See above, § 10.2(A)(8), above.

and Rights of Way Act 2000, or . . . the National Parks and Access to the Countryside Act 1949' (who is defined not to be a 'visitor' for the purposes of OLA 1957).

However, OLA 1984 makes various special provisions for the case where *Rambler* crosses land occupied by *Owner* using a right of way created by the Countryside and Rights of Way Act 2000. First, *Owner* will not owe *Rambler* a duty to protect her against a risk:

> resulting from the existence of any natural feature of the landscape, or any river, stream, ditch or pond whether or not a natural feature, or . . . a risk [that she will suffer injury] when passing over, under or through any wall, fence or gate, except by proper use of the gate or of a stile[32]

unless he has intentionally or recklessly created that risk.[33]

Secondly, if Owner *does* owe *Rambler* a duty of care under OLA 1984, the courts must, in determining whether that duty has been breached, have regard to the fact that the existence of the right of way under the 2000 Act being used by *Rambler* ought not to place an undue burden on *Owner*, and the importance of maintaining the character of the countryside.[34]

(4) *Public highway.* Someone crossing land using a public highway will not be protected either by OLA 1957,[35] or by OLA 1984.[36] However, someone who is injured as a result of the public highway being in a dangerous condition may be able to sue the highway authority that it is in charge of its maintenance under s 41 of the Highways Act 1980.[37]

(5) *Property.* The duty of care (if any) owed by an occupier of premises to someone on those premises who is not his visitor is a duty to take reasonable steps to protect them from being physically harmed by some dangerous feature of the premises: it does not require the occupier to take reasonable steps to see that anyone's property is not destroyed or damaged by that dangerous feature.

(6) *The importance of time.* An occupier of premises will only owe someone who is not his visitor a duty to take reasonable steps to protect them against a dangerous feature on his land if he knows or ought to know that people who are not his visitors may come into the vicinity of that dangerous feature. In *Donoghue v Folkestone Properties* (2003), the Court of Appeal held that whether this requirement was satisfied would depend on the *time* at which the claimant went onto the premises: it has to be shown that at *that* time, it was reasonably fore-seeable that people who were not the occupier's visitors would come into the vicinity of the dangerous feature that ended up harming the claimant. So in *Donoghue*, the claimant's claim that the defendant council owed him a duty of care to see that he did not injure himself by diving onto a submerged gridbed in the defendant's harbour was dismissed on the ground that the claimant had dived onto the gridbed in the *middle of winter* – at a time, therefore, that no one could have been expected to try to dive into the harbour. It would have been different if the diver had executed his dive in the middle of *summer*. At *that* time of year, it would have been reasonably foreseeable that trespassers *would* go near the submerged grid-bed (by jumping into the harbour at a spot over the gridbed) and so the council in *Donoghue* would have come under a duty to provide trespassers with some protection against that danger by, for example, posting up warning signs telling people not to jump into the harbour.

---

[32] Section 1(6A).
[33] Section 1(6C)
[34] Section 1A.
[35] *McGeown v Northern Ireland Housing Executive* [1995] 1 AC 233.
[36] Section 1(7).
[37] Discussed below, § 18.4.

(7) *Accepted risks.* Section 1(6) of OLA 1984 mirrors s 2(5) of OLA 1957 in that it provides that no duty is owed under OLA 1984 'to any person in respect of risks willingly accepted by that person'. This provision was applied in *Ratcliff* v *McConnell* (1999), where the claimant was a student, R, who suffered serious injuries when he dived into his college's swimming pool at the shallow end. The pool was locked up for the winter and so when R used the swimming pool he did not do so as a visitor. R sued the college's governors, seeking to recover compensation for his injuries under OLA 1984. The Court of Appeal dismissed his claim, holding that when he dived into the swimming pool he willingly took the risk that he would be killed or injured as a result. He knew when he made his dive that there was a risk that the swimming pool would be too shallow to dive in but he nevertheless went ahead with his dive.

C. The boundary between OLA 1957 and OLA 1984

It can sometimes be a difficult question which Act to apply to determine whether an occupier of premises owed a claimant a duty to protect them against a dangerous feature of those premises. Consider, for example, the **Slippery Floor Problem**:

> *Host* held a dinner party at her house. She told all her guests they could go anywhere in the house, except into the kitchen. *Guest* – suspecting that *Host* had prohibited her guests from going into the kitchen to prevent them discovering that she had not actually cooked the dinner herself but was instead serving takeaway food – walked into the kitchen and promptly slipped on the floor and suffered a severe spinal injury. *Host* had in fact told everyone not to go into the kitchen because she had had to clean up some food that she had spilled on the floor and as a result the floor was extremely slippery.

Suppose *Guest* wants to sue *Host* for compensation for his injury. But which OLA applies to determine whether or not a duty of care was owed in this case? The argument for thinking that we must look to OLA 1957 is that we want to know whether *Host* owed *Guest* a duty to take reasonable steps to *stop* him going into her kitchen, as by the time he was in the kitchen it would have been too late to save him from harm. That duty – to stop *Guest* going into the kitchen – must have been owed to *Guest before* he went into *Host*'s kitchen and *at that stage*, *Guest* was a visitor.[38] So we should look to OLA 1957 to determine whether *Host* owed *Guest* a duty to take reasonable steps to stop him going into her kitchen. The logic of this argument seems impeccable, but a majority of the House of Lords ruled in *Tomlinson* v *Congleton BC* (2004) that we should in fact look at OLA *1984* to determine whether *Host* owed *Guest* a duty to take reasonable steps to stop him going into her kitchen.[39] On this view, the 1984 Act not only determines when you have a duty to protect a *trespasser* on your land from some danger arising on your premises but also when you have a duty to take reasonable steps to stop a *visitor* of yours from entering a dangerous area of your land which she is not permitted to enter.

---

[38] Of course, as soon as he entered the kitchen, he became a trespasser: see § 10.2(A)(6), above.

[39] Applying the Act, the question of whether *Host* did owe *Guest* such a duty under the 1984 Act will largely turn on whether *Host* knew or ought to have known that despite her prohibition someone like *Guest* would attempt to enter the kitchen. If this condition is satisfied, then the courts may well find that *Host* owed *Guest* a duty to take reasonable steps to stop him going into the kitchen.

D. The difference between OLA 1957 and OLA 1984

It may be questioned whether – claims for property damage aside (which can be brought under OLA 1957, but not under OLA 1984) – the extent of protection afforded by OLA 1957 to visitors is any more extensive than the protection afforded by OLA 1984 to non-visitors. If it is not, it is hard to see why we have separate Occupiers' Liability Acts. Test it this way. Imagine that a *Visitor* is injured on premises occupied by *Owner* as a result of those premises having a dangerous *Feature, but*

1. *Owner* did not know, and had no reason to know, about *Feature*; *or*

2. *Owner* did know about *Feature* but had no reason to suppose someone like *Visitor* would go anywhere near it; *or*

3. Owner did know about *Feature* but it would have been unreasonable to expect him to do anything to protect *Visitor* against being harmed by *Feature*.

If any of (1), (2) or (3) were established, would *Visitor* be able to sue *Owner* for compensation under OLA 1957? If the answer is 'no' then *Visitor* would be *no better off* than a *Trespasser* who wanted to sue *Owner* for compensation for being injured by *Feature* and who would only be able to sue under OLA 1984 if none of (1), (2) or (3) were true in his case. We think the answer is 'no'. Given this, the only possible explanation as to why we have separate Occupiers' Liability Acts is ideological – that people would be uncomfortable with the idea that the law affords the same protection to visitors as it does to non-visitors. But (cases of property damage aside) it seems that the differences between OLA 1957 and OLA 1984 are more apparent than real.

10.4 Warnings, disclaimers, exclusions

Suppose that *Hurt* has been injured as a result of some dangerous *Feature* of land occupied by *Owner*. In this section, we are concerned with three different arguments *Owner* might make if *Hurt* sues him for damages under OLA 1957 or OLA 1984: (1) 'I warned *Hurt* about *Feature*'; (2) 'I told *Hurt* I did not accept any responsibility for his safety'; (3) '*Hurt* agreed that if he was injured on my land, he would not sue me'.

By making argument (1), *Owner* is saying that he is not liable to *Hurt* because he did not do anything wrong to *Hurt*. While he did owe *Hurt* a duty of care to protect him from being harmed by *Feature*, he did not breach that duty because by warning *Hurt* about *Feature*, he took reasonable steps to protect *Hurt* from being harmed by *Feature*.

By making argument (2), *Owner* is again saying that he is not liable to *Hurt* because he did not do anything wrong to *Hurt*. But on this occasion – unlike with argument (1) – *Owner* is saying that he did not do anything wrong to *Hurt* because he did *not* owe *Hurt* a duty of care to protect him from being harmed by *Feature*. In effect, *Owner* is arguing here that by telling *Hurt* that he did not accept any responsibility for his safety, he effectively *disclaimed* any duty of care that he might otherwise have owed *Hurt*.

By making argument (3), *Owner* is conceding that he did something wrong to *Hurt* and *Hurt* was injured as a result, but is saying that *Hurt* still cannot sue him because *Hurt* agreed that he would not sue him if he was injured. In effect, *Owner* is arguing here that *Hurt*'s agreement not to sue has effectively *excluded* the liability that *Owner* would otherwise have incurred to *Hurt* under OLA 1957 or OLA 1984.

We will now look at how far an occupier of land can rely on each of these arguments to defeat a claim for damages that is being made against him under OLA 1957 or OLA 1984.

A. Warnings

OLA 1957 makes it clear that in a case where *Visitor* has been harmed by a dangerous feature of premises occupied by *Owner*, *Owner can* rely on the fact that he warned *Visitor* of that danger to establish that he discharged 'the common duty of care' that he owed *Visitor* to see that *Visitor* would be reasonably safe in using those premises, *so long as Owner*'s warning 'was enough to enable the [claimant] to be reasonably safe'.[40] Section 1(5) of OLA 1984 says something slightly different:

> Any duty owed [under OLA 1984] in respect of a risk may, in an appropriate case, be discharged by taking such steps as are reasonable in all the circumstances of the case to give warning of the danger concerned or to discourage persons from incurring the risk.

The difference in language may reflect the fact that a trespasser who has been warned of a danger can always walk away from it, back the way he came. In contrast, a visitor might have no choice but to incur a danger, even if they have been warned of it. (For example, a babysitter might be warned that the staircase at the top of which the child she is looking after is sleeping is dangerous; but that warning will not enable her to be reasonably safe if the child starts crying and needs attention.)[41] So a warning to a trespasser always enables the trespasser to be reasonably safe; whereas this is not necessarily so with a warning given to a visitor.

So long as a warning given by the occupier *was* enough to enable the claimant to be safe, and reasonable efforts were made to bring that warning to the claimant's attention, the occupier will be able to argue that he discharged the duty of care that he owed the claimant to see that the claimant would be safe on his land, whether the duty was owed under OLA 1957 or OLA 1984. There is nothing in the Consumer Rights Act 2015 ('CRA') or Unfair Contract Terms Act 1977 ('UCTA') that would prevent the occupier relying on the fact that such a warning has been given to defeat the claimant's claim against him: in such a case, the occupier is not trying to avoid being held liable to the claimant. There is no liability to avoid: he is simply not liable.

B. Disclaimers of duty to visitors

Section 2(1) of OLA 1957 says that:

> An occupier of premises owes the same duty, the 'common duty of care', to all his visitors, except in so far as he is free to and does extend, restrict, modify or exclude his duty to any visitor or visitors by agreement or otherwise.

This suggests that an occupier can disclaim the 'common duty of care' that he would otherwise owe a visitor under OLA 1957. The Act says the occupier can do this 'by agreement or otherwise'. The '. . . or otherwise' is an implicit reference to the Court of Appeal's decision in *Ashdown* v *Samuel Williams Ltd* (1957), which said that merely notifying a visitor that you were not accepting any responsibility for their safety would be effective to disclaim the duty of care that you might otherwise owe them as an occupier of land.

---

[40] Section 2(4)(a).
[41] See, for example, *The Intruder Detection and Surveillance Fire & Security Ltd* v *Fulton* [2008] EWCA Civ 1009 (warning to employee who had to go upstairs to fit a security system that the stairs and landing at the top of the stairs had no protective bannister did not enable the employee to be reasonably safe).

There is no need to show that the visitor *agreed* to this, or that there was a contract between the visitor and the occupier which specified that the occupier would not owe the visitor a duty of care. It is, however, worth noting the facts which led the Court of Appeal in *Ashdown* to find that no duty of care was owed to the claimant in that case:

> The [claimant] saw this notice [which said that 'This property is private property. Every person . . . whilst on the said property is there entirely at his own risk . . .']; she read the first few lines of it; she knew that she went on the . . . defendants' premises at her own risk . . . We are, I think, bound to hold that she entered upon the premises by licence from the . . . defendants, and on the conditions contained in the notice.[42]

This suggests that for a notice to work to disclaim the 'common duty of care' that the occupier of land would otherwise owe a visitor: (1) the visitor has to see the notice; (2) the visitor has to understand it; and (3) the visitor has to be entering on the occupier's land by virtue of being invited or permitted to come onto the land, rather than entering the land by right. If any of these conditions are not made out (for example, if the visitor is a child, it is unlikely that conditions (1) or (2) will be made out), it is arguable that the notice will not work to release the occupier from the 'common duty of care' that he would otherwise owe the visitor under OLA 1957.

Even if these hurdles can be overcome, as we have already seen,[43] a *business* occupier of premises may still be prevented by CRA or UCTA from relying on an agreement or notice to argue that he did not owe a visitor a 'common duty of care'. This will automatically be the case where the business occupier seeks to rely on the agreement or notice to argue that because he did not owe the visitor a 'common duty of care', he is not liable for the visitor's being killed or injured. In such a case, either s 65 of CRA or s 2(1) of UCTA will apply to prevent the occupier doing this, depending on whether the visitor counts as being a 'consumer' or not. And if the business occupier attempts to argue that he is not liable for the visitor's property being damaged because an agreement or notice meant that he did not owe the visitor a 'common duty of care', then s 62 of CRA or s 2(2) of UCTA will prevent the business occupier making this argument if the agreement or notice in question was 'unfair' (s 62) or 'unreasonable' (s 2(2)) depending on whether the visitor counts as being a 'consumer' or not. Readers interested in knowing more about how these statutory provisions operate should consult a specialist work on the law of contract.

C. Disclaimers of duty to trespassers

While OLA 1957 does hold out the possibility that the 'common duty of care' imposed by it on occupiers might be disclaimed 'by agreement or otherwise', there is no similar provision in OLA 1984. If conditions (a)–(c) in s 1(3) of OLA 1984 are made out in respect of a dangerous feature on the occupier's land, then the occupier *will* owe someone who is not a visitor a duty to take reasonable steps 'to see that he does not suffer injury on the premises by reason of the danger concerned' (s 1(4)).

However, in the case where *Owner* has a prominent notice on land occupied by him saying 'Trespassers enter at their own risk', two strategies might be open to *Owner* to allow him to rely on that notice to say that he is not liable to *Trespasser*, who has been injured on *Owner*'s land as a result of that land having a dangerous *Feature*.

---

[42] [1957] 1 QB 409, 418 (per Singleton LJ).
[43] See above, §10.1.

(1) Section 1(3)(b) provides that *Owner* will only have owed *Trespasser* a duty of care under OLA 1984 if he knew or ought to have known that people like *Trespasser* were liable to come into the vicinity of *Feature*. *Owner* might try to argue that his notice meant that it was reasonable for him to think that no one like *Trespasser* would come anywhere near *Feature* – because anyone like *Trespasser* would be put off by the notice from even attempting to come onto *Owner*'s land. This is quite a weak argument, as not many people would be intimidated by a 'Trespassers enter at their own risk' notice into not going onto someone else's land.

(2) Section 1(6) provides that 'No duty is owed [under OLA 1984] to any person in respect of risks willingly accepted as his by that person . . .'. *Owner* might try to argue that if *Trespasser* saw his notice, he willingly accepted all and any risks of being injured that he would run by going onto *Owner*'s land, including the risk of being harmed by *Feature* – with the result that *Owner* would not have owed *Trespasser* a duty to protect him from being harmed by *Feature*. This is a more promising argument, but is vulnerable to the objection that it will not work in a case where *Trespasser* was injured by *Feature* in a way that he could not possibly have anticipated when he saw the notice 'Trespassers enter at their own risk'.[44]

Even if *Owner can* make an argument for saying that his notice meant that he did not owe *Trespasser* a duty to protect him against being harmed by *Feature*, it seems likely that *Owner* would be prevented from making this argument where he was an occupier of business premises as doing so would run counter to the clear intention (if not the language)[45] of CRA, s 65 and UCTA, s 2(1) that business should not be allowed to rely on notices to escape being held liable to individuals for those individuals being killed or injured.[46]

D. Exclusions

Subject to statutory provisions preventing him from doing so, a claimant can contract away his right to sue a defendant for damages if X happens so long as: (1) he has reasonably given the defendant the impression that he has agreed not to sue the defendant if X happens; and (2) he has received something in return – some *consideration* – for agreeing to do this. In light of this, let's consider the **Electrocuted Couple Problem**:

> *Husband* and *Wife* go to a rock concert put on by Promoter, planning to buy tickets on the door. At the entrance to the concert, where tickets are being sold for £50 per person, there are prominent signs saying 'No liability accepted for any harm suffered by anyone on the premises'. *Husband* thinks the price of the tickets is too high, so he decides to get into the concert some other way, which he does by going through a side door which is unlocked. *Wife* pays £50 for a ticket. *Husband* and *Wife* reunite inside the concert hall and both suffer electrocution burns as a result of stepping on a live cable that is, because of the fault of *Promoter*, insufficiently insulated.

---

[44] For example, if *Trespasser* was injured by a mantrap, or developed cancer as a result of being exposed to radiation from some illegally obtained uranium that *Owner* had left lying around his property.

[45] Technically, s 2(1) of UCTA does not apply to claims under OLA 1984 – presumably because UCTA was passed before OLA 1984 and no one remembered to update UCTA.

[46] An individual suffering some other kind of loss would not be protected under OLA 1984 anway: see above, § 10.2.

Subject to the statutory provisions contained in CRA and UCTA, we can say that *Wife* is bound by the notice saying 'No liability accepted . . .'. It was reasonably brought to her attention that *Promoter* was only willing to allow her to enter the concert hall on condition that she agreed not to sue *Promoter* if she suffered any kind of harm in the hall, and by buying a ticket, she reasonably gave the impression she was agreeing to that condition. If she did not want to agree to it, she need not have bought a ticket. And *Wife* has obtained something in return – some *consideration* – for agreeing to waive her rights to sue *Promoter* for damages under OLA 1957, by being allowed into the concert hall.

In contrast, it is much tougher to say that *Husband* is bound by the notice saying 'No liability accepted . . .'. He did not buy a ticket, and so did not give the impression that he was agreeing to this condition. And even if he did, he did not obtain anything in return for agreeing to that condition. So it seems that – again, subject to the statutory provisions in CRA and UCTA – *Promoter* can rely on the *exclusion clause* in the notice at the entrance to defeat *Wife*'s claim for damages under OLA 1957, but cannot use it against *Husband*, who will be suing *Promoter* under OLA 1984. However, there seems to be something wrong with this conclusion. Why should *Husband* benefit from his illegal act of sneaking into the concert hall? However, statute law comes to the rescue here and kicks in to ensure that, in the end, *Husband* and *Wife* will be treated equally in this case. If *Promoter* tries to rely on the exclusion clause in the notice at the entrance to defeat *Wife*'s claim for damages under OLA 1957, *Wife* can invoke s 65 of CRA to prevent him from doing this: *Promoter* will not be allowed to rely on an exclusion clause to exclude his liability for 'death or personal injury resulting from negligence'.

10.5 Liability under the general law of negligence

That concludes our discussion of occupiers' liability under OLA 1957 and OLA 1984. We now turn to situations where an occupier will be held liable to a claimant under the general law of negligence.

A. Liability to visitors

An occupier will, of course, owe people on his land a normal *Donoghue* v *Stevenson* type duty to take care not to do something *positive* that would put them in unreasonable danger of being killed or injured.[47] However, so far as *omissions* were concerned, it was thought until recently that the Occupiers' Liability Act 1957 was the only basis on which an occupier could be found to owe a visitor a *positive* duty to act to save that visitor from harm. That has now proved to be incorrect.

In *Everett* v *Comojo (UK) Ltd* (2011), the claimants were drinking at a nightclub, the Met Bar in the Metropolitan Hotel in London. A member of the club, SB, was aggrieved

---

[47] *Slater* v *Clay Cross Co Ltd* [1956] 2 QB 264, 269 (per Lord Denning MR) (example of occupier driving a car down the drive and meeting someone coming the other way). *Lear* v *Hickstead* [2016] EWHC 528 (QB) can arguably be analysed in the same way. The defendants were held to owe the claimant driver a duty of care in respect of how they organised parking on their premises during a horse show merely because (at [49]) it was foreseeable that the way they organised the parking might result in physical injury to someone like the claimant (who was injured because a ramp on his horse box that had been lifted up by unknown persons in order to clear a space for them to drive out of the defendants' premises collapsed on the claimant when he attempted to lower the ramp).

at the discourteous way in which, in his opinion, the claimants had treated their waitress. He took it on himself to remonstrate with them, more than once. Things gradually got out of control, and the claimants ended up being stabbed by an associate of SB's. Instead of suing the associate for damages, the claimants sued the defendant owners of the Met Bar. Their claim was dismissed: there was no evidence that the defendants had failed to take care to protect the claimants from being injured in the way they were. However, the importance of the case is that the Court of Appeal held that the defendants *had* owed the claimants a duty of care under the general law of negligence to protect them from being injured by a third party on the defendants' premises. Smith LJ held (with the agreement of the other two members of the court):

> I regard it as relevant that the relationship between the parties already carries with it an established duty, under the Occupiers' Liability Act 1957, in relation to the condition of the premises . . . It would be surprising if management could be liable to a guest who tripped over a worn carpet and yet escape liability for injuries inflicted by a fellow guest who was a foreseeable danger – for example in that he had previously been excluded on account of his violent behaviour and who on this occasion had been allowed in carrying an offensive weapon.[48]

Smith LJ's reasoning is hard to understand. If Parliament has legislated in the form of OLA 1957 to impose on occupiers a duty to take reasonable steps to protect visitors from dangerous features of the premises they occupy, it is hard to see how that warrants the common law imposing a duty on occupiers to protect visitors against risks from the activities of third parties on those premises. Parliament's failure to impose such a duty of care on occupiers in OLA 1957 is far more likely to indicate that Parliament did *not* want occupiers to be subject to such a duty of care, than it indicates that Parliament was happy for the courts to develop such a duty of care in parallel to the 'common duty of care' imposed by OLA 1957.

Be that as it may, *Everett* (unless and until it is overruled by the Supreme Court) at its *narrowest* stands for the proposition that an occupier will owe his visitors a duty under the common law to take care to protect them from being attacked by a third party and at its *widest* stands for the proposition that an occupier will owe his visitors a duty under the common law to take care to see that they are not injured by third parties engaging in unreasonably dangerous activities on his premises. It is uncertain at the moment just how far *Everett* goes.[49]

B. Liability to trespassers

Section 1(1) of OLA 1984 provides that OLA 1984 'shall have effect, in place of the rules of the common law, to determine' whether any duty is owed by an occupier of premises to non-visitors 'in respect of any risk of their suffering injury on the premises by reason of

---

[48] [2011] EWCA Civ 13, at [33].

[49] Para [36] of Smith LJ's judgment (which starts 'The common duty of care is an extremely flexible concept, adaptable to the very wide range of circumstances to which it has to be applied. It can be applied to the static condition of the premises and to activities on the premises . . . I think that it is appropriate . . . that it [surely not the very duty of care imposed by s 2 of OLA 1957, but rather the principles applicable to that duty] should govern the relationship between the managers of a hotel or night club and their guests in relation to the actions of third parties on the premises' and which finishes 'In a nightclub where outbreaks of violence are not uncommon, liability might well attach if a guest is injured in an outbreak of violence and there is no one on hand to control the outbreak . . . On the other hand, in a respectable members-only club, where violence is virtually unheard of . . . the duty on management may be no higher than that staff be trained to look out for any sign of trouble and to alert security staff') seems to start with the wide view and then finish with the narrow view.

any danger due to the state of the premises . . .'. So OLA 1984 leaves space for the common law to determine what duties of care occupiers owe trespassers in respect of risks of harm that do *not* result from dangers due to the state of the premises.

As usual, an occupier will owe trespassers a *Donoghue* v *Stevenson* style duty not to do a positive act that will create a foreseeable risk of a trespasser being injured, or his property being damaged.[50] So far as risks of harm that trespassers are exposed to as a result of the activities of third parties, the 'duty of common humanity' that occupiers owed trespassers before 1984 *may* still apply to determine whether an occupier owes a trespasser a duty to protect him or her against such a risk. The phrase 'duty of common humanity' comes from the case of *British Railways Board* v *Herrington* (1972), where – pre-OLA 1984 – the defendant railway company was held liable to compensate a child who had been electrocuted while walking over the defendants' railway line, which the child had access to because the defendants had allowed a fence separating the railway from a nearby meadow to fall into a dilapidated condition. But the danger there was created by the occupier[51] and situations where 'common humanity' would require an occupier to protect a trespasser against a risk of harm created by the activities of a third party may be few and far between – even assuming that the phrase 'duty of common humanity' was ever intended to apply outside cases where a trespasser was endangered by the state of the premises on which he was trespassing.

C. Liability to neighbours

An occupier of premises will owe a neighbour a duty to take reasonable steps to eliminate a dangerous situation that has arisen on his land if he knows or ought to know of that danger, and it is reasonably foreseeable that that danger threatens to damage his neighbour's land.

For example, in *Goldman* v *Hargrave* (1967), lightning struck a redgum tree on the defendant's land and set it on fire. The defendant cut down the tree but then did not do enough to put out the fire. The fire spread onto the claimant's land, causing much damage. The claimant successfully sued the defendant in negligence for compensation for the damage done to his land.[52] The Privy Council held that the defendant had owed the

---

[50] *Revill* v *Newbery* [1996] QB 567 (duty to not to fire a gun through a hole in a shed door that a trespasser was standing behind, while trying to break into the shed).

[51] Indeed, given the facts, the House of Lords had no need to invoke a 'duty of common humanity' to explain why the claimant was owed a duty of care in this case: a *Donoghue* v *Stevenson* style duty to take care not to run electricity down the defendants' line while someone might be on it would have sufficed; as would have a duty of care to avert the foreseeable danger to people like the claimant that the defendants created by running electricity down their line.

[52] The claimant could have alternatively sued the defendant in *private nuisance* for compensation for the damage done to his land (see below, § 13.9(C)) and, indeed, it is customary nowadays for claims for damage done to land as a result of dangerous situations arising on neighbouring land to be brought in private nuisance rather than negligence (see, for example, *Leakey* v *National Trust for Places of Historic Interest or Natural Beauty* [1980] QB 485 and *Holbeck Hall Hotel Ltd* v *Scarborough BC* [2000] QB 836). Where the neighbour has suffered personal injury as a result of the defendant's failure to deal effectively with a fire arising on the defendant's land, a claim in private nuisance will be unavailable as claims for private nuisance do not cover personal injuries (see below, § 13.12). So in such a case, the neighbour would have to sue in negligence under *Goldman* v *Hargrave* [1967] 1 AC 645, but such a claim may be thrown out on the basis that the claimant's personal injury is the 'wrong kind of loss' to be sued for in negligence. That is, a court might find that the duty of care arising under *Goldman* v *Hargrave* was imposed on the defendant to protect his neighbour's land from being damaged, not in order to protect his neighbour from being injured.

claimant a duty to take reasonable steps to put out the fire on his land, and that the defendant had breached that duty.[53] Decisions of the Privy Council are, of course, not binding on the English courts but the House of Lords has indicated that the decision in *Goldman* v *Hargrave* was correct.[54]

It is more uncertain whether A will owe a duty to his neighbour B to take reasonable steps to prevent his premises *becoming* a source of danger to B's land. The question was raised in *Smith* v *Littlewoods* (1987). The defendants purchased a cinema: they intended to knock it down and redevelop the land. For a few months the cinema was left unattended and unlocked. Vandals broke into the cinema and set it on fire. The fire spread to and damaged the claimants' premises. The claimants sued the defendants: they argued that the defendants had owed them a duty to take reasonable steps to keep the cinema secure, so as to prevent the cinema becoming a source of danger to their premises. The House of Lords dismissed the claimants' claim on the ground that it had not been reasonably foreseeable that the claimants' premises would be harmed if the defendants' cinema was not kept secure.[55]

In the course of deciding the case, Lords Brandon and Griffiths indicated that in the situation we are considering, A *will* owe B a duty to take reasonable steps to prevent his premises *becoming* a source of danger to B's land.[56] In contrast, Lord Goff thought that an occupier of land will *not* owe his neighbours a duty to take proactive steps to prevent his land *becoming* a source of danger to his neighbours' land: he will only owe his neighbours a duty of care in a *Goldman* v *Hargrave*-type situation where a danger *has* arisen on his land and he knows or ought to know of its existence.[57] Lord Mackay steered a middle path between these two extremes. He thought that if A occupies some premises and it is reasonably foreseeable that if those premises are not kept secure vandals will break into A's premises and start a fire which is liable to spread to B's land, then A *will* owe B a duty to take reasonable steps to keep his premises secure, thereby preventing them becoming a source of danger to B's land.[58] But Lord Mackay thought things would be different in the case where it is reasonably foreseeable that if A's premises are not kept secure, thieves will break into A's premises and use those premises to gain access to B's land and steal property from B.[59] While he did not go so far as to say that *no* duty of care would be owed in this situation,[60] he plainly thought this case more difficult than the 'fire' case just

---

[53] Had the fire been intentionally or carelessly started by the defendant, the claimant would have been entitled to sue the defendant for compensation for the damage done to his land without having to prove that the defendant was at all careless in allowing the fire to spread: see below, § 14.4(A).

[54] *Stovin* v *Wise* [1996] AC 923, 930 (per Lord Nicholls), 944 (per Lord Hoffmann).

[55] [1987] AC 241, 250 (per Lord Brandon), 251 (per Lord Griffiths), 258–59 (per Lord Mackay).

[56] [1987] AC 241, 250: '[the defendants] owed to the [claimants] a duty to exercise reasonable care to ensure that the cinema . . . did not become . . . a source of danger to neighbouring buildings owned or occupied by the claimants' (per Lord Brandon); 'the duty of care owed [by the defendants] was a duty to take reasonable care that the condition of the premises they occupied was not a source of danger to neighbouring property' (per Lord Griffiths).

[57] [1987] AC 241, 272–4, 277–9.

[58] [1987] AC 241, 258.

[59] [1987] AC 241, 268.

[60] He did think that if A came back home to find a thief boring a hole through one of his walls to gain access to B's house, then A would owe B a duty to take reasonable steps to stop the thief gaining access to B's house in this way: [1987] AC 241, 265. However, this result can easily be justified by reference to *Goldman* v *Hargrave*. In the case considered here a danger *will* have arisen on A's land which A knows about and therefore A will owe those of his neighbours who will be affected by that danger a duty to take reasonable steps to deal with it.

discussed. Puzzlingly, the fifth judge to decide *Smith* v *Littlewoods* – Lord Keith of Kinkel – expressed agreement with the judgments of Lord Mackay *and* Lord Goff, despite the clear differences between them.

So *Smith* v *Littlewoods* did not finally resolve the issue of whether an occupier of premises will owe his neighbours a duty to take reasonable steps to prevent his property becoming a source of danger to his neighbours' land. The most that can be said in light of the decisions in that case is that there was a clear majority in favour of the proposition that such an occupier *will* owe his neighbours a duty to take reasonable steps to keep his premises secure *if* it is reasonably foreseeable that if he does not vandals will break in and start a fire which is liable to spread to his neighbours' land.

D. Liability to passers-by

The area of law we have just discussed overlaps with the law of private nuisance, which area of law helps to determine the rights and duties that neighbours owe each other. We now turn to an area of law which overlaps with the law on *public* nuisance, which helps (in part) prevent people's use of highways being unreasonably interfered with.

If *Owner* occupies premises that adjoin a highway, and there is some *Fixture* attached to those premises – such as a sign or a tree – which is liable to fall into the highway if it falls into disrepair, *Owner* will owe a duty to people using the highway next to his premises to take reasonable steps to see that *Fixture* does not fall into the highway and injure them. So if *Fixture* is in an obviously dangerous condition, *Owner* will have a duty to take reasonable steps to repair it or take it down.[61] And even if *Fixture* looks perfectly sound, *Owner* will have a duty from time to time to have an expert look at it to see that it does not suffer from any latent defects which mean that it is a danger to passers-by.[62]

If *Owner* breaches the duty he owes people passing by his property to take care to see that *Fixture* does not fall into the highway, and as a result of his breach *Fixture* does fall into the highway and *Passer-By* is injured, he can be sued in negligence, but alternatively *Passer-By* could sue him for damages in public nuisance on the basis that *Owner* has adopted or continued a state of affairs that unreasonably interferes with the highway, and *Passer-By* has suffered special damage as a result.[63]

---

[61] *Tarry* v *Ashton* (1876) 1 QBD 314. The duty is non-delegable in nature. That is, if A employs someone else to repair the fixture, and that person fails to take reasonable steps to repair it properly, then A will be held to have breached his duty to take reasonable steps to repair the fixture: ibid. See above, § 7.5.

[62] *Caminer* v *Northern and London Investment Trust* [1951] AC 88 (held: occupiers not liable in negligence for injuries caused as a result of an elm tree falling into a road from their premises because the tree was apparently healthy; and, while the occupiers had failed to get anyone in to inspect the tree, even if they had, no action would have been taken to repair the tree or take it down because inspection by an expert would not have revealed that there was a problem with the tree).

[63] See below, Chapter 19.

Chapter 11
Product liability

Aims and objectives

Reading this chapter should enable you to:

(1) Understand when a product will count as being dangerously defective under the Consumer Protection Act 1987.

(2) Understand who can be held liable under the 1987 Act for harms caused by a dangerously defective product, and for what harms they can be held liable.

(3) Understand the range of defences that might be available to someone who is sued for compensation under the 1987 Act.

(4) Get a good grasp of the history behind the enactment of the 1987 Act, and the various different arguments that might be made in support of its making manufacturers and others strictly liable for harms done by dangerously defective products.

11.1 The basics

In this chapter, and for the first time in this text, we start to move outside tort law – if we conceive of tort law as being part of the law of wrongs. In this chapter, we are not concerned with a defendant being held liable for *doing something wrong;* we are concerned instead with a defendant being liable because *something has gone wrong.* More specifically, this chapter is about when a defendant can be held liable to a claimant for harm suffered by that claimant because a product has turned out to be dangerously defective in some way.

Before 1987, such a claimant only had two avenues of recourse. First, if he had bought the product from someone, he could sue the *Seller* of the product *in contract. Seller* would be held *strictly liable* under s 14 of the Sale of Goods Act 1979 if the product was not of satisfactory quality, or not fit for the purpose for which the claimant indicated to the seller he wanted the product. In such a case, *Seller* would be liable to compensate the claimant for *any and all* foreseeable losses that the claimant suffered as a result of the product being no good, including the cost of replacing the product and any pure economic losses that the claimant would not have incurred had the product not been defective.

Secondly, the claimant could sue the *Manufacturer* of the product *in negligence*. *Manufacturer* would only be held liable for the product being defective if he was *at fault* for its being defective, *and* if it was reasonably foreseeable that someone like the claimant would suffer harm to their person or other property belonging to them if the product was defective. If this were the case, the claimant would only be able to sue *Manufacturer* for compensation for any foreseeable physical injury, or damage to other property belonging to him, that he had suffered as a result of the product being defective. The claimant would *not* be entitled to sue *Manufacturer* for the cost of replacing the product, and would *not* be entitled to sue *Manufacturer* for compensation for any pure economic losses that he would not have incurred had the product not been defective.

The Consumer Protection Act 1987 gave claimants who had suffered harm as a result of a product being dangerously defective a third avenue of recourse, and one which combines elements from the first two avenues. Section 2 of the 1987 Act lays out the basic liability rule created by the Act. It provides that:

1. Subject to the following provisions of this Part, where any damage is caused wholly or partly by a defect in a product, every person to whom subsection (2) applies shall be liable for the damage.
2. This subsection applies to –
   (a) the producer of the product;
   (b) any person who, by putting his name on the product or using a trade mark or other distinguishing mark in relation to the product, has held himself out to be the producer of the product;
   (c) any person who has imported the product into a member State [of the European Union] from a place outside the member States in order, in the course of any business of his, to supply it to another.

As with a claim in contract under s 14 of the Sale of Goods Act 1979, liability under the 1987 Act is *strict*: a defendant who is sued under the 1987 Act will not be able to defend the claim by simply saying, 'I wasn't at fault for the product being defective!' or 'I wasn't at fault for what happened to the claimant!' As with a claim in negligence, a defendant can only be held liable under the 1987 Act to compensate a claimant for physical injury or harm to other property belonging to the claimant that has been suffered as a result of a product being dangerously defective.

The 1987 Act has a European origin. It was passed to give effect to Council Directive 85/374/EEC ('the Directive') which required each Member State of the European Union to take steps to ensure that under their national laws the producer of a defective product would be held liable on a 'no-fault' basis for the damage done by that product – that is, would be held liable without the necessity of showing that the producer was at fault for the existence of the defect in the product in question. Because the Consumer Protection Act 1987 was enacted in order to implement that Directive the courts are currently required to take the Directive into account in interpreting the provisions of the 1987 Act and to interpret those provisions in such a way as will give effect to the Directive and promote its objectives.[1] If and when the UK leaves the EU (as it is likely to do over the lifetime of this edition of McBride & Bagshaw) it is unlikely that the 1987 Act will be repealed; as we will see in §11.8, there are plenty of good reasons for holding manufacturers strictly liable for harms caused by defective products that will apply even if the UK

---

[1] Consumer Protection Act 1987, s 1(1).

leaves the EU. However, it is unlikely that the courts' obligation to interpret the Act in order to give effect to the Directive can survive the UK's leaving the EU – there would seem no point in doing so. As we will see, this may prove a point of some significance in applying the Act in future.

11.2 Product

Section 1(2) of the 1987 Act provides that '"product" means any goods or electricity and includes a product which is comprised in another product, whether by virtue of being a component part or raw material or otherwise.' So the term 'product' covers not only *manu-factured products* (like cars, radios and computers)[2] but also *natural products* (like coal, flowers and animals).

There is some debate over whether body parts and blood count as 'products' under the Act. It seems likely that they do – 'goods' is defined in the Act as including 'substances',[3] which would cover body parts and blood products; and Article 2 of the Directive defines the term 'product' as covering 'all moveables', which again would cover body parts and blood products. Indeed, it was conceded in the important case of *A v National Blood Authority* (2001) that contaminated blood did count as a 'product' under the Act.[4]

Opinion is more divided on the issue of whether an inaccurate map or some faulty software will count as a defective product under the 1987 Act.[5] The problem is that the map or software *qua* physical item will not be deficient in any respect. It is the information *on* the map or *in* the software that is deficient and that information does not seem to count as a 'substance' or a 'moveable'. This question has yet to be settled by the courts. It would seem an arbitrary result if, for example, an inaccurate map was not counted as being a defective product under the 1987 Act while, for example, a faulty pair of boots was regarded as defective under the Act: the danger posed by each to a mountaineer is the same. However, it may be that the language of the 1987 Act will leave the courts with little choice but to reach such a conclusion.

11.3 Defect

Section 3 of the 1987 Act provides that 'there is a defect in a product . . . if the safety of the product is not such as persons generally are entitled to expect.' The test is unhelpfully vague. However, until the recent decision of Hickinbottom J in *Wilkes* v *Depuy International Ltd* (2016), it was possible to set out the law on when a product would be regarded as defective with some degree of clarity. We'll begin by setting out where the law stood pre-*Wilkes* and then discuss what effect the decision in *Wilkes* has had on the law.

---

[2] But not buildings: s 46(3).
[3] Section 45(1).
[4] [2001] 3 All ER 289, at [17]. Blood and other human body parts and tissues are not generally regarded as 'products' under American products liability laws.
[5] See, generally, Whittaker 1989. For a negative view, see Stapleton 1994a, 333–4.

A. The law pre-*Wilkes*

While the UK courts have consistently disparaged the relevance of American products liability law in interpreting s 3,[6] it is helpful – in trying to understand the law pre-*Wilkes* – to draw on the distinction that American products liability law makes between three reasons why a product *might* be defective: that it suffers from (1) a manufacturing defect; (2) a design defect; and (3) a marketing defect.

(1) *Manufacturing defect.* A product suffers from a manufacturing defect if it does not conform to its intended design. A natural product – such as blood, or crops, which isn't manufactured – suffers from the effective equivalent of a manufacturing defect if it is contaminated with some substance which isn't intended to be present in the product. The case of *A* v *National Blood Authority* (2001)   where the claimants were infected with the hepatitis C virus as a result of receiving blood transfusions containing blood donated by people who had hepatitis C – held that a product that is more dangerous than it would otherwise be because it suffers from a manufacturing defect (or, in the words of Burton J, who decided the case, because it is a 'non-standard' product)[7] will almost always be regarded as defective under s 3. However, the fact that s 3 says that a product will be defective if its safety is not such as people are *entitled to expect* we *cannot* say that a product that is more dangerous than it would otherwise be because it suffers from a manufacturing defective will *always* be defective under s 3.

First, if everyone is generally aware that a particular product may suffer from a manufacturing defect, then it becomes much harder to argue that when that kind of product *does* suffer from that kind of manufacturing defect, the product's safety is not such as persons generally are entitled to expect. This point did not avail the defendants in *A* v *National Blood Authority* as at the time the claimants were infected, people generally were *not* aware that there was a risk that someone receiving a blood transfusion might contract hepatitis C.[8]

Secondly, if a product is designed to be much safer than anyone would expect it to be, and because of a manufacturing defect, its safety falls below its intended standard but it is *still* safer than anyone would expect the product to be, it is hard to argue that the product is not as safe as persons generally are entitled to expect. This was the position in *Tesco Stores Ltd* v *Pollard* (2006), where due to a manufacturing defect a child-resistant lock on the top of a bottle of dishwasher powder was not as strong as it should have been but was still much more difficult to open than a normal bottle top. A claim for compensation under the 1987 Act for injuries suffered by a 13-month-old child who had managed to open the top and eat some of the powder in the bottle was dismissed on the ground that the bottle was not defective.

Would it be open to a manufacturer to argue that a product that suffers from a manufacturing defect and is consequently more dangerous than it otherwise would be is *not* defective under s 3 because it would have been *very difficult* for the manufacturer to ensure that its product did not suffer from that manufacturing defect, and that persons generally are not entitled to expect that products will be free of defects that it would be very difficult to detect and eliminate? Such a plea was rejected by Burton J in *A* v *National*

---

[6] See *A* v *National Blood Authority* [2001] 3 All ER 289, at [39].
[7] Ibid, at [36].
[8] Ibid, at [65].

Blood Authority[9] – where the defendants argued that the blood that they supplied the claimants was not defective because at the time it was supplied it was impossible to detect the existence of hepatitis C in donated blood (though the risk that hepatitis C might be present in donated blood was known, at least by the defendants). This was quite right. The policy of the Act – in terms of imposing *strict* liability on manufacturers for the harms done by defective products – would be fundamentally undermined if manufacturers could escape liability by pleading that it was very difficult for them to ensure that their products did not suffer from flaws that make those products much more dangerous than they would otherwise be.

(2) *Design and marketing defects.* A product suffers from a *design* defect if it could have been designed to a higher safety standard. An example is a car that has no safety bags installed to protect someone in the front passenger seat in the event of a collision. A product suffers from a *marketing* defect if it does not carry a warning that using the product involves a particular risk, or that in certain circumstances the product will be too dangerous to use or should only be used with caution. An example is a product that does not carry a warning that a medicine should not be used if you have a certain medical condition.

In Burton J's terminology in *A v National Blood Authority*, products suffering from a design or a marketing defect count as 'standard products' – they come off the production line in exactly the state the manufacturer intended them to be, but are alleged to be defective because they could have been made safer to use.[10] Standard products are different from non-standard products in that the policy of the Act does *not* demand that a manufacturer of a product should be invariably held liable for harm resulting from the fact that the product in its *intended* state has some dangerous feature X or lacks some safety feature Y. It is not in the public interest for the law to encourage manufacturers to ensure that their products in their *intended* state have no features that might cause another harm, and are overloaded with expensive safety features.

So what approach have the courts taken to deciding whether a standard product is defective? In a case where a standard product gives the impression of being designed to a higher safety standard than would otherwise be the case, then it is very likely that the courts will find that the product is defective under s 3 as not being of the standard of safety that persons generally were entitled to expect it to be. However, if there are no general expectations as to how safe a particular product will be – in terms of the safety standards that it is designed to, and the warnings it gives – then the courts seemed to take the view that a 'standard product' would only be adjudged to be defective under the Act if *in retrospect* it would have been desirable for the product not to have some dangerous feature X or to have some safety feature Y given the costs and benefits involved in removing, or installing, that feature.

For example, in *B (a child)* v *McDonald's Restaurants Ltd* (2002), the claimants sued McDonald's for compensation under the 1987 Act when they were scalded by McDonald's coffee that was spilled on them. The coffee would not have scalded the claimants so badly had it been served at 55°C rather than the 90°C that it was actually served at. However, Field J refused to find that the coffee was defective under the Act. He held that the costs

---

[9] Ibid, at [63].
[10] Ibid, at [36].

involved in serving the coffee at this lower temperature – in the shape of a loss in custom – outweighed the benefits:

> coffee served at between 55°C and 60°C would not have been acceptable to McDonald's customers. Indeed, on the evidence, I find that the public want to be able to buy . . . coffee served hot, that is to say at a temperature of at least 65°C [the temperature at which coffee will cause a severe burn if spilled on skin] even though they know . . . that there is a risk of a scalding injury if the drink is spilled.[11]

Again, in *Worsley* v *Tambrands* (2000), the claimant claimed that a box of tampons was defective under the 1987 Act because it carried a full warning of the danger of suffering 'toxic shock syndrome' ('TSS') from using tampons in a leaflet inside the box, but the box itself only carried a direction to consult the leaflet and did not reproduce the warning in the leaflet. So if the leaflet was thrown away, the box on its own would not do enough to alert users that their use of tampons might result in their suffering TSS. Ebsworth J rejected the claimant's argument:

> TSS is a rare but potentially very serious condition which may be life threatening, but it is necessary to balance the rarity and the gravity. That balance is reasonably, properly and safely struck by the dual system of a risk warning on the box and a full explanation in the leaflet if the former is clearly visible and the latter is both legible and full.[12]

The sort of cost–benefit analysis that the courts engage in, in determining whether a 'standard product' is defective under the 1987 Act, might tempt the reader into thinking that a 'standard product' will only be defective under the 1987 Act if the manufacturer of that product could be held liable in *negligence* for the harm done by that product. The case of *Abouzaid* v *Mothercare (UK) Ltd* (2001) shows that it would be a mistake to think this.

In that case, the claimant was injured when he attempted to fit a sleeping bag onto a pushchair. The sleeping bag was to be attached to the pushchair by passing two elasticated straps attached to the sleeping bag around the back of the pushchair and buckling them together. Unfortunately, the claimant let go of one of the elasticated straps and the buckle at the end of the strap hit him in the eye. He sued the defendants who marketed the sleeping bag under their name for compensation in negligence and under the 1987 Act. The claim in *negligence* was dismissed on the ground that at the time the sleeping bag was manufactured, it was not foreseeable that marketing a sleeping bag with that kind of design would result in injury to someone like the claimant.[13] But the sleeping bag *was* held to be defective under the 1987 Act. The sleeping bag could have been designed to a higher safety standard, either by making the straps attached to the sleeping bag non-elasticated or by having one continuous elasticated strap stretch from one side of the sleeping bag to the other. And, *in retrospect*, it would have been desirable to design the sleeping bag to such a higher safety standard: it would have been quite easy to make the sleeping bag safer to use at no added cost.

So the availability of a claim in negligence against the manufacturer of a 'standard product' depends on what was foreseeable at the time the product was manufactured.

---

[11] [2002] EWHC 490, at [33].
[12] [2000] PIQR 95, 102.
[13] See above, § 5.2.

The inquiry into whether a 'standard product' is defective under the 1987 Act is not so constrained: it purely depends on whether, given what we know now, it would have been better for the product to have been designed or marketed in a different way.

B. The decision in *Wilkes* v *Depuy International Ltd* (2016)

Thus stood the law before the decision in *Wilkes*. In that case, the claimant underwent a hip replacement operation in 2007, which involved replacing the hip in his left leg with an artificial joint called a C-Stem. In 2010 it was discovered that the C-Stem had fractured and needed to be replaced. The claimant brought a claim under the 1987 Act against the manufacturer of the C-Stem, arguing that it was defective under s 3. His claim was dismissed.

The *reasoning* in *Wilkes* is obfuscatory and confusing. Obfuscatory because Hickinbottom J held that virtually all of the distinctions made in the previous section should be *disregarded* in determining whether a product counts as defective under s 3. So he held that 'the categorisation of defects into "standard"/"non-standard" . . . is unnecessary and undesirable'[14] and that 'any attempt at formal rigid categorisation of products . . . is likely to be both difficult and unwise'[15] and that 'the ease and extent to which a risk can be eliminated or mitigated may be a circumstance that bears upon the issue of the level of safety that the public generally is entitled to expect.'[16] Instead, the judge held that in 'assessing the safety of a product, the court should consider the relevant circumstances, in a suitably flexible way; no more and no less'[17] and that while this 'assessment may be difficult in practice . . . it is conceptually simple' and that the courts 'should guard against either over-complicating, or over-analysing' the process of making this assessment.[18]

The reasoning is confusing because, having rejected the relevance of the distinctions made in the previous section, the judge reintroduced them later on in his judgment when, for example, he ruled that (a) 'where a particular specimen of a product is out of specification (or otherwise "non-standard")' the fact that the product could have been designed to a higher safety standard is 'unlikely to have much, if any, weight' in assessing whether it is defective;[19] (b) 'non-compliance with any appropriate mandatory standards will provide evidence of defect; and . . . compliance with such standards . . . will provide evidence that . . . the level of safety required by the Act has been satisfied';[20] (c) there was no evidence that the C-Stem in *Willkes* suffered from 'any manufacturing defect, or other defect in the sense of the C-Stem . . . being outside the design specification';[21] (d) the C-Stem was not 'defective in design'[22] because the failure rate of C-Stems was 'very small indeed; and none of the individual reports [of such failures] suggested a "design" problem in practice'.[23]

---

[14] [2016] EWHC 3096 (QB), at [94].
[15] Ibid, at [79].
[16] Ibid, at [89].
[17] Ibid, at [96].
[18] Ibid, at [79].
[19] Ibid, at [96].
[20] Ibid, at [97].
[21] Ibid, at [115].
[22] Ibid, at [116].
[23] Ibid, at [120].

While probably correct in its *outcome*,[24] the reasoning in *Wilkes* is unfortunate, and threatens to throw the emerging jurisprudence on when a product will count as defective under s 3 back into a dark age, where no one really knows on what basis courts are reaching their conclusions as to whether a product is defective or what arguments they should make to convince a court that a given product is defective. However, it is likely that this unhappy fate will be avoided and that while future courts might pay lip service to Hickinbottom J's emphasis on the need for a 'flexible' approach that takes into account all the circumstances of the case, the real work in determining whether a product is defective will still be done by the application of the principles outlined in the previous section; this is, after all, what happened in *Wilkes* itself.

11.4 Defendants

As we have seen, where a defective product causes a claimant damage (as defined in the Act) the claimant will normally be able to sue the following people for compensation: (a) the producer of the product; (b) anyone who held themselves out as being the producer of the product; and (c) anyone who imported the product into the EU.

Section 1(2) of the 1987 Act explains who will be the 'producer' of a product. If the product was manufactured, the 'producer' of that product will be the person who manufactured it. If the product in question was not manufactured but was instead 'won or abstracted' – say the product in question was coal – 'the person who won or abstracted it' will be the producer of the product.[25] The 1987 Act goes on to specify that 'in the case of a product which has not been manufactured, won or abstracted but essential characteristics of which are attributable to an industrial or other process having been carried out (for example, in relation to agricultural produce), the person who carried out that process' will be the 'producer' of that product.

Sometimes it is difficult for a claimant to identify who (a), (b) or (c), above, are for the purposes of suing them under the 1987 Act. To help such a claimant identify who (a), (b) or (c) are, the Act gives claimants the option of suing the *supplier* of a defective product. Under s 2(3) of the Act, the supplier of a product will be held liable for the damage suffered by a claimant as a result of a product being defective if he does not identify within a reasonable period of time of being requested to do so either: (i) who (a), (b) and (c) are, in relation to that product; or (ii) who supplied the defective product to him. In this way, a claimant who wants to sue for compensation under the 1987 Act can chase up a chain of

---

[24] The facts of *Wilkes* give rise to an interesting issue as to what the approach of the courts should be where in a case like *Wilkes* it is *impossible* to tell whether the product failed because it suffered from a manufacturing defect (it failed because it suffered from some flaw the evidence of which has been destroyed by the failure of the product) or a design defect (the product's failure could have been avoided had it been designed to a higher safety standard). The decision in *Wilkes* is unsympathetic to claimants in such a case, holding (at [96]) that the burden of proof of establishing a defect is on the claimant, and if they can't prove the existence of a manufacturing defect, their claim that there was a manufacturing defect must fail and they are forced onto the much more unpromising ground of basing their case on design defect grounds.

[25] What is the position if John dies and a surgeon, Wendy, takes out his heart for transplantation purposes and the heart is given to Fred in a heart transplant operation? If the heart proves to be defective (say, for example, it is cancerous), who will count as being the 'producer' of the heart? Stapleton 1994a suggests (at 310–11) that John will be the producer because he 'manufactured' the heart. However, this seems unreal: a heart is not a manufactured product but a natural product. The better view is that Wendy is the producer because she 'won or abstracted' the heart.

supply, threatening each person in the chain that they will be held liable unless they identify who is the next highest person in the chain, until he eventually arrives at the producer of the product that harmed him.

In any given case, there may be more than one defective product that has harmed a claimant, and therefore two sets of defendants who can be sued under the 1987 Act for the harm that has been suffered by the claimant. For example, consider the following case:

> *Pedestrian* is run over by a car driven by *Driver* when one of the car's tyres explodes, and *Driver* loses control of the car. The tyre was manufactured by *Rubber*, and was fitted on the car by its manufacturer, *Automobile*. The tyre suffered from a tiny flaw which meant that when heated to a high temperature, it was liable to explode.

In this case *both* the tyre *and* the car are defective. They are both 'non-standard products' in that neither the tyre nor the car are operating in the way they were designed to operate. So *Pedestrian* will be able to sue both *Automobile* and *Rubber* for the harm that he has suffered here.

11.5 Damage

The sort of damage that can be sued for under the 1987 Act is defined in s 5(1) of the Act: '"damage" means death or personal injury or any loss of or damage to any property (including land).'

Personal injury is defined by the Act as including 'any disease and any other impairment of a person's physical *or mental condition*.'[26] The reference to 'mental condition' suggests that claimants can bring claims for psychiatric illnesses caused by defective products under the 1987 Act in circumstances where it would be impossible to bring a claim in negligence. For example, suppose that in the case we were just considering, *Bystander* witnessed *Pedestrian* being run over and was so shocked by the sight that she developed a psychiatric illness. In such a case, she could not bring a claim in negligence against anyone who was at fault for *Pedestrian*'s being run over;[27] but she might be able to sue *Automobile* and *Rubber* for compensation for her psychiatric illness under the 1987 Act.

The Act places three limits on when a claimant can sue for compensation in respect of damage to property that has occurred as a result of a product being defective:

(1) *Auto-destruction*. Section 5(2) of the 1987 Act provides that:

> A person shall not be liable in respect of any defect in a product for the loss of or any damage to the product itself or for the loss of or any damage to the whole or any part of any product which has been supplied with the product in question comprised in it.

So, in the case we have been considering, suppose that as a result of one of the tyres on *Driver*'s car exploding, not only is *Pedestrian* run over, but *Driver*'s car slams into a lamp-post and is a complete write-off. In this case, *Driver* will not be entitled to sue *Rubber* for the loss of his car because the car came with *Rubber*'s defective tyre installed as part of the car. And *Driver* will not be entitled to sue *Automobile* for the loss of his car because his

---

[26] Section 45(1) (emphasis added).
[27] See above, § 5.4.

claim against *Automobile* will be based on the argument that the car manufactured by *Automobile* was defective, and s 5(2) prevents him suing for the damage that the car did to itself as a result of being defective.

Two points about this should be noted. The first is that the law of negligence is a bit more generous to claimants in allowing them to sue for compensation where a product has been damaged because part of that product was defective. So long as the defective part of the product and the rest of the product can be viewed as two separate items of property, the law of negligence allows the owner of the product to sue whoever was at fault for the defective part of the product being defective for the damage done to the rest of the product.[28] So if, in the above case, *Rubber* was at fault for not detecting that its tyre was defective, and the defective tyre is viewed as a separate item of property from the rest of the car, then *Driver* would be able to sue *Rubber* in negligence for the damage done to the rest of the car as a result of *Rubber*'s tyre being defective.

Secondly, *Rubber* cannot be sued for the damage done to the car here because the car was supplied with their tyre as part of the car. It follows that if the car was supplied to *Driver* with a different set of tyres, and *Driver* had the tyres replaced with tyres manufactured by *Rubber*, then *Rubber* could be held liable for the damage done to the car as a result of one of their tyres exploding.

(2) *Damage to commercial property.* Article 9(b) of the Directive specified that claims for compensation for damage caused to property by a defective property should only be available if the item of property damaged was '(i) . . . of a type ordinarily intended for private use or consumption, and (ii) was used by the injured person mainly for his own private use or consumption.' This would prevent companies suing for damage to their property (as that property is not used 'mainly for . . . private use or consumption) or a private individual suing for damage to property – such as a laser or a lathe – that he *was* using for 'private use or consumption' but which is not ordinarily intended for such use.

Section 5(3) of the 1987 Act is intended to implement Article 9(b) but is badly drafted – it says that 'A person shall *not* be liable . . . for . . . damage to . . . property which . . . is *not* (i) . . . ordinarily intended for private use . . . *and* (ii) intended . . . for . . . private use'.[29] This suggests that you will only be barred by s 5(3) from bringing a claim under the 1987 Act if you have suffered damage to property that is *both* not ordinarily intended for private use *and* not intended for private use. This would open the door to companies suing for damage to company cars (because cars are ordinarily intended for private use) and private individuals suing for damage to things like lathes or lasers that they happen to have in their possession (because those things, on this occasion, are intended for private use). This was not was intended by Article 9(b) of the Directive. After Brexit, the courts will be free to choose how to interpret s 5(3) however they like, but interpreting the section to bring it into line with Article 9(b) would seem to be the better course of action even after Brexit – there seems little reason why companies should benefit from the strict products liability regime introduced by the 1987 Act.

(3) *Trivial damage to property.* Section 5(4) of the 1987 Act provides that:

> No damages shall be awarded to any person by virtue of this [Act] in respect of any loss or damage to any property if the amount which would fall to be awarded to that person . . . does not exceed £275.

---

[28] For much more discussion of this point, see above, § 5.8(E).
[29] Emphasis added.

There is a question – that has not been resolved – as to how this provision applies in a case where a defective toaster causes a small fire in a kitchen which damages curtains worth £200, and damage to the paintwork in the kitchen that will cost £250 to repair. Is the claim for compensation for this damage to property knocked out on the ground that the damages payable in respect of *each* item of damaged property do not exceed £250? Or can we aggregate the claims for damage to property here and say that the total claim for damage to property comes to £450, and is therefore unaffected by s 5(4)?

The question is one that is more likely to exercise law students and their examiners than anyone in the real world. In the real world, the owner of the toaster would claim on their household insurance, and their insurer would either write off the loss, or would make a claim for the damage (under the law on subrogation) against the manufacturer of the toaster and that claim would be settled as not worth the trouble of disputing. But, for what it is worth, we think that the language of the Act indicates that you *cannot* aggregate the claims for property damage here, and each claim will be struck out as falling short of the s 5(4) threshold. The main reason for taking this view is that the Act talks about claims for compensation in respect of 'any property' – and the use of the word 'any' here would seem to indicate that the £275 threshold is meant to apply in respect of *each* item of property that has been damaged as a result of a defective product.

11.6 Defences

Defendants who would normally be held liable under s 2(1) of the 1987 Act for damage caused by a defective product may be able to take advantage of one of the range of defences set out in s 4(1) of the Act:

(a) *That the defect was attributable to compliance with any requirement imposed by or under any enactment or with any Community obligation.*

(b) *That he did not put the product into circulation.* So say *Automobile* manufactures a car which is then stolen from their factory before it is shipped out. The car is then sold to *Driver* who is injured because the car suffers from some flaw. *Driver* will not be able to sue *Automobile* for damages under the 1987 Act because *Automobile* did not put the car into circulation.

(c) *That he did not supply the product to another in the course of business and he did not produce, brand or import it with a view to profit.* So if *Helpful* bakes some cakes for a school fair and *Father*, having bought them at the fair, is poisoned by them, *Father* will not be entitled to sue *Helpful* for damages under the 1987 Act: *Helpful* did not supply the cakes to the fair organisers in the course of a business of hers and she did not supply those cakes for profit. It would be different if the poisonous cakes were donated by a nearby *Bakery*. As *Bakery* produced those cakes in the course of business, it will not be able to take advantage of this defence if *Father* tries to sue it.

(d) *That the defect did not exist in the product at the time he supplied the product to someone else.* Go back to the case where *Driver's* car spins out of control because one of the tyres that was fitted to the car after *Driver* bought it exploded. If *Driver* attempts to sue *Automobile* under the 1987 Act for any injuries he suffered as a result of his car crashing, arguing 'Your car was defective!', Automobile will be entitled to reply, 'It wasn't defective when it left our factory; it was made defective afterwards because you fitted it with dodgy tyres.'

(e) *That the state of scientific and technical knowledge at the time when he put the product into circulation was not such as to enable a producer of that kind of product to discover the existence of the defect.*[30] The classic case where this defence – known as the 'development risks defence' – will be available is where A puts into circulation some drug that has a dangerous side-effect which no one[31] could have known about at the time the drug was marketed. Those who have suffered harm as a result of the drug's having that side effect will not be able to sue A for compensation under the 1987 Act.

It is now clear from the decision in *A v National Blood Authority* (2001) that the defence may also be available in a manufacturing defect case, where a product is defective because it does not conform to its intended design. Suppose, for example, that *Genius* manufactures computer chips, and one of the millions of chips that came off its assembly line suffered from a microscopic flaw which meant that it did not function properly when installed in a light airplane, with the result that the airplane crashed and *Pilot* was injured. *Genius might* be able to take advantage of the 'development risks defence' if it can show that the state of scientific and technical knowledge at the time it manufactured the defective chip meant that it was simply not possible to identify that chip as being defective.

However, in the *A* case, Burton J placed one very important limit on the availability of the defence in a manufacturing defect case. He held that A will not be able to take advantage of the defence if *he was aware at the time he manufactured the product that there was a risk that it might not conform to its intended design in the way it did.*[32] This limit severely curtails the availability of the development risks defence in manufacturing defect cases. For example, in the case we have been considering, *Genius* will almost certainly have been aware that there was a risk that one of its chips might suffer from a microscopic flaw. If he was – and he did not arrogantly think that there was absolutely no possibility of any of his chips being defective – then he will not be able to take advantage of the 'development risks defence' to defeat *Pilot*'s claim for damages against him under the 1987 Act.

Burton J's limit on the applicability of the development risks defence also meant that it was unavailable to the defendants in the *A* case. They sought to argue that the defence was available to them because the state of scientific and technical knowledge at the time the claimants contracted hepatitis C was not such as to enable them to

---

[30] Art 7(e) of the Directive, which s 4(1)(e) was supposed to implement, is much narrower, simply referring to the state of scientific and technical knowledge generally, and not to the state of scientific and technical knowledge that was available to producers of the product in question. The broadness of s 4(1)(e) led the European Commission to bring an action against the UK, claiming that the UK had failed in s 4(1)(e) correctly to implement the Directive. However, the European Court of Justice expressed itself content with the wording of s 4(1)(e), holding that 'there is nothing . . . to suggest that the courts in the United Kingdom, if called upon to interpret s 4(1)(e), would not do so in light of the wording and purpose of the Directive so as to achieve the result it has in view': *European Commission v UK* [1997] All ER (EC) 481, at [33]. But after Brexit, the UK courts will be free to interpret s 4(1)(e) as originally drafted, regardless of what Art 7(e) says.

[31] If, at the time A put the drug into circulation, an academic had published a paper in Manchuria revealing that the drug had this side effect, that – it seems – would not be enough to deprive A of the development risks defence: see the opinion of the Advocate-General in [1997] All ER (EC) 481, at [24]. It has to be shown that the state of *accessible* scientific and technical knowledge at the time the drug was circulated was not such as to allow the existence of the side-effect to be discovered: ibid., at [23].

[32] [2001] 3 All ER 289, at [74].

detect which of their bags of blood were contaminated with hepatitis C. Burton J held that even if this were true, the defence was unavailable because the defendants were aware at the time the claimants contracted hepatitis C that there was a risk that the blood supplied by them to people like the claimants might be contaminated with hepatitis C.

(f) *That the defect – (i) constituted a defect in a product ('the subsequent product') in which the product in question was comprised; and (ii) was wholly attributable to the design of the subsequent product or to compliance by the producer of the product in question with instructions given by the producer of the subsequent product.* It is often said that this defence will cover the case where, say, a lorry manufacturer fits tyres on one of his lorries which are completely unsuitable for that lorry with the result that when the lorry is driven the tyres blow out and an accident is caused. It is said that the tyre manufacturer will be able to take advantage of this defence if he is sued by the people involved in the accident under the 1987 Act. But it is difficult to see how he could be sued in any case by the people involved in the accident: surely his tyres were never defective?

It is worth mentioning that a defendant who is sued under the 1987 Act will *not* be able to take advantage of a defence of *volenti non fit iniuria*. So suppose that *Vain* goes to her *Doctor* for some botox injections into her face. *Doctor* warns her against having the operaton, telling her that he has heard 'on the grapevine' that there are some stocks of botox that are infected with flesh-eating viruses. *Vain* insists on going ahead with the operation. If the botox injected into *Vain*'s face *is* contaminated with flesh-eating viruses and *Vain* suffers horribly as a result then *Vain* will be entitled to sue the *Manufacturer* of the botox for compensation under the 1987 Act. It will be no defence for *Manufacturer* to say that *Vain* voluntarily took the risk that she would be infected with flesh-eating viruses when she had her injections.

It is also worth mentioning that under s 11A of the Limitation Act 1980, a defendant cannot be held liable for damage caused by a defective product unless he is sued for that damage within ten years of the product going into circulation. This does not, of course, mean that a claimant who has suffered relevant damage as a result of a product being defective will have ten years from the date the product was put into circulation to bring a claim for that damage under the 1987 Act. He will have to bring his claim within three years of the date he first suffered that damage, or the date he could have been reasonably expected to realise he had suffered 'significant damage' and to identify the person responsible for that damage.[33]

11.7 Remedies

A number of different points need to be made here about the remedies that will be made available under the 1987 Act when someone suffers some relevant damage as a result of a product being defective.

(1) *Consumers and third parties.* Although the title of the 1987 Act is the *Consumer Protection Act*, the Act operates to protect *anyone* who has suffered actionable 'damage'

---

[33] Limitation Act 1980, s 11A(4).

as a result of a product being defective. So in the example we were considering – where *Pedestrian* is run over by a car (manufactured by *Automobile*) that is spinning out of control because one of its tyres (manufactured by *Rubber*) has exploded – *Pedestrian* will be entitled to sue *Automobile* and *Rubber* for compensation for his injuries even though no one would say that he is a 'consumer'.

(2) *Range of liability.* Having said that, the 1987 Act is completely silent on the issue of whether any limits should be drawn on the range of third parties who will be entitled to sue for damages under the 1987 Act.

Suppose, for example, that in the above example, *Pedestrian*'s injuries had an adverse effect on his personality with the result that he eventually raped *Victim*. Will *Victim* be able to sue *Automobile* and *Rubber* for damages under the 1987 Act to compensate her for the fact that she was raped by *Pedestrian*? There is nothing in the Act to guide us one way or the other on this issue.

Suppose, alternatively, that *Pedestrian* was so severely injured that his *Wife* had to give up her job and look after *Pedestrian*. She was eventually so worn down by the strain of looking after *Pedestrian* that she suffered a nervous breakdown. If she sued *Automoble* or *Rubber* in negligence for compensation for her breakdown, she would lose: she would not be able to establish that either owed her a duty of care in manufacturing the tyre.[34] But could she instead sue *Automobile* and *Rubber* for compensation for her breakdown under the 1987 Act? Again, there is nothing in the Act to give us any guidance on this issue.

(3) *Fatal accidents.* Section 6(1) of the 1987 Act provides that any 'damage for which a person is liable under [the Act] shall be deemed to have been caused . . . for the purposes of the Fatal Accidents Act 1976, by that person's wrongful act, neglect or default'. So, if – in the situation we have been considering – *Pedestrian* has been killed as a result of the car spinning out of control, and had he not been killed but merely injured, he would have been entitled to sue *Automobile* and *Rubber* for damages under the 1987 Act, *Pedestrian*'s dependants may be entitled to sue those producers for damages under the Fatal Accidents Act 1976. Whether they will or not depends on who they are and what sort of loss they have suffered as a result of *Pedestrian*'s death.

(4) *Exclusion/limitation clauses.* Section 7 of the 1987 Act makes it impossible for a defendant to exclude or limit his liability under the 1987 Act. It provides that the 'liability of a person [under this Act] to a person who has suffered damage caused wholly or partly by a defect in a product, or to a dependant or relative of such a person, shall not be limited or excluded by any contract term . . .'

(5) *Remoteness of damage.* The 1987 Act leaves it completely open what rules on remoteness of damage will apply to claims under the Act. Presumably, the same rules that apply in a negligence case[35] will also apply to a claim under the 1987 Act. It would be strange if the law were to treat a negligent defendant less harshly than someone who was held strictly liable under the 1987 Act for the harm caused by a malfunctioning product. 'Strict' liability means liability without having to prove fault; it does not mean 'unlimited' liability or 'oppressively harsh' liability.

(6) *Contributory negligence.* If a claimant was partly to blame for the damage she suffered as a result of a product being defective – for example, she should have known the product

---

[34] See above, § 5.4.
[35] For which, see above, § 9.2.

was defective but carried on using it regardless – then the damages payable to the claimant may be reduced on the ground of *contributory negligence*. This is the effect of s 6(4) of the 1987 Act, which provides that where:

> any damage is caused partly by a defect in a product and partly by the fault of the person suffering the damage, the Law Reform (Contributory Negligence) Act 1945 and section 5 of the Fatal Accidents Act 1976 (contributory negligence) shall have effect as if the defect were the fault of every person liable by virtue of [this Act] for the damage caused by the defect.

11.8 Discussion

It seems to us that five arguments can be made in favour of the strict liability regime created by the 1987 Act. None of these arguments is capable of justifying *all* of the features of the 1987 Act. So they only provide a rough, and not detailed, justification of the 1987 Act. Moreover, some of these arguments – if taken to their limit – suggest that we should extend strict liability to other areas of life (such as driving on the road) where strict liability is not currently the rule. So even if these arguments roughly justify the 1987 Act, they are not necessarily given effect to by other areas of the law.

(1) *Proof problems.* The first argument in favour of the 1987 Act focuses on how difficult it can be for a consumer who has been injured by a defective product to prove that the defect was due to a manufacturer's negligence. So a strict products liability regime may be justified as the most efficient way of delivering compensation to all the claimants who should, in principle, be entitled to sue for compensation in negligence for the product-related harms they have suffered, but would find it very difficult to make out a claim were they confined to suing in negligence. Of course, such a regime also makes liable some manufacturers – such as the sleeping bag manufacturer in *Abouzaid* (2001) – who could not have been sued for compensation under the law of negligence. But given the choice between allowing an injustice to be done to many consumers (who should be allowed to sue under negligence, but cannot obtain an effective remedy under that area of law) and doing an injustice to some manufacturers, the latter option may be preferable.

(2) *Fletcher's argument.* However, it may be that a strict products liability regime is not unjust at all. This thought underlies the next two arguments in favour of strict liability for harms caused by defective products. The first such argument was made by George Fletcher in a very famous 1972 article called 'Fairness and utility in tort theory'.[36]

Fletcher argued that holding a defendant liable in tort to pay compensation to a claimant was justified where the defendant's actions exposed the claimant to a non-reciprocal risk of harm. In such a case, the defendant could justly be held liable if that risk materialised, even if he was not at fault either for exposing the claimant to a risk of harm in the first place, or the fact that that risk materialised. The fact that the defendant had exposed the claimant to a risk of harm that was not matched by any risk of harm that the claimant exposed the defendant to made it only fair that if that risk materialised, the defendant should bear the consequences. (Where the risk is reciprocal – for example, where the defendant and claimant are each driving on the same road – the only thing the defendant has to do for the claimant (and vice versa) is to take care to see that that risk does not materialise.)

---

[36] Fletcher 1972.

This argument could be adapted to support the strict products liability regime created by the 1987 Act. The risk of harm from a product being defective that manufacturers of products expose ordinary people to is not matched by any risk of harm that ordinary people expose manufacturers to. So if that risk materialises, it is only fair that the consequences of that risk materialising should be borne by the manufacturer.

(3) *Keating's argument.* Just over a quarter of a century after Fletcher published his article, another American academic, Greg Keating, made a slightly different argument in favour of strict liability that may apply to justify the 1987 Act.[37]

Keating's argument distinguishes between what he called the 'world of acts' and the 'world of activities'. In the world of acts, whether or not you suffer harm at another's hands is a matter of pure chance. But in the world of activities, risks of harm are predictable. If you continuously repeat the same activity it becomes possible to predict how likely it is that your activity is going to result in harm to someone else. And if you can predict that, then if the law holds you liable on a strict liability basis when your activity results in harm to someone else, that is not such a burden on you. You can predict how often you will be held liable and for how much, and take out insurance to cover yourself against that liability. In contrast, if someone who is harmed by your activity can only sue if you were at fault for their being harmed, they will sometimes go without a remedy, and have to bear the burden of the harm they have suffered without any support from anyone else.

So, Keating argues, in the world of activities, strict liability provides a more satisfactory way of striking the right balance between the competing demands of security (which demands that someone who has been injured always have a remedy for that injury) and the demands of freedom (which demands that people be allowed to go about their business without being held liable to anyone):

> In the world of activities . . . the choice between strict liability and negligence is a choice between a grave disruption of security and a more modest disruption of liberty. Activity liability [which means here strict liability for harms regularly associated with a particular activity] strikes a more favorable balance between the competing claims of liberty and security than negligence liability does, because activity liability disrupts the liberty of injurers less than negligence impairs the security of victims. Enterprise liability thus secures more favorable conditions than negligence liability for citizens concerned to pursue their conceptions of the good over complete lives.[38]

The application of this argument to the 1987 Act should be pretty obvious. A manufacturer of computer chips can predict how many per million of the chips that roll off its production line will turn out to be flawed. Holding the manufacturer liable for the harm done by the flawed chips will be less burdensome for it than a negligence liability regime would be for those harmed as a result of the manufacturer's chips being defective.

(4) *Deterrence.* A fourth argument in favour of a strict products liability regime is that the existence of such a regime encourages manufacturers to do as much as they can to improve the safety of their products; the idea being that under a strict liability regime, they know that they are much less likely to 'get away' with producing unsafe products than they would be under a negligence liability regime. Whether strict products liability does

---

[37] Keating 1997.
[38] Ibid, 1355.

actually encourage better safety standards among manufacturers has been the subject of recent debate.[39] The most that can be said is that the jury is still out on the question.

(5) *Making externalities internal.* The fifth and final argument in favour of a strict products liability regime is an economic one. The argument starts from the uncontroversial premise that only products that are beneficial to society should enjoy a market. A product will be beneficial if the benefits attached to its production outweigh the costs. The best way of ensuring that only beneficial products survive in the marketplace is to ensure that the price of a product reflects its real cost. If people are willing to buy a product at a price that exceeds its real cost, then that shows – almost by definition – that the benefits of that product outweigh its costs. But frequently the price of a product does not reflect its real costs. A given product may impose external costs on society which the manufacturer of the product never has to take into account in pricing that product.[40] Strict liability for harms caused by defective products is one way of ensuring that some of the externalities associated with the production of a particular product are brought home to the manufacturer, so that the price of that product will more closely reflect the real costs associated with that product.

All of these arguments seem to us to be good ones, and to put it beyond doubt that the broad effect of the 1987 Act is amply justified. (Details of the Act can, of course, be criticised.) We are more doubtful that liability under the 1987 Act or some other strict product liability regime can be justified as an example of compensation for wrongdoing, as some theorists have recently tried to argue. The most prominent such theorist is Richard Epstein, who argues[41] that if a defendant causes some harm to a claimant's person or property, then the defendant has presumptively done something wrong to the claimant: 'entering into the space of another creates the prima facie case of liability for what happens thereafter.'[42] John Goldberg and Benjamin Zipursky have also argued that:

> the case for the imposition of liability on manufacturers for product-related injuries more or less on the terms set by the current law is no different from the case for the recognition of tort law in many other instantiations. There are many reasons to have a law that . . . permits victims to respond to those who have wronged them through the courts, and deems a commercial seller that injures someone through the sale of a dangerously defective product to have committed . . . a wrong.[43]

Robert Stevens has taken a similar line, arguing that:

> a producer's duty is . . . to refrain from manufacturing defective products which cause harm[;] the fact that the manufacturer took all care in manufacturing the product does not excuse. It is not meaningless to describe the claim of a person harmed by a defective product as based upon a tort, although the manufacturer is without blame in any moral sense.[44]

All such arguments, we think, rest on a linguistic mistake: that of thinking that because we all have a right *to* bodily integrity (for example), it follows that when someone else

---

[39] See Polinsky & Shavell 2010 and Goldberg & Zipursky 2010b.

[40] For example, if burgers or chips were priced to reflect the real cost to society of their consumption, they might well become luxury items.

[41] The classic article is Epstein 1973.

[42] Epstein 2010, text at n 32.

[43] Goldberg & Zipursky 2010, at 1944.

[44] Stevens 2007, at 99.

violates our bodily integrity, they have violated our rights, and done something wrong to us.[45] The mistake is to forget that we only have a right *to* bodily integrity insofar as the law grants us rights against other people *that* they not violate our bodily integrity in various ways. And there is no reason to think that the law gives us rights against other people that *unqualifiedly* demand, as Epstein puts it, 'forbearance against physical interference with [our] person and property'.[46] Given this, we have no reason to think that a manufacturer of a defective product that has harmed a claimant's person or property has done anything legally wrong to that claimant.[47] It follows that liability under the 1987 Act is better seen as an example of 'compensation without wrongdoing' rather than as a standard example of a wrongdoer being held liable to compensate the victim of his wrong.

---

[45] See above, § 1.2.

[46] Epstein 2010, text at n 31.

[47] The fact that s 6(1) of the Consumer Protection Act 1987 explicitly creates a fiction that someone who has been killed by a defective product has been the victim of a wrong, so as to bring his case within the Fatal Accidents Act 1976, only strengthens this point.

Chapter 12
Trespass to land

Aims and objectives

Reading this chapter should enable you to:

(1) Understand in what circumstances someone will commit the tort of trespass to land.

(2) Understand who will be entitled to sue when a trespass to land has been committed, and what remedies they will be entitled to.

12.1 The basics

The tort of trespass to land provides someone who is in possession of a plot of land with a claim if someone else intrudes into that plot by, for example, marching onto it in person, or by throwing or something onto it, unless the intruder has some lawful justification for acting in this way.[1] In more precise terms: (1) A will commit the tort of trespass to land in relation to B if he crosses the boundary onto land possessed by B[2] when he has no lawful justification for doing so; and (2) A will also commit the tort of trespass to land in relation to B if he causes some object or matter to move directly onto land possessed by B when he has no lawful justification for doing so.

The language of *intruding* might make it sound as if trespasses to land have to be intentional, but this is not the case. No doubt many trespasses *are* intentional, but the key question is whether the crossing of the boundary onto B's land was a *direct* result of A's actions. Under the next two headings we explore the distinction between direct and indirect consequences of actions, and the relevance of the defendant's state of mind, before turning to justifications for trespassing, who can sue, and remedies.

---

[1] *Bocardo SA* v *Star Energy UK Onshore Ltd* [2011] 1 AC 380 at [6] (per Lord Hope): 'a trespass occurs when there is an unjustified intrusion by one party upon land which is in the possession of another.'

[2] The degree of connection that has to be established between B and the land is discussed in detail below, § 12.5.

12.2 Conduct requirements

To discuss what a defendant needs to have *done* in order to have committed the tort of trespass to land, it is helpful to distinguish between cases where she is alleged to have committed it: (a) by physically moving onto the claimant's land; (b) by causing an inanimate object to go onto the claimant's land; and (c) by causing an animal to go onto the claimant's land.

A. Physical movement

A defendant will not be held to have 'crossed' the boundary of the claimant's land unless she had sufficient control over her own movements for the action which took her body across the boundary to be attributed to her. In *Smith* v *Stone* (1647), the defendant pleaded that he had been carried across the boundary onto the claimant's land by the force and violence of others. Roll J held that this meant that the defendant had *not* committed the tort of trespass to land in relation to the claimant. A defendant might similarly avoid liability if he leapt across the boundary onto the claimant's land in an instinctive panic.[3]

B. Inanimate objects

In cases where A has caused some inanimate object or matter to move onto land possessed by B, it is orthodox to distinguish between a movement of such a thing across the boundary which is a *direct* result of A's actions (and thus within the scope of the tort) and a movement which is an *indirect* consequence of A's behaviour (outside the tort).

The primary factor which the courts use when drawing this distinction between direct and indirect consequences is the degree to which A's actions *controlled* the crossing of the boundary by the object or matter. Thus where A has placed or thrown or fired an object across the boundary, A will have committed trespass to land in relation to B. But where A has released some substance into the air, which then emanated across the boundary (for instance, where A's operations released acid fumes which then drifted on the breeze across the boundary) A will not have committed trespass to land, though B will still gain redress if he can establish that A committed the tort of private nuisance in acting as he did.[4] Similarly, if A loses control of a vehicle that he is driving so that it leaves the road and crosses onto land possessed by B this crossing is likely to be considered an *indirect* consequence of A's actions.[5]

The distinction between crossings which are a *direct* result of the defendant's actions and those which are *indirect* consequence is *not* the same as the distinction between crossings which the defendant *intended to occur* and those which he did not *intend*. In some circumstances, the connection between A's behaviour and an unintended crossing

---

[3] *Braithwaite* v *South Durham Steel Co Ltd* [1958] 1 WLR 986, 991.

[4] For the tort of private nuisance, see below, Chapter 13.

[5] Thus A will not be liable in relation to B for trespass to land, but may be liable for the tort of negligence. The situation would be different if A *chose* to drive off the highway and onto B's land in order to avoid colliding with another vehicle or a pedestrian, though here A may be able to rely on the defence of necessity.

will be so close that A will be unable to deny that the crossing was a *direct* result of his behaviour. For instance, if Brian hits a golf ball towards land possessed by Chloe with the intention that it should stop just before the boundary, then if, despite his intention, it bounces across the boundary, it is unlikely that he will be able to claim that the crossing was merely an *indirect* consequence of his behaviour: the crossing was a direct consequence of how he struck the ball. The outcome might be different, however, if the ball deflected off a passing seagull. Similarly, if a lorry driver attempts to manoeuvre his lorry under a narrow bridge, but misjudges the width of his load so that it collides with the side of the bridge, this collision would certainly be a *direct* consequence of the driver's actions even though it was not *intended*.[6]

A landowner is not generally treated as having sufficient control over the plants, trees and natural features of his land so as to make him liable for trespass if they cross onto B's land as a result of ordinary natural processes. Thus where the roots or branches of a tree on A's land gradually grow so that they cross onto B's land no trespass will be committed but A may be guilty of committing the tort of private nuisance by encroachment.[7]

C. Animals

The law on when A will commit a trespass to land in relation to B if his animals cross over onto land possessed by B is complicated. The problem is caused by the fact that animals behave less predictably than inanimate objects, so it is harder to say when their behaviour is a *direct* consequence of a person's action.

Sometimes it is unnecessary to determine whether the animal's keeper has committed trespass to land because another tort applies to the situation. For example, the possessor of *livestock* which strays onto another's land is strictly liable for *damage* done by that livestock to the land or that other's property which is on the land.[8] (Although this liability is based on the statutory provision that replaced the common law wrong of 'cattle trespass'[9] it is best understood as part of the law relating to the keeping of dangerous things[10] rather than as an aspect of the tort of trespass to land.) Further, the Animals Act 1971 makes the keepers of *dangerous* animals liable for the damage that such animals cause[11] and consequently it will not usually be necessary to determine whether they are also liable for having committed trespass to land through an incursion by such an animal.

---

[6] In *Conarken Group Ltd* v *Network Rail Infrastructure Ltd* [2010] EWHC 1852 (TCC), Akenhead J held that an owner of a bridge could sue for trespass in circumstances similar to these. But he did not consider how far the later consequences of an initial collision can be described as 'direct'. In the case the load on the lorry which had initially collided with one side of the bridge subsequently struck a vehicle which was travelling in the opposite direction, and this vehicle then struck the other side of the bridge. We think that the difficulty of determining whether the collision with the other side of the bridge was also a *direct* consequence of the lorry driver's actions helps to explain why incidents like this commonly give rise to claims in the tort of negligence, rather than trespass. The Court of Appeal subsequently upheld the conclusions that Akenhead J had reached as to the appropriate measure of damages, but did not re-consider his opinion as to the scope of the tort of trespass to land: [2011] EWCA Civ 644.

[7] *Lemmon* v *Webb* [1895] AC 1. See below, § 13.6.

[8] Animals Act 1971, s 4. A claim can also be brought for expenses reasonably incurred in keeping the livestock and ascertaining the owner.

[9] Section 1(1)(c).

[10] See below, § 14.6(C).

[11] Section 2. Which animals are considered 'dangerous' is discussed below, § 14.2.

In practice, then, the situations where it is most important to consider whether A has committed trespass to land as a result of an intrusion by animal are those involving neither 'livestock' nor 'dangerous animals'. In *Buckle* v *Holmes* (1926) – where the defendant's cat strayed onto the claimant's property and killed the claimant's pigeons and poultry – the Court of Appeal held that where an animal was neither livestock nor a 'dangerous animal', and was of a class not generally confined and unlikely to cause substantial damage on straying, such as a dog or a cat, the owner of the animal would *not* commit the tort of trespass to land whenever it strayed onto someone else's land.[12] But while this rule clearly applies to a dog or cat acting of its own volition, equally clearly it would be a tort for A to *send* such an animal onto B's land.

In *League Against Cruel Sports* v *Scott* (1986), Park J held that the master of a hunt would be liable for trespass to land if 'he either intended that the hounds should enter the land or by negligence he failed to prevent them from doing so'.[13] In so far as this makes a huntsman liable for *sending* hounds onto another's land it is uncontroversial. But the suggestion that a huntsman is liable for trespass if he negligently allows the hounds to stray is not easy to reconcile with *Buckle* v *Holmes* (1926), which was not drawn to Park J's attention.[14] Our view is that an owner of a pet dog will not commit the tort of trespass to land if all that can be said is that he has taken no steps to prevent it from straying onto someone else's land.[15] But no doubt Park J was correct to suggest that if a dog was known to stray into a neighbour's garden whenever it was let out, and its owner was apparently indifferent to this, then an intention that the dog should cross the boundary *might* be inferred from the action of letting it out.[16]

12.3 Intention and fault

Suppose A crossed the boundary onto land possessed by B. In order to establish that A committed the tort of trespass to land in so doing, B does *not* have to prove that when A crossed the boundary: (i) he *intended* to trespass on the land possessed by B; *or* (ii) he *knew or ought to have known that there was a risk* he would be trespassing on the land possessed by B. This is important in two types of case: where A is ignorant about the boundary between plots of land and where there is a disjunction between A's movements and her state of mind.

---

[12] In *Tutton* v *A D Walter Ltd* [1986] QB 61 the judge refused to treat unwanted straying bees as trespassers for the purpose of deciding whether a landowner owed their owner a duty to take care not to harm them. Suppose A, a beekeeper, released bees which strayed onto B's land and A knew they were likely to do this when he released them. Will A have committed the tort of trespass to land in relation to B? The rule expounded by *Buckle* v *Holmes* suggests that the answer is 'no'. We think it *would* be trespass to land, however, to put bees through B's letterbox, or otherwise send them onto B's property.

[13] [1986] QB 240, 251–2.

[14] In a subsequent passage Park J confined his opinion to the case '[w]here a master of staghounds takes out a pack of hounds and deliberately sets them in pursuit of a stag or hind, knowing that there is a real risk that in the pursuit hounds may enter or cross prohibited land'. This makes the case far closer to that of the golfer who hits balls towards the claimant's land with the intention that they should stop just before the boundary.

[15] The owner might, however, be liable for any consequential damage, in the tort of negligence, or under Animals Act 1971, ss 2, 3 or 8.

[16] *League Against Cruel Sports* v *Scott* [1986] QB 240, 252.

(1) *Ignorance of boundaries.* A can commit trespass to land in relation to B without intend-ing to be on B's land, and even without appreciating that there is any risk of him being there. Thus, A will commit the tort of trespass to land in relation to B if he crosses the boundary onto land possessed by B whilst lost in thick fog, even if he honestly believes that he has remained on land where he is permitted to be. An honest mistake by A is not a defence to the tort of trespass to land.

(2) *Unintended movements.* We have already seen that it has been held that A cannot com-mit the tort of battery in relation to B unless he directly applied force to B *intentionally* or *carelessly*.[17] It has been argued that a similar rule should apply with regard to the tort of trespass to land. Such a similar rule would mean that A would only commit the tort of trespass to land in relation to B if his movement – by which he crossed the boundary onto B's land – *intentionally* or *carelessly* brought him into contact with B's land.[18] It has not, however, been authoritatively settled that this is the law. The main reason why the point remains unsettled is that a defendant will not be held to have 'crossed' unless he had sufficient control over his own movements for the action which took his body across the boundary to be attributed to him. This means that even without a similar rule defendants will not usually be held liable for movements which were not intentional or careless.[19]

12.4 Defences

If A has crossed the boundary of B's land, there are many different ways in which A could establish that he had a lawful justification for the incursion. We will not attempt to provide an exhaustive catalogue. A may, for instance, seek to establish that he was merely making lawful use of a highway[20] or a private right of way, or that statute[21] or common law[22]

---

[17] See above, § 2.3, discussing the result of the decision in *Fowler* v *Lanning* [1959] 1 QB 426.

[18] In *Conarken Group Ltd* v *Network Rail Infrastructure Ltd* [2010] EWHC 1852 (TCC), Akenhead J confirmed that a trespass to land does not have to be intentional, but can be negligent. Some passages in his judgment also imply, however, that he thought that there could be no liability unless the trespass was intentional or negligent. See, for example, at [65]: 'If Y in an effective state of automatism, say, a blackout from an unknown medical condition, drives his or her car onto someone else's land, that would be unintentional and non-negligent and no trespass.' Douglas 2011 argues that a defendant should only be held to have committed trespass to land if he 'intended to make physical contact' with the land (that the claimant possessed).

[19] What sort of case might involve a non-intentional and non-negligent trespass? Suppose that *Driver* owns a garage the back wall of which is against the boundary of *Gardener's* land. Each night *Driver* parks his car by reversing it slowly into his garage until it gently touches the rear wall. He does not realise that the rear wall is actually not fixed and that each time he touches it he moves it a millimetre into *Gardener's* property. Eventually *Gardener* notices that the wall has moved into his land.

[20] The public's right to use a highway is limited: In *DPP* v *Jones* [1999] 2 AC 240 the majority held that the public's right was not limited to passing, repassing and ancillary uses, and accepted that *at least some* other reasonable, peaceful and non-obstructive uses were lawful (at 257, per Lord Irvine; 281, per Lord Clyde; and 286–7, per Lord Hutton).

[21] For example, police officers have statutory powers under ss 17 and 18 of the Police and Criminal Evidence Act 1984 to enter premises in order to make an arrest and to search after making an arrest.

[22] For example, the common law confers powers to enter premises in order to reclaim wrongfully taken personal property, in order to abate a nuisance (though sometimes notice may be required), and in order to preserve person or property from immediate danger.

conferred on him a power to enter.[23] Here we will discuss only two instances where A might be able to establish a lawful justification or excuse for crossing the boundary of B's land.

(1) *Licence (consent).* Suppose A enters B's land. A will not commit the tort of trespass to land in so doing if B has licensed him to enter. A may commit the tort of trespass to land, however, if he either exceeds the terms of the licence[24] or fails to leave within a reasonable time after the licence is withdrawn. Sometimes a contract will restrict B's power to withdraw a licence. But it is important to distinguish between cases where the withdrawal is wrongful (a breach of contract) but still effective and those where the withdrawal is ineffective.[25]

(2) *Necessity.* In *Esso Petroleum* v *Southport Corporation* (1953), the defendant shipowners dumped some oil into the sea when their ship ran aground. The defendants dumped the oil because they feared that the ship would break its back and the crew would be endangered if they did not. The oil washed up onto the claimants' foreshore. The claimants sued the defendants, claiming that they had committed the tort of trespass to land in dumping the oil.

Devlin J thought that the defendants could rely on the defence of *necessity* to justify their dumping the oil.[26] He also held, however, that the defendants would not be permitted to rely on the defence if the predicament was a result of their own negligence.[27]

The defence is available only in cases of *immediate* danger or emergency. So in *Southwark LBC* v *Williams* (1971), the Court of Appeal held that the defence did not stretch to cover the case of homeless people who made an orderly entry into empty property:

> If homelessness were once admitted as a defence to trespass, no one's house could be safe. Necessity would open a door which no man could shut. It would not be only those in extreme need who would enter. There would be others who would imagine that they were in need, or would invent a need, so as to gain entry. Each man would say his need was greater than the next man's. The plea would be an excuse for all sorts of wrongdoing. So the courts must, for the sake of law and order, take a firm stand. They must refuse to admit the plea of necessity to the hungry and the homeless: and trust that their distress will be relieved by the charitable and the good.[28]

The fact that in some circumstances necessity seems to make the defendant's decision to cause harm to the claimant justifiable does not mean that the defendant should necessarily be free from an obligation to pay compensation for the harm that he has caused.

---

[23] Where a person who is authorised by law to enter for a particular purpose afterwards abuses that authority he may be treated as a trespasser *ab initio*, that is, he may be treated as if the initial entry was unlawful. The doctrine is associated with *The Six Carpenters' Case* (1610) 8 Co Rep 146a, 77 ER 695. Although Lord Denning MR thought in *Chic Fashions Ltd* v *Jones* [1968] 2 QB 299 that the doctrine should be interred with the bones of the old forms of action, he later used the doctrine in *Cinnamond* v *BAA* [1980] 1 WLR 582.

[24] The picturesque illustration commonly given is that a person licensed to walk down the stairs becomes a trespasser if he slides down the bannisters.

[25] A text on tort is not the appropriate place to explore when licences cannot be revoked and when they will bind third parties. The interested reader should consult a standard text on land law.

[26] [1953] 2 All ER 1204. This judgment was reversed by the Court of Appeal but restored by the House of Lords: [1956] AC 218. See also *Cope* v *Sharpe (No 2)* [1912] 1 KB 496.

[27] *Esso Petroleum* v *Southport Corporation* [1953] 2 All ER 1204, 1210. See also *Rigby* v *Chief Constable of Northamptonshire* [1985] 1 WLR 1242.

[28] [1971] 1 Ch 734, 744 (per Lord Denning MR). See also *Monsanto* v *Tilly* [2000] Env LR 313.

For instance, in the American case of *Vincent* v *Lake Erie Transportation Co* (1910), the defendant's boat was moored at the claimant's dock when a severe storm arose. The crew acted to prevent the boat from getting away from the dock and being lost, but with the result that the vessel was repeatedly thrown against the dock and damaged it. A majority of the Supreme Court of Minnesota held that the claimant was entitled to compensation for the damage done. One explanation for such an outcome is that there is an *incomplete privilege* to perform an act which would otherwise be a tort in a situation of necessity – that is, the act may be performed and the claimant cannot resist or prevent this, but liability is still imposed for any *material* harm done.[29] An alternative explanation is that while a defence of necessity meant that the defendant could not be held liable to compensate the claimant in *tort*, the defendant could still be held liable in *restitution* for the damage done to the dock.[30]

12.5 Title to sue

B will be able to sue someone for trespassing on a particular piece of land if she was in *possession* of the land at the time of the alleged trespass.[31] It is important to note that possession of land is a legal concept, and is *not* synonymous with simple physical occupation. So if B's mother-in-law visits for a week then she will not take *possession* of the spare bedroom even if she physically occupies it.

In *J A Pye (Oxford) Ltd* v *Graham* (2003), Lord Browne-Wilkinson confirmed that 'there are two elements necessary for legal possession: (1) a sufficient degree of physical custody and control ('factual possession'); (2) an intention to exercise such custody and control on one's own behalf and for one's own benefit ('intention to possess').'[32] Except in the case of *joint* possessors, only one person can be in possession of a piece of land at any one time,[33] and, while the necessary degree of 'physical custody and control' will vary

---

[29] Bohlen 1926, 313; also Stevens 2007, 104. The reference to 'material' harm is intended to denote that the claimant cannot recover *simply* for the 'invasion of the right'. See also *Burmah Oil* v *Lord Advocate* [1965] AC 75, where the House of Lords treated a situation where oil installations were destroyed in wartime to prevent them falling into enemy hands as one where the acts were performed in the lawful exercise of the Royal prerogative but there was nonetheless an obligation to pay compensation. Virgo 2015 argues that English law does not correspond to US law on these points, and in England necessity currently operates in tort as an absolute defence of justification (at 148).

[30] See Weinrib 1995, 196–203.

[31] Although the rule is that the claimant must be in possession *at the time of* the trespass, if a person who is entitled to possession *enters* land, and thereby gains possession, the law will treat him as if he was in possession from the date when he became entitled to enter *and* will allow him to sue someone who has trespassed after *that* time. This doctrine is known as *trespass by relation*. See, for example, *Ocean Accident & Guarantee Corp* v *Ilford Gas Co* [1905] 2 KB 493.

[32] [2003] 1 AC 419, at [40].

[33] It is possible, however, to *split* land so that, for instance, one person possesses the surface and another person possesses the subsoil. Furthermore, the holders of certain rights over land known as *profits à prendre* can also sue for trespass to land. Thus a holder of a right to herbage, a liberty of hunting or a fishery can sue for a trespass to the land which damages the right. This rule has been applied in a modern context to hold that the company which 'owned' a genetically modified crop being grown on another's land was entitled to sue third parties for trespass to land: *Monsanto* v *Tilly* [2000] Env LR 313. By contrast, a person entitled to an easement, such as a right of way, will *not* be able to claim that A committed the tort of trespass to land in relation to her if A interfered with that right; but she may be able to claim that A committed the tort of private nuisance in relation to her in so acting: see below, § 13.7.

somewhat in accordance with the nature of the land concerned, what is looked for is *dealing* with the land in the same way that 'an occupying owner might have been expected to deal with it'.[34]

An owner of land will generally be deemed to be in *possession* in the absence of evidence to the contrary. Where the owner has granted a lease, however, and the tenant has moved onto the premises, it will be the tenant who has exclusive possession and can sue for trespass.[35] Whether a licensee (someone with permission to be on land) is treated as being in possession for the purposes of suing a third party for trespass[36] depends on the terms of the licence.[37]

Where B is in possession of land, A cannot successfully defend an action for trespass to land on the basis that someone else has a title superior to B's,[38] unless A can establish that *he* has a superior title, or that he crossed the boundary with the permission of the person with a superior title.[39] This means that B can usually safely sue if *in fact* she is in possession, even if as a matter *of law* she has no title or formal interest in the land.

(1) *Airspace.* A question that has attracted some attention is how far B can claim to be in possession of the airspace above his property so as to be able to object to A's crossing that airspace or placing something in it. The original principle was often said to be that 'the man who has land has everything above it, or is entitled at all events to object to anything

---

[34] *Powell* v *McFarlane* (1977) 38 P & CR 452, 471 (per Slade J), *approved* by the House of Lords in *J A Pye (Oxford) Ltd* v *Graham* [2003] 1 AC 419, [41] (per Lord Browne-Wilkinson).

[35] Nonetheless, a reversioner can sue where there is a trespass to land which causes either: (*a*) damage to the property which the reversioner will in time gain the right to possess; or (*b*) injury of such a permanent nature as to be necessarily prejudicial to the reversion: *Mayfair Property Co* v *Johnston* [1894] 1 Ch 508 (trespass by foundations of wall); *Jones* v *Llanrwst UDC* [1911] 1 Ch 393 (trespass by deposit of faecal matter on riverbank). The right of a reversioner to bring an immediate action is useful because the reversioner might be more willing to take the risks of litigation than a tenant with a time-limited interest and there are occasions when it is desirable for a claim in trespass to be brought sooner rather than later, for instance when it is better for repairs to be effected immediately. Technically, the claim made by the reversioner in such cases is not identical to a claim for trespass to land since the reversioner will allege that the defendant has injured his reversion rather than his land.

[36] Where the licensor throws the licensee off the land, or tries to do so, the question is generally whether the licensee has become a trespasser (after failing to leave) and not whether the licensee can sue *for* trespass to land. The question often arises where the licensee sues for a trespass to the person committed in throwing him off the land and the licensor relies on the justification of using reasonable force to expel a trespasser.

[37] In *Hill* v *Tupper* (1863) 2 H & C 121, 159 ER 51 the claimant was granted the 'sole and exclusive right or liberty' to put pleasure boats on the Basingstoke Canal, but this was held to be insufficient. By contrast in *Manchester Airport plc* v *Dutton* [2000] QB 133, the claimant was granted the right to enter and occupy the land concerned and this was held to be sufficient to allow it to obtain an order for possession against third parties who were squatting, partly on the basis that if the claimant had already entered under such a licence then it would have had sufficient possession to seek such an order. This strongly suggests that the claimant, although a licensee, would have had sufficient possession to sue for trespass. *Manchester Airport plc* v *Dutton* [2000] QB 133 was distinguished in *Countryside Residential (North Thames) Ltd* v *Tugwell* [2000] 34 EG 87, where a claimant seeking an order for possession against protesters who were camping on the site only had a licence to enter and carry out investigatory work and not one which granted 'effective control over the land'.

[38] This defence is commonly referred to as the defence of *ius tertii*.

[39] *Nicholls* v *Ely Beet Sugar Factory* [1931] 2 Ch 84, 86.

else being put over it'.[40] Thus possessors of land have successfully objected to, for instance, overhanging signs[41] and cranes.[42]

Modern cases have suggested, however, that passing over land at a height at which there can be no interference with the ordinary use of that land is not a trespass, and that all members of the public have an equal right to use this airspace.[43] Thus the modern principle seems to be that the possessor of the surface's interest only extends to the super-jacent airspace which must be controlled if the possessor is to be able reasonably to enjoy the land and put it to purposeful use.[44] Of course, the application of this principle to particular facts may still be controversial: for example, at what height over another person's land would it become a trespass to fly a small drone without their consent?[45]

Even if the modern principle represents the law, it is merely a presumption that can be displaced by unusual facts: for example, in a multi-storey building the rooms of a possessor on a higher floor may protrude over the rooms of the possessor on the ground floor, with the consequence that the ground floor possessor will be unable to assert control over the space above its premises.[46]

(2) *Underground.* Just as a trespass to land can be committed by intruding into the airspace immediately above B's land, it can also be committed by intruding into the ground beneath it.[47] In *Bocardo SA* v *Star Energy UK Onshore Ltd* (2010) – where the claimants complained that the defendants' oil pipelines had intruded into their land roughly 1,000 feet below the surface – the UK Supreme Court held that the modern principle relating to airspace – the possessor of the surface controls so much as is necessary for reasonable enjoyment and purposeful use – did *not* delimit a possessor's rights to exclude others from the space below a plot of land. Consequently, the claimants established that the defendants were trespassing on their land, even though the intrusion was occurring at a depth that could have no effect on the claimants' ordinary enjoyment of it.[48]

---

[40] *Wandsworth Board of Works* v *United Telephone Co Ltd* (1884) 13 QBD 904, 919 (per Bowen LJ). This doctrine is often presented in Latin as *cujus est solum ejus est usque ad coelum.*

[41] *Kelsen* v *Imperial Tobacco Co* [1957] 2 QB 334.

[42] *Anchor Brewhouse Developments Ltd* v *Berkley House Ltd* [1987] 2 EGLR 173.

[43] *Bernstein* v *Skyviews* [1978] QB 479. Cited with approval by the Supreme Court in *Bocardo SA* v *Star Energy UK Onshore Ltd* [2011] 1 AC 380, [26]. An overflight by a civil aircraft at a reasonable height is immune from liability under the Civil Aviation Act 1982, s 76(1).

[44] *Bernstein* v *Skyviews* [1978] QB 479. See also Gray 1991.

[45] A drone is almost certainly an 'aircraft' for the purposes of the immunity from trespass liability under the Civil Aviation Act 1982, s 76(1), but this immunity is conditional on compliance with the Air Navigation Order 2009, and this imposes limits on the use of some unmanned aircraft, particularly those that are 'equipped to undertake any form of surveillance or data acquisition'. Where the use of a drone is outside the scope of the statutory immunity it will be necessary to determine whether an overflying of property amounts to a trespass to land.

[46] *Corbett* v *Hill* (1870) LR 9 Eq 671. In *Ramzan* v *Brookwide Ltd* [2011] EWCA Civ 985, the trespass was to a 'flying freehold': the claimant owned a store room on the first floor of a building whilst the defendants owned the ground floor and the ground which supported the building.

[47] For instance, by foundations or mining. As has already been observed, encroaching tree roots are treated as a form of private nuisance.

[48] [2011] 1 AC 380, at [27] (per Lord Hope). The Supreme Court's decision in created a significant impediment to those seeking to extract shale gas by hydraulic fracturing, often called 'fracking'. As a result the UK Parliament enacted the Infrastructure Act 2015 s 43, which permits people to use 'deep-level land . . . for the purposes of exploiting petroleum or deep geothermal energy' without a need to secure the owner's consent.

12.6 Remedies

The normal remedy for a trespass to land, at least where the trespass is not on-going,[49] will be compensatory damages – damages designed to compensate the victim of the trespass for the losses resulting from it.

(1) *Unforeseeable losses.* As we have seen, the rule in the tort of negligence is that if A breaches a duty of care owed to B, B will only be allowed to claim compensatory damages for the *reasonably foreseeable losses* suffered by her as a result of A's breach.[50] Given that trespass to land is a tort that can be committed by A without his being any more blameworthy than a defendant in a negligence case, we might expect the same rule to apply where A has trespassed on B's land.

But what if A *deliberately* trespassed on B's land? For instance, consider the **Exploding Car Problem**:

> *Cheap* does not like paying to park. Consequently he sneaks his car into the underground car park possessed by *Busyco Ltd* without their permission, and ignores the notices that say that parking is only for their staff and clients. While *Cheap*'s car is in the underground car park it explodes – without any fault on *Cheap*'s part – and causes severe damage to *Busyco*'s building.

In this case, *Cheap* has obviously committed the tort of trespass to land in relation to *Busyco*. But should *Cheap* be held liable for the *unforeseeable consequences* of his trespass? On one view, the normal rule set out above will apply to determine the scope of *Cheap*'s liability and *Cheap* will only be held liable if it was reasonably foreseeable that the car might cause this kind of damage when he parked it in the car park (or if he intended the car to explode). On another view, *Cheap* will be held liable for the damage done to the car park *if* it was a direct result of his trespass, even if that kind of damage (damage by explosion) was unintended and unforeseeable; the fact that *Cheap* is a deliberate wrongdoer means he should be liable for *all* the losses directly suffered by *Busyco* as a result of his wrong.[51]

(2) *Nominal and licence fee damages.* Where A has trespassed on B's land without causing B to suffer any kind of loss, B will still be entitled to sue A for nominal damages: trespass to land is actionable *per se.*[52]

---

[49] Where the trespass is on-going, or regularly repeated, the claimant will be able to seek an injunction against the defendant. Injunctions are a discretionary remedy, and their availability is discussed in more detail below, § 13.12, and Chapter 27.

[50] See above, § 9.2.

[51] This was the view preferred by the New Zealand Court of Appeal in *Mayfair Ltd* v *Pears* [1987] 1 NZLR 459, from which our hypothetical example is drawn. (Though the court went on to find that the fire damage caused by the car bursting into flames in that case was *not* a *direct* result of the defendant's parking his car in the claimant's building.) Some support for this view might also be drawn from Lord Nicholls's judgment in *Kuwait Airways Corpn* v *Iraqi Airways Co (Nos 4 & 5)* [2002] 2 AC 883. Lord Nicholls suggested that while the normal rule is that someone who converts another's goods should only be liable for the reasonably foreseeable consequences of his conversion, if A knowingly converts B's goods, A should be held liable for *all* the losses suffered by B that were a direct consequence of A's conversion: ibid, at [103]–[104]. There is no reason to think that he would apply a different rule if A knowingly trespassed on B's land.

[52] See above, § 1.6(2), and below, § 26.2.

B may also be entitled to sue A for damages designed to make A pay B a reasonable sum for the use he has made of her land.[53] Such damages are increasingly referred to as 'user damages' in the case law,[54] though they are sometimes also called 'hypothetical negotiation damages',[55] and we refer to them as 'licence fee damages' below.[56] The fact that there is no established label for this measure of damages indicates that it is not clear *why* such damages can be claimed by B. Some argue that they are really compensatory damages – designed to compensate B for what she could have charged A for the privilege of using her land.[57] Others argue that these damages are designed to 'substitute' for the right that A has violated by trespassing on B's land.[58] We argue below that they are designed to make A compensate B for the fact that he has deprived B of the power to determine what happens with his land.[59]

Further reading

In the case of *Bocardo SA* v *Star Energy UK Onshore Ltd* (2010) Lord Hope made two references to an article discussing when the owner of the surface should be able to sue for trespass as a result of activities underground, though he did not eventually adopt its author's preferred solution: **J.G. Sprankling, 'Owning the center of the Earth' (2008) 55** *UCLA Law Review* 979. In **B Depoorter, 'Fair Trespass' (2011) 111** *Columbia Law Review* **1090**, the author discusses whether a special 'public interest' defence to trespass to land should be developed which might assist investigative journalists, among others.

---

[53] For much more detailed discussion of this aspect of the law, see below, § 25.3.

[54] *Bocardo SA* v *Star Energy UK Onshore Ltd* [2011] 1 AC 380, at [74] (per Lord Brown), [118] and [125] (per Lord Clarke).

[55] *London Borough of Enfield* v *Outdoor Plus Ltd* [2012] EWCA Civ 608, at [29]; *Stadium Capital Holdings Ltd (No 2)* v *St Marylebone Property Co Plc* [2011] EWHC 2856 (Ch), at [69].

[56] See below, § 25.1.

[57] See Sharpe and Waddams 1982.

[58] See Stevens 2007, 59f.

[59] See below, §25.1.

Chapter 13
Private nuisance

Aims and objectives

Reading this chapter should enable you to:

(1) Understand the variety of different ways in which the tort of private nuisance can be committed; in particular, by unreasonably interfering with the use and enjoyment of someone else's land, or by interfering with some right that a claimant has over a piece of land.

(2) Understand what factors the courts take into account in determining whether an emanation onto the claimant's land (such as noise, smoke, or smells) has unreasonably interfered with the claimant's use and enjoyment of land; in particular, the reasons for the emanation, whether the emanation has caused physical damage, the nature of the locality, and the degree of inconvenience caused by the emanation.

(3) Understand when a defendant will be held responsible for an interference that is serious enough to amount to a private nuisance because the defendant either (a) created or (b) authorised the interference or (c) the defendant 'adopted or continued' the nuisance because the source of the interference came from land in the defendant's control and the defendant knew or ought to have known of the problem, or potential problem, created by that source, and the defendant failed to take reasonable steps to deal with the problem.

(4) Appreciate the controversial rules about what connection with the affected land a claimant must have before they can sue for private nuisance, and what remedies they should be able to obtain.

13.1 The basics

The tort of private nuisance protects interests in, or associated with, land. Thus it is the tort which a claimant will rely on if his use and enjoyment of the house that he owns and occupies is ruined by incessant loud noise from a neighbouring factory, or its paintwork is repeatedly chipped by fragments blasted out of a nearby quarry, or the private right of way he uses to gain access to it is regularly blocked by rubble dumped by a local builder. In the next section, we will see that there is a wide variety of ways of making land less useful, and, consequently, that there are many ways of committing the tort. Nonetheless, it can, to some extent, be summarised:

> A will have committed the tort of private nuisance in relation to B if A has *created, authorised, adopted or continued* a state of affairs on land (other than land in which B has a sufficient interest) and this has an effect that unreasonably interfered, or is unreasonably interfering, with either the use and enjoyment of land in which B has *a sufficient interest*, or some right of B's that is associated with that land.

Some elements of this definition require careful elaboration. For example, in section 13.11 we will describe the rules about who can sue for a private nuisance: in summary, those with a sufficient interest in the affected land, those actually enjoying exclusive possession of the land, and those who hold various legal rights associated with the land, such as private rights of way. Similarly, in section 13.9 we will set out what must be shown in order to demonstrate that a defendant is responsible for a state of affairs, because he has *created* it, or *authorised* it, or *continued* or *adopted* it. At the core of the tort, however, is a requirement that the state of affairs (on land other than the land in which the claimant has a sufficient interest) should have an effect that amounts to an *unreasonable* interference with the claimant's use and enjoyment of his or her land.

What makes an interference an *unreasonable* interference? We provide a detailed answer in sections 13.4 and 13.5. But at this stage, we make three introductory points. First, an interference can be unreasonable even if there is no risk of people being injured or property being physically damaged. So a loud noise *can* be an unreasonable interference, even if there is no risk of it harming anyone's hearing or cracking any windows. Secondly, if an interference does not cause physical damage, then whether it is unreasonable will depend on the nature of the locality where the events take place: in some localities more disturbance is reasonable than in others. Thirdly, what is reasonable in a particular locality depends on a notion of reciprocity, or 'give-and-take': nobody should be able to complain about insubstantial interferences, or about the effects of houses being used as houses in an ordinary and convenient way, or about the effects of activities that are wholly consistent with a locality's 'established pattern of uses'. Of course, the process of applying these basic propositions to real cases can be contentious: it is not easy to fix exactly how many noisy parties, smoky bonfires, or smelly brewery-cleansings must be tolerated before a defendant will be held to have exceeded a locality's standards of ordinary 'give and take' and committed the tort of private nuisance.

13.2 Ways of committing the tort

There are many ways of committing the tort of private nuisance, even if we set to one side some peculiar forms of the tort.[1] The reasons why there are so many ways of committing the tort include that: (1) there are different ways in which a defendant can be responsible for a state of affairs; (2) there are different ways in which a state of affairs (on land other than the land in which the claimant has a sufficient interest) can have an effect on land in

---

[1] For some of the peculiar forms, see § 13.13, below.

which a claimant has a sufficient interest; and (3) there are different kinds of effects that are regarded as being sufficiently harmful for the purposes of the tort.

As we have seen, to establish that a defendant has committed the tort of private nuisance in relation to a claimant, it has to be shown that:

> the defendant created, authorised, adopted or continued a state of affairs on land (other than land in which the claimant has a sufficient interest), which had an effect that unreasonably interfered with either the use and enjoyment of land in which the claimant has a sufficient interest, or some right of the claimant's that is associated with that land.

This summary already incorporates the first important variable: (1) the three different ways in which a defendant can be responsible for the state of affairs which affected the claimant's land:[2] (a) creation; (b) authorisation; and (c) adoption or continuation.

The other two important variables are: (2) the different ways in which a state of affairs (on land other than the claimant's land) can have an effect on the claimant's land; and (3) the different kinds of effects that are regarded as being sufficiently harmful for the purposes of the tort.

With regard to (3), the different effects that are *sometimes* treated as being sufficiently harmful for the purposes of the tort of private nuisance are: (a) *violation of the boundaries*; (b) *physical damage*; (c) *reduction of amenity value*; (d) *interference with some right* associated with the claimant's land, such as a right to have water or light come onto the land, or a private right of way leading to the land. But it is important to note the word '*sometimes*': we will see below that (a) (violating the boundaries of the claimant's land) is not *always* treated as sufficiently harmful.

With regard to (2), the different ways in which a state of affairs (on land other than the claimant's land) can have an effect on the claimant's land that can amount to a private nuisance *include*: (a) something (for instance, smoke, smells, noise or electromagnetic waves) *emanating* onto the claimant's land; (b) something (for instance, branches, tree roots or a leaning wall) *encroaching* onto the claimant's land; (c) something (for instance water, air, light or TV signals) being *obstructed* from coming onto the claimant's land; (d) something (such as drug dealing or prostitution) happening near the claimant's land and thereby offending or *affronting* the claimant so as to make him unhappy about living where he does.

We can sum all this up in the table below:

Defendant	Claimant	
Create	Emanation	Violation of boundaries
Authorise	Encroachment	Physical damage to land
Adopt or Continue	Obstruction	Reduction of amenity value
	Affront	Interference with associated right

Combinations of elements from each of the three columns amount to various different ways of committing the tort of private nuisance. For example: a defendant might *create* a state of affairs (on land other than the claimant's land) which leads to an

---

[2] We use the phrase 'the claimant's land' here and below as shorthand for 'land in which the claimant has a sufficient interest, or some right of the claimant's that is associated with that land'.

emanation onto the claimant's land that *physically damages* it (which would be the case where a manufacturing process in the defendant's factory produces acidic smoke which drifts onto the claimant's land and burns holes in her roof tiles). Or: *adopting or continuing* a state of affairs which involves an *encroachment* that *violates the boundaries* of the claimant's land (which would be the case where roots from an old tree on land that the defendant has purchased grew so that they intruded into the claimant's land and the defendant knew or ought to have discovered that this was happening but did nothing about the problem).

In theory, we could put together 48 different possible combinations from the above table. However, some combinations do not exist. For example:

(1) Violation of the boundaries of a claimant's land is only usually sufficient to constitute a private nuisance[3] when it involves a physical intrusion of some permanence (such as tree roots or a leaning wall). Moreover, the laws of physics ensure that such a *physical* intrusion cannot be brought about by an *affront* or by *obstructing* something from coming onto the claimant's land. Indeed tort lawyers tend always to use the word *encroaching* to describe *how* a state of affairs can lead to a physical intrusion of sufficient permanence across the boundary of the claimant's land. So, where the defendant's tree's roots grow across the boundary into the claimant's soil, this will always be described by tort lawyers as involving an *encroachment* rather than an *emanation*.

(2) As we will see,[4] where a claim is based on something intangible, like a noise or a smell, affecting a claimant's use and enjoyment of her land it will not be enough for the claimant merely to assert that there has been a *violation of the boundaries* of her land. Moreover, no tort lawyer is likely to say that something like noise or smell has *encroached* on a claimant's land; such cases will be said to involve *emanations*.

(3) As we will see,[5] obstructing something from coming onto the claimant's land can *only* ever amount to a private nuisance if that obstruction interferes with some right of the claimant's associated with that land.

(4) A state of affairs that *affronts* the claimant can only reduce the amenity value of the claimant's land: it cannot result in physical damage, or violation of boundaries.

So, if we amend the above table to expunge the combinations that don't exist, we end up with this:

Defendant		Claimant
Create Authorise Adopt or Continue	}{	Emanation resulting in physical damage to land
		Emanation resulting in reduction of amenity value of land
		Encroachment (violation of boundaries sufficient, though it may also cause physical damage)
		Obstruction that interferes with right associated with land
		Affront resulting in reduction of amenity value of land

---

[3] Indeed, as we will see below, a simple violation of the boundaries may only be sufficient to confer on the claimant a right to *abate* the nuisance; the claimant may only be able to make a claim for substantial damages if the encroachment has caused some further damage.

[4] See below, § 13.4.

[5] See below, § 13.7.

Combining the various options in the new table gives us 15 possible ways in which someone can commit the tort of private nuisance.[6] What really matters, however, is not the exact number of ways there are of committing the tort,[7] but remembering that when we want to know whether a defendant has committed it we must assess all the *possible* combinations of: (1) the different ways in which a defendant can be responsible for a state of affairs; (2) the different ways in which such a state of affairs can have an effect on the claimant's land; and (3) the different effects that can be regarded as sufficiently harmful for the purposes of the tort.

In the rest of this chapter, we start by dividing our discussion in line with the different ways in which a state of affairs can have an effect on the claimant's land. Thus in sections 13.3 to 13.5 we present the law governing situations where a state of affairs has led to *emanations* onto the claimant's land, and then in the following three sections we deal with *encroachment*, *obstruction* and *affront*.

13.3 Emanation cases (1): establishing an interference

As we have noted, where something has emanated onto the claimant's land, the claimant has *two* ways of establishing that the emanation has caused sufficient harm with respect to her use and enjoyment of land: (1) establishing that it has reduced the amenity value of the land; or (2) establishing that it has physically damaged the land.

A. Reduction of amenity value

What is the 'amenity value' of land? Essentially, it means the day-to-day usefulness of the land. So, for example, emanations will reduce the amenity value of land being used as an ordinary house if they reduce its usefulness *as a house*, by making it harder to sleep there (loud noise at night) or harder to relax there (nauseating smells).

Usually an on-going reduction in amenity value will reduce the price for which the claimant could sell her land. But it is important to distinguish between a reduction in

---

[6] In *Hunter* v *Canary Wharf* [1997] AC 655, Lord Lloyd remarked (at 695) that 'Private nuisances are of three kinds. They are (1) nuisance by encroachment on a neighbour's land; (2) nuisance by direct physical injury to a neighbour's land; and (3) nuisance by interference with a neighbour's quiet enjoyment of land.' If this were right, then combining that with the three different ways of being responsible for a state of affairs, would give us only nine ways of committing the tort. But Lord Lloyd's statement: (1) misses out the kinds of private nuisance which involve interfering with a *right associated with land*; (2) fails to observe that where a defendant *directly* does physical damage to a claimant's land this is more likely to involve commission of the tort of trespass to land (the tort committed where a defendant damages land by going onto it or by throwing something onto it) than private nuisance, and that where physical damage gives rise to a claim in private nuisance this is usually because of *indirect* damage to the claimant's land; and (3) fails to distinguish between cases of interference by emanation and affront.

[7] It should be re-emphasised that there are also some peculiar forms of the tort of private nuisance, which we will deal with at the end of this chapter, that increase the number of ways that the tort can be committed. Moreover, to keep things simple, we have omitted some well-recognised ways of committing the tort from our tables. For example: *obstruction* is the most common way of interfering with rights associated with a claimant's land, but a claimant may also have a *right to support* associated with her land, and this can be interfered with by a *withdrawal of support*, such as by digging a hole. Some of these omitted forms of the tort will be briefly mentioned below, § 13.7.

amenity value and such a reduction in the price. The importance is evident when the emanations cease before a trial is concluded, which may occur if a defendant modifies his activities, perhaps because the claimant obtains an injunction ordering the defendant to stop the activity which was creating the emanations: in such circumstances the price for which the land could be sold may return to its previous level, but the claimant may nonetheless obtain a remedy (damages) for having suffered a loss of amenity value in the period during which the interference lasted. What this shows is that amenity value can be measured in terms of time: loss of amenity value can be for days, or months, or years, or permanent.

In the leading case of *St Helen's Smelting* v *Tipping* (1865), Lord Westbury LC referred to emanations which produce 'sensible personal discomfort' rather than those which reduce the amenity value of land. But we think there are two reasons why it is better to avoid this phrase.[8] The first reason is that emanations *very often* make land less useful because they cause *discomfort* to those who are using the land, but this is *not the only way* in which emanations can reduce the day-to-day usefulness of land. For example, if emanating electromagnetic waves mean that mobile telephones and Wi-Fi cannot be used on the claimant's land then this will reduce the amenity value even though no one will suffer any *discomfort*. The second reason is that the phrase 'sensible personal discomfort' sometimes misleads law students into thinking that the amount of damages that a defendant will be liable to pay for committing a private nuisance depends on *how many people* suffered discomfort. This is a mistake. In *Hunter* v *Canary Wharf* (1997) Lord Hoffmann made clear that damages for a private nuisance which reduces amenity value 'may be affected by the size, commodiousness and value of his property but cannot be increased merely because more people are in occupation and therefore suffer greater collective discomfort'.[9]

Can a claimant argue that an emanation reduces the amenity value of her land *even if* she uses the land in a way which means that *she* is not in fact inconvenienced? For instance, if A's factory emits nauseating smells on *weekdays* which drift into B's neighbouring cottage, then can B argue that these smells reduce the amenity value of her land *even if* B only uses the cottage at weekends? We think that the answer is 'yes': the day-to-day usefulness of B's cottage is reduced by the smells *even if* B happens not to want to use it on weekdays. The fact that B suffers no 'consequential loss' will affect the amount of damages she can claim from A.[10] But if she seeks a remedy to prevent any *continuation of* the unreasonable interference with her *right* to use and enjoy the land, A will not be able to establish that he is not committing a tort at all simply because B is personally not put out as a result of the smells coming from the factory.[11]

---

[8] Unfortunately, judges regularly echo Lord Westbury LC's phrase without discussion: for example, Lord Neuberger adopted the phrase 'personal discomfort' at the outset of his judgment in *Lawrence* v *Fen Tigers Ltd* [2014] AC 822, at [1].

[9] [1997] AC 655, 706–7.

[10] We discuss the question how the use that a claimant makes of his land will affect the damages that he can receive below, at § 13.12. In *Dobson* v *Thames Water Utilities Ltd* [2009] 3 All ER 319, Waller LJ stated (at [34]) that he was 'unable to see how there can be any damages beyond perhaps the nominal' in a situation where a claimant has not been inconvenienced at all.

[11] *Price* v *Hilditch* [1930] 1 Ch 500, 509; *Nicholls* v *Ely Beet Sugar Factory Ltd (No 2)* [1936] Ch 343. We think the position would be similar if A sneaked into B's garden and hung his washing on B's washing line on weekdays: this would amount to the tort of trespass to land even if B only used the garden at weekends.

A claimant can clearly establish that an emanation reduces the amenity value of her land even if she never *personally* visits it, but instead uses it by letting other people stay there. So, in the above example, B can sue A even if she *never* visits the cottage but uses it by renting it out to holidaymakers. The fact that it is the holidaymakers who experience the nauseous smells, and not B, will not prevent B from making a claim. B can claim because the smells have reduced the usefulness of her land *as a cottage for renting to holidaymakers*. Thus in *Andreae* v *Selfridge & Co Ltd* (1938), where a defendant's building operations unreasonably interfered with the amenity value of land used by the claimant as a hotel, the claimant did not have to establish that she had been *personally* disturbed by the noise or dust in order to recover damages covering the consequential loss of business. Indeed, it would not have mattered if the claimant had been a company, and thus incapable of being woken up at night or choked with dust.

B. Physical damage to land

Land will count as having been physically damaged if it undergoes 'a physical change which renders [it] less useful or less valuable.'[12] Moreover, physical damage to things which are *attached* to the land – buildings, fences, trees – counts as physical damage to land. Obvious examples of emanations causing physical damage include debris blasted from a defendant's quarry smashing windows, or acid smuts from a defendant's chemical works killing trees and shrubs. Less obvious examples include emanations which end up resting on the claimant's land, or become intermingled with it, and reduce its usefulness or value unless they are cleaned away. Thus, in *Hunter* v *Canary Wharf* (1997), the Court of Appeal held that the deposit of excessive dust on a carpet could amount to physical damage to the carpet, and there is no reason to think that a deposit of mud or oil on a paved area would be treated differently. Similarly, in *Blue Circle Industries* v *Ministry of Defence* (1999), the Court of Appeal was willing to hold that the intermingling of plutonium with soil so that it could not be removed amounted to a form of property damage.

If an emanation only causes damage to personal property that was present *on* the claimant's land but *not attached* to it, such as vehicles, animals or clothes, should this be treated as involving a 'reduction in the amenity value of land' or 'physical damage to land'? This question is raised by the **Dog Whistle Problem**:

> *Barker* uses his land for breeding pedigree dogs. *Grinder* operates machinery on neighbouring land which emits a high-pitched whistle. The whistle is too high-pitched for *Barker* to hear but it drives the dogs on his land into such a frenzy that they sometimes injure themselves.

We think that it cannot be said that the Dog Whistle Problem involves physical damage *to land*, and that *Barker* would have to claim that the whistling reduces the amenity value of his land by restricting his ability to use it for dog breeding. (We discuss below the separate question whether a claimant who has established that a defendant has committed private nuisance in relation to him or her can obtain damages compensating for consequential damage to personal property.)[13]

---

[12] *Hunter* v *Canary Wharf* [1997] AC 655, 676 (per Pill LJ).
[13] See below, § 15.12.

C. Personal injury

Hunter v *Canary Wharf* (1997) and subsequent decisions have made it clear that a claimant cannot sue in private nuisance for physical injuries to the person that she suffers as a result of an emanation onto her land.[14] Consider, for example, the **Blinded Gardener Problem**:

> A's factory starts to emit acidic smoke because a filter has malfunctioned. This smoke drifts onto B's land. Unfortunately, B is standing in her garden when the smoke comes onto her land, and she is permanently blinded by it. As a result, B is unable to enjoy admiring her beautiful garden, or to do any more gardening, which was previously her favourite hobby.

There is no doubt that in this situation B has suffered an interference with the way *she* uses and enjoys her land. But A is not liable to her in private nuisance because he has not made *B's land* less useful: the land itself remains just as useful for creating a beautiful garden even though *B* is no longer able to use it for that purpose.[15]

Not allowing claimants to sue in private nuisance for physical injuries to the person has advantages and disadvantages. If damages for such injuries could be recovered in private nuisance then the anomalous situation would arise that a person would find it easier to recover damages if she was injured in her garden – as in the Blinded Gardener Problem – than if she suffered the same injury in the street, or at work. Further, because only a claimant with an interest in the affected land can sue in private nuisance,[16] a second anomaly would then arise: a landowner who was injured in her garden by an emanation would be able to sue a person responsible in private nuisance for damages in respect of her injury without having to prove that the person acted carelessly; on the other hand, if the landowner's infant son (who we can assume would not have an interest in the land) were injured by the same emanation, he would have to prove carelessness on the part of the person responsible for the emanation (because he would have to use the tort of negligence). One possible solution to the second anomaly would be to let those without interests in land sue in private nuisance. But the House of Lords rejected this solution in *Hunter* v *Canary Wharf* (1997), and ruled that it was inconsistent with the *function* of the tort, which is to protect interests in land. The preferred solution to both anomalies was to insist that *nobody* could sue in private nuisance for compensation in respect of physical injuries to the person.

---

[14] [1997] AC 655, 696 (per Lord Lloyd), 707 (per Lord Hoffmann). In *Transco plc* v *Stockport Metropolitan Borough Council* [2004] 2 AC 1, a majority of the House of Lords held that damages for personal injuries could not be recovered under the rule in *Rylands* v *Fletcher* (discussed in Chapter 14, below) because the rule in private nuisance was that damages were not recoverable for this type of harm: see [9] (per Lord Bingham), [35] (per Lord Hoffmann), [52] (per Lord Hobhouse).

[15] In light of this, it is questionable whether Lawton J was correct to hold in *British Celanese Ltd* v *A H Hunt (Capacitors) Ltd* [1969] 1 WLR 959 that an isolated escape of metal foils from the defendant's land, which blew into the claimant's factory and shorted out its power supply for 12 minutes, could amount to a private nuisance. Such a short interruption to the claimant's power supply could hardly be said to have reduced the amenity value of the land. However, some temporary damage was done to the claimant's machines as a result of the power cut, and that sort of harm *might* have been capable of being counted as physical damage to the claimant's land.

[16] See below, § 13.11.

A disadvantage, however, of not allowing claimants to recover for physical injuries to the person in private nuisance cases is that this *creates* a different anomaly: if foul-smelling acidic smoke coming from A's land drifts across land belonging to B, B will find it easier to sue A for the foul smell of the smoke than for any physical injury it causes to her eyes. If the foul smell reduces the amenity value of B's land then she will be able to sue A in private nuisance for compensation *for that* without having to prove carelessness on A's part. On the other hand, carelessness on A's part must be established before B will be able to sue him (using the tort of negligence) for compensation in respect of acid burns. The impression given is that the law attaches greater importance to protecting people's land from being made less useful than it does to protecting people's physical welfare.

13.4 Emanation cases (2): reasonable interferences

Where a claimant can show that an emanation onto her land has either (1) reduced the amenity value of that land or (2) physically damaged the land, that emanation will only amount to a private nuisance if the interference was *unreasonable*. Not all interferences resulting from emanations are unreasonable. Nobody can expect that every irksome noise, smell or vibration coming onto their land will amount to a tort. Ordinary social living requires a degree of 'give and take'. Your neighbours have to put up with your singing in the shower; you, in turn, have to put up with their wailing baby.

The following three rules identify interferences that are *not unreasonable* and therefore not actionable as private nuisances:

(1) An interference will *not* be unreasonable if it is *insubstantial*, in particular, if an ordinary occupier of land in the locality would regard the interference as tolerable.

(2) An interference will *not* be unreasonable if it results from *acts 'necessary for the common and ordinary use and occupation of land and houses'*, so long as these acts are *'conveniently done'*.[17]

(3) An interference will *not* be unreasonable if it results from *the 'reasonable user' of land*.[18]

Although we will discuss each of these rules in turn it will probably already be apparent that they overlap: some people will think that the disturbance to a neighbour from a schoolboy practising the trombone for half an hour each evening is 'tolerable', others that such music practice is 'necessary for the common and ordinary use and occupation of land and houses', and still others that it is a 'reasonable user' of land in a residential area. But such overlaps cause no difficulties, because if any of the three rules is applicable then the claimant will be unable to establish that the interference is unreasonable. What this highlights is that the three rules identify interferences which are *not* unreasonable; after discussing each rule we will still have to consider what factors determine whether other interferences *are* unreasonable.

---

[17] These phrases originally come from the judgment of Bramwell B in *Bamford* v *Turnley* (1862) 3 B & S 66, 122 ER 27.

[18] In the phrase 'reasonable user' the word 'user' does not refer to the *person* who is using the land. Instead in this phrase the word 'user' means 'use', so a 'reasonable user of land' is a 'reasonable use of land'. Today, only lawyers use the word 'user' in this way.

A. Insubstantial interferences

An interference will not be unreasonable if it would be regarded as insubstantial, or tolerable, by an ordinary occupier of land.

It follows that if only a *hypersensitive occupier* could regard an interference as substantial then it will not be held to be unreasonable.[19] According to the leading case, for an interference to be actionable it must be '[an] inconvenience materially interfering with the ordinary comfort . . . of human existence, not merely according to elegant or dainty modes of living, but according to plain and sober and simple notions among the English people'.[20]

The same rule applies to interferences that can only affect 'delicate trades'. Thus in *Robinson* v *Kilvert* (1889), the claimant complained that brown paper he had been storing had been damaged by the defendant's over-heating of the room below. The court held that there had not been an unreasonable interference because the heat could only have had a detrimental effect on an 'exceptionally delicate trade'.

It is important, however, to distinguish the test for liability from the question of the *extent* of a defendant's liability once the tort of private nuisance has been established. This distinction means that once it has been established that an interference was unreasonable, and consequently that it *would* have materially interfered with an ordinary occupier's comfort or a *reasonably robust* trade, a claimant can claim even though she was actually hypersensitive or operated a delicate trade.[21] Thus in *McKinnon Industries* v *Walker* (1951), the Privy Council held that the claimant could obtain a remedy against a defendant whose factory emitted noxious fumes and sulphur dioxide. These gases would have damaged any reasonably robust neighbouring trade so the test for liability was satisfied, and the claim could proceed even though they had actually interfered with the claimant's use of land for his delicate trade as an orchid grower.

B. Interferences arising from acts that are necessary for the common and ordinary use of land, and conveniently done

Even a *substantial* disturbance will not be an *unreasonable* interference if it results from ordinary use of a house as a *house*. An example of this is provided by the case of *Southwark LBC* v *Tanner* (2001). The claimants were tenants who lived in old houses with soundproofing so inadequate that they could hear everything their neighbours did: 'their coming and going, their cooking and cleaning, their quarrels and their love-making.'[22] Lord Millett accepted that '[life] in these conditions must be intolerable'.[23] Nonetheless, the

---

[19] In *Network Rail Infrastructure Ltd* v *CJ Morris* [2004] EWCA Civ 172, the Court of Appeal suggested that it was no longer necessary to determine whether particular uses were hypersensitive since this issue had been subsumed in the more general question whether the defendant's behaviour was 'reasonable between neighbours'. We believe that the court was wrong to say this since the general question is too loose for lawyers to use in a predictable and consistent manner. Sub-rules have developed to foster predictability and consistency, and the *insubstantial interference* rule is one of these sub-rules which can help lawyers to decide whether an interference for which the defendant is responsible is an *unreasonable* interference.

[20] *Walter* v *Selfe* (1851) 4 De G & Sm 315, 322, 64 ER 849, 852 (per Knight Bruce VC).

[21] Of course, any claim for damages for past losses will be subject to the rules relating to 'remoteness of damage'. See below, § 13.12.

[22] [2001] 1 AC 1, 7.

[23] [2001] 1 AC 1, 18.

House of Lords unanimously held that this sort of interference did not amount to an actionable private nuisance. Despite the 'intolerable' effect of their everyday noises it was not unreasonable for the claimants' neighbours to make such noises.

Lord Millett expressly stated that there could be no liability if the acts causing the interference were *necessary for the common and ordinary use and occupation of land* and *conveniently done.*[24] But the test of necessity is weak here: *common and ordinary* is the phrase which governs. Babies, televisions and washing machines are not strictly *necessary* for occupation of land as a house, but they are all part of *common and ordinary occupation*, and they will not ordinarily be treated as involving unreasonable interference. *Conveniently done* is an important qualification, however. The point seems to be that to avoid liability babies, televisions and washing machines must not be arranged in ways that expose neighbours to substantial noise where it would be equally convenient to arrange them otherwise. Thus, if there was nowhere in his house that a defendant could put his washing machine without it disturbing his neighbours then the noise emanating from it (at least at times of day when washing machines are commonly used) would not be an *unreasonable* interference. But if it disturbed them only because he chose to put it in an alcove where the wall between the houses was particularly thin then the interference might be unreasonable.

C. Interferences arising from the reasonable user of land

The rule that an interference will not be unreasonable if it arises from the reasonable user of land is potentially relevant in a far broader range of cases than the two rules we have already discussed. There is considerable scope for argument, however, as to what will count as a 'reasonable user'.

(1) *Reasonable user and reasonable care.* It is important to note that saying that a defendant will not be liable for interference resulting from a 'reasonable user' is *not* the same as saying that a defendant cannot be liable if he has taken 'reasonable care' to reduce the interference to a minimum.[25] If a defendant has failed to take reasonable care to minimise the interference then this will usually prevent him from demonstrating that the interference stems from a reasonable user of land.[26] But taking reasonable care to minimise interference does not establish that the defendant's activities involve a reasonable user of land.

Suppose, for example, *Industrialist* operates a chemical factory that emits clouds of acidic gas that drift over the garden of *Restful's* nearby cottage, where it causes a nauseous smell and damages her shrubs. Here we can conclude that the operation of *Industrialist's* chemical factory is unreasonably interfering with *Restful's* use and enjoyment of her land without investigating whether the factory is being operated carelessly: *Restful* should not

---

[24] [2001] 1 AC 1, 21.

[25] In *Cambridge Water Co Ltd v Eastern Counties Leather plc* [1994] 2 AC 264 at 299, Lord Goff stated that 'if the user is reasonable, the defendant will not be liable for consequent harm to his neighbour's enjoyment of his land; but if the user is not reasonable, the defendant will be liable, even though he may have exercised reasonable care and skill to avoid it.'

[26] In *Lawrence* v *Fen Tigers Ltd* [2014] AC 822, a case involving nuisance by noise, Lord Neuberger stated, at [76]: 'the fact that it is not open to a neighbouring claimant to object to the defendant's activities simply because they emit noise does not mean that the defendant is free to carry on those activities in any way he wishes. The claimant is entitled to expect the defendant to take all reasonable steps to ensure that the noise is kept to a reasonable minimum.'

be expected to put up with nauseous smells and damaged shrubs regardless of how much *Industrialist* has invested in limiting the emanations from his factory.[27]

Some commentators argue that even if *Industrialist* has taken all reasonable precautions to minimise the emission of acidic gas he may still have been *careless* in a special way: his failure to exercise reasonable care is not in how he *operates* the chemical factory but in his decision to *locate* it where it will interfere with *Restful's* use and enjoyment of her garden. But this argument does not work: *Restful* can demonstrate that the factory is causing an unreasonable interference even if *Industrialist* proves that it is located in by far the most sensible place for it, and is being operated so as to minimise interference. We think that even if everyone agrees that such chemical factories are valuable for society, and this one has been located where it will interfere with the smallest number of people to the least extent, it should still be held that the interference that it causes – a nauseous smell and physical damage to the shrubs – is unreasonable.

How can this be? How can what is valuable and sensible be castigated as unreasonable and wrong? Our answer is that even if a chemical factory in this location is valuable and sensible *from the perspective of society as a whole*, it is unreasonable *from the perspective of Restful*, who has had her garden made unpleasant and her shrubs damaged. *Restful* can fairly argue that what is valuable and sensible *from the perspective of society as a whole* is not the same as what a neighbouring property owner must put up with by way of 'give and take', and that it is unreasonable to expect her to put up with *all* the consequences of the chemical factory without any redress.[28]

One way of thinking about what tort law is doing in this area is to think of *Industrialist* and *Restful* as having *equal rights* to use and enjoy their land.[29] If *Industrialist* can insist that the importance of his chemical factory for society as a whole means that he can operate it so as to render *Restful's* land close to useless for *her* ordinary purposes then he will not be respecting her *equal* right: he will be claiming that her right must give way to his simply because he is pursuing a project that is more important to the public. This sort of reasoning is usually rejected by private law: everyone would agree that *Industrialist* cannot seize *Restful's* cottage and evict her without redress merely because it would be valuable and sensible to extend the chemical factory onto her land. Seizing the cottage

---

[27] We discuss below how far the question whether the interference is reasonable may be influenced by the fact that *Industrialist* has obtained planning permission for his factory and may have permits 'authorising' such emissions.

[28] The argument in this paragraph demonstrates why we would not want to adopt Conor Gearty's suggestion that *all* cases involving physical damage to land should be dealt with by the tort of negligence (or under the rule in *Rylands* v *Fletcher*, discussed below, Chapter 14) rather than in private nuisance: see Gearty 1989. In contrast to Gearty, Lee 2003 argues that the label 'unreasonable' is 'unnecessary and misleading' in situations where a court is considering whether an interference which has caused physical damage to land is actionable because all that the court is really considering is whether strict liability should apply to a particular *activity*. But we do not believe that all that courts do in such cases is classify *activities*. For instance, they may also have to consider if an activity, although ordinary, was *conveniently done*, and whether the damage was merely trivial or a result of hypersensitivity.

[29] A defendant and a claimant will not have equal rights in *all* private nuisance cases. We argue below (§ 13.9(A)) that a defendant may be held liable even if he has no right to use the land where he creates the nuisance. But we have chosen to discuss the situation where defendant and claimant have equal rights because private nuisance requires rules that will be fair in *this* situation.

would clearly be a tort, even if *Restful's* land was by far the best place in the country to locate a new chemical factory. But if seizing the cottage would clearly be a tort then doing physical damage to it, or making it useless for ordinary purposes, cannot be more acceptable.

(2) *Ordinary and permitted uses.* The third rule – that an interference will not be unreasonable if it results from the 'reasonable user' of land – was formulated as an extension of the second rule, that an interference will not be unreasonable if it results from acts 'necessary for the common and ordinary use and occupation of land and houses' so long as these are 'conveniently done'. The primary reason for such an extension was to exclude from the scope of the tort the consequences of *other* uses of land – beyond use as a house – that are *wholly ordinary* in a particular locality. Where a use of land is *wholly ordinary* in a particular locality then the interference that it causes can fairly be treated as something which ought to be tolerated in that locality in accordance with a general principle of 'give and take'.[30] For example, if *Framer* and *Glazier* possess adjoining units in an industrial estate neither ought to be able to complain about daily disturbance caused by the noise of hammering or use of power tools: the noises from such wholly ordinary activities on an industrial estate clearly ought to be tolerated as part of 'give and take'.

Barr v *Biffa Waste Services Ltd* (2012) – a case where the operators of a waste tip started to process 'pre-treated waste' that was more smelly than the sorts of refuse that they had previously processed at the site – raised an important question: Will a use of land be held to be reasonable when it has been *permitted by regulators* of the activity? At first instance, Coulson J reasoned that 'the large scale tipping of waste as landfill is a necessity of modern society, and the best (perhaps the only) way in which non-recyclable waste can be disposed of without causing significant harm to the environment' and that consequently a waste tip would be a 'reasonable user' of land if it operated in accordance with permits granted by the Environment Agency.[31] In the judge's opinion, this approach avoided the 'unsatisfactory' position of common law liability for private nuisance being out-of-step with the statutory framework regulating waste tips. We think, however, that this reasoning confused: (i) what is valuable and sensible *from the perspective of society as a whole*, and (ii) what neighbouring property owners ought to put up with, by way of 'give and take', without any redress. The Court of Appeal subsequently allowed an appeal against Coulson J's judgment and confirmed: '[there] is no principle that the common law should "march with" a statutory scheme covering similar subject-matter'.[32] Carnwath LJ stated: 'An activity which is conducted in contravention of planning or environmental controls is unlikely to be reasonable. But the converse does not follow. Sticking to the rules is an aspect of good neighbourliness, but it is far from the whole story – in law as in life.'[33]

---

[30] We discuss the relevance of the character of the locality where the claimant's land is situated in detail below, § 13.5(B).

[31] [2011] EWHC 1003 (TCC), at [360] and [350].

[32] [2013] QB 455, at [46] (expressly approved by Lord Neuberger in *Lawrence* v *Fen Tigers Ltd* [2014] AC 822, at [92]).

[33] [2013] QB 455, at [76].

13.5 Emanation cases (3): establishing an unreasonable interference

So far we have established that an interference caused by an emanation will *not* be unreasonable if it is: (1) insubstantial; or (2) caused by acts 'necessary for the common and ordinary use and occupation of land and houses', so long as these acts are 'conveniently done', or (3) caused by a use of land that is wholly ordinary or well established in the locality. But what if an interference *is* substantial and is *not* caused by a wholly ordinary or well-established use of land? How will a court decide if the interference is *unreasonable*? We think that there are three helpful guidelines:

(1) If the interference reduces the amenity value of land, then a court will consider the character of the locality.

(2) If the interference reduces the amenity value of land, then a court will measure its significance by considering matters such as the time, duration, regularity and intensity of the interference.

(3) A court will consider the reasons for the interference, in particular whether the interference results from malice, negligence, or pursuit of a legitimate purpose.

These guidelines are important so we will say something about each of them in turn, before setting out a special rule, which applies where the defendant interferes with the claimant's land in defending his land against a 'common enemy' that threatens both their properties.

A. Character of the locality

We noted above that interference caused by a 'reasonable user' of land will not be unreasonable, and that uses of land that are 'wholly ordinary' in a particular locality will generally be classed as 'reasonable users'.[34] For related reasons, the character of the locality where the events occur is important when considering whether the interference caused by a use that is not 'wholly ordinary' is unreasonable, at least when the interference causes a reduction in amenity value rather than physical damage. The House of Lords identified the type of effect on the claimant's land as a significant distinction in this context in *St Helen's Smelting* v *Tipping* (1865). In this case Lord Westbury LC suggested that where there was an interference with personal sensibilities by, for instance, noise or smell, the question whether it was unreasonable would have to be judged taking into account the nature of the locality, while there would be no need to consider this if the interference caused material injury to the property.

Unfortunately, the *St Helen's* case left some loose ends. First, Lord Westbury LC at one point talks about 'material injury to property' being the condition which makes the nature of the locality irrelevant, but later describes 'sensible injury to the *value* of property' as the condition.[35] If the latter were right, then the distinction would virtually disappear, because most interferences with personal sensibilities will cause at least a temporary reduction in land *value*; nobody is likely to pay as much for a bad-smelling house or for one

---

[34] See above, § 13.4(C)(2).
[35] (1865) 11 HLC 642, at 650–1.

with a noisy factory next door. This suggests that the distinction should be between interferences which cause physical damage and those which reduce amenity value. The degree
of noise, smell, and the like which one should tolerate as part of the social rules of 'give
and take' may vary with locality, but there is no locality where it is reasonable to keep
doing things which physically damage the reasonably robust land of others.[36] In *Hunter* v
Canary Wharf (1997), Lords Hoffmann and Cooke both mentioned *St Helen's Smelting*
and the locality rule, and both expressed the key distinction as being between interferences causing 'material injury to the property' and those causing 'sensible personal
discomfort'.[37]

The second issue left unsolved by *St Helen's Smelting* is *how* to identify and classify
localities when this is necessary. Many famously quotable observations on locality, such as
the quip of Byles J that a 'swine-style might not be considered a nuisance in Bethnal
Green: but it certainly would be so in Grosvenor Square',[38] do not subdivide localities in
any detail. *Gaunt* v *Fynney* (1870) provides a fairly typical example of the 'broad brush'
sometimes used by the judiciary: in this case Lord Selborne went no further than catego-
rising Leek, Staffordshire, as a 'manufacturing town'.[39] Other cases, however, have
adopted much finer distinctions. For example, in *Adams* v *Ursell* (1913) the evidence
suggested that most of Silver Street was 'in the lowest district of Dursley . . . but that the
[claimant's] house and others near it were of a much better character.'[40] In these circumstances Swinfen Eady J granted an injunction preventing the defendant from operating a
fried fish shop in a building adjoining the claimant's, but refused to extend the injunction
so as to prevent him from opening such a shop elsewhere on the street. In *Lawrence* v *Fen
Tigers Ltd* (2014), Lord Neuberger acknowledged that 'Sometimes, it may be difficult to
identify the precise extent of the locality for the purpose of the assessment, or the precise
words to describe the character of the locality.' But despite such difficulties he warned that
'any attempt to give general guidance on such issues risks being unhelpful or worse.'[41]

In the same case, Lord Carnwath noted a further problem: 'in areas where conflicts
may arise, the character of any locality may not conform to a single homogeneous identity,
but rather may consist of a varied pattern of uses all of which need to coexist in a modern
society.'[42] Lord Neuberger agreed that the concept of a 'locality' having 'a character'
might be 'too monolithic in some cases' and suggested that it might be more useful to
describe the relevant concept as 'the established pattern of uses [of land] in the locality'.[43]
This suggests that localities may be of different sizes, and that any area where one can

---

[36] There may, however, be *occasions* when it is reasonable to do things which may cause physical damage to
the reasonably robust land of others. One example may be occasions where it is reasonable to take steps
against a 'common enemy', discussed below, § 13.5(E).

[37] [1997] AC 655, 705 (per Lord Hoffmann), 712 (per Lord Cooke). Lord Lloyd used a similar distinction
(at 695), though he did not expressly link it to *St Helen's Smelting*. Consistently with the view we
expressed above, see § 13.3(A), we would prefer to talk of interferences which 'reduce the amenity value
of land' rather than interferences which cause 'sensible personal discomfort'.

[38] Byles J made this observation during argument in *Hole* v *Barlow* (1858) 4 CB NS 334, 340; 140 ER
1113, 1116. Green 1985 has calculated that Bethnal Green was the second most impoverished area of
London in 1841 and the most impoverished in 1871.

[39] (1872–3) LR 8 Ch App 8, at 11 and 12.

[40] [1913] 1 Ch 269, 270.

[41] *Lawrence* v *Fen Tigers Ltd* [2014] AC 822, at [59].

[42] Ibid, [181].

[43] Ibid, [60].

identify a 'pattern of uses' different from those in neighbouring areas can sensibly be described as a 'locality'.

The facts of the *Fen Tigers* case raised an unusual and difficult challenge because the activities alleged to be causing a noise nuisance – operation of a stadium for various types of motor-racing and a track for moto-cross – were long-standing but unlike the activities of other occupiers of land in the surrounding, largely rural, area.[44] This meant that the Supreme Court had to decide whether the effects of activities that are *alleged* to constitute private nuisances ought themselves to be taken into account when assessing the 'established pattern of uses' in a locality. Lord Neuberger was worried that it would be artificial, and potentially unfair to the defendants, to ignore a firmly established activity altogether when characterising a locality, but, equally, it would be unfair to the claimants to treat what was alleged to be a private nuisance as defining the nature of a locality simply because it had been going on for several years. His solution was to hold that a defendant *could* rely on its own activities 'as constituting part of the character of the locality, but only to the extent that those activities do not constitute a nuisance'.[45] He conceded, however, that this might seem circular: if one has to decide whether an activity constitutes a private nuisance *before* one can decide whether it is legitimate to allow it to influence the characterisation of a locality then it is hard to see how the characterisation of the locality can be used to decide whether the activity constitutes a private nuisance.[46]

We suggest that the reason that courts attempt to characterise different localities is because different social rules of 'give and take' – what ordinary occupiers ought to tolerate – are likely to have evolved in different places, and it is these rules that are useful in deciding whether an interference should be condemned as 'unreasonable'. Consequently, we submit that a defendant should be able to rely on its own activities 'as constituting part of the character of the locality' where the continuation of those activities indicates that the community accepts that their effects *ought to be* tolerated. Where, by contrast, the activities have attracted regular protests from other residents, or where the absence of dissent can be explained otherwise than as indicating *toleration*, we suggest that it would be unfair to treat them as setting the benchmark for reasonable 'give and take' in the locality. In practice, many cases involve disputes about an *intensification* of an activity, so that its effects go beyond what has previously been tolerated.

Joanne Conaghan and Wade Mansell have raised a more general concern about setting different standards for different localities; they believe that this conceals judicial prejudice and amounts to an essentially class-based device.[47] But whilst it is certainly true that the locality principle has been used to protect the well-heeled from fish and chip shops,[48] it has also been used to protect blue-collar residential districts from industrial noise.[49] Conaghan and Mansell's core worry is probably that the locality principle leads to inhabitants of working-class housing areas having to put up with greater degrees

---

[44] Lord Neuberger described the locality as 'a sparsely populated area, with a couple of small villages and a military airfield between a mile and two miles away', ibid, [71].

[45] Ibid, [74].

[46] We do not share Lord Neuberger's belief that an 'iterative process' can resolve this circularity: ibid, [72]. Lord Carnwath appears to have also had doubts about the 'iterative process': see [190]. Steel 2017 also rejects the solution (at 162–3).

[47] Conaghan & Mansell 1999, 137.

[48] *Adams* v *Ursell* [1913] 1 Ch 269.

[49] *Halsey* v *Esso Petroleum* [1961] 1 WLR 683.

of interference than inhabitants of middle-class areas where property prices are higher. We must be careful, however, not to treat the social reality that the locality principle *imports* into the law as if it is a *consequence* of the principle.[50] Furthermore, it is worth noting that the locality principle applies equally to both claimants and defendants: thus if *Fryer* cannot use his property as a fish and chip shop because of the nature of the locality, then equally *Fryer* is protected against others carrying on activities similar to fish frying which might reduce the amenity value of *his* land. Likewise, if it is found that in a particular locality it is reasonable for *Welder* to use his land for light industry even though this interferes with *Dreamer*'s use and enjoyment of her land, then it will be equally reasonable for *Dreamer* to interfere with other people's use and enjoyment of *their land* by using *her* land for light industry. Thus while the locality principle means that there are inequalities between owners of property situated in different places, at the same time all owners in a particular locality have equal opportunities and restrictions on their use and enjoyment of land.[51]

In a recent article, Sandy Steel criticises our account of the locality principle.[52] He argues that a satisfactory account must explain why courts are *justified* in using an 'established pattern of uses', or a local rule of 'give-and-take', to determine what is reasonable: why would we want the law to absorb a particular locality's rule if that rule tolerated uses of land which were causing interference *unnecessarily* because of a failure to adopt impact-mitigation measures? We think that Steel is correct to point out that *if* the courts want to use the tort of private nuisance to ensure that land is used in the most efficient way, or in the way that best ensures that everyone has the greatest opportunity to pursue their life-plans, *then* they should not assume that relying on local rules is the best way of achieving this. But we maintain that it is sensible for the courts to enforce the settled expectations of those living in a particular locality, rather than try to use tort law to remake communities.

One suggestion that is occasionally advanced is that in classifying localities reference should be made to the opinions of planning authorities. The orthodox view, however, is that *planning permission cannot authorise a private nuisance*.[53] Private nuisance protects the private rights of a claimant, and Parliament has not granted planning authorities the power to remove private rights. Thus in *Wheeler* v *JJ Saunders Ltd* (1996), a case involving 'swine-styles' on an industrial scale (housing 800 pigs) being built with planning permission 11 metres from the claimants' holiday cottage, Peter Gibson LJ stated, 'The court should be slow to acquiesce in the extinction of private rights without compensation as a result of administrative decisions which cannot be appealed and are difficult to challenge.'[54]

---

[50] To put the same point another way, which of these statements is true? (1) Housing is more affordable in some localities *because* they are areas which are understood to be noisy, etc. (2) The law allows these areas to be subjected to additional noise, etc., *because* they are where the affordable housing is.

[51] The significance of this formal 'equality of opportunities and restrictions' should not be exaggerated. For example, in *Watson* v *Croft Promosport Ltd* [2009] EWCA Civ 15, [2009] 3 All ER 249, the Court of Appeal upheld Simon J's conclusion that the defendants could organise up to 40 days per year of noisy motor-racing without committing the tort of private nuisance, but the owners of nearby houses probably attached little value to their 'equal opportunity' to use their land to open motor-racing circuits.

[52] Steel 2017, 155–7.

[53] There are some special statutory exceptions. For example, s 158 of the Planning Act 2008 provides that an order granting development consent, which is a type of order used for nationally significant infrastructure projects, confers statutory authority to carry out the development concerned.

[54] [1996] Ch 19, 35.

This view was echoed by Lord Hoffmann in *Hunter* v *Canary Wharf* (1997),[55] and confirmed by a majority of the Supreme Court in *Lawrence* v *Fen Tigers Ltd* (2014): 'the mere fact that the activity which is said to give rise to the nuisance has the benefit of a planning permission is normally of no assistance to the defendant . . .'[56] He used the word 'normally' to allow for the possibility that in some cases a planning decision might provide a benchmark which would be useful in 'framing' the debate in a private nuisance claim, and sometimes evidence of what occurred during a planning process might be relevant to points arising in the course of a tort claim.

This orthodox view had to be reconfirmed in *Wheeler*, *Hunter* and *Fen Tigers* because doubt had been cast on it by *Gillingham BC* v *Medway (Chatham) Dock Co Ltd* (1993). This involved unusual facts: the litigant claiming that a commercial dockyard was a nuisance was the very council that had previously authorised the development. Buckley J held that the defendants were not liable because, even if a planning authority could not directly authorise a nuisance, it could 'through its development plans and decisions, alter the character of a neighbourhood. That may have the effect of rendering innocent activities which prior to the change would have been an actionable nuisance.'[57] Subsequent cases *confined* 'the *Gillingham* principle' rather than overruling it, and in *Fen Tigers* Lord Carnwath suggested it was underpinned by the rule that 'in exceptional cases a planning permission may be the result of a considered policy decision by the competent authority leading to a fundamental change in the pattern of uses, which cannot sensibly be ignored in assessing the character of the area against which the acceptability of the defendant's activity is to be judged.'[58] The majority of the Supreme Court, however, thought it was appropriate to reject the principle altogether, and to treat planning permission as primarily significant when determining what *remedy* to award to a claimant who had established that the defendant was committing private nuisance.[59]

Can the orthodox position be defended, or ought courts to recognise that planning authorities are both more expert and more democratically legitimate when choosing between competing uses of land? One objection to treating planning authorities as having power to protect new developments from tort liability, even if only by means of a 'considered policy decision', is that this would be power to reduce private rights without compensation. There is no evidence that Parliament has ever sought to grant such a power to planning authorities; indeed, it would be inconsistent with Parliament's usual practice: when it grants *statutory authority* to conduct an activity which will interfere with neighbouring land it usually requires compensation to be paid.[60] A second objection is that planning decisions may sometimes be made without all the interested parties being represented, can be based on incomplete information, and can be difficult for third parties to challenge. Maria Lee has suggested that a satisfactory compromise solution might involve

---

[55] [1997] AC 655, 710. Similarly Lord Cooke: 'compliance with planning controls is not itself a defence to a nuisance action' (at 722).

[56] [2014] AC 822, [94] (per Lord Neuberger). This approach was also supported by Lord Sumption at [156] and Lord Mance at [165]. By contrast Lord Carnwath expressed the opinion that planning permission might be relevant in a wider range of cases, and Lord Clarke expressed some support for this view.

[57] [1993] QB 343, 359.

[58] [2014] AC 822, [223].

[59] [2014] AC 822, [99].

[60] This argument is clearly set out by Lord Carnwath in [2014] AC 822, at [196].

courts *evaluating* individual planning decisions to see whether they were the result of processes likely to generate 'authoritative' decisions about the appropriate balance between public and private interests.[61] We are doubtful, however, whether enough will be gained from diverting judicial effort into appraisal of planning processes to make the game worth the candle. Moreover, this compromise does not address the absence of compensation.

B. Time, duration, regularity, intensity

The second guideline is largely a matter of common sense. The magnitude of an interference is clearly an important factor when assessing whether it is unreasonable, and this can only be assessed by considering the time, duration, regularity and intensity of the interference in question.

Thus night-time noise which interferes with sleep is far more likely to be held a nuisance than day-time noise. The unreasonableness of interfering with sleep was a major consideration in the case of *Rushmer* v *Polsue & Alferi* (1906), where a disgruntled resident persuaded North J to close down the printing presses of Fleet Street at night. When dawn breaks and when night begins are clearly matters of degree. In *Metropolitan Properties Ltd* v *Jones* (1939), Goddard LJ held that an electric motor which started at 8 am was a nuisance since 'after [that] hour an elderly gentleman is quite entitled to stay in bed, if he wants to, and have a restful time'.[62] On the other hand, in the case of *Vanderpant* v *Mayfair Hotel* (1930), the judge only granted an injunction against a hotel's noise-making between 10 pm and 8 am. Locality will also be a relevant factor: in agricultural areas no doubt the day begins rather earlier than it does in localities specialising in the accommodation of students.

On regularity, even the most innocent of noises may become a nuisance if repeated too often. Thus in *Soltau* v *De Held* (1851), the claimant succeeded in obtaining an injunction against a Roman Catholic church in Clapham which rang its chapel bell at 5 am and 6.45 am every morning, its steeple bell at 8.45 am, 6.45 pm and 7.15 pm every day, with occasional additional peals of all its bells at weekends.

C. Malice, negligence, and pursuit of a legitimate purpose

When considering whether an interference is unreasonable courts take into account *why* the interference is being caused.

An important, and disputed, question is whether proof that A *maliciously* chose to reduce the amenity value of B's land is sufficient to establish the unreasonableness of the interference.

In *Christie* v *Davey* (1893), the defendant was unfortunate enough to live next door to a 'musical family' in Brixton.[63] Their musical activities disturbed his concentration and he responded by knocking on a party wall, beating on trays, whistling, shrieking and imitating what was being played. North J decided that this alternative symphony was

---

[61] See, for example, Lee 2013, quoted by Lord Carnwath in [2014] AC 822, at [198].

[62] [1939] 2 All ER 202, 204.

[63] Mrs Christie was a teacher of music and singing; her daughter was a medallist at the Royal Academy of Music and gave lessons on violin and piano; her lodger was also a medallist in music; and her son was in the habit of playing the cello in the kitchen up until 11 at night. North J observed that Mrs Christie's husband, 'perhaps fortunately for himself, is very deaf': [1893] 1 Ch 316, 324.

an unreasonable interference and granted an injunction, stating that 'what was done by the Defendant was done only for the purpose of annoyance and in my opinion it was not a legitimate use of the Defendant's house to use it for the purpose of vexing and annoying his neighbours.'[64] It may be useful to compare this case with the *Southwark* case where a comparable degree of disturbance was not actionable because it was a product of ordinary domestic living.

A similar conclusion to that in *Christie* was reached in *Hollywood Silver Fox Farm Ltd* v *Emmett* (1936). The claimant bred silver foxes and put up a sign to advertise this. The defendant was developing one of his fields as plots for bungalows and took the view that people were less likely to buy a bungalow plot if they knew it was a mere 29 yards from where foxes were being bred. When the claimant refused to remove the sign, the defendant carried out a threat to shoot with 'black powder' to frighten the foxes and disturb their breeding. Macnaghten J held that this firing was a nuisance, emphasising the use of bird-scaring cartridges and that the defendant's intention in firing was to alarm and disturb the foxes. It is worth noting that in this case the defendant's malice meant that the interference was found to be unreasonable *even though* the claimant's activity, breeding silver foxes, was arguably *hypersensitive*.[65]

The main difficulty facing the proposition that malice *is* sufficient to make an interference *unreasonable* is that this seems inconsistent with the decision of the House of Lords in *Bradford Corporation* v *Pickles* (1895). Here it was alleged that Pickles had interfered with the groundwater percolating under his land principally because he wanted to force the Corporation, which used the water for its waterworks, to buy his land for an inflated price. In deciding the case against the Corporation their Lordships treated the question whether Pickles was malicious as irrelevant. Lord Watson, for instance, insisted that 'No use of property, which would be legal if due to a proper motive, can become illegal because it is prompted by a motive which is improper or even malicious.'[66]

It can be argued, however, that *Bradford* v *Pickles* can be distinguished from *Christie* and *Hollywood* because the *Bradford* case involved interference by *obstruction* of something heading towards the claimant's land, while *Christie* and *Hollywood* involved interference by the *emanation* of noise.[67] As we will see, in an *obstruction* case a claimant can only sue if she can show that she has a *right* to receive the benefit that has been obstructed,[68] and in the *Bradford* case the Corporation could not establish that they had a *right* to receive the water which the defendant obstructed.[69] Instead, the law treated the defendant as having an absolute right to obstruct the water. Thus it did not matter whether the defendant had acted maliciously in obstructing the water. So the House of Lords' broad statements about malice in *Bradford* v *Pickles* can be treated as being limited to situations where A prevents something going onto B's land which B

---

[64] [1893] 1 Ch 316, 326–7.

[65] The defendant's barrister argued that 'the shooting would have caused no alarm to the animals which are usually to be found on farms in Kent': [1936] 2 KB 468, 474.

[66] [1895] AC 587, 598.

[67] See Taggart 2002, 189.

[68] See, further, below, § 13.7.

[69] See, similarly, Stevens 2007, 22: 'it was held that the claimants had no (property) right to the percolating water. Without a right exigible against the rest of the world to the percolating water, no tort was committed when the supply was cut.'

had no right to receive. *By contrast*, in an *emanation* case the lawfulness of the defend-ant's activity can only be ascertained by considering whether the claimant should be expected to tolerate such interference. Here, the fact that an interference is not a conse-quence of a 'reasonable user' of land – but rather a consequence of the defendant seek-ing to injure the claimant[70] – is *highly* relevant to the question whether the emanation involves an *unreasonable* interference. There is no reason why a claimant should be expected to put up with an interference created by an emanation onto her land which a defendant has maliciously chosen to create.

The courts' strict approach to malicious emanations can be usefully contrasted with their tolerant approach to emanations caused by a defendant pursuing the sort of project that many reasonable property owners will want to pursue. Thus the courts have held that temporary disturbances associated with building works are not a nuisance, provided that the works are carried on with reasonable care and skill. In *Andreae* v *Selfridge & Co Ltd* (1938), the claimant's hotel on Wigmore Street, London, was affected by a major development by Selfridges. Lord Greene MR stated that reasonable care required restricting the hours of work, and 'using proper scientific means of avoiding inconvenience',[71] but that it was not unreasonable to use pneumatic hammers for six days to break up reinforced concrete.

D. Common enemy

Some situations recur so often that the courts have developed special rules to determine whether an interference arising out of them will be unreasonable. For example, in *Arscott* v *The Coal Authority* (2004),[72] the Court of Appeal confirmed that it is not tortious for an occupier of land to take convenient steps to protect her land against a 'common enemy', for instance flooding, even if the reasonably foreseeable consequence of these steps is to displace the problem onto a neighbour's land.[73] This rule is subject to three exceptions. First, a defendant is not permitted to protect her land by altering an established water-course. Secondly, the rule only permits steps in *anticipation* of a threat from a 'common enemy' and does not permit a defendant to cure a problem that has *already* arisen on her land by exporting the misfortune.[74] Thirdly, the defendant will not avoid liability if the protective measures were clearly excessive and the harm to the claimant was caused by their excess.

---

[70] Stevens 2007 suggests (at 23) that malice is relevant only because it demonstrates that a defendant's actions are 'pointless', or 'without social value'. We do not agree. The decision in *Hollywood* did not turn on whether there was greater 'social value' in fox-breeding or profitable bungalow-development. It turned on the *unreasonableness* of intentionally reducing the amenity value of the claimant's land when it was not *necessary* for the defendant to do so in order to use his own land in a common and ordinary way.

[71] [1938] Ch 1.

[72] [2004] EWCA Civ 892. The defendants were held not liable for raising the level of a playing field situated on a flood plain in order to protect it from flooding even though raising the field caused a flood to affect the claimants' houses more severely than it might otherwise have done.

[73] The parties in the *Arscott* case were content to treat the 'common enemy' rule as existing independently of the question whether the defendant had *unreasonably* interfered with the use and enjoyment of land in which B has a sufficient interest. We believe, however, that the 'common enemy' situation is merely one where the courts have developed clear guidance as to what is reasonable; a view apparently shared by Laws LJ: [2004] EWCA Civ 892, at [40].

[74] *Whalley* v *Lancashire and Yorkshire Railway Co* (1884) 13 QBD 131.

13.6 Encroachment cases

If branches or tree roots cross onto a claimant's land, lawyers tend to refer to such intrusions as involving 'encroachment', rather than 'emanation'. The most significant difference between 'encroachment' cases and 'emanation' cases is that it seems that any encroachment which violates the boundaries of a claimant's land *automatically* amounts to an unreasonable interference with the claimant's use and enjoyment of land. (Though of course, in practice, many occupiers of land tolerate overhanging branches and straying roots.) This is not to say that a claimant will be automatically entitled to *sue* a defendant from whose land branches or roots are encroaching: the claimant will also need to show that the defendant is *responsible* for that encroachment, an issue we deal with below.[75] Moreover, the authority of *Lemmon* v *Webb* (1895) suggests that although any encroachment by branches or roots is a private nuisance which a claimant is entitled to *abate* by cutting off the offending protuberances, he will only be able to make a claim for damages if the encroachment has caused further damage.[76]

13.7 Obstruction cases

A. Establishing a right

The summary at the start of this chapter stated that private nuisance not only protects a claimant from having the use and enjoyment of his land unreasonably interfered with, but also from unreasonable interferences with rights associated with his land. In obstruction cases – where a claimant is complaining that something has been obstructed from coming onto his land – the claimant will *only* be allowed to sue in private nuisance if the obstruction unreasonably interferes with some right that is associated with his land. If this condition is *not* satisfied, it will not matter that the obstruction reduces the claimant's enjoyment of his land, or even causes physical damage: the claimant will not be allowed to sue.

Bradford v *Pickles* (1895) and *Hunter* v *Canary Wharf* (1997) are examples of obstruction cases where the claimant could *not* show that the obstruction interfered with some right associated with his land. In *Bradford* v *Pickles*, water was percolating under the defendant's land through undefined channels and he obstructed it so that it never reached the claimants' reservoirs. It was unclear why the defendant did this: he may have simply wanted to harm the claimants, but, more likely, he was trying to persuade them to buy his land or to pay him a fee for allowing the water to continue uninterrupted through his land. The claimants' action against the defendant failed. As the water was flowing through undefined channels under the defendant's land, the claimants had no right to receive it, and could not therefore complain of its obstruction – whatever the defendant's reason for stopping it was.

In *Hunter* v *Canary Wharf*, one of the complaints was that the building of the Canary Wharf Tower interfered with the claimants' television reception because it stood between their homes and the Crystal Palace transmitter. In *Bridlington Relay Ltd* v *Yorkshire Electricity Board* (1965), Buckley J had suggested that interference with television reception

---

[75] See § 13.9.

[76] If a tree is protected by a 'tree preservation order' then the right to abate may be limited: see *Perrin* v *Northampton Borough Council* [2008] 1 WLR 1307.

could not constitute a legal nuisance because it was interference with a purely recreational facility, as opposed to interference with health or physical comfort or well-being. In *Hunter* the House of Lords expressed doubt as to whether such reasoning remained convincing in light of the increased social importance of television.[77] The majority held, however, that interference with television reception merely by building on one's own land was not actionable, because – just as a landowner has no *right* to the beautiful view that he currently enjoys from his land by looking across a neighbour's undeveloped fields – a landowner has no right to receive TV signals that would otherwise come across a neighbour's land.[78]

So when will a claimant be able to establish that she enjoys some right associated with her land to have something cross a neighbour's land without obstruction? Generally speaking, English land law is very cautious about holding that B has a right against her neighbour A that A allow some benefit to pass across or through A's land. In particular, English land law is reluctant to recognise such obligations where they cannot be precisely defined. Saying that A must not unreasonably interfere with the passage of a river which flows in a defined channel across A's land is one thing, but it is quite another thing to say that A must not unreasonably interfere with water percolating under A's land through undefined channels, or with wind that would otherwise travel onto B's land and power B's wind turbine, or with invisible electromagnetic signals that B depends on receiving for business or leisure pursuits. Alongside the problem of defining such obligations with precision is the further difficulty that such benefits could easily be obstructed by activities that the law would not want to discourage. Thus almost any building might interfere with groundwater, wind and electromagnetic signals.

The most common rights associated with land are easements, such as private rights of way. If A unreasonably interferes with B's ability to exercise her rights protected by an easement then B can sue A for having committed the tort of private nuisance. Thus if A *unreasonably* interferes with a private right of way that his neighbour, B, has over A's land, then B will be able to sue A in private nuisance for that interference.

Other rights associated with land that are commonly encountered include those relating to *light*, *water*, and *support*. We will discuss each of these briefly.

(1) Starting with *light*, a landowner may acquire through grant or prescription (as a result of having enjoyed light coming to windows in his building for a certain period of time without interruption or dispute from a neighbour) a right to freedom from such an obstruction of light as would interfere with the ordinary occupations of life.[79]

Acquiring a right to light coming through your window is one thing, but you cannot acquire by prescription a right to receive photons coming onto your land from a beautiful

---

[77] [1997] AC 655, at 684–5 (per Lord Goff), 708 (per Lord Hoffmann), 722 (per Lord Cooke).

[78] [1997] AC 655, at 685 (per Lord Goff), 699 (per Lord Lloyd), 709 (per Lord Hoffmann), 726–7 (per Lord Hope). Because *Hunter* was an obstruction case, it does not decide whether an *emanation* of electromagnetic waves *onto* B's land which interferes with B's television reception can be actionable.

[79] *Colls* v *Home & Colonial Stores Ltd* [1904] AC 179. At what point a claimant can establish that there has been an actionable interference with his right to light depends on what 'ordinary purposes' the claimant's property has been adapted for: *Allen* v *Greenwood* [1980] Ch 119, 130. There is no general right to a flow of air or wind: *Chastey* v *Ackland* [1895] 2 Ch 389, 402 (per Lindley LJ): 'no one has a right to prevent his neighbour from building on his own land, although the consequence may be to diminish or alter the flow of air over it on to land adjoining. So to diminish a flow of air is not actionable as a nuisance.' But where air flows across a defendant's land to a defined aperture in the claimant's building, like a ventilator, a right to continuation of this can be acquired as an easement: *Cable* v *Bryant* [1908] 1 Ch 259.

landscape which can be seen from your window. So if you want to acquire a right *to a view*, you must go to whoever is in a position to obstruct it and get them to enter into a *restrictive covenant* under which they agree not to build on their land. In the absence of such a covenant, there is no right to sue someone who interferes with a beautiful view.[80] In the United States, *some* courts have been willing to draw a distinction between obstructing a view (which is not usually actionable) and positively creating an ugly sight (which can be treated as analogous to an emanation). But English law has not adopted this distinction.

(2) Turning to *water*, an owner of land adjacent to a river or stream has a natural right to receive the regular flow of the stream, but this is subject to the rights of owners upstream to use the water for their domestic purposes and cattle.[81] Thus a downstream owner can make a claim in private nuisance against an upstream owner who substantially diminishes the flow of water by taking it for other purposes, or against anyone who pollutes the water. But – as *Bradford v Pickles* (1895) shows – there is no right to receive water that flows in undefined channels underneath your neighbour's land.

(3) What about *support*? For simplicity, we have talked so far of benefits being *obstructed* from coming onto the claimant's land. But a claimant might also want to sue in private nuisance because a defendant has *withdrawn* some benefit that the defendant's land would otherwise have provided for the claimant's land. The same principles apply to such cases as apply to obstruction cases: the claimant must establish a right to that withdrawn benefit before she can sue in private nuisance for its withdrawal. So if *Digger* performs excavations on his land, which have the effect of withdrawing the *support* that buildings on *Neighbour*'s land previously enjoyed from *Digger*'s land, *Neighbour* will not be able to sue *Digger* in private nuisance unless she can establish a right to that support. Under English law, *Neighbour* will not automatically enjoy such a right. The common law recognises a natural right to the support of land in its undeveloped state. But if *Neighbour* wants a right to support for a *building*, she must enter into an agreement with *Digger* which will give her what is called an *easement of support*, or acquire such a right by prescription. In the absence of such an easement *Digger* will be permitted to excavate on his own land even if this causes the collapse of a building on *Neighbour*'s land.[82]

---

[80] This was clearly stated by Lord Blackburn in *Dalton v Angus* (1881) 6 App Cas 740, 824, where he commended the reasoning that Lord Hardwicke LC used in *Attorney-General v Doughty* (1752) 2 Ves Sen 453, 28 ER 290 to explain this rule: 'I know of no general rule of common law, which warrants that, or says, that building to stop another's prospect is a nuisance. Was that the case, there could be no great towns; and I must grant injunctions to all the new buildings in this town [London].'

[81] *Miner v Gilmour* (1858) 12 Moore PC 131, 156 (per Lord Kingsdown); *John Young & Co v Bankier Distillery Co* [1893] AC 691, 698 (per Lord Macnaghten): 'A riparian proprietor is entitled to have the water of the stream, on the banks of which his property lies, flow down as it has been accustomed to flow down to his property, subject to the ordinary use of the flowing water by upper proprietors, and to such further use, if any, on their part in connection with their property as may be reasonable under the circumstances. Every riparian proprietor is thus entitled to the water of his stream, in its natural flow, without sensible diminution or increase and without sensible alteration in its character or quality.'

[82] *Dalton v Angus* (1881) 6 App Cas 740, 804 (per Lord Penzance): 'It is the law, I believe I may say without question, that at any time within twenty years after the house is built the owner of the adjacent soil may with perfect legality dig that soil away, and allow his neighbour's house, if supported by it, to fall in ruins to the ground.' See also *Ray v Fairway Motors (Barnstaple) Ltd* (1969) 20 P & CR 261. Similarly, a landowner can extract percolating groundwater from beneath his own land even if this drains water from beneath another's land and causes damage: *Popplewell v Hodkinson* (1869) LR 4 Ex 248; *Langbrook Properties Ltd v Surrey CC* [1970] 1 WLR 161.

B. Unreasonableness

We have stated that in cases of obstruction or withdrawal of a benefit the claimant will not be able to sue in private nuisance unless she can show that the obstruction or withdrawal interfered with some right associated with her land. Must the claimant also go further and show that the interference was *unreasonable*? The answer requires attention to two things. First, often the right on which the claimant bases her claim will be *defined* in such a way that any interference with it will *by definition* be unreasonable. For example, we noted above that the right to light that a claimant can acquire is a right to enough light for the ordinary occupations of life. Thus, any interference with this *right* will involve depriving the claimant of sufficient light to use her property for such ordinary purposes and will be *by definition* unreasonable.[83] The second element in the answer is that it will make a difference whether the purpose of the claim is (1) to establish that the claimant has the right that she claims to have or (2) to obtain a remedy for an interference with the right. Where the purpose of the claim is the latter, for instance where the claimant is seeking compensation, the courts will apply the rule that they do not deal with *trivial* interferences, so a claimant will have to demonstrate more than a *technical* interference with her right.

Everything we have said so far has indicated that in obstruction and withdrawal cases, the claimant will only be able to sue in private nuisance if she can show that the obstruction or withdrawal violated some *right* associated with her land. However, before leaving this topic, we should note an *expression of opinion* in *Hunter* v *Canary Wharf* (1997) which was inconsistent with this view. Lord Cooke stated that: 'The malicious erection of a structure for the purpose of interfering with television reception should be actionable in nuisance on the principle of such well-known cases as *Christie* v *Dav* . . . and *Hollywood Silver Fox Farm Ltd* v *Emmett*.'[84] This suggests a claimant does not have to establish a *right* to the benefit so long as the obstruction was *malicious*. However, the majority of the House of Lords in *Hunter* v *Canary Wharf* did not express any support for this position, which is – in any case – flat contrary to the House of Lords' decision in *Bradford* v *Pickles* (1895).

13.8 Affront cases

English law has only tentatively accepted that *affront* can amount to an actionable nuisance. Within this category the interference with the use and enjoyment of the claimant's land is caused by the mental disturbance – the affront – that comes from knowledge that nearby land is being used for a particular purpose, rather than by any emanation, encroachment or obstruction. In England this form of claim has been used principally against brothels, pornographic cinemas and sex shops.

For example, in *Laws* v *Florinplace* (1981), ten residents of an area of Pimlico, London – which enjoyed an attractive village atmosphere – sought an injunction to close down the 'Victoria Sex and Video Centre'. Vinelott J held that even if the defendant changed the business's name and altered its signs and displays, it was still arguable that the 'profound

---

[83] It is important to note that it is *not* the law that someone with a right to light can complain about *any* degree of reduction in the amount of light reaching her window.

[84] [1997] AC 655, 721. Lord Hope might be taken to have shared Lord Cooke's position, since he thought it was relevant to observe that it had not been suggested that the Canary Wharf Tower had been designed 'maliciously in order to interfere with the [claimants'] television reception' (at 726).

repugnance' caused to the claimants by knowledge of nearby trade in hard pornography could amount to sufficient interference with the use and enjoyment of their land for the purposes of the tort of private nuisance.[85]

In practice, claims such as that brought in *Laws* are rare because a claimant must demonstrate *not only* that he has suffered interference by affront *but also* that the interference was *unreasonable* when judged from the perspective of ordinary people. This limits the number of claims based on affront because it will be difficult to persuade a court that it is *unreasonable* for a defendant to carry on a *lawful* business[86] which causes no interference more severe than making people living nearby feel uncomfortable about the fact that such activities are going on in the locality.

A doctrine similar to nuisance by affront *may* explain a group of old cases in which extreme dangers, such as warehouses of gunpowder, were held to be nuisances before they had caused any physical harm.[87] It might be said that in such cases there was an *immediate* nuisance from the fear and anxiety caused to people living in the vicinity.[88] There is a tension, however, between this explanation and the rule that a claimant can only obtain an injunction to restrain an *anticipated* tort when such a tort is 'highly probable' and 'imminent',[89] since a claimant might become fearful or anxious even when a risk is 'improbable' or 'remote'. It might also be objected that this sort of reasoning could allow a claimant to establish a tort where there was no rational basis for any fear or anxiety.[90] Indeed, in *Birmingham Development Co Ltd* v *Tyler* (2008),[91] the Court of Appeal held that a defendant had not committed private nuisance by allowing a wall on its land to remain in such a condition that the claimants were advised that it might collapse and they should consequently stop working on their adjacent land: the Court held that the claim could only succeed if the fear of an imminent collapse was 'well-founded', and this required *actual* danger. In the particular case, later investigations had revealed that – contrary to appearances – the wall was actually not likely to collapse.

---

[85] See also *Thompson-Schwab* v *Costaki* [1956] 1 WLR 335, where the Court of Appeal did not accept that the defendants could only be liable for using a house as a venue for prostitution if their activity had a *physical* effect on the claimant's enjoyment of his neighbouring house. In the United States 'nuisance by affront' has also been relied on against undertakers.

[86] In *Laws* v *Florinplace* [1981] 1 All ER 659, 668, Vinelott J treated it as relevant to whether to grant an interim injunction that the defendant's business was 'at least near the boundary of the criminal law' and thought that at a full trial of the action it would be necessary to decide whether the business was lawful or not.

[87] *R* v *Lister* (1856–7) 7 Dears & B 209, 169 ER 979; *Hepburn* v *Lordan* (1865) 2 H & M 345, 71 ER 497; *R* v *Chilworth Gunpowder Co* (1888) 4 TLR 557.

[88] In *R* v *Lister* (1856–7) 7 Dears & B 209, 227, 169 ER 979, 987, Lord Campbell CJ stated that, 'the well-founded apprehension of danger which would alarm men of steady nerves and reasonable courage, passing through the street in which the house stands, or residing in adjoining houses, is enough to show that something has been done which the law ought to prevent'. It is unclear whether a series of claims in the nineteenth century against smallpox hospitals and asylums are best explained as 'nuisance by anxiety', 'nuisance by affront', or both.

[89] The Court of Appeal in *Hooper* v *Rogers* [1975] Ch 43 treated this rule as requiring no more than that the degree of probability was sufficient to make an injunction just, and the application was not premature, but even this softened version of the rule seems more stringent than the approach taken in the gunpowder factory cases.

[90] The nuisance claim against the operators of a smallpox hospital which gave rise to the appeal in *Metropolitan Asylum District Managers* v *Hill* (1881) 6 App Cas 193 is often mentioned in this context. Although the claimants' evidence included allegations as to the emanation of smells from the morgue and of a disproportionate infection rate in the vicinity of the hospital it seems that many of the fears were exaggerated.

[91] *Birmingham Development Co Ltd* v *Tyler* [2008] EWCA Civ 859.

13.9 Responsibility

Readers should now have a good understanding of what kinds of interference a claimant has to establish that he is suffering, or has suffered, in order to bring a claim in private nuisance. But to win a claim against a particular defendant the claimant will also have to show that the defendant was *responsible* for the interference – by showing that the defendant created, authorised, adopted or continued the state of affairs that caused it.

A. Creating

If A *creates* a state of affairs that brings about an unreasonable interference with B's use and enjoyment of his land then it seems straightforward that A should be liable. Thus if *Amber* lights a bonfire with old tyres piled on it, with the result that pungent smoke emanates onto *Brian's* land and fills his house, *Amber* will be responsible for the state of affairs that causes the interference, and hence liable for committing private nuisance in relation to *Brian*.

Does it matter *where Amber* creates her bonfire? If *Amber* actually goes on to *Brian's* land without his permission and builds the bonfire *there*, then this will not amount to a private nuisance in relation to *Brian*: it will be an instance of the tort of trespass to land, which we discussed in the previous chapter. But will *Amber* be liable if she creates the bonfire *anywhere else*, other than on *Brian's* land?

It is often said that private nuisance is a tort committed between *neighbours*.[92] This has led some lawyers to suggest that in order to commit the tort *Amber* must be *Brian's neighbour*, and that someone cannot be a *neighbour* unless they are the *owner* or *occupier* of nearby land. Moreover, it is sometimes claimed that a defendant has to *use this land* – that they own or occupy – as the place where they create the state of affairs that constitutes a private nuisance.[93] In *Hussain v Lancaster City Council* (2000), the Court of Appeal relied on a thesis that Professor Newark was 'prepared . . . to nail . . . to the doors of the Law Courts and to defend against all comers': 'the term "nuisance" is properly applied only to such *actionable user of land* as interferes with the enjoyment by the claimant of rights in land.'[94] Unfortunately, the Court of Appeal took this to mean that the essence of private nuisance required that 'the defendant's use *of the defendant's land* interferes with the claimant's enjoyment of the claimant's land.'[95] Thus the Court in *Hussain* thought that the claim in that case could not succeed because the people who were directly causing problems for the claimant, by serious acts of harassment, were not using *their* land to do so, but were carrying out their atrocious campaign from the street and from open ground over which they had no rights.

---

[92] See, for example, Lord Lloyd's influential summary of the tort in *Hunter v Canary Wharf* [1997] AC 655, 695. (We quoted, and criticised, this summary earlier in this chapter. See footnote 6.)

[93] Beever 2013, 125 argues that: '[The] nuisance must emanate from land over which the defendant exercises control. This is because the defendant cannot be using the land unless she has control over it.'

[94] Newark 1949, 489 (emphasis added). This thesis was approved by Lord Goff in *Hunter v Canary Wharf* (1997) but in that case the focus was on the second part of the thesis – that the interference had to be with rights in land.

[95] [2000] QB 1, 23 (emphasis added). It will not have escaped the notice of the observant reader that Professor Newark only insists that nuisance must involve *user of land*, and not that it must involve *the defendant's use of the defendant's land*.

If this is the law then *Amber* will only be liable for creating the bonfire if she does so on land that she owns or occupies. But what the Court of Appeal said in *Hussain* is not orthodoxy. Indeed, in our opinion, it is not sensible. There are plenty of cases where a defendant has been held liable for *creating* a state of affairs that caused a nuisance even though he was not the owner or occupier of the land that he created it on.[96] Quite apart from these cases, there is no reason in principle to make a claimant's degree of protection turn on the legal position of the defendant with regard to the land where she creates the relevant state of affairs.[97] A landowner deserves protection from a smoky bonfire regardless of whether it was lit by a neighbouring owner, tenant, lodger, or squatter. As Sir Christopher Staughton has pointed out,[98] it is not self-evident why a defendant who plays his stereo loudly at home may commit the tort of private nuisance in relation to his neighbour but a defendant who plays his car stereo loudly while parked outside his neighbour's house will not. Furthermore, acceptance of the Court of Appeal's opinion in *Hussain* would lead to an undesirable inconsistency between private nuisance and the tort of trespass to land: clearly a defendant can commit trespass to land without using his own land.[99]

A defendant can be held responsible for *creating* a state of affairs that interferes with a neighbour's use and enjoyment of land even if he does not *personally* do the acts that make the noise or produce the smell. Thus in *Lawrence* v *Fen Tigers Ltd* (2014) David Coventry was held liable for the noise nuisance caused by stock-car and banger racing at the stadium even though he did not personally drive all the noisy vehicles: it was sufficient that he controlled the racing activities at the stadium. The pivotal question is sometimes expressed as being whether a defendant has 'directly participated' in creating the state of affairs.[100]

Someone can also be held responsible for *creating* a nuisance even if the state of affairs that caused the problems was a side effect of his activities. In *R* v *Moore* (1832), a gunmaker possessed land where he encouraged customers to shoot at pigeons. Some of the

---

[96] Relevant cases include: *Halsey* v *Esso Petroleum* [1961] 1 WLR 683 (nuisance created from highway); *Hall* v *Beckenham Corp* [1949] 1 KB 716 (nuisance created from public park); *Bernstein* v *Skyviews* [1978] QB 479 (nuisance created from air). There is also a series of cases supporting the view that picketing can be a private nuisance, at least if it involves obstruction, violence, intimidation, molestation or threats (*J Lyons & Sons* v *Wilkins* [1899] 1 Ch 255, 267, 271–2; *Hubbard* v *Pitt* [1976] QB 142, 177, 183, 189; *Thomas* v *NUM (South Wales Area)* [1986] Ch 20, 65), and none of these suggests that the pickets must be using their own land in order to commit the tort. For *dicta* pointing the other way, see *Esso Petroleum* v *Southport Corp* [1954] 2 QB 182, 196-7 (per Denning LJ), [1956] AC 218, 242 (per Lord Radcliffe), suggesting that private nuisance cannot be committed from the sea.

[97] Beever 2013 disagrees. He argues that purpose of the tort of private nuisance is to determine *priorities* when a defendant's *use* of one plot of land interferes with a claimant's *use* of another plot of land. He submits that the central question in a private nuisance case is 'the significance of the use of the defendant's land vis-à-vis the claimant's' (at 156).

[98] *Lippiatt* v *South Gloucestershire CC* [2000] QB 51, 65.

[99] The inconvenience of the distinction can best be appreciated by remembering that it is a trespass to land to throw something directly onto B's land, and a private nuisance to release something so that it indirectly drifts onto B's land and causes an unreasonable interference. If the Court of Appeal's view was confirmed then B would seek, whenever A created an emanation from land other than his own land, to argue that the emanation was *direct* (and thus a trespass to land).

[100] In *Lawrence* v *Fen Tigers Ltd (No 2)* [2015] AC 106, the UK Supreme Court accepted that a *landlord* (or indeed anyone else, see [26]) could be responsible for a state of affairs if either he 'directly participated' in *creating* it or he *authorised* it: see, for example, Lord Neuberger at [11]. Clearly, in many circumstances where a defendant has *control* over an activity occurring on his premises it will not be necessary to distinguish between these two possibilities.

pigeons were not brought down by his customers and a nuisance resulted from the large number of people who gathered outside his premises to shoot at the strays. In response to the argument that the gunmaker had not committed nuisance because he had not *invited* this crowd, Littledale J asserted that 'If the experience of mankind must lead any one to expect the result, he will be answerable for it.'[101]

B. Authorising

A1 can commit the tort of private nuisance by *authorising* A2 to create a state of affairs that causes an unreasonable interference with B's use and enjoyment of land.

In *Hussain* v *Lancaster City Council* (2000), Malazam Hussain and his partner had bought a shop on the Ryelands estate in Lancaster. Thereafter they were subjected to over 2,000 racist attacks. Their claim listed several hundred attacks on their property (including use of petrol bombs), assaults and thefts, and named 106 alleged culprits. Many of these alleged culprits were tenants of Lancaster City Council on the Ryelands estate. Importantly, the council had power to evict these tenants from their homes if they were causing a nuisance to their neighbours, but had not done so. The claimants' case was that in these circumstances the council was liable for the state of affairs being created by its tenants.

One difficulty for the claimants was that the council was clearly not *directly participating* in the attacks. Thus it was important to determine in what other circumstances a landlord might be held responsible for a state of affairs resulting from the activities of its tenants. English law's answer, found in cases such as *Rich* v *Basterfield* (1847), is that a landlord is usually *only* liable for a state of affairs created by its *tenants* if it has *authorised* the creation of such a state of affairs.[102] Thus in *Southwark London Borough Council* v *Tanner* (2001), Lord Millett expressed the general rule as being:

> The person or persons directly responsible for the activities in question are liable; but so too is anyone who authorised them. Landlords have been held liable for nuisances committed on this basis. It is not enough for them to be aware of the nuisance and to take no steps to prevent it.[103]

What will suffice for *authorising*? Lord Millett clearly states that knowing about a problem and taking no steps to solve it is insufficient.[104] Consequently, Lancaster City Council's failure to prevent the terrible treatment of Malazam Hussain by its tenants was not enough to establish that it had *authorised* the nuisance.

A distinction can be drawn, however, between 'taking no steps to prevent a nuisance' – which is *not* 'authorising' – and granting a lease for a purpose which will *inevitably* lead to a nuisance. In the latter situation it can be said that the landlord has *authorised* the nuisance by granting the lease.

---

[101] (1832) 3 B & Ad 184, 110 ER 68. Although *R* v *Moore* was a case of public nuisance the same principle has been applied in cases of private nuisance, for example, *Walker* v *Brewster* (1867) LR 5 Eq 25 ('assemblage of idle and dissolute persons' outside a house used by defendant for twice weekly fêtes with fireworks).

[102] We explain below, under the next subheading, why we have qualified our proposition about the liability of landlords for states of affairs created by their tenants with the word '*usually*'.

[103] [2001] 1 AC 1, 22.

[104] This was also confirmed by the UK Supreme Court in *Lawrence* v *Fen Tigers Ltd (No 2)* [2015] AC 106, at [22]: 'As a matter of principle, even if a person has the power to prevent the nuisance, inaction or failure to act cannot, on its own, amount to authorising the nuisance.'

What if the landlord only knew that the tenant was *likely* to create a nuisance when the lease was granted? In *Smith* v *Scott* (1973), Pennycuick V-C stated that it might be sufficient if nuisance was 'virtually certain' to result from the purposes for which the property was let.[105] Subsequently, in *Tetley* v *Chitty* (1986), where Medway Borough Council had leased land to a go-kart club with (at least) implied permission to use it as a go-kart track, McNeill J seemed attracted by the proposition that proving reasonable foreseeability of nuisance (by noise) might be enough. In *Lawrence* v *Fen Tigers Ltd (No 2)* (2014), however, Lord Carnwath expressly rejected the suggestion that a landlord could be found to have *authorised* a nuisance when it was only a 'likely' or 'foreseeable' consequence of a lease: he insisted that a test formulated in such terms would be 'insufficiently rigorous'.[106] Consequently, we submit that a landlord will only be held to have *authorised* a nuisance by his tenants through granting them a lease where the nuisance was 'an inevitable, or nearly certain, consequence of the letting'.[107]

C. Adopting or continuing

Hussain can be contrasted with *Lippiatt* v *South Gloucestershire CC* (2000), where a group of travellers allegedly set up camp on land belonging to the council and used the site as a 'launching pad' for a series of damaging invasions of a neighbouring farmer's property. The Court of Appeal held that it was arguable that the council was liable for the nuisance resulting from the state of affairs on its land. A crucial distinction from *Hussain* is that in *Lippiatt* the travellers were *not* tenants of the council, and consequently the council continued to possess and occupy the land concerned. Orthodoxy holds that the responsibility of an *occupier of land* for a state of affairs which he did not create goes beyond responsibility for what he authorises, and extends to any state of affairs that he continues or adopts.[108] So what must B prove in order to establish that A has continued or adopted a state of affairs on land occupied by him?

In *Sedleigh-Denfield* v *O'Callaghan* (1940), the defendants owned and occupied land on which there was a drainage ditch. Middlesex County Council decided to use this ditch to drain water from a new residential development and substituted a culvert[109] for the ditch. The County Council's action was both lawless – it did not obtain permission from the owners – and incompetent – it failed to take the sensible precaution of putting in a grid to prevent the culvert becoming blocked. Three years later the culvert did block, and water which could not escape down it instead flooded the claimant's property. The House of Lords found that the defendant occupiers of the land were liable even though the state of affairs which led to the flood had been created by the trespassing and incompetent County Council.

---

[105] [1973] Ch 314, 321. He stated that such a degree of 'high probability' was necessary in order to infer that the nuisance was impliedly authorised.

[106] *Lawrence* v *Fen Tigers Ltd (No 2)* [2015] AC 106, at [56].

[107] This test was used by the majority in *Lawrence* v *Fen Tigers Ltd (No 2)* [2015] AC 106, at [15].

[108] For criticism of this area of the law, see Bright 2001, arguing that a landowner should only be held liable for actions of people on his land if he authorised or encouraged those actions.

[109] In less obscure language, a fifteen-inch pipe.

Viscount Maugham stated that an occupier in such a situation would be liable if he had 'continued' or 'adopted' the nuisance, and explained that:

> an occupier of land 'continues' a nuisance if, with knowledge or presumed knowledge of its existence, he fails to take any reasonable means to bring it to an end, though with ample time to do so. He 'adopts' it if he makes use of the erection, building, bank or artificial contrivance which constitutes the nuisance.[110]

On the facts, Viscount Maugham found that the defendants had both 'continued' and 'adopted' the nuisance. The other Law Lords did not draw such a stern distinction between 'continuing' and 'adopting'. They did, however, stress the importance of 'knowledge' or 'presumed knowledge' of the nuisance or the potential for nuisance before the occupier could be liable on this basis. In fact, although the language of 'continuing' and 'adopting' is regularly used, cases like *Sedleigh-Denfield* show that the relevant doctrine often makes defendant occupiers liable for 'failing to prevent' a nuisance from arising *as well as* for 'failing to eliminate' a state of affairs that is *already* causing problems.

Who counts as an 'occupier' who can be held responsible for 'continuing' or 'adopting' a nuisance? In *Cocking* v *Eacott* (2016) the second defendant, Mrs Waring, owned a cottage but did not reside in it; she allowed her daughter, Ms Eacott, to live there rent-free. The nuisance to the claimants, who lived next door to the cottage, resulted from the excessive barking of Ms Eacott's dog, 'Scally'. Mrs Waring submitted that she should be treated like a landlord, and only held liable if she had authorised or directly participated in the activity – keeping a noisy dog – that caused the nuisance. But the Court of Appeal upheld the trial judge's decision that Mrs Waring should be treated as an 'occupier': she 'was, in the requisite sense, both in possession and control of the property throughout her daughter's residence there'.[111]

A useful approximation of the law may be that: (i) a landlord (who has parted with possession) will usually not be an 'occupier'; (ii) a tenant who has taken possession will usually be an 'occupier'; (iii) an owner who remains in possession will usually be an 'occupier', and this will remain the case even if the owner has granted a licence to occupy to someone else; and (iv) a licensee may be an 'occupier' if he or she exercises sufficient control. But in *Cocking*, Vos LJ and Arden LJ both suggested that the precise classification of a defendant will sometimes not track the broad categories of property law, but instead require close attention to the facts: thus, sometimes a licence will leave an owner with no real, residual control, and an owner who has granted such a licence may cease to be an 'occupier'; and sometimes a lease will allow the landlord to retain sufficient control over part of the premises, such as the drains, from which a nuisance emanates.[112]

Can anyone *other than an occupier* be liable for 'continuing' or 'adopting' a private nuisance if he fails to take steps to abate a problematic state of affairs? This was considered in *LE Jones (Insurance Brokers) Ltd* v *Portsmouth City Council* (2003), a case involving

---

[110] [1940] AC 880, 894. In *Cocking* v *Eacott* [2016] QB 1080, at [25], Vos LJ suggested that Viscount Maugham's formulation was not supported by a majority in *Sedleigh-Denfield*, and that to avoid being held liable for 'continuing' a nuisance an occupier must do more than merely take 'reasonable means' to abate the problem. It appears, however, that Vos LJ was not referred to the cases of *Leakey* (1980), *Holbeck Hall Hotel* (2000) and *Marcic* (2004) that we discuss below.

[111] [2016] QB 1080, at [28].

[112] [2016] QB 1080, at [29] and [42]–[43].

damage caused by a tree which the defendant council had agreed to maintain, though it was situated on land vested in a different authority. Dyson LJ stated that:

> the basis for the liability of an occupier for a nuisance on his land is not his occupation as such. Rather, it is that, by virtue of his occupation, an occupier usually has it in his power to take the measures that are necessary to prevent or eliminate the nuisance. He has sufficient control over the hazard which constitutes the nuisance for it to be reasonable to make him liable for the foreseeable consequences of his failure to exercise that control so as to remove the hazard.[113]

Dyson LJ's test, which focuses instead on *control* over the *hazard*, rather than *occupation* of the *land*, has the potential to catch not only occupiers, but also independent contractors who manage hazards on land on behalf of occupiers, and possibly also non-occupiers, such as public officials, when they have power to intervene and deal with hazards. Indeed, Dyson LJ's test might require reassessment of the orthodox rule, discussed in the previous section, that a landlord is only responsible for a nuisance created by his tenant if he has *authorised* the tenant to act in such a way as to create a nuisance: if *power to take the measures that are necessary* is sufficient, then landlords, who are of course *not* usually in occupation, could be held liable for more than what they *authorise*. We suspect, however, that Dyson LJ may have expressed the law too boldly, and that the courts will be very cautious about extending liability beyond those in occupation.[114] Consequently, in the interests of simplicity, we have continued to use the term 'occupiers' to describe those who may be found to have adopted or continued a private nuisance.[115]

If a defendant *is* an 'occupier', then how much must she do to avoid being held responsible for a nuisance resulting from a state of affairs that she has not created? In *Sedleigh-Denfield* the potential problems could have been easily and cheaply rectified by the defendants' putting a grid in front of the pipe's opening. Moreover, the defendants might have been able to obtain the cost of installing the grid from the County Council. More difficult questions arise, however, where it will be costly for the occupier to remove the potential for nuisance.

In *Leakey* v *National Trust* (1980), the defendants owned and occupied a cone-shaped hill in Somerset called Burrow Mump. The claimants lived in cottages beneath the Mump. The hot summer and wet autumn of 1976 caused a crack which made it likely that the Mump would collapse onto the claimants' houses, and stabilising it was likely to prove expensive. The National Trust denied that it was responsible for the state of affairs created by the workings of nature. The Court of Appeal, however, held that the National Trust, as an occupier,[116] was responsible. Megaw LJ (with whom Cumming-Bruce LJ agreed) held that the *Sedleigh-Denfield* principle applied to a potential nuisance caused by the workings of nature,[117] and that if the defendant knew or ought to have known of the

---

[113] [2003] 1 WLR 427, at [11].

[114] Many of the principles determining what steps an 'occupier' must take, that we discuss in the remainder of this section, for instance those which relate contributions to the cost of dealing with a state of affairs to the degree of benefit that claimant and defendant will gain from the state of affairs being dealt with, are difficult to apply to defendants who are not occupiers.

[115] Murphy 2010b, at para 4.45, suggests that the defendant in *LE Jones (Insurance Brokers) Ltd* v *Portsmouth City Council* (2003) was actually an *occupier* and consequently there was no need to recognise 'non-occupiers with control of the hazard' as a potential category of defendants.

[116] In fact there were some doubts as to whether the National Trust really occupied the Mump, but for the purposes of the litigation it conceded that it did: [1980] QB 485, 509.

[117] [1980] QB 485, 517–24.

potential for nuisance, it was obliged to take reasonable steps to eliminate the problem. Importantly, however, the Court of Appeal also said that in judging whether particular steps were reasonably required, the defendant's capacity to find the money was relevant; as was the claimants' capacity to protect themselves from damage by erecting a barrier or providing funds for agreed works. While the occupier's duty to act reasonably is clearly subjective to this extent, Megaw LJ stressed that he did not envisage that it would be necessary to assess the wealth of the parties in anything other than an impressionistic manner.[118]

We will call the duty which an occupier must comply with, if she is to avoid being found responsible for 'continuing' a state of affairs on land that she occupies, a 'measured duty of care'.[119] Adding the word 'measured' to the usual phrase – 'duty of care' – highlights that it is a *special form* of duty of care, one which takes account of: (1) the occupier's capacity to find the money, or other resources, needed to obviate the problems, and (2) the potential victim's capacity to take steps to protect himself.

The nature of the occupier's measured duty of care with regard to problems resulting from natural forces was further explored in *Holbeck Hall Hotel Ltd* v *Scarborough Borough Council* (2000). In that case, a cliff on land belonging to the defendant council gave way and this led to the destruction of a hotel on neighbouring land belonging to the claimant. The case was particularly difficult because the defendant ought to have foreseen minor landslips damaging the claimant's rose garden and lawn, but there was no reason why it ought to have anticipated such an exceptional event as the massive slip which destroyed the hotel. In these circumstances, the Court of Appeal held that an occupier which failed to meet the measured duty to take reasonable steps to prevent a nuisance from occurring on its land should only be liable to the extent of the damage that it ought to have foreseen.[120] Further, the Court of Appeal suggested that in such a situation, where the hazard was a result of natural forces and the defendant would have gained little benefit from preserving its own land against the hazard, the defendant might have fulfilled the measured duty to act reasonably by doing no more than informing the claimants of the risk and sharing information about it.

Marcic v *Thames Water Utilities Ltd* (2004) raised the question whether a public authority responsible for sewers was responsible for flooding incidents caused by the inadequate capacity of those sewers. The Court of Appeal held that the defendants were 'in no more favourable position than a landowner on whose property a hazard accumulates by the act of a trespasser or of nature', that they ought to have known of the hazard, and that consequently, following cases such as *Sedleigh-Denfield* and

---

[118] [1980] QB 485, 526–7. In *Abbahall* v *Smee* [2003] 1 WLR 1472, where defendant and claimant occupied different floors of a building beneath a leaking roof, and the defendant sought to argue that because of her relative poverty she should not have to contribute towards the repairs, the Court of Appeal held that such an approach would be 'unjust to the point of absurdity' (at [57]) and that the costs should normally be divided in proportion to the benefit that each party would gain from the work (at [41]). The problems which may arise where a nuisance causes consequential damage while the parties are squabbling about contributions are yet to be addressed by the courts.

[119] The phrase 'measured duty of care' was used by Lord Wilberforce in *Goldman* v *Hargrave* [1967] 1 AC 645, 662, but has subsequently been regularly employed when determining whether an occupier has continued or adopted a nuisance: see, for example, *Lambert* v *Barratt Homes Ltd* [2010] EWCA Civ 681, 1.

[120] This contrasts with the usual rule of remoteness of damage (see above, § 10.2) that a defendant is liable for all damage of the same *type* as ought to have been foreseen, regardless of the *extent*.

Leakey, they would be liable unless they took reasonable steps to avoid problems arising.[121] The House of Lords, however, disagreed because such a common law duty would conflict with the statutory scheme under the Water Industry Act 1991 for enforcing the statutory obligations of 'sewerage undertakers' and controlling their prices. Lord Hoffmann, in particular, doubted whether a claimant could determine the level of service that a public utility provider must provide by invoking the occupier's common law duty not to 'continue' a state of affairs on his land which might lead to a nuisance, because a judge would not be able to determine what 'reasonable steps' ought to be taken.[122]

Given that the question whether an occupier will be responsible for a state of affairs he did not create is answered by considering whether he has fulfilled a measured duty of care, it is sometimes suggested that this group of cases properly forms part of the tort of negligence.[123] We would reject this suggestion. It is important to note that the issue is not simply about the appropriate distribution of topics within texts. If the *Sedleigh-Denfield* doctrine were *exclusively* part of the tort of negligence then this would make it impossible for a claimant to bring an action when a defendant occupier had failed to deal with a state of affairs which only had the effect of reducing the amenity value of the claimant's land.[124] Why? Because the tort of negligence imposes duties to take reasonable care not to cause *physical damage* to property, while *amenity damage* does not require any *physical* change to property. We think that the true position is that breach of the measured duty can lead to a claim for continuing a private nuisance, *and* that there is also a parallel duty of care breach of which will amount to the tort of negligence.[125]

13.10 Defences

It is appropriate at this point briefly to mention two defences that may prevent a defendant from being held liable under the law of private nuisance, and one potential 'defence' that has not yet been recognised by English law. In this section we will also mention two situations that are sometimes presented as defences, but are probably just situations where the basic conditions for liability cannot be established.

---

[121] [2002] QB 929, at [84].

[122] [2004] 2 AC 42, at [63]–[64], [70].

[123] This view is advanced by Gearty 1989, who writes of *Sedleigh-Denfield* (at 237): 'This was negligence pure and simple, confused by an ill-fitting and woolly disguise of nuisance.' See also Weir 1998a, 102–3: 'that the defendant's liability in nuisance [in *Sedleigh-Denfield*] [was] affected by considerations relevant in the tort of negligence seems beyond doubt.'

[124] An example of such a case might be an occupier failing to deal with regular noisy trespassers, or with smelly rotting rubbish tipped onto his land by trespassers.

[125] See above, § 10.5(C). The scope of the negligence duty may be important. Compensation for personal injuries can never be recovered in the tort of private nuisance (see below, § 13.12), but can be recovered in the tort of negligence. Although Megaw LJ expressed the opinion that if an occupier breached a *Goldman* v *Hargrave*-type duty of care owed to his neighbour and his neighbour suffered a personal injury as a result, then the neighbour should be able to sue the occupier for damages in negligence (see *Leakey* v *National Trust* [1980] QB 485, at 523) there is currently no binding authority as to whether 'personal injury' suffered as a result of the breach of a *Goldman* v *Hargrave*-type duty of care will count as the 'right kind of loss' to be actionable in negligence.

A. Right acquired by grant or prescription

If a claimant has granted the defendant the right to do what would otherwise amount to a private nuisance then this will clearly prevent the claimant establishing that the defendant is committing a tort, and in some circumstances such a right will 'run with the land' – that is, it will be a right that whoever owns the defendant's land at a particular point in time will have against whoever owns the claimant's land at that time.[126] Moreover, in certain situations a court will *presume* that the claimant, or a previous owner of the same land, granted the defendant such a right. The most important of these situations is where a defendant has acted in such a way as to suggest that he is asserting *a right* which could be recognised as an easement[127] for at least twenty years; here a defendant will be said to have acquired a right by *prescription*. In *Lawrence* v *Fen Tigers Ltd* (2014), the Supreme Court accepted that a defendant could acquire a right against a neighbouring landowner to continue making as much noise as would otherwise have been a private nuisance, but held that on the facts it had not been established that the defendants had been making noise *at levels that amounted to a private nuisance* for the requisite period.

B. Statutory authority[128]

A defendant will not be liable if he can demonstrate that a statute authorised him to do what would otherwise amount to an actionable nuisance. But care must always be taken to establish precisely what Parliament intended. In some cases it has been found that Parliament only intended to authorise the defendant to carry out the activity *in a way that paid reasonable regard and care to the interests of others*, and did not intend to authorise any nuisance beyond that which would be an *inevitable* consequence of conducting the activity.[129] And, in other cases, it has been found that Parliament *assumed* that the authorised activity could be conducted somewhere and under some circumstances without creating a nuisance, and consequently did not intend to permit the defendant to cause any nuisance whatsoever.[130]

C. Coming to a nuisance

It might be suggested that if B moves into a house knowing that A runs a noisy motorcycle-tuning workshop next door to it, then A should be able to raise a defence against any claim by B relating to the noise; the defence being that A 'came to the nuisance'. But it is well-established that current English law does *not* recognise such a defence.[131] In *Lawrence* v *Fen Tigers Ltd* (2014), however, Lord Neuberger drew a distinction between A's

---

[126] Readers seeking a detailed account of when rights will 'run with the land' are advised to consult a text devoted to *Land Law*.

[127] Readers seeking a detailed account of what rights *can* be recognised as easements are advised to consult a text devoted to *Land Law*. Amongst the conditions are that the *right* claimed by A must: (1) be *over* B's land; (2) benefit A's land; (3) be sufficiently clear and certain; (4) not be so extensive as to amount to a right to exclusive possession; and (5) not be a right relating solely to amusement.

[128] See Nolan 2015.

[129] See, for example, *Allen* v *Gulf Oil* [1981] AC 1001.

[130] See, for example, *Metropolitan Asylum District Managers* v *Hill* (1881) 6 App Cas 193.

[131] *Lawrence* v *Fen Tigers Ltd* [2014] AC 822, at [47], [51] and [52].

moving into a pre-existing house next door to B's noisy workshop, and A's converting a warehouse next to B's workshop into a house:

> There is much more room for argument that a claimant who builds on, or changes the use of, her property, after the defendant has started the activity alleged to cause a nuisance by noise, or any other emission offensive to the senses, should not have the same rights to complain about that activity as she would have had if her building work or change of use had occurred before the defendant's activity had started.[132]

Thus he suggested that:

> where a claimant builds on, or changes the use of, her land, . . . it may well be wrong to hold that a defendant's pre-existing activity gives rise to a nuisance provided that (i) it can only be said to be a nuisance because it affects the senses of those on the claimant's land, (ii) it was not a nuisance before the building or change of use of the claimant's land, (iii) it is and has been, a reasonable and otherwise lawful use of the defendant's land, (iv) it is carried out in a reasonable way, and (v) it causes no greater nuisance than when the claimant first carried out the building or changed the use.[133]

With respect, we think that this issue will require further discussion when a suitable case arises. We are less sure than Lord Neuberger that if B repaints motorcycles in his workshop – where this process causes very strong fumes to emanate a few metres beyond the land that he owns,[134] but fortunately causes no problems for several years because his workshop adjoins a vacant plot in an area that is otherwise residential – then A should be unable to complain of a nuisance by smell if she builds a house on this previously vacant plot. If B had parked motorcycles on part of the plot then this might equally have caused no problems whilst it was vacant, but this clearly would not establish that it would be lawful for B to continue parking there after A built her house, *unless* B succeeded in establishing a *right* to do so (acquired by prescription) and could invoke the defence discussed under the previous sub-heading.

D. Act of third party

A defendant will not be liable if he can prove that any state of affairs leading to unreasonable interference that has arisen on his land was caused by a wholly unpredictable act of a trespasser. Whilst lawyers sometimes label this as the defence 'act of a third party', we think it is really just a description of a situation where a claimant cannot establish that the claimant was responsible for the state of affairs that caused the problems. Thus, where a state of affairs created by a trespasser does not immediately cause problems for a defendant's neighbours but may do so in future, or causes interference over an extended period, we have already explained when an occupier may be held liable for 'continuing' the nuisance.[135] Further, where the trespasser's intervention was not wholly unpredictable and causes personal injury or physical damage to property, a landowner may sometimes be

---

[132] [2014] AC 822, at [53].

[133] [2014] AC 822, at [56].

[134] The position would be different if the smells from B's activities were an *established feature of the locality*. But if this was the case then the smells would not be a private nuisance at all, because it would be *reasonable* to expect A (and all other residents of the locality) to tolerate them: B would not need a special defence.

[135] *Sedleigh-Denfield* v *O'Callaghan* [1940] AC 880.

held liable in negligence for not taking reasonable precautions against the intervention: in *Smith* v *Littlewoods Organisation Ltd*,[136] Lord Goff argued that a landowner would owe his neighbour a duty to take reasonable steps to prevent a trespasser causing physical harm to his neighbour if: (1) the landowner had assumed a responsibility to his neighbour; *or* (2) the landowner was responsible for controlling the trespasser in question;[137] *or* (3) the landowner had negligently caused or permitted the creation of a source of danger which it was reasonably foreseeable that a trespasser might 'spark off';[138] *or* (4) the landowner knew or ought to have known that the trespasser in question had created a fire risk.[139]

E. Act of God

A defendant will not be liable if the state of affairs leading to unreasonable interference was caused by a wholly unpredictable and uncontrollable natural force. In *Sedleigh-Denfield* v *O'Callaghan* (1940), Lord Maugham noted that the defendants had not tried to argue that the rainfall which led to the flood was so heavy as to give rise to a defence of 'Act of God'. He suggested that this defence would, in any case, only be available when rain is 'so exceptional in amount that no reasonable man could have anticipated it'.[140] As with 'act of a third party', we think 'Act of God' is only a 'defence' in a loose sense, and is really a description of a situation where a claimant cannot establish the defendant's responsibility for the state of affairs that caused the problems. A defendant may be liable if he creates conditions that cause a problem for neighbours as a result of natural forces that *were* reasonably foreseeable,[141] or if the state of affairs created by natural events did not *immediately* lead to the interference and the defendant, as an occupier, failed to take reasonable steps to deal with a risk that he knew, or ought to have known, about.[142]

13.11 Title to sue

In *Hunter* v *Canary Wharf* (1997), the House of Lords made it clear that where a defendant created, authorised, adopted or continued a state of affairs that resulted in an unreasonable interference with the use and enjoyment of land, a claimant could still only succeed in establishing that the tort of private nuisance had been committed in relation to

---

[136] [1987] 1 AC 241. Lord Goff and Lord Mackay LC presented the law in different ways in this case, but in *Mitchell* v *Glasgow City Council* [2009] 1 AC 874, Lord Hope (at [20]-[21]) and Lord Rodger (at [56]) both stated that they preferred the approach of Lord Goff.

[137] [1987] 1 AC 241, 272.

[138] [1987] 1 AC 241, 273-4. Lord Goff's example is the storage of a quantity of fireworks in an unlocked garden shed.

[139] [1987] 1 AC 241, 274. Here the duty seems to be parallel to the measured duty of care that is considered in cases of *continuing* a private nuisance.

[140] [1940] AC 880, 886.

[141] For example, if a defendant creates a pile of refuse on his land, and the wind regularly blows the refuse onto the claimant's land, the defendant cannot avoid liability by saying that 'it is the wind that is causing the emanations, not me'.

[142] This is another situation where the relevant duty is the measured duty of an occupier to take reasonable steps to prevent conditions on his land causing nuisance to his neighbour. *Goldman* v *Hargrave* [1967] AC 645 provides a good example of a state of affairs created by a uncontrollable force of nature (red gum set alight by lightning) only causing harm to a neighbour after the occupier had a reasonable opportunity to abate the risk.

her if she had *a sufficient interest in that land*. Similarly, if her claim alleged an unreasonable interference with a right associated with land then she could only succeed if she enjoyed the relevant right.

Four questions require attention. (1) What counts as *a sufficient interest in land*? (2) If B wants to sue A for having committed the tort of private nuisance in relation to her then does B have to *prove* that she *has* a sufficient interest in the land in question, and will B be barred from suing A if A can prove that B did *not* have a sufficient interest in the land? (3) Would the law be better if a wider class of people could sue for private nuisance? (4) Might Article 8 of the ECHR compel the courts to reform this part of the law?

A. Sufficient interests in land[143]

English land law draws a distinction between interests *in land* and *personal* interests. The main distinction between these is that interests *in land* can bind third parties while *personal* interests generally do not. So if Greenacre Hall is blighted by intolerable noise created by *Drummer*, the owner of Greenacre obviously has a sufficient interest *in land* to be able to sue *Drummer* in nuisance; while *Tourist* who has purchased a ticket to visit Greenacre Hall for a guided tour does not because he has only a *personal* (contractual) interest.

In *Hunter* v *Canary Wharf* (1997), Lord Goff summarised who will be held to have a sufficient interest in land:

> [A]n action in private nuisance will only lie at the suit of a person who has a right to the land affected. Ordinarily, such a person can only sue if he has the right to exclusive possession of the land, such as a freeholder or tenant in possession, or even a licensee with exclusive possession. Exceptionally, however . . . this category may include a person in actual possession who has no right to be there; and in any event a reversioner can sue in so far as his reversionary interest is affected. But a mere licensee on the land has no right to sue.[144]

The first point that we want to highlight is that both freeholders and tenants in possession can sue. So, if Greenacre Hall has an owner–occupier, *Lord Greenacre*, then he will be able to sue for private nuisance if Greenacre Hall is affected by unreasonable noise created by *Drummer*. But if *Lord Greenacre* has leased the Hall to *Renter*, who is in possession, then *Renter* will be able to sue for private nuisance if the Hall is affected in the same way, even though *Renter* is not 'the owner'.

The fact that *Renter*, as a tenant in possession, can sue does not mean that *Lord Greenacre* cannot: *Lord Greenacre* will now have the status of 'reversioner' (that is, the person who will take back the Hall at the end of the tenancy), and a reversioner may also sue if a private nuisance has any effect on *his own* interest in land. This might be the case if, for instance, the noise created by *Drummer* was sufficiently loud to damage the windows, *Renter* was not obliged to repair them, and the building would deteriorate if they were not repaired immediately. In these circumstances the noise would have damaged the reversioner's – *Lord Greenacre*'s – interest in the land.

The interests of two classes of persons are particularly difficult to classify: (1) licensees, and (2) the spouses and children of people with interests in land. With regard to licensees,

---

[143] We will not attempt to list *all* the interests which may qualify as sufficient interests *in land*. The interested reader should consult a standard text on land law.

[144] [1997] AC 655, at 692. Later in his speech, at 694, Lord Goff held that the court should not alter the law presented in this summary.

if the licence grants exclusive possession then Lord Goff suggests that the licensee will have a 'right to the land affected' and will be able to sue. We agree that such a licensee can sue, but would attribute this to the *de facto* possession rule discussed in the next section. With regard to family members, it is clear that they will not be treated as having interests *in land* if they merely live in a house as their home.[145] Thus if *Lord Greenacre* is the owner-occupier, but allows his adult son, *Feckless*, to live in the Hall's attic, then *Feckless* will be unable to claim against *Drummer* even if the intolerable noise seriously disturbs him.

B. Proof issues

A person who *in fact* enjoys or asserts exclusive possession over a piece of land will not be required to *prove* that he has a *right* to that possession in order to sue in private nuisance. Moreover, the defendant will only be permitted to rely on the fact that the possessor has *no* right to possess the land in question[146] if either the defendant has the right to possession, or the defendant created the nuisance with the authority of the person with the right to possession. This rule has several consequences.

First, a person who enjoys exclusive possession *in fact* (often called '*de facto* possession'), but who has a defective title, will still be able to sue.[147] Secondly, a licensee who enjoys exclusive possession may be able to sue without having to convince the court that a licence granting exclusive possession creates an interest *in land*. Thirdly, a person asserting exclusive possession over something which cannot be owned as land, but which clearly is not personal property, may be able to sue.[148]

Because most[149] of those who qualify as having a title to sue in private nuisance under the first rule (those who have a *sufficient interest in the land*) will also qualify under the second rule (those who enjoy *exclusive possession in fact*), it might be thought to be a sensible simplification to treat the law as simply saying that a person who enjoys *exclusive possession in fact* can sue in private nuisance. Such a simplification is harmless as long as three points are borne in mind. First, by way of exception to the simplification, a reversioner (who is not in exclusive possession in fact of the land) can sue for interference with *his own* interest in land. Secondly, a defendant will have a good defence if he can prove that *he* has the right to possession of the land in question or is acting with the authority of the person with that right. Thirdly, it may be necessary to investigate *interests* rather than *possession* when deciding what remedy to grant. In particular, if a court wants to award damages compensating for *future* interferences in lieu of an injunction,[150] it will be important to ascertain who will suffer those future interferences.[151]

---

[145] *Hunter* v *Canary Wharf Ltd* [1997] AC 655.

[146] This is often referred to as the defence of *ius tertii*.

[147] See, for example, *Pemberton* v *Southwark London Borough Council* [2000] 1 WLR 1672. In *Metropolitan Properties Ltd* v *Jones* [1939] 2 All ER 202 the claimant, Jones, had been a tenant of the flat affected by the nuisance, but he had assigned the tenancy (and hence the right to occupy) to a person called Storer, before returning to live in the flat when Storer disappeared, leaving him (Jones) still liable for the rent. Lord Hoffmann suggested in *Hunter* v *Canary Wharf Ltd* [1997] AC 655, at 704, that Jones should have been allowed to sue on the basis of his possession *in fact*.

[148] In *Foster* v *Warblington UDC* [1906] 1 KB 648 the claimant sued for the pollution of oyster ponds on the foreshore.

[149] The obvious exception is a reversioner.

[150] For this remedy see below, § 13.12(A)(2).

[151] The fact that someone *presently* enjoys exclusive possession does not mean that such possession is likely to continue in the future.

C. Evaluation of the law

In ruling in *Hunter* that a claimant must have a sufficient interest in land to sue in private nuisance, the House of Lords overruled in part the decision of the Court of Appeal in *Khorasandjian* v *Bush* (1993), which had allowed a claimant who was living in her parents' home to bring a private nuisance claim against a defendant who was continually pestering her with telephone calls. Such a claimant would now be more likely to seek a remedy under the Protection from Harassment Act 1997 than to attempt to use the tort of private nuisance.[152] However, other claimants who might have been protected under the ruling in *Khorasandjian* may not be so lucky.

For example, in *Dobson* v *Thames Water Utilities Ltd* (2009), it was alleged that the Mogden Sewage Treatment Works had been operated so as to cause private nuisance by emanation of odours and proliferation of mosquitoes. Many of the 1,300 claimants had sufficient interests in land, but some, who had suffered just as much discomfort as a result of the odours and mosquitoes, were children living with their parents, residents of old peoples' homes, and others who did not have sufficient interests in land or exclusive possession *in fact*. In the particular case these claimants, who lacked title to claim in private nuisance, could seek damages under the Human Rights Act 1998. But this option would not have been available if the defendant had been a private company, as opposed to a 'public authority'.

Is this result satisfactory? The majority in *Hunter* v *Canary Wharf* (1997) insisted that the distinction between the *function* of private nuisance and the *function* of negligence explained the differences between the two torts[153] and why claims in private nuisance can only be brought by those with a sufficient interest in the land affected. The House of Lords argued, in summary, that private nuisance protects a claimant's interests in land, while negligence protects the personal safety of all persons regardless of whether they have interests in land. So if those without interests in land were allowed to sue in private nuisance that would 'transform it from a tort to land into a tort to the person'[154] and blur the distinction between the two torts.

Such a transformation would also conflict with the way a majority of their Lordships thought that damages should be assessed for *past* harm[155] in private nuisance cases. Lords Lloyd, Hoffmann and Hope insisted that the appropriate measure of damages (in cases not involving physical damage to the land) is the diminution in the amenity value of the land caused by the nuisance.[156] This amenity value is an amount relative to the land, not relative to how many people live on it. Lord Hoffmann said, 'Damages for nuisance recoverable by the possessor or occupier may be affected by the size, commodiousness and

---

[152] See below, § 17.5.

[153] Lord Hope pointed out one difference ([1997] AC 655, at 724), that 'the tort of nuisance is a tort of strict liability in the sense that it is no defence to say that the defendant took all reasonable care to prevent it' and Lord Hoffmann noted another ([1997] AC 655, at 707), that 'the law of negligence gives no remedy for discomfort or distress which does not result in bodily or psychiatric illness'.

[154] [1997] AC 655, 693.

[155] Damages may be claimed for *past* harm. Further, where an injunction is claimed, a court may decide to award damages for anticipated *future* harm *in lieu* of an injunction. For more details, see Chapter 27, below.

[156] [1997] AC 655, 696 (per Lord Lloyd), 706 (per Lord Hoffmann), 724 (per Lord Hope).

value of his property but cannot be increased merely because more people are in occupation and therefore suffer greater discomfort.'[157]

Their Lordships also treated both the weight of the 'transformation' argument and the persuasiveness of the damages point as reinforced by the symmetry which consequently exists between the three different effects that a private nuisance can have on someone's land: physically damaging the land, reducing its amenity value, and encroaching on its boundaries. Where a private nuisance has the effect of encroaching on the boundaries to land, or physically damaging the land, it seems obvious that the person who should be able to sue is the person with the interest in the land. Equally, it seems obvious that if that person claims damages in an encroachment or a physical damage case then these should be calculated to compensate him for the diminution in the value of his interest in the land. Thus there is a degree of consistency in holding that where the private nuisance reduces amenity value *only* those with sufficient interests in the land should be able to sue, and that *all* they can sue for is reduction of the amenity value *of the land*.

Lord Goff provided two additional practical reasons why liability in private nuisance should only extend to those with sufficient interests in land. First, he pointed out that potential claimants often reach compromises with potential defendants, for instance by permitting the nuisance to continue for a fixed period in exchange for payment. Lord Goff feared that the likelihood of such sensible arrangements would be reduced if potential defendants had to identify and deal with all the occupiers of each property affected by their activities.[158] Secondly, he suggested that if the class of those able to claim in private nuisance extended beyond the clear category of those with sufficient interests in land it would prove impossible to find any other easily definable limit. Thus he raised the awkward cases of lodgers, au pairs, resident nurses, and employees.[159]

Of the Law Lords who heard the *Hunter* case, only Lord Cooke rejected the traditional rule about title to sue. A tolerable paraphrase of Lord Cooke's reasoning might be that in modern society a domestic house, a home, is more than just an investment in real property, and it will usually be sufficiently clear whose home it is.[160] No doubt if a home is invaded by noxious fumes the owner's investment is harmed, and only the owner should be able to claim for that damage *to the investment*. But equally without doubt other occupants of the home will have suffered – their lives will have been rendered less restful and fulfilling – and should be compensated for their loss. In doctrinal terms, Lord Cooke might be said to have argued that the interests that the tort of private nuisance should protect is not merely interests in land but wider 'interests in a home'.

Lord Cooke argued that the majority's position in *Hunter* prioritised symmetry and tidiness over utility and justice.[161] We think this is unfair: the majority was motivated by the need to set down *clearly* who is protected by the law on private nuisance and for what

---

[157] Thus both Lord Hoffmann ([1997] AC 655, at 706) and Lord Lloyd ([1997] AC 655, at 698-9) expressly disapproved of the suggestion in *Bone* v *Seale* [1975] 1 WLR 797 that damages for private nuisance by smell might be assessed by drawing an analogy with awards in personal injury cases for loss of the sense of smell. Lord Hope's views were less clear. In *Lawrence* v *Fen Tigers Ltd* [2014] AC 822, at [172], Lord Clarke suggested that 'general damages' might be available in a private nuisance claim, but noted that this would be difficult to reconcile with Lord Hoffmann's approach.

[158] [1997] AC 655, 692–3.

[159] [1997] AC 655, 693.

[160] To similar effect, see O'Sullivan 1997b.

[161] [1997] AC 655, 711.

harm damages can be recovered. And clarity is not just 'tidiness'; it is important for set-tling disputes and for those who want, in advance of any dispute, to negotiate permission to develop and use land in ways which may inconvenience neighbours. Moreover, it is important to remember that many private nuisance claims do not involve interference with 'homes' but with land used for various business purposes (such as factories, shops, restaurants, concert halls, schools and hotels) and it is unclear whether Lord Cooke would have also allowed those without *interests in land* to claim in such cases.[162] On the other hand, we also think that the majority's treatment of 'homes' as simply *investments in domestic property* fails to reflect the way in which most members of our society value 'homes'. The question of who is protected by the law on private nuisance is part of a more general dispute in the law of torts between the desire to draw bright lines which will allow people to plan around the law and the desire to decide each case on its individual merits. There are no easy answers to the question of how to balance these two desires. In the area under discussion, it would be helpful to have more evidence about whether those who carry out activities which *may* create a nuisance generally *try* to negotiate in advance, or not, before deciding whether the balance struck by the majority is preferable to the bal-ance struck by Lord Cooke.[163]

D. Article 8 of the ECHR

Article 8 of the European Convention on Human Rights (ECHR) provides that 'Everyone has the right to respect for his private and family life, his home and his correspondence', and the European Court of Human Rights has held that this right *can* be violated by 'homes' being exposed to extreme noise or environmental pollution.[164] Moreover, the Court has held that even when the State has not created the noise or pollution it may nonetheless be responsible for the violation if it has failed properly to regulate private industry.[165]

We saw in Chapter 1 that several lawyers have argued that s 6 of the Human Rights Act 1998 obliges the English courts to develop the common law so as to make it compatible with the ECHR.[166] Such reasoning has been used to support the argument that the courts should extend the tort of private nuisance so that *all* those who reside in a 'home' can sue (regardless of whether they have a sufficient interest in the land) and damages should be available for any 'distress' they suffer as a result of such nuisances.[167] Three problems with this argument are worth mentioning here.

First, although the Human Rights Act 1998 obliges English courts to act compatibly with the ECHR, the cases decided by the European Court of Human Rights have *not* established that a failure by a State to create *private law actions* for children and other

---

[162] Some academics have argued that private nuisance should protect interests in land beyond 'use as a home', such as a cricket club's recreational interest in a public park where it regularly plays: Wightman 1998.

[163] If such negotiating in advance is very rare we think this would strengthen the case for accepting Lord Cooke's views.

[164] Interference with a person's 'home' by noise or pollution will not always be a violation of Article 8. An interference can be justified under Art 8.2 if it is prescribed by law and necessary in a democratic society.

[165] *Powell & Rayner* v *United Kingdom* (1990) 12 EHRR 355; *Lopez Ostra* v *Spain* (1995) 20 EHRR 277; *Guerra* v *Italy* (1998) 26 EHRR 357; *Hatton* v *United Kingdom* (2003) 37 EHRR 28. Nolan 2011c provides an excellent account of these cases.

[166] § 1.11(D). See, for example, Hunt 1998.

[167] In *McKenna* v *British Aluminium, The Times*, 25 April 2002, Neuberger J thought that it was arguable that the English courts would accept this argument.

non-owners to bring against polluters is incompatible with Article 8. The cases have established that states' failures to prevent such pollution by *regulation* or other means were incompatible with Article 8, but that is not the same as saying that every state must provide comprehensive private law actions.

Secondly, in *Dobson* v *Thames Water Utilities Ltd* (2009), the Court of Appeal held that where a child lived with his parents in a house affected by a private nuisance created by a public authority the fact that the child's parents had obtained damages for the private nuisance would be highly relevant to the question whether it was necessary to award the child damages as 'just satisfaction' for a violation of his right under Article 8. Presumably, if the parents had obtained compensation for the reduction in amenity value of their house then no further award of damages to the child under Article 8 may be necessary. If this is correct then it tends to undermine the argument that it is necessary to extend a private law claim to such children.[168]

Thirdly, extending the tort of private nuisance may not be required because to do so would actually provide children and non-owners with *far more* protection than Article 8 requires. As we have seen, the tort of private nuisance allows the owner of a house in a luxurious residential district to sue when the premises are subjected to the smell of frying fish,[169] but it seems highly unlikely that the European Court of Human Rights would regard such an owner's children as victims of a human rights violation.[170]

13.12 Remedies

There are two kinds of remedies that a claimant in a private nuisance case may seek: (1) an *injunction* to prevent *future* unreasonable interferences; and (2) *damages* to compensate for *past* unreasonable interferences. But in some cases where a claimant seeks an injunction the court may refuse this and *instead* award (3) damages *in lieu of an injunction*, which will be calculated to compensate for *future* unreasonable interferences. (We discuss (3) (damages *in lieu of an injunction*) in the section dealing with injunctions.)

A. Injunction

Where a claimant establishes that he is currently suffering an unreasonable interference with the use and enjoyment of his land, or some right associated with that land, and that the defendant is responsible for creating the state of affairs that is bringing about this interference, the claimant will *prima facie* be entitled to obtain an injunction requiring the defendant to cease doing whatever is bringing about the nuisance,[171] but whether

---

[168] Varuhas 2016, 146, argues that the reasoning in *Dobson* 'does not hold water'. He suggests that an award of compensation for private nuisance will reflect normative damage to the protected interest in the use of land and cannot provide full redress for damage to the non-proprietary interests protected by Article 8.

[169] *Adams* v *Ursell* [1913] 1 Ch 269.

[170] In *Dennis* v *Ministry of Defence* [2003] EWHC 793 (QB), Buckley J held that the amount he was awarding a landowner for private nuisance caused by noise was sufficient to amount to 'just satisfaction' of the claim by the landowner and *his wife* that their rights under Art 8 had been infringed. It seems, however, that he reached this conclusion after using the wrong method to assess damages for private nuisance, and without considering whether the amounts would always coincide. See further, Bagshaw 2004a, 41.

[171] *Lawrence* v *Fen Tigers Ltd* [2014] AC 822, [101] and [121] (per Lord Neuberger).

such an injunction will be granted, or damages awarded *in lieu* 'involves a classic exercise of discretion'.[172] Such an injunction is commonly called a *prohibitory* injunction, for the obvious reason that it prohibits the defendant from continuing to do whatever is bringing about the nuisance.[173]

The courts will not *always* award an injunction in a case where B can establish that she is the continuing victim of a private nuisance for which A is responsible. The courts may refuse to award B an injunction and award B damages *in lieu of* (instead of) an injunction.[174] Until recently it was thought that the courts would only exercise this power to *refuse* an injunction and award damages *in lieu* in 'very exceptional circumstances'.[175] But in *Lawrence* v *Fen Tigers Ltd* (2014), the Supreme Court signalled that the courts should be more ready to do so, and the choice requires 'a classic exercise of discretion' in light of the facts of the individual case.[176]

The effect of refusing to grant an injunction where a private nuisance is being committed will be to leave the defendant *in effect* free to continue committing the tort. We say '*in effect* free', rather than simply 'free', because refusing an injunction does not mean that it is not a *wrong* for the defendant to continue committing private nuisance in relation to the claimant: it remains *wrongful*, and this is why it may be appropriate to make the defendant pay damages – *in lieu of injunction* – in advance for the harm that will be caused in the future. Such damages are *in effect* a reasonable sum for the privilege of remaining free to continue committing the tort.

If a court decides to award damages in lieu of an injunction then there are (broadly speaking) two ways in which it could assess how much should be paid: it could calculate the *loss of value* of the claimant's land as a result of the nuisance continuing into the future or it could assess the *price* a reasonable person in the claimant's shoes might charge the defendant for the privilege of being allowed to continue committing the tort. The *price* might be more than the *loss of value* because it might take into account the profit the defendant could make as a result of being able to continue with his activities.[177] In *Lawrence* v *Fen Tigers Ltd* (2014), the Supreme Court left open the question which way of calculating the damages should be used: Lord Neuberger and Lord Clarke expressed

---

[172] [2014] AC 822, [120].

[173] There are three other types of injunction that are sometimes obtained in private nuisance claims: (1) *Mandatory injunctions*, which order a defendant to do something that will bring an end to a situation which is on the verge of causing significant damage to the claimant (eg *Morris* v *Redland Bricks Ltd* [1970] AC 652); (2) *Quia timet injunctions*, which order a defendant not to commit a tort that he is about to commit; (3) *Interim injunctions*, which prevent a trial from becoming pointless, for example by ordering a defendant not to do something which could lead to the claimant suffering irreparable harm before the trial. Injunctions are discussed in more detail in Chapter 27.

[174] The Chancery Amendment Act 1858, better known as Lord Cairns's Act, allowed the Court of Chancery to award damages in lieu of an injunction. This statute has been repealed, but s 50 of the Senior Courts Act 1981 preserves the court's jurisdiction to award damages in lieu of an injunction.

[175] *Watson* v *Croft Promosport Ltd* [2009] EWCA Civ 15, [44] (per Sir Andrew Morritt).

[176] *Lawrence* v *Fen Tigers Ltd* [2014] AC 822, [120].

[177] The second approach was used in *Jaggard* v *Sawyer* [1995] 1 WLR 269. In *Tamares Ltd* v *Fairpoint Properties Ltd (No 2)* [2007] 1 WLR 2167, Gabriel Moss QC held that where a court refused to grant a party an injunction to protect its right to light against a development on neighbouring land the owner of the right should normally be awarded some part of the likely profit from the development, but not so much as would have been likely to prevent the development from taking place (at [22]). In the particular case he awarded the claimant £50,000, which was slightly less than a third of the developer's expected profit and considerably *more* than the claimant's loss of amenity (assessed at no more than £3,030).

some support for the *price* approach, whilst Lord Carnwath opposed it, especially in cases where a private nuisance affected several claimants.[178]

Because an award of damages in lieu of an injunction *resembles* a forced sale of the *right* of a property owner to be free from private nuisance the courts were traditionally cautious about using their power to award damages in lieu of injunctions. In the leading case of *Shelfer* v *City of London Electric Lighting Co* (1895), A.L. Smith LJ stated:

> In my opinion it may be stated as a good working rule that – (1) If the injury to the claimant's legal rights is small, (2) And is one which is capable of being estimated in money, (3) And is one which can be adequately compensated by a small money payment, (4) And the case is one in which it would be oppressive to the defendant to grant an injunction: – then damages in substitution for an injunction may be given.[179]

However, in *Lawrence* v *Fen Tigers Ltd* (2014), the Supreme Court chose 'to signal a move away from the strict criteria derived from *Shelfer*'.[180] The primary objection raised against the criteria was that they made no reference to whether an injunction would harm the *public interest*,[181] or have serious consequences for third parties such as a defendant's employees.

In *Shelfer*, the Court of Appeal granted an injunction against the Bankside power station in London,[182] and Lindley LJ expressed the strong view that being 'in some sense a public benefactor (e.g., a gas or water company or a sewer authority)' was not 'a sufficient reason for refusing to protect by injunction an individual whose rights are being persistently infringed'.[183] But in *Lawrence* v *Fen Tigers Ltd* (2014), Lord Sumption condemned this as 'unduly moralistic', and offered a rival opinion:

> There is much to be said for the view that damages are ordinarily an adequate remedy for nuisance and that an injunction should not usually be granted in a case where it is likely that conflicting interests are engaged other than the parties' interests. In particular, it may well be that an injunction should as a matter of principle not be granted in a case where a use of land to which objection is taken requires and has received planning permission.[184]

The majority of the Supreme Court, however, refused to endorse either the proposition that 'damages are ordinarily an adequate remedy for nuisance' or that injunctions should not be granted 'in a case where a use of land to which objection is taken requires and has

---

[178] *Lawrence* v *Fen Tigers Ltd* [2014] AC 822, [128] (Lord Neuberger), [173] (Lord Clarke) and [248] (Lord Carnwath). Lord Mance, at [167], stated that he was 'broadly in agreement with Lord Neuberger' on the question of remedy whilst Lord Sumption made no mention of damages other than compensation for loss of amenity and diminished value, at [157].

[179] [1895] 1 Ch 287, 322–3. In *Jaggard* v *Sawyer* [1995] 1 WLR 269, 287, the Court of Appeal treated A.L. Smith LJ's list of four factors as having 'stood the test of time'. In *Regan* v *Paul Properties Ltd* [2007] Ch 135, the Court of Appeal held that the same approach – based on *Shelfer* – applied in 'right to light' cases.

[180] [2014] AC 822, [239] (per Lord Carnwath). Lord Sumption and Lord Clarke expressed their criticisms more forcefully: 'In my view, the decision in *Shelfer* [1895] 1 Ch 287 is out of date, and it is unfortunate that it has been followed so recently and so slavishly', [161] (per Lord Sumption).

[181] Lee 2015, points out that there was little analysis of the concept of 'public interest' in *Lawrence*, and her investigation concludes that there is no 'stable or widely accepted approach to defining public interests, or to distinguishing between public and private', at 330.

[182] The power station concerned was Bankside 'A', the coal-fired predecessor of Sir Giles Gilbert Scott's Bankside 'B'. It is the latter building that is now the Tate Modern.

[183] [1895] 1 Ch 287, 315–6.

[184] [2014] AC 822, at [161].

received planning permission'. In response to the first proposition, Lord Mance observed that 'the right to enjoy one's home without disturbance is one which I would believe that many, indeed most, people value for reasons largely if not entirely independent of money.'[185] With regard to the second, Lords Mance and Carnwath opposed a presumption against an injunction whenever a defendant's activity enjoyed the benefit of planning permission,[186] and Lord Neuberger offered only heavily-qualified support: planning permission might be a factor of 'real force in cases where it was clear that the planning authority had been reasonably and fairly influenced by the public benefit of the activity, and where the activity cannot be carried out without causing the nuisance complained of', but 'even in such cases, the court would have to weigh up all the competing factors.'[187]

The modern approach will not only allow courts to be more receptive to arguments invoking the *public interest*. A defendant will also now find it easier to resist the grant of an injunction on the basis that the damage it will do to his interests will be out of proportion to the benefits it will secure for the claimant.[188] Moreover, in all cases the behaviour of the parties can be an important factor: where a defendant has 'acted in a high-handed manner - if he has endeavoured to steal a march upon the [claimant] or to evade the jurisdiction of the court' then this will move a court towards granting an injunction, whilst if there has been a genuine dispute about the lawfulness of the defendant's activity and he 'has acted fairly and not in an unneighbourly spirit' then this will weigh in the opposite direction.[189]

Even if a court decides to exercise its discretion to grant a prohibitory injunction, it is common for such injunctions to be *suspended* for a period sufficient to give the defendant time to make alternative arrangements.

B. Damages

An injunction is the obvious remedy to seek in order to prevent a private nuisance from continuing into the future. But an injunction cannot redress the past, so claimants may also want damages to compensate for losses that have already occurred. The question of what measure of damages ought to be awarded to a claimant in a private nuisance case raises a number of difficult issues, such as what to do about claimants who used their property in ways which meant they were not inconvenienced, unforeseeable losses, and consequential damage to personal property. We will deal with each of these in turn, but will start by dealing with simple cases of physical damage to property and loss of amenity.

(1) *Simple property damage cases.* In a simple case of private nuisance causing physical damage to the land itself, or to a building on the land, the most obvious measure of damages will be either (a) the cost of repair, or (b) the diminution in capital value as a result of the physical damage. Thus if *Blaster*'s private nuisance in relation to *Graham*,

---

[185] [2014] AC 822, at [168]. An observation identified as having 'real force' by Lord Neuberger at [127] and supported by Lord Carnwath at [247].

[186] [2014] AC 822, at [167] (Lord Mance), [246] (Lord Carnwath).

[187] [2014] AC 822, at [125].

[188] [2014] AC 822, at [126] (Lord Neuberger). The Law Commission thinks the law is uncertain and has recommended that Parliament enacts a statutory discretion, structured around proportionality, to govern decisions as to whether an injunction should be granted to protect against actionable interference with rights to light: Law Commission, *Rights to Light* (Law Com No 356, 2014), Chapter 3.

[189] These factors were mentioned in a passage from Lord Macnaghten's speech in *Colls* v *Home & Colonial Stores Ltd* [1904] AC 179, 193 that was commended by Lord Neuberger in *Lawrence* v *Fen Tigers Ltd* [2014] AC 822, at [121].

the owner-occupier of a nearby house, cracks the slates on *Graham*'s roof, then the obvious measure of damages will be the cost of replacing the slates, or how much less the house can be sold as a result of having cracked slates.

(2) *Simple loss of amenity cases.* In a simple case of private nuisance causing a loss of amenity, that is, a loss of usefulness, the measure of damages will reflect the (a) the usefulness of the land, (b) the degree to which it was rendered less useful, and (c) the time for which it was rendered less useful.

For example, if *Graham* is the owner–occupier of a house, *Hector* is the owner–occupier of an office-building, and *Ian* is the owner–occupier of a horse paddock, where he keeps his horse, and all three have to stop using their land for a year because of the emanation of clouds of poisonous dust from demolition work being carried out in a reckless manner by *Jerry* on his nearby land, then *Graham*'s damages will be calculated on the basis of the loss of a year's use of a house, *Hector*'s on the basis of the loss of a year's use of an office-building, and *Ian*'s on the basis of the loss of a year's use of a horse paddock.

Importantly, the basic measure of damages in a loss of amenity case is a reflection of the amenity value of the *land* and *not* of the distress felt by those occupying the land. We have already quoted Lord Hoffmann's statement, in *Hunter v Canary Wharf* (1997) to the effect that amenity value 'may be affected by the size, commodiousness and value of his property but cannot be increased merely because more people are in occupation and therefore suffer greater collective discomfort'.[190] Three of the Law Lords who heard *Hunter* made it clear that loss of amenity value is something quantified by focusing on the loss of usefulness of the claimant's land, and not by focusing on the distress and suffering of the claimant.[191] Thus, where *Florence* and *Flora* are owner–occupiers of identical, neighbouring terraced houses, and *Stinker* committed private nuisance in relation to each of them by regularly subjecting their houses equally to the strong smell of solvents from his paint-mixing business while he was waiting for a new odour-extraction system to be delivered, we would expect *Florence* and *Flora* to each be awarded the same amount by way of damages, even if *Florence* lives in her house on her own while *Flora* shares her house with her mother, her sister, and three children.

(3) *Claimants who do not suffer any interference.* A difficult question arises where a particular claimant uses her premises in such a way that she does not suffer any interference with her use and enjoyment of them. Consider the **Two Flats Problem**:

Low Trees is a three-storey house, which has been split into three flats. *Constance* owns the top floor flat. *Drummer* owns the middle floor flat. *Flyer* owns the ground floor flat. For the past six months, *Drummer* has been practising the drums in his flat each evening, sometimes going on until after midnight. *Constance* is very disturbed by *Drummer*'s drumming – she cannot sleep and she feels unable to invite anyone to visit because the noise makes conversation impossible. *Flyer* is not disturbed at all by the drumming because she never stays in her flat. Instead, she lives in accommodation provided by her employer near her place of work. She has no inclination to visit *Low Trees* – she owns a flat there purely for investment purposes – and has no inclination to let it out to anyone else. In fact, she is only aware that *Drummer* is drumming each evening in because *Constance* told her about it, and asked for ideas as to what they could do.

---

[190] [1997] AC 655, 706–7.
[191] [1997] AC 655, 696 (per Lord Lloyd), 706 (per Lord Hoffmann), 724–5 (per Lord Hope).

In this case, both *Constance* and *Flyer* appear to be the victims of a private nuisance for which *Drummer* is responsible. His drumming is unreasonably interfering with the amenity value of both *Constance*'s flat and *Flyer*'s flat; neither of their flats is currently very useful as a flat. There seems little doubt that *Constance* could obtain an injunction requiring *Drummer* to moderate his drumming in future, and *Flyer* could also probably obtain an injunction if she proposed living in her flat or renting it out. But what could *Constance* and *Flyer* sue *Drummer* for by way of *damages*, for the nuisance he has created *for the past six months* through excessive drumming?

On the basis of the statement above – that loss of amenity value is something quantified by focusing on the loss of usefulness of a claimant's land, and not by focusing on the distress and suffering of the claimant – one might think that in Two Flats both *Constance and Flyer* will be entitled to sue *Drummer* for substantial damages; because of drummer's activities neither of their flats has been very useful as a flat for the past six months. But – if we look more closely then it seems that *Flyer* has not actually been using her flat in such a way that *Drummer*'s behaviour has reduced her ability to use and enjoy it *in this way* – as an investment – at all. So *should* we award *Flyer* substantial damages[192] in these circumstances?

We think that the answer is 'no': *Flyer* should *not* be awarded substantial damages.[193] But, this does not mean that damages for loss of amenity are *actually* for distress and suffering; rather, it reflects the fact that a claimant can only recover damages for an interference with the usefulness of land if she was actually *using* the land in a way which was interfered with. Thus the conclusion that *Flyer* should receive no compensation for *past* loss is no more controversial than concluding that a person who has paved over their garden should receive no compensation from a defendant who is responsible for a private nuisance that would typically have damaged plants and shrubs.

(4) *Unforeseeable losses.* The rule on remoteness of damage that applies to negligence cases – that losses that are an unforeseeable consequence of a tort being committed will normally be too remote to be actionable – will also apply in private nuisance cases. Consider, for example, the **Chemical Vats Problem**:

> An experiment goes wrong in *Advance*'s laboratory and results in foul-smelling smoke pouring out of the laboratory window and drifting across *Beatnik*'s land for several days. It is perfectly foreseeable that such smoke could be very unpleasant for *Beatnik* to smell, but she is away from home until after the smoke has cleared. However, *Beatnik* – unknown to *Advance* – has some vats of chemicals on her land that are exposed to the open air. She uses these vats for dyeing clothes. The smoke reacts violently with the chemicals and causes an explosion which breaks all the windows in *Beatnik*'s house.

It seems very unlikely that *Beatnik* would be entitled to sue for the physical damage to her land (broken windows) here. The decision of the Privy Council in *The Wagon Mound*

---

[192] If we do not award substantial damages then it may be the case that we cannot award nominal damages instead: it seems that private nuisance is not a tort that is actionable *per se* unless the nuisance takes the form of an interference with the right to light, or some other right associated with the claimant's land. See *Nicholls* v *Ely Beet Sugar Factory Ltd (No 2)* [1936] 1 Ch 343, 348–9.

[193] This was also the view of Waller LJ in *Dobson* v *Thames Water Utilities Ltd* [2009] 3 All ER 319, [34].

(No 2) (1967) purported to make foreseeability 'a necessary element in determining damages in . . . all cases of nuisance . . .'[194] and this position was endorsed by the House of Lords in *Cambridge Water Co v Eastern Counties Leather plc* (1994):

> [I]f a [claimant in the tort of negligence] is in ordinary circumstances only able to claim damages in respect of personal injuries where he can prove such foreseeability on the part of the defendant, it is difficult to see why, in common justice, he should be in a stronger position to claim damages for interference with the enjoyment of his land where the defendant was unable to foresee such damage.[195]

We think that a court would find that the foreseeability of damage to *Beatnik* by way of an interference with her sensibilities (the awful smell) would not prevent physical damage to windows from being too remote a consequence of *Advance*'s tort.

(5) *Consequential damages (1): damage to personal property.* The ordinary rule in tort law is that a claimant who can establish that he has been the victim of a tort committed by a defendant can recover compensatory damages for any consequential losses resulting from the tort provided that they are not too remote and not the wrong kind of loss.[196] Thus if *Blaster* commits the tort of private nuisance in relation to *Host* by using such powerful explosives in his quarry that *Host*'s nearby hotel is regularly shaken, and most of the guests who had been staying there leave in protest, *Host* is likely to be able to recover for the loss of profits associated with the early departure of the guests.

What is the position, however, if the consequential damage involves physical damage to *personal property*, as opposed to damage to the land itself, or buildings on it? For example, what would be the position if *Blaster*'s activities caused crockery to fall off the shelves in *Host*'s hotel and smash on the floor? There are certainly some cases where claimants appear to have been awarded damages in a private nuisance claim for physical harm done to their personal property.[197]

In *Hunter v Canary Wharf* (1997), Lord Hoffmann said that if a claimant's land was flooded with water coming from the defendant's land, then in addition to recovering damages for the 'injury to his land' from the flooding, the claimant might be able to recover 'damages for consequential loss' such as 'damages for chattels or livestock lost as a result [of the flood].'[198] This suggests that damages for harm to property on land but not *attached* to the land can be recovered *provided that* the physical harm is a consequence of the land itself being damaged or its amenity value being reduced. We think that this condition would be satisfied in the case of the vibrations from *Blaster*'s activities causing *Host*'s crockery to be smashed. But in any case where the condition is not satisfied, or the owner of the personal property does not have title to sue for private nuisance, then any claim for damage to personal property will have to be brought as a claim in *negligence*.

---

[194] [1967] AC 617, 640.

[195] [1994] 2 AC 264, 300 (per Lord Goff of Chieveley). In *Northumbrian Water Ltd v Sir Robert McAlpine Ltd* [2014] EWCA Civ 685, the Court of Appeal confirmed, at [18], that 'foreseeability of harm of the type suffered by the [claimant] is necessary for the defendant to be liable in damages for [private] nuisance'.

[196] See above, Chapter 9.

[197] See *Halsey v Esso Petroleum* [1961] 1 WLR 683 (claimant allowed to recover damages in private nuisance case for damage to washing and paintwork of his car resulting from acid smuts from defendants' chimney emanating onto claimant's land).

[198] [1997] AC 655, 706.

(6) *Consequential damages (2): personal injuries.* We noted above, when we discussed the Blinded Gardener Problem that the decision in *Hunter* v *Canary Wharf* (1997) made it clear that a claimant cannot sue in private nuisance for personal injuries suffered as a result of an emanation onto her land, or any other form of private nuisance.[199] Thus if *Tapster* committed private nuisance in relation to *Snorer* by creating a state of affairs that led to the flooding of *Snorer's* basement flat, and *Snorer* only awoke after inhaling such a quantity of water that she had to be hospitalised, *Snorer* would be able to recover compensation for: (a) any physical damage caused to her flat by the flooding; (b) the loss of ability to use her flat while it was flooded; (c) any consequential damage to her personal property in the flat; but not for (d) her personal injury. To recover compensation for (d), *Snorer* would have to demonstrate that *Tapster* had committed some other tort in relation to her, such as the tort of *negligence.*

13.13 Peculiar forms of the tort

There are some other torts that are treated as forms of private nuisance though they do not fit within the definition of the tort that was advanced at the start of this chapter. For example: the tort of organising a rival market within six and a half miles of a franchise or statutory market;[200] or the tort of organising a ferry service which rivals that of a person with a franchise right to operate a ferry. Such torts have often developed their own esoteric rules, such as that making the distance of six and a half miles significant, and consequently are often treated as independent torts rather than forms of private nuisance. We think that it is likely, however, that a judge asked to resolve any uncertainty about the rules applying to these torts would draw strong analogies with the tort of private nuisance.

Further reading

A classic, and highly influential, account of the proper scope of the tort of private nuisance can be found in **F.H. Newark, 'The boundaries of nuisance' (1949) 65 *Law Quarterly Review* 480.** But anyone eager to explore the modern law in more detail should start with **John Murphy,** *The Law of Nuisance* **(OUP, 2010).**

Allan Beever, *The Law of Private Nuisance* **(Hart Publishing, 2013)** is an ambitious and scholarly attempt to demonstrate that the tort is coherent, and has a distinctive role to play. Two further important essays considering private nuisance from the perspective of rights-based accounts of the law can be found in **Donal Nolan and Andrew Robertson (eds),** *Rights and Private Law* **(Hart, 2011): Chapter 16 by Donal Nolan, '"A tort**

---

[199] [1997] AC 655, 696 (per Lord Lloyd), 707 (per Lord Hoffmann). In *Transco plc* v *Stockport Metropolitan Borough Council* [2004] 2 AC 1, a majority of the House of Lords held that damages for personal injuries could not be recovered under the rule in *Rylands* v *Fletcher* (discussed in Chapter 14, below) because this was the rule in private nuisance: see [9] (per Lord Bingham), [35] (per Lord Hoffmann), [52] (per Lord Hobhouse).

[200] *Tamworth BC* v *Fazeley Town Council* (1978) 77 LGR 238; *Sevenoaks DC* v *Vinson Ltd* [1984] Ch 211; *Stoke-on-Trent City Council* v *W & J Wass Ltd* [1988] 1 WLR 1406.

against land": private nuisance as a property tort' and Chapter 17 by Richard W Wright, 'Private nuisance: a window on substantive justice'.

The story behind the leading case of *St Helen's Smelting* v *Tipping* (1865) is revealed by Brian Simpson in 'Victorian judges and the problems of social cost: *Tipping* v. *St Helen's Smelting Company* (1865)', Chapter 7 in his book *Leading Cases in the Common Law* (OUP, 1995). Ben Pontin offers a challenging and informative account of the tort's accomplishments in 'The Common Law Clean Up of the "Workshop of the World": More Realism About Nuisance Law's Historic Environmental Achievements' (2013) 40 Journal of Law and *Society* 173.

A stimulating, and accessible, account of the law from an economic perspective is provided in A.I. Ogus and G.M. Richardson, 'Economics and the environment: a study of private nuisance' (1977) 36 *Cambridge Law Journal* 284.

Maria Lee has written several interesting and important articles about private nuisance, and we think 'What is private nuisance?' (2003) 119 *Law Quarterly Review* 298 and 'Safety, regulation and tort: fault in context' (2011) 74 *Modern Law Review* 555, in particular, present significant arguments that are not adopted by our chapter.

Chapter 14
Strict liability for dangerous things

Aims and objectives

Reading this chapter should enable you to:

(1) Understand when a claimant can sue a defendant under 'the rule in *Rylands* v *Fletcher*'.

(2) Get a good grasp of current debates over why this rule exists, and whether the courts are justified in viewing liability arising under the rule as a sub-species of liability for private nuisance.

(3) Get an overview of other situations where a defendant will be held strictly liable for harm done by a dangerous thing that he is responsible for; in particular, situations where a defendant will be held strictly liable for harm done by fire spreading from his land, and for harm done by an animal that he owns or that is under his control.

14.1 The basics

In some circumstances English law imposes *strict* liability on those who are responsible for dangerous things, in particular dangerous animals and things that might escape from land and create an extraordinary problem for those with an interest in neighbouring land. It imposes these liabilities as a result of a range of rules about damage caused by animals that have been modified by statute – the Animals Act 1971 – to various degrees, 'the rule in *Rylands* v *Fletcher*', and some analogous doctrines.

All that it means to say that these liabilities are *strict*, is that they are imposed without the defendant being proved to have been at fault. Of course, the defendant *may have* behaved in an unreasonable way – he or she cannot avoid liability by confessing the he or she *was* at fault – but the claimant does not have to prove fault in order to establish the liability. In the course of our discussion of 'the rule in *Rylands* v *Fletcher*', we consider possible reasons *why* English law has chosen to impose strict liability in these areas, but not in others. Whatever the answer, it is clear that English law has 'pockets' of strict liability rather than a broad, general principle of strict liability, and consequently a considerable portion of this chapter is spent describing the rules – sometimes apparently artificial – that define the scope of these 'pockets'.

We will start by discussing 'the rule in *Rylands* v *Fletcher*', then consider analogous liability rules, and conclude the chapter with an account of the liabilities found in the Animals Act 1971.

In summary, 'the rule in *Rylands* v *Fletcher*' provides that if a person brings onto, or keeps on, some land an exceptionally dangerous or mischievous thing in extraordinary or unusual circumstances, then if that thing escapes from the land and damages another person's land, the first person will be liable to pay compensation for that damage, subject to the issue of remoteness and the possibility of defences. We will see, however, that almost every term in this summary requires some elaboration.[1]

14.2 The rule in *Rylands* v *Fletcher*: history and rationale

In the 1860s John Rylands was the leading textile manufacturer in England. He arranged for contractors to build a reservoir to provide water for the steam engines that powered the looms in one of his mills. The reservoir was built over old mine shafts which had been filled with earth, but one of these plugs of earth gave way and water escaped from the reservoir into the mine workings. It flowed through some abandoned workings and flooded a mine worked by Thomas Fletcher.

In the Court of Exchequer, Martin B found that Rylands was not liable to compensate Fletcher for the flooding to his mine.[2] He stated that 'the making of a pond for holding water is a nuisance to no one.'[3] This must be correct: a pond does not *in itself* interfere unreasonably with the interests of neighbours. But Martin B went on to say that even when the water in a pond escaped the owner of the land on which it was built should not be liable, because 'To hold the defendants liable would . . . make them insurers against the consequences of a lawful act upon their own land when they had no reason to believe or suspect that any damage was likely to ensue.'[4] As it was not reasonably foreseeable that building a reservoir on Rylands' land would result in Fletcher suffering any harm, it could not be argued that Rylands owed Fletcher a duty not to build a reservoir on his land. So it was not possible to argue that Rylands committed any kind of wrong – let alone a tort – in building the reservoir on his land.

On appeal, however, the Court of Exchequer Chamber decided the case in favour of the claimant, Fletcher. Blackburn J said,

> We think the rule of law is, that the person who, for his own purposes, brings on his land and collects and keeps there anything likely to do mischief if it escapes, must keep it in at his peril; and if he does not do so, is *prima facie* answerable for all the damage which is the natural consequence of its escape. He can excuse himself by showing that the escape was owing to the claimant's default; or perhaps that the escape was the consequence of *vis major*, or the act of God.

---

[1] We have not attempted to summarise the liability rules under the Animals Act 1971 or those that are analogous to 'the rule in *Rylands* v *Fletcher*'; any useful summary would risk being almost as long as the brief accounts of these rules that we provide in the main chapter.

[2] *Rylands* v *Fletcher* (1865) 3 H & C 774; 159 ER 737.

[3] (1865) 3 H & C 774, 792; 159 ER 737, 745.

[4] (1865) 3 H & C 774, 793; 159 ER 737, 745.

He went on to explain the justice of this rule:

> It seems but reasonable and just that the neighbour who has brought something onto his own property (which was not naturally there), harmless to others so long as it is confined to his own property, but which he knows will be mischievous if it gets on his neighbour's, should be obliged to make good the damage which ensues if he does not succeed in confining it to his own property.[5]

In the House of Lords Lord Cairns LC quoted this rule and explanation, then added, 'I entirely concur.'[6] But, he also stated that the rule would *only* apply to someone who had in the course of a *non-natural use* of his land brought onto or stored on his land something which was liable to do damage if it escaped.[7] This limit on the rule in *Rylands* v *Fletcher* – as originally formulated by Blackburn J – has been followed ever since; though, as we will see, different views have been expressed as to what will count as a *non-natural use*.

One hundred and fifty years on, lawyers continue to debate the scope of the rule in *Rylands* v *Fletcher*. But in *Transco plc* v *Stockport MBC* (2004)[8] the House of Lords provided a modern restatement of the rule, and fixed that it applies where:

1. A has brought onto, or kept on, some land an *exceptionally dangerous or mischievous thing in extraordinary or unusual circumstances*. Let's call such a thing 'T' and the land which that T was brought onto, or kept on, 'Blackacre'. The rule continues so that if:
2. T *escapes* from Blackacre and
3. T consequently *damages B's land*[9] and
4. the kind of damage that T causes is a kind that was a reasonably foreseeable consequence of such an escape, then
5. B will be entitled to sue A for compensation for that damage, unless
6. A can raise a *defence* to B's claim.[10]

Importantly, in order to sue A for compensation under the rule in *Rylands* v *Fletcher*, B will *not* have to prove that A was at fault for the escape of T from Blackacre.

Lord Hoffmann has observed that 'it is tempting to see, beneath the surface of the rule, a policy of requiring the costs of a commercial enterprise to be internalised; to require the entrepreneur to provide, by insurance or otherwise, for the risks to others which his enterprise creates.'[11] But in most contexts English law has rejected this policy and has insisted that entrepreneurs (and others) should only be liable for damage caused by their *wrongs*.

---

[5] (1866) LR 1 Ex 265, 279–80.

[6] (1868) LR 3 HL 330, 340. Lord Cranworth also supported this account of the law. Three Law Lords heard the appeal, but there is some mystery as to the identity of the third. See, generally, Heuston 1970.

[7] (1868) LR 3 HL 330, 339.

[8] Noted, Bagshaw 2004b. We will refer to this case (reported at [2004] 2 AC 1) hereafter as '*Transco*'.

[9] When we use the phrase 'B's land' in this context we intend the word 'land' to include not just the earth itself but also things attached to it, such as buildings, which count as real property. The statement that the land must be 'B's' is shorthand for the fact that in order to claim B must have a particular relationship with the land. The precise nature of that necessary relationship is discussed below, § 14.3(B). At this stage, an adequate summary is that the land will count as 'B's land' if B has a legally recognised interest in the land, and in certain circumstances it may be sufficient that B has exclusive possession of the land.

[10] This statement of the rule is based on the formulation of Lord Bingham in *Transco*, at [11].

[11] *Transco*, at [29].

Can it be said that liability under the rule in *Rylands* v *Fletcher* involves some sort of *wrong*? On this, Carleton Kemp Allen has observed that it is very hard to see how a defendant who has (without fault on his part) failed to ensure that a dangerous thing on his land stays there has necessarily done anything wrong to a claimant whose land has been damaged by that escape:

> It is often said that in respect of peculiarly dangerous things, there is a 'duty' irrespective of negligence or wilful aggression, to 'insure' neighbours and others against damage. This use of the term 'duty' is unfortunate . . . There is of course a duty of careful management of any material thing, whether it belong to the family of '*Rylands* v *Fletcher* objects' or not; but it is difficult to see that there is any 'duty' to prevent a dangerous thing escaping through causes which have nothing to do with the maintainer's fault . . . The true situation seems to be that he who maintains for his own advantage a peculiarly dangerous thing in proximity to others, necessarily imposes upon those others a risk of injury . . . greater than is to be reasonably expected in the ordinary circumstances of social life, and it is therefore just and expedient that he himself should bear the risk of making good any damage to others which results from the maintenance of the object. This is certainly a liability; but it is a confusion of ideas to [say that it involves breach of] a duty.[12]

Thus, a defendant's liability under the rule in *Rylands* v *Fletcher* is not based on any sense that the defendant committed a wrong: quoting Lord Hoffmann again, 'with hindsight, *Rylands* v *Fletcher* can be seen as an isolated victory for the internalisers. The following century saw a steady refusal to treat it as laying down any broad principle of liability.'[13]

Given that it was an *isolated* victory, and the policy reflected in the rule has been rejected in most contexts,[14] we might ask: why did the House of Lords not abolish the rule, rather than restating it? One explanation is that to overturn a case which has been part of English law for so long is thought to be 'too radical a step' for judges to take.[15] A second explanation, however, is that some judges still think that it is 'fair' to impose liability without the need to prove fault where a defendant has created an *extraordinary* risk.[16] But preserving the rule whilst simultaneously refusing 'to treat it as laying down any broad principle of liability' means that it has been confined within narrow limits. These limits, however, have proved difficult to define precisely. Indeed, the High Court of Australia castigated them as so uncertain that 'the practical application of the rule . . . is likely to degenerate into an essentially unprincipled and *ad hoc* subjective determination'.[17] Such criticism encouraged

---

[12] Allen 1931, 193–4. See also Holmes 1873, 653; Wright 1961, 86; Restatement Torts 2d (1965) §4 Comment b; Cane 1998, 165; Waddams 1998, 124–5; Goldberg & Zipursky 2016.

[13] *Transco*, at [29]. Oliphant 2005 suggests (at 118) that although the facts of *Rylands* v *Fletcher* provided an ideal testing ground for a fledgling theory of enterprise liability, an examination of the judgments gives 'no reason to believe that ideas of loss-distribution, deterrence, etc., were in the minds of the judges who participated in the decision'.

[14] For example, if B brings a peculiarly dangerous thing onto his land, and, without any fault on his part, the thing escapes from his control and injures A, who is a lawful visitor to B's land, then B is not liable to A: the cost of A's injuries are not 'internalised' to B's business: *Read* v *J Lyons & Co Ltd* [1947] AC 156.

[15] *Transco*, at [43] (per Lord Hoffmann).

[16] For instance, *Transco*, at [6] (per Lord Bingham) and [110] (per Lord Walker). Nolan 2005 (at 449) remains unconvinced: '[T]he best way forward appears to be abolition.'

[17] *Burnie Port Authority* v *General Jones Pty Ltd* (1994) 179 CLR 520, 540 (per Mason CJ, Deane, Dawson, Toohey and Gaudron JJ)

the House of Lords in *Transco* to try to 'restate [the rule] so as to achieve as much certainty and clarity as attainable'.[18]

The House of Lords sought to achieve this by declaring that the rule in *Rylands* v *Fletcher* is 'a sub-species of nuisance',[19] 'an aspect of the law of private nuisance'[20] or 'a species, or special case, of nuisance'.[21] In portraying the rule in this way, they were following in the footsteps of Lord Macmillan in *Read* v *J Lyons & Co Ltd* (1947), who took the view that *Rylands* was part of the law concerning 'the mutual duties of adjoining or neighbouring landowners'[22] and Lord Goff in *Cambridge Water Co* v *Eastern Counties Leather plc* (1994), who identified an 'historical connection with the law on nuisance' and stated that 'the rule in *Rylands* v *Fletcher* was essentially concerned with an extension of the law of nuisance to cases of isolated escape.'[23] Lord Goff's understanding was heavily influenced by Professor F H Newark's article, 'The Boundaries of Nuisance', in which Newark stated that:

> those who decided [*Rylands* v *Fletcher*] were quite unconscious of any revolutionary or reaction-ary principles implicit in the decision. They thought of it as calling for no more than a restate-ment of settled principles, and Lord Cairns went so far as to describe those principles as 'extremely simple'. And in fact the main principle involved was extremely simple, being no more than the principle that negligence is not an element in the tort of nuisance.[24]

If it is correct to say that the rule in *Rylands* v *Fletcher* is part of the law on private nui-sance, then this classification will determine who can be liable under it, who can claim, and what types of damage can be claimed for: the answers for the rule will be the same as those which have been established for the tort of private nuisance.[25] The association with private nuisance might also explain *why* defendants are held liable under the rule: they are liable because they are somehow responsible for isolated escapes which cause unreasona-ble interference with the claimant's use and enjoyment of his or her land. Unfortunately, there are three reasons for thinking that this classification is misguided:[26]

(1) Private nuisance is a tort. In contrast, liability under the rule in *Rylands* v *Fletcher* does not arise in response to someone's committing a tort: a defendant does not have to commit any kind of legal *wrong* in order to be held liable under the rule.

(2) The original rationale behind *Rylands* – internalisation of costs to commercial enter-prises – provides no justification for treating *Rylands* as – like private nuisance – a wrong that protects only interests in land, and hence distinguishing between costs from damage to neighbouring land and costs from other types of damage, such as personal injuries. Instead the internalisation rationale suggests that *Rylands* has more in common with the liability rules discussed at the end of this chapter, most of which cover types of damage beyond damage to neighbouring land.

---

[18] *Transco*, at [8] (per Lord Bingham).

[19] *Transco*, at [9] (per Lord Bingham).
[20] *Transco*, at [52] (per Lord Hobhouse).
[21] *Transco*, at [92] (per Lord Walker).
[22] *Read* v *J Lyons & Co Ltd* [1947] AC 156, 173 (per Lord Macmillan).
[23] [1994] 2 AC 264, 304.
[24] Newark 1949, 487.
[25] In the previous chapter we explained how the House of Lords in *Hunter* v *Canary Wharf* (1997) provided clear, if controversial, answers to the questions who could bring a claim for private nuisance and what kinds of damage they could claim compensation for: see above, §§ 13.11–13.12.
[26] Other scholars agree that the classification is misguided. See Murphy 2004 and Nolan 2005.

(3) The reasons provided by the House of Lords in *Transco* for preserving the rule provide no justification for limiting its operation to compensating for damage to land. For example, Lord Bingham observed that 'there is . . . a category of case, however small it might be, in which it seems just to impose liability even in the absence of fault' going on to cite the 'tragedy at Aberfan' as one such case.[27] In Aberfan, in 1966, a huge heap of waste and debris from a nearby colliery slid down a hill and buried a school, killing 116 children and 28 adults. The implication of classifying the rule in *Rylands* v *Fletcher* as a sub-species of private nuisance is that the owners of the school would be able to sue the owners of the waste heap for compensation for the damage to their buildings on a strict liability basis, while the families of the deceased would have to prove that the owners of the heap were at fault for its burying the school. Why would anyone regard *this* as 'just'?

If the rule in *Rylands* v *Fletcher* is *not* a close relation of the tort of private nuisance then the House of Lords had no good reason for restating it so that it can only protect interests in land. But unfortunately, the error involved in classifying the rule as related to private nuisance is so firmly woven into the speeches of a majority of their Lordships in *Transco* that no court below the Supreme Court can ignore it. Consequently in the next section we will assume that this erroneous classification is an unshakeable element of the current law on the scope of liability under the rule.

14.3 The rule in *Rylands* v *Fletcher*: application

Several issues need to be dealt with under this heading:

A. Who can be held liable under the rule?

The proposition that *Rylands* is part of the law concerning 'the mutual duties of adjoining or neighbouring landowners'[28] might be taken to entail that only *an owner* of land from which a dangerous thing escapes can be held liable. Weighing against this suggestion, however, are several cases where defendants who neither owned the land, nor were tenants of it, were held liable.[29] These cases suggest that liability can attach to any *occupier* of land from which the dangerous thing escaped.[30] Indeed, some *dicta* seem to go further and suggest that the person responsible for storing or collecting the mischievous substance can be liable regardless of his relation to the land.[31] Our view, consistent with our view as to who can be liable in private nuisance,[32] is that it is these *dicta* which correctly express the law.

---

[27] *Transco*, at [6].

[28] *Read* v *J Lyons & Co Ltd* [1947] AC 156, 173 (per Lord Macmillan).

[29] *Eastern & South African Telegraph Co* v *Cape Town Tramways Co* [1902] AC 381; *West* v *Bristol Tramways Co* [1908] 2 KB 14; *Charing Cross Electricity Supply Co* v *Hydraulic Power Co* [1914] 3 KB 772; *Rainham Chemical Works Ltd* v *Belvedere Fish Guano Co Ltd* [1921] 2 AC 465; *Shiffman* v *Order of St John* [1936] 1 All ER 557.

[30] In *Transco*, at [11], Lord Bingham's restatement uses the phrase 'occupier of land' to refer to the potential defendant.

[31] In *Rainham Chemical Works* v *Belvedere Fish Guano Co Ltd* [1921] 2 AC 465, Lord Sumner said (at 479) 'they cannot escape any liability which otherwise attaches to them on *storing it* [explosives] there merely because they have no tenancy or independent occupation' (emphasis added). In *Powell* v *Fall* (1880) 5 QBD 597 the escape was from the highway.

[32] See above, § 13.9.

B. Who can claim under the rule?

The conclusion that *Rylands* liability is closely related to the tort of private nuisance means that the question of who can claim under the rule should be answered in line with the answer given in *Hunter* v *Canary Wharf Ltd* (1997) to the question who can sue in private nuisance.[33] Thus to sue under *Rylands*[34] a claimant must have a sufficient interest in the land,[35] or must be enjoy *exclusive possession in fact* of the land,[36] and such a claimant can only sue for physical harm caused to the land, harm to its amenity value and consequential damage to chattels, not for personal injuries.[37]

This means that a claimant cannot use *Rylands* to recover compensation for pure economic losses that he has suffered as a result of a dangerous thing's escaping onto a third party's land. In *Cattle* v *Stockton Waterworks Co* (1875), Blackburn J was clear that in the *Rylands* case a claim could not have been made 'by every workman and person employed in the mine, who in consequence of its stoppage made less wages than he would otherwise have done'.[38] This should not be taken to mean, however, that *all* economic losses are irrecoverable under the rule in *Rylands* v *Fletcher*. Compensation for any diminution in the amenity value of land and compensation for economic losses *consequential on* physical damage to the claimant's land may be recovered under the rule in *Rylands* v *Fletcher*.[39]

C. An exceptionally dangerous or mischievous thing

Blackburn J spoke of the rule in *Rylands* v *Fletcher* as covering 'anything likely to do mischief if it escapes'. For a time, however, courts insisted that this meant things which were 'inherently dangerous'. Thus in *Hale* v *Jennings Bros* (1938), the Court of Appeal discussed whether a fairground 'chair-o-plane' was inherently dangerous, and concluded that it was because it was intended for use by 'ignorant people' who would be unaware of the dangers of fooling about in flying chairs. But when Professor Stallybrass exhaustively examined the cases he concluded that a condition of 'inherent dangerousness' was unhelpful: 'just as there is nothing which is at all times and in all circumstances dangerous so it seems that there is scarcely anything which is in all circumstances safe.'[40]

---

[33] Discussed above, § 13.11.

[34] This would have caused problems for the claimant in *Eastern & South African Telegraph Co* v *Cape Town Tramways Co* [1902] AC 381 because it was claiming for damage done to its submarine cable.

[35] Such as a fee simple in possession, a tenancy, or a reversionary interest. More detail on of what count as *sufficient* interests is to be found in the chapter on the tort of private nuisance, above, § 13.11.

[36] *Exclusive possession in fact* will be sufficient *unless* the defendant has the right to possess the land, or acted with the authority of the person with that right. But exclusive possession is not always necessary: for example, a reversioner may be able to sue. Unfortunately, Lord Bingham may have oversimplified when stating , in *Transco*, [9] and [11], that a claimant only had to be an 'occupier'.

[37] A majority in *Transco* expressly states that claims cannot be brought for personal injuries under the rule in *Rylands* v *Fletcher*: see [9] (Lord Bingham), [35] (Lord Hoffmann), and [52] (Lord Hobhouse).

[38] (1875) LR 10 QB 453, 457.

[39] The claimants in *Cambridge Water Co* v *Eastern Counties Leather* [1994] 2 AC 264 (discussed below) sought compensation for economic loss suffered by them as a result of their land suffering some kind of physical damage.

[40] Stallybrass 1929, 387.

In *Transco*, Lord Bingham reasserted the importance of a 'dangerousness' condition. He said that:

> It must be shown that the defendant has done something which he recognised, or judged by the standards appropriate at the relevant place and time, he ought reasonably to have recognised, as giving rise to an exceptionally high risk of danger or mischief if there should be an escape, however unlikely an escape may have been thought to be.[41]

He also stated that he did not think that 'the mischief or danger test should be at all easily satisfied'.[42] But, while Lords Hoffmann and Walker agreed with Lord Bingham that 'creation of an exceptional risk' was a relevant factor when applying the rule, they both treated it as related to the requirement of 'an extraordinary use of land'.[43]

D. Extraordinary use

Blackburn J's original formulation of rule in *Rylands* v *Fletcher* applied only to cases where someone brought onto land, or kept on land, something 'which was not naturally there'. As we have seen, in the House of Lords, Lord Cairns LC built on this and drew a distinction between defendants who used their land 'for any purpose for which it might in the ordinary course of the enjoyment of land be used . . . what I may term the natural user of land' and those who 'not stopping at the natural use of their close, had desired to use it for any purpose which I may term a non-natural use'.[44] So Lord Cairns LC held: (i) that liability under the rule in *Rylands* v *Fletcher* was limited to cases where someone used his land in a 'non-natural' way; *and* (ii) that someone would use his land in a 'non-natural' way if he used it in an *extraordinary* way.

The early cases do not provide any clear answer as to the original meaning of 'non-natural user'. Since the House of Lords upheld the decision in favour of Fletcher their Lordships must have concluded that a reservoir was a sufficiently non-natural use of land. Indeed, the reasoning in Blackburn J's judgment suggested that he thought that the rule covered straying cattle and escaping sewage.[45] Other early cases treated the rule as covering poisonous yew trees,[46] creosote,[47] and large quantities of electricity.[48] In *Wilson* v *Waddell* (1876), however, Lord Blackburn (as he had by then become) stated that use of land for ordinary mining operations was a natural use.

---

[41] *Transco*, at [10].

[42] Ibid.

[43] *Transco*, at [49] (per Lord Hoffmann), [103] (per Lord Walker).

[44] (1868) LR 3 HL 330, 339.

[45] In *Smeaton* v *Ilford Corp* [1954] Ch 450, Upjohn J stated that 'To collect into a sewer a large volume of sewage, inherently noxious and dangerous and bound to cause great damage if not properly contained, cannot be described, in my judgment, as a natural use of land' (at 472).

[46] *Crowhurst* v *Amersham Burial Board* (1878) 4 CPD 5. The rule does not, apparently, cover thistles which are 'the natural growth of the soil': *Giles* v *Walker* (1890) 24 QBD 656, 657.

[47] *West* v *Bristol Tramways Co* [1908] 2 KB 14.

[48] *Eastern & South African Telegraph Co* v *Cape Town Tramways Co* [1902] AC 381.

In *Rickards* v *Lothian* (1919), the Privy Council held that an escape of water from ordinary plumbing[49] did not fall within the scope of the rule. Lord Moulton said:

> It is not every use to which land is put that brings into play that [rule]. It must be some special use bringing with it increased danger to others, and must not merely be the ordinary use of land or such a use as is proper for the general benefit of the community.[50]

The last portion of this statement – 'not merely . . . such a use as is proper for the general benefit of the community' – can be interpreted as specifying that only *improper* uses of land fall within the scope of the rule in *Rylands* v *Fletcher*. By adopting this interpretation those who disliked the rule in *Rylands* v *Fletcher* could severely restrict its scope. Thus in *Read* v *J Lyons & Co* (1947), two members of the House of Lords suggested that use of land for a munitions factory in wartime might not be a 'non-natural user',[51] and in *Cambridge Water* v *Eastern Counties Leather* (1994), the trial judge held that the use of chemical solvents by a tannery in an industrial village was not a non-natural user given the benefits for local employment.

Shortly before the judgment of the House of Lords in *Cambridge Water* we might have traced a shift in the meaning of 'non-natural user' from 'not naturally there' to 'improper', via 'extraordinary'. But in that case Lord Goff spoke against any broad reading of Lord Moulton's phrase. Four points made by Lord Goff in this part of his judgment are worth particular emphasis.

First, he made clear that in his opinion 'the storage of substantial quantities of chemicals on industrial premises should be regarded as an almost classic case of non-natural use'. Secondly, he stated that the creation of employment could never be sufficient of itself to establish that a particular use of land was 'natural or ordinary'. Thirdly, he suggested that it would be less necessary *in future* to interpret the phrase 'non-natural user' narrowly in order to limit the scope of liability, because of the main ratio of the case: there can be no liability under the rule in *Rylands* v *Fletcher* for unforeseeable consequences of escapes.[52] Fourthly, he thought that the historic relationship between the rule in *Rylands* v *Fletcher* and the tort of private nuisance meant that in future the concept of 'non-natural user' might develop alongside the concept of 'reasonable user' in private nuisance.[53] The fourth point is particularly important because it suggests that the main activities which should be excluded from the scope of 'non-natural user' are those which create risks which are generally accepted as part of ordinary social give-and-take.

---

[49] The line is not easy to draw between ordinary and extraordinary plumbing but it seems to lie somewhere between *Western Engraving Co* v *Film Laboratories Ltd* [1936] 1 All ER 106, where the Court of Appeal held that the use of large quantities of water for film-washing was a non-natural user, and *Peters* v *Prince of Wales Theatre* [1943] KB 73 where a differently constituted Court of Appeal suggested that connection of water to a sprinkler system in a theatre was an ordinary and usual user. In *Transco* [2004] 2 AC 1 a water pipe carrying sufficient water for 66 flats was treated as 'entirely normal and routine' (at [13]) and thus not an 'extraordinary use', though Lord Bingham complicated the matter somewhat by stating that in his opinion the volume of water in a domestic plumbing system was also insufficient to amount to a sufficiently dangerous thing (at [10]).

[50] [1913] AC 263, 280.

[51] In the earlier case of *Rainham Chemical Works* v *Belvedere Fish Guano Co Ltd* [1921] 2 AC 465, the House of Lords had shown no hesitation in finding that making munitions during the First World War was 'certainly not the common and ordinary use of the land' (at 471, per Lord Buckmaster).

[52] These three points are to be found at [1994] 2 AC 264, 309.

[53] [1994] 2 AC 264, 299.

In *Transco*, Lord Bingham confirmed that a defendant's use of land does not have to be 'unreasonable' or 'improper' in order to fall within the scope of the rule:

> I think it is clear that ordinary user is a preferable test to natural user, making it clear that the rule in *Rylands* v *Fletcher* is engaged only where the defendant's use is shown to be extraordinary and unusual. This is not a test to be inflexibly applied: a use may be extraordinary and unusual at one time or in one place but not so at another time or in another place . . . I also doubt whether a test of reasonable user is helpful, since a user may well be quite out of the ordinary but not unreasonable, as was that of *Rylands*, *Rainham Chemical Works* or the tannery in *Cambridge Water*. Again, as it seems to me, the question is whether the defendant has done something out of the ordinary in the place and at the time when he does it.[54]

While Lord Bingham cast doubt on the utility of tests which ask whether particular uses were unreasonable or improper he offered little guidance on how to draw the line between the ordinary and extraordinary. Indeed Lord Hoffmann seemed to regard a test based around 'ordinary uses of land' as 'rather vague'.[55] He offered 'a use creating an increased risk' as the 'converse' of 'natural use',[56] stated that 'the criterion of exceptional risk must be taken seriously',[57] and, contentiously, asserted that a 'useful guide in deciding whether the risk has been created by a "non-natural" user of land is . . . to ask whether the damage which eventuated was something against which the [claimant] occupier could reasonably be expected to have insured himself'.[58]

Very few claims rely on the rule in *Rylands* v *Fletcher*, so there is very little evidence as to how the courts will sort out what counts as 'extraordinary'. In *Stannard* v *Gore* (2012), the Court of Appeal held that a defendant had not used his premises on an industrial estate in a sufficiently 'extraordinary' way when he stored more than 3,000 tyres there for use in his business.[59] Etherton LJ reasoned: 'The commercial activity carried on by Mr Stannard as a motor vehicle tyre supplier was a perfectly ordinary and reasonable activity to be carried on in a light industrial estate. There was no evidence that the number of tyres and the method of their storage was out of the ordinary for similar premises carrying on that type of activity or that they posed a foreseeable or recognised danger.'[60] With respect, we think that the focus in this reasoning on the *danger* that the defendant's activity posed to his neighbours is more convincing than the reference to what sorts of business are commonplace on industrial estates: we have just quoted Lord Goff's opinion that 'the storage of substantial quantities of chemicals on industrial premises should be regarded as an almost classic case of non-natural use'.[61] Distinguishing between ordinary and extraordinary uses of land in

---

[54] *Transco*, at [11]. Lord Scott agreed with Lord Bingham's judgment. Lord Walker expressly commended Lord Bingham's discussion of this requirement, but also commended the different approach of Lord Hoffmann!

[55] *Transco*, at [37].

[56] *Transco*, at [44].

[57] *Transco*, at [49].

[58] *Transco*, at [46]. With respect, we think that the insurability of the claimant's property is *irrelevant* to the correct classification of the defendant's activity: when a property owner insures her terraced house against destruction such insurance generally does not distinguish between a car swerving into the front wall or the local fireworks factory exploding, but that surely cannot make the local fireworks factory into an *ordinary* use of land in the locality.

[59] *Stannard (t/a Wyvern Tyres)* v *Gore* [2014] 1 QB 1.

[60] Ibid, at [68].

[61] [1994] 2 AC 264, 309.

terms of the degree of risk posed to neighbours in the event of an escape seems to us to be both consistent with precedent and straightforward to apply.

It is worth briefly making two further points about the 'extraordinary use' requirement. First, where statute has authorised a particular use of land that use will be considered as 'natural and ordinary' unless there has been negligence.[62] Secondly, Blackburn J's original formulation of the rule stated that the defendant's collection of the dangerous thing had to be 'for his own purposes'. A court would be unlikely to use this phrase to protect a defendant whose activity was intended to benefit the public generally, but might use it to protect a defendant whose activity was intended to benefit both himself and the claimant. In this situation, however, there would be an overlap with the defence of consent.

E. Escape

Liability under the rule in *Rylands* v *Fletcher* requires the dangerous thing to have *escaped* from the land where the defendant brought or kept it. Thus, in *Read* v *J Lyons & Co* (1947), the claimant was injured by an exploding shell while working as an inspector at a munitions factory, but the House of Lords held that she could not rely on the rule in *Rylands* v *Fletcher* to obtain compensation because the explosive had not escaped from the defendant's *premises*, but merely from its *control*. An escape from the defendant's land was treated as logically necessary because, in the words of Lord Macmillan, 'the doctrine of *Rylands* v *Fletcher* . . . derives from a conception of mutual duties of adjoining or neighbouring landowners, and its cogenors are trespass and [private] nuisance'.[63] Requiring an escape from the defendant's premises also ensures that the *Rylands* rule does not become entangled with the rules concerning the liability of an occupier to his or her visitors.

From the perspective of the policy of *internalising* the costs of commercial enterprises, it seems very artificial to distinguish between dangerous things escaping from land and escaping from control: why is it more worthwhile to internalise the costs of the former sort of incident? This extent to which the escape rule relies on artificial distinctions was reiterated in *Stannard* v *Gore* (2012), where the claimant's industrial unit was destroyed by a fire that had started in the defendant's adjoining unit, and which became so fierce that the fire brigade could not extinguish it before it reached the claimant's unit because it spread to stacks of tyres which the defendant was storing for use in his business.[64] The Court of Appeal held that the claimant could not rely on the *Rylands* rule here because what had escaped onto the claimant's premises – fire – was not the unusual *thing* – tyres – which the defendant had stored on his land.[65] This unexpectedly technical approach[66] to the escape

---

[62] *Transco*, at [89] (per Lord Scott). Lord Hoffmann, at [30]–[31], agreed that statutory authority for a particular use of land would prevent liability being imposed under the rule in *Rylands* v *Fletcher*, but did not state that this was because the statutory authority would make the use into a 'natural' one.

[63] [1947] AC 156, 173.

[64] Tyres do not catch fire easily, but once they are alight the fire is very difficult to extinguish.

[65] *Stannard (t/a Wyvern Tyres)* v *Gore* [2014] 1 QB 1, [48] (Ward LJ), [66] (Etherton LJ) and [164] (Lewison LJ).

[66] The Court of Appeal's approach involved departing from several first instance decisions, such as *Mason* v *Levy Auto Parts of England Ltd* [1967] 2 QB 530, *LMS International Ltd* v *Styrene Packaging and Insulation Ltd* [2005] EWHC 2065 (TCC), and *Harooni* v *Rustins Ltd* [2011] EWHC 1632 (TCC), which had accepted that the *Rylands* rule could be modified so that it could apply where a defendant 'brought onto his land things likely to catch fire, and kept them there in such conditions that if they did ignite the fire would be likely to spread to the [claimant's] land'.

requirement will prevent the *Rylands* rule from applying in most cases involving inflammable substances,[67] and possibly also in cases involving explosives.[68] The Court of Appeal, however, thought that precedent demanded that liability should not be found in any situation not covered by a strict reading of *Transco*'s formulation of the rule.[69]

F. Reasonable foreseeability

Suppose A brought a dangerous thing, T, onto his land in the course of an extraordinary use and T then escaped and caused some kind of damage to B's land. In *Rylands* v *Fletcher*, Blackburn J said that B would be entitled to sue A for compensation for this damage so long as it was a 'natural' consequence of T's escaping from A's land.[70] However, in *Cambridge Water Co* v *Eastern Counties Leather* (1994) the House of Lords decided that the modern position is that A's liability depends on it having been *reasonably foreseeable* that someone like B would suffer *that kind of harm* if T escaped from A's land.

The facts of the *Cambridge Water* case illustrate the point. The defendants ran a tanning business that used large quantities of chemicals. There were occasional spillages onto the factory floor, and as a result some of the chemicals seeped into the ground, then flowed along impermeable strata until they reached the claimants' borehole, which was over a mile away from the defendants' factory. The claimants used this borehole to obtain the water which supplied to local residents, and the chemical contamination meant that the claimants were forbidden to continue doing this.[71] The claimants sued the defendants under the rule in *Rylands* v *Fletcher* for the cost of creating a new borehole,[72] but the House of Lords dismissed their claim on the ground that no one could have foreseen that the claimants' borehole would be contaminated if the chemicals that the defendants used escaped from their land.

It should be noted that, B will *not* have to show that it was reasonably foreseeable that T *would escape* from A's land in order to bring a claim under the rule in *Rylands* v *Fletcher*,

---

[67] In *Stannard* Ward LJ accepted that liability might be imposed under the *Rylands* rule if the 'dangerous thing' that the defendant brought onto his land was some device incorporating *fire*, and the *fire* escaped, but explained that such liability would be rare in practice: see [36] (citing *Jones* v *Festiniog Railway Co* (1868) LR 3 QB 733), and [47]–[48].

[68] When an explosive substance is detonated it is rarely the substance *itself* that escapes from the defendant's land, as opposed to 'shock waves'.

[69] In *Stannard (t/a Wyvern Tyres)* v *Gore* [2014] 1 QB 1, at [19], Ward LJ went so far as to assert that 'the speech of Lord Bingham [in *Transco*] is the latest and last word on the subject'. Ironically, *Transco* did not involve a straightforward escape from the defendant's land: water escaped from a pipe on the defendant's premises and flowed to another part of the premises where it threatened to cause damage to a gas pipe which the claimant had a right to run across the defendant's premises. Lord Scott (at [78]–[80]) was adamant that even if the claimant's right to run the gas pipe across the defendant's land was a proprietary right, an easement, the claimant still could not sue the defendant because there had been no escape from the defendant's land. But the majority did not decide the case on this basis.

[70] (1866) LR 1 Ex 265, 279–80.

[71] The water may have been drinkable despite the contamination, but it fell foul of legislation that had been introduced pursuant to an EC Directive, banning the supply of water which contained even the slightest traces of the kind of chemicals that had contaminated the borehole.

[72] This claim did not fall foul of the rule in *Cattle* v *Stockton Waterworks* (1875) LR 10 QB 453 that compensation for pure economic loss may not be recovered under the rule in *Rylands* v *Fletcher*. The economic loss for which the claimants wanted to be compensated in *Cambridge Water* was consequential on the claimant's property (their borehole) being damaged.

the requirement is that it was reasonably foreseeable that *if T escaped*, someone like B would suffer the kind of harm for which she wants compensation. So suppose that A kept samples of dangerous bacteria in a laboratory on his land. Suppose further that A used such elaborate precautions to ensure that the bacteria remained in the laboratory that it was not reasonably foreseeable that the bacteria would escape from his land. Suppose further that the bacteria – against all expectation – managed to escape and damaged B's neighbouring land. In such a case, the fact that it was not reasonably foreseeable that the bacteria would escape from A's land would not be fatal to a claim by B under the rule in *Rylands* v *Fletcher*.

G. Strict liability?

Our discussion of the foreseeability rule in the previous section shows that the House of Lords in *Cambridge Water* did nothing to undermine the strictness of liability under the rule in *Rylands* v *Fletcher*. A defendant who took so many precautions that escape of a dangerous thing from his land was unforeseeable, can still be liable if an escape occurs and causes foreseeable damage to neighbouring land.

Some students find the claim that 'liability under the rule in *Rylands* v *Fletcher* is still strict' hard to accept because they assume 'strict' liability must be harsh and extensive liability. But all 'strict liability' means is that a defendant can be held liable without the claimant having to prove that he or she was at fault for what happened. There's no logical reason why 'strict liability' has to extend to providing compensation for *unforeseeable consequences*. Indeed, the remoteness rules in other parts of tort law tend only to make those who were *very much to blame* for what happened to a claimant liable for *all* the consequences of their actions, no matter how unforeseeable.[73]

Strict liability is not absolute liability. Absolute liability exists when a defendant is held liable for some harm that a claimant has suffered even though it was *impossible* for the defendant to prevent that harm occurring to the claimant. Strict liability occupies the terrain between fault-based liability and absolute liability: under a strict liability regime a defendant can be held liable without proof of fault, but will not be held liable if harm was impossible to prevent. The fact that liability under *Rylands* v *Fletcher* is strict, and not absolute, is reflected in the fact that a defendant who is being sued under the rule in *Rylands* v *Fletcher* may be able to take advantage of a number of different defences, the first three of which are roughly centred round the idea of 'impossibility of avoiding harm':

(1) *Act of a stranger.* A will have a defence to B's claim under the rule in *Rylands* v *Fletcher* if the escape from A's land resulted from the act of a person whom A could not control.[74] It seems to be assumed that a landowner has a sufficient degree of control over the anticipated activities[75] of independent contractors who he engages to bring the dangerous thing onto his premises or to store it there.[76] A defendant will not be liable, however, for

---

[73] See above, § 9.2.E.

[74] *Box* v *Jubb* (1879) 4 Ex D 76; *Rickards* v *Lothian* [1913] AC 263; *Perry* v *Kendricks Transport Ltd* [1956] 1 WLR 85.

[75] Where the independent contractor behaves in a wholly unanticipated way A may be able to avoid liability. This has been held to be the position in analogous cases involving fire. See below, § 14.4(A).

[76] In *Rylands* v *Fletcher* itself the escape seems to have been caused by the carelessness of the independent contractors who built the reservoir.

an escape resulting from the deliberate and malicious act of a stranger, unless such an act ought to have been anticipated and guarded against. So in *Perry* v *Kendricks Transport Ltd* (1956), two boys threw a lighted match into the petrol tank of a motor coach that was standing on the defendants' land, and the resulting explosion injured the claimant, who was standing outside the defendants' land, but the 'act of a stranger' defence meant that the defendants were not held liable to compensate the claimant for his injuries under the rule in *Rylands* v *Fletcher*.[77]

(2) *Act of God*. A will have a defence to B's claim under the rule in *Rylands* v *Fletcher* if the escape resulted from a wholly extraordinary natural event.[78]

(3) *Fault of the claimant*. A will have a defence to B's claim under the rule in *Rylands* v *Fletcher* if B was wholly at fault for the fact that she suffered the harm for which she is seeking compensation.[79]

(4) *Volenti*. A will have a defence to B's claim under the rule in *Rylands* v *Fletcher* if B consented to the dangerous thing being accumulated or stored by A, provided that the dangerous thing did not escape as a result of A's negligence. The thinking behind this is that if B has consented to the dangerous thing being accumulated or stored by A then she must have also accepted the risk of suffering harm if there is an escape, since if a dangerous thing is accumulated or stored there is always a possibility of an escape; but B's consent to the accumulation or storage of the dangerous thing will not have indicated willingness to accept the risk of it escaping as a result A's negligence.

This defence was applied in *Peters* v *Prince of Wales Theatre* (1943), when the defendants owned a theatre, and had leased a shop that formed part of the theatre building to the claimants, who knew that a sprinkler system was installed in the theatre building, including in the shop. Due to a severe frost, the sprinkler system burst (without the defendants being in any way at fault for this) and water poured into the claimants' shop, damaging the goods they had for sale there. The claimants sued the defendants for compensation under the rule in *Rylands* v *Fletcher*, but their claim was dismissed on the basis that they had been willing to rent the shop knowing that there was a risk that their goods might be damaged by the sprinkler system breaking down. An analogy was drawn with the rule that if A has granted possession of a parcel of land to B, and it is contemplated at the time of the grant that A will continue to use adjoining property for a particular purpose, B will not be able to complain that A's using the adjoining premises for that purpose amounts to a nuisance.[80]

The rule that negligence will vitiate B's consent to a dangerous thing being stored was applied in *Colour Quest Ltd* v *Total Downstream UK PLC* (2009), which dealt with claims

---

[77] It is now clear that the claim under the rule in *Rylands* v *Fletcher* should also have failed because the rule does not apply in personal injury cases: see above, § 14.3(B).

[78] *Nichols* v *Marsland* (1876) 2 Ex D 1, where a rainstorm was said to have been the heaviest in human memory. A different heavy storm was judged insufficiently unusual in *Greenock Corporation* v *Caledonian Railway Co* [1917] AC 556. In *Transco*, at [59], Lord Hobhouse stated that the phrase 'Acts of God' was 'used to describe those events which involved no human agency and which it was not realistically possible for a human to guard against: an accident which the defendant can show is due to natural causes, directly and exclusively, without human intervention and could not have been prevented by any amount of foresight, pains and care, reasonably to be expected of him'.

[79] *Rylands* v *Fletcher* (1868) LR 1 Ex 265, 280.

[80] *Vanderpant* v *Mayfair Hotel Co Ltd* [1930] 1 Ch 138, 162-3; *Thomas* v *Lewis* [1937] 1 All ER 137.

arising from explosions at the Buncefield Oil Storage Depot. In this case, simplifying to an extent, Total accepted that, if certain points were decided against it, then it would be liable under the rule in *Rylands* v *Fletcher* for the damage that the explosions had caused to owners of land beyond the boundaries of the Depot.[81] But Total argued that it should not be held liable for damage to the property of other oil companies which was within the boundaries of the Depot because these claimants had consented to the storage of oil in large quantities. David Steel J held that Total could not rely on this defence because the explosions had been caused by negligence that it was responsible for, and the other oil companies had not consented to *negligent* storage of oil.[82]

H. Remedies

We have already noted that the consequences of treating liability under the rule in *Rylands* v *Fletcher* as an off-shoot of the tort of private nuisance include it becoming the law that a claimant can only claim under this rule if she has suffered damage to her land (including buildings) and cannot claim compensation for personal injuries or *pure* economic losses.[83] Where a defendant is liable under the rule in *Rylands* v *Fletcher* for physical damage to a building the remedy that the claimant is most likely to obtain will be compensatory damages, and these will be calculated so as to provide *either* (1A) the cost of repair *or* (1B) the diminution in capital value of the land or building, and, in either case, also (2) redress for *consequential* economic losses.

The reader will recall that in cases of private nuisance claimants often also obtain *injunctions*, usually ordering the defendant not to continue to commit private nuisance. Can a claimant obtain an injunction in a case covered by the rule in *Rylands* v *Fletcher*? In practice, this question will rarely arise because the rule is usually relied on when there has been a *one-off* escape of a dangerous thing. But suppose: (1) a defendant is storing a dangerous thing on his land in such a way that an escape seems *imminent*, or (2) a dangerous thing is *continuing* to escape from the defendant's land and he is not taking any steps to prevent this. We think that a court would have the power to grant an injunction in both of these situations,[84] but doubt whether such an injunction would actually be granted under the rule in *Rylands* v *Fletcher*, as opposed to being granted to prevent negligence or a continuing public or private nuisance.[85]

---

[81] The correctness of this concession may have to be revisited in light of the Court of Appeal's subsequent decision in *Stannard (t/a Wyvern Tyres)* v *Gore* [2014] 1 QB 1 that a claim under the rule in *Rylands* v *Fletcher* will not be available where the *thing* which causes the damage is not the *thing* that the defendant accumulated: see above, § 14.3(E).

[82] [2009] EWHC 540 (Comm), at [405]-[406]. The Court of Appeal dealt with an appeal against part of David Steel J's decision in *Shell UK Ltd* v *Total UK Ltd* [2011] 1 QB 86, but his conclusion as to the scope of the defence of volenti under *Rylands* v *Fletcher* was not challenged.

[83] See above, § 14.3(B). We expect that the rules as to when a claimant can obtain compensation for consequential damage to chattels will be the same as those which apply in the tort of private nuisance: for an account of these rules the reader should refer back to § 13.12.

[84] See *Attorney-General* v *Cory Brothers & Co* [1921] AC 521.

[85] Why does it matter what tort such an injunction would aim to prevent? Our answer is that it matters because injunctions order people to comply with their legal duties – not to commit *wrongs* – while the rule in *Rylands* v *Fletcher*, as we have explained above (see § 14.2), imposes liability even when the defendant has not broken any duty that he owed to the claimant.

14.4 Liability rules analogous to the rule in *Rylands* v *Fletcher*

There are a number of liability rules that are analogous to the rule in *Rylands* v *Fletcher*, in that they make a defendant strictly liable for harm done by a dangerous thing under his control. The existence of these rules supplies one reason for retaining the rule in *Rylands* v *Fletcher*: abolishing the rule would put landowners who bring onto, or store on, their land something that is liable to do damage if it escapes in a better position that people who fall under the liability rules dealt with below.

A. Fire

It is commonly believed that the ancient common law made an occupier of premises *absolutely* liable for *any* damage caused by his fire (*ignis suus*) escaping from those premises. But this stern rule was altered by statute and s 86 of the Fire Prevention (Metropolis) Act 1774 now states that no action can be brought on the basis of this ancient rule 'against any person in whose house, chamber, stable, barn or other building, or on whose estate any fire shall . . . accidentally begin'. Unfortunately, the interpretation and application of this provision is not straightforward. To explain the current pattern of an occupier's liability for the spread of fire, it may be helpful to distinguish three types of situation.

(1) *A fire is negligently started on A's property and then spreads to B's property.* It has been held that the 1774 Act does not protect the occupier from liability when the fire has been *started* 'negligently' rather than 'accidentally'.[86] Importantly, this exception to the Act's protection applies even when the negligence was not the negligence of the occupier or his employee but of a guest or independent contractor. Thus a claimant who wishes to sue the occupier for damage done by a fire negligently started by a guest or independent contractor will be able to sue the occupier under the ancient common law rule and not have to rely on the tort of negligence.[87]

The 1774 Act *will* protect the occupier from being sued under the ancient common law rule, however, if the fire was started by the negligence of a *stranger*. In this context 'a "stranger" is anyone who in lighting a fire . . . acts contrary to anything which the occupier could anticipate that he would do.'[88] In rare circumstances a guest or independent contractor may become a 'stranger' for the purposes of this rule 'if his conduct in lighting a fire is so alien to your invitation that he should *qua* the fire be regarded as a trespasser'.[89] By way of illustration, in *Ribee* v *Norrie* (2001), the defendant owned a hostel and rented out bedrooms in it to various people. A fire started in the hostel's sitting room, probably as a result of a tenant dropping a smouldering cigarette onto the settee. The fire spread and damaged the adjoining house, which belonged to the claimant. The defendant was

---

[86] *Balfour* v *Barty-King* [1957] 1 QB 496. In *Stannard* v *Gore* [2014] QB 1 Lewison LJ accepted that the occupier would be liable in such circumstances but argued that this liability would not be under the ancient common law rule: 'In order to count as "ignis suus" the fire must have been made for the purpose or advantage of the occupier' (at [155]–[156]).

[87] The claimant can, of course, choose to sue the guest or the contractor in negligence.

[88] *H & N Emmanuel Ltd* v *GLC* [1971] 2 All ER 835, 839 (per Lord Denning MR).

[89] Ibid.

held liable for the fire damage to the claimant's house. He was held to have been in occupation of the hostel's sitting room when the fire was negligently started there by a tenant who had permission from the defendant to use the room, and the tenant's conduct was not 'so alien' that he could '*qua* the fire be regarded as a trespasser'; the defendant could reasonably have anticipated that a tenant using the sitting room 'might inadvertently drop a smouldering cigarette onto the settee eventually setting it on fire'.[90]

(2) *A fire is deliberately started on A's property and then spreads to B's property.* Liability in this type of situation depends on the *type of fire* and *why it spread*.

The *type of fire* is relevant because it has been held that some *deliberately lit* fires involve an 'extraordinary use' of land and consequently fall within the ambit of the rule in *Rylands* v *Fletcher*. In such cases, a claimant will not have to rely on the ancient common law rule regarding fire in order to sue, and will therefore not be affected by the 1774 Act.[91] Thus, if a case falls within the ambit of the rule in *Rylands* v *Fletcher*, then the occupier may be held liable for the escape of a deliberately lit fire from his premises even if it spreads 'accidentally'. But lighting an ordinary domestic fire in a fireplace is not an 'extraordinary use', so there will be no liability for the accidental escape of such a fire.[92]

The reasons *why the fire spread* are relevant because where a fire was started deliberately, but then spread from its original location because of the *negligence* of the occupier, his employee, his guest or his independent contractor, it has been held that the 1774 Act does not protect the occupier against being held liable under the ancient common law rule regarding damage done by fire.[93] Again, the occupier's liability does not stretch to cover liability for the negligence of a 'stranger'.[94]

(3) *Natural forces or a stranger start a fire on A's property and it then spreads to B's property.* In this situation, it seems that the 1774 Act will prevent A being held liable for the damage to B's premises *unless* the claim can be brought under the rule in *Goldman* v *Hargrave* (1967), which requires B to show that A failed to take reasonable steps to stop the fire spreading onto her property,[95] or A can be held to have acted negligently towards B by, for example, storing an inflammable substance in an unreasonably dangerous way.[96]

We should finally reflect on how far the remnant of the ancient rule relating to the escape of fire which has survived the 1774 statute *is* 'analogous to the rule in *Rylands* v *Fletcher*' since the strength of the analogy may determine questions such as who can claim under the ancient rule and what types of damage they can claim for.[97] From one perspective, this remnant *is* strongly analogous to the rule in *Rylands* because it makes an occupier liable

---

[90] (2001) 33 HLR 777, at [26] (per Ward LJ).

[91] In *Stannard* v *Gore* [2014] QB 1 Lewison LJ rejected this proposition, but the majority supported it: compare [69] (Etherton LJ) with [126] (Lewison LJ), and see also [30] (Ward LJ).

[92] *Sochacki* v *Sas* [1947] 1 All ER 344; *J Doltis Ltd* v *Issac Braithwaite & Sons (Engineers) Ltd* [1957] 1 Lloyd's Rep 522; *Johnson* v *BJW Property Developments Ltd* [2002] 3 All ER 574, at [31].

[93] *H & N Emmanuel Ltd* v *GLC* [1971] 2 All ER 835. This seems to be the opinion of Lord Denning MR (ibid, at 838; though he evinces reluctance to classify the liability rule at 839) and also the opinion of Phillimore LJ (at 842). See also *Johnson* v *BJW Property Developments Ltd* [2002] 3 All ER 574.

[94] *H & N Emmanuel Ltd* v *GLC* [1971] 2 All ER 835, 838–9 (per Lord Denning MR).

[95] *Goldman* v *Hargrave* [1967] 1 AC 645. See above, §§ 10.5, 13.9.

[96] *Stannard* v *Gore* [2014] QB 1 establishes that a claim based on the rule in *Rylands* v *Fletcher* cannot be based on the exceptional dangerousness of storing a inflammable substance *unless* it is the substance *itself* that escapes: see above, § 14.3(E).

[97] For these matters under the rule in *Rylands* v *Fletcher* see above, § 14.3(B), (F) and (H).

for escapes of fire which were not the occupier's fault, but a consequence of the negligence of a guest or independent contractor. But two distinctions may also be worth mentioning. First, under the remnant the occupier will avoid liability if he can prove that the escape was 'accidental', in the sense of not involving negligence. This is a broader defence than any available under the rule in *Rylands*.[98] Secondly, it is not clear that the ancient common law rule *only* protects neighbours against damage to their land.[99] One of the best known ancient authorities for the rule involves a claim for damage to chattels[100] and more recent judgments have also assumed that such claims were possible.[101]

B. Cattle trespass

Under s 4 of the Animals Act 1971, if livestock[102] belonging[103] to any person strays[104] onto land in the ownership or occupation of another, the person to whom the livestock belongs is liable for any damage[105] it causes to the land and property on it and for expenses reasonably incurred in impounding the livestock,[106] tracing who owns it and keeping it pending return. There is no defence covering escapes of livestock caused by malicious strangers or Acts of God, but, s 5(1) of the 1971 Act provides that a 'person [will not be] liable under [s 4] for any damage which is due wholly to the fault of the person suffering it'.[107]

Someone who suffers harm as a result of straying livestock may not have to rely on s 4 of the Animals Act 1971 to obtain compensation: other torts may be available. So if A *sends* livestock onto B's land, he will commit the tort of trespass to land, and, if A *carelessly* allows his livestock to stray when it is reasonably foreseeable that the animals will do harm to B if this occurs, he will commit the tort of negligence.[108]

C. Escape of water from the mains

Where water escapes from a pipe vested in a water undertaker, however it gets out,[109] and causes loss or damage, the undertaker shall be liable for the loss or damage.[110]

---

[98] For defences under the rule in *Rylands v Fletcher* see above, § 14.3(G).

[99] See above, § 14.3(B), for the limits on who can sue and for what under the rule in *Rylands*.

[100] *Beaulieu v Finglam* (1401) YB 2 Hen IV fo 18, pl 6.

[101] *Sochacki v Sas* [1947] 1 All ER 344, 345: 'If I happen to be on somebody else's land at a time when a fire spreads to that land and my motor car or property is destroyed, I have just as much right against the person who improperly allows the fire to escape from his land as the owner of the land on which I happen to be' (per Lord Goddard CJ).

[102] This is broadly defined in s 11. It includes cattle, horses, sheep, pigs and poultry.

[103] Animals Act 1971, s 4(2): 'For the purposes of this section any livestock belongs to the person in whose possession it is.'

[104] There is no liability where livestock strays from a highway which it was being driven along or across: Animals Act 1971, s 5(5), following the common law rule in *Tillett v Ward* (1882) 10 QBD 17. There could be liability in negligence if the drovers were careless, or under s 2 of the Animals Act 1971 if the livestock in question was known to have an unusual and dangerous tendency.

[105] Not limited to damage to land. But personal injuries are not covered by this provision.

[106] See Animals Act 1971, s 7.

[107] Damages can also be reduced for contributory negligence: s 10.

[108] The tort of negligence will allow B to claim for personal injury or property damage, subject to remoteness.

[109] There is an exception where the escape was due wholly to the fault of the person who sustained the loss or damage: Water Industry Act 1991, s 209(2).

[110] Water Industry Act 1991, s 209(1). There are some exceptions to this liability in s 209(3) and (6). Claims are not limited to claims for damage to land.

D. Nuclear installations

The licensee of a nuclear installation is liable for injuries to persons, damage to the property of others, and certain economic losses caused by occurrences involving nuclear matter or the escape of ionising radiation.[111] Licensees cannot escape liability by showing that the occurrence was the result of an Act of God or of an uncontrollable third party, though there is a defence for incidents caused by 'hostile action in the course of armed conflict'.[112]

14.5 Liability for dangerous animals

A defendant who has control of an animal may owe a duty of care to those who it is reasonably foreseeable could be injured if the animal escapes, so carelessness by the keepers of animals can lead to claims in the tort of negligence.[113] The common law, however, went further and insisted that the keeper of an animal which had a tendency to do harm was liable for any damage that the animal caused – whether the keeper was at fault for that harm or not – so long as the keeper knew that that animal had a tendency to do harm.[114] Animals were divided by species into two classes. If an animal belonged to a *dangerous species*, it would be conclusively presumed to have a tendency to do harm, its keeper would be conclusively presumed to know that it had a tendency to do harm,[115] and its keeper would be held liable for any damage that it caused. If, on the other hand, the animal belonged to a species that was by nature harmless or generally tamed or domesticated, then its keeper would only be held liable under the above liability rule if it could be specifically proved that the particular animal had a tendency to do harm and that its keeper knew that it had this tendency.

The Animals Act 1971 abolished these common law rules[116] and replaced them with the following set of liability rules:

A. Liability of the keeper of an animal belonging to a dangerous species

Section 2(1) of the 1971 Act provides that the keeper of an animal which belongs to a dangerous species is liable for the damage that it causes unless a relevant defence applies. In this context, an animal belongs to a dangerous species if two conditions are met: the species is not commonly domesticated in the British Isles; and, fully grown animals of

---

[111] Nuclear Installations Act 1965, ss 7, 11B, 11G, 11H and 12. Operators of disposal sites are subject to similar potential liability: see Nuclear Installations Act 1965, s 7B. Several important changes will be made to the statutory liability regime by the Nuclear Installations (Liability for Damage) Order 2016, and in this paragraph we have assumed that these changes have occurred, although at the time of writing (Sept. 2017) the new provisions have not been brought into force. Note, for there to be liability under the Act there does not have to be an escape from any *land* occupied by the licensee.

[112] Nuclear Installations Act 1965, s 13(4).

[113] See above, § 6.5.

[114] In this context 'harm' covers both personal injury and property damage.

[115] So, under the common law all elephants were treated as wild and dangerous, even if the elephant that actually injured a claimant was docile and tame: *Behrens* v *Bertram Mills Circus Ltd* [1957] 2 QB 1.

[116] Section 1, Animals Act 1971 provides that the Act's provisions 'replace . . . the rules of the common law imposing a strict liability . . . for damage done by an animal on the ground that the animal is regarded as ferae naturae or that its vicious or mischievous propensities are known or presumed to be known.'

that species have characteristics making it likely that they will cause severe damage, or that if they cause damage it is likely to be severe. Because this definition is narrow, Lord Walker has described the provision's relevance as 'almost entirely confined to incidents in (or following escapes from) zoos and circuses'.[117]

Section 6(3) of the 1971 Act provides that 'a person is a keeper of an animal if – (a) he owns the animal or has it in his possession; or (b) he is the head of a household of which a member under the age of sixteen owns the animal or has it in his possession'.[118] Section 6(4) of the 1971 Act qualifies this by providing that someone who takes possession of an animal 'for the purpose of preventing it from causing damage or of restoring it to its owner' will not thereby become its keeper.

B. Liability of the keeper of an animal that does not belong to a dangerous species

Section 2(2) of the 1971 Act provides that the keeper[119] of an animal which does not belong to a dangerous species will be liable for damage caused by that animal if three conditions are satisfied and no relevant defence applies. The three conditions are:

(a) the damage [was] of a kind which the animal, unless restrained, was likely to cause or which, if caused by the animal, was likely to be severe; and

(b) the likelihood of the damage or of its being severe was due to characteristics of the animal which are not normally found in animals of the same species or are not normally so found except at particular times or in particular circumstances; and

(c) those characteristics were known to that keeper or were at any time known to a person who at that time had charge of the animal as that keeper's servant or, where that keeper is the head of a household, were known to another keeper of the animal who is a member of that household and under the age of sixteen.

So, very roughly speaking, s 2(2) makes the keeper of an animal from a non-dangerous species strictly liable for harm caused by it having an uncommon, dangerous characteristic which the keeper knows about. But, as several judges have complained, s 2(2) is very difficult to interpret and apply: it has been described by Lord Denning MR as 'very cumbrously worded',[120] by Ormrod LJ as 'remarkably opaque',[121] and by Slade LJ as 'somewhat tortuous'.[122]

As the authorities stand at the moment, it seems that for s 2(2) to apply to make the keeper (K) of an animal (A) liable for some harm (H) caused by A, four conditions[123] need to be satisfied:

---

[117] *Mirvahedy* v *Henley* [2003] 2 AC 491, at [135].

[118] A keeper remains keeper of an *escaped* or *lost* animal until someone else becomes its keeper: s 6(3).

[119] The definition of 'keeper' in s 6(3) and (4), discussed in the previous paragraph, also applies to liability under s 2(2).

[120] *Cummings* v *Grainger* [1977] QB 397, 404.

[121] [1977] QB 397, 407.

[122] *Curtis* v *Betts* [1990] 1 WLR 459, 462.

[123] It should be emphasised that the language we use to describe these conditions is ours, and is used simply to try and help readers understand how s 2(2) applies. Students should not in their written work or their exams assume that the people reading their work will automatically understand what phrases such as 'the causation condition' or 'the dangerous characteristic condition' refer to, and should not therefore use those phrases without some accompanying explanation of what those phrases refer to.

(1) *The Causation Condition.* H must have been caused by A having some characteristic C.[124]

(2) *The Dangerous Characteristic Condition.* The fact that A had that characteristic C must have meant that it was likely to cause harm H, or if it caused harm H, the harm it caused was likely to be severe.[125]

(3) *The Uncommon Characteristic Condition.* It must be shown either (i) that most animals of the same species as A do not have characteristic C; or (ii) that it is only normal for animals of the same species as A to have characteristic C 'at particular times or in particular circumstances'.[126]

(4) *The Knowledge Condition.* K – or someone who had charge of A as K's servant, or someone under 16 who was a member of K's household and was also a keeper of A – must have known that A had characteristic C.[127]

A claimant wanting to sue a defendant under s 2(2) must frame their case in a way that satisfies *all* of these conditions. So, if the harm suffered by the claimant, and the characteristics of the animal that caused that harm, can be described in various different ways, the claimant must be careful to select descriptions that will satisfy all of the above four conditions.

We will now look at a number of cases to illustrate how the courts have applied and interpreted these different conditions.

In *Mirvahedy* v *Henley* (2003), the claimant was severely injured when a horse belonging to the defendants ran into his car as he drove along the A380. The horse had been kept in a field – along with two other horses – and all three horses had been scared, for some unknown reason, into bolting out of the field and running towards the A380. The characteristic that was said to have caused the harm was the horse's running in a 'mindless state of panic', ignoring obstacles in its path.[128] The issue that divided the House of Lords was whether the horse's panicked bolting satisfied the *Uncommon Characteristic Condition*. This was not a case where the claimant sought to argue that the characteristic was uncommon because there was something unusual about defendants' horse, such as that it was more likely to panic in specific circumstances than most horses;[129] it was accepted that it is completely normal for horses to panic when subjected to a severe fright, but the claimant submitted, and a majority of the House of Lords agreed, that the *Uncommon Characteristic Condition* because it was only normal for horses to have the characteristic of

---

[124] *Curtis* v *Betts* [1990] 1 WLR 459.

[125] See s 2(2)(a) and the first 17 words of s 2(2)(b). When asking whether A was 'likely' to cause H, or whether any harm was 'likely' to be severe *if* it was caused, the relevant question is not whether such consequences were 'probable', and certainly not whether they were 'more probable than not', but whether they were 'reasonably to be expected': *Freeman* v *Higher Park Farm* [2008] EWCA Civ 1185, at [33]; *Turnbull* v *Warrener* [2012] EWCA Civ 412, at [12]. This interpretation of 'likely' was also supported by Lord Scott (dissenting) in *Mirvahedy* v *Henley* [2003] 2 AC 491 at [95]–[97].

[126] See the second two lines of s 2(2)(b), quoted in the text.

[127] See s 2(2)(c).

[128] *Mirvahedy* v *Henley* [2003] 2 AC 491, at [62] and [69] (Lord Hobhouse). See also at [3] (Lord Nichols) and [157] (Lord Walker).

[129] An example of a case involving a horse which had this type of uncommon characteristic is provided by *Flack* v *Hudson* [2001] QB 698, where the horse concerned was held to have a tendency to bolt when confronted by agricultural machinery. Similarly, the *Uncommon Characteristic Condition* could be satisfied by showing that a defendant's dog was more vicious than most dogs, or was more likely to bite in specific circumstances than most dogs.

panicked bolting 'at particular times or in particular circumstances', the circumstances being 'where they have been very seriously frightened'.[130] This involved interpreting s 2(2)(b) as potentially extending strict liability to situations where animals such as horses, cows and dogs cause harm whilst behaving like typical horses, cows, and dogs, so long as the animals' tendency to behave in this way is only exhibited 'at particular times or in particular circumstances'.[131]

One point which the House of Lords did not discuss was the fact that the accident in *Mirvahedy* occurred shortly after midnight, and the defendants were unaware that their horse had bolted from its field at the time it was bolting. Does this mean the *Knowledge Condition* was not satisfied in *Mirvahedy*? The only way of rationalising the House of Lords' assumption that the *Knowledge Condition* was satisfied is to suppose that this can be satisfied by showing that A's keeper (or some other relevant individual) knew of the animal's general characteristic (*may well bolt when frightened*), and that it is not necessary to show knowledge of its specific manifestation (*is bolting* because frightened).[132]

The decision in *Mirvahedy* had the effect of extending the scope of the strict liability imposed by s 2(2), but doing so in an uneven way. Thus claimants may still fall outside the scope of the liability if either the way in which the animal injured them did not involve the manifestation of any *Uncommon Characteristic* – for example, a heavy animal tripped and fell on them[133] – or it involved a characteristic so uncommon that the keeper

---

[130] *Mirvahedy* v *Henley* [2003] 2 AC 491, at [69] (Lord Hobhouse). Other members of the majority expressed the circumstances slightly differently: see [3] (Lord Nicholls) and [157] (Lord Walker).

[131] In adopting this interpretation of s2(2)(b) the House of Lords followed the approach of the Court of Appeal in *Cummings* v *Grainger* [1977] QB 397 and *Curtis* v *Betts* [1990] 1 WLR 459, and rejected the opinions of Lloyd and Oliver LJJ in *Breeden* v *Lampard*, 21 March 1985, unreported.

[132] In support of this view, see Hale LJ's judgment in the Court of Appeal in *Mirvahedy* v *Henley* [2002] QB 769, at [31]: 'in the case of an animal who only has such a tendency in particular circumstances or at particular times, it might be thought that the keeper must know, not only of the tendency but also that the particular time or particular circumstances currently exist: for example that his bitch has just had pups or his dog was guarding his territory. Applied to this case, the keeper would have to know, not only that horses can behave in this way if frightened or panicked, but also that these horses had been frightened or panicked. Some of the above quotations from the Law Commission's Report and from Hansard might be thought to support that view. However, the Act does not. Section 2(2)(c) merely requires knowledge of the "characteristics", and not both characteristics and circumstances. In any event, if the rationale for the strict liability is the greater vigilance needed and the greater opportunity to insure brought by that knowledge then those can be employed whether or not the particular circumstances are known to exist at the time.'

[133] In *Clark* v *Bowlt* [2006] EWCA Civ 978, the claimant was injured when a horse unexpectedly moved into the path of his car whilst he was driving past it. The first instance judge got into a muddle by focusing on the horse's characteristic of being *heavy* to find that the *Dangerous Characteristic Condition* was satisfied (on the basis that the horse's weight meant that if the horse hit the car, any damage it did was likely to be severe), then focusing on the its characteristic of *asserting an inclination to go otherwise than as directed* to find that the *Uncommon Characteristic Condition* was satisfied. The Court of Appeal rejected this approach and held that the *same* characteristic had to be used to satisfy each of the conditions under s 2(2). Using that approach, the claimant lost: the horse's *weight* certainly could not satisfy the *Uncommon Characteristic Condition*, because it is normal for horses to be heavy, whilst the characteristic of 'asserting an inclination to go otherwise than as directed' was hard to describe in terms of any 'particular times' or 'particular circumstances' (at [13]), and difficult to categorise as *Dangerous*. (Disobedient horses are not particularly likely to cause harm, nor does their disobedience make it likely that the harm they cause will be severe.)

did not know of it.[134] But, many cases fall between these extremes, and in such cases, where animals cause harm by behaving in ways that are both dangerous and likely at 'particular times' or in 'particular circumstances', claimants are likely to succeed post-*Mirvahedy*. Thus in *Goldsmith* v *Patchcott* (2012), the conditions for liability were satisfied by focusing on a horse's characteristic of 'rearing and bucking when startled or alarmed', and in *Turnbull* v *Warrener* (2012)[135] the Court of Appeal thought that the conditions for liability could be satisfied by focusing on the horse's characteristic of 'refusing to slow down on command or at all when using new equipment, specifically the bitless bridle'. Indeed, in these cases the Court of Appeal opined that the expansive interpretation of s 2(2)(b) in *Mirvahedy* (2003) had led to its 'virtual emasculation' and left it without a clear purpose.[136]

The expansion of liability under s 2(2) of the 1971 Act brought about by the House of Lords' decision in *Mirvahedy* has increased the significance of the defences available to claims under the 1971 Act. There are a number of such defences, which are open to some-one who is sued under any section of the 1971 Act (not just s 2(2)):

(1) *Wholly at fault.* If B sues A for compensation for harm suffered by her under any of the liability rules set out above, A will have a defence to B's claim if B was wholly at fault for the fact that she suffered that harm.[137]

(2) *Voluntary assumption of risk.* If B has been harmed by an animal and seeks to sue A under ss 2(1) or 2(2) of the 1971 Act, A will have a defence to B's claim if B voluntarily took the risk that she would be harmed by that animal.[138] In cases where the alleged dan-gerous characteristic is a tendency of all animals of the same species to behave dangerously 'at particular times or in particular circumstances' a claimant may be treated as voluntarily taking the risk if he voluntarily interacts with such an animal with knowledge of the ten-dency: thus in *Goldsmith* v *Patchcott* (2012) the Court of Appeal upheld the conclusion that the defence applied in a case where the conditions for liability were satisfied by focus-ing on a horse's characteristic of 'rearing and bucking when startled or alarmed' because

---

[134] In *McKenny* v *Foster* [2008] EWCA Civ 173 the claimant was injured when a cow escaped from a field and collided with his car, and it was suggested that the cow had become so agitated as a result of being separated from its calf that it scaled a six-barred livestock gate and leapt across a twelve-foot cattle grid. The claimant was unsuccessful because if one focused on the cow's *agitation* at being separated from her calf, that did not satisfy the *Dangerous Characteristic Condition* – the cow's agitation did not mean that it was likely to do harm, or that any harm it did was likely to be severe – whilst if one focused on the cow's *extreme agitation*, there was a problem with the *Knowledge Condition* since the keepers were not aware that the cow was *extremely agitated*, nor is it a generally-known characteristic of cows that they sometimes get so agitated as to be able to perform near miracles such as leaping across twelve-foot cattle grids.
[135] *Turnbull* v *Warrener* [2012] EWCA Civ 412.
[136] The phrase 'virtual emasculation' is from ibid, at [23] (Maurice Kay LJ) and the statement 'It is not obvious, to me at least, what purpose section 2(2)(b) serves' is from *Goldsmith* v *Patchcott* [2012] EWCA Civ 183, at [40] (per Jackson LJ).
[137] Animals Act 1971, s 5(1). The defence of contributory negligence also applies: s 10.
[138] Section 5(2).

the claimant was an experienced, confident rider who knew that horses could buck when startled or alarmed.[139]

(3) *Trespass.* A will also have a defence if: (i) the animal in question harmed B while she was trespassing on premises on which that animal was kept; *and* (ii) *either* that animal was *not* kept on the premises for the protection of persons or property, *or* that animal *was* kept on the premises for the protection of persons or property and the keeping of the animal on those premises for that purpose was not unreasonable.[140]

The question whether a trespasser on someone else's premises who is injured by an animal might be able to sue the occupier of the premises (rather than the animal's keeper) under the Occupiers' Liability Act 1984 is not straightforward, and depends on the scope of that Act.[141]

(4) *Straying livestock.* Suppose livestock belonging to B strayed onto land belonging to someone else and was attacked there by a dog. If B sues A – the dog's keeper – for compensation for the damage done to her livestock by the dog under s 3 of the 1971 Act, A will have a defence to B's claim if: (i) the dog belonged to the occupier of the land on which the livestock was attacked; *or* (ii) the dog was authorised to be on the land on which the livestock was attacked.[142]

(5) *Act of a stranger and Act of God.* If an animal has caused B some kind of harm, and B seeks to sue A – the keeper of that animal – for compensation for that harm under the Animals Act 1971, it seems that proving that the animal acted in the way it did either because of the malicious act of a stranger or an Act of God will afford A *no defence* to B's claim. Thus, the potential liability of the keeper of a dangerous animal is wider than the liability of the storer of an inanimate dangerous thing.[143]

Standing back, the pattern of outcomes in the post-*Mirvahedy* cases make it hard to provide any kind of principled explanation as to why certain defendants (such as the defendants in *Mirvahedy*) are held liable under s 2(2), while others (such as those whose horse trips and falls onto a claimant) are not. In cases where a keeper has chosen to keep under his control an animal that he knows to be abnormally dangerous – such as a tiger or a vicious dog – then there is little problem with holding him strictly liable for the harm done by that animal's abnormally dangerous tendencies.[144] But *Mirvahedy* extends the scope of liability under s 2(2) to cases where a keeper is in control of an animal A which he knows belongs to a species that is only liable to do harm *in a certain situation S*, and which does do harm in situation S. It is hard to see why the keeper of A should be held

---

[139] The Court of Appeal, [2012] EWCA Civ 183 at [50], rejected the claimant's argument that the defence should not apply because the horse bucked more violently than she had expected: 'If the claimant, knowing of the risk which subsequently eventuates, proceeds to engage with the animal, his or her claim under the Act will be defeated. It is not a prerequisite of the section 5 (2) defence that the claimant should foresee the precise degree of energy with which the animal will engage in its characteristic behaviour.' See also, *Freeman* v *Higher Park Farm* [2008] EWCA Civ 1185.

[140] Animals Act 1971, s 5(3). In *Cummings* v *Grainger* [1975] 1 WLR 1330, O'Connor J thought that it was unreasonable for a scrap metal dealer to keep an untrained Alsatian with a known propensity to attack black people as protection for his yard, but the Court of Appeal disagreed: [1977] QB 397. It is worth noting, however, that the case arose before the Guard Dogs Act 1975 made it unlawful to keep an uncontrolled guard dog.

[141] On which see above, Chapter 10.

[142] Animals Act 1971, s 5(4).

[143] On which see above, § 14.2 and § 14.3.

[144] See above, § 12.8, for possible explanations for a strict liability regime.

liable for the harm done by A in situation S if he had no reason to know that situation S had arisen,[145] or he did know that situation S had arisen but had no opportunity to prevent A doing harm in that situation.[146]

C. Liability of the keeper of a dog that has killed or injured livestock

Section 3 of the 1971 Act provides that the keeper of a dog is liable for damage it causes by killing or injuring livestock unless a relevant defence applies.

D. Liability of a person in possession of livestock for the damage done by that livestock

Section 4 of the 1971 Act provides that the possessor of livestock is liable for certain types of damage and expenses caused by that livestock straying onto land in the ownership or occupation of another person unless a relevant defence applies.[147]

Further reading

So many articles have written about *Rylands* v *Fletcher* that some scholars feel that it is necessary to provide an excuse for adding to the library: see, for example, **Ken Oliphant, 'Rylands v Fletcher and the Emergence of Enterprise Liability in the Common Law' in H. Koziol and B. Steininger (eds), *European Tort Law* 2004 (Springer, 2005).**

From the clutch of articles written in the aftermath of the *Transco* case we would recommend **Ken Oliphant's** piece (cited above), and also **D.P. Nolan, 'The Distinctiveness of** *Rylands* v *Fletcher*' (2005) 121 *Law Quarterly Review* 421, and **J. Murphy, 'The Merits of *Rylands* v *Fletcher*'** (2004) 24 *Oxford Journal of Legal Studies* 643.

For those more interested in the story behind the leading case the best accounts are **A.W.B. Simpson, 'Bursting reservoirs: the historical context of *Rylands* v *Fletcher*'** (1984) 13 **Journal of Legal Studies 209** (a revised version appears as Chapter 8 in his book *Leading Cases in the Common Law* (Clarendon Press, 1995)) and **K.S. Abraham '*Rylands* v *Fletcher*: tort law's conscience' in R.L. Rabin and S. Sugarman, (eds), *Torts Stories* (West Law School, 2003).**

---

[145] In the 2007–8 Parliamentary Session, a Private Members' Bill was introduced that would have amended s 2(2) of the Animals Act 1971 to say that where harm was caused as a result of an animal having a 'conditional characteristic' (that is, one 'that is shared by animals of that species generally, but only in particular circumstances'), the keeper of that animal would not be held liable for that harm if he could show that 'there was no particular reason to expect that those circumstances would arise' at the time the harm was caused. The Bill, and reaction to it, revealed something of a town–country divide: it was advanced by the MP for Preseli Pembrokeshire (country) and opposed by the MP for Hendon (town). The Bill was backed by 26 votes to one in its second reading in the House of Commons, but as fewer than 40 MPs were present to vote on it, the Bill was lost. In March 2009 the Department for Environment, Food and Rural Affairs launched a consultation with the intention of changing s 2(2)(b) in the same way by using a Legislative Reform Order, as opposed to ordinary legislation, but whilst a majority of consultees favoured clarification of the Act, only a minority supported the government's proposed wording, and the matter has not been taken forward.

[146] Consider Lord Scott's example in *Mirvahedy* v *Henley* [2003] 2 AC 491, at [115], of a police horse that is jabbed in the side by a protestor and kicks out and injures an innocent bystander. (The most promising way of satisfying all the s 2(2) conditions in such a case may be to attribute some composite harm-causing characteristic to the horse – such as 'being so shocked as to kick out automatically and with great power' – that will tick all the boxes needed for a claim to be brought under s 2(2).)

[147] This provision replaces the old common law rules on liability for cattle trespass and is discussed above, § 14.4(B).

Chapter 15
Torts to personal property

Aims and objectives

Reading this chapter should enable you to:

(1) Understand when a defendant will be held liable for committing the torts of (a) conversion, and (b) trespass to goods; and when a defendant will be held liable for (c) breaching a duty as a bailee of another's goods to safeguard those goods.

(2) Understand what forms of intangible property are recognised in English law, and how they are protected (and not protected) by tort law.

(3) Understand what remedies will be available when someone commits a tort in respect of an item of tangible or intangible personal property.

15.1 The basics

We have already (in Chapters 12 and 13) looked at a couple of torts that are concerned to protect the interests of owners and possessors in land in being able to use and enjoy that land without interference from others. In this chapter we look at the torts that play the equivalent role in relation to other forms of property, which we will compendiously call *personal* property. So personal property covers all forms of property that are not land. These forms of property can be split into two – (i) *tangible* personal property (personal property that you can touch, such as a watch or hard cash), and (ii) *intangible* property (personal property that you cannot touch, such as a patent (a monopoly over the ability to exploit a particular invention), or a right to draw on a bank account).

The two primary torts that protect the enjoyment of *tangible* personal property are *trespass to goods* and *conversion*.[1] We have already seen that the law of negligence will

---

[1] It is a mistake to think that the Torts (Interference with Goods) Act 1977 replaced these torts with one generic tort of 'interference with goods' (*pace* Lord Nicholls in *Kuwait Airways Corpn v Iraqi Airways Co (Nos 4 & 5)* [2002] 2 AC 883, at [67]); what the 1977 Act did was create a generic system of remedies that would apply when *a* tort involving an interference with goods was committed.

impose duties of care on people to take care not to *destroy* or *damage* goods in someone else's possession. The torts of trespass to goods and conversion protect people against less destructive ways of someone's interfering with their enjoyment of tangible personal property, such as someone's touching or using that property, or someone's handing that property over to a third party. One thing that these torts will *not* protect is the enjoyment of tangible personal property *per se*: there is no equivalent to the tort of private nuisance (which has as its central function the protection of the *usefulness* of land being degraded by others) when it comes to tangible personal property. So, for example, if your car is on my land and I lock the gates to the land so that you cannot drive the car away, I commit no tort.[2] The fact that your car is now useless to you is neither here nor there: I have not damaged it, touched it, used it, or handed it over to anyone else. The fact that I have committed no tort in relation to your car by detaining it on my land is a major problem for you, because under English law the only way you can obtain a remedy in respect of your car is to show that I have committed a tort in respect of that car. English law does not recognise the existence of a *vindicatio* remedy: a remedy which enables you, in the case where I am in effective control of your property, to sue me for that property, or its value, *without* having to show that I have committed a tort (done anything legally wrong) in respect of that property.[3] 'He's got my car!' is not a plea that will unlock any doors to a remedy in English law. If you want to sue me, you have to show I have done something legally wrong – committed a tort – in respect of your car. As we will see, this has resulted in the tort of *conversion* becoming a tort of *strict liability* – which means that not only does the tort of conversion cover more forms of interference with tangible personal property than negligence does, it is also an easier tort to make out as fault on the part of the defendant does not have to be proved. However, this strict liability is not unfettered: the courts have recognised a number of defences that may protect a defendant who would otherwise and unfairly be held strictly liable for converting another's property.

These torts – trespass to goods and conversion – share the following structure. If A wants to establish that B has committed one of these torts in relation to A, A has to show that (i) there was *property*, (ii) in which A had a *sufficient interest*, (iii) that B *interfered* with in a relevant way, and (iv) B had no *defence* for acting as she did. What counts as a sufficient interest? Perhaps surprisingly, the fact that A *owned* the property in question (call it 'P') will not – of and in itself – suffice to show that A had a sufficient interest in that property to sue B for committing the tort of trespass to goods or conversion. What A has to show if he wants to sue B for committing the tort of trespass to goods is that A was in *possession* of P at the time B interfered with P; and if A wants to sue B for committing the tort of conversion, A has to have been in *possession* of P or have had an *immediate right* to possess P. Where ownership becomes relevant is where A's claim against B raises issues of who had the *better title* to P at the time B interfered with it. If A was not in possession of P and wants to sue B in conversion, A will have to show that he had a better title to P than B if A is going to show that he had an immediate right to possess P as against B. And if B wants to establish a defence to A's claim against her, one way to do this will be to show that she had a better title to P than A did and that justified her in acting as she did. And, of course, the best title someone can have to P is to be its owner.

---

[2] *Hartley* v *Moxham* (1842) 3 QB 701, 114 ER 675.
[3] For discussion, see McBride 2016b.

Torts that protect the enjoyment of *intangible* property share the same structure as the torts of trespass to goods and conversion, in that if A wants to establish that B has committed an intangible property tort, A will have to show that (i) there was *property*, (ii) in which A had a *sufficient interest*, (iii) that B *interfered* with in a relevant way, and (iv) B had no *defence* for acting as she did. Claims that B committed an intangible property tort in relation to A are much more likely to give rise to issues around (i) than claims that B committed a *tangible* property tort in relation to A. This is because while virtually everything you can touch is capable of amounting to 'property', lots of things you can't touch are *not* capable of amounting to property. For example, an idea – of and in itself – is not capable of amounting to property. So if you have spotted a gap in the market for a particular type of product or service, and someone else sees how well you are doing and decides to muscle in on your territory, you will have no recourse against them.[4] So what sort of intangibles are capable of amounting to property? Songs, films, the contents of books, and other original forms of expression, when put in permanent form, are the subject of *copyright* – with the result that no one else is allowed to copy them. Someone who has *patented* a new idea for an invention will have a right that no one else exploit that idea (even if they came up with it themselves, quite independently). The law provides similar protections against properly *registered designs* and *trade marks* being exploited by other people. Copyrights, patents, registered designs and trade marks make up the stuff of intellectual property law, which is the primary body of law within tort law[5] that is concerned with recognising and protecting people's property in intangibles. But the law on passing off also belongs to this area of tort law. The law on *passing off* recognises people as owning the goodwill that attaches to their name or business, and protects those people from others damaging or exploiting that goodwill.[6] The law of tort already goes some way – through the tort of *inducing a breach of contract* – towards protecting people from having their contractual rights interfered with by other people. We deal with the tort of inducing a breach of contract in Chapter 24, but in section 5(D) of this chapter, we look at whether the law of *conversion* should be extended to protect people from having their contractual rights interfered with or devalued by others. Section 2(B) of this chapter discusses whether the law of tort should get involved with protecting *virtual property* – that is, resources that are acquired and exist within the confines of a computer game that creates a virtual world for players to move around in – from being interfered with by other people.

But why should the law ever get into the business of recognising people as owning intangibles? For example, when they were starting out in the music business, Paul McCartney

---

[4] *Cadbury Schweppes Pty Ltd* v *Pub Squash Co Pty Ltd* [1981] RPC 429 (held, no tort committed by defendant who marketed a sports drink aimed at the same kind of consumer as the claimant's sports drink).

[5] Though in one of those inter-jurisdictional classificatory disputes that bedevils the law of tort, some might say intellectual property law belongs to equity and not tort law. (On the relationship between tort law and equity, see above, § 1.10.)

[6] In *Inland Revenue Commissioners* v *Muller & Co's Margarine Ltd* [1901] AC 217, Lord Macnaghten recognised (at 223) that the goodwill attached to someone's name or business was a form of property that someone could own: 'It is very difficult . . . to say that goodwill is not property. Goodwill is bought and sold every day. It may be acquired, I think, in any of the different ways in which property is usually acquired. When a man has got it he may keep it as his own. He may vindicate his exclusive right to it if necessary by process of law. He may dispose of it if he will – of course under the conditions attaching to property of that nature.'

and John Lennon thought that songs didn't belong to anyone. They thought that songs just floated around in the ether and were simply written down by people like Lennon and McCartney who had the talent to 'hear' them. As a result, they thought song writers had no more right to say that those songs were 'theirs' than anyone else did. Why does the law not take the same position and say that songs, and other intangibles, belong to no one? A number of different arguments have traditionally been made in favour of the view that the law should recognise people as having use rights and exclusivity rights over certain intangibles.

The moral argument in favour of the law's recognising that people own certain intangibles comes from John Locke's *labour theory* of property, as set out in his 1698 work *Two Treatises of Government*. According to this theory, you own something if it is the product of your labour. So if you have worked long hours writing a book or a song, or producing a film or a drug, you are entitled to say that book/song/film/drug belongs to you. The labour theory of property has great intuitive appeal in today's society – for example, the fact that song writing came so easily to Lennon and McCartney may account for why they initially did not think their songs could belong to them – and could be used as the basis of an alternative, *civil recourse*, theory as to why the law should recognise certain intangibles as being owned by individuals. The idea behind this theory is that if *Worker* feels intuitively on the basis of something like a labour theory of property that *Resource* belongs to him, *Worker* will feel aggrieved if *Interferer* fails to respect the rights *Worker* thinks he has over *Resource*, and might well feel entitled as a result to take counter-measures against *Interferer*. Given this, and in the interests of social peace, it might be wise for the law to give *Worker* what he thinks is his due, recognise that he legally owns *Resource* and give him a peaceful way of dealing with anyone like *Interferer* who might try to damage or exploit *Resource*.[7]

Utilitarian arguments for recognising that people own certain intangibles assert that we are all better off as a result of giving people use rights and exclusivity rights over some intangibles. Such arguments focus on the *stimulus to creativity* created by the prospect of obtaining use rights and exclusivity rights over one's productions, which can then be exploited to make a lot of money for the rights holder. Some have questioned the *stimulus to creativity* argument in the context of works that are cheap to produce and are labours of love. For example, the authors of this text are certainly not writing it for the royalties they earn from it, but to benefit their students and (we hope) other people's students. But there is no doubt that in the case of products that are very expensive to produce – such as films or new medicines – it would make no economic sense to attempt to produce such works if one could not recoup one's investment by exploiting the use rights and exclusivity rights that the law will give the producer over that product. At the same time, utilitarian arguments are vulnerable to objections that recognising ownership over intangibles ends up doing more harm than good, particularly in *stifling innovation*. In particular, it is argued that the patent system can be too easily abused by *Patent Trolls* who think of an invention,

---

[7] For example, in 2005, a Chinese gamer called Qiu Chengwei won a 'dragon sword' in the course of playing *Legend of Mir 3*. He lent the sword – which only existed virtually, as part of the game – to a fellow *Legend* player called Zhu Caoyuan. Chengwei then discovered that Caoyuan had auctioned off the sword on eBay to a third gamer for almost £500. The Chinese police told Chengwei that they could not do anything as virtual property was not protected under Chinese law. Chengwei then exercised his own individual brand of justice by stabbing and killing Caoyuan. Caoyuan might never have died had Chinese law done more to recognise and uphold the rights that Chengwei intuitively felt he had in this case.

patent it, do nothing to produce or market the invention, but simply sit back and wait for an honest *Inventor* to come along with the same idea who does want to produce the invention. The *Troll* will then charge *Inventor* a fee for the privilege of being allowed to go ahead and produce and market the invention. And if *Inventor* will not agree to the *Troll's* demands, the invention is never produced.

15.2 Property

A. Tangible property

We have already observed that almost anything that can be touched is capable of amounting to a piece of tangible property that can be owned or traded. The most important exception to this is ourselves – our bodies, and the parts of our bodies. While philosophers like to talk of us 'owning ourselves', and acquiring ownership of other things through our basic ownership of our own bodies, the traditional position of English law was that bodies and body parts could not amount to property. This is still the position where living bodies and body parts are concerned – they are protected by the law of trespass to the person and negligence, not by the law on conversion and trespass to goods.[8] However, where dead bodies, or body parts or fluids that have been removed from someone were concerned, the position of English law used to be that a dead body or a removed body part or fluid *would* amount to property *if* work had been done on it, either to preserve it or alter it.[9] This exception to the general rule that bodies and body parts/fluids cannot amount to property has been radically expanded by the decision of the Court of Appeal in *Yearworth* v *North Bristol NHS Trust* (2010).[10]

The claimants in that case were male cancer patients who deposited sperm with the defendant sperm bank before they underwent chemotherapy, the idea being that if the chemotherapy rendered a patient sterile, he could still have children using his donated sperm and artificial fertilisation techniques. The donated sperm was preserved by freezing it. Unfortunately, and due to the defendant's carelessness, the sperm thawed out and became useless. The claimants sued, arguing that the donated sperm was property that belonged to them, and that they were entitled to damages for the damage done to the sperm and the consequential distress and psychiatric illnesses they had suffered as a result of knowing that they could not have any more children. The Court of Appeal allowed the claimants' claims.

---

[8] Though Keren-Paz 2010b argues that it would be 'poetic justice' for a client who has sex with a woman who has been forced into working as a prostitute to be held liable for converting her body; having treated the woman's body like a tradeable piece of property, he should not be allowed to argue that her body was not in fact a piece of property.

[9] *Dobson* v *North Tyneside Health Authority* [1997] 1 WLR 596; *R* v *Kelly* [1999] QB 621; *In Re Organ Retention Litigation* [2005] QB 506, at [148] and [161]. See, generally, Matthews 1983, 196–221. Nwabueze 2007 criticises English law for taking the position that there is (usually) no tort of interference with a dead body, approvingly citing section 868 of the US Second Restatement Torts, which says that 'One who intentionally, recklessly or negligently removes, withholds, mutilates or operates upon a body of a dead person or prevents its proper interment or cremation is subject to liability to a member of the family of the deceased who is entitled to the disposition of the body.'

[10] Discussed, Lee 2009, Harmon & Laurie 2010.

The Court of Appeal could have easily found that the donated sperm amounted to property on the basis that work had been done on it to preserve it. However, the Court of Appeal thought that the rule that dead bodies or body parts/fluids would amount to property if work had been done on them was 'not entirely logical'.[11] Instead, the Court of Appeal held that the donated sperm amounted to property belonging to the claimants because:

> By their bodies, they alone generated and ejaculated the sperm . . . The sole object of their ejaculation of the sperm was that, in certain events, it might later be used for their benefit . . . [the] sperm [could not] be stored or continue to be stored without their subsisting consent [under the terms of the Human Fertilisation and Embryology Act 1990] . . . no person, whether human or corporate, other than each man [who supplied the sperm had] any *rights* in relation to the sperm which he . . . produced.[12]

The Court's finding that the donated sperm was property that belonged to the claimants seems to have rested on two facts: (a) the sperm was produced by the claimants; and (b) after it left their body, they intended to, and did, retain control over how it was disposed of.

It is not clear how far *Yearworth* goes – would it, for example, allow *Rock Star* to sue *Fan* for collecting some of his hair from the floor of the barber shop where *Rock Star's* hair has been cut, and selling that hair on eBay? But *Yearworth* would not – we think – have assisted the claimant in the very famous American case of *Moore* v *Regents of University of California* (1990).[13]

In that case, the claimant's spleen was removed at the UCLA Medical Center in the course of treating him for hairy-cell leukemia. Cancerous cells were extracted from the spleen that were then replicated in huge quantities for other doctors to experiment on in coming up with treatments for cancer. Experimenters would have to pay for these cells, and the cell-line developed from the claimant's spleen became the basis of a $3 billion dollar industry. The claimant wanted to sue for some of that money, so he argued that the doctors at UCLA had committed the tort of conversion in relation to him by using his spleen to produce a cell-line without his consent. The claim was dismissed on the ground that the claimant had no rights over the spleen once it had been extracted from his body. We think that even after *Yearworth*, the same decision would be reached here. While the spleen was produced by the claimant, the claimant did not intend to retain control over the spleen after it was extracted from his body. (Though it might be different if the claimant knew how lucrative the market was for good cell-lines and made it clear before his operation that he wanted to keep his spleen after it had been taken from his body.)

B. Intangible property

We have already set out the principal exceptions to the rule that something that cannot be touched is not normally capable of amounting to property: (1) intellectual property (in the form of copyrights, patents, and trade marks and registered design rights); (2) business goodwill; and (3) contractual rights.

---

[11] [2010] QB 1, at [45](d).
[12] [2010] QB 1, at [45](f).
[13] Discussed Harris 1986, 75–84.

An interesting question which has attracted an increasing amount of academic attention of late is whether 'virtual property'[14] – property that exists in a computer game[15] such as a weapon or currency traded within the game – should be recognised as a form of intangible property that is protected from being interfered with under English law. English law currently provides gamers with no protection against 'virtual property' being damaged or stolen by hackers or being otherwise interfered with. The effort and real world money that can be expended on acquiring virtual property[16] has led people to ask whether the law should take any steps to protect such property from being interfered with after it has been acquired.[17]

The most commonly made argument for saying that the law should get involved with protecting virtual property is a Lockean argument that in cases where virtual property has been acquired by a gamer through his expending time and skill on acquiring that property, that property should be regarded as 'his'.[18] However, it has been pointed out that the Lockean argument cannot apply here as a gamer who expends time and effort in acquiring virtual property is doing so by expending that time and effort on a game that belongs to its developers.[19] So the developers of a game have a better claim to anything that exists within the game than anyone playing that game could have, in the same way that the owner of a block of marble has a better claim to the statue that has been carved out of the block than the carver does. And the developers of games tend to make it clear in their End User Licence Agreement that they retain all and any rights they have over things that exist within the game.

Richard Bartle – the co-creator of the first ever virtual world computer game ('Multi-User Dungeon', or 'MUD') – has also argued, on utilitarian grounds, that the law should not get involved in protecting virtual property from outside interference.[20] The existence of such protection would, he argues, damage what is valuable about virtual world games. Bartle's objections are twofold. First, once legally enforceable user rights attach to virtual property that has been acquired within a game, the ability of the developers of the game

---

[14] A popular misnomer which we perpetuate here: if 'virtual property' is unprotected from being interfered with, it is hard to see how it counts as 'property'. For this reason, Nelson 2010 prefers the term 'virtual resource'.

[15] Examples of such games are: *World of Warcraft* (a fantasy wizard and orcs type game), *Ultima Online* (ditto), *EverQuest* (ditto), *Eve Online* (a science fiction game), and *Second Life* (an alternative version of our world).

[16] For example, the currency used in *Second Life* is known as the 'Linden dollar'. Linden dollars can be bought or sold for real life currency on currency exchanges. At the time of writing, the total amount of Linden dollars held by the players of Second Life comes to the equivalent of 30 million US dollars, and rising rapidly. That's a lot of money to be holding without any individual rights to sue if that money is stolen or wiped out by hackers. *New Scientist* also reported in 2009 that it was estimated that US citizens would spend $620m that year on acquiring virtual property; and in Asia, $5 *billion* would be spent on virtual property in one year alone. Countries such as South Korea and China have responded to this huge investment in virtual property in their countries by taking steps to give virtual property holders legal rights over that property that are enforceable in real life.

[17] The question is confined to cases where virtual property is stolen or destroyed as a result of people – usually computer hackers – doing things in the real world. Where virtual property is stolen or destroyed within the game, as a result of what another player has done, no one really contends that that 'virtual tort' should amount to a real tort. (It is presumed, if one player can loot another player's property within the game, then it was within the rules of the game to do that sort of thing.)

[18] See, for example, Lastowka & Hunter 2004.

[19] See Nelson 2010, at 290–1.

[20] Bartle 2004.

to change and improve the game will be radically diminished as such changes and improvements may well have negative effects for gamers who hold virtual property within the game. Such gamers could well argue that these negative effects violate their use rights.

Secondly, once legally enforceable exclusivity rights attach to virtual property, virtual property will become easily tradeable. The commodification of virtual property that exists within a computer game will, Bartle argues, damage both the virtuality and the point of the game. Virtuality will be damaged because the real world – in the shape of how rich people are in real life – will start determining who is asset-rich in the virtual world of the computer game. The point of the game will be damaged as the point of many such games is to acquire prestige and status by going on a journey within the game. The significance of acquiring such prestige and status will be lost for gamers if they know that others can acquire it simply by flexing their credit card.

Given these arguments, we think those responsible for shaping this area of the law should be very cautious about developing legally enforceable rights in relation to virtual property.

15.3 Sufficient interest

When it comes to A's suing B for committing an *intangible* property tort, the only interest that will suffice for A to sue B is *ownership* – A has to own the copyright or patent or business reputation that A is complaining B interfered with. But as we have seen, the position is more complicated where A wants to sue B for committing a *tangible* property tort in respect of a particular item of property P – in such a case, A can only sue for trespass to goods if A had possession of P, and A can only sue for conversion if A had possession of P or an immediate right to possess P.

A. Possession

When can a claimant say that she was in possession of an item of property at the time it was interfered with? The basic answer is – if she *acquired* possession before the property was interfered with, and did not *lose* possession in between acquiring possession and the property being interfered with.

(1) *Acquiring possession.* A will acquire possession of an item of property if: (a) she takes *control* of that item of property with (b) the *intention* of preventing others from taking control of that item of property.

Someone will take control of an item of property if he takes as much control over that item of property as the nature of that item of property will admit. So, for example, in *Young* v *Hichens* (1844), the claimant was fishing for pilchards and had almost encircled a shoal of pilchards with his nets when the defendant rowed through a gap in the nets and prevented the claimant from capturing the pilchards. The claimant sued the defendant, claiming that he had been in possession of the pilchards and that the defendant had disturbed his possession of the pilchards. The claim was rejected: at no time did the claimant have the pilchards completely under his control.

In contrast, in *The Tubantia* (1924), the claimants attempted to salvage the cargo of a Dutch steamship which had been sunk in the First World War and lay under 100 feet of water. The claimants located the steamship in April 1922 and spent as many days exploring the ship and salvaging its cargo as the weather permitted until November 1922 when it became impracticable to continue exploring the ship during the winter. The claimants marked the location of the ship and returned in April 1923. They then spent about 25 days exploring the ship and salvaging the cargo until July 1923 when the defendants – encouraged by rumours that the ship had been carrying treasure at the time it was sunk – started to send divers down to the ship in an attempt to locate the treasure and take it for themselves. The claimants sued the defendants, claiming that they had possession of the ship and that the defendants were acting unlawfully in disrupting their possession of the ship. The claimants' claim was allowed: they had taken as much control over the Dutch steamship as the nature of the thing and its location allowed.

Someone who takes control of an item of property will not acquire possession of that item of property unless he intends, in taking control of that item of property, to prevent other people from taking control of that item of property. If he lacks this intention, he is said to have 'custody' of the item of property in question, not 'possession'. So, for example, if *Owner* asks *Jeweller* to value a ring for her, when *Owner* gives *Jeweller* the ring, he will acquire custody but not possession of the ring.[21] When *Jeweller* takes control of the ring to inspect it he does not intend, in taking control of the ring, to prevent other people from taking control of it. Again, it is often said that employees only have custody of their work tools – they do not possess their work tools. When an employee takes control of some tools that he has been given to work with, he does not intend, in taking control of those tools, to prevent other people from taking control of those tools.[22] Of course, if an employee steals some work tools and takes them home he will acquire possession of those tools – he will have taken control of those tools with the intention of preventing other people from taking control of those tools.

(2) *Losing possession.* If A has acquired possession of an item of property, A will then lose possession of that item of property if: (a) someone else takes possession of that item of property; or (b) A intentionally abandons that item of property.

So A does *not* have to *retain control* of an item of property in order to retain possession of that item of property. For example, if *Householder* goes on holiday he retains possession of all the items of property in his house even though he does not have physical control over them while he is gone. Obviously, though, if someone breaks into *Householder*'s house while he is gone and steals some items of property from the house, *Householder* will lose possession of those items of property – someone else (the burglar) will have taken possession of those items of property. Again, suppose *Householder* employs *Oddjob* to perform some task for him and gives *Oddjob* the tools she will need to do the job. *Householder* will retain possession of the tools even after he has given them to *Oddjob* – and this is so even though *Householder* will not physically control the tools once he gives them to *Oddjob*.

---

[21] *Armory* v *Delamirie* (1721) 1 Stra 505, 93 ER 664.

[22] While this works to explain the rule that an employee only has custody of his work tools and does not possess them, the rule, it should be noted, has its origins in the definition of the now defunct crime of larceny. Someone would commit the offence of larceny if he removed goods from the possession of their owner. Under this definition, an employee who had possession of his work tools would not commit the offence of larceny if he absconded with them – by definition, if he had possession of his work tools he would not remove them from the possession of their owner (his employer) if he absconded with them. In order to ensure that employees who absconded with their employer's tools *did* commit the offence of larceny in so doing, the idea grew up that employees did not possess their work tools – they only had custody of them.

This is because when *Householder* gives the tools to *Oddjob*, *Oddjob* will merely acquire custody of the tools: she will not possess them.

B. Immediate right to possess

A will have an *immediate right* to possess goods in B's possession if A *currently* has a right to call on B to hand over those goods to her. For example, in *Gordon* v *Harper* (1796), *Landlord* leased a fully furnished flat to *Tenant*. *Tenant* owed some money and *Sheriff* – thinking that the furniture in the flat belonged to *Tenant* – seized it and sold it in execution of the debt. *Landlord* sued *Sheriff* in conversion. He lost: *Landlord* could not establish that at the time *Sheriff* seized and sold the furniture in the flat, *Landlord* had a right to call on *Tenant* to hand over possession of the furniture to him.[23] At the expiry of the lease, he would have acquired such a right but the lease had not expired at the time *Sheriff* seized and sold the furniture in question. *Tenant*, on the other hand, being in possession of the furniture at the time it was seized and sold, could have sued *Sheriff* in conversion for selling the furniture.

Let's now look at a few categories of situations in which someone *may* have an immediate right to possess an item of property.

(1) *Theft*. If *Thief* steals a watch from *Owner*, *Owner* will acquire an immediate right to possess that watch.

(2) *Evidence*. Suppose that *Fence* was in possession of stolen goods and that those goods were seized by the police in pursuit of a criminal investigation.[24] Suppose further that the true owner of the goods is untraceable and the police no longer have any statutory authority to retain those goods. In this situation, *Fence* will have an immediate right to possess the goods in question.[25] So if *Fence* demands that the police give him back the goods and the police refuse to do so, they will commit the tort of conversion.[26] It seems that this will be the case even if *Fence* actually stole the goods in question.[27]

(3) *Lost property*. If *Smeagol* has found a ring on your land which has been lost by a third party, *you* will have an immediate right to possess that ring if: (a) *Smeagol* is your employee and he found the ring in the course of his employment;[28] *or* (b) *Smeagol* is a trespasser on your land;[29] *or* (c) the ring was buried on your land;[30] *or* (d) you have 'manifested an

---

[23] However, the law protects *Landlord* by allowing him an independent action for damage to his 'reversionary interest' in the chattels sold by *Sheriff*: see Tettenborn 1994, Green 2010, and *HSBC Rail (UK) Ltd* v *Network Rail Infrastructure Ltd* [2006] 1 WLR 643.

[24] Section 19 of the Police and Criminal Evidence Act 1984 grants the police a statutory power to do this: see below, § 15.6(A)(5).

[25] It must be emphasised that this will only be the case if the police remain in custody of the goods and the true owner of the goods cannot be traced. If the police have exercised a statutory power to transfer the stolen goods to a third party, then *Fence* will no longer have any rights over the goods: *Buckley* v *Gross* (1863) 3 B & S 566, 122 ER 213. Similarly, if the stolen goods are still in the custody of the police, but the true owner can be identified, then *Fence* will have no right to demand that the goods be returned to him.

[26] *Costello* v *Chief Constable of Derbyshire Constabulary* [2001] 1 WLR 1437.

[27] Ibid, at [31].

[28] *City of London Corporation* v *Appleyard* [1963] 1 WLR 982; *Parker* v *British Airways Board* [1982] QB 1004, 1017.

[29] *Hibbert* v *McKiernan* [1948] 2 KB 142; *Parker* v *British Airways Board* [1982] QB 1004, 1017.

[30] *Waverley Borough Council* v *Fletcher* [1996] QB 334.

intention to exercise control over [your] land and the things which may be upon it or in it'.[31] If none of (a)–(d) are made out, you will have no right to possess the item of property found by *Smeagol* and he may keep it until, of course, the rightful owner turns up and claims the ring in question.[32]

(4) *Bailment.* If A holds B's property as a bailee, B will have an immediate right to possess that property if the bailment on which A holds B's property is a bailment *at will* – that is, if B has reserved the right to reclaim her property from A at any time.

If A holds B's property on a fixed-term bailment, B will normally only acquire a right to call on A to hand over possession of the property once the fixed term has elapsed. But if A misuses B's property before the term has elapsed, B may immediately acquire a right at that stage to call on A to hand over possession of the property. So, for example, suppose *Car-Hire* rented out a car to *Hirer* for six months. Two months later, *Hirer* gave the car away to *Third Party.* In such a case, *Car-Hire* will probably be able to establish that when *Hirer* gave the car away, *Car-Hire* acquired an immediate right to possess the car. As a result, *Car-Hire* will probably be able to establish that *Hirer* and *Third Party* both committed the tort of conversion in relation to *Car-Hire* when *Hirer* gave the car away to *Third Party* and *Third Party* took possession of the car.

(5) *Trusts.* Suppose A holds an item of property on trust for B. Will B have an immediate right to possess that item of property? If the property is held *solely* on trust for B then B will have a right – under the decision in *Saunders* v *Vautier* (1841) – to call on A to hand over the property to her.[33] One would have thought, then, that if A held the trust property solely on trust for B and then disposed of that property to C in breach of trust, B would be able to sue both A and C in conversion – and indeed one case held exactly that.[34]

However, if the law *did* say this, then the rule in Equity that a bona fide purchaser of trust property disposed of in breach of trust cannot be sued for the value of that property[35] would be subverted.[36] A claim in conversion would lie against the bona fide purchaser. In order to prevent this happening, the Court of Appeal has ruled in *MCC Proceeds Inc* v *Lehman Bros International (Europe)* (1998) that if trust property which is held solely on trust for B is disposed of in breach of trust, a claim in conversion will *not* lie either against the trustee disposing of the property or the recipient of the property. While B might have an immediate right to possess the trust property, that right, being *equitable* in nature, is not sufficient to allow B to bring a claim in conversion. What has to be

---

[31] *Parker* v *British Airways Board* [1982] QB 1004, 1018.

[32] Of course, if *Smeagol* takes the ring with the intention of keeping it for himself, that will be conversion – *Smeagol* is only allowed to take the ring if his intention in so doing is to restore it to its rightful owner: see below, § 15.4(B)(1).

[33] If A holds the property on trust for B and C, then B will only acquire a right to demand that A hand over the property to her if C agrees that she can do so. So B will not have an *immediate* right to demand possession of the property.

[34] *International Factors* v *Rodriguez* [1979] 1 QB 751.

[35] See *Pilcher* v *Rawlins* (1872) LR 7 Ch App 259.

[36] Though Tettenborn 1996 questions whether this is true (at 40–1). He argues that the real reason for maintaining that the beneficiary under a trust cannot bring a claim for conversion when the property is misappropriated is that to allow such a claim would expand the liabilities of: (1) innocent donees of trust property; (2) people who innocently assist a trustee to dispose of trust property; *and* (3) trustees who innocently commit a breach of trust by disposing of trust property to another.

established is that B had an immediate right to possess the trust property *under the common law* – and this B cannot do, as she merely had an equitable interest in the trust property.

15.4 Interference (1): tangible property

When it comes to the tort of trespass to goods, the kind of interference that will amount to such a tort is fairly straightforward to state: B will commit the tort in relation to A if (i) she directly interfered with goods in A's possession; (ii) she did so intentionally or carelessly.[37]

The position with the tort of conversion is much more difficult to state. Normally, a *failure to act* will not amount to conversion – but there are two significant exceptions to this rule. First, B's failure to return to A goods that A had an immediate right to possess *might* amount to the tort of conversion – and as we will see, the law on *when* such a failure to return such goods *would* amount to conversion has had a significant effect on when a *positive act* will amount to conversion. Secondly, s 2(2) of the Torts (Interference with Goods) Act 1977 provides that: 'An action lies in conversion for loss or destruction of goods which a bailee has allowed to happen in breach of his duty to his bailor . . .'.

In what follows, we will begin with when a failure to return A's goods to A will amount to conversion. We will then consider what sort of positive acts amount to conversion. And we will then look at the law on bailment, as s 2(2) of the 1977 Act has brought that area of law under the tort of conversion.

A. Failure to return

We have already seen that if B is in control of A's goods, A cannot sue B by simply claiming, 'B's got my goods!' But English law was not so perverse as to deny A any remedy in this situation. At first under the action for *detinue* (which was subject to procedural disadvantages for claimants), and subsequently under the action for *trover* (which developed in response to claimants' desires to bring a claim against people who had their goods that did not involve suing in detinue)[38] which provided the foundations for the modern-day law of conversion, the courts allowed people like A to sue people B for *wrongfully detaining* their goods by refusing to hand them over when they had been demanded from B.

However, in the case where A's watch was stolen from him and ended up in B's hands, and A went to B and said, 'That watch was stolen from me, hand it over!' the law would have been equally perverse if it had said that B would commit the tort of conversion if she failed to hand the watch over to A on the spot. Instead, the law took the position that B's refusal to hand over A's goods would only amount to conversion if B's refusal indicated

---

[37] This seems to follow from *Fowler* v *Lanning* [1959] 1 QB 426. See *National Coal Board* v *J E Evans & Co (Cardiff)* Ltd [1951] 2 KB 861, where the defendant contractors struck an underground cable belonging to the claimants when digging a trench on land belonging to the local county council. The claimants sued the defendants, claiming that they had committed the tort of trespass to goods in damaging the cable. Held: no trespass, even though the defendants had directly interfered with the claimants' cable – they had not intended to damage the cable and had not carelessly damaged the cable as they did not know and had no reason to know it was under the land on which they were digging.

[38] Detinue was finally abolished by s 2 of the Torts (Interference with Goods) Act 1977 as its functions had been completely overtaken by the part of the law of conversion under discussion here.

that she was not willing to respect A's rights over the goods.[39] In Holt CJ's words in *Baldwin* v *Cole* (1704), conversion involves 'an assuming upon one's self the property and right of disposing another's goods'.[40] So if, in our example of A's watch, B told A, 'I'm not going to give you this watch until I have taken some time to find out what the true position is' then B's initial refusal to accede to A's demand will not amount to conversion.[41] In the alternative scenario, where A gave goods to B to look after, or to look at, and then A demanded them back from B, it had always been thought that B had to give the goods back and could not say 'I must wait to inquire into whether you are really entitled to these goods.'[42] However, in *Spencer* v *S Franses Ltd* (2011), Thirlwall J held that if B was put on notice[43] that A might *not* be entitled to the goods that A has asked B to look after, or to look at, then B might be legally entitled to retain the goods for a reasonable time to see if A is the right person to whom to hand the goods.[44]

One situation where B's refusal to hand over to A goods that B readily acknowledges belong to A will *not* be wrongful is where the goods land up on B's premises without B's consent: B does not have to put himself out to return A's goods to him, or allow A onto his premises to allow A to retrieve the goods.[45] But if A deposited the goods on B's land with B's consent, B cannot subsequently refuse to hand them over without risking being sued for conversion.[46]

B. Positive acts

Holt CJ's identification of conversion with 'an assuming upon one's self the property and right of disposing another's goods' in *Baldwin* v *Cole* (1704) had fateful consequences for what kind of *positive* act would be held to amount to conversion: the courts came to think that *any* positive act of B's which 'denied' A's rights over certain goods was capable of amounting to conversion. As Lord Nicholls observed in *Kuwait Airways Corpn* v *Iraqi Airways Co (Nos 4 & 5)* (2002):

> the basic features of the tort are threefold. First, the defendant's conduct was inconsistent with the rights of the owner (or other person entitled to possession). Second, the conduct was deliberate, not accidental. Third, the conduct was so extensive an encroachment on the rights of the owner as to exclude him from use and possession of the goods.[47]

---

[39] *Isaack* v *Clark* (1615) 2 Bulstr 306; 80 ER 1143.
[40] *Baldwin* v *Cole* (1704) 6 Mod 212, 87 ER 964.
[41] *Clayton* v *Le Roy* [1911] 2 KB 1031, 1051 (per Fletcher Moulton LJ).
[42] *Armory* v *Delamirie* (1721) 1 Stra 505, 93 ER 664; *China Pacific SA* v *Food Corporation of India, The Winson* [1982] AC 939.
[43] [2011] EWHC 1269, at [295]: what is required is 'actual knowledge of facts indicating that the bailor is not in fact the owner'.
[44] Ibid, at [300]. (But on the facts of the case – where the claimant gave the defendant some embroideries, asking the defendant to investigate their history – too much time (six years) had elapsed after the embroideries were entrusted to the defendant to make it reasonable for the defendant to withhold the embroideries from the claimant on the basis that it was doubtful whether the claimant was really entitled to the embroideries.)
[45] *Miller* v *Jackson* [1977] QB 966, at 978 (per Lord Denning MR): it is not conversion to refuse to give back a cricket ball that has been hit into your back garden; *British Economical Lamp Co* v *Empire Mile End (Limited)* (1913) 29 TLR 386 (not conversion to refuse to hand back lamps left in claimants' theatre by tenants who have moved out).
[46] *Howard E Perry* v *British Railways Board* [1980] 1 WLR 1375.
[47] [2002] 2 AC 883, at [39].

This identification of conversion with 'denying' someone's rights over tangible property resulted in conversion becoming a tort of strict liability as one can act inconsistently with someone else's rights over tangible property without any intention of doing so – for example, when you accept a gift of a watch that (unknown to you and perhaps unknown to the person giving you the watch) has been stolen from someone else. Identifying conversion with 'denying' someone's rights over tangible property also meant that there are now many different types of positive act that are capable of amounting to conversion:

(1) *Taking possession.* The first way of committing the tort through a positive act is to take possession of goods that are in another's possession, with the intention of keeping them.[48] So, for example, suppose *Thief* steals some jewellery from *Rich*, and then hands the jewellery over to *Buyer*. In this case, both *Thief* and *Buyer* will have committed the tort of conversion in relation to *Rich* – *Thief* in stealing the jewellery from *Rich* and *Buyer* in taking possession of the stolen jewellery with the intention of keeping it. *Buyer*, it should be noted, will have committed the tort of conversion in this situation even if he bought the jewellery from *Thief* in perfect good faith and had no idea it was stolen.

It is essential to show – for the purpose of showing that a defendant has committed the tort of conversion under this head – that the defendant *took possession* of the claimant's goods *with the intention of keeping them*.[49] For example, in *Tear* v *Freebody* (1858), the claimant unlawfully erected a building and the defendant was given the job of tearing the building down. The defendant did so and then took the bricks and so on out of which the building was made to a stone yard, intending to retain them until he was paid for the work he had done in tearing down the building. The defendant was not entitled to do this. It was held that the defendant committed the tort of conversion in taking possession of the bricks.

In contrast, in *Club Cruise Entertainment* v *Department of Transport* (2008), a health and safety officer issued a notice detaining in port a ship in which there had been an outbreak of the norovirus. It was held that while the officer had no authority to issue this notice, he had not committed the tort of conversion in detaining the ship in port as he had not at any stage taken possession of the ship. Again, in *Fouldes* v *Willoughby* (1841), the defendant operated a ferry that ran between Birkenhead and Liverpool. The claimant took two horses on board the ferry, which the defendant refused to carry. The claimant refused to take the horses off the ferry so the defendant took hold of them and led them off the ferry and onto the shore where the defendant's brother took charge of them. The claimant stayed on the ferry which took him to Liverpool where he sent for the horses. The horses were never returned to him. The claimant sued the defendant, claiming that in taking the horses off the ferry he had committed the tort of conversion. The court doubted whether this was true: when the defendant took the horses off the ferry, he had no intention of keeping them.

---

[48] The expression 'keeping' here covers both the situation where A took possession of the goods with the intention of keeping them for himself and the situation where A took possession of the goods with the intention of giving them to a third party.

[49] See Lord Nicholls in *Kuwait Airways Corpn* v *Iraqi Airways Co (Nos 4 & 5)* [2002] 2 AC 883, at [42]: 'To constitute conversion detention . . . must be accompanied by an intention to keep the goods.' So someone who picks up a wallet in the street will not commit the tort of conversion if he picks it up with the object of restoring it to its rightful owner: *Isaack* v *Clark* (1615) 2 Bulstr 306, 312; 80 ER 1143, 1148.

(2) *Delivery into hands of third party.* The second way of committing the tort of conversion by performing a positive act is by intentionally doing something that resulted in goods in someone else's possession, or that someone has an immediate right to possess, being delivered[50] into the hands of a third party.

So, for example, *Chancer* will commit the tort of conversion if he pledges[51] *Owner's* property to *Pawn Store* when he has no lawful justification or excuse for doing so.[52] Similarly, if *Shop* gives *Agent* some goods to deliver to *Buyer* and *Agent* gives it to *Lucky* instead, *Agent* will normally be held to have committed the tort of conversion in relation to *Buyer*.

In order to make out that A has converted B's property under this head it is not necessary to show that A *physically* handed over B's property to a third party – but it must be shown that a third party obtained possession of B's property as a result of something A did.

In *Ashby* v *Tolhurst* (1937), a thief stole the claimant's car from a private parking ground which was supervised by an attendant. It was claimed that the attendant had committed the tort of conversion in allowing the thief to get away with the car. The claim was rejected. The thief did not obtain possession of the car as a result of anything the attendant did; all the attendant did was allow the thief to make good his escape once he had obtained possession of the claimant's car.

In contrast, in *Moorgate Mercantile Co Ltd* v *Finch and Read* (1962), the hirer of a car under a hire-purchase agreement lent his car to the defendant who, unknown to the hirer, used the car to smuggle watches into the country. When the defendant's activities were discovered, the car was forfeited and sold by the Customs and Excise authorities. The owners of the car argued that the defendant had committed the tort of conversion. The Court of Appeal agreed: Customs and Excise had obtained possession of the claimant's car as a result of what the defendant did – that is, smuggling watches in the claimant's car.

Similarly, in *R H Willis & Son* v *British Car Auctions Ltd* (1978), the claimants leased a car to one David Croucher under a hire-purchase agreement under which he would become the owner of the car after making a certain number of hire payments. Before Croucher had made enough hire payments to become owner of the car, he took the car to the defendant firm of car auctioneers and asked them to auction it for him. The minimum he was willing to accept for the car was £450. Unfortunately, at auction the highest bid was merely £400. The car was withdrawn but after the auction was over the auctioneers persuaded Croucher to sell the car to the highest bidder for £400 by agreeing to reduce their commission on the sale. The claimants sued the defendants, claiming that they had

---

[50] It seems that for A to have committed the tort of conversion under this head, it is essential that his actions must have resulted in B's goods being *delivered* into the hands of a third party. So if A sells, or attempts to sell, B's goods to C, that will not *of itself* amount to conversion: it is only when the goods are actually handed over to C that the tort will have been committed. See, on this, *Lancashire Waggon Co* v *Fitzhugh* (1861) 6 H & N 502, 158 ER 206; *Consolidated Company* v *Curtis & Son* [1892] 1 QB 495, 498; *Marcq* v *Christie's* [2004] QB 286, at [19]. *A fortiori*, if A goes about insisting that B's goods belong to A, that will not amount to conversion: see Torts (Interference with Goods) Act 1977, s 11(3) ('Denial of title is not of itself conversion').

[51] A will pledge B's property to C if he transfers possession of that property to C as security for a debt owed by A to C.

[52] *Pawn Store* will also be held to have converted *Owner's* property by accepting it as a pledge. See s 11(2) of the Torts (Interference with Goods) Act 1977, which provides that '[receipt] of goods by way of pledge is conversion if delivery of the goods is conversion'.

committed the tort of conversion in acting as they did. (Croucher was not worth suing as he was bankrupt.) The defendants were held liable: the Court of Appeal held that the claimants' car had been delivered into a third party's hands as a result of the actions of the defendants in reducing their commission on the sale.

(3) *Use*. The third way of committing the tort of conversion through a positive act is by using goods that are in someone else's possession, or which someone else has an immediate right to possess.[53] This has long been well acknowledged. As far back as 1591 it was observed: '[no] law compelleth him that finds a thing to keep it safely . . . but if a man findeth a thing and useth it, he is answerable, for it is conversion.'[54] Rolle's *Abridgement* took the same view: '[if] a man takes my horse and rides it and then redelivers it to me nevertheless I may have an action against him, for this is a conversion . . .'[55]

(4) *Destruction*. The fourth way of converting goods in someone else's possession, or which someone else has an immediate right to possess through a positive act is by *intentionally* doing something that results in those goods being *destroyed*. Destruction is crucial – merely damaging someone else's goods does not amount to conversion. This can create difficulty because it is sometimes difficult to tell whether a given item of property has been damaged or destroyed. If a plank of wood is sawn in two that seems to be a case of damage rather than destruction.[56] But if a cask of wine is watered, that seems to be a case of destruction.[57]

C. Bailment

By allowing 'an action [to lie] in conversion for loss or destruction of goods which a bailee has allowed to happen in breach of his duty to his bailor . . .', s 2(2) of the Torts (Interference with Goods) Act 1977 undermined any integrity that the law of conversion had, as a bailee who is sued in conversion for wrongfully allowing goods in his possession to be lost or destroyed has not necessarily acted inconsistently with the bailor's rights to the goods – she has merely failed to take sufficient care of the goods. But be that as it may, such cases now fall within the law on conversion. So what sort of cases involve a bailment? In *TRM Copy Centres (UK) Ltd* v *Lanwall Services Ltd* (2009), the House of Lords held that:

> bailment . . . embraces all situations in which possession of goods is given by one person to another upon the condition that they shall be restored to the person by whom possession has been given, or dealt with as he directs upon expiry of the agreed period of possession . . .[58]

While it is arguable that a bailment exists in *any* situation where A is voluntarily in possession of B's goods,[59] it is true that the *central case* of a bailment is the case where A has

---

[53] There seems to be an exception in the case where a bailee uses property which he holds on a bailment for another without denying the bailor's right to the return of the property.

[54] *Mulgrave* v *Ogden* (1591) Cro Eliz 219, 78 ER 475.

[55] Rolle, *Abridgement*, Action sur Case, p 5.

[56] *Simmons* v *Lillystone* (1853) 8 Ex 431, 155 ER 1417.

[57] *Richardson* v *Atkinson* (1723) 1 Stra 576, 93 ER 710.

[58] [2009] 1 WLR 1375, at [10] (per Lord Hope).

[59] There is an exception where C hands goods over to A to look after them and then sells the goods to B while they are still in A's possession. In such a case, A will only hold those goods on a bailment for B if he attorns to B (that is, if he acknowledges that he holds those goods on a bailment for B).

been *entrusted* with B's goods.[60] And that is the case we will focus on in this section. Two such cases can be distinguished:

(1) *Simple bailment.* In this case *Owner* entrusts *Bailee* with goods that belong to her. *Bailee* will hold the goods on a bailment for *Owner*, and will normally owe *Owner* a duty to take reasonable steps to ensure that those goods are not lost, stolen, destroyed, or damaged. If the goods come to some harm while in *Bailee*'s hands, the burden of proof will be on *Bailee* to show that they were not harmed as a result of his neglect.[61] If he cannot show this, he will be held to have breached the duty of care that he owed *Owner*, and will be held liable accordingly.[62]

(2) *Sub-bailment.* In this case *Owner* entrusts *Bailee* with goods that belong to her, and then *Bailee* hands the goods over to *Sub-Bailee*, for *Sub* to look after them. In this situation, *Owner* will be able to sue *Bailee* if her goods come to some harm due to *Sub*'s neglect of them. The duty of care *Bailee* will owe *Owner* is non-delegable.[63] So if *Sub* – having been entrusted with the task of looking after *Owner*'s goods – fails to protect them properly, *Sub* will put *Bailee* in breach of the duty of care he owed *Owner*, and will be held liable accordingly. *Bailee* will then be able to sue *Sub* on the basis that *Sub* was holding *Owner*'s goods on a bailment for *Bailee*, and therefore owed *Bailee* a duty to take reasonable steps to look after them, which duty he breached. Even if *Owner* never sues *Bailee*, *Bailee* will still be entitled to sue *Sub* for substantial damages for the harm done to *Owner*'s goods, which damages will then be held on trust for *Owner*.[64]

Where things get complicated is if *Owner* wants to sue *Sub directly* for the harm done to her goods. If *Sub* carelessly did something positive that foreseeably resulted in *Owner*'s goods being harmed, then *Owner* can simply sue *Sub* under the general law of negligence, arguing that *Sub* owed her, as the owner of the goods, a duty to take care not to act as he did.[65]

But let's suppose that *Sub* merely *failed to protect Owner*'s goods from being harmed. In such a case, *Owner* will only be able to sue *Sub* if he owed her a positive duty to protect her goods from being harmed. Probably the only way *Owner* will be able to do this is if she can establish that when *Sub* received her goods from *Bailee*, he not only held them on a bailment for *Bailee*, but *also* for *Owner*. If *Owner* can show this, then she may be able to argue that *Sub* owed her a duty to take reasonable steps to protect her goods from being harmed. So *Owner* will have to establish two things: (a) that *Sub* held *Owner*'s goods on a bailment for her; and (b) that the terms of that bailment required *Sub* to take reasonable steps to protect *Owner*'s goods from coming to harm.

So far as (a) is concerned, the cases are pretty clear that *Sub* will have held *Owner*'s goods on a bailment for her if and only if, when he received her goods from *Bailee*, he was aware that those goods did not belong to *Bailee*.[66] So far as (b) is concerned, if *Sub* held

---

[60] So it is debatable whether a thief who has stolen *Owner*'s goods will hold those goods on a bailment for *Owner*.

[61] See above, § 7.6.

[62] See below, § 15.7.

[63] See above, § 7.5(B)(2).

[64] *The Winkfield* [1902] P 42, 61.

[65] See above, § 5.8.

[66] *The Pioneer Container* [1994] 2 AC 324, 342 (per Lord Goff); *Marcq v Christie's* [2004] QB 286, at [49]–[50].

Owner's goods on a bailment for *Owner*, he will have owed *Owner* a duty to take reasonable steps to protect those goods from being harmed unless he: (i) made it clear to *Bailee* that he was not willing to be subject to such a duty when he accepted the goods from *Bailee*; and (ii) *Owner* authorised *Bailee* to entrust the goods to someone like *Sub* on the terms on which *Bailee* entrusted those goods to *Sub*.[67]

15.5 Interference (2): intangible property

What sort of interference with intangible property will amount to a tort depends on the type of intangible property involved.

A. Intellectual property

It is beyond the scope of this text to give a detailed account of what kind of interferences with someone else's intellectual property rights will amount to a tort – the interested reader should consult specialist works on intellectual property law. But *very roughly* if B owns the copyright in some kind of work, A will infringe that copyright if: (1) he makes a copy of that work without B's consent; *or* (2) he reproduces that work in any material form without B's consent; *or* (3) he issues copies of that work without B's consent; *or* (4) he rents or lends the work to the public without B's consent; *or* (5) he performs, shows or plays the work in public without B's consent.[68] Section 60 of the Patents Act 1977 defines the ways in which someone will be held to have infringed on someone else's patent – basically, a monopoly right to develop and exploit an invention. And someone will violate someone's registered design or trade mark if they market goods with a particular design, or under a particular mark, that is identical to, *or similar to*, the registered design or trade mark in question.[69]

B. Business goodwill

The tort of passing off protects businesses against two forms of interference with the goodwill attached to the business.

(1) *Exploitation of goodwill.* The first form of the tort is committed if A *exploits* the *goodwill* attached to B's name or business when he was not entitled to do so. What is 'goodwill'? Lord Macnaghten supplied a definition in *Inland Revenue Commissioners* v *Muller & Co's Margarine Ltd* (1901), observing that goodwill 'is a thing very easy to describe, very difficult to define. It is the benefit and advantage of the good name, reputation, and connection of a business. It is the attractive force which brings in custom.'[70]

So A will commit this form of the tort if he markets his goods or services in such a way as to create a substantial risk that people will purchase those goods or services in the belief

---

[67] *Morris* v *CW Martin Ltd* [1966] 1 WLR 716, 729 (per Lord Denning MR); *The Pioneer Container* [1994] 2 AC 324.

[68] Copyright, Designs and Patents Act 1988, ss 16–76.

[69] Registered Designs Act 1949, ss 7–7A; Trade Marks Act 1994, s 10.

[70] [1901] AC 217, 223–4.

that they are B's goods or services.[71] If he does this he will mislead people into thinking that his goods or services are supplied by B and in so doing appropriate the goodwill attached to B's name or business.[72] This is what happened in *Reddaway* v *Banham* (1896). The claimant had for some years made belting and sold it as 'Camel Hair Belting'. As a result, the name 'Camel Hair Belting' was used in the trade to refer to the belts manufactured by the claimant. The defendant began to manufacture belts made of the yarn of camel's hair and stamped the words 'Camel Hair Belting' on them. He was held to have committed the tort of passing off – in stamping 'Camel Hair Belting' on his belts he had created a substantial risk that people would purchase his belts in the belief that they were manufactured by the claimant.

Similarly, in *Reckitt & Colman Products Ltd* v *Borden Inc* (1990), the House of Lords held that Borden would commit the tort of passing off if it sold its lemon juice in lemon-shaped bottles. Reckitt & Colman had been selling its Jif lemon juice in lemon-shaped bottles for 30 years and as a result consumers tended to think that lemon-shaped bottles contained Jif lemon juice. There was therefore a substantial risk that if Borden sold *its* lemon juice in lemon-shaped bottles, consumers would purchase Borden's lemon juice in the belief that it was Jif lemon juice. Borden could not, it was found, eliminate this risk by labelling its lemon-shaped bottles to make it clear that they did not contain Jif lemon juice; the House of Lords found that, when selecting a lemon juice from a range of bottles of lemon juice on sale in a supermarket, shoppers tended not to look at the labels on the bottles of lemon juice in making their choice. So Borden's labelling its lemon-shaped bottles to make it clear that they did not contain Jif lemon juice would not eliminate the risk that shoppers would purchase Borden's lemon juice in the belief that it was Jif lemon juice.

It should be emphasised that this form of the tort may *also* be committed in situations *outside* the sort of situation we have just been considering. To establish that A committed this form of the tort it does *not* have to be established that he marketed his goods or services in such a way as to create a substantial risk that his customers would think those goods or services were B's. It merely has to be shown that A exploited the goodwill attached to B's name or business when he was not entitled to do so.

So it has been held that if A markets his goods or services in such a way as to mislead people into thinking that they are of the *same quality* as B's goods or services, he will

---

[71] See, in addition to the cases cited in the text, *Parker-Knoll Ltd* v *Knoll International Ltd* [1962] RPC 265 (held it would be passing off to market furniture under the name 'Knoll International' because doing so would create a substantial risk that people would purchase that furniture in the belief that it was marketed by Parker-Knoll); *Norman Kark Publications Ltd* v *Odhams Press* [1962] 1 WLR 380 (held the defendants would not commit the tort of passing off in relation to the claimants – the publishers of a magazine called *Today* – if they published a magazine called *Today, the New John Bull*; there was no substantial risk that people would be confused into purchasing the defendants' magazine in the mistaken belief that it was the claimants'); *Alain Bernardin et Compagnie* v *Pavilion Properties Ltd* [1967] RPC 581 (held the defendants did not commit the tort of passing off in relation to the claimants when they opened a nightclub in London called 'The Crazy Horse Saloon'; while the claimants ran an identically named nightclub in Paris, the Paris nightclub was not so well known that people in London were liable to go the defendants' nightclub in London in the mistaken belief that it was run by the claimants).

[72] Note that it is essential to show that A appropriated the goodwill specifically attached to B's name or business. If B has spotted a gap in the market and moved to fill it, A will do nothing wrong if he copies B's example and attempts to corner that part of the market himself: while it is wrong for A to appropriate the goodwill that is specifically attached to B's products, there is nothing wrong in A's borrowing B's good ideas. See n 4, above; also Cane 1996, 80–1.

commit the tort of passing off[73] – if A markets his goods by making people think that his goods are as good as B's when they are not, A will exploit the goodwill attached to the products marketed by B when he is not entitled to do so. It has also been held that a charity will commit the tort of passing off if it solicits donations under a name which is liable to make people think that they are donating money to a quite different, and well-established, charity.[74] It has further been held that a radio station committed the tort of passing off in relation to Eddie Irvine, the Formula One driver, when it misled potential advertisers on the station into thinking that Irvine was a fan of the station, thereby exploiting the goodwill associated with Eddie Irvine's name when it was not entitled to do so.[75]

It should also be noted that this form of the tort can be committed quite innocently.[76] Suppose, for example, *Nerd* opened a DVD shop in Bristol and decided to call it 'Videodrome' after the famous David Cronenberg film of that name. Suppose further that *Buff* had already had the same idea and had run for a number of years a well-regarded DVD shop in London, also called 'Videodrome'. In this situation *Nerd* may well have committed the tort of passing off in relation to *Buff* – and this is so even if *Nerd* had no idea *Buff*'s shop existed and had no intention, in naming his shop 'Videodrome', of exploiting any of the goodwill that had become attached to *Buff*'s shop.

(2) *Endangering goodwill.* The second form of the tort of passing off is committed if A markets his goods or services in such a way as to create a danger that the goodwill attached to B's name or business will be unjustifiably damaged.

This is what happened in *Associated Newspaper plc* v *Insert Media Ltd* (1991). In that case, the defendant inserted advertising material into the claimant's newspapers without the claimant's consent. The Court of Appeal held that the defendant, in so acting, had committed the tort of passing off. There was a substantial risk that people would think that the defendant's advertising material was inserted with the claimant's consent. There was therefore a substantial risk that people would associate the defendant's advertising material with the claimant and would hold it against the claimant if the advertising material proved to be dishonest or inaccurate.

---

[73] See *J Bollinger* v *Costa Brava Wine Co* [1960] 1 Ch 262 (held that the defendants committed the tort of passing off in relation to the claimant champagne manufacturers when they sold wine made in Spain or from grapes produced in Spain as 'champagne' or as 'Spanish champagne', thereby appropriating the goodwill attached to the claimants' business when they were not entitled to do so – the defendants' wine not being as good as genuine champagne); also *Erven Warnink Besloten Vennootschap* v *J Townend & Sons (Hull) Ltd* [1979] AC 731 (held that it was passing off for the defendants to manufacture a mixture of dried egg powder and Cyprus sherry under the name 'Keeling's Old English Advocaat'; if the defendants marketed their product under this name, they would appropriate the goodwill attached to genuine advocaat when they were not entitled to do so – genuine advocaat, which is made out of brandy, egg yolks and sugar, being far superior to the defendants' product).

[74] See *British Diabetic Association* v *Diabetic Society Ltd* [1995] 4 All ER 812 (held that it would be passing off for a charity to solicit contributions under the name 'The Diabetic Society' because there was a substantial risk that people would make donations to the charity in the belief that they were donating money to the quite distinct British Diabetic Association).

[75] *Irvine* v *Talksport Ltd* [2002] 1 WLR 2355

[76] It used to be a matter of debate whether someone who innocently committed the tort of passing off could be held liable to pay anything more than nominal damages to the victim of his tort, with the House of Lords reserving its position on the issue in *Marengo* v *Daily Sketch and Sunday Graphic* (1948) 65 RPC 242. However, in *Gillette UK Ltd* v *Edenwest Ltd* [1994] RPC 279, Blackburne J held that no special rule existed for defendants who innocently committed the tort of passing off: they would be held liable to pay damages to the victims of their torts in the same way as any other tortfeasors.

Similarly, in *Mirage Studios* v *Counter-Feat Clothing Company Ltd* (1991), the claimants were owners of the copyright in the Teenage Mutant Ninja Turtles. A major part of the claimants' income came from licensing other people to use images of the Teenage Mutant Ninja Turtles on products manufactured by those people. The defendants sought to cash in on the craze for the Teenage Mutant Ninja Turtles by drawing pictures of humanoid turtles and licensing various garment manufacturers to use those pictures on T-shirts and jogging clothes. It was held that the defendants had committed the tort of passing off in so acting. There was a substantial risk that people would mistake the defendants' drawings for images of the Teenage Mutant Ninja Turtles and would think that the claimants – the owners of the Teenage Mutant Ninja Turtle image – had licensed the use of those drawings on the items of clothing on which they appeared. There was therefore a substantial risk that people would associate the claimants with the items of clothing on which the defendants' drawings appeared and would therefore hold it against the claimants if those items of clothing proved to be of poor quality.

Again, in *Clark v Associated Newspapers Ltd* (1998), the *Evening Standard* was held to have committed the tort of passing off when it published a weekly column called 'The Secret Diary of Alan Clark MP'. The column was written in the same manner as Alan Clark's published diaries and amounted to a witty and exaggerated weekly fantasy as to what Alan Clark might have written in his diary that week. Although it was made clear that the diary entries were written by Peter Bradshaw, an *Evening Standard* journalist, it was held that there was a substantial risk that people would think that the diary entries were written by Alan Clark and that people would think less well of Alan Clark as a result.

C. Contractual rights

As we will see below, in Chapter 20, the tort of *inducing a breach of contract* protects contracting parties against third parties persuading the other party to their contract to breach it. In *OBG Ltd* v *Allan* (2008), an attempt was made to radically expand the types of interference with contractual rights that would attract liability in tort.

In that case, the claimant company ('OBG') got into severe financial difficulties. In order to protect his interests, one of OBG's creditors – who thought he had a charge over OBG's assets – had some receivers go in and take over OBG's business. The receivers tried to raise money to pay off OBG's debts by selling off its assets, and settling various debts that were owed to OBG for much less than the paper value of those debts. It was discovered too late that the receivers' appointment had been invalid because the creditor who had sent the receivers in did not in fact have a charge over OBG's assets. OBG was then taken over by liquidators who sued the receivers for – they claimed – wrongfully interfering with the contractual rights that OBG had against people who owed it money. It was argued that the receivers had been too lax in settling the debts that were owed to OBG, and had demanded too little in return for settling those debts.

But what sort of wrong had been committed here? Clearly not the tort of inducing a breach of contract as no breach – but rather partial performance – had been induced by the receivers' actions. So OBG's liquidators argued that the receivers had committed the tort of conversion in relation to OBG's contractual rights against its debtors. This was a novel claim, as conversion traditionally only applied to cases where a defendant interfered with a tangible thing that the claimant possessed, or had an immediate right to possess. So the issue faced by the House of Lords was whether the tort of conversion should be extended to cover cases where a defendant interfered with a contractual right that the claimant had against a third party.

The House of Lords rejected the invitation to extend the tort of conversion in this way by a majority of 3:2. The majority held that the tort of conversion only covered interferences with tangible property, and did not extend to interferences with intangible property, such as a contractual right.[77]

The minority (Lord Nicholls and Baroness Hale) made two basic arguments in favour of the view that the law of conversion should extend to interferences with contractual rights. The first argument was that if an action for conversion could not be brought here, then the paradoxical result would arise that the receivers *could* be sued in conversion for selling off OBG's physical assets, but could *not* be sued in conversion for throwing away for a song the debts that it was owed – when those debts comprised up to 70 per cent[78] of OBG's assets.[79] The second argument was that extending the tort of conversion to cover the sort of facts presented in *OBG* would involve a 'modest but principled extension of the scope of the tort'.[80] Lord Nicholls' main argument for thinking that allowing a claim for conversion in a case like *OBG* would represent a 'modest' development of the law is that the law already allows a claimant to sue a defendant for interfering with a contractual right of his where that right is embodied in documentary form.[81] The classic example of this, Lord Nicholls argued, is the case where a defendant is sued in conversion for the face value of a cheque that he has misapplied. In such a case, Lord Nicholls argued, the defendant is effectively being held liable in conversion for misappropriating the right to draw on the bank account against which the cheque was drawn. Lord Nicholls saw no reason why the law of conversion should provide a remedy when someone appropriates a contractual right that is embodied in documentary form, but should not when the right interfered with is disembodied – and extending the scope of conversion to cover interference with the second kind of right would not, he thought, represent a radical development given that the tort of conversion already protects people against interference with the first kind of right.

The majority (Lords Hoffmann, Walker and Brown) roundly rejected the minority's arguments. The majority were agreed that extending the tort of conversion to interferences with forms of intangible property such as contractual rights would represent a dramatic change in the law. Lord Hoffmann remarked scathingly, 'As for authority for such a change, it hardly needs to be said that in English law there is none.'[82] Lord Walker thought that Lord Nicholls' views 'involved too drastic a reshaping of this area of the law of tort'.[83] And Lord Brown thought that the minority's position involved 'no less than

---

[77] The decision has subsequently been followed by the Court of Appeal in *Your Response Ltd* v *Datastream Business Media Ltd* [2015] QB 41 and *The Environment Agency* v *Churngold Recycling Ltd* [2014] EWCA Civ 909.

[78] A figure arrived at by Goymour 2011, 68, presumably on the basis of the figures in Lord Nicholls' judgment ([2008] 1 AC 1, at [211]–[212]) where the debts owed to OBG were said to be worth £1,820,000 (and settled for £753,000) and the land, plant and equipment owned by OBG and sold by the receivers were worth £244,000. OBG had some other assets, such as cash in the bank, which make the sums come out right.

[79] [2008] 1 AC 1, at [221] (per Lord Nicholls): 'Why should [the receivers] be liable strictly in respect of their unauthorised dealings with some parts of the company's property but not others? This distinction makes no sense'; and [311] (per Baroness Hale): 'it makes no sense that the defendants should be strictly liable for what was lost on the tangible assets but not for what was lost on the intangibles.'

[80] [2008] 1 AC 1, at [233] (per Lord Nicholls).

[81] [2008] 1 AC 1, at [225]–[233].

[82] [2008] 1 AC 1, at [100].

[83] [2008] 1 AC 1, at [271].

the proposed severance of any link whatever between the tort of conversion and the wrongful taking of physical possession of property (whether a chattel or document) having a real and ascertainable value.'[84]

The majority's criticism of the minority was basically constitutional in nature: the minority were trying to bring about a radical change in the law when the judicial role is simply to apply and clarify the law. But four other criticisms can also be made of the minority's position.

(1) Conversion is – as currently defined – an intensely physical tort. It involves *taking possession* of, or *refusing to deliver* up, or *delivering into the hands* of a third party, or *using*, or *destroying* an *asset* in someone else's *possession*, or which someone else has an immediate right to *possess*. All the italicised expressions in the previous sentence demonstrate the real world, physical, nature of conversion. Given this, it is hard to see how the tort would be defined, or what its bounds would be, if it covered interferences with intangible property. A whole new definition of the tort would need to be created, and with that would come the threat of the tort swallowing up other areas of law that govern interferences with intangible property, such as the law on inducing a breach of contract, the law on third party liability for assisting a trustee to commit a breach of trust, and the law on intellectual property.[85]

(2) Lord Nicholls' 'If cheques, why not debts?' argument does not stand up. As Amy Goymour has painstakingly explained,[86] when D is held liable to C in conversion for the face value of a cheque that he has misapplied and which was either (a) drawn on C's bank account or (b) drawn in C's favour, it is often very difficult to say that D is really being held liable in such a case for misappropriating a right of C's. Where the cheque was (a) drawn on C's bank account, the cheque represented not a right of C's to draw on his bank account but (if anything) a right that someone else had to draw on C's bank account. Where the cheque was (b) drawn in C's favour, if the cheque was a gift to C, it will confer 'no right on [C to be paid the sum on the cheque], but merely a power to be paid the relevant sum.'[87] The cheque cases can be more easily explained: (i) as straightforward conversion cases where C sues D for the actual loss he has suffered as a result of D's misappropriating a physical asset (the paper cheque) which was in C's possession or which C had an immediate right to possess;[88] or (ii) as disguised unjust enrichment cases where C is allowed to sue D for money that D has unjustly obtained at C's expense (even though that money never technically belonged to C).[89]

(3) We will see that under the law on intellectual property, someone who innocently infringes another's copyright or patent or trade mark cannot be sued for compensatory damages.[90] If the minority's position in *OBG* had been adopted, no such defence of innocent infringement would be available to someone who converted another's contractual rights. It is not clear why a contractual right (such as a right to be paid a debt, as in *OBG*) should be given greater protection than a right in relation to intellectual property.

---

[84] [2008] 1 AC 1, at [321].
[85] See Goymour 2011, at 80.
[86] Goymour 2011, at 74 and 77.
[87] Goymour 2011, at 77.
[88] Goymour 2011, at 74–75, and 77.
[89] Lord Hoffmann's analysis at [2008] 1 AC 1, [103]–[104]; and ultimately Goymour 2011's as well, at 83–6.
[90] See below, § 15.6(C).

(4) If it were thought desirable or important to allow some remedy to OBG for having their rights to sue for money owed to it thrown away by their receivers, it was not necessary to reform the law of conversion to do it. The law on the liability of receivers could have been reformed instead, perhaps by analogy to the law on the liability of administrators of an estate who transfer assets to the wrong person.

15.6 Defences

Now that we have looked at the different ways in which someone might commit a tort in respect of personal property, we will now list some of the defences that a defendant who is being sued for committing such a tort might try to take advantage of. We begin with conversion.

A. Conversion

Conversion's nature as a tort of strict liability, and the fact that virtually any kind of dealing with another's goods is capable of amounting to conversion, means that a lot of defences to being sued for conversion have had to be recognised by the courts to prevent this tort operating in a perverse and socially disruptive way.

(1) *Consent.* This is an obvious point which requires little amplification: a claimant cannot argue that a defendant committed the tort of conversion by interfering with property in her possession or which she had an immediate right to possess if she consented to the property being interfered with in the way it was.

(2) *Animals Act 1971.* This authorises the occupier of land in certain cases to detain or destroy animals which trespass on his land. For example, s 7 gives the occupier of land powers to detain livestock trespassing on his land, and eventually to sell the livestock if no one has claimed it back. Section 9 allows an occupier of land to kill someone else's dog on his land if the dog was worrying the occupier's livestock and killing the dog was the only reasonable means of protecting the livestock.

(3) *Distress damage feasant.* If an *inanimate* item of property belonging to A is on B's land without permission and is causing damage to B's land or disrupting the operation of B's business on that land, B will be allowed: (a) to take steps to move that item of property so that it no longer causes any damage or disruption, and then (b) to detain it until A fairly compensates him for the damage or disruption caused by the presence of that item of property on his land.[91] This remedy is known as 'distress damage feasant'.[92]

(4) *Recaption.* It used to be the case that if A's property was on B's land, A would be entitled in certain circumstances to go onto B's land and recover his property. But any such power has now been abolished in English law by virtue of the Tribunals, Courts and Enforcement Act 2007.[93]

---

[91] See, for example, *The Ambergate, Nottingham and Boston and Eastern Junction Railway Company* v *The Midland Railway Company* (1853) 2 E & B 793, 118 ER 964.

[92] The remedy of distress damage feasant also used to be available when an animal of B's strayed onto A's land and caused damage or destruction: see, for example, *Sorrell* v *Paget* [1950] 1 KB 252. But s 7(1) of the Animals Act 1971 provided that the 'right to seize any animal by way of distress damage feasant is hereby abolished'.

[93] Section 65 and Sch 12.

(5) *The Police and Criminal Evidence Act 1984.* Section 19 of the 1984 Act gives a constable who is lawfully on any premises the power to seize goods that he reasonably thinks have been obtained through the commission of an offence, or that he reasonably thinks amount to evidence relevant to some offence, if he reasonably thinks it is necessary to do so to prevent the goods 'being concealed, lost, damaged or destroyed'.

(6) *Returning goods.* If A has B's goods and B has an immediate right to possess those goods, A will of course do no wrong if he returns the goods to B. What if A gives the goods to a third party, C, with instructions to return them to B? A will be allowed to do this so long as it is *reasonable* to give the goods to C for the purpose of returning them to B.

In *Elvin & Powell Ltd* v *Plummer Roddis Ltd* (1934), a conman approached the claimants – a firm of coat makers – and ordered about £350 worth of coats, asking them to be delivered to the defendants' shop. The coats were sent and the conman sent a telegram to the defendants in the claimant company's name, saying 'Goods despatched to your branch in error. Sending van to collect.' When the coats arrived at the defendants' shop, the conman turned up in a van and took the coats from them. He then disappeared. The claimants sued the defendants, claiming that they had committed the tort of conversion in handing the coats over to the conman. The claim was rejected – the defendants had only handed the coats to the conman because they wanted to return them to the claimants and it had been reasonable for them to hand the coats over to the conman for the purpose of returning them to the claimants.

This defence was not available to the defendants in *Hiort* v *Bott* (1874). In that case, the claimants mistakenly sent the defendants an invoice for barley together with a delivery order. The defendants had not in fact ordered any barley from the claimants but the invoice stated that the defendants had ordered the barley through one G. The defendants got in touch with G. He said there had been a mistake and asked them to endorse the delivery order to him so that he could have the barley delivered to the customer who actually ordered it. This the defendants did. G then used the delivery order to obtain the barley himself and absconded with it. The claimants sued the defendants, claiming that the defendants, in endorsing the delivery order, had committed the tort of conversion. The court agreed: the defendants had delivered the barley into G's hands without the claimants' consent and they had no lawful justification or excuse for doing so. They could not argue that they had delivered the barley into G's hands in order to return it to the claimants as the barley was already in the claimants' hands at the time they signed the delivery order.

(7) *The principle in Hollins v Fowler.* In *Hollins* v *Fowler* (1875), Blackburn J argued:

> I cannot find it anywhere distinctly laid down, but I submit to your Lordships that on principle, one who deals with goods at the request of the person who has the actual custody of them, in the bona fide belief that the custodier is the true owner, or has the authority of the true owner, should be excused for what he does if the act is of such a nature as would be excused if done by the authority of the person in possession . . . Thus a warehouseman with whom goods had been deposited is guilty of no conversion by keeping them, or restoring them to the person who deposited them with him, though that person turns out to have had no authority from the true owner.[94]

---

[94] (1875) LR 7 HL 757, 766–7.

So if *Thief* steals *Owner*'s dog and, pretending to *Pound* that the dog is his, asks *Pound* to look after the dog over the weekend, *Pound* will not commit the tort of conversion in relation to *Owner* if *Pound* gives the dog back to *Thief* at the end of the weekend.[95] Again, suppose *Thief* steals *Owner*'s painting and, pretending that the painting is his, hands it over to *Agent* so that she can find a buyer for it. If *Agent* cannot find a buyer and hands the painting back to *Thief*, she will not commit the tort of conversion in relation to *Owner* in so doing.[96]

(8) *Common currency.* In the interests of ensuring the smooth running of the economy, the law provides that someone who accepts stolen money paid over to him as common currency will not be liable for conversion: 'Conversion does not lie for money, taken and received as currency . . .'[97] So if *Thief* steals some money out of *Owner*'s wallet he will commit the tort of conversion. But if *Thief* takes that money and uses it to pay for some goods in *Supermarket* using that money, *Supermarket* will not commit the tort of conversion in accepting that money.

B. Trespass to goods

In the case where A has directly interfered with B's goods, many of the defences set out in the previous section may operate to prevent B suing A for committing a trespass to goods. Two further defences are worth mentioning.

(1) *Wheel clamping.* Under the common law, it used to be the case that clamping someone's car that had been parked on your land would not amount to a trespass provided you gave them sufficient warning that it would be clamped: in such a case, you could argue that they had consented to your clamping their car, or at least that they had voluntarily taken the risk that their car would be clamped.[98] However, this position has now been reversed by statute: s 54 of the Protection of Freedoms Act 2012 provides that:

1. A person commits an offence who, without lawful authority –
   (a) immobilises a vehicle . . .
   intending to prevent . . . the removal of the vehicle by a person otherwise entitled to remove it.
2. The express or implied consent . . . of a person otherwise entitled to remove the vehicle to the immobilisation, movement or restriction concerned is not lawful authority for the purposes of subsection (1).

---

[95] What would be the position if *Thief* instructed *Pound* at the end of the weekend to give the dog to *Third Party*? Would *Pound* commit the tort of conversion in relation to *Owner* if she handed the dog over to *Third Party*? The Privy Council's decision in *Maynegrain Pty Ltd* v *Compafina Bank* (1984) 58 ALJR 389 could be read as suggesting that the answer is 'no'. However, that case may rest on technicalities of the law of agency which do not apply in *Pound*'s case.

[96] *Marcq* v *Christie's* [2004] QB 286. There is an issue as to whether *Hollins* v *Fowler* goes even further and says that if *Agent* found a *Buyer* for the painting, she would not be liable for conversion if she sold and delivered the painting to *Buyer*. According to the terms of the principle in *Hollins* v *Fowler*, she should not be liable, but that may be pushing the principle too far.

[97] *Lipkin Gorman* v *Karpnale Ltd* [1991] 2 AC 548, 559 (per Lord Templeman). For similar reasons, the law provides that a bank that accepts a stolen cheque will not be liable in conversion so long as it acted in good faith and without negligence in accepting the cheque: Cheques Act 1957, s 4.

[98] See *Arthur* v *Anker* [1997] QB 564 and *Vine* v *Waltham Forest LBC* [2000] 1 WLR 2383 (driver who parked car and did not see sign warning that vehicles might be clamped because it was obscured did not voluntarily take risk that it might be clamped).

(2) *Trivial touching.* In *White* v *Withers* (2009), Ward LJ suggested that it was arguable that a trivial touching of another's goods that was 'acceptable in the ordinary conduct of daily life'[99] would not amount to a trespass to goods.[100] Even if it did, such a trespass would not give rise to a claim for anything more than nominal damages and a claim for such damages could be struck out as an abuse of process.[101]

C. Intellectual property torts

When it comes to torts in respect of intangible property, there are no specific defences applying to the tort of passing off; and the defences that might be available to a defendant who would otherwise be held liable for committing the tort of inducing a breach of contract are dealt with below.[102] Torts involving B's infringing A's intellectual property rights are, in principle, strict liability torts. But the unfairness that this can cause is mitigated by the facts that: (1) a defendant who has infringed on someone else's patent or registered design right will have a defence if he can show that he did not know, and had no reason to know, his conduct was infringing on the claimant's rights;[103] and (2) a defendant who has infringed a claimant's copyright in a work by copying that work will have a defence to being sued for *compensatory* damages if he 'did not know, and had no reason to believe, that copyright subsisted in [that] work'.[104] A further defence that applies in copyright cases and which has no analogue elsewhere in the field of property torts is the defence of 'fair use' or 'fair dealing' which – in the interests of promoting freedom of speech – allows a text like this to quote from other texts for the purpose of comment or criticism, so long as the quotations are not too extensive and no more than is required for the purpose for which we are quoting from the other text.[105]

15.7 Remedies

When one of the torts considered in this chapter is committed, the standard tort remedies of compensatory damages to compensate for losses caused by the tort, and an injunction to prevent the tort being committed again (where there is a real risk of that happening), will be available.[106] Disgorgement damages – damages designed to make the tortfeasor

---

[99] Quoting Robert Goff LJ in *Collins* v *Wilcock* [1984] 1 WLR 1172, 1178.
[100] [2009] EWCA Civ 1122, at [59]–[61].
[101] [2009] EWCA Civ 1122, at [61]. Sedley LJ seemed to agree at [72].
[102] § 20.2.
[103] Patents Act 1977, s 62(1); Registered Designs Act 1949, s 9.
[104] Copyright, Designs and Patents Act 1988, s 97(1).
[105] Copyright, Designs and Patents Act 1988, s 30.
[106] If B refuses to hand over goods to which A has an immediate right of possession, the courts have the power to order B specifically to hand those goods over to A under s 3(2)(a) of the Torts (Interference with Goods) Act 1977; but this is a power they will normally only exercise where the goods are of special value to A such that damages would not be an adequate remedy. If A could easily purchase a substitute on the open market, then B will normally be allowed to keep A's property and pay A its market value instead. See *Whiteley Limited* v *Hilt* [1918] 2 KB 808, 819 (per Swinfen Eady J); *IBL Ltd* v *Coussens* [1991] 2 All ER 133, 137 (per Neill LJ) and *Tanks and Vessels Industries Ltd* v *Devon Cider Company Ltd* [2009] EWHC 1360 (Ch), [55]–[56]. Specific restitution of goods was ordered in relation to a quantity of steel in *Howard E Perry & Co Ltd* v *British Railways Board* [1980] 1 WLR 1375, at a time when widespread industrial action meant that steel was hard to obtain.

surrender a gain made as a result of committing a tort – and licence fee damages – damages designed to make the tortfeasor pay a reasonable sum for the fact that he has committed the tort – will also be available in respect of the torts considered in this chapter.[107]

However, a very unusual remedy applies in conversion cases where the claimant who is suing in conversion has *not* recovered the property that has been converted. In such a case the claimant can sue for the market value of the property that was converted (as well as con-sequential compensatory damages for any further losses that he has suffered as a result of his property being converted) without having to prove that the defendant's tort actually caused him to lose his property. For example, consider the following case:

> *Thief* steals *Owner*'s car, who then sells it to *Gullible* for £4,000 (a fair price). *Gullible* drives the car for six months and then sells it to *Innocent* for £3,000 (a fair price). *Innocent* subsequently crashes the car and it is written-off.

In this situation, *Thief, Gullible* and *Innocent* have all committed the tort of conversion in relation to *Owner. Thief* has done so twice – first by stealing *Owner*'s car, and then by handing it over to *Gullible. Gullible* has also converted *Owner*'s car twice – first by accept-ing the car from *Thief* and then by handing it over to *Innocent. Innocent* has only con-verted the car once – by accepting it from *Gullible. Innocent*'s crashing the car does not amount to conversion as he did not do that intentionally.

As *Owner*'s car is irrecoverable, *Owner* will be able to sue *anyone* who has converted that property for *market value* damages equal to the value of the property at the time it was converted. Lord Nicholls attempted in *Kuwait Airways Corpn* v *Iraqi Airways Co (Nos 4 & 5)* (2002) to argue that *market value damages* are really compensatory in nature:

> The fundamental object of an award of damages in respect of this tort, as with all wrongs, is to award just compensation for loss suffered. Normally ('prima facie') the measure of damages is the market value of the goods at the time the defendant expropriated them. This is the general rule, because generally this measure represents the amount of the basic loss suffered by the defendant. He has been dispossessed of his goods by the defendant. Depending on the circumstances some other measure, yielding a higher or lower amount, may be appropriate.[108]

It is debatable whether this is true.[109] For example, in the case we are considering *Gullible* could argue that he has not really done anything to add to the loss suffered by *Owner* as a result of having his car stolen by *Thief* – so why should he be liable to pay *Owner* either £4,000 (the value of the car at the time *Gullible* received it from *Thief*) or £3,000 (the value of the car at the time *Gullible* passed it on to *Innocent*)? However, Lord Nicholls argued in the *Kuwait Airways* case that *Gullible*'s liability to pay market value damages to *Owner* is really compensatory because his wrong in converting *Owner*'s car lies in his *not giving the car back to Owner*: 'By definition, each person in a series of conversions

---

[107] See below, Chapter 25.
[108] [2002] 2 AC 883, at [67].
[109] For a full discussion of the basis of the right to sue for the price of the goods in conversion cases, see Tettenborn 1993.

wrongfully excludes the owner from possession of his goods. This is the basis on which each is liable to the owner.'[110] And had *Gullible* given the car back to *Owner*, either at the time he received it from *Thief* or at the time he passed it on to *Innocent*, *Owner* would have received an asset worth £4,000 or £3,000 respectively.

Whatever the basis of a converter's liability to pay the victim of his tort market value damages (in a case where the converted property has not been restored to the claimant), it is clear that in this case, *Owner* will be entitled to sue: (i) *Thief* for £4,000 (the value of the car at the time it was stolen, or handed over to *Gullible*); *or* (ii) *Gullible* for £4,000 (the value of the car at the time *Gullible* received it) or £3,000 (the value of the car at the time *Gullible* handed it over to *Innocent*); *or* (iii) *Innocent* for £3,000 (the value of the car at the time *Innocent* received it). If *Owner* sues *Thief* and recovers £4,000, his title to sue *Gullible* and *Innocent* for conversion will then be extinguished. The idea is that by recovering £4,000 from *Thief*, *Owner*'s title to the car subsequently received by *Gullible* and *Innocent* is retrospectively extinguished.[111]

The ability of a claimant in a conversion case to recover the market value of his property (provided he has not in the meantime recovered the property)[112] can create complications. For example, suppose that in the above situation, when *Gullible* received the car from *Thief*, he improved it and sold it to *Innocent* for £6,000, which was a fair price. In this situation, if *Owner* is allowed to sue *Gullible* for *market value damages* equal to the value of *Owner*'s car at the time it was sold to *Innocent* (£6,000), this would be unfair on *Gullible*. He will not receive any return for the work he did improving *Owner*'s car. To avoid this happening, s 6 of the Torts (Interference with Goods) Act 1977 provides that the damages payable to *Owner* in respect of *Gullible*'s converting *Owner*'s car by handing it over to *Innocent* will be reduced to £4,000.

Further reading

The law on when interfering with personal tangible property will amount to a tort is so thick with complication and confusion that only the most confident academics dare to write about them. Numbered among these intrepid souls are **Peter Birks ('Personal property: proprietary rights and remedies' (2000) 11** *King's College Law Journal* 1), **Andrew Tettenborn ('Damages in conversion – the exception or the anomaly?' (1993) 52** *Cambridge Law Journal* 128, and **'Trust property and conversion: an equitable confusion' (1996) 55** *Cambridge Law Journal* 36), **Sarah Green ('Understanding the wrongful interference actions' (2010) 74** *Conveyancer and Property Lawyer* 15), **Simon Douglas ('The nature of conversion' (2009) 68** *Cambridge Law Journal* 198), and **Graham McBain ('Modernising and codifying the law of bailment' [2008]** *Journal of Business Law* 1).

We have only faintly skimmed the surface of intellectual property law in this chapter. Those wishing to read more about it should consult one of the many excellent texts

---

[110] [2002] 2 AC 883, at [82].

[111] Torts (Interference with Goods) Act 1977, s 5.

[112] In which case he is confined to suing for the actual loss suffered by him as a result of the defendant's act of conversion: see *BBMB Finance (Hong Kong) Ltd* v *Eda Holdings Ltd* [1990] 1 WLR 409.

available on that subject. However, the details of intellectual property law can be quite dry, and readers might want to look elsewhere for insights into the battles around intellectual property law, particularly over film piracy and drug development. For such readers, we can warmly recommend: **James Bessen and Michael J. Meurer's** *Patent Failure* **(Princeton, 2009)**, **Marcia Angell's** *The Truth About Drug Companies* **(Random House, 2005)**, **Lawrence Lessig's** *Free Culture* **(Penguin, 2005)**, and **Michael Heller's** *The Gridlock Economy* **(Basic Books, 2008)**. **Sir Hugh Laddie's 'The insatiable appetite for intellectual property rights' (2008) 61** *Current Legal Problems* **401** is an entertaining tour of the more egregious abuses of intellectual property law in recent years. **Sarah Worthington** carefully examines the value of intellectual property law in **'Art, law and creativity' (2009) 62** *Current Legal Problems* **168. Henry C. Mitchell** is worth reading on the moral arguments for intellectual property law in his *The Intellectual Commons* **(Lexington Books, 2005)**.

Chapter 16
Defamation

Aims and objectives

Reading this chapter should enable you to:

(1) Understand what a claimant has to prove in order to sue a defendant in defamation.

(2) Understand the significance of whether a claim in defamation against a defendant is brought in libel or slander.

(3) Understand in what circumstances a defendant will be able to raise a defence against a claim brought against him in defamation.

(4) Get a good idea of what changes the recent Defamation Act 2013 has made to this area of law, and what further reforms might be desirable in this area.

16.1 The basics

Some torts are very unsocial in nature. The trespass torts and the tort of invasion of privacy (which we will be discussing in a couple of chapters' time) are based on, and give effect to, a right 'to be left alone'. By contrast, defamation is a social tort. It seeks to protect the valuable relationships we have with other people from being interfered with by third parties telling damaging lies about us. At the same time, defamation is a tort that constantly threatens to work in an anti-social way. There are two reasons for this.

First, defaming other people is something that is very easy to do, and something we do all the time. Whenever you say something negative about someone else, you are in danger of defaming them; and very few of us adhere to the maxim, 'If you can't say something nice about someone, say nothing.'[1] Secondly, it is very often very important that people be

---

[1] A maxim that was given a very human twist by President Theodore Roosevelt's daughter, Alice Roosevelt Longworth: 'If you haven't got anything nice to say about anybody, come sit next to me.'

allowed to say negative things about other people. We need to be able to tell other people that their politicians are corrupt; that their role models have feet of clay; that their prospective employees are incompetent or dishonest; that their friends and lovers are disloyal; that the medicine they are taking has dangerous side effects; that the hotel they are planning to stay at is horrible.

So if the law of defamation were allowed unbounded sway over our lives, it would potentially make tortfeasors of all of us, and severely limit our abilities to tell each other what we need to know. But it does not. The courts have long limited the reach of the law of defamation by allowing defendants who are sued for defamation a variety of defences: principally, *truth* ('What I said was substantially true'); *honest opinion* (formerly known as 'fair comment') ('I was only expressing my honest opinion'); and *privilege* ('What I said is protected under the law from being the object of a defamation claim, either because of *where* I said it (in court, in Parliament) or because of the person *to whom* I said it (because had what I said been true, it would have been my duty to tell her, or it would have been to our mutual advantage for me to tell her) or because of *what* I said (because saying what I did was in the public interest)').

Despite this, the law of defamation continues to be the subject of criticism. Taking their cue from Article 10 of the European Convention of Human Rights which provides that,

1. Everyone has the right to freedom of expression. This right shall include freedom to hold opinions and to receive and impart information and ideas without interference by public authority and regardless of frontiers . . .
2. The exercise of these freedoms, since it carries with it duties and responsibilities, may be subject to such formalities, conditions, restrictions or penalties as are prescribed by law and are necessary in a democratic society . . . for the protection of the reputation or rights of others . . .

critics argue that the law on defamation exercises an unacceptable 'chilling effect' on freedom of expression, not only here, but across the world. The main charges laid against the law of defamation run as follows:

(1) *Ease of suit.* It is argued, first, that it is just too easy in England and Wales to threaten someone who is saying something critical about you that you will sue them for defamation. Of course, you might not win your case: the defendant may be able to establish that what he said was not actually defamatory, or raise a defence to your claim. But that is not the point. If A is thinking of saying something critical about B, the fact that it would be so easy for B to respond to A's attack by threatening to sue him for defamation might well lead A to censor himself and avoid saying anything critical about B. No one could blame A for preferring a quiet life to the possibility of years of litigation, even if those years of litigation ended in success for A.

(2) *Abuses of the right to sue.* We began by saying that the law of defamation protected our relationships with other people from being damaged by third parties telling damaging lies about us. However, claims for defamation are not always brought with the intention of preserving the claimant's status in the eyes of other people.

In some cases, the claimant has not suffered any serious harm as a result of the defendant's words, but still brings a claim with the twin object of punishing the defendant for daring to say something negative about the claimant, and warning other people not to take similar liberties. If the defendant's words were published in permanent form (and therefore amounted to a *libel*), the law makes it very easy for the claimant to bring such a punitive claim against the defendant: in a libel case, the claimant can sue even if the defendant's words caused him no loss at all.

In other cases, the claimant is not even a human being. The claimant is a company, or some other organisation enjoying legal personality. The law of defamation allows 'artificial legal persons' to sue in defamation to protect their business reputation where they stand to suffer serious financial loss as a result of their reputation being unjustly besmirched. However, there is evidence that the law of defamation is now being abused by companies (particularly drug companies)[2] and other organisations to suppress criticism of the company or organisation's activities. Particularly worrying is the case of *British Chiropractic Association* v *Singh* (2011), where an article in the *Guardian* newspaper criticised the claimant association for associating itself with claims that chiropractic (manipulation of the spine) could cure a range of childhood illnesses. The claimant association chose to sue the *writer* of the article, but *not* the *Guardian*, for libel. As the Court of Appeal commented:

11. It is now nearly two years since the publication of the offending article. It seems unlikely that anyone would dare repeat the opinions expressed by Dr Singh for fear of a writ. Accordingly this litigation has almost certainly had a chilling effect on public debate which might otherwise have assisted potential patients to make informed choices about the possible use of chiropractic . . .

12. By proceeding against Dr Singh, and not the *Guardian*, and by rejecting the offer made by the *Guardian* to publish an appropriate article refuting Dr Singh's contentions, or putting them in a proper perspective, the unhappy impression has been created that this is an endeavour by the BCA to silence one of its critics . . .[3]

Although – as we will see – the claim in the *Singh* case was dismissed (the defendant, it was held, could take advantage of the defence of fair comment (now known as 'honest opinion')),[4] the Court of Appeal felt itself unable to dismiss the claim simply on the basis that it amounted to an abuse of the right to sue: 'if that is where the current law of defamation takes us, we must apply it.'[5]

(3) *Forum shopping/Libel tourism.* The courts will strike out claims for defamation as an abuse of process if they do not think that they have been brought with the serious intention of vindicating the claimant's reputation *in England*.[6] In order to satisfy this requirement, the claimant will have to show that there has been a substantial publication of material defaming the claimant in England.[7] However, the advent of the Internet has made this requirement much easier to satisfy. Defamatory statements that have been posted on the Internet from anywhere in the world are automatically available to view in England. Books that have been printed somewhere else in the world may be ordered by people living in England via Amazon or other book websites.

So a claimant who has been libelled by a defendant in the United States may no longer have to look to the US courts for a remedy. Instead, he may be able to bring a claim in England, on the basis that there has been a substantial publication of the defendant's statement in England.[8] The key advantage to suing in England, as opposed to the United States,

---

[2] See 'Anger at bid to silence heart op whistleblower' *Daily Mail*, 26 February 2009; and 'Danish scientist sued by drug firm under British libel laws to counterclaim' *The Guardian*, 16 February 2010.

[3] [2011] 1 WLR 133.

[4] Discussed below, § 16.8.

[5] [2011] 1 WLR 133, at [12].

[6] 'England' is used here and below as shorthand for 'England and Wales'.

[7] *Jameel (Yousef)* v *Dow Jones & Co* [2005] QB 946.

[8] Though there is *no* presumption that a statement posted on the Internet has been substantially published in England: *Al-Amoudi* v *Brisard* [2007] 1 WLR 113.

is this: in 1964, the US Supreme Court ruled in a case called *New York Times* v *Sullivan* that the constitutional guarantees for freedom of expression contained in the First Amendment to the US Constitution required that a public figure not be allowed to sue a defendant for defamation unless the defendant made his statement maliciously; that is, knowing that his statement was not true or having no positive belief in its truth. Public figures suing for defamation in England are not subject to the same disability: they may be able to sue a defendant in England for defamation even if the defendant honestly believed what he was saying about them was true. So a public figure in the United States who wants to sue for defamation will now try to 'forum shop' and look to bring her claim in England, rather than in the United States. However, if he or she is allowed to do this, the law of defamation will not only have a negative impact on freedom of speech in England; it will also impact on freedom of speech in the United States.

There are two significant controls on the ability of defamation claimants to engage in 'forum shopping' (or what is often called 'libel tourism'). The first we have already mentioned: the claimant has to show that there has been a substantial publication of defamatory material in England, giving him a legitimate interest in seeking to vindicate his reputation in England. If there has been no such substantial publication, his claim may be struck out on the ground that it amounts to an *abuse of process.*[9]

The second control arises where the claimant seeks to sue for defamation a defendant who lives outside the European Union. In such a case, the courts may decline to hear the claimant's case on the ground of *forum non conveniens* – in other words, on the basis that another jurisdiction provides a more appropriate forum for the claimant's case to be heard.[10] However, it is not clear whether this control adds anything to the first control. In other words, if a claimant has shown that a substantial publication of defamatory material has occurred within England, it is not clear whether the courts will *ever* decline to hear the claimant's case on the basis that there is another jurisdiction that provides a more appropriate forum for the case to be heard.[11]

(4) *Wealth.* The law of defamation, it is argued, only benefits the very wealthy, who can afford the substantial costs of bringing a defamation claim, and can afford to take the risk of being held liable for the other party's costs if they lose their claim. If this is right, then the law of defamation operates in asymmetric fashion. The *benefits* of having a law of defamation – in terms of being able to vindicate one's reputation – are mainly reserved for the very wealthy. On the other hand, the *costs* of having a law of defamation – in terms of

---

[9] Discussed further below, § 16.4(10).

[10] If the claimant is suing a defendant *who lives in the European Union* for committing a tort in England, the courts here cannot decline to hear the case on the ground of *forum non conveniens* (though they may still strike it out as an abuse of process): *Shevill* v *Presse Alliance* [1995] 2 AC 18, [1996] AC 959.

[11] See, for example, *Berezovsky* v *Michaels* [2000] 1 WLR 1004 (English courts held to be most appropriate forum to vindicate Russian businessman's reputation from being impugned by *Forbes* magazine, in an issue 800,000 copies of which were sold in the United States and only 2,000 of which were sold in England), and *King* v *Lewis* [2004] EWCA Civ 1329 (statements were posted on a California-based website accusing an American boxing promoter of being anti-semitic because he accused a New York-based lawyer who was conducting litigation against the promoter in New York of being a 'shyster lawyer' and otherwise showed disrespect towards this lawyer at Yom Kippur; held, the English courts were the most appropriate forum to hear the promoter's claim for defamation!).

chilling effects on freedom of expression, as well as increases in the price of newspapers – are borne by all of us. Why, it may be asked, should we *all* pay for an area of law that only the very wealthy really benefit from?

Two counter-arguments can be made to this. It could be argued, first, that we have no interest in reading untrue stories in the newspapers. So we all benefit from the check that the law of defamation puts on newspapers that might otherwise be tempted to rush into print with untrue and damaging stories. Secondly, it could be argued that the existence of conditional fee agreements (otherwise known as 'no win, no fee' agreements) do provide some access to justice for individuals who cannot afford legal representation out of their own pocket. So it is not true to say that it is only the very wealthy who can take advantage of the law of defamation.

Whether these counter-arguments work is a very difficult question. In relation to the first, it is not at all clear whether the public would be better or worse informed by a press operating under no constraints from the law of defamation. An unchecked press would give the public access to more information than it has at the moment – but it is uncertain what the quality of that information would be. In the absence of any evidence one way or the other, it is hard to say whether the law of defamation does help to ensure that the public is better informed than it would be in the absence of such a law.

In relation to the second argument, it should be borne in mind that a law firm will only take on a client on a conditional fee basis if there is a more than 50% chance of their winning their case. A lot of defamation cases are not so clear that either side can be confident that they have a more than a 50% chance of winning, and so the possibility of entering into a conditional fee agreement will not assist a claimant who is not very well off in a lot of defamation cases. Moreover, even if a claimant is able to find a law firm willing to take on his case, the firm – if it wins the claimant's case – will be allowed to deduct from the claimant's damages a 'success fee', which is basically designed to help the firm cover the costs of representing claimants in all the cases that it *didn't* win. So if the damages that the claimant stands to win are quite modest, the prospect of having some of those damages go into his lawyer's pockets may well make the claimant think that it is not worth his while to sue.

It seems, then, that the only way to make remedies in defamation readily accessible to ordinary claimants – other than through huge increases in publicly funded legal aid schemes, which is never going to happen[12] – is through cost regimes that markedly increase the chilling effects that the law of defamation has on freedom of expression.[13] Given this, it seems there may be no way of making remedies in defamation accessible to ordinary people at acceptable cost.

(5) *Vindication.* It is questionable how much even those who are wealthy enough to be able to take advantage of the law of defamation actually benefit from its existence. The

---

[12] The European Court of Human Rights' decision in *Steel and Morris* v *UK* (2005) 41 EHRR 22 (to the effect that, in the famous *McLibel* case, the defendants' rights to freedom of expression under Art 10 of the European Convention on Human Rights were violated as a result of their not being given sufficient publicly funded assistance to equalise the 'inequality of arms' between them and the corporate claimants in that case) seems to have been completely ignored by the UK government.

[13] For example, a 'one way costs shifting' regime – under which a claimant is encouraged to sue by being assured that if he loses his case, he will not have to bear any of the other side's costs, while if he wins, he can recover all his costs from the other side – would make it easier to sue newspapers for defamation, but in doing so might unacceptably infringe on freedom of expression.

main difficulty arises out of one of the features of the law of defamation that makes it so ease to bring a claim under it – in order to sue a defendant successfully in defamation, a claimant does not actually have to prove that what the defendant said about him was untrue. All the claimant has to do, to launch his claim, is show that the defendant said something derogatory about him – and then it is up to the defendant, if she wishes, to defend the claim by showing that what she said about the defendant was true. So if a claimant wins a defamation case, that is not necessarily because a court has found that what the defendant said about the claimant was untrue; it may be because it has not been proven, to the court's satisfaction, that what the defendant said about the claimant was true. So winning a defamation claim can just mean the allegations about the claimant were – in Scottish legal terms – 'not proven'. But 'not proven' does not provide much satisfaction to a claimant who wants to be able to say he was 'not guilty'.

What vindication for his reputation a claimant can get from winning a defamation claim tends to rest on the size of the damages he is awarded. The more unfounded the allegation, the greater the damages – or so the thinking goes. However, such thinking tends to inflate the amount of damages awarded in defamation cases, which again enhances its chilling effect on freedom of expression. Moreover, vindicating people's reputations through awards of damages tends to mean that defendants in defamation cases are held *strictly liable* to pay substantial amounts of money to successful defendants. If damages are being awarded in defamation cases simply to mark the fact that the claimant's reputation has been unjustly traduced, then it is irrelevant whether the defendant was at fault or not for damaging the claimant's reputation. But this can create injustices in cases where a defendant innocently and perfectly reasonably said something that had the effect of making the claimant look bad. In such cases, a defendant can now make an 'offer to make amends' to the claimant and thereby avert a defamation claim.[14] But the offer must be adequate, and include an offer to compensate the claimant. So even the option of making an 'offer to make amends' involves the defendant being made monetarily worse off for acting perfectly reasonably.

The charge sheet against the law of defamation is a heavy one and it is one that has impelled the UK Parliament to reform it. On 1 January 2014, the Defamation Act 2013 came into force. While the Act was hailed by the government as bringing in 'a new era of libel law that protects freedom of expression and encourages open and honest public debate, while protecting those who feel their reputations have been attacked', the reality is that the Act does not do very much to bring about fundamental change in the law of defamation.

For example, s 1 of the Act seeks to deal with the 'ease of suit' problem posed by the law of defamation by providing that 'A statement is not defamatory unless its publication has caused or is likely to cause serious harm to the reputation of the claimant.' However, this will do little to discourage the touchy and affronted from threatening to sue other people for defamation; and do nothing to encourage those who are subjected to such threats that they have nothing to worry about. Section 9 seeks to deal with the problem of 'forum shopping' (or 'libel tourism') by providing that in a case where the defendant does not live in the European Union, a British court will not 'have jurisdiction to hear [the claimant's case] unless the court is satisfied that, of all the places in which the statement complained of has been published, England and Wales is clearly the most appropriate

---

[14] Defamation Act 1996, s 2. See below, § 16.11(D).

place in which to bring an action in respect of the statement.' However, this is much the same standard as the one the courts apply already in determining whether they should decline to hear a defamation case on the ground of *forum non conveniens*.[15]

While the Defamation Act 2013 may not do much to affect the substance of the law of defamation, it will have a big impact on the language in which defamation cases are conducted: what was formerly known as the defence of 'justification' has been renamed the defence of 'truth'; the defence of 'fair comment' has become 'honest opinion'; and what was known as the defence of 'qualified privilege under the *Reynolds* test' has become, simply, a defence of 'publication on a matter of public interest'. In this chapter, we will adopt all the changes of terminology introduced by the 2013 Act, while also introducing readers to the old terms used by the pre-2014 cases so that they can make sense of those cases and their relevance now that the 2013 Act is in force.

16.2 What is defamatory?

In order to sue a defendant in defamation, a claimant has to show three things. He has to show that:

1. the defendant *published* to a third party . . .

2. . . . a statement that *referred to* the claimant . . .

3. . . . and that statement was *defamatory* of the claimant.

The third requirement is the most fundamental, and yet the most ill-defined.[16] As we have seen, s 1(1) of the 2013 Act now provides that 'A statement is not defamatory unless its publication has caused or is likely to cause serious harm to the reputation of the claimant.' This is a negative definition – it defines what is *not* defamatory, rather than what *is* – but is likely in future to be turned into a positive definition, so that a statement *will* be regarded as defamatory if, and only if, its publication has caused or is likely to cause serious harm to the reputation of the claimant.

Parliament incorporated a requirement of 'serious harm' into the definition of what is defamatory in order to protect people's rights of freedom of speech under Article 10 of the European Convention on Human Rights. Allowing claims to be made in defamation for trivial slights (such as calling a claimant 'hideously ugly'[17] or the 'worst tennis player in the world'[18]) amounts to a disproportionate interference with freedom of expression:

---

[15] In the Consultation Paper accompanying the Bill, the government expressed the view (at [85]) that the emphasis in what was then clause 7 of the Bill on '*all* the places where the statement . . . has been published' (emphasis added) will 'overcome the problem of courts readily accepting jurisdiction simply because a claimant frames their claim so as to focus on damage which has occurred in this juridiction only. This would mean that, for example, if a statement was published 100,000 times in Australia and only 5,000 times in England that would be a good basis on which to conclude that the most appropriate jurisdiction in which to bring an action in respect of the statement was Australia rather than England.' In this example, there are 20 publications in Australia for every one in England. But in *Berezovsky* v *Michaels* (above, n 11) there were *400* publications in the US for every one in England, and yet the House of Lords still accepted jurisdiction.

[16] See *Berkoff* v *Burchill* [1996] 4 All ER 1008, 1019: 'Defamation has never been satisfactorily defined. All attempted definitions are illustrative. None of them is exhaustive' (per Millett LJ).

[17] *Berkoff* v *Burchill* [1996] 4 All ER 1008.

[18] *Dee* v *Telegraph Media Group Ltd* [2010] EWHC 924 (QB).

the harm done by allowing such claims outweighs the good. However, the requirement that a statement cause, or have the potential to cause, 'serious harm' to the reputation of the claimant before it can be regarded as defamatory is not free from difficulties, and is likely to add to the cost and complexity of defamation cases. For example, consider the review of an actress' performance in a TV series that gave rise to a defamation claim in *Cornwell* v *Myskow* (1987): 'she can't sing, her bum is too big and she has the sort of stage presence that jams lavatories.' The claimant successfully argued that this was defamatory. Whether nowadays a court would say that the above statement was liable to cause 'serious harm' to her reputation is anyone's guess.

While the 2013 Act may be taken as providing a new definition of what does, and what does not, count as a defamatory statement, a number of points from the pre-2014 law of defamation on what does, and does not, count as being defamatory are likely to remain highly relevant.

(1) *Right-thinking people.* Under the pre-2014 law, a statement would only be regarded as defamatory if it would have made *right-thinking* people think less well of the claimant, or to treat the claimant less well than they otherwise would have done.[19] It is likely that this requirement will be read into the 2013 Act, so that it will be interpreted as requiring that a claimant show that a statement about the claimant caused or was likely to cause the claimant serious harm to his or her reputation *in the eyes of right-thinking* people.

So, for example, suppose *Prim* is a teetotaller but *Journo* wrote that he saw *Prim* drinking a pint of lager in a pub at the weekend. *Journo*'s statement will not be defamatory of *Prim* – a right-thinking person who read *Journo*'s statement about *Prim* would not think any the worse of *Prim* as a result. However, it would be different if *Prim* was well known to be a mentor working for Alcoholics Anonymous to help other alcoholics avoid drinking. In such a case, a right-thinking person who read *Journo*'s statement would tend to think that *Prim* was a hypocrite and would tend to think less well of *Prim* as a result. On these facts, then, it might be that *Journo*'s statement was defamatory of *Prim*, provided that she could establish that making her out to be a hypocrite had caused, or was likely to cause, serious harm to her reputation.

Again, suppose that *Drunk* calls *Beauty* 'a fat, syphilitic slag' after she turns him down for a date. Even before the 2013 Act, *Drunk*'s statement was not regarded as defamatory: the courts took the view that words of abuse were not defamatory if they were uttered and heard as such.[20] As Lord Atkin observed in *Sim* v *Stretch* (1936): 'exhibitions of bad manners or discourtesy are [not to be] placed on the same level as attacks on character.'[21] The reason is presumably that if a right-thinking person heard *Beauty* being abused by *Drunk*, he would realise that *Drunk*'s words were being uttered in anger and would therefore not take them seriously.[22] A right-thinking person would not then be led to treat *Beauty* any less well because of *Drunk*'s words. Of course, *Beauty* would be rightly and mightily offended by *Drunk*'s words – but the mere fact

---

[19] See, for example, *Thornton* v *Telegraph Media Group* [2010] EWHC 1414 (QB), at [91].

[20] *Penfold* v *Westcote* (1806) 2 B & P (NR) 335, 127 ER 656; *Fields* v *Davis* [1955] CLY 1543.

[21] *Sim* v *Stretch* [1936] 2 All ER 1237, 1242.

[22] For the same reason, Handley & Davis 2001 argue that 'words are not defamatory if they are spoken in a context where it is clear that they are in jest'. It is not clear whether the English courts would accept this. If they did not, comedians' freedom of expression would be seriously interfered with: almost all satirical depictions of public figures would be defamatory and *prima facie* actionable.

that someone has said something offensive about you does not bring your case within the law of defamation.[23]

(2) *Adverse treatment.* Under the pre-2014 law, it had long been accepted that the law of defamation was not only concerned (i) to protect people against being thought *less well of* by other people, but also (ii) to protect people against being *treated less well* (than they otherwise would have been) by other people. This meant that before the 2013 Act came into force, *Charity Worker* could sue *Newspaper* in defamation for saying that she had contracted leprosy.[24] While such an allegation would obviously not cause anyone to think less well of *Charity Worker*, it might well make people steer clear of her, or – in the language of the cases – to *shun and avoid* her.

But what is the position now? Recall that s 1(1) of the 2013 Act provides that 'A statement is not defamatory unless its publication has caused or is likely to cause serious harm to the *reputation* of the claimant' (emphasis added). Does that mean *Charity Worker* can no longer sue *Newspaper* in defamation? The answer is 'no'. The courts have taken the position that s 1 of the Defamation Act 2013 was not intended fundamentally to change the definition of what amounts to a defamatory statement, but was simply intended to place a *limit* on when someone could sue another for defamation.[25] So in *Charity Worker*'s case, the main concern of the courts would be to determine how much of an impact *Newspaper*'s allegations about her had had on her life; they would not be too concerned about *how* that impact had occurred.

For the same reason, we think that s 1(1) of the 2013 Act has not affected the pre-2014 position that a statement that exposes a claimant to ridicule by right-thinking people will be defamatory[26] – though such a claimant would have to show that they have suffered, or are likely to suffer, 'serious harm' as a result of being exposed to such ridicule. For example, in *Berkoff* v *Burchill* (1996), the majority of the Court of Appeal accepted that the journalist Julie Burchill's calling the writer–director–actor Steven Berkoff 'hideously ugly' *might* have been defamatory on the basis that it might have made 'him an object of ridicule.'[27] Nowadays Berkoff would not only have to show that Burchill's deriding his looks was liable to make him an object of ridicule in the eyes of right-thinking people, but also that he had suffered, or was likely to suffer, serious harm as a result of being made such an object of ridicule.

(3) *Procedure.* The case of *Berkoff* v *Burchill* illustrates an important point of procedure that has to be borne in mind in reading defamation cases. Between 1792 – when Fox's

---

[23] Though see *Youssoupoff* v *MGM Pictures Ltd* (1934) 50 TLR 581 (discussed, Treiger-Bar-Am 2000), where it was held that it would be defamatory to suggest in a film about the life and death of the Russian monk Rasputin that the claimant had been *raped* by Rasputin, even though it is hard to imagine right-thinking people doing anything but treating the claimant with sympathy on hearing such a statement.

[24] See *Youssoupoff* v *MGM Pictures Ltd* (1934) 50 TLR 581, at 587 (per Slesser LJ): 'not only is the matter defamatory if it brings the [claimant] into hatred, ridicule, or contempt by reason of some moral discredit on [the claimant's] part, but also if it tends to make the [claimant] be shunned and avoided and that without any moral discredit on [the claimant's] part. It is for that reason that persons who have been alleged to have been insane, or be suffering from certain diseases, and other cases where no direct moral responsibility could be placed upon them, have been held to be entitled to bring an action to protect their reputation and their honour.'

[25] *Lachaux* v *Independent Print Ltd* [2016] QB 402, at [46]

[26] *Parmiter* v *Coupland* (1840) 6 M & W 105, 108; 151 ER 340, 341–2.

[27] [1996] 4 All ER 1008, at 1018 (per Neill LJ); also at 1021 (per Phillips LJ).

Libel Act allowed civil claims to be brought for defamation – and 2014, parties to a defamation case had a right to have their case heard by a jury. In a case where a jury was used to hear the claim, it was for the jury to decide whether the words complained of *were* defamatory; the judge could only decide whether the words complained of *were capable of being* defamatory. That was the issue at stake in *Berkoff* v *Burchill*: whether calling Steven Berkoff 'hideously ugly' was *capable* of defaming him. The majority accepted that it was; but it was then for a jury to decide whether Julie Burchill's statement was *actually* defamatory. This point of procedure is now only of historical importance; though it is still, as we have said, important in making sense of the caselaw on what is, and what is not, defamatory. Section 11 of the 2013 Act abolishes the right to elect to have a defamation case heard by a jury.[28]

(4) *Business/professional defamation.* It has long been accepted that a statement casting aspersions on the way a business is run will be defamatory of the business if the effect or likely effect of that statement is to harm that business' credit or custom.[29] Likewise, it has also long been accepted that it is defamatory to cast aspersions on someone's skill or competence in practising a particular trade that is their profession.[30]

Section 1(2) of the 2013 Act has now modified the first of these rules. It provides that 'harm to the reputation of a body that trades for profit' will not count as 'serious harm' for the purposes of establishing that a statement is defamatory under s 1(1) the harm to the body's reputation 'has caused or is likely to cause the body serious financial loss'. So a statement casting aspersions on the way a business is run will be defamatory of the business if, and only if, the effect or likely effect of that statement is to harm that business' credit or custom, and in so doing cause that business serious financial loss.

The rules governing claims for defamation by businesses or professionals are very difficult to apply. In the case of a business, the law draws a distinction between: (i) damaging a business by casting aspersions on the quality of its goods or services; and (ii) damaging a business by casting aspersions on the way it is run. Only (ii) is capable of giving rise to an action for defamation.[31] A business that suffers (i) will only be able to sue if they can show the defendant's words amounted to *malicious falsehood*.[32] However, in a case where a defendant has criticised a business' goods or services as being no good, it is often difficult to determine whether the defendant's criticism carries with it a criticism of the way the business is run; after all, if the business was run well, its goods or services would normally be good.

The same difficulty afflicts cases of professional defamation. In *Drummond-Jackson* v *BMA* (1970), the British Medical Journal published a serious scientific paper casting doubt on the safety of a particular method of administering anaesthetic during dental procedures that had been developed by the claimant. The claimant sued for defamation. Lord Denning MR wanted to dismiss the claim on the ground that the paper merely

---

[28] There is a residual discretion vested in the courts to allow a defamation case to be heard by a jury, but it is hard to imagine it will ever be exercised: see *Yeo* v *Times Newspapers Ltd* [2014] EWHC 2853 (QB).

[29] *South Hetton Coal Company Ltd* v *North-Eastern News Association Ltd* [1894] 1 QB 133.

[30] *Drummond-Jackson* v *British Medical Association* [1970] 1 WLR 688, 698-9: 'words may be defamatory of a . . . professional man. . .if they impute lack of qualification, knowledge, skill, capacity, judgment or efficiency in the conduct of his . . . professional activity' (per Lord Pearson).

[31] *South Hetton Coal Company Ltd* v *North-Eastern News Association Ltd* [1894] 1 QB 133, 139.

[32] For discussion of this tort, see below, § 20.9.

criticised the claimant's *technique*, not him *personally*. However, the majority disagreed on the ground that 'A professional man's technique is . . . relatively permanent, and it belongs to him: . . . if [a dentist] use a bad technique, he is a bad dentist'.[33] It is not, however, defamatory to say of a professional person that they carry on their trade in one way rather than another if it would be legitimate for them to carry on their trade in either of those ways; so it is not defamatory to say that McBride & Bagshaw's *Tort Law* provides readers with a broad overview of the law of tort, even if the authors of that work are aiming to produce something more substantial.[34]

(5) *Bane and antidote.* In determining whether a particular statement is defamatory, regard must be paid to the context in which the statement was published, and in particular anything that was said together with the statement to neutralise or counter-act any adverse effect that it might otherwise have had.[35] And in determining whether an admittedly defamatory statement is likely to cause the claimant to suffer 'serious harm' for the purposes of s 1 of the Defamation Act 2013, regard must be had to anything that might have been said *after* the statement was made that might have neutralised or mitigated the damaging effect of the statement.[36]

(6) *The repetition rule.* Suppose *Gossip* said to *Ear*, '*Rumour* thinks/*Rumour* told me that *Jerry* is a thief'. In such a case, it will be *conclusively presumed* that a right-thinking person who heard or read *Gossip*'s statement would have concluded that *Jerry was* a thief. This rule of law is known as the 'repetition rule'.

The repetition rule applies even if it would have been clear to a right-thinking person who heard or read *Gossip*'s statement that *Gossip* was not necessarily endorsing *Rumour*'s opinion of *Jerry* – as would be the case if *Gossip* qualified his statement by saying that 'Of course, I have no way of knowing myself whether or not *Jerry* is a thief, but . . .'[37] It follows that *Gossip*'s statement in the above case *will* be defamatory of *Jerry* – it will be conclusively presumed that a right-thinking person who heard or read *Gossip*'s statement would have concluded from it that *Jerry* was a thief and would as a result have thought less well of *Jerry*.

A similar rule applies if *Accuser* said to *Ear*, 'I think *Jerry* is a thief'. Again, it will be conclusively presumed that a right-thinking person who heard or read *Accuser*'s statement would have concluded from it that *Jerry* was a thief and would therefore have thought less well of *Jerry*. It will therefore be conclusively presumed that *Accuser*'s statement was defamatory of *Jerry* – and this is so even if a right-thinking person who heard or read *Accuser*'s statement could actually have been expected to think, 'Well, *Accuser* thinks *Jerry* is a thief, but his opinion is not necessarily correct and I should wait to make up my own mind about *Jerry* instead of just blindly going along with *Accuser*'s opinions.'

Similarly, if *Suspicious* said to *Ear*, 'I have reasonable grounds to suspect *Jerry* of being a thief', it will be conclusively presumed that a right-thinking person who heard or read

---

[33] [1970] 1 WLR 688, 698 (per Lord Pearson).

[34] *Thornton v Telegraph Media Group Ltd* [2010] EWHC 1414 (QB) (not defamatory to say of a writer that she does not write to the standards of a professional journalist).

[35] *Charleston v News Group Newspapers Ltd* [1995] 2 AC 65 (newspaper headline that might have been taken as suggesting that two soap opera stars were involved in a pornographic computer game rendered non-defamatory by story below the headline, which explained that the makers of the game had used the stars' likenesses without their permission).

[36] *Cooke v MGN Ltd* [2015] 1 WLR 895.

[37] *Stern v Piper* [1997] QB 123.

Suspicious's statement would have concluded from it that there *were* reasonable grounds to suspect *Jerry* of being a thief and would have thought less well of *Jerry* as a result.[38] So, again, it will be conclusively presumed that *Suspicious*'s statement was defamatory of *Jerry* – and this is so even if a right-thinking person who heard or read *Suspicious*'s statement could actually have been expected to think, 'Well, *Suspicious* may think he has reasonable grounds to believe that *Jerry* is a thief – but what does he know? I should make up my own mind and judge *Jerry* on the evidence presented to me.'

(7) *Innuendo.* The case where *Journo* has said that he saw *Prim* drinking a pint of lager in a pub, but *Prim* works as a mentor for Alcoholics Anonymous is an example of a statement that is defamatory because it gives rise to an *innuendo* that is defamatory of *Prim*. A genuine innuendo case is where a defendant makes a statement that is innocent on its face, but would make a right-thinking person *who was possessed of certain special knowledge* think less well of the claimant. So *Journo*'s statement that he saw *Prim* drinking in a pub is totally innocent on its face, but would still make a right-thinking person think less well of *Prim* if *she knew that Prim worked as a mentor for Alcoholics Anonymous.*

In an innuendo case, the claimant can only sue the defendant if she can establish that the defendant's statement was published to one or more people who were actually possessed of the special knowledge that would make a right-thinking person who heard or read the claimant's statement think less well of the claimant. So, to take a well-known example, suppose that A said to B that he saw C coming out of a particular house the other day. Suppose further that that house happened to be a brothel. So a right-thinking person who knew the house in question was a brothel would, on hearing A's statement, tend to think less well of C as a person – he would tend to think that C used prostitutes. C will only be able to sue A for what he said to B if B *knew* that the house A said he saw C was coming out of was a brothel. Note that, so far as C is concerned, that is *all* he has to show in order to sue A for defamation. He does *not* have to show that B concluded from A's statement that C used prostitutes. He does not even have to show that B believed A's statement. All he has to show is that B had the knowledge that would make a right-thinking person who heard or read A's statement think less well of B.[39]

(8) *The single meaning rule.* Some statements are ambiguous. Suppose that A tells B that C 'made D an offer he couldn't refuse' in order to persuade D not to accept a job that one of C's clients wanted. A's statement might be taken as implying that: (i) C threatened to kill D if he took the job. But it might equally well be taken as implying that: (ii) C made D a really generous offer of alternative employment that meant D would have been crazy to accept the original job offer.

In defamation cases, the courts will not accept that statements are ambiguous in this kind of way. They are committed to the idea that *every statement has a single meaning* in the mind of a right-thinking person.[40] So if C sues A for defamation in the case we are discussing, the task of the judge deciding C's case is to discover what *single meaning* a

---

[38] *Shah* v *Standard Chartered Bank* [1999] QB 241.

[39] *Cassidy* v *Daily Mirror Newspapers Ltd* [1929] 2 KB 331 (defamatory of claimant to publish photograph of her husband with another woman with a caption saying that the man in the photo was engaged to that woman, because someone who knew claimant would infer that claimant was a liar in passing herself as married to the man in the photo, and at least one person who knew claimant had seen the photo and its caption).

[40] *Slim* v *Daily Telegraph* [1968] 2 QB 157, 172 (per Diplock LJ).

right-thinking person would have given to A's statement. Would a right-thinking person have taken A as saying (i) or (ii)? Of course, determining the answer to this question is impossible – a right-thinking person would have been uncertain what A's words meant. One might as well toss a coin to see which single meaning a right-thinking person would have ascribed to A's words. Even the courts acknowledge that the 'single meaning rule' is 'highly artificial',[41] 'the product of an accident of history resulting in a fiction that assumes that the reasonable man will understand a particular statement in only one way.'[42] However, it seems that the courts are stuck with the rule: it is too well-established to be swept away by the judges. They have, however, refused to extend it to other torts,[43] such as the tort of malicious falsehood.[44]

16.3 Reference to the claimant

Sometimes a statement is obviously defamatory, but there is an issue over whether the statement can be said to refer to the claimant. Two classes of statement need to be distinguished in this context.

A. Statements not intended to refer to the claimant

This sort of statement will be defamatory of the claimant if:

(a) a right-thinking person who *knew of the claimant and her circumstances* would have, on hearing or reading the statement in question, thought that it referred to the claimant and would, as a result, have tended to think less well of the claimant; *and*

(b) the statement in question was published to one or more people *who thought that it referred to the claimant.*

If (a) *and* (b) are true then the statement in question will be defamatory of B even though it was not intended specifically to refer to B. The question of whether a statement that was not intended specifically to refer to the claimant is defamatory of the claimant tends to come up in two contexts: (1) *mistaken identity* cases; and (2) *defamation of a class* cases.

(1) *Mistaken identity cases.* In *E Hulton & Co v Jones* (1910), the *Sunday Chronicle* carried an article describing a motor festival at Dieppe. The article featured described various figures who attended the festival including one 'Artemus Jones'. He was described as being a 'churchwarden at Peckham'. The article alleged that while he was at the festival he had consorted with a woman who was not his wife and that he was, in general, 'the life and soul of a gay little band that haunts the Casino and turns night into day, besides betraying a most unholy delight in the society of female butterflies'.

The claimant was a barrister called Artemus Jones. He sued the defendants, the publishers of the *Sunday Chronicle*, for libel. His claim was successful. It was found that friends of the claimant had seen the article in question and thought it referred to the

---

[41] *Bonnick* v *Morris* [2003] 1 AC 300, at [21] (per Lord Nicholls).
[42] *Ajinomoto Sweeteners SAS* v *Asda Stores Ltd* [2011] QB 497, at [40] (per Rimer LJ).
[43] *Ajinomoto Sweeteners SAS* v *Asda Stores Ltd* [2011] QB 497.
[44] Discussed below, § 20.9.

claimant. Moreover, it was found that a right-thinking person who knew the claimant would have thought, on reading the article, that it referred to him and would have tended as a result to think less well of him as a person. The fact that the claimant was a barrister and not a churchwarden at Peckham did not affect the issue. No doubt the fact that the claimant and the person referred to in the article shared such a distinctive name as Artemus Jones played a large part in the finding that a right-thinking person who knew the claimant would have thought on reading the article in question that it referred to him.[45]

(2) *Defamation of a class.* Suppose we wrote in this text, 'All law students are dishonest'. Could you sue us for libel? The answer is 'no'. No court would find that a right-thinking person who read the above statement would think that it applied to you, and would have tended as a result to think less well of you.[46] Why is this? The answer is that generalisations always admit of exceptions and a right-thinking person who read the above statement would not think that it applied *without exception* to *all* law students, including you.[47] It would be different if we said that, 'All the clerks who work at the Supreme Court are extremely lazy.' There are very few such clerks (one or two per Supreme Court Justice) – so our statement could be taken by a right-thinking person as applying to every single clerk employed at the Supreme Court, without exception.

So in *Knupffer* v *London Express Newspaper Ltd* (1944), an article which accused members of the 'Young Russia' party of being willing to help Hitler by building up a pro-German movement within the Soviet Union was held not to be defamatory of the claimant, who was the head of the British branch of the 'Young Russia' party. The accusations against members of the 'Young Russia' party contained in the article were far too generalised to make it reasonable to think that they applied to the claimant in particular. By contrast, in *Riches* v *News Group Newspapers Ltd* (1986), allegations that members of the Banbury CID (a police unit) had raped a woman were held to be defamatory of *all* of the members of the Banbury CID given how small the unit was.

B. Statements intended to refer to the claimant

Sometimes a defendant will make a statement that is intended to refer to the claimant, but does not specifically identify the claimant as the person being referred to. An example of the sort of statement we have in mind here is provided by a Rod Liddle article in

---

[45] See also *Newstead* v *London Express Newspaper Ltd* [1940] 1 KB 377 (claimant defamed by newspaper's account of a trial for bigamy because it referred to accused as 'Harold Newstead, thirty-year-old Camberwell man' and claimant (who was not on trial) fitted that very specific description) and *Morgan* v *Odhams Press Ltd* [1971] 1 WLR 1239 (story falsely claiming that girl had been kidnapped by members of a gang was defamatory of claimant, who had been seen with girl in time period where newspaper alleged she had been kidnapped).

[46] *Eastwood* v *Holmes* (1858) 1 F & F 347, 349, 175 ER 758, 759: '[If] a man wrote that all lawyers were thieves, no particular lawyer could sue him unless there was something to point to the particular individual' (per Willes J).

[47] See Lord Atkin's remarks in *Knupffer* v *London Express Newspaper Ltd* [1944] AC 116, 122: 'The reason why a libel published of a large or indeterminate number of persons described by some general name generally fails to be actionable is the difficulty of establishing that the claimant was, in fact, included in the defamatory statement, for the habit of making unfounded generalisations is ingrained in ill-educated or vulgar minds, or the words are occasionally intended to be a facetious exaggeration.'

The Sunday Times on 22 January 2006, describing a visit to Goodison Park to watch his team Millwall play Everton:

> My abiding memory of the Millwall midweek FA Cup replay at Everton was . . . of an incalculably dense, porky little Hitler of a Merseyside copper yapping out orders from astride his horse: 'Come on, keep up, keep up. Shut your mouth. Don't answer back. Do as you're . . . told.' And so on, interminably, throughout the duration of our five mile forced march from the football ground to Liverpool Lime Street station (where, incidentally, most of us did not want to go).'

Would the policeman who *actually did* escort the Millwall fans from Goodison Park to the railway station on horseback be entitled to sue Rod Liddle for defamation on the basis that Rod Liddle intended to describe *him* as being a 'dense, porky little Hitler of a Merseyside copper'? Or would the policeman have to show – in line with the approach adopted in cases where a statement was *not* intended to refer specifically to the claimant – that: (ii) a right-thinking person *who knew the claimant and knew of his circumstances* would have thought that the description 'densy, porky little Hitler of a Merseyside copper' applied to the claimant and would have thought less well of the claimant as a result; and (ii) the article was published to one or more people who thought that it referred to the claimant?

So far as we know, the question has not really been addressed by the courts. However, we think in principle that the policeman that Rod Liddle intended to refer to in his article should have been able to sue for defamation (subject to defences, of course) without having to establish that (i) and (ii) were true. The fact that a claimant has not been referred to by name by the defendant should not prevent him suing for defamation where he was the very person that the defendant was intending to refer to.[48]

16.4 Publication to a third party

If B wants to sue A for defamation, B will have to show that A *published* a statement that was defamatory of him to a *third party*. So, obviously, if A said *to B*, 'You are a liar and a cheat', B will not be able to sue A for defamation: A's statement was not published to a third party.

This simple requirement of publication to a third party conceals a host of difficulties, which we will now explore.

(1) *Spouses.* If A tells his wife, 'B is a liar and a cheat', B will not be able to sue A for defamation. The reason is that the courts will *not* find that A's statement in this case was published to a *third party.*[49] The courts' attitude is a throwback to the days when a husband and wife were regarded as having a common identity. While we have, of course, abandoned the idea that a husband and wife share a common identity, the courts still seem to think that someone who makes a defamatory statement to his or her spouse does not publish that statement to a third party.

---

[48] In *Jameel (Yousef)* v *Dow Jones & Co Inc* [2005] QB 946, the Court of Appeal said at [45] that: 'Where a common name is included in an article, the name itself will not suffice to identify any individual who bears that name.' However, it is submitted that this *dictum* is intended to apply only in cases where the article was *not* specifically intended to refer to the claimant.

[49] *Wennhak* v *Morgan* (1888) 20 QBD 635. The same rule will apply, of course, if a wife tells her husband something that is defamatory of another.

(2) *Secretaries.* If A dictates a letter to his secretary saying that 'B is a liar and a cheat', B may be able to sue A even if the letter is never sent. (Though there may be an issue whether s 1(1) of the 2013 Act is satisfied in B's case given that the letter was never sent.) A will have published the defamatory statements contained in the letter to a third party, namely his secretary. But if A's secretary hands back the letter to A for checking, B will not be able to sue *the secretary*. The reason is that the re-publication to A of something that A has already told his secretary will not be regarded as a publication to a third party.[50] It would be different, of course, if the secretary showed or sent the letter to someone other than A or B – in that case, B may well be able to sue the secretary for libel.

(3) *Misunderstanding.* It seems to be generally acknowledged that if A made a statement to C that was defamatory of B, A will not be held to have published that statement to a third party if C did not understand what A said because, for example, he was deaf or illiterate.

(4) *Private notes.* Suppose that A wrote down on a piece of paper 'B is a liar and a cheat' and locked the piece of paper in a desk drawer. Suppose further that C, a burglar, subsequently broke into the desk drawer and read the piece of paper. B will not be able to sue A for libel.[51] A did not publish the defamatory material to C: he did not show C the piece of paper or allow him to read it.

(5) *Unintended recipients.* If A sent a letter to B that said 'You are a liar and a cheat' and C opened the letter and read it, the courts will not hold that A published the letter to C *unless* it was *reasonably foreseeable* when A sent the letter that it would be opened and read by someone like C.[52]

(6) *Shops.* If a shop sells a newspaper or a book containing a defamatory statement, it seems that the shop will not be held to have published that statement to the person buying the book unless it knew or ought to have known that the newspaper or book in question contained a defamatory statement.[53] Such a shop would, in any case, be covered by the defence of 'innocent dissemination'.[54] But *dicta* of Eady J seem to indicate that the shop would not need to take advantage of such a defence as it could not be held in the first place to have published the defamatory statement to the purchaser of the book or newspaper.[55]

(7) *Internet search engines.* In *Metropolitan International Schools Ltd v Designtechnica Corporation* (2009), Eady J held that a company (such as Google) that administers an internet search engine will not publish to someone using that engine any defamatory statements that the searcher comes across in using that search engine. This is so even if the company knows that conducting a particular search will bring up results that contain defamatory

---

[50] *Eglantine Inn Ltd v Smith* [1948] NI 29, 33.

[51] *Pullman v Hill & Co* [1891] 1 QB 524, 527.

[52] *Pullman v Hill & Co* [1891] 1 QB 524 (letter sent to claimants' firm alleging that they had obtained money by false pretences published to third party, the clerk who opened the letter, because it was foreseeable someone like him would open and read the letter); *Huth v Huth* [1915] 3 KB 32 (letter to claimant alleging that her children were a product of an affair not published to third party butler who read the letter as it was not foreseeable that someone like him would read it); *Theaker v Richardson* [1962] 1 WLR 151 (letter to claimant alleging that she was a prostitute and ran a brothel published to third party, the claimant's husband, because it was foreseeable he would read the letter).

[53] *Emmens v Pottle* (1885) 16 QBD 354, 357 (per Lord Esher MR).

[54] Discussed below, § 16.11(A).

[55] *Bunt v Tilley* [2007] 1 WLR 1243, at [21]-[23]; *Metropolitan International Schools Ltd v Designtechnica Corporation* [2009] EWHC 1765 (QB), at [49].

statements about a claimant. The reason is that the company is not responsible for those statements coming up in response to a particular search: they have no control over what results will be yielded by a particular search.

(8) *Platforms.* What is the position if A posted the statement 'B is a liar and a cheat' on some premises which were owned or run by C? In such a case, the courts will hold that C – as well as A – published the statement to the people who read it *if* a reasonable person would think that C *approved* of the posting up of that statement. The fact that C failed to take the statement down, after having had a reasonable opportunity to do so, will entitle a reasonable person to think that C approved of the posting up of the statement, thus making C a publisher of A's statement.[56]

This 'platform principle' – so-called because in the above example, C has provided a 'platform' for A to post up his statement about B – has been applied by the courts to hold that a company which hosts a blogging site might be held to have published defamatory statements posted on a blog maintained on that site if the company failed to take reasonable steps to take those statements down after it was alerted to their existence.[57] It is difficult to see how the 'platform principle' applies in this kind of case. A reasonable person who came across a defamatory statement on a blog hosted by company X would have no basis for thinking that X approved of the posting of that statement because he or she would have no way of knowing whether or not X had been given a reasonable opportunity to take that statement down.

(9) *Printers.* We saw above that a shop that sells a book or newspaper that contains a defamatory statement will not be held to have published that statement to the purchaser of the book or newspaper if they did not know, and had no reason to know, that the book or newspaper in question contained a defamatory statement. The rule seems to be different for the printer of the book or newspaper: the printer will be held to have published to the reader of the book or newspaper any defamatory statements in the book or newspapers whatever the printer's level of knowledge about those statements.[58]

(10) *Abuse of process.* The courts reserve the power to strike out a claim in defamation if they take the view that the claimant has no legitimate interest in bringing that claim. This will be the case, the Court of Appeal laid down in the key case of *Jameel (Yousef) v Dow Jones & Co Inc* (2005) if the defamatory publications that have occurred in England do not amount to a 'real and substantial tort'.[59] Where those publications have caused minimal damage to the claimant's reputation, the courts will strike out the claimant's claim for damages on the basis that 'the game [of suing for defamation] will not be worth the candle' in terms of the cost of litigating the case and tying up the courts' time in hearing

---

[56] See *Byrne* v *Deane* [1937] 1 KB 818. A poem suggesting that the claimant had told the authorities about some illegal gambling machines in a golf club run by the defendants (with the result that the machines were removed) was posted up on the walls of the golf club. The poem was held to have been published by the defendants to whoever read the poem because there was some sign that they approved of its being posted up – the defendants had had the power to take the poem down, but none of them had. However, no claim could be made against the defendants because the poem was held not to be defamatory because a right-thinking person who read the poem would think the claimant was to be congratulated on upholding the law.

[57] *Tamiz* v *Google Inc* [2013] EWCA Civ 68.

[58] However the printer may be able to take advantage of the defence of innocent dissemination: see below, § 16.11(A).

[59] [2005] QB 946, at [70].

the case.[60] It may be that now that a claimant in a defamation case has to show – under s 1 of the Defamation Act 2013 – that the defamatory statement was likely to cause him 'serious harm' that there will be fewer cases in the future where a claimant's claim is struck out as an abuse of process: all such cases can now be struck out under s 1 instead.[61]

(11) *The multiple publication rule.* Under s 4A of the Limitation Act 1980, a claimant who wishes to sue a defendant for publishing a defamatory statement about him has to bring his claim within one year of the moment he was first entitled to sue for that publication. (As we will see in the next section, where the publication was in permanent form – and thus *libel* – the claimant is entitled to sue from the moment of publication. Where the publication is in impermanent form – and thus *slander* – the claimant is normally only entitled to sue from the moment the publication first causes him harm.)

Under the 'multiple publication rule', *every* time a defamatory statement was published, a fresh cause of action arose and the claimant had a year from the moment that cause of action arose to bring a claim. The rule went back to the case of *The Duke of Brunswick* v *Harmer* (1849), where the claimant was allowed in 1848 to sue a newspaper in defamation for an article that it had published in 1830, by the simple device of having one of his employees purchase a back copy of the newspaper and look at the article in question. It was held that the publication to the employee constituted a fresh tort, for which the claimant could sue within the limitation period for suing for defamation.[62]

This rule created difficulties for newspapers that maintain online archives. Application of the rule means that a newspaper could be sued in defamation within a year of someone accessing a defamatory article in an online archive, no matter how old the article might be. (Though it should be noted that if the article defames someone who is now dead, no claim for defamation can be brought by the deceased's estate.)[63] In order to deal with this problem, s 8 of the 2013 Act abolishes the 'multiple publication rule' in favour of a 'single publication rule' under which if a defendant has published a statement to the public that is defamatory of the claimant and that statement has subsequently been re-published in 'substantially the same' form, then the limitation period for suing the defendant for defamation runs from the date of the *first* publication. However, this rule only applies to publications after 1 January 2014,[64] so newspapers are still vulnerable to being sued under the 'multiple publication rule' in relation to newspaper stories that were produced and archived on their websites before that date.[65]

One concern about abolishing the 'multiple publication rule' is that its abolition means that a newspaper has no incentive to take down a defamatory story from its website, even after it has been successfully sued in respect of that story. This is because the fact that someone has seen the story for the first time on the newspaper's website will not – under the 'single publication rule' – give rise to a fresh cause of action against the newspaper. This concern is addressed by s 13 of the 2013 Act, which gives the courts the power to

---

[60] [2005] QB 946, at [57], quoting Eady J in *Schellenberg* v *British Broadcasting Corp* [2000] EMLR 296, 318–9. See also *Mardas* v *New York Times Co* [2008] EWHC 3135 (QB).

[61] See *Ames* v *Spamhaus Project Ltd* [2015] 1 WLR 3409, at [50].

[62] The claim would nowadays be dismissed, either on the basis that the claimant had consented to his employee seeing the defamatory article (see below, § 16.6) or on the basis that the claim amounted to an abuse of process.

[63] Law Reform (Miscellaneous Provisions) Act 1934, s 1(1).

[64] Defamation Act 2013, s 16(6).

[65] Our thanks to Ian Helme, of One Brick Court, who brought this point to our attention.

order a defendant who has lost a defamation case to remove from its website the statement that the claimant was complaining of. However, this is a draconian power that should be used sparingly, as there is a public interest in future researchers being able to find out was said about a particular person, even if what was said was untrue, or was believed to be untrue at the time.[66] It should be sufficient to order a newspaper that has published an article that was the subject of a successful claim for defamation to make a prominent note of the claim, and its success, on the online version of the article.

16.5 Title to sue

Two points need to be made under this heading.

A. Legal personality

Not everyone who is recognised in law as being a person will have a right to sue in defamation.

If the claimant is a *natural person* then there is no problem: a flesh-and-blood person may bring an action for defamation against someone else. The case of *South Hetton Coal Company Ltd* v *North-Eastern News Association Ltd* (1894) establishes that a *company* may be able to sue a defendant for libel or slander if the defendant publishes to another a statement that is defamatory of the company – but only if the statement in question has a tendency to damage the company's trading interests. Section 10(1) of the Trade Union and Labour Relations (Consolidation) Act 1992 provides that a 'trade union is not a body corporate' – so a *trade union* does not enjoy sufficient personality to bring an action for libel or slander in respect of a statement that is defamatory of the trade union.[67]

If A publishes a statement to another that is defamatory of a *public body* – such as a local authority – the public body in question will *not* be entitled to sue A for defamation. This was established by the House of Lords' decision in *Derbyshire County Council* v *Times Newspapers Ltd* (1993). In that case, *The Sunday Times* printed a couple of articles which alleged that Derbyshire County Council had acted improperly in investing funds in its superannuation fund. Derbyshire County Council sued *The Sunday Times* for libel but its claim was dismissed by the House of Lords on the ground that an action for libel could not be maintained by a public body.

The House of Lords admitted that a public body could have a legitimate interest in bringing an action for libel or slander if it were the subject of a defamatory statement. As Lord Keith of Kinkel observed, the making of a defamatory statement about a public body 'might make it more difficult [for the body] to borrow or to attract suitable staff and thus affect adversely the efficient carrying out of its functions'.[68] However, the House of

---

[66] The Duke of Brunswick's suit seems to have been very successful in suppressing the edition of *The Weekly Dispatch* that gave rise to his claim: Stephen Sedley reports that there appears to be no library on either side of the Atlantic that holds of a copy of the relevant edition of *The Weekly Dispatch* ('After Leveson', *London Review of Books*, 11 April 2013).

[67] *EETPU* v *Times Newspapers Ltd* [1980] QB 585. A trade union used to enjoy sufficient legal personality to bring an action for libel or slander: *National Union of General and Municipal Workers* v *Gillian* [1946] KB 81.

[68] [1993] AC 534, 547.

Lords felt that freedom of speech would be unreasonably infringed if the law did not assure people that they could criticise public bodies without fear of being made subject to actions for libel or slander as a result. Lord Keith remarked, 'it is of the highest public importance that a democratically elected governmental body, or indeed any governmental body, should be open to *uninhibited* public criticism. The threat of a civil action for [libel or slander] must inevitably have an inhibiting effect on freedom of speech.'[69]

The House of Lords did *not* go further in the *Derbyshire* case and say that a *politician* would have no right to sue for libel or slander if he felt that some criticism of his conduct in office was defamatory. Indeed, the House of Lords made it clear that if a defendant's criticism of a public body reflected badly on the people running the affairs of that body, those people might well be able to sue the defendant for libel or slander.[70] No doubt this can be explained on the basis that politicians have more of an interest in vindicating their reputation than public bodies do – a politician, after all, has a life inside and outside politics which can be seriously affected by the publication of a defamatory statement about him – and this warrants giving politicians a higher degree of protection from being defamed than the House of Lords was willing to afford to public bodies.

It is now clear that the *Derbyshire* decision extends to *political parties* and that a political party that feels that it has been defamed by some statement made by someone else will not be able to bring an action for libel or slander in respect of that statement;[71] though, of course, if the statement simultaneously defamed a member of that party, he or she might be able to sue for libel or slander.

B. Libel and slander

The law draws a distinction between defamation cases where a claimant is suing for *libel* and cases where a claimant is suing for *slander*. Very roughly speaking, libel involves defaming someone else by publishing a statement to another in *permanent* form. Slander involves defaming someone else by publishing a statement to another in *impermanent* form. In a libel case, the claimant does not have to prove that he has suffered any loss in order to sue the defendant. In a slander case, the claimant normally does have to prove that the defendant's publication caused him loss; if he cannot, his claim for defamation will be dismissed.

So, for example, if A *says* to C, 'B is a liar and a cheat' then that is slander. However, if A sends C a letter saying, 'B is a liar and a cheat', then that is libel. If A dictates a letter to his secretary saying, 'B is a liar and a cheat', that is slander. But if the letter is read out to a third party, that – it seems – will be libel.[72] It is submitted that if A records himself saying, 'B is a liar and a cheat' and then plays the recording back to C, that is libel: A's statement will have been published in a permanent form because it could be replayed.[73]

---

[69] Ibid.

[70] [1993] AC 534, 550.

[71] *Goldsmith* v *Bhoyrul* [1998] QB 459.

[72] *Forrester* v *Tyrell* (1893) 9 TLR 257. However, in *Osborn* v *Thomas Boulter & Son* [1930] 2 KB 226, Scrutton and Slesser LJJ both thought that reading out a defamatory letter to a third party would amount to slander. Greer LJ disagreed.

[73] Though see the discussion in *Youssoupoff* v *Metro-Goldwyn-Mayer Pictures Ltd* (1934) 50 TLR 581 as to whether the tort – if any – committed in playing a film which contained a defamatory statement in its soundtrack would be slander or libel. The Court of Appeal expressed no firm view on the issue – merely saying (at 587) that the statement would be libellous if it served to amplify or explain the visual images presented in the film.

Some statutes provide that certain statements are to be treated as having been published in permanent form. So s 166 of the Broadcasting Act 1990 provides that for 'the purposes of the law on libel and slander . . . the publication of words in the course of any programme included in a programme service shall be treated as publication in permanent form'. So if A gives a speech in a public hall in which he makes various defamatory allegations about B, that will be slander. But if A makes the same speech on radio, that will be libel. Similarly, s 4 of the Theatres Act 1968 provides that, subject to one exception, for 'the purposes of the law on libel and slander . . . the publication of words in the course of a performance of a play shall . . . be treated as publication in permanent form'. Section 7 of the 1968 Act makes it clear that this rule will not 'apply in relation to a performance of a play given on a domestic occasion in a private dwelling'.

A claimant will not always be prevented from suing a defendant for slander if she cannot prove that the defendant's publication caused her loss. There are now two cases where the courts will presume that slander has caused a claimant loss, and will not require the claimant to prove loss as a precondition of allowing her to sue. Loss will be presumed where the defendant's slander suggested: (1) that the claimant had committed a serious criminal offence; *or* (2) that the claimant was no good at her job.[74] It should be noted that in each of these cases, the claimant would find it very difficult to prove that the defendant's slander caused her to suffer loss. This is because the tendency of each of these statements would be to encourage people to 'shun and avoid' the claimant – but it would be very hard for the claimant to demonstrate that but for the defendant's statement, certain people would not have shunned and avoided the claimant.

The courts have addressed the issue of whether the rule that libel victims do not have to prove that they have suffered any loss before they can sue for libel is compatible with Article 10 of the European Convention on Human Rights. In *Jameel (Yousef)* v *Dow Jones & Co Inc* (2005), the Court of Appeal held that the fact that an *individual* could sue for libel without having to prove that the libel had caused him any loss was not incompatible with Article 10 of the ECHR:

> We believe that circumstances in which a claimant launches defamation proceedings in respect of a limited circulation which has caused his reputation no actual damage will be very rare. We reject the suggestion that the fear of such suits will have a chilling effect on the media.[75]

This point has only been made stronger by s 1 of the Defamation Act 2013.

In *Jameel (Mohammed)* v *Wall Street Europe SPRL* (2007), the House of Lords examined whether a *company* that was the victim of a libel should be able to sue in defamation without having to prove that the libel had caused it any loss. The House of Lords ruled that allowing the company to sue without proving that it had suffered any loss was not incompatible with Article 10. The majority of their Lordships in the *Jameel (Mohammed)* case thought that if A wrote that company C was run in a corrupt fashion, requiring C to prove that it had actually suffered loss as a result of A's statement might be too much to ask. Because the natural tendency of A's statement would be to cause people to 'shun and

---

[74] Defamation Act 1952, s 2. It used to be the case that loss would also be presumed where the defendant's slander suggested: (3) that the claimant had a communicable disease (*Bloodworth* v *Gray* (1844) 7 Man & Gr 334, 135 ER 140); *or* (4) that the claimant was unchaste or had committed adultery (Slander of Women Act 1891, s 1). However, these two exceptions to the rule that damage had to be proved in a slander case were abolished by s 14 of the 2013 Act.

[75] [2005] QB 946, at [39].

avoid' C's goods or services, C might find it very difficult to show that certain people who would otherwise have done business with C were put off doing business with C because of A's statement.[76] However, as we have already seen, under s 1(2) of the 2013 Act, a company suing for libel will, at the very least, have to show that the statement of which it complains is likely to cause it serious financial loss.

16.6 Consent

We will now begin to look at the various defences that might be available to a defendant who is being sued for defamation. The first defence is the rarest, but also the most obvious. If a claimant has consented to a defendant's publishing a defamatory statement about him, he cannot subsequently turn round and sue the defendant for defamation on the basis of that publication.[77]

For example, in *Chapman* v *Lord Ellesmere* (1932), a stewards' inquiry held by the Jockey Club found that a horse trained by the claimant was doped when it ran a particular race. The Jockey Club disqualified the horse and 'warned' the claimant off the course where the horse ran. The Jockey Club's decision was published in the *Racing Calendar*, the Jockey Club's official journal. The claimant sued, claiming the publication was defamatory of him. The claimant's claim was dismissed – he had consented to that publication. He was held to have consented to the publication because when he obtained a trainer's licence, he agreed to abide by the rules of the Jockey Club, and one of these rules specified that a decision of the Jockey Club could be published in the *Racing Calendar* if the Jockey Club thought it fit to do so.

Let's now consider the **Desperate Academic Problem**:

Academic – a specialist in the law of defamation and a well-respected member of the Law Faculty at Maxbrook University – had run up some very serious debts, due to his having a gambling problem. Using his knowledge of the law on defamation, he hit on an idea as to how he could get himself out of financial trouble. One day, he told *Student*, whose father was the editor of the *Daily Herald*, that for many years he had been experimenting with having sex with various different kinds of animal, and that he had concluded that goats made the most satisfying lovers. *Student* told his father this, and the *Daily Herald* ran an exclusive the next day explaining that *Academic* was a sexual deviant. In fact, *Academic* had never ever engaged in an act of bestiality. Can *Academic* sue the *Daily Herald* in defamation?

There seems something wrong about allowing *Academic* to sue in this case. He has, after all, entrapped the *Daily Herald* into defaming him. But it is not clear whether the *Daily Herald* could take advantage of any established defence in this case. The most promising

---

[76] [2007] 1 AC 359, at [26] (per Lord Bingham), [97] (per Lord Hope), and at [121] (per Lord Scott).

[77] In *Carrie* v *Tolkien* [2009] EWHC 29 (QB), the claimant was barred from suing a defendant for posting a defamatory statement about the claimant on the claimant's own website. As the claimant could have easily taken the statement down, it was held that the claimant had consented to the publication of the statement by knowingly leaving the statement up on the website.

defence is consent – *Academic* did *want* the *Daily Herald* to print this story (so that he could then sue them for thousands of pounds in damages, thereby digging himself out of his financial hole). However, *Academic* did not *agree* that the *Daily Herald* could print the story about him – and agreement may be necessary to raise a defence of consent to a claim in defamation.

16.7 Truth

Suppose A has published to another a statement that was defamatory of B because a right-thinking person who read or heard A's statement would have thought that *x* was true of B and would as a result have tended to think less well of B. In such a case, A will have a defence if B sues him for libel or slander if he can prove that *x was* true of B. If A could prove this, we used to say that A had a defence of *justification* to B's claim. Section 2 of the 2013 Act has replaced this defence with a defence of 'truth'.[78] The defence of 'truth' is indistinguishable from the old defence of justification, and so all the old cases on justification will continue be relevant to determining the scope of the new defence of 'truth'.

In order to raise this defence (of 'truth'), it will *not* be enough for A to show that his words were *literally* true – he will have to show that the impression a right-thinking person would have gained of B from A's words was a correct one. So suppose A wrote a letter in which he remarked, 'I have heard B is a liar and a cheat'. If B sues A for defamation and A wants to raise a defence of truth to B's claim, it will not be enough for A to prove that *he had actually heard* that B is a liar and a cheat and so the statement in his letter was literally true. Under the repetition rule,[79] it will be conclusively presumed that a right-thinking person who heard or read A's statement would have thought on the basis of it that B *is* a liar and a cheat – given this, if A wants to raise a defence of truth to B's claim, he will have to prove that B *is* a liar and a cheat.

Sometimes there will be some dispute as to what impression a right-thinking person would have gained from hearing or reading a given statement. In *Lewis* v *Daily Telegraph Ltd* (1964), the defendants, the *Daily Mail* and the *Daily Telegraph*, both published front-page reports which alleged that the Fraud Squad was inquiring into the affairs of the claimant, Rubber Improvement Ltd. The claimant sued both newspapers for libel. It was admitted that the reports were defamatory: a right-thinking person who read the reports would have tended to think less well of the claimant as a result. The defendants sought to rely on a defence of justification to defeat the claimant's claim. The issue was: what would the defendants have to prove to raise such a defence? This turned on what impression of the claimant would have been gained by a right-thinking person who heard about or read the reports in the newspapers. The claimant argued that a right-thinking person who heard about or read the reports in question would have concluded from them that the claimant had operated in a dishonest or fraudulent manner – so the defendants would have to prove that the claimant *had* conducted its affairs in a dishonest way if they wanted to rely on a defence of justification to defeat the claimant's claim.

The House of Lords disagreed. At best, a right-thinking person would have concluded from the stories in the defendants' newspapers that the claimant had conducted its affairs

---

[78] Defamation Act 2013, s 2(4): 'The common law defence of justification is abolished . . .'.
[79] See above, § 16.2(7).

in such a way as to give rise to a *suspicion* that it was guilty of some dishonest or fraudulent conduct. As Lord Reid observed – if someone, on reading the stories in the defendants' newspapers had observed 'Oh, if the fraud squad are after these people you can take it they are guilty' a right-thinking person would have rounded on him

> with such remarks as – "Be fair. This is not a police state. No doubt their affairs are in a mess or the police would not be interested. But that could be because [someone] has been very stupid or careless. We really must not jump to conclusions. The police are fair and know their job and we shall know soon enough if there is anything in it. Wait till we see if they [bring charges]. I wouldn't trust [the people involved in this company] until this thing is cleared up, but it is another thing to condemn [them] unheard."[80]

So, in order to establish a defence of justification to the claimant's claim, the defendants did *not* have to show that the claimant had operated its affairs in a dishonest or fraudulent manner; at best, the defendants were required to show that the claimant had operated its affairs in such a way as to give rise to a suspicion that it had acted dishonestly or fraudulently in the way it operated.

A few more points may be made about the defence of truth:

(1) *Substantial truth.* If A has published a statement to another that is defamatory of B, A does not have to prove – for the purpose of raising a defence of truth to any claim B might bring against him for libel or slander – that *every word* of what he said was correct. Section 2(1) of the 2013 Act provides – as did the old law on justification – that it is enough if A can show that what he said was *substantially true*.

So in *Alexander* v *The North Eastern Railway Company* (1865), the defendant railway company reported that the claimant had been convicted of what would now be known as 'fare-dodging' and sentenced either to pay a fine of £9 or serve three weeks' imprisonment. In fact the claimant had actually been sentenced either to pay a fine of £1 or to serve two weeks' imprisonment. The claimant sued the defendants for libel. His claim was dismissed: while the defendants' report was inaccurate in its details, it was at the same time substantially correct – the claimant *had* been convicted of fare-dodging and had been sentenced either to pay a fine or spend time in jail.

(2) *Partial truth.* Sections 2(2) and 2(3) of the 2013 Act provide that in a case where a statement complained of 'conveys two or more distinct imputations':

> If one or more of the imputations is not shown to be substantially true, the defence under this section does not fail if, having regard to the imputations which are shown to be substantially true, the imputations which are not shown to be substantially true do not materially injure the claimant's reputation'.[81]

So suppose A said to someone else, 'B is a rapist and a thief'. Suppose further that B sues A for defamation for saying that he is, one, a rapist, and two, a thief. Suppose finally that A can prove that B is a rapist, but cannot prove that B is a thief. In such a case, A will not

---

[80] [1964] AC 234, 259–60.

[81] The government proposes to repeal this provision (Defamation Bill clause 3(4)) and replace it with the following, substantially identical, provision: 'If [in a case where a claim for defamation is brought in relation to a statement which conveys two or more distinct imputations] one or more of the imputations is not shown to be substantially true, the defence under this section does not fail if, having regard to the imputations which are shown to be substantially true, the imputations which are not shown to be substantially true do not materially injure the claimant's reputation' (Defamation Bill clause 3(3)).

only have a defence of truth to B's claim against her for saying that he is a rapist; A will *also* have a defence of truth under s 2 of the 2013 Act in respect of B's claim against her for saying that B is a thief. Now that it has been established that B is a rapist, A's statement that B is a thief could hardly further injure B's reputation in the eyes of ordinary, reasonable people – B's reputation in those people's eyes will have gone about as low as it possibly could go.

But suppose B simply chooses to ignore A's statement that he is a rapist, and sues A for defamation just for saying that he is a thief. In this case, A will not be able to raise a defence of truth by showing that B is a rapist.[82] However, if B leaves A's claim that he is a rapist unchallenged, he is not likely to be awarded much by way of damages to compensate him for the harm done by A's statement that he is a thief. The courts will take the view that a rapist does not have much of a reputation to lose and therefore suffers little harm if he is unjustly accused of being a thief.[83]

(3) *Criminal conviction*. Suppose A told C, 'B is an arsonist'. In such a case, if B has been convicted for burning down someone's house, A will *normally* be able to raise a defence of truth to any claim for defamation that B might bring against A. A will *not* have to prove that B was rightly convicted of arson: the conviction will be treated in court as conclusive evidence that B *is* an arsonist.[84] *However*, if A made her allegation about B 'with malice' and B's conviction for arson counts as 'spent' under the Rehabilitation of Offenders Act 1974, then A will *not* be able to rely on B's conviction, or what B did to earn that conviction, to raise a defence of truth to B's claim for defamation.[85]

16.8 Honest opinion

English law has long taken the view that people should be free to express their views about other people without fear of being sued for defamation. The work of protecting such people was originally done by the defence of *fair comment*, which operated to protect a defendant from being sued in defamation for making statement S if: (1) S was, on its face, a statement of *opinion* rather than fact; (2) S was on a matter of *public interest*; (3) in making statement S, the defendant 'explicitly or implicitly indicate[d], at least in general terms, the facts on which it [was] based';[86] (4) those facts were true (or, at least, enough of those facts that would be sufficient to support statement S were true); and (5) the defendant honestly believed statement S to be true when he made it.[87]

---

[82] *Polly Peck (Holdings) plc* v *Trelford* [1986] 1 QB 1000.

[83] See *Grobbelaar* v *News Group Newspapers Ltd* [2002] 1 WLR 3024 (£1 awarded in damages to Bruce Grobbelaar, the ex-Liverpool and Southampton goalkeeper, who – it was found – was justifiably accused by the defendant of taking bribes to 'throw' football matches but unjustifiably accused of acting on those bribes and actually throwing football matches).

[84] Civil Evidence Act 1968, s 13(1): 'In any action for libel or slander in which the question whether the claimant did or did not commit a criminal offence is relevant to an issue arising in the action, proof that at the time when that issue falls to be determined, he stands convicted of that offence shall be conclusive evidence that he committed that offence . . .'

[85] Rehabilitation of Offenders Act 1974, ss 4(1), 8.

[86] *Joseph* v *Spiller* [2011] 1 AC 852, at [105].

[87] *Tse Wai Chun* v *Cheng* [2001] EMLR 777, at [41] (per Lord Nicholls, in the Hong Kong Court of Final Appeal); *Joseph* v *Spiller* [2011] 1 AC 852, at [67]–[69] and [108].

The defence of fair comment has now been replaced by s 3 of the 2013 Act with a defence of *honest opinion*.[88] *Like* the defence of fair comment, the defence of honest opinion only protects defendants from being sued for making a defamatory statement if that statement was a statement of opinion,[89] and in making that statement the defendant was honestly stating his or her opinion,[90] and in making that statement the defendant indicated 'whether in general or specific terms, the basis of the opinion.'[91] However, *unlike* the defence of fair comment, a defendant who wants to take advantage of the defence of honest opinion does *not* have to show that her statement of opinion was on a matter of public interest. And the defendant does not have to show that any of the facts on which she based her statement of opinion were true: all she has to show is that there did exist facts (or facts alleged to be true in a privileged statement) at the time she made her statement that would have allowed an honest person to hold the same opinion that she did.[92]

We will now look at each of the elements of the defence of honest opinion in turn.

A. Opinion, not fact

The defence of honest opinion can only apply to a statement that was, on its face, a statement of opinion, as opposed to a statement of fact. However, the distinction between what is a statement of opinion and what is a statement of fact is very hard to draw. Consider the **Dramatic Detective Problem**:

> *Detective* was called in to investigate the murder of *Rich*. After two days, *Detective* thought he had cracked the case. He summoned the 12 principal suspects into the study of *Rich*'s manor house and summed up the conversations he had had with the suspects over the past two days. He then concluded, 'I now have no doubt as to who the murderer is. Everything I have heard points to one, irrefutable, conclusion: that it was you, *Sue Rich*, it was you who killed your uncle when he threatened to reveal to the world that your fiancé was his secret love child, with the result that everyone would know you and your fiancé were in fact first cousins, and marriage between you would have become a practical impossibility.'

Assuming *Detective* has got it wrong (the butler did it), could he raise a defence of honest opinion to *Sue Rich*'s claim for defamation, arguing that his statement that she murdered her uncle was, on its face, merely a statement of opinion, rather than a statement of fact? The question is a very difficult one.

The most obvious examples of statements that, on their face, are statements of opinion rather than statements of fact are *value judgments*. A value judgment involves deciding whether something is good or bad in some way or other. So the defence of honest opinion classically protects journalists reviewing plays or books or restaurants, telling their readers whether they are any good or not. The defence also applied to an article damning the newpaper proprietor Lord Beaverbrook under the headline, 'Lower than Kemsley'. When Viscount Kemsley, the then owner of *The Sunday Times*, sued the author of the

---

[88] Defamation Act 2013, s 3(8): 'The common law defence of fair comment is abolished . . .'.
[89] Section 3(2).
[90] Section 3(5).
[91] Section 3(3).
[92] Section 3(4).

article – Michael Foot – for defamation, arguing that the headline suggested that Kemsley ran his newspapers in a dishonourable way, the House of Lords held that the headline was covered by the defence of honest (then 'fair') comment.[93] A statement that A is dishonourable, or has acted in a dishonourable way, obviously involves a value judgment and is, on its face, a statement of opinion.[94] The defence also covers defendants who comment adversely on someone else's competence: for example, saying that a doctor is 'a quack of the rankest species'.[95] It should also cover a case where a defendant disparages a medicine or course of medical treatment as useless.[96]

Another kind of statement that is traditionally treated in English law (particularly in the law of contract) as being a statement of opinion rather than fact is a *prediction* about what will happen in the future. So a newspaper's statement that an MP's constituents *would* be furious to discover that she had criticised reforms to the system for reimbursing MPs' expenses was held to be a statement of opinion, rather than fact.[97] A statement that a band could not be relied upon to fulfil its contracts would also count as a statement of opinion:[98] such a statement is a prediction as to what the band would do in future.

Neither of the preceding two paragraphs would assist *Detective* in his argument that his statement that *Sue Rich* murdered her uncle was a statement of opinion, rather than a statement of fact. Such a statement does not involve either a value judgment, or a prediction about the future. This kind of statement, rather, involves an *inference of fact* (that *Sue Rich* is guilty of murder) from other facts (the conversations *Detective* has had with the suspects in *Rich*'s murder). Whether, and when, an inference of fact will amount to a statement of opinion is a very controversial question. In *Joseph* v *Spiller* (2010), the Supreme Court seemed to take the view that an inference of fact will not be covered by the defence of honest opinion: someone who says that he thinks A is guilty of fraud because A has been charged with fraud will not be able to plead honest opinion if he is subsequently sued by A.[99]

However, there seems to be an exception (which the Supreme Court acknowledged existed) where the fact being inferred is a fact about someone else's motivations. A statement that 'A acted as he did because he . . .' will – it seems – be treated as a statement of opinion, rather than a statement of fact, even though 'the state of a man's mind is as much a fact as the state of his digestion.'[100] So in *Hunt* v *Star Newspaper Co Ltd* (1908), a newspaper story alleging that the claimant returning officer had acted in a biased way in conducting an election was held to be capable of being covered by the defence of honest

---

[93] *Kemsley* v *Foot* [1952] AC 354.

[94] See also *Joseph* v *Spiller* [2011] 1 AC 852, at [88], disapproving the suggestion that 'To say that "A is a disgrace to human nature" is an allegation of fact, but if the words were "A murdered his father and is therefore a disgrace to human nature", the latter words are plainly a comment on the former.' The defence of honest opinion would not be available for the first statement, not because it is a statement of fact rather than opinion, but because it fails the third requirement, set out above and discussed below, for the defence to be made out: that some indication be given as to the factual basis of the statement.

[95] *Dakhyl* v *Labouchere* [1908] 2 KB 325n.

[96] Compare *British Chiropractic Association* v *Singh* [2011] 1 WLR 133 ('not a jot of evidence' for the efficacy of chiropractic (manipulation of the spine) to help 'children with colic, sleeping and feeding problems, frequent ear infections, asthma and prolonged crying').

[97] *Lait* v *Evening Standard* [2010] EWHC 3239 (QB).

[98] *Joseph* v *Spiller* [2011] 1 AC 852.

[99] Ibid, at [114].

[100] *Edgington* v *Fitzmaurice* (1885) 29 Ch D 459, 483 (per Bowen LJ).

(then, 'fair') comment. In *Jeyaretnam* v *Goh Chok Tong* (1989), the leader of the Singaporean Workers' Party (WP) was invited to speak at a party conference held by Singapore Democratic Party. After giving his speech, the leader of the WP left the hall, followed by a large number of his supporters. The defendant newspaper ran a story claiming that the leader of the WP was trying to show the leader of the SDP 'who is boss' by acting in this way. It was held that this inference as to the motives for the leader of the WP's leaving the hall (he was in fact on his way to a dinner engagement) amounted to a statement of opinion capable of being protected by the then defence of fair comment.

The Court of Appeal's judgment in *British Chiropractic Association* v *Singh* (2010) seems to have created a further exception to the general rule that inferences of fact are not capable of amounting to statements of opinion. In that case, the defendant wrote an article in the *Guardian* about chiropractic medicine, in the course of which he remarked:

> The British Chiropractic Association claims that their members can help treat children with colic, sleeping and feeding problems, frequent ear infections, asthma and prolonged crying, even though there is not a jot of evidence. This organisation is the respectable face of the chiropractic profession and yet it happily promotes bogus treatments.

The Court of Appeal held that the statement that there is 'not a jot of evidence' for the efficacy of chiropractic (manipulation of the spine) in treating the children's conditions listed was one of opinion, rather than fact. The Court of Appeal argued that such a conclusion amounted to a 'value judgment'.[101] With respect, that cannot be right – any more than a statement that the Earth revolves around the Sun involves a 'value judgment'. Judgment is, of course, required to answer the question of whether there is any valid proof that chiropractic helps with the listed conditions is a difficult one – but the judgment required is not a value judgment, but a scientific judgment. However, the Court of Appeal's decision to treat the above passage as a statement of opinion rather than fact can be defended on the basis that it is not for the courts to determine whether or not there is a 'jot of evidence' to support the view that chiropractic helps treat the above children's conditions – but that is what they might have ended up doing if the above passage had been treated as a statement of fact and the author invited to justify it, or find himself liable to the British Chiropractic Association for defamation.[102]

It is not clear how far the Court of Appeal's decision in the *Singh* case goes. For example, in *Irving* v *Penguin Books & Lipstadt* (2000), the historical author David Irving sued Deborah Lipstadt and her publisher in defamation. The focus of his claim was Lipstadt's book *Denying the Holocaust*, which made a number of damaging allegations about Irving. Chief among these allegations was that Irving consistently distorted the historical record to make it conform to his agenda, which is to deny that the Holocaust happened. In that case, the defendants argued that their claims about Irving were justified, and the judge deciding the case undertook – in the words of the Court of Appeal in the *Singh* case – 'the role of historian or investigative journalist' in order to determine whether that was the case.[103] In a 333-page judgment, the judge found

---

[101] [2011] 1 WLR 133, at [26].

[102] See, in particular, the Court of Appeal's judgment at [23]: 'the material words . . . are in our judgment expressions of opinion. The opinion may be mistaken, but to allow the party which has been denounced on the basis of it to compel its author to prove in court what he has asserted by way of argument is to invite the court to become an Orwellian ministry of truth.'

[103] [2010] EWCA Civ 350, at [22].

that Lipstadt's allegations about Irving were justified. However, it may be questioned – in light of the *Singh* decision – whether the courts should get involved in adjudicating where the truth lies in such academic disputes, and it might be thought that the wiser course in the *Irving* case would have been to hold that the defendants could take advantage of a defence of honest opinion and dismiss Irving's claim for defamation on that basis.

Returning now to the **Dramatic Detective Problem**, it seems unlikely that *Detective* would be able to raise a defence of honest opinion to *Sue Rich*'s claim against him for defamation. The inference of fact that *Detective* has drawn in this case does not go to *Sue Rich*'s motives; nor does it involve the sort of exercise of scientific or historical judgment that the courts would be ill-placed and unwilling to second-guess.

B. Indication of facts

The 2013 Act follows the Supreme Court decision in *Joseph* v *Spiller* (2011) in making it clear that for a defence of honest opinion to be available to a defendant who has expressed a critical opinion about the claimant, the defendant must have identified

> at least the general nature of the facts that have led him to make the criticism. If he states that a barrister is "a disgrace to his profession" he should make it clear whether this is because he does not deal honestly with the court, or does not read his papers thoroughly, or refuses to accept legally aided work, or is constantly late for court, or wears dirty collars and bands.[104]

The object of this requirement is to ensure that the concession to free speech embodied by the honest opinion defence is not abused. The defence of honest opinion exists because the law recognises that it is valuable for people to be allowed to express their opinions so as to persuade other people to share those opinions. But if people do not make it clear, at least in general terms, what the basis of their opinions are, their opinions will become 'wholly unfocused'[105] and consequently the expression of those opinions will become less valuable and not worth protecting.

How much a defendant needs to say by way of indicating the facts that have led him to say what he did will depend on the circumstances. Where the defendant is commenting on facts that are already in the public domain – such as the production of a play, or the conduct of a well-known public figure – almost nothing need be said explicitly to indicate the basis of the defendant's comment. The basis of the comment will be obvious from the context. For example, when Michael Foot said that Lord Beaverbrook was 'Lower than Kemsley', the House of Lords held in *Kemsley* v *Foot* (1951) that Foot could take advantage of the defence of honest (then, 'fair') comment to defeat Viscount Kemsley's claim against him for defamation. Foot did not lose the defence because he had not gone out of his way to explain that Viscount Kemsley was a newspaper proprietor and that the way Kemsley ran his newspapers had given rise to Foot's comment. All that was already obvious.

In contrast, where the facts giving rise to the defendant's comment are less well-known, some general indication of what those facts are will need to be given by the defendant if he is to take advantage of the defence of honest opinion.

---

[104] [2011] 1 AC 852, at [103].
[105] [2011] 1 AC 852, at [101].

C. Truth of facts

As we have seen, under the law on fair comment, a defendant who wished to take advantage of that defence had to show that the facts or reports on which he based his statement of opinion were true (in the case of facts) or privileged (in the case of reports) – or at least enough of those facts or reports were true or privileged as would have allowed a honest person to form the same opinion as the defendant did.

What this meant was this. Suppose A said of B, 'I think B is a disgrace as a human being – despite all his wealth, he has never done anything to assist his estranged wife and child or his destitute mother.' Suppose further that B sued A for defamation. Suppose finally that while B had done nothing to support his destitute mother, he did actually help to support his wife and child. If A could show that an honest person who knew the true facts might still have thought that B was a disgrace as a human being based on the fact that he had done nothing to support his destitute mother, then A would have been able to raise a defence of fair comment to defeat B's claim.

Under the law on honest opinion, a defendant does not have to show that any of the facts or reports on which he formed his opinion were true. All that he has to show is that –

an honest person could have held the [defendant's] opinion on the basis of –

(a) any fact which existed at the time the statement complained of was published;
(b) anything asserted to be a fact in a privileged statement published before the statement complained of.[106]

So suppose that A – on hearing that B had beaten up his wife – said that 'B is a disgrace as a human being'. If B had not in fact beaten up his wife, and the report that he did was not privileged, A could not take advantage of the old defence of fair comment. But A will be allowed to take advantage of the defence of honest opinion if A can establish that before A said 'B is a disgrace as a human being', B did something (or someone said something about B that was protected by privilege) that would allow an honest person to reach that conclusion. And it will not matter if A was completely unaware of what B had done (or what someone has said about B) at the time he made his comment.

In *Joseph* v *Spiller* (2011), it was suggested that the Supreme Court adopt a very similar rule in relation to the then defence of fair comment, but the Supreme Court rejected this on the basis that it would 'radically alter the nature of the defence' without doing anything to simplify the complexity of defamation trials.[107] It is slightly surprising to see the government going where the Supreme Court feared to tread.

D. Honesty

Little needs to be said on this requirement. In the context of the defence of honest opinion, it does not matter if the defendant said what he did out of spite or ill-will. All that is required is that the defendant honestly believed that what he was saying was true when he said it.

---

[106] Defamation Act 2013, s 3(4).
[107] [2011] 1 AC 852, at [110]–[111].

16.9 Privilege

If A has published a statement to C that is defamatory of B, B will *not* be entitled to sue A for libel or slander if the statement in question was *privileged*. Certain statements will *always* be privileged – such statements are said to be *absolutely privileged*. Other statements will only be privileged provided that certain conditions are met – these statements are said to be protected by *qualified privilege*.

A. Absolute privilege

The reason why some statements are protected by absolute privilege is that there are occasions where the law places such a high priority on people being able to say what they want without *any* fear of being sued that it assures such people that what they say will *always* be privileged.

So, for example, the law places such a high priority on MPs and members of the House of Lords being allowed to say what they want to say in Parliament without fear of being sued that it assures MPs and members of the House of Lords that what they say on the floor of the House of Commons or the House of Lords will always be privileged.[108] So if A is an MP he will be able to say what he wants about B on the floor of the House of Commons without fear of being sued by B for defamation – and this is so even if A knowingly tells complete lies about B: he cannot be sued.

The following statements will also always be privileged:

(1) *Statements made in reports, papers and proceedings ordered to be published by Parliament.*[109]

(2) *Statements made in the course of judicial or quasi-judicial proceedings by anyone involved in those proceedings.* However, statements made in the course of judicial or quasi-judicial proceedings which have no relevance to those proceedings may not be privileged.[110] A court-martial will count as a 'judicial or quasi-judicial' proceeding;[111] as will disciplinary proceedings held by the Law Society.[112] So statements made in the course of either will be absolutely privileged. However, the holding of an industrial conciliation procedure will

---

[108] This follows from Art 9 of the Bill of Rights 1688 which states that 'the freedom of speech and debates or proceedings in Parliament ought not to be impeached or questioned in any court or place out of Parliament'. An exception to this rule was created by s 13 of the Defamation Act 1996 which provides that where 'the conduct of a person in or in relation to proceedings in Parliament is in issue during defamation proceedings, he may waive for the purpose of those proceedings, so far as concerns him, the protection of any enactment or rule of law which prevents proceedings in Parliament being impeached or questioned in any court or place out of Parliament'. The privilege created by Art 9 of the Bill of Rights 1688 was extended by the Court of Appeal in *Makudi* v *Baron Triesman of Tottenham* [2014] QB 839 to the case where a defamatory statement is first uttered in Parliament and then outside, and there was '(1) a public interest in repetition of the parliamentary utterance which the speaker ought reasonably to serve, and (2) so close a nexus between the occasions of his speaking, in and then out of Parliament, that the prospect of his obligation to speak on the second occasion . . . [was] reasonably foreseeable at the time of the first and his purpose on speaking on both occasions is the same or very closely related' (at [25], per Laws LJ).
[109] Parliamentary Papers Act 1840, s 1.
[110] *Seaman* v *Netherclift* (1876) 2 CPD 53, 56.
[111] *Dawkins* v *Lord Rokeby* (1875) LR 7 HL 744.
[112] *Addis* v *Crocker* [1961] 1 QB 11.

not count as a 'judicial or quasi-judicial' proceeding[113] and neither will an investigation by the European Commission into alleged breaches of European competition law.[114]

(3) *Statements made by a witness to his solicitor in preparing his testimony for court.* [115]

(4) *Statements made in the course of being questioned by someone investigating a crime; statements made at the request of someone investigating a crime.* [116]

(5) *Statements made in a report prepared by an expert which may be used in later criminal proceedings.* [117]

(6) *Statements made by an investigator to someone else in the course of investigating a crime.* [118]

(7) *Statements made to an investigator who is investigating a crime, or for the purpose of encouraging an investigator to investigate a crime.* [119]

(8) *Statements made by one officer of state to another for the purpose of discharging some official business.* [120]

(9) *Statements made in an internal memorandum circulated within a foreign embassy.* [121]

(10) *Statements made in a fair and accurate and contemporaneous report of proceedings in public before a UK court or the European Court of Justice or the European Court of Human Rights or any international crime tribunal.* [122]

B. Qualified privilege

A statement which is protected by *qualified privilege* will be privileged so long as it was *not made maliciously*. For the purposes of this area of the law, A will be held to have acted maliciously in making a statement about B if: (1) he knew that that statement was untrue when he made it; *or* (2) when he made that statement, he did not care whether it was true or not; *or* (3) he made that statement for some improper or illegitimate reason.[123] The following kinds of statements will be protected by qualified privilege:

(1) *Statements attracting qualified privilege under the duty-interest test.* The traditional rule was that if A has made a statement to C, that statement would be protected by qualified privilege if, *had the information contained in that statement been correct*, A would have had a moral or legal duty to pass that information on to C and C would have had an interest in receiving that information.

In *Watt v Longsdon* (1930), the claimant was the managing director of the Morocco branch of the Scottish Petroleum Company. The manager of the Morocco branch wrote

---

[113] *Tadd* v *Eastwood* [1985] ICR 132.
[114] *Hasselblad (GB) Ltd* v *Orbinson* [1985] QB 475.
[115] *Watson* v *M'Ewan* [1905] AC 480; *Evans* v *London Hospital Medical College (University of London)* [1981] 1 WLR 184, 191. See below, § 22.5.
[116] *Mahon* v *Rahn (No 2)* [2000] 1 WLR 2150.
[117] *X* v *Bedfordshire County Council* [1995] 2 AC 633, 755G. See below, § 22.5.
[118] *Taylor* v *Director of the Serious Fraud Office* [1999] 2 AC 177. See below, § 22.5.
[119] *Westcott* v *Westcott* [2009] QB 407. See below, § 22.5.
[120] *Chatterton* v *Secretary of State for India in Council* [1895] 2 QB 189; though perhaps not in relation to statements made by civil servants to each other: *Szalatnay-Stacho* v *Fink* [1946] 1 All ER 303.
[121] *Fayed* v *Al-Tajir* [1988] 1 QB 712.
[122] Defamation Act 1996, s 14(1).
[123] *Horrocks* v *Lowe* [1975] AC 135. See also Mitchell 1999.

to the defendant, a director of Scottish Petroleum, accusing the claimant of being drunk, dishonest and immoral. The defendant showed the letter to the chairman of the board and also the claimant's wife. The claimant sued the defendant for defamation in respect of both publications of the letter.

The allegations contained in the letter were untrue so the defendant could not defeat the claimant's action by raising a defence of justification. However, the publication to the chairman of the board was held to be privileged. *Had the information contained in the letter been correct*, the defendant would obviously have had a duty to show the letter to the chairman of the board and the chairman of the board would have had an interest in seeing the letter. This established that the publication to the chairman of the board was protected by qualified privilege and, as the defendant had not been acting maliciously in showing the letter in question to the chairman of the board, the publication of that letter to the chairman of the board was privileged.

It was different with the publication to the claimant's wife. Obviously, had the allegations in the letter been true, the claimant's wife would have had an interest in seeing the letter. However, the defendant could *not* establish that had the allegations in the letter been true, he would have had a *duty* to show that letter to the claimant's wife. The Court of Appeal refused to be drawn on the question – If A has found out that B's husband has been cheating on her and generally engaging in disreputable activities, when will A have a duty to tell B of this fact? However, the Court of Appeal thought that the nature of the defendant's relationship with the claimant's wife was not such as to make it his place to tell the claimant's wife of what her husband was supposed to have been getting up to.

Such was the position with what is called the 'duty-interest' test for qualified privilege until the decision of the Court of Appeal in *Clift* v *Slough Borough Council* (2010). In that case, the claimant – Jane Clift – felt victimised by a council employee to whom she had been trying to make a complaint about a couple who had abused and threatened her in a council park. The claimant – outraged at the employee's indifference to the abuse she had suffered – contacted an administrator in the office of the council's Chief Executive to say that she felt so 'affronted and so filled with anger' at the way the council employee had treated her that 'I would have physically attacked her if she had been anywhere near her.' This was enough to get the claimant's name entered on a 'Violent Persons Register' that the council maintained; which register was subsequently circulated to numerous council employees and council 'partner organisations'.

The claimant sued the council for defamation. The council's attempt to argue that its warning employees and partner organisations that the claimant was on the Violent Persons Register was protected by qualified privilege under the duty-interest test was upheld in part and dismissed in part at first instance. It was held that the council's warning employees who were likely to come into contact with the claimant was protected by qualified privilege as they would have an interest in knowing the claimant were violent. However, the council had gone too far in warning other employees and organisations that were never likely to come into contact with the claimant: they had no interest in knowing whether the claimant was violent or not, and so the warnings to them could not be protected by qualified privilege under the duty-interest test.

So far, so good. The council appealed. The Court of Appeal said that the issue of whether the warning to what was referred to as the 'supernumerary employees' (to save words, we will refer to them as 'SE' for short) was protected by qualified privilege under the duty-interest test was a 'puzzling question'.[124] With respect, it was not. It was as obvious as a punch in the face that the publication to the SE could *not* be protected by qualified privilege under the duty-interest test as the SE had no interest in knowing whether or not the claimant was violent. However, as the council was a *public body* – and therefore bound by the Human Rights Act 1998 – the Court of Appeal thought that it could resolve the issue of whether the council's warning to the SE was protected by qualified privilege by asking whether giving such a warning violated the claimant's Article 8 rights under the European Convention on Human Rights 'to her private and family life, [her] home and [her] correspondence'.

The Court of Appeal thought that the council *had* violated the claimant's Article 8 rights by warning the SE that the claimant was a violent person. By defaming her, they had interfered with her private life,[125] and such interference could not be justified under Article 8(2) of the ECHR. This was because while the warning to the SE may have served a legitimate purpose – that of protecting those connected with the council from violence – it did so in a disproportionate way as the SE were not likely to come into contact with the claimant.[126] So the council had acted unlawfully under the Human Rights Act 1998 in warning the SE, and could not therefore argue that it had a duty to give that warning.[127]

The Court of Appeal's decision in *Clift* is disastrous. Four criticisms can be made of it. First, and most fundamentally, it radically changes the duty-interest test (in so far as it applies to a public body) from one that rests on a hypothetical question ('*Had* the claimant been violent, would the council have had a duty to warn the SE of that fact, and did the SE have an interest in knowing that fact?') into one that rests on a real question ('Given the facts of this case as they actually were, did the council act unlawfully under the Human Rights Act 1998 in warning the SE that the claimant was violent?'). The difference this makes is well-illustrated by the following remarks of Ward LJ:

> *Ill-considered* and indiscriminate disclosure is bound to be disproportionate and no plea of administrative difficulty *in verifying the information* and limiting publication to those who truly have the need to know or those reasonably thought to be at risk can outweigh the substantial interference with the right to protect reputations.[128]

The italicised words refer to things that, traditionally, were *never* regarded as relevant to the issue of whether a publication was protected under the duty-interest test. Whether the defendant acted in undue haste in giving a third party some damaging information about the claimant was never relevant under the duty-interest test, because that test traditionally asked: *Had the information been true*, would the defendant have had a duty to tell the third party, and would the third party have had an interest in knowing it? So whether the defendant acted hastily or not in telling the third party never came into it. But it does now – so far as public bodies are concerned.

This takes us on to the second criticism of the *Clift* decision, which is that as the Human Rights Act 1998 only applies to public bodies, it is only against public bodies that one can invoke the 1998 Act to say that the duty-interest test is not satisfied. But it seems profoundly unsatisfactory for one form of the duty-interest test to apply to public bodies

---

[124] [2011] 1 WLR 1774, at [24].
[125] [2011] 1 WLR 1774, at [32].
[126] [2011] 1 WLR 1774, at [35].
[127] [2011] 1 WLR 1774, at [36].
[128] [2011] 1 WLR 1774, at [35] (emphasis added).

and a quite different form (the traditional form) to apply to private persons. In order to avoid this happening, there will be calls for the approach to *Clift* to be applied to private persons as well – that is, for a private person's publication to be deprived of protection under the duty-interest test if that publication cannot be justified under Article 8(2) of the ECHR. But it is hard to see how Article 8(2) could ever apply to a publication by a private person given that it begins by saying: 'There shall be no interference *by a public authority* with the exercise of this right . . .'.[129]

The third criticism of the *Clift* decision is that Article 8(2) of the ECHR is relatively narrow, and requiring a public body to establish that a given publication is justified under Article 8(2) before it claim that the publication is protected under the duty-interest test may be asking too much. Article 8(2) provides that a public authority's interfering with someone's 'private and family life' can only be justified if it is necessary

> in the interests of national security, public safety or the economic well-being of the country, for the prevention of disorder or crime, for the protection of health or morals, or for the protection of the rights and freedoms of others.

Suppose that, within a particular local authority, *Manager* reports to *Superior* that *Secretary* drinks so much at lunchtime that she cannot type for toffee in the afternoon. Such a report would have attracted qualified privilege under the traditional duty-interest test. After *Clift*, it is not so clear. The report does not seem to fall under any of the situations listed in Article 8(2) as warranting an interference with *Secretary*'s private life.

The fourth criticism of *Clift* is that it makes it difficult to know what effect it has on all the other situations where a statement will attract qualified privilege. If a statement that falls into one of the categories below is made by a public body and cannot be justified under Article 8(2), will it be protected by qualified privilege or not? It is very difficult to tell. We will not mention *Clift* again in going through the other sorts of statements that are protected by qualified privilege; but it should always be borne in mind that the effect of *Clift* may be that a statement that falls into one of the categories below will *not* be protected by qualified privilege if it is made by a public body and cannot be justified under Article 8(2).

(2) *Statements attracting qualified privilege under the common interest test.* If A has made a statement to C, that statement will be protected by qualified privilege if it served A's interests to make that statement to C and it served C's interests to hear it.

For example, in *Watt* v *Longsdon* (1930), the claimant *also* sued the defendant for libel in respect of a letter that the defendant wrote to the manager of the Morocco branch of Scottish Petroleum in which the defendant voiced his own suspicions about the claimant and asked the manager to obtain confirmation of the allegations contained in the manager's letter. The Court of Appeal held that the defendant's letter was protected by qualified privilege. This was because the defendant and the manager had a common interest in protecting the interests of Scottish Petroleum and this shared interest of the defendant and the manager's was served by the defendant's writing his letter to the manager and the manager's receiving it and acting on it. And as the defendant had not acted maliciously in writing to the manager, the letter was privileged.

Similarly, in *Hunt* v *Great Northern Railway Company* (1891), the claimant worked as a guard for the defendant railway company. The defendants sacked the claimant on the

---

[129] Emphasis added.

ground that he had been guilty of gross neglect of duty. The defendants inserted a notice in the monthly circular which was distributed to the defendants' employees saying that the claimant had been guilty of gross neglect of duty and had been sacked as a result. The claimant sued the defendants for libel but his case was dismissed on the ground that the statement in the monthly circular was privileged. It was protected by qualified privilege, the court held, because the publication of the statement in the monthly circular served the interests of both the defendants and the people to whom the statement was published to, the defendants' employees – in both cases, because publication of the statement let the defendants' employees know that they would be sacked if they were guilty of gross neglect of duty. And as the defendants had not acted maliciously in publishing the statement in their monthly circular – they had not, for example, published the statement in order to make the claimant unemployable or published it in the knowledge that the claimant had not been guilty of a gross neglect of duty – that statement was privileged.

Lord Denning MR thought that what we might call the common interest test could be used to establish that statements made by an employer to his secretary in dictating a letter will be protected by qualified privilege. He argued in *Bryanston Finance* v *de Vries* (1975) that as the employer and the secretary would both have an interest in getting the letter dictated by the employer written, any statements made to the secretary by the employer in dictating the letter would be protected by a qualified privilege. Such statements would therefore be privileged so long as the employer did not act maliciously in publishing them to his secretary. However, neither of the two other members of the Court of Appeal in *Bryanston Finance* agreed with Lord Denning MR on this point. They both thought the statements made in dictation would only be privileged if the publication to the intended recipient of the letter would also be privileged.

(3) *Statements attracting qualified privilege because made in self-defence.* It is well established that if someone attacks or criticises A verbally or in print, then any statements made by A in order to rebut that attack or criticism will be protected by qualified privilege.

So in *Osborn* v *Thomas Boulter & Son* (1930), the claimant – a publican – wrote to the defendants to complain about the quality of their beer. The defendants wrote back suggesting that the source of the claimant's problems with their beer was that he watered it down once it was delivered to him. The claimant sued the defendants for slander on the basis that the defendants' letter had been published not only to the claimant but also to the defendants' secretary when it was dictated to her. His claim was dismissed on the ground that the defendants' rebuttal of the claimant's attack on the quality of their beer was protected by qualified privilege and the defendants had not acted maliciously in making the allegations that they did.

In *Watts* v *Times Newspapers Ltd* (1997), *The Sunday Times* published a story which accused the claimant, Nigel Watts, of plagiarism. However, they accompanied the story with a photograph of a quite different Nigel Watts, a property developer. This Nigel Watts complained and *The Sunday Times* printed an apology in its next edition which was dictated by Nigel Watts's solicitors, Schilling & Lom. The apology repeated the original defamatory story about the claimant. The claimant sued *The Sunday Times* for libel, claiming that the apology was defamatory of him. It was held that *The Sunday Times* could not claim that their apology was privileged as they were not publishing it to rebut an attack on themselves. *The Sunday Times* then sought to make a claim in contribution against Schilling & Lom on the ground that, having dictated the terms of the apology, they were also liable to pay damages to the claimant in respect of the publication of the apology. This claim was dismissed; it was held that, vis-à-vis Schilling & Lom, the apology was privileged as it had been dictated in order to rebut the attack which *The Sunday Times* had inadvertently made on their client.

(4) *Statements attracting qualified privilege under the Defamation Act 1996.* The 1996 Act confers qualified privilege on a wide range of statements made on a matter of public concern or interest.[130] The Act splits these statements into two groups.

First, the Act provides that certain statements on matters of public concern or interest will be protected by qualified privilege '*without explanation or contradiction*'. These include: (1) statements made in a fair and accurate report of proceedings in public of a legislature or a court or a public inquiry or an international organisation or an international conference located anywhere in the world; and (2) statements made in a fair and accurate copy of or extract from any matter published by a government or a legislature or an international organisation or an international conference located anywhere in the world.[131]

Secondly, the 1996 Act provides that certain other statements on matters of public concern or interest will be protected by qualified privilege '*subject to explanation or contradiction*'. What this means is that if A, a newspaper, has published such a statement and the statement in question is defamatory of B, A will *not* be able to claim – if B sues it for defamation – that the statement was privileged if A refused or neglected to publish in a suitable manner a 'reasonable letter or statement by way of explanation or contradiction' of the statement published by A when it was requested to do so by B.[132] Statements that will be protected by qualified privilege 'subject to explanation or contradiction' include:[133] (1) statements made in a fair and accurate report of proceedings at any general meeting of a UK public company; (2) statements made in a fair and accurate copy of or extract from any document circulated to the members of a UK public company by its board or its auditors; (3) statements made in a fair and accurate report of any decision or finding made by an organisation concerned to promote a trade or a profession or a business or a game or a charitable object or general interest in art or science or religion or learning.

(5) *Peer-reviewed statements in academic or professional journals.* Section 6 of the 2013 Act provides that statements that relate to a scientific or academic matter will be protected by qualified privilege[134] provided that they were: (i) published in a scientific or academic journal;[135] and (ii) an independent review of the statement's scientific or academic merit was carried out by (a) the editor of the journal, *and* (b) one or more persons with expertise in the scientific or academic matter concerned.[136] Requirement (ii)(a) will probably ensure that this provision will have little impact: when an article is submitted to a scientific or academic journal, the editor will rarely assess the article's merit – he or she will instead send it out to be assessed by experts in the field. So it is hard to see that requirement (ii)(a) will ever be satisfied.

---

[130] Section 15(3) of the Defamation Act 1996 provides that the 1996 Act does not confer qualified privilege on matter published 'to the public, or a section of the public, . . . which is not of public concern and the publication of which [was] not for the public benefit'.

[131] For a full list, see Part I of Sch 1 of the Defamation Act 1996.

[132] Section 15(2).

[133] For a full list, see Part II of Sch I of the Defamation Act 1996.

[134] The privilege is qualified because s 6(6) provides that it will not protect publications 'shown to be made with malice.'

[135] Defamation Act 2013, s 6(1).

[136] Defamation Act 2013, s 6(3).

16.10 Public interest

Section 4(1) of the 2013 Act provides that 'It is a defence to an action for defamation for the defendant to show that – (a) the statement complained of was, or formed part of, a statement on a matter of public interest; and (b) the defendant reasonably believed that publishing the statement complained of was in the public interest.'

This defence has its origins in, and is intended to replace,[137] an important form of qualified privilege known as '*Reynolds* privilege'. '*Reynolds* privilege' was named after the House of Lords' decision in *Reynolds* v *Times Newspapers Ltd* (2001), which established that statements made in an article published in a newspaper will be protected by qualified privilege if: (i) the article was on a matter of public concern or interest *and* (ii) the newspaper acted responsibly in going ahead and publishing the article when they did and in the form that they did.[138] Such statements were said to be protected under the *Reynolds* test for qualified privilege.

It will be noted that the public interest defence laid out in s 4 of the 2013 Act is differently phrased from the *Reynolds* test for qualified privilege. A newspaper that wants to take advantage of the public interest defence will have to show that (a) the statement complained of was in an article that was on a matter of public interest and (b) the newspaper reasonably thought that publishing that article was in the public interest. Under *Reynolds*, the newspaper had to show that (i) the statement complained of was in an article on a matter of public interest; and (ii) the newspaper acted responsibly in publishing the article when they did and in the form that they did. It is submitted that there is no significant difference between (b) and (ii) – if an article is on a matter of public interest, and a newspaper acted responsibly in publishing an article when they did and in the form that they did, then it will be reasonable for them to think that publishing that article was in the public interest. If, on the other hand, the article was on a matter of public interest, but the newspaper did *not* act responsibly in publishing an article when they did and in the form that they did, then it will *not* have been reasonable for them to think that publishing that article was in the public interest.

Why, then, did Parliament not simply reproduce in section 4 the well-established requirements for *Reynolds* privilege to apply? After all, in the original Defamation Bill, on which the 2013 Act was based, that is precisely what the government did, entitling the defence 'Responsible publication on [a] matter of public interest' and setting out a number of factors to be taken into account in judging whether the defendant acted 'responsibly' in publishing the book or article complained of by the claimant.[139] The answer may lie in the desire of the sponsors of the 2013 Act to be able to boast that 'for the first time ever' English law had recognised a defence of publication 'in the public interest'. In form, this may be true: but so far as the substance of the law is concerned, *Reynolds* got there first and it is hard to see how the new public interest defence will operate any differently from the *Reynolds* defence.

To understand how *Reynolds* privilege worked, and – by extension – how the public interest defence is likely to work, *Reynolds* itself provides a good starting point. In that case, *The Sunday Times* published an article which dealt with the resignation of Albert

---

[137] Defamation Act 2013, s 4(6): 'The common law defence known as the Reynolds defence is abolished.'
[138] See *Jameel (Mohammed)* v *Wall Street Europe SPRL* [2007] 1 AC 359, at [31]–[32] (per Lord Bingham), [55] (per Lord Hoffmann), [107] (per Lord Hope), [137] (per Lord Scott).
[139] Defamation Bill, clause 2.

Reynolds, the Irish prime minister. The article alleged that Reynolds had deliberately and dishonestly misled the Irish Dáil on a particular matter and that Reynolds had been forced to resign when his colleagues found out about Reynolds's misconduct. In fact, this was not true: Reynolds never misled the Dáil and he resigned for other reasons. Reynolds sued *The Sunday Times* for libel and *The Sunday Times* claimed in its defence that its article was privileged.

The House of Lords held that the article was not privileged. While there was no doubt that the article was on a matter of public interest,[140] the House of Lords found that *The Sunday Times* did *not* act responsibly in publishing the article in the form that it did. Lord Nicholls provided a list of ten factors which could be taken into account in determining whether a newspaper acted responsibly in publishing a particular article about someone when they did and in the form that they did:

> 1. The seriousness of the [allegations made in the article]. The more serious the charge, the more the public is misinformed and the individual harmed, if [the allegations in the report were] untrue. 2. The nature of the information [in the article], and the extent to which the subject matter is a matter of public concern. 3. The source of the information. Some informants have no direct knowledge of the events. Some have their own axes to grind, or are being paid for their stories. 4. The steps taken to verify the information. 5. The status of the information. [The allegations made in the article] may already have been the subject of an investigation which commands respect. 6. The urgency of the matter. News is often a perishable commodity. 7. Whether comment was sought from the [subject of the article]. He may have information others do not possess or have not disclosed. [However, an] approach . . . will not always be necessary. 8. Whether the article contained the gist of the [subject of the article's] side of the story. 9. The tone of the article. A newspaper can often raise queries or call for an investigation. It need not adopt allegations as statements of fact. 10. The circumstances of the publication, including the timing.[141]

Taking these criteria into account, the House of Lords had little difficulty reaching the conclusion that *The Sunday Times* had not acted responsibly in publishing its article about Reynolds' resignation. The article was unjustifiably one-sided in its presentation of the reasons why Reynolds resigned. No account was given of Reynolds's explanation of why he had resigned – which Reynolds presented to the Irish Dáil on the day he resigned – when, in fairness, one would have expected such an account to have been given. Indeed, the coverage of the story behind Reynolds's resignation had been much more balanced in the Irish editions of *The Sunday Times* and this made it look like the story in the UK edition of *The Sunday Times* had been deliberately sensationalised.

Were *Reynolds* to be decided today under the new public interest defence, the same result would be reached, but different language would be used. Instead of holding that the article in *The Sunday Times* was not privileged because *The Sunday Times* did not act responsibly in publishing that article in the way it did, the courts would instead hold that the article was not protected under s 4 of the 2013 Act because while the article was on a matter of public interest, *The Sunday Times* could not have reasonably believed that publishing the article was in the public interest given the one-sided way in which the article approached the issue of the reasons why Reynolds resigned.

Four points remain to be made about the public interest defence.

---

[140] As Reynolds was one of the architects of the Northern Ireland peace process, the reasons for his resignation were of public concern and interest in the UK.
[141] [2001] 2 AC 127, 205.

A. Rationale

Let's say that A is the editor of the *Daily Herald* and one of his reporters has come to him with a damaging story about B, a famous politician. The story is clearly on a matter of the public interest – it is alleged that B has been taking bribes – but it is not 100% certain that the story is correct. So there is a risk that if A publishes the story, B might sue his newspaper for defamation and the newspaper will be unable to make out a defence of truth to defeat her claim. The public interest defence – and the *Reynolds* defence that preceded it – is intended to provide A with some reassurance that he could safely go ahead and publish the story about B even though he was uncertain whether a defence of truth could be made out if the story went to court. The law essentially promises A, 'So long as you handle the story about B *responsibly*, then your newspaper will be immune from being sued successfully by B; and this is so even if the story about B turns out to be untrue.' In making this promise, the law attempts to ensure that the law on defamation does not have a 'chilling' effect on legitimate freedom of expression by deterring editors like A from publishing stories like the story about B because they could not be 100 per cent certain they were correct. Of course, if it turned out that B was *not* taking bribes, the existence of the public interest defence will have encouraged A to publish an untrue story about B that unjustifiably besmirched her reputation. But the idea is that the risk of this happening is a price worth paying to ensure that other *true* but damaging stories on matters of the public interest are not suppressed by newspaper editors because they could not be certain that they would be able to prove that they were true in court.

B. Application

The benefits that the House of Lords hoped would flow from recognition of the *Reynolds* test for qualified privilege – in terms of emboldening editors to publish defamatory stories on matters of the public interest – were almost completely undermined by a series of first instance and Court of Appeal decisions that took a very restrictive approach to when a newspaper story would be protected by qualified privilege, thereby making it impossible for newspapers to feel confident in relation to a particular story that they could make it 'libel proof'.

The problem grew so grave that in *Jameel (Mohammed)* v *Wall Street Europe SPRL* (2007), the House of Lords felt impelled to go out of its way to make it clear that while it was for the courts to decide whether a newspaper acted responsibly in handling a particular story in the way it did, the courts had to give newspapers some latitude in determining this issue. In particular, Lord Nicholls' list of factors that should be taken into account in determining whether a newspaper acted responsibly in handling a particular story should *not* be regarded as a series of hurdles *all* of which have to be cleared before the courts will find that the newspaper acted responsibly in handling that story.[142] Lord Hoffmann suggested that the newspapers' Code of Practice, as ratified by the then Press Complaints Commission, could provide 'valuable guidance' as to whether a newspaper had acted responsibly in handling a particular story.[143] Lord Bingham went further and urged that

---

[142] [2007] 1 AC 359, at [33] (per Lord Bingham) and at [56] (per Lord Hoffmann).
[143] [2007] 1 AC 359, at [55].

in applying the *Reynolds* test, the courts should adopt something akin to the *Bolam* test for determining whether a professional acted negligently:[144]

> editorial decisions and judgments made at the time, without the knowledge of falsity which is a benefit of hindsight, are [not] irrelevant. Weight should ordinarily be given to the professional judgment of an editor or journalist in the absence of some indication that it was made in a casual, cavalier, slipshod or careless manner.[145]

Unfortunately, the lower courts refused to learn their lesson and in the subsequent case of *Flood* v *Times Newspapers Ltd* (2011) – a case involving a story alleging that a serving police officer was under investigation for taking bribes – the Court of Appeal went back to nitpicking its way through the evidence, refusing to find that the defendant's story was protected by *Reynolds* privilege if there was anything wrong – in the *Court's* opinion – in the way the defendant's newspaper approached the story. When *Flood* went to the UK Supreme Court in 2012, the Supreme Court ruled that the article complained of in *Flood* *was* protected by qualified privilege under the *Reynolds* test but did not try to revisit the attempts made in *Jameel (Mohammed)* to encourage the lower courts to be more liberal in determining when the *Reynolds* test for qualified privilege was satisfied. Instead the far-rago of inconsequential and cheeseparing distinctions indulged in by the members of the UK Supreme Court over 203 paragraphs of turgid legal prose in the *Flood* case can only have encouraged the lower courts to continue taking a legalistic approach to the scope of the *Reynolds* defence.

Now that the *Reynolds* test has been replaced by the public interest defence, will things be any better? It seems not if the courts simply take the public interest defence – as we have presented it – as being *Reynolds* under a different name. However, the change of name, the Parliamentary imprimatur given to the defence, the fact that a newspaper will be entitled to a defence under s 4 if it *reasonably believes* that publication of the statement complained of by the claimant was in a matter of public interest, and the fact that s 4(4) of the 2013 Act goes out of its way to provide that:

> [i]n determining whether it was reasonable for the defendant to believe that publishing the state-ment complained of was in the public interest, the court must make such allowance for editorial judgment as it considers appropriate.

may all encourage the courts to take a fresh approach to the scope of this defence and not be so strict in determining when a defendant can take advantage of this defence.

C. Reportage

Reportage is a 'fancy word'[146] for 'the neutral reporting without adoption or embellish-ment or subscribing to any belief in its truth of attributed allegations of both sides of a political and possibly some other kind of dispute'.[147]

An example of *reportage* is provided by the case of *Roberts* v *Gable* (2008), where the defendant newspaper *Searchlight* – which exposes the activities of parties on the far right wing of British politics – published a story reporting that there had been a falling out in

---

[144] See above, § 7.4(B).
[145] [2007] 1 AC 359, at [33]. To the same effect, see [51] (per Lord Hoffmann).
[146] *Roberts* v *Gable* [2008] QB 502, at [34] (per Ward LJ).
[147] [2008] QB 502, at [53] (per Ward LJ).

the aftermath of a London BNP (British National Party) rally with the claimants and two other individuals accusing each other of stealing the money collected at the rally. *Searchlight* did not take any sides in this dispute – its only desire was to report the fact that members of the BNP were feuding among themselves.

The claimants sued the defendant newspaper for libel, claiming that (under the repetition rule)[148] its article alleged that they *had* stolen the money collected at the BNP London rally. *Searchlight* claimed that the article was protected by qualified privilege under the *Reynolds* test. One problem with that claim was that *Searchlight* had not attempted to give the claimants an opportunity to respond to their article; nor had it attempted to find out the truth of what happened in the aftermath of the London BNP rally. However, the Court of Appeal held that this did not matter: *reportage* would be protected under the *Reynolds* test without there being any 'need to take steps to ensure the accuracy of the published information'.[149] So long as: (i) it was in the public interest to report the *fact* of the dispute being reported on; *and* (ii) the newspaper reporting on the dispute reported it in a 'fair, disinterested and neutral way' without adopting any of the allegations made in that dispute as its own;[150] *and* (iii) the newspaper acted responsibly in publishing the information about the fact of the dispute, *then* (iv) the newspaper's report would be protected by qualified privilege under the *Reynolds* test.

The special treatment of reportage under the *Reynolds* test for qualified privilege is carried over into the new public interest defence. Under s 4(3) of the 2013 Act,

> If the statement complained of was, or formed part of, an accurate and impartial account of a dispute to which the claimant was a party, the court must in determining whether it was reasonable for the defendant to believe that publishing the statement was in the public interest disregard any omission of the defendant to take steps to verify the truth of the imputation conveyed by it.

D. Scope

The *Reynolds* test for qualified privilege did not just cover statements made in articles published in newspapers. *Reynolds* privilege was also capable of protecting statements made in speeches, books, television documentaries or news programmes.[151] It could also apply to statements made in articles that have been posted in a newspaper archive on the Internet.[152] The new defence of public interest will be similarly unrestricted in its scope.

---

[148] See above, § 16.2(6).

[149] [2008] QB 502, at [61](2) (per Ward LJ).

[150] [2008] QB 502, at [61](5).

[151] *Seaga* v *Harper* [2009] 1 AC 1, at [11]: 'their Lordships . . . can see no valid reason why [*Reynolds* privilege] should not extend to publications made by any person who publishes material of public interest in any medium, so long as the conditions framed by Lord Nicholls as being applicable to "responsible journalism" are satisfied.'

[152] *Loutchansky* v *Times Newspapers Ltd (Nos 2-5)* [2002] QB 783. The Court of Appeal held that a newspaper could not claim to have acted responsibly when it placed a defamatory article originally published in its print edition in an archive on the Internet without qualifying the article in any way to make it clear that its accuracy had been challenged. See, to the same effect, *Flood* v *Times Newspapers Ltd* [2011] 1 WLR 153, holding that any *Reynolds* privilege attaching to an article on a newspaper Internet archive will be lost if reasonable steps are not taken to revise it when it becomes clear that the article is misleading.

16.11 Other defences

There are four more defences that we should mention, all designed to protect someone who has been involved in the publication of a defamatory statement about the claimant to another, but whose culpability in the matter is very low.

A. Secondary parties

As we have seen, liability for defamation can stretch beyond those who were primarily responsible for the publication of a defamatory statement and catch those who assisted in the statement's distribution such as the printers of the book or newspaper in which the statement was published, or the shop in which the book or newspaper in question was sold. Such secondary parties now have a defence to being sued in defamation under s 10 of the 2013 Act (probably the most consequential provision in the Act), which provides that:

> A court does not have jurisdiction to hear and determine an action for defamation brought against a person who was not the author, editor or publisher of the statement complained of unless the court is satisfied that it is not reasonably practicable for an action to be brought against the author, editor or publisher.

Students are always thrown by the idea, that underlies both this defence and the following defence (of 'innocent dissemination') that a defendant might be liable in defamation even if they were not the author, editor *or publisher*. If the defendant was not the publisher of the statement, then how could he be held liable in the first place? But in this context, 'publisher' does not mean the same thing as 'someone who has published a defamatory statement to another'. In this context, 'publisher'

> means a commercial publisher, that is, a person whose business is issuing material to the public, or a section of the public, who issues material containing the statement [in question] in the course of that business.[153]

and a person shall not be considered to be the

> publisher of a statement if he is only involved – (a) in printing, producing, distributing or selling printed material containing the statement; (b) in processing, making copies of, distributing, exhibiting or selling a film or sound recording . . . containing the statement; (c) in processing, making copies of, distributing or selling any electronic medium in or on which the statement is recorded, or in operating or providing any equipment, system or service by means of which the statement is retrieved, copied, distributed or made available in electronic form; (d) as the broadcaster of a live programme containing the statement in circumstances in which he has no effective control over the maker of the statement; (e) as the operator of or provider of access to a communications system by means of which the statement is transmitted, or made available, by a person over whom he has no effective control.[154]

So, for the purposes of this defence (and the defence of 'innocent dissemination' below), a printer or a bookseller or a company hosting an Internet chatroom or blog would not count as a 'publisher' and could therefore rely on s 10 if they were sued for defamation if they can show that suing one or more of the primary parties who were responsible for the dissemination of a defamatory statement is reasonably practicable.

---

[153] Defamation Act 1996, s 1(2), which is incorporated into s 10 of the Defamation Act 2013 by s 10(2).
[154] Defamation Act 1996, s 1(3), also incorporated into s 10 of the 2013 Act by s 10(2).

B. Innocent dissemination

The defence of 'innocent dissemination' is governed by s 1(1) of the Defamation Act 1996, which provides that if A has published to another a statement which was defamatory of B, A will have a defence to any claim for damages B might bring against A if: (1) A was not the 'author, editor or publisher' of the statement in question; (2) A took reasonable care in relation to its publication; *and* (3) A did not know, and had no reason to believe, that what he did would cause or contribute to the publication of a defamatory statement.[155]

Because of s 10 of the 2013 Act, someone who does not count – for the purposes either of s 1 of the 1996 Act or s 10 of the 2013 Act – as being the 'author, editor or publisher' of a defamatory statement will only be interested in taking advantage of a defence of innocent dissemination if it is not reasonably practicable to sue one or more of the people who *did* count as being the authors, editors or publishers of the defamatory statement. So the defence of innocent dissemination will come into its own where, for example, someone anonymously posts a defamatory statement on a website, or a bookseller in the UK sells a book that contains defamatory allegations about the claimant and was printed and published abroad. In such cases, the rule is that the defendant website host, or bookseller, will have a defence if he did not know and had no reason to know that he was contributing to the publication of a defamatory statement.

The defence will be lost if the defendant continues to assist in the publication of the defamatory statement after it has been brought to his attention that he is doing so and he fails to stop within a reasonable period of time. This is what happened in *Godfrey* v *Demon Internet Ltd* (2001), where the defendant company – which hosted an electronic bulletin board on the Internet – was sued in defamation when someone posted a defamatory message on the defendant's bulletin board. It was held that the defendant company could not take advantage of the defence of innocent dissemination because the presence of the message on the board had been brought to its attention and it had subsequently failed to take reasonable steps to take the message down.

One issue that was not raised in *Godfrey* was whether the defendant company could be held to have been held liable *at all* for defaming the claimant, just because a message that was defamatory of the claimant was posted on the defendant's bulletin board. This issue was addressed in *Tamiz* v *Google Inc* (2013), in which the Court of Appeal held that the 'platform principle'[156] will apply to hold a company that is running a blog service liable for statements posted on that blog if the company fails to take down those statements within a reasonable period of time of the existence of those statements being brought to its attention. In such a case, the company will become sufficiently responsible for the

---

[155] It should be remembered that a statement can still be defamatory *even if it is true*. So suppose a bookseller sold a book which contained damaging allegations about A and A wants to sue the bookseller for libel. If we want to know whether the bookseller can take advantage of the defence set out in s 1(1) of the 1996 Act we ask – did the bookseller know, or have reason to know, that the book sold by him contained damaging allegations about A? If so, he will *not* be able to take advantage of the defence set out in s 1(1) of the 1996 Act. It will not matter whether or not the bookseller in question knew, or had reason to know, that the allegations in question were *untrue* – even if he did not know, and had no reason to know, that those allegations were untrue, he will still *not* be able to take advantage of the defence set out in s 1(1) of the 1996 Act if he knew, or ought to have known, that the book contained those allegations.

[156] See above, § 16.4(8).

publication of those statements to be held liable for them in defamation *and* lose the possibility of raising a defence of innocent dissemination in respect of those statements all at the same time. However, if those statements had been posted on the internet for a sufficiently long time before they were brought to the company's attention, it might be that the company could have had a claim against it in respect of those statements struck out as an abuse of process – as happened in *Tamiz* – on the ground that any damage done by the publication of those statements was done long before the company became liable for the continued publication of those statements.

C. Operators of websites

So far as operators of websites on which defamatory statements are anonymously posted are concerned, the rule seems to be that they will be held liable in respect of those statements if: (1) the presence of those statements on their websites was brought to their attention, and (2) they failed to take reasonable steps to take those statements down. Section 5 of the 2013 Act seems to be intended to formalise the application of this rule by providing that the operator of a website on which a defamatory statement is posted will have a defence to being sued in respect of that statement *unless* (1) the author of the statement cannot be identified, *and* (2) the claimant gave a 'notice of complaint' to the operator of the website in respect of that statement, *and* (3) the operator failed to comply with statutory regulations – which will be laid down in due course by the Secretary of State for Justice – in responding to that notice of complaint. We will have to wait to see what these regulations will require operators of websites to do, but s 5(5) makes it clear that they will deal with such things as what steps the operator is expected to take in response to a 'notice of complaint' and in what sort of timescale.

D. Offer to make amends

Suppose A has published to another a statement that was defamatory of B and B wants to sue A for libel or slander. If A cannot take advantage of one of the defences set out above to defeat B's claim, he may still be able to prevent B from suing him for libel or slander by making an 'offer to make amends' to B under s 2 of the Defamation Act 1996.

Section 2 of the Defamation Act 1996 provides that if A wants to make an 'offer to make amends' to B he *must* offer

> (a) to make a suitable correction of the statement complained of and a sufficient apology to [B], (b) to publish the correction and apology in a manner that is reasonable and practicable in the circumstances, and (c) to pay [B] such compensation (if any), and such costs, as may be agreed or determined to be payable.[157]

If A only offers to do one or two of these things, then his offer will not amount to an 'offer to make amends' and will have no effect on B's right to sue A for libel or slander.

If A does make an 'offer to make amends' to B and B *accepts* the offer, B will be barred from suing A for defamation.[158] If B does *not* accept the offer, B will *still* be barred from suing A for defamation *unless*, when A published the statement which was defamatory of

---

[157] If B accepts A's offer but then they find themselves unable to agree on what should be paid to B by way of compensation, the courts will decide for them: Defamation Act 1996, s 3(5).
[158] Section 3(2).

B: (1) he knew or had reason to believe that that statement referred to B or was likely to be understood as referring to B *and* (2) he knew or had reason to believe that the statement in question was *both* false *and* defamatory of B.[159] If (1) and (2) are true then A's 'offer to make amends' will have no effect on B's right to sue A for defamation, though the fact that an 'offer to make amends' has been made and the offered correction and apology have been published will have the effect of reducing the damages payable to B even if the making of the offer did not bar B from suing A.[160]

16.12 Remedies

There are two remedies that successful claimants in defamation cases are entitled to obtain: an injunction requiring the defendant not to repeat the statement that gave rise to the claim in defamation; and damages.

Damages in defamation cases perform a vindicatory and compensatory function. The compensatory function is performed by an award that is designed to compensate the claimant for the reasonably foreseeable[161] losses that the defendant's statement caused the claimant to suffer. But damages can also be awarded in defamation cases with a view to 'send[ing] out a signal to people that there was no truth at all in the [defendant's] allegation'.[162]

> In actions of defamation . . . [n]ot merely can [a claimant] recover the estimated sum of his past and future losses, but, in case the libel, driven underground, emerges from its lurking place at some future date, he must be able to point to a sum awarded by a jury sufficient to convince a bystander of the baselessness of the charge.[163]

> [the jury] should be asked to ensure that any award they make is proportionate to the damage which the plaintiff has suffered and is a sum which it is necessary to award him to provide adequate compensation and to re-establish his reputation.[164]

Sending out such a signal may be especially important where

> as a consequence of modern technology and communication systems [defamatory] stories will have the capacity to 'go viral' more widely and quickly than ever before . . . In our judgment . . . this percolation phenomenon is a legitimate factor to be taken into account in the assessment of damages.[165]

---

[159] Section 4. *Milne* v *Express Newspapers Ltd* [2005] 1 WLR 772 makes it clear that (2) will only be true if A acted *recklessly* in publishing the statement in question. Merely showing that a reasonable person in A's position would have realised that that statement was untrue and/or defamatory will not be enough.

[160] *Cairns* v *Modi* [2013] 1 WLR 1015 (allegation that father of Baby P – who died in 2007 as a result of being abused by his mother and two men – was convicted rapist; apology and correction published two days later; parties were unable to agree on compensation to be paid under 'offer to make amends' process; held, in principle, claimant should get £100,000 but damages should be reduced by 50 per cent to reflect vindication of claimant's reputation that was effected through apology and correction).

[161] *Slipper* v *BBC* [1991] 1 QB 283; *McManus* v *Beckham* [2002] 1 WLR 2982.

[162] Per Gray J, quoted in *Purnell* v *BusinessF1 Magazine Ltd* [2008] 1 WLR 1, at [7].

[163] *Broome* v *Cassell & Co Ltd* [1972] AC 1027, 1071 (per Lord Hailsham LC).

[164] *Rantzen* v *Mirror Group Newspapers (1986) Ltd* [1994] QB 670, 696.

[165] *Cairns* v *Modi* [2013] 1 WLR 1015, at [27].

In a defamation case where a defence of truth has been pleaded and has been rejected in a reasoned judgment by a judge, the vindicatory element of any damages to be awarded to the claimant *may* be reduced to take account of the fact that the judge's judgment may go some of the way towards vindicating the claimant's reputation. But:

> The effect of such an earlier judgment depends on all the circumstances . . . there are . . . cases where the judgment will provide no or no significant or reasonable vindication. They will perhaps arise where the justification has been struck out for some technical reason in circumstances where, in truth, no consideration whatever has been given to the merits.[166]

In a case where a claimant is regarded as having little reputation to lose, an award of damages designed to vindicate the claimant's reputation will tend to reflect this, with claimants being awarded as little as £1 or one penny to make it clear of what little worth the claimant's reputation was even before he was defamed.[167] In such cases, the damages awarded to the claimant are known as 'contemptuous' or 'derisory' damages. So, for example, in *Reynolds* v *Times Newspapers Ltd* (2001), Albert Reynolds was successful in his claim against *The Sunday Times* for giving a one-sided and misleading account of the reasons why he resigned as the Irish prime minister. But he was only awarded one penny by way of damages to reflect the general disrespect in which he was held by the time his case was heard.[168]

The damages awarded to a claimant may also include a punitive element, as well as a compensatory element and a vindicatory element. Exemplary (or punitive) damages may be awarded against a defendant in a defamation case where: (1) his conduct in defaming the claimant is so outrageous as to be worthy of punishment; (2) he defamed the claimant with a view to making a gain for himself or someone else; and (3) an award of damages that did not include a punitive element would not be sufficient to punish the defendant for his behaviour.[169]

16.13 Options for reform

As we have seen, the 2013 Act represents a bit of a damp squib in terms of reforming the law of defamation. While it does make some substantive changes at the margin of the law – notably, abolishing the right to a jury trial in defamation cases, abolishing the 'multiple publication rule' (in respect of publications after 1 January 2014), and providing secondary parties who were involved in the distribution of a defamatory statement greater protection from being sued – there is nothing in the 2013 Act that will make a big difference to the law of defamation. Below we consider the merits of some more radical changes to the law.

---

[166] *Purnell* v *BusinessF1 Magazine Ltd* [2008] 1 WLR 1, at [29]-[30] (per Laws LJ).

[167] *Plato Films Ltd* v *Speidel* [1961] AC 1090.

[168] See also *Grobbelaar* v *News Group Newspapers* [2002] 1 WLR 3024 (£1 awarded in damages to Bruce Grobbelaar, the ex-Liverpool and Southampton goalkeeper, who – it was found – was justifiably accused by the defendant of taking bribes to 'throw' football matches but unjustifiably accused of acting on those bribes and actually throwing football matches).

[169] The requirements that have to be satisfied before an award of exemplary damages may be made against a defendant are discussed in much more detail below: Chapter 24.

[170] Weir 2006, 190.

(1) *Abolition.* Why not abolish the law of defamation? Tony Weir was the most forceful critic of the tort, calling it 'a blot on the lawscape',[170] 'the most difficult of all torts . . . certainly the oddest . . . odd at the very core.'[171] However, it could be argued that the social nature of the tort of defamation, in that it protects the valuable relationships we have with other people from being unjustly damaged by other people, makes the tort (at least potentially) an important guarantor of our well-being. As the European Court of Human Rights recognised in *Pfeifer* v *Austria* (2007), 'a person's reputation . . . forms part of his or her personal identity and psychological integrity'.[172] Given this, it is now increasingly accepted that damaging someone's reputation will violate their rights under Article 8 of the European Convention on Human Rights 'to respect for [their] private and family life . . .'.[173] If this is right, then the UK would violate its obligations under the ECHR to uphold people's Article 8 rights if it did not protect people's reputations from being damaged.

(2) *Declaration of falsity.* Under s 9 of the Defamation Act 1996, the courts have the power – in giving summary judgment[174] in favour of a claimant in a defamation case – to declare that the defamatory statement complained of by the claimant was false. However, there seems to be no official power to grant such a remedy in a case that goes to trial. (Though it would always be open to a judge in his judgment to make it clear that he thought the statement complained of by the claimant was false, and to order the defendant to publish a summary of his judgment under s 12 of the 2013 Act.)

As we have seen, the result is that an action for defamation is not that effective a means of vindicating a claimant's reputation. Just because a defendant has not been able to justify his allegations about the claimant does not mean they were not true. Adding the power to make an official declaration that the defendant's allegations about the claimant were false to the courts' armoury of remedies in a defamation case would provide the courts with a way of effectively vindicating the reputation of a claimant who has brought a claim for defamation. Moreover, the possibility of making an official declaration of falsity would take the pressure off courts and juries to include a vindicatory element in the damages they award to defamation claimants, thus reducing both the overall level of damages awards in defamation cases and their chilling effect on freedom of expression.

However, a declaration of falsity will not be a remedy that all claimants can pursue. It is much harder to prove a negative than a positive. In a case where A has said of B, 'B has been unfaithful to his wife', it will be almost impossible to establish that A's claim is positively false – unless, of course, B's movements have been continually monitored since he married his wife. In this sort of case, the only way to vindicate B's reputation will be through an award of damages (possibly combined with a strongly reasoned rejection of any defence of truth that A might offer to B's claim for defamation).

---

[171] Weir 2004, 519.

[172] (2007) 48 EHRR 175, at [35].

[173] *In Re Guardian News and Media Ltd* [2010] 2 AC 697, at [37]-[42] (per Lord Rodger); *Clift* v *Slough Borough Council* [2010] EWCA Civ 1484, at [32] (per Ward LJ).

[174] Under s 8, summary judgment is to be given if 'it appears to the court that there is no defence to the claim which has a realistic prospect of success, and there is no other reason why the claim should be tried.'

(3) *Liability of distributors.* Suppose there exists a book – written and published abroad – that obviously makes defamatory allegations about A. Suppose further that B, a bookseller based in the UK, is considering whether to stock and sell copies of this book. B may well think,

> Well – if I do stock and sell copies of this book and the allegations in the book prove to be incorrect, I could well be sued for libel by A. In such a case, I will be held to have published the allegations in the book to the people who buy it.[175] I probably won't have a defence under s 10 of the Defamation Act 2013 because the author and publisher are based abroad. And s 1 of the Defamation Act 1996 will not protect me because that only applies to people who unwittingly distribute material that is defamatory – and I won't fall into that category. I can't be sure that the allegations in this book are correct so I will definitely be taking a risk of being sued for libel by A if I stock and sell copies of the book. All in all, it might be best if I did not stock the book.

Now – if all booksellers react in the same way as B, there will be no market for the book about A – and this is so even if all the allegations contained in the book are completely correct. This is hardly satisfactory.

Similarly, suppose someone has anonymously posted a message on a website that is run by B. The message is obviously defamatory of A. A complains to B about the message and requests B to take it down. Again, B may well think,

> If I don't agree to A's request and the allegations made in this message prove to be untrue, I could well be sued for libel by A. Given my state of knowledge, I'll be held to be responsible for helping to publish this statement, and I won't be protected by section 1 of the Defamation Act 1996 because that only protects people who unwittingly distribute defamatory material – when I will be wittingly distributing defamatory material by allowing it to stay up on the website. I have no idea whether the allegations contained in this message are true or not so I will definitely be taking a risk of being sued for libel by A if I don't take this message down. Given this, it might be better if I withdrew this message from the website.

If B does think in this way, the message will be taken down from the website even if the allegations contained in that message were true. Again, this is hardly satisfactory.

In both these cases, the law on libel operates to 'chill' legitimate expression. In the first case, a perfectly truthful book will be rendered unmarketable by the law of libel. In the second case, B will be encouraged by the law on libel to 'censor' the message posted on his website even though it is perfectly accurate in what it says about A. What can be done to ensure that the law on libel does not have this effect? One solution would be to change the law so that it comes into line with Lord Denning MR's (unsuccessful) suggestion in *Goldsmith* v *Sperrings* (1977):

> Common sense and fairness require that no subordinate distributor – from top to bottom – should be held liable for a libel contained in it unless he knew or ought to have known that the newspaper or periodical contained a libel on the [claimant] himself; that is to say, that it contained a libel on the [claimant] which could not be justified or excused . . .[176]

---

[175] See above, § 16.4(6).

[176] [1977] 1 WLR 478, 487. The other two judges deciding the case declined to accept that Lord Denning's statement of the law was correct (on the ground that the point had not been argued before them) and it seems to have been assumed ever since that Lord Denning was wrong on this point. See, for example, *Metropolitan International Schools Ltd* v *Designtechnica Corporation* [2009] EWHC 1765 (QB), at [70] (per Eady J, arguing that even if there were still a common law defence of innocent dissemination (which was the subject of Lord Denning's *dictum* above), 'It would almost certainly not be available to a defendant who has had it drawn to his attention that the words are defamatory or, at least, arguably so').

If the law were changed in this way then, in the first case described above, booksellers could stock the book about A confident in the knowledge that if the allegations in the book proved to be untrue and they were sued for libel by A, they would have a defence to A's claim based on the fact that they did not know and had no reason to know that the allegations in the book were untrue. Similarly, in the second case described above, B could refuse to take down the message on his website, safe in the knowledge that if the allegations contained in that message proved to be untrue and A sued her for libel, she would have a defence to A's claim based on the fact that she did not know and had no reason to know that the allegations in that message were untrue.

However, the problem with giving subordinate distributors *immunity* from being sued in the way proposed by Lord Denning is that they would then have no incentive to act on *legitimate* complaints about the books they are selling, or statements that they are providing a platform for on their websites, when they might be the only people who could be expected to do anything about those complaints. Given this, it may be that the most satisfactory solution would be to grant subordinate distributors a *conditional immunity* from being sued for defamation, so that the distributor could not be sued in defamation so long as the way they handled the claimant's complaints about the material they were distributing did not show a reckless disregard for the claimant's rights.

(4) *Companies.* The social nature of the tort of defamation makes it doubtful whether companies should *ever* be allowed to take advantage of it. The justification for having a tort of defamation – that the preservation of the intimate relationships we have with other people is an important component of our well-being – simply does not translate across to a case where a company is complaining that its reputation is being damaged by imputations as to how it is run. Of course, if such imputations reflect personally on the people running the company, then they could have an action in their own names; but it is hard to see why the company *itself* should be able to sue.

Despite this, companies are still allowed to sue in defamation for statements that have 'a tendency to damage it in the way of its business'[177] and where those statements are made in permanent form, they are allowed to sue without having to prove that they have suffered any loss. (Though under s 1(2) of the 2013 Act, they will have to show that statements of which they complain are liable to cause them serious financial loss.) As we have seen, the courts – both here and in Strasbourg – have refused to find that allowing companies to take advantage of the law of defamation in this way violates people's rights to freedom of expression under Art 10 of the European Convention on Human Rights.[178]

However, there is increasing concern that companies are attempting to use the law of defamation to suppress legitimate criticism of their products or activities.[179] One creative way of ensuring that companies do not take unfair advantage of the law of defamation to limit other people's freedom of speech would be to bar companies above a particular size (whether measured by capital value, or number of employees) from suing in defamation at all.

---

[177] *Derbyshire County Council* v *Times Newspapers Ltd* [1993] AC 534, at 547 (per Lord Keith of Kinkel).
[178] See above, § 16.5. Also *Steel and Morris* v *UK* (2005) 41 EHRR 22 (holding (at [94]) that allowing a company to sue for defamation without having to prove what was said about it was false was not incompatible with Art 10).
[179] See above, § 16.1.

For example, under the Australian Uniform Defamation Laws (a catch-all term for an identical set of provisions that were adopted by all Australian states to govern claims for defamation), a company is not allowed to bring a claim for defamation unless it has fewer than ten employees (and is not a subsidiary of a larger company) or is a non-profit organisation. This approach has been criticised as arbitrary – why 10 employees? why not 20? or 30? – but it does ensure that most small businesses are able to obtain satisfactory redress through the courts when a defendant's unjustified allegations threaten to put them out of business, while at the same time forcing companies like McDonald's and Shell to rely on their public relations departments to combat any unjustified criticism of their activities.

(5) *New York Times v Sullivan (1964)*. As we have seen, in the United States, a politician – like any other public figure – will not be able to sue a defendant in defamation unless the defendant acted maliciously in saying what he did.[180]

Most judicial discussion as to whether England should adopt what is called the *Sullivan* position with regard to public figures has focussed on whether politicians should be disabled from suing for non-malicious allegations about them; the idea being that if we do not adopt *Sullivan* in relation to political figures, we can hardly apply it to any other public figures. As is well known, the House of Lords declined to adopt the *Sullivan* position in relation to politicians in *Reynolds* v *Times Newspapers Ltd* (2001), preferring to adopt the position that politicians would be able to sue a newspaper in defamation for publishing a defamatory and untrue story about them unless the story was on a matter of public interest, and was responsibly handled. Their Lordships advanced a number of reasons for taking this position.

Lord Nicholls observed that if statements about political figures were protected by qualified privilege, a politician whose reputation had been unjustly sullied by a newspaper acting in good faith would have no means of clearing his name – he would be barred from suing the newspaper for libel.[181] Lord Nicholls did not think that this was satisfactory:

> Once besmirched by an unfounded allegation in a national newspaper, a reputation can be damaged for ever, especially if there is no opportunity to vindicate one's reputation. When this happens, society as well as the individual is the loser . . . It is in the public interest that the reputation of public figures should not be debased falsely. In the political field, in order to make an informed choice, the electorate needs to be able to identify the good as well as the bad.[182]

Lords Nicholls and Cooke both observed that if statements about politicians were automatically protected by qualified privilege, one could have no confidence that newspapers – especially the tabloid press – would act responsibly in using this new won freedom to make statements about politicians free from the fear that they would be sued as a result of what they said.[183] They did not elaborate on this point but they must have feared that the press would use this freedom to print damaging stories about political figures based on the slenderest of materials and to print damaging stories about politicians which were of no conceivable public interest.

---

[180] See above, § 16.1(3).
[181] [2001] 2 AC 127, 201.
[182] [2001] 2 AC 127, 201.
[183] [2001] 2 AC 127, 201–2 (per Lord Nicholls), 219 (per Lord Cooke).

Lords Cooke and Steyn observed that if political speech were protected by qualified privilege, a politician who was defamed by a story in a newspaper would find it
very difficult to establish that the newspaper acted maliciously in publishing that
story.[184] This is for two reasons. First, malice is in itself a difficult thing to prove.
Secondly, English law does not compel journalists to prove their sources for a story –
thus making it very difficult for a claimant to show that a story had no source and was
simply made up. Given these difficulties of proving malice, politicians would have very
little protection against being defamed if political speech were protected by qualified
privilege – such speech would be *de facto* absolutely privileged; a politician who was
defamed by a particular story would in effect find it impossible to sue for libel in
respect of that story.

Finally, Lord Steyn advanced another argument against holding that all statements
about politicians are protected by qualified privilege. He thought that such a rule might
violate the European Convention on Human Rights, under which the resolution of competing rights and interests – such as the right to freedom of speech and the interest in
preserving one's reputation undamaged – is to be done on a case-by-case basis rather than
by laying down general rules which apply in a wide variety of cases.[185]

While the law of defamation does not protect political speech *as such*, it does protect
some statements about political figures. In particular, statements that express someone's
honest opinion about a politician and statements about politicians that are protected
under the new public interest defence set out in s 4 of the 2013 Act are protected under
UK law. Given this, *in theory* most forms of political speech will be protected under the
law in the United Kingdom and those forms of political speech which will not be protected – malicious speech, tittle-tattle and the publication of irresponsible and untrue
stories about politicians – are perhaps not worthy of protection. However, *in practice* the
law on defamation can still have the effect of chilling legitimate political speech if an editor is encouraged to 'sit on' a damaging story about a politician because he simply does
not have any confidence that the courts will find that he acted responsibly in handling
that story and consequently hold that that story was protected by a public interest defence
under s 4 of the 2013 Act.

As we have seen,[186] the House of Lords attempted in *Jameel (Mohammed)* v *Wall
Street Journal SPRL* (2007) to reassure editors in this regard and tried to ensure that
the courts would in future adopt a more 'journalist friendly' approach to determining
whether a story was handled in a responsible fashion than they have in the past. However, if the courts are incapable of embracing properly the liberalisation of defamation
law that the House of Lords' decision in *Reynolds* was intended to effect it may be that
the only way to ensure that the law of defamation does not have the effect of chilling
legitimate speech about politicians is to adopt a modified *Sullivan* position in relation to
politicians and rule that *all* speech about politicians (other than speech about their private lives that clearly has no bearing on the public interest) is protected by qualified
privilege.

---

[184] [2001] 2 AC 127, 210 (per Lord Steyn), 219–20 (per Lord Cooke).
[185] [2001] 2 AC 127, 211.
[186] See above, § 16.11.

Further reading

Those wanting to explore further the case for reforming the law of defamation may be interested to read:

Barendt, 'Libel and freedom of speech in English law' [1993] *Public Law* 449;

Barendt, 'What is the point of libel law?' [1999] *Current Legal Problems* 110;

Loveland, 'Political libels – whose right is it anyway?' (2000) 53 *Current Legal Problems* 333;

Coad, '*Reynolds* and public interest – what about truth and human rights?' (2007) 18 *Entertainment Law Review* 75;

Coad, '*Reynolds, Flood* and the King's new clothes' (2011) 22 *Entertainment Law Review* 1; and

Howarth, 'The cost of libel actions: a skeptical note' (2011) 70 *Cambridge Law Journal* 397.

Tony Weir's attacks on the law of defamation in his little book on tort law (*An Introduction to Tort Law*, 2nd ed (Clarendon Press, 2006), Chapter 12) and/or his casebook (*A Casebook on Tort*, 10th ed (Sweet & Maxwell, 2004), 519–23) are not to be missed.

Paul Mitchell's *The Making of the Modern Law of Defamation* (Hart Publishing, 2005) tells us how we got where we are today.

The colourful nature of defamation cases means that they have always attracted interest from journalists and non-specialist publishers, and that interest has resulted in some interesting books: **Adam Raphael's** *My Learned Friends* (**Virgin Books, 1989**) (an account of the Jeffrey Archer libel action and other libel cases); **Alan Watkins'** *A Slight Case of Libel* (**Duckworth, 1990**) (an account of Michael Meacher's libel action against Watkins and his newspaper, *The Observer*, for accusing Meacher of exaggerating his working-class background; Meacher lost); **John Vidal's** *McLibel: Burger Culture on Trial* (**Pan Books, 1997**); and **Dominic Carman's** *No Ordinary Man: A Life of George Carman* (**Hodder & Stoughton, 2002**) (a biography of the famous libel lawyer, by his son).

Chapter 17
Invasion of privacy, harassment and abuse

Aims and objectives

Reading this chapter should enable you to:

(1) Understand the development of a tort of misuse of private information, and when that tort will have been committed.

(2) Appreciate how this area of law is developing; in particular, its extension from cases of disclosure of private information to situations where someone has wrongfully obtained access to private information about someone else.

(3) Understand when someone can sue another under the Protection from Harassment Act 1997.

(4) Understand the current scope of, and debate around, the tort in *Wilkinson* v *Downton*.

17.1 The basics

Some scholars believe tort law's core concern is to protect people's freedom to decide how they will live their lives, and what they will do with the things that belong to them, free from interference by other people. For these scholars tort law is principally concerned to protect people from being killed, from having their bodies physically maimed or restrained, and from having their property taken or physically damaged. But people need more than protection from physical harm and restraint in order to feel free to choose the lives they want to live. For example, they may need to be able to hide information about some aspects of their lives from the world at large, so as to avoid a constant sense of being scrutinised, judged, or laughed at. And they may need to feel confident about going out of their front doors, or heading to work, and not fear that they will be constantly followed, hectored and belittled. Some people have 'thick skins', but for many of us a life where we were constantly stared at, criticised and mocked would be intolerable. This chapter deals with some areas of tort law that help protect people from their lives being made intolerable in such ways. In each area we will observe similar challenges for the law; challenges related to the difficulty of protecting people's freedom to enjoy the lives that they want to live, whilst not impinging too far on the freedom of others to do ordinary, human things, like sharing information, opinions and gossip, taking an interest in what is going on, debating values, and telling jokes.

A. Protection of privacy

English law recognises privacy as a value which underpins various rules of tort law (for instance, parts of the torts of trespass to land, private nuisance, defamation, and malicious falsehood). However, English law has *not* elevated the protection of privacy to the status of a legal principle from which judges can directly derive conditions of tortious liability.[1] To put the same point another way, English law has *not* recognised a *general* 'over-arching, all-embracing cause of action for "invasion of privacy"'.[2]

During the last two decades, however, and partly under the influence of the Human Rights Act 1998, the judges have developed a civil wrong, called misuse of private information. This wrong was initially recognised in order to deal with a *specific form* of invasion of privacy: disclosure of information about a claimant that ought to have been kept secret. Most of our discussion of misuse of private information deals with this form of invasion (wrongful disclosure). But more recently still, the judges have gone further and imposed civil liability for a second *specific form* of invasion of privacy: wrongfully obtaining access to private information. So, after describing misuse of private information as it applies in disclosure cases, we will go on to discuss when obtaining access to private information amounts to misuse. (Whilst it seems somewhat awkward to refer to *obtaining* information as *misusing* information, the courts regard the development as an extension of the tort of *misuse of private information*.) After identifying the current limits of the tort, we will assess the likelihood of its future extension to cover further specific forms of invasion of privacy.

Misuse of private information[3] has attracted public attention because it is the tort that is used to prevent newspapers from publishing salacious information about the sex lives of celebrities. But its scope is wider than this; it has also been invoked by others who have attracted media attention, such as prominent businesspeople, victims of crime, people who suffer from unusual illnesses, and the children of famous parents. As we have just noted, the courts currently recognise that a defendant can misuse private information by

---

[1] In *Wainwright* v *Home Office* [2004] 2 AC 406, Lord Hoffmann suggested (at [31]–[33]) that English law should not give effect to a general principle such as 'the unjustified invasion of another's privacy is always actionable' because the detailed attention of a legislator would often be necessary in order to fashion conditions of liability and appropriate defences in the very different areas where the value of privacy might be invoked. He mentioned regulation of the use of images recorded by CCTV cameras as an example of an area where detailed legislation would be more appropriate than a judicial attempt to derive a solution from a broad principle.

[2] *Campbell* v *MGN Ltd* [2004] 2 AC 457, at [11] (per Lord Nicholls).

[3] In the previous edition of this text we called the tort 'wrongful disclosure of private information', but the label 'misuse of private information' is now more common in legal practice: *Murray* v *Express Newspapers plc* [2009] Ch 481, at [24](ii) (per Sir Anthony Clarke MR) 'the essence of the tort is better encapsulated now as misuse of private information'; *Imerman* v *Tchenguiz* [2011] Fam 116, at [65]: '[T]here is now a tort of misuse of private information' (per Lord Neuberger MR); *Vidal-Hall* v *Google Inc* [2015] 1 WLR 4534.

either *disclosing* it or *obtaining access* to it, but for the purpose of an introductory summary we will begin with cases involving disclosure. In such cases, in summary, the tort will be committed by A in relation to B where:

1. A discloses information about B to C

2. it is information that B reasonably expects to remain private,

3. A knows, or ought to know this, and

4. the circumstances are *not* such that A's being left free to disclose the information to C is more important than protecting B's interest in the information remaining private.[4]

Thus if *Tabloid* published details about a sexual encounter between *Rocker* and *Groupie* it is very likely that *Tabloid* will have committed the tort of misuse of private information in relation to *Rocker*. (Indeed, if *Groupie* is not the source of the information that *Tabloid* published then it is very likely that *Tabloid* will have committed the tort in relation to *Groupie* as well.) But we cannot say for certain that *Tabloid* will have committed the tort in this situation without investigating the facts in more detail since in some circumstances *Tabloid* will be able to establish: (a) that the information was not private at all (perhaps because it had already been widely published by others); or (b) that publishing the information served some public interest that is more important than the protection of *Rocker's* (and perhaps *Groupie's*) privacy. An example of such a public interest justification for publication would be if the story went no further than necessary to correct a false impression that *Rocker* has conveyed to the public.

Where a court finds that the tort has been committed it can award damages, and may also grant an injunction prohibiting further publication of the private information, unless that would be a futile gesture. In practice, however, many of the cases dealt with by the courts involve claims for injunctions in advance of any widespread publication, where the claimant's aim is to prevent publication of private information.

We noted above that liability for misuse of private information by *wrongfully obtaining access* to it was recognised later than for misuse by disclosure. Because few cases have considered this form of invasion of privacy, it is more difficult to summarise the scope of this extension to the tort with any certainty. So far the courts have held that A will commit a tort in relation to B if he intentionally obtains information by secretly looking at a document or copying it, or listening to a recorded message, knowing that B reasonably expects this information to be private, and the circumstances are not such that A's interest in obtaining the information is more important than B's interest in it remaining private. Thus *Nightjar*, *Rocker's* wife, may commit the tort in relation to *Rocker* if she sneaks into his office and makes copies of financial documents that he always refused to show her. In *Gulati* v *MGN Ltd* (2015) the defendants accepted that it was similarly a tort to listen covertly to private messages on someone's answerphone.[5] It is possible that in the future the wrong will be extended beyond obtaining access to information in documents and recordings, so as to cover obtaining information by eavesdropping or surveillance.

---

[4] The type of *misuse* of private information that most frequently leads to claims is *disclosure* of that information. Indeed, it is not easy to identify actionable forms of *misuse* that do not involve *disclosure*, so, for the sake of simplicity, our summary only covers this.

[5] The Court of Appeal was asked to rule on the correct approach for assessing damages in such cases, rather than on whether the behaviour was tortious: *Gulati* v *MGN Ltd* [2017] QB 149.

B. Protection from harassment

Until 1997, it was not a tort in England – of and in itself – to harass someone else. Of course, someone who harassed someone else might commit another tort in the course of so doing. For example, harassing someone by constantly threatening them with imminent violence would amount to an assault; harassing someone by continually calling them at home would amount to a private nuisance (so long as the person being called had an interest in the home where the calls were received).[6] But harassment *per se* did not amount to a tort. However, things are very different nowadays. We now have not one, but two sets of statutory provisions that make it a tort to harass someone else.

Section 1(1) of the Protection from Harassment Act 1997 provides that 'A person must not pursue a course of conduct – (a) which amounts to harassment of another, and (b) which he knows or ought to know amounts to harassment of the other.' That breach of this provision will amount to a tort is made clear by s 3(1) of the 1997 Act, which provides that an 'actual or apprehended breach . . . may be the subject of a claim in civil proceedings by the person who is or may be the victim of the course of conduct in question.'

In this chapter we will focus on the Protection from Harassment Act 1997, but it is worth noting that the protection against being harassed provided by the 1997 Act has now been added to by the Equality Act 2010.[7] The structure of this Act is quite complex. Part 2 of the Act lays out various forms of 'prohibited conduct', including 'harassment' (s 26). For the purposes of that provision, someone (A) will 'harass' someone else (B) if he engages in any of three specific forms of conduct, *and* that conduct has the purpose or effect of violating B's dignity, or has the purpose or effect of creating an 'intimidating, hostile, degrading, humiliating or offensive environment for B'. The three specific forms of conduct are: (i) engaging in 'unwanted conduct' related to a 'protected characteristic'; (ii) engaging in 'unwanted conduct' of a 'sexual nature'; and (iii) treating someone less favourably because they have submitted to or rejected 'unwanted conduct' of a 'sexual nature or that is related to gender reassignment or sex'. For the first specific form, 'unwanted conduct', the 'protected characteristics' are: age; disability; gender reassignment; race; religion or belief; sex; sexual orientation.

Parts 3–7 of the Act define who is not allowed to engage in the 'prohibited conduct' laid out in Part 2, and in what ways. Those who fall under the Act are: service providers (Part 3); people who deal with, or have an interest in, premises (Part 4); employers (Part 5); education providers (Part 6); and, associations (Part 7). So, for example, ss 101(4) and 102(3) of the Act (which belong to Part 7 of the Act) provide that an association must not 'harass' a member of the association, or someone seeking to be a member of the association, or an associate member of the association, or a guest of the association, or someone seeking to be a guest of the association.

Part 9 of the Act sets out what happens if a defendant breaches a provision laid out in Parts 3–7 of the Act, that required the defendant not to engage in conduct that is 'prohibited' under Part 2 of the Act. Section 119(2) of the Act provides that a defendant who

---

[6] *Hunter* v *Canary Wharf Ltd* [1997] AC 655, disapproving *Khorasandjian* v *Bush* [1993] 1 QB 727 (which had ruled that an interest in the premises where the calls were received was not necessary to bring a claim in private nuisance against a defendant who was harassing you by continually calling you at home).

[7] Some forms of harassment could give rise to civil claims under earlier equality legislation, on the basis that in the circumstances the harassment amounted to direct discrimination: see, e.g. *Jones* v *Tower Boot Co Ltd* [1997] ICR 254, on when harassment by employees might amount to discrimination by their employer.

'harasses' someone else contrary to a provision in Parts 3, 4, 6 or 7 of the Act can be sued in tort in the county court by the victim of that harassment, and the court can award any of the remedies usually available in a tort claim. That leaves workplace harassment (governed by Part 5 of the Act), which will be dealt with by an employment tribunal, but can also lead to an award of compensation (s 124(2)). In applying these provisions, Part 8 makes clear that an employer is liable for what is done by its employee in the course of employment, a principal is liable for what is done by its agent with authority, and the individual employee or agent may also be held liable for their conduct where it amounts to a contravention of the Act by their employee or principal.

C. The tort in *Wilkinson* v *Downton*

In *Wilkinson* v *Downton* (1897), the defendant told the claimant that her husband had met with a serious accident and that both his legs had been broken. In fact, as the defendant knew, this was not true. It seems the defendant intended a practical joke, but the claimant was so upset that she became physically ill. The claimant subsequently sued the defendant for compensation. Wright J held that the defendant's conduct amounted to a tort, and the claimant was entitled to sue the defendant for compensation. However, the elements of the defendant's conduct that Wright J fastened on as establishing that the defendant had committed a tort – that the defendant had 'wilfully done an act calculated to cause physical harm to the plaintiff . . . and has in fact thereby caused physical harm to her' when there was 'no justification' for what he did[8] – did not fall within any established definition of when a tort would be committed. So lawyers treated Wright J as having recognised a wholly new form of wrongdoing – which came to be known as 'the tort in *Wilkinson* v *Downton*'.

Over a century later, in *Wainwright* v *Home Office*, Lord Hoffmann noted that 'commentators and counsel' had been 'unwilling to allow [the tort in] *Wilkinson* v *Downton* to disappear beneath the surface of the law of negligence'.[9] The idea behind this comment was that *if* the tort in *Wilkinson* v *Downton* is *only* committed when a defendant intentionally or recklessly causes someone to suffer physical injury or psychiatric illness – a position close to that taken by the Court of Appeal in *Wong* v *Parkside Health NHS Trust* (2003) – then it is hard to see why we need the tort in *Wilkinson* v *Downton*: anyone who intentionally or recklessly causes someone to suffer physical injury or psychiatric illness can nowadays be sued in negligence.[10] In *O (a child)* v *Rhodes* (2016), however, the Supreme Court reaffirmed the independent status of the tort in *Wilkinson* v *Downton* and clarified when it would be committed by defining the conduct element, mental element and consequence element that a claimant must prove. The conduct element is 'words or conduct directed towards the claimant for which there is no justification or reasonable excuse', the mental element is that the defendant intended, at least, 'to cause at least severe mental or emotional distress', and the consequence element is that the claimant has suffered 'physical harm or recognised psychiatric illness'. We discuss the decision in *Rhodes* in more detail in the final section of this chapter.

---

[8] [1897] 2 QB 57, 589.

[9] [2004] 2 AC 406, at [41].

[10] A former Professor of Law at Oxford University used to say that if A poisoned B's drink and B was made sick as a result of drinking the poison, the only tort B could sue A under was the tort in *Wilkinson* v *Downton*. But there seems no reason why B could not sue A in negligence here: A owed B a duty to take care not to poison her drink and he clearly breached that duty by putting poison in her drink. Negligence liability covers intentional acts, as well as careless acts: see above, § 3.2.

17.2 Misuse of private information: disclosure

The case of *Campbell* v *MGN* (2004)[11] concerned the publication in the *Daily Mirror* of the information that Naomi Campbell was a drug addict, was seeking treatment through Narcotics Anonymous, some details of her treatment, and a photograph of her at a place where a Narcotics Anonymous meeting took place. She conceded that the *Daily Mirror* was entitled to disclose *some* of this information to the world, in particular that she was a drug addict and was seeking treatment. But she contended that the defendant had committed a tort in relation to her by publishing the other details and the photograph. The House of Lords unanimously confirmed that someone (A) will commit a tort[12] in relation to someone else (B) if he unjustifiably discloses to a third person (C) information which A knows or ought to know is private information about B. By a bare majority of three to two the House of Lords held that the *Daily Mirror* had committed this tort in publishing the details of Naomi Campbell's treatment and the photograph.

A. The independence of the new tort

Most of the judges involved in developing this new tort *said* that they were not actually creating a new tort but were *extending* the long-established equitable wrong of breach of confidence. But we think that it was always artificial to pretend that what was happening was the 'evolution' of breach of confidence, an equitable wrong. The traditional features of breach of confidence played no significant role in cases involving the wrongful disclosure of *private* information. For instance, the 'cause of action has now firmly shaken off the limiting constraint of the need for an initial confidential relationship'[13] and the narrow limits on the defences to the equitable wrong do not apply in cases protecting privacy.[14] Moreover, judges who were asked to settle disputes about features of the new wrong generally referred to human rights law and analogies with torts like libel and slander rather than to any principles developed by the Courts of Equity. Most courts now treat the civil wrong committed by the *Daily Mirror* in *Campbell* as a *new and independent tort* – the tort of misuse of private information.[15]

One advantage of treating wrongful disclosure of private information as an independent tort is that it avoids confusion with the *original* form of the equitable wrong of breach of

---

[11] Reported at [2004] 2 AC 457; and referred to henceforth as '*Campbell*'.

[12] Strictly speaking only one of their Lordships refers to the wrong as a 'tort' (Lord Nicholls at [14]). But matters have moved on, and most judges now refer to the wrong as the 'tort of misuse of private information'. Any reader who still doubts whether the wrong is a 'tort' can instead treat the next three parts of this chapter as dealing with *extensions of* an equitable wrong for pragmatic reasons. See above, § 1.9.

[13] *Campbell*, at [14] (per Lord Nicholls).

[14] *Theakston* v *MGN* [2002] EMLR 137, at [66].

[15] Although the majority of the House of Lords in *Campbell refused* to treat wrongful disclosure of private information as an independent tort – and this refusal could have significant practical consequences, particularly in the field of remedies – subsequent Court of Appeal decisions have referred to 'the rechristening of the tort as misuse of private information' and treated Lord Nicholls's opinion (*Campbell*, at [14]) on this point as orthodox: *McKennitt* v *Ash* [2008] QB 73, at [8]. (In subsequent footnotes we will refer to this case as *McKennitt.*) See also *Lord Browne of Madingley* v *Associated Newspapers Ltd* [2008] QB 103, at [21]–[22], and *Vidal-Hall* v *Google Inc* [2015] 1 WLR 4534, where the Court of Appeal held that misuse of private information was a 'tort' for the purposes of the Civil Procedure Rules relating to service outside the jurisdiction.

confidence, which continues to exist. The *original* form of breach of confidence deals with situations where abstract information, which need not be private information – such as a trade secret – is disclosed to someone on the condition that it will remain confidential.[16] Some lawyers might argue, however, that treating the two wrongs as *independent* tends to exaggerate the differences between them. Indeed in *Imerman* v *Tchenguiz* (2011), the Court of Appeal stated that 'the law should be developed consistently and coherently in both privacy and "old fashioned confidence" cases, even if they sometimes have different features.'[17] Moreover, in practice cases often arise where claimants rely on both wrongs simultaneously. This makes it important to consider how judges treat cases where the information that the defendant has disclosed is arguably both private information within the scope of the new tort *and* information that the defendant was told or discovered in the course of a confidential relationship with the claimant. The answer is that in such cases a claimant gains an advantage by demonstrating that a duty of confidence in the *original* form attaches to the information since: (i) if the information is *also* private the original duty of confidence will add weight to the claim that it is appropriate to restrict a defendant's right to free expression,[18] and (ii) if the information is *not* private then the claimant will only be able to win if she can demonstrate a duty of confidence in the original form.

B. Article 8 of the ECHR

The most important influence on the development of the new tort has been and remains the right to privacy contained in Article 8 of the European Convention on Human Rights (ECHR). Although s 6 of the Human Rights Act 1998 does not impose a duty on *private individuals* to act compatibly with Convention rights,[19] it does impose such a duty on public authorities, including the courts. Further, the European Court of Human Rights has held that Article 8 requires States to do more than merely ensuring that public authorities do not *themselves* perform acts that violate privacy: States must also assist private individuals who want to preserve their privacy against other private individuals. As the Court expressed the point in *Von Hannover* v *Germany* (2005):

> although the object of Article 8 is essentially that of protecting the individual against arbitrary interference by the public authorities, it does not merely compel the State to abstain from such interference: in addition to this primarily negative undertaking, there may be positive obligations inherent in an effective respect for private or family life. These obligations may involve the adoption of measures designed to secure respect for private life even in the sphere of the relations of individuals between themselves.[20]

---

[16] In *Douglas* v *Hello! Ltd (No 3)* [2008] 1 AC 1, a majority of the House of Lords accepted that a private event could be organised in such a way as to make the information that would be disclosed by a *photographic* image of the event into a commercial secret, which could be protected by the wrong of breach of confidence, and this could clearly cover what a particular person *looked like during the event*. The protection provided by this aspect of the wrong of breach of confidence is *separate* from the duty not to publish photographic images which disclose *private* information.

[17] *Imerman* v *Tchenguiz* [2011] Fam 116, at [67]. This case is discussed in detail below, § 17.7.

[18] For instance, when considering the unauthorised publication of Prince Charles's travel journals the Court of Appeal stated that '[b]oth the nature of the information and of the relationship of confidence under which it was received weigh heavily in the balance in favour of Prince Charles': *HRH Prince of Wales* v *Associated Newspapers Ltd* [2008] Ch 57, at [71].

[19] See above, § 1.8.

[20] (2005) 40 EHRR 1, at [57].

Clearly one way of assisting private individuals to preserve their privacy against other private individuals is by recognising a tort, and this is what the English courts have done. Indeed they have modelled this new tort on the assumption that 'the values underlying Articles 8 and 10 are not confined to disputes between individuals and public authorities'.[21] It is important to note, however, that the courts have *not* simply made *all* behaviour what would amount to a violation of Article 8 if done by a State into a tort if done by a private individual. This point needs emphasis because Article 8 protects privacy in many contexts well beyond the boundaries of the new tort. For example, Article 8 has been relied on compel States to recognise the new genders of those who have undergone gender-reassignment[22] and to prohibit States from retaining DNA samples taken from innocent people.[23] The new tort was initially *limited* to protecting claimants against *wrongful disclosure of private information* in situations where the balance between Articles 8 and 10 means that such protection is justifiable,[24] and has now, as we will see, been extended to cover *wrongfully obtaining access to private information*.

C. The structure of the new tort

The new tort has an unusual structure because, at least in situations involving *disclosure,* it exists at the meeting point of *two* human rights: *Teller's* disclosure to *Reporter* of private information about *Striker may* infringe *Striker's* right to privacy, but a restriction on *Teller* making such a disclosure *may* infringe the right to free expression of *Teller, Reporter* and the public generally.[25] Neither of these human rights is pre-eminent, so 'the proportionality of interfering with one has to be balanced against the proportionality of restricting the other'.[26]

The term 'balancing' is shorthand for a more complex process, and one which requires an 'intense focus' on the particular facts of the case.[27] In order to impose tort liability only when that is appropriate given the competing rights at stake, the court is likely to find it convenient to proceed by asking the following questions:

(1) Is the information about B which A has disclosed to C sufficiently *private* to come within the potential ambit of the tort?

(2) If the information is sufficiently private, how important is it to protect this aspect of B's privacy?

(3) Was A's disclosure of the information to C *expression* within the ambit of Article 10?

(4) If so, how important is it not to restrict this sort of expression?[28]

---

[21] *Campbell,* at [18] (per Lord Nicholls). Article 10 is, of course, the provision which defines the right to free expression in the ECHR. See also at [50] (per Lord Hoffmann), 'I can see no logical ground for saying that a person should have less protection against a private individual than he would have against the state for the publication of personal information for which there is no justification.'

[22] *Goodwin v United Kingdom* (2002) 35 EHRR 18.

[23] *S and Marper v United Kingdom* (2008) 48 EHRR 50.

[24] The degree of correspondence is strong. Buxton LJ expressed the relationship as follows in *McKennitt,* at [11]: 'Those articles are now not merely of persuasive or parallel effect but . . . are the very content of the domestic tort that the English court has to enforce.'

[25] It is important to remember that both the *publisher* of the information and the *recipient* have a right to free expression.

[26] *Campbell,* at [140] (per Baroness Hale). See also [113] (per Lord Hope) and [167] (per Lord Carswell).

[27] *Re S (A Child) (Identification: Restrictions on Publication)* [2005] 1 AC 593, at [17] (per Lord Steyn).

[28] Importance must be assessed considering the interests of both *publisher* and *recipient.*

(5) Using the answers to (2) and (4), will making A liable amount to a *proportionate* restriction on A's and C's freedom of expression in order to protect B's privacy *or* will not holding A liable constitute a *proportionate* limit on the protection of B's privacy in order preserve freedom of expression?

It *may* also sometimes be necessary to ask a further question:

(6) Did A know, or ought A to have known, that the information was sufficiently private?

We have expressed these six steps in the terms that will be appropriate if a court is dealing with a case where the information has already been published. In practice, however, cases are often brought to try to *prevent* widespread publication, and consequently a court will often have to amend questions (1) and (3) so that they ask about possible future disclosure. For example, question (1) will become: (1) Is the information about B which A *is about to* disclose to C sufficiently *private* to come within the potential ambit of the tort?

    In many cases, of course, it will not be necessary to go through all these steps. Often it will be obvious that *if* the information about B is sufficiently *private* to come within the potential ambit of the tort – question (1) – then B ought to win the case, since no significant value associated with free expression will be served by disclosing the information to C.

D. Private information

What sorts of information are sufficiently private to come within the ambit of the tort? The basic test is whether B had a 'reasonable expectation of privacy' in relation to the information that A disclosed to C.[29] Some simple points can be made about this test.

(1) *A reasonable expectation of privacy is consistent with limited disclosure.* People can have a 'reasonable expectation of privacy' with regard to information even if it is not totally secret: what matters is whether they can reasonably expect to retain some control over its dissemination.[30] Thus, when *Poorly* goes to *Doctor* and describes his symptoms he will be aware that medical professionals usually record such information and can properly share it with colleagues and assistants, but it would nonetheless usually be reasonable for *Poorly* to expect to retain control over whether the information is disclosed to his wife, his employer, or a journalist. In practice, most[31] cases are likely to involve information which the claimant has revealed to a lover or disclosed to a limited circle of family, friends or colleagues.[32] Thus the relevant expectation is as to whether B ought to be able to control in what circumstances, if ever, the information will be released more widely.

---

[29] *Campbell*, at [21] (per Lord Nicholls), [85] (per Lord Hope), [134] (per Baroness Hale).

[30] In *Campbell*, at [51], Lord Hoffmann said that the new tort 'focuses upon the protection of human autonomy and dignity – *the right to control the dissemination of information about one's private life* and the right to the esteem and respect of other people' (emphasis added).

[31] Exceptional cases can be imagined; for instance, where *Snapper* takes a photograph of *Tripper* falling over in the street and sells it to *Tabloid* this may disclose information that *nobody* previously *knew*: exactly what *Tripper* looks like when he's falling over.

[32] In *Browne of Madingley (Lord)* v *Associated Newspapers Ltd* [2008] QB 103, at [61], the Court of Appeal identified 'an important distinction between information which is made available to a person's circle of friends or work colleagues and information which is widely published in a newspaper.'

(2) *A reasonable expectation of privacy can exist even when information has been published widely.* In *PJS* v *News Group Newspapers Ltd* (2016),[33] the Supreme Court had to deal with a case where the claimant, who worked in the entertainment industry – as did his partner – and who had young children, sought an injunction to prevent further disclosure of information about his adulterous sexual encounters with AB, including participation in a 'three-way' with AB and CD. After an interim injunction had been obtained in England, a magazine in the United States had published the story, as had newspapers in Canada and Scotland, and it had appeared on various websites. Nonetheless, the Supreme Court granted a further interim injunction. Lord Mance accepted that even when private information had been published in foreign newspapers and on the Internet, a claimant might be subjected to a wholly different degree of intrusion and distress if the same story appeared, perhaps illustrated with photographs, on the front of a national tabloid and precipitated a 'media frenzy'. Thus he drew a distinction between material protected by a traditional 'duty of confidence', which would cease to be 'confidential' once it was in the 'public domain', and truly private information, such as details of a sexual encounter, which would remain private even if there had been significant disclosure. Indeed, Lord Mance went so far as to say that even publishing private information to someone who already knew the information might involve the commission of a further tort, particularly if the second disclosure occurred in a different medium.[34]

The Court of Appeal had previously suggested republishing a photograph that conveyed private information might amount to a further tort. In *Douglas* v *Hello! Ltd (No 3)* (2006) the Court of Appeal explained:

> In so far as a photograph does more than convey information and intrudes on privacy by enabling the viewer to focus on intimate personal detail, there will be a fresh intrusion of privacy when each additional viewer sees the photograph and even when one who has seen a previous publication of the photograph is confronted by a fresh publication of it. To take an example, if a film star were photographed, with the aid of a telephoto lens, lying naked by her private swimming pool, we question whether widespread publication of the photograph by a popular newspaper would provide a defence to a legal challenge to repeated publication on the ground that the information was in the public domain.[35]

This said, there is an important distinction between whether publication or republication will be a tort, and whether it would be appropriate for a court to exercise its discretion to grant an injunction: at some point information or a photograph will have been published so widely that it would be pointless for a court to make an order prohibiting further publication: for example, Eady J ruled that an injunction before trial would be futile in *Mosley* v *News Group Newspapers Ltd* (2008), where edited footage of a sado-masochistic sex session involving the claimant had been viewed on the Internet more than 1.4 million times before the injunction was sought.[36]

---

[33] Reported at [2016] AC 1081; and referred to henceforth as '*PJS*'.

[34] *PJS*, at [32].

[35] *Douglas* v *Hello! Ltd (No 3)* [2006] QB 125, at [105].

[36] [2008] EWHC 687 (QB). See also *PJS*, at [33]. Our reference is to the judgment in Max Mosley's unsuccessful claim for an interim injunction. His subsequent successful claim for damages is discussed below at §17.8. In the later case of *Mosley* v *Google Inc* [2015] EWHC 59 (QB), at [3], Mitting J stated that Max Mosley obtained a permanent injunction against the defendant newspaper group at the same time as being awarded damages, but there is no express mention of this in the judgment in the damages claim: [2008] EWHC 1777 (QB).

(3) *'The law of privacy is not intended for the protection of the unduly sensitive'.*[37] 'The question is what a reasonable person of ordinary sensibilities would feel if she was placed in the same position as the claimant and faced with the same publicity'.[38] So a claim cannot be based on the publication by *Tabloid* of information about *Diva* that a reasonable person would not be worried about maintaining any degree of control over. For example, if *Diva* is inexplicably sensitive about other people finding out the date of her birthday this will not mean that *Tabloid* will commit a tort if it discloses the date to its readers.

The ordinary sensibilities rule is qualified to an extent, however, by the further rule that the reasonableness of the expectation of privacy as to information about a particular feature is judged from the perspective of people who share the same feature. Thus in *Campbell* the question whether it was reasonable for Naomi Campbell to expect that the details of her treatment should be kept private was assessed from the perspective of a reasonable drug addict receiving treatment.[39]

(4) *The reasonable expectation test is objective.*[40] The reasonable expectation test does not depend on the claimant establishing what she personally expected; many celebrities *in fact expect* atrocious behaviour from tabloid newspapers and others, and children can claim to have been victims of the tort even if they are much too young to understand the concept of 'privacy'.[41] The crucial issue is whether a reasonable person in the claimant's position *ought to be able to* expect privacy. But this, of course, is often a controversial question, since reasonable people may have different views as to what should remain private. For example, *ERY* v *Associated Newspapers Ltd* (2016) raised the question whether a prominent businessman could establish a reasonable expectation of privacy with respect to the information that he had been investigated for financial crime and interviewed under caution.[42] Ought a reasonable businessperson be able to keep such information out of the newspapers? Similarly, in the New Zealand case of *Andrews* v *Television New Zealand Ltd* (2009), the claimants were involved in a car accident in which their car left the road, and some months later the defendant broadcast film of them while they were trapped in the vehicle awaiting rescue as part of a television series called 'Fire Fighters': would an English court have held that they could reasonably expect such pictures not to be published?[43] We do not think that there is any easy solution to the problems caused by uncertain and inconsistent expectations.

(5) *Relevant factors.* In *Murray* v *Express Newspapers Ltd* (2009) the Court of Appeal provided the following summary of the factors which are most important when considering whether a claimant has a reasonable expectation of privacy:

> . . . the attributes of the claimant, the nature of the activity in which the claimant was engaged, the place at which it was happening, the nature and purpose of the intrusion, the absence of consent and whether it was known or could be inferred, the effect on the claimant and the circumstances in which and the purposes for which the information came into the hands of the publisher.[44]

---

[37] *Campbell*, at [94] (per Lord Hope).
[38] *Campbell*, at [99] (per Lord Hope).
[39] *Campbell*, at [98] (per Lord Hope), [136] (per Baroness Hale).
[40] *Murray* v *Express Newspapers plc* [2009] Ch 481, at [35].
[41] For example, in *Weller* v *Associated Newspapers Ltd* [2016] 1 WLR 1541 (henceforth, '*Weller*'), two of the claimants were ten months old when the relevant photographs of them were published.
[42] See also *ZXC* v *Bloomberg LP* [2017] EWHC 328 (QB).
[43] The judge, Allan J, held that the claimants could establish that they had a reasonable expectation of privacy, but eventually gave judgment for the defendants because of another point.
[44] [2009] Ch 481, at [36].

This summary was specifically formulated to address the question in cases involving photographs, but a similarly broad account of the relevant factors would be necessary to summarise the test used in cases involving *stories* rather than *images*. Our reading of the cases suggests that courts have treated the following six factors as relevant when considering whether a claimant had a 'reasonable expectation of privacy':

(i) *The nature of the information.* Certain types of information, for example information relating to sexuality[45] or health,[46] can be straightforwardly classified as private as a result of their *private nature.* Equally, at the other end of the spectrum, information as to what occurred during the formal proceedings of public institutions, such as in Parliament or a court, will generally not be private information.[47]

(ii) *The form in which the information was kept.* Certain ways of storing information, such as in a private diary or a confidential file, add weight to a claimant's assertion that it was reasonable for him to expect that the contents would not be generally published.

(iii) *The relationship between the claimant and the person who discloses the information.* There is clearly a stronger expectation that information discovered in the course of a relationship will be kept private when the parties are husband and wife, priest and penitent, or doctor and patient, than when they are storekeeper and customer, or journalist and celebrity.[48] In other words, the *nature of the relationship* which led to B holding information about A can affect whether A has a reasonable expectation of privacy with respect to that information.[49]

---

[45] The category of 'sexuality' includes information about a person's gender identification, sexual orientation and sexual life: *PG* v *United Kingdom* [2001] ECHR 546, at [56]. The 'salacious details' of any sexual encounter will generally be private information, but that on occasion a claimant will be unable to establish that he or she could reasonably expect no publicity to be given to the bare fact of a sexual relationship: eg *Donald* v *Ntuli* [2011] 1 WLR 294.

[46] The category 'health' includes 'information about a person's health and treatment for ill-health', *Campbell* at [145] (per Baroness Hale), though *trivial matters* will not be protected: ibid, at [157] (per Baroness Hale), 'the privacy interest in the fact that a public figure has a cold or a broken leg is unlikely to be strong enough to justify restricting the press's freedom to report it'.

[47] In *Khuja* v *Times Newspapers Ltd* [2017] UKSC 49, the information relating to the claimant was that he had been arrested in the course of an inquiry into sexual offences against children, but subsequently released without being charged. The claimant's attempt to prevent the publication of this was significantly impeded, however, by the fact that the matters that had aroused suspicion against him, and the fact that he had not been identified by the complainant, had been mentioned in a criminal trial of others for related offences. Lord Sumption, in a judgment that gained the support of a majority in the Supreme Court, held that the claimant could not have a reasonable expectation of privacy with regard to proceedings in an open court that had been conducted without any attempt to shield his identity (at [34]).

[48] For example, in *McKennitt* at [14]–[18], [24], the Court of Appeal thought that the relevant information *might* have been private in *nature* anyway, but held that the conclusion that it should be protected from disclosure became irresistible once account was taken of the fact that the information had only become available to the defendant in the course of a close friendship between herself and the claimant.

[49] The interplay between the nature of the relationship and the nature of the information is apparent in *Lord Browne of Madingley* v *Associated Newspapers Ltd* [2008] QB 103, where Lord Browne, the group chief executive of BP plc, sought to restrain the defendants from publishing information received from Jeff Chevalier, who had been Lord Browne's homosexual partner for four years. Eady J, at first instance, held that the relationship was such that Lord Browne was entitled to expect that any comments he made to Jeff Chevalier about his business colleagues, and the content of conversations at dinner parties and the like, would remain private. But Eady J concluded, and the Court of Appeal upheld this, that Lord Browne could not expect the fact that he had provided Jeff Chevalier with assistance from BP plc's staff and resources, or the mere fact of the relationship, or the fact that he had discussed BP plc's business with his lover, to remain private.

(iv) *How the information was obtained.* If the information had to be obtained by subterfuge or trickery this will add weight to the argument that it was private.[50]

(v) *The claimant's previous behaviour.* A claimant's previous behaviour may indicate that he has waived any right to keep information about some aspect of his life private, and a claimant cannot reasonably expect people to refrain from publishing information about him if he has led them to believe that he is content for such information to be published.[51] But the fact that a claimant has voluntarily disclosed to the public some measure of information about a private topic will not be taken to mean that he has waived protection for all further information relating to that topic. The contrary suggestion, sometimes referred to as the 'zone' or 'zonal' argument, has been discredited.[52] In some circumstances, however, a claimant's previous disclosures about some aspect of his life may mean that it is in the public interest for other information about the same aspect of his life to be published in order to correct a 'false impression'.

(vi) *The likely consequences of the disclosure.*[53] Privacy is closely linked with autonomy and liberty. Thus information is more likely to be classified as private if its disclosure would be likely to restrict a person's ability to live the life that he chooses. For example, the European Court of Human Rights has emphasised that one of the reasons why information that a person is HIV-positive is private is that publication of such information 'may dramatically affect his or her private and family life, as well as the individual's social and employment situation, by exposing that person to opprobrium and the risk of ostracism.'[54]

In *Weller* (2015), the Court of Appeal suggested that the likely consequences of disclosure might be of particular importance in a case involving photographs of the children of a celebrity because of the potential risk to their security and the prospect that they might suffer from embarrassment or bullying at school.[55]

Real cases usually require a combination of these factors to be assessed, and it is often difficult to identify any particular factor as *decisive*. Thus a claimant's reasonable expectation is often established by 'an interdependent amalgam of circumstances'.[56] For instance,

---

[50] Lord Hoffmann suggested, in *Campbell* at [75], that it might be a violation of privacy to publish a photograph obtained by intrusion because to do so demonstrated that apparently private space was not inviolate.

[51] The Court of Appeal in *McKennitt*, at [35]–[36], suggested that *Woodward* v *Hutchins* [1977] 1 WLR 760 might be a rare example of such a doctrine being applied: Bridge LJ, at 765, explained the outcome of that case as turning on the principle that 'those who seek and welcome publicity of every kind bearing upon their private lives so long as it shows them in a favourable light are in no position to complain of the invasion of their privacy by publicity that shows them in an unfavourable light'. But in *McKennitt* Buxton LJ described as 'cruelly insensitive' (at [54]) the suggestion that Loreena McKennitt's controlled disclosures about the effect on her of her fiancé's drowning prevented a claim based on the defendant's publication of a detailed description of her pitifully grief-stricken reaction.

[52] See, *McKennitt*, above; *RocknRoll* v *News Group Newspapers Ltd* [2013] EWHC 24 (Ch), at [19]: 'that discredited zone argument' (per Briggs J).

[53] This factor will also be significant when weighing the *importance* of respecting the claimant's expectation of privacy (see below at §17.3(G)). But the likely consequences may establish the expectation, for example, where a defendant publishes which branch of a supermarket a celebrity claimant shops in each Thursday night or that the claimant has won the lottery.

[54] *Z* v *Finland* (1997) 25 EHRR 371, at [95]–[96]; *Armonienė* v *Lithuania* (2009) 48 EHRR 53, at [40].

[55] *Weller* [2016] 1 WLR 1541, at [64].

[56] *HRH Prince of Wales* v *Associated Newspapers Ltd* [2008] Ch 57, at [36] (per Lord Phillips CJ).

when considering whether the Prince of Wales had a reasonable expectation of privacy with respect to a journal recording his impressions on a visit to Hong Kong, the Court of Appeal stated, 'It is not easy in this case, as in many others, when concluding that information is private to identify the extent to which this is because of the nature of the information, the form in which it is conveyed and the fact that the person disclosing it was in a confidential relationship with the person to whom it relates.'[57]

(6) *The substantial offence test.* Because of the difficulty of applying the reasonable expectation test in borderline cases some judges have advocated the use of a alternative test based on a reasonable person's reaction to the publication. For instance, in *Campbell* Lord Hope stated that 'the broad test is whether disclosure of the information about the individual ("A") would give substantial offence to A, assuming that A was placed in similar circumstances and was a person of ordinary sensibilities'.[58] This echoes a suggestion made by Gleeson CJ in the High Court of Australia that a 'useful practical test' is whether the 'disclosure or observation of information or conduct would be highly offensive to a reasonable person of ordinary sensibilities'.[59]

Other judges, however, have criticised this test. For instance, in *Campbell* Lord Nicholls was concerned that the 'highly offensive' test raised the threshold of liability higher than the 'reasonable expectation' test, and that a person's reaction to a publication might reflect factors relevant to the later stages of an inquiry into whether a defendant could be held liable for disclosing private information (for instance, whether the publication was justified by free speech values) and not just whether the information was potentially private.[60] A further problem with a test based on a reasonable person's reaction to the publication is that such a test is unlikely to work when the information is about someone who does not understand the significance of privacy, such as a disturbed adult[61] or a very young child.[62] These criticisms mean that the substantial offence test is not a reliable guide to the sorts of information potentially protected by the tort, though some judges may continue to use it *alongside* the reasonable expectation test.

(7) *Photographs.* Where a photograph depicts the claimant in a private space then it will generally be straightforward to establish that it was reasonable for her to expect that it would not be published without her consent, and the claimant's position will be stronger still if the photograph was obtained by subterfuge or trickery, or reveals intimate information. But how does the reasonable expectation test apply when the photograph depicts the claimant in a public place?

If a person goes to a public place then she clearly accepts that other people will be able to look at her and thereby obtain certain information about her. But a photograph will often capture more information than even a careful observer would perceive, will preserve that information in a potentially permanent form, and can be used to communicate more information more widely than mere words easily could. For instance, if *Gossip* wanted to

---

[57] Ibid.

[58] *Campbell*, at [92].

[59] *Australian Broadcasting Corporation* v *Lenah Game Meats Pty Ltd* (2001) 208 CLR 199, at [42].

[60] *Campbell*, at [22]. See also [135] (per Baroness Hale).

[61] In *T* v *BBC* [2007] EWHC 1683 (QB) the claimant was an 18-year-old who was incapable of giving informed consent, and whose reactions to appearing in a television documentary were likely to be unpredictable and inconsistent, but on balance negative.

[62] In *Murray* v *Express Newspapers plc* [2009] Ch 481 the claimant, the son of the author J.K. Rowling, was two years old at the time of the relevant publication.

let *Friend* know about a dress that *Star* wore on a visit to a theme park with her children (in order to criticise her for choosing to wear such a dress) then showing *Friend* a photograph of *Star* wearing the dress would communicate more information more quickly and convincingly than trying to describe it verbally. But if observers – such as other visitors to the theme park – can see a person at a particular moment, then how can she claim to have a reasonable expectation of privacy as to what would appear on a photograph taken at that moment? Could *Star* complain about the photograph being published on a website that specialises in 'celebrity stories'?

In *Campbell* Lord Hoffmann suggested that:

> The famous and even the not so famous who go out in public must accept that they may be photographed without their consent, just as they may be observed by others without their consent.[63]

But he thought that they could nonetheless object to some photographs taken in public being made available to the world at large.[64] The House of Lords drew an apparent distinction between photographs taken in public places of people doing mundane things – Baroness Hale, for instance, stated that there was nothing essentially private about what Naomi Campbell 'looks like if and when she pops out to the shops for a bottle of milk'[65] – and photographs containing information that a reasonable person would want to maintain control over – for instance what the person looks like when in extreme distress or when eating messy food. Thus Lord Hoffmann stated that:

> the widespread publication of a photograph of someone which reveals him to be in a situation of humiliation or severe embarrassment, even if taken in a public place, may be an infringement of the privacy of his personal information.[66]

The European Court of Human Rights, however, has expressed a different view as to whether the publication of innocuous photographs taken in public can breach Article 8. In *Von Hannover* v *Germany* (2005), the Court held that Germany had violated Article 8 by permitting the publication in German magazines of photographs showing Princess Caroline of Monaco in the course of everyday activities such as visiting a market and riding a bicycle. An influential factor was that Princess Caroline had been subject to near-continuous observation by press photographers and it is easy to see how the innocuous nature of each photograph, judged individually, did not reflect the effect of such a campaign on her privacy. The Court's response was to treat the publication of *each* photograph, no matter how innocuous, as potentially violating Article 8: 'In the present case there is no doubt that the publication by various German magazines of photos of the applicant in her daily life either on her own or with other people falls within the scope of her private life.'[67]

---

[63] *Campbell*, at [73]. In *Murray* v *Express Newspapers plc* [2007] EWHC 1908 (Ch), at [37], Patten J stated that 'A photograph taken by a member of the public which remains the property of that person and is at most shown to family and friends does not infringe any right of privacy because it does not lead to any real public exposure of the events portrayed.' Although Patten J's judgment was overturned on appeal, [2009] Ch 481, this opinion was not discussed by the Court of Appeal.

[64] *Campbell*, at [74]–[75]. See also at [122] (per Lord Hope).

[65] *Campbell*, at [154]. This was applied in *John* v *Associated Newspapers Ltd* [2006] EWHC 1611 (QB), when Eady J refused to grant an interim injunction to prevent the defendant from publishing a photograph of Sir Elton John in the street, wearing a tracksuit and baseball cap, opening his front gate.

[66] *Campbell*, at [76].

[67] (2005) 40 EHRR 1, at [53].

In *Murray* v *Express Newspapers plc* (2007) and (2009), the English courts had to confront the apparent inconsistency between *Campbell* and *Von Hannover* when faced with a claim arising from a photographic agency supplying a newspaper with a photograph taken in public of David, the 19-month-old son of the author J.K. Rowling, being pushed in his pushchair by his parents. At first instance Patten J struck out David's claim as unarguable on the basis that even after *Von Hannover* 'there remains an area of innocuous conduct in a public place which does not raise a reasonable expectation of privacy.'[68] The Court of Appeal, however, restored David's claim because they thought that it was arguable that he had a reasonable expectation that he would 'not be targeted in order to obtain photographs in a public place for publication which the person who took or procured the taking of the photographs knew would be objected to on behalf of the child.'[69] In *Weller* (2015), which involved photographs of the children of Paul Weller, taken whilst they were out shopping and then relaxing in a café, the Court of Appeal confirmed that a child might be able to establish a reasonable expectation of privacy in a broader range of everyday situations than an adult: Lord Dyson MR emphasised that the consequences of publication of innocuous photographs might be more serious for a child, because they might be bullied or their security put at risk, and that, particularly in a case involving a young child, it could not be said that the child had willingly gone into an environment where he or she was likely to be stared at and photographed.[70] Moreover, he suggested that a distinction should be drawn between truly quotidian activities – such as heading to a local store to buy milk – and 'family activities' that form part of a protected sphere of family life, such as an outing to a local park, swimming pool, shopping street or café.[71]

(8) *Iniquity.* The case law governing the long-established equitable wrong of breach of confidence took the view that there could be no protection for 'iniquity'.[72] But it seems that a claimant can reasonably expect *some* 'iniquitous behaviour' to remain private, and that consequently a defendant will have to justify publishing such information. For example, in *Campbell* (2004) Lord Hoffmann said that 'use of drugs' was a matter in respect of which 'even a public figure would ordinarily be entitled to privacy'.[73] And in *CC* v *AB* (2006),[74] and several subsequent cases,[75] it has been held that there is no general rule that an adulterer cannot obtain an injunction to restrain the publication of matters relating to his adulterous relationship. In *Mosley* v *News Group Newspapers Ltd* (2008), a case involving sado-masochistic sex, Eady J questioned whether the 'iniquity' exception could ever be applied 'to

---

[68] [2007] EWHC 1908 (Ch), at [68]. A similar claim, involving a photograph of the 18-month-old twins of a television personality was rejected by the New Zealand Court of Appeal: *Hosking* v *Runting* [2005] 1 NZLR 1. In New Zealand, however, the publication of private facts is only actionable when 'the publicity given to those private facts that would be considered highly offensive to an objective and reasonable person.'

[69] [2009] Ch 481, at [57].

[70] [2016] 1 WLR 1541, at [63]–[64]. We are inclined to suggest that the potential consequences for a child's development and integration into the world of being regularly targeted by the paparazzi are far more serious than the potential security threat and risk of being bullied.

[71] Ibid, at [61].

[72] *Gartside* v *Outram* (1857) 26 LJ Ch 113. For the relationship between the long-established equitable wrong of breach of confidence and the tort of misuse of private information see above at § 17.2(A).

[73] *Campbell*, at [36].

[74] [2006] EWHC 3083 (QB), at [30].

[75] See, for example, *ETK* v *News Group Newspapers Ltd* [2011] EWCA Civ 439.

sexual activity, fetishist or otherwise, conducted between consenting adults in private'.[76] By contrast, in *X* v *Y* (2004) Mummery LJ held that a person's sexual activity in a transport café lavatory 'did not take place in his private life nor was it within the scope of application of the right to respect for it'[77] apparently because it amounted to a criminal offence.

Even where a person's behaviour is so iniquitous that he could have no *immediate* expectation of privacy with regard to it the experience of other jurisdictions warns against the stark position that such a person can *never*, even after the passage of time, develop a right to prevent further publication of details of his behaviour.[78] With the passage of time, a person's legitimate interest in maintaining the benefit of successful rehabilitation may come to outweigh any possible public benefit to be gained by further publication, and in such circumstances a person may reasonably expect his past iniquities not to be re-published.[79] Moreover, even when a person cannot claim that the *mere fact* of his past offending ought to remain private he may be able to object to its publication alongside other information, such as his address, where this is likely to lead to harassment and possibly violence.[80]

E. Companies

Should a company be able to sue for invasion of privacy if, for instance, information about its private operations is published? The simplest way of answering this question would be to say 'yes' – tort law applies the same rules to claimants whether they are human beings or artificial legal persons.[81] But if we look deeper then it seems that many of the reasons

---

[76] *Mosley* v *News Group Newspapers Ltd* [2008] EWHC 1777 (QB), at [106].

[77] [2004] EWCA Civ 662, at [53]. See also [69]–[71] (per Dyson LJ). Brooke LJ dissented on this point.

[78] *Melvin* v *Reid*, 121 Cal App 285 (1931), is a famous example from California: the claimant had been a prostitute and had been acquitted of shooting her pimp and lover in 1918, but had subsequently married and been accepted into 'respectable society'. She successfully sued when her past was revealed in a popular movie. (The movie, called 'The Red Kimona' on its credits, but 'The Red Kimono' on posters, was successful in the United States but banned by the British Board of Film Censors.)

[79] In C-131/12 *Google Spain* v *AEPD and Mario Costeja Gonzalez* [2014] QB 1022, the Court of Justice of the European Union held that under the Data Protection Directive (Parliament and Council Directive 95/46/EC of 24 October 1995) a person might be able to rely on a 'right to be forgotten' against a search engine that provided links to old newspaper reports mentioning proceedings taken against him several years before for the recovery of social security debts. Clearly this case did not *directly* decide anything about the scope of the English tort of misuse of private information. Moreover, the Court thought that it was significant that search engines can effectively provide a 'profile' of someone whenever a search is made for a particular name, and search engine operators may have no justification for making the information concerned available *beyond* the fact that a searcher has used the claimant's *name* as a search term. In the case the information concerned had appeared in a newspaper, but was no longer generally known, and the 'publisher' could not identify any particular reason why the information should be made available beyond the fact that it was true.

[80] *CG* v *Facebook Ireland Ltd* [2016] NICA 54. In this case M had created a Facebook page – 'Keeping our kids safe from predators' - on which he published details about XY's prior offending including a photograph, and other users had posted comments identifying where XY might have been living. The Court doubted that the claimant's photograph would have been private information if it had been published on its own, but held, at [49], that 'in view of the campaign of harassment and threatened violence to the offender, the identification of the locality in which he was living, his name, photograph and the circumstances of the offending this was cumulatively information in respect of which the respondent had a reasonable expectation of privacy because of the risk that those who wished to do him harm could have established his whereabouts in order to do so.'

[81] The wrong of breach of confidence clearly protects the interests of companies in preserving their industrial secrets and the like.

for creating a privacy tort, such as protecting human autonomy and dignity, and facilitating love, friendship and community, do not apply to artificial legal persons.

In *R* v *Broadcasting Standards Commission*, ex p *BBC* (2001), the Court of Appeal held that the Commission was entitled to uphold a complaint by Dixons (a company) that the BBC had infringed its privacy unjustifiably by carrying out covert filming in one of its stores. Lord Woolf MR pointed out that companies could engage in private activities which should be protected from unwarranted intrusion, such as board meetings. But both he and Hale LJ drew attention to the fact that Article 8 of the ECHR did not refer to a 'right to privacy' in general but only to a 'right to respect for his private and family life, his home and correspondence'. Thus the fact that Dixons succeeded in this case may not be a good guide to the scope of the new tort because its development has been strongly tied to Article 8.

Extending the new tort to protect companies would also be inconsistent with the opinion of three members of the High Court of Australia who expressly held in *Australian Broadcasting Corporation* v *Lenah Game Meats* (2001) that Australia's emergent tort of invasion of privacy was for 'the benefit of natural, not artificial, persons'.[82] Similarly, companies are not protected under the United States Rest 2d, Torts, §652I: 'an action for invasion of privacy can be maintained only by a living individual whose privacy is invaded.'[83]

By contrast, others have argued that companies should be able to sue for invasions of privacy because they can sue for libel and slander, and allowing them to sue for invasions of privacy will prevent them from seeking to distort other torts to prevent unwanted publications about their private activities. A further reason for allowing companies to sue may be that their interests in keeping information from being published will often be hard to separate from the privacy interests of their employees and clients. For instance, in *Green Corns Ltd* v *Claverley Group Ltd* (2005), a claimant company sought to prevent the defendant from publishing the addresses of properties being used by the claimant company to house disturbed children and their carers and the weight of the privacy claim was treated as an aggregation of the weight of the claims that could have been brought by the company, the children and the carers.

F. Measuring the importance of protecting privacy

The importance of protecting people against the disclosure of particular private information can be measured by reflecting on the reasons which are commonly given for such protection: to protect autonomy,[84] human dignity[85] and personality,[86] and to facilitate the formation of *special* relationships such as love, friendship and community.[87] The

---

[82] (2001) 208 CLR 199, at [132].

[83] American Law Institute (1965), emphasis added. It seems that the protection offered by Art 8 of the ECHR does *not* end with an individual's death: see *Plon* v *France* (58148/00), 18 May 2004, unreported.

[84] In this context 'autonomy' refers to a person's freedom to choose what sort of life they are going to live. For confirmation of the claim that 'autonomy' underpins the tort of misuse of private information, see, for example, *Weller* at [31] and [61].

[85] See, for example, Bloustein 1964, 1003, 'The man who is compelled to live every minute of his life among others and whose every need and thought, desire, fancy or gratification is subject to public scrutiny, has been deprived of his individuality and human dignity.'

[86] *Von Hannover* v *Germany* (2005) 40 EHRR 1, at [50]: 'the guarantee afforded by Article 8 of the Convention is primarily intended to ensure the development, without outside interference, of the personality of each individual in his relations with other human beings.'

[87] See, for example, Fried 1968; also Feldman 1997.

significance of the interference can usually be assessed by considering the importance of claimants being able to retain control over such information in order to enjoy the advantages that protection of privacy provides, and the seriousness of the effects of any intrusion. Thus, in *Campbell* the majority in the House of Lords attached particular weight to the fact that publication of the details of Naomi Campbell's treatment might cause *harm* by disrupting her treatment.[88]

Where the publication of the information will have effects on the private and family lives of people other than the immediate claimant these effects must be considered by the judge when measuring the importance of preserving privacy. Thus in *ETK v News Group Newspapers Ltd* (2011) where the anonymous claimant, a man who worked in the entertainment industry, sought to prevent publication of the fact that he had been involved in an adulterous affair with *X*, a woman who worked in the same industry, the Court of Appeal held that the judge should have given weight to the privacy interests of the claimant's wife and children and *X*, as well as the claimant's interest.[89] Indeed, Ward LJ suggested that the factor which 'tipped the balance' and made it appropriate to grant an injunction was the interests of the children in avoiding 'playground ridicule' and in the preservation of the stability of the marriage while their parents pursued a reconciliation.[90]

G. Freedom of expression

Although it is *logical* to ask whether the defendant's disclosure of the information amounted to 'expression' within the ambit of Article 10 we might expect it to be rare for the answer to be 'no'.

One unusual situation where the defendant's behaviour may not count as 'expression' is where the disclosure is *unintentional,* such as where *Medic* permits *Tabloid* to obtain private information about *Starlet* by forgetfully leaving *Starlet*'s medical records on a train. But this example raises the awkward question of what is meant by 'disclosure' in the context of the new tort: all the cases considered so far in England have involved deliberate publication so the courts have not provided any guidance as to whether the tort covers accidental or careless disclosures.[91]

In most cases, since the defendant's disclosure *will* amount to 'expression', it will be necessary to move on to an assessment of how valuable the defendant's conduct is likely to be, since it is well-established that some types of expression are much more important to protect than others. In *Campbell* Baroness Hale said:

> There are undoubtedly different types of speech, just as there are different types of private information, some of which are more deserving of protection in a democratic society than others. Top of the list is political speech. The free exchange of information and ideas on matters relevant to the organisation of the economic, social and political life of the country is crucial to any

---

[88] *Campbell*, at [98] and [119] (per Lord Hope), [130] and [165] (per Baroness Hale), [169] (per Lord Carswell).

[89] [2011] 1 WLR 1827, at [14].

[90] [2011] 1 WLR 1827, at [17]–[22].

[91] In *TLT v Secretary of State for the Home Department* [2016] EWHC 2217 (QB), Mitting J assessed damages in a claim arising from the Home Office's unintentional publication of the personal details of 1,598 people involved in the 'family returns' process. (The process by which people with children who have no right to remain in the United Kingdom are returned to their country of origin.) The defendant conceded, however, that it was liable for misuse of private information.

democracy . . . This includes revealing information about public figures, especially those in elective office, which would otherwise be private but is relevant to their participation in public life. Intellectual and educational speech and expression are also important in a democracy, not least because they enable the development of the individuals' potential to play a full part in society and in our democratic life. Artistic speech and expression is important for similar reasons, in fostering both individual originality and creativity and the free-thinking and dynamic society we so much value.[92]

Expression which is not political, intellectual, educational or artistic, such as mere gossip, is still protected to an extent, because it may play an important role in preserving social networks and in making newspapers financially viable. But it will be far easier to justify a restriction on the publication of mere gossip[93] to protect privacy than a restriction on political debate.

(1) *Public interest.* An influential factor in measuring the importance of preserving free expression is whether it was in the public interest for the information to be disclosed to the people to whom the defendant disclosed it. But 'public interest' is obviously a broad concept which cannot be *defined* with any precision. Indeed in *A* v *B* (2003) the Court of Appeal simply stated that 'in the majority of situations whether the public interest is involved or not will be obvious' and that where it is not obvious the factor is 'unlikely to be decisive'.[94] The European Court of Human Rights has been more forthcoming:

> the public interest relates to matters which affect the public to such an extent that it may legitimately take an interest in them, which attract its attention or which concern it to a significant degree, especially in that they affect the well-being of citizens or the life of the community. This is also the case with regard to matters which are capable of giving rise to considerable controversy, which concern an important social issue, or which involve a problem that the public would have an interest in being informed about.[95]

And the Independent Press Standards Organisation's Editors' Code of Practice (January 2016) includes a helpful catalogue of the practical situations where defendants regularly raise 'the public interest' as a justification for disclosure:

> The public interest includes, but is not confined to:
> - Detecting or exposing crime, or the threat of crime, or serious impropriety.
> - Protecting public health or safety.
> - Protecting the public from being misled by an action or statement of an individual or organisation.
> - Disclosing a person or organisation's failure or likely failure to comply with any obligation to which they are subject.

---

[92] *Campbell*, at [148]. See also *Khuja* v *Times Newspapers Ltd* [2017] UKSC 49, where the claimant was seeking to restrict the freedom of the media to report part of what had been said in open court during a criminal trial, and the Supreme Court emphasised the importance of the freedom to publish information about court proceedings.

[93] In *Von Hannover* v *Germany* (2005) 40 EHRR 1, the European Court of Human Rights treated (at [65]) the preservation of freedom to publish photographs of Princess Caroline of Monaco's daily activities as relatively unimportant when 'the sole purpose was to satisfy the curiosity of a particular readership regarding the details of the applicant's private life, [and the photographs] cannot be deemed to contribute to any debate of general interest to society despite the applicant being known to the public'.

[94] [2003] QB 195, at [11](viii).

[95] *Couderc* v *France* [2015] ECHR 992, at [103] (citations omitted).

- Disclosing a miscarriage of justice.
- Raising or contributing to a matter of public debate, including serious cases of impropriety, unethical conduct or incompetence concerning the public.
- Disclosing concealment, or likely concealment, of any of the above.
- There is a public interest in freedom of expression itself.

Mosley v *News Group Newspapers Ltd* (2008) provides an example of a case where newspaper editors and the courts expressed different views about the scope of 'the public interest'. In this case Eady J rejected the defendants' submission that they could rely on the public interest in exposing 'serious impropriety' as a justification for disclosing the claimant's 'immoral, depraved and to an extent adulterous' participation in a sado-masochistic sex session.[96] He held that a belief that such behaviour was 'depraved' did not justify telling the world that someone had behaved in that way. He drew an important distinction:

> Everyone is naturally entitled to espouse moral or religious beliefs to the effect that certain types of sexual behaviour are wrong or demeaning to those participating. That does not mean that they are entitled to hound those who practise them or to detract from their right to live life as they choose.[97]

This opinion was not shared by Paul Dacre, Editor-in-Chief, of the *Daily Mail*:

> Since time immemorial public shaming has been a vital element in defending the parameters of what are considered acceptable standards of social behaviour, helping ensure that citizens – rich and poor – adhere to them for the good of the greater community. For hundreds of years, the press has played a vital role in that process. It has the freedom to identify those who have offended public standards of decency – the very standards its readers believe in – and hold the transgressors up to public condemnation.[98]

No doubt different views can be held as to whether 'public shaming' by tabloid newspapers ever advances the public interest. We expect, however, that other judges will follow the approach of Eady J and hold that 'the fact . . . that someone's tastes are unconventional or "perverted", does not give the media *carte blanche*.'[99]

(2) *Public figures.* In *A* v *B* (2003), Lord Woolf CJ suggested that public figures must accept a greater degree of disclosure of information than ordinary individuals:

> because of his public position [a public figure] must expect and accept that his actions will be more closely scrutinised by the media . . . Whether you have courted publicity or not you may be a legitimate subject of public attention. If you have courted public attention then you have less ground to object to the intrusion which follows. In many of these situations it would be overstating the position to say that there is a public interest in the information being published. It would be more accurate to say that the public have an understandable and so a legitimate interest in being told the information.[100]

---

[96] [2008] EWHC 1777 (QB), at [124]. The quoted words are from the judge's summary of the defendants' barrister's argument. The defendants also argued that their publication was in the public interest because the sex session had a 'Nazi theme', but Eady J held that it was simply untrue that the session had any such theme.

[97] [2008] EWHC 1777 (QB), at [127].

[98] Paul Dacre, Speech to the Society of Editors, 9 November 2008.

[99] [2008] EWHC 1777 (QB), at [128].

[100] [2003] QB 195, at [11](xii).

In *Campbell* the Court of Appeal analysed this passage and insisted that Lord Woolf CJ was not intending to say that once a person was identified as a legitimate subject of public attention then *any information of any type* about that person could be published, and this is also the position taken by the European Court of Human Rights. We think that there are four important ways in which a person's status as a 'public figure' can alter a court's assessment of the value of the expression of private information about that person.

First, a person's status as a 'public figure' may be related to them having undertaken a significant public role, for example as a politician or military officer, and their role may increase the public interest associated with the disclosure of information of some relevance to their suitability for the position. For example, in the litigation arising after the publication of Susan Kuronen's book about her nine-month relationship with Matti Vanhanen, then the Prime Minister of Finland, the European Court of Human Rights agreed that Mr Vanhanen's position meant that it was valuable to inform the public about how the couple met through an Internet dating site and how swiftly their relationship developed, since these facts could be relevant to his judgment, but that there was no substantial value in disclosing information about his sexual behaviour.[101]

Secondly, a person's status as a 'public figure' may stem from them having done things that give rise to what Lord Woolf described as the public having 'an understandable and so legitimate interest' in their life choices. In *Axel-Springer AG v Germany* (2012),[102] the European Court of Human Rights considered a case arising from the publication in a German tabloid of the fact that an actor, famous for playing a detective in a popular television series, had been arrested at the Munich Beer Festival for possession of cocaine. The Strasbourg Court held that the actor was sufficiently well known to be a 'public figure', and that the fact that his television character was a police officer increased the public interest in publication of the information that he had been arrested for a criminal offence.[103]

Thirdly, a person's status as a 'public figure' may be associated with them having made public statements about themselves, and in such circumstances there may be a special public interest in any false impressions created by those statements being corrected. Thus in *A v B* (2003) Lord Woolf CJ stated that, 'where a public figure chooses to make untrue pronouncements about his or her private life, the press will normally be entitled to put the record straight.'[104]

Fourthly, where a 'public figure' has become a 'role model' some judges appear to appear to have recognised a special public interest in the publication of information that tends to suggest that they have behaved disreputably. The logic behind this is opaque: if 'role models' can influence young people then why should the law make it easier for the public to learn about their disreputable behaviour? In *Campbell* the Court of Appeal stated that it did 'not see why it should necessarily be in the public interest that an individual who has been adopted as a role model, without seeking this distinction, should be demonstrated to have feet of clay'.[105] Subsequent cases have tended to restrict the scope of the 'role model' doctrine to situations where a claimant has accepted a publicly significant

---

[101] *Ruusunen v Finland* [2014] ECHR 35, at [49]; *Ojala v Finland* [2014] ECHR 36, at [54].
[102] *Axel-Springer AG v Germany* [2012] ECHR 227.
[103] Ibid, at [99].
[104] [2003] QB 195, at [43]. See also, for example, *Campbell*, at [58] (per Lord Hoffmann).
[105] [2003] QB 633, at [41]. See also *Campbell*, at [151] (per Baroness Hale).

position, such as by becoming a teacher or a vicar, so that it tends to merge with what we presented above as the first consequence of 'public figure' status.[106] Further, in *AMC* v *News Group Newspapers Ltd* (2015), where the defendant was seeking to publish X's story of her sexual relationship with a footballer, who also had a long-term girlfriend, Laing J suggested it was important to consider the 'breadth' of the claimant's status as a role model; she accepted that the claimant might be a role model for sportsmen and aspiring sportsmen, but held that this did not mean it was in the public interest to publish information about his sexual activities. Being a successful footballer did not make him 'an example in every sphere of his existence': 'He is not a role model for cooks, or for moral philosophers.'[107]

(3) *Contribution to a debate of general interest.* The important case of *Von Hannover* v *Germany* (2005) arose out of the publication in German magazines of photographs of Princess Caroline of Monaco depicting her in the course of ordinary tasks like going shopping and playing tennis. The German courts had concluded that such publications were not wrongful because the public has a legitimate interest in being allowed to judge whether the personal behaviour of a 'figure of contemporary society *par excellence*' ('*absolute Person der Zeitgeschichte*') convincingly tallies with his behaviour during official engagements. But the European Court of Human Rights held that the application of this doctrine to the case of Princess Caroline had left her with insufficient protection for her right to privacy when 'the interest of the general public and the press is based solely on her membership of a reigning family whereas she herself does not exercise any official functions'.[108] The Court insisted that 'the public does not have a legitimate interest in knowing where the applicant is and how she behaves generally in her private life even if she appears in places that cannot always be described as secluded and despite the fact that she is well known to the public'[109] and suggested that 'the decisive factor in balancing the protection of private life against freedom of expression should lie in the contribution that the published photos and articles make to a debate of general interest.'[110]

Subsequent English cases, such as *Mosley* v *News Group Newspapers* (2008) have echoed this final phrase, and elevated whether a publication made a 'contribution to a debate of public interest' into a pivotal issue.[111] Unsurprisingly, Eady J concluded in that case that the many thousands of people who watched the edited footage of the claimant's sado-masochistic encounter on the defendant's website were not 'prompted by a desire to participate in a "debate of general interest" of the kind contemplated in *Von Hannover*.'[112]

Importantly, however, the European Court of Human Rights has decided later cases in such a way as to suggest that the key phrase – 'contribution to a debate of public interest' – should not be read too narrowly; in particular, it seems that the ordinary meaning of the

---

[106] In *Ferdinand* v *MGN Limited* [2011] EWHC 2454 (QB), at [89]–[94], Nicol J reasoned that the position of the claimant, a Premiership footballer, had been changed by his voluntary decision to accept the captaincy of the England football team, since this 'carried an expectation of high standards'.

[107] *AMC* v *News Group Newspapers Ltd* [2015] EWHC 2361 (QB), at [20].

[108] *Von Hannover*, at [72].

[109] *Von Hannover*, at [77].

[110] *Von Hannover*, at [76].

[111] [2008] EWHC 1777 (QB), at [131]. See also *ETK* v *News Group Newspapers Ltd* [2011] 1 WLR 1827, at [23].

[112] [2008] EWHC 1777 (QB), at [132].

word 'debate' may be misleading. Thus in *Couderc* v *France* (2015), the European Court of Human Rights decided it would be:

> useful to emphasise that the press's contribution to a debate of public interest cannot be limited merely to current events or pre-existing debates. Admittedly, the press is a vector for disseminating debates on matters of public interest, but it also has the role of revealing and bringing to the public's attention information capable of eliciting such interest and of giving rise to such a debate within society.[113]

Consistently with this, it seems that there will generally be a public interest in publishing information about public events, or other matters of general interest. In *Von Hannover (No 2)* v *Germany*,[114] the Court upheld the decision of the German courts that it had been acceptable to publish photographs of Princess Caroline on a skiing holiday alongside an article about the illness of her father, Prince Rainier III, then the reigning prince of Monaco. The Court apparently accepted that the Prince's illness was a 'matter of general interest', and that there was some value for 'public debate' in reporting how 'the prince's children reconciled their obligations of family solidarity with the legitimate needs of their private life, among which was the desire to go on holiday.'[115] Similarly, in *Von Hannover (No 3)* v *Germany*,[116] the Court accepted that there was a public interest in publishing a story about celebrities, including the Von Hannovers, choosing to make their holiday homes available for rent, accompanied by a photograph of Princess Caroline and her husband on holiday.

(4) *Autobiography.* In some cases the person who wishes to publish the information argues that the court should attach weight to her freedom 'to tell her story'. This freedom will be given substantial weight where disclosure is important for self-development or to preserve reputation, perhaps by 'setting the record straight'. But the freedom will be given significantly less weight if it seems that the defendant is primarily interested in being paid, or wants to disclose information to inflict pain by way of revenge.[117] The weight accorded to the freedom will also vary according to how far the defendant's story is *about* the defendant. Thus the Court of Appeal in *McKennitt* v *Ash* (2008) held that the freedom had to give way to the claimant's privacy interest where the story to be told involved mainly private facts about the claimant's life that the defendant had learnt or observed while in a relationship with the claimant rather than genuinely '*shared* experiences'.[118]

(5) *Errors.* How should a court approach a case where the reason that a defendant thought that it was justifiable to publish private information was based on an error of fact? Consider, for example, the **Deceptive Appearances Problem**:

---

[113] *Couderc* v *France* [2015] ECHR 992, at [114].

[114] *Von Hannover (No 2)* v *Germany* (2012) 55 EHRR 15.

[115] Ibid, at [117]–[118].

[116] *Von Hannover (No 3)* v *Germany* [2013] ECHR 835.

[117] In *CC* v *AB* [2006] EWHC 3083 (QB), at [35]–[36], Eady J drew a distinction between a husband disclosing that his wife had been involved in an adulterous affair with the defendant when 'discussing his wife's adultery with a close friend, or with members of the family, or (if he needed to do so) with a family doctor, counsellor or social worker, or with his lawyers' and selling the information to the tabloids for money or revenge. In *Donald* v *Ntuli* [2011] 1 WLR 294 the Court of Appeal regarded the defendant's claim that she needed to tell the story of her relationship with Howard Donald, a member of 'Take That', for reasons of self-development and personal autonomy as 'an ex post facto dignification', at [23].

[118] [2008] QB 73, at [50]–[52], relying on findings reported at [31]–[32].

Tabloid received an anonymous tip-off that *Politico*, a government minister who had made speeches extolling the virtue of 'traditional marriage and monogamy', regularly invited a prostitute to his family home while his wife was away. To confirm the story, *Tabloid*'s photographer hid outside *Politico*'s family home, and took pictures of *Politico*'s wife leaving the house in the early evening, then a younger woman arriving at 9 pm and leaving just after midnight. *Tabloid*'s inquiries established that the younger woman was 18 years old and employed by an 'escort agency', so it published a story, illustrated with the pictures, accusing *Politico* of hiring a teenage prostitute. *Tabloid* believed that it was in the public interest to expose *Politico*'s hypocrisy. But when he read the story *Politico* called a press conference and disclosed that the younger woman is in fact his daughter, and that she visited him while his wife, her mother, was away because his wife strongly disapproves of her job.

No doubt *Politico* could sue *Tabloid* for libel in this situation. But his prompt rebuttal of *Tabloid's* accusation may mean that his reputation has not been significantly damaged. Nonetheless, *Politico*, his wife, and daughter, may all be distressed by the way in which *Tabloid* has revealed aspects of their family affairs that they could reasonably expect to remain private. So if *Politico* sues *Tabloid* for misuse of private information how will a court deal with *Tabloid's* claim that its story was valuable 'free expression'?

In *Mosley* v *News Group Newspapers* (2008), Eady J was clear that the defendants could not avoid liability for publishing private information about the claimant's participation in a sado-masochistic sex session merely by establishing that they honestly believed that the events had a Nazi-theme and involved mockery of victims of the Holocaust. Indeed he held that 'the public interest is to be determined solely by the court *ex post facto*',[119] and that consequently his finding that there was no Nazi-theme or mockery was decisive. He acknowledged, however, that in the tort of libel the defence associated with *Reynolds v Times Newspapers Ltd* (2001) allowed a defendant to avoid liability for publishing a *false* and *defamatory* story on a matter of public interest if the error was consistent with 'responsible journalism',[120] and that there was an argument for drawing an analogy between libel and the wrongful disclosure tort. In *Mosley* (2008), however, it was unnecessary to reach a final view on this matter since Eady J found that the defendants' judgment about the nature of the sex session 'was not based on enquiries or analysis consistent with "responsible journalism"' but 'made in a manner that could be characterised, at least, as "casual" and "cavalier"'.[121]

Returning to the Deceptive Appearances Problem, this requires a decision as to whether a defendant can rely on an aspect of the public interest when he has made an error, at least if that error was 'reasonable in the circumstances'. The strongest argument in favour of treating expression as valuable, even if it is mistaken, is that news is often a perishable commodity and it is often difficult for journalists, and others, to ascertain what the truth is *in advance*; consequently, free expression might be seriously 'chilled' if only

---

[119] [2008] EWHC 1777 (QB), at [171].

[120] This has now been replaced by a statutory defence of 'publication on a matter of public interest': Defamation Act 2013 s 4. See above, at § 16.10.

[121] [2008] EWHC 1777 (QB), at [170]. The terms 'casual' and 'cavalier' are quoted from the account of the *Reynolds* defence in *Jameel (Mohammed) v Wall Street Journal Sprl* [2007] 1 AC 359, at [33] (per Lord Bingham).

those who 'get it right' can avoid liability. The most convincing counter-argument invokes the impossibility of restoring privacy: where false defamatory material has been published about *Politico* – the province of libel – his reputation can be restored by general recognition that it was false, but nothing can undo the fact that after *Tabloid*'s story many people will know private details about *Politico*'s family life. A compromise position might be to recognise that *reasonable* stories can be valuable, even if mistaken, but to take the severity of the potential consequences for *Politico* into account when deciding whether the defendant's mistaken belief was 'reasonable'.[122]

H. Striking the balance

Suppose that A has disclosed to C information about B that is sufficiently private *potentially* to attract the protection of the tort considered here. How will the courts strike the balance between the desire, on the one hand, to protect B's privacy and the desire, on the other hand, not to limit disproportionately A's freedom of expression? It is hard to give any useful *general* guidance on this issue: there must always be an 'intense focus' on the particular facts of the case.[123] However, two points can be made.

(1) *The dual perspective approach.* In deciding which right is to prevail in this case – A's right to freedom of expression or B's right to privacy – a court must take account of the fact that *neither* right should be subjected to a disproportionate restriction. So if the court is considering making A liable – thus restricting A's freedom of expression in order to protect B's privacy – it must ask if the restriction it is considering imposing on A's right to freedom of expression is rational, fair, not arbitrary and the minimum restriction necessary to protect B's right to privacy. In order to decide whether this is the case it will often be helpful for the court *also* to consider the case from the converse perspective; that is, to consider – if B's privacy is *denied* protection in order to protect A's right to freedom of expression, will this restriction on the protection of B's right to privacy be rational, fair, not arbitrary and the minimum restriction necessary to protect A's right to freedom of expression? The reason for this is that since one right must prevail, and neither right should be subject to any disproportionate restriction, the court will *only* be able to hold A *liable* if doing so amounts to a proportionate restriction on A's right to freedom of expression in order to protect B's privacy; while, at the same time, it will *only* be able to hold that A is *not* liable if turning down B's claim amounts to a proportionate limit on the protection of B's right to privacy in order to protect A's right to freedom of expression. Adopting a dual perspective approach allows the court to compare the *relative merits* of these two possible conclusions.[124]

---

[122] In *Mosley* v *United Kingdom* [2011] ECHR 774, the European Court of Human Rights ruled that it was not necessary for the United Kingdom to enact a law requiring newspapers to inform the subjects of their stories about them in advance of publication. Max Mosley argued, unsuccessfully, that such prior notification was required so that a claimant could obtain an injunction against a mistaken or otherwise unjustifiable story before irreparable damage was done.

[123] *Re S (A Child) (Identification: Restrictions on Publication)* [2005] 1 AC 593, at [17] (per Lord Steyn).

[124] A summary of the dual perspective approach is set out by Baroness Hale in *Campbell*, at [141], and it also seems to have been the approach used by Lord Hope, at [105], with the agreement of Lord Carswell, at [167]. Some subsequent cases have used the label 'parallel analysis' to refer to the same approach.

(2) *Practical reality.* In striking a balance between protecting people's privacy and people's rights to freedom of expression, the courts must be careful to ensure that they are not devising standards which real journalists cannot be reasonably expected to meet. For instance, a real journalist cannot be expected to produce a justification for every choice of phrasing or supporting detail. In *Campbell* all of their Lordships recognised:

> the importance of allowing a proper degree of journalistic margin to the press to deal with a legitimate story in its own way, without imposing unnecessary shackles on its freedom to publish detail and photographs which add colour and conviction.[125]

Thus a judge setting the balance must be careful not to hold a defendant liable merely because he or she would have presented the story in a different way, and must take account of the advantages which come with detailed argument and hindsight.

Having made these points, let's consider a concrete example, the **Drunken Student Problem**, so as to get a better 'feel' for how the courts will strike the balance:

> *Student* gets so drunk celebrating the end of her exams that she collapses in the street and has to be treated by paramedics. The incident is recorded by CCTV cameras belonging to *University*, and *University* later uses the images in a video it shows to new students to warn them about the dangers of binge drinking. *Watcher*, one of the new students, recognises *Student* as the daughter of *Rocker*, a famous musician with a reputation for 'hard living'. *Watcher* tells *Tabloid* that images of *Rocker*'s daughter are being used by *University* to warn of the dangers of binge drinking, and *Tabloid* publishes this story under the headline 'Rocker's Daughter Makes Him Proud'.

Here, *Student* may want to bring claims for misuse of private information against *University*,[126] *Watcher* and *Tabloid*.

To claim against *University*, it will be necessary for *Student* to establish that the images contain information about her that a reasonable person would want to retain control over. Since she is apparently recognisable it is likely that the images will convey what she looked like during a distressing and humiliating episode which is something that a reasonable person would want to retain control over, at least to the extent of preventing a record of it being released to a wide audience. However, her willingness to expose this information about herself to those present in a public street will diminish her ability to claim that her interest in maintaining control over the information is very weighty.

To claim against *Watcher* and *Tabloid*, it will be necessary for *Student* to establish that the information about her that they publish – that she collapsed as a result of consuming too much alcohol, was filmed in these circumstances, and images of her are being shown to others as a warning – are private facts that a reasonable person would expect not to be published to the general public. To establish such a reasonable expectation *Student* may argue that (i) the information was in part about her need for medical treatment, and

---

[125] *Campbell*, at [169] (per Lord Carswell). Lord Nicholls and Lord Hoffmann thought that this factor was decisive in favour of the defendants, but the majority disagreed.

[126] If *University* is a public authority within the Human Rights Act 1998 *Student* could claim against it under that statute and thereby seek to circumvent the limits on the new tort. In this example we assume that it is a *private* institution.

(ii) the fact that her father is a celebrity should not mean that she is entitled to less protection for her privacy than a child of ordinary parents. And against *Watcher* she may be able to rely on an additional argument based on the relationship between students attending *University*: it may be the case that students attending *University* generally recognise a duty not to tell stories about each other's disreputable behaviour to outsiders. But again, the weight of her claim will be reduced by her willingness to expose this information about herself to those present in a public street.

From the point of view of expression, *University* may seek to argue that the violation of *Student*'s privacy is proportionate to the public interest in expressing an important social message in a graphic and effective manner. The court will want to investigate, however, whether it was *necessary* to violate *Student*'s privacy in order to express this message effectively, or whether the same message could have been delivered just as effectively using actors or by disguising *Student*'s identity.[127] On balance it seems unlikely that *University* will be able to justify using the images.

Tabloid may argue that its story contributed to more than one 'debate of general interest', such as those about how to reduce binge-drinking and about whether the children of 'hard-living' celebrity parents are more likely than others to behave in irresponsible ways. No doubt such debates could be pursued without giving publicity to the specific incident involving *Student*, but *Tabloid* can argue that specific examples attract the attention of their readers. In *Goodwin* v *News Group Newspapers* (2011) Tugendhat J quoted from a speech of Lord Rodger:

> stories about particular individuals are simply much more attractive to readers than stories about unidentified people. It is just human nature . . . A requirement to report it in some austere, abstract form, devoid of much of its human interest, could well mean that the report would not be passed on. Ultimately, such an approach could threaten the viability of newspapers and magazines, which can only inform the public if they attract enough readers and make enough money to survive.[128]

In practice, we think that the most important factor in determining the weight of *Tabloid*'s free expression arguments is whether it appears to the judge that the story made some contribution to any such debate,[129] as opposed to being mere gossip satisfying curiosity about the life of a celebrity's child.

---

[127] In *Peck* v *United Kingdom* (2003) 13 BHRC 669, the European Court of Human Rights held that a local authority's disclosure to the media of CCTV footage showing the applicant in a public place with a large knife in order to increase the effectiveness of a new CCTV system 'pursued the legitimate aim of public safety, the prevention of disorder and crime and the protection of the rights of others' (at [67]), but interfered with the applicant's privacy to a disproportionate extent because no attempt was made to secure his consent and too little was done to ensure that his identity was properly masked (at [85] and [87]). Similarly, in *T* v *BBC* [2007] EWHC 1683 (QB), while Eady J recognised that there was a genuine public interest in the subject of adoption and that the BBC's proposed documentary intended to deal with the subject in a serious and informative way, he doubted whether it was necessary to *identify* T, a vulnerable young adult, when portraying her final meeting with her child.

[128] [2011] EWHC 1437, at [110], quoting from *In re Guardian News and Media Ltd* [2010] 2 AC 697, at [63] (per Lord Rodger).

[129] In *Couderc* v *France* [2015] ECHR 992, at [110], the European Court of Human Rights made clear that the disclosure of private information would be treated as of substantial value as expression provided that the disclosure was concerned with a debate of public interest, the article did not have to be *devoted* to contributing to that debate, and that what mattered was whether it was *capable* of contributing to a debate, not whether it actually achieved its objectives.

We would expect the weight of *Watcher*'s free expression arguments to be no greater than the weight of *Tabloid*'s, unless *Watcher* had some reason for thinking that *Tabloid* would use the information in some other way. Indeed, *Watcher*'s case may be weaker than *Tabloid*'s from the perspective of free expression, if, for example, she had no desire to contribute to any debate and simply wanted to be paid for supplying a story.

I. Fault elements

Where a claim is brought against a publisher who has obtained information *indirectly* the question may arise whether the publisher *knew or ought to have known* that the information was private.[130] Cases have arisen, for example, where an agency has supplied photographs to a newspaper, which then published them under the mistaken impression that they depicted events occurring in a public place. In such cases, where A has provided information about B to C, and C has published it, it will be C's knowledge of the nature of the information which is in issue if B sues C.[131]

It seems, however, that the courts may define what a *media defendant* 'ought to know' so widely that any requirement for knowledge or constructive knowledge will be rendered nugatory. In the *Campbell* case, the Court of Appeal held that 'the media can fairly be expected to identify confidential information about an individual's private life which, absent good reason, it will be offensive to publish'.[132] We suspect, however, that in future difficult cases may arise which require the courts to delve deeper into the question whether an innocent publisher can be liable for committing the misuse of private information tort. Consider, for example, the **Unreliable Paparazzi Problem**:

> *Actress* has recently had a baby and has told the world that she will abandon her celebrity lifestyle and concentrate on caring for her child. *Snapper* photographs her in St Tropez carrying suitcases and without her baby, and sells the picture to *Tabloid*, explaining that 'it was a hotel, and she was arriving for a holiday'. This explanation is untrue: *Actress* was arriving at a private retreat that specialises in discreetly treating those suffering from post-natal depression. *Tabloid* publishes the picture under the headline: 'Normal service resumed: *Actress* off on holiday without her baby'. *Actress* is extremely distressed by publication of the photograph since she believes several of her celebrity acquaintances will recognise the private retreat and realise that she must have developed post-natal depression.

Some people might argue that it would be harsh to hold *Tabloid* liable for misuse of private information by publishing the information that *Actress* has developed post-natal depression, at least if there was no reason why they should have doubted *Snapper*'s explanation. Others, however, might argue that a professional media organisation must take responsibility for what it publishes, and *Actress*'s right to privacy should not be diminished just because *Tabloid* has been misled by *Snapper*. On balance, we would support allowing *Tabloid* to avoid liability if it could demonstrate that it had a 'reasonable belief'[133] that its publication wholly innocuous, or that it was in the public interest because it prevented the public from being misled.

---

[130] *Campbell*, at [85] (per Lord Hope), [134] (per Baroness Hale).

[131] Of course, if B only sues A then C's knowledge will be irrelevant.

[132] *Campbell* v *MGN Ltd* [2003] QB 633, at [68].

[133] The phrase 'reasonable belief' is intended to echo a key component of the defence to the tort of libel found in s 4 Defamation Act 2013.

J. Remedies

(1) *Compensatory and aggravated damages.* Where a defendant has wrongfully disclosed private information the claimant will normally be entitled to claim compensatory damages. But how are such damages calculated?

In *Mosley* v *News Group Newspapers Ltd* (2008), Eady J noted that whatever sum he awarded could not *restore* the claimant's privacy in any meaningful sense: 'Accordingly, it seems to me that the only realistic course is to select a figure which marks the fact that an unlawful intrusion has taken place while affording some degree of *solatium* to the injured party'.[134] In *Gulati* v *MGN Ltd* (2015),[135] the Court of Appeal upheld the trial judge's decision that general compensatory damages could be calculated to compensate a claimant for both the extent to which they lost control of the private information concerned and any distress associated with the misuse of their private information. The Court also approved the judge's general approach, which included three important principles: damages should be higher where the information misused was more private or intimate, and where the consequences, such as distress or disruption of life, were more severe, and where the claimant was more sensitive, and hence more affected.[136]

Damages may also be increased where the defendant's actions aggravate the injury. In *Mosley* v *News Group Newspapers Ltd* (2008), one of the factors that led Eady J to make a high award, £60,000, was that the defendants had aggravated the wrong by persisting in their claim that the sex session had a 'Nazi theme'. Equally, however, the award was apparently reduced because the claimant was *himself* responsible to some extent for the embarrassment and distress he suffered.[137]

(2) *Disgorgement damages.* In Chapter 25, we clarify what we mean by 'disgorgement damages' and explain when they are available in tort law. We note there that because the tort of misuse of private information developed from the equitable wrong of breach of confidence this makes it likely that disgorgement damages will be available as a remedy that can be obtained against defendants who commit the tort. Indeed, in *Douglas* v *Hello! Ltd (No 3)* (2006), the Court of Appeal accepted that if the defendants in that case had made a profit from publishing unauthorised photographs of the claimants' wedding celebrations, then the claimants would have been entitled to sue the defendants for a sum equal to that profit.[138]

(3) *Exemplary damages.* In *Mosley* v *News Group Newspapers Ltd* (2008), Eady J held that exemplary damages could not be awarded for a *misuse of private information*, even if a defendant had committed the wrong deliberately after calculating that by doing so he

---

[134] [2008] EWHC 1777 (QB), at [231].

[135] *Gulati* v *MGN Ltd* [2015] EWCA Civ 1291, [2017] QB 149.

[136] Ibid at [74], approving the approach of the judge that they set out earlier, at [32].

[137] [2008] EWHC 1777 (QB), at [226]. Eady J did not expressly confirm that he had reduced the claimant's award to reflect the extent to which 'a casual observer' would have regarded the claimant's behaviour 'as reckless and almost self-destructive'. But he said that: 'It could be thought unreasonable to absolve him of all responsibility for placing himself and his family in the predicament in which they now find themselves. It is part and parcel of human dignity that one must take at least some responsibility for one's own actions.'

[138] [2006] QB 125, at [249]. The claimants in *Gulati* v *MGN Ltd* [2017] QB 149, elected not to seek 'restitutionary damages'.

would make a profit in excess of what he might have to pay by way of compensatory damages.[139] He based this conclusion on three arguments: (1) the wrong is an equitable wrong – breach of confidence – and therefore authorities which say that exemplary damages can be awarded in cases of tort are not directly applicable; (2) the wrong has directly incorporated elements from the European Convention on Human Rights, particularly Articles 8 and 10, and consequently it would be odd to graft onto it an approach to measuring damages which is not used by the Strasbourg court; (3) the possibility of an award of exemplary damages is not necessary in a democratic society, and would 'chill' free speech to a disproportionate extent.[140]

We disagree with all three of these arguments. Briefly: (1) misuse of private information has now been recognised as an independent tort, and it is not sensible to make the availability of a measure of damages turn on something as irrelevant as whether a cause of action was historically developed by the Courts of Equity; (2) the Strasbourg Court is concerned with awarding 'just satisfaction' to injured parties against States, and not with deciding what measures are necessary *within* a State to ensure that private bodies respect the law and victims feel they have received sufficient recourse;[141] (3) many States which have signed the European Convention have decided that it is necessary to impose *criminal penalties* for invasions of privacy, and provided that awards of exemplary damages are set at an appropriate level and only imposed when calculating contempt for the law has been *clearly* demonstrated, we cannot see why their availability will have an unjustifiable effect on free expression.[142]

(4) *Injunctions.* In Chapter 27 we discuss the different types of injunction that are potentially available, and set out the tests which determine when they will be granted. With regard to cases of *misuse of private information*, if a claimant successfully proves at trial that the defendant has committed this tort then a court will grant an injunction prohibiting him from committing it again, unless this would be pointless, either because the information is now in the public domain or there is no prospect of the defendant committing the tort in the future.

More often, however, a claimant seeks an injunction *before* widespread disclosure of private information has taken place. In such situations the claimant will usually seek an *interim* injunction requiring the defendant not to disclose the information before trial (or before a further order of the court). Four issues require further discussion here.

    (i) *The freedom of expression issue.* Because an injunction which prohibits disclosure will usually prohibit *expression* courts must be particularly cautious before granting such an order. Indeed in s 12(3) of the Human Rights Act 1998, Parliament stated that:

        No . . . relief [affecting the exercise of the Convention right to freedom of expression] is to be granted so as to restrain publication before trial unless the court is satisfied that the applicant is likely to establish that publication should not be allowed.

---

[139] This is one of the situations when exemplary damages *can* usually be awarded in tort law: see, below, at § 30.2.
[140] [2008] EWHC 1777 (QB), at [172]–[197].
[141] In *Gulati* v *MGN Ltd* [2017] QB 149, the Court of Appeal rejected the submission that awards of compensatory damages for misuse of private information should be comparable to awards made by the Strasbourg Court for violations of Article 8.
[142] For further discussion of the utility of exemplary damages and when they should be awarded, see Chapter 24.

It was held in *Cream Holdings Ltd* v *Banerjee* (2005) that this means that an interim injunction which prohibits expression should usually only be granted where a claimant can demonstrate that he is more likely than not to establish at trial both that the defendant is liable and that a *final* injunction is appropriate. Moreover, to make this judgment a court must reach a provisional view on disputes of fact and questions of law. This makes it more difficult for a claimant to obtain an interim injunction that will restrict expression than to obtain one which will restrict commission of some tort that does not involve expression.

(ii) *The effect on third parties issue.* Where an interim injunction has been granted against a defendant, a third party will commit contempt of court if it knows this and nonetheless publishes information that thwarts the purpose of the injunction. This is commonly called the *Spycatcher* doctrine, because this was the name of the book which gave rise to the litigation which established it.[143] In practice, this means that a claimant who has obtained an interim injunction against an individual defendant will commonly serve this on a range of news organisations so as to prevent them from disclosing the information concerned.

While the *Spycatcher* doctrine will protect a claimant *until* trial, once he obtains a *final* injunction a third party cannot commit contempt of court by thwarting the purpose of an *interim* injunction.[144] Of course, once a *final* injunction has been granted news organisations may be *aware of the risk* that publishing particular information will be a tort. But in some circumstances the possibility of a tort claim may be insufficient to prevent them from yielding to temptation; certainly such a prospect is likely to be less of a deterrent than the threat of proceedings for contempt of court. In circumstances such as these, provided that a court considers that the step is necessary and proportionate in order to protect a claimant's privacy, it can grant an injunction *contra mundum* (that is, against the world), prohibiting *everyone* from disclosing the private information in future.[145]

(iii) *The anonymity issue.* When a court has decided that an interim injunction should be granted prohibiting disclosure of private facts it may also need to restrict how the case should be reported, since otherwise the way in which it is reported might undermine the injunction. Such a restriction on reporting can achieved by granting a claimant (and sometimes other parties as well) anonymity. Such an order, however, is a far more serious matter than an ordinary interim injunction since it will impinge on the principle of *open justice*, a fundamental constitutional principle that helps to ensure the integrity and legitimacy of the legal system.

In *H* v *News Group Newspapers Ltd* (2011) the Court of Appeal held that what a judge must do in such a case is: (a) decide whether it is *necessary* to place some restriction on the free reporting of legal proceedings in order to protect a claimant's privacy, and if the answer is 'yes', then (b) decide what is the least restrictive way of protecting the claimant's privacy.[146] The Court of Appeal suggested that

---

[143] See *Attorney-General* v *Newspaper Publishing Plc* [1988] Ch 333 and *Attorney-General* v *Times Newspapers Ltd* [1992] 1 AC 191.

[144] *Jockey Club* v *Buffham* [2003] QB 462.

[145] *OPQ* v *BJM* [2011] EWHC 1059 (QB).

[146] [2011] 1 WLR 1645, at [21]–[22].

usually if a claimant is granted anonymity then it will be possible for the judge to include more detail in her judgment about why an interim injunction is being granted, and that will usually involve less of a restriction on *open justice* than allowing the claimant to be named but limiting what details about the claim can be reported.[147]

(iv) *The super-injunction issue.* The label 'super-injunction' is appropriately used for an *interim* injunction which prohibits the party against which it is obtained from disclosing to others that a claim has been made and an *interim* injunction obtained. Thus if *Striker* makes a claim of misuse of private information against *Dancer* and obtains a *super-injunction* against her, then she will be prohibited from telling others that a claim has been made against her and an injunction granted. Although this is the appropriate use of the label 'super-injunction', English newspapers often use the label for all *anonymised injunctions.*

It seems to be generally agreed that *super-injunctions* are a legitimate *interim* remedy when they are granted for a short period in order to prevent accomplices, or the like, from being 'tipped off'. But greater controversy surrounds the granting of *super-injunctions* simply in order to prevent newspapers and the public from speculating about what private information might be being protected. Because *super-injunctions* involve such a significant restriction on *open justice* – they permit the workings of the justice system to be hidden from public view, at least temporarily – a Committee, chaired by Lord Neuberger MR, was asked to consider them.[148] Its conclusion was that there might be some situations beyond prevention of 'tipping-off' when it would be appropriate to grant a *super-injunction*, but that one should 'only be granted following intense scrutiny by the court in the individual case, and only when it is strictly necessary as a means to ensure that justice is done.'[149]

17.3 Misuse of private information: access

In *Imerman* v *Tchenguiz* (2011), the claimant, Vivian Imerman, shared the office premises of his two brothers-in-law, Robert and Vincent Tchenguiz, and used the computer system which served the offices for his personal and business purposes. The claimant's wife, Elizabeth, petitioned for divorce in December 2008, and in January and February 2009 her brothers, Robert and Vincent, accessed the server which supported the computer system and made electronic copies of emails and other documents stored by the claimant. The brothers primarily did this because they were worried that the claimant would conceal his assets to reduce what their sister would receive as a result of the divorce. The brothers later sent printed copies of the documents to their solicitor, and some were subsequently sent on to the solicitors who were handling the divorce. The claimant sought

---

[147] [2011] 1 WLR 1645, at [25].

[148] *Report of the Committee on Super-Injunctions: Super-Injunctions, Anonymised Injunctions and Open Justice* (20 May 2011).

[149] Ibid, at 2.38. Super-injunctions do not appear to be at all common: the Ministry of Justice's statistics report that only one such injunction was granted at the Royal Courts of Justice between August 2011 and June 2014. But academics have pointed out the Ministry's statistics for ordinary privacy injunctions are unreliable.

the return of the documents, and injunctions prohibiting the brothers from disclosing, copying or using any information contained in them. The Court of Appeal granted the injunctions, and held, in a judgment delivered by Lord Neuberger MR, that A would commit a wrong in relation to B if she intentionally and secretly obtained information in respect of which she must have appreciated that B had an expectation of privacy.[150]

The Court of Appeal referred to the wrong that they recognised in *Imerman* as 'breach of confidence', and stated that 'the normal equitable rules apply'.[151] But, the wrong was founded on the claimant's expectation of *privacy*, and, as we have noted above,[152] if a defendant *discloses* private information he is now regarded as having committed the tort of *misuse of private information*, despite liability for such disclosures *developing* within 'breach of confidence'. Thus we think that wrongfully obtaining access to private information can also now be treated as an instance of the tort of *misuse of private information*. This classification is consistent with the subsequent case of *Gulati* v *MGN Ltd* (2015), where the claimants obtained damages for 'phone-hacking', involving unlawfully obtaining private information from their voicemail, and their claims were described as having been for *misuse of private information*.

The classification of wrongfully obtaining access to private information as an instance of misuse of private information also fits with the reasoning that persuaded the Court of Appeal in *Imerman* that the defendants' behaviour was wrongful. That reasoning proceeded in two steps: (1) If there is information about B that A would be under a duty not to disclose if she *accidentally* came to learn it, then (2) A will commit a wrong if she intentionally and secretly *obtains* it.[153] This reasoning equates the private information that it is a tort to disclose with the private information it is wrongful to obtain intentionally and secretly, reinforcing the sense that what has developed is a tort which covers two ways of misusing *private information*. Such an understanding would also have the advantage of making clear that 'the dual perspective approach', which has been used to determine whether some countervailing interest makes it justifiable to disappoint a claimant's expectation that information will remain private, could be used in both settings: disclosure and access.

Whilst we think that the wrong that the Court of Appeal recognised in *Imerman* ought to be treated as an instance of the tort of misuse of private information, and that consequently the rules that we set out when discussing *disclosure* cases, such as those that determine when a claimant has a 'reasonable expectation of privacy' will be equally applicable to *access* cases, there are four elements that require further discussion:

(1) *Intention.* The wrong is said by the Court of Appeal to require the *intentional* acquisition of private information. Thus if *Daydreamer* accidentally opens mail that has been erroneously delivered to his house instead of his neighbour's he may be under a duty not to publish what he sees, but he will not have committed the tort of *misusing* private information.[154]

---

[150] [2011] Fam 116, at [68].

[151] Ibid, at [74].

[152] At § 17.2.A

[153] Ibid.

[154] You will recall that we noted above, at §17.2(I), that it is unclear whether a defendant can be held to have misused private information by *unintentionally* disclosing it, such as by leaving it on a train. Thus, it may turn out that *misuse* of private information can never be committed accidentally.

(2) *Secretly.* In our opinion the Court of Appeal should not have incorporated *secrecy* into the definition: we think that the brothers' behaviour in *Imerman* (2011) would still have been wrongful if they had *openly* copied the documents from the server (after taking steps to prevent the claimant from deleting them).

(3) *Obtained information.* If a defendant copies documents, reads another person's correspondence, or listens to another person's voice-mail then it is obvious that he has 'obtained information', and in such situations we can then proceed to ask whether the claimant had a reasonable expectation of privacy with regard to the information obtained. But could it be said that the two prison officers 'obtained information' in *Wainwright* v *Home Office* (2004) when they forced *Alan* to undress in front of them, the information being 'what *Alan* looks like naked'?[155] Of course, it is doubtful if the prison officers remembered this information for more than an instant, and they also did not obtain it secretly. But we can see, however, that if 'obtained information' is read broadly then the misuse tort will be capable of covering a wide range of forms of intrusion: perhaps, taking photographs of people on private property using a long-range lens, or spying on someone when they are taking a shower.[156]

(4) *Justification.* In cases which involve *disclosure* any justification relied on by the defendant is likely to depend on the value of 'expression'. Cases where a defendant wants to *justify* intentionally *obtaining access* to private information are likely to raise two issues. First, defendants may seek to rely on values other that 'expression'; for example, the defendants in *Imerman* were (it seems) seeking to prevent the claimant from hiding assets from someone who might have had a legitimate claim to them, which is not a goal primarily focused on expression. Secondly, courts will have to deal with the problem that defendants are likely to have to obtain private information *before* they can actually be sure whether obtaining it was justified. Consider, for example, the **Concerned Sister Problem**:

> Two years ago *Brother* successfully completed a drug rehabilitation programme and stopped using heroin. *Sister* thinks that *Brother* has recently started to behave erratically, and is concerned that he may be using heroin again, particularly since she often lets him babysit her young children. When *Brother* was using heroin he communicated with his dealer using email, and since *Sister* knows *Brother*'s password, she decides to log into his email account. From his emails she discovers that *Brother* is gay, and has been in a dispute with his boyfriend about whether he should tell his family. *Brother* is not using heroin again.

If the justification test is applied with the benefit of hindsight then it seems that *Sister* will have no defence: she had no justification for obtaining access to information about *Brother*'s sexuality. (Moreover, although she did not intend to obtain access to information about *Brother's* sexuality it will be difficult for her to argue that she did not intend to obtain access to any private information.) But when we discussed the Deceptive Appearances Problem,[157] we noted that the courts might develop a doctrine which would allow a defendant to avoid liability for *disclosing* private information if the disclosure would have been justifiable had the circumstances been as he mistakenly – but 'reasonably' – believed. A similar choice would face the courts in cases involving *obtaining* private information.

---

[155] Discussed above, §17.1.

[156] In *C* v *Holland* [2012] 3 NZLR 672, Whata J held that it was a tort in New Zealand for a defendant to film a claimant intentionally and secretly when she was taking a shower. But he did not define the tortious behaviour in terms of *obtaining information* but in terms of *intruding on seclusion*.

[157] Above, at § 17.2(G)(5).

17.4 Cases not involving wrongful disclosure or access

We have already mentioned that some aspects of privacy may be protected by torts dealt with elsewhere in the text (for instance, by the torts of trespass to land, private nuisance, defamation, and malicious falsehood). But these and the tort of misuse of private information, discussed above, do not between them provide comprehensive protection for privacy. For example, *Star*, a celebrity, may feel that his privacy is invaded by: (1) *Fan* disturbing his meal in a restaurant to seek a 'selfie' and an autograph; (2) *Bore*, who occupies the seat next to him on an aeroplane, spending the entire flight outlining the conspiracy that prevented *Bore* from becoming famous; and (3) *Laugh*, a popular comedienne, amusing her television audience by confessing that *Star* is the regular subject of her sexual fantasies. Should the English law of torts attempt to deal with any forms of invasion of privacy *other than* intentionally obtaining access to and disclosing private information?

In the United States of America, a fourfold division of forms of invasion of privacy is commonly used: (1) unreasonable intrusion into private situations; (2) unreasonable publication of private facts; (3) publicity unreasonably placing the claimant in a 'false light'; (4) appropriating the claimant's name or likeness for private advantage.[158] The English tort of misuse of private information clearly covers 'unreasonable publication of private facts', and, as we explained above, its extension to 'intentionally obtaining access to private information' *may* allow it to cover some forms of 'unreasonable intrusion into private situations'. But many forms of intrusion do not involve any misuse of *information*; nor does casting 'false light'. So – in order to allow English law to deal with all the forms of invasion of privacy that tort law covers in the United States we would have to develop further *limited* torts to cover: (1) intrusion that does not involve obtaining access to private information; (2) placing the claimant in a 'false light'; and (3) appropriating the claimant's name or likeness. In the remainder of this section we will consider whether there are *distinct* problems with developing each of these limited torts.

A. Intrusion

A tort dealing with this form of invasion would encompass behaviour such as *Fan* disturbing *Star*'s meal in a restaurant in order to seek a 'selfie' and an autograph, or perhaps simply staring at him, or surreptitiously snapping a picture of him with a camera-phone.[159] While many people would castigate *Fan*'s behaviour in these scenarios, perhaps calling it 'outrageously rude', the question whether a new tort should be created to cover it is controversial.

We will see in the next section of this chapter that Parliament has enacted that a 'course of conduct', but not a one-off event, can amount to *harassment* under the Protection from Harassment Act 1997. This means that English law can probably already deal with any individual who *repeatedly* intrudes on someone else's privacy, such as a paparazzi photographer who follows *Star* around. The scope of the 1997 Act *might* also suggest that Parliament believes that single instances of intrusive behaviour are too trivial to warrant civil litigation. This said, celebrities may face a special problem because the cumulative effect of intrusive behaviour by unconnected people is intolerable: for example, where *Fan* is just one of many

---

[158] See, for instance, Prosser 1960; Rest 2d, Torts § 652A.
[159] We noted above that *staring* or *taking photographs* might amount to *misuse of private information* – but only if *obtaining information* is defined broadly. See above, § 17.3(3).

people who treat *Star* in a similar way, one can easily imagine how *Star* and his family could be affected. But it would be very difficult to design a tort to protect people against the cumulative effect of intrusions without impinging severely on the freedom of others to do ordinary, human things, like taking an interest in who else is eating in the same restaurant.

B. False light

A tort dealing with this form of invasion would cover behaviour such as publishing the false information that the claimant was romantically involved with a celebrity, or a falsely exaggerated (but non-defamatory) version of a dramatic event involving the claimant. Clearly, if *Tabloid* published the information that *Cinders*, a single woman, was dating *Prince Chaming*, a single man, this would usually not be defamatory of *Cinders* even if it was wholly false;[160] it would undoubtedly, however, to subject *Cinders* to a significant degree of public attention, and it is easy to see why she might want to be protected from this. But the issue whether a tortious duty should be created to confer such protection raises two subsidiary questions: (1) Whether the degree of annoyance and inconvenience likely to be suffered by someone subjected to such attention is sufficiently significant to warrant such a step, given that there cannot be a duty to avoid all potentially annoying forms of conduct;[161] (2) Whether the existence of such a duty might unduly restrict the activities of those who want to retell recent events in a dramatically engaging manner, such as the authors of docudramas and unauthorised biographies. It would certainly be a burden on modern historians and unauthorised biographers if they could be liable for non-defamatory factual errors that attract public attention, and we think that the complexity of the current law of libel – a product of both complex case law and detailed statutes – provides a good reason why courts should be cautious about presuming that they have the capacity to develop a new privacy tort in this area.

C. Appropriation of personality

A tort dealing with this form of invasion would extend over behaviour such as using a photograph of a person in an advertisement without his consent. For instance, if an airline published an advertisement for its flights using the picture of a person recently involved in a criminal case and the slogan 'for a quick getaway fly with our airline'[162] then the person depicted might be able to claim.[163] Similarly, this tort might cover a case where a

---

[160] It might be defamatory in unusual circumstances: for instance, if *Starlet* was a nun.

[161] Such a duty would be unsatisfactory because it would impinge on so many aspects of ordinary social life. It would be extraordinarily ironic if many everyday encounters became subject to legal regulation in the interests of protecting *privacy*!

[162] EasyJet issued similar advertisements during 2003.

[163] Some celebrities already enjoy some protection from having their images appropriated by advertisers, because the extension of the tort of passing off in *Irvine* v *Talksport Ltd* [2002] 1 WLR 2355 (discussed above, §15.5(B)) protects a celebrity who has acquired a valuable reputation or goodwill from *misrepresentations* which enable a defendant to make use of or take advantage of that reputation (at [38], per Laddie J). See also, *Fenty* v *Arcadia Group Brands Ltd* [2015] EWCA Civ 3, at [43], where Kitchin LJ summarised the requirements for a claim as being: 'He must show that he has a relevant goodwill, that the activities of the defendant amount to a misrepresentation that he has endorsed or approved the goods or services of which he complains, and that these activities have caused or are likely to cause him damage to his goodwill and business.'

photograph of a teenager taken in a public place without her consent was used to illustrate a magazine article.[164] It might also help to deal with even more problematic forms of exploitation of another's image, such as designing a sex robot to look like a real person without their consent. From a privacy perspective the utility of the tort would be that it would secure for people control over *how* their images and identities are used, and prevent these being treated as mere tools by others.

One difficulty with creating a tort to cover this form of invasion of privacy would be defining the scope of a claimant's protected interest. Where a photograph of the claimant is used in an advertisement the matter seems straightforward, but more difficult cases might involve use of archetypes, or of a less distinctive catchphrase, mannerism or vocal characteristic.[165] It might be possible to get round this problem by defining the tort so that it covered only *intentional* appropriation, but this would not avoid all difficulties.[166] A further difficulty would be defining the situations where use of a person's image without consent is justifiable. For instance, photographs are commonly used without the consent of those depicted to illustrate legitimate news stories, in protest and in satire.[167] In Germany a person's image is protected, but the courts have had to define the exceptions: for instance, the Bundesgerichtshof had to determine *when* it was permissible for Greenpeace to use the name and picture of the president of a chemical company on a campaign poster.[168] No doubt English courts could solve similar disputes, but it is important to note that extending tort law to cover this form of invasion of privacy would be likely to involve a move away from the traditional preference for clear legal duties in contexts which could impinge on the liberty of commercial actors.[169]

17.5 Protection from Harassment Act 1997

(1) *The basic provision.* Section 1(1) of the 1997 Act provides that:

A person must not pursue a course of conduct –

    (a) which amounts to harassment of another, and
    (b) which he knows or ought to know amounts to harassment of another.

---

[164] *Aubry* v *Editions Vice-Versa Inc* [1998] 1 SCR 591.

[165] Cases from the United States have involved the use of a television presenter's catchphrase to market a portable toilet (*Carson* v *Here's Johnny Portable Toilets Inc*, 698 F 2d 831 (1983)), the use of a singer who sounded like Bette Midler to advertise cars (*Midler* v *Ford Motor Co*, 849 F 2d 460 (1988)), and the use of a robot dressed like a gameshow hostess to advertise videorecorders (*White* v *Samsung Electronics America Inc*, 971 F 2d 1395 (1992)).

[166] For instance, if the defendant argued that he intended to invoke a *generic* athlete of the 1970s while the claimant argued that his individual image was appropriated. (In 2003 David Bedford, the athlete who held the world record for the 10,000 metres from 1973 until 1977, became involved in a dispute with a directory enquiries company which he claimed had appropriated his image.)

[167] The short phrase 'for private advantage' used in the summary of the tort recognised in the United States clearly does not go very far towards answering the difficult issues raised, since newspapers and satirists generally seek to make a profit.

[168] BGH, 12 October 1993, NJW 1994, 124 (Federal Court of Justice, Germany).

[169] In *Von Hannover* v *Germany* (2005) 40 EHRR 1, the European Court of Human Rights held (at [72]) that states have undertaken a 'positive obligation under the Convention to protect private life *and the right to control the use of one's image*' (emphasis added). See also [57]. One way in which the United Kingdom could fulfil this obligation would be for the *courts* to create a new tort making appropriation of personality actionable.

Section 1(3) provides someone who engages in such a conduct with a defence if that conduct:

(a) . . . was pursued for the purpose of preventing and detecting crime,

(b) . . . was pursued under any enactment or rule of law or to comply with any condition or requirement imposed by any person under any enactment, or

(c) . . . was reasonable [in the circumstances].

(2) *A crime and a tort.* Someone who violates s 1 of the 1997 Act will commit a crime (s 2) and a tort (s 3). This is unusual. Normally, the sort of crimes which make up the core of the criminal law involve committing a tort *with* the sort of *mens rea* (or fault element) that makes committing that tort worthy of punishment.[170] Not so here: anyone who commits the tort of harassment created by the 1997 Act will also commit a crime; no added fault element need be established for the crime of harassment to have been committed. This creates a difficulty for the courts. In interpreting the 1997 Act for the purposes of deciding whether a claimant can sue a defendant in tort for harassment, the courts have to keep one eye out for the fact that their decision will also have implications for whether people can be criminally punished for acting in the way the defendant did.

(3) *Threshold of seriousness.* It is for this reason that the courts have decided that a defendant's conduct has to pass a threshold of seriousness before he will be held to have committed the tort of harassment under the 1997 Act. Lord Nicholls held in *Majrowski* v *St Guy's and St Thomas's NHS Trust* (2007) that this threshold of seriousness would only be passed if the defendant's conduct was 'offensive and unacceptable':

> . . . irritations, annoyances, even a measure of upset, arise at times in everybody's day-to-day dealings with other people. Courts are well able to recognise the boundary between conduct which is unattractive, even unreasonable, and conduct which is oppressive and unacceptable. To cross the boundary from the regrettable to the unacceptable the gravity of the misconduct must be of an order which would sustain criminal liability under s 2.[171]

This suggests that whether a defendant's conduct is regarded as 'offensive and unacceptable' should be determined according to whether it is worthy of punishment. But in the subsequent case of *Veakins* v *Kier Islington* (2009), the Court of Appeal made it clear that whether a defendant's conduct was 'offensive and unacceptable' should be decided independently of whether it was the sort of conduct that a prosecutor might want to prosecute.[172]

One sort of conduct that is obviously 'offensive and unacceptable', and that the 1997 Act was designed to address, is 'stalking'. But the Act has been used to deal with a wide range of abuses, including cases where the alleged harassing conduct took the form of communications, publications or broadcasts, which might be protected as 'expression' by Article 10 of the European Convention on Human Rights (ECHR). Where a court has to determine whether such conduct is sufficiently serious it must consider whether it is 'so unreasonable that it is necessary and proportionate to prohibit or sanction the speech in pursuit of one of the aims listed in article 10.2 [ECHR]'.[173]

(4) *Alarm and distress.* Section 7(2) of the 1997 Act provides that 'References to harassing a person include alarming the person or causing the person distress.' The use of the word 'include' suggests that a defendant can be held liable under the 1997 Act for harassment

---

[170] See above, §1.12.
[171] [2007] 1 AC 224, at [30].
[172] [2009] EWCA Civ 1288, at [15].
[173] *Trimingham* v *Associated Newspapers Ltd* [2012] 4 All ER 717, at [53].

even if his conduct did not cause alarm or distress. (If you said that the people at the dinner *included* 'Andy and Mary', that would suggest that there were *more* people at the event than just Andy and Mary.) This interpretation of the scope of 'harassment' was accepted by Baroness Hale in *Majrowski* v *St Guy's and St Thomas's NHS Trust* (2007).[174] But whilst conduct *can* be harassment even if it does not cause alarm or distress, conduct *cannot* be harassment of A unless it prompts a reaction in A that is consistent with it having been *harassment* of him:[175] if B attends a series of public appearances made by A, a foreign film star visiting London, and at each B asks A an obscene and impertinent question, but A does not understand English and believes that B is just another of his fans, then it cannot be said that B has harassed *A*.[176]

If 'harassing a person *include[s]* . . . causing the person distress' then are *all* courses of conduct that cause distress to A harassment of A? The answer to this question must be 'no', since otherwise the effect of s 7(2) would be to circumvent the requirement that a defendant's conduct must be sufficiently serious: behaviour that is less serious than 'offensive and unacceptable' can easily *cause distress*. As Lord Phillips MR stated in *Thomas* v *News Group Newspapers* (2001), 'There are many actions that foreseeably alarm or cause a person distress that could not possibly be described as harassment.'[177] But how is this answer consistent with the wording of s 7(2)? The answer provided by Lord Phillips MR was that the purpose of this provision was to help to define what the *effect* of the conduct must be, if the conduct was to be harassment, rather than defining what types of conduct might be actionable.

(5) *Targeting and calculating.* In *Thomas* v *News Group Newspapers* (2001) Lord Phillips MR went on to offer a partial definition of 'harassment': 'It describes conduct targeted at an individual which is calculated to produce [alarm or distress] and which is oppressive and unreasonable.'[178] We should briefly consider what he meant by 'targeted at an individual' and 'calculated to produce' a harmful effect.

The issue of 'targeting' was considered by the Court of Appeal in *Levi* v *Bates* (2015). In this case B had pursued a dispute with L in part through writing columns for the matchday programmes of Leeds United Football Club; in one of these he suggested that

---

[174] *Majrowski* v *St Guy's and St Thomas's NHS Trust* [2007] 1 AC 224, at [66]: 'conduct might be harassment even if no alarm or distress were in fact caused.' See also Briggs LJ in *Levi* v *Bates* [2016] QB 91, at [33], '. . . usually, but not limited to, alarm and distress.'

[175] Some support for this can be found in *University of Oxford* v *Broughton* [2008] EWHC 75 (QB), where Treacy J refused to grant an injunction against demonstrators who were chanting slogans outside the building used by the University for graduation ceremonies; he noted, at [36]: 'Not only is there an absence of evidence to show alarm, fear or distress, but the demeanour of those present at the ceremony did not appear to bear out the assertion that they were people undergoing harassment.'

[176] A person cannot have been harassed by behaviour that he knew nothing about: *Shakil-Ur-Rahman* v *ARY Network Ltd* [2016] EWHC 3110 (QB), at [117].

[177] *Thomas* v *News Group Newspapers* [2001] EWCA Civ 1233, at [29]. In *Levi* v *Bates* [2016] QB 91, at [28], Briggs LJ offered the example of a sportscar driver regularly speeding in a particular neighbourhood as an illustration of a course of conduct that might cause alarm and distress (for example, to the parents of young children) but would not be harassment.

[178] *Thomas* v *News Group Newspapers* [2001] EWCA Civ 1233, at [30]. We have adjusted this quotation by replacing the words 'the consequences described in section 7' with [alarm or distress], since these are the consequences described in section 7(2). As we noted under the previous heading, however, s 7(2) does not provide an exhaustive definition of how a person must react to a course of conduct if it is to be classed as 'harassment'.

readers might have questions for L, and published L's home address, whilst in another, after raising questions, he told readers that they could find L's home telephone number in the phonebook. The question which the Court of Appeal had to answer was whether by pursuing the dispute in this way B had harassed not just L, but also *L's wife*, who lived at the same address and had the same telephone number. Briggs LJ treated conduct as 'targeted at A' if it was 'aimed at' or 'directed at' A.[179] His judgment includes two further important points, however. First, he held that a person could claim even if they were a victim of harassment that 'targeted' someone else, provided that the effect on them was reasonably foreseeable and direct.[180] This was sufficient to mean that Mrs L could claim against B. Secondly, Briggs LJ held that a person who suffered distress or anxiety simply out of sympathy for a close relative or friend who was being harassed could not claim, because the effect on them would have been insufficiently direct.[181]

What then did Lord Phillips MR mean when he stated that the defendant's course of conduct must have been 'calculated' to cause the claimant alarm or distress.[182] Importantly, he did not mean that the defendant must have *intended* to bring about such an effect. This is clear from the fact that s 1(1) of the 1997 Act expressly provides that someone can be held liable for harassment if he merely 'ought' to have known that his conduct amounted to harassment, and s 1(2) provides that it will be held that a person ought to have known this 'if a reasonable person in possession of the same information would think the course of conduct amounted to harassment of the other'. Moreover, requiring that a defendant must have *intended* to cause alarm or distress would hamper the prospects of the 1997 Act in addressing stalking: those who indulge in this form of behaviour quite frequently intend to benefit their targets, and do not understand themselves to be causing anxiety and distress. We think that when Lord Phillips MR stated that harassment required a course of conduct 'calculated' to cause anxiety and distress what he meant was that it must be conduct of a sort that a reasonable person would recognise as likely to cause such consequences.[183]

(6) *Course of conduct.* One of the key – and most difficult – requirements for establishing liability under the 1997 Act is that it has to be shown that the defendant engaged in a *course of conduct* that amounted to harassment of the claimant. This makes it obvious that a one-off act cannot amount to harassment under the 1997 Act.[184] (The position is quite different under the Equality Act 2010.[185]) But where a defendant has done X, and later on Y, when will his doing X and Y be held to amount to a *course of conduct*?

---

[179] *Levi* v *Bates* [2016] QB 91, at [28]. See also Longmore LJ, at [55]–[57].

[180] Ibid, at [34].

[181] Ibid, at [33]. Longmore LJ expressed agreement with the reasoning of Briggs LJ, at [57]. Ryder LJ reached a decision in favour of Mrs L by a different route: he held, at [52], that 'targeting is an objective concept that includes a situation where the conduct complained of is not only intended to harm a particular victim, but would also foreseeably harm another person, because of her proximity to the intended victim.'

[182] [2001] EWCA Civ 1233, at [30].

[183] See also May LJ referring to conduct that is 'calculated, *in an objective sense,* to cause distress' (emphasis added) in the Court of Appeal in *Majrowski* v *Guy's and St Thomas's NHS Trust* [2005] QB 848, at [82].

[184] Though see *Kelly* v *DPP* [2003] Crim LR 43, where it was held that leaving three messages on someone's answering machine – all of which were listened to on the same occasion – could amount to a 'course of conduct' under the 1997 Act.

[185] For a very brief account, see above, § 17.1(B).

The fact that X and Y are the same, or similar, forms of behaviour will not suffice to turn doing X and doing Y into a course of conduct. For example, in *R v Hills* (2001), it was held that hitting one's live-in girlfriend once in April and then again in October could not be said to amount to a 'course of conduct'. And in *R v Curtis* (2010), the Court of Appeal held that the defendant's hitting, or threatening to hit, his live-in girlfriend on six different occasions in a nine month period of co-habitation did not amount to a 'course of conduct'.[186] So what will turn two or more separate actions into a course of conduct? The cases provide very little guidance on this issue, but it might be suggested that doing X, and later on Y, amounts to a 'course of conduct' if X and Y were each done with the intention of achieving a particular goal that was not achieved by doing X alone.

So if *Unhappy* is co-habiting with *Miserable*, and *Unhappy* starts screaming at *Miserable* one day with the sole object of making her feel bad that day, and then he does the same thing a month later, that is not a 'course of conduct'. The first screaming fit achieved its goal, and there is therefore no connection between the first and second screaming fits, even though each fit was aimed at the same goal. But if *Unhappy* starts screaming at *Miserable* one day with the object of making her so miserable that she will leave him – thus allowing him move in the new object of his affections – and, when he does not initially achieve this goal, he starts screaming at her again a week later in order to give her some more encouragement to leave him, his two screaming fits will amount to a 'course of conduct'. Importantly, as we have already noted, a defendant can commit harassment against someone even if he did not intend to cause any harm; thus the intention that links a series of events into a 'course' of conduct need not be an intention to harm the claimant.

In *Iqbal v Dean Manson Solicitors* (2011), the Court of Appeal emphasised that not every element in a 'course of conduct' need be experienced as harassment for that 'course of conduct' to amount to harassment. This is right: if *Dumped* rings *Ex* to ask her how things are going for her, she may think nothing of that call. But if he then rings her the following day to ask exactly the same question, it may become apparent that the first phone call was part of a 'course of conduct' that amounts to harassment.

(7) *Scope of liability.* *Jones v Ruth* (2011) is the leading case on the scope of a defendant's liability to pay damages to a claimant under the 1997 Act. The Court of Appeal ruled in that case that damages will be payable to the victim of harassment even in respect of harms that were not a foreseeable consequence of that harassment. The decision was based in part on the fact that foreseeability of harm is not mentioned in the Act as placing a limit on a defendant's liability to pay damages under the Act; but the fact that harassment involves some form of deliberate conduct also must have played a part in the Court's decision to adopt the rule on remoteness of damage that usually applies in fraud cases and other cases of deliberate malfeasance.

(8) *Defences.* As we have seen,[187] a defendant who has engaged in a course of conduct that amounts (as he knows or ought to know) to harassment may have a defence under s 1(3) to being sued for harassment.

The UK Supreme Court dealt with the issue of when a defendant could take advantage of a defence under s 1(3)(a) (that the defendant was acting 'for the purpose of

---

[186] *Pratt v DPP* [2001] EWHC 483 (Admin) (holding that losing one's temper with one's wife once at Christmas and subsequently in March amounted to a 'course of conduct') always looked wrong and the result (though nothing said in the decision) in *Curtis* seems to confirm that it was wrong.
[187] Above, §17.5(1).

preventing or detecting crime') in *Hayes* v *Willoughby* (2013). The defendant in that case obsessively wrote hundreds of letters to the authorities, claiming that his former employer was guilty of various financial crimes. The majority held that the defendant could only take advantage of s 1(3)(a) if there was 'some logical connection' between the evidence available to him and his conduct, and that the defence would not be available to a defendant whose conduct was dominated by 'arbitrariness, . . . capriciousness or . . . reasoning so outrageous in its defiance of logic as to be perverse.'[188] Applying that standard, the majority held that the defendant was not entitled to a defence under s 1(3)(a).

The question of when a newspaper that had run a campaign targeted at a particular individual could take advantage of the defence of 'reasonable conduct' under s 1(3)(c) was considered by the Court of Appeal in *Thomas* v *News Group Newspapers Ltd* (2001). Lord Phillips MR explained that a newspaper would only be held to have acted unreasonably in running a series of articles criticising a particular individual if the campaign amounted 'to an abuse of the freedom of the press which the pressing social needs of a democratic society require should be curbed'.[189]

As a test for determining when a newspaper will be held to have acted unreasonably in running a campaign against a particular individual, this is unsatisfactory: it is likely to have a 'chilling' effect on newspapers' legitimately exercising their right to freedom of expression. This is because the test is so vague that a newspaper which is thinking of running a campaign against an individual will find it hard to know whether it will or will not be held liable under the 1997 Act if it runs the campaign.[190] As a result, it may well choose to 'pull' the campaign rather than run it and take the risk of being sued (or prosecuted) under the 1997 Act. It would have been more satisfactory if the Court of Appeal in *Thomas* had adopted the test set out in the second American Restatement of Torts for determining when the infliction of severe emotional distress will be tortious, and ruled that a newspaper which ran a series of articles targeted at a particular individual could only be held to have acted unreasonably in so doing if its running that campaign was so 'extreme and outrageous' that it went beyond 'all possible bounds of decency . . . and [was] utterly intolerable in a civilized society'.[191] (Which test would probably have been satisfied in the *Thomas* case anyway, given the newspaper's concession in that case that the articles were aggressive and inflammatory, and the Court of Appeal's finding that the articles were probably racist.)

(9) *Companies as defendants.* The defendant in the *Thomas* case was a company – News Group Newspapers Ltd. There is no problem with a company being sued personally under the 1997 Act, or on the basis that it is vicariously liable for an employee's committing the tort of harassment under the 1997 Act.

---

[188] [2013] 1 WLR 935, at [14] (per Lord Sumption); see also at [22] (per Lord Mance).

[189] [2001] EWCA Civ 1233, at [50]. It was conceded in *Thomas* that this test would be satisfied if a newspaper campaign was calculated to stir up racial hatred.

[190] The decision of the first instance court in *Trimingham* v *Associated Newspapers Ltd* [2012] 4 All ER 717 (declining to find the *Daily Mail* liable for harassment after publishing numerous articles mentioning the claimant and the history of her relationship with the disgraced Liberal Democrat politician Chris Huhne) provides no reassurance on this score: the fact that it took 281 paragraphs for the judge to reach his conclusion shows just how difficult it is for newspapers to know whether they are protected by s 1(3)(c).

[191] Rest 2d, Torts, §46, Comment *d*.

For a company to be held *personally* liable under the 1997 Act, it has to be shown that *the company* engaged in a course of conduct which it knew or ought to have known amounted to harassment. This creates a problem (already encountered earlier in this text)[192] about – whose acts should we look at in order to determine what the company did? In *Ferguson* v *British Gas* (2010), the Court of Appeal held that the traditional answer – we look at the actions of those who are the company's 'directing mind or will' – was not meant by Parliament to apply in the context of the 1997 Act. Instead, a company will be held to have engaged in a course of conduct that amounted to harassment if someone employed to act on behalf of the company (at whatever level) engaged, on behalf of the company, in a course of conduct that amounted to harassment.

So far as *vicarious liability* is concerned, in *Majrowski* v *Guy's and St Thomas's NHS Trust* (2007), the House of Lords confirmed that, unless Parliament provides otherwise, the principle that an employer will be vicariously liable in respect of an employee's torts that were committed in the course of his employment applies just as much to statutory torts as it does to common law torts, such as negligence or assault. So an employer will be held vicariously liable if one of his employees commits the tort of harassment in relation to someone else in the course of his or her employment.[193]

(10) *Companies as claimants.* Section 7(5) of the 1997 Act makes it clear that only a natural person, and not a company, can claim to be a victim of harassment: 'References to a person, in the context of the harassment of a person, are references to a person who is an individual.'

Section 7(5) was not part of the 1997 Act when it was originally passed. But in *Daiichi Pharmaceuticals UK Ltd* v *Stop Huntingdon Animal Cruelty* (2004), it was held that a company could not seek an injunction against people attempting to disrupt the running of its business on the basis that *it* was the victim of harassment, because Parliament only intended s 1(1) of the Act to prohibit harassing human beings. Parliament responded by amending the 1997 Act[194] so as to create, in s 1(1A), a new prohibition on harassing two or more people (who could be, for example, a company's employees, customers or shareholders) with the object of inducing someone, including potentially a company, not to do something that it is required to do or to do something that it is under no obligation to do, and, in s 3A, a new right for any target of a breach of s 1(1A), which can include a company, to seek an injunction.[195]

17.6 The tort in *Wilkinson* v *Downton*

(1) *O (a child) v Rhodes (2016).* This case arose when James Rhodes, the well-known concert pianist, sought to publish a book, which detailed – among other things – the trauma he had suffered as a result of being sexually abused at school.[196] Rhodes' ex-wife – who

---

[192] See above, §7.5(C).

[193] On when someone can be said to have committed a tort in the course of his or her employment, see below, §31.4.

[194] By means of the Serious Organised Crime and Police Act 2005, s 125.

[195] *SmithKline Beecham* v *Avery* [2009] EWHC 1488 (QB). Note that breach of s 1(1A) will not give rise to a right to sue for damages (s 3 of the 1997 Act only applies to an actual or apprehended breach of s 1(1) of the Act: s 3(1)).

[196] The book has now been published; it is titled *Instrumental: A Memoir of Madness, Medication and Music.*

was living in the United States with their son, O, aged 11 and suffering psychological problems of his own – objected to this. Her concern was that publishing the book might cause severe emotional distress or psychological harm to their son if, for example, he found references to its contents online.[197] She initiated a claim, in O's name, for an injunction, claiming that Rhodes would commit a tort in relation to O (either the tort of negligence, or the tort in *Wilkinson* v *Downton*) by publishing the book without substantially editing the sections which graphically described his abuse and subsequent incidents of self-harm. The application for an injunction was dismissed, and the claims struck out, at first instance, but the Court of Appeal allowed an appeal; it rejected the claim in negligence, but held that it was arguable that the claim under the tort in *Wilkinson* v *Downton* could succeed, and granted an injunction. In turn, the Supreme Court reversed the Court of Appeal's decision, holding that Rhodes would not commit the tort in *Wilkinson* v *Downton* if he published his book in its unexpurgated form. Importantly, however, they did not reach this conclusion by abolishing the tort in *Wilkinson* v *Downton*, but by clarifying the elements required in order to establish it. Thus the Supreme Court's judgments provide an authoritative account of the tort.

Baroness Hale and Lord Toulson gave the leading judgment (with which Lord Clarke and Lord Wilson agreed). They held that to establish that tort in *Wilkinson* v *Downton* has been committed by A in relation to B 'a conduct element, a mental element, and a consequence element' must all be proved:[198] 'The conduct element requires words or conduct directed towards the claimant, for which there is no justification or reasonable excuse';[199] the 'necessary mental element is intention to cause physical harm or severe mental or emotional distress';[200] and, the consequence element requires that the claimant have suffered 'physical harm or [a] recognised psychiatric illness'.[201] In the instant case, they found that if Rhodes published his book then he would not commit the tort because neither the conduct element nor the mental element would be satisfied.[202]

Baroness Hale and Lord Toulson held that the conduct element would not be made out because there was 'every justification for the publication', once that question was assessed from the perspective of the book being 'directed towards' a general audience: 'A person who has suffered in the way that [Rhodes] has suffered, and has struggled to cope with the consequences of his suffering in the way that he has struggled, has the right to tell the world about it. And there is a corresponding public interest in others being able to listen to his life story in all its searing detail.'[203] Lord Neuberger delivered a separate judgment (with which Lord Wilson also agreed), in which he expressed concern about making the outcome dependent on a public interest in Rhodes' story being told: he wanted to avoid judges assessing which books it would be valuable for the public to be able to read, and thought it would have been better to hold that a claimant could not

---

[197] The parties were agreed that a copy of the book was unlikely to come into O's possession, but his mother thought that he might come across reviews and references if he searched for information about his father online: [2016] AC 219, at [19]–[20].

[198] [2016] AC 219, at [73].

[199] Ibid, at [74].

[200] Ibid, at [87].

[201] Ibid, at [73].

[202] Ibid, at [90].

[203] Ibid, at [74]–[76]. The Court of Appeal had erroneously assessed the question of justification by focusing on the position of O, who was at risk of suffering psychiatric harm.

restrain publication of a book which referred to him only in unobjectionable terms, and was not intended or expected to do him harm.[204] But we do not think that Baroness Hale and Lord Toulson intended to invite judges to assess the merits of particular books: they said it was 'difficult to envisage any circumstances in which speech which is not deceptive, threatening or possibly abusive, could give rise to liability', which suggests that they expected the publication of almost all works of both non-fiction and fiction to be justifiable, and they expressly rejected the notion of judges taking editorial control over how authors express their stories.[205]

(2) *Was the tort worth preserving?* Given that the Supreme Court restated the elements of the tort in *Wilkinson v Downton* in narrow terms, were there sufficient reasons to refrain from abolishing it altogether? In *Wainwright v Home Office* (2004) Lord Hoffmann explained the reasoning in *Wilkinson v Downton* (1897) as a ruse to get round a limit that then existed on liability in negligence – that a claimant could not sue in negligence for physical injuries caused by a defendant's causing the claimant to be upset – and as therefore having been made redundant by the removal of that limit in *Dulieu v White & Sons* (1901). Underpinning his reasoning was a recognition that the tort of negligence has expanded since 1897, and provides an appropriate platform for considering when we should take reasonable care to avoid harming each other's physical health or psychiatric welfare.[206] But in *Rhodes*, Baroness Hale and Lord Toulson dismissed Lord Hoffmann's explanation as an 'interesting reconstruction [which] shows the pitfalls of interpreting a decision more than a century earlier without a full understanding of jurisprudence and common legal terminology of the earlier period'.[207] Further, they insisted that 'negligence and intent are very different fault elements and there are principled reasons for differentiating between the bases (and possible extent) of liability for causing personal injury in either case'.[208]

There are two ways of understanding this explanation of the value of the tort in *Wilkinson v Downton*: Baroness Hale and Lord Toulson could be arguing that it is valuable to have a separate tort for instances of intentional harm-causing even when the tort of negligence is available, or that it is valuable to have a tort which can impose liability on explanation of intentional harm-causing even when for some reason the tort of negligence is not available. To substantiate the first argument it would have to be shown that the separate tort could provide a more appropriate range of remedies than those available in cases of negligence: for instance, tort law tends to be more willing to award aggravated damages or exemplary damages in cases involving intentional harm-causing,[209] and also

---

[204] Ibid, at [96]–[97]. We suspect that what Lord Neuberger meant to highlight by saying that the book only referred to O in 'unobjectionable terms' was that the book did not defame O, or misuse private information about him.

[205] Ibid, at [78]–[79].

[206] In *Rhodes*' case there was an unusual 'gap' in the tort of negligence: the defendant did not owe a duty of care to O because he was O's father, and the law has been reluctant to impose duties of care between parents and children other than in contexts where uncontroversial standards of care are available, such as driving. Clearly, however, the Supreme Court did not preserve the tort in *Wilkinson v Downton* primarily to deal with claims between parents and their children.

[207] Ibid, at [62].

[208] Ibid, at [63].

[209] This said, there is no good reason why these remedies cannot be available *within* the law of negligence. However, because of the really bad decision of Woolf J in *Kralj v McGrath* [1986] 1 All ER 54, aggravated damages cannot currently be awarded in negligence cases.

tends to use a more generous rule of remoteness of damage. We think, however, that the second explanation is more plausible. Importantly, liability in negligence depends on it being reasonably foreseeable to someone such as the defendant that his words or actions might cause physical injury or psychiatric harm, but the version of the tort in *Wilkinson* v *Downton* that Baroness Hale and Lord Toulson adopted can impose liability on a defendant who *intended* to cause physical harm *or severe mental or emotional distress*.

Is there a class of people who go out and do unjustifiable things *with the intention of causing severe distress*, but in circumstances where they had no particular reason to foresee the possibility of the physical harm or psychiatric injury that they actually caused? Perhaps there is, and it's a class that includes: the defendant in the original case of *Wilkinson* v *Downton* (1897), who told Mrs Wilkinson a shocking (but untrue) tale about injuries to her husband as a 'practical joke'; the defendants in *Janvier* v *Sweeney*,[210] who made a shocking allegation against Mlle Janvier in order to get a private audience with her and try to persuade her to show them someone else's private letters; and, people who set out to cause serious distress to others simply because they want to upset them. But opinions may differ as to whether it is a particularly large class, or one that it is worth having a special tort to deal with. As Lord Hoffmann noted in *Wainwright* v *Home Office* (2003), Parliament chose to require a 'course of conduct' before a claim for damages could be made under the Protection from Harassment Act 1997; should an intention to cause severe distress be enough to make a single 'boorish incident' actionable?[211]

Clearly, this restated version of the tort in *Wilkinson* v *Downton* invites the question whether it ought to be extended further so as to cover cases where the person who the unjustifiable words or behaviour were directed at suffers *only* severe pure distress (that is, severe distress not consequent on physical injury and not amounting to a recognised psychiatric illness). Baroness Hale and Lord Toulson did not express a view on this question because no one in the case had argued that the tort in *Wilkinson* v *Downton* extended so far.[212] Lord Neuberger, however, offered some support for such an extension, saying that 'there is much to be said' and that 'there is plainly a powerful case' that significant pure distress should be actionable under the tort.[213]

Were liability under the tort in *Wilkinson* v *Downton* to extend to cases where a defendant causes a claimant to suffer pure distress, there would be a stonger case for treating the tort as distinct from the tort of negligence as it is extraordinarily difficult to sue a defendant in negligence for causing you to suffer pure distress. (As the law stands at the moment, the only circumstances in which you can do so is when you have a concurrent claim in contract against the defendant for causing you to suffer pure distress because the defendant contractually undertook to take care in dealing with some matter and part of the object of his making that undertaking was to save you from distress.) However, such an extension might intrude too far into everyday social interactions. To quote Lord Hoffmann again: 'In institutions and workplaces all over the country, people constantly do and say things with the intention of causing distress and humiliation to others. This shows lack of consideration and appalling manners but I am not sure that the right way to deal with it is always by litigation.'[214]

---

[210] *Janvier* v *Sweeney* [1919] 2 KB 316.
[211] [2004] 2 AC 406, at [46].
[212] [2016] AC 219, at [73].
[213] Ibid, at [116] and [119].
[214] *Wainwright* v *Home Office* [2004] 2 AC 406, at [46]

Further reading

If we were asked to select three articles from the last two decades that usefully analyse the issues confronting the developing law on invasion of privacy then we would opt for three by **Nicole Moreham: 'The protection of privacy in English common law: a doctrinal and theoretical analysis'** (2005) 121 *Law Quarterly Review* 628; **'Privacy in public places'** (2006) 65 *Cambridge Law Journal* 606 and **'Beyond information: physical privacy in English law'** (2014) 73 *Cambridge Law Journal* 350. Dr Moreham is also one of the editors of an excellent practitioners' work, which is invaluable for anyone seeking to explore the *details* of the law: **Warby and Moreham (eds),** *Tugendhat and Christie: The Law of Privacy and the Media,* **3rd edn (Oxford University Press, 2016).**

Looking beyond tort law, for those interested in exploring the problems faced by anyone brave enough to attempt to *define* 'privacy' we would recommend **Daniel J. Solove's** *Understanding Privacy* (**Harvard University Press, 2008**).

Chapter 18
Breach of statutory duty

Aims and objectives

Reading this chapter should enable you to:

(1) Understand the factors that the courts will take into account in determining whether a claimant who has suffered harm as a result of a defendant's breaching a statutory duty will be able to sue the defendant for compensation for that harm by bringing a claim for 'breach of statutory duty' against the defendant.

(2) Get a good grasp of some of the situations where it is established that a claim for breach of statutory duty can be brought against a defendant; in particular, under the Highways Act 1980.

18.1 The basics

We have already seen a number of different situations where a defendant who has breached a statutory duty can be sued for damages by a claimant. So, for example, a defendant who has – contrary to s 1 of the Protection from Harassment Act 1997 – unreasonably subjected a claimant to a course of conduct that he knows, or ought to know, amounts to harassment, can be sued for damages by that claimant under s 3 of the 1997 Act. The same point applies to breaches of statutory duties imposed on defendants by the Occupiers' Liability Acts 1957 and 1984, the Copyright, Designs and Patents Act 1988, and the Human Rights Act 1998.

All of these are examples of situations where a claimant can sue a defendant for *breach of statutory duty* – in other words, for breaching a duty that arises under an Act of Parliament, not under the common law. But not every breach of statutory duty ('SD' for short) is civilly actionable – that is, capable of entitling someone to sue the person committing the breach for the sort of remedies (damages or an injunction) dealt with in this text. In fact, most SDs are not enforceable by private persons. Most SDs are *only* enforceable by the *State*, either by bringing a criminal prosecution against a defendant for breaching a SD, or by obtaining an order from the courts (known as a *public law remedy*) requiring the defendant to stop acting unlawfully, or to undo the effect of his earlier unlawful conduct.

This chapter is concerned with situations where a claimant can bring a civil action to enforce a SD that a defendant is subject to.[1] We can distinguish three different situations where a claimant might be interested in bringing such an action:

A. Breach of duty owed to no one in particular

The first situation is where a defendant has breached a SD that was imposed on him for the benefit of the community as a whole. The general rule here is that the defendant's breach will *not* be civilly actionable. There are two exceptions to this rule.[2]

The first is where the defendant's breach amounts to a *public nuisance*. In that case, anyone who has suffered *special damage* as a result of the defendant's breach of duty will be entitled to sue the defendant for compensation for that damage. (We will talk about public nuisance in the chapter immediately following this one.) The second is where the defendant is a public official and he has committed the tort of *misfeasance in public office* in acting as he did. (We will talk about the tort of misfeasance in public office in Chapter 21, below.)

An example of the general rule set out here is provided by *Lonrho Ltd v Shell Petroleum (No 2)* (1982), where the claimant argued that its businesses in Southern Rhodesia (now Zimbabwe) had been unnecessarily disrupted as a result of the defendants' propping up the government of Southern Rhodesia by illegally supplying oil to Southern Rhodesia, in breach of sanctions that had been imposed on that country by the UK in response to Southern Rhodesia's unilaterally declaring itself independent of the UK. The claimant argued that but for the defendants' actions, the Southern Rhodesian government would have collapsed much more quickly than it did, sanctions would have been lifted much earlier than they were, and the claimant's businesses in Southern Rhodesia would have done much better than they did under the weight of sanctions. The claimant's claim for compensation was dismissed. The SD breached by Shell in this case was imposed for the benefit of the UK as a whole, which had an interest in bringing down the Rhodesian government through the use of sanctions. It was therefore owed to no one in particular.

The SD that was breached in *Lonrho* was clearly imposed for the benefit of the community as a whole, and not for any particular individual's benefit. However, not all cases are so clear-cut. For example, in *X v Bedfordshire County Council* (1995), the claimants were five children who suffered years of abuse at home. Despite being alerted to this, the relevant local authority failed to initiate proceedings to take the claimants into care, thereby breaching various SDs which required it to intervene to protect 'at risk' children. The claimants sued the local authority for compensation in respect of the losses they had

---

[1] For a claim that failed because the defendant was *not* subject to the SD that was breached, see *Campbell v Peter Gordon Joiners Ltd* [2016] AC 1513, where the claimant argued that the defendant director was subject to a SD to ensure that the company had adequate insurance against workplace injuries because he was subject to a criminal penalty if the company breached that SD. The UK Supreme Court held that the only person who was subject to this SD was the company; the criminal penalty for the director was merely intended to help ensure that the *company* complied with *its* SD.

[2] The High Court of Australia suggested a further exception in *Beaudesert Shire Council v Smith* (1966) 120 CLR 145, holding (at 160) that if A's breach of statutory duty was intentional, and B suffered loss as an inevitable consequence of A's breach, then B would be able to sue A for compensation for that loss. However, the House of Lords ruled in *Lonrho v Shell Petroleum (No 2)* [1982] AC 173, at 188 that this was *not* the law in England. (Nor is it now the law in Australia: *Northern Territory v Mengel* (1995) 185 CLR 307.)

suffered as a result of the local authority's breaches of statutory duty. The House of Lords dismissed the claim on the basis that the SDs breached in this case had not been imposed for the benefit of any particular individuals, such as children at risk of being abused, but were 'all concerned to establish an administrative system designed to promote the social welfare of the community'.[3]

Again, in *Cutler* v *Wandsworth Stadium* (1949), the claimant was a bookmaker who sued a dog racing track for breaching its SDs under s 11 of the Betting and Lotteries Act 1934 'not [to] . . . exclude any person from the track [because] he proposes to carry on bookmaking on the track' and to 'take such steps as are necessary to secure that . . . there is available for bookmakers space on the track where they can conveniently carry on bookmaking in connexion with dog races run on the track on that day'. The House of Lords dismissed the claimant's claim, holding that the SDs arising under s 11 of the 1934 Act were not imposed for the benefit of bookmakers like the claimant, but for the benefit of members of the general public who might want to lay a bet at the races, and whose interests might be prejudiced if the owners of racing tracks had a monopoly over betting at their tracks.

B. Breach of a duty owed to a third party

The second situation is where a defendant has breached a SD that was imposed on him for the benefit of someone other than the claimant. The general rule here is that the claimant will *not* be entitled to bring an action for breach of statutory duty against the defendant. (However, the defendant might have committed some *other* tort in relation to the claimant in acting as he did. This possibility is explored in the chapter on the 'Economic Torts', two chapters on from this one.) An example of the general rule is provided by *Wingrove* v *Prestige & Co Ltd* (1954).[4] The defendants in that case breached a statutory duty to ensure that the scaffolding they used was 'suitable and safe', with the result that the claimant – a council employee who was supervising the defendants' work as they built a school for the council – was blinded in both eyes. The claimant's claim for compensation was dismissed: the statutory duty that the defendants breached had been imposed for the benefit of the defendants' employees, not the claimant.

C. Breach of a duty owed to the claimant

The third situation where a claimant might be interested in bringing a claim for breach of statutory duty against a defendant is where the SD breached by the defendant was imposed on him for the benefit of the claimant, or the benefit of a limited class of people that included the claimant. In this sort of case, the rule is that the defendant's breach of duty *will* be civilly actionable by the claimant, so long as: (1) the defendant's breach has resulted in the claimant suffering the kind of loss that the SD breached by the defendant was imposed on him in order to avoid; and (2) Parliament intended that a breach of the SD that the defendant breached should be civilly actionable.

---

[3] [1995] 2 AC 633, 747 (per Lord Browne-Wilkinson).
[4] See also *Bretton* v *Hancock* [2005] EWCA Civ 404 (statutory duty on car owner to ensure that people he allows to drive his car are adequately insured is imposed for the benefit of people who might be physically injured as a result of the car being driven negligently, not for the benefit of people who might be interested in bringing a claim in contribution against the driver).

(1) *Wrong kind of loss.* We are already quite familiar with the idea that you cannot sue in tort for a loss suffered as a result of a breach of duty if the loss is the wrong kind of loss – not the sort of loss that the duty breached was imposed in order to avoid.[5] And we have already mentioned[6] *Gorris* v *Scott* (1874), the leading case that establishes that that rule applies to actions for breach of statutory duty. That was the case where the defendant shipowner failed – in breach of his statutory duty to do so – to keep the claimant's sheep in pens while he was transporting them, with the result that the sheep were washed overboard when a big wave crashed onto the deck of the defendant's ship. It was held the claimant could not bring a claim for breach of statutory duty against the defendant for the loss of his sheep as the SD breached by the defendant in that case was imposed on him in order to stop disease spreading among the sheep, not to protect them from being washed overboard.

(2) *Parliamentary intention.* If a defendant has breached a SD owed to the claimant, and the claimant has suffered the right kind of loss as a result, the claimant will still not be entitled to bring a claim for breach of statutory duty against the defendant unless Parliament intended that breach of the defendant's SD should be civilly actionable. As Lord Browne-Wilkinson observed in *X* v *Bedfordshire County Council* (1995):

> The basic proposition is that in the ordinary case a breach of statutory duty does not, by itself, give rise to any private law cause of action. However a private law cause of action will arise if it can be shown, as a matter of construction of the statute, that the statutory duty was imposed for the protection of a limited class of the public *and that Parliament intended to confer on members of that class a private right of action for breach of that duty.*[7]

Whether or not Parliament could be said to have intended that breach of a particular SD should be civilly actionable depends, the courts say, on the proper construction of the statute that created that SD. However, it can often be very difficult to determine what Parliament's intentions were in creating a particular SD, as to whether breach of that SD should be civilly actionable. Sometimes Parliament makes it clear that breach of a particular SD should not be civilly actionable.[8] Sometimes – as is the case with the Occupiers' Liability Acts, or the Human Rights Act, or the Protection from Harassment Act – Parliament makes it clear that breach of a particular SD should be civilly actionable. But more often than not Parliament does not make it clear one way or the other whether it intended that the breach of a SD which exists for the benefit of a limited class of people should be civilly actionable if one of those people suffers the right kind of loss as a result of the breach of that SD. In such cases – what we can call *hard cases* – Lord Denning MR despairingly observed that 'you might as well toss a coin to decide'[9] what Parliament's intentions were. However, we should not be so quick to despair. There are in fact two different approaches available to us to determine in a hard case whether or not Parliament intended breach of a particular SD should be civilly actionable. Those two approaches are the subject of the next section.

---

[5] See above, § 9.3.

[6] See above, § 9.1(2).

[7] [1995] 2 AC 633, 731–2 (emphasis added).

[8] For example, s 9 of the Post Office Act 1969 provides that 'It shall be the duty of the Post Office . . . to provide throughout [the British Islands] . . . such services for the conveyance of letters . . . as satisfy all reasonable demands for them' but section 9(4) of the Act makes it clear that a breach of this duty will *not* be civilly actionable: 'Nothing in this section shall be construed as imposing upon the Post Office . . . any form of . . . liability enforceable by proceedings before any court.'

[9] *Ex parte Island Records* [1978] 1 Ch 122, 135A.

18.2 Resolving hard cases

The first approach to determining in a hard case whether or not Parliament intended that breach of a particular SD should be civilly actionable is exemplified by the Supreme Court decision in *Morrison Sports Ltd* v *Scottish Power Plc* (2010). In that case, the claimants owned properties that had been damaged by a fire which had originated from an electricity meter cupboard. The claimants brought an action for breach of statutory duty against the defendant electricity supplier, arguing that the fire was the result of the defendant's breach of its statutory duty under reg 17 of the Electricity Supply Regulations 1988 to ensure that its works were 'so constructed, installed, protected . . . used and maintained as to prevent danger . . . so far as is reasonably practicable.' Through a close analysis of the history of the 1988 Regulations, and the scheme of statutory duties set up by the Regulations, the Supreme Court concluded that Parliament did not intend that a breach of reg 17 should be civilly actionable:

> Looked at as a whole . . . the scheme of the legislation, with its carefully-worked out provisions for various forms of enforcement on behalf of the public, points against individuals having a private right of action for damages for contravention of regulations made under it.[10]

While the courts always adopt this kind of *analytical approach* nowadays to the question of whether – in a hard case – Parliament intended that breach of a particular SD should be civilly actionable, this approach is of no use to students who will often by asked to determine whether a claimant can bring a claim for breach of statutory duty when the SD that has been breached has been *made up*, and very limited information about that fictional SD is supplied to the student. In determining whether breach of that kind of SD was intended to be civilly actionable, a different approach is needed – one we will call the *presumption approach*.[11]

Under the *presumption approach*, we start off by presuming that if a defendant has breached a SD that was imposed on the defendant for the benefit of the claimant and that claimant has suffered the right kind of loss as a result of that breach (the sort of loss that the breached SD was imposed in order to avoid), then Parliament intended that the claimant should be able to bring a claim for breach of statutory duty against the defendant. We then look to see whether there is any reason to think that Parliament did *not* in fact intend that breach of the SD that was breached by the defendant would be civilly actionable. If we can find sufficient indicators that Parliament did *not* intend that breach of that SD would be civilly actionable, then that is what we will conclude, and find that the claimant will not be able to bring an action for breach of statutory duty against the defendant. If we cannot make a convincing case for thinking that Parliament did not intend that breach of the defendant's SD would be civilly actionable, we will conclude that Parliament intended that breach of that SD should be civilly actionable and find that the claimant can bring a claim for breach of statutory duty against the defendant.

In looking for indications that Parliament did *not* intend that breach of the SD breached by the defendant would be civilly actionable, we look at a wide number of factors.

(1) *Alternative means of enforcement.* As Lord Rodger observed in the *Morrison* case:

> if a statute provides some means, other than a private law action for damages, of enforcing any duty which it imposes, that will normally indicate that the statutory right was intended to be enforceable by those means and not by private right of action.[12]

---

[10] [2010] 1 WLR 1934, at [37].
[11] Following Stanton 2003, 25–6.
[12] [2010] 1 WLR 1934, at [29].

In the *Morrison* case itself, the extensive powers given to the relevant Secretary of State to enforce proper observance of the regulations in question in *Morrison* counted heavily against the Supreme Court finding that breach of those regulations was intended to be civilly actionable. In *Scally v Southern Health and Social Services Board* (1992), the House of Lords held that an employer's breach of his statutory duty to give his employees a written statement detailing the particulars of their contracts of employment was not intended by Parliament to be civilly actionable. This was because Parliament had specified precisely what should happen when that statutory duty was breached: an affected employee would have the right to go to a tribunal to get the terms of his employment detailed there.

The existence of a criminal penalty for breach of a given SD may count as an indication that Parliament intended that breach of that SD should be sanctioned through the criminal law, and not through a civil action. However, the existence of such a penalty will not be a *conclusive* indication that Parliament did not intend that breach of the SD in question should be civilly actionable, as well as the sort of thing that could give rise to a criminal prosecution. For example, in *Groves v Wimborne* (1898), the claimant's employer breached the statutory duty he owed the claimant under s 5 of the Factory and Workshop Act 1878 to ensure that all dangerous machinery used by the claimant was securely fenced. As a result of this breach, the claimant was injured by some unfenced cogwheels. Section 82 provided that an employer breaching his duty under s 5 could be fined. No provision was made in the Act for anyone to bring a civil claim for breach of the duty created by s 5. Despite this, the Court of Appeal still found that when Parliament created the statutory duty contained in s 5 of the 1878 Act, it intended that a breach of that duty should be civilly actionable. Vaughan Williams LJ observed that:

> where . . . a remedy is provided in cases of nonperformance of the statutory duty, that is a matter to be taken into consideration for the purpose of determining whether [Parliament intended that breach of that duty should be civilly actionable], or whether [Parliament] intended that there should be no other remedy than the statutory remedy; *but it is by no means conclusive or the only matter to be taken into consideration for that purpose.*[13]

(2) *Floodgates.* Among the other matters 'to be taken into consideration' is whether finding that breach of a given SD is civilly actionable would create an oppressive burden of litigation for those who are subject to that SD.

For example, in *Atkinson v The Newcastle and Gateshead Waterworks Company* (1877), the defendants supplied Newcastle and surrounding towns with water. Under the Waterworks Clauses Act 1847, they had a statutory duty to install fire hydrants and supply water to those hydrants at a certain pressure. They breached this duty with the result that firefighters could not obtain any water from one of the defendants' fire hydrants to put out a fire in the claimants' house. As a result, the claimants' house burned down. The claimants brought a claim for breach of statutory duty against the defendants. Their claim was rejected. The Court of Appeal thought that when Parliament created the duty breached by the defendants it could not have intended that a breach of that duty should be civilly actionable:

> it certainly appears a startling thing to say that a company undertaking to supply a town like Newcastle with water, would not only be willing to be put under [a statutory] duty to supply gratuitously for the purpose of extinguishing fire an unlimited quantity of water at a certain

---

[13] [1898] 2 QB 402, 416 (emphasis added). See also *Phillips v Britannia Hygienic Laundry Co* [1923] 2 KB 832, 841 (per Atkin LJ).

pressure . . . but would further be willing in their contract with [P]arliament to subject themselves to the liability to actions by any number of householders who might happen to have their houses burnt down in consequence [of the company's non-performance of this duty]; and it is, *a priori*, equally improbable that [P]arliament would think it a necessary or reasonable bargain to make . . . [T]he company would virtually become gratuitous insurers of the safety from fire, so far as water is capable of producing that safety, of all the houses within the district over which their powers were to extend.[14]

(3) *The public interest.* It is also material to ask whether it would be contrary to the public interest for breach of a given SD to be civilly actionable. If so, we can safely assume that Parliament did not intend that breach of that SD should be civilly actionable.

This was one of the considerations that led the House of Lords to conclude in *X* v *Bedfordshire County Council* (1995) that when Parliament imposed duties on local authorities to safeguard the welfare of children in their jurisdiction, Parliament did not intend that the breach of those duties should be civilly actionable. As Lord Browne-Wilkinson observed:

> the Acts in question are all concerned to establish an administrative system designed to promote the social welfare of the community. The welfare sector involved is one of peculiar sensitivity, involving very difficult decisions how to strike the balance between protecting the child from immediate feared harm and disrupting the relationship between the child and its parents. Decisions often have to be taken on the basis of inadequate and disputed facts. In my judgment in such a context it would require exceptionally clear language to show a parliamentary intention that those responsible for carrying out these difficult functions should be liable in damages if, on subsequent investigation with the benefit of hindsight, it was shown that they had reached an erroneous conclusion and therefore failed to discharge their statutory duties.[15]

(4) *Useful purpose.* We could also ask whether finding that a breach of a given SD is civilly actionable would serve some useful purpose. If the answer is 'no' then that may indicate that when Parliament created that SD, it did *not* intend that a breach of that duty would be civilly actionable.

For example, in *McCall* v *Abelesz* (1976), the claimant let a room in a house owned by the defendants. Through no fault of the claimant the authorities cut off the supply of gas and electricity to his room and the defendants did nothing to get the supply reconnected in the hope that if the gas and electricity supply to the claimant's room remained cut off, the claimant would be persuaded to take up alternative accommodation that they were offering him. The defendants owed the claimant a statutory duty not to do this under statutory provisions forbidding landlords from harassing their tenants into giving up their tenancies. The claimant brought a claim for breach of statutory duty against the defendants. The claim was dismissed by the Court of Appeal. One of the reasons the Court of Appeal gave for finding that Parliament did not intend that the SD breached by the defendants would be civilly actionable was that making breach of this duty civilly actionable would serve little useful purpose. A tenant who was being harassed by his landlord would usually have a range of remedies available to him, and so there would be little point in adding one more remedy on top of those.

Again, in *Cullen* v *Chief Constable of the Royal Ulster Constabulary* (2003), the claimant was arrested under suspicion of being involved in an act of terrorism. During his time in

---

[14] (1877) 2 Ex D 441, 445–6.
[15] [1995] 2 AC 633, 747.

police custody, the police denied him access to a solicitor and in doing so committed a breach of statutory duty. The claimant suffered no loss as a result of being denied access to a solicitor but still sued the police for nominal damages. A bare majority of the House of Lords held that the claim should be dismissed. The majority thought that Parliament had not intended that the SD breached by the police in this case would be civilly actionable even if the victim of the breach suffered no loss as a result of the breach. The best explanation of this decision is that no useful purpose would be served if denial of access to a solicitor were actionable *per se*. Of course, if unlawfully denying someone access to a solicitor were actionable *per se*, then someone who was denied access to a solicitor could bring a claim in tort against the police straightaway, without having to wait for the denial of access to cause him some kind of loss. He would thereby be provided with a speedy means of getting a court to determine whether or not he was entitled to a solicitor. However, someone who is denied access to a solicitor while in custody *already* has a speedy means of getting a court to determine whether or not he is entitled to see a solicitor – he can make an application for judicial review of the decision to deny him access.[16]

(5) *State of mind.* One factor which the courts have taken into account in the past in determining – in a hard case – whether Parliament intended that breach of a particular SD would be civilly actionable is whether the existence of that SD was dependent on the person who was subject to that duty having a certain state of mind. If it was, the courts have taken that as indicating that Parliament did *not* intend that breach of that SD would be civilly actionable.

For example, s 2(2) of the Child Care Act 1980 provided that 'Where it *appears* to a local authority' that a child needed to be taken into care, the authority would have an SD to do so. One of the reasons the House of Lords gave in *X* v *Bedfordshire County Council* (1995) for thinking that Parliament did not intend that breach of this statutory duty would be civilly actionable was that if it were, the following paradoxical result would obtain. An *Incompetent* local authority that thought a child in its area needed to be taken into care but then failed to follow through and take the child into care would be subject to an action for breach of statutory duty. In contrast, a *Callous* local authority that perversely refused to recognise that a child in its area needed to be taken into care could not be sued for breach of statutory duty because it would not have the state of mind required for that duty to kick in. So *Incompetent* local authorities would be treated more severely under the law than *Callous* local authorities, if breach of the statutory duty in s 2(2) of the Child Care Act 1980 were civilly actionable.

Again, s 65 of the Housing Act 1985 provides that if a housing authority is '*satisfied*' that an applicant for accommodation needed to be accommodated then the authority has

---

[16] [2003] 1 WLR 1763, at [34]–[40] (per Lord Hutton). Lords Bingham and Steyn dissented, on the ground (at [20]) that someone who is denied access to a solicitor will hardly be in a position to make an application for judicial review to get a court to determine whether the denial of access is lawful or not. However, it is hard to see how being allowed to sue for nominal damages would assist such a detainee – the lack of access to a solicitor would make it just as difficult for him to bring a claim in tort against the police. The only possible advantage of allowing claims for nominal damages to be made in cases like *Cullen* is that if such claims could be made, then a detainee who was denied access to a solicitor while in custody would be able to bring a claim in tort against the police months or years after he was detained for the *sole* purpose of having it established in a public forum whether or not the police acted lawfully in denying him access to a solicitor. But it is hard to see what *useful* purpose would be served in allowing him to do this.

an SD to accommodate him. In *O'Rourke* v *Camden London Borough Council* (1998), Lord Hoffmann thought that when Parliament enacted this section, it could not have intended that a breach of this duty would be actionable in tort. If it *had* had such an intention then the following 'anomalous' result would obtain: 'a housing authority which accepts it has a duty to house the applicant but does so inadequately will be liable in damages, but an authority which perversely refuses to accept it has any such duty will not.'[17] As Lord Hoffmann observed, 'This seems to me wrong.'[18]

By attending to factors such as the five set out above, most hard cases where Parliament has not expressly made it clear whether or not it intended that breach of a given SD would be civilly actionable can be resolved using the *presumption approach*. The following sections will not be concerned with hard cases. In the following sections we will look at some statutory duties breach of which, Parliament has made it clear, *will* be civilly actionable.

18.3 Health and safety at work

An employer cannot be sued for breach of statutory duty if he breaches the general duty that he will owe all of his employees under s 2 of the Health and Safety at Work Act 1974 'to ensure, so far as is reasonably practicable, the health, safety and welfare at work of all his employees'. This is because s 47(1)(a) of the 1974 Act makes it clear that breach of *that* duty will not be civilly actionable.

Section 15 of the 1974 Act gives the government power to create statutory regulations governing health and safety in the workplace, and it *used* to be the case that s 47(2) of the 1974 Act provided that a breach of a duty arising under these regulations would be civilly actionable unless the regulations provide otherwise. This has now been completely reversed by s 69 of the Enterprise and Regulatory Reform Act 2013, which amended s 47(2) to say that a breach of duty under health and safety regulations will *not* be civilly actionable unless those regulations expressly provide it should be. As all of the health and safety regulations that were passed between 1974 and 2013 were created in the expectation that their breach would automatically be civilly actionable, it is unlikely that any of them expressly provide that breach of those regulations will be civilly actionable. The result is that virtually none of these regulations can now be relied on to bring a claim against an employer – a result that seems to have been intended by the government to reduce the costs to businesses of operating in the UK under UK law, but which also may have placed the UK in violation of EU law as many modern health and safety regulations were passed in response to European directives. (However, this last point will become academic in the event of the UK leaving the EU.)

One set of regulations that seem to be unaffected by s 69 of the 2013 Act are the Management of Health and Safety at Work Regulations 1999, which require an employer, among other things, to make a 'suitable and sufficient assessment of . . . the risks to the health and safety of his employees to which they are exposed whilst they are at work' and to take 'preventive and protective measures' to protect the health and safety of his employees on the basis of that risk assessment.[19] It used to be that a breach of duty under

---

[17] [1998] AC 188, 196.
[18] Ibid.
[19] Regs 3–4.

the 1999 Regulations would not be civilly actionable[20] but this has now been reversed by the Management of Health and Safety at Work and Fire Precautions (Workplace) (Amendment) Regulations 2003.[21] As virtually any accident at work can be said to be attributable to an employer's failure to implement a 'suitable and sufficient' risk assessment, it is likely that the 1999 Regulations will provide a fertile source of litigation.

18.4 Highways

Under s 41(1) of the Highways Act 1980, the highway authority for a particular highway will owe the users of that highway 'a [statutory] duty to maintain the highway'.[22] Section 41(1A) provides that 'In particular, a highway authority are under a duty to ensure, so far as is reasonably practicable, that safe passage along a highway is not endangered by snow or ice.'[23]

A breach of these duties will give rise to an action for breach of statutory duty. However, s 58(1) of the 1980 Act provides that in

> an action for damages against a highway authority in respect of damage resulting from their failure to maintain a highway . . . it is a defence . . . to prove that the authority had taken such care as in all the circumstances was reasonably required to secure that the part of the highway to which the action relates was not dangerous for traffic.

So, in effect, a user of a highway who is injured or whose property has been harmed[24] because the relevant highway authority failed to ensure that the highway was properly maintained will *not* be able to sue the highway authority for damages *if* the highway authority can prove that it took reasonable steps to see that the highway in question would be reasonably safe to travel on. (In cases of harm caused by a highway authority's failure to clear the highway of snow or ice, it seems unlikely that the highway authority will need to take advantage of s 58(1) as its duty in relation to snow or ice is already, under s 41(1A), limited to doing what is *reasonably practicable* to clear the highway of snow or ice.)

---

[20] This was by virtue of Reg 22(1), which provided that 'Breach of a duty imposed by these Regulations shall not confer a right of action in any civil proceedings.'

[21] The 2003 Regulations do this in a somewhat backhanded way, amending Reg 22 of the 1999 Regulations so that it says: 'Breach of a duty imposed on an employer by these Regulations shall not confer a right of action in any civil proceedings insofar as that duty applies for the protection of persons not in his employment.' Thus, but only by implication, a breach of a duty arising under the 1999 Regulations *will* be actionable if an *employee* was affected by the breach. The somewhat grudging wording of the new Reg 22 is no doubt attributable to the fact that the government was forced into changing the old Reg 22 on the ground that the old Reg 22 failed properly to implement EU health and safety directives.

[22] It has been held that this duty does not go so far as to require the highway authority to erect traffic signs along the highway to reduce the risk of accidents: *Lavis* v *Kent County Council* (1992) 90 LGR 416; *Gorringe* v *Calderdale MBC* [2004] UKHL 15.

[23] This provision was inserted by s 111 of the Railways and Transport Safety Act 2003 and has the effect of reversing the decision of the House of Lords in *Goodes* v *East Sussex County Council* [2000] 1 WLR 1356, which held that a highway authority will *not* be required under s 41 to keep the highways under its jurisdiction free from ice.

[24] It appears no action can be brought under the Highways Act 1980 for pure economic loss resulting from a highway authority's breach of its duty to maintain the highway: *Wentworth* v *Wiltshire CC* [1993] QB 654.

18.5 Defective premises

Section 1(1) of the Defective Premises Act 1972 provides that:

> A person taking on work for or in connection with the provision of a dwelling[25] (whether the dwelling is provided for by the erection or by the conversion or enlargement of a building) owes a duty –
>
> (a) if the dwelling is provided to the order of any person, to that person; and
> (b) without prejudice to paragraph (a) above, to every person who acquires an interest (whether legal or equitable) in the dwelling;
>
> to see that the work which he takes on is done in a workmanlike or, as the case may be, professional manner, with proper materials and so that as regards that work the dwelling will be fit for habitation when completed.[26]

It is quite clear that a breach of this duty will be civilly actionable: both ss 1(5) and 2(1) of the 1972 Act contemplate that someone who breaches this duty may be sued by a victim of the breach who has suffered loss as a result – where 'loss' includes pure economic loss incurred in repairing defects in the building and is, indeed, primarily intended to cover this kind of loss given the fact that such loss is normally irrecoverable by the subsequent purchaser of a house from the builder of that house.

Further reading

In *R v Saskatchewan Wheat Pool* [1983] 1 SCR 205, the Supreme Court of Canada ruled that it would no longer recognise a free-standing right to sue a defendant for damages based on the fact that the defendant had breached a statutory duty owed to the claimant. A claim for such damages would have to be brought under the law of negligence (with the breach of duty going to indicate fault on the part of the defendant) or nothing. Academics periodically discuss whether the UK courts should abolish the action for breach of statutory duty. For us, the proposal (as stated) is a non-starter: if we recognise the sovereignty of Parliament, we have to also recognise that Parliament has the power to make certain breaches of statutory duty civilly actionable. Whether the courts should adopt a hardline position that a breach of statutory duty will not be civilly actionable if Parliament has not expressly indicated that it will be is another matter. Certainty would indicate that the courts should. On the other hand, justice may demand that an inadvertent failure by Parliament to say that it wants a breach of a given SD to be civilly actionable should not count against someone's being able to bring a claim for breach of that SD if it is plain that that is what Parliament actually wanted to happen. Anyone who is interested in exploring this topic further should definitely read **Neil Foster's 'The merits of the civil action for breach of statutory duty' (2011) 33** *Sydney Law Review* **67** as well as **James L.R. Davis' 'Farewell to the action for breach of statutory duty?' in Mullany and Linden (eds),** *Torts Tomorrow: A Tribute to John Fleming* **(LBC Information Services, 1998).**

---

[25] On what kind of work can be said to have been done 'in connection with the provision of a dwelling' see *Jenson v Faux* [2011] 1 WLR 3038 (work done refurbishing basement did not amount to 'the provision of a dwelling' – the work must be so extensive that it amounts to the provision of a new dwelling, wholly different from the old).

[26] Why did we not mention this duty when setting out the situations in which it has been established one person will owe another a duty of care? (See above, Chapters 5–7.) The reason is that the duty set out in s 1(1) of the 1972 Act is *not* a duty of care – it is much stricter than that. It requires someone who takes on work in connection with the provision of a dwelling to *ensure* that the work is done in a workmanlike manner, with proper materials and done in such a way that the house will be fit for habitation.

Chapter 19
Public nuisance

Aims and objectives

Reading this chapter should enable you to:

(1) Understand what amounts to a 'public nuisance' and in what circumstances a claimant can sue a defendant who is responsible for a 'public nuisance' for compensation for harm that she has suffered as a result.

(2) Understand when a defendant will be held responsible for a 'public nuisance' because he created, authorised, adopted or continued the state of affairs that amounted to a 'public nuisance'.

(3) Understand in what respects liability for 'public nuisance' is different from liability for 'private nuisance'.

(4) Understand the debates around whether liability for 'public nuisance' is anomalous, and whether it could be reconceptualised to make it more coherent with the rest of the law of tort.

19.1 The basics

A defendant will commit a public nuisance if:

1. he creates, authorises, adopts or continues a state of affairs which

2. unreasonably interferes with *either* (a) a public right *or* (b) the comfort, convenience or safety of the public,

3. he knew, or ought to have known (because the means of knowledge were available to him), that would be the consequence of what he did or omitted to do.

Public nuisance is an anomalous tort, if it is a tort at all.[1] Why? For a start public nuisance is a crime. But crimes *also* being torts is not particularly unusual, though it may surprise someone who misguidedly equates tort law with the tort of negligence. Many well-established torts are also crimes: assault and battery, for example. What makes public nuisance anomalous is what *sort* of wrong it is.[2] The duty that someone breaches when they commit a public nuisance is a duty imposed for the benefit of the public as a whole, not for the benefit of any particular individual. And tort law normally deals – as we have seen just in the last chapter – with breaches of duties owed to particular individuals.

So how did public nuisance end up in the contents pages of tort texts? The answer is 'By accident – and not just one accident, but two.' As John Spencer's excellent article 'Public nuisance – a critical examination' explains, the first accident was the responsibility of medieval legal writers who associated public nuisance (a crime) with private nuisance (a well-established tort) simply because they shared half a name and dealt with somewhat similar problems:

> it became usual for legal writers who were explaining private nuisance to add a discussion of nuisances to public rights of way either immediately before or afterwards. When the concept of private nuisance later grew to include stinking neighbours out with pigs as well as flooding them and blocking up their access, the writers naturally added to their discussion of obstructing the highway a sentence or two on depasturing pigs in city streets – a practice all too common in days when citizens used the streets as dustbins as well as highways – and which like blocking the highway was a criminal matter for the local courts.[3]

The second accident was the fault of the judges. As Spencer explains: 'It was once a settled rule that no civil action lay for damage resulting from a [public] nuisance, [public] nuisances being exclusively a matter for criminal proceedings.'[4] But once the medieval legal writers had *linked* public and private nuisances, someone asked – Why aren't public nuisances civilly actionable like private nuisances are? In a classic example of the dangers of

---

[1] For discussion, see Merrill 2011 – though note his distinctly American perspective: in the US government bodies have historically used public nuisance to bring civil actions on behalf of the public in a wider range of circumstances than in the UK, and Merrill's concern is to determine whether public nuisance claims should be brought *by government bodies*. This perspective is encapsulated in another article's claim that the 'essence' of public nuisance 'is to allow governments to use the tort system to stop quasi-criminal conduct that, while not illegal, is unreasonable given the circumstances and could cause injury to someone exercising a common, societal right': Schwartz & Goldberg 2006, 541. In England the Court of Appeal discouraged local government bodies from using civil injunctions to deal with quasi-criminal conduct where they could seek an anti-social behaviour order (ASBO) instead: *Birmingham City Council* v *Shafi* [2009] 1 WLR 1961. Parliament subsequently created a new form of civil injunction which various public authorities could obtain to deal with anti-social behaviour: Anti-social Behaviour, Crime and Policing Act 2014, Part 1. Indeed, there is now a substantial catalogue of orders which are *not* part of tort law, but are available to public authorities seeking to deal with various forms of misbehaviour: other examples include Community Protection Notices, Public Spaces Protection Orders (see Anti-social Behaviour, Crime and Policing Act 2014, Part 4) and injunctions to prevent gang-related violence, known colloquially as a 'gangbos' (Police and Crime Act 2009, Part 4, as expanded by Serious Crime Act 2015).

[2] Neyers 2017 provides a very different 'interpretation' of public nuisance as a tort. We discuss his views in detail below, § 19.5.

[3] Spencer 1989, 58.

[4] Spencer 1989, 73.

reaching the right conclusion but for the wrong reasons, the judges did *not* say – Public nuisances are not civilly actionable because they are wrongs *to the public*, and not to any particular private individual. Instead, the reason:

> given in 1535 by Baldwin CJ in a case where the [claimant] tried unsuccessfully to sue the defendant for damages for blocking the public highway was that 'if one person shall have an action for this, by the same reason every person shall have an action, and so he shall be punished a hundred times on the same case' . . .[5]

And this *floodgates argument* for the non-actionability of *public* nuisances left room for the judges (including Fitzherbert J, in the very same case in 1535)[6] to accept that exceptionally, a claimant who had suffered *special damage* – over and above that suffered by everyone else – *was* entitled to sue the defendant who was responsible for a public nuisance. Allowing *that exceptional claimant* to sue would not open the floodgates to hundreds of other actions against the defendant for the same thing.

So something that had nothing to do with tort law ended up in the tort texts: and we are now stuck with the rule that if a defendant commits a public nuisance – as defined at the start of the section – then a claimant can bring a civil claim for damages against him if: (4) the claimant suffered special damage as a result of that state of affairs.

The next three sections explain the key elements in the definition: (a) what sorts of things will be held to unreasonably interfere with *either* a public right *or* the comfort, convenience or safety of the public; (b) when a defendant will be held responsible for a state of affairs as a result of having created, authorised, adopted or continued it; and (c) what will count as special damage. A final section considers the proposals that Jason Neyers has made for 'reconceptualising' public nuisance so as to make it fit better with the rest of tort law.[7]

19.2 Unreasonable interference

So many things have been held to be public nuisances that it is difficult to provide a help-ful definition which covers them all.[8] Most texts rely on Archbold's definition, according to which A will commit the crime of public nuisance if he:

> commits an act not warranted by law, or omits to discharge a legal duty, where the effect of the act or omission is to endanger the life, health, property, [morals,] or comfort of the public or to obstruct the public in the exercise of rights common to all Her Majesty's subjects.[9]

---

[5] Spencer 1989, 73.

[6] For criticism of Fitzherbert J's *dictum*, see Newark 1949, 483.

[7] See Neyers 2017.

[8] Spencer 1989 scathingly criticises the current scope of the concept of a 'public nuisance'.

[9] Archbold's definition was approved by the House of Lords in R v *Rimmington*, R v *Goldstein* [2006] 1 AC 459, subject to removal of the reference to morals (per Lord Bingham at [36], per Lord Rodger at [45]), which is why we have put that word in square brackets. Archbold's definition follows *Stephen's Digest of the Criminal Law*, 9th edn (1900), at 184: 'A common nuisance is an act not warranted by law or an omission to discharge a legal duty, which act or omission obstructs or causes inconvenience or damage to the public in the exercise of rights common to all His Majesty's subjects.'

But this is very vague. What, for instance, is 'an act not warranted by law'?[10] The Second US Restatement of Torts notes that English judicial decisions have held that public nuisance covers:

> interference with the public health, as in the keeping of diseased animals . . . ; with the public safety, as in the case of storage of explosives in the midst of a city . . . ; [with the public morals, . . . ;] with the public peace, as by loud and disturbing noises; with the public comfort, as in the case of widely disseminated bad odors, dust, and smoke; with the public convenience, as by obstruction of a public highway or navigable stream; and with a wide variety of miscellaneous public rights of a similar kind.[11]

This catalogue usefully illustrates the breadth of public nuisance in practice. Of course, it is not the case that *any degree* of interference with these public interests will be sufficient to constitute the wrong. For example, it is clearly not the law in that a defendant commits public nuisance whenever he stortes the slightest amount of explosives in a city, otherwise it would be a crime for a competent professional to store the powerful fireworks required for a public display.[12] Similarly, a defendant will not commit a public nuisance whenever he obstructs the highway to a minor extent.[13] What is crucial is whether the explosives are stored *to an unreasonable extent or in an unreasonable way*, and whether the highway is obstructed *to an unreasonable extent*.[14] Thus we suggest that someone who commits a public nuisance breaches one or both of the following two overlapping duties:

(PND1) a duty not to create, authorise, adopt or continue a state of affairs which *interferes unreasonably with a public right*;

(PND2) a duty not to create, authorise, adopt or continue a state of affairs which *interferes unreasonably with the comfort, convenience or safety of the public*.

A. Unreasonable interference with public rights

Claims based on breach of duty PND1 raise the question of what counts as a public *right*. Some of the uncertainties as to the scope of public nuisance flow from the fact that it is easy to use the word *right* in a loose sense. It is important not to assume that there is a

---

[10] In *R v Rimmington, R v Goldstein* [2006] 1 AC 459, the House of Lords held that the definition of public nuisance is not so vague that it violates human rights standards because it is (at [36]): 'clear, precise, adequately defined and based on a discernible rational principle. A legal adviser asked to give his opinion in advance would ascertain whether the act or omission contemplated was likely to inflict significant injury on a substantial section of the public exercising their ordinary rights as such: if so, an obvious risk of causing a public nuisance would be apparent; if not, not.

[11] Restatement of Torts 2d, §821B, comment b.

[12] *R v Lister* (1856–7) 7 Dears & B 209, 169 ER 979; *R v Chilworth Gunpowder Co* (1888) 4 TLR 557.

[13] *Trevett v Lee* [1955] 1 All ER 406, CA (temporarily placing a hosepipe across a country lane).

[14] Support for this proposition can be found in the Court of Appeal decision of *Harper v G N Haden & Sons Ltd* [1933] Ch 298 concerning whether builders' scaffolding which obstructed a pavement amounted to a public nuisance. Lord Hanworth MR said (at 302): 'A temporary obstruction to the use of the highway . . . does not give rise to a legal remedy where such obstruction is reasonable in quantum and in duration.' Romer LJ drew an express parallel with the standard of unreasonableness in private nuisance cases and stated (at 317): 'The law relating to the user of the highway is in truth the law of give and take.' However, in the more recent case of *Westminster City Council v Ocean Leisure Ltd* [2004] EWCA Civ 970, the Court of Appeal treated Lord Hanworth's dictum as too wide (at [24]). The Court preferred (at [42]) the view that a limited restriction on the ability of the public to use the highway will be lawful if the restriction is a consequence of a reasonable incident of use of the highway, for instance parking, or of reasonable access to or maintenance of premises alongside the highway.

right to all benefits which are widely enjoyed: for example, there is no *right* to attach 'lost cat' notices to lamp-posts, or to hand out leaflets in the street. The rights which are most often relied on in public nuisance cases are the right to free passage along public highways and the right to free navigation along a public river.[15]

To illustrate how the law is applied in practice, we will focus on unreasonable interferences with the right to free passage along public highways. Free passage will be unreasonably interfered with if the highway is unreasonably *obstructed* or users of it are unreasonably *endangered*. So, what will count as an actionable *obstruction*? And what will count as an actionable *endangerment*?

(1) *Obstruction.* Whether an obstruction to the highway is *unreasonable* depends on the degree of interference and the reasonableness of causing such an obstruction. Obstructions are commonly physical, but need not be: for example, in *Wandsworth LBC* v *Railtrack PLC* (2001) the obstruction took the unusual form of users being discouraged from using a particular footpath by the risk of falling pigeon excrement: Gibbs J held this amounted to a public nuisance even without consideration of the possible health risks.

There are three situations where a defendant will be able to establish that any obstruction that he has caused was not unreasonable. The first is where the obstruction was *insubstantial*, and unlikely to inconvenience the public: for example, erecting a lamp-post on a pavement.[16] The second situation is where the obstruction resulted from the *defendant's* reasonable use of the highway:

> No member of the public has an exclusive right to use the highway. He has merely a right to use it subject to the reasonable user of others, and if that reasonable user causes him to be obstructed he has no legal cause of complaint.[17]

Thus it is not a public nuisance to block a highway with a cart in order to unload it,[18] but it is a public nuisance to block it so regularly as effectively to prevent its use by others.[19] The third situation is where the obstruction results from exercise of a right to gain access to premises alongside the highway, or to do building work on premises alongside the highway.[20] The courts have generally been reluctant to treat obstructions as *reasonable* outside these three situations; in particular, obstructions cannot be defended simply by appealing

---

[15] Neyers 2017 identifies the public right to fish in tidal waters as a further significant public right.

[16] *W H Chaplin & Co Ltd* v *Mayor of Westminster* [1901] 2 Ch 329.

[17] *Harper* v *G N Haden & Sons Ltd* [1933] Ch 298, 317 per Romer LJ. See also, *Herring* v *Metropolitan Board of Works* (1865) 19 CB NS 510, 144 ER 886.

[18] *R* v *Jones* (1812) 3 Camp 230, 231; 170 ER 1364, 1365: 'A cart or wagon may be unloaded at a gateway; but this must be done with promptness' (per Lord Ellenborough).

[19] *R* v *Cross* (1812) 3 Camp 224, 227, 170 ER 1362, 1363: 'No one can make a stable yard of the king's highway' (per Lord Ellenborough, finding against the proprietors of the Greenwich stagecoach which made two 45-minute stops each day near Charing Cross). But it seems that in rare circumstances even this may be reasonable: *Dwyer* v *Mansfield* [1946] 1 KB 437, where the obstruction was caused by queues at a greengrocer's shop during wartime rationing. Whilst it has been established that it can be lawful to use a highway as the location for a protest, in the leading case – *DPP* v *Jones* [1999] 2 AC 240 – the protest did *not* obstruct users of the highway, and where there is a substantial obstruction it will be difficult for protesters to show that their activities are lawful: *Mayor of London* v *Hall* [2011] 1 WLR 504; *Mayor of London* v *Samede* [2012] EWCA Civ 160, at [49].

[20] *Westminster City Council* v *Ocean Leisure Ltd* [2004] EWCA Civ 970, where the state of affairs (that would have been a public nuisance had it not been authorised by statute) involved obstruction of the highway in order to build a new footbridge across the River Thames.

to some advantage that might flow to the public interest from their continuation.[21] More-over, no right to continue an obstruction of the highway can be acquired by long use.[22]

(2) *Endangerment.* As we have said, a state of affairs which unreasonably endangers users of the highway will amount to an unreasonable interference with free passage. It might be thought that where a claimant has been injured on a highway he ought really to sue the defendant for committing the tort of negligence.[23] After all, negligence is the tort which is – in large part – built around the existence of duties to others to avoid creating unreason-able risks of physical injury.[24] But there is no rule that prevents a claimant from bringing a claim in public nuisance, rather than negligence, if she has been injured as a result of a defendant creating, authorising, continuing or adopting a state of affairs that poses an unreasonable danger to users of the highway. This absence of such a rule probably reflects the fact that many states of affairs that are dangerous involve a degree of *obstruction*, and there is no doubt that unreasonable obstruction of the highway can give rise to a claim for public nuisance.[25]

B. Interference with the public's comfort and convenience

Claims based on a breach of duty PND2 raise the difficult question of how we draw the line between situations where we say 'this has interfered with the comfort, convenience or safety of *some individuals*' and those where we say 'this has interfered with the comfort, convenience or safety of *the public*'. We think that the line depends on two factors: (1) how many people were affected, or potentially affected, and (2) whether the effect on them was 'common'. We will discuss each of these factors in turn, and then consider: (3) when an interference with comfort, convenience or safety will be *unreasonable*; and (4) whether a breach of duty PND2 requires more than a single, isolated incident.

(1) *How many people were affected?* In *Attorney-General* v *PYA Quarries* (1957), Denning LJ refused to stipulate that some minimum number of people had to be affected, and instead said that for an interference to amount to a public nuisance it would have to be

> so widespread in its range or so indiscriminate in its effect that it would not be reasonable to expect one person to take proceedings on his own responsibility to put a stop to it, but that it should be taken on the responsibility of the community at large.[26]

---

[21] In *R* v *Train* (1862) 2 B & S 640, 121 ER 1129, the King's Bench ruled that a tramway in Lambeth was a public nuisance since it withdrew part of the highway from ordinary use. As Crompton J pointed out, the effect of such a ruling was merely to insist that those who wanted to promote such projects had to obtain a private Act of Parliament. Some 'technical' obstructions may, however, be held to be reasonable because they 'enable the public to exercise their right with greater facility and more convenience', such as a barrier preventing unauthorised vehicles from using a towpath: *Attorney-General* v *Wilcox* [1938] 3 All ER 367, 372 (liability found on the facts).

[22] *R* v *Cross* (1812) 3 Camp 224, 227, 170 ER 1362, 1363: 'It is immaterial how long the practice may have prevailed, for no length of time will legitimate a nuisance' (per Lord Ellenborough). But if an obstruction pre-dates dedication of the road as a highway then the dedication may be treated as subject to the reservation of the obstruction being continued: *Fisher* v *Prowse* (1862) 2 B & S 770, 121 ER 1258.

[23] See *Hunter* v *Canary Wharf* [1997] AC 655, 692. The question whether private nuisance *should* be restricted to exclude claims for personal injuries is discussed in detail below, §13.4(D).

[24] For an account of the principle that foreseeability of physical injury gives rise to a duty of care, this being the duty that underlies most negligence claims arising from accidents on highways, see above, §5.2.

[25] Neyers 2017 suggests (at 114) that it should *only* be possible to sue for personal injuries in public nuisance when the harm is consequential on an unreasonable obstruction.

[26] [1957] 2 QB 169, 191.

This statement has been regularly cited and has made its way into almost all tort texts. But in our opinion, it must be treated with caution.

Our caution towards Denning LJ's statement stems from its apparent assumption that every public nuisance by breach of PND2 is also a private nuisance to a large number of claimants.[27] This overlooks the fact that the public interest (protected by public nuisance) is *not* simply a conglomeration of private interests *in land* (protected by private nuisance). Many cases of public nuisance do not involve interferences with private interests *in land* at all. For instance, in *R v Madden* (1975), the Court of Appeal stated that the crime of public nuisance could be committed by making a hoax bomb threat if a considerable number of persons was affected, but there was no suggestion that those affected had to be possessors of land able to sue for private nuisance. And in the important case of *Corby Group Litigation Claimants* v *Corby BC* (2009), the claimants established that the defendant was responsible for a state of affairs that unreasonably endangered the *health* of the public, rather than one that unreasonably interfered with private interests *in land*.[28]

Instead of considering the reasonableness of expecting *individuals* to sue, we think a better test would ask: is the interference 'so widespread in its range or so indiscriminate in its effect' that it is appropriate to treat it *as a wrong to the community at large*? This modification preserves an important element in Denning LJ's statement: the interference can amount to a wrong to the *community* because *either* it is (1) 'widespread in its range' *or* (2) 'indiscriminate in its effect'.

For the avoidance of doubt, although it is *not* the case that *every* public nuisance is made up of multiple instances of private nuisance, *some* public nuisances will involve widespread effects that can *also* give rise to claims in private nuisance. If the interference in question has caused any claimant to suffer *both* special damage and an unreasonable interference with land in which she has a sufficient interest, then she can claim in *both* public nuisance and private nuisance.[29] Claims for public nuisance and private nuisance are not mutually exclusive.[30]

We still have to answer the question of *how many* people, in practice, must be inconvenienced or discomforted, or subjected to an indiscriminate risk, before a defendant will be held to have breached duty PND2.[31] In *Attorney-General v PYA Quarries* (1957), Romer LJ

---

[27] This assumption can best be seen by going through the following steps. (1) Denning LJ's test for a public nuisance depends on whether it *would be reasonable to expect* an individual to sue. (2) The question whether it is *reasonable to expect* an individual to sue assumes that the individual *could sue*. (3) The most obvious thing individuals could be suing for is private nuisance.

[28] The reference here is to the first instance trial: [2009] EWHC 1944 (TCC). Before this trial was held the Court of Appeal ruled on whether the public nuisance claim should be 'struck out': *Corby Group Litigation Claimants* v *Corby BC* [2009] QB 335.

[29] For example, in the case of *Jan de Nul (UK) Ltd* v *AXA Royale Belge SA* [2000] 2 Lloyd's Rep 700 (upheld on appeal, [2002] 1 Lloyd's Rep 583) Jan de Nul (UK) Ltd conducted dredging operations in Southampton Water in such a way as to cause silt to be deposited elsewhere in the estuary. Some of the users who were inconvenienced by this *possessed* parts of the river bed and could have sued in private nuisance, while others could only have sued for public nuisance by interference with the public right of navigation or the public right to take fish.

[30] See *Colour Quest Ltd* v *Total Downstream UK PLC* [2009] EWHC 540 (Comm), at [432]–[434]. The Court of Appeal dealt with an appeal against part of David Steel J's decision in *Shell UK Ltd* v *Total UK Ltd* [2011] 1 QB 86, but his conclusion on this point was not re-examined.

[31] Where the defendant breaks duty PND1 – that is, 'interferes unreasonably with a public right' – there is no need for any minimum number of people to be affected. As Denning LJ said in *Attorney-General* v *PYA Quarries* [1957] 2 QB 169, 191, 'Take the blocking up of a public highway or the non-repair of it. It may be a footpath very little used except by one or two households. Nevertheless, the obstruction affects everyone indiscriminately who may wish to walk along it.'

suggests that a judge should ask whether 'the neighbourhood' is affected and should then consider whether 'the local community within that sphere comprises a sufficient number of persons to constitute a class of the public'.[32] On the particular facts of the *PYA Quarries* case, the Court of Appeal held that there were no grounds for interfering with the trial judge's conclusions that flying rocks which disturbed 30 petitioners and vibrations which prompted fewer complaints were both sufficiently widespread. It is common to cite *R v Lloyd* (1802) as a case on the other side of the line: there the defendant was acquitted of public nuisance when the noise he made as a tinsmith disturbed only three addresses in Clifford's Inn.

(2) *Was the effect 'common'?* Whether there has been a wrong to the community at large depends in part on *how many* people were affected – the issue we explored under the previous sub-heading – but also on whether the effect on them was 'common'. We do not, of course, mean 'common' as opposed to rare, but 'common' in the sense of 'shared'. This requirement is illustrated by *R v Rimmington* (2006).[33] Here the House of Lords held that a defendant had not committed the crime of public nuisance by sending out 538 letters and packages containing racially offensive material. The defendant had offended a large number of people; but the effect on them was not 'common'.[34] The outcome might have been different if the defendant had set up a loudspeaker system through which he broadcast racially offensive material so that it could be heard simultaneously by 538 people in a particular area. In such a case all the people living in the local community would have been subjected to the 'common' annoyance of disturbance by the defendant's obnoxious broadcasts. So far, most English cases have involved injuries that were 'common' because they affected a sufficient number of people in a particular geographical location; the appellate courts have not had to decide whether public nuisance can also protect communities that are not defined by geographical propinquity.[35]

An effect does not cease to be 'common' just because a significant number of *individual* interests are simultaneously affected. Thus the explosion at the Buncefield Oil Storage Depot in 2005 disrupted over 600 nearby businesses, led to 2,000 people being evacuated from their homes, and damaged houses throughout the St Albans district. In the litigation that followed David Steel J ruled that the fact that many of the claimants could sue for *private* nuisances was not inconsistent with there also having been a 'common injury' sufficient to give rise to a claim for public nuisance:

> 'while a private owner's right to the enjoyment of his own land is not a right enjoyed by him in common with other members of the public, nonetheless any illegitimate interference, being the very same interference contemporaneously suffered by other members of the public, constitutes a common injury satisfying the public nature of a public nuisance'.[36]

(3) *Unreasonable interference.* Not every interference with comfort, convenience or safety will amount to a wrong, even if it is widespread and common; for example, the fact that

---

[32] [1957] 2 QB 169, 184–5.

[33] *R v Rimmington, R v Goldstein* [2006] 1 AC 459.

[34] Similarly, the House of Lords held that making obscene telephone calls to a large number of different people will not amount to a public nuisance.

[35] Suppose, for instance, that a defendant was responsible for a state of affairs that interfered with the 'comfort, convenience or health' of the users of a particular online service, perhaps by interrupting all those who were playing a popular online game by streaming violent pornography to their computers.

[36] *Colour Quest Ltd v Total Downstream UK PLC* [2009] EWHC 540 (Comm), at [430]. The Court of Appeal dealt with an appeal against part of David Steel J's decision in *Shell UK Ltd v Total UK Ltd* [2011] 1 QB 86, but this point was not re-examined.

residents near major football stadia will regularly be disturbed by chanting fans, does not mean that they are victims of public nuisance. In such cases, the pivotal question is whether the interference is *unreasonable*.

Many of the factors that courts take into account when considering whether an interference is unreasonable parallel those taken into account in private nuisance cases;[37] for example: (a) an *insubstantial* interference will not be unreasonable; (b) an interference resulting from a *wholly ordinary use of land* will not be unreasonable; (c) when considering whether an interference is unreasonable a court will ignore any amplification of its effects that can be attributed to the *hypersensitivity* of those affected; (d) what is unreasonable will be considered in the context of what is ordinarily to be expected in such a *locality*, that is 'the established pattern of uses [of land] in the locality'; and (e) the significance of an interference will vary in accordance with how regularly it occurs, the time when it occurs, its duration and intensity. Thus in *Shoreham-by-Sea UDC v Dolphin Canadian Proteins Ltd* (1973),[38] in considering whether the smell emanating from the defendant's factory amounted to a public nuisance, Donaldson J took into account that it was situated in 'an industrial area' – 'the local inhabitants are not entitled to expect to sit in a sweet-smelling orchard' – and that mechanical failure or human error would almost inevitably lead to the emission of offensive smells two or three times a year, but concluded that the particular smell's frequency and strong, unattractive character meant that it was a public nuisance. But while *many* of the factors have parallels in the tort of private nuisance it must be borne in mind that in private nuisance the essential question is what a landowner in a particular locality ought to be expected to tolerate, while in public nuisance the essential question is whether the state of affairs is such that it should be condemned as a *wrong to the community*.[39]

(4) *Isolated incidents.* Can an isolated incident amount to a public nuisance? In *Stone v Bolton* (1949), Oliver J answered: 'an isolated act of hitting a cricket ball on to a road, cannot, of course, amount to a nuisance . . . nuisance must be a state of affairs'.[40] Professor Newark agreed, though he seems to have worried that otherwise a skidding bus might constitute a public nuisance.[41] If Oliver J's opinion represents the law,[42] then it is necessary

---

[37] See above, §§ 13.4–13.5.

[38] *Shoreham-by-Sea UDC v Dolphin Canadian Proteins Ltd* (1973) 71 Local Government Reports 261.

[39] This may mean that planning permission should be treated as more relevant in cases of *public* nuisance than in cases of *private* nuisance. But this point has not been explored in the cases (for instance, *Lawrence v Fen Tigers Ltd* [2014] AC 822) or in recent academic commentary: for example, Parpworth 2008, Bishop & Jenkins 2011.

[40] [1949] 1 All ER 237, 238e. This point was not discussed when the case reached the House of Lords: [1951] AC 850.

[41] Newark 1949, 486, 488. There are more convenient ways of avoiding inconsistency with the tort of negligence in road accident cases. Thus it could be argued that (1) it is not an unreasonable use of the highway to drive a reasonably safe bus on it, (2) such buses sometimes skid without anyone having been careless, and (3) consequently, the non-careless skidding of a bus is not an unreasonable interference with the safety of other road users.

[42] It is doubtful whether the case law is consistent with Oliver J's opinion. Thus public nuisance can cover situations where a mass of snow suddenly falls off a roof onto a claimant (*Slater v Worthington's Cash Stores (1930) Ltd* [1941] 1 KB 488, decided by Oliver J!), where a building next to the highway suddenly collapses (see, for instance, *Wringe v Cohen* [1940] 1 KB 229 and *Mint v Good* [1951] 1 KB 517) and where an isolated incident, such as the discharge of oil, creates a longer term interference (see, for example, *Southport Corporation v Esso Petroleum Co Ltd* [1954] 2 QB 182, 197 per Denning LJ). Perhaps, the first two situations can be explained on the basis that the mass of snow and buildings were public nuisances *before* they collapsed because of the *danger* they posed to users of the highway.

to determine: (1) how long a single incident (for example, a flood) must last in order to amount to a 'state of affairs'; and (2) whether, and, if so when, a series of single incidents can amount to a 'state of affairs'. In our opinion there is no good reason of principle for getting enmeshed in such arcane questions. Rather courts should concentrate on the central question whether there was an unreasonable interference or not.[43]

19.3 Responsibility

Where a claimant has suffered special damage (a term still to be explained) caused by a public nuisance, he will only be entitled to sue a defendant for damages if the defendant *created, authorised, adopted or continued* the state of affairs that caused the problems. It is convenient to split these ways of establishing a defendant's responsibility into two.

A. Creating or authorising

A person who *creates* a state of affairs that amounts to a public nuisance can be held responsible for it. And a person who *authorises* someone else to create such a state of affairs can *also* be held responsible for it. But in both situations the defendant will only be responsible if he knew, or ought to have known (because the means of knowledge were available to him[44]), that such an interference would be the consequence of what he did or omitted to do.

The importance of knowledge (or means of knowledge) in establishing responsibility was determined by the House of Lords in the criminal case of *R v Goldstein* (2006). The defendant in this case had enclosed a small amount of salt in a letter which he posted. This was intended as a harmless joke, but some of the salt leaked from the envelope in a postal sorting office and because of fears that it might be anthrax the building was evacuated and the police called in. The House of Lords held that a defendant is only responsible for a public nuisance which 'he knew, or ought to have known (because the means of knowledge were available to him), would be the consequence of what he did or omitted to do'.[45] Applying this test, the House of Lords held that Goldstein should not have been convicted because it had not been proved that he ought to have known that the salt would escape.

The House of Lords adopted this test from the Court of Appeal in *R v Shorrock* (1994), which had itself adopted it from Lord Wright in *Sedleigh-Denfield v O'Callaghan* (1940). The relevant passage in Lord Wright's speech states:

> Though the rule has not been laid down by this House, it has I think been rightly established in the Court of Appeal that an occupier is not prima facie responsible for a nuisance created without his knowledge and consent. If he is to be liable a further condition is necessary, namely,

---

[43] In *Colour Quest Ltd v Total Downstream UK PLC* [2009] EWHC 540 (Comm), David Steel J ruled (at [408]–[421]) that there is no rule preventing a claim in *private* nuisance being based on a 'single isolated escape', and the defendants did not attempt to argue that such a rule existed in *public* nuisance. The Court of Appeal dealt with an appeal against part of David Steel J's decision in *Shell UK Ltd v Total UK Ltd* [2011] 1 QB 86, but this point was not re-examined.

[44] In *Sedleigh-Denfield v O'Callaghan* [1940] AC 880, 904, Lord Wright treated the phrase 'means of knowledge' as equivalent to what an occupier should have realised 'with ordinary care in the management of his property'. If we can generalise from this that 'means of knowledge' refers to 'the capacity to know through the exercise of reasonable care', then this guidance is likely to be useful.

[45] [2006] 1 AC 459, at [39] (per Lord Bingham) and [56] (per Lord Rodger).

that he had knowledge or means of knowledge, that he knew or should have known of the nuisance in time to correct it and obviate its mischievous effects . . . The responsibility which attaches to the occupier because he has possession and control of the property cannot logically be limited to the mere creation of the nuisance. It should extend to his conduct if, with knowledge, he leaves the nuisance on his land. The same is true if the nuisance was such that with ordinary care in the management of his property he should have realised the risk of its existence. This principle was affirmed in *Barker* v *Herbert*[46] . . .[47]

In this passage, Lord Wright was only purporting to discuss what had to be proved as to the defendant's state of mind in order to establish liability in cases where the defendant was an *occupier of land* who had *not* created or authorised the nuisance. *Sedleigh-Denfield* involved a flood arising from work done on the defendant's land by a trespasser, and earlier in his speech Lord Wright had bluntly stated that: 'If the work had been done by or on behalf of the [defendant], the conditions requisite to constitute a cause of action for damages for a private nuisance, would be beyond question complete.'[48] Similarly, *R* v *Shorrock* (1994) involved potential responsibility of an occupier for a public nuisance caused by the acts of others on his land: an 'acid house party' attended by between 3,000 and 5,000 people in one of the defendant farmer's fields, after he had gone away for the weekend. The farmer appealed against his conviction on the grounds that the judge ought to have directed the jury that actual knowledge had to be proved: he had only permitted an acquaintance to use the field for a 'disco' to raise money for charity. But the Court of Appeal held that the trial judge's direction in accordance with Lord Wright's speech had been correct.

If knowledge is now required even in a case where a defendant *created or authorised* the state of affairs that amounted to a public nuisance then the House of Lords *changed the law* in *Goldstein*'s case: a rule that was developed for one group of cases – those where the defendant is an occupier of land who did *not* create or authorise the state of affairs concerned – was extended to another group of cases – those where the defendant creates or authorises the state of affairs. But some subsequent cases *seem* to have overlooked that the House of Lords may have changed the law in this way. For example, in the litigation arising from the explosion at the Buncefield Oil Storage Depot nobody seems to have argued that the claimants' public nuisance claim required them to show that the defendant knew (or ought to have known) that an explosion 'would be the consequence' of what they did (overfilling a storage tank with petrol).[49]

A controversial line of cases suggests that a defendant may be responsible, even if he has not *personally* created or authorised a public nuisance, if he has engaged a contractor to perform some task which involves an obstruction of the highway or endangers users of the highway, and the *contractor* has created an *unreasonable* obstruction or *unreasonably* endangered other users of the highway. The cases, which frequently use the term 'non-delegable duty', indicate that in these circumstances the defendant will be responsible for the public nuisance created by the contractor unless the contractor's behaviour was collateral to what he was instructed to do.[50] This rule has been relied on principally against

---

[46] [1911] 2 KB 633. Lord Wright expressly notes that this was a *public* nuisance claim.
[47] [1940] AxC 880, 904–5.
[48] [1940] AC 880, 902.
[49] *Colour Quest Ltd* v *Total Downstream UK PLC* [2009] EWHC 540 (Comm).
[50] *Hardaker* v *Idle DC* [1896] 1 QB 335; *Penny* v *Wimbledon Urban District Council* [1899] 2 QB 72; *Holliday* v *National Telephone Co* [1899] 2 QB 392.

bodies with special statutory powers allowing them to arrange for the digging up of the highway. In *Rowe* v *Herman* (1997), the Court of Appeal suggested that the rule would not make a householder liable if builders she engaged failed to put lights on a skip which they placed in the road.[51] Thus it seems possible that this rule applies *only* to those with special statutory powers.

B. Adopting or continuing

An owner or occupier of land can also be held responsible for an interference caused by a state of affairs arising on land that is *owned*[52] or *occupied*[53] by her if she *continues* or *adopts* the state of affairs in question.[54] She will be held to have continued or adopted the state of affairs in question if: (1) she knew, or ought to have known (because the means of knowledge were available to her), that such a state of affairs would be the consequence of what she did or omitted to do; and (2) a reasonable owner or occupier in her position would have taken steps to prevent the state of affairs from arising or to deal with it once it had arisen.

Owners and occupiers can be held to have *continued* or *adopted* a state of affairs directly caused by trespassers.[55] Thus in *Attorney-General* v *Tod Heatley* (1897) the owner of a building site in Westminster was held to have continued a public nuisance by failing to take sufficient steps to remove dead dogs, cats, fish and offal which had been dumped on the site by unknown trespassers.[56]

Owners and occupiers are also often held to have *continued* or *adopted* a state of affairs directly caused by natural processes. For instance, if a tree on A's land falls into the highway, A may be held liable for the interference if she had carelessly failed to inspect it to determine whether or not it was likely to fall.[57]

Where a *building falls into disrepair* and endangers the public the approach of the courts to deciding whether the owner or occupier is responsible for the public nuisance tends to be stern: 'there must be some fault on the part of someone or other for that to happen'.[58] Further, if a defendant is aware of the disrepair, or ought to be, her duty to take reasonable steps to deal with the problem will be *non-delegable*; as a result, if contractors appointed by the defendant carelessly fail to deal with the problem, she will still be held liable.[59] She will avoid liability, however, if she can establish that the danger was

---

[51] [1997] 1 WLR 1390, 1394.

[52] In *Mint* v *Good* [1951] 1 KB 517 the Court of Appeal held that the rule set out in the text applied to owners who were not in possession as well as to occupiers.

[53] For instance, a tenant at will can be held liable under this rule: *R* v *Watts* (1703) 1 Salk 357, 91 ER 311.

[54] The Court of Appeal has held that a Highway Authority does not count as an owner or occupier of a highway for the purpose of these rules: *Ali* v *City of Bradford MDC* [2010] EWCA Civ 1282. Thus a Highway Authority will not be liable for public nuisance if it fails to use its powers to clear debris from a highway.

[55] *Barker* v *Herbert* [1911] 2 KB 633.

[56] A decision which was approved by the House of Lords in *Sedleigh-Denfield* v *O'Callaghan* [1940] AC 880, and held still to represent the law by the Court of Appeal in *Wandsworth LBC* v *Railtrack PLC* [2002] QB 756, [26].

[57] *Noble* v *Harrison* [1926] 2 KB 332; *Caminer* v *Northern & London Investment Trust Ltd* [1951] AC 88; *British Road Services* v *Slater* [1964] 1 WLR 498.

[58] *Mint* v *Good* [1951] 1 KB 517, 526–7, per Denning LJ. Though in *Wringe* v *Cohen* [1940] 1 KB 229, 233, the Court of Appeal suggested that where premises were undermined by 'a secret and unobservable operation of nature, such as subsidence under or near the foundations' the owner or occupier might not be liable.

[59] *Tarry* v *Ashton* (1876) 1 QBD 314.

purely the result of 'latent defects'. Historically, this non-delegable duty was probably related to the rule in *Rylands* v *Fletcher*.[60] Now, however, only an extraordinary use of land will fall within the ambit of that rule, while public nuisance covers more everyday cases of premises falling into disrepair. The public nuisance duty is also distinct in that where the complaint is of unreasonably endangering users of the highway those who have suffered special damage will be able to make claims, while claims under the rule in *Rylands* v *Fletcher* must be made by persons with sufficient interests in neighbouring land,[61] and cannot redress personal injuries.

19.4 Special damage

If A is responsible for a public nuisance and B has suffered some harm as a result, B will only be entitled to sue A for damages if that harm counts as 'special damage'. For these purposes 'special damage' means damage which is different in nature *or* extent to that suffered by the other members of the public affected by the nuisance. Thus if A creates a public nuisance by unreasonably obstructing a highway, but all that B suffers is the inconvenience of having to turn around and use a different route, then B probably will not have suffered 'special damage'.[62] But if B trips on the obstruction and is injured, or her personal property is damaged, then she will have suffered 'special damage'. The difficulty comes with deciding how to deal with cases that fall between these extremes. We will discuss four situations which have caused difficulty.

A. Special costs from obstruction

In some cases courts have decided that a claimant suffered 'special damage' because the obstruction suffered by all was, in practice, far more inconvenient for the claimant. The best example of this is provided by *Rose* v *Miles* (1815)[63] where the defendant was alleged to have moored a barge across a public navigable creek and the claimant had to incur the expense of unloading goods from his barges and conveying them by land. The court seems to have thought that the claimant's damage was 'special' to him because he had

---

[60] See Chapter 14 for a discussion of this rule. It will be noted that Blackburn J played a pivotal role in both *Rylands* v *Fletcher* and *Tarry* v *Ashton*, and that both cases involved independent contractors carrying out operations on the defendants' land.

[61] In *Wringe* v *Cohen* [1940] 1 KB 229 the Court of Appeal held that the non-delegable duty only attached to 'premises on a highway' but that both passers-by and owners of adjoining property could take advantage of the duty. It seems to us, however, that it would be implausible for an *adjoining owner* to claim that he had been a victim of unreasonable interference with the public right to use the highway. Consequently, we think that if the owner of *adjoining property* has a claim at all it certainly is not a claim for *public* nuisance. Perhaps it may be a claim for continuing a *private* nuisance (see above, § 13.9(C)). In *Mint* v *Good* [1951] 1 KB 517, 527, Denning LJ stated that the decision in *Wringe* v *Cohen* was 'clearly correct in regard to the responsibility of an occupier to *passers-by*' (emphasis added).

[62] Neyers 2017 disagrees. At 104 he argues that any *actual* (not merely theoretical) interference with the claimant's right to use a highway which causes *economic* loss is actionable. See also Neyers and Botterell 2016, at 1043: 'actual pecuniary loss'. But we do not think that it is sensible to formulate the rule so that every haulage firm that has a vehicle delayed by a lengthy and unreasonable obstruction of a motorway will have suffered *special* damage; nor can we see any reason for distinguishing the *economic* losses of a delayed haulier from the *non-economic* losses of guests prevented from reaching a wedding ceremony.

[63] See also *Walsh* v *Ervin* [1952] VLR 361.

already loaded his goods before the time of the obstruction and consequently he was unable to avoid the extra expenses. Dampier J said, 'If this be not a particular damage, I scarcely know what is'.[64]

A similar approach was taken in *Jan de Nul (UK) Ltd* v *AXA Royale Belge SA* (2000), where Moore-Bick J considered the liability of a dredging company responsible for siltation interfering with freedom of navigation in an estuary. He held that in such circumstances,

> any significant interference with an individual's commercial operations or the enjoyment of private rights resulting from the obstruction to navigation would in my judgment represent damage over and above that suffered by the public at large and would be sufficient to support an action.[65]

B. Interference with customers

The question whether B will have suffered 'special damage' if an obstruction interferes with his ability to receive customers at his place of business is controversial. In *Iveson v Moore* (1699), the claimant alleged that he had lost customers and the profits of his colliery because of the obstruction of the highway near his colliery. The Court of King's Bench split 2:2 on whether this was sufficiently 'special damage'. But it seems that the case was later argued before all the judges of the Common Pleas and Exchequer, and their opinions unanimously supported the claimant's claim.[66] Similarly, in *Wilkes* v *Hungerford Market Co* (1835) a bookseller successfully claimed that the loss he suffered through his customers being inconvenienced by an obstructed highway was sufficiently distinct to constitute 'special damage'. The correctness of *Wilkes* was doubted by Lord Chelmsford LC in *Ricket* v *Metropolitan Railway* (1867), but treated as correct by Greer LJ in *Blundy, Clark & Co Ltd* v *London North Eastern Railway* (1931):

> Where a [claimant] has property near a highway which he uses for the purposes of his business, and the highway . . . is unlawfully obstructed, and he is thereby put to greater expense in the conduct of his business, or suffers loss by the diminution of his business, he is entitled to recover damages as a person who has suffered special or peculiar damage beyond that which has been suffered by other members of the public wanting to use the highway.[67]

---

[64] (1815) 4 M & S 101, 104; 105 ER 773, 774. 'Particular damage' is a term that some judges and authors use instead of 'special damage'.

[65] [2000] 2 Lloyd's Rep 700, [44]. This point was not challenged on appeal: [2002] 1 Lloyd's Rep 583.

[66] It is worth noting that in this case the defendant was a rival colliery owner and it was alleged that he obstructed the road with the aim of harming the claimant. In such a situation a modern claimant might prefer to rely on the tort of intentional infliction of harm by unlawful means (discussed in Chapter 20) rather than alleging public nuisance. Such a claimant would have to establish that the means used were 'unlawful' (see below, §20.4) and that the defendant was 'aiming' to cause harm to him. It would not be necessary, however, to demonstrate 'special damage'.

[67] [1931] 2 KB 334, 369. See also *Lyons, Sons & Co* v *Gulliver* [1914] 1 Ch 631; *Walsh* v *Ervin* [1952] VLR 361; and *Colour Quest Ltd* v *Total Downstream UK Plc* [2009] EWHC 540 (Comm), at [459]: 'I conclude that there is long standing and consistent authority in support of the proposition that a claimant can recover damages in public nuisance where access to or from his premises is obstructed so as to occasion a loss of trade attributable to obstruction of his customers' use of the highway and liberty of access' (per Steel J). Stevens 2007 objects to *Wilkes* (at 186–8) because he believes that the bookseller's claim was not based on interference with *his own* right to use the highway but interference with the rights of his *customers*. See also Neyers and Diacur 2011. This assumes, however, that a person's right to use the highway does not include a right to use it as a way of *being reached* by customers, guests, etc. Similarly, courts have allowed the occupiers of piers and those with businesses at the water's edge to bring cases based on interference with public rights of navigation when the difficulty was in *being reached* by others: *Jan de Nul (UK) Ltd* v *AXA Royale Belge SA* [2000] 2 Lloyd's Rep 700 (upheld on appeal, [2002] 1 Lloyd's Rep 583).

Jason Neyers and Eric Andrews have argued that B *will* have suffered 'special damage' when he, or his servant or agent, has been obstructed and this has caused harm to the profits of B's business, or when the obstruction has reduced the value of B's premises, but that any loss B suffers as a consequence of the obstruction or diversion of potential customers will be too remote.[68] But in our opinion their suggested distinction between a loss of profits caused by the obstruction or diversion of potential customers (not 'special damage' according to Neyers and Andrews) and a fall in the value of business property (can be 'special damage') is irredeemably unstable;[69] we prefer Greer LJ's formulation of the rule.

C. Costs of removing the public nuisance

In *Winterbottom* v *Lord Derby* (1867), the Court of Exchequer held that the claimant could not rely on the expense he had incurred in removing an obstruction as 'special damage' since otherwise any person could give to himself the opportunity to sue. But in *Tate & Lyle Industries Ltd* v *GLC* (1983),[70] the House of Lords held that the claimant *could* claim for the expense it had incurred in dredging the River Thames in order to remove the obstruction to free navigation for which the defendant was responsible. The majority of the House of Lords seems to have held that the 'special damage' was not the cost of dredging itself, but the special loss that the claimant suffered because ships of particular dimensions were unable to progress up the channel. This is important, because it clarifies that the claimant had suffered 'special damage' *before* the dredging was undertaken, and thus does not conflict with the decision in *Winterbottom*.

The cost of removing a public nuisance may be 'special damage' where it falls on a body that fulfils a statutory function by doing so. In *Jan de Nul (UK) Ltd* v *AXA Royale Belge SA* (2002), the Court of Appeal held that where a dredging company had caused quantities of silt to be deposited in such a way as to interfere with the public right of navigation in a river, a harbour authority could sue that company in public nuisance for the cost of dredging the river bed, if either it was its duty to do this dredging or it had a statutory power to do so.[71]

D. Personal injuries

There is no real dispute over whether personal injuries can be sufficiently 'special' to an individual claimant. Instead, the debate is over whether personal injuries should be actionable at all in public nuisance cases.

---

[68] Neyers and Andrews 2016. Their argument follows the approach of Stevens 2007, described in the previous footnote, and is supported by detailed analysis of *Ricket* v *Metropolitan Railway Co* (1867) LR 2 HL 175 and subsequent cases.

[69] The instability results from the fact that the value of property that is only suitable for retail business uses will depend critically on public access; it would frequently be impossible to determine how far a reduction in value was caused by obstruction of B's employees and agents and how far by obstruction of B's customers. In any case, we cannot see any *practical justice* in public nuisance offering better protection to a pizza restaurant that primarily offers a delivery service (obstruction of employees and agents) than to one which primarily caters for eat-in customers.

[70] Lord Diplock disagreed with the majority and argued that 'special damage' arising from the claimant's choice about how it used public rights could not be the basis for a claim for public nuisance ([1983] 2 AC 507, 547). On *Tate & Lyle Industries Ltd* v *GLC* (1983), see Neyers and Botterell 2016 and Neyers 2010.

[71] [2002] 1 Lloyd's Rep 583, at [60]. For a similar case involving a highway authority see *Louth District Council* v *West* (1896) 65 LJ (QB) 535.

The Court of Appeal addressed this question in *In re Corby Group Litigation* (2009). The claimants in the case were children who claimed that they were born suffering from various deformities because the defendant council's programme of reclaiming and detoxifying land formerly belonging to the British Steel Corporation had released toxic materials which affected them while they were in their mothers' wombs. One of the grounds on which the claimants sued the defendant was public nuisance. The defendant applied to have this particular aspect of their claim struck out, arguing that compensation for personal injuries could not be obtained for public nuisance, by analogy with the position in private nuisance established by the House of Lords in *Hunter* v *Canary Wharf Ltd* (1997)[72] and *Transco plc* v *Stockport Metropolitan Borough Council* (2004).[73]

The Court of Appeal held that there was nothing in those two decisions that would entitle them to depart from the long line of precedents[74] where damages were awarded for personal injuries in public nuisance cases. The Court of Appeal went on to doubt the argument of the counsel for the defendant – borrowed from F.H. Newark's article 'The boundaries of nuisance' – that public nuisance was, like private nuisance, concerned to protect claimants' interests in exercising 'rights over land in the amplest manner'.[75] Dyson LJ argued that:

> [t]he essence of the right that is protected by the crime and tort of public nuisance is the right not to be adversely affected by an unlawful act or omission whose effect is to endanger the life, safety, health etc of the public.[76]

Given this, he found it hard to understand why damages for personal injury should not be recoverable in a public nuisance case.[77]

19.5 Is public nuisance irretrievably anomalous?

In the section at the start of this chapter, we presented the orthodox view that the duties that someone breaches when they commit public nuisance are imposed for the benefit of the public as a whole, not for the benefit of any particular individual, and we explained how two mistakes led to the establishment of such an odd, or anomalous, tort. Through the subsequent sections, we have sought to describe the law as it is currently applied by the courts in England and Wales. But at this point it may be worth returning to the form of

---

[72] Discussed above, §13.11. In *Hunter* v *Canary Wharf* [1997] AC 655, at 692, Lord Goff drew attention 'to the fact that although, in the past, damages for personal injury have been recovered at least in actions of public nuisance, there is now developing a school of thought that the appropriate remedy for such claims as these should lie in our now fully developed law of negligence, and that personal injury claims should be altogether excluded from the domain of nuisance.'

[73] Discussed above, §14.3(B).

[74] See, for example, *Castle* v *St Augustine's Links* (1922) 38 TLR 615, and, more recently, *Mistry* v *Thakor* [2005] EWCA Civ 953.

[75] See Newark 1949, 489.

[76] [2009] QB 335, at [29].

[77] [2009] QB 335, at [30]. At a subsequent trial, *Corby Group Litigation Claimants* v *Corby BC* [2009] EWHC 1944 (TCC), the claimants demonstrated that the defendant was responsible for a public nuisance, and that the toxic materials that were emitted had the ability to cause the type of limb defects that all except two of the claimants complained of. In April 2010 the defendant dropped plans to appeal, and reached a settlement with the claimants: Ben Quinn, 'Poisoned children win compensation fight against Corby borough council' (published on guardian.co.uk, 16 April 2010).

the tort in order to emphasise two consequences of its anomalous nature. First, a claimant who has suffered 'special damage' as a result of the crime of public nuisance being committed may be able to bring a civil claim for compensation, but those who have suffered 'special damage' as a result of other crimes will not be able to bring similar claims. Secondly, if various forms of 'pure economic losses' – such as losses resulting from interference with customers – are recoverable in public nuisance, then there will be unexplained inconsistency with when similar losses are recoverable in the tort of negligence.

In a recent article, Jason Neyers has suggested that public nuisance could be reconceptualised so as to make it cohere with the rest of tort law; this could be done by limiting its scope so that it only protects rights to use public highways (including navigable rivers) and to fish in tidal waters.[78] These rights can be formulated so that they are analogous to two types of rights that are protected by the tort of private nuisance – easements and profits à prendre – and restricting public nuisance to their protection would have various advantages: for example, the wrong would no longer be intolerably broad and vague, and the requirement of 'special damage' could be understood as demanding no more than that the harm flowed from an unreasonable interference with *the claimant's* 'public right'.

Would we recommend a court to reconceptualise public nuisance in the way suggested by Neyers? Clearly, real advantages can flow from the law being made more coherent: it may become easier to describe the legal rules as reflecting a *moral* position rather than being a product of pragmatic compromises, or even mistakes, and less time and money may have to be spent clarifying distinctions. But, equally, the pursuit of coherence can sometimes require the abolition of causes of action that have proved practically useful, or have produced outcomes that people generally regard as just. Where a defendant's activities blight the life of a whole community, as with the 'acid house party' in *R v Shorrock* (1994), might it be practically useful and just for those who have suffered 'special damage' to remain able to obtain a remedy without having to rely on the assistance of public officials?

Further reading

The most important article about public nuisance remains **J.R. Spencer, 'Public nuisance – a critical examination' (1989) 48 *Cambridge Law Journal* 55**. Readers will want to assess for themselves whether the House of Lords in *R v Rimmington; R v Goldstein* (2006) sufficiently addressed the concerns raised in it. But the pre-eminence of Professor Spencer's analysis has come under challenge from a series of articles written by Professor Neyers, culminating, at the time of writing, in **J. Neyers, 'Reconceptualising the tort of public nuisance' (2017) 76 *Cambridge Law Journal'* 87**.

---

[78] See Neyers 2017.

Chapter 20
The economic torts

Aims and objectives

Reading this chapter should enable you to:

(1) Understand when someone will be held to have committed the torts of: (a) inducing a breach of contract, (b) causing loss by unlawful means; (c) intimidation; (d) lawful means conspiracy; (e) unlawful means conspiracy; (f) deceit; (g) malicious falsehood.

(2) Get a good grasp of the debates around whether any of torts (a), (c), (e), (f) and (g) are examples of, or sub-species of, tort (b) and what implications that has for the shape of torts (a), (c), (e), (f) and (g).

(3) Understand the development of these torts, and why it is the case that a single person who maliciously causes another harm, using lawful means to do so, will not commit a tort; while two or more people who combine together to cause another harm maliciously, using lawful means to do so, will commit a tort.

20.1 The basics

In this chapter, we deal with six torts that are conventionally grouped under the name 'the economic torts':

(1) *Inducing a breach of contract.* This tort is primarily committed where A intentionally persuades C to breach a contract that C has with B. In such a case, A will normally be found to have committed the tort of inducing a breach of contract in relation to B, and will be held liable to compensate B for any losses that she has suffered as a result of C's breach.

(2) *Causing loss by unlawful means.* As currently defined, this tort is committed where A intentionally causes loss to B by committing (or threatening to commit) a civil wrong – a breach of contract, a tort, or an equitable wrong – in relation to C, which interferes with C's liberty to deal with B.

(3 and 4) The *conspiracy* torts: *lawful means conspiracy* is committed where A and C combine together to inflict loss on B for no legitimate reason; *unlawful means conspiracy* is committed where A and C combine together to inflict loss on B using unlawful means to do so.

The final two torts that we will be discussing in this chapter both involve deceiving some-one else:

(5) *Deceit*. This is committed where A deliberately lies to B with the object of inducing B to do *x*, B is induced by A's lie to do *x*, and B suffers loss as a result.

(6) *Malicious falsehood*. This tort is committed where A deliberately tells a lie to C about B and B suffers loss as a result.

There is a seventh economic tort – the tort of *passing off*. The principal way in which A will commit this tort is if people are induced to buy A's goods because he is selling them in a way that makes it look like they are made by B. We have already discussed this tort[1] and will not talk about it again here.

These torts are known as 'the economic torts' because they are *normally* committed by one person causing another to suffer some form of pure economic loss, and there are few, if any, other torts that protect claimants against defendants inflicting pure eco-nomic loss on them.[2] However, the label 'the economic torts' is regrettable, for three reasons.

First, the label might misleadingly suggest that these torts can *only* be committed by causing another person to suffer some form of pure economic loss. Consequently, the question of whether these torts might operate to protect a claimant against (say) the infliction of pure distress by someone else tends not even to be raised. (We will, however, discuss this question below in section 20.10.)

Secondly, grouping these torts under a common label leads many lawyers to think that 'the economic torts' must have something *more* in common with each other than the fact that they all *normally* involve one person inflicting some kind of pure economic loss on another. And so in books and articles we find wistful references to the fact that the eco-nomic torts have so far 'lacked their Atkin'[3] – the genius who will finally discern the principle that underlies all the economic torts and unify them as a single tort.

These tendencies to mono-mania must be resisted. There is no good reason to think that the torts gathered together in this chapter have anything in common except for the accidental fact of the kind of loss that *normally* tends to be suffered by someone who is a victim of one of these torts. All attempts to find a unifying principle that underlies all of these torts have failed. For example, it has been suggested[4] that all of the economic torts give effect to a rule that A will commit a tort in relation to B if he intentionally causes B to suffer some kind of loss using unlawful means. So – according to this view – all of the economic torts are examples of, or species of, the tort of *causing loss by unlawful means*. But this view is unsustainable. It does not have to be shown that A had an intention to harm B in order for it to be established that A committed the tort of inducing a breach of contract in persuading C to breach his contract with B. Nor does it have to be shown that there was anything unlawful about the methods (means) that A used to persuade C to breach his contract with B. The same is true of the deception torts. To establish that

---

[1] See above, §15.5(B).
[2] It is important to remember that a claimant's economic loss counts as being *pure* economic loss when it is *not* a consequence of the claimant's person or property being harmed.
[3] See Wedderburn 1983, at 229.
[4] See Weir 1997.

A committed one of those torts in relation to B, it does not have to be shown that A acted as he did because he was trying to harm B.[5]

Thirdly, giving these torts the name 'the *economic* torts' tends to ghettoise them as being primarily about money and business, and about regulating what businesses can do to each other by way of competition.[6] As a result, 'the economic torts' are not thought of as being centrally important to the law of tort, and in many law schools are not even mentioned to first year law students. This is regrettable, not least because they raise fundamental issues about the limits of individual freedom under the law. *Allen* v *Flood* (1898) – a key case on the economic torts that we discussed in the opening chapter[7] – was ranked by Tony Weir as 'arguably the most important case' in his *A Casebook on Tort*:

> The case is important because it is about freedom. It holds that, whatever morality might say, in law one is free to beggar one's neighbour provided one neither does anything unlawful oneself nor gets anyone else to do anything unlawful.[8]

The decision that the House of Lords reached in *Allen* v *Flood* was crucial in determining the scope of the torts now known as 'the economic torts'. In the case, you may recall, the claimants were employed on a day-to-day basis to do woodwork on a ship. The defendant was a union delegate of the ironworkers, and they objected to the hiring of the claimants because they had done ironwork on another ship, and the ironworkers regarded this as their exclusive province. The defendant told the claimants' employer that if the claimants were asked to come back to work the next day then the ironworkers working on the same ship would not turn up for work (they were entitled not to turn up, since they were also employed on a day-to-day basis). The claimants' employer gave in to this threat and told the claimants their services were no longer required.

A nine judge House of Lords ruled, by six to three, that the claimants could *not* sue the defendant for putting them out of work.[9] The defendant had not induced the claimants' employer to breach any contract that the employer had with the claimants, and while the defendant had intentionally harmed the claimants, he had not used unlawful means to do so. There was, Lord Herschell held, a 'chasm' between using lawful means to harm someone else and unlawful means:[10]

> In my opinion a man cannot be called upon to justify either act or word merely because it interferes with another's trade or calling; any more than he is bound to justify or excuse his act or word under any other circumstances, unless it be shewn to be *in its nature wrongful*, and thus to require justification.[11]

---

[5] See, in relation to the tort of deceit, *Polhill* v *Walter* (1832) 3 B & Ad 114, 110 ER 43. The fact that the tort of deceit can be committed without any intention to harm the victim of the deceit means that Weir 1964 (at 226), Cane 1996 (at 152, n. 9) and Sales & Stilitz 1999 (at 432) are *wrong* to suggest that deceit can be seen as an instance of the tort of using unlawful means to harm another.

[6] See Carty 2010, 2–4. Deakin and Randall 2009 go so far as to argue (at 533) that the torts *should* only protect specified economic interests: 'unless a direct interference with trade, business or employment is made out, a vital element of the wrong is missing, even if loss or damage is also present'.

[7] See above, §1.2.

[8] Weir 2004, 604.

[9] For an account of the litigation see Heuston 1986.

[10] The point is actually slightly better put by Lord Reid in *Rookes* v *Barnard* [1964] AC 1129, at 1168–9: 'I agree with Lord Herschell [in *Allen* v *Flood* [1898] AC 1, at 121] that there is a chasm between doing what you have a legal right to do and doing what you have no legal right to do.'

[11] [1898] AC 1, 139 (emphasis added).

Lawyers still debate as to whether the House of Lords made the right choice in *Allen* v *Flood* by deciding that intentionally harming someone else will *not* amount to a tort unless independently unlawful means are used to inflict the harm. Some American states made a different choice. For example, in *Tuttle* v *Buck* (1909), the claimant worked as a barber in the village of Howard Lake, Minnesota, whilst the defendant was a wealthy local banker. The claimant complained that the defendant had developed a grudge against him and had opened up a rival barbershop in the village, with the intention of driving him out of business. The Supreme Court of Minnesota held that:

> To divert to one's self the customers of a business rival by the offer of goods at lower prices is in general a legitimate mode of serving one's own interest, and justifiable as fair competition. But when a man starts an opposition place of business, not for the sake of profit to himself, but regardless of loss to himself, and for the sole purpose of driving his competitor out of business, and with the intention of himself retiring upon the accomplishment of his malevolent purpose, he is guilty of a wanton wrong and an actionable tort.[12]

The legal philosopher John Finnis agrees: 'A sound tort law identifies as tortious every act *intended* precisely to cause harm to another person . . .'[13] As we will see, English law has gone some way towards adopting Finnis' position in relation to *conspiracies* to harm someone else: an agreement between *Chum* and *Mate* to harm *Target*, if carried out successfully, will amount to a tort if there was *no good reason* for the conspirators to have sought to harm *Target*. Such lack of good reason is most easily made out where the conspirators acted out of sheer malice towards *Target*.

For what it is worth, we think that the House of Lords was right in *Allen* v *Flood not* to adopt the position that it is a tort intentionally to harm someone else for no good reason. This is for four reasons.

(1) *The difficulty of ascertaining someone's motives.* It can be very difficult to determine *why* someone acted as they did. But such an inquiry would have to be made in order to apply a rule under which it is a tort intentionally to harm someone else for no good reason.[14] As we are not blessed with the ability to peer inside other people's souls, we would do well to steer clear of legal rules that require us to do this.

(2) *Legitimacy of reasons.* Even if we could determine in a given case why a defendant intentionally harmed a claimant, it might be a controversial question whether the defendant had a *good* reason for having done so.[15] For example, suppose A drove B out of business because B had beaten up A's son – would A have had a good reason for acting in the way he did? What if A acted as he did because B had attempted to seduce A's wife, or insulted A? These are very difficult questions and it is not clear the courts are the right institutions to answer them.[16] Under the ruling in *Allen* v *Flood* these questions never arise. If A

---

[12] (1909) 107 Minn Rep 145 (per Elliott J). The law in Minnesota has subsequently become far closer to that set out in *Allen* v *Flood*: in *Gieseke ex rel Diversified Water Diversion, Inc* v *IDCA, Inc*, 844 NW 2d 210 (2014), at 219, the Minnesotan Court of Appeals held that interference with a prospective economic advantage was only actionable when the means used were 'either independently tortious or in violation of a state or federal statute or regulation'.

[13] Finnis 2002, 46 (emphasis in original). See also Dietrich 2000.

[14] See Restatement 2d, Torts, §870, Comment *i*.

[15] See Weir 1997, 74–5.

[16] Had *Allen* v *Flood* [1898] AC 1 gone the other way, it would have been – at that time – up to a jury to determine these issues, and distrust of juries' abilities to determine correctly whether or not someone had a *good* reason for intentionally harming someone else undoubtedly influenced the House of Lords.

intentionally ruins B using *unlawful means* to do so he will commit a tort – the question of whether or not A had a good reason for acting as he did never arises because you can never be said to have a good reason for breaking the law.[17]

(3) *Certainty.* The third reason emerges out of the first two: if the law said that A will commit a tort in relation to B if he intentionally harms B for no good reason, the law would become intolerably uncertain. Were the law to take the *Tuttle* v *Buck* position, A would not be able to tell with any degree of certainty whether or not his driving B out of business would amount to a tort or not. Maybe it would, maybe it wouldn't – it would all depend on how the courts, acting after the event, construed his motives and evaluated the reasons why he harmed B. This is unsatisfactory: as Tony Weir asks, 'Is it not important that people should be able to be told in advance what they may or may not do . . . ?'[18]

(4) *Freedom.* In *Wainwright* v *Home Office* (2004), the House of Lords considered whether to recognise a new tort that A would commit in relation to B if he intentionally caused B distress without any good reason for doing so. Lord Hoffmann, delivering the leading judgment, cautioned against taking this step:

> In institutions and workplaces all over the country, people constantly do and say things with the intention of causing distress and humiliation to others. This shows lack of consideration and appalling manners but I am not sure that the right way to deal with it is always by litigation . . . it might not be in the public interest to allow the law to be set in motion for one boorish incident.[19]

It seems likely that people also constantly do and say things with the intention of causing pure economic losses to others – consider, for example, how many bad ratings are posted on 'review' websites to punish businesses for trivial or imaginary infractions. If people had to be ready to justify all such expressions of opinion in court then their freedom would be significantly curtailed. Under the ruling in *Allen* v *Flood*[20] no such concern arises. If A intentionally causes B to suffer some kind of harm, A will only commit a tort in relation to B if the means he uses to inflict that loss are already means that are unlawful, or means (for instance, deliberate lies) which are dealt with by one of the other 'economic torts'.

Whether these four arguments are correct or not, we hope it is now clear to the reader just how important the torts dealt with in this chapter are, and how significant the issues governing their contours can be. We will now turn to look at each tort in turn.

---

[17] Though Parliament has taken the view that a trade union official who uses unlawful means to inflict harm on an employer in the course of a trade dispute should not be held liable for so acting: see the Trade Union and Labour Relations (Consolidation) Act 1992, s 219 (summarised below, §22.4).

[18] Weir 1997, 68.

[19] [2004] 2 AC 406, at [46]. In the United States, where a tort of intentionally causing another emotional distress without lawful justification or excuse is widely recognised, this concern is addressed by requiring that the defendant's conduct has been so 'extreme and outrageous' that it goes beyond 'all possible bounds of decency . . . and [is] utterly intolerable in a civilized community': see Rest 2d, Torts, §46, Comment *d*.

[20] Strangely, *Allen* v *Flood* was not cited at all in *Wainwright* v *Home Office* even though, had the House of Lords declared that it is a tort intentionally to cause another distress without lawful justification or excuse, they would have created a large exception to the principles laid down in *Allen* v *Flood*.

20.2 Inducing a breach of contract

A will have committed the tort of inducing a breach of contract in relation to B *if*:

1. B had a contract with a third party, C; *and*

2. A induced C to breach that contract;[21] *and*

3. A was in a certain state of mind – defined below – when A induced C to breach that contract; *and*

4. A had no justification for acting as he did.

So – in *Lumley* v *Gye* (1853), Johanna Wagner, a well-known soprano, made a contract with Lumley to sing at Her Majesty's Theatre, and not to sing anywhere else. Gye, a rival opera impresario, was alleged to have persuaded Wagner to sing at the Royal Italian Opera – and therefore to break her contract with Lumley. The Court of Queen's Bench held that if Gye *had* persuaded Wagner to break her contract with Lumley then Gye would have committed a tort in relation to Lumley.[22]

The tort in *Lumley* v *Gye* is usually described as either 'procuring a breach of contract' or 'inducing a breach of contract'. At one time it was thought that the tort might extend beyond situations where A induced C to *breach* her contract with B – for instance, to situations where A made it *impossible* for C to perform her contract with B. In such situations, C's failure to perform might not actually amount to a *breach* of contract: non-performance as a result of forces beyond C's control might be expressly excused under the contract's terms or A's intervention might have *frustrated* the contract. The apparent extension of the tort to cover situations where there was no breach led to suggestions that it should renamed 'interference with contract'.[23] But in *OBG Ltd* v *Allan* (2008),[24] the House of Lords held that it was an error to think that the tort in *Lumley* v *Gye* extends to situations where A has made it impossible for C to perform her contract with B. Since *OBG*, it is clear that A will *not* commit a tort in relation to B by making it impossible for C to perform her contract with B *unless* he uses *unlawful means* to make it impossible *and* he intends to cause harm to B. And then the tort A will commit in relation to B will be the tort of *causing loss by unlawful means* – the tort discussed in the next section[25] – *not* the tort of *inducing a breach of contract*.

We will now look at the elements required to commit the tort of inducing a breach of contract.

A. Breach

The House of Lords' decision in *OBG* made it clear that C's committing an *actionable breach of contract* is a necessary element of the tort discussed here.[26] The tort was explained

---

[21] The term 'induce' as used in this chapter does not bear its normal meaning of 'cause' or 'bring about': see below, §20.2(B).

[22] In fact, at the later trial of the facts, a jury found that Gye had not committed the tort because he had honestly believed that Wagner was at liberty to terminate her agreement with Lumley: for further details, see Waddams 2001.

[23] For instance, Fleming 1998, 756–7.

[24] The case is reported at [2008] 1 AC 1, and is referred to hereafter as '*OBG*'.

[25] See below, § 20.3.

[26] Ong 2008 points out (at 731) that the courts have not clarified 'how severe the breach of contract must be before tortious liability is imposed.' We think that this is because there is no severity threshold. But Deakin and Randall 2009 (at 538) would not allow the tort to cover breaches where there was an exemption clause (or significant limitation clause) in the contract.

as involving a form of *secondary liability* and, for A's liability to be secondary, C must also be liable: 'No *secondary liability* without primary liability.'[27]

So A will not have committed the tort discussed here if he persuaded C to *terminate* her contract with B in a *lawful* manner, as there will be no primary liability in this situation.[28] This is consistent with the famous case of *Allen* v *Flood* (1898), which we have just discussed, and which established that A will not commit a tort in relation to B if he persuades C by lawful means *not to make* a contract with B.

The decision in *OBG* also seems to indicate that it is *not* a tort to persuade someone to rescind a contract that is voidable.[29] In *Proform Sports Management Ltd* v *Proactive Sports Management Ltd* (2006), Judge Hodge QC had to consider the separate question whether it is a tort to persuade someone to *breach* a contract which *could have been* lawfully avoided by the party who was induced to breach it.[30] His conclusion was that there was no good reason for imposing a duty not to induce a breach of any contract which *could be* lawfully avoided by the party who was induced to breach it.

B. Inducing

What sort of thing does A have to do before he will be found to have *induced* C to breach a contract with B? A number of different forms of conduct can be distinguished.

(1) *Persuading.* There is no doubt that if A has *persuaded* C to break a contract with B then A will be held to have induced C to breach that contract. Some commentators have argued that the tort should extend no further than this: 'liability should attach under *Lumley* v *Gye* only when the defendant has persuaded the [claimant's] contractor deliberately to break his contract.'[31] Persuasion in this context could involve either an enticing offer or an unattractive threat – either 'carrot or stick'.[32] However, below we consider some cases when A has been held to have induced C to breach her contract with B even though it would be difficult to describe the part he played in bringing about that breach as *persuasion*.

---

[27] *OBG*, at [44] (per Lord Hoffmann). See also [5] (per Lord Hoffmann), [172] (per Lord Nicholls), [320] (per Lord Brown).

[28] The position was less clear before *OBG*. In *Torquay Hotel Co Ltd* v *Cousins* [1969] 2 Ch 106, Winn LJ stated *obiter* (at 147): 'For my part I think that it can at least be said, with confidence, that where a contract between [B and C] exists which gives [C] an optional extension of time or an optional mode for his performance of it, or of part of it, but, from the normal course of dealing between them, [B] does not anticipate such postponement, or has come to expect a particular mode of performance, [inducing C] to exercise such an option should, in principle, be held actionable if it produces material damage to [B].' This view was contrary, however, to that expressed by Morris LJ in *DC Thomson & Co Ltd* v *Deakin* [1952] Ch 646, 702. The High Court of Australia accepted in *Sanders* v *Snell* (1998) 196 CLR 329, at [23], that Morris LJ had correctly stated the law on this point.

[29] There is clear authority that someone will not commit the tort discussed here if he induces someone not to perform a contract which is void: *Joe Lee Ltd* v *Lord Dalmeny* [1927] 1 Ch 300. On whether it is a tort to induce someone to rescind a voidable contract, in *Greig* v *Insole* [1978] 1 WLR 302, at 333, Slade J found the authorities conflicted but decided to assume that it was not.

[30] The party could have avoided the contract because he was a minor when he entered it and it did not fall into any of the exceptional classes of contract which are binding on minors. The contract involved the footballer Wayne Rooney appointing the claimant company as his exclusive representative in contract negotiations and transfers for two years for a management fee calculated as a percentage of his earnings.

[31] Weir 1997, 35. See also Carty 2010, 37: 'Persuasion . . . is the necessary link'.

[32] Weir 1997, 34. Likewise, in *OBG*, [20], Lord Hoffmann treats persuasion to breach a contract by a threat of assault as falling within the tort of inducing a breach of contract *as well as* potentially falling within the tort of three-party intimidation.

(2) *Advising*. Suppose that *Singer* has contracted to sing at a theatre in London, but that *Aunt* has advised her not to go to London because a wealthy relative is dying and this relative is likely to give bequests only to family members who pray at his bedside. If *Singer* takes this advice and breaks her contract, should *Aunt* be held to have induced the breach?

Those who argue that *Aunt* should not be held to have induced *Singer* to breach her contract assert that there is an important distinction between *creating* a reason to break a contract and *pointing out* that a reason exists.[33] But Winn LJ showed no sympathy for such a distinction when it was pressed in *Torquay Hotel* v *Cousins* (1969), and suggested that a father who told his daughter that her fiancé had been convicted of indecent exposure would have induced her to break her engagement even if the information was true.[34] Certainly there would be a risk, if the courts drew a distinction between persuasion and advice, that the line between making a soprano a generous offer to *persuade* her to break her contract and merely *advising* her that such an offer was likely to be available if she broke her contract would be difficult to draw in practice.

(3) *Harbouring*. Can A be said to have induced a breach of a contract between B and C if C's breach of that contract happened *before* A became involved? Suppose, for example, that *Soprano* contracted to perform exclusively for *Impresario*, but then walked out on *Impresario* in breach of contract, and was later engaged by *Rival*. Can *Rival* be said to have induced *Soprano* to breach her contract with *Impresario*? It seems that the English courts have taken the view that *Rival can* be held liable if *Soprano*'s breach of her contract with *Impresario* was still 'retrievable'.[35] This is often referred to as liability for 'harbouring' – the idea being that in the case just described, *Rival*, by providing *Soprano* with a 'harbour', might have made it less likely that *Soprano* would return and perform for *Impresario*.[36]

(4) *Facilitating*. In *British Motor Trade Association* v *Salvadori* (1949), C sold a car to A, in breach of a contractual undertaking that C had made with B that he would not sell the car to anyone within a year of purchasing it. A argued that C had been willing to sell the car and break his contract with B without any influence from him, and that consequently he could not be said to have induced the breach. Roxburgh J held, however, that C could not break the contract *not to sell* without *someone* being willing to buy, and that 'any active step taken by a defendant . . . by which he facilitates a breach' was sufficient to fall within the scope of the tort.[37] Some commentators have expressed strong doubts about this statement because the courts have refused to adopt a general principle that anyone who assists another to commit a tort will be held liable.[38] But in *One Money Mail Ltd* v *Ria Financial Services* (1995), where W had contracted to work exclusively with O, but R, knowing this, entered an agreement with W that meant that he was in breach of his exclusivity obligation, the Court of Appeal held that R had procured W's breach: Longmore LJ stated that by

---

[33] Carty 2010, 37, citing Hart and Honoré 1985, 54.

[34] [1969] 2 Ch 106, 147. Of course, in such a case the father might be able to rely on the defence of justification. In *Camden Nominees Ltd* v *Slack (or Forcey)* [1940] Ch 352, Simonds J was equally clear that 'advice which is intended to have persuasive effects is not distinguishable from inducement', but also held that a person who provided advice could rely on the defence of justification if the law recognised a moral duty to give the advice.

[35] *Blake* v *Lanyon* (1795) 6 TR 221, 101 ER 521; *De Francesco* v *Barnum* (1890) 63 LT 514.

[36] As we will see, *Rival* will only commit the tort if he *intended* to bring about a breach. Moreover, if it is clear that *Soprano* would never have returned to perform for *Impressario* then *Rival's* 'harbouring' will not have caused *Impresario* any actionable loss: *Jones Brothers (Hunstanton) Ltd* v *Stevens* [1955] 1 QB 275.

[37] [1949] Ch 556, 565.

[38] See below, §30.2.

intentionally, and knowingly, making a contract with W, 'which was or made provision for the very act which was a breach of [W's] contract with [O]', R did more than merely 'assisting' the breach; R combined with W to do the very thing that was a breach.

(5) *Inconsistent dealing.* We use the label 'inconsistent dealing' to cover those situations where A does something that puts C in breach of a contract with B, usually after A has previously made a deal with C that removes C's power to control whether he performs the contract with B and instead allocates that power to A. Two examples may help.

First, suppose that *Owner* contracts with *Neighbour* that no building will be erected during *Neighbour's* lifetime on Whiteacre, a plot of land that belongs to *Owner*. *Owner* then sells Whiteacre to *Rich*. Secondly, suppose *Owner* owns a boat ('*Whitesail*') which she hires to *Neighbour* for two years. Before the end of this period, *Owner* sells *Whitesail* to *Rich*. Clearly in each example *Owner* has relinquished her power to control whether the contract is performed – having sold Whiteacre and *Whitesail* to *Rich* it is *Rich* who now can decide whether to build on Whiteacre or to take *Whitesail* back from *Neighbour*. But will the courts treat *Rich* as being at liberty to do these things? Or might it be a tort for *Rich*, at least if he knows about the contracts that *Owner* has made, to build on Whiteacre[39] or to take *Whitesail* back?

We think that it would be better *not* to treat 'inconsistent dealing' as falling within the scope of the tort. If it were within the scope then there would be a risk of the tort being inconsistent with the special set of rules about when a covenant relating to land can be enforced against a subsequent owner of the land.[40] There might also be inconsistency with the rules that establish that where a contract between A and B creates an *equitable interest* in an item of property then this will bind a subsequent purchaser of the property unless he was a bona fide purchaser for value without notice.[41] Thus we think a good case can be made for drawing a line between (1) A doing something with the intention of *facilitating* a breach of contract by C,[42] and (2) A acquiring property from C then dealing with it in a way which will mean that a contract made by C is breached.[43]

(6) *Preventing performance.* Suppose A *prevented* C from performing a contract with B and B suffered some kind of financial loss as a result, and A did this knowing of the contract and intending that C should be unable perform it. In *OBG* the House of Lords decided that A will *not* commit a tort in relation to B by making it impossible for C to perform her contract with B *unless* he uses *unlawful means* to make performance impossible *and*

---

[39] The Whiteacre scenario is similar to the situation in *Sefton (Earl)* v *Tophams* [1965] Ch 1140, where Stamp J found that the defendant would have committed the tort of inducing a breach of contract if he built. The Court of Appeal continued an injunction against the defendant, requiring him not to build, without finding that the defendant would commit the tort of inducing a breach of contract if he did build, and the House of Lords did not consider this point: *Sefton (Earl)* v *Tophams* [1967] 1 AC 50.

[40] For these rules see, Smith 2014, Chapter 24.

[41] *Swiss Bank Corp* v *Lloyds Bank Ltd* [1982] AC 584, 598, 613. When such an equitable interest will arise is a controversial question. Compare *Lord Strathcona SS Co* v *Dominion Coal Co* [1926] AC 108 with *Port Line Ltd* v *Ben Line Steamers Ltd* [1958] QB 146.

[42] *British Motor Trade Association* v *Salvadori* [1949] Ch 556, discussed in the previous section.

[43] If this view is correct it follows that *Rich* should not be held liable for *inducing a breach of contract* in either of our two examples. Carty 2010, 55 argues that 'inconsistent transactions should not be seen as tortious per se'. Indeed she would also exclude 'facilitating', and perhaps 'harbouring' from the scope of the tort. See also Smith 1977.

intends to cause harm to B.[44] And then the tort A will commit in relation to B will be the tort of *causing loss by unlawful means* – the subject of the next section – not the tort of *inducing a breach of contract*.

Since A will not be held to have *induced* C to breach a contract if A takes steps which prevent C from performing, it follows that A will also not be held to have *induced* C to breach a contract if A *omits to take steps which would have enabled C to perform*. Thus if *Speculator* contracts to sell a painting to *Investor*, and *Owner*, who currently owns the painting, refuses to sell it to *Speculator*, then *Owner* will not have committed a tort in relation to *Investor even if Owner*'s only reason for refusing to sell was because he wanted to cause *Speculator* to be in breach of his contract with *Investor*.

The two main arguments[45] in favour of fixing the limit on what counts as 'inducing' between *persuading* (potentially within the tort) and preventing (always outside the tort) are that it is easier to draw this line than any alternative[46] and that there is a moral difference between seducing C into committing a wrong and merely rendering C unable to perform.[47] But the clarity of the persuasion/prevention distinction should not be exaggerated: there are some forms of behaviour which must be assessed, particularly *harbouring* and *facilitating*, that cannot be easily described as *either* persuasion *or* prevention.[48] Similarly, the significance of the moral difference should not be overplayed: B may find it difficult to share the philosopher's view that if A persuades C to break her contract with B by *threatening* to have her tied up[49] he commits a different wrong from D who prevents C from performing by *actually* tying her up. But while B may think that he suffers the same harm – non-fulfilment of his contractual expectation – *OBG* treats A and D as having committed different torts in relation to B.

---

[44] This point was expressed most clearly by Lord Nicholls: *OBG*, at [178]–[180]. Lord Hoffmann did not make the same point *explicitly*. But such a point is consistent with Lord Hoffmann's insistence that there can be no liability for inducing breach of contract unless there has been a breach of contract, because preventing performance will not always result in a breach. In *Meretz Investments NV v ACP Ltd* [2008] Ch 244 the Court of Appeal confirmed that preventing performance could not amount to inducing a breach of contract and that Lord Hoffmann had not intended to disagree with Lord Nicholls on this point.

[45] A wider range of arguments for and against such a distinction are reviewed in Bagshaw 2000.

[46] The principal alternative is to draw a line between *direct* and *indirect* interferences with contract. But this distinction is not easy to draw and was expressly condemned as 'unsatisfactory' by Lord Hoffmann in *OBG*, at [38].

[47] Simester and Chan 2004 argue (at 152) that *persuading* C to break a contract is essentially different from *preventing* C from performing because only the former 'attacks the very status of [the contractual] undertaking as a reason-generating promise'. But while this argument identifies a way in which *persuasion* is different from *prevention* it does not explain why the law of torts ought to *use* the distinction. Similarly, Stevens 2007 (at 280) offers an explanation more likely to appeal to an outside observer than to the victim: 'Where the promisor has no choice [because he has been prevented from performing], the damage to the convention of promising, and consequently our ability to place trust in one another, is not undermined to the same degree [as it is when the defendant induces a voluntary breach by the promisor].'

[48] Neyers 2009 argues (at 174–5) that in order to make the tort of inducing breach of contract consistent with a corrective justice account of the law it would be better if the law held that A had induced a breach of contract by C only where A has 'intentionally appropriated' B's right to C's performance of the contract.

[49] Recall that for Weir and Lord Hoffmann *persuasion* can involve 'carrot or stick': see above, n 32.

C. Fault elements

Suppose A induced C to breach a contract that she had made with B. A will not have committed the tort of inducing a breach of contract unless he also had the *requisite state of mind* when he brought about the breach.

So what must A's state of mind have been? The short answer is that when A induces C to breach the contract A must: (1) *know* that he is inducing a breach of contract *and* (2) *intend* to induce a breach of contract. But both of these elements require further discussion.

(1) *Knowledge that a breach is being induced.* In *OBG*, Lord Hoffmann explained:

> To be liable for inducing a breach of contract, you must know that you are inducing a breach of contract. It is not enough that you know that you are procuring an act which, as a matter of law or construction of the contract, is a breach. You must actually realise that it will have this effect.[50]

This means that if A mistakenly but genuinely believes that what he is procuring will *not* amount to a breach of contract then he will not be liable, even if that belief is unreasonable.[51] In one of the cases heard by the House of Lords alongside *OBG* –*Mainstream Properties Ltd* v *Young* – two employees of the claimant had told the defendant that they were at liberty to purchase a particular plot of land for development. That was wrong; it was a breach of their contracts with their employer, the claimant, for them to divert the purchase to their joint venture with the defendant. But because the defendant believed what he had been told – that the two employees were at liberty to do what they did – he was not liable for inducing a breach.[52] Of course, the two employees were liable; they broke their contracts. Any mistake they made as to their contractual obligations, even if honest and reasonable, could not help them.

While a defendant who mistakenly believes that he is *not* bringing about a breach will not commit the tort, a defendant who makes a conscious decision not to find out how things stand will be liable. In *Emerald Construction* v *Lowthian* (1966), the defendants, who were officers of a building trade union, sought to persuade the main contractor building the Fiddlers Ferry power station to terminate a labour-only subcontract.[53] The defendants knew of the subcontract but were not aware of its terms. The main contractor terminated the subcontract and committed a breach of contract in so doing; the subcontract did not permit the main contractor to terminate it in the way that it did. The defendants were held liable for inducing a breach of contract even though they had not known

---

[50] *OBG*, at [39].

[51] *British Industrial Plastics* v *Ferguson* [1940] 1 All ER 479, HL.

[52] In *Meretz Investments NV* v *ACP Ltd* [2008] Ch 244, the Court of Appeal dealt with a case where the defendant had received legal advice about the action which brought about a breach of contract; he had *not* been advised that the action would not induce a breach, but had been advised that he was *legally* entitled to act in this way. The Court concluded, at [124], that a defendant's honest belief that he was *legally* entitled to act in a particular way was sufficient to preclude his state of mind being held to have been an intention to induce a breach of contract. This seems doubtful, particularly since it might have the effect of protecting from liability a range of defendants who *mistakenly* believe themselves to enjoy a defence of justification.

[53] The defendants objected to workers being employed on labour-only subcontracts because the subcontractor (in this case, a company with only two shareholders, a joiner and his wife) tended to have no assets, and as a result any workers employed by the subcontractor would have no effective recourse if the subcontractor went bust.

for certain that the main contractor would commit a breach of the subcontract if it terminated it. Lord Denning MR remarked:

> Even if they did not know the actual terms of the contract, but had the means of knowledge – which they deliberately disregarded – that would be enough. Like the man who turns a blind eye. So here, if the officers deliberately sought to get this contract terminated, heedless of its terms, regardless of whether it was terminated by breach or not, they would do wrong. For it is unlawful for a third person to procure a breach of contract knowingly, or recklessly, indifferent whether it is a breach or not.[54]

This passage was quoted with approval by Lord Hoffmann in *OBG*.[55] He made clear that the crucial line was to be drawn between an honest belief – even if it stems from gross negligence – that a breach would not be induced, and a conscious decision not to confirm a suspicion that a breach would be induced.

(2) *Intention to induce a breach.* A will only have committed the tort of inducing a breach of contract in relation to B *if* when A induced C to breach her contract with B he *intended to induce a breach of contract.* So, what counts as 'intention' in this context? The simple answer is that A will be held to have intended to induce a breach of contract *if* A *aimed* to induce C to commit a breach of contract, either as an end in itself or (much more commonly) as a means of achieving some other end. But A will not be held to have intended to induce a breach of contract if such a breach was merely an unaimed-for *side effect* of A's actions, albeit one which A knew was very likely to occur as a consequence of his actions. There are three points of detail that we must clarify.

First, where a defendant sets out to achieve his end by means of inducing a breach of contract then he will be held to have intended to induce a breach of contract *even if* he would have preferred it to have been possible to achieve his end in some other way. Thus if *Antville FC* persuaded *Cobweb* to break his contract with *Bugtown FC*, by persuading *Cobweb* to refuse to play for *Bugtown FC* until they agree to transfer him to *Antville FC*, then it will not assist *Antville FC* for them to claim that they would have much preferred the transfer to have been arranged without such steps being taken by *Cobweb*.

Secondly, a difficult issue concerns the position of a defendant who aims to achieve a particular end but is unsure what means will be necessary to achieve it. For instance in *Emerald Construction* v *Lowthian* (1966), as we have seen, the defendants' end was to *terminate* a labour-only subcontract but they were not sure if the main contractor would have to *breach* the subcontract in order to achieve this. Lord Denning MR's comments, quoted above, suggest that he thought that defendants could commit the tort if they suspected that it might be necessary for a contract to be breached in order to achieve their end but went ahead without investigating whether this was the case because they did not care. Given that Lord Hoffmann cited these comments with approval in *OBG*,[56] it seems likely that a defendant will be held to have intended to induce a breach of contract by C if he intends to induce

---

[54] [1966] 1 WLR 691, 700–1.

[55] *OBG*, at [40]–[41].

[56] *OBG*, at [40]–[41]. At this point in his speech Lord Hoffmann is discussing 'knowledge' rather than 'intention', but there would be little point in holding that turning a blind eye to whether a contract would have to be broken is sufficient to constitute 'knowledge' if such reckless indifference could not also constitute 'intention'. Moreover, in a later passage in his speech (at [69]–[71]), Lord Hoffmann seems to assume that it would be actionable for A to encourage C to terminate a contract with B with reckless indifference as to whether C will have to breach this contract.

C to *take whatever means are necessary* to achieve a particular end, and he knows that it may be necessary for C to breach a contract with B, but he does not care. This is not, of course, to say that a defendant will be held to have intended to induce a breach of contract by C whenever he was recklessly indifferent as to whether a consequence of his conduct would be to persuade C to breach a contract with B. There is an important difference between being recklessly indifferent between different means that may be necessary in order to achieve your object and being recklessly indifferent as to the likely *consequences* of achieving your object.

Thirdly, in deciding what a defendant intends it is necessary to distinguish carefully between what is *part of* the defendant's end or means and what is *a consequence of* achieving that end or using those means. An outcome will count as *part of* the defendant's end if it is 'simply the other side of the same coin' *and* the defendant knows that this is the case.[57] An example of such a situation may be provided by the facts of *Lumley* v *Gye*: suppose Gye knew that Wagner had made a valid contract with Lumley not to sing elsewhere than at Her Majesty's Theatre. If so, when persuading her to sing for him at the Royal Italian Opera, he could *not* say that he intended to persuade her to sing at the Royal Italian Opera but did not intend to persuade her to break her contract with Lumley: in the circumstances, singing at the Royal Italian Opera would be the very same thing as breaking her exclusive engagement with Lumley.

(3) *Summary.* So – to sum up: to find that A committed the tort of inducing a breach of contract in inducing C to breach her contract with B, it will have to be established that when A acted as he did:

(a) he *knew* that he was inducing a breach of contract; *and*
(b) he *intended* to induce a breach of contract.

But (a) will also be satisfied if A *suspected* that he might be inducing a breach of contract, but deliberately chose not to find out. And (b) will be satisfied if A intended to achieve an end by whatever means were necessary, and A did not care that the necessary means might involve a breach of contract by C.

(4) *Intention to harm.* We have just summarised the fault requirements for the tort of inducing breach of contract. It may be worth emphasising that it does *not* have to be shown that A *intended to harm* B when he acted as he did. This was confirmed by the House of Lords in *South Wales Miners' Federation* v *Glamorgan Coal Co Ltd* (1905),[58] where the defendant miners' union had induced miners to break their contracts of employment in order to raise the price of coal (at the time the wages of miners were pegged to the price of coal) and argued that this would *benefit* the claimant colliery owners rather than harming them. The House of Lords held that the defendants' expectation that the claimants might benefit from their actions was irrelevant because to establish the tort it was sufficient to demonstrate an intention to induce the claimants' employees to breach their contracts.

D. Absence of justification

Suppose A has induced C to breach her contract with B. Suppose further that A did so with the requisite mental element. If A had a *justification* for inducing C to breach her contract with B, the courts will *not* find that A committed the tort of inducing a breach of

---

[57] *OBG*, at [134] (per Lord Hoffmann), [167] (per Lord Nicholls).
[58] [1905] AC 239. This case was cited with approval as authority for this point by Lord Hoffmann in *OBG*, at [8].

contract in acting as he did. Importantly, the pivotal question is *not* whether *C's breach of contract* was justified but whether *A's inducing C to breach* her contract was justified.

English law has recognised the validity of both legal and moral justifications for inducing a breach. A can establish a *legal* justification if he had a legal right which was inconsistent with B's contractual rights and was superior or equal in status to those contractual rights. A simple example of this situation would be if Johanna Wagner had foolishly made two contracts with rival impresarios promising to sing exclusively for each. In such circumstances either impresario would be justified in seeking to persuade Johanna Wagner to break her contract with the other.

A more complex example is provided by *Edwin Hill* v *First National* (1989). In this case, the defendant was a finance company which had loaned money to a property developer to enable him to purchase Wellington House for development. Unfortunately the project stalled and the developer became unable to repay. This meant that the defendant had the power to force the sale of Wellington House. Instead of exercising this power of sale, the defendant agreed to finance the project itself, but, as a condition of doing so, insisted that the developer should break his contract with the architects who he had previously engaged. The architects then sued the defendant for inducing the developer to breach this contract. The defendant claimed that it had been justified in doing so.

The complexity in the case comes from the fact that although the defendant had a (superior) legal right in the form of its power to force the sale of Wellington House, it had not actually exercised *this* power. It had instead used the bargaining position that this power provided in order to put together a different deal (which included the breach of contract). Despite this complexity the Court of Appeal thought that the defendant could rely on the defence of justification. Two explanations were provided. First, the court identified the legal right which the defendant had, which might justify it in interfering with the architects' contractual right against the developer, as the right to receive payment of what was due. Given this, one could say that the defendant acted reasonably[59] to protect its right to be repaid the money it had lent the developer. Secondly, the court pointed out that the end result was no worse for the architects than if the power to force the sale had been exercised and that in such circumstances it made no sense for the law to prohibit a different deal which was better for both defendant and developer.

To establish a defence of *moral* justification the defendant must show that he was impelled to act by a sense of moral duty. It is not sufficient merely to claim that there were good reasons for inducing a breach, still less that the person breaking the contract might gain some valuable benefit from doing so: 'The fact that their motives were good in the interests of those they moved to action does not form any answer to those who have suffered from the unlawful act.'[60] In practice, the defence of moral justification has been successfully deployed very infrequently. A rare example is provided by *Brimelow* v *Casson* (1924), where the defendant induced theatre proprietors to break their contracts with a stage show producer in order to pressurise him into paying higher wages to the chorus girls he engaged. The supposed moral necessity was provided by the belief that the wages were so low that his employees were being forced into lives of immorality and prostitution.

---

[59] The reasonableness of changing architects was not considered in detail. But it should have been, because it is important to establish some inconsistency between the architect's right to the continuation of his contract and the defendant's right to be repaid.

[60] *South Wales Miners' Federation* v *Glamorgan Coal Co Ltd* [1905] AC 239, 252 (per Lord James). See also *Greig* v *Insole* [1978] 1 WLR 302, 341.

E. Is it a tort?

We have now described the various elements required to establish the tort of inducing a breach of contract. However, two issues in relation to this tort still need discussing. First of all, is inducing a breach of contract a tort at all, or is it some other form of liability masquerading as a tort?

In *OBG*, the House of Lords held that liability for inducing a breach of contract is not an *independent* tort but is actually a form of *accessory* liability – the defendant is held liable because he participated in the contract-breaker's wrong.[61] This point has been used as a foundation for arguing that liability for inducing a breach of contract should be studied alongside liability for participating in torts committed by others, and should be reformulated to make it conform to a *general* model of *accessory* liability for torts.[62] One concern about this, however, is that most versions of a *general* model treat a defendant who is an *accessory* to another's tort as if he *also* committed the same tort, and is *jointly* liable for it.[63] Of course, if liability for inducing a breach of contract is a form of *accessory* liability it may remain convenient to *talk about it* as if it were a tort because it sounds so odd to say that a person who was never a party to a contract is *jointly* liable for breaching it. But there are at least three reasons for doubting whether a defendant who has induced a breach of contract will, even after the *OBG* case, *be treated* as if he is jointly liable for having breached a contract.[64]

(1) *Different remedies.* Suppose that A has induced C to breach her contract with B. If A's liability to B in this situation is genuinely *secondary* in nature – and does not arise out of the fact that A committed a tort in relation to B in acting as he did – then it follows that the remedies available against A should be similar to those available against C. But the available evidence suggests that *different remedies* will be available against A and C.[65]

(2) *Different defences.* If a defendant's liability for inducing a breach of contract is genuinely *secondary* it seems odd that the defendant can rely on a defence of *justification* to escape being held liable even when the contract-breaker has undoubtedly committed the

---

[61] *OBG*, at [5] (per Lord Hoffmann), [172] (per Lord Nicholls), [320] (per Lord Brown). Similar views were expressed by academics before the *OBG* case: see Sales 1990, 503–4. The law on when someone will be held secondarily liable as an accessory to a tort committed by someone else is dealt with in Chapter 30, below.

[62] Carty 1999, 506–10; Carty 2010, 319–320; Davies 2015, 172–176, seeks to associate the tort of inducing breach of contract with 'general principles of accessory liability which operate throughout the common law' which he identifies, but argues most strongly for 'fusion' of the tort with accessory liability for breach of equitable, fiduciary obligations.

[63] Davies 2015, 284, is an exception, in that he argues for a *general* model that does not involve *joint* liability: 'Whilst such liability is clearly parasitic upon the occurrence of a primary wrong, the nature of the accessory's wrong is distinct from that of the primary wrongdoer. This best explains the different conduct elements, mental elements, defences and remedies which are available against the primary wrongdoer and accessory.'

[64] Deakin and Randall 2009, Neyers 2009 and Lee 2009 also conclude that the tort is not an instance of secondary liability, though their reasons diverge from ours.

[65] The cases where damages have been assessed do not seem to have proceeded by considering how much would be awarded in an action for breach of contract. See e.g. *Goldsoll v Goldman* [1914] 2 Ch 603, 615–16. Indeed, in *Lumley v Gye* (1853) 2 E & B 216, 230, one of the reasons that Crompton J gave for the existence of the tort was that the measure of damages might be different from that in an action for breach of contract. Moreover, as Stevens 2007 has pointed out (at 277), courts readily grant injunctions against defendants ordering them not to *induce* employees to breach their contracts of employment while they would not usually grant injunctions against the employees ordering them not to breach the same contracts. See also Davies 2015, Chapter 8.

wrong of breach of contract. In such a case, after all, the defendant may have knowingly and intentionally *persuaded* the contract-breaker to commit the wrong.

(3) *Vicarious liability for inducing breach.* Suppose that A induces C to breach her contract with B – and that A, in so acting, was acting in the course of his employment by E. If A's liability for inducing C to breach her contract with B were genuinely secondary in nature then B could not sue *E* for damages in respect of the losses suffered by him as a result of C's breach.[66] But it seems likely that if *Lackey* was employed by *Impresario* and in the course of his employment *Lackey* persuaded *Soprano* to breach her contract with *Rival* the courts *would* want to hold *Impresario* vicariously liable for *Lackey*'s wrong.

Is there an alternative way of explaining the existence of the tort? Robert Stevens has written:

> The better view is that all contractual rights carry with them a right good against everyone else that they do not induce the infringement of the contractual right. The secondary right is accessory to the primary right and its infringement is a free-standing tort.[67]

This explanation insists that a defendant who induces someone to breach a contract is *not* jointly liable for committing the same wrong as the contract-breaker. It is not, however, an explanation that can draw any support from the *OBG* case.[68]

F. Should the tort exist?

The second issue that we still need to discuss is whether defendants should be held liable *at all* for inducing other people to breach their contracts. Some legal commentators[69] have condemned the existence of a tort of inducing a breach of contract. The foundation for their criticisms is that if A has committed the tort by inducing C to breach her contract with B, B will be able to make a claim for breach of contract against C. Why, they ask, should B be given a claim against A as well?

Part of the answer may be that occasionally a claim against A will be more attractive than a claim against C. For instance, in *South Wales Miners' Federation* v *Glamorgan Coal Co Ltd* (1905), the defendant organisation had persuaded miners in South Wales to break their contracts with the coal companies which employed them and stop working for a one-day protest. Regardless of what we may think about such protests, we can easily imagine why the coal companies did not want to sue the people who had broken their contracts, the miners. It would not have been good for labour relations to have made legal claims against the miners as soon as they returned to work. There might also have been doubts about whether the miners would have had the money to pay for any losses suffered

---

[66] There is no precedent for an employer being held vicariously liable for an employee's breach of contract – whether that breach of contract was personally committed by the employee or whether the employee has been held to have committed that breach of contract because he was an accessory to it.

[67] Stevens 2007, 281. Bagshaw 2000 identifies (at 132–7) some reasons for recognising such 'a right good against everyone else'. Lee 2009 argues (at 524) that the claimant's right is a right to 'exclusive access (vis-á-vis third parties) to the peremptory status of the promisor's promise'.

[68] The explanation is also rejected by Beever 2016, 111–14. He also rejects the accessory liability account, at 108–11.

[69] See, for example, Howarth 2005b; and Fridman 2009, at 234: 'what was done in 1853 was something that was contrary to precedent and a step in the wrong direction, and . . . capable of producing undesirable consequences.'

through stopping production for a day. Furthermore, from the point of view of the coal companies we can see why the defendant organisation might appear to have been 'the real authors of the mischief'.[70] The miners would not have stopped work for the protest without the encouragement of the defendant organisation. To use a biblical metaphor, the defendant organisation played a role similar to that of the serpent in the Garden of Eden.[71]

But showing why victims of a breach of contract would *like* a tort of inducing a breach of contract to exist is not enough to satisfy all of its detractors. One common criticism is that the tort fails to advance economic efficiency because it tends to discourage the *efficient breach* of contracts. A second indictment is that the tort reduces the capacity of workers to organise effective industrial action and consequently facilitates their oppression by powerful employers. Can these criticisms be answered?

(1) *Efficient breach.* The notion of 'efficient breach' is based on the idea that it may be better for the wealth of society as a whole if particular contracts are broken.[72] Suppose, for example, that *Seller* owns the only widget in the world and contracts to sell it to *Buyer*, who will use it to generate 40 units of wealth each year. *Seller* then discovers that *Rival* could use the widget to generate 50 units of wealth each year and is therefore willing to pay *Seller* more for the widget than *Buyer* is. In such a case, *it might be thought* that it would be better for society as a whole if *Seller* breaks his contract with *Buyer*, pays her compensation for the loss of profits resulting from her not getting the widget, and sells the widget to *Rival* instead.[73] But the existence of the tort of inducing a breach of contract means that it would be wrongful for *Rival* (or anyone else) to *persuade Seller* to break his contract with *Buyer* in order to ensure that the widget goes to the person who can make the most productive use of it.

So far, it looks as if the critics of the tort might have a good case. But we have ignored two things. First, the tort does not stop *Rival* negotiating with *Buyer* and *Seller*[74] to try to persuade them to cancel their contract so that the widget can be sold to him – indeed, if *Rival* can use the widget to make more money than *Buyer* can, then *Rival* should be capable of making very attractive offers to both *Buyer* and *Seller* to induce them to cancel their contract. Secondly, in our discussion we have assumed that everyone knows how much *Rival* and *Buyer* can make with the widget. In real life such information is often not available. In particular, it is unlikely that *Seller*, if approached by *Rival*, will be in a position to know who is likely to make best use of the widget. Consequently, it might again

---

[70] [1905] AC 239, 246 (per Lord Macnaghten).

[71] In *McGill* v *Sports and Entertainment Media Group* [2017] 1 WLR 989, a football agent sued a rival agent for inducing a footballer to breach a contract with him, after settling a breach of contract claim with the footballer for an amount far lower than his loss. The claimant's explanation included the opinion that whilst the footballer had been tempted, the rival agent and the club involved in the transfer were 'the real perpetrators'.

[72] For a presentation of the doctrine of 'efficient breach' see Posner 2003, 119–21. But note that Posner has argued that the existence of the tort can be justified in most of the circumstances in which it is used: Landes & Posner 1987, 224.

[73] See, for example, Perlman 1982, at 128, 'In cases of [inducing breach of contract by] otherwise lawful acts, tort liability works at cross-purposes with contract policies. Contract remedies seem to promote efficiency, whereas the addition of inducer liability inhibits efficient outcomes.'

[74] If *Rival* wants the identical widget which *Seller* has contracted to supply to *Buyer* he may be able to negotiate solely with *Buyer* – but in other cases, where, for instance, *Seller* has contracted to supply the output of his widget factory to *Buyer*, and *Rival* instead wants *Seller*'s factory to make slightly different widgets for him, all three parties will have to be involved in the negotiations.

be better to encourage *Rival* to negotiate with both *Buyer* and *Seller*. A further benefit of encouraging such negotiations, rather than allowing *Rival* to persuade *Seller* to break his contract with *Buyer*, is that a negotiated cancellation will avoid the courts having to spend valuable time calculating how much by way of damages *Seller* should pay *Buyer* in the aftermath of his breaching his contract to sell the widget to her.[75]

(2) *Industrial oppression*. One answer to the second criticism of the tort of inducing a breach of contract that was advanced above might be: the tort can only be relied on where there is a *contract*, and an employee must have voluntarily (to the extent that the law of contract demands) *agreed* to the terms of his contract of employment, so there is only limited scope for an employee to argue that he is oppressed by others being prohibited from *persuading* him to breach terms that he has agreed to. But this answer only really works at a formal level. In practice, we know that employees (and others) frequently have little control over the terms of the contracts that they enter. No one thinks that the South Wales miners had much opportunity to influence the terms of the contracts being offered when they applied for their jobs. Moreover, Parliament has recognised that in practice employees are empowered by the possibility of *collective* industrial action, which frequently depends on an organiser *persuading* multiple employees to break their contracts simultaneously, and has consequently provided a statutory immunity for economic torts committed in the furtherance of trade disputes.[76] So there is no doubt but that the existence of the tort of inducing breach of contract improves the position of employers relative to their employees. The core issue is whether this effect can be justified by the advantages that flow from providing additional protection for contractual rights: for many people and companies their contractual rights are one of their most valuable assets.[77]

20.3 Analogous torts

If inducing breach of contract is a tort, perhaps because it is a form of *accessory* liability which is *talked about* as a tort because it *sounds* odd to say that a person who was never a party to a contract is *jointly* liable for breaching it,[78] we should consider whether there are similar torts covering the inducing of other similar wrongs.

English cases have recognised liability for inducing the violation of obligations which are somewhat similar to contractual obligations. For example, the Court of Appeal held in a case involving an employment relationship that was governed by statute rather than contract, that A could commit a tort in relation to B by inducing C to breach a statutory obligation to work provided that such a breach by C could give rise to a civil action by B.[79]

---

[75] See Macneil 1982, at 957–60, for discussion of how it can only be determined whether a breach will be 'efficient' in the light of 'transaction costs' – that is, broadly speaking, the relative costs of negotiations and of sorting out breaches.

[76] This immunity is now conditional on certain procedures being followed in the organisation of the industrial action: see below, §22.4.

[77] See further, Bagshaw 2000, at 132–7.

[78] Normally, where A has procured B to commit a tort against C the law holds that A and B are *jointly* liable for committing the tort against C. See below, Chapter 30.

[79] *Associated British Ports* v *Transport and General Workers' Union* [1989] 1 WLR 939, 952, 959–60, 964–5. Liability for inducing a breach of a statutory duty is not confined to statutory duties similar to employment obligations: *Meade* v *Haringey LBC* [1979] 1 WLR 637.

It may also be a tort for A to persuade C to break a duty to grant a particular private law remedy to B.[80]

By contrast, in *Metall und Rohstoff AG* v *Donaldson Lufkin & Jenrette Inc* (1990), the Court of Appeal refused[81] to recognise that it was a tort to induce someone to commit a breach of trust, principally to avoid any conflict with the well-developed equitable wrong of dishonestly assisting another to commit a breach of trust.[82] The position with respect to inducing breach of other equitable duties is less clear. In *PK Airfinance SARL* v *Alpstream AG* (2015), Christopher Clarke LJ was willing to contemplate that it might be a tort to induce a breach of the equitable duty that a mortgagee owes to the mortgagor and others with a contingent interest in the security.[83]

20.4 Causing loss by unlawful means

A will have committed the tort of *causing loss by unlawful means*[84] in relation to B if:

1. A caused B to suffer some kind of loss;
2. by interfering with the freedom of a third party, C, to deal with B; and
3. the means by which A interfered with C's freedom to deal with B were unlawful; and
4. A acted in the way he did with the intention of harming B.

This tort developed as a *generalisation* of two more narrowly defined torts. The first of these torts will be committed by A in relation to B if A uses *unlawful threats* in order to intimidate a third party, C, into not dealing with B, or ceasing to deal with B.[85] This tort is usually referred to as *three-party intimidation*.[86]

The second of these torts will be committed by A in relation to B if A makes use of *unlawful means* in order to interfere with a third party, C's, *performance of a contract* with B. For instance, in *Merkur Island Shipping Corp* v *Laughton* (1983), the claimants owned a ship, the *Hoegh Apapa*, which docked at Liverpool. The defendant union officials made it impossible for the claimants to perform their charter-contract with C to 'prosecute . . . voyages with the utmost despatch', and under the terms of the charter-contract C was not obliged to pay hire for the days when the ship was trapped in Liverpool. The defendant union officials achieved this by persuading the employees of a tug company to break their

---

[80] This was assumed by the Court of Appeal in *Law Debenture Corp* v *Ural Caspian Ltd* [1995] Ch 152, although it went on to hold that there was no right to an equitable remedy until it had been granted. The matter is somewhat complicated, however, by the fact that the reasoning of the court invokes both (1) a *broader* version of the tort of inducing breach of contract than is authoritative after the *OBG* case, and (2) the case of *Acrow (Automation) Ltd* v *Rex Chainbelt Inc.* [1971] 1 WLR 1676, which was founded on a *broader* version of the tort of causing loss by unlawful means than is authoritative after the *OBG* case.

[81] [1990] 1 QB 391, at 481.

[82] See *Royal Brunei Airlines* v *Tan* [1995] 2 AC 378. See also Davies 2015, 126–31.

[83] *Airfinance SARL* v Civ 1318, at [310] and [312].

[84] In *OBG*, this tort is referred to by Lord Hoffmann, Baroness Hale and Lord Brown as 'the tort of causing loss by unlawful means', but by Lord Nicholls as 'interference with a trade or business by unlawful means or, more shortly, the tort of unlawful interference'. We discuss below, § 20.10, whether the tort should cover only economic losses associated with 'trade or business' interests.

[85] *Garret* v *Taylor* (1620) Cro Jac 567, 79 ER 485; *Tarleton* v *M'Gawley* (1790) Peake NPC 270, 170 ER 153.

[86] The qualifying term *three-party* is necessary because a tort of *two-party* intimidation *may* also exist. See below, § 20.5.

contracts of employment with the tug company by refusing to assist the tug company in fulfilling its obligation to tow the ship from its berth; in other words the means used by the defendants to cause loss to the claimants was commission of the tort of inducing breach of contract *in relation to the tug company.*

The claimants sued the defendants, arguing that the defendants had a committed a tort in relation to the *claimants* in indirectly interfering with their ability to perform their charter-contract and were therefore liable to compensate them for the loss of hire.[87] The House of Lords agreed, referring to the tort committed by the defendants as 'the common law tort of actionable interference with contractual rights'.[88] But the House of Lords also stated that the case could fit within the general tort of 'interfering with the trade or business of another person by doing unlawful acts'.[89] Persuading the tug company's employees to break their contracts of employment was identified as the necessary 'unlawful means'. At one time this tort, 'actionable interference with contractual rights', was treated as an *extension* of the tort of inducing breach of contract. But in *OBG*, the House of Lords firmly stated that this had been an error, and it was part of the tort of *causing loss by the use of unlawful means.*

Between them then, the two narrowly defined torts of *three-party intimidation* and *actionable interference with contractual rights* provided a good basis for recognising a more general tort. The tort of *actionable interference with contractual rights* had developed with a focus on a particular way in which a claimant might suffer loss (interference with his contractual rights), but a central element in the tort's make-up was a requirement for the use of *unlawful means.* By contrast, the tort of *three-party intimidation* put no limit on the way in which a claimant might suffer loss – but also required a particular type of *unlawful means* (unlawful threats). So together the two narrowly defined torts suggested that it ought to be a tort to use *unlawful means* (including, but not limited to, unlawful threats) to cause loss (including, but not limited to, interference with contractual rights), though some features of this general tort of *using unlawful means to cause loss,* such as what might count as 'unlawful means', what the defendant's state of mind would have to be, and what varieties of loss it would protect against, remained to be settled. We will discuss each of these features below.

A. Unlawful means

In defining what amounts to 'unlawful means' for the purpose of the tort of causing loss by the use of unlawful means, the law draws on definitions of what is unlawful found in other areas of the law.

(1) *Tort.* It is clear that if A has caused B to suffer some kind of loss by committing a *tort* in relation to C which interferes with C's freedom to deal with B, A will be found to have caused B to suffer that loss through the use of unlawful means.[90]

In *OBG*, Lord Hoffmann stated that A's behaviour would also amount to 'unlawful means' if the only reason that it did not amount to a *tort* in relation to C was that C did not suffer any kind of actionable loss.[91] An example of this extension of the meaning of

---

[87] Recall: because the claimants could not conduct the voyage, C was not required to pay hire to the claimants.

[88] [1983] 2 AC 570, 609.

[89] Ibid.

[90] In *Marex Financial Ltd* v *Sevilleja* [2017] EWHC 918 (Comm), Knowles J held that it was at least arguable that breach of a fiduciary duty would count as unlawful means for the purpose of this tort.

[91] *OBG*, at [49]–[50].

'unlawful means' may be provided by *Lonrho* v *Fayed* (1990) where it was alleged that the defendant had caused loss to the claimant by using the unlawful means of a deceitful statement to the Secretary of State for Trade and Industry, but this had not amounted to a tort in relation to the Secretary of State because *he* had not suffered any actionable loss as a result of this statement. It seems that Lord Hoffmann thought that this extension was also wide enough to cover cases where A *threatened to commit a tort* in relation to C but did not have to go through with the threat because C 'gave in' and caused loss to B in the way which A sought.[92]

(2) *Breach of contract.* The question whether a *breach of contract* will amount to 'unlawful means' for the purposes of the tort discussed here might seem to be more difficult. If A has breached a contract with C in order to harm B, one can clearly castigate what A has done as unlawful vis-à-vis C, but is there any reason to treat A's action as unlawful means vis-à-vis B? The law of contract would not, after all, usually give B any right to insist on a contract between A and C being performed.[93] Nonetheless, it was decided in *Rookes* v *Barnard* (1964) that a threat to break a contract was an unlawful threat for the purposes of the tort of three-party intimidation, which tort – as we have seen – forms part of the *general* tort. A major strand in the reasoning which supported this conclusion was that there was 'no difference in principle between a threat to break a contract and a threat to commit a tort'.[94] In *OBG* Lord Hoffmann also stated that 'In principle, the cases establish that intentionally causing someone loss by interfering with the liberty of action of a third party in breach of contract with him is unlawful.'[95] In other words, a *breach of contract* will count as 'unlawful means' for the purposes of the tort discussed here, and so will a *threat to breach a contract*.

(3) *Crime.* Will the commission of a *criminal offence* count as 'unlawful means' for the purposes of the tort discussed here? This question causes no problems when the behaviour that constitutes the criminal offence could also be actionable as a tort, because we have already seen that all torts count as unlawful means.[96] The answer is difficult, however, when we think about minor crimes such as regulatory offences.[97] Here the main controversy flows from the fact that the definition of 'unlawful means' helps to determine what, for instance, traders can do to each other by way of competition, while Parliament may have defined certain things as minor crimes for reasons completely different from any considerations of what should be legitimate behaviour between competitors.

---

[92] *OBG*, at [49], 'In the case of intimidation, for example, the threat will usually give rise to no cause of action by the third party because he will have suffered no loss. If he submits to the threat, then, as the defendant intended, the claimant will have suffered loss instead. It is nevertheless unlawful means. But the threat must be to do something which *would* have been actionable if the third party had suffered loss.' There is a risk that this definition of which threats will count as 'unlawful means' will prove to be too narrow. For instance, if A threatens C that he will kill C's spouse unless C acts in a way which will cause loss to B, and C submits, then the threat which C will have used will *not* have been a threat of behaviour which would have been actionable by C if he suffered loss.

[93] For an exception, see the Contracts (Rights of Third Parties) Act 1999.

[94] [1964] AC 1129, 1168 (per Lord Reid).

[95] *OBG*, at [48].

[96] Neyers 2009 suggests (at 188–97) that the tort would be easier to justify from a corrective justice perspective if *only* serious criminal offences, and not civil wrongs, were treated as 'unlawful means'.

[97] An overlapping question is whether the breach of a statutory duty will count as 'unlawful means' for the purposes of the tort discussed here if the breach of the duty in question is *not* civilly actionable.

For example, many competitors try to persuade each other's customers to switch allegiances by sending out small free gifts with advertising slogans. If *Upstart* decided to try and take customers from *Rival* by sending *Rival*'s customers free calculators, would we want to say that *Upstart* committed the tort of using unlawful means to harm another in relation to *Rival* if its campaign was successful – and caused loss to *Rival* – but it later turned out that the batteries in these calculators contained a chemical which can cause severe pollution, so that it was a statutory offence to supply them? The dilemma here is that 'unlawful means' is meant to be a clearly defined concept and consequently there is an attraction to the answer that *all* criminal offences should count as 'unlawful means'. On the other hand, however, if the role of the tort is to help define what methods it is wrongful for A to use against C in an attempt to take business from B, it makes a nonsense of the tort to allow it to cover methods which nobody thinks are improper. Does anyone think if *Upstart* sends *Rival*'s customers defective calculators (instead of good quality calculators) he is behaving wrongfully vis-à-vis *Rival*?

The question whether *criminal offences* should count as 'unlawful means' divided the House of Lords in the *OBG* case. Lord Hoffmann held that they should not:

> In my opinion, and subject to one qualification, acts against a third party count as unlawful means only if they are actionable by that third party. The qualification is that they will also be unlawful means if the only reason why they are not actionable is because the third party has suffered no loss.[98]

By contrast, Lord Nicholls preferred the view that 'In this context the expression "unlawful means" embraces all acts that a defendant is not permitted to do, whether by the civil law or the criminal law'.[99] In discussion, he qualified this view by suggesting that committing a criminal offence might *only* count as unlawful means if: (a) the defendant's crime was committed 'against' the claimant, *or* (b) the defendant intentionally caused loss to the claimant by committing (or threatening to commit) a crime against a third party in order to cause a loss to the claimant 'through the *instrumentality* of'[100] that third party.[101]

A majority in the House of Lords expressly adopted Lord Hoffmann's view.[102] There seem to be three reasons why the majority made this choice.

---

[98] *OBG*, at [49]. Lord Hoffmann explained that the qualification included cases where A had done everything necessary to commit a tort in relation to C but C had suffered no loss *and also* cases where A had threatened to use unlawful means on C but never had to go through with the threat because C surrendered to it and acted in a way which harmed B.

[99] *OBG*, at [162].

[100] *OBG*, at [159] (emphasis in original).

[101] *OBG*, at [159]–[162]. The relevant passages are not easy to follow. The House of Lords seems to have been concerned to define the tort of causing loss by the use of unlawful means so that it would *not* catch a delivery company gaining an advantage over its rivals by offering a faster service premised on its agents ignoring speed limits and traffic lights. With reference to a similar example Lord Nicholls states, at [160], that the reason that this would not be a tort is because 'The couriers' criminal conduct is not an offence committed against the rival company in any realistic sense of that expression'. The example is an unusual one because it involves a *promise* to third parties – potential customers – to commit crimes to their advantage, rather than the more familiar variation of a *threat* to commit crimes to their disadvantage. If we consider the more familiar variation – *threats* to commit crimes – it is not clear why anyone who thought the tort ought to cover threats to commit crimes would single out threats to commit crimes 'against' third parties for special treatment: for example, what if a defendant intentionally intimidated third parties into not trading with the claimant by *threatening* to commit blasphemy or to be cruel to animals?

[102] *OBG*, at [266]–[270] (Lord Walker), [302] and [306] (Baroness Hale), [320] (Lord Brown). It was also adopted by the Supreme Court of Canada: *AI Enterprises Ltd* v *Bram Enterprises Ltd* [2014] 1 SCR 177.

First, let's return to the example of *Upstart* trying to take customers from *Rival* by sending her customers free calculators, where this scheme involves a criminal offence because the calculators' batteries contain a potentially polluting chemical. Lord Hoffmann thought that this sort of example demonstrated that it would be *arbitrary* to allow the question of whether *Upstart* had committed a tort in relation to *Rival* to turn on the question whether a criminal offence had been committed. In this example the aspect of *Upstart*'s scheme which is criminal – the content of the calculator batteries – has no effect on the likelihood of the free gifts influencing *Rival*'s customers to cease trading with her.

Lord Nicholls might respond by claiming that he agrees that in this example *Upstart* should not be liable. But he would reach this conclusion *not* by denying that *Upstart*'s offence amounts to 'unlawful means', but by insisting that (in his view) the tort requires a crime *against Rival*'s customers, which enables *Upstart* to cause loss to *Rival* 'through the instrumentality of' the customers: here neither condition – crime *against* customers, instrumentality – is made out. But this response leads to the second reason why the majority in *OBG* might have chosen to reject Lord Nicholls's position: if it were to be adopted, we would have to define these additional terms – 'against C', 'instrumentality' – and this might be very difficult. Suppose, for example, that the night before *Salesman* is due to pitch for a multi-million pound contract for the company he works for, *Rival* supplies *Salesman* with copious quantities of illegal drugs so that *Salesman* will be in no condition to impress anyone the next day, and *Rival* can pick up the contract instead. Would we say in this situation that *Rival* has committed a crime *against Salesman*? It is very hard to say – *Rival*'s crime here is regarded by some people as 'victimless', by others as an offence 'against society', and by a third group of people as an example of the law trying to protect people like *Salesman* from themselves.

A third reason for choosing Lord Hoffmann's position was that many crimes are created by statute and it would be undesirable to treat Parliament as having extended the scope of the law of tort in the absence of any evidence that Parliament intended its legislation to be used in this way. Sometimes, for example, Parliament may have enacted broad criminal offences in the knowledge that prosecutors will only choose to enforce them when it is in the public interest to do so: would it be appropriate for the courts to treat such offences as extending the scope of tort liability?

(4) *Two-party cases.* In *OBG*, Lord Walker predicted that neither Lord Hoffmann's nor Lord Nicholls' judgments would be regarded as 'the last word on this difficult and important area of the law.'[103] His prediction came true within ten months when, in the conspiracy case of *Revenue & Customs Commissioners* v *Total Network* (2008), members of the House of Lords suggested *obiter* that Lord Nicholls' approach to the question of what amounted to unlawful means for the purpose of the tort discussed here might be adopted in a *two-party case*, that is where a defendant intentionally caused loss to a claimant directly, rather than by interfering with a third party's freedom to deal with the claimant.[104] In making this suggestion, their Lordships focused on the following passage in Lord Hoffmann's speech in *OBG*:

> I would only add one footnote to this discussion of unlawful means. In defining the tort of causing loss by unlawful means as a tort which requires interference with the actions of a third party

---

[103] *OBG*, at [269].
[104] [2008] 1 AC 1174, at [43] (per Lord Hope), [99] (per Lord Walker), [124] (per Lord Mance], [223] (per Lord Neuberger). From here on we will refer to this case as simply *Total Network*.

in relation to the [claimant], I do not intend to say anything about the question of whether a claimant who has been compelled by unlawful intimidation to act to his own detriment, can sue for his loss.[105]

Though the first sentence in this paragraph refers to 'unlawful means', we suspect that Lord Hoffmann did not mean to suggest that in *two-party cases* a different test of unlawful means should be adopted: he was pointing out that the *next* requirement (which we discuss under the next sub-heading) for the tort of causing loss by unlawful means might not apply in two-party cases. It remains to be seen whether the suggestions in *Total Network* that 'unlawful means' might have a different meaning in *two-party cases* than it does in *three-party cases* (where the majority's view in *OBG* remains authoritative) will be taken up by the courts.

B. Interference with a third party's freedom

A claimant's economic interests often depend on third parties being willing and able to deal with him. For example, if B runs a business then he will clearly lose money if his customers take their business elsewhere or his employees resign or his suppliers refuse to sell him what he requires or if it becomes impossible for any of these groups to deal with him. This said, the customers, employees and suppliers *will often* be at liberty to act in this way *without* committing any civil wrong to B. (The most obvious exception is where by acting in this way the customers, employees or suppliers will be breaching a *contract* with B.)

In circumstances where B's economic interests depend on third parties remaining willing and able to deal with him, he will be vulnerable to A taking steps to *interfere* with that willingness or ability. For instance, he will be vulnerable to A scaring off his potential customers by threats of violence or preventing his suppliers from making deliveries by damaging their vehicles. A, of course, is likely to owe a duty *to the potential customers* not to act violently towards them and a duty *to the suppliers* not to damage their vehicles. But the tort of *causing loss by unlawful means* implies the existence of a further duty, owed *to B*, not to use such unlawful means in order to cause loss to him.

So, for example, if *Driver* runs down *Striker*, a professional footballer, with the intention of causing economic loss to *Club*, which employs *Striker*, then *Club* will be able to make a claim against *Driver* on the basis that *Driver*, in acting as she did, committed the tort of causing loss by unlawful means in relation to *Club*. Such a claim will be supplementary to *Striker*'s claim for the wrong done *to him* when *Driver* ran him down. Moreover, such a claim is permitted even though *Club* could *not* claim for its losses if all that happened was that *Driver negligently* ran down *Striker*. It is a crucial feature of the tort that *Driver* must have acted as she did with the *intention* of causing loss to *Club*.

In *OBG*, Lord Hoffmann distinguished between situations where A uses unlawful means to *interfere with the freedom* of a third party to deal with B and situations where A uses unlawful means to *reduce the value* to B of his relationship with a third party.[106] For instance, in the case of *RCA Corp* v *Pollard* (1983), the claimant had the exclusive right

---

[105] *OBG*, at [61].

[106] *OBG*, at [51], 'Unlawful means therefore consists of acts intended to cause loss to the claimant by interfering with the freedom of a third party in a way which is unlawful as against that third party and which is intended to cause loss to the claimant. It does not in my opinion include acts which may be unlawful against a third party but which do not affect his freedom to deal with the claimant.' It must be noted, however, that earlier in his speech, at [47], Lord Hoffmann described the 'essence of the tort' as 'interference *with the actions of a third party* in which the claimant has an economic interest' (emphasis added), and it may be possible to alter someone's actions without reducing their freedom.

to exploit records made by Elvis Presley and the defendant sold 'bootleg' recordings made at concerts without the consent of Elvis. Lord Hoffmann stated that, assuming that this behaviour amounted to 'unlawful means',[107] and *even if* the defendant had used such means with the intention of causing loss to the claimant,[108] he would still *not* have committed the tort of causing loss by unlawful means in relation to the claimant. This is because the defendant's conduct did not interfere with the ability of Elvis's estate to perform its contract with the claimant.[109]

What forms of conduct will 'interfere with the freedom' of a third party? The examples discussed by Lord Hoffmann in the *OBG* case suggest that the list includes:

1. Making it *impossible* for a third party to behave in a particular way towards B, including preventing a third party from performing a contract with B;

2. *Threatening* a third party to persuade him to behave in a particular way towards B; and

3. *Misleading* a third party to lead him to behave in a particular way towards B.

In situations (2) and (3), the threat or misleading statement can be used *either* to cause a third party to refrain from dealing with B *or* to take some *positive steps* which will cause loss to B. It is unclear whether the list should also include:

4. Making it *less attractive* for a third party to behave in some way towards B which would be advantageous to B, with the result that the third party chooses not to act in that way; and

5. Making it *more attractive* for a third party to behave in some way towards B which would be disadvantageous to B, with the result that the third party chooses to act in that way.

Arguably, using unlawful means to *steer* a third party's behaviour should be covered because it is sufficiently similar to using a misleading statement or a threat of unlawful conduct to do so. Thus it is arguable that (4) and (5) should also be treated as situations which may involve *interference* with the freedom of a third party. But in *British Airways* v *Emerald Supplies* (2015) the Court of Appeal cast some doubt on this. In this case, to simplify, the defendant airline was alleged to have used unlawful means to increase the price that it could charge to freight-forwarders, with the effect that freight-forwarders charged higher prices to the claimants, who were shippers of freight. The outcome of the case turned on other issues, but the Court of Appeal commented: 'We are very doubtful whether action which simply increases the price at which freight services can be acquired by the claimants can be said to affect the freedom of freight forwarders to deal with the shippers.'[110] We have fewer doubts: if a defendant threatened a third party in order to force it to raise the price that it charged a claimant, we think it would be fair to hold that the defendant had interfered with the freedom of the third party to deal with the claimant.

---

[107] The behaviour was clearly criminal and might have also amounted to the tort of breach of statutory duty in relation to Elvis Presley: see *Lonrho Ltd* v *Shell Petroleum Co Ltd (No 2)* [1982] AC 173, at 187 (per Lord Diplock).

[108] Carty 2010 argues (at 97–8) that the requirement of 'interference with a third party's freedom' would have been unnecessary if the House of Lords in *OBG* had insisted that the tort required 'targeted harm'. But this would mean that a bootlegger that had the primary goal of damaging a record company's profits would be liable to the record company.

[109] *OBG*, at [53]. In *Secretary of State for Health* v *Servier Laboratories Ltd* [2017] EWHC 2006 (Ch), Roth J struck out a claim of causing loss by unlawful means because the alleged means – deceiving the European Patent Office and the High Court – did not interfere with the liberty of those bodies to deal with the claimants.

[110] [2015] EWCA Civ 1024, at [129].

One curious consequence of the requirement for A's use of unlawful means to interfere with the freedom of a third party to deal with B is that in certain circumstances A may be liable to B for *threatening to do x* to C, even though he would *not* have been liable if he had *actually done x* to C. For instance, suppose *Publisher* has the contractual right to publish a book that *Author* is about to complete. If *Jealous* defames *Author* by calling him a 'Nazi sympathiser', with the result that the contractual right to publish *Author*'s book is rendered valueless (as no one is likely to buy a copy until *Author* clears his name), *Publisher* will be unable to sue *Jealous* even if *Jealous*'s intention when he defamed *Author* was to cause loss to *Publisher*. This is because *Jealous*'s defamatory words will not have interfered with *Author*'s liberty to deal with *Publisher*. By contrast, if *Jealous threatens Author* that he will defame him unless *Author* terminates his relationship with *Publisher*, then if *Author* gives in to this threat, *Publisher* will be able to sue *Jealous*, at least if *Jealous*'s intention when he threatened *Author* was to cause loss to *Publisher*.

C. Intention to cause loss

B will only be able to base a claim on A's use of unlawful means to interfere with a third party's freedom to deal with him if A acted in the way he did with the intention of causing loss to B. So we must ask what state of mind will count as 'intention' in this context.

The simple answer to this is that A will have intended to cause loss to B if he aimed to cause B loss, either as an end in itself or as a means of achieving some other end. But A will not be held to have intended to cause loss to B if such loss was merely a unaimed-for side effect of A's actions, albeit one that he knew was very likely to occur. There are four points of detail that we must clarify.

(1) *Undesired losses.* If causing loss to B was either A's end or the means by which he was seeking to achieve that end then A *will* have intended to cause loss to B *even if* A would have preferred not to have been put in a position where he had to pursue such an end or would have preferred not to have had to resort to such means to achieve his end.[111] For instance, the defendants in the case of *Rookes* v *Barnard* (1964) used unlawful means – a threat to commit a breach of contract – to persuade BOAC to dismiss the claimant, Rookes. The defendants might have preferred Rookes to have resigned his post voluntarily so that they did not have to persuade his employer to dismiss him – indeed, they might have preferred to avoid the dispute that led to them targeting Rookes – but such preferences would not negate the fact that when they threatened BOAC they intended to cause loss to Rookes.

(2) *The other side of the coin.* A defendant will be held to have aimed to cause a claimant loss if the claimant's suffering a loss was 'simply the other side of the same coin' as the defendant's achieving his aim, and the defendant knew that this was the case.[112] For instance, if *Chancer* threatens to break *Owner*'s legs unless *Owner* burns a particular photograph, and *Chancer* knows that *Owner* was about to donate this photograph to *Gallery*, then *Chancer* cannot simultaneously maintain that he intended to have the photograph destroyed but also did not intend to prevent *Gallery* from obtaining it. The courts will find that it was part of *Chancer*'s aim to prevent *Gallery* from obtaining the photograph, as *Gallery*'s being prevented from obtaining it was – as *Chancer* knew – the inevitable flipside of his achieving his aim of having it destroyed.

---

[111] *OBG*, at [165] (per Lord Nicholls).
[112] *OBG*, at [134] (per Lord Hoffmann), [167] (per Lord Nicholls). Carty (2010), 82–4, criticises this aspect of the decision.

In *Douglas* v *Hello! (No 3)* (2008), one of the appeals heard by the House of Lords alongside *OBG*, the defendants and claimants were respectively the publishers of two rival celebrity magazines, *Hello!* and *OK!* The claim resulted from the defendants' publishing unofficial photographs of the wedding of Michael Douglas and Catherine Zeta-Jones in *Hello!* shortly before the claimants were due to publish official photographs in *OK!* The trial judge found that the defendants had not intended to cause loss to the claimants on the basis of evidence from the controlling shareholder of *Hello!*'s Spanish holding company that his intention was only to avoid a loss of sales for *Hello!* and not to reduce sales of *OK!* But Lord Hoffmann identified this as a situation where the loss to *OK!* was necessarily intended because it was simply the flipside of the preserved sales of *Hello!*, presumably because a substantial proportion of the preserved sales would be to purchasers who would otherwise have bought *OK!* instead.[113]

Lord Hoffmann distinguished this situation from one where a customer suffered loss as a result of action directed against its supplier.[114] If, for instance, *Saboteur* used unlawful means to prevent *Airline* from operating its flights, with the intention of causing loss to *Airline*, although *Saboteur* would probably know that some passengers would suffer loss as a result of his activities he would *not* be held to have intended to cause passengers to suffer such losses because he could achieve his aim – causing loss to *Airline* – even if all passengers unexpectedly reached their destinations on time. In such a case any loss suffered by passengers would *not* be the inevitable flipside of the defendant's achieving his aims. The situation would, of course, be different if one of the defendant's objectives was to inflict loss on the passengers *in order to* prompt them to put pressure on *Airline*.

In *WH Newson Holding Ltd* v *IMI plc* (2013) the Court of Appeal had to confront a situation where, to simplify somewhat,[115] the defendants, who supplied copper tubes, *intended* to make a gain by acting unlawfully in a way which would maintain prices above the competitive level, but did not care whether the claimant, an *initial* purchaser of such tubes, suffered a corresponding loss (by paying too much), or whether the *initial* purchaser would succeed in passing the extra cost down a chain to a *subsequent* purchaser. The court held that in such a case it could not be said that the defendants necessarily intended to cause loss to the *initial* purchaser. One way of generalising the decision in the case may be to say that where a defendant knows that *someone* will lose as the inevitable flipside of him achieving his goal (making a gain), but does not know or care who, from

---

[113] *OBG*, at [134]. Suppose that a substantial number of readers usually buy only one magazine or the other, and that the defendants knew that. The defendants might say that they *could* achieve their aim – maintain sales of their own magazine – *without* reducing sales of the claimant's magazine, provided that more readers than usual bought *both* magazines. But it is hard to believe that the defendants really intended to preserve their sales only by persuading *more* readers to buy two magazines; surely they intended to persuade some readers not to switch to their rival's publication.

[114] *OBG*, at [64]. Lord Hoffmann cited, *Barretts & Baird (Wholesale) Ltd* v *Institution of Professional Civil Servants* [1987] IRLR 3, and said of it: 'I think Henry J was right . . . when he decided a strike by civil servants in the Ministry of Agriculture in support of a pay claim was not intended to cause damage to an abattoir which was unable to obtain the certificates necessary for exporting meat and claiming subsidies. The damage to the abattoir was neither the purpose of the strike nor the means of achieving that purpose, which was to put pressure on the government.'

[115] The simplification is necessary because the precise point in the case was whether an intention to harm the claimants could be inferred from the finding of the European Commission that the defendants 'had entered into a cartel in order to distort competition and thereby to promote their own interests'.

within a substantial and diverse class, then it will not be possible to say that the defendant *intended* to cause a loss to the person who ends up suffering it.[116]

(3) *No need for an intent to cause the type of loss suffered by the claimant.* In *OBG*, Lord Hoffmann repeatedly stated that what is required is an intention to cause loss to the claimant rather than an intention to cause the particular type of loss which the claimant ends up suffering. This might be significant if, for instance, *Rival* made threats of violence against *Trader's* potential customers with the intention of persuading them not to trade with *Trader*, but *Trader* avoided this type of loss either by paying for additional security for his potential customers. It would be unsatisfactory if *Rival* could avoid liability by objecting that the type of loss which *Trader* suffered was different from the type that he intended to cause.

(4) *Breach of contract cases.* The state of mind that the tort of causing loss by unlawful means requires – an intention to cause loss to B – is different from the state of mind required in order to establish the tort of inducing a breach of contract. We saw above that to show that a defendant has committed the tort of inducing a breach of contract it is necessary to show that he intended *to induce a breach of contract*, and a defendant will not avoid liability by demonstrating that he honestly expected the breach to cause no loss.[117] The distinction is potentially significant because where a defendant causes loss to a claimant by persuading a third party to break a contract with the claimant he may commit a tort if he intended *to induce a breach of contract*, while if a defendant causes loss to a claimant by preventing a third party from performing a contract with the claimant, he will only commit a tort if he *intended to cause loss* to the claimant.

20.5 Two-party cases

We have seen that in the *OBG* case the House of Lords defined the tort of causing loss by unlawful means so that A could only commit it in relation to B if he interfered with C's freedom to deal with B. In other words, the tort was defined so as to cover only situations involving *three* parties.

It might be thought that there is no need for a similar tort in situations involving only *two* parties. Why? Because the tort requires unlawful means, and, this usually requires a 'civil wrong' – a tort or a breach of contract, so in situations involving only two parties the claimant might be expected simply to sue for this 'civil wrong'.[118] But

---

[116] See also *British Airways* v *Emerald Supplies* [2015] EWCA Civ 1024 where the Court of Appeal stated, at [152], that it was bound by the discussion of intention in *Newson* and 'we respectfully agree with it'. The position will, of course, be different if the defendant knows who will necessarily suffer the loss by *description*, for example 'whoever owns *this* business': the fact that the defendant does not know the person's *name* will not prevent a finding that the defendant intended to cause the person loss.

[117] See above, § 20.2(C)(4).

[118] Could a claimant obtain a greater measure of damages by framing his claim as one for a two-party version of the tort of causing loss by unlawful means rather than simply relying on the 'civil wrong'? For instance, if B could show that A intentionally caused loss to him by breaching a contract with him then perhaps he could obtain a greater measure of damages than would usually be awarded for a breach of contract, since, for example, exemplary damages are not available for a breach of contract but are available for an intentional tort. It must be doubtful, however, whether the courts would be willing to establish a two-party version of the tort simply in order to allow a claimant to circumvent the rule that exemplary damages are not available for breach of contract. In an attempt to avoid such a consequence, Carty 2010 argues (at 118–19) that an actual breach of contract should only constitute 'unlawful means' in a case involving *three* parties, while Sales & Stilitz 1999 argue (at 424) that in a *two* party case, a threat to break a contract should constitute 'unlawful means' but an actual breach of contract should not.

we have also seen that a defendant will be held to have used unlawful means if he has *threatened* to commit a 'civil wrong', but has not had to do so because the person threatened *submits*. This means that there is at least one situation involving *two* parties where the claimant cannot simply sue for a 'civil wrong': where A threatens B that he will commit a civil wrong in relation to B unless B acts in some way that will cause him loss, and A makes his threat with the intention of causing B to suffer loss. Would A commit a tort in relation to B in this situation if B submitted to the threat and acted in such a way as to cause himself some loss?

There is good evidence that such a tort of *two-party intimidation* exists. The Court of Appeal recognised its existence in *Godwin* v *Uzoigwe* (1993) and awarded £20,000 to a teenager who had been coerced into working without pay for two and a half years by the defendant's violence and mistreatment. It was also recognised by Lord Devlin in *Rookes* v *Barnard* (1964): 'an action will doubtless lie at the suit of a trader who has been compelled to discontinue his business by means of threats of personal violence made against him by the defendant with that intention'.[119] And although in the *OBG* case Lord Hoffmann defined the tort of causing loss by unlawful means so that it required three parties, he expressly stated that he was not discussing 'the question of whether a claimant who has been compelled by unlawful intimidation to act to his own detriment, can sue for his loss'.[120]

One reason why Lord Hoffmann did not simply *confirm* the existence of the tort may have been the uncertainty which surrounds some elements of it. Three factors, cumulatively, suggest that a two-party tort might not comprise elements precisely parallel to those found in the three-party tort.

First, threats are often made in two-party situations where there is a genuine dispute. For example, if A threatens to breach a contract with B unless B pays him a sum of money which is not due, it may be the case that A *honestly believes* that all he is threatening is to exercise his right to refuse to perform until he receives a sum that he is owed. If B pays the sum in this situation, then the law may have an interest in treating the payment as the settlement of a dispute rather than completion of a tort.

Secondly, and relatedly, where B makes a contract with A after a threat, or pays money to A after a threat, the doctrines of duress and economic duress determine whether A can enforce that contract, or will have to repay the money. Clearly it would be unsatisfactory if when these doctrines provide that a contract is enforceable, or money can be retained, tort law could insist that B should be compensated by A for the loss caused by the threat.[121]

Thirdly, in a two-party situation B may have an opportunity to refuse to submit, and to see if he can force A to withdraw the threat, whilst in a three-party situation C's response is out of B's hands. Thus a tort of two-party intimidation should *perhaps* be defined so as to require a claimant not to submit too readily, so as to avoid insignificant threats becoming actionable.

---

[119] [1964] AC 1129, 1205. Lord Devlin was quoting, with approval, from the contemporary edition of *Salmond on The Law of Torts*.

[120] *OBG*, at [61].

[121] In *Dawson* v *Bell* [2016] EWCA Civ 96, at [32], the Court of Appeal accepted that where the effect of pressure on a party was insufficient to substantiate a claim of economic duress, it could not amount to the tort of two-party intimidation.

20.6 Lawful means conspiracy

In the mid-1880s, a group of shippers entered into an association in order to try to squeeze rival shippers out of the China tea shipping market. They offered discounts on freight charges to shipping agents who only ever used ships owned by association members, and agreed between themselves that if a non-association ship tried to find a cargo of tea, they would immediately send association ships to the same port to offer to carry the cargo at a cheaper freight rate, even if they had to carry it at a loss. The defendants in the action were members of this association.

The claimants owned ships which had previously taken part in the China tea trade, and indeed had been part of the association in previous years, but had been excluded in 1885 because they only sent their ships to China for the three-week tea season when shipping was most profitable while the other association members operated shipping links all year round. Despite being excluded, the claimants sent their ships to China to load tea during the 1885 season. The association responded by sending ships to undercut their rates, and the claimants were forced to reduce their rates so far that they made a loss in order to get any cargo at all.

The claimants then sued, but the House of Lords held in *Mogul Steamship Co Ltd* v *McGregor, Gow & Co* (1892) that the defendants had not committed a tort in relation to the claimants. Lord Watson explained that although the defendants had agreed to band together and pursue the course of action which caused loss to the claimants

> If neither the end contemplated by the agreement [between members of the association], nor the means used for its attainment were contrary to law, the loss suffered by the [claimants] was *damnum sine injuria*.[122]

This sentence reflects the fact that there are *two* forms of tort involving a conspiracy. One form depends on the *end* contemplated by the agreement being unlawful; the other form depends on the *means* used to attain the end being contrary to law. The claimants lost in the *Mogul* case because they could not establish that the defendants had committed either form of conspiracy tort.

Although the claimants *alleged* that the defendants had used unlawful means against them, they failed to substantiate this: they failed to prove that unlawful threats were made, and although the contract which held the association together might have been unenforceable, the *making of* such an agreement was not, at that time, unlawful. With regard to the 'end contemplated', Lord Watson dismissed the suggestion that this had been unlawful:

> There is nothing in the evidence to suggest that the parties to the agreement had any other object in view than that of defending their carrying trade during the tea season against the encroachments of the [claimants] and other competitors, and of attracting to themselves custom which might otherwise have been carried off by these competitors. That is an object which is strenuously pursued by merchants great and small in every branch of commerce; and it is, in the eye of the law, perfectly legitimate.[123]

The argument that the object of the conspiracy in *Mogul* was lawful because the defendants in *Mogul* were seeking to promote their business interests proved to have momentous consequences. In later cases, it was held that where the *predominant purpose* of a conspiracy was *not* to promote the conspirators' business interests, but was simply to hurt the claimant, then the conspiracy would have an unlawful object and would be actionable.

---

[122] [1892] AC 25, 42. '*Damnun sine injuria*' means 'damage which it is not a legal wrong to inflict'.
[123] Ibid.

So *Mogul* contemplated the existence of two forms of actionable conspiracy: the first sort of conspiracy, where the *illegitimacy of the end* of the conspiracy was pivotal, became known as *lawful means conspiracy*,[124] the second, where the *unlawfulness of the means* was pivotal, as *unlawful means conspiracy*. We will discuss *lawful means conspiracy* first.

A. Definition

A defendant will commit the tort of *lawful* means conspiracy in relation to a claimant where:

1. someone intentionally harmed the claimant; and

2. in so doing, they were acting in pursuance of a plan that had been agreed upon by the defendant and one or more other people; and

3. the parties to that agreement had no good reason for seeking to harm the claimant.

Below we will discuss these three elements in turn, and then consider some criticisms that have been raised against this tort.

B. Intention to harm

We discussed when a defendant would be found to have intended to cause loss to a claimant in detail when we were describing the tort of causing loss by unlawful means. Consequently, here we will simply state that A will have intended to cause harm to B if he aimed to cause B harm, either as an end in itself or as a means of achieving some other end. But A will not be held to have intended to cause harm to B if such harm was merely an unaimed-for side effect of A's actions, albeit one that he knew was very likely to occur. Anyone who wants a more detailed account should refer back to section 20.4(C).

C. Agreement

There can be no conspiracy unless there was an agreement to harm the claimant which was subsequently carried out. So, if *Boss* takes against *Enemy* and orders his employees to spend their days ringing up *Enemy*'s customers and attempting to talk them out of doing further business with *Enemy*, *Boss* cannot be said to have committed the tort of *lawful means conspiracy* as he has not reached an *agreement* with his employees that they will try to harm *Enemy*.[125]

D. Absence of good reason

The illegitimacy of the end – the goal – of the conspiracy is the most important element in the tort of *lawful means* conspiracy.

---

[124] Lord Walker referred to this tort as 'unlawful object' conspiracy in *Total Network* [2008] 1 AC 1174, at [66] and [73]. Sales LJ has suggested that it might be more accurate to refer to it as 'conspiracy to injure by non-unlawful means': *JSC BTA Bank* v *Ablyazov (No 14)* [2017] EWCA Civ 40, at [8].

[125] See *Crofter Hand Woven Harris Tweed Co* v *Veitch* [1942] AC 435, 468 (per Lord Wright). On the other hand, see Viscount Simon LC, at 441: 'It was argued that the [defendant] Mackenzie should not be regarded as acting in combination with the [defendant] Veitch, so as to establish the element of agreement between them in the tort of conspiracy, because Veitch held the responsible position of Scottish area secretary to the union, whereas Mackenzie was only branch secretary for Stornoway. This, I think, is an unsound contention. The respective position of the two men in the hierarchy of trade union officials has nothing to do with it. *Even if Mackenzie could be regarded as only obeying orders from his superior, the combination would still exist if he appreciated what he was about*' (emphasis added).

Most modern cases have adopted the language of Viscount Simon LC in *Crofter Hand Woven Harris Tweed Co* v *Veitch* (1941) and proclaim that liability depends on whether the conspirators' 'predominant purpose' was 'to damage another person' (tortious) or 'the lawful protection or promotion of any lawful interest of the combiners [*ie* conspirators]' (not tortious).[126] But when conspirators have set out to harm a claimant as a way of achieving some further end it is difficult to answer the question 'which of their goals was *predominant?*' If the intended harm was the means they planned to use to achieve their intended end, then how could one be *predominant* over the other? If the courts always concluded in such case that the defendants could not be liable, because the intention to cause harm to the claimant simply could not be 'predominant', then the 'predominant purpose' test might be tolerable. But, in fact, courts tend to discount goals that they regard as *illegitimate* when deciding which goal was 'predominant', and this is why we claim that the question that liability *actually* turns on is whether the conspirators had a *good reason* for harming the claimant.

Support for our position can be found later in Viscount Simon LC's speech in *Crofter*. In this case, the defendants were trade union officials, who had instructed dockers (union members) not to handle yarn that was being imported onto the island of Lewis for weaving into tweed, or cloth that had been woven from imported yarn. The union's goal was to improve the economic position of the spinning mills that produced yarn on the island, since these mills employed mainly union members, and improving their economic position would secure better wages for their employees. But in order to achieve this goal the defendants were intentionally harming the economic position of the claimants, whose businesses involved importing yarn and selling tweed woven from it. Viscount Simon LC concluded: 'The result [the defendants] aimed at achieving was to create a better basis for collective bargaining, and thus directly to improve wage prospects. A combination with such an object is not unlawful, because the object is the legitimate promotion of the interests of the combiners.'[127] But Viscount Simon LC also stated that the defendants would not have been able to avoid liability if they had agreed to damage the claimants' businesses in order to gain a large donation to union funds from the spinning mill owners.[128] Our claim is that it makes no sense to say that the gain for union members was 'predominant' in the actual case, but that harm to the claimants would have been 'predominant' *if* the union had been seeking a donation instead: the real difference between the two appears to be that an offer of payment is not a good enough – *legitimate* – reason for setting out to harm someone.[129]

---

[126] [1942] AC 435, 445. Viscount Simon LC's 'predominant purpose' test was cited as orthodox by Lord Scott, at [56], and Lord Walker at [74] and [76], in *Revenue & Customs Commissioners* v *Total Network SL* [2008] 1 AC 1174. See also *Lonrho plc* v *Fayed* [1992] 1 AC 448, 465 (per Lord Bridge of Harwich).

[127] [1942] AC 435, 447.

[128] Ibid, 446.

[129] Regrettably, some courts have not noticed that the 'predominant purpose' test requires an evaluation of the conspirators' reasons for harming a claimant: for example, in *JSC BTA Bank* v *Ablyazov (No 14)* [2017] EWCA Civ 40, Sales LJ stated that lawful means conspiracy was unavailable against participants in an (alleged) conspiracy to thwart attempts to recover money stolen from the claimants, because the defendants' goal of retaining the money for themselves was inconsistent with them having the predominant purpose of causing loss to the claimants. Lord Neuberger identified the same difficulty in *Revenue & Customs Commissioners* v *Total Network SL* [2008] 1 AC 1174, where the conspirators had defrauded the claimant, and their intention to gain looked as if it might be inconsistent with them having a predominant purpose of harming the claimant: his suggested solution, at [228], that the intention to harm the claimant was simply the 'obverse' of the conspirators' intention to gain, and thus harm to the claimant *was* the conspirators' *predominant* purpose, might ensure an appropriate outcome, but at the price of a contortion of language.

What reasons *are* good enough? *Crofter* holds that improving the 'wage prospects' of union members is a good enough reason for union officials to agree to act so as to harm a claimant, and the *Mogul* case (1892) makes it clear that protecting your own business interests is an acceptable reason for intentionally harming someone else.[130] On the other side of the line, in the foundational case of *Quinn v Leathem* (1901) union officials were held liable for having damaged the claimant's business (by persuading his best customer to stop dealing with him), where they wanted the claimant to employ only union members, but would not let him pay for his current employees to join: their purpose was to punish the claimant, and not to advance the legitimate interests of the union.[131]

If, on a moral scale, intentionally harming someone for vindictive or malicious reasons is at one end, and intentionally harming someone to advance competitive industrial or business interests is somewhere in the middle, intentionally harming someone for altruistic reasons would be at the other end of the scale. Thus it comes as no surprise that in *Scala Ballroom (Wolverhampton) Ltd v Ratcliffe* (1958) the Court of Appeal held that acting in accordance with an agreement to harm someone using lawful means that was entered into for altruistic reasons did not amount to the tort of lawful means conspiracy. In this case the claimants were proprietors of a ballroom and operated what was called a 'colour bar', a rule that excluded people who were not white from the dance floor. At the same time, they allowed black musicians to play in the orchestra. The defendants were officials of the Musicians' Union. They attempted to bring the claimants' discriminatory practices to an end by warning the claimants that members of the Musicians' Union would not be allowed to play at the claimants' ballroom while the policy of racial discrimination continued. The Court of Appeal held that the defendants had committed no tort in so acting.

What is the position if the defendant and his co-conspirators had different reasons for seeking to harm the claimant? The law seems to say that if the defendant had a good reason for seeking to harm the claimant, he will still have committed the tort of lawful means conspiracy if he *knew* his co-conspirators did not have a good reason.[132] If the defendant had a bad reason for seeking to harm the claimant, there will be no actionable conspiracy for him to join if all his co-conspirators had a good reason, unless at least one of his co-conspirators knew that the defendant had a bad reason.

E. Criticisms

Two criticisms are commonly made of the tort of lawful means conspiracy.

The first is that the existence of this tort cannot stand beside the decision of the House of Lords in *Allen v Flood* (1898). As Lord Diplock observed in *Lonrho Ltd v Shell Petroleum (No 2)*, 'Why should an act which causes economic loss to A but is not actionable at his

---

[130] See also *Sorrell v Smith* [1925] AC 700 (union of retail newsagents attempt to limit the competition in their area by agreeing not to deal with any wholesaler who supplies newspapers to an 'unauthorised' newsagent; no lawful means conspiracy committed when the members of the union switched their trade away from the claimant wholesaler, who had supplied an 'unauthorised' newsagent).

[131] This was the explanation of the case provided by Lord Walker in *Total Network* [2008] 1 AC 1174, at [73]. See also *Huntley v Thornton* [1957] 1 WLR 321 (tort of lawful means conspiracy committed against a fitter and turner who had broken a strike for one day only and subsequently found he could not obtain work anywhere due to lawful threats that the union had made to prospective employers).

[132] *Crofter Hand Woven Harris Tweed Co Ltd v Veitch* [1942] AC 435, 495 (per Lord Porter). See also *Huntley v Thornton* [1957] 1 WLR 321 (two union officials committed no tort in helping other union officials prevent the claimant getting work as they had no idea the other union officials were doing this out of petty vindictiveness).

suit if done by B alone become actionable because B did it pursuant to an agreement between B and C?'[133]

The second is that the existence of this tort plunges the courts into all the difficulties regarding ascertaining people's motives for acting, then evaluating their reasons, that the decision of the House of Lords in *Allen* v *Flood* helped the courts avoid in cases where a single defendant, acting alone, intentionally causes harm to a claimant. For example, in *Quinn v Leathem* (1901), it must have been very difficult to determine why the defendants victimised the claimant. On the one hand, it was argued that they acted as they did because they were outraged at the way the claimant had stood up to them and they wanted to teach him a lesson. On the other hand, it could just as well have been argued that the defendants had sought to harm the claimant in order to promote the interests of their trade union, by making it clear to everyone that anyone who failed to go along with their demands would incur severe sanctions.

Both of these criticisms seem to us to be convincing, but there is no realistic possibility of the tort of lawful means conspiracy disappearing from our law.[134] In the *Total Network* case, the House of Lords expressed itself very content with the existence of lawful means conspiracy as a tort, with Lord Scott arguing that it was an example of a situation where 'the conduct of the authors of the harm had been sufficiently reprehensible to require the conclusion that they ought to be held responsible for the harm'[135] and Lord Walker arguing that the law is acting in a 'principled' way in holding people liable where their 'object is simply to do harm, and not to exercise [their] own just rights.'[136] And, as we will now see, in *Total Network* the existence of the lawful means conspiracy tort was allowed to have a big effect on the definition of when someone would commit the tort of unlawful means conspiracy.

20.7 Unlawful means conspiracy

A defendant will commit the tort of *unlawful* means conspiracy in relation to a claimant where:

1. someone intentionally harmed the claimant using unlawful means to do so; *and*

2. in so doing, they were acting in pursuance of a plan that had been agreed upon by the defendant and one or more other people.

The main differences between this tort and the lawful means conspiracy tort are that for this tort: (a) it has to be shown that the claimant was harmed using unlawful means, and (b) this was part of the conspirators' plan, and (c) it does *not* have to be shown that the conspirators had no good reason for harming the claimant.

We do not need to say anything more about the third of these differences, but below we will discuss the first two in turn.

---

[133] [1982] AC 173, 188.

[134] In *Lonrho Ltd* v *Shell Petroleum (No 2)* [1982] AC 173, 188–9, Lord Diplock stated that the tort 'must I think be accepted by this House as too well-established to be discarded however anomalous it may seem today' but 'unhesitatingly' chose to confine it to the 'narrow limits that are all that common sense and the application of the legal logic of the decided cases require'.

[135] *Total Network*, at [56].

[136] *Total Network*, at [77], quoting Bowen LJ in *Mogul Steamship Co Ltd* v *McGregor, Gow & Co* (1888) 23 QBD 598, at 616.

A. Unlawful means

The most controversial issue in relation to unlawful means conspiracy has been what counts as 'unlawful means'. In *Powell* v *Boladz* (1998), Stuart-Smith LJ held that the 'unlawful means' had to be an actionable wrong, such as a tort, in relation to the claimant.[137] But in *Total Network*, the House of Lords said that this was wrong.

Total Network concerned what is known as a 'carousel fraud' against the UK tax authorities. Such a fraud involves those behind the scheme creating a situation where one company is obliged to pay the taxman VAT that it has charged and a second company is entitled to a rebate of VAT that it has (notionally) paid; if the second company cashes in its rebate and the first 'disappears' without paying what it owes, then those behind the scheme will have made a gain at the taxman's expense.[138]

The claimant in *Total Network* was the Revenue & Customs Commissioners, who had lost almost £2m as a result of 13 such 'carousel frauds' involving mobile phones. The defendant was one of the parties to the fraud – a Spanish company from whom the mobile phones had been bought. Lawful means conspiracy was not pleaded.[139] Instead, the claimant based its case on unlawful means conspiracy, and alleged that the unlawful means by which the claimant had been harmed was a common law crime – cheating the Revenue. Thus the courts had to decide whether that crime amounted to 'unlawful means' for the purpose of the tort of unlawful means conspiracy. Two arguments were made for why it did not.

(1) *Unlawful means conspiracy as accessory liability.* The first argument was that unlawful means conspiracy gives effect to a form of accessory liability, where A is held liable for a wrong committed by B in relation to C because A agreed with B that B should commit that wrong to C. If this view of unlawful means conspiracy were correct, then if B had not in fact done any civil wrong to C, but had instead caused loss to C by committing some crime, there would have been no basis for making A liable as an accessory – B would have done no primary civil wrong to C to which A could be an accessory. The House of Lords firmly rejected this view – the *secondary liability view* – of unlawful means conspiracy as 'unsustainable'.[140]

The main problem[141] with the *secondary liability view* is that in a case of *conspiracy to commit a tort against C*, where A and B agree that B should intentionally cause loss to C by committing a simple tort in relation to C, such as battery or deceit, the *secondary liability view* renders the tort of unlawful means conspiracy completely redundant. In such a case, if you want to make A liable for C's loss you can simply do so on the basis that A is an accessory to B's tort.[142] The House of Lords thought that there would have been no point in the

---

[137] [1998] Lloyd's Rep Med 116, 126. The same conclusion was reached by Laddie J at first instance in *Michaels* v *Taylor Woodrow Developments Ltd* [2001] Ch 493.

[138] The carousel frauds in *Total Network* exploited rules that provide that VAT is not chargeable on imports into the UK from other EU countries, or on exports from the UK into other EU countries, but is chargeable on sales between companies in the UK: a common scheme involves an import of high value goods, one of more sales of these within the UK, then their export, with the goods ending up where they started (hence the label 'carousel').

[139] See above, n 128.

[140] *Total Network*, at [103] (per Lord Walker). Also [123] (per Lord Mance) and [225] (per Lord Neuberger).

[141] We also set out a second problem below, § 30.2.

[142] Accessory liability is discussed below, Chapter 30.

law recognising a tort of unlawful means conspiracy if it only helped claimants who could already obtain the same remedies using the rules about accessory liability for torts.

(2) *The argument from* OBG *v* Allan *(2008)*. The second argument was that only a few months before, in *OBG* (2008), the House of Lords had held that for the purposes of the tort of causing loss by unlawful means, 'unlawful means' meant an actionable wrong (or one that would have been actionable had the victim suffered some loss as a result). It was argued that for the sake of consistency, the same test for 'unlawful means' should apply in unlawful means conspiracy cases.

The House of Lords had two reasons for rejecting this argument. Their first reason was that *OBG* was distinguishable because Lord Hoffmann's opinion as to what can amount to 'unlawful means' for the purpose of the tort of causing loss by unlawful means might not have been intended to apply in *two-party cases*, that is cases where a defendant intentionally caused a claimant harm directly rather than by interfering with a third party's freedom to deal with the claimant.[143] (*Total Network* was in this sense a *two-party case*, since the conspirators defrauded the claimant directly, without the intervention or manipulation of any intermediary.[144])

The second reason was provided by the existence of the tort of lawful means conspiracy. Lord Neuberger expressed it very well:

> a claim based on conspiracy to injure can be established even where no unlawful means, let alone any other actionable tort, is involved . . . [G]iven the existence of that tort, it would be anomalous if an unlawful means conspiracy could not found a cause of action where, as here, the means 'merely' involved a crime, where the loss to the claimant was the obvious and inevitable, indeed in many ways the intended, result of the sole purpose of the conspiracy, and where the crime involved, cheating the revenue, has as its purpose the protection of the victim of the conspiracy.[145]

Lord Hope and Lord Scott expressed similar views.[146] To paraphrase, the House of Lords treated the tort of *lawful means conspiracy* as demonstrating that combining together for the purpose of harming a claimant is behaviour that is *almost* tortious, but requires an additional element to make it wrongful: that additional element could be an absence of good reason (for *lawful means conspiracy*) or the use of unlawful means (for *unlawful means conspiracy*). In the latter case, however, *crimes*, being more obviously unlawful than *torts* or *breaches of contract*, should be treated as a sufficient additional element.

Is any crime sufficient? In the passage from Lord Neuberger's speech that we quoted in the previous paragraph he referred to the crime having as its purpose the protection of

---

[143] See *Total Network*, at [43] (per Lord Hope), [99] (per Lord Walker), [124] (per Lord Mance), [223] (per Lord Neuberger).

[144] This basis for distinguishing *OBG* may prove significant if a case ever arises where conspirators agree to cause harm to claimant by using unlawful means against that claimant's customers, suppliers or employees, since such a case will involve a conspiracy that operates through an effect on the liberty of third parties to deal with the claimant.

[145] *Total Network*, at [221]. Lord Neuberger uses the label 'conspiracy to injure' for the tort we refer to as 'lawful means conspiracy'.

[146] *Total Network*, at [44] (per Lord Hope: 'If . . . it is in the fact of the conspiracy that the unlawfulness resides, why should that principle not apply here? As a subspecies of the tort of unlawful means conspiracy, the case is virtually indistinguishable from the tort of conspiracy to injure') and at [56] (Lord Scott).

the victim of the conspiracy. Lord Mance's speech suggested that this might be a requirement before a crime could count as 'unlawful means'.[147] But most of the judges in the
House of Lords did not express opinions supporting this, and in *Digicel (St Lucia) Ltd* v
Cable & Wireless plc (2010) Morgan J said that he inclined to the view that *all crimes*
should be sufficient.[148]

What might count as 'unlawful means' other than crimes and civil wrongs? In *JSC
BTA Bank* v *Ablyazov (No 14)* (2017), the Court of Appeal considered whether breach of
a court order, amounting to contempt of court, could count as 'unlawful means' for the
purposes of the tort. They approached this question by assessing where such behaviour
fell on a 'scale of reprehensibility', and concluded that it could amount to 'unlawful
means'.[149] In *Digicel (St Lucia) Ltd* v *Cable & Wireless plc* (2010), however, Morgan J held
that a non-actionable breach of a non-criminal statute ought not to be treated as 'unlawful means';[150] the contrary conclusion would have risked the tort of unlawful means conspiracy being used to circumvent the limits on the tort of breach of statutory duty.[151]

In *Total Network* Lord Walker, in particular, emphasised that the tort would not be
committed whenever a defendant happened to use 'unlawful means' in accordance with
the conspirators' plan, the unlawful conduct must also have been *instrumental* in causing
the claimant loss: 'in the phrase "unlawful means" each word has an important part to
play. It is not enough that there is an element of unlawfulness somewhere in the story.'[152]
So, for example, suppose that in *Lonrho Ltd* v *Shell Petroleum (No 2)* (1982),[153] Shell and
other oil companies had agreed, 'This is our chance to do down our enemy Lonrho. The
longer we can keep the Rhodesian government propped up by supplying it with oil in
breach of the sanctions imposed on Rhodesia, the more likely it is that Lonrho will go
bust because its business interests in Rhodesia will remain frozen.' On Lord Walker's
view, that would *not* amount to an unlawful means conspiracy.[154] What makes Shell and
the other companies' sanctions-breaking unlawful (it is contrary to the interests of the
UK, which wants to bring the Rhodesian government down) is not what would be helping it and the other companies do down Lonrho.

B. Part of the conspirators' plan

The breadth of what can now constitute 'unlawful means' for the purpose of the tort of
unlawful means conspiracy has given prominence to a new and difficult question: will a
defendant have committed this tort if he did not realise that the proposed means were
unlawful? This question can easily arise when the law is obscure, and in some cases the
defendants have even received legal advice to the effect that their proposed plan of action
was *lawful*. Two views can be found in the cases that have addressed the matter: one line
of cases takes the view that a defendant who joins a conspiracy knowing about the

---

[147] *Total Network*, at [120].
[148] [2010] EWHC 774 (Ch), Annex I [54].
[149] [2017] EWCA Civ 40, at [45]–[49].
[150] *Digicel (St Lucia) Ltd* v *Cable & Wireless plc* [2010] EWHC 774 (Ch), Annex I [55]–[62]. This issue
appears to have been anticipated by Lord Walker in *Total Network*, at [96].
[151] For these limits, see above, § 18.1(C).
[152] *Total Network*, at [96].
[153] Discussed above, § 18.1(A).
[154] *Total Network*, at [95].

elements of the conspirators' plan that *in fact* amount to 'unlawful means' can be liable, and gains no assistance from a mistake as to how the law will classify such behaviour;[155] a second line of cases holds that a defendant must know that the proposed means *are unlawful*, or, at least, cannot be liable if he honestly believes them to be lawful.[156] We are tentative about predicting which view will be accepted by the appellate courts: the first view has the advantage of simplicity, in that it does not require courts to investigate what each defendant knew about the law, but the second view tends to ensure that only those whose behaviour seems 'reprehensible' become liable as conspirators.[157]

20.8 Deceit

A will have committed the tort of deceit (or fraud) in relation to B if:

1. he made a representation of fact to B which was untrue; *and*
2. when he made that representation to B he did not honestly believe that it was true; *and*
3. he intended, in making that representation to B, to induce B to act in a particular way; *and*
4. B was induced to act in that way by A's representation; *and*
5. B suffered loss as a result.[158]

It is worth saying more about three elements of this tort.

A. Representation of fact

(1) *Conduct.* Someone can obviously make a representation of fact by words or writing, but they can also do so by conduct. If A has conducted himself in such a way that B *reasonably* inferred from A's conduct that *x* was true, then it is fair to say that A represented to B that *x* was true.[159]

(2) *Representation of opinion.* A representation of opinion always carries with it a representation of fact that can ground an action for deceit. This is because if A says to B, 'I think that *x* is true' he makes a representation that it is a fact that he thinks *x* is true. So if A says to B 'I think that *x* is true' when he does not actually think *x* is true then A makes an untrue representation of fact to B – he represents to B that he thinks *x* is true when this

---

[155] See *First Subsea* v *Balltec Ltd* [2014] EWHC 866 (Ch), at [157], and authorities cited therein.

[156] See *Digicel (St Lucia) Ltd* v *Cable & Wireless plc* [2010] EWHC 774 (Ch), Annex I [117], and authorities cited therein.

[157] In *JSC BTA Bank* v *Ablyazov (No 14)* [2017] EWCA Civ 40, [2017] 2 WLR 1563, the Court of Appeal appears to have assumed that a defendant could not be liable for conspiring to cause harm by helping someone to disobey a court order unless the defendant knew of the order (at [56]).

[158] There is no further requirement that A's representation must have been made in a commercial context: see *P* v *B* [2001] 1 FLR 1041 and *Magill* v *Magill* (2006) 226 CLR 551 (both cases allowing a claimant to bring an action for deceit against his ex-partner, claiming that she lied to him in telling him that he was the father of her child).

[159] *Ward* v *Hobbs* (1878) 4 App Cas 13 (driving pigs to market did not amount to representation that pigs of good quality and free from illness: see Lord Selborne's observation (at 29): '[t]o say that every man is always to be taken to represent, in his dealings with other men, that he is not, to his knowledge, violating any statute, is a refinement which . . . would not I think appear reasonable to any man').

is not true. Some judges have gone further and said that if A says to B 'I think that x is true' when A is in a much better position than B to know whether or not x is true, then A's representation 'I think that x is true' will amount to a representation of fact that there is *good reason* to believe that x is true.[160] Some judges have gone even further than this and said that in such a case, A's representation 'I think that x is true' will amount to a representation of fact that x *is* true.[161]

(3) *Representation of intention.* Similarly, a representation of intention always carries with it a representation of fact that can ground an action for deceit.[162] This is because if A says to B, 'I intend to do x', he makes a representation that it is a fact that he currently has an intention to do x. So if A says to B 'I intend to do x' when he has no such intention, A makes an untrue representation of fact – he represents to B that it is currently his intention to do x when this is not true. Bowen LJ put the point memorably: 'There must be a misstatement of an existing fact [for an action in deceit to be maintained]: but the state of a man's mind is as much a fact as the state of his digestion.'[163]

(4) *Ambiguous representations.* What if a representation is ambiguous? In *Smith* v *Chadwick* (1884), a company's prospectus claimed that the 'present value of the turnover or output of the entire works is over £1m per annum'. This was ambiguous: it could have meant that the company's entire works *had actually* produced £1m worth of produce in one year (which was not true) or it could have meant the company's entire works were *capable* of producing £1m worth of produce in one year (which was true). The claimant was induced by this statement to buy shares in the company. He then sued the directors of the company in deceit, seeking to recover the money he had paid for the shares.

To succeed in his claim the claimant would have had to show: (i) that he understood the statement in the company's prospectus to mean that the company's entire works had actually produced £1m worth of produce in one year;[164] (ii) that the directors had intended to encourage people like the claimant to think this; (iii) the directors did not honestly believe that the company's entire works had actually produced £1m worth of produce in one year;[165] and (iv) the directors intended, by encouraging people to believe that the company's entire works had actually produced £1m worth of produce in one year, to induce people to buy shares in the company. As things turned out, the claimant's claim failed: he could not prove that (i) was true.

B. Lack of honest belief

In *Derry* v *Peek* (1889), Lord Herschell observed that, 'in order to establish an action of deceit, there must be proof of fraud, and nothing short of that will suffice . . . fraud is proved when it is shewn that a false representation has been made (1) knowingly, or

---

[160] *Brown* v *Raphael* [1958] 1 Ch 636
[161] *Bisset* v *Wilkinson* [1927] AC 177.
[162] See, for example, *East* v *Maurer* [1991] 1 WLR 461 (untrue representation by seller of hairdressing salon that he did not intend to work regularly in another nearby salon that he owned).
[163] *Edgington* v *Fitzmaurice* (1885) 29 Ch D 459, 483
[164] The claim could not have succeeded if the claimant had understood the statement in the company's prospectus to mean that the company's entire works were capable of producing £1m worth of produce in one year because, in that case, he would not have been deceived when he bought shares in the company – just like the claimant in *Ship* v *Crosskill* (on which see below, §20.8(D)).
[165] *Akerhielm* v *De Mare* [1959] AC 789, 805.

(2) without belief in its truth, or (3) recklessly, careless whether it be true or false.'[166] But if (1) is true, (2) is true. And if (3) is true, (2) is true. So we can reduce Lord Herschell's statement down to: 'fraud is proved when it is shewn that a false representation has been made . . . without belief in its truth' without losing anything.

What if a defendant believed that a fact was true at the time that he made a representation but subsequently discovered that it was not true? So, suppose that A made a representation of fact to B intending to induce B to do *x*, and B was induced to do *x* by that representation. And suppose further that at the time A made that representation, he honestly believed that it was true but before B did *x*, A discovered that his representation was untrue. The law, as it stands now, seems to say that if A did not warn B in time that his representation was untrue, then A committed the tort of deceit.[167]

C. Inducement

The courts will hold that A's representation of fact to B induced B to do *x* if A's representation *played some part* in B's decision to do *x*.[168]

In *Smith v Chadwick* (1884), the claimants claimed that they were induced to buy shares in a company because its prospectus falsely represented that G was a director of the company. This claim was dismissed. The claimants could not have been induced to buy shares in the company by the representation in the prospectus that G was a director of the company because, by their own admission, the claimants had never heard of G before the prospectus was issued. The representation in the prospectus that G was a director of the company could not therefore have played any part in the claimants' decision to take up shares in the company.

Sometimes it is very difficult to know whether a given person was induced to act in a certain way by a representation that was made to him or her – for example where *Driver* buys a car after *Trader* tells *Driver* that the car has just passed its MOT. To assist them in in determining whether *Trader*'s representation played any part in *Driver*'s decision to buy the car, the courts have taken the position that they will *presume Driver*'s decision was influenced by *Trader*'s representation if (i) the representation was intended to influence *Driver* into buying the car, (ii) it would have been reasonable for *Driver* to be so influenced; and (iii) *Driver* bought the car after *Trader* made his representation.[169] Clearly all these requirements will be satisfied in *Driver*'s case, with the result that *Trader* will have to rebut the presumption that his representation played some part in *Driver*'s decision to buy the car.

---

[166] *Derry* v *Peek* (1889) 14 App Cas 337, at 374.

[167] *Brownlie* v *Campbell* (1880) 5 App Cas 925; *Briess* v *Woolley* [1954] AC 333.

[168] It does *not* have to be shown that B would not have done *x but for* A's representation: *Downs* v *Chappell* [1997] 1 WLR 426 (action for deceit available when claimants bought bookstore having been shown a set of accounts for the bookstore which made the bookstore out to be a lot more profitable than it was: the fact that the state of the accounts played some part in the claimant's decision to buy the bookstore was enough to ground an action for deceit – it was irrelevant that the claimants might well have bought the bookstore anyway had they never seen the accounts).

[169] *Smith* v *Chadwick* (1884) 9 App Cas 187, 196 per Lord Blackburn: 'if it is proved that the defendants with a view to induce the claimant to enter into a contract made a statement to the claimant of such a nature as would be likely to induce a person to enter into a contract, and it is proved that the claimant did enter into the contract, it is a fair inference of fact that he was induced to do so by the statement.'

D. A difficult scenario

An interesting problem arises where a fact that was untrue when the representation was made later becomes true. Suppose that A made a representation of fact to B intending to induce B to do x and B was induced to do x by that representation. Suppose further that A's representation of fact was – to A's knowledge – untrue at the time he made it, but, by the time B came to do x, A's representation of fact was no longer untrue. In such a case, B cannot sue A in deceit: at the time she did x she was not deceived.[170]

20.9 Malicious falsehood

As a general rule, A will commit the tort of malicious (or injurious) falsehood in relation to B if he maliciously makes a false statement to C that refers to B or B's property and B suffers loss as a result.

The term 'maliciously' needs some explanation. A will have acted maliciously in making a false statement to C if: (1) he knew the statement was untrue when he made it; *or* (2) he did not care whether or not the statement was true when he made it; *or* (3) he made that statement for some dishonest or improper reason.[171]

A couple of examples of this tort being committed will help to illustrate its role. In *Ratcliffe v Evans* (1892), the *County Herald*, a Welsh newspaper, incorrectly said that the claimant had ceased to trade as an engineer and boilermaker and that the claimant's firm had ceased to trade. As a result the claimant experienced a loss of business. He was held entitled to sue the *County Herald* on the ground that it had committed the tort of malicious falsehood. The *County Herald* had not acted in good faith in publishing its story about the claimant and the claimant had suffered loss as a result of its publication.

In *Khodaparast v Shad* (2000), the claimant was an Iranian woman who worked in an Iranian community school. She had an affair with the defendant and when she brought it to an end, he sought to take revenge by circulating photocopies of pages from pornographic magazines which appeared to contain photographs of the claimant advertising telephone sex services. In fact the claimant had nothing to do with telephone sex services; the defendant's photocopies were made by photocopying pages from pornographic magazines on which he had artfully superimposed revealing pictures of the claimant that he had taken during their affair. As a result of the defendant's circulating these photocopies, the claimant was dismissed from her job. She successfully sued the defendant for committing the tort of malicious falsehood – the defendant had maliciously misled people into thinking that she was involved in telephone sex services and she had suffered loss as a result.[172]

Four further points can be made about the tort of malicious falsehood:

(1) *The difference between malicious falsehood and defamation.* There are three significant differences.

First, malicious falsehood extends to cases where a defendant causes a claimant loss by making non-defamatory statements about the claimant to third parties. For example, the

---

[170] *Ship* v *Crosskill* (1870) LR 10 Eq 73 (representation in share prospectus that half of company's share capital already subscribed not true at time prospectus was issued, but was true when claimant was induced by prospectus to buy shares in company).

[171] *Dunlop* v *Maison Talbot* (1904) 20 TLR 579.

[172] The House of Lords refused leave to appeal: [2001] 1 WLR 126

statement in *Ratcliffe* v *Evans* (above) was not defamatory of the claimant – right-thinking people would not think less well of the claimant on hearing that he had closed down his business – but that did not prevent a finding that the defendant had committed the tort of malicious falsehood in making that statement.

Secondly, to bring an action for malicious falsehood, you have to prove that the statement you are complaining of was untrue; to bring an action for defamation, all you need do is prove that the statement you are complaining of was defamatory – it is for the defendant to prove that it was true.

Thirdly, to bring an action for malicious falsehood, you have to prove that the defendant acted maliciously in making the statement which you are complaining about; in an action for defamation, you will not normally need to show that the defendant acted maliciously to succeed in your claim.

If a defendant maliciously published a false and defamatory statement about you to someone else and you suffered loss as a result, you will be able to sue either for malicious falsehood or defamation, depending on which way of presenting your action is more advantageous.[173]

(2) *Presumption of loss.* The normal rule in a malicious falsehood case is that the claimant has to prove that the defendant's statement caused her to suffer some kind of loss. However, s 3(1) of the Defamation Act 1952 qualifies this rule. It provides that in an action for malicious falsehood:

it shall not be necessary to allege or prove special damage –

(a) if the words upon which the action is founded are calculated to cause pecuniary damage to the claimant and are published in writing or other permanent form; or

(b) if the said words are calculated to cause pecuniary damage to the claimant in respect of any office, profession, calling, trade or business held or carried on by him at the time of the publication.

(3) *An exception to the rule.* A claim for malicious falsehood will not be available in a case where *Trader* has lured customers away from *Rival* by alleging that his goods are of better quality than *Rival*'s: the courts will not want to get into the business of adjudicating whether or not *Trader*'s boasts were justified or not.[174] However, if *Trader* alleges to *Rival*'s customers that *Rival*'s goods suffer from specific defects, an action for malicious falsehood may be available to *Rival* as the courts will have no problem determining in this case whether or not *Trader*'s allegations were correct.[175]

---

[173] *Joyce* v *Sengupta* [1993] 1 WLR 337. The 'serious harm' test in s 1 Defamation Act 2013 does not apply to claims for malicious falsehood, but it seems that to avoid a claim being struck out a claimant may have to show that he has 'sufficient prospect of recovering a substantial sum by way of damages to justify continuing the proceedings to trial': *Tesla Motors Ltd* v *BBC* [2013] EWCA Civ 152.

[174] See the remarks of Lord Herschell LC in *White* v *Mellin* [1895] AC 154, 164–5: 'My Lords, I cannot help saying that I entertain very grave doubts whether any action could be maintained for an alleged disparagement of another's goods, merely on the allegation that the goods sold by the party who is alleged to have disparaged his competitor's goods are better either generally or in this or that particular respect than his competitors' are . . . I think it is impossible not to see that . . . a very wide door indeed would be opened to litigation, and that the Courts might be constantly employed in trying the relative merits of rival productions, if an action of this kind were allowed.'

[175] *De Beers Abrasive Products Ltd* v *International General Electric Co of NY* [1975] 1 WLR 972.

(4) *Ambiguous representations.* In *Ajinomoto Sweeteners SAS* v *Asda Stores Ltd* (2011), the defendant supermarket had marketed its own brand of health foods. The packaging of these health foods said 'No hidden nasties' and 'No artificial colours and flavours and no aspartame.' (Aspartame is an artificial sweetener often used as a substitute for sugar in low calorie foods.) The claimant manufactured aspartame. It sued the defendant in malicious falsehood, claiming that the combination of these statements on the defendant's packaging amounted to a false representation that aspartame might be harmful. The defendant argued that in making these statements on its packaging, it was merely saying that its health foods were suitable for customers who objected to foods that contained aspartame.

The Court of Appeal rejected the contention that it should – as happens in defamation cases[176] – find that the statements on the packaging had one single meaning, and attempt to determine what that meaning was. Instead, they held that if reasonable consumers might understand the packaging in two ways then the court should go on to consider malice with regard to each of these meanings.

In the later case of *Cruddas* v *Calvert (No 2)* (2015), however, the Court of Appeal qualified the position reached in *Ajinomoto* by insisting that a defendant could not be malicious with regard to an understanding of his words that he did not intend to convey. The case involved a newspaper article that had one meaning, which was true, but might also be misunderstood by some cynical readers as expressing a more serious allegation, which was, as the authors knew, untrue. Jackson LJ stated:

> In my view, if (a) an article has one correct meaning which is true but is susceptible to a second incorrect interpretation by some cynical readers which is untrue, (b) the author intends the article to convey its correct meaning but foresees that some cynical readers will place upon it the incorrect interpretation, then that does not constitute malice for the purpose of malicious falsehood.[177]

The position now reached, it seems, is that where a statement has two meanings, then a court should consider whether the defendant was malicious with regard to either of these, but a defendant will not have to show that he honestly believed (was not malicious with regard to) all the misunderstandings of his words that he can foresee.

20.10 Recoverable harm

So far, we have presented the economic torts in the way that most lawyers think of them – as a way for claimants to recover compensation for pure economic loss that they have suffered.[178] (Where that loss usually takes the form of a loss of profits or business or wages.) However, in this final section we question the assumption that the economic torts are purely *economic* in nature and ask whether the torts examined in this chapter could be used to claim for other forms of loss. We begin, however, by considering the argument of Deakin and Randall[179] that the economic torts should only protect economic interests associated with 'trade, business or employment'.

---

[176] See above, § 16.3(10).
[177] [2015] EWCA Civ 171, at [111].
[178] Injunctions are often also sought as a remedy where commission of an economic tort is imminent, continuing, or regularly repeated. See below, Chapter 27 for discussion of injunctions.
[179] Deakin & Randall 2009.

A. Trade, business and employment

In their challenging article,[180] Deakin and Randall argue that the economic torts should only protect economic interests associated with 'trade, business and employment'.[181] Their reasoning is that the primary role of the economic torts is to 'maintain the integrity of the competitive process' and consequently courts should focus on designing torts to achieve this goal, without the distraction of protecting interests that are not associated with it.

We think that there are three reasons why the economic torts should not be re-fashioned and confined in the way that Deakin and Randall suggest.

Firstly, Deakin and Randall do not provide much evidence that any problems that the courts have had in deciding the scope of the economic torts have been caused by a failure to focus on cases involving competition. Difficult questions, such as how to define the requisite mental states and what should count as 'unlawful means', are not easy to answer even in cases that obviously involve business competition.

Secondly, adoption of Deakin and Randall's proposal would oblige the courts to fix the scope of their limiting concept: 'trade, business and employment'. *This* would not be straightforward. For example, they think that a central question in the *Total Network* case should have been whether the claimant, the collector of tax, came 'within the range of claimants with relevant economic interests at stake in the competitive process'.[182] What should the answer have been?

Thirdly, as we argue in the next two sections, we think that there are good reasons for recognising that 'the economic torts' can protect a wider range of interests than those that are *purely economic*.

B. Personal injury and property damage

We think that a claimant could sue for personal injury or property damage that was caused as a result of several of these torts being committed if a suitable case arose.

Suppose, for example, that *Doctor* had made a contract with *Patient*, promising to visit him in a remote location and provide some form of treatment necessary to prevent his health from deteriorating, and *Weevil* intentionally persuaded *Doctor* to breach this contract with the result that *Patient*'s health deteriorated. In such a case we can see no strong argument for preventing *Patient* from suing *Weevil* for the tort of *inducing a breach of contract* and recovering damages for the deterioration of his health. Why would tort law distinguish between contracts that confer purely economic benefits and contracts which are designed to protect property or health?[183]

Variations on the same example can be used to test whether the other economic torts also ought to be available to be used where a claimant has suffered personal injury or property damage. Suppose, for instance, that *Doctor* has not made a contract with *Patient* but routinely visits him at the remote location each Monday to provide the necessary treatment. If *Weevil* prevented *Doctor* from visiting by, for example, threatening to punch her if she visits, then why - assuming that *Weevil* can be shown to have the requisite mental element (intention to harm *Patient*) – should *Patient* not be able to sue *Weevil* for the tort of *causing loss by unlawful means* (intimidation)?

---

[180] Ibid.

[181] Ibid, 533. Sometimes they say 'trade, business and livelihood' instead.

[182] Deakin & Randall 2009, 534.

[183] Deakin and Randall might argue for such a limit: see Deakin and Randall 2009, 537–8. We discussed their views in the previous section.

No doubt the main reason why it is rarely asked whether claimants can sue for personal injury or property damage using the economic torts is that it is *assumed* that in such cases *Weevil* could be straightforwardly held liable in negligence for what he did. But we are not sure that this is straightforward. Suppose, for example, *Weevil* commits the tort of trespass to land by parking his car on *Doctor*'s land, and as a result blocks *Doctor* from getting her own car onto the public highway. Suppose further that *Doctor* asks *Weevil* to move his car, and explains that she needs to set off to visit *Patient* in order to provide him with crucial treatment. In such circumstances it is not straightforward to establish that *Weevil* will owe a duty to *Patient* to move his car, so as to be potentially liable in negligence, because *not moving* the car might be classified as an omission. But surely it ought to amount to a tort (causing loss by unlawful means), if *Weevil* decides not to move his car, and thus continues to commit the tort of trespass, with the intention of thereby causing harm to *Patient*.

We must acknowledge, however, that there is currently clear authority concerning the tort of *malicious falsehood* which confines it to protecting claimants against economic harm.[184]

C. Pure distress

Even if the economic torts will rarely be required in cases involving personal injury or property damage, we must discuss whether a claimant could bring a claim for *pure distress* using any of the torts discussed in this chapter. This issue is important because, as we have seen, *pure distress* – that is, mental suffering not serious enough to qualify as a psychiatric illness and which does not result from the sufferer's experiencing some other loss, such as personal injury or property damage – is hardly ever actionable in negligence. We will consider each tort in turn.

(1) *Inducing a breach of contract.* In a case where a claimant can sue a contract-breaker for damages for pure distress, we can see no reason why the claimant should not also be able to sue anyone who culpably induced the breach for such damages.

(2) *Causing loss by unlawful means.* In *OBG*, Lord Hoffmann said that the 'essence' of this tort 'appears to be (a) a wrongful interference with the actions of a third party in which the claimant *has an economic interest* and (b) an intention thereby to cause loss to the claimant.'[185] He later said that this tort was 'designed *only* to enforce basic standards of civilised behaviour in *economic competition*, between traders or between employers and labour.'[186] These *dicta* strongly suggest that the tort of causing loss by unlawful means will only ground an action for economic loss.

Consider, for example, the **Tiger Kidnapping Problem**:[187]

Gangster rings up *Bank Manager* at work and tells him that he has kidnapped *Manager*'s wife and children. He instructs *Manager* to take £100,000 out of the bank's vault and deposit it at a location that will be given to *Manager* at a later stage. If he follows the instructions precisely, *Manager* will be reunited with his family. *Manager* does so, but it is many hours before his wife and children are found by the police, and he is informed they are safe. Until then, and since receiving *Gangster*'s 'phone call, *Manager* has been undergoing horrendous mental suffering, worrying about his family. That suffering did not, however, amount to a recognised psychiatric illness.

---

[184] Carty 2010, 216–18.
[185] *OBG*, at [47] (emphasis added).
[186] *OBG*, at [56] (emphasis added).
[187] The crime described in the problem is known generally as '*tiger* kidnapping' because of the amount of stalking and planning that is required beforehand to pull the crime off.

Although *Gangster* has committed a wrong (false imprisonment) in relation to *Manager*'s family here, and he committed that wrong with the object of causing *Manager* mental distress (as a means of persuading *Manager* to obey *Gangster*'s instructions), it seems that *Gangster* will *not* have committed the tort of causing loss by unlawful means to *Manager* here, because *Manager* did not have an *economic* interest in his family's welfare, and *Gangster*'s scheme did not really interfere with the family's freedom to 'deal' with *Manager*.

There are, however, some *three-party cases* where the claimant will only have suffered pure distress and which will fit Lord Hoffmann's definition of when the tort of causing loss by unlawful means will be committed in a three party case. In their excellent article, 'Intentional infliction of harm by unlawful means', Daniel Stilitz and Philip Sales suggest the example of a case where a defendant who was in a dispute with a train company wrongfully interferes with the running of the company's trains. They observe that if the passengers sought to sue the defendant on the basis that he had committed causing loss by unlawful means in relation to them (because he aimed to disrupt the passengers' journeys as a way of putting pressure on the train company to settle the dispute), 'It would be invidious . . . if the business passengers could recover, but those on a day trip could not.'[188] A passenger who was planning to spend the day at the seaside with his family but whose journey was ruined by the defendant's actions could bring himself within Lord Hoffmann's definition of the *three-party* version of the intentional harm tort, as the defendant's actions have interfered with the train company's freedom to provide its services to the passenger. We see no reason why such a passenger should not be able to sue for having his day ruined.

So far as possible *two-party* forms of the tort of causing loss by unlawful means are concerned – that is, cases where a defendant directly causes harm to a claimant without going through a third party – the picture is mixed. On the one hand, in *Godwin* v *Uzoigwe* (1993), the Court of Appeal gave damages for distress to a claimant who had been bullied into working for the defendants for two and a half years. On the other hand, in *Mbasogo* v *Logo Ltd* (2007) – where the head of state of Equatorial Guinea tried to sue for damages for pure distress resulting from the defendants' financing (allegedly) an abortive coup attempt against him – the Court of Appeal refused to extend the tort of causing loss by unlawful means to this kind of harm because they thought that doing so might have the side effect of granting victims of harassment a common law right to sue for such harassment, thereby undermining the rules for when such a claim could be brought under the Protection from Harassment Act 1997. But the Court did accept – in line with the decision in *Godwin* v *Uzoigwe* – that intimidation was a 'paradigm' example of a tort where compensation could be awarded for injury to feelings.[189]

(3) *Lawful means conspiracy.* It seems very unlikely that damages for pure distress could be sued for using this tort. There are two objections. The first is the *anomaly objection* – if a defendant acting alone could not be sued for damages for pure distress for intentionally causing a claimant to suffer pure distress, it would seem wrong that he could be sued if he did what he did pursuant to an agreement with another. The second is what we can call

---

[188] Sales & Stilitz 1999, 431.
[189] [2007] QB 846, at [97].

the *Wainwright objection* – so-called because it reflects a concern raised by Lord Hoffmann in *Wainwright* v *Home Office* (2004):

> In institutions and workplaces all over the country, people constantly do and say things with the intention of causing distress and humiliation to others. This shows lack of consideration and appalling manners but I am not sure that the right way to deal with it is always by litigation.[190]

Allowing damages for pure distress to be sued for in lawful means conspiracy would open the doors to claims being made for 'lack of consideration and appalling manners' so long as it could be shown that more than one person was in on a plan to treat the claimant that way.

(4) *Unlawful means conspiracy.* There are three arguments against damages for pure distress being available in cases of unlawful means conspiracy. First, the *anomaly objection*, raised in our discussion of *lawful means conspiracy*, will apply whenever the unlawful means are such that a claimant could not bring a tort claim if they were deployed against him by a defendant acting on his own. Secondly, the rule ought to be the same for both forms of conspiracy tort, particularly since *Total Network* (2008) treated them as closely related to one another, and we have argued above that damages for pure distress should not be available in lawful means conspiracy claims. Thirdly, the Court of Appeal held in *Mbasogo* v *Logo Ltd* (2007) that damages for pure distress are not available in an unlawful means conspiracy case for reasons which we outlined above, when discussing cases of *causing loss by unlawful means.*

(5) *Deceit.* Allowing claims for pure distress in deceit might also fall foul of the *Wainwright objection*, as it would open the doors to litigation against pranksters who induced a claimant to humiliate themselves by telling them a lie. (For example, telling a new employee, 'Next Friday is "Batman Day" in this office – everyone comes in dressed as a character from Batman' and the employee duly turns up for work on Friday dressed as the Penguin . . .) Given this, we think the better view is that damages for deceit cannot be given for pure distress.[191]

(6) *Malicious falsehood.* It was assumed by Eady J in *Quinton* v *Peirce* (2009) – a case concerning an election leaflet criticising the claimant, who was standing for election – that damages could only be awarded in malicious falsehood if the defendant's falsehood resulted in the claimant suffering 'actual financial loss'.[192] So being distressed by the loss of one's seat as a council member would not be an adequate foundation for a claim in malicious falsehood – but loss of the right to claim expenses as a council member might be![193]

In *Ajinomoto Sweeteners SAS* v *Asda Ltd* (2011), the Court of Appeal said that it did not 'find at all helpful' the suggestion that malicious falsehood was a purely economic tort, and suggested that it was concerned to protect 'the reputation of property, typically in the

---

[190] [2004] 2 AC 406, at [46].
[191] Carty 2010 argues (at 194) that damages for distress *can* be sued for in deceit, citing *Shelley* v *Paddock* [1980] QB 348. In that case, the claimant was deceived into paying the defendant £9,420 to purchase a house in Spain which the defendant had no power to transfer into her name. The trial judge awarded the claimant £500 for the distress she had suffered as a result of losing her money. However, the distress in that case was not *pure*, as it was consequent on the economic loss the claimant had suffered as a result of the defendant's deceit.
[192] [2009] EWHC 912 (QB), at [86]. Similarly, in *Joyce* v *Sengupta* [1993] 1 WLR 337, 347–9, Sir Donald Nicholls V-C said *obiter* that 'injury to feelings alone will not found a cause of action in malicious falsehood.'
[193] [2009] EWHC 912 (QB), at [85].

form of the goodwill of a business.'[194] We do not think, however, that the Court intended to imply that this was its exclusive domain.[195] When one contemplates the facts of *Khodaparast* v *Shad* (2000), it would be natural to think that the claimant should have been awarded some kind of remedy even if she had been merely upset by her ex-boyfriend leading everyone to believe that she was a telephone sex worker, and had not lost her job.[196] However, allowing a claim to be made for pure distress in a case like *Khodaparast* again runs into the *Wainwright objection* – and might also increase the likelihood of claimants attempting to use the tort of malicious falsehood in situations where libel would be more appropriate.

Further reading

Anyone interested in exploring this area of law further should consult **Hazel Carty's** *An Analysis of the Economic Torts*, **2nd edn (OUP, 2010)**. While rendered slightly out of date by recent developments, **Tony Weir**'s discussions of the economic torts in his *An Introduction to Tort Law*, **2nd edn (Clarendon, 2006), Chapter 13**, and the 'Introduction' to **Part VIII ('Deception and other wrongful conduct')** of his *A Casebook on Tort*, **10th ed (Sweet & Maxwell, 2004)** are impeccably clear and extremely stimulating. Also somewhat out of date, but significant as a roadmap for an untaken journey, is **Philip Sales and Daniel Stilitz's 'Intentional infliction of harm by unlawful means' (1999) 115** *Law Quarterly Review* **411.** Getting more up to date, we have already referred to **Deakin and Randall's 'Rethinking the economic torts' (2009) 72** *Modern Law Review* **519. David Howarth's 'Against** *Lumley* v *Gye*' **(2005) 68** *Modern Law Review* **195** and **Jason Neyers' 'The economic torts as corrective justice' (2009) 17** *Torts Law Journal* **164** are also worth reading, not least because they promulgate views very different from those found in our chapter.

---

[194] [2011] QB 497, at [28].

[195] The statement was made in the context of rejecting a *bad* argument for distinguishing between malicious falsehood and defamation: the facts of the case did not require the court to consider the full range of interests protected by the former tort.

[196] In *Khodaparast* v *Shad* [2000] 1 WLR 618 the Court of Appeal upheld the trial judge's decision to award the claimant *aggravated damages* to reflect the 'injury to her feelings', at [42] and [44].

Chapter 21
Abuse of power or position

Aims and objectives

Reading this chapter will enable you to:

(1) Understand when a defendant will be held to have committed the torts of (a) malicious prosecution, and (b) maliciously instituting civil proceedings.

(2) Understand when a defendant will be held to have committed the tort of misfeasance in public office, noting, in particular, the two forms of this tort and the debates about their scope.

(3) Know when the Human Rights Act 1998 makes public authorities liable to pay compensation for acting incompatibly with people's rights under the European Convention on Human Rights.

21.1 The basics

Cases like *Allen* v *Flood* (1898)[1] demonstrate the unwillingness shown by the English common law courts[2] when asked to make it a tort to abuse *private* power (in the case of *Allen* v *Flood*, the power to withhold one's labour when under no contractual obligation

---

[1] And also the earlier case of *Bradford* v *Pickles* [1895] AC 587, where the defendant landowner was held to have had a perfect right to take as much as he liked of water flowing under his land in undefined channels, even though he was only appropriating that water in order to annoy the claimants into whose reservoirs it would have otherwise flowed. *Bradford* v *Pickles* is not, however, as good an example of the courts' unwillingness to impose liability for 'abuse of rights' as *Allen* v *Flood*, because there is an alternative analysis of why the claimants were not entitled to sue in *Bradford* v *Pickles*. According to this analysis, the claimants could not sue because you cannot complain that your use of land has been interfered with as a result of something being prevented from coming onto your land unless you had a *right* to receive that thing – and the claimants in *Bradford* v *Pickles* had no *right* to receive any of the water that was flowing under the defendant's land. So it could be argued that the claimants could not sue in *Bradford* v *Pickles* not because the defendant had a perfect right to take as much as he liked of the water flowing under his land, but because the claimants had no right to receive that water. See further § 13.5(C) and § 13.7, above.

[2] As we have already seen (see above, § 1.10), the Courts of Equity were much more interventionist, restraining people from relying on their strict legal rights when it would be 'unconscionable' to do so. But they never asserted a power to make someone pay damages for abusing their legal rights.

to work). However, when it came to abuse of *public* power, or *quasi-public* power,[3] the courts revealed themselves to be much more willing to intervene. There are two well-established torts that seek to stop public powers being abused.

The first of these torts focuses on a specific power – the power to bring criminal prosecutions. Abuse of that power, by either a public official or a private citizen, will amount to the tort of *malicious prosecution*. It has also now spawned a new tort – recently recognised by the UKSC – of maliciously bringing unsuccessful civil proceedings against someone else.

The second well-established tort applies specifically to public officials, and makes it a tort – the tort of *misfeasance in public office* – for a public official to abuse his powers when he knows that a particular claimant is likely to suffer loss as a result.

The legislature has also addressed misuse of public power, and the Human Rights Act 1998 imposes liability where a public authority has acted in a way that is incompatible with a person's rights under the European Convention on Human Rights.

21.2 Malicious prosecution

A will have committed the tort of malicious prosecution in relation to B if:

1. A prosecuted B for committing a criminal offence; *and*

2. the prosecution ended in B's favour;[4] *and*

3. A had no reasonable and probable cause to prosecute B for that offence; *and*

4. A acted maliciously in prosecuting B for committing that offence.[5]

Five points should be made about this tort:

(1) *Prosecution.* In order to show that A has committed the tort of malicious prosecution in relation to B, it is first necessary to show that A prosecuted B for committing a criminal offence. This requirement will obviously be satisfied if A is a private citizen and brings a private prosecution against B for committing an offence. Similarly, if A works for the Crown Prosecution Service and in that capacity prosecutes B for committing an offence.

Outside these simple cases, the House of Lords has made it clear that A will be held to have prosecuted B for committing a criminal offence if he was *directly responsible* for B's being prosecuted for committing that offence.[6] So, for example, if *Informer* supplied information to the police which indicated that *Suspect* had committed some offence and *Suspect* was subsequently prosecuted for that offence, *Informer* will only be held to have 'prosecuted' *Suspect* if: (i) *Informer* supplied his information to the police with the intention of persuading the police to prosecute *Suspect*; *and* (ii) the facts of *Suspect*'s case were

---

[3] It may be that the conspiracy torts can be seen in this way – as an attempt by the courts to ensure that the *quasi-public* power to associate with other people and to pursue common goals is not abused.

[4] That is, B was not found guilty of committing that offence or B was found guilty of committing that offence but her conviction was subsequently reversed.

[5] For a general discussion of the tort, see Fridman 1963.

[6] *Martin* v *Watson* [1996] 1 AC 74.

such that it was impossible for the police to exercise any independent judgment as to whether or not *Suspect* should be prosecuted.[7]

However, even if (i) and (ii) are satisfied, and *Informer* maliciously supplied false information about *Suspect* to the police, he may still be protected from being sued for malicious prosecution by the decision of the Court of Appeal in *Westcott* v *Westcott* (2009), which held that statements made to the police for the purpose of encouraging them to investigate a crime were protected by absolute immunity, which means they cannot be made the basis of a tort claim under any circumstances.

(2) *Termination of prosecution in claimant's favour.* The courts will refuse to say that A committed the tort of malicious prosecution in prosecuting B for committing a particular criminal offence if B was found guilty of committing that offence and her conviction has not yet been reversed. This is to stop B from reopening the question of whether or not her conviction was valid by bringing an action for malicious prosecution against A.[8]

(3) *Reasonable and probable cause.* A *Prosecutor* will only have had reasonable and probable cause to prosecute *Defendant* for an offence if, when he brought the prosecution: (i) *Prosecutor* thought that *Defendant* had probably committed that offence;[9] *and* (ii) it was reasonable for *Prosecutor* to think this, given the evidence available to him at the time he prosecuted *Defendant*.[10] If (i) or (ii) are missing, there will be no reasonable and probable cause for the prosecution.[11]

---

[7] *Mahon* v *Rahn (No 2)* [2000] 1 WLR 2150, at [269]. Also *Martin* v *Watson* [1996] 1 AC 74 (W's allegation that M had indecently exposed himself to her capable of giving rise to action for malicious prosecution). In *H* v *AB* [2009] EWCA Civ 1092 – a case where the subject of an overturned conviction for rape sued the woman who claimed he had raped her for malicious prosecution – Sedley LJ held that: (i) the defendant could not be sued for malicious prosecution because the police had approached her, not the other way round; and (ii) even if the defendant had approached the police, claiming that she had been raped, she could only be sued for malicious prosecution if she had done something 'improper . . . designed to cause . . . [the] authorities to take a course [they] would not otherwise have taken' (at [46]–[47]).

[8] *Basébé* v *Matthews* (1867) LR 2 CP 684, 687 (per Byles J): 'there is [no] doubt that the criminal proceeding must be determined in favour of the accused before he can maintain an action for malicious prosecution. If this were not so, almost every case would have to be tried over again upon its merits . . . It makes no difference that the party convicted has no power of appealing.'

[9] See Lindley J in *Shrosbery* v *Osmaston* (1877) 37 LT 792, 794: 'if a man believes that another is not guilty of a criminal charge, and prosecuted unsuccessfully, I confess I have the greatest difficulty in seeing that such a man can be held to have reasonable and probable cause for prosecuting.' But it does not have to be shown that *Prosecutor positively believed* that *Defendant* was guilty: *Tempest* v *Snowden* [1952] 1 KB 130, 139 (per Denning LJ), *Glinski* v *McIver* [1962] AC 726, 758 (per Lord Denning). All that has to be shown is that he thought *Defendant* was *probably* guilty.

[10] *Glinski* v *McIver* [1962] AC 726, 766 (per Lord Devlin): 'there must [have been] cause (that is, sufficient grounds . . .) for thinking that [*Defendant*] was probably guilty of the offence imputed.'

[11] It may be more difficult than one might think to show that either (i) or (ii) are missing. Most of the leading cases on 'reasonable and probable cause' are cases where 'reasonable and probable cause' was established: *Hicks* v *Faulkner* (1878) 8 QBD 167 (not unreasonable to rely on own memory of events in support of view that claimant had committed an offence); *Dawson* v *Vansandau* (1863) 11 WR 516 (not unreasonable to rely on testimony of purported accomplice to form view that claimant had probably committed offence); *Abbott* v *Refuge Assurance Co Ltd* [1962] 1 QB 432 (not unreasonable to rely on not obviously defective advice from counsel that prosecution of claimant would probably succeed).

(4) *Malice.* It seems that *Prosecutor* will act maliciously in prosecuting *Defendant* for committing a criminal offence if his predominant purpose in prosecuting B for committing that offence is *not* to ensure that justice is done to B with respect to that offence.[12]

It was suggested in *Glinski* v *McIver* (1962) that the police prosecuted the claimant for conspiracy to defraud not

> in order to bring him to justice for that offence, but to punish the claimant for having a week before given evidence, which the police believed then to have been perjured, for the defence in the case of *Reg* v *Comer*.[13]

On another reading of the facts in *Glinski* v *McIver*, the police prosecuted the claimant in order to induce him to admit that he had perjured himself in the *Comer* case the week before. Even on this reading, the police acted maliciously in prosecuting the claimant: their object in prosecuting the claimant was not to ensure that justice was done to the claimant – if the claimant had admitted his perjury, they would have dropped the prosecution.

(5) *Analogous torts.* There are a couple of torts that are strongly analogous to the tort of malicious prosecution. A will commit a tort if he maliciously and without reasonable and probable cause procures the issue of either (i) a warrant for B's arrest,[14] or (ii) a search warrant authorising the police to search B's premises.[15]

21.3 Malicious or abusive civil proceedings

If the law is willing to make it a tort to procure, maliciously and without reasonable and probable cause, the issue of an arrest warrant or a search warrant, then does it also make it a tort maliciously and without reasonable and probable cause to invoke the powers of the civil law against a particular person? The courts have in the past given an uncertain answer to this question, ruling that maliciously instituting civil proceedings will *not* amount to a tort *per se*,[16] but may do so if the launching of proceedings involved obtaining property to which the defendant knew he was not entitled.[17] Finally, in *Willers* v *Joyce* (2016), the UKSC ruled – by a majority of 5:4 – that a defendant who was responsible for civil proceedings being brought against a claimant could be sued in tort by the claimant if the proceedings were launched without reasonable cause, were ultimately dismissed, and the defendant acted maliciously in having those proceedings brought against the defendant. In the majority, Lord Toulson observed that it 'seems instinctively unjust for a person to suffer injury as a result of the malicious prosecution of legal proceedings for which there is no reasonable ground, and yet not be entitled to compensation for the injury intentionally caused by the person responsible for instigating it.'[18] It remains to be seen

---

[12] See Alderson B's observation in *Stevens* v *Midland Counties Railway* (1854) 10 Ex 352, 356; 156 ER 480, 482: 'Any motive other than that of simply instituting a prosecution for the simple purpose of bringing a person to justice, is a malicious motive on the part of the person who acts in that way.'

[13] [1962] AC 726, 766 (per Lord Devlin).

[14] *Roy* v *Prior* [1971] AC 470.

[15] *Reynolds* v *Commissioner of Police of the Metropolis* [1985] QB 881, 886; *Gibbs* v *Rea* [1998] AC 786, 797; *Keegan* v *Chief Constable of Merseyside Police* [2003] 1 WLR 2187.

[16] *Quartz Hill Consolidated Gold Mining Co* v *Eyre* (1863) 11 QBD 674; *Gregory* v *Portsmouth City Council* [2000] 1 AC 419.

[17] *Grainger* v *Hill* (1834) 4 Bing NC 212, 132 ER 769; *Gilding* v *Eyre* (1861) 10 CB NS 592, 142 ER 584.

[18] [2016] UKSC 43, at [43].

whether the tort created in *Willers* v *Joyce* will extend to the malicious launch of *disciplinary proceedings* against a claimant.[19] Lord Toulson's observation seems to cover this further way of harming a claimant, but it might prove difficult to fix *which* disciplinary proceedings are sufficiently similar to being subject to a civil claim.[20] The courts may also have to consider whether the new tort should extend to cases where civil litigation is maliciously initiated by A against C in order to harm B.[21]

21.4 Misfeasance in public office

Public officials have a special capacity to cause harm by abusing their official powers or neglecting their official duties.

> The rationale of the tort [of misfeasance in public office] is that in a legal system based on the rule of law executive or administrative power 'may be exercised only for the public good' and not for ulterior and improper purposes.[22]

In many situations, a public official who abuses his or her powers will commit one of the other torts discussed in this text. For instance, if a public official physically detains someone when he has no lawful authority to do so, he will commit the tort of false imprisonment. Similarly, a public official will commit the tort of conversion if she seizes someone else's property when she has no lawful authority to do so. But there are situations where an abuse of power by a public official will not fall within the ambit of any other tort, such as where a public official refuses to grant a licence to someone when such a licence would normally have been granted,[23] or orders someone not to carry out a profitable activity when such an order should not have been given, or neglects to fulfil his or her official duties.[24] The existence of the tort of misfeasance in public office helps to fill these gaps.

---

[19] In *Gregory* v *Portsmouth City Council* [2000] 1 AC 419 the House of Lords refused to extend the tort of malicious prosecution to the malicious initiation of *private* disciplinary proceedings.

[20] In *Gregory* v *Portsmouth City Council* [2000] 1 AC 419, at 430–431, Lord Steyn noted that some disciplinary proceedings are far more formal and serious than others, with a range stretching from the tribunals that hear cases relating to medical practitioners and solicitors, to the disciplinary committees of local sports clubs.

[21] In *Land Securities plc* v *Fladgate Fielder* [2010] Ch 467, before the decision in *Willers* v *Joyce*, the Court of Appeal refused to extend the tort of abuse of process to a case where it was alleged that A had sought to stymie B's business plans and cause B economic loss by bringing an application for judicial review of a local authority's decision to grant B planning permission.

[22] *Three Rivers DC* v *Governor and Company of the Bank of England (No 3)* [2003] 2 AC 1 (henceforth, *Three Rivers (No 3)*), 190 (per Lord Steyn, quoting Nourse LJ in *Jones* v *Swansea CC* [1990] 1 WLR 54, 85).

[23] Many of the cases on misfeasance in public office involve abuses of licensing powers. For example, *Roncarelli* v *Duplessis* [1959] SCR 121 involved an abuse of the power to grant liquor licences to restaurants, *David* v *Abdul Cader* [1963] 1 WLR 834 involved an abuse of the power to licence cinemas, and *Three Rivers (No 3)* involved allegations of abuse of the power to license banks. Another group of cases involve alleged abuses of planning powers: see, for example, *Dunlop* v *Woollahra MC* [1982] AC 158 and *Barnard* v *Restormel BC* [1998] 3 PLR 27. Recently, many claims have alleged abuse of powers relating to immigration and asylum.

[24] Some of the claims in *Three Rivers (No 3)* involved allegations that the defendant had deliberately decided not to perform the duties imposed on it by the statutes which made it the regulator of deposit-taking institutions. In *Odhavji Estate* v *Woodhouse* [2003] 3 SCR 263, the Supreme Court of Canada expressly rejected the argument that the tort only covered the abuse of powers. The Court held (at [30]) that the tort should cover both abuse of powers and neglect of duty because they were 'equally inconsistent with the obligation of a public officer not to intentionally injure a member of the public through deliberate and unlawful conduct in the exercise of public functions'.

So, A, a public official, will commit the tort of misfeasance in public office in relation to B if:

1. in bad faith he abuses his powers or neglects his duties with the specific intention of injuring B *and* B suffers material damage; *or*

2. in bad faith he acts in a way that he knows is beyond his powers or is inconsistent with his duties, *when* he knows that this is likely either to injure B or to injure a class of people of which B is a member, *and* B suffers material damage.

In *Three Rivers DC v Bank of England (No 3)* (2003),[25] the members of the House of Lords expressed different views as to whether (1) and (2), above, are two different forms of the tort. Lord Steyn stated that it was 'conducive to clarity to recognise' that (1) and (2) are *alternative forms* of the tort with a 'unifying element of conduct amounting to an abuse of power accompanied by subjective bad faith'.[26] By contrast, Lord Millett argued that 'the two limbs are merely different ways in which the necessary element of intention is established'.[27] On this question we prefer the view of Lord Steyn since we doubt whether anything properly called an 'intention to injure' can be inferred from proof of (2). We would describe the relationship between the two forms in this way – form (2) is an *extension* of the scope of the tort beyond form (1).

Several elements of the definition are worth further discussion.

(1) *Public official.* This is defined broadly. Best CJ was of the opinion that 'every one who is appointed to discharge a public duty, and receives a compensation in whatever shape, whether from the Crown or otherwise, is constituted a public officer'.[28] Most cases involve officers who are members of the executive, but the Court of Appeal of New Zealand has held that the tort can also be committed by a judge.[29] Public bodies, such as local councils, can be liable, as well as individual public officials.[30] If A is a public official, he can commit the tort of misfeasance in public office by abusing *any* of the powers attached to his post: 'It is not the nature of the power which matters. Whatever its nature or origin, the power may be exercised only for the public good. It is the office on which everything depends.'[31] Thus an official who works for a particular public body can commit the tort by abusing the powers which come from the public body being a landlord,[32] or which come from the fact that the body has the capacity to make contracts, and not just by abusing the special statutory and prerogative powers that the public body may have.[33] Indeed, a public official may

---

[25] The House of Lords dealt with the issues raised by this case in two separate sets of speeches that are reported sequentially at [2003] 2 AC 1. Only the second set of speeches used numbered paragraphs. Thus our references to the first set of speeches use page numbers and our references to the second set use paragraph numbers.

[26] [2003] 2 AC 1, 191–2.

[27] [2003] 2 AC 1, 235.

[28] *Henly v Mayor of Lyme* (1828) 5 Bing 91, 107, 130 ER 995, 1001. In *Stockwell v Society of Lloyd's* [2008] 1 WLR 2255 the Court of Appeal concluded that Lloyd's was *not* a public officer for the purposes of the tort.

[29] *Rawlinson v Rice* [1998] 1 NZLR 454.

[30] Further, a public body may be held vicariously liable if one of its employees commits the tort of misfeasance in public office: *Racz v Home Office* [1994] 2 AC 45. For the rules governing when an employer will be vicariously liable in respect of its employees' torts, see below, Chapter 31.

[31] *Jones v Swansea CC* [1990] 1 WLR 54, 85 (per Nourse LJ).

[32] As was the case in *Jones v Swansea CC* where the claimant alleged that the council had maliciously refused to allow a change of user of premises that she leased from the council.

[33] Aronson 2011 argues that it would be better to focus the tort on abuse of *public power* rather than the defendant's *office*. Thus he would extend liability to abuse of *public power* by government contractors.

also be able to commit the tort by using his or her position to lay claim to powers that he or she does not legally have. In the Australian case of *Northern Territory* v *Mengel* (1995), the defendant public officials committed the tort by asserting a power to stop the Mengels transporting their cattle to market when, in fact, they had no such power.

(2) *Acts and omissions*. Obviously, a public official can commit the tort of misfeasance in public office by performing a *positive act* that is unlawful, such as issuing an unlawful order. The defendant's unlawful positive act must be identified with care, since a pivotal issue will be A's state of mind *when* performing that act.[34]

Does the tort also cover situations where public officials *fail to act*, knowing that this is likely to lead to B suffering some kind of harm? Inconsistent answers to this question were provided in *Three Rivers (No 3)*, where some of the claims were based on *failure* to revoke a licence.[35] Lord Hobhouse stated that:

> If there is a legal duty to act and the decision not to act amounts to an unlawful breach of that legal duty, the omission can amount to misfeasance for the purpose of the tort . . . What is not covered is a mere failure, oversight or accident.[36]

This answer suggests that two separate conditions must be fulfilled before an omission can amount to misfeasance: there must be (1) a breach of a *legal duty* to act, and (2) a *decision* not to act. Lord Hutton also seemed to support (2) and said that where the claim was based on an omission it 'must be a deliberate one involving an actual decision'.[37] By contrast, Lord Hope stated 'I would reject the argument that proof of conscious decisions to act or not to act is required. In my view the tort extends to a deliberate or wilful failure to take those decisions.'[38]

We think that condition (1) must be satisfied when a claim is based on an omission because the tort of misfeasance requires *unlawful* behaviour, and an omission will not be unlawful unless there was a duty to act. It is important to remember, however, that public law insists that where an official has a *power* to act: (a) that official will be under a legal *duty* to exercise the power if, in the circumstances, it would be utterly unreasonable[39] not to do so, and (b) that official will be under a legal duty *to consider* whether to use that power or not. Lord Hope's reason for rejecting condition (2) was that he thought it would benefit a defendant who repeatedly procrastinated and refused to make a decision. But we think it is arguable that such a refusal could be described as a *decision* to breach legal duty (b).[40]

---

[34] *Calveley* v *Chief Constable of the Merseyside Police* [1989] AC 1228, 1240.

[35] *Three Rivers (No 3)*, involved claims that the Bank of England, as regulator of deposit-taking institutions, was liable to compensate depositors who lost money on the collapse of the Bank of Credit and Commerce International (BCCI). The claims alleged that the Bank of England had acted unlawfully in licensing BCCI and in not intervening sooner to control its activities.

[36] *Three Rivers (No 3)*, at 230. See also 237 (per Lord Millett).

[37] *Three Rivers (No 3)*, at 228.

[38] *Three Rivers (No 3)*, at [69].

[39] Those who have studied administrative law will be familiar with this concept being called '*Wednesbury* unreasonableness', after the case of *Associated Provincial Picture Houses Ltd* v *Wednesbury Corp* [1948] 1 KB 223.

[40] The House of Lords in *Three Rivers (No 3)* split 3:2 over whether the claims should be permitted to proceed to trial. The dissentients, Lord Hobhouse (at [172]–[173]) and Lord Millett (at [191]) regarded the claims based on omissions to revoke the licence as flawed by a failure to establish a legal duty to revoke. Lord Hope was willing to allow the case to proceed on the basis of the general allegation that 'the Bank deliberately ran away from its responsibility as the relevant supervisory authority' (at [68]).

(3) *State of mind.* The state of mind which it must be proved a public official had at the time of his unlawful act or omission is different for the two forms of the tort. To prove that A has committed form (1) of the tort in relation to B, B must prove that A 'specifically intended' to injure B (or a class of persons of which B was a member) when he misused his powers or neglected his duty. It is probably also necessary to show that A knew that it was unlawful to injure B – otherwise the tort could cover a case where A honestly believed that punishing B was legally authorised.[41]

Suppose now that B wants to establish that A committed form (2) of the tort of misfeasance in public office. What will B have to prove was A's state of mind when he acted in this way? The answer to this question is complicated, because B must prove A had a particular state of mind *towards the unlawfulness of his act* and a particular state of mind *towards the risk of B being injured.* As to the *unlawfulness,* in the *Three Rivers (No 3)* case Lord Steyn said that 'only reckless indifference in a subjective sense will be sufficient'.[42] So, at the very least, B will have to 'prove that [A] acted with a state of mind of reckless indifference to the illegality of his act'.[43] This means that B must show that A knew that the act was unlawful, or suspected that it was unlawful but did not bother to check because he did not care whether it was or not.

As to A's state of mind *towards the risk of B being injured,* Lord Steyn said that at the very least B must prove that A acted 'in the knowledge that his act would probably injure [B] or a person of a class of which [B] was a member'.[44] But again, proof of actual knowledge is not necessary and it will be sufficient for B to prove that A suspected that injury to B would probably be caused but did not bother to check further because he did not care.

In *Akenzua* v *Secretary of State for the Home Department* (2003), the Court of Appeal considered whether Lord Steyn's statement that A must know that 'his act would probably injure [B] or a person of a class of which [B] was a member' meant that the tort could not catch a defendant who unlawfully acted in a way which endangered people indiscriminately. The Court held that a defendant could be liable even if he did not contemplate harm to an identifiable *group of persons,* provided that the *way in which the harm was caused* was the same sort of way as the defendant had in contemplation at the time of his unlawful act or omission. Thus if A unlawfully released C from detention knowing him to be an arsonist, A might be liable to B if she was injured by a fire started by C, but not if she was injured by C's negligent driving.

(4) *Bad faith.* The speeches in *Three Rivers (No 3)* did not settle the role 'bad faith' plays in the tort of misfeasance in public office. Lord Hope suggested that 'bad faith' was *demonstrated* by proof of the relevant state of mind.[45] So, for him at least, 'bad faith' is not an *additional* ingredient. By contrast, Lord Hutton treated 'bad faith' as requiring an evaluation of the defendant's *motive.*[46] If a bad motive is a necessary extra ingredient, then a public official who knowingly acts unlawfully, knowing that the claimant will probably be injured, can nonetheless avoid liability if he acts for the purest of motives, for instance, because he believes

---

[41] The formulation of the tort in *Three Rivers (No 3)* does not mention this element, but both forms of the tort require 'bad faith' and in our opinion it is obvious that 'bad faith' requires not just an intention to injure but also knowledge that such injury is not lawful.

[42] *Three Rivers (No 3)*, at 193.

[43] ibid.

[44] *Three Rivers (No 3)*, at 196.

[45] *Three Rivers (No 3)*, at [44].

[46] *Three Rivers (No 3)*, at [121]–[125].

that his unlawful behaviour is in the public interest. This has been criticised on the ground that 'there should be no encouragement given to [public officials] to dream up arguments as to why it was a good idea to deliberately choose not to comply [with legislation]'.[47] But Lord Hutton's view gives more weight to the *function* of the tort as being to control *abuse* of the official's position. So whilst an official's pure motive clearly cannot make his unlawful behaviour lawful, it may be enough to keep it outside the scope of this tort.

(5) *Lord Steyn's error?* In *Three Rivers (No 3)* Lord Steyn stated that:

> in both forms of the tort the [state of mind] required *must be directed at the harm complained of,* or at least to harm of the type suffered by the plaintiffs.[48]

If Lord Steyn's statement is correct what follows? Consider the **Unpredictable Criminal Problem**:

Turnkey, a corrupt prison officer, unlawfully releases *Fist* from prison before the end of his sentence, knowing that *Fist* has vowed to take revenge on *Citizen*, whose testimony led to *Fist* being imprisoned. *Turnkey* knows that it is very likely that *Fist* will physically attack *Citizen* but he does not care. *Fist* goes to *Citizen*'s house with the intention of attacking her, but after breaking in, he finds that *Citizen* owns several valuable paintings and decides it would be better to steal these and make a new life for himself. *Fist* steals *Citizen*'s paintings.

The difficulty raised by this problem stems from the fact that *Turnkey*, the public official, expected *Fist* to cause one *type* of harm to *Citizen* – physical injuries – but *Fist* has actually caused a different *type* of harm – loss of personal property. If we apply Lord Steyn's rule, *Turnkey* will not be held liable to compensate *Citizen* for the harm suffered by her as a result of *Turnkey*'s act of misfeasance; his state of mind was *not* directed at 'the harm complained of, or at least to harm of the type suffered by' *Citizen*. This result is contrary to the usual rules about the extent of a defendant's liability for committing an *intentional* tort.[49] Moreover, Lord Steyn did not expressly consider how the law should deal with facts like these. Consequently there are grounds for arguing that Lord Steyn made an error. In our opinion, he should have said that in order to have committed the tort of misfeasance in public office in relation to *Citizen*, *Turnkey* must, when misusing his powers, have intended *Citizen* to suffer harm, or known that *Citizen* would probably suffer harm, or suspected that *Citizen* would probably suffer harm and not cared, but that if *Turnkey* has committed the tort, the separate and further question of what damages are recoverable should be governed by the usual rules governing the extent of an intentional tortfeasor's liability.[50]

(6) *Material damage.* In *Watkins* v *Secretary of State for the Home Department* (2006), the House of Lords considered whether three prison officers had committed the tort of misfeasance in public office in relation to Watkins, a serving prisoner, when they unlawfully

---

[47] Stanton 2003, 134.

[48] *Three Rivers (No 3)*, at 195–6 (emphasis added).

[49] An intentional tort is one which can only be committed deliberately. On the rules governing the extent of an intentional tortfeasor's liability, see above, § 9.2(E).

[50] In *Watkins* v *Secretary of State for the Home Department* [2006] 2 AC 395, at [72], Lord Rodger referred to these rules in connection with the tort of misfeasance in public office. He did not draw attention, however, to their inconsistency with Lord Steyn's statement in *Three Rivers (No 3)*.

and in bad faith opened his correspondence. The case was difficult because the officers' acts caused Watkins no 'material damage', that is, no economic loss or physical or mental injury.[51] Indeed the trial judge had found that Watkins appeared 'to thrive on these conflicts'. The House of Lords concluded that the three prison officers had not committed the tort in relation to Watkins *because* he had not suffered 'material damage'. One factor that seems to have influenced the judges was that they did not want the tort to be available as a vehicle for claimants whose sole object was to punish public officials through obtaining awards of punitive damages.[52]

21.5 Liability under the Human Rights Act 1998

Section 6(1) of the HRA makes it unlawful for a 'public authority to act in a way which is incompatible with a Convention right', except where s 6(2) applies. So: if A, a public authority, acts in a way which is incompatible with a 'Convention right' in circumstances where s 6(2) does not apply and B suffers loss as a result, B may be able to claim damages from A under s 8 of the 1998 Act in respect of that loss. This raises a number of issues which we will deal with in this section.

A. Public authority

The HRA does not define 'public authority'. It states that courts and tribunals *are* 'public authorities',[53] and that neither of the Houses of Parliament, nor any person exercising functions in connection with proceedings in Parliament, is a 'public authority'.[54] Beyond these classes, however, the Act merely provides that the term 'public authority' *includes* 'any person certain of whose functions are functions of a public nature'[55] *but* that such a person will not be a 'public authority' by virtue only of this provision 'if the nature of the act is private'.[56]

After reading this provision it might be thought that the key test is whether A is a 'person certain of whose functions are functions of a public nature'. This, however, is not what Parliament intended.[57] Parliament intended that there should be two classes of 'public authorities': *core* or *pure* public authorities, such as government departments, local authorities, the police and the armed forces,[58] which are treated as 'public authorities' for *all* activities, and *hybrid* or *functional* authorities, which are only treated as 'public

---

[51] In the later case of *Karagozlu v Metropolitan Police Comr* [2007] 2 All ER 1055 the Court of Appeal held that a claim for misfeasance in public office could also be based on a 'loss of liberty', including the loss of residual liberty that a prisoner would suffer if unlawfully moved from an open prison to a closed prison. See also *Iqbal v Prison Officers Association*, [2010] QB 732, at [41]–[42].

[52] For further discussion of the case, see below, § 26.2.

[53] HRA, s 6(3)(a). For discussion of liability for judicial acts see below, at § 21.5(F).

[54] Section 6(3)(b).

[55] Ibid.

[56] Section 6(5).

[57] When interpreting a statute it is Parliament's intention which is crucial. Here, however, the statements of government ministers who were involved in steering the HRA onto the statute book provide the best evidence of Parliament's intentions.

[58] These are the examples given by Lord Nicholls in *Aston Cantlow and Wilmcote with Billesley Parochial Church Council v Wallbank* (henceforth '*Aston*') [2004] 1 AC 546, at [7].

authorities' with regard to acts which are part of their public functions, as opposed to acts of a private nature.[59] In the parliamentary debates leading to the passing of the 1998 Act, Railtrack plc[60] was regularly used as an example of a *hybrid* or *functional* authority. Thus the Lord Chancellor suggested that Railtrack would have to act compatibly with 'Convention rights' when carrying out its *public* functions in relation to safety, but not when performing *private* acts as a property developer.[61] The Home Secretary identified churches as further authorities which might be treated as *hybrid*.[62] Another example might be a private security company which provides services to corporate clients (private acts) and also runs a 'private' prison (public function).

How do the courts determine whether a body is a *core* or *pure* 'public authority'? In *Aston Cantlow* v *Wallbank* (2004), Lord Nicholls said that the 'nature' of such bodies was 'governmental', and that factors leading to such a classification were likely to include 'the possession of special powers, democratic accountability, public funding in whole or in part, an obligation to act only in the public interest, and a statutory constitution'.[63] As we noted above, examples of *core* public authorities include government departments, local authorities, the police and the armed forces. Thus when these bodies act incompatibly with a person's 'Convention rights' they may be liable.

The test for whether a body is a *hybrid* public authority, because some of its functions are 'of a public nature', has proved more difficult for judges to agree on. In *Aston Cantlow* v *Wallbank* (2004), Lord Nicholls concluded that 'there is no single test of universal application' which can determine whether a particular function is 'of a public nature' because of 'the diverse nature of governmental functions and the variety of means by which these functions are discharged today'.[64] He went on, however, to identify several *relevant* factors, and subsequent cases have also adopted a 'factor-based' approach. Within such an

---

[59] In *Aston* the two classes are referred to (at [11]) as 'core public authorities' and 'hybrid public authorities'. But in its reports the Joint Committee on Human Rights, *The Meaning of Public Authority under the Human Rights Act, Seventh Report of the Session 2003–4* (HL Paper 39, HC 382) and *The Meaning of Public Authority under the Human Rights Act, Ninth Report of the Session 2006–7* (HL Paper 77, HC 410), uses the terms 'pure' and 'functional'. For evidence that two classes were intended see, for example, Lord Irvine of Lairg LC, Hansard (HL Debates), 24 November 1997, col. 784, 'There are obvious public authorities . . . which are covered in relation to the whole of their functions by [s 6(1)]. Then there are some bodies some of whose functions are public and some private. If there are some public functions the body qualifies as a public authority but not in respect of acts which are of a private nature.' See also Jack Straw MP, Home Secretary, Hansard (HC Debates), 16 February 1998, col. 775.

[60] The private company in which the infrastructure of the railway system was vested after privatisation. In 2001, Railtrack was put into administration, changed its name, and was bought by Network Rail Ltd.

[61] Hansard (HL Debates), 24 November 1997, col. 784. Many of Railtrack's duties relating to the *regulation* of safety were removed by the Railways (Safety Case) Regulations 2000 (SI 2000/2688) and in *Cameron* v *Network Rail Infrastructure Ltd* [2007] 1 WLR 163 Sir Michael Turner held that the company was not *thereafter* a 'public authority' under the Human Rights Act.

[62] Hansard (HC Debates), 20 May 1998, col. 1020. At col. 1017 he stated that 'the two most obvious examples' of churches carrying out *public* functions 'relate to marriages and to the provision of education in Church schools'. Despite pressure Parliament did not exclude churches from the scope of s 6 but instead sought to allay concerns by accepting the amendment which became s 13 of the HRA. In *Aston* the House of Lords confirmed that parochial church councils, an emanation of the Church of England, were a hybrid body.

[63] *Aston*, at [7]. He drew attention to Oliver 2000, where it is suggested (at 492) that the test for a *core* public authority should 'place emphasis on whether it enjoys special powers and authority, and whether it is under constitutional duties to act only in the public interest which are "enforceable", *inter alia*, via mechanisms of democratic accountability'.

[64] *Aston*, at [12].

approach '[a] number of factors may be relevant, but none is likely to be determinative on its own and the weight of different factors will vary from case to case'.[65] Note, the question whether a particular function is 'of a public nature' can be important in two ways: (1) a body cannot be a *hybrid* public authority *at all* unless *at least one* of its functions is 'of a public nature'; and (2) such a body will cease to be a public authority whenever it is performing a private act, but an act is unlikely to be classified as 'private' if it is central to the performance of one of its public functions.[66]

So what factors are relevant to determine if a function is 'of a public nature'? To answer this question it is necessary to look in detail at the case of *YL* v *Birmingham City Council* (2008), where the House of Lords had to decide whether Southern Cross Healthcare Ltd (SCH), a private company operating a care home for profit, was performing a function 'of a public nature' by providing YL, an elderly sufferer from Alzheimer's disease, with residential care in its care home. Most of the fees for YL's care were being paid by Birmingham City Council, which had a statutory duty to 'make arrangements for providing' residential care for YL. Consequently, the case raised the important general question whether companies and charities delivering services under contracts with pure public authorities, usually local government bodies, are *hybrid* or *functional* 'public authorities'.[67] A majority of the House of Lords held that SCH, when caring for YL, was *not* carrying out 'functions of a public nature'.[68]

Recall, in *Aston*, Lord Nicholls identified one relevant factor as being 'the extent to which in carrying out the relevant function the body is publicly funded'.[69] The majority in the *YL* case accepted that 'public funding' is relevant, but they thought that it was important to distinguish between a company which was seeking to make a profit by receiving a commercial fee under a contract with a public authority and one receiving a 'subsidy' from public funds.[70] A 'subsidy' would point towards the body carrying out 'functions of a public nature' while obtaining commercial fees, equal to what private clients were be charged for the same service, would not.

The majority in the *YL* case also agreed with Lord Nicholls that a second relevant factor is 'the extent to which in carrying out the relevant function the body . . . is exercising statutory powers'.[71] But this pointed against SCH being a hybrid authority, since it had no special powers, and provided similar residential care for both publicly funded and privately funded clients; the majority thought it would be anomalous if SCH were treated as performing a public function when caring for a publicly funded client but a private function when caring for a privately funded one.[72]

---

[65] *YL* v *Birmingham City Council* (henceforth, '*YL*') [2008] 1 AC 95, at [5] (per Lord Bingham). Although Lord Bingham was in the minority with regard to the outcome of the appeal his general description of a 'factor-based' approach is *not* what divided the House of Lords. The matters which did divide the court are discussed in the next paragraphs of the text.

[66] There is no simple answer to the question how closely connected with a 'public function' an act must be in order to prevent it from being a 'private act'.

[67] Important cases *before* the *YL* case included *Poplar Housing and Regeneration Community Association Ltd* v *Donoghue* [2002] QB 48 and *R (Heather)* v *Leonard Cheshire Foundation* [2002] 2 All ER 936. These were criticised in Craig 2002.

[68] The majority comprised Lord Scott, Lord Mance and Lord Neuberger. Lord Bingham and Baroness Hale dissented.

[69] *Aston*, at [12].

[70] *YL*, at [27] (per Lord Scott), [105] (per Lord Mance), [165] (per Lord Neuberger).

[71] *Aston*, at [12] (per Lord Nicholls); *YL*, at [28] (per Lord Scott), [102] (per Lord Mance), [160] (per Lord Neuberger).

[72] *YL*, at [117]–[119] (per Lord Mance), [151] (per Lord Neuberger).

Lord Nicholls in *Aston* held that it was also appropriate to consider 'the extent to which in carrying out the relevant function the body . . . is taking the place of central government or local authorities, or is providing a public service'.[73] The majority in the *YL* case, however, were cautious about how these factors might be understood. They suggested that very little weight could be attached to the fact that a function had *previously been performed* by a *core* public authority, or *could have been performed* by a *core* public authority instead of being 'contracted out'. Lord Mance noted that the fact that a function was *sometimes* performed by *core* public authorities did not establish that it was a *'public* function' because the HRA applies to *all* functions, public or private, when they are performed by *core* public authorities,[74] and Lord Neuberger emphasised the very wide range of functions undertaken by *core* public authorities.[75] In contrast, the minority in the *YL* case attached considerable importance to whether the state had 'assumed responsibility' for seeing that a particular task was performed[76] and to whether it was in the public interest for it to be performed, which might be demonstrated by the task being regulated by the state.[77]

In summary, the effect of the majority's decision in the *YL* case was to establish that, in general,[78] profit-seeking bodies that perform services for public authorities under contracts which lead to them being paid commercial fees will *not* count as 'public authorities', and consequently cannot be held liable under HRA 1998 for acting incompatibly with people's 'Convention rights'.[79]

Even if a body will sometimes be a *hybrid* public authority, because *some* of its functions are 'of a public nature', it is necessary to consider whether the particular 'act' that is alleged to be incompatible with a Convention right is 'private', because s 6(5) HRA 1998 provides that a body will not count as a *hybrid* public authority 'if the nature of the act is private'.[80]

---

[73] *Aston*, at [12].

[74] *YL*, at [110] (per Lord Mance), 'it is a fallacy to regard all functions and activities of a core public authority as inherently public in nature', citing Oliver 2004.

[75] *YL*, at [144] (per Lord Neuberger), 'Apart from anything else, there must be scarcely an activity which cannot be carried out by some core public authority.' See also [30] (per Lord Scott).

[76] *YL*, at [7] and [15] (per Lord Bingham), [66] (per Baroness Hale).

[77] The majority doubted the significance of regulation – see, for example, *YL*, at [116] (per Lord Mance), 'Regulation by the state is no real pointer towards the person regulated being a state or governmental body or a person with a function of a public nature, if anything perhaps the contrary' – and performance of a function being in the 'public interest' – see, for example, *YL*, at [134] (per Lord Neuberger): 'The fact that a service can fairly be said to be to the public benefit cannot mean, as a matter of language, that it follows that providing the service itself is a function of a public nature. Nor does it follow as a matter of logic or policy. Otherwise, the services of all charities, indeed, it seems to me, of all private organizations which provide services which could be offered by charities, would be caught by section 6(1).' To the contrary, [9] (per Lord Bingham) and [67] (per Baroness Hale).

[78] The actual result in the *YL* case was subsequently reversed by Parliament in the Health and Social Care Act 2008, s 145(1), subsequently replaced by the Care Act 2014, s 73; but the general test for how to identify a *hybrid* public authority was not altered.

[79] Several scholars have argued that the House of Lords *ought* to have interpreted s 6 HRA so as to cover a much wider range of bodies. For example, Palmer 2008, at 604: 'Considering the intention of the HRA "to bring rights home," the decision in *YL* is disappointing. It will not encourage a culture of human rights to flourish but, rather, will excuse private institutions and actors that exercise public functions from fully implementing basic human rights standards. Human rights values must traverse the public–private divide if there is to be a change of culture in institutions delivering public services.' For an impressive analysis of the issues from a comparative perspective see Donnelly 2007.

[80] This makes it very important to distinguish between *core* and *hybrid* public authorities: *all* of the acts of *core* public authorities must be compatible with Convention rights (unless s 6(2) applies), but the *private* acts of *hybrid* public authorities fall outside the HRA 1998.

This issue caused considerable disagreement in the Court of Appeal in *R (Weaver)* v *London & Quadrant Housing Trust* (2010), where the defendant was a registered social landlord and the claim arose out of it seeking possession from a tenant who had not paid her rent.[81] All the parties accepted that registered social landlords have *some* functions 'of a public nature', since they have special statutory powers with regard to anti-social behaviour and the like. But since the defendant had not exercised any of these special powers against the claimant their existence clearly did not determine whether seeking possession for non-payment of rent was a 'private' act, and consequently outside the scope of the HRA 1998. A majority in the Court of Appeal divided the decision as to whether an act is 'private' into two stages. First, a court must determine if the act was 'in pursuance of, or at least connected with, performance of functions of a public nature'.[82] This means that the 'factor based' approach from *Aston* and *YL* must be applied to the particular function that the act was connected with in order to decide if *that* function was 'of a public nature'. Secondly, the degree of connection between the act and the function must be determined. Thus an act that is 'inextricably linked' to a function 'of a public nature' will be a public act, while an act that is 'purely incidental or supplementary' to that function may still be 'private'.[83] Applying this to the facts, the majority concluded that 'management of social housing' by a registered social landlord *was* a function 'of a public nature' – emphasising that registered social landlords receive a significant subsidy from public sources and enter 'allocation agreements' giving local authorities substantial control over who obtains tenancies – and the act of terminating the claimant's tenancy *was* sufficiently linked to that function to make it a public act. They suggested, however, that other acts, such as terminating a contract with a window-cleaner or builder, would be very likely to be classified as 'private', because they would be far less closely connected to the public functions of the landlord.[84]

B. What actions of public authorities will be incompatible with Convention rights?

The scope of this text does not allow us to deal with this issue comprehensively or in detail; the interested reader should consult a standard work on the HRA. However, a few preliminary points can be made here.

(1) *Convention rights.* The term 'Convention rights' refers to the rights and fundamental freedoms set out in Articles 2 to 12 and 14 of the ECHR and in Articles 1 to 3 of the First Protocol and Articles 1 to 2 of the Sixth Protocol.[85] Many of these 'Convention rights' stretch beyond the interests currently protected by the law of tort. To pick two examples,

---

[81] The claimant alleged that the defendant had violated her right to respect for private and family life under Article 8.

[82] [2010] 1 WLR 363, at [95] (per Lord Collins). The two judges in the majority differed in the importance they attached to this issue: Elias LJ thought that it was highly relevant to the classification of the relevant act while Lord Collins thought that it was an 'essential pre-requisite' to a conclusion that the act was 'public'.

[83] See [76] (per Elias LJ) and [102] (per Lord Collins).

[84] See [76] (per Elias LJ) and [96] (per Lord Collins). The third judge, Rix LJ, doubted whether 'management' of social housing by registered social landlords was a function 'of a public nature' at all, and also thought that 'management' could be sub-divided so that even if 'allocation' of social housing was a 'public function' the termination of an individual tenancy was a 'private' act (see [160]).

[85] These articles are all set out in Sch 1 to the HRA.

there is no tort designed to protect directly a person's right to a fair trial (Article 6) or a person's right to family life (part of Article 8). Further, some 'Convention rights' offer greater protection for particular interests than is provided by the law of tort.[86] It seems likely that public authorities will act in ways that are incompatible with many, if not all, of these 'Convention rights', and that when they do so questions of liability to pay compensation will arise.[87]

(2) *Qualified rights.* It is important to bear in mind that not all of the 'Convention rights' are *absolute*. Many of them *expressly* permit restrictions, provided that such restrictions can be demonstrated to be 'prescribed by law' and 'necessary in a democratic society' in order to fulfil certain listed purposes. Where a public authority's act falls within a permitted restriction it will not be incompatible with the 'Convention right'. Moreover, even some of the rights that are not *expressly* qualified, such as the right to a fair trial (Article 6), turn out not to make *absolute* demands when they are interpreted by the ECtHR.

(3) *Acts and omissions.* Under the HRA 'failures to act' by a public authority are treated as 'acts' for the purpose of determining whether an authority has acted in a way which is incompatible with a 'Convention right'.[88] This provision is particularly important in those contexts where it has been held that a Convention right imposes a *positive* obligation on states.

For instance, in *Osman* v *United Kingdom* (1999), the European Court of Human Rights ('ECtHR' for short) ruled that Article 2 imposed a positive obligation on a state to protect an individual whose life was at risk from criminal acts, and that this included an obligation on the police to 'do all that could be reasonably expected of them to avoid a real and immediate risk to life of which they have or ought to have knowledge'.[89] Similarly, in *Z* v *United Kingdom* (2001), the ECtHR held that there was a parallel positive obligation under Article 3 on local authorities to take all steps that could reasonably be expected of them to avoid a real and immediate risk of ill-treatment of children of which they knew or ought to have had knowledge.[90]

There is, however, an important exception to the rule that the HRA generally covers omissions as well as acts: s 6(6) makes it clear that a failure to introduce a proposal for legislation cannot be treated as an unlawful 'act'. So a Minister will not act unlawfully under the HRA if all he or she fails to do is to propose a Bill to better protect a Convention Right.

---

[86] A good example is provided by Article 2, the right to life. In *Osman* v *United Kingdom* [1999] 1 FLR 193, the ECtHR held that Article 2 puts a broader duty on police to take steps to deal with threats to life by criminals than is imposed on the police by the common law. In other contexts, a duty of care will exist in parallel with an 'operational duty' to protect people from dying under Art 2: this will be the case where a patient with known suicidal tendencies is being treated in an NHS hospital (see *Savage* v *South Essex Partnership NHS Foundation Trust* [2009] 1 AC 681 (patient detained pursuant to s 3 of the Mental Health Act 1983) and *Rabone* v *Pennine Care NHS Trust* [2012] 2 AC 72 (patient treated at hospital as voluntary patient)) or, arguably, where a soldier is being equipped to fight in a war (see *Smith* v *Ministry of Defence* [2014] AC 52).

[87] In practice, some of the 'Convention rights' are violated by public authorities far more often than others. One field of activity where claims for damages under the HRA are frequently seen is 'where local authorities have infringed the right of parents under Article 8 to respect for their family life by shortcomings in the procedures by which they have taken children into care or kept them in care': see, for example, *Re P* [2007] EWCA Civ 2.

[88] HRA, s 6(6).

[89] [1999] 1 FLR 193, 223. On the facts, though, the European Court of Human Rights found that there had not been a violation of Article 2.

[90] [2001] 2 FLR 612, at [73].

C. Section 6(2)

Section 6(2) of the 1998 Act provides that a public authority will not be liable for an act which violates a 'Convention right' if:

(a) as the result of one or more provisions of primary legislation, the authority could not have acted differently; or

(b) in the case of one or more provisions of, or made under, primary legislation which cannot be read or given effect in a way which is compatible with the Convention rights, the authority was acting so as to give effect to or enforce those provisions.

This subsection means that it is not unlawful for a public authority to perform a statutory duty, even if this leads to a violation of a 'Convention right'. In such circumstances the most that a UK court will be able to do is to declare that the statutory provision is incompatible with a 'Convention right'. Similarly, a public authority will not be liable for enforcing or giving effect to an incompatible statute or delegated legislation, where that legislation cannot be given effect to in any way which is compatible. Of course, if it is possible to interpret the statute so that it does not impose a duty which will lead to the violation of a 'Convention right', or in such a way that it can be enforced or given effect without any such right being violated, then s 3 of the 1998 Act obliges a UK court to adopt this interpretation,[91] and as a result the protection that s 6(2) might have provided for a public authority will evaporate.

D. The availability of remedies: victims

If a public authority has acted incompatibly with a 'Convention right' a claimant will only be able to obtain damages, or any other remedy, if he or she was a 'victim' of the public authority's unlawful act.[92] The HRA expressly relies on the definition of 'victim' developed in individual claims to the ECtHR under Article 34 of the ECHR.[93] A person will have no difficulty in establishing that she is a 'victim' if she has been 'directly affected' by the public authority's unlawful act. In certain circumstances, however, the ECtHR has also allowed claims by 'indirect victims', for instance, close relatives of a person whose right to life was violated.[94] Thus in *Rabone* v *Pennine Care NHS Foundation Trust* (2012), the UK Supreme Court held that the parents of a patient who had killed herself counted as 'victims' of the breach of Article 2 of the ECHR that the doctor had committed in allowing her to go home from hospital when it was unsafe to leave her on her own. This opened the door to the parents' obtaining an award of £5,000 each in respect of the violation of Article 2, in circumstances where they would not have been allowed to sue for damages for bereavement under the Fatal Accidents Act 1976.[95]

---

[91] See above, § 1.8.

[92] HRA, s 7(1). See, generally, Miles 2000.

[93] Section 7(7).

[94] In *Savage* v *South Essex Partnership NHS Foundation Trust* [2010] EWHC 865 (QB), at [91], Mackay J reported that decisions of the ECtHR have treated the range of relatives having 'the necessary standing to bring a claim based on an Article 2 violation' as including: 'siblings...; parents...; the... son of the deceased...; and a nephew.....'.

[95] Such damages are only payable to the parents of a *minor* who has been wrongfully killed (see below, § 28.5), and the patient in *Rabone* was 24 when she died.

Companies and other associations with legal personality can be 'victims',[96] but *core* public authorities cannot be.[97]

E. The quantification of damages: principles

Where a court finds that a public authority has acted incompatibly with a 'Convention right' it may only award damages if it is a type of court which can award damages in civil proceedings.[98] Section 8(3) of the HRA states that a court should not award damages unless, taking account of all the circumstances of the case, it 'is satisfied that the award is necessary to afford just satisfaction to the person in whose favour it is made'.[99] In considering whether an award is *necessary*, and, if it is, the amount, courts are instructed to 'take into account the principles applied by the European Court of Human Rights in relation to the award of compensation under Article 41 of the Convention'.[100] This instruction might seem relatively loose, since it is an instruction 'to take into account', not 'follow', and refers to 'principles', not 'detailed practice'. But in *R (Greenfield)* v *Secretary of State for the Home Department* (2005) the House of Lords unanimously held that domestic courts should follow the Strasbourg court's guidance with regard to both *when* an award should be made and the *amount* because 'the purpose of incorporating the Convention in domestic law through the 1998 Act was not to give victims better remedies at home than they could recover in Strasbourg but to give them the same remedies without the delay and expense of resort to Strasbourg.'[101]

Before the HRA came into force the Law Commission carried out a survey of the 'principles' applied by the ECtHR,[102] and concluded that 'the only principle which is clearly stated in the Strasbourg caselaw is that of *restitutio in integrum*'.[103] That is: the victim should be returned, as far as possible, to the position that he or she would have been in had there not been a breach of a 'Convention right'. The Court of Appeal has described this as 'the fundamental principle' and has derived from it the proposition that 'where the breach of a Convention right has clearly caused significant pecuniary loss, this will usually be assessed and awarded'.

This leaves open, however, the question of how the courts should deal with cases where a victim has suffered non-pecuniary loss. In an important recent book, Jason Varuhas has argued that the English courts ought to have adopted 'a "vindicatory", tort-based approach . . . to the decision whether to award damages, to assessment of quantum and to the kinds of damages available to remedy violations.'[104] He contrasts this with the approach that has actually been adopted, which compels English courts to pay close attention to the Strasbourg case law, arguing that this is unhelpful because the ECtHR's

---

[96] Provided that the right that they are asserting is one which can be enjoyed by such a body.

[97] *Aston*, at [8]: 'A core public authority seems inherently incapable of satisfying the Convention description of a victim' (per Lord Nicholls).

[98] HRA, s 8(1). The Family Court can award damages (*Re H (a child: breach of Convention rights: damages)* [2014] EWFC 38, at [64]) but magistrates and the Crown Court probably cannot do so.

[99] See, generally, Fairgrieve 2001.

[100] Section 8(4).

[101] [2005] 1 WLR 673, at [19]. This approach was confirmed by the UKSC in *R (Faulkner)* v *Secretary of State for Justice* [2013] 2 AC 254. Varuhas 2016 criticises this approach.

[102] Law Com. No. 266, *Damages Under the Human Rights Act 1998* (2000).

[103] Ibid, para 3.78.

[104] Varuhas 2016, 1. He regards an award as 'vindicatory' if it affirms the inherent worth of an interest, its normative importance within a hierarchy of norms, and that it ought to be treated with respect (p. 4).

'approach is influenced by its status as a subsidiary, supranational institution' and 'its Article 41 jurisprudence is renowned for its lack of principle, consistency, coherence and "parsimonious" reasoning.'[105] Such criticisms of the ECtHR's jurisprudence are not without foundation, but the Law Commission identified five specific factors which appear to have been regularly taken into account by the ECtHR in determining whether or not to make an award of damages, and how to fix on an appropriate amount.[106]

(1) *A finding of a violation may constitute 'just satisfaction'.* Where an applicant has not suffered pecuniary loss as a result of a breach, the ECtHR has sometimes concluded that the mere decision that there was a violation is sufficient to constitute 'just satisfaction'. This conclusion is most common in cases where convicted criminals have claimed that while they were being investigated or tried there were violations of a procedural type.[107]

(2) *The degree of loss suffered must be sufficient to justify an award of damages.* Although the ECtHR has generally been more willing to award damages for forms of mental distress falling short of psychiatric injury than English courts dealing with tort claims, it has also usually insisted that something beyond mere annoyance or frustration must be shown before an award of damages will be appropriate.[108] Consistently with this, in *R (KB)* v *London and South and West Region Mental Health Review Tribunal* (2004), Stanley Burnton J concluded that mental health patients who had suffered frustration and distress because of inordinate delay in processing their claims to mental health review tribunals in violation of Article 5(4) were only entitled to compensation for significant distress, which he took to be distress at the level that might be recorded in clinical notes.

But while the ECtHR has been more willing to award damages for mental distress than English courts dealing with tort claims this difference is largely offset by the fact that the ECtHR does not tend to make awards for an invasion of a right *per se*. Thus English courts in tort claims often give damages for harms such as 'loss of liberty' without looking for any form of further *consequential* loss, while the ECtHR will in parallel situations only award damages for mental distress or other forms of *consequential* loss.[109]

In cases involving bereavement, it seems it will not be difficult to establish sufficient loss to justify an award of damages. In *Savage* v *South Essex Partnership NHS Foundation Trust* (2010), Mackay J made an award of £10,000 to the adult daughter of a mother who

---

[105] Varuhas 2016, 6.

[106] Law Com. No. 266, para 4.44.

[107] In *R (Greenfield)* v *Secretary of State for the Home Department* [2005] 1 WLR 673, the House of Lords decided that no damages should be awarded to a prisoner whose Article 6 'Convention right' was violated when a deputy controller, who was not an independent and impartial tribunal, decided that he had committed a prison disciplinary offence. The court concluded, however, a procedural violation could lead to an award of damages if the violation led to the claimant being 'deprived of a real chance of a better outcome' (at [14]–[15]) or caused 'anxiety and frustration' (at [16]).

[108] *Silver* v *United Kingdom* (1991) 13 EHRR 582. In *R (Greenfield)* v *Secretary of State for the Home Department* [2005] 1 WLR 673, the House of Lords did not suggest that feelings of 'anxiety and frustration' had to reach any particular pitch before an award of damages could be made *but* nonetheless refused to make an award to the claimant in the case confronting them. The court apparently attached weight to the facts that although the claimant had demonstrated 'structural bias' the conduct of the adjudication was exemplary and he was not treated in an unexpected way or differently from anyone else (see [29]). Compare *R (Sturnham) (Nos 1 and 2)* v *Parole Board* [2013] 2 AC 254, where Lord Reed suggested (at [66]) that the stress and anxiety caused by a delay of three months in the holding of a hearing by the Parole Board would be likely to be sufficient to justify an award of damages, but a shorter delay would not ordinarily have a sufficiently serious effect on an applicant.

[109] For further analysis of this distinction see Steele 2008, 630–4.

had committed suicide, acknowledging that the award could 'never compensate her for the loss of her mother and can only be a symbolic acknowledgement that the defendant ought properly to give her some compensation to reflect her loss'.[110] In *Rabone* v *Pennine NHS Trust* (2012), Lord Dyson upheld an award of £5,000 each to parents whose 24 year old suicidal daughter had killed herself after being allowed to leave hospital, emphasising the closeness of the parents to their daughter and the added distress they would have suffered, knowing that if the hospital authorities had listened to their warnings about their daughter's condition she might still be alive.[111] Indeed, he thought £5,000 each might be too low, but the parents had not asked for the award to be increased on appeal.[112]

(3) *The seriousness of the violation will be taken into account.* Substantial awards have been made for both pecuniary and non-pecuniary losses where there has been a serious violation, for instance, deliberate torture.[113] At the same time, however, the ECtHR has expressly refused to award aggravated or exemplary damages.[114]

(4) *The conduct of the public authority may be taken into account.* This includes both the conduct giving rise to the claim and any record of previous violations by the state. As noted above, the ECtHR does not award 'exemplary damages', but it tends to be more generous in compensating for non-pecuniary loss when the behaviour of a public authority has been particularly reprehensible[115] or forms part of a pattern of violations.[116] In *Anufrijeva* v *Southwark LBC* (2004), the Court of Appeal held that the wording of s 8 precluded awarding exemplary damages.[117]

The question has been asked whether a claimant must show that a breach of Convention rights was the result of a public authority's blameworthy conduct in order to obtain damages.[118] The simple answer must be 'no'. But the more detailed answer will add the qualifications that *in some circumstances* the claimant will have to show fault on the part of the public authority in order to establish that the authority acted incompatibly with a particular Convention right,[119] and *in some circumstances* the blameworthiness of the

---

[110] [2010] EWHC 865 (QB), at [97].

[111] [2012] 2 AC 72, at [87].

[112] [2012] 2 AC 72, at [88].

[113] *Aksoy* v *Turkey* (1997) 23 EHRR 553.

[114] Discussed in Chapter 24, below.

[115] Two cases involving the United Kingdom provide good examples of this factor in action: *Halford* v *United Kingdom* (1997) 24 EHRR 523 (£10,000 awarded for stress caused by phone-tapping); *Smith and Grady* v *United Kingdom* (2000) 29 EHRR 493 (£19,000 awarded for non-pecuniary loss suffered as a result of investigation and dismissal from the armed forces because of sexual orientation).

[116] Cases involving excessive length of legal proceedings in Italy provide the best example of this factor in action: Law Com. No. 266, paras 3.52–3.53.

[117] [2004] QB 1124, at [55]. The House of Lords has suggested, however, that one reason why an award of damages may be appropriate, rather than a finding of a violation being held to be just satisfaction, is if 'there is felt to be a need to encourage compliance [with their duties under the Convention] by individual officials or classes of official: *R (Greenfield)* v *Secretary of State for the Home Department* [2005] 1 WLR 673, at [19].

[118] Fairgrieve 2001, 698.

[119] For instance, where the Convention right imposes a positive obligation to take *reasonable* steps to protect someone's life under Article 2, a claimant will only be able to show that an omission to take steps was incompatible with Article 2 if it would have been *reasonable* to take such steps. In *Savage* v *South Essex Partnership NHS Foundation Trust* [2009] 1 AC 681, Baroness Hale suggested (at [100]) that in judging what steps it would have been reasonable to take to prevent someone from committing suicide it would be necessary to take into account the importance of that person's liberty and autonomy and the available resources.

public authority may be decisive in demonstrating that damages are necessary as 'just satisfaction'.

(5) *The conduct of the applicant will be taken into account.* An award will be reduced where the applicant's conduct made a violation more likely or contributed to the damage suffered as a result of a violation.[120] There is also some evidence of a general reluctance to compensate criminals for violations of their 'Convention rights'.[121]

The Law Commission's review concluded that in most cases courts awarding damages under the HRA would award amounts similar to what might have been awarded had the claim been for a tort.[122] But in *R (Greenfield)* v *Secretary of State for the Home Department* (2005), as we noted above, the House of Lords insisted that courts should pay attention to the level of awards made by the ECtHR and 'should not aim to be significantly more or less generous than [that] court might be expected to be'.[123] This means that claimants must frequently accompany their claims with schedules listing the awards made by the ECtHR in comparable cases.[124] Before the HRA came into force Lord Woolf stated, extra-judicially, that awards made by English courts under s 8 for non-pecuniary losses should be 'moderate',[125] and this comment has been judicially endorsed.[126] Is there a good reason for moderation? Some explanation may be found in a principle identified by Lord Woolf CJ in *Anufrijeva* v *Southwark LBC* (2004): 'in considering whether to award compensation and, if so, how much, there is a balance to be drawn between the interests of the victim and those of the public as a whole.'[127] This suggests that a victim's interest in receiving compensation for a violation of his or her 'Convention rights' is something that a court should weigh against the interest of the wider public in the continued funding of public services.

F. Liability for judicial acts

Section 9(3) of the HRA states that 'In proceedings under this Act in respect of a judicial act done in good faith, damages may not be awarded otherwise than to compensate a person to the extent required by Article 5(5) of the Convention'.

---

[120] In *McCann* v *United Kingdom* (1996) 21 EHRR 97, the ECtHR found a violation of Article 2 (right to life) with respect to three IRA terrorists suspected of planning a bomb attack on Gibraltar, but refused to award compensation because of the applicants' behaviour.

[121] Law Com. No. 266, para. 3.57 discusses the different views on this matter.

[122] Law Com. No. 266, para 4.97. In *Anufrijeva* v *Southwark LBC* [2004] QB 1124, Lord Woolf CJ instructed courts making awards for kinds of harm not commonly compensated for in tort law to consider the level of awards for such harm commonly made by the Parliamentary Ombudsman and Local Government Ombudsman.

[123] [2005] 1 WLR 673, at [19]. Awards in cases brought against the UK, or countries with a similar cost of living, are most relevant: *R (Sturnham)* v *Parole Board (Nos 1 and 2)* [2013] 2 AC 254, at [39].

[124] *R (Sturnham)* v *Parole Board (Nos 1 and 2)* [2013] 2 AC 254, at [99]–[103].

[125] Woolf 2000, 434.

[126] *Anufrijeva* v *Southwark LBC* [2004] QB 1124, at [73]. Lord Woolf also stated extra-judicially that awards should be 'normally on the low side by comparison to tortious awards', but in the same paragraph that endorsed his call for 'moderate' awards for non-pecuniary loss the Court of Appeal said that the 'on the low side' comment 'should in future be ignored'. In *R (Greenfield)* v *Secretary of State for the Home Department* [2005] 1 WLR 673, [19], the House of Lords suggested that damages under the HRA might seem modest alongside tort awards because in HRA cases the finding of a violation would always be 'an important part' of a claimant's remedy.

[127] [2004] QB 1124 at [56].

Article 5(5) provides that 'Everyone who has been the victim of arrest or detention in contravention of the provisions of this Article [5] shall have an enforceable right to compensation.' In practice, the ECtHR has not interpreted Article 5 as being violated whenever a judge has made an error and imposed an inappropriate prison sentence. But where imprisonment follows conviction at a trial that was vitiated by 'gross and obvious irregularity' or a 'flagrant denial of justice' that a judge was responsible for, a claimant may seek damages.[128]

Where a judicial act has not led to imprisonment but interference with some other 'Convention right', such as Article 8 (family life), s 9(3) will be important, since it precludes an award of damages if the act was done in good faith.[129] To an extent, it may be possible to circumvent this by attributing the violation to the act of some other public authority, for instance, a public prosecutor. But this will not always be possible, because s 9(5) defines 'judicial act' as including 'an act done on the instructions, or on behalf, of a judge'.

G. Liability for legislative acts

For the avoidance of doubt it is worth stating that because the term 'public authority' does not include 'either House of Parliament or a person exercising functions in connection with proceedings in Parliament'[130] there will be no liability under s 8 of the HRA for the passing of legislation which violates a 'Convention right'. Further, because, as we noted above, 'act' does not include 'a failure to (a) introduce in, or lay before, Parliament a proposal for legislation, or (b) make any primary legislation or remedial order',[131] there will be no liability under s 8 of the HRA for a ministerial failure to correct legislation which violates a 'Convention right'.

Further reading

Some see the torts dealt with in this chapter as examples of defendants being held liable for an 'abuse of rights': see, for example, **Jason Neyers, 'Explaining the inexplicable? Four manifestations of abuse of rights in English law' in Nolan and Robertson (eds), *Rights and Private Law* (Hart Publishing, 2011), Chapter 11**. The difficulty with this view is that it is hard to see that there is a *right* to bring an unjustified prosecution, or a *right* in a public body to act unlawfully. For this reason we prefer to characterise these torts as being directed at abuses of *power*, rather than abuses of *right*.

On the tort of misfeasance in public office we particularly recommend **Mark Aronson, 'Misfeasance in public office: a very peculiar tort' (2011) 35 *Melbourne University Law Review***, which discusses significant questions about the future of the tort, and draws on a wealth of knowledge about both public and private law in a range of Commonwealth jurisdictions. **John Murphy** continues his long march through tort law, trying to show that popular (but wrong?) theories of tort law do not marry with established tort law doctrines, in his **'Misfeasance in public office: a tort law misfit?' (2012) 32 *Oxford Journal of Legal Studies* 51**.

---

[128] *Webster v Lord Chancellor* [2016] QB 676; *LL v Lord Chancellor* [2017] EWCA Civ 237.
[129] It will be difficult to infer a lack of good faith from a judicial error in the absence of evidence of an ulterior motive: *Webster v Lord Chancellor* [2016] QB 67, at [34].
[130] HRA, s 6(3)(b).
[131] Section 6(6).

So many interesting books and articles have been written about the Human Rights Act 1998, claims for damages under it, and its relation to tort law, that it seems invidious to highlight only two. Nonetheless, we think that **Jenny Steele, 'Damages in tort and under the Human Rights Act: remedial or functional separation?' (2008) 67** *Cambridge Law Journal* **606** discusses some particularly important questions about the relationship between tort remedies and remedies under the 1998 Act, whilst Jason Varuhas provides comprehensive analysis and provocative answers to similar questions in his outstanding book *Damages and Human Rights* (**Hart Publishing, 2016**).

Chapter 22
Defences

Aims and objectives

Reading this chapter should enable you to:

(1) Understand what we, and other academics, mean by a 'defence' to being sued in tort, and how the different defences might be classified.

(2) Get a good grasp of the full range of defences that might be raised to a claim in tort, in particular, the defences of (a) *volenti non fit injuria*; and (b) illegality. (The 'defence' of contributory negligence is dealt with in Chapter 23.)

22.1 The basics

In this chapter, we look at some general pleas that a defendant in a tort case might be able to make to defeat the claim that is being made against him. Some of these pleas involve the defendant in denying that he is liable to the claimant because he did nothing wrong to him. A defence such as *volenti non fit injuria* ('no wrong is done to the willing') is of this type. Unsurprisingly, we are already very familiar with this defence as it is an important feature of all of the torts set out in this text that the claimant did not consent to be treated in the way he was. Other defences take the form of the defendant arguing he is not liable to the claimant because, even if he did something wrong to the claimant, the claimant still cannot sue him for reasons of public policy, or the proper administration of justice.[1]

---

[1] Goudkamp 2013 draws a more subtle distinction between 'denials' (where the defendant claims 'I did no wrong' and which are not defences at all in his book), 'justifications' (where the defendant claims 'I did wrong but I was justified in what I did'), and 'public policy defences'. In our view, there are no such thing as 'justifications', in the sense that Goudkamp (following John Gardner in this respect) is using that term. It makes no sense to say 'I did wrong but I was justified in doing what I did' and this nonsense is not saved through observations that 'wrongdoing calls for justification if anything does'. No: what calls for justification is conduct that we would *normally* regard as wrong in the absence of justification. If there are no such things as 'justifications' in the way Goudkamp is using that term, then on his view, the only things that genuinely count as defences are 'public policy defences'. However, it is convenient to also deal in this chapter with factors giving rise to what Goudkamp calls 'denials' – where the defendant is allowed to claim that, ultimately, he did no wrong to the claimant – as they apply across the board to all torts and would therefore – if they were not decanted into a general 'Defences' chapter – have to be mentioned over and over again in every chapter dealing with particular torts.

We will not seek rigorously to classify all the defences set out below as either being 'no wrong defences' (arguing 'I did no wrong') or 'public policy defences' (arguing 'Even if I did do something wrong, considerations of the public interest require that I not be held liable for what I did').[2] (To save words, from now on we will call a 'no wrong defence', a 'NWD'; and a 'public policy defence', a 'PPD'.) It seems to us that there are some defences that could be classified either way. For example, when a trade union calls its members out on strike, thereby inducing them to breach their contracts of employment, the trade union cannot be sued for inducing a breach of contract, provided it has followed the proper procedures before calling the strike. It is hard to tell, in such a case, whether the trade union's *immunity* from being sued in this case should be classified as an NWD ('We did no wrong in calling our members out on strike') or as a PPD ('We did wrong, but we cannot be sued for it because public policy dictates that the interests of trades unions in being allowed to call strikes over their grievances should prevail over the interest employers have in keeping their employees working').

Difficult though the distinction might be to apply in concrete cases, the distinction is important for the purpose of evaluating whether or not a particular defence should be recognised or not. NWDs need no justification – if the defendant did not do anything wrong to the claimant, he should not be held liable to the claimant, and that is that. But PPDs are in need of very strong justification if they are to be recognised. This is because 'the rule of public policy that has first claim on the loyalty of the law [is] that wrongs should be remedied.'[3] We have already come across this *dictum* before, as a factor that the courts consider in determining whether or not one person owed another a duty of care.[4] We attacked the relevance of this factor to the inquiry as to whether the defendant owed a duty of care to the claimant – because it presupposes precisely what is at issue in that inquiry: whether the defendant did anything wrong to the claimant. But this *dictum* comes into its own in this chapter, so far as PPDs are concerned. If the defendant *has* done something wrong to the claimant, that is something – as we will see later on, when we consider the basis of claims for compensatory damages – that calls out to be repaired or rectified.[5] The existence of PPDs leaves the hole created by the defendant's tort unfilled. And that is something that requires substantial justification.[6]

---

[2] There seems to be no room in tort law – as there is in criminal law – for an *excusatory* defence of 'I did wrong, but the circumstances in which I committed are such that it would be unfair to hold me liable to the claimant.' For discussion, see Goudkamp 2013, 82–101, Goldberg 2015, and Edelman and Dyer 2015.

[3] See *X v Bedfordshire CC* [1995] 2 AC 633, at 663 (per Sir Thomas Bingham MR); *Gorringe v Calderdale MBC* [2004] 1 WLR 1057, at [2] (per Lord Steyn); *A v Essex CC* [2004] 1 WLR 1881, at [43]; *D v East Berkshire Community NHS Trust* [2005] 2 AC 373, at [24]–[25] (per Lord Bingham).

[4] See above, § 4.3(L).

[5] See below, § 23.7.

[6] As a result a PPD that is overbroad is liable to be found to contravene Article 6(1) of the ECHR (which provides that in the determination of his civil rights and obligations . . . everyone is entitled to a fair and public hearing within a reasonable time by an independent and impartial tribunal established by law.' Whether Article 6(1) extends to an NWD, and if so when, is a matter of debate: see *Fayed v United Kingdom* (1994) 18 EHRR 393 at [65], *Matthews v Ministry of Defence* [2003] 1 AC 1163, at [35], [79], and *Roche v United Kingdom* (2006) 42 EHRR 30. For an extended discussion of the effect of these cases, see previous editions of this text. As the issue of whether Article 6(1) extends to an NWD seems not to have troubled the courts of late, the discussion has been dropped from this edition.

So in going through the defences set out below, it is worth asking yourself – is this defence an NWD or a PPD? And if it is a PPD, ask yourself whether the reasons for the defence justify overriding the normal right that the victim of a tort would have to seek some kind of remedy from the person who committed that tort.

22.2 Lack of capacity

We start with a defence that very rarely applies. It is very rare for a person to be able to plead that they lacked the capacity to commit a tort. Three types of person who might want to make such a plea can be distinguished.

A. Children[7]

Under the criminal law, children under the age of 10 are incapable of committing crimes.[8] The same is not true of tort law. A child who has fulfilled all the requirements for a tort to have been committed will have committed that tort, whatever their age. This position is of very long standing. For example, in *Jennings* v *Rundall* (1799), Lord Kenyon CJ remarked, '. . . if an infant commit an assault, or utter slander, God forbid that he should not be answerable for it in a Court of Justice.'[9]

The seeming harshness of tort law in subjecting children to the same legal require-ments as adults is substantially mitigated by the fact that in so far as foreseeability of harm is a prerequisite either to finding a defendant has committed a tort or to holding the defendant liable for the consequences of a tort that he or she has committed, the courts will take into account the defendant's age in judging what sort of harm was reasonably foreseeable.[10] So, for example, we have already seen that in *Mullin* v *Richards* (1998)[11] – where Mullin and Richards, both 15-year-old schoolgirls, were playfully fencing with plastic rulers when one of the rulers shattered and Mullin was blinded in her right eye – Richards was held not to have committed the tort of negligence in play fighting with Mullin as a typical 15 year old could not have been expected to foresee that Mullin would be injured as a result of their play. In so ruling, the Court of Appeal followed the approach of the High Court of Australia in *McHale* v *Watson* (1966), where a 12-year-old was being sued in negligence for throwing a spike at a wooden post. Unfortunately, the spike cannoned off the post and hit the claimant in the eye. The High Court found that the defendant was not liable in negligence for the claimant's injury as it would not have been

---

[7] See Bagshaw 2001, Goudkamp 2013, 184–86.

[8] Children and Young Persons Act 1933, s 50.

[9] (1799) 8 TR 335, 337; 101 ER 1419, 1421–2.

[10] The courts will also not allow a claim in tort to be made against a child where doing so would subvert the rules protecting children from being bound by contracts. So a claim in tort cannot be made against a child who has purportedly hired a horse and ridden it for longer than the contract of hire permitted as the contract of hire was not binding on the child (*Jennings* v *Rundall* (1799) 8 TR 335, 101 ER 1419), but a claim in tort can be made against a child who has purportedly hired a horse and injured it by making it do something that the child could foresee was dangerous (*Burnard* v *Haggis* (1863) 14 CB (NS) 45, 143 ER 360).

[11] Discussed above, § 5.2.

reasonably foreseeable to a typical 12-year-old that throwing the spike would result in injury to the claimant:

> It is, I think, a matter for judicial notice that the ordinary boy of twelve suffers from a feeling that a piece of wood and a sharp instrument have a special affinity. To expect a boy of that age to consider before throwing the spike whether the timber was hard or soft, to weight the chances of being able to make the spike stick in the post, and to foresee that it might glance off and hit the girl, would be, I think, to expect a degree of sense and circumspection which nature ordinarily withholds till life has become less rosy.[12]

B. Persons suffering from mental illness

Tort law does not make any special exceptions for people suffering from mental illness.[13] If such a person has fulfilled all the requirements for committing a tort, then he will be held to have committed that tort. So, for example, in *Morriss* v *Marsden* (1952), the defendant suffered from schizophrenia and attacked the claimant, the manager of a hotel at which the defendant was staying. The court found that the defendant knew what he was doing at the time he attacked the claimant, but his mental condition meant that he did not know what he was doing was wrong. Under the criminal law, the defendant would have been found not guilty 'by reason of insanity' of committing an offence against the person in attacking the claimant.[14] However, the defendant *was* found to have committed the tort of battery in attacking the claimant as he had the requisite intention to commit that tort – an intent to apply force to the claimant's person – and was held liable to pay the claimant almost £6,000 in damages.[15]

It does not seem – in terms of determining what was reasonably foreseeable to the defendant in a tort case – that the courts will make the same concession to defendants who are mentally ill as they do to children. That is, they will *not* judge what was reasonably foreseeable by adopting the point of view of a reasonable person with the defendant's mental incapacities.[16] However, the objectivity of the standard of care that defendants are expected to live up to in performing a task such as driving will be relaxed where a defendant's mental incapacity meant that he was incapable of driving to the same standard as a ordinary, reasonable driver *and* the onset of that incapacity was sudden and could not have been foreseen by the defendant.[17]

C. The Crown

It used to be believed that 'The King can do no wrong', with the result that it used to be the case that it was simply not possible to bring a claim in tort against the 'Crown' – a term which includes the monarch, government departments, and heads of government departments acting in an official capacity. (Of course, an employee of the Crown could

---

[12] (1966) 115 CLR 199, at 216.
[13] See Goudkamp 2011b, and Goudkamp 2013, 166–84, for arguments that insanity should be a defence to being sued in tort.
[14] This is under the *M'Naghten* rules on when a criminal defendant will be found not guilty by reason of insanity, under which rules a defendant will be able to take advantage of a defence of insanity if he was suffering from 'a disease of the mind' which meant either that he did not know what he was doing, or if he did know what he was doing, that he did not know it was wrong (legally *and* morally).
[15] A huge sum of money at that time: worth approximately £135,000 in today's money.
[16] See Moran 2003, 18–26.
[17] *Mansfield* v *Weetabix* [1998] 1 WLR 1263.

always be held personally liable if he or she had committed a tort in relation to the claimant.) The Crown Proceedings Act 1947 abrogated this rule to some extent. Section 2 of the Act provides that the Crown can be sued in tort, in the same way that an ordinary person can be: (1) in respect of torts committed by its servants or agents; (2) in respect of a breach of a duty of care it owes one of its employees as that employee's employer; (3) in respect of a breach of a duty attaching to 'the ownership, occupation, use or control of property'; or (4) in respect of the breach of a statutory duty which is binding on people 'other than the Crown and its officers' and breach of which is normally actionable in tort. Otherwise the old rule of Crown immunity from being sued in tort remains.

22.3 Political immunities

A number of immunities to being sued in tort serve a political function, of allowing states and their agents to act free from the fear that their actions might result in their being sued in tort. For example, the defence of *act of state* classically applies in a case where the Crown, or someone whose acts have been authorised or ratified by the Crown, has deliberately injured a claimant who is not British and where the injury occurred outside British territory.[18] It is doubtful whether 'act of state' could be successfully pleaded to defeat the claim of a British citizen who is injured abroad,[19] and impossible that the plea could be successfully made where anyone – whether British or not – is injured on British soil.[20] In such cases, an attempt might be made to defeat the claim by relying on s 11 of the Crown Proceedings Act 1947, which provides that the Crown cannot be sued in tort for exercising its powers under the royal prerogative or under statute. However, it has been held that the Crown enjoys no powers under the royal prerogative to seize or destroy a British subject's property without compensating the property owner for the loss of his property.[21] English law also recognises the existence of *sovereign*[22] and *diplomatic*[23] *immunities* which protect foreign states and their diplomats from being sued in tort for actions performed on UK soil.

---

[18] See, for example, *Buron v Denman* (1848) 2 Exch 167, 154 ER 450, where Rear Admiral Joseph Denman burned down some depots at the mouth of the Gallinas river in Africa (on the current border between Sierra Leone and Liberia) where almost 850 slaves were being held. The Spanish slave dealer who owned the depots sued for damages. Denman's actions having been ratified by the Crown, it was held that the claim must be dismissed on the ground of 'act of state'. It is questionable, though, whether UK law would even apply nowadays to such a case (that is, the case where a foreigner has suffered some kind of harm outside the UK): see the Private International Law (Miscellaneous Provisions) Act 1995, Part III. (Though see *Bici v Ministry of Defence* [2004] EWHC 786 (QB), where it was agreed that two Albanian Kosovars who had been shot at by UK soldiers working for the UN in Kosovo could have their claims for damages against the UK government tried under UK law.) It is different with the Human Rights Act 1998, which can apply to protect foreigners living outside the UK: *R (Al-Skeini) v Secretary of State for Defence* [2008] 1 AC 153 and *R (Smith) v Oxfordshire Assistant Deputy Coroner* [2011] 1 AC 1. In those cases, the Supreme Court ruled that the Human Rights Act 1998 applied in UK military bases on foreign soil. The European Court of Human Rights has recently gone much further by ruling in *Al-Skeini v United Kingdom* (7 July 2011) that the European Convention on Human Rights applies not just in UK military bases abroad, but more generally in territories or areas which are controlled by the UK, or over which the UK has assumed some governmental powers.

[19] *Nissan v Attorney-General* [1970] AC 179, 213 (per Lord Reid).

[20] *Johnstone v Pedlar* [1921] 2 AC 262.

[21] *Attorney-General v De Keyser's Royal Hotel* [1920] AC 508; *Burmah Oil Co Ltd v Lord Advocate* [1965] AC 75; *Nissan v Attorney-General* [1970] AC 179, 227–8 (per Lord Pearce).

[22] See the State Immunity Act 1978.

[23] See the Diplomatic Privileges Act 1964.

22.4 Trade union immunity

If A, a trade union member, has committed a tort in relation to B, B will be barred from bringing a claim in tort against A under s 219 of the Trade Union and Labour Relations (Consolidation) Act 1992 Act *if:* (1) A committed his tort in the 'contemplation or furtherance of a trade dispute';[24] *and* (2) the tort committed by A was one of the following torts: inducing a breach of contract, interfering with the performance of a contract, interfering with B's business using the unlawful means of threatening a breach of contract, lawful means conspiracy; *and* (3) none of the qualifications to s 219 of the 1992 Act apply in A's case.[25]

22.5 Witness immunity

The basic rule is that the testimony a witness gives in court cannot give rise to a claim in tort against that witness. The reason for giving witnesses such an immunity from being sued in tort is the importance the law attaches to witnesses in judicial proceedings being able to say what they want in court free from the fear that they might be sued for what they say.[26] Witness immunity will normally protect witnesses from being sued for defamation, but it will also protect them from being sued for conspiracy (where the claimant's claim will be that the testimony was given with the object of harming the claimant, in furtherance of a conspiracy to injure the claimant),[27] or even negligence (where the claimant's claim will be that the witness acted carelessly, and breached a duty of care owed to the claimant, in giving the testimony she did). Witness immunity will also protect an actual or potential witness from being sued for pre-trial statements made to lawyers who are building a case.[28] The reason for this is that the protection given to witnesses for what they say in court would be easily eroded if claimants could simply refocus their claims on what the witness said before trial.

An important limit on the scope of witness immunity was created by the decision of the Supreme Court in *Jones* v *Kaney* (2011), which dealt with whether witness immunity

---

[24] Section 244 of the 1992 Act defines a 'trade dispute' as involving a 'dispute between workers and their employer which relates wholly or mainly' to such things as – the workers' terms and conditions of employment, the employer's actions in firing or refusing to engage one or more workers; matters of discipline; a worker's membership or non-membership of a trade union; facilities for officials of trade unions.

[25] *Very broadly speaking*, s 219 will not work to protect A from being sued by B if: (1) A's tort was committed by him in the course of picketing which was not rendered lawful by s 220 of the 1992 Act (s 219(3)); (2) A's tort was committed because B proposed to employ a non-union member or refused to discriminate against a non-union member (s 222); (3) A's tort was committed because B dismissed an employee for unofficial trade union action (s 223); (4) B was not party to the trade dispute in the furtherance of which A's tort was committed (s 224, though A will still be protected if his tort was committed in the course of lawfully picketing B's premises); (5) A's tort was committed in order to pressure B into recognising a trade union (s 225).

[26] Witnesses who knowingly give false testimony in court are, of course, liable to be prosecuted for perjury. However, the prospect of a prosecution for perjury is not likely to have any 'chilling' effect on what (honest) witnesses say in court. Witnesses will know that prosecutions for perjury are very rare and are only brought in blatant cases of dishonesty, so there is little or no likelihood of a witness who gives his testimony in good faith being prosecuted for perjury.

[27] *Marrinan* v *Vibart* [1963] 1 QB 528.

[28] *Watson* v *M'Ewan* [1905] AC 480 (no claim for defamation would be allowed in respect of statements about the claimant made to the barrister who was acting for the claimant's wife, and gathering evidence for the wife's impending divorce proceedings).

protected an *expert witness* who was hired by the claimant to give his views about a case the claimant was involved in. The Supreme Court ruled by five Justices to two that witness immunity does not apply to expert witness. In *Jones* v *Kaney* itself, the claimant was negligently run over by a drunk driver. The claimant sued for compensation claiming that she had, among other things, suffered post-traumatic stress disorder (PTSD) as a result of being run over. There was some dispute over whether the claimant was actually suffering from PTSD, and the claimant hired the defendant to give her view as a consultant clinical psychologist. The defendant initially agreed that the claimant was suffering from PTSD but after a judge ordered the defendant and an expert witness on the other side to come up with a joint opinion, the defendant signed a report prepared by the other expert witness which said that the claimant was *not* suffering from PTSD and was deliberately exaggerating some of his symptoms. Faced with this joint report, the claimant's claim for damages was settled for a lot less than it might have been. The claimant sued the defendant in negligence, alleging that as he had hired her to work for him as an expert witness, she had owed him a duty to do that work with a reasonable degree of care and skill and had breached that duty in simply going along with the opinion of the expert witness on the other side. The Supreme Court ruled that there was no reason why expert witnesses should be protected by witness immunity. Holding that expert witnesses could be sued by their clients in negligence would not, they thought, have an adverse effect either on the quality of the testimony given by expert witnesses,[29] or the willingness of expert witnesses to give evidence in court.

While the Supreme Court's decision in *Jones* v *Kaney* has limited the scope of witness immunity – at least in so far as claims against *expert* witnesses by their *clients* are concerned – there are other authorities that have *extended* witness immunity to protect defendants from being sued for statements that have been made in the course of an *investigation* into actual or alleged criminal offences. For example, in *X* v *Bedfordshire County Council* (1995), Lord Browne-Wilkinson held that a psychiatrist who was employed by the police to determine who had sexually abused a child could not be sued in negligence for mistakenly reporting that the child had been sexually abused by the child's mother's lover; her report was protected by witness immunity.[30] In *Taylor* v *Director of the Serious Fraud Office* (1999), the defendant was a lawyer in the Serious Fraud Office. She suspected that the claimant, a lawyer practising in the Isle of Man, was engaged in a major fraud with one F. She wrote to the Attorney-General of the Isle of Man, requesting his assistance in her investigation. When F was eventually charged and prosecuted, the Serious Fraud Office's files on him were disclosed to F. These files included a copy of the defendant's letter which F showed to the claimant. The claimant sued the defendant for libel. The claim was dismissed; it was held that the statements made in the letter were protected by witness immunity. In *Westcott* v *Westcott* (2009), the Court of Appeal held that witness immunity covered the case where the defendant made a complaint to the police about the claimant, thus triggering an investigation into the claimant; though this may have gone too far and is hard to reconcile with other authorities which hold out the possibility that such a complainant might, in the right circumstances, be sued for false imprisonment or malicious prosecution.[31]

---

[29] Indeed, Lord Brown thought that being exposed to the risk of being sued in negligence might improve the quality of such testimony, as expert witnesses would become more cautious about making bold claims on behalf of their client that would later prove impossible to sustain: [2011] UKSC 13, at [67].

[30] [1995] 2 AC 633, 755.

[31] See above, §§ 2.2, 21.2.

The House of Lords has placed one limit on this extension of the law on witness immunity to cover statements made in the course of an investigation, holding in *Darker* v *Chief Constable of the West Midlands Police* (2001) that the law on witness immunity does not protect an investigator from being sued on the basis that he committed a tort *by encouraging other people to fabricate evidence or by concealing evidence.*

22.6 Abuse of process

If A has committed a tort in relation to B, B will sometimes be barred from suing A for compensatory damages on the ground that B will only be able to establish that she is entitled to sue A for such damages by bringing into question – in other words, by making a *collateral attack* on – the correctness of an earlier decision of the courts. In such a case, B may be barred from suing A for compensatory damages on the ground that bringing such an action would involve an *abuse of process.* It is hard to tell *when* B will be barred from suing A on this basis but the following test may be suggested: B will be barred from suing A on the ground of abuse of process if it would not be legitimate to allow B to challenge the correctness of the earlier judicial decision by bringing a claim in tort against A.

For instance, in *Hunter* v *Chief Constable of the West Midlands Police* (1982), the claimants were the Birmingham Six. They had been convicted of causing two bomb explosions which killed 21 people and injured 161 others. They were convicted largely on the basis of written and oral confessions that they made while in police custody. At their trial, they had claimed that these confessions had been beaten out of them. The trial judge held a hearing on the matter and concluded that the claimants had not been beaten by the police and held that their confessions were admissible in evidence. After the claimants were convicted, they sued the police for assault. Their claims were struck out on the ground that they involved an abuse of process. The claimants' claims sought to challenge the correctness of the trial judge's decision that the claimants had not been beaten and, in the absence of any fresh evidence that was unavailable to the trial judge at the time he made his decision, it would not be legitimate to allow the claimants to attack the correctness of that earlier decision by bringing a claim in tort against the police.

Similarly, in *Smith* v *Linskills (a firm)* (1996), the claimant was convicted of aggravated burglary at the Crown Court and sent to prison. On his release, the claimant sued the defendants, the solicitors who had acted for him during his trial, claiming that they had breached the duty they owed him to represent him with a professional degree of care and skill. The claimant's claim was dismissed on the ground that it amounted to an abuse of process. The claimant's claim involved an attack on the correctness of his conviction – he could only show that the defendants' negligence had caused him to suffer some kind of loss by showing that 'if his criminal defence had been handled with proper care he would not, and should not, have been convicted'.[32] In the absence of any fresh evidence that was unavailable to the Crown Court when the claimant was convicted, it would not be legitimate to allow the claimant to cast doubt on the correctness of his conviction by bringing a claim in tort against the defendants.

In contrast, in *Walpole* v *Partridge & Wilson (a firm)* (1994), the claimant was convicted of obstructing a veterinary officer in the execution of his duty in that he tried to prevent the officer taking blood samples from the pigs at his farm. The claimant instructed

---

[32] [1996] 1 WLR 763, 768–9.

the defendants, his solicitors, to appeal against the decision. He thought that as the officer had no reason to suspect that his pigs were diseased, he had not committed any offence in attempting to prevent the officer taking blood samples from them. The defendants failed to lodge an appeal in time and the claimant sued them in negligence. The Court of Appeal refused to strike out the claimant's claim on the ground that it amounted to an abuse of process. While the premise of the claimant's claim was that his conviction would have been overturned on appeal and therefore that he should not have been convicted in the first place, the claimant's claim that he should not have been convicted in the first place was based on a point of law which was not considered by the court which convicted the claimant. Given this, it was not illegitimate to allow the claimant to bring a claim in tort against the defendants even though the bringing of such a claim would inevitably challenge the correctness of his conviction.

All these cases concerned claimants who claimed to have been convicted of some *criminal* offence due to the negligence of their lawyers.[33] What is the position if, say, A, a barrister, represented B in a *civil case* and B lost her case? Could B sue A in negligence for damages, alleging that A failed to conduct her case with a professional degree of care and skill and that had A conducted her case properly she would have won the case? The question was considered in *Arthur J S Hall* v *Simons* (2002), which established that a barrister who represented a client in court would owe that client a duty to represent that client with a reasonable degree of care and skill. Lord Hoffmann thought that in the situation just described, any claim by B would *not* normally be struck out as involving an abuse of process.[34]

22.7 Death

It used to be the rule at common law that if A committed a tort in relation to B and A subsequently died, B would be barred from suing A (or, more accurately, A's estate) for compensatory damages. Similarly, it used to be the rule at common law that if A committed a tort in relation to B and B subsequently died, B (or, more accurately, B's estate) would be barred from suing A for compensatory damages in respect of the losses suffered by B as a result of A's tort before she died. These rules were, for the most part, abolished by s 1(1) of the Law Reform (Miscellaneous Provisions) Act 1934. However, the 1934 Act left the old common law rules intact in one respect. Section 1(1) of the 1934 Act provides that 'this subsection shall not apply to causes of action for defamation'. So suppose that

---

[33] An attempt by a still convicted criminal to sue an expert witness who had been hired to give testimony on his behalf at his trial would also founder on the shoals of abuse of process: *Jones* v *Kaney* [2011] UKSC 13, at [60] (per Lord Phillips).

[34] [2002] 1 AC 615, 706–7. He did suggest one exception. Suppose *Barrister* represented *Client* in a defamation case where *Angry* was suing *Client* for defaming her. Suppose further that C admitted that her statements about A were defamatory but claimed that they were true. Suppose finally that B did not do a very good job of arguing C's case with the result that the court found that C's statements were not true and found for A, awarding substantial damages against C. In such a case, Lord Hoffmann suggested, if C then sought to sue B in negligence, her claim might be struck out on the ground that it amounted to an abuse of process. In order to make out her claim against B, C would have to show that but for B's negligence, the courts would have accepted that her statements about A were true. So C's claim would amount to an attack on the correctness of the court's decision that her statements about A were not true. Lord Hoffmann thought it might be improper to allow C to attack this decision. This must be right: it would surely be wrong to allow C to bring an action against B which, if successful, would have the effect of blackening A's name without giving A any opportunity to defend herself.

Journo libelled *Celeb* and shortly after this happened *Celeb* died. In such a case, *Celeb*'s estate will be barred from suing *Journo* for damages. Alternatively, suppose that *Journo* died before *Celeb* could sue her for damages. *Journo*'s death will mean that *Celeb* cannot sue *Journo*'s estate for damages; though *Celeb*'s independent action against *Journo*'s newspaper for publishing her story about him will still survive.

22.8 *Volenti non fit injuria*

A. The rule

The rule that *volenti non fit injuria* ('no wrong is done to the willing') applies in two situations.

1. A claimant cannot complain that a defendant committed a tort in relation to her by acting in a particular way if the claimant fully consented to the defendant's acting in that way.

2. If a defendant has committed a tort in relation to a claimant and the claimant has suffered some kind of loss as a result, the claimant will normally be barred from suing the defendant for compensation for that loss on the ground that *volenti non fit injuria* if she willingly took the risk that *she would suffer that kind of loss in the way that she suffered it.*

We are already very familiar with the law on *volenti* as it applies in the first situation.[35] That the defence of *volenti* applies in the second situation is more controversial,[36] and so its application in this kind of case will be discussed in detail here.

A good example of the defence of *volenti* being applied in the second kind of situation is provided by the case of *Morris* v *Murray* (1991). In that case, Morris and Murray went drinking together. At the end of the evening Murray suggested that they go for a ride in his light aircraft. Both men were quite drunk at this stage but Morris agreed to Murray's suggestion. Once both men were inside the plane, Murray – in his drunken state – just managed to get the plane airborne but it crashed soon after. Morris was badly injured and Murray was killed. Morris sued Murray's estate for damages in respect of his injuries, claiming that Murray had been negligent in the way he had piloted the plane.

The Court of Appeal dismissed Morris's claim.[37] In climbing into the plane he had willingly taken a risk that Murray would fail to pilot the plane properly and that he would be injured as a result. It would have been different, it might be suggested, if – once Morris and Murray were airborne – Murray had suddenly been overcome by suicidal feelings and had deliberately targeted the plane at the ground. While Morris willingly took the risk when he climbed into the plane that he would be injured as a result of the plane being badly piloted, he did not willingly take the risk that he would be injured as a result of Murray's deliberately crashing the plane into the ground. Given this, in our alternative scenario, Morris would not have been barred from suing Murray's estate for damages on the ground that *volenti non fit injuria.*

---

[35] See above, §§ 1.4, 5.2.

[36] For example, Jaffey 1985 does not think that *volenti* applies at all in the second situation, arguing that the defence will only be available if the claimant expressly agreed that the defendant's conduct would not be actionable before he did what he did. However, this view is too narrow; it is certainly not consistent with the authorities mentioned below.

[37] The House of Lords refused leave to appeal: [1991] 1 WLR 1362.

That this is correct is confirmed by the decision of the Court of Appeal in *Slater* v *Clay Cross Co Ltd* (1956). In that case, the defendants operated a railway which passed through a tunnel. For many years, local residents walked through the tunnel to get to a village. One day the claimant happened to be walking through the tunnel when she was hit by one of the defendants' trains and was injured. The claimant sued the defendants, claiming that the defendants' driver had been negligent in the way he had driven the train; he had not kept a proper look-out and so on. The defendants argued that the claimant's claim should be dismissed on the ground that when the claimant walked through the tunnel she had voluntarily taken a risk that she would be hit by an oncoming train. However, the Court of Appeal dismissed this argument, holding that when the claimant walked through the tunnel she did not willingly take a risk that a train driver would *negligently* run into her.

It should be emphasised that for the *volenti* defence to be raised in the sort of situation we are discussing here, it must be shown that the claimant – who is seeking compensation for some loss that she has suffered – *willingly* took the risk that she would suffer that loss in the way that she did. So in *Haynes* v *Harwood* (1935) the defendant negligently left some horses unattended in the street.[38] A boy threw a stone at the horses and as a result they bolted. The claimant, a nearby police constable, threw himself in the way of the horses and seized their reins and brought them under control – but in doing so he suffered various personal injuries. The claimant successfully sued the defendant in negligence for compensation for his injuries. The Court of Appeal held that the defence of *volenti non fit injuria* was not available here. While the defendant had taken the risk when he tried to stop the horses bolting that he would be injured, he did not *willingly* take that risk – he had only acted as he did because it was an emergency.

B. Exceptions to the rule

A couple of exceptions and one non-exception to the rule that *volenti non fit injuria* are worth mentioning.

(1) *Paternalistic duties.* If A owes B a duty to stop B harming herself, then if A breaches that duty with the result that B harms herself, A will not be able to defeat B's claim for damages on the ground that *volenti non fit injuria*. While B – when she harmed herself – willingly took the risk that she would suffer that harm in the way she did, if the *volenti* defence were available to A here A's duty would become meaningless. A would be completely free to breach it, safe in the knowledge that if B took advantage of his breach to harm herself, he would be able to raise a *volenti* defence to any subsequent claim she might bring against him for compensation for the harm she had suffered.[39]

(2) *Traffic accidents.* Section 149(3) of the Road Traffic Act 1988 provides that, 'The fact that a [passenger] has willingly accepted as his the risk of negligence on the part of the [driver] shall not be treated as negativing any . . . liability of the [driver].'[40] This meant

---

[38] 'Negligently' because it was reasonably foreseeable that the horses might bolt and injure passers-by if they were left unattended in the street.

[39] *Reeves* v *Commissioner of Police of the Metropolis* [2000] 1 AC 360, 375–6 (per Lord Jauncey of Tullichettle).

[40] So the result in *Morris* v *Murray* would have been different if Murray had invited Morris to come for a drive in his car and had driven the car so badly that it crashed with the result that Morris was injured. In such a case, s 149(3) of the Road Traffic Act 1988 would have applied to prevent Morris's claim being barred on the ground that *volenti non fit injuria*.

that a defence of *volenti* was unavailable in *Pitts* v *Hunt* (1991), where the claimant and defendant stole a motorbike and took it for a joyride. The defendant drove the motorbike and the claimant sat behind him. The defendant – with the encouragement of the claimant – drove the bike faster and faster, and finally crashed the bike. While the claimant was *volenti* as to the risk of being injured in the way he was, his claim for damages in respect of the injuries he suffered in the crash could not be dismissed on that ground because of the statutory provision preventing the defence of *volenti* applying in that case.[41] The provision is an unprincipled one, designed to ensure that the costs of looking after the victims of motor accidents stay with insurance companies and are not shifted onto the State through the National Health Service and disability allowances.

(3) *The 'fireman's rule'.* This is the non-exception. Some American states have adopted what is known as the *fireman's rule* under which someone whose job involves running the risk of suffering a particular kind of loss cannot seek to recover compensatory damages if he actually suffers that kind of loss in doing his job.[42]

So if *Fool* negligently starts a fire in his house and *Fireman* is injured in the course of fighting the fire, then – under the *fireman's rule* – *Fireman* will be barred from suing *Fool* for damages. Again, the *fireman's rule* would operate to bar a police officer who developed a psychiatric illness as a result of what he saw or heard in dealing with a particularly traumatic incident from suing the person responsible for causing that incident for damages.

The reason for the rule is clear enough: if you have been paid to run a particular risk, you should not complain if that risk materialises and you suffer loss as a result. However, in *Ogwo* v *Taylor* (1988) the House of Lords refused to adopt the *fireman's rule* in English law and allowed a fireman to sue a householder for damages in respect of injuries suffered by him in fighting a fire negligently started by the householder.[43] The House of Lords had another opportunity to adopt the 'fireman's rule' in *Frost* v *Chief Constable of West Yorkshire Police* (1999) where – it will be recalled – the claimant policemen sought to recover damages in respect of the psychiatric illnesses they claimed to have developed as a result of the work they did helping out in the aftermath of the Hillsborough tragedy. However, their Lordships again showed no sign that they were in any way inclined to adopt the *fireman's rule.*

22.9 Exclusion of liability

Three cases where a defendant (D) might be able to rely on a contractual term to defeat a claim in tort that has been made against him by a claimant (C) need to be distinguished.

---

[41] The claimant's claim was, however, dismissed on the ground of illegality: see below, § 22.10.

[42] California: *Walters* v *Sloan*, 571 P 2d 609 (1977); Michigan: *Kreski* v *Modern Wholesale Electric Supply Co*, 415 NW 2d 178 (1987) (though see also *Miller* v *Inglis*, 567 NW 2d 253 (1997) and *Gibbons* v *Caraway*, 565 NW 2d 663 (1997), holding that the 'fireman's rule' does not apply in cases where defendant wilfully and wantonly created a risk that the claimant would be injured).

[43] [1988] AC 431, 449, approving *Salmon* v *Seafarer Restaurants Ltd* [1983] 1 WLR 1264.

A. Term in contract between D and C

If there is a term in a contract between D and C that, properly interpreted, excludes or limits C's right to sue D for the tort that he has committed, then D will normally be able to take advantage of that term to defeat C's claim against him (if the term is an exclusion clause) or limit his liability to C (if it is a limitation clause).

We say 'normally' because there are statutory limits on when a defendant will be able to take advantage of a contract term to defend a claim in tort that is being made against him:

1. *Section 2(1) of the Unfair Contract Terms Act 1977* ('UCTA') and *section 65 of the Consumer Rights Act 2015* ('CRA') provides that a term that purports to exclude or limit a business's liability in negligence for death or personal injury will always be invalid. (Which section applies depends on whether the term in question is in a 'consumer contract'[44] – if it is, then s 65 applies; if it does not, s 2(1) applies.)

2. *Section 2(2) of UCTA* provides that a term that is *not* in a 'consumer contract'[45] and that purports to exclude or limit a business's liability in negligence for any other kind of loss (such as property damage or economic loss) will be invalid if it is unreasonable.

3. *Section 3 of the Misrepresentation Act 1967* provides that a term that purports to exclude or limit someone's (not necessarily just a business's) liability for misrepresentation will be invalid if it is unreasonable.

4. *Section 62 of CRA* provides that a term in a contract between a business and a consumer will be invalid if it counts as 'unfair', which it will if 'contrary to the requirement of good faith', the existence of the term caused a 'significant imbalance' in the parties' rights and obligations under the contract to the detriment of the consumer.

5. *Section 149 of the Road Traffic Act 1988* provides that a term in a contract between a driver and a passenger that purports to exclude or limit the driver's liability for injuring the passenger will be invalid.

Readers wishing to find out more about how these provisions will apply in practice should consult a specialist text on contract law.

B. Term in a contract between C and a third party

In this sort of case, D wants to take advantage of a term in a contract between C and a third party which purports to exclude or limit C's right to sue D for the tort that he has committed. So, for example, if C has employed *Shipper* to deliver some goods for him to C's new home, *Shipper* might have inserted into his contract with C a provision saying that C would not be entitled to sue any of *Shipper*'s employees for negligently damaging those goods. So if D, one of *Shipper*'s employees, does negligently damage those goods, and is subsequently sued by C, D will want to take advantage of the term in the contract between C and *Shipper* to defeat C's claim against him.

Traditionally, the doctrine of *privity of contract* – which said that someone could not take advantage of, or be burdened by, a contract to which he was not party – would stand in D's way here. As D was not a party to the contract between C and *Shipper*, he

---

[44] UCTA, s 2(4)(a). A 'consumer' is defined in s 2(3) of the CRA as 'an individual acting for purposes that are wholly or mainly outside that individual's trade, business, craft or profession.'

[45] UCTA, s 2(4)(a).

could not take advantage of the term in that contract that had been inserted for his benefit. Attempts were made to get round this by, for example, finding that there existed a contract between C and D which included this term,[46] or by saying that C could not sue D because the existence of the term in the C-*Shipper* contract meant that C had willingly taken the risk of his goods being negligently damaged by D.[47] However, such arguments were always quite artificial and the need to make them has been substantially reduced by the Contracts (Rights of Third Parties) Act 1999, which has created a major exception to the doctrine of privity.

Under the 1999 Act, D will be able to take advantage of a term in a contract to which he is not a party if: (1) D is expressly identified in the contract as being someone who should be able to take advantage of that term; or (2) the term purports to be for D's benefit and the parties to the contract have *not* indicated that D should *not* be able to take advantage of that term. While the 1999 Act is primarily concerned with allowing third parties to a contract to *sue* when that contract has been breached, s 1(6) of the Act makes it clear that the Act also applies to cases where a third party to a contract *who is being sued* wants to take advantage of a term in that contract to defend the claim that is being made against him.

So, in the concrete example we are considering, the 1999 Act will probably apply here to allow D to take advantage of the term in the contract between C and *Shipper* to exclude or limit his liability to C. However, D may still be barred from relying on that term to exclude or limit his liability to C by one of the statutory provisions set out above.[48]

C. Term in a contract between D and a third party

In this sort of case, a third party has agreed in a contract with D that if something goes wrong, D will not be liable or his liability will be limited to a certain amount. Something has gone wrong and C, as a result, is entitled in principle to sue D in tort for what has happened. D wants to take advantage of the term in his contract with the third party to say either that C cannot sue him, or that his liability to C is limited to a certain amount.

Understandably, D will find it very hard to do this. The courts are highly resistant to the notion that provisions in a contract which might have been made without C's knowledge or agreement could limit C's rights to sue D in tort. However, there are occasions where C will be bound by a term in a contract to which she was not a party (provided, of course, that the term is not rendered invalid by the statutory provisions set out above).

For example, if *Keeper* held C's goods as a bailee for C, and C authorised *Keeper* to hand those goods over to D for safekeeping on terms which limited D's liability in the event that the goods were lost or damaged, then C will be bound by any such terms in the contract between *Keeper* and D.[49] Again, where C is essentially suing D in tort for failing to perform properly a contract with a third party – as is the case with a claim for pure economic loss under *White* v *Jones* (1999)[50] or *Junior Books Ltd* v *Veitchi* (1983)[51] – then C will be bound by any terms in the contract between D and that third party which

---

[46] *New Zealand Shipping Co Ltd* v *A M Satterthwaite & Co Ltd, The Eurymedon* [1975] AC 154.
[47] *Scruttons Ltd* v *Midland Silicones Ltd* [1962] AC 446, 488–9 (per Lord Denning, dissenting); *Norwich City Council* v *Harvey* [1989] 1 WLR 828.
[48] Contracts (Rights of Third Parties) Act 1999, s 3(6).
[49] *Morris* v *C W Martin* [1966] 1 QB 716, 729 (per Lord Denning MR); *The Pioneer Container* [1994] 2 AC 324.
[50] See above, § 5.12.
[51] See above, § 5.10.

specified what the scope of D's liability would be if he breached that contract.[52] C cannot pick and choose: she cannot sue D for failing to perform a responsibility that he assumed in a contract and ignore the terms on which he was prepared to assume that responsibility.[53]

22.10 Illegality

In medieval times, someone who was declared to be an 'outlaw' had all his civil rights suspended. The result was that anyone could do anything they liked to an outlaw, without any legal sanction at all. The outlaw was outside the law's protection. Outlawry as an institution has long fallen into disuse, but it remains the case that people who have committed criminal offences will sometimes enjoy less protection under the law of tort than the rest of us do. The law on when the defence of *illegality* (otherwise known as the defence of *'ex turpi causa non oritur actio'*, or *'ex turpi causa'* for short)[54] will apply to prevent C suing D in tort has been made very uncertain as a result of the UK Supreme Court's decision in *Patel* v *Mirza* (2016) and requires very careful discussion. We'll begin by setting out some cases where a defendant might *want* to raise a defence of illegality to defeat a claim in tort that has been made against her, before discussing whether the defendant would be *allowed* to raise a defence of illegality both under the law as it existed before *Patel* v *Mirza* and after *Patel* v *Mirza*.

A. Some cases raising illegality issues

There are a wide range of cases where a defendant might try to rely on a defence of illegality; here are a few.

1. *Convicted Rapist.* C suffers a head injury as a result of D's negligence that causes C's personality to change for the worse and C subsequently attacks and rapes T. C is sent to prison, and wants to sue D for compensation for his loss of liberty.

2. *Sued Rapist.* Same as *Convicted Rapist*, but C's rape of T results in her suing him for damages, and C sues D in tort seeking to be compensated for the money that he is going to have to pay T by way of damages.

3. *Injured Burglar.* C, a professional burglar who makes £5m a year from burgling high-class hotels, is negligently run over by D. C's injuries are so extensive that he has to give up being a burglar, and he sues D for compensation for his resulting loss of earnings.

4. *Injured Refugee.* C enters the UK and claims asylum. While her application for asylum is being considered she is forbidden from taking up any paid employment. In breach of this requirement, she starts working in D's factory where she earns £1,000 a month.

---

[52] *White* v *Jones* [1995] 2 AC 207, 268 (per Lord Goff); *Junior Books Ltd* v *Veitchi Co Ltd* [1983] 1 AC 520, 546 (per Lord Roskill).

[53] Though in a *Junior Books* type situation it might be different if D got the job of working as a subcontractor on a job that *Contractor* was doing for C by assuring C that he would do an excellent job and would take full responsibility if his work turned out to be imperfect, and then secretly inserted a provision in his contract with *Contractor* specifying that he could not be sued, or only sued for a limited amount, if his work was not up to scratch.

[54] 'From a shameful cause, no action will arise.'

Due to D's negligence, C is seriously injured while working in the factory and is unable to carry on working there. C sues D for compensation for (i) her injuries, and (ii) the loss of earnings that she would have made had she carried on working at the factory.

5. *Injured Prostitute.* C earns £5m a year working as a high-end prostitute. D attacks C and injures her so severely that she is longer able to work as a prostitute; she sues D for compensation for her resulting loss of earnings.

6. *Joint Criminal Venture.* D and C attempt to open a bank safe using explosives. D carelessly drops the explosives, and C is injured in the ensuing explosion. C seeks to sue D for compensation for his injuries.

7. *Excessive Force.* C attempts to grab D's handbag. In order to get C to let go of the handbag, D takes a gun out of her pocket and shoots C in the face. C wants to sue D for compensation for his injuries.

8. *Stolen Handbags.* C is arrested with a number of handbags in his possession that the police know to be stolen. The police seize the handbags as evidence but are unable to trace the owners. C – having served a short time in prison for theft – demands that the police return the handbags to him. The police refuse, and C sues the police in conversion for the value of the handbags.

9. *Stolen Cocaine.* C is in possession of a quantity of cocaine that D steals from C and consumes. C sues D in conversion for the 'street value' of the cocaine that D took.

B. The law pre-*Patel* v *Mirza*

The pre-*Patel* v *Mirza* law on when a claimant would be prevented from suing a defendant in tort because the claimant had engaged in some kind of illegal behaviour rested on a mix of common, judge-made, law and statute law.

The common law on when a defendant could take advantage of a defence of illegality was restated by Lord Hoffmann in *Gray* v *Thames Trains Ltd* (2009). Lord Hoffmann followed counsel for the defendants in that case by distinguishing between a 'wider' and a 'narrower' form of the common law defence of illegality.[55]

The narrower form of the defence says that 'you cannot recover for damage which is the consequence of a sentence imposed on you for a criminal act.' This form of the defence is based on the need for consistency across the legal system: if the criminal law has imposed a particular punishment on an offender, the civil law would subvert what the criminal law is trying to do if it allowed the offender to sue for damages to compensate him for the harm caused to him by that punishment.[56]

The wider form of the defence says that 'you cannot recover for damage which is the consequence of your own criminal act'. Lord Hoffmann did not seem to place any qualification on this wider form of the defence, other than to insist that the damage of which the claimant complains should truly be *caused* by the claimant's act.[57] However, as Lord Hoffmann noted, other judges have been much more cautious, and have only been willing to say that the wider form of the defence of illegality will apply where 'The facts which

---

[55] [2009] 1 AC 1339, at [29] and [32].
[56] [2009] 1 AC 1339, at [37].
[57] [2009] 1 AC 1339, at [54].

give rise to the claim [are] inextricably linked with . . . criminal conduct [which is] sufficiently serious to merit the application of the [defence].'[58] Lord Hoffmann thought that
this wider version of the defence was

> justified on the ground that it is offensive to public notions of the fair distribution of resources
> that a claimant should be compensated (usually out of public funds) for the consequences of his
> own criminal conduct.[59]

This seems weak. This form of the defence of illegality is more likely to be based on the
ground that it is offensive for someone who has previously flouted the law to then turn round
and demand that *his* legal rights be respected. The wider form of the defence of illegality was
supplemented by s 329 of the Criminal Justice Act 2003, which was designed to provide
'justice' for the victims of crime who had gone 'over the top' in injuring a criminal who was
threatening them, or who had broken into their house.[60] Section 329 would ensure – it was
thought – that the injured criminal would not be able to sue for compensation for his injuries. Provided that D – in committing the tort of assault, battery or false imprisonment in
relation to C – had not responded to B's committing an imprisonable offence in a 'grossly
disproportionate' way, D would be entitled to a defence to C's suing D in tort.

Let's now see how the narrower and wider form of the defence of illegality applied to deal
with the sort of cases we have set out in the previous section. C's claim for compensation for
the loss of his liberty in *Convicted Rapist* would have been ruled out by the narrower form
of the defence: the law would contradict itself if on the one hand it sought to punish C for
raping T, and on the other hand it mitigated the severity of that punishment by allowing C
to sue D for damages to compensate him for the fact that he had been imprisoned.[61] The
House of Lords' decision in *Gray* v *Thames Train Ltd* (2009) indicates that this principle of
non-contradiction would also apply if C sought to sue D for damages to compensate him for
any loss of earnings suffered by him during his period of imprisonment: the loss of earnings
is also part of C's punishment and cannot be mitigated by the law of tort.

All of our other hypotheticals would fall to be disposed of under the wider form of the
defence of illegality, and turn on whether there is a *sufficiently close* connection between
C's criminal conduct and either the tort that D committed in relation to C, or any loss
that C suffered as a result of D's tort. In hypotheticals like *Sued Rapist*,[62] *Injured Burglar*,

---

[58] *Vellino* v *Chief Constable of Manchester Police* [2002] 1 WLR 218, at [70] (per Sir Murray Stuart-Smith).
[59] [2009] 1 AC 1339, at [51].
[60] In fact, as the case of *Adorian* v *Commissioner of Police of the Metropolis* [2009] 1 WLR 1859 exposed, the
principal beneficiaries of s 329 were the *police*, who would attempt to rely on s 329 to defeat claims in
tort that were made against them as a result of their using excessive force in arresting people.
[61] See *Clunis* v *Camden and Islington Health Authority* [1998] QB 978 (claimant not allowed to sue
defendant health authority for damages in respect of his imprisonment for manslaughter on grounds of
diminished responsibility, where the claimant was arguing that he would never have killed anyone had the
health authority taken better care of his mental health). *Meah* v *McCreamer* [1985] 1 All ER 367
(claimant sexually assaulted two women as a result of a personality change caused by a car crash that
occurred as a result of the defendant's negligence; Woolf J *allowed* his claim to be compensated for the
fact that he had been imprisoned for the acts of sexual assault) had previously gone the other way, but as
the defence of illegality had not (strangely) been raised in that case, it was easily distinguished by the
Court of Appeal in *Clunis*.
[62] See *Meah* v *McCreamer (No 2)* [1986] 1 All ER 943 (following on from *Meah* v *McCreamer* (previous
footnote), claimant was sued by the victims of his sexual assaults for damages, and was held – by Woolf J – *not*
to be entitled to sue the defendant for compensation for the damages he would have to pay those victims).

Joint Criminal Venture,[63] and *Stolen Cocaine*[64] it is easy enough to find that such a sufficiently close connection exists with the result that D would be entitled to raise a defence of illegality to C's claim. Other cases are more marginal. In *Excessive Force*, whether there is a 'sufficiently close connection' between D's tort and C's crime in trying to steal D's handbag to allow D to raise a defence of illegality to C's claim for damages would depend, both at common law[65] and under s 329 of the Criminal Justice Act 2003, on whether D's shooting C in the face was a grossly excessive or disproportionate response to C's actions. On the facts of the case, it would seem that the courts would find that D's actions were excessive and that D would not be entitled to the wider form of the defence of illegality.[66] In *Injured Refugee*, the fact that C would not have been injured had she not been illegally employed by D would probably not allow D to take advantage of the wider form of the defence of illegality to defeat C's claim for compensation for her injuries. As C's status as an illegal employee had nothing to do with the fact that she ended up being injured – she would still have been injured whatever her status – there would not be a sufficiently close connection between her injuries and her illegal conduct in getting employment at D's factory.[67] However, the fact that earnings C would have made had she not been injured were inextricably bound up with her working illegally would prevent her suing for compensation for the loss of those earnings.[68]

Injured Prostitute and *Stolen Handbags* were probably the most difficult hypotheticals to resolve under the law on illegality as it stood pre-*Patel* v *Mirza*. The difficulty raised by *Injured Prostitute* is that it is not actually illegal to earn money as a prostitute. However,

---

[63] See Lord Asquith's treatment of the identical hypothetical in *National Coal Board* v *England* [1954] AC 403, at 429. Also *Pitts* v *Hunt* [1991] 2 QB 24, where the defendant and claimant were engaged in the joint criminal ventures of joyriding and speeding, with the result that the defendant negligently crashed the motorbike he and the claimant were on, and the claimant was injured. Held: the defendant could rely on a defence of illegality to defeat the claimant's claim for damages. A similarly close connection between the claimant's injuries and a joint criminal venture between the defendant and claimant was made out in *Joyce* v *O'Brien* [2014] 1 WLR 70, where the claimant and defendant stole some ladders, placing them in the back of a van, and the defendant drove away so quickly that the claimant – who was in the back of the van, holding the ladders in place (as they were too long to close the back door of the van) – fell out of the van and was injured. Such a connection did not exist in *Delaney* v *Pickett* [2012] 1 WLR 2149, where the defendant and claimant were transporting some cannabis by car with the aim of selling it, and the defendant negligently crashed the car, injuring the claimant. As there was no connection between the defendant's negligence and his and the claimant's joint criminal enterprise, the defence of illegality did not apply to defeat the claimant's claim. Goudkamp 2012 goes far too far in suggesting that the decision in *Delaney* is inconsistent with the decision in *Pitts*.

[64] *Bowmakers Ltd* v *Barnet Instruments Ltd* [1945] KB 65, 72; *Webb* v *Chief Constable of Merseyside Police* [2000] QB 427, 444 (per May LJ).

[65] See *Cross* v *Kirkby*, *The Times*, 5 April 2000, holding that even if the defendant had used unreasonable force in defending himself against a hunt saboteur who was threatening the defendant with a baseball bat, the force was not so excessive as to deprive the defendant of a defence of illegality to the claimant's action for damages against the defendant in respect of his injuries.

[66] See *Revill* v *Newbery* [1996] QB 567 (no defence of illegality where the defendant shot the claimant burglar through a hole in the door of the shed on the defendant's allotment, in response to the claimant's attempt to break into the shed).

[67] See *Hounga* v *Allen* [2014] 1 WLR 2889 (no defence of illegality to claims that the defendant employers had tortiously harassed and discriminated against the claimant).

[68] See *Hewison* v *Meridian Shipping Services Pte Ltd* [2002] EWCA Civ 1821 (crane operator who had illegally obtained employment by concealing his epilepsy from his employers could not sue for loss of earnings that resulted from his being unable to carry on working as a crane operator because he was injured as a result of the defendant's negligence).

in *Nayyar* v *Denton Wilde Sapte* (2009), Hamblen J held that the defence of illegality 'can extend to immoral as well as illegal acts'[69] and on that basis would have prevented a company suing a defendant in negligence for advising them to pay someone a bribe (which did not have the intended effect) even if paying the bribe had not happened to amount to a criminal offence. And in *Les Laboratoires Servier* v *Apotex* (2014), the UK Supreme Court held that:

> The *ex turpi causa* principle is concerned with claims founded on acts which are contrary to the public law of the state and engage the public interest. The paradigm case is . . . a criminal act. In addition, it is concerned with a limited category of acts which, while not necessarily criminal, can conveniently be described as 'quasi-criminal' because they engage the public interest in the same way . . . [T]his additional category of non-criminal acts giving rise to the defence includes cases of dishonesty or corruption . . . some anomalous categories of misconduct, such as prostitution, which without itself being criminal are contrary to public policy and involve criminal liability on the part of secondary parties; and the infringement of statutory rules enacted for the protection of the public interest and attracting civil sanctions of a penal character . . .[70]

but went on to hold that the principle was not engaged in the case where a claimant was suing for money it would have made by violating a Canadian patent held by a third party had it not been restrained from doing so by an interim injunction obtained by the defendant that was later discharged. On the basis of these authorities, it seems that a defence of illegality *would* have been available in *Injured Prostitute* under the law on illegality as it stood pre-*Patel* v *Mirza*.

Stolen Handbags would seem to fall under the wider form of the defence of illegality in that C's claim in conversion against the police for the value of the handbags in the police's possession is inextricably bound up with his criminal act in stealing the handbags in the first place. However, in *Webb* v *Chief Constable of Merseyside Police* (2000), the Court of Appeal held that the defence of illegality will *not* apply in a case like *Stolen Handbags*. Once the statutory powers under which the stolen handbags (or, on the facts of *Webb*, the proceeds of drug trafficking) had been seized ceased to apply, the handbags had to be returned to C. The constitutional importance of not allowing property to be expropriated by the State unless authorised by statute overrode any other consideration militating against finding for C in a case like *Stolen Handbags*.[71]

C. The decision in *Patel* v *Mirza*[72]

Patel v *Mirza* (2016) was *not* a tort case; a fact that will prove to be of some significance in trying to assess the significance of the decision in that case for tort law. In *Patel* v *Mirza*, Patel paid Mirza £620,000 for the purpose of betting on movements in the price of shares in the Royal Bank of Scotland ('RBS'), relying on insider information that Mirza expected to receive regarding a government announcement about RBS. This kind of trading on insider information is, of course, illegal. As it happened, Mirza did nothing with the money that Patel paid him as no announcement was made about RBS; but neither did

---

[69] [2009] EWHC 3218 (QB), at [92] (criticised, Goudkamp 2011a).
[70] [2015] AC 430, at [25].
[71] If returning property to C would help C commit a criminal offence, then refusing to return that property will not amount to a tort (*Chief Constable of Merseyside Police* v *Owens* [2012] EWHC 1515 (Admin)). See, generally, Goudkamp and Mayr 2015.
[72] [2017] AC 467 (henceforth, '*Patel*').

he repay Patel the value of the money Patel paid him. So Patel sued Mirza. The UKSC unanimously held that Patel's claim should be allowed to succeed and that Mirza could not raise a defence of illegality to Patel's claim. However, the UKSC disagreed over when a defendant should and should not be allowed to rely on a defence of illegality.

Lord Toulson gave the majority judgment. He took the view that the law on illegality, as it had been developed by the courts, was both unclear and potentially arbitrary in the way it operated, and that it was open to the UKSC to lay down fresh guidance on how the defence of illegality should operate in future. He proceeded to lay down such fresh guidance. The two most important paragraphs in his judgment, for the purposes of trying to understand how Lord Toulson thought the defence of illegality should operate in future, are paragraphs [99] and [101]. In paragraph [99], Lord Toulson identified:

two broad discernible policy reasons for the common law doctrine of illegality as a defence to a civil claim. One is that a person should not be allowed to profit from his own wrongdoing. The other, linked, consideration is that the law should be coherent and not self-defeating, condoning illegality by giving with the left hand what it takes with the right hand.

In paragraph [101], Lord Toulson observed that:

one cannot judge whether allowing a claim which is in some way tainted by illegality would be contrary to the public interest, because it would be harmful to the integrity of the legal system, without (a) considering the underlying purpose of the prohibition which has been transgressed, (b) considering conversely any other relevant public policies which may be rendered ineffective or less effective by denial of the claim, and (c) keeping in mind the possibility of overkill unless the law is applied with a due sense of proportionality.

Factors (b) and (c) are factors that militate *in favour* of allowing a claimant to sue a defendant despite the fact that the claimant's claim might be tainted with illegality, and it is clear from Lord Toulson's discussion in paragraph [102] that he saw factor (a) in the same way: that a claim that might be tainted with illegality should still be allowed if denying it on the ground of illegality would undermine the purpose of the prohibition that has been transgressed.[73]

If this is right, this suggests that Lord Toulson thought that illegality cases should be resolved by application of the following algorithm[74] where one *first* asks (1) Would allowing the claimant's claim allow the claimant to profit from her wrongdoing, or result in the law becoming incoherent and self-defeating? and if the answer is 'yes' then one asks *secondly* (2) Should the claimant's claim still be allowed because denying it would: (a) undermine the point of the statutory provision that has been transgressed in this case, or (b) render

---

[73] At paragraph [102], Lord Toulson made it clear that he regards *Hardy* v *Motors Insurers' Bureau* [1964] 2 QB 745 as a case where a claim tainted by illegality was allowed because of factor (a). The defendant Motor Insurers' Bureau ('MIB') argued that it should not have to indemnify the claimant against the injuries suffered by him as a result of being deliberately run down by an uninsured driver because a contract to indemnify someone against the consequences of a deliberate criminal act is unlawful. It was held that the MIB should pay up because not to do so would undermine the point of the prohibition under the Road Traffic Act 1960 against driving uninsured – which is to ensure that someone who is injured by a motorist has a good claim against someone for their injuries.

[74] Using the term 'algorithm' might seem inconsistent with Lord Toulson's disdain in *Patel* v *Mirza* for a 'rule-based' (at [82] onwards) or 'mechanistic' (at [101]) approach to the defence of illegality, but we should *not* interpret Lord Toulson as having given up completely on the idea that the law (that is, rules) governs how the defence of illegality applies. Instead Lord Toulson is resistant to a rules-based or mechanical approach to answering the two questions in his algorithm.

some other relevant public policies less effective, or (c) have a disproportionate effect on the claimant given the seriousness of the claimant's unlawful conduct and the relative culpability of the defendant and the claimant for the claimant's unlawful conduct.[75] *Only* if the answer to (1) is 'yes' and the answer to (2) is 'no' should the claimant's claim be dismissed on the ground of illegality.[76]

D. The effect of *Patel* v *Mirza*

In assessing the effect of *Patel* v *Mirza* on the defence of illegality as it applies in tort law, two questions need to be answered. First, does Lord Toulson's algorithm apply *at all* in tort cases? Secondly, if Lord Toulson's algorithm does apply to tort cases, how does it apply in cases such as those set out above?

On the first question, in *Henderson* v *Dorset Healthcare University NHS Foundation Trust* (2016), the claimant stabbed her mother to death in a paranoid schizophrenic state, and was consequently detained in hospital under the Mental Health Act 1983. She sued the defendant health authority for damages, arguing that had the defendants taken more care of her, her mental state would not have deteriorated to the point where she stabbed her mother to death. Jay J refused to apply Lord Toulson's algorithm to determine whether the claimant's claim should be denied on the ground of illegality, arguing that under the rules of precedent anything Lord Toulson said in *Patel* v *Mirza* was *obiter* in so far as it applied to tort law, and he was bound by decisions such as that of the Court of Appeal in *Clunis* v *Camden and Islington Health Authority* (1998) and the House of Lords in *Gray* v *Thames Train Ltd* (2009) to find that the claimant's claim was barred on the ground of illegality. Against this, Lord Toulson's judgment was meant to apply to *all* private law cases raising illegality issues[77] and the fact that no less than *nine* Supreme Court Justices were assembled finally to thrash out the correct approach to adopt in private law cases involving a possible defence of illegality means that it is likely that the UKSC would take a dim view of a court taking a technical approach to the question of what sort of cases *Patel* v *Mirza* applies to. Given this, it is likely that the courts will take the view in future that Lord Toulson's algorithm *does* apply in tort cases.

Turning to the second question, application of Lord Toulson's algorithm turns out to narrow the application of the defence of illegality as compared with the law pre-*Patel* v *Mirza*. C's claim for damages would still be denied on the basis of illegality in *Convicted Rapist* – allowing the claim would engage Lord Toulson's second policy concern underlying the law on illegality and none of factors (a)–(c) would militate in favour of allowing C's claim. A defence of illegality would also be available in *Injured Burglar*: Lord Toulson's first policy concern about not allowing claimants to profit from their wrongdoing would be affected by allowing the claim to be made, and none of (a)–(c) apply to indicate that C's claim should be allowed. But claims like those made in *Sued Rapist*, *Joint Criminal Venture*, and *Excessive Force* should *all* be allowed under the law of

---

[75] *Patel*, at [107].

[76] In *Patel* v *Mirza* itself, Lord Toulson thought that the defence of illegality did not apply because the answer to question (1) was no: *Patel*, at [115]–[116].

[77] See *Patel*, at [2] ('Illegality has the potential to provide a defence to civil claims of all sorts, whether relating to contract, property, tort or unjust enrichment, and in a wide variety of circumstances' and Lord Toulson's frequent citation in his judgment of authorities on the application of the defence of illegality in tort at [18], [28], [38], [55], [72], and [111].

illegality as restated by Lord Toulson. In none of these cases does allowing C's claim mean either that C is allowed to profit from his wrongdoing, or that the law is rendered incoherent or self-defeating. (Though in *Excessive Force* a defence will still be available under s 329 of the Criminal Justice Act 2003 so long as C sues D for committing a trespass against his person, as opposed to bringing a claim in negligence.) The same applies to C's claim for compensation for her injuries in *Injured Refugee*. When it comes to C's claim for compensation for her loss of earnings in *Injured Refugee*, it might be thought that allowing C to make such a claim would render the law self-defeating (as undermining the law's prohibition on C from getting paid employment) – thus providing us with a positive answer to the first question in Lord Toulson's algorithm. But when we turn to the second question, it may be that denying C's claim for her loss of earnings might be regarded as 'disproportionate' given the straitened circumstances that resulted in her seeking to be employed at D's factory. Allowing C's claim in *Stolen Handbags* and *Stolen Cocaine* would violate Lord Toulson's first policy concern, but it may be that denying the claim in *Stolen Handbags* would (b) render some other relevant public policies less effective (the policy against allowing the state to appropriate people's property without statutory authorisation), while none of considerations (a)–(c) indicate that C's claim should still be allowed in *Stolen Cocaine*. Finally, it seems that the fact that C was not engaged in any kind of unlawful conduct in *Injured Prostitute* means that her claim for loss of earnings *cannot* be defeated on the basis of illegality post-*Patel* v *Mirza*: Lord Toulson's judgment assumes that the defence of illegality only applies where the claimant has acted unlawfully.[78]

The following table sums up the difference between the application of the defence of illegality after *Patel* v *Mirza* as compared with the law pre-*Patel* v *Mirza*, where a tick indicates that the defence of illegality *would* be available and a cross indicates that it would *not* be available.

	Pre-*Patel* v *Mirza*	Post-*Patel* v *Mirza*
Convicted Rapist	√	√
Sued Rapist	√	x
Injured Burglar	√	√
Injured Refugee	x (claim for injury) √ (claim for loss of earnings)	x x? (claim for loss of earnings)
Injured Prostitute	√	x
Joint Criminal Venture	√	x
Excessive Force	√ (if force not grossly disproportionate)	x (but still defence under CJA 2003 if force not grossly disproportionate and claim brought for trespass to person)
Stolen Handbags	x	x
Stolen Cocaine	√	√

---

[78] Paragraphs [99] and [101] of Lord Toulson's judgment in *Patel* v *Mirza*, ibid, make it tolerably clear that Lord Toulson did not envisage any role for the defence of illegality outside a case where a claimant has 'transgressed' a 'prohibition' – that is, acted unlawfully.

22.11 Limitation

In the interests of justice, the law places time limits on when a tort claim can be brought against a defendant. If those limits are exceeded, the defendant will normally be able to raise a defence of *limitation* to the claim being made against him. When we say 'In the interests of justice' we refer both to: (1) the fact that it may become very hard to do justice in a case that is heard long after the facts of that case occurred, when relevant documents may have been lost and memories may be impaired; and (2) the fact that it would be unjust to potential defendants to tort claims to allow them to go through their lives, year after year, with the prospect that they might be sued in tort constantly hanging over them: at some point, people are entitled to face, and plan for, the future free of the burden of what they might have done in the past.

The law on when a claimant will be barred on grounds of limitation from suing a defendant in tort is very complicated and a detailed account is beyond the scope of this text. However, a brief summary of the law in this area can be given. The *general rule* is that if A has committed a tort in relation to B, B will be barred from suing A for committing that tort if she does not sue A within *six years* of the date she was first entitled to obtain a remedy in respect of A's tort.[79]

However, this general rule is subject to various qualifications.

A. Ignorance

What if B was first entitled to obtain a remedy in respect of A's tort in August 2009 – but she only found out that she was entitled to obtain such a remedy in January 2013? As a general rule, if it was A's *fault* that B did not know she was entitled to sue A for committing his tort until January 2013, then the limitation period will be extended and B will have six years from January 2013 to bring an action against A, not six years from August 2009.[80]

---

[79] Limitation Act 1980, s 2. Assume that A committed his tort in January 2012. If that tort was actionable *per se* (that is, the tort committed by A was actionable even if it did not cause B to suffer any actionable loss), then B will normally have until January 2018 to sue A for committing that tort. The reason for this is that because A's tort was actionable *per se* B was entitled to obtain a remedy in respect of that tort as soon as it was committed. If, on the other hand, A's tort was not actionable *per se* (that is, the tort committed by A was only actionable if it caused B to suffer an actionable loss), then B will *normally* have six years from the date she first suffered an actionable loss as a result of A's tort to sue A for committing that tort. So if A's tort was not actionable *per se* and B first suffered an actionable loss as a result of A's tort in June 2013, B will *normally* have until June 2019 to sue A for committing that tort. The reason for this is that because A's tort was not actionable *per se*, the first time B was entitled to obtain a remedy in respect of A's tort was in June 2010. In *Hedley Byrne* cases – where the claimant is entitled to sue the defendant in negligence for pure economic loss – it can be very difficult to say when exactly the claimant first suffered a pure economic loss for which she could sue. See, for example, *Shore* v *Sedgwick Financial Services Ltd* [2008] EWCA Civ 863 (time to bring a claim started running as soon as claimant invested in inferior pension scheme on defendant's advice, not when the value of his investment depreciated) and *Law Society* v *Sephton & Co* [2006] 2 AC 543 (solicitor misappropriated client money and Law Society had to pay out to clients from Solicitor's Compensation Fund; sued defendant accountants for misrepresenting state of solicitor's accounts and lulling Law Society into false sense of security about solicitor's honesty; time to bring claim started running from moment Law Society had to pay out to defrauded clients, not moment when it failed to strike off solicitor or moment when solicitor misappropriated client money).

[80] Limitation Act 1980, ss 32(1)(b), 32(2). It appears this qualification to the general rule does not apply to actions under the Defective Premises Act 1972: *Warner* v *Basildon Development Corp* (1991) 7 Const LJ 146.

If it wasn't A's fault that B was left in ignorance for so long that she was entitled to sue A, then B will normally be stuck – the limitation period for suing A having elapsed in June 2011, she will be barred from suing A. However, it is different if the tort committed by A was *negligence* and A's negligence caused B to suffer various actionable losses which B only found out she could sue for in January 2013. In such a case, B will have three years to sue A from the date that she first believed[81] that she was entitled to a remedy against A.[82]

B. Physical injury

If A has committed a tort in relation to B and B has suffered some kind of physical injury as a result, a special limitation regime will often apply to B's action against A under s 11 of the Limitation Act 1980. Section 11 will apply in cases where a claim is made for physical injury resulting from 'negligence, nuisance or breach of duty'.[83] If s 11 applies to B's claim against A, then B will normally have three years from the date she was injured as a result of A's tort to sue A for damages in respect of that injury.

There are two exceptions to this rule. First, if it took B some time for her to realise that she had suffered a 'significant injury'[84] and to identify A as being the person whose act or omission was responsible for her suffering that injury, then she will have three years from the date she believed[85] that A was responsible for her suffering a significant injury to sue him for that injury.[86] Secondly, if the applicable limitation period for suing A in respect of B's injury has elapsed, the courts may nevertheless allow B to sue A for compensation for her injury under s 33 of the Limitation Act 1980 if it would be 'equitable' to do so.[87]

C. Sexual abuse

The House of Lords has had to decide on two different occasions whether the victim of sexual abuse comes within the special limitation regime created by s 11 of the Limitation Act 1980 – that is, the limitation regime that applies where the victim of 'negligence, nuisance or breach of duty' suffers physical injury as a result. The question is of vital importance because victims of sexual abuse tend only to bring claims many years after they were abused, and as a result their claims will normally fail on the ground of limitation unless they come within the special limitation regime described above. If they do, then claims for sexual abuse that have been brought years after the acts of abuse might not be defeated on grounds of limitation if it would be 'equitable' to allow the claims to continue under s 33 of the Limitation Act 1980 despite the lapse of time between the acts of abuse and the bringing of the claim.

---

[81] On what amounts to a sufficient belief to set the clock running against a claimant, see *AB* v *Ministry of Defence* [2013] 1 AC 78.

[82] Limitation Act 1980, s 14A. This rule is not meant to prejudice the limitation period for suing A that B would enjoy under the general rule that you have six years to sue from the first time you were entitled to sue the defendant.

[83] Section 11(1).

[84] Section 14. On when the victim of sexual abuse can first be said to have realised that they have suffered a 'significant injury' see *A* v *Hoare* [2008] 1 AC 844, at [34]–[35] (per Lord Hoffmann), [66]–[68] (per Lord Carswell); and *B* v *Nugent Care Society* [2010] 1 WLR 516, at [108]–[114].

[85] See n 79, above.

[86] Section 11(4)(b) in combination with s 14.

[87] Section 33.

In the first case dealing with this issue – *Stubbings* v *Webb* (1993) – the House of Lords decided that the phrase 'negligence, nuisance or breach of duty' did not cover the case where one person sexually abused another. In particular, the House of Lords did not think that the phrase 'breach of duty' covered a case involving a trespass to the person. Lord Griffiths remarked:

> I should not myself have construed breach of duty as including a deliberate assault. The phrase lying in juxtaposition with negligence and nuisance carries with it the implication of a breach of duty of care not to cause personal injury, rather than an obligation not to infringe any legal right of another person. If I invite a lady to my house one would naturally think of a duty to take care that the house is safe but would one really be thinking of a duty not to rape her?[88]

The issue came back to the House of Lords in *A* v *Hoare* (2008). The House of Lords refused to follow *Stubbings* v *Webb* and held that a trespass to the person *did* involve a breach of duty, as that phrase is used in s 11 of the Limitation Act 1980.[89] As Lord Hoffmann observed, 'there could be no moral or other ground for denying to a victim of intentional injury the more favourable limitation treatment [under s 11 of the 1980 Act] for victims of injuries caused by negligence.'[90]

Right though that undoubtedly is, the decision in the *Hoare* case placed a possibly unwelcome burden on the courts to decide in sexual abuse cases where the cases were brought years after the acts of abuse whether it would be 'equitable' to allow those cases to continue under s 33 of the Limitation Act 1980. In the *Hoare* case, Lord Brown went out of his way to warn that:

> By no means everyone who brings a late claim for damages for sexual abuse, however genuine his complaint may in fact be, can reasonably expect the court to exercise the section 33 discretion in his favour. On the contrary, a fair trial (which must surely include a fair opportunity for the defendant to investigate the allegations . . .) is in many cases likely to be found quite simply impossible after a long delay.[91]

However, it would require remarkable steeliness on the part of a trial judge not to be swayed by the opprobrium he would undoubtedly receive if he concluded that it would not be 'equitable' to allow a claim for sexual abuse to be brought years after the acts of sexual abuse occurred. In the *Hoare* case itself – where the defendant attempted to rape the claimant in 1988, was sentenced to life imprisonment, was released in 2005, having won £7m on the National Lottery on day release in 2004, and was sued by the claimant when she heard the news about his lottery win – Coulson J held that it would be 'equitable' to exercise his discretion under s 33 to allow the claimant to sue the defendant for trespass to the person, some 17 years after the trespass occurred, because the defendant had not been worth suing up until 2004.[92]

---

[88] [1993] AC 498, at 508.
[89] Approving the views of Lord Greene MR in *Billings* v *Riden* [1945] KB 11, at 19 that 'trespass to the person . . . is certainly a breach of duty'; and Adam J in the Australian case *Kruber* v *Grzesiak* [1963] VR 621, at 623 that 'do not all torts arise from breach of duty – the tort of trespass to the person arising from the breach of a general duty not to inflict direct and immediate injury to the person of another either intentionally or negligently in the absence of lawful excuse?'
[90] [2008] 1 AC 844, at [14].
[91] [2008] 1 AC 844, at [86].
[92] *A* v *Hoare* [2008] EWHC 1573 (QB).

In the subsequent case of *B* v *Nugent Care Society* (2010), the Court of Appeal considered when the courts should exercise their discretion under s 33 to allow a 'late' claim for damages for sexual abuse to be brought. The Court made it clear that relevant factors to be considered included:

(1) The quality of the evidence that was now likely to be available to determine whether the claimant has a good claim against the defendant. The narrower the basis of the claimant's claim the more likely it is that the lapse of time in bringing the claim will not prevent the courts from properly disposing of his case.[93]

(2) The reasons for the claimant's delay in bringing the case. Particularly relevant will be the issue of 'whether the claimant, taking into account his psychological state in consequence of the injury, could reasonably have been expected to institute proceedings.'[94]

(3) The strength of the claimant's case, as it appears at the preliminary hearing to determine whether the discretion under s 33 should be exercised:

> if the claimant's case is beset by inconsistencies and the claimant shows himself in evidence to be unreliable, the court may conclude that the delay is likely to prejudice the defendant in [that he will be] put to the trouble and expense of successfully defending proceedings and then not [be] able to recover costs . . . In those circumstances . . . it may well be that it would not be equitable to allow the claimant to proceed. On the other hand, if the evidence of the claimant is compelling and cogent that the abuse occurred, and it is said that it was the abuse that inhibited him from commencing proceedings, that is surely a compelling point in favour of the claimant.[95]

(4) The size of the claimant's claim. The smaller the claimant's claim is, the less compelling his case will be for arguing that it would be 'equitable' to allow the claim to be brought despite the lapse of time in bringing the claim.[96]

D. Defamation, malicious falsehood and deceit

If A has committed one of these torts in relation to B, a special limitation period will apply. In cases of defamation and malicious falsehood, B will normally have only a year to sue A from the moment she was first entitled to obtain a remedy in respect of A's tort.[97] In the case of deceit, B will have six years from the time A's deceit first came to light to sue A.[98]

22.12 Contributory negligence

This defence is often discussed in tort texts in this kind of chapter. However, there is an important distinction between this defence and all the other defences we have considered so far. The defences we have looked at so far operate to bar a claimant from suing a defendant. Contributory negligence does not: it merely operates to reduce the amount of

---

[93] [2010] 1 WLR 516, at [14]–[15].
[94] [2010] 1 WLR 516, at [16]; also [43]–[44].
[95] [2010] 1 WLR 516, at [22].
[96] [2010] 1 WLR 516, at [63].
[97] Section 4A. However, the limitation period may be extended under s 14A. If the applicable limitation period for B's suing A has expired, the courts may still allow B to sue A if it would be 'equitable' to do so: s 32A.
[98] Section 32(1)(a).

compensatory damages a claimant can sue a defendant for in respect of some loss the claimant has suffered if the claimant is judged also to have been at fault for the fact that that loss has been suffered. Accordingly, we will postpone any discussion of contributory negligence until the chapter on 'Compensatory Damages' below.[99]

Further reading

The indispensable text in this area is, now, **James Goudkamp**, *Tort Law Defences* (**Hart Publishing, 2013**). A close second is **Dyson, Goudkamp and Wilmot-Smith (eds)**, *Defences in Tort* (**Hart Publishing, 2015**), which provides state of the art reflections on the full range of tort defences from some of the best tort law academics writing today.

A lot of writing on defences focuses on the illegality defence, but has now been rendered largely out of date by the UKSC's decision in *Patel* v *Mirza*. A forthcoming volume of essays on *Illegality after Patel* v *Mirza*, edited by Sarah Green and Alan Bogg, should provide a good starting point for discussing this area of law in light of *Patel* v *Mirza*.

On *volenti*, see **A.J.E. Jaffey**, '*Volenti non fit injuria*'(1985) 44 *Cambridge Law Journal* 87 and **Mark Lunney**, '**Personal responsibility and the "new"** *volenti*' (2005) 13 *Tort Law Review* 76.

---

[99] See § 23.5.

Chapter 23
Compensatory damages

Aims and objectives

Reading this chapter should enable you to:

(1) Get a good grasp of the different ways in which the tort system delivers compensatory damages to the victim of a tort, and in cases where such damages are awarded by giving the victim a lump sum designed to compensate her for losses suffered both in the past and losses that might potentially be suffered in the future, how that lump sum is assessed.

(2) Understand when the compensatory damages payable to the victim of a tort will be reduced because (a) she received a benefit as a result of that tort being committed, or (b) she was partly to blame for that tort being committed.

(3) Understand in what situations the victim of a tort may recover damages in respect of losses suffered by third parties who have suffered harm as a result of that tort being committed.

(4) Begin to get a good understanding of the various different theories that have been offered as to why the law requires a tortfeasor to pay compensatory damages to the victim of his tort.

23.1 The basics

This chapter is concerned with the victim of a tort's right to sue for compensatory damages in respect of the actionable losses that that tort has caused her to suffer, and may cause her to suffer in the future. The rights of a third parties to a tort to sue for compensation for losses they have suffered as a result of that tort being committed will be dealt with in Chapters 28 and 29.

Much of the work that should be done in this chapter has already been done. We have looked at when the victim of a tort can argue that that tort has *caused* her loss in Chapter 8, and set out the rules on when a loss suffered by the victim of a tort as a result of that tort being committed will be *actionable* in Chapter 9. With those fundamental matters of principle already settled, much of this chapter is quite technical in nature.

In the next section we look at the different ways in which the victim of a tort might be compensated for the past, present and future actionable losses that that tort has caused, or might cause, her to suffer. Traditionally, the victim of a tort has been awarded a *lump sum* to cover all these losses. As this sum is intended to cover future losses as well as past and present losses, it is invariably speculative in nature. In order to avoid this speculation, new methods for awarding compensatory damages have been developed in recent years, such as making *periodical payments* of damages.

Having looked at these different techniques for awarding compensatory damages, we will go on to take a much more detailed look in section 23.3 at how, in a case where a claimant is to be compensated through the award of a lump sum, the courts go about assessing how much the claimant should, in principle, be awarded. We say 'in principle' because any damages award (however made) to a claimant is liable to be reduced because, for example: (1) the claimant was *partly to blame* for the losses she has suffered, or is liable to suffer, as a result of the defendant's tort; or (2) the claimant has received some kind of *benefit* from the defendant's tort which should go to offset the damages she would normally be entitled to sue the defendant for. In sections 23.4 and 23.5, we look at when compensatory damages normally payable to a claimant will be reduced because of either (1) or (2).

So far, we have been assuming when the victim of a tort sues for compensatory damages, she will be simply suing for damages in respect of the losses that *she* has suffered as a result of that tort being committed. However, there are occasions when she will be entitled to sue for damages in respect of the losses suffered by *third parties* to the tort (which damages will then be held *on trust* for those third parties) in section 23.6.

In section 23.7, we look at the various theories that have been presented to explain why the victim of a tort is entitled to sue for compensatory damages. Most such theories are either *economic* or *rights-based* in nature. An *economic* theory says that the victim of a tort is allowed to sue for compensatory damages because it makes economic sense to allow her to sue for such damages. *Rights-based* theories take a variety of forms. One theory says that the victim of a tort is allowed to sue for compensatory damages as a 'second best' way of giving her what she had a legal right to in the first place, and was deprived of when that tort was committed. Another theory – 'civil recourse theory' – says that the victim of a tort is allowed to sue for compensatory damages because she has a moral right to seek redress for that wrong, and allowing her to sue for compensatory damages provides her a civilised way of achieving that redress.

23.2 Techniques

Where A has committed a tort in relation to B, the courts will normally aim – in awarding compensatory damages to B – to give B a *lump sum* sufficient to compensate her for the actionable losses that A's tort *has caused* her to suffer and the losses that A's tort *may* cause B to suffer in the future.

So in the case where *Driver* negligently runs over *Injured* and one of *Injured*'s legs has to be amputated as a result, *Driver*'s tort will have *caused Injured* to suffer (i) physical injury, (ii) pain and distress, and (iii) loss of income (arising out of *Injured*'s not being able to work while her injuries are treated). But *Driver*'s tort *may* cause *Injured* to suffer economic loss in the future – if *Injured* loses her current job in the future, the fact that she has only one leg may make it difficult for her to find alternative employment.

So the lump sum payable to *Injured* in this situation will be designed to compensate her for: (1) the fact that *Driver*'s tort has *caused* her to suffer physical injury, distress and economic loss; *and* (2) the fact that *Driver*'s tort *may* cause her to suffer economic loss in the future because her capacity to find alternative employment if she loses her current job has been diminished.[1] Inevitably, in awarding damages designed to compensate *Injured* for (2), she will not be awarded damages equal to the *full* amount of money she would lose if she lost her job and found it difficult, because of her disability, to find alternative employment. Because there is a chance that she will not lose her job, the damages payable to *Injured* will be *discounted* to take account of that chance. However, this creates a problem.

The problem arises out of the fact that once *Injured* is awarded a lump sum in damages that is designed to compensate her for (1) and (2), *that is it*. If the lump sum proves inadequate to cover the losses that *Injured* has suffered as a result of *Driver*'s tort, she will not be able to go back to court to obtain a larger amount. Similarly, if it proves that *Driver* has overpaid and the lump sum award turns out in fact to be larger than was necessary to compensate *Injured* for the losses that she has suffered as a result of *Driver*'s tort, then *Driver* will not be able to go back to court to claw back the overpayment.

Now – because the lump sum payable to *Injured* in this case will be designed in part to compensate her for (2), that lump sum will *inevitably* either undercompensate or overcompensate *Injured* for the losses she has suffered as a result of *Driver*'s tort.[2] Either *Injured* will at some stage in the future lose her job and find it difficult to find alternative employment because she has only one leg – in which case the lump sum award will undercompensate her because that part of the award which was designed to compensate her for the fact that this might happen was discounted to take account of the possibility that *Injured* might *not* lose her job. Or *Injured* will never lose her current job and will sail on to retirement, with her earning capacity undisturbed by the fact that she has only one leg – in which case *Injured* will be overcompensated, because the lump sum paid to her included an element designed to compensate her for the possibility that she might suffer a loss that, as things turned out, she never did.

Given this problem, the law has started to move towards different systems of awarding damages, such as awards of *provisional damages* (under which the victim of a tort is awarded an initial lump sum with the option of going back to court and suing for

---

[1] Damages that are designed to compensate the victim of a tort for the fact that she may suffer economic loss in future because the tort has reduced her capacity to find alternative employment are known as damages for 'loss of earning capacity' or '*Smith* v *Manchester* damages' after one of the cases in which such damages were awarded: *Smith* v *Manchester* (1974) 17 KIR 1. In the situation we are considering, such damages will only be awarded to *Injured* if there is in fact a *real or substantial* risk that she will lose her job in the future and that her disability will make it difficult for her to find alternative employment: *Moeliker* v *Reyrolle* [1977] 1 All ER 9.

[2] See Lord Scarman's remarks in *Lim* v *Camden Area Health Authority* [1980] AC 174, at 182–3: '[There are] insuperable problems implicit in a system of compensation for personal injuries which (unless the parties agree otherwise) can yield only a lump sum assessed by the court at the time of judgment. Sooner or later . . . if the parties do not settle, a court (once liability is admitted or proved) has to make an award of damages. The award, which covers past, present, and future injury and loss, must, under our law, be of a lump sum assessed at the conclusion of the legal process. The award is final; it is not susceptible to review as the future unfolds, substituting fact for estimate. Knowledge of the future being denied to mankind, so much of the award as is to be attributed to future loss and suffering – in many cases the major part of the award – will almost surely be wrong. There is really only one certainty: the future will prove the award to be either too high or too low.' See also Lord Steyn in *Wells* v *Wells* [1999] 1 AC 345, at 384.

further damages if the tort causes her loss in future),[3] *periodical payments* (under which the victim of a tort whose economic prospects and life expectancy have been reduced by the tort is awarded a yearly sum to compensate her for her diminished earnings that is to be paid for her for however long she ends up living),[4] and *flexible periodical payments* (under which the yearly payments made to the victim of a tort whose economic prospects and life expectancy have been reduced by the tort can be varied to take account of the actual effect the tort has had on the victim's earning capacity).[5] Despite the advantages involved in making awards of damages in these new and more flexible ways, it should be noted that there are some disadvantages involved in making awards of damages in these ways.

First, all the parties to litigation will have an interest in not letting litigation 'drag on'. The victim of a tort's ability to get on with her life will be impeded if she is left in constant uncertainty as to how much compensation she will get in respect of the losses suffered by her as a result of that tort being committed. At the same time, the tortfeasor (or his insurer) will have an interest in knowing as soon as possible what his total liability to the victim of his tort is going to be for the purpose of financial planning.

Secondly, the victim of a tort may well have other reasons for preferring to receive a lump sum award designed to compensate her for *all* the losses that she has suffered as a result of that tort being committed and the losses that she may suffer in the future as a result of that tort being committed, rather than receiving small periodic payments designed to compensate her for the losses that, it turns out, she has suffered as a result of that tort being committed. She will be able to do more things with a lump sum: for instance, armed with a lump sum award of damages, she could purchase a business which would be out of her financial reach if she received her damages in small periodic payments over a number of years.[6]

23.3 Assessment

In this section, we will look at some typical cases where the victim of a tort might sue the person who committed that tort for compensatory damages and see how the courts assess how large the lump sum that is payable to the victim of the tort should be.

---

[3] Senior Courts Act 1981, s 32A (as amended by Administration of Justice Act 1982, s 6). Under rule 25.7 of the Civil Procedure Rules 1998, the courts are only allowed to exercise this power in cases where the defendant is insured or is a public authority – the idea being that in such cases, there is no real injustice to the defendant in having the possibility of a further award of damages being made against him sometime in the future hanging over his head.

[4] Damages Act 1996, s 2. See Lewis 2007.

[5] Damages (Variation of Periodical Payments) Order 2005.

[6] At the same time, the victim of a tort who has suffered large losses as a result of that tort being committed might not want to shoulder the burden of managing the large lump sum that she will be awarded to compensate her for her losses. If this is the case *and* liability is undisputed *and* the person who committed the tort in question is insured, the victim of the tort will have the option of entering into what is called a 'structured settlement' with the tortfeasor's insurer. Under this arrangement, a proportion of the damages that would be paid to the victim of the tort in a lump sum if she went to court are paid over to the victim of the tort upfront and the rest is invested by the tortfeasor's insurer in annuities that will produce a regular, tax-free, yearly income for the victim of the tort.

A. Physical injury

Let us consider first a standard case where *Driver* negligently caused a crash in which *Pedestrian* ('P') was injured. P's injuries were such that she has become permanently disabled and, as a result, she has had to take a job which pays less than the job she was working in before the crash. P had to take six months off work so as to have her injuries treated with the result that she did not receive any wages for those six months. P opted to have her injuries privately treated and as a result she incurred substantial medical bills. So *Driver*'s negligence will have caused P to suffer a mixture of *non-pecuniary* and *pecuniary* losses.

(1) *Non-pecuniary losses.* P's *non-pecuniary* losses include: (a) the *physical injury* that P sustained in the car crash; (b) the consequential *pain and suffering* P experienced as a result of being injured; (c) the *inconvenience* that P's disability causes her to suffer in trying to get around and cope with life generally; (d) the *loss of amenity* (or enjoyment of life) that P's disability will cause her to suffer.

Inevitably, the process of determining how much P should be paid to compensate her for the fact that she has suffered losses (a)–(d) is arbitrary in the sense that there is no demonstrably correct answer as to how much P should be awarded so as to compensate her for the fact that she has suffered these losses. We could easily award P £10,000 or we could award her £20,000; neither figure seems more appropriate. In assessing the figure payable, the courts will merely seek to be *consistent*. As a result, a body of case law has been built up on how much will be customarily awarded to compensate people who suffer certain 'standard' injuries and consequential non-pecuniary losses, details of which can be found in advanced works on damages.[7]

Whatever sum is payable to P to compensate her for the fact that she has suffered losses (a)–(d), it will normally be discounted somewhat to take account of the possibility that had P not become disabled as a result of *Driver*'s negligence, she might have become disabled at some stage in the future. So if P was 'doomed' to become disabled even if *Driver* had not been negligent, then the damages payable to P to compensate her for the fact that she has suffered losses (a)–(d) will be substantially reduced.[8]

(2) *Pecuniary losses.* P's *pecuniary* losses include: (e) the income she lost as a result of having to take six months off work to have her injuries treated; (f) the money P spent on having her injuries privately treated; (g) the loss of income she has suffered and will suffer as a result of having to take a job that pays less than the one she had before she was injured.

Assessing the amount payable to P in respect of the future loss of income that she will probably suffer as a result of *Driver*'s negligence is very problematic, given our inability to be certain either about what would have happened to P in the future had she not been injured by *Driver* but also our uncertainty about what will now happen to P in the future. Let us suppose that before she was injured, P was earning £20,000 a year net of tax. P's disability means that she is now in a job where she earns £12,000 a year net of tax. Let us further assume that P was 40 when she was injured.

---

[7] See, for example, *Heil* v *Rankin* [2001] QB 272 (updating the standard amounts paid in personal injury cases in response to worries that serious injuries 'worth' over £10,000 on the old scale had been compensated too conservatively in the past).
[8] *Jobling* v *Associated Dairies Ltd* [1982] AC 794.

It is *not* possible to say that had P not been injured she would probably have earned £8,000 a year more than she is currently earning up until retirement age (65) and that she should therefore be awarded (£8,000 × (65 – 40) =) £200,000 to compensate her for the future loss of income that she will probably suffer as a result of A's negligence. This is for three reasons.

First, P might not live until 65. If P's medical health is such that an actuary would predict that P will not survive beyond 60, then the damages payable to P in respect of the loss of income that she will probably suffer in the future as a result of P's negligence should be assessed on the basis that P will die at 60.

Secondly, P might not have continued to earn £20,000 a year net of tax but for P's negligence for the rest of her expected working lifespan. P might have been sacked, or been made redundant and found it difficult to find alternative employment. The damages payable to P to compensate her for the loss of income that she will probably suffer in the future as a result of A's negligence should be adjusted to take account of these possibilities.

Thirdly, suppose that we estimate that P will probably work for 20 more years and that, but for *Driver*'s negligence, P would have earned £8,000 a year more over those years than she actually will. The damages paid to P *now* in respect of the loss of income that she will probably suffer in the future as a result of *Driver*'s negligence should not equal the total amount of extra income P would probably have earned over her expected working lifespan, that is, (£8,000 × 20 =) £160,000. If they did, then P could invest the damages and earn a yearly income with them – made up of interest plus yearly withdrawals of portions of the capital sum invested – which would exceed the yearly income loss suffered by her as a result of *Driver*'s negligence. So awarding P damages equal to the total amount of extra income P would have obtained over her expected lifespan had *Driver* not negligently injured her would overcompensate P: it would make P better off than she would have been had *Driver* not been negligent. To avoid this possibility, the damages payable to P should amount to a capital sum which, when properly invested, will yield P an annual income – made up of interest plus a proportion of the capital sum – equivalent to £8,000 a year for 20 years; at the end of which 20 years the capital sum will be used up. This capital sum will be considerably smaller than £160,000.

So one way of assessing how much P should be paid to compensate her for the loss of income that she will probably suffer in the future as a result of *Driver*'s negligence would be to proceed as follows. First, ask: What is the difference between what P is earning now net of tax and what she would have been earning now net of tax had *Driver* not been negligent? (Say this is £8,000.) Then ask: How much of a working life has P probably got left to her? (Say this is 20 years.) Next, multiply £8,000 by 20 to get a rough idea of how much the total loss of income will be that P will suffer over the rest of her working life as a result of *Driver*'s negligence: this gives us £160,000. Next, discount that sum to take account of the possibility that had *Driver* not been negligent, P would have been sacked or made redundant and might not have earned as much as £8,000 more over the rest of her working life than she will now earn over the rest of her working life. So if we discount £160,000 by 25 per cent, this gives us a figure of £120,000, equivalent to a loss of income of £6,000 a year over the rest of P's expected working life.

Then we assess what sort of capital sum, properly invested, would produce a yearly income stream – made up of interest plus a proportion of the capital sum – of £6,000 a year over 20 years. Obviously this depends a lot on how we might expect P to invest the capital sum awarded. In *Wells* v *Wells* (1999), the House of Lords ruled that in assessing the damages payable in respect of future loss of income it must be assumed that the payee will invest the damages in very safe, low-interest investments such as government index-linked bonds. The capital sum we finally come up with (say £112,000) is the sum P should be paid to compensate her for the loss of income that she will probably suffer in the future as a result of *Driver*'s negligence.

Instead, the courts adopt a slightly different method of assessing how much P should be paid by way of damages to compensate her for the loss of income that she will probably suffer in the future as a result of *Driver*'s negligence. This method is known as the *multiplier method*. What the courts do is assess the difference between what P now earns net of tax and what she would have been earning now net of tax had *Driver* not been negligent. This figure (here, £8,000) is known as the *multiplicand*. They then multiply the multiplicand by a figure (known as the *multiplier*) which takes into account: (a) the number of years that P can be expected to suffer that yearly loss of income; (b) the possibility that P would not actually have earned as much in the future as she was earning at the time *Driver* injured her; and (c) the fact that P is being awarded damages *now* in respect of future income loss and can therefore be expected to earn interest with those damages which will help to cover that future income loss.

The end result is exactly the same as is yielded by the approach suggested in the above paragraph (the courts might be expected to apply a multiplier of about 14 in the above case,[9] resulting in a damages award of £112,000). The multiplier approach simply represents a slightly different way of going about assessing the damages payable to P in respect of the loss of income that she will probably suffer in the future as a result of *Driver*'s negligence.

B. Loss of life expectancy

Suppose A has negligently injured B. Suppose further that B was 35 when she was injured and before she was injured she could have been expected to live to 70. However, B's injury now means that she can only be expected to live to 45.

B will, of course, be entitled to sue A for damages in respect of: her injury and any consequential non-pecuniary losses suffered by her as a result of that injury; any medical expenses incurred by her as a result of being injured; and any loss of income that she has suffered or is likely to suffer as a result of A's injuring her between the date of her injury and the date of her death (now anticipated to occur at 45).

It is, however, well established that B will *also* be entitled to sue A for damages in respect of the money she could have earned during the years that are now 'lost' to her as a result of A's negligence[10] provided that such an award would not be too

---

[9] Of course, if B had been younger when she was injured, a higher multiplier would be used to assess the damages payable to her. In practice, the courts will rarely apply a multiplier greater than 17 or 18 in assessing how much should be paid to compensate someone for a future loss of income.

[10] *Pickett* v *British Rail Engineering Ltd* [1980] AC 126, overruling *Oliver* v *Ashman* [1962] 2 QB 210. Section 1(1)(a) of the Administration of Justice Act 1982 prevents victims of torts who have suffered a 'loss of expectation of life' suing for damages to compensate them for that fact (so no action for loss of amenity can be brought in respect of the pleasures that a victim of a tort would have enjoyed in the years that are now 'lost' to her as a result of that tort being committed). However, s 1(2) of the same Act provides that s 1(1)(a) does not apply to actions for 'damages in respect of loss of income'.

speculative.[11] This is a bit puzzling: what earthly good would awarding B such damages do her? However, the point of awarding B such damages is *not* actually to compensate B but to ensure that any dependants of B – who would have been supported by B in the years that are now 'lost' to her – do not lose out as a result of B's expectation of life being reduced.[12] B can sue for damages in respect of the money she would have earned in the years that are now lost to her and thereby create a fund that will help to support her dependants after she dies.[13]

C. Property damage

Let us now consider what the position is if *Driver* negligently damages property belonging to *Owner*. Assuming that the damage to property is actionable, how do we go about determining how much *Owner* should be paid so as to compensate him for the fact that his property has been damaged?

The courts' answer is: *As a general rule, Owner* should be paid damages equal to the amount of money it would have cost *Owner* to repair the property in question had he repaired that property at the time it was first reasonable for him to do so.

So, for example, in *Dodd Properties (Kent) Ltd* v *Canterbury City Council* (1980), the defendants built a multi-storey car park beside a building owned by the claimants. The building work took place in 1968. Due to the defendants' negligence in carrying out pile-driving operations for the foundations, serious structural damage was done to the claimants' building. The claimants could have repaired the building in 1970 when it would have cost £11,375 to repair the building, but could not afford to do so and decided to hold off doing any repairs until they had sued the defendants – by which time the cost

---

[11] It was for this reason that the Court of Appeal ruled in *Croke (a minor)* v *Wiseman* [1982] 1 WLR 171 that damages for the years that have been 'lost' could *never* be awarded to a young child whose life expectancy has been reduced by the defendant's tort. The Court of Appeal expressed some unhappiness with this decision in *Iqbal* v *Whipps Cross University Hospital NHS Trust* [2007] EWCA Civ 1190 (life expectancy of infant reduced to 41 due to negligence of defendants when he was being born) but held that as *Croke* was not 'manifestly wrong', they were bound by it.

[12] However, B will be entitled to sue A for damages in respect of the money she would have earned in the years that are now lost to her even if she has no dependants who would have been supported by her in those years.

[13] See Lord Diplock's explanation of the decision in *Pickett* v *British Rail Engineering Ltd* in *Gammell* v *Wilson* [1982] AC 27, at 64–5; also Lord Phillips MR in *Gregg* v *Scott* [2005] 2 AC 176, at [177]–[181]. An alert student might raise the following objection to this explanation. 'Surely after B dies, B's dependants will be entitled in any case to bring a claim for loss of support against A under the Fatal Accidents Act 1976? So why would the law go to such lengths to allow B to protect her dependants while she is still alive?' However, if B sues A for damages before she dies, B's dependants will lose any rights they might otherwise have had to sue A under the 1976 Act – and B will almost certainly want and need to sue A before she dies in order to get some compensation for the losses that she is *currently* suffering as a result of A's negligence. However, on this point, see: (1) Lord Phillips MR in *Gregg* v *Scott* [2005] 2 AC 176, arguing at [182] that 'It would be much better if [B] had no right to recover for such loss of earnings [that would have been made in the 'lost years'] and the dependants' right to claim under [s] 1(1) of the Fatal Accidents Act 1976 subsisted despite the claimants' recovery of damages for his injury. I am not persuaded that this result could not be achieved by a purposive construction of that section.' (2) Section 3 of the Damages Act 1996, which provides that 'The award of provisional damages [to the victim of a tort] shall not operate as a bar to an action in respect of that person's death under the Fatal Accidents Act 1976', though the award may be taken into account in judging how much a claimant bringing a claim under the 1976 Act has in fact lost by way of a loss of support.

of doing the repairs had risen to £30,327. The Court of Appeal held that the claimants had acted reasonably in delaying repairing their building until they had sued the defendants and therefore awarded the claimants £30,327 in damages.[14]

The general rule set out above is subject to three exceptions.

(1) If, when *Owner*'s property was damaged, it would have been *cheaper to replace* it rather than repair it then the compensation for the damage done to *Owner*'s property will *usually* be assessed by reference to the cost of replacing it rather than repairing it. The cost of repair measure of compensation will still be used if the property in question was so special to *Owner* that it would have been unreasonable to expect him to have replaced it rather than repaired it.

So in *O'Grady* v *Westminster Scaffolding Ltd* (1962), the defendant negligently damaged the claimant's 1938 MG motor car. The claimant could have bought a replacement car for about £185 but his MG was his 'pride and joy' and so he decided to keep it and spent about £250 repairing it. It was held that the claimant was entitled to damages for the damage done to his car assessed according to the cost of repair measure: given his special attachment to his car, it would have been unreasonable to expect him to have scrapped it and bought a replacement car.[15]

(2) If the property that was damaged by *Driver*'s negligence was *valueless* to *Owner* – for example, *Owner* was going to scrap it – then *Owner* will not be entitled to recover the cost of repairing that property from *Driver*.

(3) If the property that was damaged by *Driver*'s negligence was *in need of repair anyway* and performing that repair work would at the same time repair the damage done by *Driver*'s negligence, *Owner* will not be entitled to recover anything for the cost of repairing the damage done to his property by *Driver*'s negligence.

So in *Performance Cars Ltd* v *Abraham* (1962), the defendant negligently drove his car into the claimant's Rolls-Royce. The front wing of the claimant's Rolls-Royce was damaged as a result. It was agreed that in order to repair the damage the whole of the lower part of the Rolls-Royce would need to be resprayed. However, at the time of the collision, the rear wing of the Rolls-Royce was already damaged and *that* damage could only be repaired by respraying the whole of the lower part of the Rolls-Royce. The Court of Appeal held that the claimant was not entitled to sue the defendant for anything by way of damages: at the time of the accident, the Rolls-Royce was already in need of a respray and carrying out that respray would, as well as repairing the damage to the rear wing of the Rolls-Royce, at the same time repair the damage done by the defendant to the front wing of the Rolls-Royce.

Now let's consider the situation where *Driver* has negligently damaged a car belonging to *Owner*, and *Owner* is entitled to sue *Driver* for the reasonable costs of repairing that car. While the car is being repaired, *Owner* will be deprived of the use of that car, and will be entitled to sue for damages in respect of that. However, the basis on which such damages should be assessed has occasioned some controversy. If *Owner* has hired a replacement car, and has acted reasonably in hiring the car at the rate he did, then

---

[14] See also the Privy Council decision in *Alcoa Minerals of Jamaica Inc* v *Broderick* [2002] 1 AC 371, which endorsed the decision in *Dodd Properties*.
[15] Contrast *Darbishire* v *Warran* [1963] 1 WLR 1067, where the claimant's car – which had been damaged by the defendant's negligence – would have cost £80 to replace, but the claimant – out of inertia – instead had the car repaired at a cost of £192. Held, the claimant could only sue the defendant for £80.

Owner can sue for the costs of hiring that replacement car.[16] But other cases are not so simple.

The first variation we can call *No Hire*. In this variation, *Owner* never hired a replacement car: he simply used another car that he had in his garage to get around, or borrowed a replacement from his neighbour. The second variation we can call *Unreasonable Hire*. In this variation, *Owner* hired a replacement car but it was unreasonable for him to do so. For example, while his car was being repaired, *Owner* was going on holiday anyway, so had no need for a replacement car – but he hired one anyway, which he left outside his house while he was away. In both the *No Hire* and *Unreasonable Hire* case, *Owner* will *not* be entitled to sue for the costs of hiring a replacement car.[17] But can he get anything for the fact that he has been deprived of the use of his car while it is being repaired?

The Court of Appeal ruled in *Beechwood Birmingham Ltd* v *Hoyer Group UK Ltd* (2011) that in a *No Hire* or *Unreasonable Hire* case, we need to distinguish between cases where *Owner* is a private person and where *Owner* is a company. Damages for the loss of the use of a car that belongs to a *company* while it is being repaired will – in a *No Hire* or *Unreasonable Hire* situation – equal the interest payable on the capital value of the car for the period that it is being repaired.[18] In contrast, where the owner of the damaged car that is being repaired is a private person, damages for the loss of the use of the damaged car while it is being repaired will simply aim to compensate *Owner* for any inconvenience he may suffer as a result of being deprived of the use of that car.[19] So in the situation where *Owner* is on holiday anyway while his car is being repaired, no such damages will be payable.

23.4 Reduction (1): receipt of benefit

In this section, we look at when the compensatory damages payable to the victim of a tort will be reduced because the victim obtained some benefit from that tort being committed. The *general rule* is that the damages payable to the victim of a tort will be reduced to take account of a benefit that she has obtained as a result of that tort being committed, unless there is some good reason why they should not be. We will now look at a range of benefits that the victim of a tort might obtain from that tort being committed and see which will work to reduce the damages payable to the victim, and which will not.

A. Savings on food and other necessities

Suppose that *Careless* negligently injured *Unlucky*, with the result that *Unlucky* had to stay for a few weeks in a private hospital, having his injuries treated. Suppose further that

---

[16] *Lagden* v *O'Connor* [2004] 1 AC 1067. *Bee* v *Jenson* [2007] 4 All ER 791 seems to suggest (at [15] and [22]) that *Owner* can recover the cost of hiring the replacement car even if someone else covered the cost for him. It is not clear that the suggestion is limited to the situation considered in *Bee*, where an insurer covers the cost of hiring the replacement car; and if it is not so limited (and a friend paid for the replacement car) whether any damages payable for the cost of hire would be held on trust for the person who actually incurred that cost.

[17] In *Unreasonable Hire*, this will be either because *Owner's* unreasonable hiring of a replacement car broke the chain of causation between *Driver's* negligence and the expenses incurred by *Owner* in hiring the replacement car, or because *Owner* unreasonably failed to mitigate the loss suffered by him as a result of *Driver's* negligence in unreasonably incurring the expense of hiring a replacement car.

[18] [2011] QB 357, at [52].

[19] [2011] QB 357, at [48]–[49].

while he was in the hospital, the hospital provided him with meals. *Careless* will of course be liable to compensate *Unlucky* for the medical bills he has incurred in being treated.

However, in this situation *Careless*'s negligence will have resulted in *Unlucky* receiving a benefit: while he was in hospital, he did not have to buy his own food. *Careless*'s liability will be reduced to take account of this saving that *Unlucky* has made.[20] So suppose that *Unlucky*'s medical bills came to £10,000; but in the time *Unlucky* was in hospital, he would have spent £500 on buying food for himself. On these figures, *Careless* will only be liable to pay *Unlucky* £9,500 in compensatory damages – *Careless*'s *prima facie* liability to pay *Unlucky* £10,000 in damages will be reduced to take account of the fact that *Unlucky* saved £500 that he would otherwise have spent on buying food for himself while he was in hospital.[21]

The same point will apply if, had *Unlucky* not been in hospital, he would have spent money on necessities that were provided by the hospital, such as washing *Unlucky*'s clothes. The damages payable to *Unlucky* will be reduced to take account of this saving.

B. Compensation payments from other defendants liable in tort

Suppose that *Driver* negligently ran over *Pedestrian*'s leg, but a failure to treat the leg properly in hospital by *Doctor* resulted in *Pedestrian* ('P') losing the leg. Suppose that £100,000 would be sufficient to compensate P for the loss of his leg. Each of *Doctor* and *Driver* will be liable to pay this sum to P. If *Doctor*'s settles P's claim against him for a certain sum of money, this will reduce the amount of money P is entitled to sue *Driver* for: the compensation payment from *Doctor* will count as a benefit that P has received as a result of *Driver*'s tort.

The difficult question is by how much *Driver*'s liability to P will be reduced. Obviously, if *Doctor*'s compensation payment to P came to £100,000, then *Driver* will not be liable to pay P anything. P will be fully compensated for the losses that she suffered as a result of *Driver*'s tort and will therefore not be entitled to sue *Driver* for anything.[22] But what if *Doctor*'s compensation payment came to only £80,000? The normal rule is that P will be entitled to sue *Driver* for £20,000 – the balance of the uncompensated loss that she suffered as a result of *Driver*'s tort. However, there are two situations in which *Doctor*'s compensation payment to P of £80,000 will have the effect of extinguishing *entirely Driver*'s liability to P.

(1) It used to be the case that if A and C were *jointly liable* to compensate B for the losses suffered by her, then any compensation payment by C to B would have the effect of discharging A's liability to B. However, the position nowadays is a bit more complicated.

If C's compensation payment was made because B won a *judgment* against C, then C's payment will not have the effect of extinguishing B's rights to sue A for compensation: A will

---

[20] *Shearman* v *Folland* [1950] 2 KB 43.

[21] Of course, *Unlucky*'s medical bills will almost certainly include a charge for the food *Unlucky* received while he was in hospital but that is immaterial. At the same time as *Unlucky* was paying the hospital for the food that the hospital served him, he was saving money which he would have spent had *Careless* not injured him on buying food for himself.

[22] However, *Doctor* will be entitled to make a claim in contribution against *Driver*, forcing *Driver* to shoulder a 'just and equitable' share of the burden of compensating P for the losses she has suffered: see above, § 4.3(F)(2).

therefore be liable to make up any shortfall in the compensation paid by C to B.[23] If, on the other hand, C's compensation payment was made to B under a settlement that he reached with B, then the old rule will apply – and A's liability to B will be extinguished – *unless* B's settlement with C preserved her rights to sue A for damages in respect of the losses suffered by her:[24] in which case, A will again be liable to make up any shortfall in the compensation C has paid B.

As it happens the law on joint liability will not apply in *Driver*'s case. This is because joint liability will only arise where one defendant is vicariously liable, or liable as an accessory, for another's tort.[25] Neither apply here: *Driver* and *Doctor*'s torts were committed independently of each other. So in this situation *Driver* and *Doctor* will be *jointly and severally* liable to compensate P for the loss of her leg.[26]

(2) Even though *Doctor* and *Driver* were *jointly and severally* liable to compensate P for the loss of her leg, a compensation payment of £80,000 by *Doctor* to P will still have had the effect of extinguishing *Driver*'s liability to P if P treated *Doctor*'s payment of £80,000 to her as *fully compensating* her for the loss of that leg. This odd rule owes its existence to the decision of the House of Lords in *Jameson* v *Central Electricity Generating Board* (2000). The rule exists for the protection of *Doctor* who, having settled P's claim against him, might find – if P subsequently dies because of medical complications arising out the loss of his leg – that *Driver* has been found liable to pay a substantial sum to P's dependants for the loss of support that they have suffered as a result of P's death, and that *Driver* now wants *Doctor* to contribute to his liability. In the interests of allowing *Doctor* to wash his hands of any further liabilities that he might incur as a result of what has happened to P, the House of Lords ruled in *Jameson* that if *Doctor*'s compensation payment to P is treated by P as fully compensating P for the loss of her leg, P will then lose her right to sue *Driver* for compensation for the loss of her leg. This means that if P subsequently dies of complications arising out of the loss of his leg, P's dependants will not be able to sue *Driver* for loss of support under the Fatal Accidents Act 1976 (and *Doctor* will not have to fear *Driver* subsequently making a contribution claim against him). This is because P's dependants will not be able to show – as they are required to under the 1976 Act – that had P lived longer, she would have been entitled to sue *Driver* for damages.[27]

---

[23] Civil Liability (Contribution) Act 1978, s 3: 'Judgment recovered against any person liable in respect of any . . . damage shall not be a bar to an action . . . against any other person who is . . . jointly liable with him in respect of the same . . . damage.'

[24] *Gardiner* v *Moore* [1969] 1 QB 55.

[25] See Chapters 30–31, below.

[26] See *The Koursk* [1924] P 140. In that case, two ships – the *Clan Chisholm* and the *Koursk* – collided with each other. The collision occurred as a result of the negligence of both the owners of the *Clan Chisholm* and the negligence of the defendants, the owners of the *Koursk*. As a result of the collision, the *Clan Chisholm* collided with the claimants' vessel, the *Itria*, which sank. In this case the owners of the *Clan Chisholm* and the defendants, the owners of the *Koursk*, were each liable in tort to compensate the claimants for the loss of the *Itria*: each of them committed the tort of negligence in relation to the claimants and the *Itria* would not been sunk had not each of them been negligent. However, as their negligent acts were unconnected, the owners of the *Clan Chisholm* and the defendants were not *jointly* liable to compensate the owners of the *Itria* for the loss of the *Itria*; they were jointly and severally liable. So when the owners of the *Clan Chisholm* made a compensation payment to the owners of the *Itria*, that did not have the effect of extinguishing the liability of the defendants to the owners of the *Itria*. The defendants were still liable to compensate the owners of the *Itria* for the balance of the uncompensated loss that they had suffered as a result of the sinking of the *Itria*.

[27] See below, § 28.3.

C. Redundancy payments

Suppose that *Careless* negligently injured *Employee* and as a result *Employee* was unable to continue in her job and was made redundant. Any redundancy payment received by *Employee* on leaving her job will operate to reduce the damages payable by *Careless* to *Employee*.[28]

D. Social security payments

Suppose that A negligently injured B and B was incapacitated as a result. Suppose that as a result of her being incapacitated, B received quite a lot of money in social security payments. The Social Security (Recovery of Benefits) Act 1997 establishes that the social security payments that B received as a result of her being incapacitated in the first *five* years after A injured her will be taken into account in determining the damages payable to B; however, any subsequent social security payments will be disregarded. At first sight, the Act seems to work in A's favour. However, the Act also provides that if A makes a compensation payment to B, he will be liable to compensate the State for *all* the social security payments that B received as a result of her being incapacitated in the first five years after A injured her. This can cause injustice if A is not wholly to blame for the fact that B was injured.

E. Gifts

The damages payable to the victim of a tort will *not* be reduced to take account of the value of any gifts that she received from sympathetic friends and relatives who wanted to help or comfort her in the aftermath of the tort. Suppose, for example, that *Driver* negligently ran over *Builder* and as a result *Builder* was laid up for a while. *Friend* gave *Builder* £500 'to tide you over until you are back on your feet and able to work again'. The damages payable to *Builder* will not be reduced to take account of the £500 that *Builder* has received from *Friend*, even though *Builder* would not have received that money but for *Driver's* tort. There are two reasons for this. First, if the damages were reduced, then *Friend's* gift would end up working to benefit *Driver*, not *Builder*. As the gift was made for *Builder's* benefit, and not *Driver*, this would be unfair. Secondly, if the damages were reduced, *Friend* might be discouraged from helping *Builder* out, on the basis that in the long run, his helping *Builder* would only benefit *Driver*.

F. Insurance payments

Generally speaking, any insurance payments received by the victim of a tort (P) committed by D will *not* be taken into account in determining what damages are payable to P.[29]

---

[28] *Colledge* v *Bass Mitchells & Butlers Ltd* [1988] 1 All ER 536.

[29] *Bradburn* v *Great Western Railway Co* (1874) LR 10 Ex 1. What is the position if A negligently destroys B's property, B obtains the value of the property from his property insurer, and then sues A for damages equal to the value of the property? B will be entitled to recover the full value of the property from A but B's insurance company will then have a charge over those damages for the value of the insurance money it paid out to B: *Lord Napier and Ettrick* v *Hunter* [1993] AC 713. The reason why B's insurance company will have a charge over the damages is to prevent double recovery. Contracts of insurance against physical injury are different: and claimant who is tortiously injured where her injury is covered by an insurance policy will be entitled to pocket the insurance money *and* the damages. The concern about double recovery will not apply here as the courts acknowledge that it is impossible to determine what would amount to an 'adequate' level of compensation for the physical injury suffered by the claimant – so people should be left free to insure their persons so as to 'boost' the amount of money they will be able to recover if someone tortiously injures them.

The reason is that if such payments had the effect of reducing the damages payable to P, then the premiums paid on P's insurance policy would have the effect of benefiting D, and not P.[30] Three points may be made about this:

1. There could be no objection to the insurance payment to P going to reduce D's liability to P if D repaid P all the premiums paid on P's insurance policy.[31] However, no court has ever taken this path.

2. What would have been the position if D had paid the insurance premiums on P's insurance policy? There would then be no injustice in allowing D to reduce his liability to P by the amount of the insurance payout to P, and indeed the cases indicate that in this situation, D's liability will be reduced by the amount of the payout.[32]

3. What would have been the position if a *Third Party* had paid the premiums on P's insurance policy? The cases seem to indicate that in this kind of situation the damages payable to P *should* be reduced by the amount of the insurance payout to P.[33] However, this seems over-simple. We can imagine two variations on this kind of situation.

   In the first case, *Third Party* intended, when he paid the premiums, that P and no one else should get the benefit of those premiums. In such a case, it would be unfair – unfair on *Third Party* – for the court to allow D to take advantage of the payment of those premiums and hold that D's liability should be reduced by the amount of the payout to P.

   In the second case, *Third Party* paid the premiums because he was contractually obliged to do so under an arrangement with P and, in paying the premiums, *Third Party* had no intention one way or the other as to who should benefit from the payment of those premiums. If this had been the case, it would *not* be unfair to allow D to take advantage of the payment of those premiums and hold that his liability to P should be reduced by the amount of the payout to P.

G. Windfall payments

In *Needler Financial Services Ltd v Taber* (2002), the defendants negligently advised the claimant to switch pension schemes. The claimant did so and lost out as a result: the pension scheme that he switched into (with the Norwich Union) was not as profitable as his original pension scheme. He sued the defendants for damages. The defendants admitted liability but claimed that the damages payable to the claimant should be reduced because the claimant received a windfall payment of about £7,800 when the Norwich Union demutualised. Sir Andrew Morritt V-C held that this benefit – which the claimant had received as a result of the defendants' negligent advice – should *not* be taken into account in determining the damages payable to the claimant. It is hard to understand why it should not have been. However, one possible explanation is that the claimant might have already spent the windfall payment that he received from the Norwich Union. If he had,

---

[30] See *Shearman v Folland* [1950] 2 KB 43, 46 (per Asquith LJ): 'If the wrongdoer were entitled to set-off what the wrongdoer was entitled to recoup or had recouped under his policy, he would, in effect, be depriving the claimant of all benefit from the premiums paid by the latter and appropriating that benefit to himself.'

[31] *Bristol & West Building Society v May, May & Merrimans (No 2)* [1998] 1 WLR 336, 356.

[32] *Gaca v Pirelli General plc* [2004] 1 WLR 2683.

[33] *Hussain v New Taplow Paper Mills* [1988] 1 AC 514, 527; *Hodgson v Trapp* [1989] 1 AC 807, 819; *Bristol & West Building Society v May, May & Merrimans (No 2)* [1998] 1 WLR 336, 358–9.

then taking that windfall payment into account in determining the damages payable to the claimant would have made him, through no fault of his own, worse off overall – which would have been unfair to the claimant.

H. Gains made through the exercise of skill and judgment

In *Hussey* v *Eels* (1990), the defendants fraudulently induced the claimants to buy their house. The house was, to the defendants' knowledge, affected by subsidence but the defendants told the claimants that to their knowledge the property had not been subject to subsidence. The claimants purchased the defendants' house for approximately £53,000. The true value of the house was about £36,000 as repairing it would have cost in excess of £17,000. So the defendants' fraud caused the claimants to lose £17,000. However the claimants, having discovered the problem with subsidence, then began to turn things around. They decided not to have the house repaired. Instead, they demolished it and sought planning permission to build two bungalows on the vacant plot. This was granted and the claimants then sold the land to a developer with the planning permission for £78,500.

So – having initially lost £17,000, the claimants' ingenuity meant that they made a gain of £42,500 on selling the land on which their house was originally built: they obtained £78,500 in return for an asset which was originally worth £36,000 in their hands. The claimants then sued the defendants for the original £17,000 that they had lost in buying the defendants' house. The defendants claimed that the £42,500 profit that the claimants made on selling the land on which the house was built should be taken into account in assessing the damages payable to the claimants. So in effect they argued that they should not be held liable to the claimants at all. The Court of Appeal rejected the defendants' claim. This was quite right: had the claimants' profit been taken into account, all the work and planning they did in improving the value of their land would have redounded to the benefit of the defendants. So the defendants were correctly held liable to pay the claimants £17,000 in damages.

I. Psychic benefits

In *Wise* v *Kaye* (1962), Sellers LJ remarked that:

> The complete loss of sight may bring, and I think often does, a serenity and calm of life which might lead to a happiness hitherto unknown, but I cannot think that a defendant is entitled to pray that in aid in order to reduce the damages he has to pay to the sufferer. [Similarly if] [i] nfirmity which cripples and incapacitates a man . . . [brings] him a sympathy and attention which reveals in him an inward comfort which he has never previously known [making him] happier than he has ever been.[34]

23.5 Reduction (2): contributory negligence

Section 1(1) of the Law Reform (Contributory Negligence) Act 1945 provides that where:

> any person suffers damage as the result partly of his own fault and partly of the fault of any other person or persons . . . the damages recoverable in respect thereof shall be reduced to such extent as the court thinks just and equitable having regard to the claimant's share in the responsibility of the damage.

---

[34] [1962] 1 QB 638, 651.

Section 4 of the 1945 Act provides that:

> 'fault' means negligence, breach of statutory duty or other act or omission which gives rise to
> liability in tort or would, apart from this Act, give rise to a defence of contributory negligence.

A number of different points need to be made about the scope of the defence of contributory negligence.[35]

A. Defendant's conduct

The 1945 Act says that the defence of contributory negligence can be pleaded where the damage suffered by the claimant was 'the result . . . partly of the fault of [some] other person' where 'fault' is defined as meaning 'negligence, breach of statutory duty' or some other form of conduct which, before 1945, would have given rise to a defence of contributory negligence. So contributory negligence will *not* be available as a defence to *all* torts. There will be some torts where the fact that the claimant was partly to blame for the fact that she suffered the loss she did will not go to reduce the damages payable to the claimant. If the tort committed by A was conversion or amounted to an intentional trespass to B's goods, then the defence will not apply;[36] nor will it if the tort committed by A was deceit[37] or involved dishonesty of any kind[38] (as will be the case if the tort committed by A was conspiracy or inducing a breach of contract). In *Standard Chartered Bank* v *Pakistan National Shipping Corporation (Nos 2 and 4)* (2003), Lord Rodger of Earlsferry stated that 'contributory negligence [has] never been a defence open to a defendant who . . . intended to harm the [claimant]'.[39] Although a defendant may assault or batter a claimant without necessarily having an intention to harm the claimant,[40] the Court of Appeal ruled in *Pritchard* v *Co-operative Group Ltd* (2011) that 'the 1945 Act cannot, in principle, be used to reduce damages in cases where claims are based on assault and battery . . .'.[41]

B. Claimant's conduct

If A has committed a tort in relation to B to which the defence of contributory negligence applies, then the compensatory damages payable to B will be reduced if it was 'partly [her] own fault' that she suffered the losses she did as a result of A's tort. The House of Lords made it clear in *Reeves* v *Commissioner of Police of the Metropolis* (2000) that 'fault' does not just cover an inadvertent act by the victim of a tort that contributed to her own loss – it also covers a deliberate act (here, self-harm) that contributed to the losses that the victim of a tort suffered as a result of that tort being committed.[42] However it should be noted that

---

[35] On which, see generally Gravells 1977 and Steele 2013. For an attack on the idea that damages payable to a claimant in tort should *ever* be reduced for contributory negligence, see Stevens 2015.

[36] Section 11 of the Torts (Interference with Goods) Act 1977 provides that 'Contributory negligence is no defence in proceedings founded on conversion, or on intentional trespass to goods.'

[37] *Alliance & Leicester Building Society* v *Edgestop Ltd* [1993] 1 WLR 1462; *Standard Chartered Bank* v *Pakistan National Shipping Corporation (Nos 2 and 4)* [2003] 1 AC 959.

[38] *Corporacion Nacional de Cobre* v *Sogemin* [1997] 1 WLR 1396.

[39] [2003] 1 AC 959, at [45].

[40] See above, § 2.3.

[41] [2012] QB 320, at [62] (per Aikens LJ), disapproving Lord Denning MR's suggestion to the contrary in *Murphy* v *Culhane* [1977] QB 94, at 98–9.

[42] [2000] 1 AC 360, at 370 (per Lord Hoffmann), 377 (per Lord Jauncey), 383 (per Lord Hope), 385 (per Lord Hobhouse)

where A has committed a tort in relation to B and that tort has resulted in B suffering some kind of loss because B did something deliberate *after* A committed his tort, B may be barred *completely* from suing for that loss, either on the basis that B's deliberate act broke the chain of causation between A's tort and B's loss,[43] or on the basis that B's deliberate act meant she failed to mitigate the loss suffered by her as a result of A's tort.[44]

In judging whether the losses suffered by the victim of a tort were 'partly [her] own fault', one first asks whether the victim of a tort did anything to contribute to the fact that she suffered those losses, and if she did, one then asks whether a reasonable person of her age[45] and in her physical condition[46] would have acted in the way she did. Subject to one doubt, if a reasonable person of the victim's age and in the victim's physical condition would not have acted as she did, then we would find that the losses suffered by the victim were 'partly [her] own fault'.

The one doubt arises in the case where the victim of a tort suffered from a mental illness that led her to do something that contributed to the losses that she suffered as a result of that tort. For example, consider the **Horrible Seat-Belt Problem**:

> *Teen* suffered from a mental illness that meant that she could not bear the feeling of a seat-belt against her body. One day, she was travelling in the back of a car that *Driver* negligently crashed into. *Teen* was badly injured in the crash. Had she been wearing a seat belt, she either would not have been injured at all, or her injuries would have been substantially mitigated.

Should the damages payable to *Teen* by *Driver* be reduced for contributory negligence? There is no doubt that a reasonable person of *Teen*'s age and in her physical condition would have been wearing a seat-belt at the time of the crash. But does that mean we should say that *Teen*'s injuries were 'partly [her] own fault'? There is authority that says 'yes' to this question, and holds that the damages payable should be reduced for contributory negligence.[47] However, the case of *Corr* v *IBC Vehicles Ltd* (2008)[48] (which we discuss in detail below) indicates that we should adopt a more nuanced approach. If *Teen*'s mental illness meant that she literally had *no choice* whether or not to wear the seat-belt, then the Law Lords in *Corr* were agreed that the damages payable to *Teen* should not be reduced for contributory negligence. On the other hand, if *Teen*'s mental illness meant that she *could* have worn a seat-belt, but it would have been *very difficult* for her to do so, then three of the Law Lords in *Corr* were agreed that the damages payable to *Teen* should be reduced for contributory negligence to recognise 'the element of choice'[49] that *Teen* enjoyed in this case. (Though the damages payable to *Teen* will not be reduced by anywhere near as much as they would have been in the case where *Teen* did not have any good reason not to wear a seat-belt.)

---

[43] See above, § 8.11.
[44] See above, § 9.6.
[45] *Yachuk* v *Oliver Blais Co Ltd* [1949] AC 386, *Gough* v *Thorne* [1966] 1 WLR 1387.
[46] *Daly* v *Liverpool Corporation* [1939] 2 All ER 142.
[47] *Baxter* v *Woolcombers Ltd* (1963) 107 SJ 553.
[48] Reported at [2008] 1 AC 884, and referred to as '*Corr*' below.
[49] *Corr*, at [52] (per Lord Mance).

C. Assessment of reduction

(1) *Two-party cases.* If A has committed a tort in relation to B but can raise a defence of contributory negligence to reduce the damages payable to B in respect of the losses suffered by B as a result of A's tort, the courts determine by how much the damages payable to B should be reduced by assessing the *comparative blameworthiness* of A and B for the losses suffered by B. So if they were equally to blame for the fact that B suffered those losses, the damages payable will be reduced by 50 per cent;[50] if A was four times as much to blame as B for the losses suffered by B, the damages will be reduced by 20 per cent.[51]

(2) *Three-party cases.* The position is a bit more complicated in a case which involves two tortfeasors. Suppose that *Careless* and *Heedless* each committed a tort in relation to *Silly* and *Silly* suffered various losses as result but *Silly* was partly to blame for the fact that he suffered those losses. We determine by how much the damages payable to *Silly* should be reduced by lumping *Careless* and *Heedless* together and asking: as compared to *Silly*, how much to blame were *Careless* and *Heedless together* for the losses suffered by *Silly*?

So in *Fitzgerald* v *Lane* (1989), *Pedestrian* ('P') walked across a road when the lights were against him. He was struck by a motor car being negligently driven by *Driver One*. While he was lying in the road he was struck by a motor car which was negligently driven by *Driver Two*. It was held that *One* and *Two both* caused P to suffer the injuries he suffered as a result of the second collision[52] and so P was entitled to sue either *One* or *Two* or both for compensation for the fact that he received those injuries. However, P was partly to blame for the fact that he suffered those injuries: he would not have been injured had he not acted unreasonably by walking across the road when the lights were against him. Given this, the damages payable to P were liable to be reduced for contributory negligence. It was found that P was twice as much to blame as *each* of *One* and *Two* for the injuries that he suffered in the second collision – that is, P was 50 per cent to blame for what happened, *One* was 25 per cent to blame, and *Two* was 25 per cent to blame. It followed that P was just as much to blame for the injuries that he suffered as *One* and *Two* were *together*. The damages payable to the claimant were therefore reduced by 50 per cent.

D. Self-harm

The question of whether the defence of contributory negligence should be applied in a case where the victim of a tort has deliberately harmed herself (in the worst case, killed herself) and the person who committed that tort is being sued for the loss resulting from that act of self-harm has troubled the courts.

Let us first of all consider the case where the victim of a tort was mentally ill when he or she harmed herself. In *Corr* v *IBC Vehicles* (2008), an employee injured in workplace accident caused by his employer's negligence developed post-traumatic stress disorder with the result that he eventually killed himself. The Law Lords were deeply divided over

---

[50] The deduction made in *Reeves* v *Commissioner of Police of the Metropolis* [2000] 1 AC 360 (prisoner took advantage of defendants' negligence to commit suicide).

[51] The deduction made in *Froom* v *Butcher* [1976] QB 286 (claimant's failure to wear seat-belt contributed to the injuries she suffered in car accident caused by defendant's negligence).

[52] For an explanation of this point, see above, § 8.1.

whether the damages payable to the employee's dependants in respect of his death should be reduced on the ground of contributory negligence. Lords Bingham and Walker thought that the fact that the employee killed himself in a depressed state meant that he was not *at all* to blame for his death and thought that the damages payable to the employee's dependants should *not* be reduced *at all* for contributory negligence.[53] The other Law Lords – Scott, Mance, and Neuberger – disagreed. They took the view that *if* the employee was not an automaton at the time he killed himself,[54] then his death was, in part, something for which he was responsible, and the damages payable to the employee's dependants in respect of that death should be reduced for contributory negligence. Lord Scott would have been in favour of the damages being reduced by 20 per cent in *Corr*.[55] Lords Mance and Neuberger thought that as the questions of (i) whether the employee was in an autonomous state at the time he killed himself, and if so, (ii) what his degree of responsibility for his own death was, had not been addressed at first instance, it would be inappropriate for them to make a finding on those questions. So they decided that the damages in *Corr* should not be reduced for contributory negligence;[56] but because of a lack of evidence rather than a matter of principle.

Given the willingness of three of the five Law Lords in *Corr* to allow a defence of contributory negligence to be pleaded against someone who was *mentally ill* but still enjoyed some degree of autonomy when they harmed themselves, it is clear that the decision of the House of Lords in *Reeves* v *Commissioner of Police of the Metropolis* (2000) – which dealt with the case where someone of *sound mind* harmed themselves – remains good law. In *Reeves*, someone who had been charged with credit card fraud and was remanded in police custody and was known to be a suicide risk took advantage of the police's carelessness to kill himself in his cell. The prisoner – 'surprising thought it might seem'[57] – was found to have been of sound mind when he killed himself. The House of Lords held that the damages payable to the prisoner's dependants in respect of his death should be reduced by 50 per cent for contributory negligence, as the prisoner was as much responsible for his death as the police were.

E. Contributory negligence and *Hedley Byrne*

Two problems need to be addressed under this heading. First, will a defendant who has breached a duty of care owed to another under one of the principles in *Hedley Byrne* be entitled to rely on the defence of contributory negligence to reduce the damages payable to that other? Secondly, if he is, how does the defence of contributory negligence interact with the limit placed by the *SAAMCO* principle on what damages can be sued for in a *Hedley Byrne* case?

On the first question, suppose that A advised B that a car that she was thinking of buying was in good condition and that he indicated to her that she could safely rely on his advice. Suppose further that she did rely on A's advice and bought the car. However, the car later proved to be so defective that it was not worth repairing and had to be given away to some scrap metal merchants. If B sues A in negligence, can A attempt to raise a defence

---

[53] *Corr*, at [22] (per Lord Bingham), [44] (per Lord Walker).
[54] *Corr*, at [31] (per Lord Scott), [51] (per Lord Mance), [65] (per Lord Neuberger).
[55] *Corr*, at [32].
[56] *Corr*, at [47] (per Lord Mance), [70] (per Lord Neuberger).
[57] *Corr*, at [64] (per Lord Neuberger).

of contributory negligence to B's claim on the basis that she was partly to blame for the fact that she lost the money she spent on the car because it was very foolish of her to rely on his advice? It is unlikely that A would be allowed to make such an argument.[58] Having earlier indicated to B that she could safely rely on his advice, it is likely that A would be prevented (estopped) from subsequently arguing that B was foolish to rely on his advice for the purpose of raising a defence of contributory negligence to her claim for damages.

However, if the *extent* of the losses suffered by B as a result of acting on A's advice was partly B's fault, then there is no reason why A should not be allowed to raise a defence of contributory negligence to reduce the damages payable to B. This was what happened in *Platform Home Loans* v *Oyston Shipways Ltd* (2000), a case which also dealt with the interaction between the *SAAMCO* principle and the defence of contributory negligence. Simplifying the facts of the case slightly, the claimant lent £1m to a Mr Hussain secured by a mortgage of Hussain's home. The home was negligently valued by the defendant as being worth £1.5m: it was in fact worth only £1m. Four years later, Hussain defaulted on repaying the loan and the claimant sought to recoup the money he had lent by selling Hussain's house, which was worth only £400,000 at that stage. So the claimant lost £600,000 as a result of the defendant's negligence.[59] But two points complicated the case.

The first was that under the *SAAMCO* principle, the claimant should only have been entitled to sue the defendant for £500,000 – that was the loss that the claimant had suffered that was attributable to the fact that it had loaned money to Hussain on inadequate security.[60] The second point was that the claimant was – as compared with the defendant – 20 per cent to blame for the fact that he lost the money he did on the loan to Hussain. The reasons for this were: (1) he had failed to check whether or not Hussain was a credit risk; and (2) he had loaned Hussain more than was reasonable given the defendant's valuation of Hussain's house. So the defendant was entitled to raise a defence of contributory negligence to reduce the damages that he had to pay the claimant.

The problem faced by the courts in the *Platform Home Loans* case was – how did these two points relate to each other? Do you say that the defendant was *prima facie* liable to pay the claimant £600,000, deduct 20 per cent for contributory negligence, turning the defendant's liability into one to pay the claimant £480,000, and then allow the claimant to claim for the whole of that on the basis that doing so would not violate the *SAAMCO* principle (under which the most the claimant could have sued the defendant for was £500,000)? Or do you say that the *SAAMCO* principle means that the defendant was *prima facie* liable to pay the claimant £500,000 and then knock 20 per cent off *that* figure, turning the defendant's liability into one to pay the claimant £400,000? The Court

---

[58] See *Gran Gelato Ltd* v *Richcliff (Group) Ltd* [1992] Ch 560, 574 (per Sir Donald Nicholls V-C), doubting whether the damages payable to a claimant in a *Hedley Byrne* case could be reduced for contributory negligence where it was alleged that the claimant was contributorily negligent because she should not have done the very thing that she was advised to do by the defendant.

[59] It was established that if the defendant had taken care in his valuation, he would have accurately valued the house as being worth only £1m; as a result, the claimants would have offered to lend Mr Hussain only £700,000 and he would have declined the loan.

[60] Had the claimant lent the £1m to Hussain on adequate security – that is, in return for a mortgage of a house worth £1.5m – when Hussain defaulted, the security would have been worth £900,000 and the claimant would have lost £100,000 on the loan. So £100,000 of the £600,000 loss suffered by the claimant would have been suffered by the claimant anyway, even if he had lent Hussain money on adequate security. Therefore, £500,000 of the money lost by the claimant was lost by the claimant because he lent money to Hussain on inadequate security.

of Appeal preferred the latter approach; but the House of Lords ruled that the former approach was correct. In so doing, the House of Lords reinterpreted the *SAAMCO* principle as one which does not determine *which* of the losses suffered by a claimant in a *Hedley Byrne* case can be sued for by that claimant, but as one which places a 'cap' on the potential liability of a defendant to a claimant in a *Hedley Byrne* case. It is, however, doubtful whether that interpretation of the *SAAMCO* principle is reconcilable with the reasons for its adoption by Lord Hoffmann in the *SAAMCO* case.

F. Contributory negligence and *White* v *Jones*

Suppose that A asked C to prepare a will for him under which B would inherit £9,000. C prepared the will but only had one person witness A's signing the will, thus making the will invalid. A – who had some knowledge of the law relating to wills – thought that more than one witness was required but did not raise any objections because he thought C 'knew best'. Shortly afterwards, A died and his will was declared to be invalid with the result that B did not receive her legacy. B will, of course, be able to sue C for damages under the principle in *White* v *Jones* (1995),[61] but will C be able to raise a defence of contributory negligence to her claim on the basis that *A* was partly to blame for the fact that B did not receive her legacy? The question was raised in *Gorham* v *British Telecommunications plc* (2000). Of the three members of the Court of Appeal who decided that case, Pill and Schiemann LJJ preferred to leave the matter to be decided another day,[62] though Pill LJ thought the argument that a defence of contributory negligence should be available in this kind of case had its 'attractions'.[63] Sir Murray Stuart-Smith thought that the defence *would* be available in this kind of case.[64]

G. One final limit

Suppose that A has committed a tort in relation to B and B has suffered various losses as a result, for which she was partly to blame – she would not have suffered those losses had she not acted unreasonably in some way. It seems to be the case that if the reason why B suffered those losses has nothing to do with the reason why it was unreasonable for B to act in the way she did, A will not be able to raise a defence of contributory negligence to B's claim to be compensated for those losses.

So, for example, in *Jones* v *Livox Quarries Ltd* (1952), Denning LJ considered whether the defence would be available in the following case. A negligently fires a gun and the bullet fired from the gun happens to hit and injure B while she was dangerously perched on the back of a moving lorry. Now – it was clearly unreasonable for B to stand on the back of the lorry and had she not done this she would not have been hit by the bullet: it was because she was on the lorry that she was in the wrong place at the wrong time. Does this mean that A can raise a defence of contributory negligence to any claim B makes against him for damages? Denning LJ thought not.[65] But the only explanation as to why the defence would not be available here is that the reason why it was unreasonable for B to perch on the back of the lorry had nothing to do with the reason why B was hit by the bullet.

---

[61] Discussed above, § 5.12.
[62] [2000] 1 WLR 2129, 2144 (per Pill LJ), 2145 (per Schiemann LJ).
[63] [2000] 1 WLR 2129, 2144.
[64] [2000] 1 WLR 2129, 2149.
[65] [1952] 2 QB 608, 616.

In *Westwood* v *The Post Office* (1974), the claimant worked for the Post Office at a telephone exchange. His place of work was a three-storey building with a flat roof. Workers at the exchange, including the claimant, would frequently take short breaks on the roof although they were not authorised to do so and not permitted to gain access to the roof. While on his way back from one such break on the roof, the claimant fell through a defective trapdoor and was injured. The claimant sued the Post Office for damages in respect of his injuries, claiming that he had been injured because the Post Office had breached the duty it owed him under s 16 of the Offices, Shops and Railway Premises Act 1963 to ensure that the floors in the claimant's workplace were of sound construction. The Post Office admitted liability but sought to raise a defence of contributory negligence to the claimant's claim. The Post Office argued that the claimant was partly to blame for his injuries because he would not have been injured had he not acted unreasonably in trespassing on the flat roof of the telephone exchange. The House of Lords held that no defence of contributory negligence could be raised here: the reason why the claimant was injured (he trod on a trapdoor which was not soundly constructed) had nothing to do with the reason why it was unreasonable for the claimant to trespass on the flat roof of the telephone exchange (he had no business being up there).

In *St George* v *Home Office* (2009), the claimant – who was addicted to alcohol and drugs – was sentenced to four months in prison. On arrival at the prison, he informed the staff that he was prone to epileptic seizures when in withdrawal from alcohol and drugs. Despite this, he was allocated the top bunk in his cell. While lying on the top bunk, the claimant had a withdrawal-induced epileptic seizure, fell off the bunk, and hit his head on the floor. The head injury caused the claimant to have continual seizures for over an hour, and he suffered severe brain damage as a result. He successfully sued the prison authorities in negligence for allocating him a top bunk when they knew he was prone to epileptic seizures when withdrawing from alcohol and drugs. An attempt to plead that the damages payable to the claimant should be reduced for contributory negligence, on the ground that the claimant was to blame for the fact that he was addicted to alcohol and drugs in the first place, was dismissed. The reason why the claimant suffered brain damage in this case (withdrawing from alcohol and drugs resulted in his suffering an epileptic seizure) had nothing to do with the reason why it was unreasonable for the claimant to get addicted to alcohol and drugs (addictions are enslaving).

23.6 Third party losses

So far, we have been looking at cases where the victim of a tort wants to sue for compensation for losses that *she* has suffered as a result of that tort being committed. Occasionally, however, the law will allow the victim of a tort to sue for compensatory damages in respect of losses that have been suffered by a *third party* as a result of that tort being committed. We have already seen an example of this.

If A has committed a tort in relation to B and B has been so badly injured as a result that her expectation of life has been reduced, she will be allowed to sue A for damages in respect of the money she would have earned and not spent on herself in the years that are now 'lost' to her.[66] The point of allowing B to sue for such damages is essentially to

---

[66] See above, § 23.3(B). Though no such damages will be awarded if B is so young that any estimate as to how much she earned in the years that are now 'lost' to her would be purely speculative: *Gammell* v *Wilson* [1982] AC 27, 78 (per Lord Scarman, suggesting there might be an exception in the case where a child was already earning money at the time her expectation of life was cut short as a result of someone's negligently injuring her; which would be the case if the child was a movie star).

ensure that any dependants that B has, who would have been supported by her in the years that are now 'lost' to her, do not lose out as a result of A's tort. By allowing B to sue A for damages in respect of the money she would have earned in the years that are now 'lost' to her, the law enables B to set up a fund which will look after her dependants after she has died.

Another example is provided by what we can call the *principle in Donnelly v Joyce.*[67] (Though '*Hunt* v *Severs* damages'[68] is also a popular way of referring to the damages awarded under this principle.) This principle applies in the following kind of situation. Suppose that A tortiously injured B and B, as a result, was incapacitated and needed to be looked after. Suppose further that C – a friend or relative[69] of B's – looked after B without charging her anything for the work done by him in looking after her.[70] The principle in *Donnelly v Joyce* says that in this situation, B will be entitled to sue A for damages equal to the value of the work that C did in looking after B.[71] That such damages are designed to compensate C for the effort he put in looking after B is shown by two things.

First, the damages payable will depend on what sort of sacrifices were incurred by C in looking after B; the greater the sacrifices, the greater the damages payable.[72]

---

[67] After the decision in *Donnelly* v *Joyce* [1974] QB 454.

[68] After the decision in *Hunt* v *Severs* [1994] 2 AC 350 (ironically, no damages were actually awarded in *Hunt* v *Severs*).

[69] It is uncertain whether the principle in *Donnelly* v *Joyce* will apply in the situation where a complete stranger looks after the victim of a tort without charging her anything for doing so. In Scotland, only care provided by a relative is covered by their version of the principle in *Donnelly* v *Joyce*: Administration of Justice Act 1982, s 8. It seems implicit in *Islington LBC* v *University College London Hospital NHS Trust* [2005] EWCA Civ 596 (noted, Stanton 2007a) that the position is the same in England (though care provided by friends is also covered). In that case, the claimant local authority sought to sue the defendant hospital in negligence for the money it had spent providing residential care to Mrs J, a woman who had had a stroke as a result of the defendant's negligence. The claim was dismissed – the defendant had not owed the claimant a duty of care. It seemed to be assumed that suing in negligence was the only way for the claimant to recover the money it had spent caring for Mrs J; that is, Mrs J could not have sued herself for the costs of her care by the claimant. But, on the other hand, Clarke LJ wondered (at [45]) whether if Mrs J had been looked after by a friend, the friend could have compelled Mrs J to have made a claim for the cost of her care by the friend, and if so, whether Islington LBC could have done so as well.

[70] If C had *charged* B for looking after her, then A would of course be liable to compensate B for the money she spent on getting C to look after her – so long, of course, as the money she paid C for looking after her was reasonable.

[71] So – in *Donnelly* v *Joyce* [1974] QB 454 itself, the claimant was a child who was negligently injured by the defendant and as a result needed to spend six months at home having his injuries treated. The claimant's mother took time off work to look after the claimant. The claimant was allowed to sue the defendant for damages equal to the value of the work done by the claimant's mother in looking after him.

[72] *Housecroft* v *Burnett* [1986] 1 All ER 332, 343. However, the damages payable will not be allowed to exceed the going market rate for the kind of services that C provided B: ibid. So, for example, suppose *Careless* negligently injured *Wife* and *Wife's* injuries were so serious that she needed to be looked after 24 hours a day for six months. *Husband* – who earned £400 a hour working as a lawyer – decided to quit his legal practice to look after *Wife* full time for the six months she was laid up, thereby forgoing roughly £400,000. *Wife* would not be able to sue *Careless* for that £400,000; instead she will be limited to suing *Careless* for the market value of the services provided by her husband in looking after. The reason why *Wife* will not be able to sue *Careless* for £400,000 under the principle in *Donnelly* v *Joyce* is that by having her husband look after her, she and *Husband* will have failed to mitigate the loss suffered by them as a result of *Careless's* tort: it would have been much cheaper to hire a nurse to look after *Wife* and have *Husband* carry on working.

Secondly, if B does sue A for damages equal to the value of the work done by C in looking after her, she will hold those damages on trust for C.[73] This feature of the law had an unexpected effect in *Hunt* v *Severs* (1994), where the defendant in that case negligently injured his girlfriend in a car accident and then spent a lot of time looking after her while she was incapacitated. The girlfriend then sued the defendant for damages, which would – in effect – be paid by the defendant's liability insurer. The House of Lords held that the girlfriend could *not* sue the defendant for damages in respect of the work that he had done in looking after her because if such damages were awarded to her, they would have to be paid straight back to the defendant. So the principle against *circuity of actions* worked against a finding of liability in this case. (Of course, in reality, the girlfriend and the defendant would have benefited a great deal from an arrangement where the defendant had to pay damages to his girlfriend in respect of the care she had received and then the girlfriend had to pay those damages straight back to the defendant. As the damages would have come from the defendant's liability insurer in the first place, allowing the girlfriend to sue for the care she had received would have been a way of enriching the defendant at his insurer's expense.) The logic of the decision is impeccable, but it has been criticised on the ground that its effect is to encourage a husband who has negligently injured his wife to contract out her care to a complete stranger rather than looking after her himself. The Law Commission has accordingly recommended that the result in *Hunt* v *Severs* be reversed.[74]

There are other situations where the victim of a tort will be entitled to sue for damages in respect of losses suffered by third parties to that tort – though it must be emphasised that these situations are exceptional in nature; the normal rule is that the victim of a tort is confined to suing for compensatory damages in respect of the losses that *she* has suffered as a result of that tort being committed. So –

(1) If A tortiously injures a housewife with the result that she can no longer do any housework, she will be entitled to sue A for damages in respect of the work done by any members of her family in filling in for her.[75]

(2) If B regularly looked after C, a family member, but is now no longer able to do so because she was tortiously injured by A, with the result that another family member has to look after C, B will be entitled to sue A for damages equal to the value of the work she used to do in looking after C.[76]

---

[73] It is a difficult question whether B will also hold her *right to sue* A for those damages on trust for C; if she does, then C will be allowed to *compel* B to sue A for those damages. Degeling 2003 takes the view that, as the law stands, C will not be able to compel B to sue. However, she goes on to argue that C *should* be subrogated to B's rights to sue A for damages in respect of the cost of caring for her – which would allow C to sue A for such damages in B's name.

[74] Law Comm No 262, *Damages for Personal Injury* (1999), paras 3.67–3.76.

[75] *Daly* v *General Steam Navigation Co Ltd* [1981] 1 WLR 120. But if A negligently injures a businessman and as a result the businessman can no longer run his business and has his wife fill in for him, he will not be able to sue A for damages in respect of the work done by his wife running the business for him: *Hardwick* v *Hudson* [1999] 1 WLR 1770.

[76] *Lowe* v *Guise* [2002] QB 1369. Rix LJ suggested in that case (at [38]) that the damages, once paid over, 'may' be held on trust for the family member who took B's place in looking after C. What if C responded to B's being incapacitated by paying someone else to look after him, C? Presumably in that case the damages payable to B might then be held on trust for C.

(3) If A negligently damages B's car and C – a friend of B's – lends B a replacement car while his car is being repaired, then B *may* be entitled to sue A for damages equal to the rent that he would normally have had to pay to rent that kind of replacement car.[77]

23.7 Theories

Having looked at the law governing the victim of a tort's right to sue the person who committed that tort for compensatory damages, we will now address an issue which lies at the heart of tort law: *why* does the law give the victim of a tort a right to sue for compensatory damages? In order to sharpen the discussion, we will consider a hypothetical situation adapted from Jeremy Waldron's excellent essay 'Moments of carelessness and massive loss':

> As *Fate* drove his car through a shopping district, he took his eyes off the road, turning his head for a moment to look at the bargains advertised in a shop window. Distracted by a bargain advertised in a shoe shop, he failed to notice that the traffic ahead of him had slowed down. His car ploughed into a motorcycle ridden by *Hurt*. *Hurt* was gravely injured: his back was broken so badly that he would spend the rest of his life in a wheelchair. When the police arrived, *Fate* readily admitted he had been driving carelessly. *Hurt* successfully sued *Fate* for £5 million to cover his medical costs, to compensate him for the extreme pain in which he would live for the rest of his life, and to make up the earnings he could have expected from the career he was pursuing at the time.[78]

The question we want to address here is – *why* is *Hurt* entitled to sue *Fate* for compensation for the losses that he has suffered as a result of what *Fate* has done?

A. Economic theories

In the 1970s, the most popular explanations as to why someone like *Hurt* is entitled to sue for compensatory damages were economic in nature. The idea was that *Hurt* is allowed to sue *Fate* for compensatory damages, because giving him such a right produced economically beneficial results.

According to one such theory,[79] the person who could have avoided the accident in which *Hurt* was injured was *Fate*: by keeping a proper look-out, *Fate* could have easily avoided hitting *Hurt*. By telling *Fate* that if he does not keep a proper look-out, he will be held liable to pay compensatory damages to *Hurt*, the law gives *Fate* an incentive to keep a proper look-out, and ensures that *Fate* will keep a proper look-out and avoid hitting

---

[77] The point was left open in *Giles* v *Thompson* [1994] 1 AC 142, at 166–167. However, it is implicit in the House of Lords' decision in *Dimond* v *Lovell* [2002] 1 AC 384 that such a claim will be available to B, and may even be available where C was not a friend but a complete stranger. No such claim could be made on the facts of *Dimond* v *Lovell*, however – where the replacement car was provided by a finance company under a hire agreement that was void under the Consumer Credit Act 1974 – because to allow such a claim would have subverted the 1974 Act.

[78] Waldron 1995, 387 (paraphrased).

[79] Calabresi 1970.

Hurt unless it makes economic sense for him not to pay proper attention to what is happening in front of him. This will be the case if he can make more money by focussing on something other than the traffic ahead of him (for example, a business deal that has to be concluded right there and now on *Fate*'s mobile phone) than he would have to pay out if his failure to keep a proper look-out resulted in someone like *Hurt* being injured.

The problem with all such economic theories of tort law – and the reason why they have fallen into disrepute nowadays – is that they assume that tort law is made up of *liability rules*: rules which are intended to give people an incentive to act in economically sensible ways by telling them 'If you do *x*, then you will have to pay price *P*'. But – in the language of adherents to such explanations of tort law – tort law is made up of *property rules*.[80] That is, tort law is made up of rules which tell people 'Don't do *x*' or 'Do *x*', and what we need to explain is why violation of one of *those* rules gives rise to a right on the part of the person for whose benefit that rule exists to sue for compensatory damages.[81] We cannot explain this right by recharacterising the rules of tort law as liability rules – by imagining that, in the case we are considering, the law actually permitted *Fate* to drive badly so long as he could make driving badly pay by making more money from driving badly than he would have to pay out to those injured by his bad driving. The law does not *ever* permit *Fate* to drive badly, and an explanation of the basis of *Fate*'s liability to pay compensatory damages to *Hurt* that forgets that fact is missing something important.

B. Next best theories

The same accusation cannot be made of the next explanation as to why *Hurt* is allowed to sue *Fate* for compensatory damages. According to this explanation, allowing *Hurt* to sue *Fate* for such damages is the next best way of upholding the right that *Fate* violated by carelessly crashing into *Hurt*. This is because paying compensatory damages to *Hurt* puts him – so far as money can do such a thing – in the position he would have been in had *Fate* been more careful. Ernest Weinrib, John Gardner, Robert Stevens, and Arthur Ripstein have all advanced such *next best theories* of the foundation of a victim of a tort's right to sue the person who committed that tort for compensatory damages:

> When [a] defendant . . . breaches a duty correlative to the [claimant's] right, the [claimant] is entitled to reparation. The remedy reflects the fact that even after the commission of the tort the defendant remains subject to the duty with respect to the [claimant's] right. The defendant's breach of . . . duty . . . does not, of course, bring the duty to an end . . . With the materialization of wrongful injury, the only way the defendant can discharge his or her obligation respecting the [claimant]'s right is to undo the effects of the breach of duty . . . Thus tort law places the defendant under the obligation to restore the [claimant], so far as possible, to the position the [claimant] would have been in had the wrong not been committed.[82]

> When I fail to perform a duty that I owe to someone, there is something that I still owe that person afterwards. Strictly speaking, I still owe him performance of the duty, which continues to bind me. But if it is too late to perform – the dirty deed is done – I now owe him the next best thing. I owe it to him to put him back, so far as it can now be done, into the position he would have been in if I had done my duty in the first place.[83]

---

[80] See Calabresi and Melamed 1972.
[81] See, generally, Nance 1997.
[82] Weinrib 1995, 135.
[83] Gardner 2011, text at n 20.

> Where [a] wrong has been committed, the secondary obligation to pay money imposed upon the wrongdoer can be seen as the law's attempt to reach the 'next best' position to the wrong not having been committed by him in the first place. Where the defendant is required to make good the claimant's . . . loss . . . this is the law's attempting to reach this nearest approximation of the wrong not having occurred.[84]

> Damages are not awarded to compensate for the awful things that people do to each other, but rather to make it as if [people] had the means that they would have had if others had not wrongfully deprived them of them.[85]

The difficulty with all such *next best theories* is that they conceal a problem that needs to be addressed. It is *tempting* to think that because it is justified for the law to impose on *Fate* a duty to take care not to crash into *Hurt* (or, to put it another way, give *Hurt* a right that *Fate* take care not to crash into him), the law is *also* justified – now that that primary duty/right has been violated – in requiring *Fate* to repair his violation by putting *Hurt* back in the position he would have been in had that duty/right not been violated. But, like most temptations, this is one that needs to be resisted. The reason for this is that repairing *Fate*'s breach of duty/violation of right is *a lot* more burdensome than observing the primary duty/right that was violated in this case. Requiring *Fate* to pay *Hurt* £5m pounds is unimaginably more burdensome than requiring *Fate* to keep a proper look-out while he is driving his car. So it would be wrong to think that *just because* the primary duty that *Fate* owed *Hurt* (or the right *Hurt* had against *Fate*) is justified, then requiring *Fate* to repair his violation of that duty/right is *also* justified. What we need is an argument that it would *not be unfair* on *Fate* to require him to repair that violation – and the above theorists do not supply us with such an argument.[86] But someone *has* made such an argument, and we will look at whether that argument works right now.

C. Outcome responsibility

Tony Honoré's theory of 'outcome responsibility' – first presented in his *Law Quarterly Review* article 'Responsibility and luck: the moral basis of strict liability'[87] – purports to offer an explanation as to why it might *not be unfair* to impose a liability on *Fate* to compensate *Hurt* for the losses that he has suffered here.[88]

---

[84] Stevens 2007, 59.

[85] Ripstein 2007a, 1968.

[86] Of course, *Fate* will have been carrying liability insurance which means that requiring her to pay *Hurt* £5 million will not impose an undue burden on her. However, it is not clear that this gets the 'second-best' theorists off the hook. Liability insurers only undertake to cover the insured's legal liabilities. The legal liabilities therefore come first, and have to be justified without reference to the fact that they might end up being insured against. So if we are to explain why it would not be unfair to make *Fate* pay *Hurt* £5 million, as part of a project of justifying imposing such a liability on *Fate*, we must do so on the basis that that liability will be borne by *Fate* and ignore the possibility that it might end up being insured against.

[87] Honoré 1988.

[88] Honoré is careful not to say that he is offering a reason why *Fate should* be held liable to *Hurt* here: his theory 'does not entail that whenever a harmful outcome is properly allocated to someone this justifies imposing on him a strict liability to compensate for that outcome' (Honoré 1988, 541): it merely explains why it might be *not unfair* to hold *Fate* liable to *Hurt* here for *other reasons*. (For Honoré, these other reasons normally reduce to saying that *Fate* was at fault for what happened to *Hurt*, or that what *Fate* did carried with it a special risk of *Hurt* suffering harm: see Honoré 1988, 542.)

Honoré argues that we live in a society that generally allocates 'credit and esteem and . . . discredit and resentment'[89] according to the outcomes of our actions. When our actions go well, we make money and enjoy a good reputation. When our actions go badly, we lose money and incur other people's resentment. This is so even though it is often just a matter of luck whether our actions go well or badly. But the fact that our society operates a system of outcome responsibility will not be unfair so long as its operation is 'impartial, reciprocal and over a period beneficial':

> It must apply impartially to all those who possess a minimum capacity for reasoned choice and action. It must be reciprocal in that each person is entitled to apply it to others and they to him. It must work so as to entitle each person to potential benefits which are likely on the whole to outweigh the detriments to which it subjects him. This makes it unfair to apply the system to the incapable, for whom there is no likely surplus of benefit over detriment. But for the capable the three conditions are normally satisfied. All those who possess a minimum capacity stand to profit from the system of outcome-allocation most of the time . . .[90]

Seen as part of a general social system in which credit and discredit are allocated to us according to the outcomes of our actions, and under which we all end up winning more credit than we lose, it is not unfair on *Fate* to impose on him a duty to compensate *Hurt* that has the effect of allocating the responsibility for what has happened to *Hurt* to *Fate*. Indeed, *Fate* should welcome being subjected to such a system of outcome responsibility. It is only by ascribing outcomes – good and bad – to *Fate* that *Fate* acquires the characteristics of a person: someone who has 'a history, an identity, and a character.'[91]

The fairness of holding *Fate* liable for what has happened to *Hurt* here crucially depends – according to Honoré's theory – on whether *Fate* is likely to be a long-term winner under a system of outcome responsibility, where credit and demerit attaches to *Fate* according to the outcome of his actions. Honoré assumes that *Fate* is likely to be a long-term winner, but it is not clear that this is so. As Stephen Perry observes,

> the claim that the system of [outcome responsibility] is beneficial to all [people who 'possess a minimum capacity for reasoned choice and action] seems to be, empirically, false. We all know people, or know of people, who apparently possess whatever minimum capacity is required to get by in the world and be properly regarded as a person, who nonetheless seem to be (and to be destined from the outset to be) life's perennial losers.[92]

Fate could very easily turn out to be one of those long-term 'losers' once he is saddled with a £5m debt. We can test Honoré's assumption that people of minimum capacity will turn out to be long term winners under a system of outcome responsibility another way. Suppose we applied Honoré's system of outcome responsibility to *Hurt*'s choice to go out riding on a motorbike the day *Fate* would be distracted while driving behind *Hurt*, and allocated the responsibility for the outcome of *Hurt*'s choice to *Hurt*, so that he was not entitled to sue anyone for being permanently disabled as a result of *Fate*'s running into him.[93] Having done

---

[89] Honoré 1988, 540.

[90] Honoré 1988, 540–1.

[91] Honoré 1988, 543.

[92] Perry 2001, 67.

[93] Honoré would not personally be in favour of doing this as there seems to be no positive reason for making *Hurt* responsible for the outcome of his choice. But that does not matter. If Honoré's assumption that everyone of minimum capacity benefits under a system of outcome responsibility, then the assumption should hold in this situation or any other situation where outcome responsibility applies.

this, do we think that *Hurt* is still likely to be a long-term winner from living under a system of outcome responsibility? It seems very doubtful that *Hurt* will be a long-term winner: it is much more plausible to think that he will end up being a long-term loser.

So Honoré's optimism is unjustified. Some perfectly capable but unlucky people can end up being long-term losers under a system of outcome responsibility; and we have no reason to think that *Fate* would not be one of those people were he held accountable for the outcome of his choice to go out driving on the day when traffic would slow down while he was distracted by an advertisement in a nearby shop window. The truth is that outcome responsibility only *seems* fair because it is surrounded by a battery of institutions (the family, the State, insurance, employment law) that help to catch people who lose out under outcome responsibility. Outcome responsibility *on its own* is unfair, and cannot explain *on its own* why it is not unfair to hold *Fate* liable to pay *Hurt* £5 million in the situation we are considering.

If this is right, Tony Honoré's theory of outcome responsibility does not work to explain why it would not be unfair to make *Fate* pay *Hurt* £5m, so as to force him to do the 'next best' thing to what he should have done in the first place. It follows that theorists who advance 'next best' theories as to why we make people pay compensatory damages still have to explain why it would not be unfair to make someone do the 'next best' thing to what they should have done in the first place, even when doing the 'next best' thing is hugely more burdensome than doing what they should have done in the first place. And it is not clear that such an explanation can be offered.

D. Civil recourse theory

Finally, we come to the theory of tort liability that John Goldberg and Benjamin Zipursky have been developing over last 20 years or so: the civil recourse theory of tort law.[94] This theory makes a number of connected claims, which we can set out as follows:

(1) There are some moral wrongs that morally entitle the victim of one of those wrongs to seek some form of redress against the perpetrator of that wrong. We can call such a wrong, 'a redress-entitling wrong'.[95]

(2) However, the State – in order to preserve a monopoly of force within society – prevents the victim of a redress-entitling wrong from taking direct action against the perpetrator of that wrong to obtain redress for the fact that that wrong has been committed.

(3) As a result, victims of redress-entitling wrongs have a right against the State that it provide them with a peaceful means of seeking redress against the person or persons who have committed those wrongs against them.

(4) Tort law exists to provide victims of redress-entitling wrongs with such a peaceful means of seeking redress. The function of tort law is to determine when someone has been the victim of a redress-entitling wrong and to provide a means of redress where something that is recognised as a redress-entitling wrong by the law of tort has been committed.

---

[94] Citing all the articles in which this theory has been developed would not assist the reader very much, such is Goldberg and Zipursky's prodigious productivity. Key articles (in chronological order) are: Zipursky 1998a, Goldberg & Zipursky 2002, Zipursky 2003, Goldberg & Zipursky 2010a.

[95] Note that the phrase 'redress-entitling wrong' is a phrase we have coined to make it easier to set out and understand Goldberg and Zipursky's civil recourse theory of tort law: it is not a phrase that occurs in Goldberg and Zipursky's work.

So in the situation we are considering, *Hurt* is entitled to sue *Fate* for £5 million because the law recognises that *Fate* has committed a redress-entitling wrong in this situation, and allowing *Hurt* to sue *Fate* for compensatory damages is the law's way of providing *Hurt* with a civilised, peaceful and orderly way of obtaining redress for *Fate*'s wrong.

It seems to us that there are three problems with the civil recourse theory of tort law. First of all, it is not clear that the side of our characters that wants to obtain redress for wrongs that other people do to us is a particularly attractive one, or one that the State should pander to by providing each of us with a civil means of obtaining redress from those that the State thinks have committed a redress-entitling wrong in relation to us.[96] However, it may be that forgiving those who trespass against us is beyond most of us, and that the State would be faced with a serious social problem if it did not do something to help us obtain some redress against those who have seriously wronged us. So this first objection does not provide a clinching argument against the truth of the civil recourse theory of tort law.

The second objection is more serious. The objection is that the State's catalogue of wrongs that it recognises as torts does not correspond with any plausible list of what we might regard as being redress-entitling wrongs. The lack of match-up is on both sides: there are torts that are so trivial it is hard to believe the State seriously thinks they are redress-entitling wrongs, and there are redress-entitling wrongs (if there are any redress-entitling wrongs) that the State does not recognise as torts. For example, if *Hiker* innocently wanders onto *Owner*'s land, no one would seriously think that *Owner* was entitled at a moral level to seek some redress for what *Hiker* has done: but *Hiker*'s conduct will still amount to the tort of trespass to land. On the other side of the line, if *Social Services*, on virtually no evidence, seize *Child* from his *Parents* and give the child up to be adopted, with the result that *Parents* are then legally disabled from ever regaining custody of *Child*, most people would regard *Social Services*' conduct as a classic example of a redress-entitling wrong, and would not be at all surprised if *Parents* wanted to maim the people responsible for what *Social Services* did. But *Social Services*' conduct will not amount to a tort to the *Parents*.[97]

The third objection is that it is not clear why the means of redress that the State provides to the victim of (what the State perceives to be) a redress-entitling wrong should take the form of holding the person who committed that wrong liable to pay *compensation* to the victim of his wrong. Holding the person who committed that wrong liable to pay a fixed sum to the victim of his wrong – assessed according to the nature of the wrong and how it was committed – would provide an alternative way of allowing the victim of wrong a way of making the person who committed that wrong pay for what he did, and this alternative means of civil recourse might work in a much fairer way in a case like *Fate*'s where a momentary lack of attention has resulted in a huge loss.

E. Conclusion

Our conclusion from reviewing these various theories is a pessimistic one: there is no completely satisfactory way of explaining why *Fate* is held liable to pay compensatory damages to *Hurt* in the case we are considering. Our guess is that the explanation that comes

---

[96] See Finnis 2002, 656.

[97] See above, § 1.3.

closest to being 'correct' is a *next best theory*, but allowing the victim of a tort to claim *full* compensation for the losses he has suffered as a result of a tort being committed cannot be justified in today's society (where the losses that might be suffered by the victim of a tort are potentially massive), and is only tolerated because of the existence of liability insurance.

Further reading

Many of the articles referred to in the further reading to Chapter 1 are also relevant to this chapter.

In discussing the various theories as to why a tortfeasor is held liable to pay compensatory damages to the victim of his tort, we have not used the phrases *corrective justice* or *distributive justice*. This would puzzle many tort theorists who think that a tortfeasor is required as a matter of 'corrective justice' to compensate the victim of his tort. But when one asks what corrective justice requires, the normal answer is – that wrongful losses be rectified, or that wrongdoers are made to repair their wrongs. (The notion of 'corrective justice' comes from Aristotle's *Nicomachean Ethics* – actually, a set of notes on some lectures on ethics delivered by Aristotle round about 350BC, and prepared by or dedicated to his son Nicomachus. This fact has given rise to countless and utterly pointless articles discussing what Aristotle really meant by 'corrective justice' and whether theorist X's account of corrective justice is compatible with what Aristotle had to say about it.)

But if this is right, then appeals to 'corrective justice' do not tell us anything about why tortfeasors are held liable to pay compensatory damages to the victims of their torts: 'Why does the law require a wrongdoer to undo the harmful consequences that his wrong has had on the victim of his wrong?' 'Because corrective justice demands it' 'And what does corrective justice demand?' 'That wrongdoers undo the harmful consequences that their wrongs have had on the victims of their wrongs' 'Oh . . .' Still, for those wishing to explore the notion of corrective justice further, **John Gardner's 'What is tort law for? Part 1: the place of corrective justice' (2010, available on SSRN)** is as good a place as any to start. **Scott Hershowitz's 'Harry Potter and the trouble with tort theory' (2011) 63** *Stanford Law Review* **67 (also available on SSRN)** wonderfully explores the limitations of corrective justice and economic accounts of the basis of tort law.

Principles of distributive justice – which tell us how things that need to be distributed should be distributed – are relevant to tort law in two ways: (1) they are relevant to the issue of who is given what rights under tort law; (2) insofar as principles of distributive justice are relevant to how much wealth people should have (something some people would dispute as they do not think wealth is something that is up for distribution) they may limit how much one person can sue another for in tort, where allowing a claim in tort would have unacceptable effects on the distribution of wealth. (1) is not really relevant to this chapter, and – as we have just observed – it is debatable whether distributive justice has anything to do with (2). **Tsachi Keren-Paz** explores the relevance of distributive justice to tort law in his monograph *Torts, Egalitarianism and Distributive Justice* **(Ashgate Publishing, 2007)**; the book was reviewed by **William Lucy in (2009) 72** *Modern Law Review* **1048** and by **Ariel Porat in (2009) 29** *Legal Studies* **509**.

The judges have eagerly seized on the language of corrective and distributive justice to make sense of what they are doing in deciding tort cases: see, for example, **Lord Steyn's**

'Perspectives of corrective and distributive justice in tort law' in (2002) 37 *Irish Jurist* 1. (The awkwardness of the title may bespeak a lack of confidence in the concepts of corrective and distributive justice.) It is also worth reading the reflections of another Law Lord, **Lord Scott**, on 'Damages' in [2007] *Lloyd's Maritime and Commercial Law Quarterly* 465.

Tony Weir's 'All or nothing' (2003–4) 78 *Tulane Law Review* 512 is a typically brilliant survey of the trend across the whole of the common law, including tort law, away from either awarding a claimant *everything* he is suing for or *nothing*, towards awarding a claimant *some* of what he is suing for.

Chapter 24
Aggravated and exemplary damages

Aims and objectives

Reading this chapter should enable you to:

(1) Understand what aggravated and exemplary damages are, and when they will be awarded.

(2) Get a good grasp of the debates around what function is performed by awards of such damages.

24.1 The basics

Where a tortfeasor is liable to pay the victim of his tort compensatory damages, or nominal damages (in the case where the tort is actionable *per se* and the victim has suffered no loss as a result of that tort being committed), *aggravated* damages may also be awarded to the victim of the tort if the tortfeasor has behaved in an *arrogant and high-handed* way, either in committing that tort, or in the way he treated the victim of the tort after it was committed.

While awards of aggravated damages have attracted little criticism, the same is not true of awards of exemplary damages – damages that are designed to punish people who have knowingly or recklessly violated other people's rights. The power that the courts currently enjoy in civil cases to award exemplary damages against a tortfeasor whose conduct was so outrageous as to be worthy of punishment has long been regarded with suspicion, as undermining the protections that the criminal law affords to those whom the State wishes to punish.

In *Rookes* v *Barnard* (1964), the House of Lords made a major effort to place major limits on this power, ruling that exemplary damages could only be awarded in tort where: (1) the defendant was a public body and acted in an 'arbitrary, oppressive or unconstitutional manner' in committing a tort; or (2) the defendant committed a tort because he figured he would make more money from committing that tort than he would have to pay out in compensatory damages to the victim of that tort; or (3) a statute authorised award of such damages. But within those limits, the power to award exemplary damages in tort cases remained.

Since 1964, academic and judicial opinion has been deeply divided on the future of exemplary damages. Nobody seems that happy with *Rookes* v *Barnard*. Some argue that the *Rookes* v *Barnard* limits on when exemplary damages should be abolished, pointing out that no other common law jurisdiction has followed the House of Lords' example in *Rookes* v *Barnard* and sought to limit its powers to award exemplary damages in civil cases. Others regret that the House of Lords in *Rookes* v *Barnard* 'was willing to wound and yet afraid to strike'[1] down the institution of exemplary damages altogether. We will make our position clear in the final section of this chapter.

24.2 Aggravated damages

A. Arrogant and high-handed conduct

The principal requirement that has to be satisfied before a claimant can sue a defendant in tort for aggravated damages is that the claimant has to show that the defendant treated her in an arrogant and high-handed way, either (1) in the way he acted in committing a tort in relation to the claimant; or (2) in the way he treated the claimant after he had committed the tort. When will a claimant be able to show that either (1) or (2) are true?

(1) *Conduct in committing the tort.* A defendant who *knowingly* committed a tort can be said to have acted in an arrogant and high-handed way in committing that tort.[2] The authorities also indicate that someone who has *unknowingly* committed a tort can still be said to have acted in an arrogant and high-handed way in committing that tort if he *humiliated or insulted* the victim of that tort in committing the tort in question. So, for example, in *Thompson* v *Commissioner of Police of the Metropolis* (1998), the Court of Appeal held that police officers who commit the tort of false imprisonment by arresting someone when they are not entitled to do so can be sued for aggravated damages if, in making the arrest, they humiliated the person being arrested or otherwise behaved in a 'high-handed, insulting, malicious or oppressive manner [in conducting] the arrest',[3] and this is so even if the police officers thought they were entitled to make the arrest in question and therefore did not knowingly commit the tort of false imprisonment in making the arrest.

(2) *Conduct after the tort was committed.* In *Sutcliffe* v *Pressdram Ltd* (1991), the Court of Appeal held that if A has wrongfully defamed B, A will act in an arrogant and high-handed manner in dealing with B's claims to be compensated for the actionable losses suffered by her as a result of A's defaming her if: (i) he fails to make any or sufficient apology for and withdrawal of his defamatory statement; (ii) he repeats the statement; (iii) he tries to deter B from proceeding with her claim against A; (iv) he tries to defeat B's claims by persisting, 'by way of a prolonged or hostile cross-examination of [B] or in turgid

---

[1] Alexander Pope, *An Epistle to Dr Arbuthnot* (1734).

[2] See, for example, *Thompson* v *Hill* (1870) LR 5 CP 564 (deliberately committing tort of private nuisance by blocking off light) and *McMillan* v *Singh* (1984) 17 HLR 120 (wrongfully ejecting tenant in order to make more money from renting premises).

[3] [1998] QB 498, 516.

speeches to the jury, in a plea of justification which is bound to fail';[4] (v) he tries to give wider publicity to his defamatory statement in the preliminaries to the trial of B's action against A or in the trial itself;[5] (vi) he engages in a general persecution of B.[6]

In *Alexander* v *Home Office* (1988), the Court of Appeal held that if A commits a tort by unlawfully discriminating against B on grounds of her race, A will act in an arrogant and high-handed way in dealing with B's claims to be compensated for the actionable losses suffered by her as a result of A's discrimination if: (1) he makes untrue and injurious allegations about B in an attempt to establish that his acts of discrimination against B were not racially motivated; *or* (2) he conspicuously fails to acknowledge that his acts of discrimination against B were unjustified.[7] Similarly, if A commits the tort of false imprisonment by arresting B when he had no right to do so, he will act in an arrogant and high-handed way in dealing with B's claims to be compensated for the losses suffered by her as a result of A's falsely imprisoning her if he attempts, through making untrue allegations about B, to justify his arrest of B.[8]

B. Negligence

It seems to be that aggravated damages will not be awardable against a defendant who is being sued for *negligence*.[9] There seems to be no good reason why this should be so. After all, someone can breach a duty of care owed to another in an arrogant and high-handed manner. (For example, suppose an employer deliberately refused to install necessary safety equipment in his factory on the ground that his employees' safety didn't matter to him.) In *Kralj* v *McGrath* (1986), Woolf J said that:

> it would be wholly inappropriate to introduce into claims . . . for . . . negligence, the concept of aggravated damage. [Making such damages available in negligence cases would] be wholly inconsistent with the general approach to damages in this area, which is to compensate the [claimant] for the loss that she has actually suffered, so far as it is possible to do so, by the award of monetary compensation and not to treat those damages as being a matter which reflects the degree of negligence . . . of the defendant.[10]

But this just begs the question as to whether damages in negligence should be purely compensatory in nature.

---

[4] [1991] 1 QB 153, 184.

[5] See, for example, *Ley* v *Hamilton* (1935) 153 LT 384 (aggravated damages awarded against defendant who had libeled claimant by alleging he had embezzled money, and while not seeking to rely on defence of justification in trial, claimed in cross-examination that claimant *had* embezzled money).

[6] [1991] 1 QB 153, 184.

[7] [1988] 1 WLR 968, 979.

[8] *Thompson* v *Commissioner of Police of the Metropolis* [1998] QB 498, 518.

[9] Aggravated damages have been awarded for: (i) assault or battery in *W* v *Meah* [1986] 1 All ER 935; (ii) false imprisonment in *Thompson* v *Commissioner of Police of the Metropolis* [1998] QB 498; (iii) defamation in *Ley* v *Hamilton* (1935) 153 LT 384, and *Sutcliffe* v *Pressdram Ltd* [1991] 1 QB 153; (iv) trespass to land in *Drane* v *Evangelou* [1978] 1 WLR 455 and *McMillan* v *Singh* (1984) 17 HLR 120; (v) private nuisance in *Thompson* v *Hill* (1870) LR 5 CP 564; (vi) intentionally inflicting harm on another using unlawful means in *Messenger Newspapers Group Ltd* v *National Graphical Association* [1984] IRLR 397; (vii) deceit in *Archer* v *Brown* [1985] QB 401; (viii) malicious falsehood in *Khodaparast* v *Shad* [2000] 1 WLR 618 (ix) malicious prosecution in *Thompson* v *Commissioner of Police of the Metropolis* [1998] QB 498; (x) discriminating against another on grounds of race in *Prison Service* v *Johnson* [1997] ICR 275; and (xi) discriminating against another on grounds of sex in *Ministry of Defence* v *Meredith* [1995] IRLR 539.

[10] [1986] 1 All ER 54, 61e–g.

In *AB* v *South West Water Services Ltd* (1993), Sir Thomas Bingham MR said: 'I know of no precedent for awarding damages for indignation aroused by a defendant's conduct [where the defendant has merely acted negligently or committed some other non-intentional tort].'[11] But the fact that there is no precedent for awarding aggravated damages in a negligence case is a poor justification for refusing to award such damages when they are merited.

However, it may be that the courts are moving towards the position that in appropriate cases, aggravated damages may be awarded in negligence cases. In *Ashley* v *Chief Constable of Sussex Police* (2008),[12] the police were sued in negligence and assault and battery for shooting a man dead in the course of a drugs raid on his house. It was argued that the police had been negligent in organising the raid on the man's house, and had committed an unlawful trespass to his person when they shot him. The defendant chief constable was willing to settle the claim in negligence, and pay the dead man's estate aggravated damages as part of that settlement. In regard to that concession, Lord Scott observed that aggravated damages 'would not *normally* be available in a negligence claim.'[13] Lord Neuberger went further:

> I cannot see why [aggravated] damages should not . . . be recoverable in some categories of negligence claims . . . It appears to me that it would be reminiscent of the bad old days of forms of action if the court held that the Ashleys' claim could result in aggravated damages if framed in battery, but not if framed in negligence.[14]

C. Companies

After some to-ing and fro-ing in the caselaw on the issue of whether a company that has been treated in an arrogant and high-handed manner by tortfeasor can sue for aggravated damages, the Court of Appeal has now made it clear that companies can *never* sue for aggravated damages.[15]

D. Theories

Issues of whether aggravated damages can be sued for in negligence aside, the law is clear as to when aggravated damages will be available. What is less clear is *why* the law allows the victim of a tort who has been treated in an arrogant and high-handed way by the person who committed that tort to sue him for aggravated damages. Three theories may be considered.

(1) *Compensation for distress.* There are many *dicta* in the cases which take the view that aggravated damages are really compensatory in nature, and they are designed to compensate the victim of a tort for any *distress* that she has been caused as a result of

---

[11] [1993] QB 507, 532. It is necessary to insert the passage in square brackets because otherwise Sir Thomas Bingham's remarks may be read as indicating that aggravated damages may *never* be awarded to the victim of a tort. See Smith J's remarks in *Prison Service* v *Johnson* [1997] ICR 275, at 286–7: '[It has been suggested] that Sir Thomas Bingham MR was [in *AB* v *South West Water Services Ltd*] making a statement of general application that there is not or should not be any such thing as an award of aggravated damages . . . [However it must be] realised that those remarks were made in the context of a claim for damages . . . based upon the torts of negligence, non-intentional nuisance and non-intentional breach of statutory duty . . . [Sir Thomas Bingham MR's] dicta were not [therefore] of general application and were not intended to change the law relating to aggravated damages . . .'.

[12] Discussed in detail above, § 2.7.

[13] [2008] 1 AC 962, at [23] (emphasis added).

[14] [2008] 1 AC 962, at [102].

[15] *Eaton Mansions (Westminster) Ltd* v *Stinger Compania de Inversion SA* [2013] EWCA Civ 1308.

the way that tort was committed, or as a result of the way she was treated in the aftermath of that tort.[16] However, there are two problems with this view.

First, there is no requirement that the claimant in a tort case show that the defendant's conduct *upset* or *distressed* her before she can be awarded aggravated damages. If the claimant was merely *indignant* or *outraged* at the defendant's conduct, aggravated damages may still be payable to the claimant. Outrage is not the same as distress. Secondly, in some cases where the claimant *was* distressed at the arrogant and high-handed way in which she was treated by the defendant, the court dealing with her claim made her an award of damages for her distress and gave her a *separate* award of aggravated damages.[17] If aggravated damages were meant to compensate for distress, the court would be guilty of double counting here.

(2) *Civil recourse theory.*[18] There is no doubt that we feel entitled to hit back at those who treat us as though we are worthless, and it might be argued that suing for aggravated damages provides us with a civilised, peaceful and orderly way of achieving this goal. On this view, aggravated damages exist to assuage the outrage we feel at the way a tortfeasor has treated us, by allowing us a peaceful way of hurting the tortfeasor for treating us with contempt. As Windeyer J observed in the Australian case of *Uren* v *John Fairfax & Sons Pty Ltd* (1965): 'the satisfaction that the [claimant] gets [from an award of aggravated damages] is that the defendant has been made to pay for what he did.'[19] The difficulty with this view is that it tends to obliterate the distinction between aggravated damages and exemplary damages, that we will look at in the next chapter. However, it could be argued in response that there is in fact no real distinction between the two forms of damages,[20] and we should stop acting as though there is one.

(3) *Dignity.* Theorists who are unhappy with the first two explanations have tended to argue that aggravated damages are awarded to compensate the victim of a tort for the injury to his *dignity* that has been occasioned by the way in which that tort was committed.[21] As John Murphy argues:

> wherever an individual is subjected to conduct that constitutes or implies some form of disregard for the innate values associated with personhood – be it their deliberate humiliation or objectification (in the sense of treatment as though a mere thing or object) – that person can be said to have suffered an affront to his or her dignity. It is the explicit or implicit treatment of another in a manner which undermines or demeans their human status or moral worth that comprises an affront to dignity. It is treating them as though they were somehow worth less than oneself, or simply worthless.[22]

---

[16] *Rookes* v *Barnard* [1964] AC 1129, 1221 (per Lord Devlin); *McCarey* v *Associated Newspapers Ltd (No 2)* [1965] 2 QB 86, 104–5 (per Pearson LJ); *Broome* v *Cassell & Co Ltd* [1972] AC 1027, 1124 (per Lord Diplock); *Archer* v *Brown* [1985] QB 401, 424–5 (per Peter Pain J); *Thompson* v *Commissioner of Police of the Metropolis* [1998] QB 498, 512. See also Scott 2007.

[17] See *Duffy* v *Eastern Social Health and Services Board* [1992] IRLR 251 (£15,000 damages awarded for distress, as well as £5,000 in aggravated damages). Also *Deane* v *Ealing LBC* [1993] ICR 329, 335.

[18] Discussed in detail above, § 23.7(D).

[19] (1965–66) 117 CLR 118, 151.

[20] Murphy 2010a does point out (at 355) that there may be a distinction where the victim of a tort dies: in such a case exemplary damages cannot be sued for by the victim's estate (see below, § 24.3(B)(4)), but the House of Lords saw no problem in *Ashley* with allowing the dead man's estate to sue for aggravated damages in that case.

[21] Beever 2003a; Murphy 2010a. Birks 1996a argues that aggravated damages are not compensatory but instead mark the fact that a tortfeasor has, in the way he treated the victim of his tort, committed the distinct tort of using unlawful means to treat someone with less than an 'equality of respect'.

[22] Murphy 2010a, 360.

This theory chimes in well with the requirement that it be shown that the defendant treated the claimant in an 'arrogant and high-handed manner' before aggravated damages will be awarded against him. However, one problem with this theory is that John Murphy's explanation of the concept of dignity suggests that someone's dignity can be injured without their being aware of it. If, *in fact*, A has treated B as 'worthless' then A has injured B's dignity, whether B is aware of it or not. (Suppose, for example, that A turned B's application for a job down because she was a woman, but he convinced her that he had turned it down because she lacked the necessary qualifications.) But it is not clear that aggravated damages can be awarded simply on the basis that the victim of a tort has suffered an *objective* insult to her dignity.

For example, in *Ministry of Defence* v *Meredith* (1995), the defendants unlawfully sacked the claimant when she became pregnant. The claimant sued the defendants for compensatory *and* aggravated damages. As part of her case, she sought to obtain discovery of documents that would indicate whether or not the defendants had *known* they were acting unlawfully in sacking her because she was pregnant. The Employment Appeal Tribunal held that the claimant was not entitled to discovery of those documents as they had no relevance to her claim. They obviously had no relevance to her claim for compensatory damages; and they had no relevance to her claim for aggravated damages as – they held – she would *only* have been entitled to claim such damages from the defendants if she *already knew* that the defendants had acted in an arrogant and high-handed manner in sacking her.

Again, in *Ashley* v *Chief Constable of Sussex Police* (2008), the deceased knew nothing about the circumstances leading up to his shooting before he was shot dead by the police. So he could not have known whether the drugs raid on his house had been organised or conducted by the police in an 'arrogant and high-manner'. Lord Carswell thought this fact made it difficult to see how the police could be sued for aggravated damages.[23]

If – as these cases suggest – something more than an objective injury to the claimant's dignity is required before aggravated damages can be awarded, this tends to undermine the strength of dignity-based explanations of such awards. If an on-going *awareness* that you have been treated with contempt by the defendant is required, then we seem to tip back towards the idea that aggravated damages are awarded to assuage the victim of a tort's outrage at having been treated with contempt, and satisfy their desire to see the tortfeasor pay for treating them that way. If this is right aggravated damages are simply a form of exemplary damages.

24.3 Exemplary damages

A. Requirements

A number of different requirements have to be satisfied before an award of exemplary damages can be made against a tortfeasor.

(1) *Desert*. The most fundamental requirement is that the defendant must *deserve* to be punished for what he has done. But when will this be the case? In *A* v *Bottrill* (2003) – a Privy Council case – the minority (Lords Hutton and Mustill) argued that exemplary

---

[23][2008] 1 AC 962, at [80]. Lord Neuberger was willing to award aggravated damages on the basis that it was reasonably foreseeable that 'a negligently mishandled armed police raid could result in just the sort of mental distress and shock that aggravated damages are intended to reflect'. But if no such mental distress or shock was experienced because the deceased in *Ashley* was shot dead before he could gather his thoughts, it is hard to see how aggravated damages could be awarded in this case.

damages should only be awarded against a tortfeasor who was *aware* that his conduct amounted to a tort. But the majority took a more expansive approach, holding that exemplary damages could be awarded against a tortfeasor who was unaware that he was doing anything wrong at the time he acted if his conduct was so *outrageous* as to be worthy of condemnation.

So in *Bottrill*, the claimant had four cervical smear tests over four years. In each case, the smear test was examined by the defendant pathologist and in each case he gave the claimant a clean bill of health. However, the defendant failed in each case to inspect the claimant's smear test properly. Had he done so, he would have spotted that the claimant was in danger of developing cervical cancer and the claimant would have received treatment that would have prevented the cancer developing. However, because the claimant's smear tests were not properly examined, the claimant's condition went untreated and she developed cervical cancer. The Privy Council held, by a 3:2 majority, that exemplary damages could be awarded against the defendant.[24] While the defendant may have *thought* that he was adopting an adequate procedure for inspecting the claimant's smear tests, he had acted so outrageously in adopting a procedure for inspecting smear tests that had a 50 per cent error rate[25] that his conduct was worthy of punishment.

It is now clear that the English courts are following the approach laid down by the majority of the Privy Council in *Bottrill* and asking themselves whether the defendant's conduct was so outrageous as to be worthy of punishment. For example, in *Muuse* v *Secretary of State for the Home Department* (2010),[26] the claimant was detained by the Home Office after serving four months in custody for a criminal damage offence. The Home Office was not entitled to do this: the claimant was a Dutch national who could not be deported from the UK, or detained in the UK once his prison sentence had been served. Unfortunately, no one who handled the claimant's case could be bothered to ascertain his true nationality – despite the claimant's repeated protestations that he was Dutch and the fact that he had actually handed over to officials a Dutch ID card in his name – and handled his case on the basis that he was a Somali national. Even if he had been, the claimant's case was still handled improperly: he was detained without any of the correct procedures for notifying him of the grounds of detention having been followed. Eventually the claimant was released, after having been detained for about four months.

The judge at first instance found the Home Office liable for false imprisonment, and awarded the claimant £27,500 in exemplary damages. The Court of Appeal upheld the award, expressly disapproving the suggestion that 'malice, fraud, insolence [or] cruelty' has to be shown before exemplary damages may be awarded against a defendant.[27] It is enough to show that the defendant's conduct was so 'outrageous' as to be worthy of

---

[24] As the case occurred in New Zealand, she was not allowed to sue the defendant for compensation for the fact that she developed cervical cancer: that was covered under the New Zealand Accident Compensation Scheme (summarised below, § 32.3(A)). However, s 396 of the Accident Insurance Act 1998 preserved the powers of the courts in New Zealand to award exemplary damages against defendants in personal injury cases.

[25] That is, the procedure failed to recognise the signs of cancer in every other smear test inspected that objectively did show signs of cancer.

[26] Noted, Stanton 2010, Varuhas 2011.

[27] [2010] EWCA Civ 453, at [71].

punishment.[28] So in *Muuse*, while no one involved in handling the claimant's case may have been *aware* they were unlawfully detaining the claimant, their 'manifest incompetence', their repeated and unexplained failures to follow proper procedures, and the Home Office's systemic failure to put any checks in place on officials acting incompetently meant that the claimant's detention was so 'outrageous' as to be worthy of punishment.[29]

(2) *Rookes v Barnard*. Even if a tortfeasor's conduct in committing that tort was so outrageous as to be worthy of punishment, exemplary damages can only be awarded against him if his case falls into one of the situations in which the House of Lords held in *Rookes v Barnard* (1964) that exemplary damages can be awarded. The House of Lords held[30] in *Rookes v Barnard* that if A has committed a tort, exemplary damages can only be awarded against him if:

(i) A was a 'servant of the government' at the time he committed his tort and he acted in an 'oppressive, arbitrary or unconstitutional' manner in committing that tort;[31]

(ii) A committed his tort because he figured that he would make more money committing that tort than he would have to pay out in damages to the victim of that tort; or

(iii) statute law authorises an award of exemplary damages to be made against someone who has committed the kind of tort that A committed.

We will now look at each of these categories in turn.

(i) *Torts committed by public officials*. It is clear from the judgments in *Broome v Cassell & Co Ltd* (1972) that the phrase 'servant of the government' should be construed broadly: it covers anyone 'purporting to exercise powers of government, central or local, conferred on them by statute or at common law'.[32] So the police would be counted for these purposes as being servants of the government; as would officials of a local authority. In *AB v South West Water Services Ltd* (1993), the Court of Appeal held that a nationalised corporation which supplied water to the inhabitants of Camelford was not a 'servant of the government' for the purpose of determining whether or not it could be sued for exemplary damages; it did not exercise any governmental powers but was merely a commercial operation.[33]

(ii) *Gain-seeking torts*. Lord Devlin made it clear in his judgment in *Rookes v Barnard* that this category does not just cover cases where someone deliberately commits a tort because he thinks that he will make more money by committing that tort than he will have to pay the victim of the tort in compensatory damages:

> It extends to cases in which [someone deliberately commits a tort in order] to gain . . . some object – perhaps some property which he covets – which either he could not obtain at all or not obtain except at a price greater than he wants to put down.[34]

---

[28] [2010] EWCA Civ 453, at [70], quoting Lord Hutton in *Kuddus v Chief Constable of Leicestershire* [2002] AC 122, at [89].

[29] [2010] EWCA Civ 453, at [73]–[74].

[30] Or rather Lord Devlin: he was the only Law Lord in *Rookes v Barnard* to address the issue of when exemplary damages could be awarded against a defendant in a tort case. The other Law Lords were content to indicate that they agreed with this aspect of Lord Devlin's judgment.

[31] [1964] AC 1129, 1226.

[32] [1972] AC 1027, 1130 (per Lord Diplock). See also 1077–8 (per Lord Hailsham LC) and 1087–8 (per Lord Reid).

[33] [1993] QB 507, 525 (per Stuart-Smith LJ), 532 (per Sir Thomas Bingham MR).

[34] [1964] AC 1129, 1227.

For example, in *Drane* v *Evangelou* (1978), the defendant let some premises to the claimant. He then unlawfully evicted the claimant from the premises so that they could be occupied by his in-laws. It was held that the case fell within *Rookes* v *Barnard*'s second category of situations where exemplary damages could be awarded: the defendant deliberately committed the tort of trespass because he thought he would gain more by committing that tort – possession of the premises occupied by the claimant – than he would have to pay the claimant in damages.

For a case to fall under this category, it does not have to be shown that the defendant did a precise calculation as to how much he stood to gain and lose from committing his tort.[35] It is enough to show the tort was committed with a view to a gain: from that it can be inferred that the tortfeasor calculated he could make more than he would lose from committing the tort.[36]

(iii) *Statutory authorisation.* There are very few examples of statutes which authorise the victim of a tort to sue the person who committed that tort for exemplary damages. Until recently, the only real example was s 13(2) of the Reserve and Auxiliary Forces (Protection of Civil Interests) Act 1951, which provides that exemplary damages may be awarded against someone who converts goods that are covered by the Act. However, in 2012, Leveson LJ published his *An Inquiry into the Culture, Practices and Ethics of the Press* in which he recommended that a new independent press regulator be set up by Parliament. He further recommended that once the regulator was set up, in order to encourage members of the press to sign up to be regulated by this regulator, exemplary damages should be awarded against defendant newspapers and other publishers who had not signed up to be so regulated and had been found liable for defaming someone else or invading their privacy (however innocently) on the wholly specious ground that:

> a refusal to participate in a regulatory body might itself be evidence of a deliberate decision to stand outside any approved regulatory regime which itself could go towards the demonstration of outrageous disregard [of the claimant's rights] . . .[37]

A sufficient majority was found in Parliament to implement Leveson LJ's recommendations in the Crime and Courts Act 2013. Sections 34 to 39 of that Act seek to regulate awards of exemplary damages against members of the press, with s 34 giving members of the press who have agreed to be regulated by an 'approved regulator' a limited immunity from being sued for exemplary damages, and allowing exemplary damages to be awarded against members of the press who have not so agreed but only where 'the defendant's conduct has shown a deliberate or reckless disregard of an outrageous nature for the claimant's rights'.[38] Section 35(3) then provides that in determining whether or not exemplary damages should be awarded under s 34, the court *must* take into account whether the defendant could have signed up to be regulated by the 'approved regulator' and its reasons for not so signing up. Section 61 provides that ss 34 to 39 of the Act will only come into force a year after an approved regulator has been set up by Royal Charter. An approved regulator was created in November 2014 with the result that ss 34 to 39

---

[35] *Broome* v *Cassell & Co Ltd* [1972] AC 1027, 1078–9 (per Lord Hailsham LC), 1094 (per Lord Morris).
[36] *John* v *Mirror Group Newspapers Ltd* [1997] QB 586, 619A.
[37] Leveson 2012, Part J, § 5.11 (p. 1511).
[38] Section 34(6)(a).

of the Act came into force in November 2015, but *all* members of the press have refused to sign up to be regulated by the approved regulator.[39] It remains to be seen whether that refusal will result in exemplary damages becoming widely available against members of the press.

(3) *Compensatory and aggravated damages not enough to punish.* If a defendant's conduct in committing a tort was so outrageous as to be worthy of punishment, *and* the circumstances in which he committed that tort fall within one of the three *Rookes* v *Barnard* categories of situation where exemplary damages may be awarded, exemplary damages will still not be awarded against the defendant if requiring him to pay compensatory and aggravated damages to the victim of his tort will punish him adequately for what he has done.[40]

(4) *No double punishment involved.* Until recently, it had been thought that exemplary damages could not be awarded against a defendant who had been criminally punished for his conduct.[41] The reason for this is pretty obvious: the law should not punish people twice for the same offence. If a defendant's conduct has already been the subject of criminal punishment, it is inappropriate for the civil to come in and add to his punishment.

This seemed obvious until the decision of the Court of Appeal in *Borders* v *Commissioner of Police of the Metropolis* (2005), and the decision of Treacy J in *AT* v *Dulghieru* (2009). In the *Borders* case, £100,000 was awarded in exemplary damages against a book thief who had already been sentenced to 30 months in prison for his activities. In the *AT* case, the two defendants had been involved in a sex trafficking network which had resulted in the four claimants in *AT* being forced to have sex with clients over one or two months. £60,000 in exemplary damages was awarded against the defendants, even though they had already been sentenced to long terms in prison for their activities.

These cases are an illustration of the saying that 'ideas have consequences'. And really bad ideas have really bad consequences. The really bad idea[42] here – endorsed by Sedley LJ in the *Borders* case,[43] and adopted by Treacy J in the *AT* case[44] – is that exemplary damages that are awarded under the second *Rookes* v *Barnard* head are not really designed to punish the defendant for his behaviour, but are really a form of disgorgement damages, designed to strip the defendant of the profits he has made from committing a tort. (Disgorgement damages are discussed in the next chapter.) So if this is true, then there can be no objection to awarding exemplary damages against a defendant under the second head in *Rookes* v *Barnard* even though the defendant has already been criminally punished for his behaviour, as the award of exemplary damages under that head is not intended to punish, but to strip the defendant of the gains he has made from his behaviour.

---

[39] They have instead set up a new independent press regulator – known as the Independent Press Standards Organisation (IPSO) – to replace the old, discredited Press Complaints Commission.

[40] *Rookes* v *Barnard* [1964] AC 1129, at 1228: jury is only allowed to award exemplary damages against a defendant in a tort case if 'the sum which they have in mind to award as compensation (which may, of course, be a sum aggravated by the way in which the defendant has behaved . . .) is inadequate to punish him for his outrageous conduct . . .'.

[41] See, for example, *Archer* v *Brown* [1985] QB 401 (no award of exemplary damages against a defendant who had committed the tort of deceit because he had already been sent to prison for his fraud).

[42] First propounded by restitution scholars casting around for authorities that would support the idea that there was such a thing as gain-based damages under the common law. See, for example, Edelman 2006, at 149.

[43] [2005] EWCA Civ 197, at [25]-[27].

[44] [2009] EWHC 225, at [68].

Why is it such a bad idea to say that exemplary damages awarded under the second head in *Rookes* v *Barnard* are really a form of disgorgement damages? There are two reasons. First, and most importantly, it's just *not true*. There is no reason to think that a defendant *actually* has to have made a gain from his tort for exemplary damages to be awarded against him under the second head in *Rookes* v *Barnard*. All that has to be shown is that he *aimed* to make a gain. And even if he did make a gain from his tort, there is no reason to think that the exemplary damages that will be awarded against him under the second head in *Rookes* v *Barnard* will precisely match the gain that he has made.[45] As we will see, exemplary damages that are awarded against a defendant are designed to make the defendant 'smart'. How much is required to do that will depend on the defendant's overall resources, not the size of the gain that he made from committing his tort.

Secondly, legal fictions are always and everywhere a bad idea in the long run. Awarding disgorgement damages under the heading of exemplary damages can only result in the law becoming confused and unprincipled. For example, until *AT* v *Dulghieru*, there had been no authority in English law that allowed disgorgement damages to be sued for in a case involving a trespass to the person, and at the time *AT* v *Dulghieru* was decided, two significant Court of Appeal cases had set their face against any extensions being made in awards of disgorgement damages.[46] So allowing an award of what was meant to be, effectively, disgorgement damages in the *AT* case raised important issues of precedent and principle, that were never addressed at all by Treacy J in *AT* because the damages were being awarded as 'exemplary damages' rather than 'disgorgement damages'. If Treacy J had thought it desirable to award disgorgement damages in the *AT* case, he should have proceeded by declining to award exemplary damages (on the basis that the defendants had already been punished for their conduct) and then made an award of disgorgement damages, having first explained how such an award was justified in principle and consistent with the authorities that were binding on him.

B. Further points

Here are four more important points about the law on exemplary damages:

(1) *Quantum of damages.* In a case where it would be appropriate to award exemplary damages against a defendant, the damages payable will be just enough to bring the entire amount of damages that the defendant has to pay to the claimant up to a level sufficient to punish him for his conduct.[47]

This general rule is subject to two qualifications. First, in *Holden* v *Chief Constable of Lancashire* (1987), the Court of Appeal held that the exemplary damages payable to the victim of a tort might be reduced if he or she provoked the person who committed that tort into committing that tort.[48]

Secondly, in a case where a defendant's conduct has resulted in his committing torts in relation to multiple claimants, the Court of Appeal held in *Riches* v *News Group Newspapers* (1986) that the size of the exemplary damages payable by the defendant should be

---

[45] For example, £60,000 represented about half of what the defendants might have been expected to make from forcing the claimants in the *AT* case to have sex with clients. See, further, Keren-Paz 2010a.

[46] *Devenish Nutrition Ltd* v *Sanofi-Aventis SA* [2009] Ch 390; *Forsyth-Grant* v *Allen* [2008] EWCA Civ 505.

[47] What level of damages will be sufficient to punish A for committing his tort will, of course, depend on his means and how badly he behaved in committing his tort: *Rookes* v *Barnard* [1964] AC 1129, 1228.

[48] [1987] 1 QB 380, 388 (per Purchas LJ).

assessed by: (a) assessing how much of a sum the defendant would have to pay to punish him for his conduct; (b) subtracting from that the total sum of compensatory and aggravated damages that the defendant must pay to *all* the claimants; (c) and awarding the difference between (a) and (b) as exemplary damages against the defendant, shared out in equal shares between the claimants.[49]

(2) *Standard of proof.* In a criminal case, a defendant can only be found guilty and punished if it is proved *beyond a reasonable doubt* that he committed the offence with which he is charged. But, as we have seen already in the context of the law on causation,[50] that in civil cases, a defendant can be held liable if it is proved *on the balance of probabilities* that the defendant committed a tort and caused the claimant actionable harm. It seems right that the courts should only award exemplary damages against a defendant who has *clearly* done what he is alleged to have done. Having said that, there is no English case – so far as we know – where exemplary damages have been awarded against a defendant where there was any doubt about what the defendant had done.

(3) *Vicarious liability.* If *Employee* has committed a tort in the course of his employment, the *Victim* of that tort will be entitled to sue the employee's *Employer* for whatever *Victim* could sue *Employee* for by way of compensatory and aggravated damages.[51] But if exemplary damages may be awarded against *Employee*, could they also be awarded against *Employer*? One would have thought that, in principle, the answer should be 'no' – why should *Employer* be punished for what his *Employee* has done?[52] But a number of cases seem to assume that if *Employee* is liable to pay *Victim* exemplary damages, then so should *Employer*.[53]

(4) *Death.* Section 1(2)(a)(i) of the Law Reform (Miscellaneous Provisions) Act 1934 provides that if the victim of a tort dies before she has had a chance to sue the person who committed that tort for damages, any right she might have had to sue the tortfeasor for exemplary damages will die with her.

---

[49] It seems that the exemplary damages will be split equally between the claimants even if one claimant was more affected by the defendant's conduct than the others. So the exemplary damages payable in *AT* v *Dulghieru* [2009] EWHC 225 were split equally among the four claimants in that case, even though two of the claimants had each been forced to work as prostitutes for two months, and the other two for a month each.

[50] See above, § 8.4.

[51] See below, § 31.1.

[52] See *Kuddus* v *Chief Constable of Leicestershire* [2002] 2 AC 122, at [137].

[53] See *Lancashire County Council* v *Municipal Mutual Insurance Ltd* [1997] QB 897 (not improper for local authority to insure against exemplary damages because such awards could be made against it under the law on vicarious liability, and if such an award were made, it would not be to blame for the conduct that was being punished); *Thompson* v *Commissioner of Police of the Metropolis* [1998] QB 498 (not only can exemplary damages be awarded against an employer under the law on vicarious liability, they could actually exceed the exemplary damages that the employee would be liable to pay because the employer would have more means than the employee); *Muuse* v *Secretary of State for the Home Department* [2010] EWCA Civ 453 (exemplary damages awarded against Home Office because of 'manifest incompetence' of its employees). See also *New South Wales* v *Ibbett* [2006] HCA 57, where the High Court of Australia upheld an award of exemplary damages against the State of New South Wales on the ground that it was vicariously liable for two police officers' torts (trespass to land and assault), holding (at [51]) that the award was necessary to bring home to the State that police officers employed by the State had to be trained not to engage in the sort of conduct that the police officers in *Ibbett* had engaged in.

C. Reform

In order to assess whether the law on exemplary damages is in need of reform, we need to determine whether it serves any useful purpose. It could be argued that awards of exemplary damages serve not one, but two useful functions.

(1) *Vindicating the rule of law.* The House of Lords in *Rookes* v *Barnard* (1964) clearly thought that awards of exemplary damages served a useful purpose in giving people an incentive to obey the law.[54] This was why they limited such awards to cases where a public official had acted outrageously in committing a tort, and cases where someone had committed a tort figuring he could make more money by committing that tort than he would have to pay out in damages. In each of these cases, the standard incentives that the tortfeasor has to obey the law are significantly weakened. In the second case, the prospect of having to pay compensatory and aggravated damages to the victim of his tort will not put the tortfeasor from committing his tort. In the first case, the public official might think it unlikely that his outrageous behaviour will receive any sanction from his superiors or the police. The tendency of the State to look after its own was remarked on by the Court of Appeal in the *Muuse* case:

> There has been no Parliamentary or other enquiry into Mr Muuse's case. No Minister or senior official has been held accountable. We were not told of any internal or other enquiry conducted by the Permanent Secretary or Head of the Immigration Directorate (or as it now is the UK Border Agency). The only way in which the misconduct of the Home Office has been exposed to public view and his rights vindicated is by the action in the High Court.[55]

The Court of Appeal went on to observe that:

> Given the absence of Parliamentary accountability for the arbitrary and unlawful detention of Mr Muuse, the lack of an enquiry and the paucity of the measures taken by the Home Office to prevent a recurrence, it is difficult to see how such arbitrary conduct can be deterred in the future and the Home Office made to improve the way in which the power to imprison is exercised other than by the court making an award of exemplary damages . . . [The] award of [such] damages . . . has a real role in restraining the arbitrary use of executive power and buttressing civil liberties, given the way the United Kingdom's Parliamentary democracy in fact operates.[56]

(2) *Civil recourse theory.* We saw in the previous section that it is normal for people to feel entitled to strike back at those who treat them with contempt. It could be argued that allowing a claimant to sue a defendant in tort for exemplary damages when conditions (1) ('desert'), (3) ('compensatory and aggravated damages not enough to punish') and (4) ('no double punishment involved') in section 24.3(A), above, are satisfied gives the claimant a civilised, peaceful and orderly way of satisfying his natural desire to see the defendant pay for treating her in such an outrageous fashion.[57] While we might be

---

[54] See *Rookes* v *Barnard* [1964] AC 1129, 1226 ('an award of exemplary damages can serve a useful purpose in vindicating the strength of the law'); also *Kuddus* v *Chief Constable of Leicestershire* [2002] 2 AC 122, at [63] (per Lord Hutton): 'the power to award exemplary damages . . . serves to uphold and vindicate the rule of law because it makes clear that the courts will not tolerate such conduct.'

[55] [2010] EWCA Civ 453, at [75].

[56] [2010] EWCA Civ 453, at [77].

[57] See Zipursky 2005 (at 151–61), defending awards of exemplary damages on the ground that, on occasion, the victim of a tort has a 'right to be punitive' towards the person who committed that tort, because of the manner in which it was committed. See Stevens 2007, at 85–7, and Sebok 2007 for similar arguments.

initially skeptical as to whether awards of exemplary damages play a role in allowing a claimant to ensure the defendant gets what he deserves for treating her with contempt, it should be noted that this view of exemplary damages explains s 1(2)(a)(i) of the Law Reform (Miscellaneous Provisions) Act 1934, which prevents exemplary damages being awarded to the estate of the victim of a tort who died after that tort was committed. If the victim of a tort is no longer around, there is no longer anyone whose desire to strike back at the person who committed that tort needs to be assuaged.

Now that we have identified the functions played by awards of exemplary damages, we can canvass the two main options for reform of this area of the law.

(1) *Abolition*. This is not a possibility we should seriously entertain.[58] Abolishing awards of exemplary damages would clearly weaken the force of the rule of law among those defendants at whom *Rookes* v *Barnard* currently directs such awards. Purists like Allan Beever object to the damage done to the 'integrity' of tort law by allowing claimants to make claims for exemplary damages on the basis that allowing such claims to be made is in the public interest.[59] Why should only the *victim* of a tort be allowed to sue for such damages? Why should it only be *damages* that can be sued for? However, impurity is not always a bad thing. Pearls come from a bit of grit that finds its way into an oyster shell. It seems that we would be throwing away a valuable pearl if in the interests of purity, we abolished the ability of civil courts to award exemplary damages.

(2) *Reversing Rookes v Barnard*. Should we follow the example of other common law jurisdictions and get rid of the *Rookes* v *Barnard* limits on when exemplary damages may be awarded in a tort case?

Rule of law considerations do not strongly indicate that there is a problem with *Rookes* v *Barnard*. Where a private actor is thinking about committing a tort, but not for gain, the existing incentives that he has to obey the law (the prospect of having to pay damages to the victim of his tort, and possible criminal prosecution for what he has done, as well as extra-legal sanctions such a losing his job) will usually prove sufficient to keep him straight; and where they do not, it is not clear that the prospect of an award of exemplary damages will make any difference.

From the point of view of an adherent to civil recourse theory, *Rookes* v *Barnard* looks more problematic – it stands in the way of a claimant suing for exemplary damages to make a defendant pay for treating her in an outrageous fashion, when the defendant was a private person and his tort was not committed for gain. However, even from this perspective, something can be said for *Rookes* v *Barnard*. It might be argued that there is something especially outrageous about committing a tort for financial gain or in your capacity as a public servant. Public servants are supposed to work for us, not against us. And treating someone's interests as less important than making a financial gain for yourself is especially insulting. So it might be argued that in the situations currently covered by *Rookes* v *Barnard*, a claimant's desire to strike back at the defendant for what he has done will be especially strong; and there is not much of a case for extending the availability of exemplary damages to cases where the desire to see the defendant pay for what he has done will be less strong.

---

[58] Nor is it a realistic possibility anymore given the Crime and Courts Act 2013, discussed above, § 24.3(A)(2)(iii).

[59] Beever 2003a.

Further reading

John Murphy's piece on aggravated damages – 'The nature and domain of aggravated damages' (2010) 69 *Cambridge Law Journal* 353 – is well worth reading in full and currently represents the state of the art in thinking about the nature and function of aggravated damages. Students should never pass up the chance to read anything by Peter Birks, and they should definitely not miss the chance to read 'Harassment and hubris: the right to an equality of respect' (1997) 32 *Irish Jurist* 1, even though we would disagree with his claim that there exists a distinct tort of committing some other tort in an arrogant or high-handed manner, and that aggravated damages are awarded in response to that distinct tort.

The case for and against abolishing awards of exemplary damages is considered in Birks (ed), *Wrongs and Remedies in Private Law* (OUP, 1996) (see the chapters by McBride ('Punitive damages') and Burrows ('Reforming exemplary damages')) and Rickett (ed), *Justifying Private Law Remedies* (Hart Publishing, 2008) (see the chapters by Edelman ('In defence of exemplary damages') and Beever ('Justice and punishment in tort: a comparative theoretical analysis')).

Chapter 25
Disgorgement and licence fee damages

Aims and objectives

Reading this chapter should enable you to:

(1) Identify the difference(s) between disgorgement damages and licence fee damages.

(2) Understand when such damages will be awarded against a tortfeasor.

(3) Get a good grasp of the various different theories as to why the courts award such damages in cases where someone has committed a tort.

25.1 The basics

In previous editions of this text, this chapter was entitled 'Gain-Based Damages'. This reflected our view that the two types of damages awards which we deal with in this chapter – *disgorgement damages* (damages designed to make a tortfeasor give up to the victim of his tort the monetary value of any gain he has made as a result of committing that tort) and *licence fee damages* (damages designed to make a tortfeasor pay a reasonable sum for the fact that he has committed a tort)[1] – were both concerned to make a tortfeasor account for a gain he had made as a result of committing a tort. However, that is no longer our view.

---

[1] What we are calling 'licence fee' damages have also been referred to as 'user damages', 'reasonable fee damages', 'negotiating damages' (see *Lunn Poly Ltd* v *Liverpool and Lancashire Properties Ltd* [2006] EWCA Civ 430, at [22] (per Neuberger LJ)), 'hypothetical negotiation damages' (see above, § 12.6, fn 55) and '*Wrotham Park* damages'. We prefer Peter Jaffey's suggestion (Jaffey 2007, at 100; also Jaffey 2011) that these damages should be called 'licence fee damages': 'user damages' wrongly suggests these damages are only available in cases where someone has made use of someone else; 'reasonable fee damages' is too wide as there are many other contexts where someone is allowed to sue another for a reasonable fee; 'negotiating damages' or 'hypothetical negotiation damages' is not good English; and '*Wrotham Park* damages' is too obscure.

While disgorgement damages are undeniably gain-based, our view now is that licence fee damages are compensatory in nature – but they compensate for a different kind of loss from the kind of loss that normal compensatory damages are designed to cover. Normal compensatory damages are designed to compensate the victim of a tort for some material, tangible loss that she has suffered as a result of that tort being committed, such as pain and suffering or a loss of income. Licence fee damages are not like that. They are designed to compensate the victim of a tort for an immaterial, intangible loss that she has suffered as a result of that tort being committed – the loss of the ability to determine what should happen to her and the things under her control.[2]

This is all fairly abstract, so let's sharpen it up by considering the following two situations:

> Thief steals *Owner's* horse and sells it to *Third Party* for £10,000. *Owner* can sue *Thief* for the £10,000 made from selling his horse.[3]
>
> *Chancer* goes for a ride on *Owner's* horse without *Owner's* permission, and brings the horse back to *Owner* in good condition. *Owner* can sue *Chancer* for a reasonable sum for the use he has made of the horse.[4]

In the first situation, *Owner* is entitled to sue *Thief* for disgorgement damages – damages designed to make *Thief* give up the equivalent of the £10,000 he has made from wrongfully selling *Owner's* horse. In the second situation, *Owner* is entitled to sue *Chancer* for licence fee damages – damages designed to make *Chancer* pay a reasonable sum for the fact that he has taken a ride on *Owner's* horse.

It is our contention that while the disgorgement damages that *Thief* is liable to pay *Owner* are undoubtedly gain-based, the licence fee damages that *Chancer* is liable to pay *Owner* are compensatory. However, the licence fee damages that *Chancer* is liable to pay *Owner* are not designed to compensate *Owner* for any material, tangible loss that he might have suffered as a result of *Chancer's* going for a ride on his horse. As Lord Shaw pointed out in *Watson, Laidlaw & Co Ltd* v *Potts, Cassels and Williamson* (1914), *Chancer* is liable to pay *Owner* licence fee damages even if *Chancer* can argue that, 'The horse is none the worse [for my riding on it]; it is the better for the exercise.'[5] Our contention is that the licence fee damages that *Chancer* is liable to pay *Owner* are designed to compensate *Owner* for the fact that he has been deprived of the power to decide whether or not his horse should be taken out for a ride – a power which the law acknowledge that he should have, and the deprivation of which the law responds to by making *Chancer* pay *Owner* licence fee damages. So while *Owner* may have suffered no material, tangible loss as a result of *Chancer's* tort, he has suffered a loss in the plane of the law – the loss of something which the law wanted him to have.

---

[2] This new view of the nature of licence fee damages was set out almost simultaneously and independently in McBride 2014, 272–4, and Barker 2014.

[3] See below, § 25.2.

[4] See below, § 25.3.

[5] [1914] SC (HL) 18, 31.

It should be immediately noted that this analysis is not accepted by everyone. The academic literature reveals three other views of the nature of licence fee damages:

(1) *Licence fee damages are a form of disgorgement damages.* This is the view adopted by most restitution lawyers (in particular, Andrew Burrows).[6] The idea is that when *Chancer* takes *Owner's* horse for a ride, he does make a gain – he gets to enjoy a ride on *Owner's* horse. Making *Chancer* pay *Owner* a reasonable sum for going for a ride on *Owner's* horse is a way of making him give up that gain. On this view of things, there is no reason for distinguishing between disgorgement damages and licence fee damages: licence fee damages are simply a form of disgorgement damages and this chapter should accordingly be entitled 'Disgorgement Damages'.

(2) *Licence fee damages are restitutionary damages.* This view is most closely associated with James Edelman, who argued in his influential book *Gain-Based Damages*[7] that what we are calling disgorgement damages and what we are calling licence fee damages were distinct in that a tortfeasor who is held liable to pay disgorgement damages is made to give *up* to the victim of his tort a gain that he has made from a third party by committing that tort, while a tortfeasor who is held liable to pay licence fee damages is made to give *back* to the victim of his tort a gain that he has made from that victim by committing that tort. So, in the above examples, when *Thief* is held liable to pay *Owner* disgorgement damages, he is held liable to give up to *Owner* a gain he has made from whoever he sold *Owner's* horse to. In contrast, Edelman contends, when *Chancer* is held liable to pay *Owner* licence fee damages he is required to give *back* to *Owner* a gain that he has made *from Owner*: the gain being, as per the analysis in (1), above, the privilege of going for a ride on *Owner's* horse. So Edelman argued that what we are calling licence fee damages should really be called 'restitutionary damages' because they require a tortfeasor to make restitution of a gain that he has made from the victim of his tort.

(3) *Licence fee damages are normal compensatory damages.* This view was advanced over 30 years ago by Sharpe and Waddams, who argued that in allowing *Owner* to sue *Chancer* for licence fee damages, the law is concerned to compensate *Owner* for a material, tangible loss that he has suffered as a result of *Chancer's* taking his horse for a ride without asking for *Owner's* permission.[8] The material, tangible loss *Owner* has suffered is the loss of the chance to charge *Chancer* a fee for going for a ride on *Owner's* horse. So if we ask, 'What would have happened had *Chancer* not acted wrongfully in riding on *Owner's* horse, but obtained *Owner's* permission?' the answer is '*Owner* would now be better off by £x – the amount *Owner* would have charged *Chancer* for going on a ride on his horse.' So by making *Chancer* pay *Owner* £x, we put *Owner* in the material position he would have been in had *Chancer* not committed a tort in going for a ride on *Owner's* horse – just as we do in any other case where we award the victim of a tort compensatory damages.

None of these alternative analyses appeal to us. The problem with (1) and (2) is that just as *Chancer* cannot avoid being held liable to pay licence fee damages to *Owner* by pointing out that *Owner* has not suffered any loss as a result of his riding on *Owner's* horse, neither

---

[6] See Burrows 2008.
[7] Edelman 2002b.
[8] See Sharpe and Waddams 1982. See also, to the same effect, Giglio 2007; *WWF* v *WWF* [2006] EWHC 184 (QB), at [137] (per Peter Smith J); and *Devenish Nutrition* v *Sanofi-Aventis* [2009] Ch 390, at [40]–[41] (per Arden LJ).

can *Chancer* avoid being held liable to pay licence fee damages by pointing out that he did not in fact make a gain by riding on *Owner*'s horse – as would be the case if *Owner*'s horse proved to be so unruly that *Chancer* had a thoroughly miserable experience riding on her and ended up falling off the horse and breaking his leg.[9] The problem with (3) is that *Owner* will be entitled to sue *Chancer* for licence fee damages even if, had *Chancer* asked *Owner* for permission to go for a ride on *Owner*'s horse, *Owner* would have: (a) happily allowed *Chancer* to ride on the horse for free; or (b) refused to allow *Chancer* to ride on the horse at any price. Where (a) or (b) are true, it is extremely difficult to see how we can characterise the award of licence fee damages to *Owner* as being designed to compensate *Owner* for the loss of the money he would have made from *Chancer* had *Chancer* asked *Owner* permission to go for a ride on his horse.

No doubt the debates about the nature of disgorgement and licence fee damages will provide fodder for academics for some years to come, but there is equally no doubt about the existence of these heads of damages in English law and the need in a text such as this to give an account of when these damages will be payable by a tortfeasor. It is to this task that we now turn.

25.2 Disgorgement damages

A. The law

Disgorgement damages are available for the following torts:

(1) *Conversion.* In *Kuwait Airways Corpn* v *Iraqi Airways Co (Nos 4 & 5)* (2002), Lord Nicholls remarked that 'all those who convert [someone else's goods] should be accountable for the *benefits* they receive';[10] and indeed it has long been established that disgorgement damages may be claimed against someone who commits the tort of conversion.

So, for example, in *Oughton* v *Seppings* (1830) the defendant, a sheriff's officer, sold a pony cart belonging to the claimant, thinking that it belonged to the claimant's tenant, whose property he was authorised to seize and sell to pay off a debt owed by the tenant. The defendant was held liable for the value of the money he obtained in return for the claimant's pony.[11] In *Oughton*, the defendant converted the claimant's property by selling it. May disgorgement damages be awarded against a defendant who converts another's property by *using* it? In such a case, English law normally awards licence fee, and not disgorgement, damages against the defendant.[12] However, there is an American case where disgorgement damages were awarded. In *Olwell* v *Nye & Nissen* (1946), the defendant

---

[9] See McBride 2014, 254.

[10] [2002] 2 AC 883, at [79] (emphasis added).

[11] Of course, the defendant no longer had that money – he would have handed it over to Winslove's creditors. However, it is generally accept that there is no defence of what is called '*change of position*' to a claim for disgorgement damages against a wrongdoer: see *Lipkin Gorman* v *Karpnale* [1991] 2 AC 548, 580 (per Lord Goff). This is rough on a defendant who has *innocently* converted someone else's property, and Lord Nicholls suggested in the *Kuwait Airways* case that a defence of change of position should be available to such a defendant: [2002] 2 AC 883, at [79].

[12] See McInnes 2003, at 712: '[The] precedents consistently indicate that while the defendant is required to give up his entire gain if he wrongfully *sells* the claimant's property, he merely is required to pay a hiring fee [i.e. licence fee damages] for improper *usage*' (at 712).

converted a machine belonging to the claimant by using it in his factory. It was held that the claimant was entitled to sue the defendant for the profits the defendant had made by using that machine.

(2) *Passing off.* Disgorgement damages may be awarded against someone who has *deliberately* committed the tort of passing off.[13] So in *My Kinda Town* v *Soll* (1982), the defendants deliberately dressed up their restaurant in such a way that people would be deceived into thinking that the defendants' restaurant was a branch of a chain of restaurants run by the claimants. Slade J held that the claimants were entitled to sue the defendants for the money they had made by passing off their restaurant as being one of the claimants' restaurants: a difficult sum to quantify as it was uncertain how many of the defendants' customers had been lured into their restaurant because they thought it was run by the claimants.

(3) *Infringement of intellectual property rights.* Disgorgement damages (under the name 'account of profits') may be awarded against someone who infringes another's copyright[14] or someone who infringes another's design right.[15] In the case where a defendant has infringed another's patent, disgorgement damages may be awarded if the defendant knew or ought to have known of the existence of the patent at the time he infringed it.[16]

(4) *Invasion of privacy.* The equivalent of disgorgement damages are routinely awarded against defendants who commit equitable wrongs such as a breach of trust, a breach of fiduciary duty, or a breach of confidence.[17] The fact that the new tort of wrongful disclosure of private information has its origins in the equitable wrong of breach of confidence makes it likely that disgorgement damages will be routinely awarded against defendants who commit this tort. Indeed, in *Douglas* v *Hello! Ltd (No 3)* (2006), the Court of Appeal accepted that if the defendants in that case had made a profit from publishing unauthorised photographs of the claimants' wedding celebrations, then the claimants would have been entitled to sue the defendants for a sum equal to that profit.[18] However, it was found that the defendants had paid so much for the photographs, they did not in the end make a profit from the extra sales of their magazine that resulted from their publishing the photographs.[19]

It is currently *uncertain* whether disgorgement damages will be available for *trespass to land*. Such damages were awarded in *Edwards* v *Lee's Administrators* (1936). That case concerned a long cave that contained some very interesting rock formations. The entrance to the cave was on the defendants' land and they would charge people to enter the cave

---

[13] *Edelsten* v *Edelsten* (1863) 1 De G J & S 185, 46 ER 72.

[14] Copyright, Designs and Patents Act 1988, s 96(2). It is not thought that s 97(1) of the 1988 Act affects this point. That subsection provides that: 'Where in action for infringement of copyright it is shown that at the time of the infringement the defendant did not know, and had no reason to believe, that copyright subsists in the work to which the action relates, the claimant is not entitled to damages against him, but without prejudice to any other remedy.' It is thought that the reference to *damages* in this section is a reference to *compensatory* damages.

[15] Section 229(2). Again, it is not thought that s 233(1) of the 1988 Act – which provides that the owner of a design right which has been infringed will not be entitled to sue the person who infringed the design right for damages if he did not know of, and had no reason to know of, the existence of the design right infringed by him – affects this point.

[16] Patents Act 1977, s 62(1).

[17] See, for example, *Attorney-General* v *Guardian Newspapers Ltd (No 2)* [1990] 1 AC 109.

[18] [2006] QB 125, at [249].

[19] [2006] QB 125, at [245].

and look around. Unfortunately, a third of the cave stretched under the claimants' land, with the result that the defendants committed the tort of trespass to land whenever they allowed customers to view that part of the cave that was under the claimants' land. The claimants were allowed to sue the defendants for damages equal to the money the defendants had made by allowing people to look at that part of the cave that was under the claimants' land. It has been doubted whether the same approach would be adopted under English law.[20] James Edelman has argued that *Livingstone* v *Rawyards Coal Company* (1880) is authority for the proposition that if A *deliberately and in bad faith* trespasses on B's land and makes a gain as a result, he will be liable to pay disgorgement damages to B.[21] However, the only statement in the case that can be taken as supporting that idea is the following:

> There is no doubt that if a man furtively and in bad faith robs his neighbour of property . . . the person [will be held liable for] the value of the whole of the property which he has so furtively taken, and . . . no allowance [will be made] in respect of what he has so done as would have been justly made to him if the parties had been working by agreement, or if, as in the present case, they had been the one working and the other permitting the working through a mistake.[22]

But that statement is considering the case where A has stolen B's property (a case of conversion), rather than the case where A trespasses on B's land and makes a profit for himself as a result without actually stealing anything from B.

It seems *fairly clear* that disgorgement damages will *not* be available for private nuisance.[23] The UK Supreme Court had the chance to consider whether disgorgement damages should be awarded against someone who committed the tort of private nuisance in *Lawrence* v *Fen Tigers Ltd* (2014) but made no suggestion that such damages should be available. They *did* discuss the basis on which damages *in lieu* of an injunction should be awarded against someone committing the tort of private nuisance, and whether such damages – when awarded – should include an element to reflect any gain made by the tortfeasor.[24] However, as we will see, damages *in lieu* of an injunction cannot be characterised as disgorgement damages, and the fact that the Supreme Court Justices did not even think that disgorgement damages might be available on a free-standing basis against someone who has committed the tort of private nuisance, makes it very difficult for the time being for anyone to argue that it is the law in the UK that such damages might be claimed in a private nuisance case.

---

[20] See McInnes 2003, at 712: '[It] is quite likely that an English claimant, in the same circumstances, would be limited to reasonable rental value [i.e. licence fee damages]'; to the same effect, Cooke 1994, 428–9; also *Severn Trent Water Ltd* v *Barnes* [2004] EWCA Civ 570 (disallowing anything but an award of licence fee damages against a defendant who had trespassed on the claimant's land by laying a water mains under the land); and *Stadium Capital Holdings Ltd* v *St Marylebone Property Co Ltd* [2010] EWCA Civ 952 (trespass by fixing advertisement hoarding to claimant's wall; held, first instance judge should *not* have awarded damages equal to entire amount of profit made from hoarding).

[21] Edelman 2006, at 147.

[22] (1880) 5 App Cas 25, at 34 (per Lord Hatherley).

[23] *Stoke-on-Trent CC* v *Wass* [1988] 1 WLR 1406 (disgorgement damages not available against trader who committed tort of private nuisance by running market in area where claimants had exclusive right to run market); *Forsyth-Grant* v *Allen* [2008] EWCA Civ 505 (disgorgement damages not available against defendant who profited by building two houses that interfered with claimant's right to light).

[24] Lords Neuberger and Clarke thought it was arguable that damages *in lieu* of an injunction should include such an element in [2015] AC 106, at [128] and [173] respectively. Lord Carnwath was more skeptical at [248].

The Court of Appeal's decision in *Devenish Nutrition* v *Sofia-Aventis* (2009) seems to make it *very* clear that – until the UK Supreme Court rules otherwise – disgorgement damages will *not* be available for the following *non-proprietary* torts:[25] breach of statutory duty, deceit, trespass to the person, and defamation. A claim for disgorgement damages for breach of statutory duty was explicitly ruled out in *Devenish Nutrition*. A claim for such damages in the case of deceit was ruled out by the Court of Appeal in *Halifax Building Society* v *Thomas* (1996), where the defendant obtained a mortgage by lying about his indebtedness to the claimant building society and was held entitled – once the building society affirmed the mortgage by foreclosing it and forcing a sale of the house that the defendant bought with the mortgage – to keep any profits from the increase in the value of the house after the defendant had bought it.[26] No attempt to disapprove *Thomas* was made in *Devenish Nutrition*. By holding itself unable to award disgorgement damages in any cases other than proprietary torts, the Court of Appeal has effectively ruled out for itself the possibility of making such awards in trespass to the person or defamation cases. (However, in such cases, an award of exemplary damages may well be available.)

B. Confusions about the law

Thus stands the law at the moment on which torts may give rise to an award of disgorgement damages. However, some restitution scholars would like to suggest that disgorgement damages are available for a much wider range of torts. In order to make that suggestion they point to the following areas of law. However – as we will see – none of these areas of law deal with when the victim of a tort can sue the person who committed that tort for disgorgement damages. Suggestions to the contrary are confused, and confusing.

(1) *Rookes v Barnard*. It is suggested, first, that exemplary damages that are awarded under the second head in *Rookes v Barnard* (1964) are really disgorgement damages, as such damages are awarded against a tortfeasor who committed his tort with the object of making a gain for himself. However – as we have already seen[27] – the facts that (a) no actual gain has to have been obtained by a tortfeasor for damages under the second head in *Rookes* v *Barnard* to be awarded against him, and (b) there is no requirement that exemplary damages awarded under the second head should precisely equal any gain made by the tortfeasor through committing his tort, make it impossible to characterize exemplary damages under the second head as being disgorgement damages.

(2) *Damages in lieu of an injunction*. It is suggested, secondly, that damages awarded *in lieu* of an injunction are really disgorgement damages, and this suggestion is sometimes relied on to make the further suggestion that disgorgement damages *may* be awarded against someone who commits the tort of private nuisance.

---

[25] It is true, as Burrows 2011 notes at 659, that in *Devenish Nutrition* Longmore LJ took the view that there was no authority binding on the Court of Appeal that held that disgorgement damages could only be awarded in cases of a 'tortious claim[] for breach of a proprietary right' (at [145]) and went on to say (at [148]) that 'an account of profits outside the established categories is only to be made [and therefore by implication *can* be made] in "exceptional" cases' but Longmore LJ was in the minority on this point.

[26] See also *Renault UK Ltd* v *Fleetpro Technical Services Ltd* [2007] EWHC 2541 (QB), where the judge refused to award disgorgement damages against a defendant who, by deceit, persuaded the claimant to manufacture and sell to him some cars that he then sold on at a profit.

[27] See above, §24.3(A)(2).

The reason why damages *in lieu* of an injunction *seem* to be a form of disgorgement damages is this. Consider a situation where *Farmer* is, in principle, entitled to an injunction to stop *Industrialist* polluting *Farmer*'s land with so much smoke from *Industrialist*'s factory, but, for one reason or another, the courts award *Farmer* damages *in lieu* of an injunction instead. The practice of the courts up until now[28] has been to assess how much to award *Farmer* in damages by seeing how much *Farmer* and *Industrialist* would *hypothetically* agree *Farmer* should be paid for giving up his right[29] to an injunction, were each party to negotiate in good faith and not hold out grimly for the best possible deal for themselves. Were such a *hypothetical bargain* to be entered into, *Farmer* would insist on *Industrialist* paying him enough money to cover any losses he might suffer as a result of *Industrialist*'s pollution *but he would also* want *Industrialist* to add something on top of that to give *Farmer* a share of any gain *Industrialist* might make from being allowed to carry on polluting *Farmer*'s land. It is only fair that if *Farmer* is giving up his right to an injunction, that he should get a proportion of the profits that *Industrialist* will make as a result of not being subject to that injunction. It is because damages *in lieu* of an injunction contain this gain-based element that some people argue that they are a form of disgorgement damages.

However, damages *in lieu* of an injunction will only give *Farmer a share* of the profits made by *Industrialist* as a result of polluting *Farmer*'s land. This simple fact makes it impossible to characterise damages *in lieu* of an injunction as being a form of disgorgement damages, as disgorgement damages strip a tortfeasor of *the whole* of the gain he has made by committing a tort. The better view is that damages *in lieu* of an injunction are *compensatory*: they exist to compensate *Farmer* for the fact that he has been forced to sell his right to an injunction by giving him a fair price for giving up that right.[30] So there is no inconsistency between the cases in which damages *in lieu* of an injunction that included a gain-based element were routinely awarded in private nuisance cases,[31] and cases in which it was denied that disgorgement damages could be awarded to the victim of a private nuisance.[32] The two sets of authorities are dealing with completely different things.

(3) *Attorney-General v Blake.* Finally, it is suggested that the decision of the House of Lords in *Attorney-General* v *Blake* (2001) has some implications for the availability of disgorgement damages against a tortfeasor. *Blake* was a landmark case in which the House of Lords held that gain-based damages might be awarded against a defendant who had committed a *breach of contract*. Lord Nicholls, giving the leading judgment, could see no

---

[28] It is still uncertain whether the *obiter dicta* in the UK Supreme Court in *Lawrence* v *Fen Tigers Ltd* [2015] AC 106 (at [128], [172]–[173] and at [248]) on the factors to be taken into account in assessing the amount of damages to be awarded *in lieu* of an injunction will have any effect on this practice.

[29] Technically, no one has a right to an injunction (injunctions are awarded as a matter of discretion by the courts) but for the purposes of the hypothetical bargain, it is assumed that *Farmer* does have such a right, which gives him a bargaining chip and something to sell in his negotiations with *Industrialist*.

[30] *Carr-Saunders* v *Dick McNeil Associates Ltd* [1986] 1 WLR 922, 931; *Jaggard* v *Sawyer* [1995] 1 WLR 269, 291; *Stoke-on-Trent County Council* v *Wass* [1988] 1 WLR 1406, 1420.

[31] *Carr-Saunders* v *Dick McNeil Associates Ltd* [1986] 1 WLR 922, *Tamares Ltd* v *Fairpoint Properties Ltd* *(No 2)* [2007] EWHC 212 (QB).

[32] *Stoke-on-Trent City Council* v *W & J Wass Ltd* [1988] 1 WLR 1406, *Forsyth-Grant* v *Allen* [2008] EWCA Civ 505.

reason why the victims of proprietary torts could sue for gain-based damages while the victim of a breach of contract could not:

> it is not easy to see why, as between the parties to a contract, a violation of a party's contractual rights should attract a lesser degree of remedy than a violation of his property rights.[33]

But, by the same reasoning, it could be suggested that it is not easy to see why wrongfully harming someone's person or reputation should attract a lesser degree of remedy than violating someone's contractual rights – so if *Blake* makes disgorgement damages available in the last case, then they should also be available in cases of battery or defamation. Some support was expressed for this idea in *Devenish Nutrition*, where the Court of Appeal argued that:

> The overall holding in *Blake*'s case is that the law on remedies . . . should be coherent and that the same remedies should be available in the same circumstances, even if the cause of action is different.[34]

Despite this, Arden and Tuckey LJJ took the view that disgorgement damages could not be awarded for the defendant's committing the tort of breach of statutory duty in *Devenish Nutrition* because they were bound by Court of Appeal authority that such damages could only be awarded in tort where a proprietary tort had been committed.

The case of *Devenish Nutrition* seems to have neutralised the effect *Blake* might otherwise have had on the availability of disgorgement damages against tortfeasors, at least so far as the Court of Appeal and lower courts are concerned. It follows that only the UK Supreme Court can usher us into the bold new world which *Blake* points us towards, where disgorgement damages are available against all wrongdoers, regardless of the nature of their wrong.

C. Theories

In deciding whether or not to take that bold step, the UK Supreme Court must first decide why we would *ever* award disgorgement damages against a wrongdoer in the first place. It is only if we know that, that we can determine when disgorgement damages should be awarded against a wrongdoer. In this section, we will look at some of the arguments that have been advanced for awarding disgorgement damages against wrongdoers and see, in relation to the arguments that seem to have some merit, what they imply as to when disgorgement damages should be made available against a wrongdoer.

(1) *A wrongdoer should not be allowed to profit from his wrong.* It is a popular argument among restitution scholars that awards of disgorgement damages are based on the idea that a wrongdoer should not be allowed to profit from his wrong.[35] The argument may be popular, but it is also a really bad argument. It is equivalent to saying that 'Wrongdoers are not allowed to profit from their wrongs [through the award of disgorgement damages] because they should not be allowed to profit from their wrongs.' This is not an argument: it is a bare assertion.

---

[33] [2001] AC 268, 283.
[34] [2009] Ch 390, at [4] (per Arden LJ).
[35] See, for example, Burrows 2011, at 623: 'Restitution for a wrong directly reflects the idea that "no person shall profit from his or her wrong".'

(2) *Deterrence.* It is another popular argument among some restitution scholars that awards of disgorgement damages are designed to deter people from committing wrongs.[36] The idea is that you will be less likely to commit a wrong in relation to someone else if you know that you will not be allowed to keep any gain that you might make from committing that wrong. There are two problems with this argument.

First, it is highly unlikely that the availability of awards of disgorgement damages would put anyone off committing a wrong from which they stood to make a gain. The reason is that *all* disgorgement damages do is strip you of the gain you have made by wronging someone else. So even in a world where disgorgement damages are widely available, it would still make sense to wrong other people in order to make gains for yourself because there will always be a chance – and probably a good chance   that you will be allowed to hang onto those gains, either because your wrongdoing will go undetected or because you will not be sued for disgorgement damages even if your wrongdoing is detected.

Secondly, if awards of disgorgement damages were designed to deter people from committing wrongs, it is hard to understand why, in tort at least, disgorgement damages (a) may be awarded against tortfeasors who have innocently committed a tort (such as the defendant in *Oughton* v *Seppings* (1830)), and (b) may be awarded in cases where there exist ample other remedies (such as a substantial award of compensatory damages, or the possibility of an award of exemplary damages) that should be sufficient to put a putative tortfeasor off the idea of committing a tort. While in *Attorney-General* v *Blake* (2001), the House of Lords ruled that disgorgement damages should only be available in a breach of contract case where other remedies are 'inadequate',[37] there has *never* been a similar limit on disgorgement damages being awarded in tort and Longmore LJ warned his colleagues in *Devenish Nutrition* v *Sanofi-Aventis* (2009) against being seduced by *Blake* into importing such a limit into tort law: 'The concept of damages being an inadequate remedy . . . is a treacherous one if it is used as a supposedly principled reason for the disgorgement of profits.'[38]

(3) *Waiver of tort.* In his article 'As if it had never happened',[39] Arthur Ripstein argues that we can justify awards of disgorgement damages against a tortfeasor on the basis that making such an award makes it as though the tortfeasor's tort never happened. The idea is this. Suppose that *Thief* sells *Owner*'s car to a third party for £5,000. *Owner* could sue *Thief* on the basis that *Thief* acted wrongfully in selling the car and obtain various remedies – such as compensatory damages, and possibly exemplary damages – on that basis. But alternatively, *Owner* could choose to treat *Thief* as though *Thief* was acting on *Owner*'s behalf in selling his car, and thereby treat *Thief* as though *Thief* did nothing wrong in selling the car. But if *Thief was* acting on *Owner*'s behalf in selling the car, then *Thief* owes *Owner* £5,000 – the money he made from selling the car. So allowing *Owner* to sue *Thief* for that money is the logical consequence of treating *Thief* as though he did nothing wrong in selling *Owner*'s car.

---

[36] See, for example, Edelman 2002b.
[37] [2001] AC 268, 285.
[38] [2009] Ch 390, at [148]. Arden and Tuckey LJJ's flirtations in the same case with the idea that disgorgement damages should only be available in tort where other remedies are inadequate can be found at [2009] Ch 390, [4] and [104].
[39] Ripstein 2007a.

Ripstein's article resurrects a very old explanation of why disgorgement damages are awarded against tortfeasors – that in certain cases where a tort has been committed, the victim of the tort is entitled to 'waive the tort' and treat the tortfeasor as though he had acted lawfully, with all the consequences that doing so logically entails. The idea that the recovery of disgorgement damages in tort cases was based on 'waiver of tort' came under fierce attack from restitution scholars, who insisted that disgorgement damages were awarded against a tortfeasor because he had done something *wrong*, not because he was being treated as though he had not done anything wrong.[40] However, if awards of disgorgement damages *are* based on the 'waiver of tort' idea, then there would be certain torts for which disgorgement damages could *never* be claimed. For example, in the case of *AT* v *Dulghieru* (2009), where the claimants were forced by the defendants to have sex with clients, the claimants would not have been able to sue the defendants for disgorgement damages equal to the profits the defendants made by renting the claimants' bodies out, on the basis that the defendants were acting on their behalf by renting them out as it is unlawful to act as a prostitute's pimp. Similarly, if *Thug* were paid £5,000 to beat *Snitch* up, it would not be possible for *Snitch* to sue *Thug* for that £5,000 on the basis that *Thug* was acting on *Snitch*'s behalf in beating him up in return for £5,000: such an arrangement is simply not lawful and so *Snitch*'s case could not be decided on the basis that such an arrangement had existed in that case.

It seems to us that this last explanation of why tortfeasors can never be sued for disgorgement damages is also the best explanation. If this is right, then it would be a major error for the UK Supreme Court to take the position that disgorgement damages may be awarded in any case where a tortfeasor has made a gain from committing a tort. There could be no reason for taking such a wide view of when disgorgement damages will be available to the victim of a tort.

25.3 Licence fee damages

Licence fee damages are available for the following torts:

(1) *Conversion.* It is well established that licence fee damages may be awarded against someone who has committed the tort of conversion.[41]

So, for example, if A has converted B's property by using it, B will be entitled to sue A for damages designed to make A pay B a reasonable sum for the use he has made of B's property.[42] What if A did not *use* B's property but converted it by doing something to

---

[40] Such scholars would usually point to *United Australia Ltd* v *Barclays Bank Ltd* [1941] AC 1 as definitively establishing that awards of disgorgement damages were not based on a 'waiver of tort' as the House of Lords ruled in that case that, in an appropriate case, the victim of a tort could make alternative claims for compensatory damages and disgorgement damages and did not have to elect which remedy to go for until the time of judgment when she would know how much she could obtain under each remedy. It was argued that if one's ability to sue for disgorgement damages was based on a 'waiver of tort', then picking and choosing one's remedy in this way should be impossible: you would have to decide *first* whether you were going to sue on the tort or waive your claim, and then launch your claim.

[41] See *Kuwait Airways Corpn* v *Iraqi Airways Co (Nos 4 and 5)* [2002] 2 AC 883, at [87] (per Lord Nicholls).

[42] See, for example, *Strand Electric Engineering Co. Ltd* v *Brisford Entertainments* [1952] 2 QB 246 (defendants converted claimants' switchboards by using them in various theatre productions staged at the defendants' theatre; they were held liable to pay the claimants a reasonable sum for the use they had made of the switchboards).

prevent B getting hold of it? It does not matter: B will still be entitled to sue A for damages designed to make A pay B a reasonable sum for the *dominion* he has enjoyed over B's property.[43]

(2) *Trespass to land.* It is also well established that licence fee damages may be awarded against someone who has committed the tort of trespass to land.

So – if *Tenant* stays in *Landlord's* house beyond the term of the lease, *Landlord* will be entitled to sue *Tenant* for a reasonable sum – known as *mesne*[44] *profits* – for the use *Tenant* made of *Landlord's* house by staying in it beyond the term of his tenancy.[45]

More generally, if A commits the tort of trespass to land by using B's land without his consent for some purpose, B will be entitled to sue A for damages designed to make A pay B a reasonable sum for the use he has made of B's land.[46] The sum payable normally equals the going market rate for the use A has made of B's land, though that measure was displaced in favour of a lower sum in the unusual case of *Ministry of Defence* v *Ashman* (1993).[47] Where there is no going market rate, the sum payable is assessed by imagining how much A and B would have agreed A should have to pay for using B's land, assuming that they had each been bargaining in good faith and trying to reach a reasonable agreement.[48]

What if A commits the tort of trespass to land not by using B's land but by preventing B gaining access to his land? A will still have to pay B a reasonable sum for the dominion he has enjoyed over B's land while B was kept out. So in *Inverugie Investments Ltd* v *Hackett* (1995), the claimant leased 30 apartments in a hotel in the Bahamas but was then kept out of them for 15 years by the defendants, who owned the hotel. During those 15 years, the defendants let the apartments out to guests but at any one time only about 40 per cent of the apartments were let out. So the defendants used only about 40 per cent of the claimant's apartments during the 15 years they kept him out of them. However, during

---

[43] So if A takes one of B's chairs away for a year but does not use it, B will be entitled to sue A for damages designed to make A pay B a reasonable sum for the dominion he has enjoyed over the chair for a year – and this is so even if B did not miss the chair at all in the year A had it: *Mediana (Owners of Steamship)* v *Comet (Owners of Lightship)* [1900] AC 113, 117 (per Earl of Halsbury LC).

[44] Pronounced 'mean'.

[45] *Swordheath Properties* v *Tabet* [1979] 1 WLR 285; *Ministry of Defence* v *Ashman* [1993] 2 EGLR 102; *Ministry of Defence* v *Thompson* [1993] 2 EGLR 107.

[46] See *Whitwham* v *Westminster Brymbo Coal & Coke Company* [1896] 2 Ch 538 (defendants who committed the tort of trespass to land by tipping refuse from their colliery onto the claimants' land held liable to pay the claimants a reasonable sum for the use they had made of the claimants' land); and *Penarth Dock Engineering Co* v *Pounds* [1963] 1 Lloyd's Rep 359 (defendant committed the tort of trespass to land by keeping his boat tied up in the claimants' docks; he was held liable to pay the claimants a reasonable sum for the use he had made of their land).

[47] In that case the defendant was a military wife whose husband left her, and she was forced to stay on in military quarters as the local council could not re-house her and her children. Hoffmann J refused to hold the defendant liable to pay the going market rate for living in quarters like the ones she was trespassing on, and instead only held her liable to pay the rent she would have had to pay had she been in council accommodation.

[48] See *Bocardo SA* v *Star Energy UK Onshore Ltd* [2011] 1 AC 380 (trespass to claimant's land by allowing pipelines to intrude under the claimant's land, while extracting oil from under the land; held, had the claimant and defendants bargained in good faith as to how much the defendants should pay the claimant to be allowed to drill under his land, the defendants would not have ended up paying very much as they could at any point obtained a licence from the Crown entitling them to insert pipelines under the claimant's land).

those 15 years they enjoyed dominion over all the claimant's apartments, 365 days a year. Accordingly, it was held that the claimant was entitled to sue the defendant for damages designed to make the defendants pay the claimant the going rate for renting apartments like the claimant's 365 days a year for 15 years.

(3) *Private nuisance.* The Court of Appeal decision in *Forsyth-Grant* v *Allen* (2008) seems to indicate that in an 'exceptional' case (Patten J, with Mummery LJ agreeing)[49] or an 'appropriate' case (Toulson LJ),[50] licence fee damages may be awarded against a defendant who commits the tort of private nuisance. In such a case, the damages would be 'calculated by reference to the price, which the defendant might reasonably be required to pay for a relaxation of the claimant's rights so as to avoid an injunction.'[51]

(4) *Inducing a breach of contract.* It seems that licence fee damages *may* be awarded against someone who commits the tort of inducing a breach of contract. So, for example, in *Lightly* v *Clouston* (1808), the defendant persuaded the claimant's apprentice to work as a mariner on his ship instead of working on board the claimant's ship. Mansfield CJ held that the claimant was entitled to compel the defendant to pay him a reasonable sum for the work that his apprentice did for the defendant.[52] However, these cases may be based on an old-fashioned idea that someone's servants were his property.

(5) *Non-proprietary torts.* Depending on how one reads the Court of Appeal's decision in *Devenish Nutrition* v *Sofia Aventis* (2009), the Court of Appeal *may* have ruled out licence fee damages being awarded in *any* case involving a non-proprietary tort. It depends on whether one thinks that the Court of Appeal, in ruling out awards of disgorgement damages for non-proprietary torts, was also ruling out the award of licence fee damages for such torts. We can test whether licence fee damages should be awarded in cases where a non-proprietary tort has been committed by asking whether we should allow such a claim to be made in the case where *Thug* beats up *Snitch*. We would suggest there are two serious problems in the way of allowing licence fee damages to be awarded in such a case.

First, we cannot assess what a 'reasonable sum' might be for the privilege of being allowed to beat someone else up. And it would be contrary to public policy for the courts to engage in the exercise of imagining *Thug* and *Snitch* bargaining to determine how much *Thug* should pay *Snitch* for the privilege of beating him up. Any such bargain would be unenforceable in real life as contrary to public policy – so giving effect to such a 'hypothetical bargain' would also be contrary to public policy. The same point applies even more strongly to a case where a claimant has been forced by a defendant to have sex with someone else, as in *AT* v *Dulghieru* (2009). The courts would bring themselves into disrepute if they attempted to determine what a 'reasonable sum' might be for hiring out your body for sex.

Secondly, if it is correct that licence fee damages are – as we have argued – compensatory, in that they are designed to compensate the victim of a tort for being deprived of a power to decide what would happen to her and the things under her control that she was supposed to have under the law, it would be hard to argue for allowing such damages to be awarded in case like the one where *Thug* beats up *Snitch* or a case like *AT* v *Dulghieru*. To award such damages in these kinds of cases would send out the message that it is

---

[49] [2008] EWCA Civ 505, at [31]–[32].
[50] [2008] EWCA Civ 505, at [38].
[51] [2008] EWCA Civ 505, at [32] (per Patten J).
[52] See also *Foster* v *Stewart* (1814) 3 M & S 191, 105 ER 582.

possible to put a money value on the freedom to decide whether or not to allow someone to hit you, or the freedom to decide who you will have sex with. However, a civilised society will regard these freedoms as being beyond price and will refuse to allow them to be 'monetised' by awarding licence fee damages when they are violated.[53] In such cases, the victim of a tort must seek other remedies.

Further reading

The areas of law dealt with in this chapter are usually discussed in texts on the law of restitution under the title 'Restitution for Wrongs'. However, discussion of the law on 'restitution for wrongs' got off to a bad start in the UK through adoption of two assumptions: (1) that in all restitution for wrongs cases, the wrongdoer is stripped of a gain he has made from his wrong; and (2) that all restitution for wrongs cases can be explained as giving effect to the principle that 'no wrongdoer should profit from his wrong'. The academic literature on the areas of law covered in this chapter has yet to recover fully from these two historic errors, and should as a result be approached with care and scepticism.

James Edelman's monograph *Gain-Based Damages* (Hart Publishing, 2002) was a major achievement, in that it brought into question whether (1) and (2) were true, but only at the expense of endorsing another major misconception: (3) that awards of disgorgement damages are designed to deter people from wronging others.

Craig Rotherham is emerging as a major thinker on this area of law: see his 'The conceptual structure of restitution for wrongs' (2007) 66 *Cambridge Law Journal* 172; '*Wrotham Park* damages and accounts of profits: compensation or restitution?' [2008] *Lloyd's Maritime and Commercial Law Quarterly* 25; 'The normative foundations of restitution for wrongs: justifying gain-based relief for nuisance' in Robertson and Tang (eds), *The Goals of Private Law* (Hart Publishing, 2009); 'Gain-based relief in tort after *Att-Gen* v *Blake*' (2010) 126 *Law Quarterly Review* 102.

On the nature of licence fee damages, it is well worth reading Burrows, 'Are "damages on the *Wrotham Park* basis" compensatory, restitutionary or neither?' in Saidov and Cunnington (eds), *Current Themes in the Law of Contract Damages* (Hart, 2008), Jaffey, 'Licence fee damages' (2011) 19 *Restitution Law Review* 95, Barker, 'Damages without loss – can Hohfeld help?' (2014) 34 *Oxford Journal of Legal Studies* 1, and McBride, 'Restitution for wrongs' in Mitchell and Swadling (eds), *The Restatement Third – Restitution and Unjust Enrichment: Critical and Comparative Essays* (Hart, 2014).

Sarah Worthington's 'Reconsidering disgorgement for wrongs' (1999) 62 *Modern Law Review* 219 is also worth reading.

---

[53] See, further, McBride 2014, 274–5, and 279–80. For a different view, see Keren-Paz 2010b.

Chapter 26
Nominal and vindicatory damages

Aims and objectives

Reading this chapter should enable you to:

(1) Understand what vindicatory damages are, and the history of their gradual recognition as a distinct form of damages.

(2) Get a good grasp of the (currently very uncertain) state of the law on whether such damages can ever be awarded against a tortfeasor, and if so when.

(3) Form an intelligent view on whether such damages should ever be available in a tort case.

26.1 The basics

If the victim of a tort has suffered no loss as a result of that tort being committed, he or she might still be entitled to sue the person who committed that tort for *nominal damages* – usually £5.[1] Whether she will be entitled to sue for such damages will depend on whether the tort that she is the victim of is *actionable per se* – that is, actionable without her having to prove that she has suffered any loss as a result of that tort. The following torts are actionable *per se*: torts involving a trespass to someone's person;[2] trespass to land;

---

[1] See, for example, *Brandeis Goldschmidt & Co v Western Transport* [1981] QB 864, 874; *Watkins v Secretary of State for the Home Department* [2004] EWCA Civ 966, at [61]. Until the 1980s, the conventional sum awarded in making an award of nominal damages was £2: see, for example, *Child v Stenning* (1879) 11 Ch D 82; *Sykes v Midland Bank Executor & Trustee Co* [1971] 1 QB 113. The press release accompanying the Supreme Court decision in *Lumba v Secretary of State for the Home Department* [2011] UKSC 12 – in which the claimants were awarded nominal damages – said that the claimants in that case were only awarded £1 in nominal damages; but the judgments in the case make no mention of the sum that should be awarded in nominal damages.

[2] That is, assault, battery and false imprisonment.

private nuisances involving an interference with someone's right to light or other rights attached to his land.[3]

Nominal damages are awarded for a variety of reasons, principally to allow a claimant who has been the victim of a tort committed by the defendant to have it publically established that the defendant's conduct amounted to a legal wrong, and – by obtaining a verdict in her favour – to prevent the defendant obtaining a licence to commit the same wrong in future (as might happen, for example, if the defendant is in the habit of walking across the claimant's land in a way that causes no harm to the land, and could acquire a right by prescription to walk across the land if allowed to do so without objection for a number of years).[4] However, the fact that nominal damages only amount to £5 means that they are an unsatisfactory remedy where C is the victim of a very serious tort that is actionable *per se* and the circumstances are such where aggravated or exemplary damages are available against D. For example, if C is tricked into having sex with D by being led to believe that D is her boyfriend (and D is similarly tricked into having sex with C by being told that C wants to sleep with him), allowing C to sue D for battery and obtain £5 in nominal damages from D seems inadequate to acknowledge the seriousness of the wrong that C suffered in this case. Hence the need for *vindicatory damages*, which are designed to vindicate a claimant's rights by making a defendant pay the claimant a significant sum for the mere fact that he has violated the claimant's rights. The availability of such damages in English law is a matter of serious controversy. In recent years, an increasing number of judges[5] and academics[6] have argued that: (1) at least in some tort cases, a claimant should be able to claim vindicatory damages; and (2) a number of established damages awards should be re-analysed as being vindicatory in nature. In other words, they argue that we *should* allow claimants to sue for vindicatory damages (at least in some tort cases), and that we *already do* allow claims for vindicatory damages to be made in some tort cases (though we may currently and inaccurately call such damages something else (such as 'compensatory' or 'gain-based') when they are claimed).

A major impetus behind this development has been the widespread adoption of human rights legislation. In a case where A's human rights have been violated but A has suffered no or very little loss as a result (for example, where A's telephone has been unlawfully tapped by the police, or where A has been unlawfully denied access to a solicitor while in custody), allowing A to sue the government for a small sum in compensatory damages would seem to make a mockery of his rights. Hence the suggestion that in this sort of case, A should be allowed to sue for vindicatory damages – a significant sum to mark the significance of the violation of his rights that has occurred in this case.[7] However, it is still not clear whether vindicatory damages have a place in the law of tort. The issue of

---

[3] See *Nicholls* v *Ely Beet Sugar Factory Ltd (No 2)* [1936] 1 Ch 343, 348–9.

[4] See, for example, *Bower* v *Hill* (1835) 1 Bing NC 549, 555; 131 ER 1229, 1231.

[5] See Scott 2007.

[6] Notably, Stevens 2007, 59–91.

[7] See *Att-Gen of Trinidad and Tobago* v *Ramanoop* [2006] 1 AC 328, at [19]; *James* v *Attorney General of Trinidad and Tobago* [2010] UKSC 23, at [35]; *Inniss* v *Attorney-General of Saint Christopher & Nevis* [2008] UKPC 42, at [27]; *Vancouver* v *Ward* [2010] 2 SCR 28, at [25]–[29]; *Taunoa* v *Attorney General* [2007] NZSC 70, at [109], [255], [372].

whether the victim of a tort can sue for vindicatory damages was addressed by the Supreme Court in the recent case of *Lumba* v *Secretary of State for the Home Department* (2011),[8] and – as we will see – the Supreme Court Justices could not reach agreement on this issue.

26.2 Nominal damages

A. Torts that are and are not actionable *per se*

As has already been observed, the trespass torts and the tort of private nuisance when it involves an interference with someone's rights to light, or other rights attached to the claimant's land, are torts that are actionable *per se*. The classic example of a tort that is *not* actionable *per se* is negligence. So if *Driver*'s bad driving results in his *almost* running over *Pedestrian, Pedestrian* will *not* be entitled to sue *Driver* for nominal damages. Private nuisances not involving an interference with someone's right to light or other rights attached to his land do not seem to be actionable *per se*.[9] It is unclear whether the tort of trespass to goods is actionable *per se*. Ancient authority indicates that it is not,[10] but the Court of Appeal assumed – though without the benefit of any argument on the matter – that trespass to goods could be actionable *per se* in *White* v *Withers* (2009).[11] The House of Lords has made it clear that the tort of misfeasance in public office is not actionable *per se*.[12] It seems that it will be very rare for the breach of a statutory duty owed to another to be actionable *per se*.[13]

Libel is often said to be a tort that is actionable *per se*. This is because if A publishes to C a statement referring to B that is defamatory of B, B will still be entitled to sue A for damages even if she cannot show that she suffered any loss as a result of A's publication. However, the better analysis of what is going on in a libel case such as B's is that B does not have to *prove* that she has suffered any loss as a result of A's libel. Instead, it will be *presumed* that she did suffer some loss as a result of A's libel and it will be up to a jury or a judge to put a figure on how much of a loss she suffered.[14] If the loss suffered by B seems to the jury or judge to be very small because, for example, C did not believe A's statement or because B was of such bad character that she had no reputation to lose, then B will not

---

[8] Reported at [2011] UKSC 12, and referred to below as '*Lumba*'.

[9] Though see *Dobson* v *Thames Water Utilities Ltd* [2009] EWCA Civ 28, where it was suggested (at [34]) that a claimant might be entitled to sue in private nuisance, but obtain no more than nominal damages where the nuisance had not caused them an *actual* loss of amenity.

[10] *Slater* v *Swann* (1730) 2 Stra 872, 93 ER 906.

[11] [2009] EWCA Civ 1122, at [62] (per Ward LJ), and [71] (per Sedley LJ).

[12] *Watkins* v *Secretary of State for the Home Department* [2006] 2 AC 395.

[13] In *Cullen* v *Chief Constable of the Royal Ulster Constabulary* [2003] 1 WLR 1763 (discussed above, § 18.2), Lord Hutton held that the breach of a statutory duty owed by A to B might be actionable *per se* if the statutory duty was contained in a written constitution, but if the duty in question was imposed by an ordinary statute, A's breach of that duty would only be actionable if it caused B to suffer 'loss or injury of a kind for which the law awards damages' (ibid, at [47], quoting *Pickering* v *Liverpool Daily Post* [1991] 2 AC 370, at 420 (per Lord Bridge)).

[14] To the same effect, see Mitchell 2005, 53.

be awarded very much by way of damages[15] – but the damages paid to her will still be *compensatory in nature, not nominal.*[16]

B. Theories

Why are some torts actionable *per se* and other torts only actionable if the victim can show that she has suffered some loss as a result of that tort being committed? Some people think that the reasons for this are *deep*; other people think that the reasons are relatively *shallow*.

(1) *Shallow theories.* A theory as to why some torts are actionable *per se* and others are not is *shallow* if it explains the distinction on purely pragmatic grounds. So such a theory might say that the tort of trespass to land is actionable *per se* because that enables landowners to stop harmless trespassers acquiring a licence to go over their land; while negligence is not actionable *per se* because there does not seem to be much point in allowing *Pedestrian* to sue *Driver* for *almost* running her over. Such a theory might go on to say that libel is actionable *per se* (if it is) because that enables the subject of defamatory but harmless allegations that have been published in permanent form to get a judgment that she can point to should anyone in the future see those allegations and be tempted to think less well of her. But you will not normally be entitled to sue for slanderous but harmless words, because the fact that those words are not in a permanent form means that it is unlikely that people will revisit those words in future and need to be told that those words were the subject of a successful claim for defamation.

Some support for the idea that the reasons why some torts are actionable *per se* and others not are relatively shallow is provided by the decision of the House of Lords in *Watkins* v *Secretary of State for the Home Department* (2006), where their Lordships gave relatively shallow reasons why misfeasance in public office should not be actionable *per se*. They did not see any real need for the tort to be made actionable *per se*: abuses of public power that did not cause any harm could be sanctioned through disciplinary proceedings, and corrected through applications for judicial review.[17] They were also concerned that making the tort actionable *per se* would unlock the door to exemplary damages being awarded in cases where a claimant had not suffered any loss as a result of an abuse of public power: they doubted whether exemplary damages should be awarded in such a case.[18]

(2) *Deep theories.* A theory as to why some torts are actionable *per se* and others not is *deep* if it explains the distinction as resting on fundamental ideas about the nature of a tort or the basis of tort liability.

For example, Robert Stevens concedes that the reasons why torts such as slander (in most of its forms) and misfeasance in public office are not actionable *per se* are shallow in nature.[19] But he thinks the reason why negligence is not actionable *per se* is *deep*. The reason why *Pedestrian* cannot sue *Driver* for nominal damages in the case where *Driver* almost runs over *Pedestrian* is that *Driver* has done nothing wrong – committed

---

[15] In *Newstead* v *London Express Newspaper* [1940] 1 KB 377, the claimant was awarded one farthing. In *Reynolds* v *Times Newspapers Ltd* [2001] 2 AC 127, the claimant was awarded one penny.

[16] If the damages payable to B are extremely small because she had no reputation to lose when A libelled her, they will be known as *contemptuous* or *derisory* damages.

[17] [2006] 2 AC 395, at [26] (per Lord Bingham), [65] (per Lord Rodger), [81] (per Lord Carswell).

[18] [2006] 2 AC 395, at [32] (per Lord Hope), [64] (per Lord Rodger), [81] (per Lord Carswell).

[19] Stevens 2007, 88.

no tort – to *Pedestrian*. The only duty of care *Driver* owed *Pedestrian* was a CPR-focused duty to take care not to injure *Pedestrian* by driving carelessly.[20] As *Driver*'s bad driving did not result in injury to *Pedestrian*, *Pedestrian* cannot say that *Driver* has done anything wrong to her in this case.

26.3 Vindicatory damages

A. Examples?

A number of possible examples of awards of vindicatory damages can be given.

(1) *Other awards of damages.* Some theorists analyse other types of damages that we have already discussed as being truly vindicatory in nature.[21] For example, *nominal* damages look vindicatory in nature: it can be argued that they exist to mark the fact that the claimant's rights have been violated, and to mark the courts' disapproval of that fact, it is hard to see why they exist. Some theorists – as we have seen – re-analyse *compensatory* damages as serving a vindicatory purpose: that of giving the claimant in money form what he was entitled to in the first place from the defendant.[22] Robert Stevens argues that *exemplary* damages are vindicatory in nature,[23] quoting in support Lord Nicholls in *A v Bottrill* (2003): '[Exemplary damages] serve as an emphatic vindication of the [claimant's] rights.'[24] John Goldberg takes a similar view of exemplary damages. In *Huckle v Money* (1763), the claimant printer was falsely imprisoned under a general warrant for six hours (and treated to beef steaks and beer while imprisoned!) by royal agents, because the claimant had been involved in producing a newspaper that was critical of the government. A jury awarded the claimant £300 in damages (about £22,500 in today's money). Only about £20 of that award (about £1,500 in today's money) could be justified as genuinely compensatory. The Court of King's Bench refused to set aside the award:

> the small injury done to the plaintiff, or the inconsiderableness of his station and rank in life did not appear to the jury in that striking light in which the great point of law touching the liberty of the subject appeared to them at the trial; they saw a magistrate over all the King's subjects, exercising arbitrary power, violating Magna Charta, and attempting to destroy the liberty of the kingdom, by insisting upon the legality of this general warrant before them; they heard the King's Counsel, and saw the solicitor of the Treasury endeavouring to support and maintain the legality of the warrant in a tyrannical and severe manner. These are the ideas which struck the jury on the trial; and I think they have done right in giving exemplary damages.[25]

John Goldberg argues that the exemplary damages in this case were awarded in order to satisfy or vindicate the claimant's rights: 'the jury acted appropriately "in giving exemplary damages" because a relatively large award accurately reflected the enormity of the wrong that the victim had suffered at the hands of his government captors.'[26]

---

[20] On CPR-focused duties of care, see above, § 5.5.

[21] Cf. Witzleb & Carroll 2009, at 42: 'vindication of the [claimant's] legal right is the effect and purpose of *all* private law remedies' (emphasis added).

[22] See above, § 23.7(B).

[23] Stevens 2007, 85–8.

[24] [2003] 1 AC 449, at [29].

[25] (1763) 2 Wils KB 205, 206–7; 95 ER 768, 769.

[26] Goldberg 2006, 460–1.

(2) *Ashby v White* (1794). In *Ashby* v *White*, the electors of Aylesbury were called upon to elect two people to represent them in Parliament. Ashby was entitled to vote in the election and duly turned up to vote. Unfortunately, the four constables – including White – who were charged with conducting the election refused to allow Ashby to vote, and refused to count his vote. Ashby sued, claiming that he had a right to vote and that the constables had committed a tort in acting as they did. His claim was turned down in the Court of King's Bench by four votes to one. However, the House of Lords reversed this decision (by 50 votes to 16), preferring the opinion of the judge who dissented in the Court of King's Bench: Holt CJ. It is plain from Holt's judgment that he thought Ashby had to be given a remedy in this case in order to vindicate his right to vote:

> it is a great privilege to vote for a Parliament man, and sure every one that has that great privilege has a right in it; and if so, of necessary consequence he has an action to vindicate and maintain that right . . . it is a vain thing to imagine that there should be a right without a remedy . . .[27]

What is interesting is how much Ashby sued for in damages, and was presumably awarded when his case was reinstated in the House of Lords. He sued for £200, which is the equivalent of about £11,000 in today's money. Such a sum could not possibly be equivalent to any loss he suffered as a result of being denied the right to vote. The damages Ashby would have recovered on winning his case therefore look vindicatory in nature: they were awarded in order to ensure that Ashby's right to vote was not made meaningless. As Holt CJ remarked, 'the encouraging of remedies for injuries is the most effectual way to make these officers honest and observant of the constitutions of their cities and boroughs'.[28]

(3) *Property torts.* In *Mediana (Owners of Steamship)* v *Comet (Owners of Lightship)* (1900), Lord Halsbury LC observed that: 'the unlawful keeping back of what belongs to another person is of itself a ground for real damages, not nominal damages at all.'[29] In support of this proposition, he gave as an example:

> Supposing a person took away a chair out of my room and kept it for twelve months, could anybody say you had a right to diminish the damages by shewing that I did not usually sit in that chair, or that there were plenty of other chairs in the room?[30]

In such a case, he thought substantial damages would be payable (calculated by reference to how much it would cost to rent a chair for a year) even if no actual loss had been suffered by the claimant as a result of being deprived of the chair. The argument for analysing these damages as vindicatory in nature goes as follows.

People's property rights would become much weaker if people were only held liable to pay compensatory damages on violating them. In cases where the violation caused no material loss at all, the right would melt away and become ineffectual. In order to stop this happening, it could be argued that the law adopts the position that vindicatory damages are the *normal* remedy when someone's property rights are violated, and compensatory damages are awarded *on top* of vindicatory damages when a violation of someone's property

---

[27] (1794) 6 Mod 45, 53; 87 ER 810, 815.
[28] (1794) 6 Mod 45, 55; 87 ER 810, 817.
[29] [1900] AC 113, 118.
[30] [1900] AC 113, 117.

rights caused the property owner special loss. This is the position adopted by Robert Stevens,[31] citing two strong cases in favour of this position.[32] Stevens' position has come under attack from Andrew Burrows,[33] who thinks that when a property tort has been committed, the normal remedy should be compensation, and that the awards of what look like non-compensatory damages in property tort cases are really examples of a defendant tortfeasor not being allowed to take advantage of arrangements that the claimant entered into that allowed her to transfer the loss from the tort to someone else, or to avoid the loss that that tort would otherwise have caused her to suffer.[34]

(4) *Trespass to the person.* In *Ashley* v *Chief Constable of Sussex Police* (2008), Ashley was shot dead during a police raid on his house. In the course of his judgment, Lord Scott suggested that vindicatory damages might be awardable to Ashley's estate.[35] The suggestion is an attractive one because it fills whatever otherwise might be regarded as a loophole in the law. The loophole is illustrated by the **Murdered Tramp Problem**:

> *Tramp* lives on the streets and has no job and no prospects. One night, *Killer* walks up behind *Tramp* and shoots him through the head. *Tramp* dies instantly.

In this sort of case, if *Killer* cannot be sued for vindicatory damages, it does not seem that he will be liable to pay damages to *anyone* in this case. *Tramp* has no dependants who could sue for damages under the Fatal Accidents Act 1976. And *Tramp*'s estate cannot sue for damages under the Law Reform (Miscellaneous Provisions) Act 1934, as *Killer*'s tort in shooting *Tramp* caused *Tramp* no loss before he died. It might be thought that is unsatisfactory: that if we leave *Killer* to be dealt with by the criminal law, and leave his case untouched by tort law, we will be giving the poor and homeless less protection under the law than we would give the rich and privileged.

(5) *Defamation.* We have already seen that damages in defamation cases have a vindicatory function: part of the reason for giving a claimant substantial damages at the end of a defamation case is to send out a signal to the public at large that what was said about the claimant was untrue.[36] However, it is not clear that such damages are vindicatory in the sense that that term is being used here. Damages in defamation cases are intended, in

---

[31] Stevens 2007, 73–4. Though Stevens would use the word 'substitutive' rather than 'vindicatory' in this context, and strongly disapprove of the pragmatic explanation advanced in the text for the availability of vindicatory/substitutive damages in this context, arguing that the claimants are entitled to vindicatory/substitutive damages as of right (see above, § 23.7(B)).

[32] *The Sanix Ace* [1987] 1 Lloyds Rep 465 (owner of goods being shipped to buyer entitled to sue in respect of negligent damage to goods even though buyer agreed to pay full price for the goods whatever condition they were in when they were delivered to him); *Mediana (Owners of Steamship)* v *Comet (Owners of Lightship)* [1900] AC 113 (claimants entitled to sue for a reasonable sum for loss of use of lightship which was negligently damaged by defendants and needed to be repaired, even though the claimants had a spare lightship which they used while the damaged lightship was out of action and did not have to hire a replacement).

[33] Drawing on the arguments of Edelman 2009, 213–16.

[34] Burrows 2011, 638–40.

[35] [2008] 1 AC 962, at [22]. None of the other Law Lords who decided *Ashley* expressed agreement with Lord Scott on this issue.

[36] See above, § 16.12.

part, to vindicate the claimant's *reputation*, not to vindicate his *right that the defendant not unjustly defame him.*[37]

(6) *Invasion of privacy.* In *Mosley* v *News Group Newspapers* (2008), Eady J held that the damages payable for a wrongful invasion of privacy could include a vindicatory component 'to ensure that an infringed right is met with "an adequate remedy".'[38] So in a case where a wrongful invasion of privacy had caused little or no loss, substantial damages could still be awarded to a claimant 'to [mark] the fact that an unlawful intrusion has taken place.'[39]

(7) *Rees v Darlington Memorial Hospital NHS Trust (2004).* The most obvious example of vindicatory damages being awarded in the law of negligence is the House of Lords' decision in *Rees* v *Darlington Memorial Hospital NHS Trust* (2004) that a claimant who gives birth to an unwanted baby due to a defendant's negligence will be entitled to sue the defendant for a fixed sum of £15,000. Although such a sum is supposed to compensate the claimant for the 'loss of autonomy' she will suffer as a result of having to bring up an unwanted child, Lord Hope convincingly criticised this view of the award in *Rees* on the basis that it makes no sense to compensate for such a loss through a *fixed* award.[40] However, Lord Bingham argued that the fixed sum of £15,000 was not intended to be compensatory at all:

> The conventional award would not be, and would not be intended to be, compensatory. It would not be the product of calculation. But it would not be a nominal, let alone a derisory, award. It would afford some measure of recognition of the wrong done.[41]

Lord Bingham's emphasis on 'the wrong done' suggests that the fixed sum award made in *Rees* is vindicatory in nature – intended both to mark the fact that the claimant in a wrongful birth or wrongful pregnancy case has suffered a wrong and to ensure that the defendant incurs some sanction for violating the claimant's rights to be treated properly by the defendant.[42]

(8) *Chester v Afshar (2005).* Another example of vindicatory damages being awarded in the law of negligence is provided by the case of *Chester* v *Afshar* (2005). In that case, it will be recalled, the claimant was partially paralysed when an operation carried out by the defendant resulted in her suffering nerve damage in her back.[43] The defendant had wrongfully failed to warn the claimant of the very small (1–2 per cent) risk that the operation would result in her suffering such harm. Lord Hoffmann, in the minority, took the view that the claimant's claim for compensation for her paralysis should be dismissed, but that

---

[37] The distinction is marked by Eady J in his judgment in *Mosley* v *News Group Newspapers* [2008] EWHC 1777 (QB), at [216].

[38] Ibid.

[39] [2008] EWHC 1777 (QB), at [231].

[40] [2004] 1 AC 309, at [71]–[73].

[41] [2004] 1 AC 309, at [8].

[42] Nolan 2007b objects (at 79) to this analysis on the ground that negligence is not actionable in the absence of proof of damage: so 'while torts such as battery can vindicate rights in the absence of harm, negligence cannot'. Meh. If duties of care are conduct-focused (as we have argued, above § 4.5) and a duty of care has been breached without causing the claimant harm, there may still be reasons why the courts should make an award to mark the fact that the claimant's rights (the flipside of the duties owed to her) have been breached. If those reasons exist, why should the courts be prevented from responding to them simply because there is a mantra that 'damage is the gist of negligence'?

[43] The case is discussed in detail above, at § 8.10.

there was a case for awarding her a 'modest solatium'.[44] Such an award looks vindicatory in nature – it is intended to give the claimant something for the fact that her right to be treated properly by the defendant (which right encompasses a right to be told about the risks associated with her operation) has been violated.

The majority – it could be argued – took a different route to vindicating the claimant's right to be treated properly. Even though the defendant's failure to treat the claimant properly did not *cause* her to become paralysed,[45] the majority still allowed the claimant to sue the defendant for compensation for her paralysis in order to ensure that her right to be treated properly did not become meaningless. As Lord Hope observed, in terms reminiscent of Holt CJ's judgment in *Ashby* v *White*, over 200 years earlier:

> The function of the law is to enable rights to be vindicated and to provide remedies when duties have been breached. Unless this is done the duty is a hollow one, stripped of all practical force and devoid of all content. It will have lost its ability to protect the patient and thus to fulfil the only purpose which brought it into existence. On policy grounds therefore I would hold that the test of causation is satisfied in this case.[46]

However, as the Court of Appeal recently pointed out in *Shaw* v *Kovac*, if the majority's approach in *Chester* v *Afshar* was intended to vindicate the claimant's right to choose whether or not to have her operation, it has the weakness of *not* allowing the claimant the ability to sue at all where the operation went well.[47]

B. The *Lumba* decision

The case of *Lumba* v *Secretary of State for the Home Department* (2011) provided the Supreme Court with an ideal opportunity to clarify the position of vindicatory damages in the law of tort. A majority of the Supreme Court held that the claimants had been falsely imprisoned by the government in being detained pursuant to a secret and blanket policy that was inconsistent with the government's official position as to when people like the claimants would be detained. At the same time, the Supreme Court took the view that the claimants had not suffered any loss as a result of being falsely imprisoned as they could have been legitimately detained even under the government's announced policy. So the Supreme Court had a choice between awarding the claimants merely nominal damages for being falsely imprisoned, or awarding them something more substantial by way of vindicatory damages to mark the fact that their rights not to be falsely imprisoned had been violated by the government.

The result of the *Lumba* case was a signal lack of clarity as to when vindicatory damages will be available in tort. Of the six Supreme Court Justices who thought the claimants had been falsely imprisoned, three (Lords Walker and Hope and Lady Hale) thought the claimants should be awarded vindicatory damages, and three (Lords Dyson, Collins and Kerr) thought that the claimants should be awarded nominal damages. Because the remaining three Supreme Court Justices who decided *Lumba* (Lords Phillips, Brown and Rodger) were in favour of giving the claimants nothing at all on the ground that they had

---

[44] [2005] 1 AC 134, at [34].

[45] Because there was a merely coincidental connection between the defendant's wrong and the claimant's paralysis: see above, § 8.10.

[46] [2005] 1 AC 134, at [87].

[47] [2017] EWCA Civ 1028, at [71].

not been falsely imprisoned, the claimants ended up merely getting nominal damages. On the issue of when vindicatory damages should be available in tort:

(1) Lord *Dyson* thought that vindicatory damages should *never* be available: he could see 'no justification for letting such an unruly horse loose on our law.' 'Undesirable uncertainty would result' from opening the door to such awards being made, both in terms of for what torts vindicatory damages would be available, and as against which defendants. He thought that the purpose of vindicating claimants' rights was adequately served through remedies such as compensatory damages, declarations that a wrong had been committed, and awards of exemplary damages.[48]

(2) Lord *Collins* agreed, arguing that there was no authority that justified 'a conclusion that there is a separate head of vindicatory damages in English law' and there was no case for recognising one here.[49] The award of a fixed sum of £15,000 in wrongful birth and wrongful pregnancy cases 'served a vindicatory purpose' but did not amount to 'vindicatory damages'.[50]

(3) Lord *Phillips* (dissenting on the issue of whether the government had falsely imprisoned the claimants) said that had he 'agreed with Lord Dyson on liability, I would have shared his approach to damages. I also endorse Lord Collins' conclusions in relation to vindicatory damages.'[51]

(4) Lord *Brown* (also dissenting on the issue of whether the tort of false imprisonment had been committed in *Lumba*) did not say anything about vindicatory damages in his judgment. However, he did make it clear that he thought the position taken by *Dyson*, *Collins* and *Kerr* – ruling that the claimant *had* been falsely imprisoned but ruling that only nominal damages should be awarded him because he had suffered no loss as a result of being falsely imprisoned – made no sense. He thought that *if* the claimant had been falsely imprisoned (and was aware he was being imprisoned)[52] then he should be awarded substantial damages.[53] It was for this reason that he thought that the UK Supreme Court should find that the claimant had *not* been falsely imprisoned.[54] One way of reading this aspect of Lord *Brown*'s judgment is that he agreed with *Walker*, *Hope* and *Hale* that if someone was falsely imprisoned but suffered no material loss as a result then they should still obtain a substantial award by way of vindicatory damages.[55] But another way of reading Lord *Brown*'s judgment is that he thought that if someone had been falsely imprisoned, they would always be due substantial *compensatory* damages for the loss of liberty they had thereby suffered. In support of this second reading, Lord *Brown* went out of his way to express agreement with Lord *Dyson*'s judgment on every aspect except the issue of whether the claimant had been falsely imprisoned – and, of course, Lord *Dyson*'s judgment was hostile to awards of vindicatory damages ever being made.[56]

(5) Lord *Rodger* agreed with Lord *Brown*.

---

[48] *Lumba*, at [101].
[49] *Lumba*, at [237].
[50] *Lumba*, at [236].
[51] *Lumba*, at [335].
[52] *Lumba*, at [344].
[53] *Lumba*, at [343]-[345].
[54] *Lumba*, at [342], [346].
[55] For this reading, see Varuhas 2014, at 282.
[56] *Lumba*, at [362].

(6) Lord *Kerr* did not rule out the possibility that vindicatory damages could be available in tort, but thought that 'such an award could only be justified where the declaration that a claimant's right has been infringed provides insufficiently emphatic recognition of the seriousness of the defendant's default.' He thought that was not the case here: 'The defendant's failures have been thoroughly acknowledged and exposed.'[57]

(7) Lord *Walker* seemed to take the view that vindicatory damages should be available in cases where a claimant's 'constitutional rights' have been violated or where there has been 'an assault on individual's person or reputation'. He was in favour of awarding £1,000 in vindicatory damages to each of the claimants in *Lumba*.[58]

(8) Lord *Hope* seemed to think that vindicatory damages should be available in tort where a claimant had suffered a serious violation of her 'fundamental rights'. He thought *Lumba* (unlike *Rees* v *Darlington Memorial Hospital NHS Trust* (2004))[59] was such a case:

> the conduct of the officials in this case amounted . . . to a serious abuse of power and it was deplorable. It is not enough merely to declare that this was so. Something more is required, and I think this is best done by making an award of damages that is not merely nominal.[60]

Lord *Hope* was content to agree with Lord *Walker*'s suggested damages of £1,000 for each claimant 'although I, for my part, would have arrived at a substantially lower figure.'[61]

(9) Lady *Hale* seemed to think that vindicatory damages should be available where 'important rights' of the claimant had been violated. As examples of such 'important rights' she instanced 'the rights to bodily integrity and personal autonomy, the right to limit one's family and to live one's life in the way planned' (which rights justified a vindicatory award in *Rees*)[62] and 'the right to be free from arbitrary imprisonment by the state.'[63] Accordingly, she thought that *Lumba* was an appropriate case for an award of vindicatory damages:

> perhaps £500 rather than the £1,000 suggested by Lord Walker, designed to recognise that the claimant's fundamental constitutional rights have been breached by the state and to encourage all concerned to avoid anything like it happening again.[64]

None of the judgments in *Lumba* on whether and when vindicatory damages will be available in tort are at all impressive. Lords Hope and Walker and Lady Hale's vacillation on the issue of how much the claimants in *Lumba* should have been awarded only strengthens Lord Dyson's argument that undesirable uncertainty might be injected into the law by the widespread availability of vindicatory damages; as does their failure to agree on what sort of rights the violation of which should give rise to a right to sue for vindicatory damages. On the other hand, Lords Dyson, Collins and Phillips failed to address the argument that vindicatory damages are *already* being awarded by the courts, and their existence cannot simply be wished away. In particular, Lord Collins' assertion that the conventional award of £15,000 in a wrongful birth or a wrongful pregnancy case serves a 'vindicatory purpose' but does not amount to a form of vindicatory damages is mystifying.

---

[57] *Lumba*, at [256].
[58] *Lumba*, at [195].
[59] Lord Hope reaffirmed his opposition to the conventional award in *Rees* in *Lumba*, at [180].
[60] *Lumba*, at [176].
[61] *Lumba*, at [180].
[62] *Lumba*, at [216].
[63] *Lumba*, at [217].
[64] Ibid.

C. After *Lumba*

Since *Lumba* was decided, the courts have tended to assume that vindicatory damages cannot be awarded under English law in an ordinary tort case. In *Weller* v *Associated Newspapers Ltd* (2014), it was held at first instance that vindicatory damages could not be awarded against a defendant who had committed the tort of misuse of private information. In *Bostridge* v *Oxleas NHS Foundation Trust* (2015), the Court of Appeal refused to allow vindicatory damages to be awarded to a patient who had been unlawfully detained in a hospital when, had the proper procedures been followed, he could have been lawfully detained. And in *Shaw* v *Kovac* (2017), the Court of Appeal held that an award of vindicatory damages could not be made to a patient who had been subjected to medical treatment without being given the opportunity to make an informed choice as to whether or not to have that treatment.

However, the fact that claims for vindicatory damages were made in cases like *Weller*, *Bostridge* and *Shaw* suggests that the issue as to whether such damages *should* be made available in tort cases is still a live one, and one worth discussing here. Our discussion can begin with Lord Dyson's criticism of the suggestion that vindicatory damages should be awarded in *Lumba*:

> If they were awarded here, then they could in principle be awarded in any case involving a battery or false imprisonment by an arm of the state. Indeed, why limit it to such torts? And why limit it to torts committed by the state?[65]

These are good questions that we want to address here. *In principle*, we see no reason why vindicatory damages should not be made available whenever someone has committed a tort and the standard remedies for that tort do not provide an adequate sanction for that tort being committed. We think that vindicatory damages have a useful role to play in ensuring that *no one* feels that they can ride roughshod over *any* of the rights that the law of tort recognises us as having against other people.

However, *in practice*, we recognise that making vindicatory damages so widely available is liable to overburden the courts' limited resources with a multiplicity of tort claims. Given this, we would suggest that the availability of vindicatory damages be limited to cases where the standard remedies for a particular tort will almost always tend to be quite weak and limited. This will be the case where tort law provides us with rights that are designed to protect intangible interests of ours – in particular, our interest in being able to *choose* for ourselves what happens to us and what happens to our property. Where what we can call a *choice right* is violated by someone else, the standard remedies for committing a tort are liable to be particularly weak because it will be hard for a claimant to prove that being deprived of a particular choice has actually made her financially worse off in any way. In such cases, vindicatory damages have a vital role to play in ensuring that people are not allowed to override the law's decision that a particular choice should be made by the claimant and not by anyone else, and it is not an accident that they have been made available in the past in cases involving the violation of a choice right like *Ashby*, *Rees*, and *Chester* v *Afshar*.

So we think vindicatory damages should be available for torts involving the appropriation of someone else's property; invasion of privacy; battery (where the battery involves unwanted medical treatment or physical attention); false imprisonment (where the

---
[65] *Lumba*, at [101].

imprisonment involves preventing someone going where they have the power and desire to go); and negligence (where the negligence results in someone not being able to make an informed choice about their medical treatment, or having an unwanted baby). In contrast, we do not think that a particularly strong case can be made for extending the availability of vindicatory damages to cases of wrongfully damaging someone else's property or person or reputation. In such cases, the standard remedies for committing a tort will normally prove sturdy enough to provide sufficient sanction for the defendant's wrongdoing.

Turning to the second question posed by Lord Dyson – whether vindicatory damages should be limited to cases of torts committed by the State – again, *in principle*, we see no reason why vindicatory damages should not be made available against *anyone* who has committed a tort where the standard remedies for that tort are not likely to provide an adequate sanction for that kind of wrongdoing. However, *in practice*, it has to be admitted that the concern underlying awards of vindicatory damages – that the law provide an adequate sanction for violating someone else's rights – is magnified in cases where a defendant is wealthy or powerful enough not to have to worry very much about the consequences of violating someone else's rights. In such cases, it is especially important that vindicatory damages be made available so that even the richest and most powerful defendant will be given pause for thought before trampling on someone else's rights. So in practice, we think that vindicatory damages should be made available in cases where the state or a company or an employee of the State or a company has committed one of the torts set out in the previous paragraph. In cases where a private individual, not working for the state or a company, has committed one of those torts, we think the case for making vindicatory damages available against such a defendant is not especially strong.

Further reading

Anyone wishing to explore the law on vindicatory damages still further must read **Robert Stevens'** chapter on **'Remedies' (Chapter 4)** in his *Torts and Rights* (OUP, 2007), **Normann Witzleb and Robyn Carroll's 'The role of vindication in tort damages'** (2009) 17 *Tort Law Review* 16, **Kit Barker's 'Private and public: the mixed concept of vindication in torts and private law'** (in Pitel, Neyers and Chamberlain (eds), *Tort Law: Challenging Orthodoxy* (Hart Publishing, 2013)) and **Jason Varuhas' 'The concept of "vindication" in the law of torts: rights, interests and damages'** (2014) 34 *Oxford Journal of Legal Studies* 253.

Chapter 27
Injunctions

Aims and objectives

Reading this chapter should enable you to:

(1) Distinguish between the different kinds of injunction that may be granted in a tort case.

(2) Understand the principles governing the award of interim and final injunctions.

(3) Discuss whether injunctions should be made more, or less, readily available in cases where a defendant's conduct threatens the safety of a claimant's person or violates a claimant's property rights.

27.1 The basics

An injunction is 'a court order prohibiting a person from doing something or requiring a person to do something'.[1] In some circumstances, a claimant will seek an injunction to prevent a defendant from committing a tort in relation to him or her.[2] In particular, a claimant may find this remedy attractive if the defendant is continuously doing something that amounts to a tort, or regularly does something that amounts to a tort, or seems to be on the verge of doing something that will amount to a tort.

For example, if *Breeze* regularly lands his hot air balloon on *Mown*'s land, continuing to do so despite knowing that *Mown* objects, then *Mown* may want to seek an injunction that will order *Breeze* not to commit the tort of trespass to land by landing his balloon on *Mown*'s land in the future. If such an injunction is issued against *Breeze* then he is very likely to obey it; a defendant who ignores a court order will be in contempt of court

---

[1] Civil Procedure Rules, glossary. The general authority of the High Court to grant injunctions is found in Senior Courts Act 1981, s 37(1).

[2] Injunctions are also available in many circumstances outside tort law. For example, s 34 of the Policing and Crime Act 2009 empowers a court to award a 'gang injunction' to help prevent gang-related violence. Clearly many of the things that a 'gang injunction' can prohibit a person from doing, such as wearing particular gang-related articles of clothing in particular places, would not amount to *torts* if the person concerned was to do them. This chapter is focused on injunctions *in tort law*.

and can be punished, even imprisoned.[3] Moreover, if *Mown* expects *Breeze* to continue trespassing, then it may be to his advantage to obtain an injunction once and for all, rather than having to return to court to seek damages for each of *Breeze's* future trespasses.

Regularly repeated and continuing torts are common examples of situations where claimants may have good reasons for seeking injunctions. Another example is where, if the defendant goes ahead and commits a tort, the claimant is likely to suffer some form of harm that can never be fully redressed by an award of damages. For example, if *Diva* learns that *Redtop* is about to commit the tort of misuse of private information in relation to her, by publishing intimate text messages from her stolen phone, then she is likely to want a remedy that will prevent this tort from being committed: obtaining damages *after* publication will never re-establish *Diva's* privacy, and she may already have more money than she knows how to spend.

The examples concerning *Mown* and *Diva* explain why injunctions can be an attractive remedy for claimants. But they also indicate why courts must be cautious about granting this remedy: injunctions restrict the liberty of those they are granted against in a far more direct way than awards of damages, and may sometimes impose disproportionate burdens on those who are subject to them. Let's use the hot air balloon case to illustrate the restriction of liberty: suppose that *Breeze* claims that the nature of hot air ballooning makes it very difficult for him to know where the wind will blow him, and consequently, if he is ordered *never* to land on *Mown's* land, on pain of punishment for contempt of court, he will have to stop launching his balloon anywhere near *Mown's* land, even though most of his flights cause no problems because the owners of most nearby farms are happy for him to land in their fields. If so, *Breeze* may ask: 'Is is really appropriate to grant a remedy that will restrict my liberty so severely just to avoid an occasional minor annoyance to *Mown*?' And let's use *Diva's* case to illustrate the risk of a defendant being subject to a disproportionate burden: suppose that *Redtop* can show that if it is ordered not to publish *Diva's* text messages it will have to recall and pulp a large number of newspapers that it has already printed and distributed to wholesalers, and this will cause it financial loss out of all proportion to the amount of damages that *Diva* might expect to be awarded if the texts are published. These concerns – about effects on liberty and disproportionate burdens – help to explain why courts do not automatically grant injunctions whenever a tort has been committed. Instead, injunctions are a 'discretionary' remedy.

Saying that injunctions are a discretionary remedy does not, of course, mean that a court has a *free* choice as to whether to grant one or not; it simply means that courts will not *automatically* grant them. Instead each court must make a judgment about whether an injunction is appropriate in the particular circumstances, taking into account the suitability of *other* possible remedies. Moreover, certain rules – some of which we discuss in sections 27.3 and 27.4 – guide the courts: for example, an injunction will not be granted unless the court can clearly specify what the defendant must cease doing (or must do), or if a claimant delays too long before seeking it.

---

[3] Contempt of Court Act 1981, s 14. In *JSC BTA Bank* v *Ablyazov (No 8)* [2013] 1 WLR 1331, at [102]–[109], the Court of Appeal dismissed an appeal against a lengthy sentence of imprisonment for civil contempt and made clear that such a sentence might be used legitimately both to punish a litigant for not complying with a court order and to encourage future compliance.

27.2 Classification of injunctions

(1) *Interim and final injunctions.* Injunctions granted as a remedy at the conclusion of a trial are referred to as *final* or *perpetual* injunctions. English civil procedure also allows a party to seek an injunction to protect his or her position before trial. Such injunctions are referred to as *interim* (formerly *interlocutory*) injunctions.[4] *Interim* injunctions are particularly important where there is a risk that a claimant will suffer *irreparable* damage if the defendant is not prevented from doing something which is arguably a tort. But *interim* injunctions also give rise to special concern because they restrict a defendant's liberty *before* it has been established whether what he is doing, or proposes to do, is, or will be, a tort. (In Chapter 17, we discuss in detail some special issues relating to interim injunctions which arise most commonly in cases of misuse of private information. In particular, we discuss the courts' approach when an interim injunction will restrict free expression, their effect on third parties, when the parties will be anonymised, and when, if ever, it will be appropriate to grant a super-injunction, to forbid disclosure of the fact that such an injunction has been obtained.[5])

(2) *Mandatory and prohibitory injunctions.* If an injunction instructs someone to take positive action, for example, to repair a wall, then it is called a *mandatory* injunction. Whilst if an injunction instructs someone to cease behaving in a particular way, for example, to stop harassing their former partner, it is called a *prohibitory* injunction. The distinction is one of substance rather than form. A good rule of thumb is that if complying with an injunction requires the expenditure of money then it is, in substance, *mandatory*. English courts are more cautious about granting *mandatory* injunctions than *prohibitory* injunctions.[6]

(3) *Quia timet injunctions.* Most injunctions will instruct someone not to *continue* committing a tort. It is also possible, however, for a claimant to obtain an injunction if she can establish that she is *about* to be the victim of a tort. Such an injunction, known as a *quia timet* injunction, will order the defendant not to commit the tort. For example, in *Litchfield-Speer* v *Queen Anne's Gate Syndicate (No 2) Ltd* (1919), Lawrence J granted an injunction to restrain the defendants from erecting a building, which, had it been built, would have amounted to a private nuisance to the claimants because its presence would have unreasonably interfered with their right to light.

27.3 When will an interim injunction be granted?

We have already noted that interim injunctions are particularly important where A proposes to do something – *x* – which will cause damage to B *before* there is time to hold a trial to determine whether *x* will be a tort to B, and where that damage could not be properly reversed by an award of damages. In such a case, B can seek an *interim* injunction against A, ordering him not to do *x* until after a trial (or until a subsequent order). But since A may dispute that doing *x* will be a tort to B, and even insist that preventing him from doing *x* will cause *him* irreparable damage, we must establish what test a court will use when deciding whether to grant such an injunction.

---

[4] We will not discuss certain specialised interim injunctions, such as 'asset freezing injunctions', which help to ensure that money is still available if a defendant is eventually held liable to pay damages.

[5] See above, § 17.2(J)(4).

[6] The reasons for this are explained below, § 27.4.

A. The 'balance of convenience' test[7]

The general rule is that B must do three things before an interim injunction will be granted:

1. B must establish that there is a serious question to be tried as to whether if A does x he will commit a tort to her.[8]

2. B must undertake that if an interim injunction *is* granted against A, but it is later found that x would *not* have been a tort to her, she will compensate A for any losses he suffers as a result of the injunction.[9]

3. B must establish that the 'balance of convenience' favours granting an interim injunction.

The 'balance of convenience' is determined by balancing B's need to be protected against any harm (which could not be adequately compensated in damages) that she might suffer if A is allowed to do x against A's need to be protected against any harm (which could not be adequately compensated in damages under B's undertaking) that he might suffer if he is prevented from doing x. Where it is doubtful whether damages will be an adequate remedy for B if it transpires that x is a tort *and* doubtful whether an award under B's undertaking will adequately compensate A if it transpires that x is not a tort, then a court may have to assess the relative strength of the parties' cases before deciding whether an interim injunction should be granted.[10]

Thus if *Lux* wants to cut down a tree on land that he believes that he owns so as to allow more light to reach his windows, and *Eco* claims that the tree is actually on her land so cutting it down will be a tort to her, then the court must assess: (1) whether *Eco* could be adequately compensated if the tree is cut down, but it turns out to have been her tree, and (2) whether *Lux* could be adequately compensated if he is prevented from cutting down the tree until after a trial where it is held that it is his tree. Clearly, a pivotal question will be whether *Lux* will suffer *any* harm, and if so what, if he is ordered to delay. If the court decides that neither party could be compensated adequately, then it will have to reach a provisional view about the merits of the case, that is whether *Eco* will more likely than not to be able to prove that the tree is on her land, so cutting it down will be a tort.

---

[7] This test was set out by Lord Diplock in *American Cyanamid* v *Ethicon Ltd* [1975] AC 396, and is commonly referred to as 'the *American Cyanamid* test'. For its detailed application, and the criticisms that have been made of it, the reader is advised to consult a specialist text on civil procedure.

[8] This is not a high hurdle. In *American Cyanamid* v *Ethicon Ltd* [1975] AC 396, Lord Diplock explained (at 407) that there was a 'serious question to be tried' if the claim was not 'frivolous or vexatious'. He also stated: 'It is no part of the court's function at this stage of the litigation to try to resolve conflicts of evidence on affidavit as to facts on which the claims of either party may ultimately depend nor to decide difficult questions of law which call for detailed argument and mature considerations. These are matters to be dealt with at the trial.' Zuckerman 2013 (at 10.43) suggests that many judges are reluctant to use such a *low* hurdle when they feel able to reach a preliminary view on the merits, so there is a 'widespread but unstated practice' of using a *higher* hurdle: 'as every lawyer should know, a clear probability of success on the merits is bound to figure in judges' calculations when they come to decide whether to grant interim relief.'

[9] Civil Procedure Rules, Practice Direction 25, 5.1(1).

[10] *National Commercial Bank Jamaica Ltd* v *Olint Corpn Ltd (Practice Note)* [2009] UKPC 16, [2009] 1 WLR 1405, at [18]: 'Among the matters which the court may take into account are the prejudice which the [claimant] may suffer if no injunction is granted or the defendant may suffer if it is; the likelihood of such prejudice actually occurring; the extent to which it may be compensated by an award of damages or enforcement of the cross-undertaking; the likelihood of either party being able to satisfy such an award; and the likelihood that the injunction will turn out to have been wrongly granted or withheld, that is to say, the court's opinion of the relative strength of the parties' cases.'

B. Exceptions

There are four situations which commonly arise in tort cases where the courts will *not* use the 'balance of convenience' test:

(1) *Time is of the essence.* In some situations ordering A not to do something until trial will effectively preclude him from ever doing it, since he may only want to do it at a particular time. So in these cases the grant or refusal of an interim injunction will effectively determine the whole case. An example might be where *Airline* seeks an order that *Union* should not organise some industrial action. If *Airline* obtains an interim injunction, then *Union* will be unable to use the industrial action to pursue its goal, and by the time a full trial can be arranged neither party may think it is worth spending money to establish whether what *Union* proposed to do would have *actually* been a tort to *Airline*. In such an exceptional case a judge considering whether to grant an interim injunction must assess not merely whether there is a serious question to be tried, but whether *Airline* will be likely to obtain a *final* injunction if there is a trial.[11]

(2) *Defamation cases.* '[T]he importance of leaving free speech unfettered is a strong reason in cases of libel for dealing most cautiously and warily with the granting of interim injunctions.'[12] This caution is reflected in the rule[13] that interim injunctions will not generally be granted in cases where B claims that a proposed publication by A will libel or slander her[14] but A intends to argue at trial that his statement is not defamatory,[15] or intends to put forward a defence of truth,[16] honest opinion,[17] privilege,[18] or publication on matter of public interest. If, however, it is clear that the defence is doomed to fail, an interim injunction may still be granted.[19]

(3) *Freedom of expression cases.* Section 12(3) of the Human Rights Act 1998 provides that:

> No . . . relief [affecting the exercise of the Convention right to freedom of expression] is to be granted so as to restrain publication before trial unless the court is satisfied that the applicant is likely to establish that publication should not be allowed.

This provision has not altered the common law rule discussed in the previous paragraph, which applies in cases of libel and slander.[20] But it means that the 'balance of convenience'

---

[11] *NWL Ltd* v *Woods* [1979] 1 WLR 1294, 1306–7.

[12] *Bonnard* v *Perryman* [1891] 2 Ch 269, 284 (per Lord Coleridge).

[13] Commonly referred to as 'the rule in *Bonnard* v *Perryman*'.

[14] Similar rules probably apply to the tort of malicious falsehood, and courts will be careful not to allow the rules to be evaded by claims that the publication may amount to some other tort, such as lawful means conspiracy (discussed in Chapter 20, above): see *Gulf Oil (Great Britain) Ltd* v *Page* [1987] Ch 327, 333–4; *Femis-Bank* v *Lazar* [1991] Ch 391.

[15] *Coulson* v *Coulson* [1887] 3 TLR 846.

[16] This was the rule with respect to the common law defence of justification (*Bonnard* v *Perryman* [1891] 2 Ch 269), and is almost certainly still the law now that the Defamation Act 2013 s 2 has replaced this with a defence of truth.

[17] This was the rule with respect to the common law defence of fair comment on a matter of public interest (*Fraser* v *Evans* [1969] 1 QB 349, 360), and is almost certainly still the law now that the Defamation Act 2013 s 3 has replaced this with a defence of honest opinion.

[18] *Quartz Hill Consolidated Mining Co* v *Beal* (1882) 20 Ch D 501; *Harakas* v *Baltic Mercantile and Shipping Exchange Ltd* [1982] 1 WLR 958.

[19] *Holley* v *Smyth* [1998] QB 726, holding that a claimant may adduce evidence to show that a defence of justification (now, truth) is bound to fail; *Herbage* v *Pressdram* [1984] 1 WLR 1160, 1164, discussing a situation where there was overwhelming evidence of malice which would negate a defence of qualified privilege.

[20] *Greene* v *Associated Newspapers Ltd* [2005] QB 972.

test also *does not* apply in further situations where an interim injunction is sought to prevent a wrong involving publication, such as misuse of private information.[21] In *Cream Holdings Ltd* v *Banerjee* (2005), the House of Lords noted the difficulty of defining 'likely' in s 12(3) because its test must be applied in such a wide range of situations. In some cases (for instance, those involving allegedly private business information) the claimant might be seeking to protect a purely financial interest, but in others (for instance, those involving protecting the new identity of a former spy) the claimant might be seeking to protect his right to life. Lord Nicholls' solution was to hold that Parliament intended the word 'likely' to be able to change meaning: 'likely' usually requires a 'likelihood of success at the trial higher than the commonplace *American Cyanamid* standard of 'real prospect'", but not when it is necessary to depart from this, such as when publication could lead to very severe consequences.[22] The higher degree of likelihood of success that is usually required is that the claim will 'more likely than not' succeed at trial.[23]

(4) *Trade disputes.* The fourth exception is where A claims that his proposed course of action will be performed in contemplation or furtherance of a trade dispute. In such a case, before granting an interim injunction a court must consider the likelihood that A will be able to establish the defence of trade union immunity[24] at trial.[25]

27.4 When will a final injunction be granted?

A. General principles

The remedy of injunction was initially developed in the Courts of Equity and consequently it conforms to general *equitable* principles about remedies. The central general principle is that remedies developed by the Courts of Equity (known as 'equitable remedies') are 'discretionary'. What this means is that even where a claimant has established the conditions sufficient to be awarded such a remedy a court will not necessarily grant it – it can still choose not to. In practice, courts' choices generally follow well-developed rules. Thus an injunction will not be awarded where this would be oppressive,[26] where the claimant does not have 'clean hands',[27] where the claimant is unwilling to 'do equity',[28] where the claimant initially allowed the defendant to do what she is now seeking an injunction against,[29]

---

[21] Discussed in Chapter 17, above. In *A* v *B* [2003] QB 195, at [11], the Court of Appeal set out guidance for judges deciding whether to grant an interim injunction to prevent commission of this tort.

[22] [2005] 1 AC 253, at [20].

[23] [2005] 1 AC 253, at [22].

[24] The immunity is found in Trade Union and Labour Relations (Consolidation) Act 1992, ss 219–220. These provisions are discussed above, at § 22.4.

[25] Trade Union and Labour Relations (Consolidation) Act 1992, s 221(2).

[26] This concept is discussed below, § 27.4(C).

[27] This basis for refusing an injunction allows a court to take account of any misconduct by a claimant. Of course, the courts will not refuse to grant an injunction because of trivial misconduct.

[28] This basis for refusing an injunction allows a court to consider whether the claimant is willing to perform any duties that she owes the defendant.

[29] An injunction might be refused on this basis if, for instance, B stood by and watched A expend money on a project before objecting to it and seeking an injunction. In *Jaggard* v *Sawyer* [1995] 1 WLR 269 the claimant warned the defendants that their proposed action was wrongful, but did not seek an interim injunction. The Court of Appeal treated this failure to seek an interim injunction as relevant to the decision whether to grant a final injunction: 283 (Sir Thomas Bingham MR), 289 (Millett LJ).

or where the claimant has delayed too long. Similarly, an injunction will more probably be granted where a defendant has 'acted in a high-handed manner – if he has endeavoured to steal a march upon the [claimant] or to evade the jurisdiction of the court.'[30]

The most important rule when a court is deciding whether to grant a *final* injunction ordering a defendant not to continue committing a tort, or not to repeat the commission of one, is that such an injunction should only be granted if there is a sufficient basis for believing that without it there will be a continuation or repetition, and justice will not be done by waiting and then ordering the defendant to pay damages to the claimant for any continued, or repeated, tort.[31] In practice, this means that injunctions are rarely sought in cases involving torts that are usually committed by isolated impacts, such as negligence, because the prospect of repetition is low,[32] and are more frequently sought in cases involving torts committed by interference with someone's interests over a longer period, such as private nuisance. It is worth emphasising, however, that injunctions are intended to deal with *future* tortious behaviour, so where a defendant's wrongdoing started in the past but is also on-going, a claimant can claim *both* damages for past injury *and* an injunction for the future.

Courts are generally more cautious about granting mandatory injunctions than prohibitory injunctions, for two principal reasons. First, if a mandatory injunction is granted, the court must specify exactly what positive steps the defendant must take to comply with it. Where this is impossible, for example because no one is sure what engineering works will be necessary to reverse the consequences of the defendant's wrongdoing, a mandatory injunction will be refused.[33] Secondly, there is a worry that mandatory injunctions can be wasteful, where it will cost A much more to comply than the value of anything B will gain as a result. This risk of waste leads courts to look with special care at whether damages could be an *adequate* remedy for any future harm, and how much it will cost a defendant to obey a mandatory injunction.[34]

---

[30] *Colls* v *Home and Colonial Stores Ltd* [1904] AC 179, 193 (Lord Macnaghten). Approved by Lord Neuberger in *Lawrence* v *Fen Tigers* [2014] AC 822, [121].

[31] The question when, if ever, damages are an adequate remedy for an ongoing property tort led to a division of opinion in the Supreme Court in *Lawrence* v *Fen Tigers* [2014] AC 822: Lord Sumption (at [161]) offered some support for the opinion that 'damages are ordinarily an adequate remedy for nuisance', whilst Lord Mance (at [168]) disagreed, and stated that 'the right to enjoy one's home without disturbance is one which I would believe that many, indeed most, people value for reasons largely if not entirely independent of money.' Lord Carnwath (at [247]) supported Lord Mance's position, and Lord Neuberger (at [127]) stated that he saw 'real force' in it.

[32] Cf Lord Denning MR's remark in *Miller* v *Jackson* [1977] QB 966, 980: 'there is no case, so far as I know, where [an injunction] has been granted to stop a man being negligent.' This is disputed, however, in McBride 2004, pointing to the American cases of *Shimp* v *New Jersey Bell Telephone Co.*, 368 A 2d 408 (1976) and *Smith* v *Western Electric Co*, 643 SW 2d 10 (1982), where in each case an injunction was granted against an employer, compelling him to comply with the duty of care he owed his employees to take reasonable steps to see that they would be reasonably safe in working for him.

[33] *Redland Bricks Ltd* v *Morris* [1970] AC 632, 667–8. Prohibitory injunctions must also be sufficiently clear: in *O (a child)* v *Rhodes* [2016] AC 219, the Court of Appeal granted an injunction prohibiting publication of a book in a form which included 'graphic accounts' of sexual abuse, self-harm, and mental illness, but Baroness Hale and Lord Toulson held, at [79], that this was too unclear, and violated the principle that 'Any injunction must be framed in terms sufficiently specific to leave no uncertainty about what the affected person is or is not allowed to do.'

[34] *Redland Bricks Ltd* v *Morris* [1970] AC 632, 666.

B. Final injunctions affecting freedom of expression and other Convention Rights

Where a court is considering whether to grant any relief which, if granted, might affect the exercise of the Convention right to freedom of expression then:

> The court must have particular regard to the importance of the Convention right to freedom of expression and, where the proceedings relate to material which the respondent claims, or which appears to the court, to be journalistic, literary or artistic material (or to conduct connected with such material), to –
>
> (a) the extent to which –
>   (i) the material has, or is about to, become available to the public; or
>   (ii) it is, or would be, in the public interest for the material to be published;
> (b) any relevant privacy code.[35]

Clearly an injunction ordering someone not to publish something may affect free *expression* to a greater extent than awarding damages *after* its publication. Thus before granting such an injunction a court will want to be convinced that the proposed interference is supported by 'relevant and sufficient grounds', will respond to a 'pressing social need' and will not interfere to any greater extent than what is necessary to achieve its legitimate aim. The Court of Appeal has held that s 12(4) does not require *extra* weight to be given to the listed factors, and merely draws attention to contexts where free expression is of special importance, and to 'considerations which may none the less justify restricting that right'.[36] Moreover, the provision is not intended to suggest that one Convention right (Article 10, free expression) has priority over other Convention right (e.g. Article 8, privacy).[37]

Convention Rights are not only relevant where injunctions are sought to prevent *publication*. For instance, people occupying land in order to protest have invoked Article 10 (free expression) and Article 11 (freedom of assembly) to try to prevent injunctions being granted to landowners who wanted to evict them. In such cases, the courts have accepted that they must assess whether granting an injunction might have 'the effect of preventing any effective exercise of freedom of expression' or [of destroying] 'the essence of the right'.[38] But where protesters occupy land without its owner's permission for lengthy periods the 'rights of others' will often make it legitimate to grant an injunction despite the effects on free expression and assembly. Thus, when considering a claim relating to a camp erected by the 'Occupy Movement' outside St Paul's Cathedral in London, the Court of Appeal stated: 'it is very difficult to see how [the protesters' Article 10 and 11 rights]

---

[35] Human Rights Act 1998, s 12(4).

[36] *Ashdown* v *Telegraph Group Ltd* [2002] Ch 149, [27].

[37] The court should not give either right precedence, should focus intensely 'on the comparative importance of the specific rights being claimed in the individual case', should take account of 'the justifications for interfering with or restricting each right' and should apply the proportionality test to each right: *In re S (a child) (Identification: Restrictions on Publication)* [2005] 1 AC 593, at [17].

[38] These phrases are from the judgment of the European Court of Human Rights in *Appleby* v *United Kingdom* (2003) 37 EHRR 783, at [47], when rejecting a claim that the Convention rights of the applicants had been violated as a result of national law empowering the private owners of a shopping centre to forbid them from protesting on the premises about local issues. Importantly, the Court held that a state might be subject to a positive obligation to enhance opportunities for protest in circumstances where private property rights had such substantial effects, such as where a private corporation owned *all* the land in a municipality.

could ever prevail against the will of the landowner when they are continuously and exclusively occupying public land, breaching not just the owner's property rights . . . , but significantly interfering with the public and Convention rights of others, and causing other problems (connected with health, nuisance, and the like)'.[39]

C. Damages in lieu of final injunctions

If B applies for a final injunction ordering A not to continue committing, or repeat, a tort to B in the *future*, the choice for the court is not simply between granting the injunction or leaving B, for the time being,[40] without a remedy. It may refuse to grant the injunction but award B damages *in lieu of* (instead of) the injunction.[41]

Refusing to grant an injunction in a case where A will continue committing a tort in relation to B in the future might appear to leave A *free* to continue committing that tort. But this is not correct: refusing an injunction does not mean that it ceases to be *wrongful* for A to continue committing the tort, and if A does continue doing so then B will be able to return to court for damages for any further harm. Nonetheless, having to return to court repeatedly is unlikely to suit either party. So a court *can* make A pay damages to B – *in lieu of injunction* – *in advance*. Such damages are an immediate remedy for a tort to B that will occur in the future – and are consequently different from damages to compensate for harm already caused by past wrongdoing.

How should damages *in lieu of injunction* be calculated? One obvious approach is to estimate the loss that B will suffer if A continues to commit the tort concerned. In *Lawrence* v *Fen Tigers Ltd* (2014), the Supreme Court suggested that where an injunction was refused in a case of private nuisance 'damages [in lieu of injunction] are conventionally based on the reduction in the value of the claimant's property as a result of the continuation of the nuisance.'[42] But other cases have identified an alternative that might sometimes be appropriate; this asks how much a reasonable person in the claimant's shoes might charge the defendant for the privilege of being allowed to continue committing the tort?[43] The alternative differs from a simple estimate of *future loss*, because the price that a reasonable person might charge could include a fair share of however much a defendant stands to *gain* if he is able to continue acting wrongfully towards the claimant. In the *Fen Tigers* case, the Supreme Court expressly left open the question whether this alternative measure is appropriate in private nuisance cases, and, if so, when: Lord Neuberger and Lord Clarke both thought it arguable that the alternative should sometimes be used, but Lord Carnwath doubted its practical utility in cases where there is no stable 'market' for the type of right concerned, since this will make it hard to fix a 'reasonable price', and also where the defendant's on-going wrong will affect far more people than just the claimants.[44]

---

[39] *City of London Corporation* v *Samede* [2012] EWCA Civ 160, at [49]. See also *Mayor of London* v *Hall* [2011] 1 WLR 504.

[40] If no injunction is granted and A *does* continue to commit, or repeat, the tort in the future then B will be able to come back to court to seek *damages* at that stage.

[41] The Chancery Amendment Act 1858, better known as Lord Cairns's Act, allowed the Court of Chancery to award damages in lieu of an injunction. This statute has been repealed, but s 50 of the Senior Courts Act 1981 preserves the court's jurisdiction to award damages in lieu of an injunction.

[42] *Lawrence* v *Fen Tigers Ltd* [2014] AC 822, [101], [157] and [172]. Further damages may, of course, be available to compensate for *past* losses.

[43] *Jaggard* v *Sawyer* [1995] 1 WLR 269.

[44] *Lawrence* v *Fen Tigers Ltd* [2014] AC 822 at [128]–[131] (Lord Neuberger), [173] (Lord Clarke) and [248] (Lord Carnwath).

Until *Lawrence* v *Fen Tigers Ltd* (2014), it was widely thought that where a continuing tort would affect a claimant's interest in *land,* for example a continuing private nuisance or trespass, then a court would grant an injunction *unless* this would be 'oppressive' to the defendant.[45] This approach was associated with the leading case of *Shelfer* v *City of London Electric Lighting Co* (1895), where A.L. Smith LJ stated that it was a 'good working rule' that damages should be awarded in lieu if the injury to the claimant's rights was small, easy to assess in monetary terms and to compensate by a small payment, *and* it would be oppressive to grant an injunction.[46] The *Shelfer* approach respected owners' rights to control use of their property, and avoided any impression that the courts were willing to 'licence' wrongs in exchange for payment of a 'fee' (damages in lieu). But in the *Fen Tigers* case, the Supreme Court changed the law in two significant ways. First, it decided 'to signal a move away from the strict criteria derived from *Shelfer*'.[47] So instead of concentrating on 'oppression', the choice whether to grant or refuse an injunction requires 'a classic exercise of discretion' in light of the facts of the individual case.[48] The second significant change was to make clear that the public interest can be an important influence on whether to refuse an injunction. Thus Lord Neuberger stated that it would be relevant whether an injunction would 'involve a loss to the public or a waste of resources on account of what may be a single claimant', and that a court ought to take account of the fact that a 'defendant's business may have to shut down if an injunction is granted' and 'that a number of the defendant's employees would lose their livelihood', though he cautioned that 'in many cases' this last factor 'may well not be sufficient to justify the refusal of an injunction'.[49]

27.5 Reform

In this section we will consider two ways in which it has been argued that the law relating to injunctions ought to be reformed.

A. Should *quia timet* injunctions be granted more readily?

John Murphy argues that a court should have power to grant an injunction against A where he wantonly or recklessly acts in such a way as to create an unjustifiable risk to B's physical well-being.[50] This would require a change in the law because currently a court would probably say that A had not yet committed a tort in relation to B (because the most

---

[45] *Watson* v *Croft Promosport Ltd* [2009] EWCA Civ 15, [44] (per Sir Andrew Morritt).

[46] [1895] 1 Ch 287, 322–3. In *Jaggard* v *Sawyer* [1995] 1 WLR 269, 287 (per Millett LJ), the Court of Appeal treated A.L. Smith LJ's list of four factors as having 'stood the test of time'.

[47] [2014] AC 822, [239] (per Lord Carnwath). Lord Sumption expressed his criticisms more forcefully: 'the decision in *Shelfer* [1895] 1 Ch 287 is out of date, and it is unfortunate that it has been followed so recently and so slavishly' (at [161]) and Lord Clarke 'entirely agree[d]' with him about this (at [171]).

[48] *Lawrence* v *Fen Tigers Ltd* [2014] AC 822, [120].

[49] *Lawrence* v *Fen Tigers Ltd* [2014] AC 822, [124]–[126]. Lord Sumption (at [161]) seemed attracted by the more radical propositions that 'damages are ordinarily an adequate remedy for nuisance', 'an injunction should not usually be granted in a case where it is likely that conflicting interests are engaged other than the parties' interests' and 'an injunction should as a matter of principle not be granted in a case where a use of land to which objection is taken requires and has received planning permission.'

[50] Murphy 2007b.

obviously applicable tort, negligence, is not complete until damage has been caused to B) and, as we have seen, an injunction will only be granted *before* a tort is committed if a tort that will cause serious damage is imminent.[51] Murphy's proposal might allow an injunction to be granted in the **Regular Menace Problem**:

> *Newt* and *Gary* are neighbours. Most mornings, *Newt* plays with his young son on a communal paved area in front of their houses. And nearly every morning *Gary* drives out of his garage and across the paved area with a mobile phone awkwardly gripped between ear and shoulder. Several times *Gary* has narrowly avoided running over *Newt* and his son, apparently so distracted by his telephone call that he has not noticed them. *Newt* protests to *Gary* about his dangerous and unlawful behaviour, but *Gary* just shrugs. *Newt* forms the view that *Gary* poses an unjustifiable risk to his safety and that of his son.

Murphy argues that we should we change the law to allow *Newt* to obtain an injunction against *Gary* because it is important to protect people like *Newt* and his son from physical harm[52] and equally important to prevent people like *Gary* from wantonly or recklessly ignoring the duties of care that tort law imposes on them. We agree that these goals are important. But there are two counter arguments to consider.

First, if injunctions could be granted to people facing a significant risk of being injured by a tort, rather than just to those who are at *imminent* risk, then many more people will become eligible to seek injunctions. Tort claims are expensive to process, and who can say whether the extra cost of dealing with additional applications for injunctions will in fact be counter-balanced by a reduction in the number of injuries?

Secondly, granting such injunctions will create something like a 'two-tier' criminal law: most drivers caught using mobile phones while driving near *Newt* and his son will face the ordinary criminal penalties, but if an injunction is granted and then *Gary* is caught doing the same thing, he will face more serious punishment for contempt of court. Why, *Gary* might ask, should a private citizen like *Newt* – who has not been injured – be able to increase the penalties that another citizen will face?

B. Should final injunctions be granted less often in cases involving property torts?

Legal economists, in particular, have asked whether the granting of final injunctions in cases involving property torts, in particular private nuisance,[53] prevents land from being used in the most productive way.

---

[51] Murphy accepts that this is the law, quoting Chitty J's statement (in *Attorney-General* v *Manchester Corporation* [1893] 2 Ch 87, at 92) that: 'The principle which I think may be properly and safely extracted from the *quia timet* authorities is, that the [claimant] must shew a strong case of probability that the apprehended mischief will, in fact, arise.'

[52] Oddly, Murphy 2007b suggests that one reason that the law does not currently grant injunctions in situations such as the Regular Menace Problem is because courts are more ready to grant injunctions to protect property. We do not think that this is the explanation: we think that *Newt* would find it no easier to obtain an injunction against an unjustifiable risk that *Gary* might be posing to his garden fence.

[53] The academic work discussed in this section was conducted *before* the Supreme Court changed the law on when injunctions will be granted in *Lawrence* v *Fen Tigers Ltd* [2014] AC 822. (See above, § 27.4(C).) But the analysis of the underlying issues remains relevant and valuable.

Professor Coase's answer, presented in a famous article,[54] was that if 'bargaining costs' are ignored, then the initial decision in a private nuisance case will have no effect on how land is actually used. Whatever the decision, the parties will end up using their land in the most profitable way: if the party engaged in the more profitable use wins the case then all will be fine, and if the party engaged in the less profitable use wins the case then the losing – more profitable – side will bargain with the winner so as to reverse the result. All the court's decision will determine is how the profits garnered from using the land in that (more profitable) way are shared between the parties.[55]

In the real world, of course, there are 'bargaining costs', and these make it important whether a court chooses to grant an injunction or not: for example, if a court grants an injunction to B against A even though A's use of land is more profitable than B's, A will be unable to use his land in the more profitable way *if* 'bargaining costs' prevent him from reaching an appropriate agreement with B.

An example might help to illustrate this point: suppose that *Host* runs a hotel and obtains an injunction against *Promo* ordering him not to hold a noisy rock festival on his land because it will disturb *Host*'s guests to such a degree that she will lose all her business for a week. If *Promo* will make ten times as much profit from the festival than *Host* can make from her hotel in a week then ideally *Promo* ought to reach an agreement with *Host* which will allow the festival to go ahead and leave them both better off than if the injunction was complied with. But if 'bargaining costs' are high, say because *Host*'s accounts are a mess and she has no idea how much she will lose if she closes her hotel, then there is a risk that the parties will not reach an agreement.[56]

Legal economists[57] commonly argue that if 'bargaining costs' between *Promo* and *Host* are *low* then an injunction should be granted. This way, the parties can reach whatever agreement is appropriate and the courts will not have to spend time trying to estimate *Host*'s likely losses or how much a reasonable hotel owner would charge a festival Promo for the right to make so much noise.[58] If, however, 'bargaining costs' are high, it may be better to refuse to grant *Host* an injunction and instead award her damages *in lieu*. If these damages are calculated correctly, *Promo* will only go ahead and hold the festival if he can make more money from it than the court calculates that *Host* ought to receive to cover her losses.

If this is correct then it means that – from the perspective of ensuring that land is used in the most productive way – courts should only grant final injunctions *readily* if they think that 'bargaining costs' are low. Such evidence as there is suggests that 'bargaining costs' between parties in the aftermath of private nuisance cases *are* actually high.[59] Thus a careful study of 20 American nuisance cases found that there was no serious bargaining after judgment in any of them.[60] This was in part because the litigation seemed to have

---

[54] Coase 1960.

[55] Of course, the fairness of the distribution of the profits is a perfectly legitimate concern for English law. It is worth remembering throughout this section that economic efficiency is not all-important.

[56] Of course, a court that did not grant an injunction to *Host*, but awarded damages *in lieu*, would have to try to estimate her losses, which would be difficult given the state of the accounts.

[57] See, for instance, Ogus & Richardson 1977; Tromans 1982.

[58] As we explained above, § 27.4(C), these are the two measures courts might use to calculate damages *in lieu of* injunction.

[59] Thus offering some support for the changes that the Supreme Court made to the law in *Lawrence* v *Fen Tigers Ltd* [2014] AC 822, summarised above, § 27.4(C).

[60] Farnsworth 1999.

resulted in animosity between the parties; also, winning claimants often seemed unwilling to treat their rights – for example, to freedom from noise, or freedom from smell – as things which could be commodified and sold.

This last point is, of course, important. If most claimants who obtain final injunctions as a remedy for a property tort think that the rights which are being protected are *priceless*, then this tends to challenge the very premise of any inquiry into whether the courts' readiness to grant such injunctions may prevent land from being used in the most productive way: how can anything be more productive than protecting what is priceless?

Further reading

In his thought-provoking article, **'Rethinking Injunctions in Tort Law' (2007) 27** *Oxford Journal of Legal Studies* **509, John Murphy** laments that there is so little academic writing about injunctions in tort law. Fortunately his article helps to fill the gap. Anyone inclined to research the law on the topic in depth would probably be well-advised to start with the relevant chapter – Chapter 29, written by **Andrew Tettenborn** – in *Clerk and Lindsell on Torts* **(21st edn, 2014)**. But for a very different perspective on the role of injunctions, that has stimulated many academic articles in the United States, we would recommend **Guido Calabresi and A. Douglas Melamed, 'Property Rules, Liability Rules, and Inalienability: One View of the Cathedral' (1972) 85 Harvard Law Review 1089.**

Chapter 28
Wrongful death claims

Aims and objectives

Reading this chapter should enable you to:

(1) Understand who will count as being a dependant of the victim of a tort who has died as a result of that tort being committed.

(2) Understand how, through the Fatal Accidents Act 1976, English tort law provides remedies to such dependants; in particular, the remedies of a claim for loss of support and a claim for bereavement.

(3) Understand how the damages that are awarded to a claimant who is suing for loss of support are assessed.

(4) Understand who is allowed to bring a claim for bereavement and how the damages payable to the claimants in a bereavement case are assessed, and what that might tell us about the nature of such damages.

28.1 The basics

We saw, all the way back in Chapter 1, how tort law remedies are usually only made available to the *victim* of a tort.[1] Third parties who suffer losses as a result of a tort that has been committed in relation to someone else are usually left to bear those losses themselves.[2] The most important exception to this rule – by far – is created by the Fatal Accidents Act 1976.

That Act enables a *Dependant* of the *Victim* of a tort who has died as a result of that tort being committed to sue the person who committed that tort for: (a) any *loss of support* that *Dependant* has suffered as a result of *Victim*'s death; (b) *bereavement damages*, in the case where *Dependant* and *Victim* were married or where *Victim* was *Dependant*'s child

---

[1] See above, § 1.5.
[2] For further examples, see Stanton 2007a.

and still a minor; and (c) *Victim's funeral expenses,* in the case where *Dependant* paid for those expenses.

The general conditions that have to be satisfied before a *wrongful death* claim can be brought against a defendant under the 1976 Act are:

1. the defendant – or someone for whose actions the defendant is liable[3] – must have committed a tort *in relation to the deceased*;

2. that tort must have *caused* the deceased's death, and the death must have been a *non-remote* consequence of that tort;[4]

3. had the deceased not died, she would have been entitled to sue the defendant for damages.

If (1), (2) and (3) are made out, then a dependant of the deceased's *may* be entitled to bring a *wrongful death* claim under the 1976 Act for loss of support, bereavement damages or funeral expenses.

All of this needs much more explanation, which we aim to provide in this chapter.

28.2 Dependant

In a case where A has committed a tort in relation to B and B has died as a result, s 1(3) of the 1976 Act tells us who B's 'dependants' will be. In terms of blood relatives, B's parents or grandparents, any children of B, any nieces/nephews, and any cousins will count as dependants. Anyone B treated as being his/her parent, or his/her child will also count. Other non-blood relatives who will count as being B's dependants are any wives/husbands/civil partners (current or former), and anyone who was living with B as his/her wife/husband at the time of B's death and had been so living for at least two years before B's death.[5]

28.3 The parasitical nature of wrongful death claims

A dependant's ability to bring a claim under the 1976 Act is conditional on it being shown that had the deceased not been killed as a result of the defendant's tort, she would have been entitled to sue the defendant for damages. This limit on the right to sue a defendant for wrongful death covers – somewhat uneasily – two entirely different situations, which need to be considered separately.

---

[3] See Chapters 30 and 31 below, for an account of when someone can be held liable for a tort committed by someone else.

[4] Section 1(1) of the 1976 Act merely says that 'If death is *caused* by any wrongful act . . . the person who would have been liable had death not ensued shall be liable to an action for damages . . .' (emphasis added). However, it has been accepted by both the Law Commission (Law Com No 263, *Claims for Wrongful Death* (1999), para 2.4) and the courts (*Corr* v *IBC Vehicles Ltd* [2008] 1 AC 884) that a wrongful death claim cannot be brought under the 1976 Act if the deceased's death was a remote consequence of the defendant's tort.

[5] An attempt to claim that the two year limit on cohabitees being able to bring a wrongful death claim under the 1976 Act was incompatible with Article 8 (right to privacy and family life) of the European Convention on Human Rights was dismissed by the Court of Appeal in *Swift* v *Secretary of State for Justice* [2014] QB 373.

(1) *Instantaneous death.* Suppose that A's tort caused B to die instantaneously. In order to see whether a dependant of B's can to sue A under the 1976 Act, we have to ask: had B survived the tort that killed her and *merely been injured by it,* would she have been entitled to sue A for damages? If the answer is 'no' – because, for example, A could have raised a defence of illegality to any claim for personal injury that B might have brought against him – then no claim for wrongful death can be brought against A under the 1976 Act.[6]

(2) *Tort causing injury which results in death some time after.* Suppose that A's tort caused B to suffer some kind of injury and B died some time after that because she suffered that injury. In order to see whether a dependant of B's is entitled to sue A under the 1976 Act, we have to ask: had B not died when she did *but had lived a little longer,* would she have been entitled to sue A for damages in respect of her injury? If the answer is 'no' – because, for example, before B died she had already obtained a compensation payment from A in respect of that injury,[7] or a compensation payment from a third party that had the effect of extinguishing her right to sue A for damages in respect of that injury[8] – then no claim for wrongful death can be brought against A under the 1976 Act.[9]

The parasitical nature of claims under the 1976 Act is also reflected by the fact that s 5 of the 1976 Act provides if – had the deceased sued the defendant for damages – the damages payable to the deceased would have been reduced for contributory negligence, then any damages awarded under the 1976 Act 'shall be reduced to a proportionate extent'.

28.4 Loss of support

As we have seen, there are basically three kinds of claims that can be brought under the 1976 Act by a dependant who has suffered loss as a result of the victim of a tort's death. The most important is the claim for *loss of support.*

A. Requirements

In order to bring a claim for loss of support under the 1976 Act, a dependant of the deceased has to show that:

(1) there was a reasonable prospect that had the deceased not died, the dependant would have obtained some kind of financial benefit from the deceased in the future; *and*

(2) the dependant would have obtained that benefit by virtue of the fact that he was a dependant of the deceased's.

---

[6] See *Murphy* v *Culhane* [1977] QB 94; though it is questionable whether the case would now be decided the same way after *Patel* v *Mirza* [2017] AC 467 (see above, §22.10).

[7] Section 3 of the Damages Act 1996 provides that if A's payment to B took the form of provisional damages, then that payment will not bar anyone from bringing a claim against A under the Fatal Accidents Act 1976.

[8] See above, § 23.4, for discussion of when this will be the case.

[9] See, for example, *Read v The Great Eastern Railway Company* (1868) LR 3 QB 555. In that case, the claimant's husband was injured as a result of the defendant railway company's negligence. The claimant's husband died of his wounds but not before he accepted a sum of money from the defendants in full and final settlement of all his claims against the defendants. Once the claimant's husband died the claimant brought a claim for loss of support against the defendants. Her claim was dismissed: at the time of her husband's death, he was not entitled any more to sue the defendants for damages.

The following cases demonstrate these rules in action. For example, in *Franklin* v *The South Eastern Railway Company* (1858), the claimant's son was killed as a result of the defendants' negligence. At the time his son was killed, the claimant was getting old and infirm but was not receiving any assistance from his son, who was earning 3s 6d a week at the time he was killed. It was held that had the son not been killed there was a reasonable prospect that as the claimant grew older and weaker, the son would have paid the claimant some money so as to assist him financially. As a result the claimant was held entitled to bring an action for loss of support against the defendants.

In *Barnett* v *Cohen* (1921), the claimant's four-year-old son was killed as a result of the defendant's negligence. The claimant brought an action for loss of support against the defendant, claiming that had his son not been killed and had instead grown up to earn a living, his son would have paid him some money to assist him financially. The claim was dismissed: the claimant had not established that there was a reasonable prospect he would have received such assistance from his son had his son not been killed and grown up instead. This was for two reasons. First, the age of the claimant's son when he was killed made it impossible to predict what would have happened had he not been killed as a result of the defendant's negligence. Secondly, the claimant was a very wealthy man (earning £1,000 a year at the time of his son's death) and it was therefore hardly likely that the claimant's son would have had any reason to give the claimant anything by way of financial assistance if he had been allowed to grow up.

In *Davies* v *Taylor* (1972), the claimant's husband was killed in a road accident that was caused by the defendant's negligence. At the time the claimant's husband died, the claimant and her husband were separated and the claimant's husband was in the process of divorcing the claimant for adultery. The claimant brought an action for loss of support against the defendant, claiming that had her husband not been killed, there was a reasonable prospect her husband would have spent money on her. The claimant's claim was dismissed: had the claimant's husband not been killed, the claimant's husband would only have spent money on the claimant if they had been reconciled and the claimant had not established that there was a reasonable prospect that she and her husband would have been reconciled had he not been killed as a result of the defendant's negligence.

In *Berry* v *Humm* (1915), the defendant negligently knocked down and killed the claimant's wife. At the time of her death, the claimant's wife stayed at home and did all the domestic chores while her husband worked in the docks. Had the claimant's wife not been killed there was every prospect that the claimant's wife would have continued to do work around the claimant's house for free, thereby conferring a financial benefit on the claimant. As a result, the claimant was held entitled to bring a claim for loss of support against the defendant.

In *Burgess* v *Florence Nightingale Hospital for Gentlewomen* (1955), the claimant and his wife were professional dance partners. The claimant's wife was killed as a result of the defendant's negligence. There was a reasonable prospect that had the wife not been killed the claimant and his wife would have continued to dance together and would have earned a certain amount of prize money. However, as this money would have been obtained by the claimant because he was his wife's *dancing partner*, not because he was *married* to her, it was held it could not be sued for in bringing a claim for loss of support.[10]

---

[10] See also *Malyon* v *Plummer* [1964] 1 QB 330 (claimant who lost salary as a result of collapse of business owned by her and her husband after her husband's death could only sue for proportion of salary that did *not* reflect the value of the services she provided the business), and *Cox* v *Hockenhull* [2000] 1 WLR 750 (claimant could not sue for loss of invalidity care allowance that was paid to him as his wife's full-time carer and which he no longer received after wife was negligently killed in a car accident – the allowance was paid to claimant not because he was his wife's husband but because he was his wife's carer).

B. Limits

Two limits on a dependant's ability to bring a claim for loss of support under the 1976 Act should be noted.

(1) *Illegality.* No claim for loss of support can be made in respect of any proceeds of crime that the dependant would have received from the deceased had the deceased not been killed.[11]

(2) *No loss of benefit.* No claim for loss of support can be brought if the deceased's death did not actually prevent the dependant receiving a financial benefit that she would have received had the deceased not died.

In *Auty* v *National Coal Board* (1985), the claimant's husband was killed due to the defendants' negligence. Her husband was 55 when he died. When he died the claimant received a widow's pension under the Mineworkers' Pension Scheme. Had the claimant's husband not been killed, there was a reasonable prospect that he would have died before retiring at 65 and the claimant would have received a widow's pension. The claimant brought an action for loss of support against the defendants and included in her claim a claim for the fact that had her husband not been killed as a result of the defendant's negligence there was a reasonable prospect he would have died before retiring and she would have received a widow's pension. This element of her claim was thrown out: her husband's death had not actually prevented her from receiving a widow's pension due to her husband's dying in service as when he died as a result of the defendants' negligence, she did receive a widow's pension.

This case can be contrasted with *Welsh Ambulance Services NHS Trust* v *Williams* (2008), where the claimants' husband and father was killed when an ambulance belonging to the defendants negligently crashed into his car. The deceased was a businessman who operated a very substantial family business from which the claimants benefited a great deal financially. After his death, the deceased's son and one of his daughters took over the running of the business and managed to keep it going as a successful enterprise from which they and their mother and their sister obtained a substantial income. Counsel for the defendants argued that this meant that no claim for loss of support could be made against the defendants: as things had turned out, the claimants were just as well off after the deceased's death as they had been before. This argument was rejected at first instance. The Court of Appeal upheld the decision of the first instance judge, holding that:

> He was correct when he said that nothing that a dependant (or for that matter anyone else) could do after the death could either increase or decrease the dependency. The dependency is fixed at the moment of death; it is what the dependants would probably have received as benefit from the deceased, had the deceased not died. What decisions people make afterwards is irrelevant.[12]

The value of the benefit that the claimants were receiving from the deceased at the time of his death was valued at the cost of replacing his services in running the family business, and this is what the claimants were awarded.

What we might call the *Williams principle* that the value of someone's dependency is fixed at the moment of death and cannot be affected by what happens afterwards might

---

[11] *Burns* v *Edman* [1970] 2 QB 541 (no claim allowed for £20 a week allowance that claimant usually received from her husband – who was negligently killed in car accident – as the £20 invariably represented the proceeds of crime).

[12] [2008] EWCA Civ 81, at [50].

also be said to underlie the decision of the Court of Appeal in *Hay* v *Hughes* (1975). In that case, the parents of two boys were killed in a motor accident caused by the defendant's negligence. The boys were then taken in by their grandmother and looked after by her. The boys were held entitled to sue for the loss of care that they would have received (free of charge) from their parents until they were grown-up. The fact that they were now getting the same sort of care, free of charge, from their grandmother was held not to affect their right to sue the defendant. An alternative explanation of the decision in this case was that allowing the boys to sue for the loss of care from their parents was the Court of Appeal's roundabout way of making up for the fact that the law, strangely, does not allow children to bring claims for bereavement damages when one or both of their parents die.

The *Williams principle* also seems to underlie s 3(3) of the 1976 Act which provides that:

> In an action under this Act where there fall to be assessed damages payable to a widow in respect of the death of her husband there shall not be taken into account the re-marriage of the widow . . .

So a widow who remarries within six months of her husband's death and gets everything from her new husband that she was accustomed to getting from her deceased husband will still be entitled to sue in full for the loss of financial benefits that she stood to receive from her first husband had he not died.

Some whiffs of disapproval of the *Williams* principle can be gleaned from the decision of the UK Supreme Court in *Cox* v *Ergo Versicherung AG* (2014). Lord Sumption – giving the leading judgment – observed that he would prefer to leave open the question of whether what we have been calling the *Williams* principle provided a 'correct or helpful analysis' of the way the 1976 Act was supposed to work and indicated that he viewed s 3 of the 1976 Act as marking 'a departure from the ordinary principles of assessment [of damages] in English law, which can fairly be described as anomalous.'[13]

C. Assessment

The rules on assessing how much can be sued for by way of loss of support where A and B were married and childless,[14] and both A and B were earning money, and A died as a result of the defendant's tort, are quite complex.

It is assumed that had A not died, he would have spent a third of his earnings exclusively on himself, a third exclusively on B, and a third on joint expenditures from which both A and B profited. And B would have done the same: spent a third of her earnings exclusively on herself, a third on A, and a third on joint expenditures from which both A and B profited. So had A not died, B would have profited from two-thirds of A's earnings and two-thirds of her earnings.

---

[13] [2014] AC 1379, at [10].

[14] For simplicity, we assume that A and B are childless, but even if they do have children, the rules for assessing loss of support remain much the same. It is assumed that before A died, a third of A and B's income went on A, and the rest on B and the children and any joint expenditures from which all the family benefited. And now that A has died, all of B's money will go on her and the children. So the net loss of support suffered by B and the children as a result of A's death will be calculated by taking two-thirds of A and B's projected joint income in the future and deducting from that B's projected income in the future.

Now that A has died, B will no longer receive anything from A's earnings, but *all* of her own earnings will now be spent on herself instead of a third being spent exclusively on A. So the *net* loss of support that B will suffer each year as a result of A's death is calculated by:

1. adding together the yearly income that A and B could each have been expected to earn in the future;

2. multiplying (1) by two-thirds to put a value on the financial support B could have expected to receive each year in the future had A not died; and

3. deducting from (2) the income that B can be expected to earn in the future to give the difference between the financial support that B could have expected to receive each year in the future had A not died and the financial support that B will now receive each year in future given that A has died.

B's award for loss of support will aim to give her a lump sum which, if appropriately invested, will give her the value of (3) each year for the rest of her life.[15]

In assessing the damages payable to a dependant for loss of support, s 4 of the 1976 Act provides that *no* reduction will be made in respect of any benefits that the dependant has received as a result of the deceased's death. So, for example, if – in the case we have just been considering – on A's death, the mortgage on A and B's house was paid off with the result that B no longer has to make any mortgage payments, that will *not* go to reduce the amount of damages payable to B for loss of support.[16]

There seem to be two situations where the courts will still reduce the damages payable to a claimant under the 1976 Act because they have received a benefit from the deceased's death.

(1) *Receipt of benefit from defendant.* In *Hayden* v *Hayden* (1992), the claimant's mother was killed as a result of the negligence of the defendant, the claimant's father, in driving the car in which they were travelling. The defendant gave up his job to look after the claimant full-time. The claimant sued the defendant (in reality, his liability insurer) for the loss of her mother's services in caring for her. It was held that the damages payable to the claimant should be reduced to take account of the value of the care that she was now receiving from the defendant and that she would not have received had her mother not died.

However, the decision of the Court of Appeal in *Arnup* v *White* (2008) has made it very difficult to say that benefits received *from the defendant* as a result of the deceased's death will go to reduce the damages for loss of support that are payable to a claimant under the 1976 Act. In that case, the claimant's husband was killed at work as a result of his employer's negligence. Shortly after his death, the claimant received cheques for £129,600 and £100,000, the first from a death in service benefits scheme set up by the defendant, and the second from a trust fund set up by the defendant. The Court of

---

[15] See § 23.3, above, for discussion as to how such a lump sum is calculated.

[16] See *Pidduck* v *Eastern Scottish Omnibuses Ltd* [1990] 1 WLR 993 (payment of widow's allowance to claimant on death of her husband not to be taken into account in assessing damages payable to widow under 1976 Act); *McIntyre* v *Harland & Wolff plc* [2006] 1 WLR 2577 (payments made by employer's provident fund to claimant's husband before he died, and which then formed part of his estate that claimant inherited, should be disregarded in assessing damages payable to claimant under 1976 Act).

Appeal strictly applied s 4 and held that these benefits were not to be taken into account in assessing the damages payable for loss of support to the claimant. A payment by the defendant to the claimant after the deceased's death would only go to reduce the damages payable to the claimant under the 1976 Act if the payment was made subject to the stipulation that he 'wishes to have it taken into account when damages are assessed . . . Then it will not be a benefit, caught by section 4, it will be a conditional payment on account.'[17]

Where the decision in *Arnup* leaves the decision in *Hayden* v *Hayden* is very hard to say. *Hayden* was cited in argument in *Arnup*, but was not mentioned by the Court of Appeal.

(2) *Adoption.* In *Watson* v *Willmott* (1991), the claimant's mother was killed in a car accident caused by the defendant's negligence. The claimant's father, depressed at the death of his wife, committed suicide and the claimant was adopted. The claimant sued for the loss of care that he would have received from his parents (free of charge) until he was grown-up. The damages payable to the claimant were reduced to take account of the value of the care he had received and would receive from his adoptive parents. The court felt it was authorised to depart from the rule set out in s 4 of the 1976 Act by virtue of para 3 of Sch 1 of the Children Act 1975 under which 'An adopted child shall be treated in law . . . where the adopters are a married couple, as if he had been born as a child of the marriage'. As such, the decision in *Watson* v *Willmott* is to be confined strictly to the case where a child's parents have been killed as a result of a tort committed in relation to them and the child has been subsequently adopted.

28.5 Bereavement

The second kind of action that can be brought under the 1976 Act is a claim for bereavement damages. Section 1A of the Fatal Accidents Act 1976 provides that such damages can be sued for by:

(a) . . . the wife or husband or civil partner of the deceased; and
(b) where the deceased was a minor who was never married or a civil partner –

    (i) . . . his parents, if he was legitimate; and
    (ii) . . . his mother, if he was illegitimate.

The damages payable for bereavement are fixed at £12,900. They cannot vary according to how upset the claimant was at the deceased's death. This leads Tony Weir to argue that the damages payable for bereavement are:

> not designed as compensation for grief but [are] simply . . . a replacement in money for a life lost. The lump sum is standard because people are equal, not because they are equally regrettable.[18]

Weir's view is supported by the fact that £12,900 is the maximum a defendant can be held liable to pay by way of bereavement damages. So if more than one claimant is entitled to claim such damages – which will be the case where a legitimate child with two parents still alive is killed as a result of the defendant's tort – the lump sum has to be shared out between them. Double the grief does not result in double the damages for bereavement.

---

[17] [2008] EWCA Civ 447, at [26].
[18] Weir 2006, 215.

28.6 Funeral expenses

Section 3(5) of the 1976 Act provides that:

> If the dependants [of the victim of a tort who was killed as a result of that tort being committed] have incurred funeral expenses in respect of the deceased, damages may be awarded in respect of those expenses.

Such a claim will of course be available only if the conditions that have to be satisfied before a claim can be brought under the 1976 Act are satisfied.

28.7 Limitation

Section 12(2) of the Limitation Act 1980 provides that, in the case where the victim of a tort has died as a result of that tort having been committed, a claimant will not be able to bring an action under the 1976 Act more than three years after the *later* of the following two dates: (1) the date the victim of the tort died; (2) the date the claimant first learned, or could have reasonably been expected to learn, that the victim of the tort had died. Section 33 of the Limitation Act 1980 creates an exception to this rule: it provides that a claimant who attempts to bring a claim under the 1976 Act outside the limitation period set out in s 12(2) may be allowed to do so if it would be 'equitable' to do so.

28.8 Non-wrongful death

The 1976 Act is meant only to apply in cases where the victim of a *tort* has died as a result of that tort being committed. The requirement that a *wrong* must have been committed before a claim can be brought under the 1976 Act can sometimes create problems.

For example, if A's cat caused B some kind of physical harm due to the cat's having an uncommon characteristic, known to A, that meant the cat was likely to cause that sort of harm, A will be held strictly liable to compensate B for that harm under s 2(2) of the Animals Act 1971.[19] A's liability in this case is not based on his having done anything *wrong* to B. Section 2(2) merely sets up a liability rule: if B is harmed, then A is liable. But if B dies as a result of his injuries, we might well want his dependants to be able to bring a claim for wrongful death against A. In order to allow them to do this – to bring a claim for wrongful death even though no wrong has necessarily been committed – s 10 of the Animals Act 1971 provides that 'For the purposes of the Fatal Accidents Acts . . . any damage for which a person is liable under sections 2 to 4 of this Act shall be treated as due to his fault.'

The same trick is pulled in relation to the Consumer Protection Act 1987, which again sets up a liability rule: if you are injured as a result of a product being dangerously defective, then the producer will be liable for your injury.[20] In order to allow the dependants of someone who has been killed by a dangerously defective product to bring a claim for loss of support under the Fatal Accidents Act 1976 – again, to bring a wrongful death claim where no wrong has necessarily been committed – s 6(1) of the Act sets up a fiction that 'Any damage for which a person is liable under [the Act] shall be deemed to have been caused . . . for the purposes of the Fatal Accidents Act 1976, by that person's wrongful act, neglect or default.'

---

[19] See above, § 14.5.
[20] See above, § 11.1.

Chapter 29
Other third-party claims

Aims and objectives

Reading this chapter should enable you to:

(1) Get a good grasp of the (very limited) situations outside the Fatal Accidents Act 1976 where a third party who has suffered loss as a result of that tort being committed will be allowed to sue for damages in respect of that tort.

(2) Understand when a claim for damages may be brought under the Congenital Disabilities (Civil Liability) Act 1976, and why such damages may not be claimed in a 'wrongful life' case.

29.1 The basics

Having dealt with the Fatal Accidents Act 1976 in the previous chapter, this chapter is about the remaining few exceptions to the general rule that only the victim of a tort can obtain a remedy in respect of that tort. What exceptions there are are attributable either:

1. to the fact that a child that has been injured in the womb will sometimes be unable to argue that he or she was the victim of a tort and would as a result be left without a remedy for his disabilities were the general rule applied to his case; or

2. the State using its law-making powers to protect itself from being left without a remedy when it has spent money looking after the victim of a tort; or

3. a perception that there is something unsatisfactory about applying the general rule to a situation where the victim of a tort has suffered no loss, but a third party has.

29.2 Congenital disabilities

The Congenital Disabilities (Civil Liability) Act 1976 ('CDCLA' for short) allows a child that has been born disabled to sue a defendant for damages in respect of its disabilities if those disabilities were caused by a tort that the defendant committed in relation to one or both of the child's parents.

It is arguable that the 1976 Act is unnecessary, at least in the following type of case:

> *Pregnant* is involved in a car *Accident* that was a foreseeable result of *Defendant*'s carelessness. The foetus inside *Pregnant*'s womb is injured in the accident, but *Pregnant* does not miscarry and carries the foetus to term, when she gives birth to a disabled baby *Boy*.

This is because the Court of Appeal decided in *Burton* v *Islington Health Authority* (1992) that in this kind of case *Boy* would be able to sue *Defendant* in negligence for his disabilities, arguing that the defendant owed him – while he was in *Pregnant*'s womb, in the form of a foetus – a duty to take care not to cause *Accident* as it was reasonably foreseeable that if *Defendant* caused *Accident*, *Boy* would be born disabled. In *Burton*, it was argued that no such duty of care could have been owed by *Defendant* to *Boy* while he was in *Pregnant*'s womb because at that point he was just a foetus and enjoyed no legal personality. So arguing that such a duty of care was owed by *Defendant* would be like arguing that *Defendant* owed a duty to *Pregnant*'s car not to cause *Accident* on the basis that it was reasonably foreseeable that if he did so, the car would be damaged. The Court of Appeal disagreed:

> while there are cases . . . which establish the general proposition that a foetus enjoys, while still a foetus, no independent legal personality . . . [there] are other contexts . . . in which the English courts have adopted as part of English law the maxim of the civil law that an unborn child shall be deemed to be born whenever its interests require it . . .[1]

So the Court of Appeal thought that there was no problem in finding that, in the case we are considering, *Defendant* owed *Boy* a duty to take care not to cause *Accident*, even though at the relevant time *Boy* was merely a foetus. *Boy* could argue that: 'When I was in my mother's womb, you owed me a duty to take care not to cause *Accident* because it was reasonably foreseeable that if you did, I would be born disabled as a result. You breached that duty and I have suffered the right kind of loss as a result – I have been born disabled, as opposed to being killed in the womb. So pay up.'

The existence of the CDCLA makes it unnecessary for such an argument to be made anymore.[2] Moreover, the CDCLA applies in cases where the law of negligence cannot go – for example, to cases where a defendant was not at fault for a child's disabilities, or cases where a child's disabilities were due to something that the defendant did before the child was even conceived. The CDCLA does all this by creating an exception to the general rule that you can only sue for compensation for losses suffered as a result of a tort being committed if you were a victim of that tort. It basically provides that a child that has been born disabled will be entitled to sue a defendant for damages in respect of his or her disabilities if:

1. the child's disabilities are the result of the defendant committing a tort in relation to either of its parents which had the effect of impairing their ability to have a normal, healthy child,[3] *or*

---

[1] [1992] 3 All ER 833, 838 (per Dillon LJ).
[2] In *Burton*, the claimants were all children who were not entitled to sue under the CDCLA as the events giving rise to their disabilities had all occurred before the Act came into force.
[3] Section 1(2)(a).

2. the child's disabilities are the result of the defendant committing a tort in relation to the child's mother during her pregnancy or while the child was being born,[4] *or*

3. the child's disabilities are the result of the defendant committing a tort in relation to the child's parents when artificially inseminating the child's mother.[5]

A number of different points need to be made about the CDCLA.

(1) *Wrongful life.* A child can only sue under the CDCLA if its *disabilities* are attributable to a tort that the defendant has committed in relation to one of its parents. So no action can be brought by the child under the CDCLA in the case where *Doctor* scans a pregnant *Mother* to see if her child is disabled, *Doctor* negligently fails to spot that the child is disabled and fails to give *Mother* the opportunity of having the child aborted, and *Mother* ends up giving birth to a disabled child. While *Doctor* will be liable to pay damages to *Mother* in this case,[6] he will not be liable to pay the child damages under the CDCLA. The child's being *born* is attributable to the *Doctor*'s negligence here, not the child's being *disabled*.

Any claim that the child might make here is known as a claim for 'wrongful life'. The child's claim is basically: 'Had you not been negligent, I would not have been born and so I would not be suffering these disabilities.' The courts have made it clear that they will not countenance claims for 'wrongful life' being made under the CDCLA.[7] Not only does the wording of the Act not cover this kind of case,[8] the courts think that it would be wrong in principle to allow claims for 'wrongful life' to be brought.[9] The courts will not accept that a child that has escaped being aborted and has been born alive can claim that he or she has suffered a loss as a result. In their view, the gift of life is so immense that it outweighs any number of disabilities that might come with that gift – so the courts simply will not allow a claimant to say, 'It would have been better for me had I never existed.'

(2) *Assumption of risk.* Under ss 1(4) and 1A(3) of the CDCLA, no claim can be brought by a *Child* that has been born disabled if the defendant's tort occurred *before the child was conceived* and at least one of the child's parents were aware at that time that the defendant's tort might have the effect of causing *Child* to be born disabled. The idea is that if the child's parents or one of the child's parents consciously took a risk of having a disabled child as a result of what the defendant did, that is their responsibility, not the defendant's.

---

[4] Section 1(2)(b).

[5] Section 1A.

[6] See above, § 9.5.

[7] *McKay* v *Essex Area Health Authority* [1982] 1 QB 1166, 1178 (per Stephenson LJ), 1186–7 (per Ackner LJ), 1192 (per Griffiths LJ).

[8] While s 1(1) does simply refer to a child being 'born disabled' as a result of the defendant's actions – a phrase that would cover a wrongful life case – s 1(1) makes it clear that the defendant's actions have to fall within s 1(2), which says that the defendant's actions must have: '(a) affected either parent of the child in his or her ability to have a normal, healthy child; or (b) affected the mother during her pregnancy . . . so that the child is born with disabilities which would not otherwise have been present.' The case of the *Doctor* who negligently fails to spot that *Mother* is pregnant with a disabled child does not fall within (a) or (b). *Child* may be born with disabilities as a result of *Doctor*'s negligence, but it can hardly be said that those disabilities 'would not otherwise have been present' had *Doctor* not been negligent. The disabilities would not have existed had *Doctor* not been negligent – but only because the child bearing those disabilities would not have existed either. For a different view of the scope of the CDCLA, see Ellis & McGivern 2007.

[9] In addition to *McKay* v *Essex Area Health Authority* [1982] 1 QB 1166, see the High Court of Australia's decision in *Harriton* v *Stephens* (2006) 80 AJLR 791 (criticised, Teff 2007).

There is an exception under s 1(4) where the defendant is the *father*. So suppose *Husband* gave *Wife* some weedkiller in an attempt to kill her, but the dose was too small to affect her, or even be noticeable. If he was aware that even that small dose might cause any child she subsequently conceived to be disabled, and he did not tell her about that, then if *Wife* subsequently conceives a *Child* with *Husband* and *Child* is born disabled, then *Child* can sue *Husband* for damages for his disabilities under the CDCLA.

(3) *Action against the mother.* Section 1(1) of the CDCLA makes it clear that claims cannot be brought under the CDCLA against the mother of a disabled child. (The wording of the various provisions of the Act probably make it impossible for the mother to fall under any of them in any case.) There is one exception to this, though. This is created by s 2 of the CDCLA, which provides that:

> A woman driving a motor vehicle when she knows (or ought reasonably to know) herself to be pregnant is to be regarded as being under the same duty to take care for the safety of her unborn child as the law imposes on her with respect to the safety of other people; and if in consequence of her breach of that duty her child is born with disabilities which would not otherwise be present, those disabilities are to be regarded as damages resulting from her wrongful act and actionable at the suit of the child.

As we have already explained,[10] the reason for this provision lies in its opening words. 'A woman driving a motor vehicle' will be carrying liability insurance, and so any damages award to her child for the disabilities he or she is born with as a result of her bad driving will not come from her, but her liability insurer.

(4) *Defective product.* Because a defendant's liability under the Consumer Protection Act 1987 for damage caused by a dangerously defective product is not contingent on its being shown that the defendant did anything *wrongful* in producing or supplying that product,[11] special provision had to be made in s 6(3) of the 1987 Act to allow a child who had been born disabled as a result of a product being dangerously defective to bring a claim for his disabilities under the CDCLA. Section 6(3) basically provides that if a child is born disabled as a result of a product being dangerously defective under the 1987 Act, the child will be able to sue a defendant for compensation for his disabilities under the CDCLA if the defendant would have been held liable to the child's parents under the 1987 Act had the product harmed one of them.

The framers of the 1987 Act would have been especially aware of the need to make provision for the effects of dangerously defective products on unborn children as one of the most notorious cases of dangerously defective products causing harm in the second half of the twentieth century was provided by the drug thalidomide, that was licensed in the UK in 1958 as a cure for morning sickness in pregnant women. Soon after it was licensed, women who had taken thalidomide while pregnant gave birth to disabled children. The connection between thalidomide and the disabilities was quickly established, and the drug was withdrawn in 1961, but not before 2,000 babies were born with thalidomide-linked disabilities, of which about 1,500 subsequently died.

Were a comparable tragedy to occur again today as a result of a drug affecting babies in the womb, the children that were born with disabilities might be able to sue

---

[10] See above, § 1.15(B)(3).
[11] See above, § 11.8.

the producers of the drug under the CDCLA, on the basis that the producers would have been liable to their mothers under the Consumer Protection Act 1987 had the drug harmed them. However, the producers might be able to escape liability by invoking the 'development risks defence',[12] under which they could not be held liable to anyone for the harm done by their drug if the state of scientific and technical knowledge at the time the drug was marketed was not such as to enable the drug's defective nature to be discovered. (A provision that would have arguably protected the manufacturers of thalidomide.)

29.3 Recovery of state losses

In two situations, the State is allowed to sue someone who has committed a tort for compensation in respect of the losses that it has suffered as a result of that tort being committed.

(1) *The Social Security (Recovery of Benefits) Act 1997. Roughly speaking*, this Act provides that someone who has made a compensation payment to the victim of a tort will be held liable to the State for the value of *all* the social security payments that have been made to the victim of that tort as a result of her being a victim of that tort.[13]

(2) *The Health and Social Care (Community Health and Standards) Act 2003.* Section 150 of this Act covers the situation where B, the victim of a tort, has suffered some kind of injury ('physical or psychological')[14] as a result of that tort being committed. If B has received treatment on the National Health Service (NHS) for that injury, or has been provided with an ambulance service on the NHS as a result of suffering that injury, then anyone who makes a compensation payment to B in respect of that injury will be liable to pay charges to the NHS for the treatment, or ambulance services, received by B. If B was partly to blame for her injury so that the compensation payable to her is liable to be reduced for contributory negligence, the charges payable in respect of the NHS services received by B will be reduced by a corresponding amount.[15]

---

[12] Discussed further above, § 11.6(5).

[13] Space does not allow us to say more than this. For a *very* detailed treatment of the Act, see Lewis 1999, 113–222.

[14] Section 150(5) provides that '"Injury" does not include any disease.'

[15] Section 153(3).

Chapter 30
Accessory liability

Aims and objectives

Reading this chapter should enable you to:

(1) Understand what significance the law attaches to the fact that someone was an accessory to a tort committed by someone else.

(2) Understand in what situations someone will be held to have been an accessory to another person's tort.

(3) Get a good grasp of the debate surrounding whether the law should (as it does not, currently) say that someone who knowingly assisted someone else to commit a tort was an accessory to that tort.

30.1 The basics

So far, we have assumed that there is only *one* way of committing a particular tort: you commit the tort of negligence by breaching a duty of care owed to another; the tort of battery by unlawfully and directly applying force to another's person; the tort of defamation by making a defamatory and untrue statement about another person to a third party; and so on.

In fact, there are *two* ways of committing a tort: committing a tort yourself, or by being an accessory to a tort committed by someone else. So you will commit the tort of battery if you hit B unlawfully; but you'll also commit the tort of battery if you successfully encourage A to hit B unlawfully. In the second situation, you will be held to have committed the tort of battery because you were an accessory to the battery carried out by A. So if A hits B with your encouragement, B will be able to sue you, or A, or both you and A, for damages; and you and A will be *jointly* liable to pay the damages that are due to B.[1]

There are basically four ways in which you can become an accessory to somebody else's tort: (1) by *procuring* the tort; (2) by *authorising* the tort; (3) by *ratifying* the tort;

---

[1] The significance of two or more people being *jointly* liable to pay damages to a claimant was explored above: see § 23.4(B).

(4) as a result of the tort having been committed in furtherance of a *common design* that you and the tortfeasor agreed to carry out. The next section will explore these different ways of becoming an accessory to a tort committed by someone else.

30.2 Requirements

(1) *Procuring.* In *John Hudson & Co Ltd* v *Oaten* (1980), Oliver LJ said, 'A man who procures the commission by another person of a tortious act becomes liable because he then becomes principal in the commission of the act. It is his tort.'[2]

In *CBS Songs* v *Amstrad* (1988), Lord Templeman made it clear that 'A defendant may procure [someone to commit a tort] by inducement, incitement or persuasion.'[3] He then went on to observe that 'Generally speaking, inducement, incitement or persuasion to [commit a tort] must be by a defendant to an individual tortfeasor and must identifiably procure a particular [tort] in order to make the defendant liable as a joint [tortfeasor].'[4] Two points need to be made about this way of becoming an accessory to a tort.

First, if A has committed a tort by doing *x*, C can only be held to have procured A to commit that tort if his words of inducement, incitement or persuasion *played some part* in A's decision to do *x*. It would be going too far to demand that it be shown that A would *not* have done *x but for* C's words; but it must be shown that A took C's words into account in deciding to do *x*.

Secondly, if something C said to A led A to commit a tort by doing *x*, C can only be held to have procured A to commit that tort if C *intended to encourage* A to do *x* when he spoke to A. So, for example, suppose *Friend* told *Husband* that his wife was having an affair. As a result, *Husband* beat his wife up, thereby committing the tort of battery. *Friend* can only be said to have procured *Husband* to commit the tort of battery if, when he told *Husband* of his wife's affair, he intended to encourage *Husband* to beat his wife up.

(2) *Authorisation.* If A commits a tort by doing *x*, and C has granted A permission to do *x* then C will be held to be an accessory to A's tort.[5]

It does not have to be shown that A would not have committed his tort but for C's giving him permission. For example, if *Landlord* has agreed that *Tenant* can use the house for *Tenant's* band to rehearse in, it is no defence – when *Landlord* is sued by his neighbours for private nuisance – for *Landlord* to argue that had he not given his permission, *Tenant* would still have used the house for band rehearsals.

However, if A has committed a tort by doing *x*, C can only be held to have been an accessory to A's tort under this head if C had the authority, or purported to have the authority, to permit A to do *x*.[6] So if *Teen* produces an illegal copy of a CD or a DVD on her computer, the manufacturer of that computer cannot be said to have 'authorised' *Teen* to commit this

---

[2] 19 June 1980 (unreported), quoted by House of Lords in *Credit Lyonnais NV* v *ECGD* [2000] 1 AC 486, 497–8.
[3] [1988] AC 1013, at 1058.
[4] Ibid.
[5] For further discussion of this point in relation to the tort of private nuisance, see above, § 13.9(B).
[6] See *CBS Inc* v *Ames Records & Tapes Ltd* [1982] Ch 91, at 106 (per Whitford J): 'authorisation can only come from somebody having or purporting to have authority . . . an act is not authorised by somebody who . . . does not purport to have any authority which he can grant to justify the doing of the act.'

breach of copyright because the manufacturer does not have, and does not pretend to have, the authority to permit *Teen* to produce illegal CDs and DVDs on her computer.[7]

(3) *Ratification.* If A commits a tort by doing *x*, and C subsequently treats A as though A did *x* on C's behalf, then C will be held to be an accessory to A's tort.

For example, in *Hilbery* v *Hatton* (1864), a ship called *John Brooks* was stranded off the coast of Africa. A man called Ward – who owned cargo on board the ship – unlawfully took charge of the ship and sold it to the defendants' agent, a man called Thompson, who was principally employed by the defendants to buy palm oil for them. Thompson subsequently wrote to the defendants announcing that he had purchased *John Brooks* for them; presumably, he thought the defendants could use the ship in their business. The defendants wrote back, approving the purchase. It was held that Thompson had committed the tort of conversion in buying, and taking possession, of the ship, and that the defendants also committed the tort of conversion when they approved the purchase of the ship on their behalf.

(4) *Common design.* In *The Koursk* (1924), the Court of Appeal endorsed the proposition that 'Persons are said to be joint tortfeasors when their respective shares in the commission of the tort are done in furtherance of a common design.'[8] The UK Supreme Court's decision in *Fish & Fish Ltd* v *Sea Shepherd UK* (2015) helps to clarify what is required for A to be held to have committed B's tort as an accessory under this head: '[A] must have acted in a way which furthered the commission of the tort by [B]; and [A] must have done so in pursuance of a common design to do or secure the doing of the acts which constituted the tort.'[9]

Some have argued that liability for committing the tort of unlawful means conspiracy[10] has its origins in this rule of accessory liability.[11] However – as the House of Lords observed in *Revenue & Customs Commissioners* v *Total Network SL* (2008) – this is incorrect.[12] Suppose that *Rogue* and *Villain* agree to imprison a famous opera *Singer* so as to disrupt a performance of *Le Nozze di Figaro* which *Impresario* is putting on. *Rogue* subsequently kidnaps *Singer* and the opera performance has to be cancelled.

It is well established that in this situation *Impresario* can bring a claim for unlawful means conspiracy against both *Rogue* and *Villain*. It is not clear how *Impresario*'s claim can be rationalised as being based on a form of accessory liability. Clearly, *Rogue* committed the tort of false imprisonment in kidnapping *Singer*, and *Villain* will be liable to *Singer* for false imprisonment as an accessory to *Rogue*'s tort. But that does not explain the basis of *Impresario*'s claims against *Rogue* and *Villain* as it was *Singer* who was the victim of *Rogue*'s act of false imprisonment, not *Impresario*.

It is possible to argue that in kidnapping *Singer*, *Rogue* committed the tort of intentional infliction of harm by unlawful means[13] in relation to *Impresario*, and that *Villain* is an accessory to *that* tort. Given this, one could argue that the real reason why the courts

---

[7] *CBS Songs* v *Amstrad plc* [1988] AC 1013, 1053–5.

[8] [1924] P 140, 151, 156, 159. (*The Koursk* is discussed further above, § 23.4, fn 26.)

[9] [2015] AC 1229, at [21] (per Lord Toulson). See also Lord Sumption's formulation at [37] ('[A] will be liable if . . . (i) he has assisted the commission of the tort by [B], (ii) pursuant to a common design with [B], (iii) to do an act which is, or turns out to be, tortious'; and, to almost identical effect, Lord Neuberger's formulation at [55].

[10] Discussed above, § 20.7.

[11] For arguments that the tort of unlawful means conspiracy is rooted in this rule of accessory liability, see Sales 1990, and Stevens 2007, 249.

[12] [2008] 1 AC 1174, at [103] (per Lord Walker) and [225] (per Lord Neuberger).

[13] Discussed above, § 20.4.

allow *Impresario* to sue *Rogue* and *Villain* for unlawful means conspiracy is that *Rogue* committed the tort of intentional infliction of harm by unlawful means in relation to *Impresario*, and *Villain* is an accessory to that tort. However, this seems implausible – the tort of unlawful means conspiracy existed long before the tort of intentional infliction of harm by unlawful means was explicitly recognised by the courts.

30.3 Limits

The decision of the House of Lords in *CBS Songs* v *Amstrad plc* (1988) makes it clear that merely assisting someone to commit a tort will *not* make you an accessory to that tort.[14] So in the *Amstrad* case, CBS Songs argued that Amstrad were liable for all the breaches of copyright that were committed by people who used stereos manufactured by Amstrad to produce copies of cassette tapes bought in the shops. The House of Lords held that this would only be the case if Amstrad had procured or authorised people to make these copies, or that these copies were produced as part of a common design between Amstrad and their customers. The mere fact that Amstrad was helping its customers commit breaches of copyright by manufacturing their stereos was not enough to make it liable as an accessory for those breaches of copyright.

The fact that there is no accessory liability for assisting someone to commit a tort creates a puzzle in the law. The puzzle is that it *is* an equitable wrong dishonestly to assist someone else to commit a breach of trust.[15] Moreover, someone who aids or abets someone to commit a crime will be held to have committed that crime.[16] So why is the common law so reluctant to impose liability in tort on someone who assists someone else to commit a tort?[17] The answer may lie in the fact that there are a huge number of perfectly legitimate actions that may end up assisting someone to commit a tort. Some random examples are: selling someone a knife or a bottle of bleach, creating a computer on which DVDs or CDs can be created, giving someone lessons in self-defence, and telling someone where a particular person lives or what their phone number is.

Paul Davies argues that we can impose liability for assisting someone else to commit a tort without unacceptable side effects if we only make people liable for assisting a tort if they *knew* that their actions would have the effect of assisting that *particular* tort to be committed.[18] Under this formula, A would be held liable if he saw B beating up C, and A threw a knife to B, which B then used to stab C. In a case where a defendant like Twitter knows that it is assisting *Gossip* to unlawfully violate *Celebrity*'s privacy by maintaining the Twitter account on which *Gossip* is revealing *Celebrity*'s secrets, Davies argues that Twitter should be liable unless it can take advantage of a defence of *justification*.[19] Such a defence

---

[14] See also *Credit Lyonnais NV* v *Export Credit Guarantee Department* [2000] 1 AC 486, discussed below, § 31.7.

[15] Authorities on the modern form of this wrong are: *Royal Brunei Airlines* v *Tan* [1995] 2 AC 378, *Twinsectra Ltd* v *Yardley* [2002] 2 AC 164, and *Barlow Clowes International* v *Eurotrust International* [2006] 1 WLR 1476.

[16] Accessories and Abettors Act 1861, s 8.

[17] This reluctance carries over into the law of negligence, where the courts take a very cautious approach to finding that a defendant owed a claimant a duty of care not to do something that enabled a third party to commit a tort in relation to the claimant: see above, § 5.3.

[18] Davies 2015, 200–2, 213–21. Dietrich 2011 takes a very similar position (at 247).

[19] Davies 2015, 214–15.

might well be available to it if it can show that 'despite knowing that [its] product would be used to commit [breaches of privacy], it was reasonable for [Twitter] nevertheless to provide the product given the substantial lawful uses to which that product could be put.'[20]

There are two problems with Davies' position. The first is that while he insists that *actual* knowledge that you are assisting someone else to commit a tort should be required before assistance liability is imposed,[21] the courts have in the past found themselves incapable of sticking to such a position. Once liability based on actual knowledge is allowed, the courts invariably expand liability to cases of 'Nelsonian knowledge' (turning a blind eye to the effects of one's actions),[22] and once they have made that move away from requiring actual knowledge, they are unable to find any natural stopping place in determining what sort of knowledge will make a defendant liable and what will not. The law on liability for knowingly assisting someone to commit a tort would soon turn into the same sort of legal quagmire that, for example, the law on when someone will be held liable for knowingly receiving assets disposed of in breach of trust has become.[23]

Secondly, Davies argues that any unacceptable side effects caused by adopting an expanded definition of what amounts to culpable knowledge that your actions will assist someone else to commit a tort can be avoided through making a defence of justification available to defendants. However, as Davies himself points out, 'the contours of the defence of justification have not been clearly defined'.[24] Given this, the prospect of possibly being able to take advantage of a defence of justification is likely to provide little reassurance to companies like Twitter or Craigslist, that would want to know in advance whether they could be held liable for assisting someone to commit an invasion of privacy, or to commit a rape, when the services they provide are abused.

It seems that if the law were to open the door to defendants being held liable simply on the basis that they assisted someone to commit a tort, the law would soon become unacceptably uncertain and inhibit many perfectly legitimate activities.[25] Not holding A liable in a case where he throws a knife to B, which is then used to stab C, is a price we have to pay in the interests of legal certainty and the public welfare.

Further reading

The leading work on this area of law is now **Paul Davies'** *Accessory Liability* (**Hart Publishing, 2015**). Those who are unable to lay their hands on Davies' book could usefully consult his earlier article **'Accessory liability for assisting torts'** (2011) 70 *Cambridge Law Journal* 353. It is also worth reading **Carty, 'Joint tortfeasance and assistance liability'** (1999) 19 *Legal Studies* 489 and **Dietrich, 'Accessorial liability in the law of torts'** (2011) 31 *Legal Studies* 231.

---

[20] Davies 2015, 243.

[21] Davies 2015, 208–9.

[22] Called 'Nelsonian knowledge' because at the Battle of Copenhagen in 1801, Vice-Admiral Nelson disregarded a signal to retreat from his commanding officer by looking with his blind eye through a telescope at the flags signalling that he should retreat and remarking 'I really see do not see the signal!'

[23] See *Fish & Fish Ltd* v *Sea Shepherd UK* [2013] 1 WLR 3700, at [44] (per Beatson LJ).

[24] Davies 2015, 226.

[25] A criticism that can already be levelled at the criminal law, which does make people criminally liable for culpably assisting someone else to commit a crime.

Chapter 31
Vicarious liability

Aims and objectives

Reading this chapter should enable you to:

(1) Understand in what ways vicarious liability is distinct from other forms of liability for harm caused by a third party's acts or omissions (such as accessory liability, or liability arising out of the breach of a non-delegable duty of care).

(2) Get a good grasp of the full range of situations where one person will be held vicarious liable in respect of a tort committed by someone else; in particular, the case where an employee will be held vicariously liable in respect of a tort committed by an *employee* 'in the *course of his employment*'.

(3) To understand when someone will be held to have been working for someone else as that person's *employee*.

(4) To understand the history of the tests for determining whether an employee who has committed a tort did so in the course of his employment; in particular, the original Salmond test for determining this issue and the change in the law caused by the decision of the House of Lords in *Lister* v *Hesley Hall Ltd* (2002).

(5) To understand when an employee is likely to be held to have committed a tort 'in the course of his employment' under the new *Lister* test; in particular, the idea that this test will be satisfied if *either* the employee was acting 'in the course of his employment' under the old Salmond test *or* there was a special risk attached to the employee's employment that he would commit the tort that he committed.

(6) To understand the new category of situation where someone (A) will be held to be vicariously liable in respect of a tort committed by someone else (B): where there existed a relationship 'akin to employment' between A and B, and B committed his tort in the course of working for A; and to understand when the courts are likely to find that a relationship 'akin to employment' existed.

31.1 The basics

Vicarious liability is not accessory liability. In a situation where A has committed a tort in relation to B and C is vicariously liable in respect of that tort, C will *not* be held to have committed that tort.[1] But the courts will treat C *as though* he had committed that tort along with A. So if B can sue A for compensatory damages, she will also be able to sue C for such damages.[2]

Three points need to be emphasised about this form of liability:

A. Joint liability

In the situation where C is vicariously liable in respect of a tort that A has committed in relation to B, A and C will be *jointly* liable to pay damages to B. So if B releases A from liability, all her rights to sue C for damages will usually also be extinguished.[3]

B. Vicarious liability and personal liability

It is very easy to get into the habit of thinking that whenever A does something that results in C being held liable in tort to pay damages to B, that is an example of vicarious liability. But if we are to think clearly about the law on vicarious liability, we have to resist this temptation. Consider the **Fur Coat Problem** (though it is not really a problem at all):

> *Rich* entrusts her fur coat to *Store*'s care, and *Store* gives the coat to *Shifty* to look after. *Shifty* then steals the coat.

It is well established that in this situation, *Rich* will be entitled to sue *Store* for damages for the loss of her coat.[4] At first sight, this looks like an example of vicarious liability.[5] *Shifty* has done something wrong by stealing the coat, and *Store* ends up being held liable to compensate *Rich* for the loss caused by *Shifty*'s wrong, as though *Store* had stolen the coat itself.

But appearances mislead. The real reason that *Store* is liable to *Rich* here is that it owed *Rich* a non-delegable duty[6] to take reasonable steps to safeguard *Rich*'s coat and *Shifty*'s actions put *Store* in breach of this duty: *Store* gave *Shifty* the job of looking after the coat and *Shifty* failed to look after the coat properly.[7] So *Store* is not held liable to pay *Rich*

---

[1] Though some would dispute this. See § 31.6(6), below, for further discussion of this point.

[2] Birks 1995 observes at 41 that: 'A "vicarious" liability is a liability which one person takes over from another, and as such [is] not his but that other's, just as a "vicar" was originally a person in holy orders who occupied a place which was not his but the rector's whose substitute he was.' This is not quite right: A's liability to pay damages to B is not shifted on to C, but is shared with C.

[3] See above, § 23.4(B).

[4] *Morris* v *CW Martin & Sons Ltd* [1966] 1 QB 716.

[5] It was assumed that this is an example of vicarious liability in *Lister* v *Hesley Hall Ltd* [2002] 1 AC 215, at [19] (per Lord Steyn), [46] (per Lord Clyde), [57] (per Lord Hobhouse), [75]–[76] (per Lord Millett). See also *Dubai Aluminium Co Ltd* v *Salaam* [2003] 2 AC 366, at [129] (per Lord Millett).

[6] Any reader currently unacquainted with the concept of a non-delegable duty of care should read § 7.5(B), above, before proceeding further.

[7] See Weir 2006, 111–12. Also *New South Wales* v *Lepore* (2003) 212 CLR 511, at [127] (per Gaudron J) and at [147], [161] (per McHugh J).

damages here under the law on vicarious liability. It is *personally liable* under the law of bailment (or negligence, or conversion, as one prefers) to compensate *Rich* for the loss that she has suffered as a result of *Store*'s breach of the duty of care it owed *Rich* to take reasonable steps to safeguard her coat.

There are some who argue that even though the law may say that *Store* has committed a tort here, and that is what *Store* is being held liable for, what is *really* going on is that *Store* is being held vicariously liable in respect of *Shifty*'s tort. So, for example, Gleeson CJ, of the High Court of Australia, urged in *Leichhardt Municipal Council v Montgomery* (2007) that the law should 'frankly acknowledge' that in cases where someone is held liable for breaching a non-delegable duty of care owed to another, 'what is involved is not the breach by the defendant of a special kind of duty, but an imposition upon a defendant of a special kind of vicarious [liability].'[8]

With all due respect to Gleeson CJ, and those who think like him,[9] the law on when someone will be held liable for breaching a non-delegable duty of care *cannot* be subsumed within the law on vicarious liability.[10] Consider the **Slippery Canteen Floor Problem:**

Part of the floor of the canteen at *Boss*'s factory is slippery because someone spilled a drink on it. *Boss* tells one of his employees, *Lackey*, to clean up the spillage. *Lackey* fails to do so for no good reason. Subsequently, another one of *Boss*'s employees, *Unlucky*, slips on the spilled drink and breaks his leg.

It is well established that in this situation, *Unlucky* will be entitled to sue *Boss in negligence* for damages for his broken leg. *Lackey*'s failure to clean up the spillage put *Boss* in breach of the non-delegable duty he owed *Unlucky* to take reasonable steps to see that the canteen would be safe for her to use. We *cannot* re-explain *Boss*'s liability in this case as being a form of vicarious liability because *Lackey* did not do anything wrong *to Unlucky* in failing to clean up the spillage. *Lackey* did not owe *Unlucky* a duty to clean up the spillage. So if *Boss* is held liable here, it can only be because *Boss* did something wrong to *Unlucky*, not because *Lackey* did something wrong to *Unlucky*.

C. Vicarious liability and accessory liability

Consider the following two situations:

1. *Boss* successfully encourages *Tough* to beat *Victim* up.

2. *Tough*, *Boss*'s employee, beats *Victim* up with the result that *Boss* is held vicariously liable for *Tough*'s battery.

In situation (1), *Boss* will be held to have committed the tort of battery in relation to *Victim*. In situation (2), *Boss* will *not* be held to have committed the tort of battery, but will otherwise be treated by the courts *as though* he had beaten *Victim* up and will

---

[8] [2007] HCA 6, at [24].
[9] See, for example, Williams 1956b; Fleming 1998, 434.
[10] Stevens 2007, 118.

consequently be held liable to pay damages to *Victim*. But what practical difference does it make whether *Boss* is held to have committed the tort of battery, or is treated *as though* he has committed the tort of battery? There are two potential effects:

First, in situation (1), *Boss* is a wrongdoer and a court may award exemplary damages – damages designed to punish *Boss* for his conduct – against him. In situation (2), it would be much more controversial to award exemplary damages against *Boss*. After all, if *Boss* is not *actually* a wrongdoer – but is merely treated for one reason or another as though he were one – how can it be legitimate to punish him for what he has done in this situation?

Secondly, because *Boss* is an actual wrongdoer in situation (1), there is a possibility that someone else – say, *Chief* – might be vicariously liable in respect of *Boss*'s wrong to *Victim*. So it might end up that *Victim* could sue *three* people for damages in situation (1): *Tough* (for battery), *Boss* (for battery), and *Chief* (on the basis that he is vicariously liable for *Boss*'s battery). In situation (2), because *Boss* is not an *actual* wrongdoer, no one else can be held vicariously liable for what *Boss* has done in this situation. So *Victim* will be confined to suing *Tough* and *Boss* for damages here.[11]

31.2 Situations of vicarious liability

There are many different situations in which one person will be vicariously liable in respect of a tort committed by another:

1. *Employment.* If A is B's *employer*, A will be vicariously liable in respect of a tort committed by B if that tort is committed by B 'in the course of his employment'.[12]

2. *Relationship akin to employment.* The UK Supreme Court has recently recognised that if B commits a tort in the course of working for A, then A will be vicariously liable in respect of that tort even if B is not technically A's employee – it will be enough if A and B's relationship is 'sufficiently akin' to that of the relationship between an employer and an employee.[13]

3. *Police.* If A is the chief police officer in charge of an area in which B, a police officer, is working, A will be vicariously liable in respect of a tort committed by B in performing his functions as a police officer.[14]

4. *Agency.*[15] If A appoints B to act as his agent,[16] and B commits a tort while acting within the actual or ostensible scope of her authority as A's agent, A will be vicariously liable in respect of B's tort.[17]

---

[11] See *Credit Lyonnais Bank Nederland NV* v *Export Credit Guarantee Department* [2000] 1 AC 486 (discussed below, § 31.8).

[12] It used to be the case that if an employee of the Crown committed a tort in the course of his employment, the Crown would not be held vicariously liable in respect of that tort. That rule has now been abolished by s 2(1)(a) of the Crown Proceedings Act 1947.

[13] *Various Claimants* v *Catholic Child Welfare Society* [2013] 2 AC 1.

[14] Police Act 1996, s 88.

[15] See Watson & Noonan 2009.

[16] An 'agent' is someone who acts as someone else's representative for legal purposes.

[17] *Lloyd* v *Grace, Smith & Co* [1912] AC 716 (for an alternative explanation of the decision in this case, see above, § 7.5(B)); *Uxbridge Permanent Benefit Building Society* v *Pickard* [1939] 2 KB 248; *Armagas Ltd* v *Mundogas Ltd, The Ocean Frost* [1986] AC 717.

5. *Car owners.* Suppose that A requested B to perform some task for him which required B to drive A's car. Suppose further that in performing that task B negligently crashed A's car and in so doing injured C. It has been held – perhaps by analogy to the above rule dealing with vicarious liability for the acts of one's agents – that in this situation, A will be vicariously liable in respect of B's negligence.[18]

6. *Partnership.* Under s 10 of the Partnership Act 1890, the partners in a firm will be vicariously liable in respect of a tort committed by one of the partners in that firm so long as the partner in question was acting 'in the ordinary course of the business of the firm'.[19]

7. *Joint venture.* If A and B embark on a joint venture, and B commits a tort in the course of furthering that venture, then A will be vicariously liable in respect of B's tort.

In *Brooke v Bool* (1928), the defendant let to the claimant a shop on the ground floor of a house next door to the defendant's home. The claimant agreed that each day the defendant could enter the shop after the claimant had left it to check that it was securely locked up. One night a lodger in the defendant's home told the defendant that he thought he could smell gas coming from the claimant's shop. The defendant and the lodger both went to investigate. They inspected a gas pipe which passed down a wall in the claimant's shop, the defendant inspecting the lower half of the pipe and the lodger the upper half. The lodger used a naked light to inspect his half of the gas pipe. Unfortunately, the upper half of the gas pipe was leaking gas and when the gas came into contact with the lodger's light there was an explosion which damaged the claimant's goods. The lodger had been negligent in using a naked light to inspect the gas pipe and the defendant was held to be vicariously liable in respect of the lodger's negligence: he and the lodger had been engaged in a joint venture (checking for a gas leak) and the lodger had been attempting to further that venture when he acted as he did.[20]

Of these seven situations in which one person will be held vicariously liable in respect of a tort committed by someone else, the most important by far is the first. (Though the second may come to assume increasing importance in the future and may in time threaten

---

[18] See *Ormrod v Crosville Motor Services Ltd* [1953] 1 WLR 1120 (criticised, Brooke-Smith 1954). The defendant asked O to drive his car down to Monte Carlo so that the defendant could drive it in a motor rally there. In doing so, O negligently crashed the car into a bus. It was held that the defendant was vicariously liable in respect of O's negligence. *Ormrod* did *not* apply in *Klein v Caluori* [1971] 1 WLR 619, where F borrowed the defendant's car without his consent; when the defendant discovered this, he told F to bring the car back. As F was driving the car back, he negligently crashed into the claimant's car. Held, the defendant was not vicariously liable in respect of F's negligence because F was not performing a task for the defendant in bringing the car back – the job of bringing the car back was always F's to perform, not the defendant's. Neither did it apply in *Morgans v Launchbury* [1973] AC 127, where the defendant's husband went to the pub in the defendant's car. Realising he was too drunk to drive himself home, he had C drive him home in the defendant's car. On the way home, C drove the car so negligently that the claimants were injured. It was held that the defendant was not vicariously liable in respect of C's negligence as the defendant did not ask C to drive her husband home. See also *Nelson v Raphael* [1979] RTR 437.

[19] It is worth noting that vicarious liability used to arise in the context of a very different kind of partnership: a husband used to be held vicariously liable in respect of any torts committed by his wife, but that rule was abolished by s 3 of the Law Reform (Married Women and Joint Tortfeasors) Act 1935.

[20] Stevens 2007, at 248–9, seems to treat this case as an example of accessory liability, but as there was no agreement between the defendant and the lodger that the lodger should use a naked light to inspect the pipe (and no encouragement from the defendant that the lodger should do so), we would prefer to see it as an example of vicarious liability. Even Carty 1999 (at 500) concedes that if *Brooke v Bool* is an example of accessory liability, it is 'probably at the outer limits' of such liability.

the previously well-established rule that if A gets B to do some work for him as an *independent contractor*, A will *never* be vicariously liable in respect of a tort committed by B, even if B commits that tort in the course of doing the work that A has hired him to do.)[21]

The rule that an employer will be held vicariously liable for a tort committed by one of her employees if that tort was committed in the course of the employee's employment raises two key issues: (1) When can someone be said to be someone else's *employee?* and (2) When can a tort committed by an employee be said to have been committed *in the course of his employment?* Most of the rest of this chapter will be devoted to answering these questions.

31.3 Who is an employee?

Suppose that A committed a tort while working for C. When can we say that A was working for C as an employee of C's?[22] The basic answer is – we look at the nature of the contract between A and C that governed A and C's relationship. If it was a contract *of service* then A was working for C as an *employee*. If it was a contract *for services* then A was working for C as an *independent contractor*.

This does not get us very far. (Though it does emphasise that you can only be said to be working for someone else as their employee if you are contractually bound to work for them. So a wife who types up some documents for her husband as a favour to him is not acting as an employee in typing the documents.)[23] We need to know how to determine whether A's contract with C is a contract of service or a contract for services.

For a long time, the courts thought the distinction between a contract of service and a contract for services lay in the amount of *control* the contract gave C over *how* A did his work. If C was allowed under the contract to dictate how A did his work, then it was a contract of service. If, on the other hand, the contract merely specified what work A was supposed to do, and it was left up to A to decide how to do it, then it was a contract for services.[24] However, the courts have now rejected the 'control test' as an unsatisfactory means of

---

[21] Of course, if A was subject to a non-delegable duty and he gave B – an independent contractor – the job of discharging that duty, then B might put A in breach of that duty and A might incur some sort of liability as a result. However, as has already been made clear, that liability will be personal in nature, not vicarious.

[22] See, generally, Kidner 1995.

[23] See *Carmichael* v *National Power plc* [1999] 1 WLR 2042 (tour guides who worked for defendant on casual basis, turning up for work as and when they were required to do so, could not claim to be employees of the defendant as they were under no obligation to turn up for work when they were asked to do so).

[24] See *Performing Right Society Ltd v Mitchell & Booker (Palais de Danse) Ltd* [1924] 1 KB 762 (finding that a dance hall band was employed by the owner of the dance hall because the contract under which they worked gave the owner 'the right of continuous, dominant and detailed control on every point, including the nature of the music to be played [by the band]' (at 771)). See also *Yewens* v *Noakes* (1880) 6 QBD 530, 532–3: 'A servant is a person who is subject to the command of his master as to the manner in which he shall do his work' (per Bramwell LJ) and *Honeywill and Stein Ltd* v *Larkin Brothers Ltd* [1934] 1 KB 191, 196: 'The determination whether [someone] is a servant . . . on the one hand or an independent contractor on the other depends on whether or not the employer not only determines what is to be done, but retains control of the actual performance, in which case the doer is a servant . . . ; but if the employer, while prescribing the work to be done, leaves the manner of doing it to the control of the doer, the latter is an independent contractor' (per Slesser LJ).

determining whether a contract to do work for someone else is a contract of service or a contract for services. In cases where an employee has very specialised skills, an employer cannot hope to control how the employee does her work: but the employee remains an employee for all that.[25] The modern approach to this issue[26] is more impressionistic. We look at a range of different factors and form an impression as to whether we are dealing with a contract of service or a contract for services. Relevant factors will include:

(1) *Scope of duty.* A key difference between employees and independent contractors is that employees are employed to work for a particular period of time, whereas independent contractors are normally hired to perform a particular job – how long they take over it is up to them.[27]

The fact that an independent contractor can be hired to work for a particular period of time (for example, a nanny being hired to babysit for a certain number of hours in the evening) means this factor cannot provide a foolproof method of determining whether a contract is a contract of service or a contract for services. However, if C hires A to perform a particular job, and leaves A completely free to determine how he will do that job and how long he will spend on it, it is almost inevitable that A will be classified as an independent contractor, rather than an employee.

(2) *Payment.* Following on from the last point, employees are paid according to the time they have worked for their employer. In most cases, they are paid *wages* (an amount per week worked) or a *salary* (an amount per month worked).[28] Independent contractors, by contrast, are normally paid a *fee* for doing a particular job. Again, payment by way of a fee would almost inevitably indicate that the person receiving the fee should be classified as an independent contractor rather than an employee. But a contract providing for payment for time worked will not always be a contract of service.[29]

(3) *Personal nature of duty.* Contracts of employment are like prison sentences: the work to be done under the contract has to be done by the employee, and cannot be done by

---

[25] See *Gold* v *Essex County Council* [1942] 2 KB 293, 305 (per Mackinnon LJ, giving the example of the master of a ship).

[26] 'Modern' is a relative term here. The approach set out here dates back to Lord Thankerton's judgment in *Short* v *J W Henderson Ltd* (1946) 62 TLR 427, setting out (at 429) 'four indicia' that we should look at in determining whether a given contract is a contract of service or a contract for services. See also Cooke J's judgment in *Market Investigations Ltd* v *Minister of Social Security* [1969] 2 QB 173, 184–5 (endorsed by the Privy Council in *Lee Ting Sang* v *Chung Chi-Keung* [1990] 2 AC 374, at 382), setting out a range of factors to be considered in determining whether someone who has contracted to work for another is 'in business on his own account' (if yes, he is an independent contractor; if no, he is an employee).

[27] See *WHPT Housing Association Ltd* v *Secretary of State for Social Services* [1981] ICR 737, 748 (per Webster J): 'the difference between a contract of service and one for services must reside, essentially, in the terms of the principal obligation agreed to be undertaken by the employee – a word which I use without begging the question. In a contract of service . . . the principal obligation undertaken by the employee is to provide himself to serve: whereas in a contract for services the principal obligation is not to provide himself to serve the employer but his services for the use of the employer.'

[28] One of Lord Thankerton's 'four indicia' of whether A is working for C under a contract of employment was whether the contract provided for A to be paid a wage (see above, n 26).

[29] See, for example, *Argent* v *Minister of Social Security* [1968] 1 WLR 1749, where a school drama teacher (an actor who was normally out of work) was paid on an hourly basis, but was still found to be an independent contractor by virtue of the fact that whenever he found a paying job as an actor he would take a 'leave of absence' from his school duties in order to perform. This was not a vicarious liability case and the decision might have gone the other way had the teacher sexually abused a student and the issue was whether the school was vicariously liable for his actions. We could well expect the courts' decisions as to who is an employee and who is not to depend on the context in which that question arises.

anyone else. In contrast, an independent contractor will usually be free to subcontract the work to be done under the contract to somebody else. The important thing, where some-one hires an independent contractor to work for him, is that the job be done; not who will do it. However, there are exceptions: if C hires A to paint his portrait, A will be an inde-pendent contractor, but will also be required under the contract to paint the portrait himself and will not be allowed to delegate the job to anyone else.

(4) *Identity of the person for whom the work is being done.* Employees are not usually employ-ers. So if A is working for C, and C earns his money by working as employee for D, it will not usually be the case that A is an employee of C's. It is far more likely to be the case that A is an independent contractor, hired by C to help out with some job that C is too busy – because of his employment commitments – to do himself. However, there are (as usual) exceptions. Some employees (usually bankers or lawyers!) are paid so much they can afford to pay for a nanny to live with their family to help out with looking after children and doing various domestic chores. Such a live-in nanny would count as being an employee, rather than an independent contractor – she will be paid to work for a particular period of time; her contractual obligations are personal to her and cannot be discharged by anyone else; her major source of income will be from the family that she looks after (see (6), below); and the family for which she works will have a great deal of control over how she does her job (see (7), below).

(5) *Identity of the person doing the work.* The fact that employees are rarely employers (see (4), above) gives us an additional ground for distinguishing between a contract of service and a contract for services. If A contracts to do work for C, and A employs people to help him do that work, then A will normally be working for C as an independent con-tractor, and not as an employee.[30] And if A is a company, then A will definitely be an independent contractor. Companies can only be employers, or independent contractors, or both: they can never be employees. Only human beings can be employees.

(6) *Source of income.* Employees normally rely on their employer as their sole, or primary, source of income. In contrast, independent contractors normally earn money by working for a range of different people.

The courts have sought to articulate this relatively simple point in a variety of differ-ent ways. For example, in *Stephenson Jordan & Harrison Ltd v MacDonald & Evans* (1951), Denning LJ suggested that 'under a contract of service, a man is employed as part of the business and his work is done as an integral part of the business: whereas under a contract for services his work, although done for the business, is not integrated into it but is only accessory to it.'[31] Cooke J's suggestion in *Market Investigations* v *Minister of Social Security* (1969) that an independent contractor was 'in business on his own account' and that an employee was not[32] may be taken as making much the same point.

---

[30] Cooke J suggested in *Market Investigations* v *Minister of Social Security* [1969] 2 QB 173, at 185 that someone who 'hires his own helpers' would tend to be regarded as an independent contractor.

[31] (1951) 69 RPC 10, 22. See also *Bank voor Handel en Scheepvart NV* v *Slatford* [1953] 1 QB 248, where Denning LJ suggested (at 295) that 'the test of being a servant does not rest nowadays on submission to orders. It depends on whether the person is part and parcel of the organisation.' This test was criticised for being unduly vague by MacKenna J in *Ready Mixed Concrete (South East) Ltd v Minister of Pensions and National Insurance* [1968] 2 QB 497, at 524.

[32] See above, n 26.

(7) *Control.* While the courts have rejected the idea that you can determine whether A's contract to work for C is a contract of service or a contract for services by looking solely at how much control C is allowed to exercise under the contract over how A does his work, the degree of control that C has over A under the contract is still a relevant factor to be looked at in determining whether A is an employee of C's or an independent contractor.[33] Employees *are* normally subject to more control than independent contractors are.

(8) *Equipment.* A final factor that the courts will look at in determining whether A's contract to work for C is a contract of service or a contract for services is whether C supplies A with the equipment that he needs to do his work.[34] Employees tend to turn up to work and have the equipment they need to do their job supplied to them by their employer. By contrast, independent contractors tend to supply their own equipment. Again, this factor is not determinative – it is possible to think of cases that go the other way (for example, a chef who is an employee but turns up to work with his own knives and other cooking equipment; and a motivational speaker who visits firms as an independent contractor to speak to their employees, but expects the firms to provide all the presentational equipment he requires to do his job).

The table below sums up this section. Where A contracts to do work for C, we take into account a variety of different factors in determining whether A is an employee (working for C under a contract of service) or an independent contract (working for C under a contract for services):

Factors to be considered	The question to be asked:	The answer:	
		YES	NO
Scope of duty	Is A required to work for a particular time for C?		
Payment	Will A be paid according to how long he has worked for C?		
Nature of duty	Is A under a duty to carry out the work himself?		
Nature of C	Is C an employee himself?		
Nature of A	Is A an employer himself?		
Source of income	Is C A's primary source of income?		
Control	Does the contract give C control over how A does his work?		
Equipment	Does C provide A with the equipment he needs for his work?		

The more ticks that appear in the shaded boxes, the more likely it is that A is an employee of C's, rather than an independent contractor.

---

[33] See, for example, *Montgomery* v *Johnson Underwood Ltd* [2001] EWCA Civ 318 (held, a temp is not employed by the employment agency which places her with various employers on a temporary basis because the employment agency had no control over how she did her work) – though note again that this was not a vicarious liability case, but an unfair dismissal case (where again the issue of whether someone is an employee (and thus qualifies for various employment rights) is very important). The inconvenience of burdening temp agencies with unfair dismissal legislation may well have played an important part in the courts' decision not to find that the worker here was an employee.

[34] This factor was mentioned by Cooke J as a relevant factor in *Market Investigations* v *Minister of Social Security* [1969] 2 QB 173, 185.

31.4 Course of employment

We can now turn to the second of the two issues raised by the rule that an employer will be held vicariously liable in respect of a tort committed by one of his employees if that tort was committed *in the course of the employee's employment*: when we can we say that a tort was committed in the course of an employee's employment?

A. The Salmond test

Before the decision of the House of Lords in *Lister* v *Hesley Hall Ltd* (2002), one would use the *Salmond test* to determine whether an employee's tort was committed in the course of his employment. Under this test – set out by the great tort lawyer Sir John Salmond in the first edition of his *Law of Torts* – an employee's tort will have been committed in the course of his employment if it was:

> either (a) a wrongful act authorised by [the employee's employer], or (b) a wrongful and unauthorised mode of doing some act authorised by [the employee's employer][35]

To put the test another way, under the Salmond test, an employee's tort will have been committed in the course of his employment if *the employee did something he was employed to do by committing that tort*.

For example, in *Poland* v *John Parr & Sons* (1927), a carter who was employed by the defendants to accompany a cart carrying sugar bags as it travelled through Liverpool hit a claimant schoolboy who he mistakenly thought was trying to steal a bag from the cart. The boy fell under the impact of the blow and one of the wheels of the cart rolled over the boy's foot, breaking it. It was held that the defendants were vicariously liable in respect of the carter's battery. The carter had been acting in the course of his employment in hitting the claimant because he was doing something he was employed to do – prevent people stealing sugar from the cart – by hitting the claimant. True, the defendants may have been horrified at the *way* in which the claimant went about his job of preventing people stealing sugar; they may even have expressly forbidden him from using force to prevent people stealing sugar from the cart. But that is immaterial under the Salmond test. The only issue is whether the employee was doing something he was employed to do by committing the tort: whether he was allowed or forbidden to act in the way he did makes no difference.

Similarly, and much more recently, in *Bernard* v *Attorney-General of Jamaica* (2004) – a Privy Council case – a policeman wanted to use a public payphone to call for assistance but the claimant – who was using the payphone at the time – refused to hang up. The policeman took out his gun (the case occurred in Jamaica) and shot the claimant through the head. (Amazingly, the claimant survived the shooting.) The policeman's employers were found to be vicariously liable for the policeman's battery. The policeman had been doing something he was employed to do – freeing up the payphone so that he could call for assistance – by committing his tort. Getting hold of the phone by shooting the person

---

[35] Salmond 1907, 83. It should be pointed out that an employer will be held liable as an accessory for an employee's tort if the tort was committed with the employer's authority (see above, § 30.2(2)), and so there is no need in this kind of case (situation (a) in the Salmond test) to say that the employer will be held vicariously liable in respect of his employee's tort.

currently using it was completely uncalled for and unauthorised, but that is – again – immaterial under the Salmond test.[36]

In contrast, in *Heasmans v Clarity Cleaning Co* (1987), the claimants engaged the defendant cleaning company to clean its offices. One of the cleaners employed by the defendants to clean the claimants' offices made a number of long-distance telephone calls on the claimants' telephones while cleaning their offices, thereby committing the tort of conversion. The claimants sued the defendants, claiming that they were vicariously liable in respect of their cleaner's acts of conversion. The claim was dismissed on the ground that, under the Salmond test, the cleaner did not act in the course of his employment when he made his international telephone calls. The cleaner was not doing anything he was employed to do by making the international telephone calls.[37]

For the most part, the Salmond test for determining whether or not an employer would be vicariously liable in respect of a tort committed by one of his employees was straight-forward to apply. However, in certain marginal cases there were difficulties – arising out of the fact that it is not always clear how widely or narrowly we should characterise what an employee was employed to do. For example, in *London County Council v Cattermoles (Garages) Ltd* (1953), the defendants employed one Preston to work in their garage. One of Preston's duties was to move cars that had been left at the garage when they were in the way of other cars using the garage. He was told to move any cars by hand as he did not have a driving licence. Preston was instructed to move a van which was obstructing access to the defendants' petrol pumps. Preston got into the van and drove it into the road. However, he did not keep a proper lookout in driving the van into the road and it collided with the claimant's vehicle. The claimant sued the defendants claiming that they were vicariously liable in respect of Preston's negligence.

The case turned on the question: What was Preston employed to do? If he was employed to move cars in the defendants' garage *by hand* then Preston did *not* do anything he was

---

[36] See also *Limpus v London General Omnibus Company* (1862) 1 H&C 526; 158 ER 995 (bus company vicariously liable for bus driver's breaking of speed limit while driving buses on route); *Rose v Plenty* [1976] 1 WLR 141 (defendant employers vicariously liable in respect of milkman's negligent driving in driving milk float on his round); *Brown v Robinson* [2004] UKPC 56 (in an attempt to maintain order in a crowd of people waiting to get into a football stadium, a security guard got into an altercation with the claimant which resulted in his shooting the claimant; held that defendant employers of the security guard were vicariously liable for the shooting as the security guard acted as he did to maintain some discipline in the crowd).

[37] See also *Warren v Henleys Ltd* [1948] 2 All ER 935 (a petrol pump attendant struck a customer in the course of an altercation about whether or not the customer had paid for petrol taken from the petrol pump; held, that the employers of the attendant were not vicariously liable in respect of the battery committed by the attendant as the attendant did not do anything he was employed to do by striking the customer); *Keppel Bus Co v Sa'ad bin Ahmed* [1974] 1 WLR 1082 (bus conductor swore at passenger and then hit him when the passenger protested; held, bus company not vicariously liable in respect of conductor's battery as he did not do anything he was employed to do in hitting the passenger); *Deatons Pty Ltd v Flew* (1949) 79 CLR 370 (defendant hotel owners not vicariously liable in respect of tort committed by employee tending bar in hotel when she reacted to lewd suggestion by a patron of the bar by throwing beer, and subsequently an empty glass, in his face); *Storey v Ashton* (1869) LR 4 QB 476 (two employees of defendant's went by horse and cart to deliver some wine to a customer of the defendant's; on the way back, one employee persuaded the other to make a diversion and pick up a cask of wine from the first employee's brother-in-law; held, defendant not vicariously liable in respect of negligent way in which second employee drove horse and cart on the way to the home of the first employee's brother-in-law as second employee not employed to drive horse and cart to that destination).

employed to do by *driving* the van into the road without keeping a proper lookout. If he was simply employed to *move* cars in the defendants' garage, then Preston *did* do something he was employed to do by driving the van into the road without keeping a proper lookout. The Court of Appeal took a wide view of what Preston was employed to do in this case and found that Preston was employed to move cars in the defendants' garage. So the court concluded that Preston *was* acting in the course of his employment when he drove the van into the road without keeping a proper lookout.

It should also be noted that the application of the Salmond test in particular cases to determine whether an employer was vicariously liable in respect of a tort committed by one of his employees was sometimes affected by the following legal rule: In any proceedings between a claimant and an employer of an employee who has committed a tort, the employer will be *estopped* (or prevented) from denying that the employee in question was employed to do *x* if the employer led the claimant to believe that the employee was employed to do *x* and the claimant relied on that belief.

For example, in *Conway v George Wimpey & Co Ltd* (1951), the defendant building company took on some construction work at an airport and to help out their employees they had some of their employees drive lorries around the perimeter of the airport – the idea being that if any of the defendants' employees wanted a lift to another area of the airport, they could hitch a lift on one of these lorries. The claimant – who was not one of the defendants' employees – hitched a ride on one of these lorries and was injured as a result of the fact that the driver was negligent in driving the lorry. The Court of Appeal applied the Salmond test and held that the defendants were *not* vicariously liable in respect of their driver's negligence because he was not employed to give rides to people like the claimant: he was only employed to give rides to the employees of the defendant company who were working at the airport.

But it would have been different if the defendants had led the claimant to believe that their drivers were employed to give rides to *anyone* working in the airport and the claimant had relied on that belief by hitching a ride on one of the defendants' lorries. In such a case – when the claimant sued the defendants on the basis that they were vicariously liable in respect of their driver's negligence – the defendants would have been estopped (or prevented) from denying that their driver was employed to give rides to people like the claimant. The defendants would therefore have been unable to deny that their driver was acting in the course of his employment when he drove the claimant to his chosen destination in a negligent fashion. As it happened, the defendant company had done nothing to induce the claimant to believe that its lorry driver was employed to pick up people like him and give them lifts to where they wanted to go and so the defendant company was not estopped from denying that its lorry driver was employed to pick up people like the claimant.

This principle of estoppel is often said[38] to underlie the decision of the House of Lords in *Lloyd v Grace, Smith & Co* (1912).[39] In that case, the claimant owned two cottages. She was dissatisfied with the income she received from her assets and consulted the defendant firm of solicitors for advice. Her case was handled by one Sandles, the managing clerk of the firm. He tricked her into transferring the two cottages to him. The House of Lords

---

[38] See *Dubai Aluminium Co Ltd* v *Salaam* [2003] 2 AC 366, at [28] (per Lord Nicholls); *New South Wales* v *Lepore* (2003) 212 CLR 511, at [108]–[111] (per Gaudron J) and [232] (per Gummow and Hayne JJ).

[39] For an alternative explanation of the case, see above, § 7.5(B).

held that the defendants were liable to compensate the claimant for the losses suffered by her as a result of Sandles's deceit. It is possible to argue that the source of the defendants' liability in this case was that they were vicariously liable in respect of Sandles's deceit – and the reason why they were vicariously liable in respect of Sandles's deceit was that they were estopped from denying that Sandles did something he was employed to do when he persuaded the claimant to sign over her cottages to him. After all, the defendants did lead the claimant to believe that Sandles was acting with their authority in *whatever* he did in relation to the claimant's affairs and the claimant relied on that belief by allowing Sandles to handle her affairs.

B. The decision in *Lister* v *Hesley Hall Ltd*

We are now in a position to understand the radical change in the law that was brought about by the decision of the House of Lords in *Lister v Hesley Hall Ltd* (2002). In that case, the defendants ran a boarding house for children who attended a nearby school. The defendants employed a married couple, Mr and Mrs Grain, to run the boarding house and maintain discipline. Unfortunately, Mr Grain used his position to sexually abuse a number of the children staying at the boarding house. The claimant sued the defendants for compensation, claiming that the defendants were vicariously liable in respect of the torts committed by Grain when he sexually abused them.

Had the Salmond test been applied to determine whether or not Grain was acting in the course of his employment when he sexually abused the claimants, the claimants' claims for compensation would certainly have been dismissed. There was no way it could be said that Grain did something he was employed to do by sexually abusing the claimants. Indeed, in an earlier case the Court of Appeal had applied the Salmond test to determine whether a local education authority was vicariously liable in respect of the torts committed by a deputy headmaster in sexually assaulting a student when they were on a school trip together, and had concluded that the deputy head had not been acting in the course of his employment when he sexually assaulted the student.[40]

However, the Salmond test was *not* applied in the *Lister* case to determine whether or not Grain was acting in the course of his employment when he sexually abused the claimants. The House of Lords swept that test away. In its place, the House of Lords adopted a quite different test for determining whether or not an employee was acting in the course of his employment when he committed a tort. This test was first adopted by the Supreme Court of Canada in the cases of *Bazley v Curry* and *Jacobi v Griffiths* (both 1999).[41] Under this test, an employee will be held to have acted in the course of his employment when he committed a tort if that tort was:

> so closely connected with his employment that it would be fair and just to hold the [employee's employer] vicariously liable [in respect of that tort].[42]

---

[40] *Trotman* v *North Yorkshire County Council* [1999] LGR 584.

[41] Noted, Cane 2000a.

[42] *Lister* v *Hesley Hall Ltd* [2002] 1 AC 215 (henceforth '*Lister*'), at [28] (per Lord Steyn). See also [70] (per Lord Millett: 'What is critical is . . . the closeness of the connection between the employee's duties and his wrongdoing'). An alternative formulation of the same test was offered by Lord Nicholls in *Dubai Aluminium Co Ltd* v *Salaam* [2003] 2 AC 366, at [23]: 'the wrongful conduct must be so closely connected with acts the . . . employee was authorised to do that, for the purpose of the liability of the . . . employer to third parties, the wrongful conduct *may fairly and properly be regarded* as done by the [employee] while acting in the ordinary course of the . . . employee's employment' (emphasis in original).

The House of Lords held that under *this* test – what we might call the 'sufficiently close connection' test, Grain *had* acted in the course of his employment when he sexually abused the claimants.[43] Their main reason for so finding was that the defendants had owed the claimants a duty to look after them; that they tried to discharge that duty by having Grain look after the claimants; and Grain conspicuously failed to look after the claimants when he sexually abused them.[44]

Three criticisms may be made of the House of Lords' decision in *Lister*:

(1) *Constitutionality.* It may be wondered whether the House of Lords acted entirely constitutionally in sweeping aside a test for determining whether an employee acted in the course of his employment when he committed a tort that had stood the test of time for almost a century. It was surely a job for Parliament, acting in conjunction with the Law Commission, to bring about such a radical change in the law on vicarious liability.[45]

Perhaps recognising this, their Lordships in *Lister* attempted to argue that there was nothing *new* about the 'sufficiently close connection' test that they adopted in *Lister*.[46] They argued that there were plenty of cases where this test had *already* been used to determine whether an employee acted in the course of his employment in committing a tort. Unfortunately, it could be argued that two of the cases mentioned – *Morris* v *C W Martin & Sons Ltd* (1966) and *Photo Production v Securicor* (1980) – are not vicarious liability cases at all but cases where the defendant was put in breach of a non-delegable duty of care by the acts of one of his employees.[47] A similar analysis could be made of the third case mentioned by their Lordships – *Lloyd* v *Grace, Smith & Co* (1912).[48] But even if that case *is* regarded as a vicarious liability case, the decision in that case is compatible with the Salmond test for determining whether an employee acted in the course of his employment in committing a tort and cannot be read as supporting the 'sufficiently close connection' test adopted by their Lordships in *Lister*.[49]

(2) *Necessity.* Had the House of Lords wanted to rule in favour of the claimants in *Lister*, they had no need to alter the law on vicarious liability to do so. They could have easily found that the defendants in *Lister* were *personally* liable to compensate the claimants for the harm they suffered as a result of being sexually abused by Grain. Their Lordships could have reached this conclusion using the device of a non-delegable duty of care. They could have ruled that: (1) the defendants owed the claimants a non-delegable duty of care to look after them; (2) the defendants gave Grain the job of looking after the claimants; and (3) Grain put the defendants in breach of the non-delegable duty of care that they

---

[43] They also found that under this test the deputy headmaster in the *Trotman* case (see above, n 40) *had* been acting in the course of his employment when he sexually assaulted the student in that case and, accordingly, the House of Lords overruled the Court of Appeal's decision in that case that the local education authority was not vicariously liable in respect of the torts committed by the deputy head in sexually assaulting the student.

[44] *Lister*, at [25]–[28] (per Lord Steyn), [50] (per Lord Clyde), [59]–[61] (per Lord Hobhouse), [82]–[83] (per Lord Millett).

[45] It was argued by counsel for the defendants that 'Any radical expansion or development of liability in this area of law should be left to Parliament' (*Lister*, at 218) but that argument was ignored by their Lordships.

[46] *Lister*, at [15] (per Lord Steyn), [69] (per Lord Millett). Cf. *New South Wales* v *Lepore* (2003) 212 CLR 511, at [319]: '[The House of Lords] did not depart from precedent in establishing the "close connection" analysis. They merely developed and elaborated the traditional approach' (per Kirby P).

[47] For such an explanation, see above, § 7.5(B).

[48] Ibid.

[49] See above, § 31.4(A).

owed the claimants when, by sexually abusing the claimants, he failed to look after the claimants properly. It is hard to understand why the House of Lords did not decide *Lister* in this way – particularly as these were the *very* reasons why Lord Hobhouse, for one, found that there *was* a 'sufficiently close connection' between the torts committed by Grain in the *Lister* case and what he was employed to do so as to make the defendants *vicariously* liable in respect of those torts:[50]

> Whether or not some act comes within the scope of the servant's employment depends upon an identification of what duty [of the employer's][51] the servant was employed by his employer to perform . . . If the act of the servant which gives rise to the servant's liability to the [claimant] amounted to a failure by the servant to perform that duty, the act comes within 'the scope of his employment' and the employer is vicariously liable.[52]

(3) *Certainty.* The third criticism that may be made of the House of Lords' decision in *Lister* is that the 'sufficiently close connection' test is so vague and open-ended that it is now very hard to tell when exactly an employee will be held to have committed a tort in the course of his employment.[53] As Lord Nicholls observed in *Dubai Aluminium Co Ltd* v *Salaam*:

> the 'close connection' test . . . affords no guidance on the type or degree of connection which will normally be regarded as sufficiently close to prompt the legal conclusion that the risk of the wrongful act occurring, and any loss resulting from the wrongful act, should fall on the firm or employer rather than the third party who was wronged . . . [Under the 'sufficiently close connection' test, the] crucial feature or features, either producing or negativing vicarious liability, [will] vary widely from one case or type of case to the next. Essentially the court makes an evaluative judgment in each case, having regard to all the circumstances . . .[54]

It is not clear that the judges who decided *Lister* would regard the lack of certainty inherent in the 'sufficiently close connection' test as a problem; they might even regard it as a virtue. It is obvious that in the *Lister* case, their Lordships wanted to come up

---

[50] See Glofcheski 2004, 27; also *New South Wales* v *Lepore* (2003) 212 CLR 511, at [208]: 'The analyses of Lord Hobhouse and Lord Millett [in *Lister*] have strong echoes of non-delegable duties' (per Gummow and Hayne JJ).

[51] It is quite clear from Lord Hobhouse's judgment (in particular [54]-[55]) that the word 'duty' here refers to a duty that the *employer* is subject to, not a duty that the employee is subject to. In the situation he is discussing, the employee is given the job of performing the employer's duty.

[52] *Lister*, at [59]. See also [50] (per Lord Clyde), and [82] (per Lord Millett). The House of Lords did not feel it necessary to explain *why* it is 'fair and just' to hold an employer vicariously liable in respect of a tort committed by one of his employees in this situation: Lord Steyn thought that it was a clear case where vicarious liability should be imposed (at [28]).

[53] Cf. Callinan J's criticisms of the 'sufficiently close connection' test for determining whether an employee committed a tort in the course of his employment in *New South Wales* v *Lepore*: '[If such a test were to be adopted in Australia] [d]istinguishing between [cases where there was a "sufficiently close connection" between an employee's tort and what he was employed to do and cases where there was not] would be very difficult. Cases would, as a practical matter, be decided according to whether the judge . . . thought it "fair and just" to hold the employer liable. Perceptions of fairness vary greatly. The law in consequence would be thrown into a state of uncertainty. I would not therefore be prepared to adopt their Lordships' or any like test' (ibid, at [345]). Only one of the seven judges who decided *New South Wales* v *Lepore* in the High Court of Australia expressed any enthusiasm for the 'sufficiently close connection' test (Kirby P). Callinan, Gaudron, Gummow, Hayne JJ and (less clearly) Gleeson CJ all held that Australian courts should continue to use the Salmond test to determine whether an employee committed a tort in the course of his employment. McHugh J declined to express an opinion on the issue.

[54] [2003] 2 AC 366, at [25]–[26].

with a test for when an employee would be held to have acted in the course of his employment in committing a tort that would allow them to do 'practical justice'[55] in individual cases.[56] But, as Lord Millett observed in *Lister*, it is doubtful whether anyone can come up with a test that is sufficiently flexible as to allow the courts to do 'practical justice' in individual cases but at the same time sufficiently precise so as 'to enable the outcome of a particular case to be predicted'.[57] Any test which did work in a predictable fashion would be 'rigid and possibly inappropriate . . . as a test of liability' in particular cases.[58]

C. Application of the *Lister* test before the UKSC's decision in *Mohamud* (2016)

Under the *Lister* test for determining whether an employee's tort was committed in the course of his or her employment, the courts have to ask – Was there a sufficiently close connection between the employee's tort and what he or she was employed to do so as to make it 'fair and just' that the employer should be held vicariously liable in respect of the employee's tort? Until the UKSC's recent decision in *Mohamud v Wm Morrison Supermarkets plc* (2016), the courts seemed to have agreed that the 'sufficiently close connection' requirement will be satisfied if: (a) the employee's tort would have counted as having been committed in the course of his or her employment under the Salmond test,[59] *or* (b) there was a *special risk* associated with the employee's job that the employee would commit the particular kind of tort that the employee committed.

The idea that the 'sufficiently close connection' requirement will be satisfied if (b) is true[60] comes from the decisions of the Supreme Court of Canada in *Bazley v Curry* and *Jacobi v Griffiths* (both 1999),[61] which Lord Steyn made clear in *Lister* should form the 'starting point' of any inquiry into whether there was a 'sufficiently close connection' between what an employee was employed to do and a tort committed by the employee.[62] This requirement was held to be satisfied in *Bazley v Curry* (1999), where the defendants unknowingly employed a paedophile to work in a home for disturbed children and the paedophile used his position to sexually abuse some of the children in the home. It was held that there was a special risk that people who work in children's homes will sexually assault the children there. This is because, McLachlin J explained, people who work in children's homes occupy a position of 'power and intimacy' in relation to the children at the homes – as a result, if they have paedophiliac tendencies, they will feel emboldened to

---

[55] *Lister*, at [16] per Lord Steyn.
[56] For a fine critique of judicial attempts to do 'practical justice' in individual cases, see Beever 2003b.
[57] *Lister*, at [66].
[58] Ibid.
[59] It can hardly be supposed that for nearly 100 years before *Lister* was decided, the courts acted unfairly or unjustly by holding employers vicariously liable for their employees' torts when the Salmond test was satisfied. But see Lord Millett's observation in *Dubai Aluminium Co Ltd v Salaam* [2003] 2 AC 366 that 'the Salmond test is only that – a test. It is not a conclusive definition of the circumstances in which vicarious liability arises. *Even if it is satisfied, the facts, taken as a whole, may nevertheless show that the employee was not acting in the course of his employment*' (at [128], emphasis added).
[60] See, generally, Brodie 2010.
[61] The decisions actually talk in terms of an 'increased or materially enhanced . . . risk' (*Bazley v Curry* [1999] 2 SCR 534, at [39] (per McLachlin J)) but it is simpler to use the term 'special risk'.
[62] [2002] 1 AC 215, at [27].

sexually abuse the children in their care and the children in their care will be more likely to submit to being assaulted without complaint.[63]

In contrast, there was no such special risk in *Jacobi* v *Griffiths* (1999). In that case, the defendants set up a club for children. They employed a Harry Griffiths to act as programme director at the club. His job was to organise recreational activities at the club and the occasional outing. Griffiths used his position to befriend a couple of the children who used the club and he ended up inviting them to his home, where he sexually assaulted them. The Supreme Court of Canada held, by four to three, that there was *not* a 'sufficiently close connection' between what Griffiths was employed to do and the torts that he committed in sexually assaulting the children.

The fact that Griffiths had been employed to work at the club had of course given him the opportunity to sexually assault the children, but that was not enough to establish the requisite connection between his torts and what he was employed to do.[64] There was no special risk that someone employed in Griffiths' capacity would sexually abuse children who used the club: there was no special reason to think that someone employed to work as a programme director at a children's club would develop a relationship of 'power and intimacy' with the children at the club that might embolden him to assault the children at the club and lead them to submit to the assaults without complaint.[65]

The fact that the Supreme Court of Canada divided four to three in *Jacobi* over whether the special risk requirement was satisfied in that case indicates that it will often be very difficult to tell whether or not there was a special risk associated with what an employee was employed to do that he would commit a particular kind of tort. The difficulty lies in distinguishing between cases where an employee's employment creates a *special risk* that an employee will commit a particular kind of tort and cases where an employee's employment merely gives him a *good opportunity* to commit a particular kind of tort. All of the judges in *Lister*, *Bazley* v *Curry* and *Jacobi* were agreed that a 'sufficiently close connection' between an employee's tort and what he was employed to do would *not* be established in a case where an employee's employment merely gave him a good opportunity to commit that tort.[66]

So how can we draw the line between *special risk* cases and *good opportunity* cases? The post-*Lister* case law seemed to identify three categories of situation where we could say that there was a special risk attached to an employee E's doing a particular job J that they would commit a particular tort T.

(1) *Special skills.* The first category of situation is where E's job J gave him a particular set of skills that he drew on to commit tort T. It may be that the decision in *Mattis* v *Pollock* (2003) can be explained on this basis. In that case, the claimant was stabbed by a nightclub bouncer employed by the defendants; the bouncer had earlier had an altercation with

---

[63] [1999] 2 SCR 534, at [44]. See also *New South Wales* v *Lepore* (2003) 212 CLR 511, at [216] (per Gummow and Hayne JJ).

[64] If the same case occurred in the United Kingdom, could a court find the defendants vicariously liable for the programme director's acts of sexual abuse using the 'delegation' idea set out above? It depends on whether it could be said that the programme director in *Jacobi* v *Griffiths* was employed by the defendants in that case to discharge the duty the defendants owed the children at the club to take reasonable steps to see that they were reasonably safe in using the club.

[65] [1999] 2 SCR 570, at [79]–[86] (per Binnie J).

[66] *Lister*, at [45] (per Lord Clyde), [59] (per Lord Hobhouse), [65] (per Lord Millett); *Bazley* v *Curry* [1999] 2 SCR 534, at [40] (per McLachlin J); *Jacobi* v *Griffiths* [1999] 2 SCR 570, at [81] (per Binnie J).

the claimant and was seeking to take revenge on him for this. The Court of Appeal held that the defendants *were* vicariously liable in respect of the bouncer's attack on the claimant. Part of the reason why the court found that there was a 'sufficiently close connection' between the bouncer's tort and what he was employed to do was that 'he was encouraged and expected to perform his duties in an aggressive and intimidatory manner, which included physical manhandling of customers.'[67]

(2) *Trust and confidence.* The second category of situation is where E's job J meant that she occupied a special position of trust and confidence that enabled her to commit tort T. The finding of a 'sufficiently close connection' between Grain's acts of sexual abuse in *Lister* and what he was employed to do can be explained on this basis. The position of authority that Grain occupied in the boarding house meant that it was far easier for him to get the children staying at the boarding house to do what he wanted them to do than it would have been for, say, a handyman employed to do odd jobs around the boarding house.[68]

The line of post-*Lister* cases holding that church organisations can be held vicariously liable for acts of sexual abuse carried out by priests working for those organisations – *Maga* v *Trustees of the Birmingham Archdiocese of the Roman Catholic Church* (2010), *E* v *English Province of our Lady of Charity* (2012), and *Various Claimants* v *Catholic Child Welfare Society* (2012) – can also be explained on this basis, at least where the abused claimant was seeking the priest's counsel (as in *Maga*), or where she was living in a home run by the church and visited by the priest (as in *E*), or where he was being taught by the priest (as in *Various Claimants*). In each such case, the priest would occupy a position of trust and confidence in relation to the claimant that would make the claimant tend to comply with the priest's suggestions and overtures.

The case of *Weir* v *Chief Constable of Merseyside Police* (2003) can also be explained on this basis. In that case, the defendant chief constable was held vicariously liable in respect of an assault committed by an off-duty police officer on the claimant in a police van which the officer had borrowed in order to help a friend move some belongings. (The police officer suspected that the claimant had attempted to pilfer some of the friend's belongings while they were awaiting removal.) The Court of Appeal's main reason for finding the defendant vicariously liable in respect of the officer's assault was that, before he took the claimant into the police van and assaulted him, 'he . . . confirmed to, and the [claimant] understood, that he was a police officer'.[69]

(3) *Aggravation.* The third category of case covers situations where E's job J carried with it certain aggravations or annoyances that meant E was very likely at some stage to commit tort T. The case of *Gravil* v *Carroll* (2008) provides an excellent example of this third type of case.[70] The case arose out of a rugby match between Halifax RFC and Redruth

---

[67] [2003] 1 WLR 2158, at [30].

[68] See *Jacobi* v *Griffiths* [1999] 2 SCR 570, at [45] (per Binnie J); also *EDG* v *Hammer* [2003] 2 SCR 459, at [36] (per Arbour J).

[69] [2003] EWCA Civ 111, at [12] (per Rt Hon Sir Denis Henry).

[70] As may the pre-*Lister* case of *Fennelly* v *Connex South Eastern Ltd* [2001] IRLR 390, where an initial altercation between a passenger and a ticket inspector over the passenger's failure to produce his ticket escalated and the ticket inspector ended up putting the passenger into a headlock. The Court of Appeal held that the inspector's employers were vicariously liable in respect of the tort committed by the inspector in laying his hands on the passenger. It may be the aggravation involved in dealing with fare dodgers and generally hostile members of the public means there is a special risk that ticket inspectors will end up 'losing it' in the way that the employee in *Fennelly* did.

RFC in 2005. Andrew Gravil was playing for Halifax when he was punched by Richard Carroll, a Redruth player, in a melee that developed following a scrum. Gravil sued Redruth RFC for damages, claiming that they were vicariously liable in respect of Carroll's battery. The Court of Appeal held that there was a sufficiently close connection between Carroll's employment and his punch:

> . . . the throwing of punches is not uncommon in situations like this, when the scrum is breaking up after the whistle has gone. Indeed, they can fairly be regarded as an ordinary (though undesirable) incident of a rugby match.[71]

In *Wallbank* v *Fox Designs Ltd* (2012), the claimant was injured by a fellow employee who had reacted badly to the claimant's criticising his performance and attempting to show the employee how he should do his job. The Court of Appeal held that there was a 'sufficiently close connection' between the employee's battery and what he was employed to do on the ground that:

> The possibility of friction is inherent in any employment relationship, but particularly one in a factory, even a small factory, where instant instructions and quick reactions are required. Frustrations which lead to a reaction involving some violence are predictable. The risk of an over-robust reaction to an instruction is a risk created by the employment.[72]

D. The UKSC's decision in *Mohamud* (2016)

So stood the law on when the *Lister* 'sufficiently close connection' test would be satisfied before the UKSC's decision in *Mohamud* v *Wm Morrison Supermarkets plc* (2016). In that case, the claimant called in at a petrol station at one of the defendant's supermarkets and asked the staff on duty – including a Mr Amjid Khan – whether he could print off some documents using a USB stick. Khan told him to get lost, and as the claimant went back to his car, Khan followed him, subjecting the claimant to racial abuse, and ended up beating the claimant up. The claimant argued that the defendant was vicariously liable for Khan's assault.

Under the law set out in the previous section, the courts should *not* have found that Khan's assault was committed in the course of his employment. They *should* have found that there was *no* 'sufficiently close connection' between Khan's assault and what he was employed to do because (a) the Salmond test was not satisfied, and (b) there was no special risk attached to working as a petrol station attendant that the attendant will end up racially abusing and beating up a customer.[73] Perhaps for this reason, counsel for the claimant in *Mohamud* argued that the UKSC should *abandon* the *Lister* test for when an employee's tort would be held to have been committed in the course of his or her employment in favour of an even wider test that – counsel hoped – would cover *Mohamud*'s case.

In its decision in *Mohamud*, the UKSC refused to abandon the *Lister* test but found that there *was* a sufficiently close connection between Khan's assault and what he was employed to do. Lord Toulson gave the leading judgment. His only basis for finding that the *Lister* test was satisfied in this case seemed to be that (1) Khan's telling the claimant

---

[71] [2008] EWCA Civ 689, at [23].
[72] [2012] EWCA Civ 25, at [54].
[73] This was, indeed, the conclusion of the Court of Appeal in deciding *Mohamud*: [2014] EWCA Civ 116.

that they did not print out documents for customers and Khan's beating the claimant up formed a 'seamless episode', and (2) Khan told the claimant never to come back to the petrol station, and thereby purported to issue an instruction on behalf of his employer.[74] It hardly needs to be said that this is a desperately thin basis on which to find that the *Lister* test has been satisfied and leaves everyone completely uncertain as to when the courts will and will not find that that test has been satisfied.

It may be that in applying the *Lister* test in future, the courts will simply ignore *Mohamud* as a bizarre aberration and return to the principles set out in the previous section. But if they take *Mohamud* seriously, it seems to have recognised a third category of situation where the *Lister* test will be satisfied so that there will be a 'sufficiently close connection' between an employee's tort and what the employee was employed to do if (a) the Salmond test is satisfied, *or* (b) there was a *special risk* associated with the employee's job that the employee would commit the particular kind of tort that the employee committed, *or* (c) the employee's tort was committed *in the workplace or somewhere they were employed to work.*[75]

31.5 Vicarious liability for non-employees

As we saw in section 31.2, above, it has long been the case that a defendant could be held vicariously liable for a tort that was committed by someone who was not actually their employee. However, the range of situations where this could happen were kept narrowly circumscribed to specific situations, such as where an agent or partner or police constable committed a tort. This area of vicarious liability has now been rendered dangerously unstable by the UK Supreme Court's decision in *Various Claimants* v *Catholic Child Welfare Society* (2013), which holds that a defendant can be held vicariously liable for a tort committed by a non-employee who was working for him so long as their relationship was sufficiently 'akin to that between an employer and an employee'.[76]

Delivering the only judgment in the *Various Claimants* case, Lord Phillips held that the relationship between A and B would be sufficiently 'akin to that between an employer

---

[74] [2016] AC 677, at [47]. Students wishing to save some time in their studies and who have been told to read *Mohamud* will be grateful to know that this is the only paragraph worth reading in Lord Toulson's judgment.

[75] If (c) is correct then *Weddall* v *Barchester Healthcare Ltd* [2012] EWCA Civ 25 (held, no vicarious liability for employee attacking manager at work, because employee harboured intense dislike of manager) and *Heasmans* v *Clarity Cleaning Company* [1987] ICR 949 (see above, text at n 36) would count as wrongly decided. The correctness of *Heasmans* in the post-*Lister* climate had already been brought into question in *Brink's Global Services Inc* v *Igrox Ltd* [2010] EWCA Civ 1207, at [31], [37] (held, vicarious liability for acts of employees in stealing silver bars that employees had been told to fumigate). Torts committed outside the workplace, or where one is employed to work, would only come under the 'sufficiently close connection' test if (a) or (b) were satisfied. See *Allen* v *Chief Constable of Hampshire* [2013] EWCA Civ 967 (no vicarious liability where A, a police officer, harassed woman who was involved with another police officer, B, because B used to go out with A) and *Attorney-General of British Virgin Islands* v *Hartwell* [2004] 1 WLR 1273 (no vicarious liability where A, a police officer, fires gun into bar – hitting a tourist in the bar – where ex-girlfriend of police officer is sitting with another man). In neither case was there any connection between the wrongdoing police officer's loss of control and the nature of their job.

[76] [2013] 2 AC 1, at [47]. The suggestion that there might be vicarious liability in such a situation was originally made (in the UK) by Ward LJ in *E* v *English Province of Our Lady of Charity* [2013] QB 722.

and an employee' if their relationship possessed the 'same incidents' as those that 'make it fair, just and reasonable to impose vicarious liability' on an employer.[77] Lord Phillips identified those incidents as being:

> (i) the employer is more likely to have the means to compensate the victim than the employee and can be expected to have insured against that liability; (ii) the tort will have been committed as a result of activity being taken by the employee on behalf of the employer; (iii) the employee's activity is likely to be part of the business activity of the employer; (iv) the employer, by employing the employee to carry on the activity will have created the risk of the tort committed by the employee; (v) the employee will, to a greater or lesser degree, have been under the control of the employer.[78]

Of these incidents, (ii) and (iv) do not really go to the relationship between A and B, but rather to whether B can be fairly said to have committed a tort in the course of working for A. So in identifying whether A and B's relationship was one 'akin to employment', the most crucial factors are likely to be: (1) whether A is carrying on an enterprise in an organised and regular way; (2) whether, when B was working for A, B was seeking to further the goals of that enterprise rather than his own private goals; and (3) whether A had the power to direct B what to do in seeking to further those goals. Focusing on these factors is consistent with Lord Phillips' judgment in *Various Claimants*, which found that there was a relationship 'akin to employment' between the defendant institute and various lay brothers of the Catholic Church who were members of the institute and who had been sent by the institute to work at one of its schools, where – it was alleged – they had sexually abused children attending the school:

> In the context of vicarious liability the relationship between the teaching brothers and the institute had many of the elements, and all the essential elements, of the relationship between employer and employees. (i) The institute was subdivided into a hierarchical structure and conducted its activities as if it were a corporate body. (ii) The teaching activity of the brothers was undertaken because the provincial directed the brothers to undertake it . . . (iii) The teaching activity undertaken by the brothers was in furtherance of the objective, or mission, of the institute. (iv) The manner in which the brother teachers were obliged to conduct themselves as teachers was dictated by the institute's rules.[79]

So far, it has been held that there existed a relationship 'akin to employment' between a defendant and a tortfeasor in the following contexts:

(1) *'Borrowed' employees.* In a 'borrowed' employee situation, B is an employee of C's, and then B is sent by C to work for A. While B was working for A, he committed a tort. It has long been established that in this situation, A might be held vicariously liable for B's tort even though B was not technically his employee.

In the *Various Claimants* case, Lord Phillips endorsed[80] Rix LJ's view in *Viasystems (Tyneside) Ltd* v *Thermal Transfer (Northern) Limited* (2006), that A should be held vicariously liable for B's tort if B was 'so much a part of the work, business or organisation [of A's] that it is just to make [A] answer for [B's tort].'[81] If this test is satisfied in relation to A, so that A might be held vicariously liable for B's tort, what is the position in relation to C, B's actual employer? Until the *Viasystems* case was decided, it had always been assumed

---

[77] [2013] 2 AC 1, at [47].
[78] [2013] 2 AC 1, at [35].
[79] [2013] 2 AC 1, at [56].
[80] [2013] 2 AC 1, at [45].
[81] [2006] QB 510, at [79].

that if A could be held vicariously liable for B's tort, then C could not be. However, in *Viasystems* it was decided that there could be 'dual' vicarious liability, where both an actual employer and borrowing employer could be held vicariously liable for a borrowed employee's tort. This would be the case where: 'the employee in question . . .is so much a part of the work, business or organisation of *both* employers that it is just to make *both* employers answer for his [tort].'[82]

This test for dual vicarious liability was satisfied in *Viasystems* itself, where B was an apprentice metalworker, learning his trade under the supervision of a 'fitter', C was a firm that supplied metalworkers to help out on building sites, and A was a firm that had been engaged to install some airducts in the claimants' factory. C supplied A with a fully trained 'fitter' to work on the installation job, and sent B along with the 'fitter' to help out. While B was fetching some equipment, he carelessly set off the factory sprinkler system, which caused a flood. It was held that while B was working on the installation job, he was effectively so much a part of both A and C's businesses that it would be just to hold them both vicariously liable for B's negligence.

The test for dual vicarious liability was held *not* to be satisfied in *Hawley* v *Luminar Leisure Ltd* (2006), where B was a nightclub 'bouncer', C was a firm that supplied bouncers to nightclubs, and A was a firm that operated a nightclub. B was sent by C to work at A's nightclub. One evening, a fracas broke out outside A's nightclub, and in the course of dealing with the fracas, B punched the claimant in the face. It was held that A – as the borrowing employer – could be held vicariously liable for B's battery on the basis that B was working as part of A's enterprise when he punched the claimant on the nose, but that C would not be liable. In the *Various Claimants* case, Lord Phillips indicated that he disagreed with this result: 'the facts of [*Hawley*] could have supported a finding of dual vicarious liability.'[83]

(2) *Priests.* The main impetus behind the courts' developing the law on when someone can be held vicariously liable for a tort committed by someone who was in a relationship 'akin to employment' with the defendant has been to find a way of holding churches and parishes vicariously liable for torts committed by priests working in those churches and parishes. Priests are not employees: they have no contract with their parishes requiring them to work a certain set of hours and their income is not governed by a contract either. Instead, priests are office-holders: they are appointed to an office (usually that of parish priest) within the church by someone more senior within the church and their duties in that office are set by custom and expectation rather than contract law. (Another, perhaps more familiar, example of an office holder is that of the Prime Minister, who has a salary as Prime Minister but no contractual duties on his or her side that would allow us to say that the Prime Minister is an employee of the Crown.) In *E* v *English Province of our Lady of Charity* (2013), the Court of Appeal held that even though a priest is not an employee, the bishop of a parish in which the priest worked (and where the priest had been alleged to have committed various acts of sexual abuse) could be held vicariously liable for the priest's torts on the basis that: the bishop exercised a great deal of control over how the priest did his work; the priest's work was central to the enterprise being carried on by the bishop, within which enterprise the priest held an established position; and the priest was not engaged in his own enterprise, but fully committed to furthering the goals of the bishop's enterprise.[84]

---

[82] Ibid (emphasis added).
[83] [2013] 2 AC 1, at [46].
[84] [2013] QB 722, at [72] (per Ward LJ) and [123] (per Davis LJ).

(3) *Volunteers.* The *Various Claimants* case would fall within this category: the alleged tort-feasors in that case were people who had volunteered to work for the defendant institute (known as the 'Institute of the Brothers of the Christian Schools' or the 'De La Salle Brothers'), had become members of the institute, and had been sent to work by the defendant institute in a school that was effectively run by the institute. As we have seen, the UK Supreme Court found that there was a relationship 'akin to employment' between the institute and the alleged tortfeasors, based on the fact that the alleged tortfeasors were working to further the institute's objectives and not their own when they worked for the institute, and the high degree of control the institute exercised over the alleged tortfeasors in terms of determining what they did for the institute. There is little doubt that the same factors would lead future courts to find that there exists a relationship 'akin to employment' between a charity shop and people who volunteer to work in the shop on a casual basis.

(4) *Prisoners.* The idea that a defendant can be held vicariously liable for a tort committed by someone who was in a relationship 'akin to employment' with the defendant was recently applied by the UKSC in *Cox* v *Ministry of Justice* (2016) to a case where a prisoner negligently injured the prison's catering manager while he was helping unload food supplies to the prison. The high degree of control exercised by the prison over the prisoner and the fact that he could not have been said to have been helping unload food supplies to the prison for his own purposes made the UKSC's finding of a relationship 'akin to employment' almost inevitable.

(5) *Social services.* The same could not be said of the UKSC's decision in *Armes* v *Nottinghamshire County Council* (2017), where a majority found that the social services enjoyed a sufficient degree of control over foster carers with whom the social services had placed children that there existed a relationship 'akin to employment' between the social services and foster carers, with the result that the social services would be held vicariously liable for any acts of child abuse performed by those foster carers.

  Giving the majority judgment, Lord Reed observed that: 'The local authority controlled who the foster parents were, supervised their fostering, and controlled some aspects of day to day family life, such as holidays and medical treatment.'[85] Lord Hughes dissented on the ground that it was questionable how far foster carers could be said to be operating as an integral part of whatever 'enterprise' we can say that the social services are engaged in: 'The foster carers do not do what the authority would otherwise do for itself: they do something different, by providing an upbringing as part of a family.'[86] The fact that the UKSC was willing to extend the notion of a relationship 'akin to employment' to a case where 'children are in reality committed to independent carers'[87] and Lord Reed's observations in *Armes* that in the context of claims that a defendant is vicariously liable for torts committed by someone who is in a relationship 'akin to employment' with the defendant 'it is important not exaggerate the extent to which control is necessary for the imposition of vicarious liability to be justified' and that '[i]t is not necessary for there to be micro-management, or any high degree of control, in order for vicarious liability to be imposed'[88] may open the door for a future and wide-ranging assault on the principle that a defendant will not be held vicariously liable for the acts of the defendant's independent contractors.

---

[85] [2017] UKSC 60, at [65].
[86] Ibid, at [88].
[87] Ibid.
[88] [2017] UKSC 60, at [65].

31.6 Theories of vicarious liability

The areas of law we have dealt with in the two preceding sections – the law on when someone will be held to have committed a tort in the course of his employment by another under the *Lister* test, and the law on when a defendant will be found to have had a relationship 'akin to employment' with a tortfeasor – rest almost entirely nowadays on notions as to when it would be 'fair, just and reasonable' to find an employer vicariously liable for an employee's tort. An employee will only be held to have committed a tort in the course of his employment by another under the *Lister* test if that tort was 'so closely connected with [the employee's] employment that it would be fair and just' to make the employee's employer vicariously liable in respect of that tort.[89] A defendant will only be found to have had a relationship 'akin to employment' with a tortfeasor where their relationship have the 'same incidents' as those which make it 'fair, just and reasonable to impose vicarious liability' on an employer.[90]

Given this, it is vital to know *why* it is ever 'fair, just and reasonable' to hold an employer vicariously liable in respect of a tort committed by an employee. If we knew *why* it is 'fair, just and reasonable' to do this, we could then tell *when* it would be 'fair, just and reasonable' to hold an employer vicariously liable for an employee's torts and then use that knowledge to inform both our application of the *Lister* test and our decisions as to when to find that there existed a relationship 'akin to employment' between a defendant and a tortfeasor. As we will see, we do not lack for answers to the question why it is ever 'fair, just and reasonable' to hold an employer vicariously liable for an employee's tort – however, the answers are either unsatisfying[91] or they indicate that the law on vicarious liability does *not* currently apply in a 'fair, just and reasonable' way.

(1) *Deep pockets.* It is argued, first of all, that in a case where *Employee* commits a tort in the course of employment, it is 'fair, just and reasonable' to hold *Employer* vicariously liable for that tort because doing so will allow the victim of *Employee*'s tort to recover damages from someone worth suing.[92] This theory does not work: there is nothing 'fair, just and reasonable' about giving effect to a principle of 'can pay, will pay'. Moreover, if the law on vicarious liability were designed to give the victim of a tort a

---

[89] *Lister* v *Hesley Hall Ltd* [2002] 1 AC 215, at [28].

[90] *Various Claimants* v *Catholic Child Welfare Society* [2013] 2 AC 1, at [47].

[91] Cf. *Hollis* v *Vabu Pty Ltd* (2001) 207 CLR 21, at [35] (per Gleeson CJ, Gaudron, Gummow, Kirby and Hayne JJ): 'a fully satisfactory rationale for the imposition of vicarious liability . . . has been slow to appear'; also *New South Wales* v *Lepore* (2003) 212 CLR 511, at [106] (per Gaudron J, remarking on the 'absence of a satisfactory and comprehensive jurisprudential basis for the imposition of liability on a person for the harmful acts or omissions of others'), and [299] (per Kirby P: 'The history of the imposition of vicarious liability demonstrates that the foundation of such liability has been uncertain and variable').

[92] This theory goes back to Willes J's judgment in *Limpus* v *London General Omnibus Company* (1862) 1 H&C 526, 529; 158 ER 995, 998 ('It is well-known that there is virtually no remedy against the driver of an omnibus, and therefore it is necessary that, for injury resulting from an act done by him in the course of his master's service, the master should be responsible; for there ought to be a remedy against some person capable of paying damages to those injured by improper driving') and was recently, and surprisingly, revived by Lord Phillips in *Various Claimants* v *Catholic Child Welfare Society* [2013] 2 AC 1, at [34] ('The policy objective underlying vicarious liability is to ensure, in so far as it is fair, just and reasonable, that liability for tortious wrong [sic] is borne by a defendant with the means to compensate the victim.' See also Baty 1916, 152; Atiyah 1967, 22; Feldthusen 1998, 224–5.

cash-rich defendant to sue, it is hard to see why the victim of a tort is only allowed to sue the tortfeasor's employer when the tort was committed *in the course of the employee's employment.*[93]

(2) *Loss spreading.* It is argued, secondly, that it is 'fair, just and reasonable' to hold *Employer* vicariously liable for a tort committed by *Employee* in the course of his employment because doing so will shift the loss caused by that tort onto the shoulders of someone who can then spread the loss throughout the community – either by recovering the loss from *Employer*'s liability insurer, which will then spread the loss to all its customers through higher premiums; or by spreading the loss among *Employer*'s customers in the form of higher prices.[94]

A variant on this loss spreading argument is made by Tony Weir, who argues that vicarious liability seems to be designed to allow losses to be shifted from human beings (in the shape of the victims of torts) to companies (in the shape of employers), which are in a better position to absorb and spread those losses:

> [S]uppose that one were challenged to produce formal rules with the substantial effect that companies must pay for people but not *vice versa*. One could hardly do better than lay down that liability should attach to employers but not to customers, that one should be liable for one's permanent staff but not for any other bodies whom or which one might pay to do things or get things done – in brief, that there should be liability for employees but not for independent contractors.[95]

This explanation again suffers from problems. There seems nothing 'fair, just and reasonable' about shifting a loss onto someone else simply because he or she can absorb and spread it more easily than the person currently suffering that loss. And if a desire to spread losses did underlie the law on vicarious liability, it is hard to see why the loss suffered by the victim of a tort committed by an employee will *only* be shifted and spread if the tort was committed in the course of an employee's employment.

(3) *Relative blame.* In *Hern v Nichols* (1700), Holt CJ explained that *Employer* will be held vicariously liable in respect of a tort committed by *Employee* in the course of his employment because 'seeing somebody must be a loser [as a result of a tort committed by an employee] it is more reason that he that employs and puts a trust and confidence in [the employee] should be a loser than a stranger'.[96] But if this is right it is hard to see why someone who engages someone else to work for him as an independent contractor should not be vicariously liable in respect of any torts committed by that contractor in doing the work he is engaged to do.

(4) *Deterrence.* It is also said that holding *Employer* vicariously liable in respect of a tort committed by *Employee* in the course of his employment will encourage *Employer* to take

---

[93] Fleming 1998 argues (at 410) that the law does not hold employers liable for torts committed by their employees outside the course of their employment because it does not want to 'foist an undue burden on business enterprise'. But there is more than a whiff of *ex post facto* rationalisation about this explanation.

[94] See *Bazley v Curry* [1999] 2 SCR 534, at [31]: 'the employer is often in the best position to spread the losses [caused by an employee's tort] through mechanisms like insurance and higher prices, thus minimizing the dislocative effect of the tort within society' (per McLachlin J).

[95] Weir 2004, 269.

[96] (1700) 1 Salk 289, 91 ER 256. See also *Bazley v Curry* [1999] 2 SCR 534, at [50] and [54] (per McLachlin J).

steps to see that his employees do not act wrongfully while they work for him.[97] For example, in *Gravil* v *Carroll* (2008), the Court of Appeal justified imposing vicarious liability on the defendant rugby club for a punch thrown by their player in a melee following a scrum on deterrence based grounds:

> There is an obvious temptation for clubs to turn a blind eye to foul play. They naturally want their side to win and, no doubt, to play hard to do so. The line between playing hard and playing dirty may be seen as a fine one. The temptation for players to cross the line in the scrum may be considerable unless active steps are taken by clubs to deter them from doing so . . . It is . . . striking that here the club did not take any disciplinary action against [their player]. Perhaps it would have done if it had appreciated that there was a risk of liability in such cases in the future.[98]

The difficulty with all such explanations of vicarious liability is that it makes no difference *at all* to an employer's liability whether or not he has taken all reasonable steps, or has done everything he can, to prevent his employees committing torts while working for him. Suppose that in *Gravil* v *Carroll* (2008) the defendant rugby club had regularly disciplined any of their players who stepped out of line on the field of play. That would have made no difference to their vicarious liability for any future infractions.

(5) *Enterprise risk.* Another explanation as to why the law will sometimes hold *Employer* vicariously liable in respect of a tort committed by an *Employee* in the course of his employment goes as follows. Elementary fairness dictates that if you seek to make money from engaging in some activity and other people suffer loss as a result of your engaging in that activity, you should compensate them for that loss – if you want to obtain the gains resulting from engaging in that activity, then you should bear the losses as well.

This principle of fairness applies here.[99] An employer sets up in business for himself, and employs people to work for him and make money for him. If the sort of work an employee is employed to do carries with it a special risk that the employee will commit a particular kind of tort, when that risk materialises, it is only fair that the employer should bear the loss resulting from that risk materialising.[100]

---

[97] See *Bazley* v *Curry* [1999] 2 SCR 534, at [32]–[33]: 'Fixing the employer with responsibility for the employee's wrongful act, even where the employer is not negligent, may have a deterrent effect. Employers are often in a position to reduce accidents and intentional wrongs by efficient organization and supervision . . . Beyond the narrow band of employer conduct that attracts direct liability in negligence lies a vast area where imaginative and efficient administration and supervision can reduce the risk [of wrongdoing by the employer's employees]. Holding the employer vicariously liable for the wrongs of its employee may encourage the employer to take such steps and, hence, reduce the risk of future harm' (per McLachlin J). Also *New South Wales* v *Lepore* (2003) 212 CLR 511, at [305] (per Kirby P); Pollock 1882, 130.

[98] [2008] ICR 1222, at [26]–[27].

[99] It may also underlie the Consumer Protection Act 1987, in so far as it makes a manufacturer who manufactures goods for profit liable for the harm caused by any of his goods being defective. See Stapleton 1994a, 185–217; Waddams 1998, 124-5. The 1987 Act is discussed in detail above, in Chapter 11. The rule in *Rylands* v *Fletcher* (discussed above, Chapter 14), might also be said to rest on this principle of fairness: Cane 1999, 202.

[100] Cf. *Dubai Aluminium* v *Salaam* [2003] 2 AC 366, at [21]: 'The . . . legal policy [underlying the law on vicarious liability] is based on the recognition that carrying on a business enterprise necessarily involves risks to others. It involves the risk that others will be harmed by wrongful acts committed by the [employees] through whom the business is carried on. When those risks ripen into loss, it is just that the business should be responsible for compensating the person who has been wronged' (per Lord Nicholls). See also *Lister* v *Hesley Hall Ltd* [2002] 1 AC 215, at [65] (per Lord Millett); *Bazley* v *Curry* [1999] 2 SCR 534, at [22], [30] (per McLachlin J); *New South Wales* v *Lepore* (2003) 212 CLR 511, at [303] (per Kirby P); *Majrowski* v *Guy's and St Thomas's NHS Trust* [2007] 1 AC 224, at [9] (per Lord Nicholls); Pollock 1882, 122.

This explanation of the law on vicarious liability makes sense of the current state of the law, post-*Lister*, as to when an employer will be held vicariously liable for a tort committed by one of his employees. However, it suffers from a major flaw. The law on vicarious liability applies to *all* employers, and not just employers who are in business for themselves and out to make a profit for themselves.[101] Moreover, the extension of the law on vicarious liability to cases involving relationships 'akin to employment' has primarily affected non-profit making bodies such as churches, charities, and prisons. If the 'enterprise risk' idea does underlie the current law on vicarious liability, it is hard to see how extending the law to make it *easier* to sue non-profit making bodies is 'fair, just and reasonable'.

(6) *Master's tort.* We began this chapter by saying that vicarious liability is not accessory liability – that is, an employer whose employee has committed a tort in the course of his employment is not held to have committed a tort *himself* but is instead treated *as though* he had committed the employee's tort along with the employee. There is, however, a very old theory of vicarious liability – known as the 'master's tort' theory – which says that this is not true. In the case where *Employee* commits a tort in the course of his employment (so the theory goes) *Employer* is held liable because *he* has committed a tort. *Employer* is held to have done what *Employee* did, and is held liable accordingly. So suppose *Employee* punched *Victim* in the course of his employment. Because the punch occurred in the course of *Employee*'s employment, the punch is attributed to *Employer*. So *Employer* is held to have punched *Victim* and as a result is held liable in battery to pay damages to *Victim*.

The master's tort theory of vicarious liability has long been unfashionable.[102] However, it has recently been revived by academics who are hostile to policy-based explanations of tort law in general, and the sort of policy-based explanations of vicarious liability that have been canvassed above and found wanting. Chief among these academics is Robert Stevens, whose book *Torts and Rights* (2007) contains a powerful defence of the 'master's tort' theory of vicarious liability:

> A close analogy is with the rules of games. In the 1966 World Cup Final, the person whose phys-ical actions caused the last goal to be scored was Geoff Hurst. However, the rules of the game also attribute his physical actions to his team, England. Both Geoff Hurst and England scored the goal. Beyond the selection of 11 players, it is not possible for either side to choose for itself who can score its goals, or perhaps more pertinently commit a foul. If a player kicks the ball into his own team's net, this will be considered to be an own goal. It does not matter that he was acting contrary to the express instructions of his team manager; nor does it matter if he did so deliberately in a fit of anger. If the words or actions of another person are attributed to the defendant, and those actions infringe the claimant's rights, the defendant will be liable. The law, like the game of football, has rules for determining this.[103]

However, there are a number of problems with the 'master's tort' theory.

---

[101] *Bazley* v *Curry* [1999] 2 SCR 534, at [47]–[56]; *Gravil* v *Carroll* [2008] ICR 1222, at [9].

[102] Until recently, the last defence of the 'master's tort' theory of vicarious liability could be found in Williams 1956a. Recent decisions have had no hesitation in (implicitly) rejecting this theory of vicarious liability: see *Dubai Aluminium Co Ltd* v *Salaam* [2003] 2 AC 366, at [155] (per Lord Millett): '[In a vicarious liability case] [t]he employer is not a wrongdoer; he is not liable in respect of his own conduct. He is answerable for his employee's wrongdoing, and his liability is coextensive with that of his employee. He is personally innocent, but he is liable because his employee is guilty.' To the same effect, see also *Majrowski* v *Guy's and St Thomas's NHS Trust* [2007] 1 AC 224, at [7] and [15] (per Lord Nicholls), and [68] (per Baroness Hale).

[103] Stevens 2007, 261.

First, the fact that we *can* attribute the acts of an employee to an employer does not establish that we *should*. Robert Stevens attempts to counter this argument by saying that:

> the liability of corporate bodies for misfeasance demonstrates that rules for the attribution of words and actions are *indispensable* . . . Corporations are legal constructs and do not exist in the physical world. When we refer to the conduct of a corporation, this is a form of shorthand for the acts of a corporation's human agents, usually its employees.[104]

But not all employers are corporations – so why should a living, breathing employer be fixed with any of the actions of his employees?

Secondly, we *already have* a set of rules for attributing actions to corporations. We discussed them above, in the chapter on 'Breach of duty'.[105] According to those rules, a corporation is normally only held to have done what those who represent its 'directing mind and will' have done. Given this, why would the law on vicarious liability supply us with a *second* set of rules for attributing actions to corporations, according to which a corporation is supposed to have done whatever *any* of its employees, however lowly and subordinate, have done so long as those employees were acting in the course of their employment?

Thirdly, the 'master's tort' theory of vicarious liability tells us *nothing* about *what* rules we should adopt for attributing an employee's actions to his employer. Given this, the 'master's tort' theory of vicarious liability gives us no basis for criticising or praising the decision to find vicarious liability in cases like *Lister* or *Maga* and the decision not to find vicarious liability in a case like *Jacobi* v *Griffiths*. All the 'master's tort' theory tells us is that when vicarious liability is found, it is because the employee's actions were attributed to his employer; and when vicarious liability was not found, the employee's actions were not attributed to his employer. It tells us nothing about when we *should* attribute an employee's actions to his employer and when not.

Fourthly, the 'master's tort' theory of vicarious liability is inconsistent with a fairly basic fact about vicarious liability. An employer whose employee has punched someone else in the course of employment is *not* held liable for 'battery'. He is instead held liable on the basis that he is vicariously liable in respect of the *employee's* battery.

The truth is that vicarious liability is a bit of a mystery: something without which hardly any tort cases would be brought to court, but the existence of which has no rational justification. It is an area of law that is desperately in need of reform and rationalisation.[106]

31.7 Two final points

A couple of final points about the law on vicarious liability remain to be made:

A. Contribution and indemnity

Suppose that A has committed a tort and B is vicariously liable in respect of that tort. Suppose further that B is held liable to pay compensatory damages to the victim of A's tort. In such a case B will be entitled to bring a claim in contribution against A under the

---

[104] Stevens 2007, 262 (emphasis in original).
[105] See above, § 7.5.
[106] Amazingly, the Law Commission – that cannot stop fiddling with certain areas of law, such as the criminal law – seems never to have thought it worth its while to have a look at the law on vicarious liability.

Civil Liability (Contribution) Act 1978 because they were both liable to make the compensation payment that B made. This will allow B to recover from A a 'just and equitable' *proportion* of the compensation payment that he made.

However, if the reason why B was vicariously liable in respect of A's tort was that A was her employee and he committed his tort in the course of his employment by B, then B will be entitled to bring a claim for breach of contract against A: he will have invariably breached his contract of employment in committing his tort. If B does bring a claim for breach of contract against A, she will be allowed to sue A for damages equal to the *entire* amount of money that she had to pay out to the victim of A's tort: the entire amount will count as a loss that B has suffered as a result of A's breach of contract.

So – in *Lister* v *Romford Ice and Cold Storage Co Ltd* (1957), Lister, who was employed by the claimants as a lorry driver, drove his lorry into a slaughterhouse yard to pick up some waste. Lister's father accompanied him and got out of the lorry before Lister had parked it. In parking the lorry, Lister negligently knocked down and injured his father. Lister's father sued the claimants, claiming that they were vicariously liable in respect of his son's negligence, and recovered £1,600 from the claimants in compensatory damages. The claimants then sued Lister, claiming that he had breached his contract of employment when he negligently knocked down his father and that they were therefore entitled to sue him for damages equal to the £1,600 that they had to pay out to Lister's father as a result of Lister's negligence. The House of Lords allowed the claim, agreeing that Lister had breached his contract of employment in negligently knocking down his father: they found that there was an implied term in Lister's contract of employment with the claimants that he would perform his duties under his contract of employment with reasonable skill and care and that when Lister negligently knocked down his father he breached that implied term.

B. Vicarious liability for the acts of accessories

We have already noted that if A has committed a tort in relation to B, and C is an accessory to A's tort with the result that the courts will hold that A's tort was committed by both A *and* C, then it may be possible for *someone else* to be vicariously liable in respect of the tort that the courts will hold C has committed.[107] The decision of the House of Lords in *Credit Lyonnais* v *Export Credit Guarantee Department* (2000) emphasises that if, in this situation, C's employer is to be held vicariously liable for C's tort, then *all* of the actions that made C an accessory to A's tort have to have been committed in the course of C's employment.

In the *Credit Lyonnais* case, the claimants were defrauded of a substantial amount of money by one Mr Chong. The fraud worked like this. Chong forged some bills of exchange – promises to pay for goods received – and offered them for sale to the claimants. Obviously the claimants wanted some assurance that they would be paid under the bills of exchange before they bought them. This is where Chong's accomplice, a man called Mr Pillai, came in. Pillai was employed by the defendants, a government agency called the Export Credit Guarantees Department. Pillai – who knew very well that Chong's bills of exchange were forged – arranged for the defendants to guarantee that they would pay the claimants 90 per cent of the value of the bills of exchange if they were not paid. Encouraged by this guarantee, the claimants paid Chong £10m for the bills of exchange. Chong then disappeared. The bills of exchange were worthless. So was the defendants' guarantee: it was

---

[107] See above, § 30.1.

conditional on the claimants' having taken reasonable steps to assure themselves that the bills of exchange were genuine, and the claimants had not done this. The claimants sued the defendants for damages, claiming that Pillai had committed a tort in acting as he did, and that the defendants were vicariously liable for that tort.

But what tort had Pillai committed? Pillai had not committed the tort of deceit through his own actions because the claimants had not been deceived by the defendants' guarantee. Chong *had* committed the tort of deceit in relation to the claimants. Was Pillai an accessory to Chong's deceit, so that it could be said that Chong's deceit was committed by both Chong *and* Pillai? The answer was 'yes' – Chong deceived the claimants as part of a common design agreed on between Pillai and Chong.[108] Unfortunately, when Pillai and Chong agreed on their scheme for defrauding the claimants, Pillai was not acting in the course of his employment by the defendants. The only thing Pillai did in the course of his employment was have the defendants issue their guarantees to the claimants. Pillai's doing this *did* help Chong defraud the claimants but, unfortunately for the claimants, merely helping someone commit a tort does not make you an accessory to that tort.[109] So Pillai had not done anything in the course of his employment that made him an accessory to Chong's tort. As a result, Pillai had not committed any tort in the course of his employment for which the defendants could be held vicariously liable.[110]

Further reading

The undoubted master of this area of law is **Paula Giliker**: see her **'Rough justice in an unjust world'** (2002) 65 *Modern Law Review* 269, **'Making the right connection: vicarious liability and institutional responsibility'** (2009) 17 *Torts Law Journal* 35, and **'Lister revisited: vicarious liability, distributive justice, and the course of employment'** (2010) 126 *Law Quarterly Review* 521. She has also written a monograph on *Vicarious Liability in Tort: A Comparative Perspective* (CUP, 2010). However, **Phillip Morgan** is giving her a close run for her money: see his **'Recasting vicarious liability'** (2012) 71 *Cambridge Law Journal* 615, **'Ripe for reconsideration: foster carers, context, and vicarious liability'** (2012) 20 *Torts Law Journal* 110 (available on academia.edu), **'Close connection and police torts'** (2013) 29 *Professional Negligence* 233 and **'Vicarious liability on the move'** (2013) 129 *Law Quarterly Review* 139.

Po Jen Yap's article **'Enlisting close connections: a matter of course for vicarious liability'** (2008) 28 *Legal Studies* 197 is also worth reading for an excellent summary of the law post-*Lister*.

The old 'master's tort' theory of vicarious liability is discussed in **Glanville Williams'** **'Vicarious liability: tort of the master or tort of the servant?'** (1956) 72 *Law Quarterly Review* 522 and wonderfully revived in **Robert Stevens'** *Torts and Rights* (OUP, 2007), Chapter 11.

---

[108] For this ground of accessory liability, see above, § 30.2.

[109] See above, § 30.3.

[110] An argument that there is a tort of 'assisting someone to commit a tort' which Pillai committed in the course of his employment by the defendants was rejected by the House of Lords: see above, § 20.3.

Chapter 32
Loss compensation schemes

Aims and objectives

Reading this chapter should enable you to:

(1) Distinguish between different types of loss compensation schemes.

(2) Begin to get a grasp of the details of four real-world loss compensation schemes.

(3) Discuss whether any part (or the whole) of tort law might be adequately replaced by such a scheme.

32.1 The basics

We do not think that tort law is purely a scheme for getting compensation to those who deserve it. But many people do think this. They ask whether tort law might be better replaced with an *alternative* loss compensation scheme. This chapter is intended to help with such discussions, by setting out a variety of different possible loss compensation schemes and discussing their merits and demerits.

32.2 Features of loss compensation schemes

The dominant model for a loss compensation scheme involves the State compelling contributions to a fund, with the fund then paying compensation to a defined range of claimants. A variety of schemes can be based on this simple model, but there are five principal variables.

(1) *Conditions for entitlement.* A common feature of all schemes is that the claimant's ability to prove that a *particular defendant was at fault* is *not* a condition for entitlement to claim against the fund. Thus such schemes are often referred to as *no-fault compensation schemes.* But beyond this common feature there are many possibilities. An ambitious *general* scheme might attempt to assist all victims of serious adverse events, including illness; a less ambitious *general* scheme might attempt to assist all victims of *accidents*; and a sector-limited scheme might attempt to assist only victims of a particular type of accident or adverse event, e.g. road accidents or adverse events during medical treatment. Schemes might be further refined by making particular categories of people ineligible to claim, e.g. victims of self-inflicted injury or drivers who were drunk when injured.

(2) *Contributors and their contributions.* There is a range of options as to who is compelled to contribute to the fund and in what proportions. For instance, a State could seek to compel contributions by risk creators in proportion to the risks that they create, or it could seek to compel contributions from potential claimants in proportion to the potential benefits that they might claim, or it could add the cost to the burden of general taxation, or it could adopt some combination of these approaches.

(3) *Levels of compensation.* There is scope for defining the level of compensation to be paid by the fund. Some schemes pay compensation at a level equivalent to what would be awarded in a successful tort claim, while others provide limited payments (e.g. only 80 per cent of lost earnings). Some more complicated schemes, particularly those which involve contributions from potential claimants, allow contributors to select their own possible level of compensation when their contributions are calculated.[1]

(4) *Relationship to tort claims.* A fourth variable is the relationship between the scheme and tort claims. In some jurisdictions where a loss compensation scheme has been set up, it operates parallel to tort law,[2] while in others tort law has been abolished for incidents within the scope of the scheme. A more complicated option involves the scheme becoming the *exclusive* way of dealing with minor injuries, but being supplemented by the possibility of tort claims for more serious injuries.[3]

(5) *Who administers the fund.* The fifth variable is who administers the fund. Although such funds are usually created by statute,[4] they can be operated either by a public body or by private organisations such as insurance companies. More complicated possibilities are also sometimes used. For instance, where contributions are paid by potential injurers (such as, employers) to a scheme which will cover possible injuries to a fixed class (such as, their employees), a public body may operate the scheme for small employers, whilst large employers can opt out if they take full responsibility themselves for providing equivalent benefits to their employees.[5]

Clearly when it comes to designing or evaluating a scheme these five variables cannot be considered in isolation from each other. For instance, the wider the scope of entitlement to

---

[1] A greater contribution is demanded in exchange for the promise of a higher level of compensation.

[2] Where a loss compensation scheme operates parallel to tort law it will be necessary to define the exact relationship between the two types of claims. One possibility is to reduce the tort claim by any amount recovered under the scheme. An alternative is not to reduce the tort claim, but instead to allow the operators of the scheme to recoup any tort damages paid to compensate for loss that the scheme had already compensated. The Criminal Injuries Compensation Scheme, which pays compensation to those suffering personal injuries as a result of being a victim of crime, or seeking to prevent a crime or apprehend a criminal, is an example of a scheme which is supplementary to tort law. Such victims are entitled to sue the perpetrators in tort if such a course is likely to be worthwhile.

[3] For an example of a scheme like this see the discussion below of road traffic accident schemes in use in some American states.

[4] Of course operators of activities may set up contractual insurance pools to supplement tort rights. Many climbing gyms, for instance, require users to buy insurance to cover all accidents and mishaps.

[5] A variation on this model is used in New Zealand.

claim, and, in particular, the further that the entitled group extends beyond those who might be able to claim in tort, the greater the pressure to cap the level of payments and the greater the pressure to raise some share of the contributions from the potential beneficiaries. As a second example, it is where the entitled group is limited to victims of a particular type of accident that it may be most practical to compel contributions from risk creators, to quantify awards in line with tort, and to abolish tort claims. The interrelationship of the five factors should become clearer as we consider four specific schemes.

32.3 Four loss compensation schemes

A. The New Zealand Accident Compensation Scheme

This came into operation on 1 April 1974, and has been regularly amended since then. The 1974 scheme covered all personal injuries suffered in accidents and tort law claims were abolished for injuries falling within it.[6] Contributions were raised from three groups: employers paid a levy on wages (and the self-employed made similar payments) to cover the costs of injuries to earners (other than in road accidents); owners of motor vehicles paid a levy to cover the costs of injuries in road accidents; and the government funded the costs of injuries to non-earners, such as students, the unemployed, the retired and visitors from abroad. The level of compensation was reasonably close to tort law: the scheme covered a victim's medical expenses, 80 per cent of their loss of earnings (up to a maximum cap[7]) after the first week, and also provided a lump sum for pain, suffering and loss of amenity.

One criticism of the 1974 scheme was that it was unfair to make employers pay contributions to cover the cost of *all* accidental injuries suffered by their employees, including those not associated with work. A second criticism was that it was unfair not to distinguish between employers with good and bad safety records when setting contribution levels. A third criticism was that it was unfair to treat the victims of accidents more generously than those who fell ill and those born with disabilities.

The scheme has been amended to respond to the first and second criticisms. Thus employees now pay a special contribution towards the cost of non-work injuries which is collected from them alongside their income tax, and the levy on employers takes into account how many claims have been made by their employees in the previous three years.[8] The third criticism has proved more difficult to meet, however, and the only significant move in that direction has been the extension of the scheme to cover injuries caused by medical 'treatment injuries'.[9]

---

[6] Claims for exemplary damages can still be brought.

[7] At the time of writing (August 2017), the cap on payment for loss of earnings is approximately £1,100 per week.

[8] For large employers the 'experience rating' scheme operates by comparing the employers' claims record against others in the same industry, or similar industries: those with better-than-average records receive a discount (up to 50 per cent off) on their levy for the next year, and those with worse-than-average records pay an additional percentage (up to 75 per cent more).

[9] 'Treatment injuries' are adverse medical events causally linked to treatment (including non-treatment and diagnosis) by a registered health professional, as opposed to adverse events which are a necessary part or ordinary consequence of treatment. Thus injury caused by an allergic reaction to a medicine will be covered, but an ordinary side effect will not be. For assessment see Oliphant 2007.

Some other significant changes to the scheme have also been tried but then reversed. Thus at one stage lump sum payments were abolished and replaced by 'independence allowances'. This, however, has been reversed, and other attempts are being made to encourage rehabilitation. A second experiment was 'privatisation' of the scheme by allowing private insurance companies to compete to provide scheme-style cover to employers. But this has also been reversed and the scheme is once again administered by the Accident Compensation Corporation,[10] a Crown entity.

B. Road traffic accident schemes in use in some American states[11]

It is often argued that there are strong reasons for introducing a limited scheme covering personal injuries suffered in road accidents because: (i) drivers are already used to paying for insurance which covers the cost of some[12] such personal injuries; (ii) the class of people who create the risk of road accidents and might be expected to pay for them (that is, drivers) are also by-and-large those who might make most claims from a compensation scheme;[13] but (iii) it is costly and slow to sort out road accidents through the tort system, and (iv) there are significant classes of victims who excite sympathy but are left uncompensated by tort (for example, children who unpredictably run into the road). Given these factors any scheme which will cost drivers no more than current insurance premiums while offering better protection for victims could gain popular support.

The model scheme which is most common in the United States involves contributions from road users and is administered by private insurance companies. Under the scheme all victims of road accidents are entitled to compensation even if they cannot prove that another driver was at fault, but in exchange for this wider-than-tort entitlement the level of compensation is reduced to below the tort level for victims of *minor* accidents. Usually tort claims are abolished for these minor accidents. Private insurance companies sell membership of these schemes alongside other insurance policies, and pay out on claims.[14] Thus drivers pay their insurers amounts covering the risk that they will be injured in a road accident (and the risk that they will have to compensate a person who is not a driver and will consequently not have his own policy), while claims are made by injured drivers

---

[10] Details of the history and operation of the New Zealand scheme can be found at http://www.acc.co.nz/

[11] We concentrate on American schemes because they are well established and have been carefully studied. Similar schemes are also in place, however, in several Canadian provinces, Australian states, and European countries, e.g. France.

[12] Not all. Currently it is not compulsory in England and Wales for a driver to insure against injury to *himself* or *herself*, though it is compulsory to insure against the possibility of *negligently* injuring a *third party*. Nonetheless, many drivers purchase insurance against injury to themselves.

[13] To spell this out: the risk of road accidents is created by drivers, and people injured in road accidents are generally also drivers (even though they may be travelling as passengers or be pedestrians at the time when they are injured).

[14] Insurers often sell drivers a 'package' which includes: (1) scheme membership, often called 'personal injury protection' (PIP); (2) liability insurance, covering the risk of being held liable in tort for causing personal injuries not covered by the scheme; and (3) insurance covering property damage, which is usually outside the scheme.

against their insurers, and by injured non-drivers against insurers in accordance with a priority list.[15]

Three arguments are commonly raised against such schemes. The first objection is that it seems unfair that where a victim was undoubtedly injured by the negligence of another driver the scheme leaves her with less compensation than tort law would have provided if it had not been abolished. This objection is often augmented by the fact that when it is a driver who was undoubtedly injured by the negligence of another then the scheme adds insult to injury by making the innocent victim claim on her own policy (perhaps forfeiting a no-claims bonus).

This first objection can be partially met by preserving the possibility of a tort claim if the injury suffered goes above a certain level of seriousness. This means that no victim suffering a *serious* injury will be left significantly worse off by the scheme. Unfortunately, however, the use of seriousness hurdles, especially if seriousness is measured by the cost of medical treatment, creates an incentive for fraud, in the form of exaggerated medical bills.[16]

The second objection is that drivers who drive badly, and know that this is the case, will still be able to claim compensation for their own injuries if they cause an accident and will not have to pay damages to other motorists, except (perhaps) those suffering serious injuries. Given this, the incentive to drive carefully may be reduced, and accident rates may rise. Studies trying to determine whether the introduction of no-fault schemes has led to an increase in accident rates have yielded mixed results, and are discussed in the final section of this chapter.

The third objection is that experience has shown that what motorists must pay in no-fault states is not always less than what they would have to pay in states that kept ordinary tort law. Thus the authors of a major study in 2010 reported that:

> between the 1980s and 2006, both average liability premiums and premium growth were higher in no-fault states than other states, particularly tort states. These differences persist after adjusting for property-damage costs to account for variation in general inflation and accident prevalence across states. We also found that states that repealed no-fault laws saw substantial drops in liability premiums. Taken together, these facts indicate that no-fault has been a more expensive auto-insurance system.[17]

The reasons why no-fault schemes have proved more expensive than their designers expected are not clear. The authors of the same study conclude that no-fault schemes do not lead to more accidents, nor make injured people more willing to claim, but instead lead to claimants seeking a greater amount on average for medical expenses.[18]

---

[15] Different American states have different 'priority lists', which require a pedestrian or cyclist injured by a vehicle to claim against the first *available* no-fault insurer on the list. As an example, the list for an injured pedestrian in a particular jurisdiction might be: (1) pedestrian's own insurer; (2) pedestrian's spouse's insurer; (3) insurer of a relative who the pedestrian lives with; (4) vehicle owner's insurer; (5) vehicle driver's insurer; (6) residual insurance fund. (This list is a considerably *simplified* version of the list that is used in Michigan.)

[16] After Massachusetts raised its tort threshold from $500 to $2,000 in 1988, the median number of treatment visits rose from 13 to 30 per auto injury claim: Marter & Weisberg 1992, 488.

[17] Anderson, Heaton & Carroll 2010, at 76.

[18] Ibid, 131–2.

Twelve American states have no-fault road accident schemes.[19] All of these allow tort claims to be brought if the victim's injury exceeds a particular threshold of severity, with seven expressing that threshold in terms of the medical bills ($2,000 in Massachusetts, $4,000 in Minnesota) and five using a phrase such as 'serious injury' (New York) or 'significant and permanent loss of an important bodily function' (Florida).[20] Usually such a threshold is sufficient to keep most claims out of tort law.[21] When the claim is below the threshold then the schemes differ as to the level of compensation provided. In New York, for instance, the scheme covers hospital and medical expenses and 80 per cent of lost wages up to a maximum of $2,000 per month for a period not exceeding three years, subject to a total cap of $50,000. In Florida, by contrast, the scheme covers only 80 per cent of hospital and medical expenses up to a maximum of $10,000, and then only if the injured person has suffered an 'emergency medical condition' (otherwise the maximum is $2,500). Moreover, it is only if any of the $10,000 is left that a claim can be made for loss of earnings, and then only for 60 per cent. Michigan is the only state which has extended its no-fault scheme beyond personal injuries: it also covers up to $1 million of damage to the property of others, with the exception of moving or improperly parked cars.

C. Vaccine damage schemes

Many vaccines that are routinely administered have a small risk of very serious adverse consequences. The Vaccine Damage Payments Act 1979 set up a scheme under which people who have been left severely disabled[22] by vaccination are awarded a lump sum, currently £120,000. This is clearly far less than such a child might expect to be awarded if the disability was caused by a tort, but an award does not preclude a tort claim. The scheme is funded by the state from general revenue and administered by the Department for Work and Pensions. The justification for such a scheme was explained by the Pearson Commission: 'There is a special case for paying compensation for vaccine damage where vaccination is recommended by a public authority and is undertaken to protect the community.'[23]

The United Kingdom scheme is far less generous than the scheme operating in the United States. In the United States, the National Childhood Vaccine Injury Act of 1986 established a Federal *no-fault* scheme to compensate those injured by certain listed childhood vaccines, whether administered in the private or public sector. Awards under the

---

[19] As of February 2014. In nine of these states the no-fault scheme is mandatory, while in three a driver can choose whether to participate in the no-fault scheme (in which case her insurance premium will be lower) or to keep full tort rights. At the peak of the popularity of no-fault road schemes during the late 1970s, 16 states had some form of no-fault scheme.

[20] The New York Law provides a more detailed definition of 'serious injury' and the phrase we have quoted from the legislation in Florida is only one part of that state's severity threshold.

[21] Estimated to be kept out of tort law in 1997, 58 per cent of claims in Kentucky, 70 per cent in Colorado, 78 per cent in New York and 66 per cent in Florida: Insurance Research Council 1999.

[22] This requires at least 60 per cent disability: Vaccine Damage Payments Act 1979, s 1(4) (as amended). The interpretation of this requirement was considered by the Court of Appeal in *G (A Minor) v Secretary of State for Work and Pensions* [2017] 1 WLR 1956. The sum of £120,000 was set by the Vaccine Damage Payments Act 1979 Statutory Sum Order 2007 (SI 2007/1931).

[23] Pearson 1978, para. 1398.

scheme are substantial, covering medical and rehabilitative expenses, and in certain cases, pain and suffering and future lost earnings.[24] Eligibility and appropriate compensation are decided by the US Federal Court of Claims[25] but legal fees are covered provided that there was a reasonable basis for the claim and it was made in good faith, and many hearings are simplified by the statutory presumption that the victim is eligible if he suffered an 'adverse event' appearing in the 'Vaccine Injury Table'.[26] The scheme is funded by an excise tax of 75 cents on each dose of covered vaccine. One of the reasons why a generous scheme exists is that before its creation tort claims led to vaccine prices soaring and several manufacturers halted production. A vaccine shortage resulted and public health officials became concerned about the return of epidemic disease. The statute requires victims to file claims for compensation under the *no-fault* scheme before commencing tort litigation, and if a claimant accepts an award under the US scheme he is precluded from pursuing a tort claim.

D. Professor Atiyah's first-party insurance scheme

Patrick Atiyah has suggested that 'the personal injury tort system should be abolished, but *not* replaced by a universal state compensation system. Instead, we should be willing to leave its replacement largely to the operation of the free market.'[27] He predicted that many people would choose to go into the market to buy insurance covering themselves against income lost as a result of non-trivial accidents (regardless of who, if anyone, was at fault) but usually would not buy coverage for pain and suffering or medical costs. Moreover, such people would consider carefully how far they needed protection for loss of income.[28] Perhaps the government would have to intervene to compel people to buy a *minimum level* of coverage against common types of serious accidents, such as road accidents, but in other spheres of life, for instance the workplace, institutions such as unions might arrange convenient mass cover.

It is worth describing Atiyah's proposals in terms of the five factors which we used when discussing designs for loss compensation schemes: contributions are paid by potential victims in proportion to the degree of risk that they face, and they choose for themselves what events they want to be covered against and what level of compensation they want should such events occur; these choices will be made at the time of buying a policy from a private insurance company, such private companies administering the scheme, and tort law will be abolished for personal injuries.

Many students' first reaction to Atiyah's proposals is that it is unfair to make potential victims pay for their own protection, partly because many could not afford to do so. But it may be the case that the costs of liability policies (that is, of potential tort claims) are already passed on to potential victims in the form of higher prices for products and services, and that the price of one of Atiyah's insurance policies (at least if a low level of general coverage is chosen) will be *cheaper* for potential victims than the total of all these

---

[24] The average award is currently (fiscal year 2017, to August) approximately US$380,000 (with a maximum of $250,000 in cases of death).

[25] At first instance by 'special masters' appointed by the Court.

[26] This lists particular 'adverse events' and 'time windows' for each vaccine covered by the scheme.

[27] Atiyah 1996, 35. See also Atiyah 1997, Chapter 8.

[28] For example, professional footballers might conclude that if they were injured in an accident they could 'get by' in future on less than £90,000 per week.

passed-on costs.[29] Moreover, Atiyah's scheme would almost certainly be cheaper to administer and claimants would be compensated more quickly.

This should not suggest, however, that we think that Atiyah's proposals should be accepted without further debate. At the very least there are major practical issues to be thought through concerning the position of those who could not reasonably be expected to buy policies, such as children and the insane, and those who foolishly failed to buy any cover, or bought far less cover than they later turned out to need. We also think that there are broader issues to be considered when evaluating loss compensation schemes which are intended to replace tort law, and these are considered in the next section.

32.4 Evaluation of loss compensation schemes

To evaluate a particular scheme we recommend considering it from five perspectives.

First, the *fairness of the funding arrangements* should be considered. It is commonly argued that there are justifications for internalising the costs associated with particular risks to those that create the risks,[30] and this could support a particular approach to funding. But other approaches might also be justified, for instance, by someone who believes that it is fair to redistribute resources from profit-making enterprises to potential victims of the industrial society.

Secondly, the *cost of administering the scheme* should be considered, including consideration of the costs of collecting contributions and of deciding whether claimants are entitled to claim. Clearly with a sector-limited scheme, such as one covering only the victims of road accidents, there may also be costs involved in determining which claims properly fall within the scheme and which do not.

Thirdly, the *fairness of the definition of those qualified to claim* should be considered. Here an important issue may be whether there is a sufficient reason for distinguishing between those qualified to claim and others who suffer similar injuries or have equivalent disabilities but are not entitled to assistance from the fund.

Fourthly, the *effect of the scheme on accident rates* should be considered. Many defenders of tort law argue that it plays a role in reducing the number of accidents to an efficient

---

[29] In particular, it may be cheaper for a low earner to buy an *Atiyah*-policy which offers him better coverage than to buy an ordinary *liability*-policy. For instance, imagine that the chance for all drivers of being involved in a serious collision with another car is 1 in 1,000 per year; and that the chance of that accident being caused by your own negligence is 40 per cent, by the other driver's negligence 40 per cent, and by nobody's negligence 20 per cent. Imagine further, that in such accidents both drivers have to take one year off work. Now let us consider the position of A, who earns £10,000 per year, which is less than the £30,000 per year earned by the average driver. The cost of an *Atiyah*-policy for A will reflect his risk of being a victim, which is £10 (1/1,000 x £10,000). The cost of a *liability*-policy for A will reflect his risk of negligently injuring another, which is £12 (40% x 1/1,000 x £30,000). Of course, the average driver's *Atiyah*-policy will be more expensive (£30) than a *liability*-policy (£12), but that is because an *Atiyah*-policy will compensate him for his loss of earnings in 100 per cent of accidents, while a liability-policy will only help him in 40 per cent of accidents (those in which he incurs a liability). Moreover, the example has been kept artificially simple by considering *only* loss of earnings. Currently a *liability*-policy also has to cover possible claims for pain and suffering and private medical care. If we added to the example the extra fact that all such accidents involve £20,000 of pain and suffering and £25,000 of medical bills then the average driver's earnings-only-*Atiyah*-policy would be the same price (£30) as his current *liability* policy (40% x 1/1,000 x £75,000 = £30).

[30] If people who create risks do not bear the costs of those risks then they may tend to create *more* risks.

minimum, or (to put the same point a different way) in deterring inefficient risk-creating behaviour.[31] Consequently, if a scheme is promoted with the intention of abolishing tort law it will be necessary for its promoters to explain whether they believe that the scheme will continue to provide such incentives (as might be the case if contributions to the scheme's funding are truly proportionate to risk created), whether such incentives will be sufficiently provided by some other area of law (e.g. criminal law), or whether they believe that the beneficial effect of tort law on accident rates was always exaggerated and will not be much missed.

Fifthly, it must be considered whether *tort law performs any irreplaceable tasks* which a loss compensation scheme would not perform.

(1) *Fairness of the funding arrangements.* Some questions concerning the fairness of funding arrangements, such as whether it is fair to redistribute the cost of accidental injuries from the rich to the poor, require deeper analysis of competing models of justice than is appropriate in a tort text. That said, many of the proposals for schemes which have not attracted support have been unpopular because their funding arrangements did not actually achieve what the proponents of the scheme anticipated. For instance, at one time advocates of road-accident schemes proposed that contributions should be by way of a levy on petrol, a so-called 'pay-at-the-pump' scheme.[32] These advocates thought that it would be fair for those who drove further to pay more since they would be likely to be involved in more accidents. In fact this was a false premise, since accident rates are more closely related to traffic density than to mileage,[33] and if the scheme had been put into practice then those driving long distances in rural areas would have subsidised the accident costs of those making short journeys in busy cities!

(2) *Cost of administration.* It has sometimes been suggested that the main problem with ambitious state-run schemes, such as the New Zealand scheme, is that they create massive bureaucracies which cost too much to operate. But, in fact, the bureaucracies that are created are many times less costly than the networks of professionals and officials who are required to operate the tort system. The real problem with ambitious state-run schemes is that the *total* cost of achieving their goals is high. Let us imagine (for the sake of argument) that the tort system compensates only 20 per cent of accident victims, that the total compensation bill is £n per year, and that the administration costs are a further 40 per cent on top of the total compensation bill. Given these figures we can say that the tort system costs £1.4n per year. So what might an accident compensation scheme cost by comparison? Let us assume that such a scheme will compensate 90 per cent of accident victims, will pay them each only 75 per cent of what they would have received had they won a tort claim and will cost only 10 per cent on top of the total compensation bill to administer. Such a compensation scheme requires £3.7n per year.[34] So it requires more than

---

[31] This is not to say, of course, that tort liability exists *in order to* deter wrongful behaviour. Our intention is merely to consider what effect a switch to a loss compensation scheme might have on incentives to behave reasonably.

[32] The Pearson Commission recommended a 'pay-at-the-pump' scheme (Pearson 1978, paras 1054, 1057) though this was intended as a supplement to tort law rather than an alternative.

[33] Though there are more *fatalities* per mile driven on rural roads, perhaps because of the speed of collisions and the distance to hospitals.

[34] This figure is derived in the following way: If compensating 20 per cent of victims at tort law levels costs £n, then compensating 90 per cent of victims at 75 per cent of tort law levels will cost £3.38n (n x 4.5 x 0.75). Add to that administration costs of 10 per cent (£0.338n) and the total is £3.7n (£3.38n + £0.338n).

two-and-a-half times as much as the tort system in total despite the fact that it is paying less per claimant and is more administratively efficient.

Some people find it baffling that a more efficient system which pays less per claimant ends up being more expensive. But the key to avoiding bafflement is to realise that the current tort system leaves such a high proportion of accident victims uncompensated.[35] Currently members of this large group obtain medical care through the NHS, but beyond that are left to struggle through life as best as they can with assistance from savings, family, charities and the social security safety net. A major cost of any ambitious loss compensation scheme is that many in this group will now qualify for the far better benefit of an award at 75 per cent of tort levels and such awards add up. Of course, arguments *can* be made for helping this group. But the proposition, 'we should pay more tax to ensure better provision for those injured in accidents which they cannot show were caused by anyone else's fault' is not uncontroversial.

(3) *Fairness of qualification.* Those who have advocated loss compensation schemes have often relied on the argument that because claimants can only obtain remedies in tort law if they prove that the defendant's breach of a duty caused them compensatable damage, and because the breach and causation elements of such claims are often difficult to prove in practice, many claimants who were *in fact* victims of torts are *in practice* unable to obtain remedies. Thus some of the beneficiaries of loss compensation schemes are persons who *ought to have been* compensated in tort law.

It is usually impossible, however, to define those entitled to claim so as to include *only* persons who *ought to have been* compensated in tort law; any attempt to do so is likely to make it costly to determine whether any particular individual is entitled or not. Consequently, it is common to define the class of those entitled to claim in terms of the type of accident which *caused* their injuries, such as 'victims of road accidents' or 'victims of vaccine'. It is not easy to explain why it is fair for accident victims generally, or victims of specific types of accidents, to be treated better than those who fall ill or who are born with disabilities. But, as the discussion under the previous sub-heading suggests, one of the major problems with compensation schemes has been their *total cost.* Consequently, whilst it might be fair to extend qualification beyond accident victims to others in need this would probably cost more than most governments would be willing to raise by way of taxation.[36]

(4) *Effect on accident rates.* Some studies have suggested that no-fault road accident schemes lead to higher accident rates.[37] For instance, Cummins, Weiss and Phillips modelled the effect of road accident schemes in the United States and concluded that no-fault

---

[35] Harris 1984 found (at 51) that tort damages were recovered by 19 per cent of work accident victims, 29 per cent of road accident victims, and 2 per cent of victims of other accidents. Because accidents in the home make up such a high proportion of all accidents the overall figure was that 12 per cent of accident victims obtain tort compensation.

[36] In 1989 the New Zealand government (Labour) announced that the compensation scheme would be extended to cover those incapacitated by sickness or disease, but the Labour Party lost the election in 1990 to the National Party and no such change was made when the scheme was reformed in 1992.

[37] There is less evidence available as to the effect that schemes might have on accident rates in sectors other than road accidents. Rubin and Shepherd 2007, have suggested that several reforms aimed at *reducing* tort damages in the United States have led to a *reduction* in death rates. Their explanation for this effect is that many tort claims are directed at defendants who are in the business of reducing risks, for instance medical professionals and the producers of pharmaceuticals and safety devices, and reforms which reduce the exposure of such defendants to heavy liability bills may lead to their services and products becoming both cheaper and more widely available.

is associated with higher fatality rates than tort: two models yielded estimates of 12.8–13.8 per cent and 7.2–7.5 per cent higher than tort.[38] A subsequent empirical study by Cohen and Deheija estimated that no-fault led to a 10 per cent increase in fatalities.[39] These effects seem severe, but are actually more moderate than McEwin's estimate of 16 per cent higher fatalities in Australia and New Zealand.[40] By contrast Loughran concluded that his comparison of fatal accident, car damage and negligence rates in tort and no-fault states cast 'serious doubts on contentions that no-fault auto insurance as implemented in the United States has led to greater driver negligence and higher accident rates'.[41] He pointed out that most people avoid driving negligently because they do not want to risk being injured, that if they thought that others were driving less safely they might alter their own behaviour so as to drive more safely, and that because most road accidents involve damage to cars and most no-fault schemes do not cover property damage tort law still provides some incentives. Likewise, a study by Heaton and Helland which used data relating to non-fatal accidents found 'little evidence that no-fault coverage is associated with more numerous accidents . . . Overall, our results suggest that the behavioural adjustments of drivers induced by no-fault, if any, are modest and affect accident severity more than accident incidence.'[42]

(5) *Effect on tort law's functions.* Does tort law perform any tasks that a loss compensation scheme cannot perform? It will be recalled that tort law is made up of two parts, each of which performs a different function. The duty-imposing part of tort law helps to determine what duties we owe each other; while the remedial part of tort law determines what remedies will be available when one of these duties is breached. Obviously no loss-compensation scheme could perform the first function – that of helping to determine what duties we owe each other. So if tort law were abolished outright in favour of a loss-compensation scheme, the task of determining what duties we owe each other would have to be shouldered by other parts of the law, such as criminal law and contract law. Whether this would be a good thing or a bad thing is too complex a question to be addressed in this text.

What of the remedial part of tort law? *Currently*, the remedial part of tort law performs a number of different tasks:

(a) Requiring wrongdoers to *repair* their wrongs by putting the victim of a tort in (roughly) the position he or she would have been in had that wrong not been committed.

(b) In a case where a tort has been committed in a particularly outrageous manner, satisfying the victim of a tort's perception that the person who committed that tort must be made to pay for the fact that he has ridden roughshod over the victim's rights.

(c) Giving the victim of a tort that is being committed on an ongoing basis the ability to bring that wrongdoing to an end by allowing him or her to obtain an injunction, requiring the person who is committing that tort to stop what he or she is doing.

---

[38] Cummins, Weiss & Phillips 2001, 455.
[39] Cohen & Deheijia 2004, 360, 382.
[40] McEwin 1989.
[41] Loughran 2001.
[42] Heaton & Helland 2008, 20. A similar conclusion was reached by Winkler 2017, 44, in an article which establishes that state interference in the setting of prices for insurance, particularly prohibition of 'experience rating', appears to reduce incentives to take care in a much more significant way.

The existence of a loss-compensation scheme would mean that the law no longer needed to perform function (a) in respect of losses covered by that scheme. The existence of the scheme would mean that there was nothing for a tortfeasor to repair, in so far as his tort had caused the victim of that tort to suffer a loss compensated by the scheme. But a loss-compensation scheme cannot perform the other tasks – (b) and (c) – that the remedial part of tort law currently performs. Given this, we suggest that any proposal to abolish tort law *altogether* in favour of a loss-compensation scheme would be seriously defective. Before such a proposal could be countenanced, some other mechanism would need to be found to perform tasks (b) and (c).

Further reading

Patrick Atiyah's work has been tremendously influential in this area. **P.S. Atiyah, *The Damages Lottery* (Hart Publishing, 1997)** manages to be powerful, provocative, and easy to read. **Peter Cane** is now the author of ***Atiyah's Accidents, Compensation and the Law* (8th edn, Cambridge University Press, 2013)**, which continues to challenge orthodox visions of tort law. **Don Dewees, David Duff and Michael Trebilcock, *Exploring the Domain of Accident Law – Taking the Facts Seriously* (Oxford University Press, 1996)** collects and analyses a vast amount of data about tort law and alternative schemes; it is an essential source for anyone considering what the benefits and pitfalls of replacing tort law with an alternative scheme might be. With respect to the automobile schemes that operate in parts of the USA we particularly recommend **Gary Schwartz, 'Auto no-fault and first party insurance: advantages and problems' (2000) 73 *Southern California Law Review* 611.**

Bibliography

Abraham, K.S. 2003. '*Rylands* v *Fletcher*: tort law's conscience' in Rabin and Sugarman 2003, 207–28.

Allen, C.K. 1931. *Legal Duties and Other Essays in Jurisprudence*. Clarendon Press.

Allen, J. 2009. 'Variable standards of care in negligence' *Tort Law Review* 17:5.

Ames, J.B. 1908. 'Law and morals' *Harvard Law Review* 22:97.

Andenas, M. and Fairgrieve, D. 2000. eds. *Judicial Review in International Perspective: II*. Kluwer Law International.

Anderson, J.M., Heaton, P. and Caroll, S.J. 2010. *The US Experience With No-Fault Automobile Insurance: A Retrospective*. RAND Institute for Civil Justice.

Armour, J. 1999. 'Corporate personality and assumption of responsibility' *Lloyd's Maritime and Commercial Law Quarterly* [1999]:246.

Aronson, M. 2011. 'Misfeasance in public office: a very peculiar tort' *Melbourne University Law Review* 35:1.

Atiyah, P.S. 1967. *Vicarious Liability in the Law of Torts*. Butterworths.

———. 1996. 'Personal injuries in the twenty-first century: thinking the unthinkable' in Birks 1996b, 1–46.

———. 1997. *The Damages Lottery*. Hart Publishing.

Bagshaw, R. 1999. 'The duties of care of emergency service providers' *Lloyd's Maritime and Commercial Law Quarterly* [1999]:71.

———. 2000. 'Inducing breach of contract' in Horder 2000, 131–50.

———. 2001. 'Children through tort' in Fionda 2001, 127–50.

———. 2004a. 'Private nuisance and the defence of the realm' *Law Quarterly Review* 120:37.

———. 2004b. 'Rylands confined' *Law Quarterly Review* 120:388.

———. 2004c. 'Children as actionable damage' *King's College Law Journal* 15:117.

———. 2009a. 'Negligently making business activities illegal: *Jain* v *Trent Strategic Health Authority*' *Torts Law Journal* 17:295.

———. 2011a. 'Causing the behaviour of others and other causal mixtures' in Goldberg 2011.

———. 2011b. 'The edges of tort law's rights' in Nolan and Robertson 2011, 405–32.

Bailey, S.H. 2010. 'Causation in negligence: what is a material contribution?' *Legal Studies* 30:167.

Bailey, S.H. and Nolan, D. 2010. 'The *Page* v *Smith* saga' *Cambridge Law Journal* 69:495.

Baker, T. 2005. 'Liability insurance as tort regulation: six ways that liability insurance shapes tort law in action' *Connecticut Insurance Law Journal* 12:1.

Barendt, E. 1993. 'Libel and freedom of speech in English law' *Public Law* [1993]:449.

———. 1999. 'What is the point of libel law?' *Current Legal Problems* [1999]:110.

Barker, K. 1993. 'Unreliable assumptions in the law of negligence' *Law Quarterly Review* 109:461.

———. 2008. 'Economic loss and the duty of care: a study in the exercise of legal justification' in Rickett 2008, 175–203.

———. 2013. 'Private and public: the mixed concept of vindication in torts and private law' in Pitel, Neyers and Chamberlain 2013, 59–94.

———. 2014. 'Damages without loss – can Hohfeld help?' *Oxford Journal of Legal Studies* 34:1.

Barker, K., Grantham, R. and Swain, W. 2015. eds. *The Law of Misstatement: 50 Years on from Hedley Byrne* v *Heller*. Hart Publishing.

Bartle, R. 2004. 'Virtual worldliness: what the imaginary asks of the real' *New York School Law Review* 49:19.

Baty, T. 1916. *Vicarious Liability*. Clarendon Press.

Beever, A. 2003a. 'The structure of aggravated and exemplary damages' *Oxford Journal of Legal Studies* 23:87.

_____. 2003b. 'Particularism and prejudice in the law of tort' *Tort Law Review* 11:146.

_____. 2007. *Rediscovering the Law of Negligence*. Hart Publishing.

_____. 2008. 'Justice and punishment in tort: a comparative theoretical analysis' in Rickett 2008, 249–98.

_____. 2009. 'Transferred malice in tort law?' *Legal Studies* 29:400.

_____. 2013. *The Law of Private Nuisance*. Hart Publishing.

_____. 2016. *A Theory of Tort Liability*. Hart Publishing.

Beitz, C. 2009. *The Idea of Human Rights*. Oxford University Press.

Benson, P. 1995. 'The basis for excluding liability for economic loss in tort law' in Owen 1995, 427–58. Bingham, Lord. 2010. 'The uses of tort' *Journal of European Tort Law* 1:3.

Bird, C. 2007. 'Harm versus sovereignty: a reply to Ripstein' *Philosophy and Public Affairs* 35:179.

Birks, P.B.H. 1995. 'The concept of a civil wrong' in Owen 1995, 31–51.

_____. 1996a. *Harassment and Hubris: The Right to an Equality of Respect*. University College, Dublin.

_____. 1996b. ed. *Wrongs and Remedies in the 21st Century*. Oxford University Press, Oxford.

_____. 1997a. ed. *The Classification of Obligations*. Clarendon Press.

_____. 1997b. ed. *Privacy and Loyalty*. Clarendon Press.

_____. 2000a. 'Personal property: proprietary rights and remedies' *King's College Law Journal* 11:1.

_____. 2000b. 'Rights, wrongs and remedies' *Oxford Journal of Legal Studies* 20:1

Bishop, P. and Jenkins, V. 2011. 'Planning and nuisance: revisiting the balance of public and private interests in land-use development' *Journal of Environmental Law* [2011]:285.

Bjorge, E. 2011. 'Torture and "ticking bomb" scenarios' *Law Quarterly Review* 127:196.

Bloustein, E. 1964. 'Privacy as an aspect of human dignity: an answer to Dean Prosser' *New York University Law Review* 39:962.

Bohlen, C. 1926. 'Incomplete privilege to inflict intentional invasions of property and personality' *Harvard Law Review* 39:307.

Bright, S. 2001. 'Liability for the bad behaviour of others' *Oxford Journal of Legal Studies* 21:311.

Brodie, D. 2010. *Enterprise Liability and the Common Law*. Cambridge University Press.

Brooke-Smith, B.J. 1954. 'Liability for the negligence of another' *Law Quarterly Review* 70:253.

Buckland, W. 1935. 'The duty to take care' *Law Quarterly Review* 51:637.

Burrows, A. 1996. 'Reforming exemplary damages' in Birks 1996b, 153–74.

_____. 2004. *Remedies in Contract and Tort*, 3rd edn. Oxford University Press.

_____. 2008. 'Are "damages on the *Wrotham Park* basis" compensatory, restitutionary or neither?' in Saidov and Cunnington 2008.

_____. 2011. *The Law of Restitution*, 3rd edn. Oxford University Press.

Burrows, A. and Peel, E. 2003. eds. *Commercial Remedies: Current Issues and Problems*. Oxford University Press.

Burrows, A. and Rodger, Lord. 2006. eds. *Mapping the Law: Essays in Memory of Peter Birks*. Oxford University Press.

Butler, R. 2003. 'SAAMCO in practice' in Burrows and Peel 2003, 71–90.

Butler, S. 2006. ed. *Discovering the Law*. Law Matters Publishing.

Calabresi, G. 1970. *The Cost of Accidents*. Yale University Press.

Calabresi, G. and Melamed, D. 1972. 'Property rules, liability rules and inalienability: one view of the cathedral' *Harvard Law Review* 85:1089.

Campbell, D. 2015. 'The curious case of the dog that did bark in the night-time: what mischief does *Hedley Byrne* v *Heller* correct?' in Barker, Grantham and Swain 2015.

_____. 2016. 'The absence of negligence in *Hedley Byrne*' *Law Quarterly Review* 132:266.

Cane, P. 1982. 'Justice and justifications for tort liability' *Oxford Journal of Legal Studies* 2:30.

_____. 1996. *Tort Law and Economic Interests*, 2nd edn. Clarendon Press, Oxford.

_____. 1998. 'Retribution, proportionality and moral luck in tort law' in Cane and Stapleton 1998, 141–74.

_____. 1999. 'Fault and strict liability for harm in tort law' in Swadling and Jones 1999, 171–206.

———. 2000. 'Vicarious liability for sexual abuse' *Law Quarterly Review* 116:21.

———. 2001. 'The temporal element in law' *Law Quarterly Review* 117:5.

———. 2004. 'The doctor, the stork and the court: a modern morality tale' *Law Quarterly Review* 120:23.

———. 2013. *Atiyah's Accidents, Compensation and the Law*, 8th edn. Cambridge University Press.

Cane, P. and Gardner, J. 2001. eds. *Relating to Responsibility*. Hart Publishing.

Cane, P. and Stapleton, J. 1998. eds. *The Law of Obligations: Essays in Honour of John Fleming*. Oxford University Press.

Carty, H. 1999. 'Joint tortfeasance and assistance liability' *Legal Studies* 19:489.

———. 2010. *An Analysis of the Economic Torts*. 2nd edn. Oxford University Press.

Chambers, R., Mitchell C. and Penner J. 2009. eds. *Philosophical Foundations of the Law of Unjust Enrichment*. Oxford University Press.

Clark, T. and Nolan, D. 2014. 'A critique of *Chester* v *Afshar*' *Oxford Journal of Legal Studies* 34:659.

Coad, J. 2007. '*Reynolds* and public interest – what about truth and human rights?' *Entertainment Law Review* 18:75.

———. 2011. '*Reynolds*, *Flood* and the King's new clothes' *Entertainment Law Review* 22:1.

Coase, R. 1960. 'The problem of social cost' *Journal of Law and Economics* 3:1.

Cohen, A. and Dehejia, R. 2004. 'The effect of automobile insurance and accident liability laws on traffic fatalities' *The Journal of Law and Economics* 47:357.

Coleman, J. and Shapiro, S. 2002. eds. *The Oxford Handbook of Jurisprudence and Philosophy of Law*. Oxford University Press.

Conaghan, J. and Mansell, W. 1999. *The Wrongs of Tort*, 2nd edn. Pluto Press.

Cooke, E. 1994. 'Trespass, mesne profits and restitution' *Law Quarterly Review* 110:420.

Cooke, Lord. 1991. 'An impossible distinction' *Law Quarterly Review* 107:46.

Cornford, T. 2008. *Towards a Public Law of Tort*. Ashgate Publishing.

Cummins, J.D., Weiss, D. and Phillips, M. 2001. 'The incentive effects of no-fault automobile insurance' *Journal of Law and Economics* 44:427.

Dalphond, P. 2002. 'Duty of care and the supply of alcohol' *Supreme Court Law Review (2d)* 17:97.

Davies, P.S. 2011. 'Accessory liability for assisting torts' *Cambridge Law Journal* 70:353.

———. 2015. *Accessory Liability*. Hart Publishing.

Davis, J.L.R. 1998. 'Farewell to the action for breach of statutory duty?' in Mullany and Linden 1998, 69–83.

Deakin, S. and Randall, J. 2009. 'Rethinking the economic torts' *Modern Law Review* 72:519.

Degeling, S. 2003. *Restitutionary Rights to Share in Damages: Carers' Claims*. Cambridge University Press.

Depoorter, B. 2011. 'Fair trespass' *Columbia Law Review* 111:1090.

Dewees, D., Duff, D. and Trebilcock, M. 1996. *Exploring the Domain of Accident Law – Taking the Facts Seriously*. Oxford University Press.

Dicey, A.V. 1908. *Introduction to the Study of the Law of the Constitution*, 7th edn. Macmillan.

Dietrich, J. 2000. 'Lawful coercive threats and the infliction of harm' *Torts Law Journal* 8:187.

———. 2011. 'Accessorial liability in the law of torts' *Legal Studies* 31:231.

Donnelly, C. 2007. *Delegation of Governmental Power to Private Parties: A Comparative Perspective*. Oxford University Press.

Douglas, S. 2009. 'The nature of conversion' *Cambridge Law Journal* 68:198.

———. 2011. 'Re-examining trespass', unpublished manuscript on file with the authors.

D'souza, D. 2002. *Letters to a Young Conservative*. Basic Books.

Duff, D. and Trebilcock, M. 1996. *Exploring the Domain of Accident Law – Taking the Facts Seriously*. Oxford University Press.

Dugdale, T. 2000. 'The impact of SAAMCO' *Professional Negligence* 16:203.

Duncan Wallace, I. 2000. '*Donoghue* v *Stevenson* and "complex structures": *Anns* revisited?' *Law Quarterly Review* 116:530.

Dworkin, R. 1986. *Law's Empire*. Fontana Publishing.

Dyson, A., Goudkamp, J. and Wilmot-Smith, F. 2015. eds. *Defences in Tort*. Hart Publishing.

Dyson, M. 2014. ed. *Unravelling Tort and Crime*. Cambridge University Press.

Economides, K. 2000. et al. eds. *Fundamental Values*. Hart Publishing.

Edelman, J. 2002. *Gain-Based Damages*. Hart Publishing.

——. 2006. 'Gain-based damages and compensation' in Burrows and Rodger 2006, 141–60.

——. 2008. 'In defence of exemplary damages' in Rickett 2008, 225–48.

——. 2009. 'The meaning of loss and enrichment' in Chambers, Mitchell and Penner 2009, 211–41.

Edelman, J. and Dyer, E. 2015. 'A defence of duress in the law of torts?' in Dyson, Goudkamp and Wilmot-Smith 2015, 159–182.

Ellis, E. and McGivern, B. 2007. 'The wrongfulness or rightfulness of actions for wrongful life' *Tort Law Review* 15:135.

Elvin, J. 2003a. 'Liability for negligent refereeing of a rugby match' *Law Quarterly Review* 119:560.

——. 2003b. 'The duty of schools to prevent bullying' *Tort Law Review* 11:168.

Epstein, R.A. 1973. 'A theory of strict liability' *Journal of Legal Studies* 2:151.

——. 2010. 'Towards a general theory of tort law: strict liability in context' *Journal of Tort Law* 3:Article 6

Evans, H. 2001. 'The scope of the duty revisited' *Professional Negligence* 17:147.

Fairgrieve, D. 2001. 'The Human Rights Act 1998, damages and tort law' *Public Law* [2001]:695.

Farnsworth, W. 1999. 'Do parties to nuisance cases bargain after judgment? A glimpse inside the cathedral' *University of Chicago Law Review* 66:373.

Feldman, D. 1997. 'Privacy-related rights and their social value' in Birks 1997b, 15–50.

Feldthusen, B. 1998. 'Vicarious liability for sexual torts' in Mullany and Linden 1998, 221–43.

Ferran, E. 2011. 'Corporate attribution and the directing mind and will' *Law Quarterly Review* 127:239.

Finnis, J. 2002. 'Natural law: the classical tradition' in Coleman and Shapiro 2002, 1–60.

——. 2011. *Natural Law and Natural Rights*, 2nd edition. Clarendon Press.

Fionda, J. 2001. ed. *Legal Concepts of Childhood*. Hart Publishing.

Fleming, J. 1997. 'Preventive damages' in Mullany 1997, 56–71.

——. 1998. *The Law of Torts*, 9th edn. LBC Information Services.

Fletcher, G. 1972. 'Fairness and utility in tort theory' *Harvard Law Review* 85:537.

Fordham, M. 2010. 'Saving us from ourselves – The duty of care in negligence to prevent self-inflicted harm' *Torts Law Journal* 18:22.

Foster, N. 2011. 'The merits of the civil action for breach of statutory duty' *Sydney Law Review* 33:67.

Fridman, G.H.L. 1963. 'Compensation of the innocent' *Modern Law Review* 26:481.

——. 2009. '*Lumley* v *Gye* and the (over?) protection of contracts' in Neyers, Bronaugh and Pitel 2009, 225–35.

Fried, C. 1968. 'Privacy' *Yale Law Journal* 77:475.

Gardner, J. 2010. 'What is tort law for? Part 1: the place of corrective justice', available on SSRN.

——. 2011. 'Punishment and compensation: a comment', available on SSRN.

Gearty, C. 1989. 'The place of private nuisance in a modern law of torts' *Cambridge Law Journal* 48:214.

Giglio, F. 2007. 'Restitution for wrongs: a structural analysis' *Canadian Journal of Law and Jurisprudence* 20:5.

Giliker, P. 2002. 'Rough justice in an unjust world' *Modern Law Review* 65:269.

——. 2009. 'Making the right connection: vicarious liability and institutional responsibility' *Torts Law Journal* 17:35.

——. 2010a. *Vicarious Liability in Tort: A Comparative Perspective*. Cambridge University Press.

——. 2010b. 'Lister revisited: vicarious liability, distributive justice, and the course of employment' *Law Quarterly Review* 126:521.

Glofcheski, R. 2004. 'A frolic in the law of tort: expanding the scope of employers' vicarious liability' *Tort Law Review* 12:18.

Goff, R. 1983. 'The search for principle' *Proceedings of the British Academy* 69:169.

——. 1986. *Judge, Jurist and Legislature.* Child and Co Oxford Lecture.

Goldberg, J. 2002. 'Unloved: tort law in the modern legal academy' *Vanderbilt Law Review* 55:1501.

——. 2006. 'Two conceptions of tort damages: fair vs full compensation' *DePaul Law Review* 435.

——. 2008. 'Ten half-truths about tort law' *Valparaiso University Law Review* 42:1221.

——. 2015. 'Tort law's missing excuses' in Dyson, Goudkamp and Wilmot-Smith 2015, 53–64.

Goldberg, J. and Zipursky, B. 2001. 'The Restatement (Third) and the place of duty in negligence law' *Vanderbilt Law Review* 54: 657.

——. 2002. 'Unrealized torts' *Virginia Law Review* 88:1625.

——. 2006. 'Seeing tort law from the internal point of view: Holmes and Hart on legal duties' *Fordham Law Review* 75:1563.

——. 2009. 'Intervening wrongdoing in tort: The Restatement (Third)'s unfortunate embrace of negligent enabling' *Wake Forest Law Review* 44:1211.

——. 2010a. 'Torts as wrongs' *Texas Law Review* 88:917.

——. 2010b. 'The easy case for products liability law' *Harvard Law Review* 123:1919.

——. 2016. 'The strict liability in fault and the fault in strict liability' *Fordham Law Review* 85:743.

Goldberg, R. 2011. ed. *Perspectives on Causation.* Hart Publishing.

Gordley, J. 1998. 'Responsibility in crime, tort and contract for the unforeseeable consequences of an intentional wrong: a once and future rule?' in Cane and Stapleton 1998, 175–208.

Goudkamp, J. 2011a. '*Ex turpi causa* and immoral behaviour in the tort context' *Law Quarterly Review* 127:354.

——. 2011b. 'Insanity as a tort defence' *Oxford Journal of Legal Studies* 31:727.

——. 2012. 'The defence of illegality in tort law: wither the rule in *Pitts* v *Hunt*?' *Cambridge Law Journal* 71:481.

——. 2013. *Tort Law Defences.* Hart Publishing.

Goudkamp, J. and Mayr, L. 'The doctrine of illegality and interference with chattels' in Dyson, Goudkamp and Wilmot-Smith 2015, 223–46.

Goymour, A. 2011. 'Conversion of contractual rights' *Lloyd's Maritime and Commercial Law Quarterly* [2011]:67.

Gravells, N. 1977. 'Three heads of contributory negligence' *Law Quarterly Review* 93:581.

Gray, K. 1991. 'Property in thin air' *Cambridge Law Journal* 50:255.

Gray, N. and Edelman, J. 1998. 'Developing the law of omissions: a common law duty to rescue?' *Torts Law Journal* 6:240.

Green, D.R. 1985. 'A map for Mayhew's London: the geography of poverty in the mid-nineteenth century' *London Journal* 11:115.

Green, S. 2010. 'Understanding the wrongful interference actions' *Conveyancer and Property Law* 74:15.

——. 2014. *Causation in Negligence.* Hart Publishing.

——. 2017. '*Fairchild* and the single agent criterion' *Law Quarterly Review* 133:25.

Haberfield, L. 1998. '*Lowns* v *Woods* and the duty to rescue' *Tort Law Review* 6:56.

Handford, P. 2007. 'Psychiatric injury in breach of a relationship' *Legal Studies* 27:26.

Handley, E. and Davis, G. 2001. 'Defamation and satire: *Hanson* v *Australian Broadcasting Corporation*' *Torts Law Journal* 9:1.

Harmon, S. and Laurie, G. 2010. '*Yearworth* v *North Bristol NHS Trust*: property, principles, precedents and paradigms' *Cambridge Law Journal* 69:476.

Harris, D. 1984. et al. *Compensation and Support for Illness and Injury.* Oxford University Press.

Harris, J. 1986. 'Who owns my body?' *Oxford Journal of Legal Studies* 16:55.

Hart, H.L.A. 1994. *The Concept of Law.* 2nd edn. Clarendon Press.

Hart, H.L.A. and Honoré, A.M. 1985. *Causation in the Law*, 2nd edn. Oxford University Press.

Hartstone, J. 2008. 'Confusion, contradiction and chaos within the House of Lords post *Caparo* v *Dickman*' *Tort Law Review* 16:8.

Heaton, P. and Helland, E. 2008. *No-Fault Insurance and Automobile Accidents: RAND Working Paper WR-551-ICJ.* RAND Institute for Civil Justice.

Herring, J. and Palser, E. 2007. 'The duty of care in gross negligence manslaughter' *Criminal Law Review* [2007]:24.

Hershowitz, S. 2011. 'Harry Potter and the trouble with tort theory' *Stanford Law Review* 63:67.

Heuston, R.F.V. 1970. 'Who was the third Law Lord in *Rylands* v *Fletcher*?' *Law Quarterly Review* 86:160.

———. 1986. 'Judicial prosopography' *Law Quarterly Review* 102:90.

Hill, T. 1991. 'A lost chance for compensation in the tort of negligence by the House of Lords' *Modern Law Review* 54:511.

Hoffman, D. 2011. ed. *The Impact of the UK Human Rights Act on Private Law*. Cambridge University Press.

Hoffmann, Lord. 2005. 'Causation' *Law Quarterly Review* 121:592.

———. 2009. 'Reforming the law of public authority negligence' *Bar Council Law Reform Lecture*

———. 2017. 'Review of Steel, *Proof of Causation in Tort Law*' *Law Quarterly Review* 133:516.

Holmes, O.W. 1873. 'The theory of torts' *American Law Review* 7:652.

Honoré, A.M. 1988. 'Responsibility and luck: the moral basis of strict liability' *Law Quarterly Review* 104:530.

Hope, Lord. 2003. 'James McGhee – a second Mrs Donoghue?' *Cambridge Law Journal* 62:587.

Horder, J. 2000. ed. *Oxford Essays in Jurisprudence 4th Series*. Clarendon Press.

Howarth, D. 1997. 'Is there a future for the intentional torts?' in Birks 1997a, 233–81.

———. 2005a. 'Poisoned wells: "proximity" and "assumption of responsibility" in negligence' *Cambridge Law Journal* 64:23.

———. 2005b. 'Against *Lumley* v *Gye*' *Modern Law Review* 68:195.

———. 2006. 'Many duties of care – or a duty of care? Notes from the underground' *Oxford Journal of Legal Studies* 26:449.

———. 2011. 'The cost of libel actions: a skeptical note' *Cambridge Law Journal* 70:397.

Hoyano, L. 2002. 'Misconceptions about wrongful conception' *Modern Law Review* 65:883.

Hunt, M. 1998. 'The "horizontal" effect of the Human Rights Act' *Public Law* [1998]:422.

Hyman, D. 2005. 'Rescue without law: an empirical perspective on the duty to rescue' *Texas Law Review* 84:653.

Insurance Research Council. 1999. *Injuries in Auto Accidents: An Analysis of Auto Insurance Claims*. Insurance Research Council.

Jackson, R. 2009. *Review of Civil Litigation Costs*. The Stationery Office.

Jaffey, A.J.E. 1985. '*Volenti non fit injuria*' *Cambridge Law Journal* 44:87.

Jaffey, P. 2007. *Private Law and Property Claims*. Hart Publishing.

———. 2011. 'Licence fee damages' *Restitution Law Review* 19:95.

Jolowicz, J.A. 2008. 'Civil litigation: what's it for?' *Cambridge Law Journal* 67:508.

Keating, G. 1997. 'The idea of fairness in the law of enterprise liability' *Michigan Law Review* 95:1266.

Kelly, R. 1967. 'The inner nature of the tort action' *Irish Jurist (New Series)* 2:279.

Keren-Paz, T. 2007. *Torts, Egalitarianism and Distributive Justice*. Ashgate Publishing.

———. 2010a. '*AT* v *Dulghieru* – compensation for victims of trafficking, but where is the restitution?' *Torts Law Journal* 18:87.

———. 2010b. 'Poetic justice: why sex slaves should be allowed to sue ignorant clients in conversion' *Law and Philosophy* 29:307

Kessler, D.P. and McClellan, M. 1996. 'Do doctors practise defensive medicine?' *Quarterly Journal of Economics* 111:353.

Kidner, R. 1995. 'Vicarious liability: for whom should the "employer" be held liable?' *Legal Studies* 15:47.

Kimel, D. 2003. *From Promise to Contract: Towards a Liberal Theory of Contract*. Hart Publishing.

Klar, L. 1998. 'Downsizing torts' in Mullany and Linden 1998, 305–20.

Koenig, T.H. and Rustad, M.L. 2001. *In Defense of Tort Law*. New York University Press.

Koziol, H. and Steininger, B. 2005. eds. *European Tort Law 2004: Tort and Insurance Yearbook*. Springer.

Laddie, H. 2008. 'The insatiable appetite for intellectual property rights' *Current Legal Problems* 61:401.

Landes, W.M. and Posner, R.A. 1987. *The Economic Structure of Tort Law*. Harvard University Press.

Lastowka, F.G. and Hunter, D. 2004. 'The law of the virtual worlds' *California Law Review* 92:1.

Lee, J. 2009. 'The fertile imagination of the common law: *Yearworth* v *North Bristol NHS Trust*' *Torts Law Journal* 17:130.

Lee, M. 2003. 'What is private nuisance?' *Law Quarterly Review* 119:298.

———. 2011. 'Safety, regulation and tort: fault in context' *Modern Law Review* 74:555.

———. 2013. 'Nuisance and regulation in the Court of Appeal' *Journal of Planning & Environmental Law* [2013]:277.

———. 2015. 'The public interest in private nuisance: collectives and communities in tort' *Cambridge Law Journal* 74:329.

Lee, P.W. 2009. 'Inducing breach of contract, conversion and contract as property' *Oxford Journal of Legal Studies* 29:511.

Leveson, B. 2012. *An Inquiry Into the Culture, Practices and Ethics of the Press*. The Stationery Office.

Lewis, R. 1999. *Deducting Benefits from Damages for Personal Injury*. Oxford University Press.

———. 2007. 'Tort law in practice: appearance and reality in reforming periodical payments of damages' in Neyers, Chamberlain and Pitel 2007, 487–508.

Lewis, R., Morris, A. and Oliphant, K. 2006. 'Tort personal injury claims statistics: is there a compensation culture in the United Kingdom?' *Torts Law Journal* 14:158.

Loughran, D. 2001. *The Effect of No-Fault Automobile Insurance on Driver Behaviour and Automobile Accidents in the United States*. Rand Corporation.

Loveland, I. 2000a. 'Political libels – whose right is it anyway?' *Current Legal Problems* 53:333

———. 2000b. *Political Libels*. Hart Publishing.

Low, K. 2010. 'Equitable title and economic loss' *Law Quarterly Review* 126:506.

Lucy, W. 2009. Review of Keren-Paz, *Torts, Egalitarianism and Distributive Justice*. *Modern La Review* 72:1048.

Lunney, M. 2005. 'Personal responsibility and the "new" *volenti*' *Tort Law Review* 13:76.

MacDonald, A. 1936–1938. '*Hollywood Silver Fox Farm* v *Emmett*' *Alberta Law Quarterly* 2:99.

Machin, E.A. 1954. 'Negligence and interest' *Modern Law Review* 17:405.

Macneil, I. 1982. 'Efficient breach of contract: circles in the sky' *Virginia Law Review* 68:947.

Marter, S. and Weisberg, H. 1992. 'Medical expenses and the Massachusetts automobile Tort Reform Law: a first review of 1989 bodily injury liability claims' *Journal of Insurance Regulation* 10:462.

Mason, J.K. 2002. 'Wrongful pregnancy, wrongful birth and wrongful terminology' *Edinburgh Law Review* 6:46.

Matthews, P. 1983. 'Whose body? People as property' *Current Legal Problems* [1983]:193.

McBain, G. 2008. 'Modernising and codifying the law of bailment' *Journal of Business Law* [2008]:1.

McBride, N.J. 1996. 'Punitive damages' in Birks 1996b, 175–202.

———. 2004. 'Duties of care: do they really exist?' *Oxford Journal of Legal Studies* 24:417.

———. 2006. 'Tort law' in Butler 2006, 26–35.

———. 2011. 'Rights and the basis of tort law' in Nolan and Robertson 2011.

———. 2014. 'Restitution for wrongs' in Mitchell and Swadling 2014.

———. 2016a. '*Michael* and the future of tort law' *Professional Negligence* 32:14.

———. 2016b. 'Vindicatio: the missing remedy?' *Singapore Academy of Law Journal* 28:1052.

———. 2017. 'Employer's liability in negligence for defamation, again' *Professional Negligence* 33:216.

McBride, N.J. and Hughes, A. 1995. '*Hedley Byrne* in the House of Lords: an interpretation' *Legal Studies* 15:376.

McBride, N.J. and Steel, S. 2012a. 'Suing for the loss of a right to sue: why *Wright* is wrong' *Professional Negligence* 28:27.

———. 2012b. 'The 'Trigger' litigation' *Professional Negligence* 28:245.

———. 2014. *Great Debates in Jurisprudence*. Palgrave Macmillan.

McEwin, I.R. 1989. 'No-fault and road accidents: some Australasian evidence' *International Review of Law and Economics* 9:13.

McInnes, M. 2003. 'Interceptive subtraction, unjust enrichment and wrongs – a reply to Professor Birks' *Cambridge Law Journal* 62:697.

Merkin, R. 2010. 'Tort and insurance: some insurance law perspectives' *Professional Negligence* 26:194.

———. 2012. 'Tort, insurance and ideology: further thoughts' *Modern Law Review* 75:301.

Merrett, L. 2009. 'Costs as damages' *Law Quarterly Review* 125:468.

Merrill, T.W. 2011. 'Is public nuisance a tort?' *Journal of Tort Law* 4(2):4.

Miles, J. 2000. 'Standing under the Human Rights Act 1998: theories of rights enforcement and the nature of public law adjudication' *Cambridge Law Journal* 59:133.

Mitchell, H.C. 2005. *The Intellectual Commons.* Lexington Books.

Mitchell, C. and Mitchell, P. 2010. eds. *Landmark Cases in the Law of Tort.* Hart Publishing.

Mitchell, C. and Swadling, W. 2014. eds. *The Restatement Third: Restitution and Unjust Enrichment: Critical and Comparative Essays.* Hart Publishing.

Mitchell, P. 1999. 'Malice in qualified privilege' *Public Law* [1999]:328.

———. 2005. *The Making of the Modern Law of Defamation.* Hart Publishing.

Moore, M. 2009. *Causation and Responsibility.* Oxford University Press.

Moran, M. 1997. 'Rethinking *Winnipeg Condominium*: restitution, economic loss, and anticipatory repairs' *University of Toronto Law Journal* 47:115.

———. 2003. *Rethinking the Reasonable Person.* Oxford University Press.

———. 2010. 'The reasonable person: a conceptual biography in comparative perspective' *Lewis and Clark Law Review* 14:1233.

Moreham, N. 2005. 'The protection of privacy in English common law: a doctrinal and theoretical analysis' *Law Quarterly Review* 121:628.

———. 2006. 'Privacy in public places' *Cambridge Law Journal* 65:606.

———. 2014. 'Beyond information: physical privacy in English law' *Cambridge Law Journal* 73:350.

Morgan, J. 2006. 'The rise and fall of the general duty of care' *Professional Negligence* 22:206.

———. 2015. 'Liability for independent contractors in contract and tort: duties to ensure that care is taken' *Cambridge Law Journal* 74:109.

Morgan, P. 2012a. 'Recasting vicarious liability' *Cambridge Law Journal* 71:615.

———. 2012b. 'Ripe for reconsideration: foster carers, context, and vicarious liability' *Torts Law Journal* 20:110.

———. 2013a. 'Vicarious liability on the move' *Law Quarterly Review* 129:139.

———. 2013b. 'Close connection and police torts' *Professional Negligence* 29:233.

Morris, A. 2007. 'Spiralling or stabilising? The compensation culture and our propensity to claim damages for personal injury' *Modern Law Review* 70:349.

———. 2011. '"Common sense common safety": the compensation culture perspective' *Professional Negligence* 27:82.

Moyn, S. 2010. *The Last Utopia: Human Rights in History.* Harvard University Press.

———. 2014. *Human Rights and the Uses of History.* Verso.

Mulheron, R. 2010. 'Trumping *Bolam*: a critical legal analysis of *Bolitho*'s "gloss"' *Cambridge Law Review* 69:609.

———. 2012. 'Rewriting the requirement for a "recognised psychiatric injury" in negligence claims' *Oxford Journal of Legal Studies* 32:77.

Mullany, N. 1997. ed. *Torts in the Nineties.* LBC Information Services.

———. 1998. 'Liability for careless communication of traumatic information' *Law Quarterly Review* 114:380.

Mullany, N. and Handford, P. 1993. *Tort Liability for Psychiatric Damage.* LBC Information Services.

Mullany, N. and Linden, A.M. 1998. eds. *Torts Tomorrow: A Tribute to John Fleming.* LBC Information Services.

Mullender, R. 2000. 'Negligence, the personal equation of defendants and distributive justice' *Tort Law Review* 8:211.

———. 2005. 'The reasonable person, the pursuit of justice, and negligence law' *Modern Law Review* 68:681.

———. 2008. 'Negligence law and the concept of community' *Tort Law Review* 16:85.

_____. 2011. 'Blame culture and political debate: finding our way through the fog' *Professional Negligence* 27:64.

Murphy, J. 2004. 'The merits of *Rylands* v *Fletcher*' *Oxford Journal of Legal Studies* 24:643.

_____. 2007a. 'Juridical foundations of common law non-delegable duties' in Neyers, Chamberlain and Pitel 2007, 369–91.

_____. 2007b. 'Rethinking injunctions in tort law' *Oxford Journal of Legal Studies* 27:509.

_____. 2010a. 'The nature and domain of aggravated damages' *Cambridge Law Journal* 69:353.

_____. 2010b. *The Law of Nuisance*. Oxford University Press.

_____. 2012. 'Misfeasance in public office: a tort law misfit?' *Oxford Journal of Legal Studies* 32:51.

Nance, D. 1997. 'Guidance rules and enforcement rules: a better view of the cathedral' *Virginia Law Review* 83:837.

Nelson, J.W. 2010. 'The virtual property problem: what property rights in virtual resources might look like, how they might work, and why they are a bad idea' *McGeorge Law Review* 41:281.

Newark, F.H. 1949. 'The boundaries of nuisance' *Law Quarterly Review* 65:480.

Neyers, J. 2009. 'The economic torts as corrective justice' *Torts Law Journal* 17:162.

_____. 2010. '*Tate and Lyle Food Distribution Co Ltd* v *Greater London Council (1983)*' in Mitchell and Mitchell 2010, 227–50.

_____. 2011. 'Explaining the inexplicable? Four manifestations of abuse of rights in English law' in Nolan and Robertson 2011, 309–30.

_____. 2017. 'Reconceptualising the tort of public nuisance' *Cambridge Law Journal* 76:87.

Neyers, J. and Andrews, E. 2016. 'Loss of custom and public nuisance: the authority of *Ricket*' *Lloyd's Maritime and Commercial Law Quarterly* [2016]:135.

Neyers, J. and Botterell, A. 2016. '*Tate & Lyle*: pure economic loss and the modern tort of public nuisance' *Alberta Law Review* 53:1031

Neyers, J., Bronaugh, R. and Pitel, S. 2009. eds. *Exploring Issues in Contract Law*. Hart Publishing.

Neyers, J., Chamberlain, E. and Pitel, S. 2007. eds. *Emerging Issues in Tort Law*. Hart Publishing.

Neyers, J. and Diacur, J. 2011. 'What (is) a nuisance?' *Canadian Bar Review* 90:215.

Nolan, D. 2004. 'Psychiatric injury at the crossroads' *Journal of Personal Injury Law* 1:1.

_____. 2005. 'The distinctiveness of *Rylands* v *Fletcher*' *Law Quarterly Review* 121:421.

_____. 2007. 'New forms of damage in negligence' *Modern Law Review* 70:59.

_____. 2009. 'Causation and the goals of tort law' in Robertson and Tang 2009, 165–90.

_____. 2011a. 'The liability of public authorities for failure to confer benefits' *Law Quarterly Review* 127:260.

_____. 2011b. '"A tort against land": private nuisance as a property tort' in Nolan and Robertson 2011, 457–88.

_____. 2011c. 'Nuisance' in Hoffman 2011, 165–94

_____. 2013a. 'Deconstructing the duty of care' *Law Quarterly Review* 129:559.

_____. 2013b. 'Negligence and human rights law: the case for separate development' *Modern Law Review* 76:286.

_____. 2013c. 'Varying the standard of care in negligence' *Cambridge Law Journal* 72:651.

_____. 2015. 'Nuisance, planning and regulation: the limits of statutory authority' in Dyson, Goudkamp, and Wilmot-Smith 2015, 183–206.

Nolan, D. and Robertson, A. 2011 eds. *Rights and Private Law*. Hart Publishing.

Nwabueze, R. 2007. 'Interference with dead bodies and body parts: a separate cause of action in tort?' *Tort Law Review* 15:63.

Ogus, A. and Richardson, G. 1977. 'Economics and the environment – a study of private nuisance' *Cambridge Law Journal* 36:284.

Oliphant, K. 2005. '*Rylands* v *Fletcher* and the emergence of enterprise liability in the common law' in Koziol and Steininger 2005, 81–120.

_____. 2007. 'Beyond misadventure: compensation for medical injuries in New Zealand' *Medical Law Review* 15:357.

Oliver, D. 2004. 'Functions of a public nature under the Human Rights Act' *Public Law* [2004]:329.

Ong, B. 2008. 'Two tripartite economic torts' *Journal of Business Law* [2008]:723.

Orr, G. 1995. 'Is an innkeeper her brother's keeper? The liability of alcohol servers' *Torts Law Journal* 3:239.

O'Sullivan, J. 1997a. 'Negligent professional advice and market movements' *Cambridge Law Journal* 56:19.

———. 1997b. 'Nuisance in the House of Lords – normal service resumed' *Cambridge Law Journal* 56:483.

———. 1999. 'Liability for fear of the onset of future medical conditions' *Professional Negligence* 15:96.

Owen, D. 1995. ed. *Philosophical Foundations of Tort Law*. Clarendon Press.

Palmer, S. 2008. 'Public functions and private services: A gap in human rights protection' *International Journal of Constitutional Law* 6:585.

Parpworth, N. 2008. 'Public nuisance in the environmental context' *Journal of Planning and Environmental Law* [2008]:1526

Pearson, Lord. 1978. *Royal Commission on Civil Liability and Compensation for Personal Injury*. HMSO.

Pedain, A. 2005. 'Requiem for a fairytale' *Cambridge Law Journal* 64:11.

Peel, E. 2003a. 'SAAMCO revisited' in Burrows and Peel 2003, 55–70.

———. 2003b. '"Loss of a chance" revisited: *Gregg* v *Scott*' *Modern Law Review* 66:623.

Perlman, H. 1982. 'Interference with contract and other economic expectancies: a clash of tort and contract doctrine' *University of Chicago Law Review* 49:61.

Perry, S. 1992. 'Protected interests and undertakings in the law of negligence' *University of Toronto Law Journal* 42:247.

———. 2001. 'Honoré on responsibility for outcomes' in Cane and Gardner 2001, 61–80.

Pitel, S., Neyers, J. and Chamberlain, E. 2013. *Tort Law: Challenging Orthodoxy*. Hart Publishing.

Polinsky, A.M. and Shavell, S. 2010. 'The uneasy case for products liability' *Harvard Law Review* 123:1437.

Pontin, B. 2013.'The common law clean up of the "workshop of the world": more realism about nuisance law's historic environmental achievements' 40 *Journal of Law and Society* 173.

Porat, A. 2009. Review of Keren-Paz, *Torts, Egalitarianism and Distributive Justice*. *Legal Studies* 29:509.

Porat, A. and Stein, A. 2003. 'Indeterminate causation and apportionment of damages: an essay on *Holtby*, *Allen* and *Fairchild*' *Oxford Journal of Legal Studies* 23:667.

Posner, R.A. 1972. 'A theory of negligence' 1 *Journal of Legal Studies* 29.

———. 2003. *Economic Analysis of Law*. 6th edn. Aspen. Postema, G. 2001. ed. *Philosophy and the Law of Torts*. Cambridge University Press.

Priaulx, N. 2007. *The Harm Paradox: Tort Law and the Unwanted Child in an Era of Choice*. Routledge.

Priel, D. 2014. 'Tort law for cynics' *Modern Law Review* 77:703.

Prosser, W. 1960. 'Privacy' *California Law Review* 48:383.

Rabin, R. 1999. 'Enabling torts' *DePaul Law Review* 49:435.

Rabin, R. and Sugarman, S. 2003. eds. *Torts Stories*. West Law School. Rawls, J. 1971. *A Theory of Justice*. Harvard University Press.

Reece, H. 1996. 'Losses of chance in the law' *Modern Law Review* 59:188.

Rickett, C. 2008. ed. *Justifying Private Law Remedies*. Hart Publishing.

Ripstein, A. 1998. 'Some recent obituaries of tort law' *University of Toronto Law Journal* 48:561.

———. 2006a. 'Private order and public justice: Kant and Rawls' *Virginia Law Review* 92:1391.

———. 2006b. 'Beyond the harm principle' *Philosophy and Public Affairs* 34:215.

———. 2007a. 'As if it had never happened' *William and Mary Law Review* 48:1957.

———. 2007b. 'Tort law in a liberal state' *Tort Law Journal* 1:Article 3.

———. 2009. *Force and Freedom: Kant's Legal and Political Philosophy*. Harvard University Press.

———. 2015. *Private Wrongs*. Harvard University Press.

Ripstein, A. and Zipursky, B. 2001. 'Corrective justice in an age of mass torts' in Postema 2001, 214–49.

Robertson, A. 2011. 'Rights, pluralism and the duty of care' in Nolan and Robertson 2011.

——. 2013. 'On the function of the law of negligence' *Oxford Journal of Legal Studies* 33:31.

Robertson, A. and Tang, H.W. 2009. *The Goals of Private Law*. Hart Publishing.

Rotherham, C. 2007. 'The conceptual structure of restitution for wrongs' *Cambridge Law Journal* 66:172.

——. 2008. '*Wrotham Park* damages and accounts of profits: compensation or restitution?' *Lloyd's Maritime and Commercial Law Quarterly* [2008]:25.

——. 2009. 'The normative foundations of restitution for wrongs: justifying gain-based relief for nuisance' in Robertson and Tang 2009, 389–418.

——. 2010. 'Gain-based relief in tort after *Att-Gen* v *Blake*' *Law Quarterly Review* 126:102.

Rubin, P.H. and Shepherd, J.M. 2007. 'Tort reform and accidental deaths' *The Journal of Law and Economics* 50:221.

Rudden, B. 1991–1992. 'Torticles' *Tulane Civil Law Forum* 6/7:105.

Saidov, D. and Cunnington, R. 2008. eds. *Current Themes in the Law of Contract Damages*. Hart Publishing.

Sales, P. 1990. 'The tort of conspiracy and civil secondary liability' *Cambridge Law Journal* 49:491.

Sales, P. and Stilitz, D. 1999. 'Intentional infliction of harm by unlawful means' *Law Quarterly Review* 115:411.

Salmond, J. 1907. *Law of Torts*. Sweet and Maxwell.

Schwartz, G. 1991. 'The myth of the Ford Pinto case' *Rutgers Law Review* 43:1013.

——. 2000. 'Auto no-fault and first party insurance: advantages and problems' *Southern California Law Review* 73:611.

Schwartz, V.E. and Goldberg, P. 2006. 'The law of public nuisance: maintaining rational boundaries on a rational tort' *Washburn Law Journal* 45:541.

Scott, Lord. 2007. 'Damages' [2007] *Lloyd's Maritime and Commercial Law Quarterly* 465.

Sebok, A. 2007. 'Punitive damages: from myth to theory' *Iowa Law Review* 92:957.

Seneviratne, M. 2001. 'The rise and fall of advocates' immunity' *Legal Studies* 21:644.

Sharpe, R.J. and Waddams, S.M. 1982. 'Damages for lost opportunity to bargain' *Oxford Journal of Legal Studies* 2:290.

Shmueli, B. 2010. 'Love and the law, children against mothers and fathers: or, what's love got to do with it' *Duke Journal of Gender Law and Policy* 17:131.

Simester, A. and Chan, W. 2004. 'Inducing breach of contract: one tort or two?' *Cambridge Law Journal* 63:132.

Simpson, A.W.B. 1984. 'Bursting reservoirs: the historical context of *Rylands* v *Fletcher*' *Journal of Legal Studies* 13:209.

——. 1995. *Leading Cases in the Common Law*. Oxford University Press.

Smith, J.C. and Burns, P. 1983. '*Donoghue* v *Stevenson* – the not so golden anniversary' *Modern Law Review* 46:147.

Smith, R. 1977. 'The economic torts: their impact on real property' *Conveyancer and Property Lawyer* 41:318.

——. 2014. *Property Law*. 8th edn. Pearson Education.

Smith, S. 2011. 'The normativity of private law' *Oxford Journal of Legal Studies* 31:215.

Solomon, R. and Payne, J. 1996. 'Alcohol liability in Canada and Australia: sell, serve and be sued' *Tort Law Review* 4:188.

Solove, D. 2008. *Understanding Privacy*. Harvard University Press.

Spencer, J. 1989. 'Public nuisance – a critical examination' *Cambridge Law Journal* 48:55.

Sprankling, J.G. 2008. 'Owning the center of the Earth' *UCLA Law Review* 55:979.

Stallybrass, W.T.S. 1929. 'Dangerous things and non-natural user of land' *Cambridge Law Journal* 3:376.

Stanton, K. 2003. et al. *Statutory Torts*. Sweet and Maxwell.

——. 2007a. 'Pure economic loss: back to basics in the 21st century' *Tort Law Review* 15:5.

——. 2007b. 'Decision-making in the tort of negligence in the House of Lords' *Tort Law Review* 15:93.

——. 2009. 'Burying the dead: developing a modern approach to vicarious liability' *Tort Law Review* 17:9

——. 2010.'Tort and wrongful detention' *Tort Law Review* 18:69.

Stapleton, J. 1991. 'Duty of care and economic loss: a wider agenda' *Law Quarterly Review* 107:249.

_____. 1994. *Product Liability*. Butterworths.

_____. 1995. 'Duty of care: peripheral parties and alternative opportunities for deterrence' *Law Quarterly Review* 111:301.

_____. 1998. 'Duty of care factors: a selection from the judicial menus' in Cane and Stapleton 1998, 59–95.

_____. 2002a. 'Comparative economic loss: lessons from case-law-focused "middle theory"' *University of California, Los Angeles Law Review* 50:531.

_____. 2002b. 'Lords a-leaping evidentiary gaps' *Torts Law Journal* 10:276.

_____. 2013. 'Unnecessary causes' *Law Quarterly Review* 129:39.

_____. 2015. 'An "extended but-for" test for the causal relation in the law of obligations' *Oxford Journal of Legal Studies* 35:697.

Stapleton, J. and Steel, S. 2016. 'Causes and contributions' *Law Quarterly Review* 132:363.

Stauch, M. 2001. 'Risk and remoteness of damage in negligence' *Modern Law Review* 64:191.

Steel, S. 2012. 'Causation in English tort law: still wrong after all these years' *University of Queensland Law Journal* 31:243.

_____. 2014. 'Defining causal counterfactuals in negligence' *Law Quarterly Review* 130:564

_____. 2015. *Proof of Causation in Tort Law*. Cambridge University Press.

_____. 2017. 'The locality principle in private nuisance' *Cambridge Law Journal* 76:145.

Steel, S. and Ibbetson, D. 2011. 'More grief on uncertain causation in tort' *Cambridge Law Journal* 70:451.

Steele, J. 2008. 'Damages in tort and under the Human Rights Act: remedial or functional separation?' *Cambridge Law Journal* 67:606.

_____. 2013. 'Law Reform (Contributory Negligence) Act 1945: collisions of a different sort' in Arvind and Steele 2013, 159–86.

Stevens, R. 2005. 'An opportunity to reflect' *Law Quarterly Review* 121:189.

_____. 2007. *Torts and Rights*. Oxford University Press.

_____. 2015. 'Should contributory fault be analogue or digital?' in Dyson, Goudkamp and Wilmot-Smith 2015, 247–64.

Stevens, R. (2). 1964. '*Hedley Byrne* v *Heller* – judicial creativity and doctrinal possibility' *Modern La Review* 27:121.

Steyn, Lord. 2002. 'Perspectives of corrective and distributive justice in tort law' *Irish Jurist* 37:1.

Stigglebout, M. 2009. 'The scope and rationale of the principle that the defendant "take his victim as he finds him"' *Tort Law Review* 17:140.

Swadling, W. and Jones, G. 1999. eds. *The Search for Principle: Essays in Honour of Lord Goff of Chieveley*. Oxford University Press.

Tadros, V. 2011. 'Independence without interests?' *Oxford Journal of Legal Studies* 31:193.

Taggart, M. 2002. *Private Property and Abuse of Rights in Victorian England*. Oxford University Press.

Tan, K.F. 1981. 'A misconceived issue in the tort of false imprisonment' *Modern Law Review* 44:166.

Teff, H. 1998. 'Liability for negligently inflicted psychiatric harm: justifications and boundaries' *Cambridge Law Journal* 57:91.

_____. 2007. 'Condoning wrongful suffering' *Tort Law Review* 15:7.

Tettenborn, A. 1993. 'Damages in conversion – the exception or the anomaly?' *Cambridge Law Journal* 52:128.

_____. 1994. 'Reversionary damage to chattels' *Cambridge Law Journal* 53:326.

_____. 1996. 'Trust property and conversion: an equitable confusion' *Cambridge Law Journal* 55:36.

_____. 2000a. 'Professional negligence: free riders and others' in Economides 2000, 295–311.

_____. 2000b. 'Components and product liability: damage to "other property"' *Lloyd's Maritime and Commercial Law Quarterly* [2000]:338.

Thomson, J. 2013. ed. *Juridical Review – Donoghue* v *Stevenson: The Paisley Papers*. W Green.

Tomlinson, E.A. 2000. 'The French experience with duty to rescue: a dubious case for criminal enforcement' *New York Law Journal of International and Comparative Law* 20:451.

Treiger-Bar-Am, L.K. 2000. 'Defamation law in a changing society: the case of *Youssoupoff* v *Metro-Goldwyn-Mayer*' *Legal Studies* 20:291.

Tromans, S. 1982. 'Private nuisance – prevention or payment' *Cambridge Law Journal* 41:87.

Tunc, A. 1972. 'Tort law and the moral value' *Cambridge Law Journal* 30:247.

Turner, P. 2010. 'Consequential economic loss and the trust beneficiary' *Cambridge Law Journal* 69:444.

Turton, G. 2016. *Evidential Uncertainty in Causation in Negligence*. Hart Publishing.

Varuhas, J.N.E. 2009. 'A tort-based approach to damages under the Human Rights Act 1998' *Modern Law Review* 72:750.

———. 2011. 'Exemplary damages: "public law" functions, *mens rea* and quantum' *Cambridge Law Journal* 70:284.

———. 2014, 'The concept of "vindication" in the law of torts: rights, interests and damages' *Oxford Journal of Legal Studies* 34:253.

———. 2016. *Damages and Human Rights*. Hart Publishing.

Veitch, E. and Miers, D. 1975. 'Assault on the law of tort' *Modern Law Review* 38:139.

Waddams, S. 1998. 'New directions in products liability' in Mullany and Linden 1998, 119–29.

———. 2001. 'Johanna Wagner and the rival opera houses' *Law Quarterly Review* 117:431.

Waldron, J. 1995. 'Moments of carelessness and massive loss' in Owen 1995, 387–408.

Warby, M. and Moreham, N. 2016. *Tugendhat and Christie: The Law of Privacy and the Media*. 3rd edn. Oxford University Press.

Watson, S. and Noonan, C. 2009. 'The widening gyre of vicarious liability' *Torts Law Journal* 17:144.

Wedderburn, Lord. 1983. 'Rocking the torts' *Modern Law Review* 46:224.

Weinrib, E. 1980. 'The case for a duty to rescue' *Yale Law Journal* 90:247.

———. 1995. *The Idea of Private Law*. Harvard University Press.

———. 2012. *Corrective Justice*. Oxford University Press.

———. 2016. 'Causal uncertainty' *Oxford Journal of Legal Studies* 36:135.

Weir, J.A. 1964. 'Chaos or cosmos? *Rookes*, *Stratford* and the economic torts' *Cambridge Law Journal* 23:225.

———. 1989. 'Governmental liability' *Public Law* [1989]:40.

———. 1995. 'A damnosa hereditas' *Law Quarterly Review* 111:357.

———. 1997. *Economic Torts*. Clarendon Press.

———. 1998. 'The staggering march of negligence' in Cane and Stapleton 1998, 97–138.

———. 2003–4. 'All or nothing' *Tulane Law Review* 78:512.

———. 2004. *A Casebook on Tort*. 10th edn. Sweet and Maxwell.

———. 2006. *An Introduction to Tort Law*. 2nd edn. Clarendon Law Series, Oxford.

Weston, C.A.R. 1999. 'Suing in tort for loss of computer data' *Cambridge Law Journal* 58:67.

Whittaker, S. 1989. 'European product liability and intellectual products' *Law Quarterly Review* 105:125.

———. 1997. 'The application of the "broad principle of Hedley Byrne" as between parties to a contract' *Legal Studies* 17:169.

Wightman, J. 1998. 'Nuisance – the environmental tort? *Hunter* v *Canary Wharf* in the House of Lords' *Modern Law Review* 61:870.

Williams, G. 1956a. 'Vicarious liability: tort of the master or servant?' *Law Quarterly Review* 72:122.

———. 1956b. 'Liability for independent contractors' *Cambridge Law Journal* 15:180.

Williams, K. 2001. 'Medical Samaritans: is there a duty to treat?' *Oxford Journal of Legal Studies* 21:393.

———. 2005. 'State of fear: Britain's compensation culture reviewed' *Legal Studies* 25:499.

Winfield, P. 1926. 'The history of negligence in the law of torts' *Law Quarterly Review* 42:184.

———. 1934. 'Duty in tortious negligence' *Columbia Law Review* 34:41.

Winkler, K.E. 2017. 'Safety effects of no-fault auto insurance' *Journal of Personal Injury Law* [2017]:38.

Witting, C. 2000. 'Negligent inspectors and flying machines' *Cambridge Law Journal* 59:544.

_____. 2001. 'Distinguishing between property damage and pure economic loss in negligence: a personality thesis' *Legal Studies* 21:481.

Witzleb, N. and Carroll, R. 2009. 'The role of vindication in torts damages' *Tort Law Review* 17:16.

Woolf, Lord. 2000. 'The Human Rights Act 1998 and remedies' in Andenas and Fairgrieve 2000, 429–36.

Worthington, S. 1999. 'Reconsidering disgorgement for wrongs' *Modern Law Review* 62:218.

_____. 2009. 'Art, law and creativity' *Current Legal Problems* 62:168.

Wright, C. 1961. 'The English law of torts – a criticism' *University of Toronto Law Journal* 11:84.

Wright, R. 1995. 'The standards of care in negligence law' in Owen 1995, 249–75.

_____. 2003. 'Hand, Posner and the myth of the "Hand Formula"' *Theoretical Inquiries in Law* 4:145.

_____. 2011a. 'The NESS account of natural causation: a response to criticisms' in Goldberg 2011.

_____. 2011b. 'Private nuisance law: a window on substantive justice' in Nolan and Robertson 2011, 489–522.

Yap, P.J. 2008. 'Enlisting close connections: a matter of course for vicarious liability?' *Legal Studies* 28:197.

_____. 2009. 'Pure economic loss and defects in the law of negligence' *Tort Law Review* 17:80.

Zipursky, B. 1998. 'Rights, wrongs and recourse in the law of torts' *Vanderbilt Law Review* 51:1.

_____. 2003. 'Civil recourse, not corrective justice' *Georgetown Law Journal* 91:695.

_____. 2005. 'A theory of punitive damages' *Texas Law Review* 84:105.

_____. 2007. 'Sleight of Hand' *William and Mary Law Review* 48:1999.

Zuckerman, A. 2013. *Zuckerman on Civil Procedure – Principles of Practice*. 3rd edn. Sweet and Maxwell.

Index of problems

Index